THE MASTER REFERENCE COLLECTION

NEW
DICTIONARY
THE(OF)OLOGY

EDITORS:
Sinclair B. Ferguson
David F. Wright
CONSULTING EDITOR:
J. I. Packer

INTERVARSITY PRESS
DOWNERS GROVE, ILLINOIS 60515
LEICESTER, ENGLAND

Inter-Varsity Press
38 De Montfort Street, Leicester LE1 7GP, England
P.O. Box 1400, Downers Grove, Illinois 60515, U.S.A.

Inter-Varsity Press, England, is the publishing division of the Universities and Colleges Christian Fellowship (formerly the Inter-Varsity Fellowship), a student movement linking Christian Unions in universities and colleges throughout the United Kingdom and the Republic of Ireland, and a member movement of the International Fellowship of Evangelical Students. For information about local and national activities in Great Britain write to UCCF, 38 De Montfort Street, Leicester LE1 7GP.

InterVarsity Press, U.S.A., is the book-publishing division of InterVarsity Christian Fellowship, a student movement active on campus at hundreds of universities, colleges and schools of nursing. For information about local and regional activities, write Public Relations Dept., InterVarsity Christian Fellowship, 6400 Schroeder Rd., P.O. Box 7895, Madison, WI 53707-7895.

Distributed in Canada through InterVarsity Press, 860 Denison St., Unit 3, Markham, Ontario L3R 4H1, Canada.

Unless otherwise stated, quotations from the Bible are taken from the HOLY BIBLE: NEW INTERNATIONAL VERSION. Copyright © 1973, 1978 by the International Bible Society, New York. Used in USA by permission of Zondervan Bible Publishers, Grand Rapids, Michigan, and published in Great Britain by Hodder and Stoughton, Ltd.

Set in 10/11 pt Sabon
Typeset in Great Britain by Input Typesetting Ltd, London SW19 8DR

UK ISBN 0-85110-636-6
US ISBN 0-8308-1400-0

Printed in the United States of America

British Library Cataloguing in Publication Data

New dictionary of theology.
    1. Theology—Dictionaries
    I. Ferguson, Sinclair B.   II. Wright, David F.
    230'.03'21   BR95

UK ISBN 0-85110-636-6

Library of Congress Cataloging in Publication Data
New dictionary of theology/editors, Sinclair B. Ferguson, David F. Wright: consulting editor, J. I. Packer.
    p. cm.—(The Master reference collection)
    Bibliography: p.
    ISBN 0-8308-1400-0
    1. Theology—Dictionaries.   I. Ferguson, Sinclair B.   II. Wright, David F.   III. Packer, J. I. (James Innell)   IV. Series.
BR95.N38 1988
    230'.03'21—dc19   87-30975
                                   CIP

19	18	17	16	15	14	13	12	11	10	9	8	7	6	5	4	3	2	1
99	98	97	96	95	94	93	92	91	90	89	88							

Contents

Preface

'Everything a theologian does in the church', said Martin Luther, 'contributes to the spread of the knowledge of God and the salvation of men.' That may not sum up every Christian's attitude to theologians and theology, but it strikes the right note. The root meaning of 'theology' is 'speaking about God'. What Christian theology seeks to do is to spell out the significance of God's revelation, supremely in Jesus Christ, of himself and his provision and purposes for his world and the men and women he has made. Theology does this in different ways, some of which are suggested by qualifying epithets such as 'biblical', 'historical' and 'systematic'. Yet all the various methods and models of theology aim to set forth an ordered understanding of the revealed mind of God – about himself, about us his creatures in his world, and about the way he plans us to live in fellowship with himself and one another. The Christian whose diet has no theological content is likely to suffer from stunted or unbalanced growth instead of developing maturity of mind and heart.

This *Dictionary* is intended to provide the enquiring reader with a basic introduction to the world of theology – its themes, both majestic and minor, its famous formulations and its important historical moments, its distinguished – and notorious – exponents, past as well as present, its sources, disciplines and styles, its technical vocabulary, its ebb and flow in movements, schools and traditions, and its interaction with other currents of thought and religion. While the common standpoint of the editors and contributors is allegiance to the supreme authority of the Scriptures, and their shared concern to set forth a biblical basis for theological knowledge and judgment, no attempt has been made to exclude or minimize diversity of interpretation within these boundary marks.

The production of a volume like this would never have been possible without the contributions of many individuals over many months. Special mention must be made of Richard Bauckham, who helped in the planning stages, and of the successive theological editors of IVP, David Preston, Claire Evans and David Kingdon. The last-named has borne the heat and burden of the main part of the day. Their reward, and ours, in part will be the knowledge that this *Dictionary* fulfils its purpose – to promote an informed and biblically controlled approach to thinking and speaking about God and his works.

Sinclair B. Ferguson
David F. Wright

How to use this Dictionary

This introduction provides some guidance as to how this *Dictionary* can be used to the best advantage.

Cross-references

It has been editorial policy in this *Dictionary* to group smaller topics together and treat them in a single longer article. For example, **BIOETHICS** includes contraception, genetic engineering and euthanasia – but not **ABORTION**, which has merited an independent article; the various Reformation and post-Reformation 'Confessions of Faith' are similarly collected under **CONFESSIONS OF FAITH**, and many matters are subsumed under **EUCHARIST**. Cross-referencing is therefore important. Four methods are in use:

1. Numerous one-line entries refer the user to the title of the article or articles where the topic is treated: *e.g.*

    MASCALL, ERIC, see Anglo-Catholic Theology.

    COMMON GRACE, see Grace.

2. An asterisk after a word or a phrase indicates that further relevant information will be found in the article under that title. It is equivalent to the abbreviation *q.v.* Readers should note:

    a. The *form* of the word asterisked will not always be precisely the same as that of the title of the article to which the asterisk refers. For example, 'Trinitarianism*' directs the reader to the article on **TRINITY**, 'kenotic*' to **KENOTICISM** and 'mysticism*' to **MYSTICAL THEOLOGY**.

    b. The asterisk sometimes applies to two or three words rather than to the word asterisked. Thus 'covenant theology*' sends you to the article **COVENANT THEOLOGY** and 'Thomas Aquinas*' to the entry **THOMAS AQUINAS**, not 'Aquinas'.

3. A reference in brackets in the body of an article such as '(see Angels*)' or '(*cf.* Oecolampadius*)' speaks for itself.

4. A cross-reference at the end of an article is also self-explanatory: *e.g.*

    See also: Anabaptist Theology.

Abbreviations

A list of abbreviations used in the *Dictionary* will be found on pp. x–xiii.

Authorship of articles

The authors (in a few cases, co-authors) of articles are indicated by their initials at the foot of each article. A full list of authors will be found on pp. xiv–xix, in alphabetical order of initials, not of surnames.

Bibliographies

Guidance for further study has been provided for virtually every article, sometimes in the body of the article itself, but in most cases at the end. Writings by the subject of the article are placed first. The works listed in a Bibliography may include studies which take up a different position from that of the contributor of the article.

Bible versions

Quotations from the Bible are from the New International Version, unless specified otherwise.

Transliteration

The following systems have been adopted throughout the volume:

Hebrew

א	= ʾ	ד	= ḏ	י	= y	ס	= s	ר	= r
ב	= b	ה	= h	כ	= k	ע	= ʿ	שׂ	= ś
ב	= ḇ	ו	= w	כ	= ḵ	פ	= p	שׁ	= š
ג	= g	ז	= z	ל	= l	פ	= p̄	ת	= t
ג	= ḡ	ח	= ḥ	מ	= m	צ	= ṣ	ת	= ṯ
ד	= d	ט	= ṭ	נ	= n	ק	= q		

Long Vowels			Short Vowels	Very Short Vowels
(ה)ָ = â	ָ = ā		ַ = a	ֲ = ᵃ
ֵ = ê	ֶ = ē		ֶ = e	ֱ = ᵉ
ִ = î			ִ = i	ְ = ᵉ (if vocal)
וֹ = ô	ֹ = ō		ָ = o	ֳ = ᵒ
וּ = û			ֻ = u		

Greek

α	= a	ι	= i	ρ	= r	ῥ	= rh
β	= b	κ	= k	σ, ς	= s	ʽ	= h
γ	= g	λ	= l	τ	= t	γξ	= nx
δ	= d	μ	= m	υ	= y	γγ	= ng
ε	= e	ν	= n	φ	= ph	αυ	= au
ζ	= z	ξ	= x	χ	= ch	ευ	= eu
η	= ē	ο	= o	ψ	= ps	ου	= ou
θ	= th	π	= p	ω	= ō	υι	= yi

Arabic

١	= ʾ	خ	= ḫ	ش	= š	غ	= ġ	ن	= n
ب	= b	د	= d	ص	= ṣ	ف	= f	ه	= h
ت	= t	ذ	= ḏ	ض	= ḍ	ق	= ḳ	و	= w
ث	= t	ر	= r	ط	= ṭ	ك	= k	ى	= y
ج	= ǧ	ز	= z	ظ	= ẓ	ل	= l	ة	= t
ح	= ḥ	س	= s	ع	= ʿ	م	= m		

Abbreviations

1. Books and journals

ACW
Ancient Christian Writers
(Westminster, MD, and
London, *etc.*, 1946–)

ANCL
*Ante-Nicene Christian
Library*, 25 vols. (Edinburgh,
1866–97)

ANF
Ante-Nicene Fathers (re-
edition of of *ANCL* in 10
vols., Buffalo and New York,
1885–96, and Grand Rapids,
MI, 1950–51)

AV(KJV)
Authorized Version (King
James'), 1611

BJRL
*Bulletin of the John Rylands
Library* (Manchester,
1903–)

BS
Bibliotheca Sacra (New York,
etc., 1843–)

BTB
Biblical Theology Bulletin
(Rome, 1971–)

CBQ
Catholic Biblical Quarterly
(Washington, DC, 1939–)

CC
Christianity and Civilization
(Tyler, TX, 1982–)

CCCM
*Corpus Christianorum,
Continuatio Medievalis*
(Turnhout, 1966–)

CCG
*Corpus Christianorum, Series
Graeca* (Turnhout, 1977–)

CCL
*Corpus Christianorum, Series
Latina* (Turnhout, 1935–)

CD
Church Dogmatics, Karl
Barth, 4 vols. in 13 + index
vol. (ET, Edinburgh,
1936–81)

CG
Christian Graduate (London,
etc., 1948–83)

CH
Church History (Scottdale,
PA, *etc.*, 1932–)

CHLGEMP
*Cambridge History of Later
Greek and Early Medieval
Philosophy*, ed. A. H.
Armstrong (Cambridge,
1967)

CPG
Clavis Patrum Graecorum, ed.
M. Geerard (Turnhout,
1983–)

CPL
Clavis Patrum Latinorum, ed.
E. Dekkers and A. Gaar
(Turnhout, ²1961)

CT
Christianity Today
(Washington, 1956–)

CTJ
Calvin Theological Journal
(Grand Rapids, MI, 1966–)

DBS
*Dictionnaire de la Bible,
Supplement*, ed. L. Pirot *et al.*
Paris, 1928–)

DCB
*Dictionary of Christian
Biography*, ed. W. Smith and
H. Wace, 4 vols. (London,
1877–87)

DNB
*Dictionary of National
Biography*, ed. L. Stephen and
S. Lee *et al.* (London, 1885–)

DSp
Dictionnaire de Spiritualité,
ed. M. Viller *et al.* (Paris,
1937–)

DTC
*Dictionnaire de théologie
catholique*, ed. A. Vacant *et al.*,
15 vols. (Paris, 1903–50)

EBT
*Encyclopaedia of Biblical
Theology*, ed. J. B. Bauer, 3
vols., (³1967; ET, London,
1970)

EC
Encyclopedia of Christianity,
vols. 1–4 (no more
published), eds. E. H. Palmer,
G. G. Cohen and P. E.
Hughes (Wilmington, DL, and
Marshalton, DL, 1964–72)

EP
Encyclopedia of Philosophy,
ed. P. Edwards, 8 vols. (New
York, 1967)

EQ
Evangelical Quarterly
(London, *etc.*, 1929–)

ERE
*Encyclopaedia of Religion and
Ethics*, ed. J. Hastings,
13 vols. (Edinburgh,
1908–26)

ExpT
Expository Times (Aberdeen,
etc., 1889–)

FC
Fathers of the Church (New
York, *etc.*, 1947–)

FP
Faith and Philosophy
(Wilmore, KY, 1984–)

HBT
Horizons in Biblical Theology
(Pittsburgh, PA, 1979–)

HDB
Dictionary of the Bible, ed. J.
Hastings, 5 vols. (Edinburgh,
1898–1904)

HR
History of Religions (Chicago,
1961–)

HTR
Harvard Theological Review
(New York, *etc.*, 1908–)

IBD
*The Illustrated Bible
Dictionary*, ed. J. D. Douglas
et al., 3 vols. (Leicester, 1980)

ICC
*International Critical
Commentary* (London, *etc.*,
1895–)

IDB
*The Interpreter's Dictionary
of the Bible*, ed. G. A. Buttrick
et al., 4 vols. (New York and
Nashville, TN, 1962)

IDBS
IDB, Supplement, 1976

IJT
Indian Journal of Theology
(Serampore, *etc.*, 1952–)

Int
Interpretation (Richmond,
VA, 1947–)

IRB
*International Reformed
Bulletin* (London, 1958–)

ISBE
*International Standard Bible
Encyclopaedia*, ed. J. Orr, 5
vols. (Chicago, ²1930), new
edition, ed. G. W. Bromiley
(Grand Rapids, MI, 1979–)

JAAR
*Journal of the American
Academy of Religion*
(Chambersburg, PA, 1967–)

JBL
Journal of Biblical Literature
(Boston, *etc.*, 1881–)

JEH
*Journal of Ecclesiastical
History* (London, 1950–)

JETS
*Journal of the Evangelical
Theological Society* (Wheaton,
IL, 1969–)

JNES
*Journal of Near Eastern
Studies* (Chicago, 1942–)

JR
Journal of Religion (Chicago,
1921–)

JSOT
*Journal for the Study of the
Old Testament* (Sheffield,
1976–)

JSSR
*Journal of the Scientific Study
of Religion* (Wetteren, *etc.*,
1961–)

JTS
Journal of Theological Studies
(Oxford, 1899–)

JTSA
*Journal of Theology for
Southern Africa*
(Braamfontein, 1972–)

LCC
Library of Christian Classics,
26 vols. (London and
Philadelphia, 1953–70)

LCL
Loeb Classical Library
(London and Cambridge,
MA, 1912–)

LW
Luther's Works ('American
edition'), ed. J. Pelikan and
H. T. Lehmann (Philadelphia
and St Louis, MO, 1955–)

MC
Modern Churchman (London,
1911–)

MQR
Mennonite Quarterly Review
(Goshen, IN, 1927–)

NBD
New Bible Dictionary, ed. J.
D. Douglas *et al.* (Leicester,
²1982)

NCE
New Catholic Encyclopedia,
ed. W. J. McDonald, 17 vols.
(New York, 1967–79)

NIDNTT
*The New International
Dictionary of New Testament
Theology*, ed. C. Brown, 3
vols. (Exeter, 1975–8)

NovT
Novum Testamentum
(Leiden, 1956–)

NPNF
*A Select Library of Nicene and
Post-Nicene Fathers of the
Christian Church*, First Series,
ed. P. Schaff, 14 vols. (New
York, 1886–90); Second
Series, ed. H. Wace and P.
Schaff, 14 vols. (New York,
1890–1900); new edition
(Grand Rapids, MI, 1980)

NRT
Nouvelle revue théologique
(Tournai, *etc.*, 1879–)

NTS
New Testament Studies
(Cambridge, 1954–)

ODCC
*The Oxford Dictionary of the
Christian Church*, ed. F. L.
Cross and E. A. Livingstone
(Oxford, ²1974)

PG
Patrologia Graeca, ed. J. P.
Migne, 162 vols. (Paris, 1857–66)

PL
Patrologia Latina, ed. J. P.
Migne, 221 vols. (Paris,
1844–64)

PTR
Princeton Theological Review
(Philadelphia, 1903–29)

RAV
Revised Authorized Version,
1982, = New King James'
Version, anglicized 1987.

RB
Revue Biblique (Paris, 1892–)

RBén
Revue Bénédictine
(Maredsous, 1884–)

RGG
*Die Religion in Geschichte
und Gegenwart*, ed. K. Galling,
7 vols. (Tübingen, ³1957–65)

RJ
Reformed Journal (Grand
Rapids, MI, 1951–)

RR
The Reformed Review
(Holland, MI, 1947–)

RSV
Revised Standard Version:
NT, 1946; OT, 1952;
Common Bible, 1973

SBT
Studies in Biblical Theology
(London, 1958–76)

SCJ
Sixteenth Century Journal
(Kirksville, MO, 1970–)

SJT
Scottish Journal of Theology
(Edinburgh, *etc.*, 1948–)

SL
Studia Liturgica (Rotterdam,
1962–)

SM
Sacramentum Mundi, ed. K.
Rahner *et al.*, 5 vols. (New
York, 1968–70)

SP
Studia Patristica (Berlin, *etc.*,
1957–)

TDNT
*Theological Dictionary of the
New Testament*, ed. G. W.
Bromiley, 10 vols. (Grand
Rapids, MI, 1964–76), ET of
*Theologisches Worterbuch
zum Neuen Testament*, ed. G.
Kittell and G. Friedrich
(Stuttgart, 1932–74)

Th
Theology (London, 1920–)

Them
Themelios (Lausanne,
1962–74; new series,
London, *etc.*, 1975–)

Tr
Transformation (Exeter,
1984–)

TRE
*Theologische
Realenzyklopädie*, ed. G.
Krause *et al.* (Berlin, NY,
1977–)

TS
Theological Studies
(Woodstock, MD, 1940–)

TSFB
*Theological Students'
Fellowship Bulletin* (London,
1951–75)

TU
*Texte und Untersuchungen
zur Geschichte der
altchristlichen Literatur*
(Leipzig, *etc.*, 1882–)

TynB
Tyndale Bulletin (London,
etc., 1956–)

VC
Vigiliae Christianae
(Amsterdam, 1947–)

VT
Vetus Testamentum (Leiden,
1951–)

USQR
*Union Seminary Quarterly
Review* (New York, 1945–)

WTJ
*Westminster Theological
Journal* (Philadelphia,
1938–)

ZAW
*Zeitschrift für die
alttestamentliche Wissenschaft*
(Geissen, *etc.*, 1881–)

ZKG
*Zeitschrift für
Kirchengeschichte* (Gotha,
etc., 1877–)

ZTK
*Zeitschrift für Theologie und
Kirche* (Tübingen, 1891–)

Editions are indicated by small
superior figures: [2]1982.

2. Early Christian works

EH
Eusebius, *Ecclesiastical
History*

Ep.
Polycarp, *Epistles to the
Philippians*

Eph.
Ignatius, *Ephesians*

Strom.
Clement of Alexandria,
Stromateis

Trall.
Ignatius, *Trallians*

3. Biblical books

Books of the Old Testament
Gn., Ex., Lv., Nu., Dt., Jos.,
Jdg., Ru., 1, 2, Sa., 1, 2 Ki.,
1, 2 Ch., Ezr., Ne., Est., Jb.,
Ps. (Pss.), Pr., Ec., Song, Is.,
Je., La., Ezk., Dn., Ho., Joel,
Am., Ob., Jon., Mi., Na.,
Hab., Zp., Hg., Zc., Mal.

Books of the New Testament
Mt., Mk., Lk., Jn., Acts,
Rom., 1, 2 Cor., Gal., Eph.,
Phil., Col., 1, 2 Thes., 1, 2
Tim., Tit., Phm., Heb., Jas.,
1, 2 Pet., 1, 2, 3 Jn., Jude, Rev.

4. General abbreviations

ad loc.	*ad locum* (Lat.), at the place	Lat.	Latin
b.	born	lit.	literally
c.	*circa.* (Lat.), about, approximately	*loc. cit.*	*loco citato* (Lat.), in the place already quoted
cf.	*confer* (Lat.), compare	LXX	Septuagint (Gk. version of OT)
ch. (chs.)	chapter(s)		
col. (cols.)	column(s)	Macc.	Maccabees (Apocrypha)
d.	died	mg.	margin
Ecclus.	Ecclesiasticus (Apocrypha)	MS (MSS)	manuscript(s)
ed. (eds.)	edited by, edition, editor(s)	n.d.	no date
Eng.	English	n.s.	new series
ET	English translation	NT	New Testament
et al.	*et alii* (Lat.), and others	*op. cit.*	*opere citato* (Lat.), in the work cited above
EVV	English versions		
f. (ff.)	and the following (verse(s), etc.)	OT	Old Testament
		par.	and parallel(s)
fl.	*floruit* (Lat.), flourished	repr.	reprinted
Ger.	German	tr.	translated, translation
Gk.	Greek	v. (vv.)	verse(s)
Heb.	Hebrew	*viz.*	*videlicit* (Lat.), namely
ibid.	*ibidem* (Lat.), the same work	vol. (vols.)	volume(s)
idem	*idem* (Lat.), the same author	vss	versions

List of contributors

A.A.H. A. A. Hoekema, A.B., A.M., B.D., Th.D., Emeritus Professor of Systematic Theology, Calvin Theological Seminary, Grand Rapids.

A.C.T. A. C. Thiselton, B.D., M.Th., Ph.D., Principal, St John's College, University of Durham.

A.D. A. Dallimore, B.Th., D.D., formerly Pastor, Cottam Baptist Church, Ontario.

A.F.H. A. F. Holmes, B.A., M.A., Ph.D., Professor of Philosophy, Wheaton College, Illinois.

A.N.S.L. A. N. S. Lane, M.A., B.D., Lecturer in Christian Doctrine, London Bible College.

A.S.W. A. S. Wood, B.A., Ph.D., F.R.Hist.S., formerly Principal, Cliff College, Calver, Derbyshire.

A.T.B.McG. A. T. B. McGowan, B.D., S.T.M., Minister of Causewayend Church, Aberdeen.

A.V. A. Vos, A.B., M.A., Ph.D., Professor of Philosophy, Western Kentucky University.

B.D. B. Demarest, B.Sc., M.Sc., M.A., Ph.D., Professor of Systematic Theology, Denver Seminary, Colorado.

B.E.F. B. E. Foster, M.A., M.Div., Ph.D., Pastor of Calvary Lutheran Church, Lemmon, South Dakota.

B.J.N. B. J. Nicholls, M.A., B.D., M.Th., D.D., Presbyter, St John's Church, Mehrauli, and the Church of the Epiphany, Gurgaon, Delhi.

B.K. B. Kristensen, B.A., M.A., Lecturer, College for Social Work, Ede, The Netherlands.

B.R.R. Bong Rin Ro, B.A., B.D., S.T.M., Th.D., Dean of Asia Graduate School of Theology, Taichung, Taiwan

C.A.B. C. A. Baxter, B.A., Ph.D., Lecturer, St John's College, Nottingham.

C.A.R. C. A. Russell, Ph.D., D.Sc., C.Chem., F.R.S.C., Professor of History of Science and Technology, The Open University, Milton Keynes.

C.B. C. Brown, M.A., B.D., PhD., Professor of Systematic Theology, Fuller Theological Seminary, Pasadena, California.

C.D.H. C. D. Hancock, M.A., B.A., Ph.D., Chaplain, Magdalene College, Cambridge.

C.E.A. C. E. Armerding, A.B., B.D., M.A., Ph.D., Principal, Professor of Old Testament, Regent College, Vancouver.

C.H.P. C. H. Pinnock, B.A., Ph.D., Professor of Christian Interpretation, McMaster Divinity College, Hamilton, Ontario.

C.M.C. C. M. Cameron, B.A., B.D., Ph.D., Minister of St Ninian's Parish Church, Dunfermline.

C.M.N.S. C. M. N. Sugden, M.A., M.Phil., Registrar, Oxford Centre for Mission Studies.

C.O.B. C. O. Buchanan, M.A., formerly Principal of St John's College, Nottingham; (Suffragan) Bishop of Aston, Birmingham.

C.P.D. C. P. Duriez, B.A., General Books Editor, Inter-Varsity Press, Leicester.

C.P.W. C. P. Williams, M.A., B.D., M.Litt., Ph.D., Vice-Principal, Trinity College, Bristol.

C.S. C. Seerveld, Ph.D., Senior Member in Philosophical Aesthetics, Institute for Christian Studies, Toronto.

C.W. C. Wigglesworth, B.Sc., Ph.D., B.D., M.B.E., formerly Lecturer in Practical Theology, Aberdeen University; General Secretary of the Board of World Mission and Unity, The Church of Scotland, Edinburgh.

D.A.Ha. D. A. Hagner, B.A., B.D., Th.M., Ph.D., Professor of New Testament, Fuller Theological Seminary, Pasadena, California.

D.A.Hu. D. A. Hughes, B.A., B.D., Ph.D., Regional Coordinator, Tear Fund, Wales; formerly Senior Lecturer in Religious Studies, Polytechnic of Wales.

D.C.D. D. C. Davis, B.A., M.A., B.D., D.Theol., Professor of Church History, Westminster Theological Seminary, Philadelphia.

D.C.T.S. D. C. T. Sheriffs, B.A., B.D., M.A., D.Litt., Lecturer in Old Testament, London Bible College.

D.D.S. D. D. Sceats, M.A., Rector of Colton, Staffordshire; formerly lecturer in Church History and Historical Theology, Trinity College, Bristol.

D.F.K. D. F. Kelly, B.A., B.D., Ph.D., Associate Professor of Theology, Reformed Theological Seminary, Jackson, Mississippi.

D.F.W. D. F. Wright, M.A., Senior Lecturer in Ecclesiastical History, New College, University of Edinburgh.

D.Ga. D. Garlington, B.A., M. Div., Th.M., Ph.D., Lecturer in Biblical Studies, Toronto Baptist Seminary.

D.Gu. D. Guthrie, B.D., M.Th., Ph.D., formerly Vice-Principal, London Bible College.

D.G.D. D. G. Deboys, B.D., M.Litt., Librarian, Tyndale House, Cambridge.

D.G.J. D. G. Jones, B.Sc., M.B.B.S., D.Sc., Professor of Anatomy, University of Otago, Dunedin.

D.G.P. D. G. Preston, M.A., Ph.D., formerly Senior Lecturer in French, Ahmadu Bello University, Zaria, Nigeria.

D.H.F. D. H. Field, B.A., Vice-Principal, Oak Hill College, London.

D.J.T. D. J. Tidball, B.A., B.D., Ph.D., Minister of Mutley Baptist Church, Plymouth, England; formerly Director of Studies, London Bible College.

D.K.C. D. K. Clark, B.A., M.A., Ph.D., Associate Professor in Theology and Philosophy, Toccoa Falls College, Georgia.

D.L. D. Lyon, B.Sc., Ph.D., Senior Lecturer in Social Analysis, Bradford and Ilkley College, West Yorkshire, and visiting research fellow, Leeds University.

D.L.B. D. L. Baker, B.A., Ph.D., Lecturer in Biblical Studies, HKBP Theological Seminary, Pematang Siantar, Indonesia.

D.L.W. D. L. Williams, B.A., Post-graduate student, St John's College, Cambridge.

D.M. D. Macleod, M.A., Professor of Systematic

Theology, Free Church College, Edinburgh.

D.M.MacK. The late D. M. MacKay, B.Sc., Ph.D., F.Inst.P., formerly Professor of Communication, University of Keele.

D.P.K. D. P. Kingdon, M.A., B.D., Theological Books Editor, Inter-Varsity Press, Leicester; formerly Principal, The Irish Baptist College, Belfast.

D.W.A. D. W. Amundsen, B.A., M.A., Ph.D., Professor of Classics, Western Washington University.

D.W.Be. D. W. Bebbington, M.A., Ph.D., Lecturer in History, University of Stirling.

D.W.Br. D. W. Brown, A.M., B.D., Ph.D., Professor, Christian Theology, Bethany Theological Seminary, Oak Brook, Illinois.

D.W.C. D. W. Clowney, B.A., M.A., B.D., Assistant Professor of Apologetics, Westminster Theological Seminary, Philadelphia.

E.D.C. E. D. Cook, B.A., M.A., Ph.D., M.A., Fellow, Green College, Oxford; Director of the Whitefield Institute, Oxford.

E.E. E. Evans, B.D., Ph.D., Presbyterian Minister, Merthyr Tydfil.

E.E.E. E. E. Ellis, B.Sc., M.A., B.D., Ph.D., D.D., Professor of New Testament, Southwestern Baptist Theological Seminary, Fort Worth, Texas.

E.F. E. Ferguson, B.A., M.A., S.T.B., Ph.D., Professor, Abilene Christian University, Texas.

E.M.Y. E. M. Yamauchi, B.A., M.A., Ph.D., Professor of History, Miami University, Oxford, Ohio.

E.P.C. E. P. Clowney, B.A., Th.B., S.T.M., D.D., Professor of Practical Theology, Emeritus, and former President, Westminster Theological Seminary, Philadelphia; Associate Pastor, Trinity Presbyterian Church, Charlottesville, Virginia.

F.F.B. F. F. Bruce, M.A., D.D., F.B.A., Emeritus Rylands Professor of Biblical Criticism and Exegesis, University of Manchester.

F.L. F. Lyall, M.A., LL.B., LL.M., Ph.D., Professor of Public Law, University of Aberdeen.

F.P.C. F. P. Cotterell, B.D., B.Sc., Ph.D., Fellow of the Institute of Linguists, Director of Overseas Studies, London Bible College.

G.A.K. G. A. Keith, M.A., D. Phil., School teacher, Ayr.

G.D.D. G. D. Dragas, B.D., Th.M., Ph.D., Senior Lecturer in Patristics, University of Durham.

G.G.S. G. G. Scorgie, B.Th., M.A., Ph.D., M.C.S., Assistant Professor of Theology, Canadian Bible College, Regina.

G.H.T. G. H. Twelftree, B.A., M.A., Ph.D., Minister of the Uniting Church in Australia, Adelaide.

G.L.B. G. L. Bray, B.D., M.Litt., D.Litt., Lecturer in Christian Doctrine, Oak Hill College, London.

G.M. G. Maier, Dr. Theol., Rektor, Albrecht Bengel Haus, Tübingen.

G.M.M. G. M. Marsden, B.A., B.D., M.A., Ph.D., Professor of the History of Christianity in America, The Divinity School, Duke University, Durham, North Carolina.

G.M.R. G. M. Rosell, B.A., M.Div., Th.M., Ph.D., Vice-President for Academic Affairs, Dean of the Seminary and Professor of History, Gordon-Conwell Theological Seminary, South Hamilton, Massachusetts.

G.R.B.-M. G. R. Beasley-Murray, M.A., Ph.D., D.D., formerly James Buchanan Harrison Professor of New Testament Interpretation, Southern Baptist Theological Seminary, Louisville, Kentucky.

G.W.B. G. W. Bromiley, M.A., Ph.D., D.Litt., D.D., Emeritus Senior Professor of

Church History and Historical Theology, Fuller Theological Seminary, Pasadena, California.

G.W.K. G. W. Kirby, M.A., formerly Principal, London Bible College.

G.W.M. G. W. Martin, M.A., B.D., B.A., Ph.D., Principal, Scottish Baptist College, Glasgow.

H.B. H. Burkhardt, Lecturer in Systematic Theology at St Chrischona Theological Seminary, Basel, Switzerland.

H.D.McD. H. D. McDonald, B.A., B.D., Ph.D., D.D., formerly Vice-Principal, London Bible College, and Senior Lecturer in Philosophy of Religion and Historical Theology.

H.H. H. Harris, B.A., Dip.Mus., B.D., D.Theol., Christian scholar, Teversham, Cambridge.

H.H.D. H. H. Davis, B.A., Ph.D., Lecturer in Sociology, University of Kent.

H.H.R. H. H. Rowdon, B.A., Ph.D., Senior Lecturer in Church History, London Bible College.

H.J.L. H. J. Loewen, Ph.D., M.Div., B.A., B.Th., Associate Professor of Theology and Chairman of the Division of Theological and Historical Studies, Mennonite Brethren Biblical Seminary, Fresno, California.

H.M.C. H. M. Conn, B.A., B.D., Th.D., Litt.D., Professor of Missions, Westminster Theological Seminary, Philadelphia.

H.O.J.B. H. O. J. Brown, B.A., S.T.B., S.T.M., Ph.D., Forman Professor of Theology and Ethics, Trinity Evangelical Divinity School, Deerfield, Illinois.

H.W.S. H. W. Smart, B.Sc., Ph.D., Freelance writer, Montrose, Scotland.

I.B. I. Breward, M.A., B.D., Ph.D., Professor of Church History, Ormond College, Parkville, Victoria, Australia.

I.D.B. I. D. Bunting, M.A., Th.M., Kingham Hill Fellow, Oak Hill College, London.

I.Ha. I. Hamilton, B.A., B.D., M. Phil., Minister of Loudoun Church of Scotland, Ayrshire.

I.He. I. Hexham, B.A., M.A., Ph.D., Assistant Professor, Department of Religious Studies, University of Calgary, Alberta.

I.H.Ma. I. H. Marshall, M.A., B.D., B.A., Ph.D., Professor of New Testament Exegesis, University of Aberdeen.

I.H.Mu. I. H. Murray, B.A., General Editor, Banner of Truth Trust, Edinburgh.

I.McP. I. McPhee, B.A., M.A., Ph.D., Editor, Trinity Press, Ontario.

I.S. I. Sellers, M.A., M.Litt., Ph.D., Senior Lecturer, North Cheshire College, Warrington.

I.S.R. I. S. Rennie, B.A., M.A., Ph.D., Dean and Professor of Church History, Ontario Theological Seminary.

J.A. J. Atkinson, M.A., M. Litt., Dr.Theol., Canon Theologian of Sheffield Cathedral.

J.A.E.V. J. A. E. Vermaat, Drs. (Leiden), Writer and journalist.

J.A.K. J. A. Kirk, B.D., B.A., M. Phil., A.K.C., Associate Director of the London Institute for Contemporary Christianity and Theologian Missioner of the Church Missionary Society.

J.A.P. J. A. Punshon, M.A., Quaker Studies Tutor, Woodbrooke College, Selly Oak, Birmingham.

J.B. J. Barrs, B.A., M.Div., Tutor, L'Abri Fellowship, Liss, Hampshire.

J.B.R. J. B. Root, B.A., M.A., Vicar of St James' Church, Alperton, Middlesex.

J.B.Wa. J. B. Walker, M.A., B.D., D.Phil., Principal, Queen's College, Birmingham.

J.B.We. J. B. Webster, M.A., Ph.D., Professor of Systematic Theology, Wycliffe College, Toronto.

J.D.De. J. D. Dengerink, LL.D., formerly Professor of

Christian Philosophy at the Universities of Groningen and Utrecht, The Netherlands.

J.D.Do. J. D. Douglas, M.A., B.D., S.T.M. Ph.D., Editor and writer.

J.E.C. J. E. Colwell, B.D., Ph.D., Minister of King's Church, Catford, London.

J.G. J. Goldingay, B.A., Ph.D., Vice-Principal and Lecturer in Old Testament, St John's College, Nottingham.

J.G.McC. J. G. McConville, M.A., B.D., Ph.D., Lecturer in Old Testament and Hebrew, Trinity College, Bristol.

J.H.E. J. H. Elias, B.Sc., B.D., Senior Lecturer in Religious Studies, Polytechnic of Wales.

J.H.G. J. H. Gerstner, B.A., M.Div., Th.M., Ph.D., D.D., L.H.D., Professor Emeritus, Pittsburgh Theological Seminary, Pennsylvania.

J.I.P. J. I. Packer, M.A., D. Phil., Professor of Historical and Systematic Theology, Regent College, Vancouver.

J.I.Y. J. Isamu Yahamoto, B.A., M.A., Managing Editor of Public Management Institute, San Pablo, California.

J.M.F. J. M. Frame, A.B., B.D., M.Phil., Associate Professor of Apologetics and Systematic Theology, Westminster Theological Seminary, California.

J.N.D.A. J. N. D. Anderson, O.B.E., M.A., LL.D. (hon.), D.D., Q.C., F.B.A., formerly Professor of Oriental Laws and Director of the Institute of Advanced Legal Studies in the University of London.

J.N.I. J. N. Isbister, M.A., Ph.D., Director of Training, Enterprise Counselling Services Ltd., Oxford.

J.P. J. Philip, M.A., Minister of Holyrood Abbey Church of Scotland, Edinburgh.

J.P.B. J. P. Baker, M.A., B.D., Rector of Newick, Lewes, East Sussex.

J.S.W. The late J. Stafford Wright, formerly Principal, Tyndale Hall, Bristol; Canon of Bristol Cathedral.

J.T. J. Tiller, M.A., B.Litt., Chancellor and Canon-Residentiary, Hereford Cathedral.

J.W. J. Wilkinson, B.D., M.D., F.R.C.P., M.F.C.M., D.T.M.&H., Community Medicine Specialist, Lothian Health Board, Edinburgh.

J.W.C. J. W. Charley, M.A., Vicar, Great Malvern St Mary, Worcestershire.

J.W.G. J. W. Gladwin, B.A., General Secretary to the General Synod of the Church of England's Board for Social Responsibility, London.

J.W.W. J. W. Ward, B.D., B.Sc., M.Sc., Director of Studies, Elim Bible College, Nantwich, Cheshire.

J.Y.A. J. Y. Amanu, B.A., Th.M., Research Associate, Dallas Theological Seminary, Dallas, Texas.

K.Be. K. Bediako, B.A., M-ès-L., Doct.3ᵉ cycle, Ph.D., Director, Akrofi-Christaller Memorial Centre for Mission Research and Applied Theology, Accra, Ghana.

K.Bo. K. Bockmuehl, Dr. Theol., Professor of Theology and Ethics, Regent College, Vancouver.

K.G.H. K. G. Howkins, M.A., B.D., Senior Lecturer in Religious Studies, Hertfordshire College of Higher Education.

K.R. K. Runia, B.D., M.Th., Th.D., Professor of Practical Theology, Reformed Seminary, Kampen, The Netherlands.

L.L.M. L. L. Morris, Ph.D., M.Th., M.Sc., formerly Principal, Ridley College, Melbourne, Australia.

L.P.Z. L. P. Zuidervaart, B.A., M.Phil., Ph.D., Associate Professor of Philosophy, Calvin College, Grand Rapids, Michigan.

M.A.J. M. A. Jeeves, M.A., Ph.D., F.B.Ps.S., F.R.S.E., Vice-Principal of the University of St Andrews and Professor of Psychology.

M.A.N. M. A. Noll, B.A., M.A., Ph.D., Professor of History, Wheaton College, Illinois.

M.C.G. M. C. Griffiths, M.A., D.D., Principal, London Bible College.

M.D. M. Dowling, B.A., B.D., M.Th., Ph.D., Lecturer in Church History and Historical Theology, Irish Baptist College, Belfast.

M.D.G. M. D. Geldard, M.A., Vicar of St John the Divine, Liverpool.

M.F.G. M. F. Goldsmith, M.A., Lecturer at All Nations Christian College, Ware.

M.G.B. M. G. Barker, M.B., Ch.B., F.R.C.P.Ed., F.R.C.Psych., D.P.M. Consultant Psychiatrist, Bristol and Weston Health Authority.

M.J.H. M. J. Harris, M.A., Dip.Ed., B.D., Ph.D., Professor of New Testament Exegesis and Theology, Trinity Evangelical Divinity School, Deerfield, Illinois.

M.J.N.-A. M. J. Nazir-Ali, formerly Bishop of Lahore; Director in Residence, Oxford Centre for Mission Studies; Theological Consultant to the Archbishop of Canterbury.

N.J. N. Jason, B.A., B.D., M.A., Ph.D., Pastor of Christ Church (Church of South India), Madras, India.

N.J.S. N. J. Smith, B.A., B.D., D.D., Part-time Lecturer in Missiology at the University of South Africa, Pretoria; minister of the Dutch Reformed Church in Africa, Mamelodi, Pretoria; formerly Professor in Missiology at the Theological Seminary, University of Stellenbosch, South Africa.

N.L.G. N. L. Geisler, B.A., M.A., Th.B., Ph.D., Professor of Systematic Theology, Dallas Theological Seminary, Dallas, Texas.

N.M.deS.C. N. M. de S. Cameron, M.A., B.D., Ph.D., Warden of Rutherford House, Edinburgh.

N.P.F. N. P. Feldmeth, AB., Th.M., Ph.D., Adjunct Assistant Professor of Church History, Fuller Theological Seminary, California.

N.R.N. N. R. Needham, B.D., Librarian, Rutherford House, Edinburgh.

N.S. N. Sagovsky, B.A., Ph.D., Dean of Clare College, Cambridge.

N.T.W. N. T. Wright, M.A., D.Phil., Lecturer in New Testament Studies, Oxford University; Chaplain and Tutor in Theology, Worcester College, Oxford.

N.Y. N. Yri, B.D., M.Th., Dr.Theol., Professor of New Testament Studies, Lutheran Theological College, Tanzania.

O.M.T.O'D. O. M. T. O'Donovan, M.A., D.Phil., Regius Professor of Moral and Pastoral Theology, University of Oxford; Canon of Christ Church.

O.R.B. O. R. Barclay, M.A., Ph.D., formerly General Secretary of the Universities and Colleges Christian Fellowship, Leicester.

P.A.L. P. A. Lillback, B.A., Th.M., Ph.D., Pastor of Bethany Orthodox Presbyterian Church, Oxford, Pennsylvania.

P.D.L.A. P. D. L. Avis, B.D., Ph.D., Vicar of Stoke Canon, Exeter.

P.D.M. P. D. Manson, B.Sc., B.D., Tutor in Pastoral Studies, Spurgeon's College, London.

P.E. P. Ellingworth, M.A., B.A., Ph.D., Translation Consultant, United Bible Societies, Aberdeen.

P.F.J. P. F. Jensen, M.A., B.D., D.Phil., Principal of Moore College, Sydney, Australia.

P.H. P. Helm, M.A., Reader in Philosophy, University of Liverpool.

P.H.L. P. H. Lewis, Minister of Cornerstone Evangelical Church, Nottingham.

P.J.A.C. P. J. A. Cook, B.A., M.A., Ph.D., Chaplain and Senior Lecturer in Religious Studies, Stranmillis College of Education, Belfast.

P.M.B. P. M. Bechtel, M.A., Ph.D., Emeritus Professor of English, Wheaton College, Illinois.

P.M.J.McN. P. M. J. McNair, M.A., D.Phil., Ph.D., Serena Professor and Head of the Department of Italian, University of Birmingham.

P.M.K. P. M. Krishna, B.A., LL.B., M.Litt., Ph.D., Dip. in Indian Philosophy and Religions, formerly Professor of Oriental Studies, University of Durban, Westville, South Africa.

P.M.W. P. M. Walters, M.A., Ph.D., Research Director, Keston College.

P.N.H. P. N. Hillyer, B.D., Ph.D., formerly Lecturer in Theology, Bishop's College, Calcutta.

P.P.J.B. P. P. J. Beyerhaus, D.Th., Director of the Institute of the Discipline of Missions and Ecumenical Theology, Tübingen University.

P.R.F. P. R. Forster, M.A., B.D., Ph.D., Senior Tutor, St John's College, Durham.

P.T. P. Toon, M.A., M.Th., D.Phil., Director of Post-Ordination Training, Diocese of St Edmundsbury and Ipswich.

R.B. R. Brown, M.A., B.D., M.Th., Ph.D., Minister of Victoria Drive Baptist Church, Eastbourne; formerly Principal, Spurgeon's College, London.

R.B.G. R. B. Gaffin Jr., A.B., B.D., Th.M., Th.D., Professor of New Testament, Westminster Theological Seminary, Philadelphia.

R.D.K. R. D. Knudsen, A.B., Th.B., Th.M., S.T.M., Ph.D., Associate Professor of Apologetics, Westminster Theological Seminary, Philadelphia.

R.D.P. R. D. Preus, Ph.D., D.Theol., President of Concordia Theological Seminary, Fort Wayne, Indiana.

R.E.F. R. E. Frische, Pastor at the Deaconesses' House, Bern, and Lecturer at the Preachers' College, St Crischona, Basel.

R.F.G.B. R. F. G. Burnish, J.P., B.A., M.Th., Ph.D., Minister of Powerscourt Road Baptist Church, Portsmouth.

R.G.C. R. G. Clouse, B.D., M.A., Ph.D., Professor of History, Indiana State University.

R.G.H. R. G. Hower, B.D., S.T.M., Th.D., Associate Professor of Church History, Evangelical School of Theology, Myerstown, Pennsylvania.

R.J.B. R. J. Bauckham, M.A., Ph.D., Reader in the History of Christian Thought, University of Manchester.

R.J.S. R. J. Song, B.A., Research Student, Corpus Christi College, Oxford.

R.K. R. Kearsley, B.D., Ph.D., Lecturer in Systematic Theology, Bible Training Institute, Glasgow.

R.L.G. R. L. Greaves, B.A., M.A., Ph.D., F.R.Hist.S., Professor of History, Florida State University.

R.L.S. R. L. Sturch, M.A., D.Phil., Rector of Islip, Oxfordshire.

R.M.P. R. M. Price, B.A., M.T.S., M.Phil., Ph.D., Instructor, Montclair State College, Upper Montclair, New Jersey.

R.M.V. R. M. Vince, M.A., B.D., M.Th., M.Sc., Headmaster of St Mark's Day School, Shreveport, Louisiana.

R.N. R. Nicole, M.A., Th.D., Ph.D., formerly Professor of Theology, Gordon-Conwell Theological Seminary, Massachusetts.

R.N.C. R. N. Caswell, M.A., Ph.D., formerly Head of Religious Education, The Academical Institution, Coleraine, Northern Ireland.

R.P.G. R. P. Gordon, M.A., Ph.D., Lecturer in Divinity, University of Cambridge.

R.P.M. R. P. Martin, B.A., M.A., Ph.D., Director of Graduate Studies Program and Professor of New Testament, Fuller Theological Seminary, Pasadena, California.

R.S.G. R. S. Greenway, B.A., B.D., Th.M., Th.D., Executive Director of the Board of World Ministries of the Christian Reformed Church of North America, Grand Rapids, Michigan.

R.S.W. R. S. Wallace, M.A., B.Sc., Ph.D., Professor Emeritus of Biblical Theology, Columbia Theological Seminary, Decatur, Georgia.

R.T.B. R. T. Beckwith, M.A., B.D., Warden of Latimer House, Oxford.

R.T.J. R. T. Jones, D.Phil., D.D., D.Litt., Principal, Coleg Bala-Bangor, Bangor.

R.W.A.L. R. W. A. Letham, B.A., M.A., Th.M., Ph.D., Lecturer in Christian Doctrine, London Bible College.

R.W.C. R. W. Cowley, M.A., B.D., D.D., Course Leader of Non-Stipendiary Ministry Training Course, Oak Hill College, London.

S.B.F. S. B. Ferguson, M.A., B.D., Ph.D., Associate Professor of Systematic Theology, Westminster Theological Seminary, Philadelphia.

S.H.T. S. H. Travis, M.A., Ph.D., Lecturer in New Testament, St John's College, Nottingham.

S.J.S. S. J. Smalley, B.D., M.Th., formerly Lecturer in Historical and Contemporary Theology, University of Manchester.

S.N.L. S. N. Lieu, M.A., D.Phil., F.R.A.S., F.R.Hist.S., Lecturer in Ancient History, University of Warwick.

S.N.W. S. N. Williams, M.A., Ph.D., Professor of Theology, United Presbyterian Theological College, Aberystwyth.

S.P.K. S. P. Kanemoto, B.S., M.S., M.A., M.Div., Th.M., Lecturer, Tokyo Christian College; Lecturer, Kyoritsu Christian Institute, Japan.

S.R.P. S. R. Pointer, A.B., M.A., Ph.D., Assistant Professor of History, Trinity College, Deerfield, Illinois.

S.S.S. S. S. Smalley, M.A., B.D., Ph.D., Dean of Chester Cathedral.

T.A.N. T. A. Noble, M.A., B.D., Dean, British Isles Nazarene College, Didsbury, Manchester.

T.G.D. T. G. Donner, B.D., Ph.D., Lecturer in Historical Theology, Seminario Bíblico de Colombia.

T.H. T. Howard, B.A., M.A., Ph.D., Professor of English, St John's Seminary, Boston, Massachusetts.

T.J.N. T. J. Nettles, B.A., M.Div., Ph.D., Associate Professor of Church History, Mid-America Baptist Theological Seminary, Memphis, Tennessee.

T.L. T. Longman III, B.A., M.Div., M.Phil., Ph.D., Associate Professor of Old Testament, Westminster Theological Seminary, Philadelphia.

T.R.A. T. R. Albin, B.A., M.A., Minister of the United Methodist Church, USA.

T.W.J.M. T. W. J. Morrow, M.A., B.D., M.Th., Ph.D., Minister of Lucan Presbyterian Church, Co. Dublin, Republic of Ireland.

V.K.S. V. K. Samuel, B.Sc., M.Litt., General Secretary, Evangelical Fellowship in the Anglican Communion.

W.C.K. W. C. Kaiser, Jr. A.B., B.D., M.A., Ph.D., Academic Dean and Vice-President of Education; Professor of Semitic Languages and Old Testament at Trinity Evangelical Divinity School, Deerfield, Illinois.

W.D.B. W. D. Beck, B.A., M.A., Ph.D., Professor of Philosophy, Liberty Baptist College, Lynchburg, Virginia.

W.G.M. W. G. Morrice, M.A., B.D., S.T.M., Ph.D., New Testament Tutor and Librarian, St John's College, Durham.

W.J.R. W. J. Roxborogh, B.E., B.D., Ph..D., Lecturer in Church History and New Testament, Seminari Theoloji, Malaysia, Kuala Lumpur.

W.N.K. W. N. Kerr, B.A., B.D., Th.D., Ph.D., Professor of Church History, Gordon-Conwell Theological Seminary, Massachusetts.

W.R.G. W. R. Godfrey, A.B., M.Div., M.A., Ph.D., Professor of Church History, Westminster Theological Seminary, California.

W.W.C. W. W. Chow, B.Sc., B.D., M.A., Ph.D., Dean, China Graduate School of Theology, Hong Kong.

W.W.G. W. W. Gasque, B.A., B.D., M.Th., Ph.D., E. Marshall Sheppard Professor of Biblical Studies at Regent College, Vancouver.

A

ABELARD, PETER (1079–1142), (or more accurately, Abailard), was born near Nantes, of Breton parents. He was probably the most brilliant thinker of the 12th century, but his life was repeatedly marred by tragedy.

Abelard studied first under Roscelin (d. *c.* 1125), a thoroughgoing nominalist,* then under William of Champeaux (*c.* 1070–1121), an equally thoroughgoing realist. While Roscelin was accused of regarding universals as mere words with no reality of their own, William maintained that the universal is more real than the individuals and in fact exists independently of them. Abelard took a mediating position, seeing universals as mental concepts. They have no existence independent of particular individuals, but they are not arbitrary names. A universal, like 'dog', is real, but it is not something that exists independently of individual dogs. It precedes individual dogs in that, when God planned the creation of dogs, the universal idea of 'dog' was in his mind; it exists in individual dogs; and it exists in our minds when we have the concept of 'dog'. This view came to be generally accepted and closed the debate until the time of William of Ockham.*

Abelard did not merely disagree with his teachers, he actively opposed them. He attacked Roscelin's doctrine of the Trinity,* which verged on tritheism.* He opposed William's realism and set himself up as a rival lecturer at Paris, forcing William to leave Paris and rethink his position on universals. Abelard later meted out the same treatment to Anselm of Laon (d. 1117), with whose exegetical methods he disagreed. After leaving Laon, Abelard returned to Paris where he committed his worst indiscretion. He lodged with Fulbert, a canon of Notre Dame, whose attractive and intelligent niece Héloise he tutored. Héloise gave birth to a baby boy. Fulbert later took revenge in a terrible incident in which Abelard was castrated.

In 1122 Peter wrote *Sic et Non* (*Yes and No*). In this book he considers 158 different theological questions, juxtaposing apparently contradictory passages from the Bible, the fathers and other authorities. His aim was not, as once was supposed, to discredit these authorities. He was rather commending reason as the arbiter to reconcile conflicting authorities and, if necessary, to choose between them. He did not invent this method. Gratian (died not later than 1179), an expert in canon law,* used this approach with great success in his *Concord of Discordant Canons*. Abelard's novelty lay in its application to theology and the documents of revelation.

Behind *Sic et Non* lay Abelard's basic approach to theology. Anselm,* like Augustine,* had followed the method of faith seeking understanding: 'I believe in order that I may understand' (see Faith and Reason*). Abelard reversed this, introducing the method of doubt. The way to find the truth is to doubt, to ask questions. In the preface to *Sic et Non* Abelard stated that 'by doubting we come to enquire and by enquiring we reach truth'. Doubt* he sees not so much as sin (the traditional view) as the necessary beginning of all knowledge. Theology had become a science instead of a meditation, as in the tradition of monastic theology.*

In his commentary on Rom. 3:19–26, Abelard applied this method to the doctrine of the atonement.* He questioned the meaning of the statement that we are redeemed by Christ's death. He ridiculed the idea, already declining in popularity since Anselm, that the devil has any rights over mankind. If anything, Satan's seduction of the human race gives *us* the right of redress over *him*. The death of Christ was not offered to Satan as a ransom for mankind. The ransom was paid to God, not to Satan.

But Abelard goes on to question the need for any ransom at all. How could God demand the death of an innocent man, much less the death of his own Son? How could God be reconciled to the world by such a death? Abelard looks elsewhere for the significance of the cross. He sees it as a supreme example of God's love for us, which awakens a response of love in us. Abelard points here towards the 'moral influence theory' of the atonement, which sees its value in its effect upon us.

The idea that the cross awakens a loving response on our part is true as far as it goes, but manifestly fails to do full justice to Rom. 3:19–26. But was Abelard actually seeking to

1

limit the atonement to *merely* an example of love? Elsewhere he continues to use traditional language of Christ bearing the punishment for our sins. Some hold that such passages cannot be taken seriously in the light of the commentary on Romans. Others see such passages as proof that Abelard did not wish to reduce the cross to merely an example of love. It may be significant that while he denies that a ransom was paid to Satan, he only asks *why it was necessary* for a ransom to be paid to God. Perhaps, as with *Sic et Non*, his aim is to stimulate rational enquiry rather than discredit scriptural teaching.

Abelard's innovative brilliance, combined with his contempt for those who were his elders but not his betters, launched him on a collision course with disaster. His *On the Divine Unity and Trinity* was condemned in his absence at the Council of Soissons in 1121 and burnt. This did not permanently affect his career. But he managed to incur the wrath of Bernard of Clairvaux,* who was appalled by his rationalistic approach and accused him of inventing a fifth gospel. Abelard was summoned before a council at Sens in 1140 and condemned. He appealed to Rome, but Bernard had already secured the ear of the pope with his treatise *The Errors of Peter Abelard*. Abelard became a monk at the abbey of Cluny and died in 1142.

Bibliography

Works: PL 178 and CCCM 11–12. *Sic et Non*, ed. B. B. Boyer and R. McKean (Chicago, 1976–77); *A Dialogue of a Philosopher . . .*, tr. P. J. Payer (Toronto, 1979); *Ethics*, tr. D. E. Luscombe (Oxford, 1971).

Studies: L. Grane, *Peter Abelard* (London, 1970); J. R. McCallum, *Abelard's Christian Theology* (Oxford, 1948); R. E. Weingart, *The Logic of Divine Love. A Critical Analysis of the Soteriology of Peter Abailard* (Oxford, 1970).

A.N.S.L.

ABORTION is the loss or expulsion from the womb of a living foetus before it has reached the stage of viability. Many abortions occur spontaneously (miscarriages), whereas others are deliberately induced. It is the latter which are the focal point of contemporary theological and ethical debate.

Traditionally, Christian opinion has strongly resisted the deliberate termination of any pregnancy. Tertullian* is typical of early authorities in denouncing abortion as 'a precipitation of murder', because 'he also is a man who is about to be one' (*Apologia* 9). Augustine* took a slightly softer line by positing a critical point of 'ensoulment' (sixty to eighty days after conception), before which abortion was a criminal but not a capital offence, but such a dualistic approach is now widely discredited.

The chief theological ground for a strict anti-abortion stance is the conviction that every human being is made in God's image from the time of conception (*cf*. Gn. 1:27). Life-taking, like life-giving, is God's prerogative, and man needs a special mandate to end any human being's physical existence. Permission to kill is given by Scripture in carefully defined circumstances as a response to injustice (specifically murder and war, *cf*. Gn. 9:6; 1 Ki. 2:5–6), but no foetus has done anything to deserve the death penalty. Abortion, therefore, is morally bad.

Biblical support for this conclusion is often found in the OT's allusions to life before birth (*e.g.* Ps. 139:13–17; Je. 1:5; Ec. 11:5) and in the NT's use of the Greek word *brephos* to describe both a foetus and a child (Lk. 1:41; 2:12). These references assume continuity of personhood on both sides of birth.

A rigid 'no abortion' policy has been challenged in three ways. First, the Roman Catholic Church (which is otherwise implacably opposed to abortion) allows for a pregnancy to be terminated, under the ethical law of 'double effect', when a procedure intended to save the mother-to-be's life (such as hysterectomy for cancer) results in the death of the foetus.

Secondly, some Protestant theologians argue that the foetus is a potential person, rather than an actual person with potential. While a foetus demands care and respect at any stage of its existence, its claim to life is proportional to its stage of development. Plausible though this theory sounds, it does not easily square with the Bible's stress on personhood's continuum, and it is by no means simple to apply in practice.

Thirdly, and most radically, Christian situationists contend that love alone must dictate the decision whether or not to abort in a particular case. Compassion for the woman (if her life or health is threatened) or for the unborn child (if he or she is likely to be born deformed or defective) may dictate the ending of a pregnancy. Furthermore, they argue, because love must always choose the maximum benefit for the greatest number, abortion may be indicated when the baby is unwanted by the family, by society – or, for that matter, by an overcrowded world.

Situation ethics has come under heavy fire from Christians who accept Scripture's authority. Nowhere does the Bible teach that love replaces divine principle or overrides divine law. Nor does it support the utilitarian assumption that the best actions can be calculated by counting heads.

Nevertheless, the situationist's stress on compassion is a salutary and biblical reminder that those who oppose abortion on principle are obliged to find practical, loving alternatives for women with unwanted pregnancies (cf. Jas. 2:14–17).

See also: BIOETHICS; ETHICS.

Bibliography

R. F. R. Gardner, *Abortion* (Exeter, 1972); O. M. D. O'Donovan, *The Christian and the Unborn Child* (Bramcote, Nottingham, 1973); M. Potts, P. Diggory, J. Peel, *Abortion* (Cambridge, 1977); M. J. Gorman, *Abortion and the Early Church* (Downers Grove, IL, 1982).

D.H.F.

ABSOLUTION, see GUILT AND FORGIVENESS.

ACCOMMODATION or condescension, is a basic principle underlying all of God's revelation to man. It means that God speaks to us in a form that is suited to the capacity of the hearer, like a father addressing a small child or a teacher with a young pupil. The supreme instance of accommodation is the incarnation,* where God speaks to us in the most fitting way possible – as a human being himself. Again, in the Scriptures* God's word comes to us in a human way – through human authors, using human language, addressed to particular human situations. In the ministry of the word and sacraments God speaks to us and communicates himself to us, but in a form that is suited to our present condition – through human agents and through earthly elements such as bread and wine.

Accommodation, rightly understood, means not that God communicates falsehood to us but that he communicates truth to us in a manner which is necessarily less than perfect. Ezekiel recognized the limitations of his vision of God: 'This was the appearance of the likeness of the glory of the LORD' (Ezk. 1:28). Paul acknowledged the imperfection of all our present knowledge of God, concluding that 'Now we see but a poor reflection' (1 Cor. 13:9–12). The biblical message comes to us in human language and in the thought forms of particular times – not because the writers 'got it wrong' but because that was the only way that God's word could come to such as us. In his condescension God chooses to submit his truth to the limiting process of being reduced to a humanly comprehensible level rather than preserve it pure in heaven.

The idea of accommodation was common in the early fathers (e.g. John Chrysostom, c. 344/354–407) and was revived by Calvin* and others.

Bibliography

F. L. Battles, 'God was Accommodating Himself to Human Capacity', *Interpretation* 31 (1977), pp. 19–38; J. B. Rogers (ed.), *Biblical Authority* (Waco, TX, 1977), pp. 19–29.

A.N.S.L.

ADAM. 1. From the Heb. *'ādām*. In most of the OT the word is generic, meaning 'man', 'men' or 'mankind' (e.g., Ps. 73:5; Is. 31:3). In Gn. 1 – 5, however, it denotes, either specifically or as a proper name ('Adam'), the first human being. The first woman, Eve, is formed from his body (Gn. 2:22; 3:20). Male and female, they are, in distinction from all other creatures, made by God in his own 'image'* or 'likeness' (Gn. 1:27; 5:1–2; see Anthropology,* Creation,* Feminist Theology,* Image of God*). As such they are good and without sin; but together they subsequently sin and bring God's curse on themselves and the entire creation (Gn. 3; see Fall,* Sin*). Outside of these chapters Adam is mentioned elsewhere in the OT only once, in a genealogy in 1 Ch. 1:1 (possibly also, Jb. 31:33; Ho. 6:7); it remains for the NT, especially Paul, to explain his significance. Yet, plainly, what Gn. 1 – 3 teaches about Adam not only underlies but profoundly controls the entire OT: the origin and unity of mankind by descent from Adam and Eve, the uniqueness of man as made in God's image, man as dependent upon and accountable to God, the origin of sin and death, and the nature of sin, not as a virtually inevitable natural phenomenon but as man's wilful transgression of God's law.

2. The NT refers to Adam in five places (Lk. 3:38; Rom. 5:14; 1 Cor. 15:22, 45; 1 Tim. 2:13–14; Jude 14). Several other passages contain unmistakable allusions. In Lk. 3:38 he is at the head of the genealogy of Jesus: 'the son of Adam, the son of God'. In contrast to Matthew, who takes Jesus' genealogy back only to Abraham (Mt. 1:1), Luke's lengthening probably intends to point to Jesus as the last Adam (see below). Further, Luke's placing of the genealogy, not at the very beginning of his gospel like Matthew, but in the midst of the narration, just before his account of the temptation (Lk. 4:1–13), suggests a comparison: while Adam succumbed to a single temptation by Satan, within the favourable circumstances of the garden of Eden, Jesus successfully resists Satan's multiple seductions under difficult desert conditions. 1 Tim. 2:13–14 refers to Adam and Eve in order to regulate the assemblies of the church. Women may not teach or exercise authority over men in the congregation, not because women are morally weaker or otherwise inferior to men, but because of the order of creation and the disorder introduced at the fall: Adam, not Eve, was created first; Eve, not Adam, was deceived first. Elsewhere allusion is made to Adam as created in God's image (1 Cor. 11:7–9; Jas. 3:9), to his sin and fall (Rom. 1:21–23; 3:23). Acts 17:26 (Paul in his Areopagus sermon) teaches the origin and unity of the human race in Adam: 'From one man he made every nation of men . . .'

3. Rom. 5:12–19 and 1 Cor. 15:21–22, 45–49 contrast Adam with Christ and at the same time identify the latter as the last Adam (explicitly in 1 Cor. 15:45, 47). The effect of this contrast is to open up the widest possible outlook on the work of Christ. In 1 Cor. 15 Adam is the great counterpart to the resurrected Christ: as death has come through the man, Adam, in whom all die, so resurrection-life has come through the man, Christ, in whom all (believers) will be made alive (vv. 21–22). As the reversal of the death brought by Adam at the beginning of history, Christ's resurrection is not merely an isolated event in the past but has a profound corporate significance for the future: he is the 'firstfruits' of the great resurrection-harvest, in which believers will have a place, at the end of history (v. 20; see Resurrection, General,* Resurrection of Christ*).

The carefully developed antithetical parallelism of verses 42–49, starting with the differences between the dead ('sown') body and the believer's resurrection body (vv. 42–44a), broadens in verses 45–49 to include Adam and Christ. Not only do they exemplify these bodies, respectively, but also they are key, representative figures, heads over contrasting orders of existence. Adam is 'first' (vv. 45, 47), there is no-one before him; Christ is 'second' (v. 47), there is no-one between Adam and him; Christ is 'last' (v. 45), there is no-one after him. By virtue of creation (not because of the fall, note the use of Gn. 2:7 in v. 45b), Adam became 'a living being' (psychē)' and so represents the 'natural' (psychikos, vv. 44, 46) or 'earthly' (vv. 47–49) order, subject now, since his fall, to death. By resurrection (cf. vv. 20, 21b, 22b), Christ, 'the last Adam', became (economically, not ontologically) 'life-giving Spirit' (v. 45c; pneuma here refers to the Holy Spirit; see esp. 2 Cor. 3:6: 'the Spirit gives life', and the only other NT occurrence of the 'natural' – 'spiritual' contrast in 1 Cor. 2:14–15); as such he represents the corresponding 'spiritual' (vv. 44, 46), 'heavenly' (vv. 47–49) order of eschatological life. In view ultimately are two creations, the original become 'perishable', contrasted with the final and 'imperishable' (v. 42), each with an Adam of its own. The resurrected Christ, in the power of the Spirit, is the head of nothing less than a new creation (cf. 2 Cor. 5:17). Yet this antithesis is not an ultimate dualism.* In Christ's resurrection God's original purposes for creation have been attained. Where Adam failed, the last Adam has succeeded. The consummation intended for the 'natural' order has been realized in the 'spiritual', resurrection order. The image of God, distorted by Adam's sin, has been restored in Christ; in fact, as resurrected, he is the eschatological image of God (see 2 Cor. 4:4; Col. 1:15). As believers now bear 'the likeness of the earthly man' (Adam), so when they are raised bodily they will bear 'the likeness of the man from heaven' (v. 49), the image of the exalted Christ (cf. Phil. 3:20).

Conformity to this image is the goal of their predestination* (Rom. 8:29), a conformity which presently is already being realized in them (2 Cor. 3:18; Eph. 4:23–24).

The representative, determinative significance of Adam and Christ is also a major theme in Rom. 5:12–19. Adam is 'a pattern of the one to come' (v. 14) because his sin brings the world under the 'reign' (v. 17) of sin, condemnation and death, in antithesis to the 'reign' of righteousness,* justification* and life secured for all (believers) by Christ. A perennially debated question is exactly how 'through the disobedience of the one man the many were made sinners' (v. 19a). In view of the sustained emphasis on the *one* sin of the *one* man (vv. 15–19), as well as the antithetically parallel way, here as elsewhere (see esp. Rom. 4:1–8), in which believers are justified, all men are sinners not only because they inherit a sinful nature from Adam but primarily because his sin is imputed to them, or reckoned as theirs.

4. Especially since the Enlightenment,* the *historicity* of Adam has been questioned or denied. Where an evolutionary understanding of the origin of man is accepted (see Creation*), Gn. 1 – 3 are usually read as a myth,* a parable illustrating the human condition in general. Typically (*e.g.* K. Barth,* H. Berkhof*), the 'before' and 'after' sequence of creation and a historical fall is transposed into a timeless dialectic between 'above' (creation as good, man as free) and 'below' (man as sinful). However, there is no exegetical or literary evidence to suggest that these chapters are intended as any less historical than the patriarchal narratives in the later chapters. Moreover, the NT writers plainly view Adam historically, as the first human being (see the passages listed above, in 2.). Rom. 5 and 1 Cor. 15 teach an essential, inseparable tie between the historical reality of Christ's work and the historical reality of Adam's fall. The biblical understanding of creation, of man, of the person and work of Christ and of salvation is rooted in the historicity of Adam.

Bibliography

K. Barth, *CD* IV. 1, pp. 504–513; H. Berkhof, *Christian Faith* (Grand Rapids, MI, 1979); J. Murray, *The Epistle to the Romans*, 1 (Grand Rapids, MI, 1959); H. Ridderbos, *Paul* (Grand Rapids, MI, 1975); J. P. Ver-steeg, *Is Adam a 'Teaching Model' in the New Testament?* (Nutley, NJ, 1978); G. Vos, *The Pauline Eschatology* (1930; Grand Rapids, MI, 1979).

R.B.G.

ADIAPHORA. This concept (from the Greek for 'things indifferent') was explored controversially particularly by Lutheran* theologians in the mid-16th century at a time when the Protestant movement was threatened by Catholic power in Germany. The basic question related to the status of certain ceremonies and rites, both public and private, which are neither commanded nor forbidden by the word of God in Scripture, and which have been introduced, it was claimed, into the church for the sake of good order, decorum and discipline. One party, led by Philip Melanchthon,* held that in a period of persecution one may, with a clear conscience, at the insistence of the enemy, restore certain things such as the rite of confirmation.* The other party, led by Matthias Flacius (1520–75), contended that under no circumstances could this be done with a clear conscience. In the *Formula of Concord* (1577), ch. X is entitled, 'The ecclesiastical rites that are called "Adiaphora" or things indifferent', where a middle way is proposed. In times of persecution, concessions are not to be offered but at other times 'the community of God in every place and at every time has the right, authority and power to change, to reduce, or to increase ceremonies according to its circumstances, as long as it does so without frivolity and offence but in an orderly and appropriate way . . . for good order, evangelical decorum and the edification of the church'.

The issue of adiaphora was also contentious in England in the 16th century and in Lutheran pietism* in the 17th century, and in strong or weak forms has often arisen in churches which take the word of God as authoritative.

Bibliography

C. L. Manschreck, *Melanchthon, The Quiet Reformer* (New York and Nashville, 1958); B. J. Verkamp, *The Indifferent Mean. Adiaphorism in the English Reformation to 1554* (Athens, OH, 1977).

P.T.

ADOPTION, see SONSHIP.

ADOPTIONISM. The term is most commonly applied to the notion that Jesus was merely an ordinary man of unusual virtue or closeness to God whom God 'adopted' into divine Sonship. This exceptional elevation, which in primitive adoptionism was usually associated with the event of Christ's baptism, involves nevertheless only a special divine activity upon or in Jesus, not the personal presence in him of a second member of the Trinity* bearing the proper name of Word (Logos*) or Son.

Although early material on adoptionism is scant, it seems clear that the movement first became prominent in the teachings of Theodotus, an erudite leather-merchant active in Rome about AD 190. He taught that the 'Spirit' or 'Christ' descended upon Jesus at baptism, initiating miraculous powers in one who was, though supremely virtuous, just an ordinary man. Theodotus was an offence to his critics for defining Jesus as a 'mere man' (*psilos anthrōpos* – hence the label 'psilanthropism'), a term underlined by the adoptionist's own description of his previous lapse from faith as denial 'not of God but of a man'. According to Hippolytus,* Theodotus 'determined to deny the divinity of Christ'. Artemon, a convert in Rome to the teaching of Theodotus, sought to establish the historical pedigree of adoptionism; the significant response of one contemporary, held by some scholars to be Hippolytus, was to demonstrate that each of the early Christian apologists* 'proclaim Christ both God and man'.

The most famous heir to the early adoptionist tradition is Paul of Samosata who, in most of the early witnesses, is firmly linked with the teaching of Artemon. Paul was finally condemned for his views at the Synod of Antioch (AD 268). We have no contemporary record of his doctrine but it is plain that he was understood to teach that Jesus was 'by nature an ordinary man' (*koinou tēn physin anthrōpou*). In the next century he was accused by the church historian Eusebius* of holding a demeaning view of Christ and thus denying both 'his God and his Lord'. It was his misdemeanour, alleged Eusebius, to draw back from acknowledging that the Son of God came down from heaven, confessing instead that Jesus was 'from below'.

Modern Christologies* sometimes defend themselves, with some justness, from the suspicion of adoptionism by consciously renouncing certain untenable features of the original movement, such as its impersonal interpretation of the divine presence with Jesus, its neglect of divine initiative over against human achievement and its blurring of the NT distinction between Christ's Sonship and the adoptive counterpart in believers. These unsound traits, however, were, at least in the minds of the movement's critics, quite secondary to the inadequately expressed identity accorded in adoptionism to the Jesus borne by Mary. Its really characteristic error was to deny the divine origin and identity of Jesus, calling him a mere man, a failing combated by the later title *Theotokos* (God-bearer) for Mary.*

Adoptionism (or Adoptianism) is technically the title also for a less well-known movement in the Spanish church of the 8th century, condemned for making Christ's manhood participate in his dignity as Son only by adoption.

See also: MONARCHIANISM.

Bibliography
A. Grillmeier, *Christ in Christian Tradition*, vol. 1: *From the Apostolic Age to Chalcedon AD 451* (London, ²1975); J. N. D. Kelly, *Early Christian Doctrines* (London, ⁵1977).

R.K.

AESTHETICS is the study of general features of the arts and aesthetic experience. 'The arts' include drama, music, painting, poetry and many other fields. Aesthetics has been a branch of philosophy since its christening by A. Baumgarten (1714–62) in the 1700s. But important contributions have also come from other academic disciplines, as well as from artists and art critics.

Contemporary aesthetics includes theory of the aesthetic, philosophy of the arts and philosophy of arts criticism (G. Dickie). For Christians the most significant issues arising in these areas concern 1. aesthetic responsibility, 2. approaches to art, 3. social frameworks and 4. relationships between theology and philosophy. This article summarizes each issue in turn.

Aesthetic responsibility

To speak of 'aesthetic responsibility' is to challenge traditional aesthetics. Since I.

Kant's* influential *Critique of Judgment* (1790), aesthetic experience has often been regarded as a sanctuary from both natural necessity and moral obligation. In extreme positions 'aesthetic experience' of 'beauty' or of 'aesthetic objects' has become a matter of enjoyment for enjoyment's sake. One of the first provocative Christian challenges came from L. Tolstoy.* When he rejected 'beauty' as a defining feature of art, Tolstoy rejected 'aesthetic experience' itself as a poor excuse for irreligious, elitist hedonism.

Two Christian philosophers have recently challenged the traditional notion of beauty without rejecting 'aesthetic experience' as such. Distinguishing more carefully than Tolstoy between *aesthetic* and *artistic* excellence, both philosophers argue that all human beings have aesthetic responsibilities. N. Wolterstorff makes a case for aesthetic excellence in cities and churches. C. Seerveld urges Christians to lead an 'obedient aesthetic life' in their families, dwellings and social interactions. Although disagreeing about the main features of aesthetic objects, both philosophers see the aesthetic dimension as one in which we are created to give God praise and called to seek Christ's renewal.

Approaches to art

Authors who retain traditional notions of beauty tend to condemn recent high art. This tendency is evident in writings by H. R. Rookmaaker (1922–1977) and F. A. Schaeffer.* Works by Picasso (1881–1974), Samuel Beckett (b. 1906) and Ingmar Bergman (b. 1918) do not display the pleasurable proportion, integrity and brightness that Thomas Aquinas* associated with beauty. The lack of such features is often taken to signal artistic defects and cultural decay. Other authors, however, such as Harvey Cox (b. 1929) and Amos Wilder in *The New Orpheus*, praise some of modern art for its artistic power, its ability to unsettle comfortable Christianity and its highlighting of social needs.

Linked to such divergent assessments are different theologies of culture.* How Christians practise and view the arts depends in part on how they relate to their culture and society. Isolationists tend to ward off contemporary art as something dangerous to their faith. Synthetic and accommodating Christians are inclined to use Christian teachings to justify contemporary art, either as a liturgical means of worship or as something good in itself. Transformational Christians usually expect Christians to promote renewal within contemporary arts.

Two philosophical issues here concern art's characteristic features and art's proper roles within human life. Some response to these issues, no matter how vague, is already assumed in specific decisions about which works to promote or how to use arts in worship. Thus, for example, Tolstoy's rejection of Shakespeare and commendation of Charles Dickens assumes that art's main task is to communicate feelings.

Following H. Osborne we may distinguish three types of Western philosophies about art. Instrumental theories understand art as a means of improvement, indoctrination, education or emotional expression. Referential theories understand art as an imitation, reflection or projection of actual, ideal or imaginative realities. Formalist theories understand works of art as autonomous creations whose intrinsic worth lies in their formal and aesthetic properties.

Each type of theory fails to do justice to wide ranges of artistic projects and roles within human life. A comprehensive Christian philosophy of the arts would try to correct and incorporate all three theories. Such a philosophy would note, for example, that instrumental theories often underestimate the intrinsic worth of the arts; referential theories often ignore the non-cognitive functions of art; and formalist theories often treat works of art as if they were nothing more than isolated objects of secular devotion.

Social frameworks

It cannot be denied that many works do function as isolated objects of secular devotion. This fact has led some Christians to repudiate the 'religion' of art spawned by 19th-century Romanticism.* A more fruitful approach seems to lie in analysing the social frameworks within which contemporary arts operate. Wolterstorff has described salient features of Western society's 'institution of high art'. This characteristic pattern of making and using art contributes directly to the isolation of high art and to aesthetic impoverishment in everyday life. Wolterstorff urges Christians to participate thoughtfully in the institution of high art and to liberate life from high art's spell.

Though helpful, Wolterstorff's approach largely ignores Western society's institution of low art. Yet a good deal of our aesthetic impoverishment is prompted by popular music, film and advertising. These arts operate within what T. Adorno has called 'the culture industry'. In this institution commercial success is the primary goal. Even high arts in museums and concert halls seem to have become locked into an international culture industry. Christian criticisms of the arts and involvements in them might make little redemptive difference unless we address the economic basis for social frameworks of contemporary arts.

Theology and philosophy

Christian artists and art critics often turn to theology for guidance. By itself, however, theology may prove insufficient. After noting that we have 'no Christian philosophy of the arts', for example, Dorothy Sayers tries to derive most of her own aesthetics from a lay theology of creation. But her use of this *theology* is itself heavily indebted to a *philosophy*, namely R. G. Collingwood's *The Principles of Art* (Oxford, 1938).

No doubt theology should provide touchstones for reflections about the arts and aesthetic experience. To become more serviceable for art and life, however, such reflections need to be refined by philosophy, to which aesthetics belongs. Protestants have long been hampered by their lack of a cogent aesthetics. The aesthetics needed would be informed by Scripture, theology and Christian traditions but would remain genuine philosophy. Used in conjunction with theological reflections, work in aesthetics by Christian philosophers could help free us to serve God and our neighbours more fully in matters artistic and aesthetic.

See also: BALTHASAR, HANS URS VON.

Bibliography

T. W. Adorno, *Aesthetic Theory* (London, 1984); M. C. Beardsley, 'Aesthetics, History of' and J. Hospers, 'Aesthetics, Problems of', *Encyclopedia of Philosophy*, vol. 1 (New York, 1967), pp. 18–56; G. Dickie, *Aesthetics: An Introduction* (Indianapolis, 1971); G. S. Heyer, *Signs of Our Times* (Grand Rapids, MI, 1980); H. Küng, *Art and the Question of Meaning* (New York, 1981); J. Maritain, *Creative Intuition in Art and Poetry* (Cleveland, OH, 1953); H. Osborne, *Aesthetics and Art Theory* (New York, 1970); H. R. Rookmaaker, *Art Needs No Justification* (Leicester, 1978); *idem, Modern Art and the Death of a Culture* (London, 1970); D. L. Sayers, *Christian Letters to a Post-Christian World* (Grand Rapids, MI, 1969); F. A. Schaeffer, *Art and the Bible* (Downers Grove, IL, 1973); *idem, How Should We Then Live?* (London, 1980); N. A. Scott, Jr., ed., *The New Orpheus* (New York, 1964); C. Seerveld, *Rainbows for the Fallen World* (Toronto, 1980); *idem*, 'Relating Christianity to the Arts', *CT* (November 7, 1980); *idem, A Turnabout in Aesthetics to Understanding* (Toronto, 1974); L. Tolstoy, *What Is Art?* (1896; Indianapolis, MN, 1960); G. Van der Leeuw, *Sacred and Profane Beauty* (New York, 1963); N. Wolterstorff, *Art in Action: Toward a Christian Aesthetic* (Grand Rapids, MI, 1980); L. Zuidervaart, 'Toward a Shared Understanding of the Arts', *Pro Rege* 11 (Dordt College, Sioux Centre, IA, December 1982), pp. 18–25.

L.P.Z.

AFRICAN CHRISTIAN THEOLOGY.

The rapid spread of Christianity in Africa in the 20th century has been one of the notable features of modern Christian history. For some time now it has been acceptable even to speak of a shift in Christianity's geographical and cultural centre of gravity. The heartlands of the faith are no longer in the old Christendom of Western Europe and its extension in North America, but rather are to be found in the 'Southern' continents: Latin America, parts of Asia and the Pacific, and particularly tropical Africa.

This phenomenal rate of expansion of Christianity in Africa has led to an awareness that the Christian faith as professed by Africans ought to find expression in terms that arise out of African cultural values and life-experience. The effort to think through faith in Christ in terms which reflect authentically African perspectives has produced 'the quest for an African (Christian) theology' since the mid-1950s.

Admittedly, a certain amount of spontaneous 'theologizing' goes on in the life and witness of Africa's Christian communities and this is probably most evident in the so-called African Independent Churches.* However, African theology in its academic and literary form has emerged largely from the Departments of Religion in the various universities on the continent. It is worth noting that the vast majority of Africa's theological academics are also ordained churchmen who maintain an active association with their churches. Already one can discern some positive achievements of this first flowering of African theological reflection.

The agenda of African theology is quite startling. The historical roots of African Christianity lie in the modern missionary enterprise from the West. Given the generally negative Western evaluation of indigenous African religions, it has come as a surprise that virtually all of Africa's leading theologians, though trained in theology according to Western models, have concentrated their research and writing on those very religious traditions of the African 'past' which were considered to be theologically insignificant. This concern with the African pre-Christian religious heritage assumed such proportions that one observer of the African theological scene ventured to suggest that an effect of this concentration of interest was that 'areas of traditional Christian doctrine which are not reflected in the African past disappear or are marginalized' (Adrian Hastings). The titles of significant publications by some of the leading theologians of the continent confirm this emphasis. An important question raised by African theological writing to date is how to account for this high level of interest that Africa's Christian theologians have manifested in the pre-Christian religious traditions of Africa, and often of the particular writer's own people.

To the extent that the Western missionary picture of pre-Christian Africa was that of a religious *tabula rasa*, the writings of African theologians may be said to have consisted in 'demonstrating that the African religious experience and heritage were not illusory and that they should have formed the vehicle for conveying the Gospel verities to Africa' (Desmond Tutu). The central theme of this African theological literature has been the nature of African pre-Christian religious life and values and their 'relationship of continuity rather than discontinuity with Christian belief' (Hastings). This attempt at rehabilitating the African pre-Christian religious consciousness has been carried out as a self-consciously Christian and theological effort, and can thus be said to have also been an attempt to define the nature of African Christian identity. This is so since the kind of study that the African theologian makes of traditional religion differs significantly in outlook from that made by the anthropologist. Neither can it be compared with 'a clinical observation of the sort one might make about Babylonian religion; he is handling dynamite, his own past, his people's present' (A. F. Walls).

The viewpoints of the major protagonists of this theological interpretation of the African pre-Christian religious heritage are by no means identical in all respects. E. Bolaji Idowu (Nigeria) is most noted for the position that the African experience of God in the pre-Christian tradition is essentially the same as in Christian belief. Idowu arrives at this conclusion by drastically reducing all 'lesser divinities' in the Yoruba pantheon, for example, to the status of manifestations or refractions of the Supreme God. The African world of divinity becomes, according to Idowu, one of 'diffused monotheism' (*Olódùmarè*, p. 204), so that, in the final analysis, 'in Africa, the real cohesive factor of religion is the living God' (*African Traditional Religion*, p. 104). Idowu, therefore, not only insists that Africa's 'old' religions are a proper (though by no means the sole) source for African Christian theology; his approach also tends towards the conclusion that African Christian experience does little more than bring into sharper focus the sense of God which African tradition had all along.

The writings of John Mbiti (a Kenyan who was Director of the Ecumenical Institute of the World Council of Churches from 1972 to 1980) reflect a more settled Christian self-consciousness, though they are equally concerned with the theological interpretation of Africa's pre-Christian heritage in religion. Mbiti has written of himself, 'It is with a deep Christian faith that I feel conscious of myself, that I respond to the universe and that I try to make something out of life' (Preface to his *Poems of Nature and Faith*, Nairobi, 1969).

For Mbiti it is important not only to recognize that 'historically Christianity is very much an African religion' (*African Religions and Philosophy*, pp. 229f.), but also to distinguish between the phenomenon of Christianity, in its cultural embodiment as the missionary religion brought to Africa, and the

Christian faith, which as religious faith is capable of being apprehended by Africans in African terms without undue difficulty. This means that the task of constructing an African theology on the basis of an African experience of the Christian faith can proceed without anxiety or self-justification. This outlook stamps Mbiti's writings with a feeling of freedom, which in the context of the quest by African theologians for an appropriate sense of identity, is quite remarkable.

Like, Idowu, Mbiti also places positive value on the African pre-Christian heritage of religion, but only as *praeparatio evangelica*, as indicative of the African preparedness for the gospel, 'that final and completing element that crowns their traditional religiosity and brings its flickering light to full brilliance'. Mbiti, therefore, achieves a more profound integration of 'old' and 'new' than Idowu, and the vindication of an African theological point of view reflecting African cultural sensitivities, which Idowu affirms largely as a concomitant of African religious self-consciousness, is defended by Mbiti on the basis of African Christian experience itself. No other major African theologian uses the expression 'Christian Africa' in speaking of 20th-century Africa as freely as Mbiti.

The generally sympathetic interpretation of the pre-Christian religious tradition and its integration into African Christian experience indicated in the writings of Idowu and Mbiti are echoed by the majority of Africa's theologians. The only notable exception is the late General Secretary of the Association of Evangelicals of Africa and Madagascar, Byang Kato. Kato postulated a radical discontinuity between the pre-Christian tradition and Christian belief. However, the prospects for fruitful dialogue with those on the 'other side' were ended with his sudden death in 1975. No other African theologian has espoused quite as extreme a view as Kato.

African theology has overturned virtually every negative verdict passed on African tradition by the ethnocentric perspective of the earlier Western missionary estimate of Africa. Now there are indications that African Christian theology is ready to take up themes and subjects which belong within the mainstream of Christian debate and reflection, like Christology,* soteriology, and biblical hermeneutics.* It is likely that this development would not have been possible without

an effective treatment in the first instance of the question of identity.

See also: BLACK THEOLOGY.

Bibliography

K. Appiah-Kubi and Sergio Torres (eds.), *African Theology en route* (New York, 1979); K. Bediako, 'Biblical Christologies in the context of African Traditional Religion' in V. Samuel and C. Sugden (eds.), *Sharing Jesus in the Two-Thirds World* (Bangalore, 1983), pp. 115–175; K. Dickson and P. Ellingworth (eds.), *Biblical Revelation and African Beliefs* (London, 1969); A. Hastings, *African Christianity – An Essay in Interpretation* (London, 1976); E. B. Idowu, *Olódùmarè – God in Yoruba Belief* (London, 1962); idem, *African Traditional Religion – A Definition* (London, 1973); B. H. Kato, *Theological Pitfalls in Africa* (Kisumu, 1975); J. S. Mbiti, *African Religions and Philosophy* (London, 1969); idem, *Concepts of God in Africa* (London, 1970); idem, *New Testament Eschatology in an African Background* (London, 1970); idem, *The Prayers of African Religion* (London, 1975); C. Nyamiti, *African Tradition and the Christian God* (Eldoret, Kenya, n.d.); idem, *Christ as our Ancestor – Christology from an African perspective* (Gweru, 1984); J. S. Pobee, *Toward an African Theology* (Nashville, 1979); H. Sawyerr, *Creative Evangelism – Towards a New Christian Encounter with Africa* (London, 1968); D. Tutu, 'Whither African Theology?' in E. W. Fashole-Luke *et al.* (eds.), *Christianity in Independent Africa* (London, 1978), pp. 364–369; A. F. Walls, 'Towards understanding Africa's place in Christian history' in J. S. Pobee, (ed.), *Religion in a Pluralistic Society* (Leiden, 1976), pp. 180–189.

K.Be.

AFRICAN INDEPENDENT CHURCHES, THEOLOGY OF. A notable feature of the phenomenal growth of Christianity in Africa in the 20th century has been the emergence of the so-called African Independent Churches. In 1968 a survey identified six thousand such churches with a total membership of nearly ten million spread over thirty-four countries on the continent and giving every indication that their numbers were still on the increase. A sign of their importance is the fact that these churches are now being considered as a fourth Christian strand alongside the Roman Catholic, Orthodox and Protestant traditions. They are in most cases the results of breakaways from mission churches. They testify to the vitality of an African genius in religion and a capacity to adapt a missionary faith to African needs and situations.

It is probably not the case that all the movements which are grouped under this general name qualify as genuinely Christian churches. It can be shown that some of them are non-Christian religious movements which use Christian symbols, or else teach heterodox forms of Christianity. However, it is undeniable that a large portion of them are properly Christian churches and reveal in their various ways an apprehension of the Christian faith in African terms.

When the 'quest for an African Christian theology' got under way in the mid-1960s, it was to the Independent Churches that some of Africa's academic theologians looked for signs of an authentically Africanized Christianity. Yet these churches have little, if any, explicit theology. Rather, they demonstrate the liveliness and power of Christian faith in which a theology is undoubtedly implicit.

While these churches display a tendency towards the use of ritual and symbolism reminiscent of the practice of African traditional religion, they also manifest a radical Bible-centredness which points to a consciousness of being in direct continuity with prophetic and apostolic times; hence their expectation that the power and gifts of prophets* and apostles* must be available to them.

This radical biblicism needs to be distinguished from the fundamentalism* of other Christian groups. For the African Independents' approach does not stem from a rationally conceived 'doctrine' of the inspiration of Scripture; rather, the Bible in the vernacular is the *living* word of the *living* God who therefore is bound to demonstrate his *living* power in *living* experience. Healing,* prophetic guidance, protection against evil spirits, revelation through dreams – these are simply the demonstration that the God of Moses, of Elijah and of Paul is available today to all who call upon him. In this sense, the Independents have been compared to the Radical Reformation* in 16th-century Europe; they have been called modern Africa's Anabaptists.*

Since in these churches Christian faith is validated more in demonstration of power* than in rational articulation of belief, some of them also tend to be imprecise on a doctrine such as the Trinity.* A sense of the absolute Lordship of Jesus may in one of them overshadow the Father, whereas in others, the intense awareness of the Spirit of power may appear to obscure the person of Christ. But even here it may be asked whether the 'distinction of persons' (see Hypostasis*) in Western Christian theology is closer to the biblical picture than the Independents' inclination to apprehend the activity of 'the three' in their unity and interchangeability.

The African Independent Churches may be said to be marked more by a spirituality* than by a theology, a spirituality which, though reflecting the sense of the spirituality of the whole of life in African traditional culture, yet transposes African life into a new 'key' by a radical faith in Christ.

One cannot assume that the Independents will remain content with an implicit theology. Some of them, like the important Kimbanguist Church in Zaire (a member of the World Council of Churches), have established their own theological faculties with curricula similar to those operated by the mission-related churches. Others welcome the assistance of the mission-related churches in the training of their leaders or participate in ecumenical training for the ministry. In the process, the peculiarly 'African' spirituality of these churches is already becoming their contribution to the emergence of an African Christian theology* which transcends denominational barriers.

Bibliography

David B. Barrett, *Schism and Renewal in Africa: An Analysis of Six Thousand Contemporary Religious Movements* (Nairobi and London, 1968); M. L. Daneel, 'Towards a *theologia africana?* The Contribution of Independent Churches to African Theology', *Missionalia* 12 (1984), pp. 64–89; G. M. Bengt Sundkler, *Bantu Prophets in South Africa* (London, ²1961); idem, *Zulu Zion and some Swazi Zionists* (Uppsala and London, 1976); Harold W. Turner, *History of an African Independent Church*, 2 vols. (Oxford, 1967); F. B. Welbourn and B. A. Ogot, *A Place to Feel at Home: A Study of Two*

Independent Churches in Western Kenya (London, 1966).

K.Be.

AGAPE, see LOVE; NYGREN, ANDERS.

AGNOSTICISM. A term coined by T. H. Huxley (1825–95) to express the view that the evidence for God's existence is balanced by the evidence against, and thus that the only consistent position on the question is a suspense of judgment. In so far as agnosticism is based on an ethic of belief which requires that only those propositions should be believed for which there is sufficient evidence, the agnostic position was interestingly challenged by William James (1842–1910), who argued that it was rational to believe upon insufficient evidence when the choice involved was 'living, momentous and forced'.

Agnosticism in fact, if not in name, is one consequence of Kant's* arguments about human knowledge being bounded by the categories of time and space. God, beyond time and space, is the unknowable. This is more of an agnosticism about God than about the question of whether or not he exists. More recently this older debate about the limit of human knowledge has been superseded by the positivist-inspired claims that the very language used to speak of God is cognitively meaningless, because unverifiable (see Logical Positivism;* Religious Language*).

Agnosticism has always been an element in theology which wishes to observe the limits of divine revelation and to eschew speculation, and to recognize that talk of God contains analogical* elements.

P.H.

ALBERTUS MAGNUS (*c.* 1193–1280). A scholar, saint and bishop of the medieval church who was born in Bavaria sometime between 1193 and 1206. He entered the Dominican* order in 1223 and studied at the universities of Padua and Bologna. During 1228–40 he taught at convents in Germany where he composed a series of commentaries on the *Sentences* of Peter Lombard.* He attended the University of Paris, earning his doctorate there and becoming a master from 1245 to 1248. It was at this time that Thomas Aquinas* was one of his students and his assistant. In 1248 he was sent to Cologne to establish a new curriculum for his order. Later he became Bishop of Regensburg (1260–62). After leaving his administrative duties he spent the remainder of his life in Cologne as a writer, teacher and controversialist.

Albert was one of the major leaders in the movement known as scholasticism.* Broadly defined, this is an intellectual product of the medieval universities that attempted to harmonize faith and reason.* There were mystical scholastics like Bernard* and Bonaventura,* empirical scholastics such as Robert Grosseteste (*c.* 1175–1253) and Roger Bacon (*c.* 1214–92), and there was the rational scholasticism of Albert and Aquinas. The rational scholastics, like contemporary Jewish and Arab scholars, sought by means of reason to reconcile their faith with the philosophy of ancient pagan writers, especially Aristotle.*

Albert was attracted by the scientific works of Aristotle which were being translated and studied in the European universities for the first time. He mastered this material in a series of works which have been republished in twenty-eight volumes (1890–99). He is credited with establishing the study of nature as a legitimate concern for Western Christian intellectuals. The encyclopaedic approach of the times led him to deal with a wide range of subjects in the natural sciences, including geography, psychology, physics, botany, zoology and mineralogy. His major books on religious thought are commentaries on Lombard's work, explanations of the major and minor prophets and a book of theology (*Summa theologiae*). His work differs from that of many other scholastics because he does not comment on each line of the text but instead paraphrases the work and adds his own observations. He was not as successful at developing a synthesis between Christianity and Aristotelian thought as was his student, Thomas Aquinas, but he did insist on the integrity of both the area of revelation* and the realm of reason. He taught the importance of secular learning but affirmed that such knowledge cannot ultimately contradict divine revelation.

In a sense Albert was unique, living during the 'golden age of scholasticism' and, despite an enormously busy and varied life, mastering the most advanced knowledge of his day. Impatient with others who lacked his understanding, he combined his reading of scientific works with observations of nature, constantly trying to fit the details into coherent schemes. His achievements were recognized by his contemporaries, many of whom believed that they were due to magic. He was canonized in 1931 and became the patron of those who study the natural sciences.

Bibliography
S. M. Albert, *Albert the Great* (Oxford, 1948); Thomas Maria Schwertner, *St Albert the Great* (Milwaukee, WI, 1932); James A. Weisheipl (ed.), *Albertus Magnus and the Sciences: Commemorative Essays* (Toronto, 1979).

R.G.C.

ALBIGENSES. A medieval dualistic* sect, ultimately heir to Manichaean* teaching, that spread along the trade routes from the Middle East and became popular in northern Italy and southern France during the 11th and 12th centuries. At times called the Cathars, the followers of this group were known as Albigenses because their greatest strength centred in the town of Albi. They taught that there was a god of light (spirit) and a god of darkness (matter). The perfect life, one devoid of material things, could be approached by a rigorous asceticism* including abstaining from meats and sex, and condemning the medieval church. They also objected to the orthodox teaching about Christ because they did not believe that the Son of God could be incarnate as a man.

Albigenses were divided into the 'perfect' who closely followed the teaching of the group and the 'believers' who could continue to live normal lives until their deathbeds, at which time, if they repented, they could be assured of salvation. At first, the papacy tried to bring them back into the church through peaceful means such as sending special preachers into southern France to convert them. However, in 1208 a papal representative was murdered in Toulouse provoking Innocent III (1160–1216) to call a crusade which crushed the movement.

Bibliography
S. Runciman, *The Medieval Manichee* (Cambridge, 1947).

R.G.C.

ALEXANDRIAN SCHOOL. Alexandria was the intellectual centre of the early Roman Empire, especially noted for philological studies and for syncretism* in religion and philosophy. Gnostic* teachers (such as Basilides, Carpocrates and Valentinus) were active in Alexandria from the early 2nd century. *The Epistle of Barnabas*, one of the apostolic fathers,* with its non-literal interpretation of the OT, may come from Alexandria.

The orthodox Alexandrian literary tradition begins with Clement of Alexandria,* a student of Pantaenus (d. *c.* 190). Clement operated a private school in Alexandria, in which he picked up the work of the 1st-century Jewish philosopher Philo* of Alexandria in undertaking to reconcile the biblical revelation with the Greek educational heritage.

The towering figure of the Christian Alexandrian intellectual enterprise was Origen.* He was doing private teaching when asked by Bishop Demetrius to undertake the church's catechetical instruction of candidates for baptism. Later he assigned the elementary teaching to Heraclas and undertook more advanced instruction in what amounted to a private university. The opposition of Bishop Demetrius forced Origen to move to Caesarea. Through his pupil Gregory Thaumaturgus (*c.* 213–*c.* 270), Origen's thought passed to the 4th-century Cappadocians.

Intellectual concerns influenced by Origen, although accompanied by a disavowal of Origen himself, continued in the later 3rd-century bishops of Alexandria, Heraclas and Dionysius (d. 264/5). The latter, known as the Great, applied the literary criticism developed in Alexandria to argue that the apostle John was not the author of the book of Revelation. His emphasis on the distinction between the three divine persons, in opposition to modalism (see Monarchianism*) provoked a rebuke from Dionysius, Bishop of Rome, on behalf of the divine unity. He took a moderate position on readmitting to communion those who lapsed in persecution, and he rejected the rebaptism* of heretics.

The Arian* controversy of the 4th century may be understood, in its early stages, as a conflict between two wings of Origenist thought. Arius, a presbyter in Alexandria, pursued the subordinationist tendency in Origen's doctrine of the Godhead, taking the metaphor of begetting in a literal sense. Bishop Alexander and his successor

Athanasius* developed the implications of the Godhead being of the same nature and removed temporal distinctions from the realm of eternity.

The most celebrated teacher in Alexandria in the 4th century was Didymus the Blind (d. 398), the last great head of the catechetical school and amazingly learned in spite of becoming blind at the age of four. Didymus advocated the Nicene doctrine of God, especially extending it to the Holy Spirit. Many of his extensive doctrinal writings and commentaries have perished because, as a result of his defence of the orthodoxy of Origen, he shared in the condemnation of the latter at the Council of Constantinople in 553. Origen remained controversial in Alexandria, receiving strong opposition from Bishop Theophilus (385–412). His successor, Cyril,* Bishop of Alexandria from 414 to 444, continued the Alexandrian emphasis on the deity of Christ in the Nestorian* controversy. In his interpretation of Scripture he preferred the term *theoria* for the hidden meaning discerned by speculation.

The special concerns of the Alexandrian school of thought may be listed as four: 1. the place of the teacher and free intellectual enquiry in the church; 2. the relation of faith and reason;* 3. the interpretation of Scripture (see Hermeneutics*); and 4. Christology.*

1. The independent teacher, outside the church's hierarchy, maintained himself longer in Alexandria than in other Christian centres. Origen was one of the last, and he received ordination to the presbyterate from bishops in Palestine. He and Clement before him emphasized a spiritual hierarchy in the church based on the understanding of Scripture and spiritual qualities. The intellectual and administrative tasks were often combined in the bishops of Alexandria, and Heraclas, Dionysius, and probably Peter (d. 311) were heads of the catechetical school before becoming bishops. The erudite and ascetic Didymus was a layman.

2. The great task of the teachers at Alexandria was the reconciliation of the Christian faith with pagan learning. Clement claimed the concept of *gnosis* (see Gnosticism*) for orthodoxy and developed the idea of the Christian Gnostic who was faithful to the church but integrated Greek wisdom, education and spirituality into his religion. Origen had the most encyclopaedic knowledge of any early Christian teacher, but his total system had elements felt by many to be incompatible with the Bible. The Christian philosophy of Alexandria was developed during the formative stages of Neoplatonism (see Platonism*) and was permeated by its perspective.

3. Crucial to the accommodation of the Bible to Greek learning was allegorical exegesis, a method developed by the Stoics* and at home among scholars in Alexandria. It had been applied to the Jewish Bible by Philo of Alexandria. Origen found three levels of meaning in biblical texts: historical, moral and allegorical (spiritual). His varied terminology led later interpreters to systematize interpretation on four levels: literal, allegorical, moral and anagogical. Didymus and Cyril simply made a distinction between literal and spiritual senses. The same Spirit that inspired the text guided the interpreter in finding hidden spiritual meanings.

4. Origen's thought provided for the divine nature of Father, Son and Holy Spirit, while clearly marking the distinctions between the three. Athanasius emphasized their unity as one God. The Alexandrians' tendency was to stress the divinity in Christ. 'The Word became flesh' (Jn. 1:14) was their key text. Thus Cyril of Alexandria and his successors opposed the Antiochene* division between the divine and human in Christ by insisting on the unity of his person in which the Word is the subject of Christ's every activity. The term *theotokos* ('God-bearer') had been in use in Alexandria for Mary* before Cyril made it a watchword of his opposition to Nestorius. Even in the Christological controversies with Antioch, the Alexandrians understood their stress on the unity of the incarnate Word as an important defence of the Nicene creed and refutation of Arian arguments. The unity of Christ not only shaped the Alexandrian Christology, but it also provided a scheme for interpreting the gospels. Although safeguarding the unity of Christ's person, the Alexandrian approach led to Monophysitism,* which appealed to Cyril as its theological mentor.

Bibliography

In addition to the bibliographies accompanying articles on individuals mentioned, note the following: C. Bigg, *The Christian Platonists of Alexandria* (Oxford, ²1913); E. Molland, *The Conception of the*

Gospel in the Alexandrian Theology (Oslo, 1938); R. V. Sellers, *Two Ancient Christologies* (London, 1940); R. B. Tollinton, *Alexandrian Teaching on the Universe* (London, 1932); Robert Wilken, 'Alexandria: A school for Training in Virtue' in Patrick Henry (ed.), *Schools of Thought in the Christian Tradition* (Philadelphia, 1984).

E.F.

ALIENATION is the experience of being a stranger, 'away from home', estranged from others and from oneself. In the NT the verb *apallotrioō* (to estrange or alienate) is found only in Eph. 2:12, 4:18 and Col. 1:21, and always in the passive (see Stott, p. 90). Paul refers both to mankind's alienation from God and from his fellow man. These fundamental estrangements are overcome in the cross of Christ (see Atonement*).

Alienation is also a theme of the Scriptures as a whole. Adam's eviction from Eden, Cain's wandering as a fugitive, Israel's servitude in Egypt and later exile in Babylon, all symbolize an alienation that is the lot of mankind. In Lk. 15 Jesus' parable of the prodigal son gives 'a microcosmic anatomy of estrangement' (Jones, p. 176).

The word 'alienation' appears in English from 1388, and for centuries meant either transfer of ownership or insanity. Then, from the 1940s, the word was used increasingly to describe social and cultural estrangement. Influences include the vast disorientation caused by World War II, and the writings of Weber,* Kierkegaard* and Tillich.* A major source was the newly published *Economic and Philosophical Manuscripts* of Marx.*

Hegel* and Feuerbach* had seen alienation as part of man's developing self-consciousness, whereas Marx saw it as an urgent social and economic problem. For him, man was alienated in religion, under the state, but supremely in his labour. 'For Marx and Kierkegaard, the world in which Hegel felt "at home" had become alien' (Löwith, p. 173). It would seem that we are inheritors of that world. Alienation, an important concept in social psychology, has its roots in a basic theological reality: that mankind is alienated from God, creation, his fellows and himself.

Bibliography
EB (1974 ed.), vol. 1, pp. 574–576; G. V. Jones, *The Art and Truth of the Parables* (London, 1964); K. Löwith, *From Hegel to Nietzsche: the Revolution in Nineteenth-Century Thought* (London, 1965); B. Ollman, *Alienation: Marx's Conception of Man in Capitalist Society* (Cambridge, 1976); J. R. W. Stott, *The Message of Ephesians: God's New Society* (Leicester, 1979); R. M. Vince, *Alienated Man: The Theme of Alienation in the Writings of Karl Marx and Søren Kierkegaard* (unpublished MTh dissertation, King's College, London, 1980).

R.M.V.

ALLEGORY, see Hermeneutics.

ALTHAUS, PAUL (1888–1966). One of the most significant 20th-century Lutheran theologians, Althaus had a long teaching career at the University of Erlangen. Most of his work is characterized by profound engagement with the thought of Luther.* Along with contemporaries such as Werner Elert (1885–1954), under the influence of his teachers Holl* and Carl Stange (1870–1959), Althaus represents a shift from a purely historical interest in Luther to a use of Luther as a fertile theological stimulus. His reinstatement of Luther as a theologian corrects earlier Ritschlian* accounts, notably over the centrality of Luther's doctrine of justification and his theology of the cross*, though Althaus is critical of what he sees as Luther's excessive pessimism over sin and of his eucharistic theology. Althaus' own dogmatics, *Die christliche Wahrheit* (*Christian Truth*), represents a major alternative to Barth's* Christocentric understanding of revelation.* Among his other writings are an eschatology, an ethics and a much-used commentary on Romans.

Bibliography
Works in ET: *The Ethics of Martin Luther* (Philadelphia, 1972), see Foreword; *The Theology of Martin Luther* (Philadelphia, 1966).

H. Grass, in *TRE* 2, pp. 329–337; W. Lohff in L. Reinisch (ed.), *Theologians of our Time* (Notre Dame, IN, 1964), pp. 48–64.

J.B.We.

AMBROSE (*c.* 339–97) had a Christian upbringing in an aristocratic Roman family. He followed an administrative career, and at the age of thirty was appointed governor of Liguria-Aemilia, with his residence in Milan. In 374 this city was thrown into turmoil over an episcopal election. By popular acclamation Ambrose was designated the new bishop.

In office, Ambrose proved a resolute opponent of Arianism.* Being proficient in Greek, he could render the best of Eastern Nicene theology into clear Latin. The fruits of this work were his *On the Faith* and *On the Holy Spirit*. He was also involved politically in the demise of Arianism. He took initiatives to eliminate Arianism from Illyricum; while in the 380s he was pressurized in Milan itself by the mother of the boy emperor, Valentinian II, to hand over a church to Arian adherents in the city. Ambrose, whose own life was threatened, succeeded in his resistance only because of the support of the Milanese population. He based his stance on the argument that 'a temple of God could not be surrendered by a bishop'.

This was not the only occasion when Ambrose asserted the independence of the church from imperial control. In the reign of Theodosius I, who had been responsible for an indiscriminate massacre at Thessalonica, Ambrose effectively excommunicated the emperor until he did public penance for his crime. Theodosius accepted ecclesiastical discipline. But on other occasions Ambrose's assertion of ecclesiastical authority was not so felicitous. The bishop of Callinicum had inspired some monks to burn down the local synagogue. Theodosius wanted the synagogue rebuilt by the bishop, but was restrained by Ambrose on the ground that a Christian emperor ought not to show favour to unbelieving Jews. Ambrose took this position because he did not distinguish between personal duties and the duties of public office. But in general Ambrose's contribution to ecclesiastical authority in the West was good. He established that there were separate spheres of authority for church and state. In some areas too, the emperor was bound by the instruction of the church.

Ambrose was keenly concerned with the practical duties of episcopacy, among which he gave pre-eminence to scriptural instruction. He acquired considerable repute as a preacher (in which capacity he contributed significantly to the conversion of Augustine*) while his writings were well-suited to help ordinary believers. Ambrose did not originate much new theological thought, though he did adumbrate the doctrine of original sin,* and in eucharistic* theology he was the first in the West to speak of a change in the nature of the elements. This quasi-creative act was brought about by the priest, acting in Christ's stead, when he repeated the words used by Christ at the Last Supper. Ambrose was a prominent pioneer in the West of allegorical exegesis (see Hermeneutics*), Christian Neoplatonism and ascetic* theology.

A set of commentaries on the Pauline epistles was included among most manuscripts of Ambrose. Their real author, called Ambrosiaster by Erasmus, was a rough contemporary of Ambrose. This commentary exercised an important influence on the developing doctrine of original sin by interpreting Rom. 5:12 as involving the whole human race in Adam's sin and a consequent legacy of corruption for all Adam's descendants.

See also: STOICISM.

Bibliography
F. H. Dudden, *The Life and Times of St Ambrose*, 2 vols. (Oxford, 1935); H. von Campenhausen, *The Fathers of the Latin Church* (London, 1964).

G.A.K.

AMBROSIASTER, see AMBROSE.

AMES, WILLIAM, see PURITAN THEOLOGY.

AMYRALDISM. This word is derived from the Latin form of the name of Moise Amyraut (1596–1664), perhaps the most eminent and influential professor of the French Protestant Academy of Saumur. This was established in 1598 by a decision of the national synod of the French Reformed Churches. It enjoyed the special favour of Philippe Duplessis-Mornay (1549–1623), governor of Saumur and one of the noblest and most influential Protestant leaders at the turn of the century. Achieving wide acclaim in France and in foreign countries for the brilliance of its faculty, it attracted a very considerable number of students until it was abolished by order of King Louis XIV at the revocation of the Edict of Nantes in 1685.

The school was known also for its encouragement of progressive ideas and its special consideration to people of nobility or wealth. In philosophy this was made apparent by the vigorous advocacy of Ramist* over against Aristotelian* logic which remained the standard in more traditional institutions like Sedan, Geneva, or Leiden. In theology, the influence of John Cameron (1579–1625) was a dominant feature, even though he taught there only between 1618 and 1621. During that time, however, he managed to exercise a very great influence on three of his students, Louis Cappel (1585–1658), Josué de la Place (Placaeus, 1596–1655), and Moise Amyraut mentioned above.

Each of these three was involved in controversy over teachings which tended to broaden the Reformed* orthodoxy represented for instance in the Synod of Dort.* Cappel was embroiled in a discussion relating to the presence of the vowel points in the original Hebrew text and contended against Johann Buxtorf of Basel, that these were a later addition made by the Masoretes (see Biblical Criticism*) to facilitate the reading of Scripture by people who had little knowledge of Hebrew. Later scholarship has vindicated him in this, although it remains true that the text without vowel points constitutes a clear standard of truth. Placaeus promoted the theory of mediate imputation, according to which Adam's* descendants were not adjudged guilty of the first sin of Adam but were born corrupt as a result of that sin and incurred God's displeasure by virtue of this corruption. The National Synod of Charenton (1645) expressed reservations in this area, although theologians of Saumur insisted that it had not condemned Placaeus' view.

Moise Amyraut was undoubtedly the most celebrated theologian of this school and served from 1633 to the time of his death in 1664. He was involved in a severe controversy relating to the scope of divine grace, predestination* and the extent of Christ's atonement.* Amyraut intended to soften the edges of the traditional orthodox Reformed view and thus to relieve difficulties in the controversy with Roman Catholics and facilitate a reunion of Protestants in which Reformed and Lutheran could join ranks. In his *Traité de la Prédestination* (1634) he claimed that God, moved by his love for mankind, had appointed all human beings to salvation provided they repent and believe. He sent his Son, the Lord Jesus Christ, to die for the sins of all mankind in order to implement this purpose. However, since human beings would

not on their own initiative repent and believe, God then chose to bestow a special measure of his Spirit to some only, who are the elect. Grace thus is seen as universal in the provision for salvation but as particular in the application of it. In viewing matters in this fashion, Amyraut thought that he could continue to adhere to the Canons of Dort and at the same time provide a picture of God's benevolence that would be more faithful to Scripture and indeed to Calvin* than the thoroughly particularistic approach that characterized Reformed orthodoxy in the second quarter of the 17th century.

Amyraut's views were supported by his colleagues in Saumur and by the pastors of the influential Reformed Church of Charenton near Paris. He was strenuously opposed by Pierre du Moulin of Sedan (1568–1658), André Rivet of the Netherlands (1572–1651), and Friedrich Spanheim of Geneva and Leiden (1600–49). At the National Synod of Alençon (1637) he was admonished, but not condemned for heresy. The controversy raged until 1661, with three periods of special intensity: 1634–37, 1641–49 and 1655–61. In the last period Amyraut did not participate in the debates carried out by Jean Daillé (Dallaeus 1594–1670) and Samuel Desmarets (Maresius, 1599–1673).

Various assessments of the impact of the Salmurian theology have been offered. It seems apparent that it tended to weaken the unity of Reformed thought and to open the door to increasing departures from Reformed orthodoxy. It may have influenced King Louis XIV and his counsellors into thinking that there was no intrinsic incompatibility between the Reformed faith and Roman Catholicism. He was thus led to believe erroneously that the revocation of the Edict of Nantes would not produce great turmoil in France. The three Saumur professors together produced the large work *Theses Theologicae Salmurienses* (4 parts in 2 vols., 1664 and again in 1665) which became a frequently used manual for the study of theology.

One of Amyraut's students and successors at Saumur, Claude Pajon (1625–85), carried the trend further by positing that the Spirit's work of regeneration* is merely an illumination of the mind which brings about, of necessity, a change in the direction of the human will (congruism; see Merit*). This stance, strenuously opposed by Pierre Jurieu

(1637–1713), increased misgivings about Saumur's orthodoxy. In 1675 J. H. Heidegger in concert with F. Turretin (1623–1687) and L. Gernler issued the *Formula Consensus Helvetica* designed specifically as an anti-Salmurian document, but the influence of Saumur was felt in all the countries to which French Protestants fled after the revocation of the Edict of Nantes.

Bibliography

On Saumur the fullest treatment is still to be found in P. Daniel Bourchenin, *Etude sur les Académies protestantes en France au XVIIe et au XVIIIe Siècles* (Paris, 1882). The researches of Jean Paul Pittion at Trinity College, Dublin are very valuable but difficult of access.

Brian Armstrong, *Calvinism and the Amyraut Heresy* (Madison, WI, 1969); François Laplanche, *Orthodoxie et Prédication* (Paris, 1965); J. Leith, *Creeds of the Churches* (Richmond, VA, ³1982); Roger Nicole, *Moyse Amyraut. A Bibliography* (New York and London, 1981); P. Schaff, *Creeds of Christendom*, vol. 1 (London, 1877), pp. 477–489; B. B. Warfield, *The Plan of Salvation* (Grand Rapids, MI, 1942). Note also the PhD theses by J. Moltmann at Göttingen (1951) and L. Proctor at Leeds (1952).

R.N.

ANABAPTIST THEOLOGY.

The Anabaptists, together with other groups known today as the revolutionaries, spiritualists and evangelical rationalists, belonged to the radical wing of the Protestant Reformation.* Contemporary scholarship makes a distinction between the 'revolutionary Anabaptists' who were associated with the Zwickau Prophets, Thomas Müntzer (*c.* 1490–1525) and the later violent Münsterites, and the 'evangelical Anabaptists' who found their origin in Conrad Grebel (*c.* 1498–1526), Hans Hut (d. 1527), Pilgram Marpeck (d. 1556) and Menno Simons (1496–1561). The latter had their beginnings in Zurich in Switzerland and spread to South Germany, Moravia and the Netherlands with considerable homogeneity between each region. More recent studies, however, have contended for the multiple origins and diversity of the Anabaptist movement in these various centres, rather than for the monogenesis of a norma-

tive movement in Switzerland. Accordingly, the theology of this movement cannot be characterized without allowing for exceptions and paradoxes. But its basic theological emphases are clearly discernible.

The Anabaptists did not consciously do theology in the classical sense, even though they accepted the substance of the Christian creeds.* Their theology was much more occasional in nature. It was largely an exposition of Bible doctrine as it applies to life. In this manner they developed a theological focus of their own alongside and in reaction to magisterial Protestantism.

One of the central points of difference between the Anabaptists and the mainline Reformers relates to the question of human nature and salvation. Whereas the Reformers defined sin* as bondage of the will,* the Anabaptists, rejecting the Augustinian* interpretation of the sovereignty of God, viewed sin as a loss of capacity or a serious sickness. For them there is no real repentance and commitment without the freedom of the will. Consequently, Anabaptist theology is not regulated by the concept of sin as much as by the concept of wilful obedience. Salvation is not simply a certitude of being saved from damnation but a walking in newness of life. The emphasis is more on regeneration* of the new being in Christ than on justification* by faith (*Rechtfertigung*). God in effect makes us righteous (*Gerechtmachung*) in Christ and then accepts us on the basis of that righteousness.* In order to ensure a sinless Christ as a basis for a strong doctrine of salvation, Dutch and North German Anabaptism held to a questionable view of the celestial origin and nature of Christ's flesh. This view was later superseded by a more traditional Christology.*

The attendant theology of the church* as a visible fellowship of obedient disciples, exhibiting the way of suffering love, was another of the controlling features of Anabaptist theology which diverged from magisterial Protestantism most emphatically. Various concepts of the church prevailed among the Anabaptists: church as congregation, as inner spiritual reality, as intentional community and as kingdom of God.* However, at the centre was the idea of the church as a believers' fellowship (*Gemeinde*) versus the church as a state church (*Volkskirche*).

The practice of adult baptism* was essential to the Anabaptist view of the church. Their rejection of infant baptism was based on the lack of NT evidence for such a practice. For them believers' baptism was the consequence of understanding the church as a voluntary fellowship, consisting of those who had experienced conversion and who were baptized upon the confession of their faith. It was a distinguishing mark of separation from the world and of commitment to Christian discipleship.

The central aspects of Anabaptist ecclesiology were actual personal conversion,* holy living, suffering in the Spirit of Christ, practice of love* and non-resistance, separation from the world,* full community in the church, obedience to the great commission, maintenance of church discipline,* rejection of the use of power by Christians and of involvement in political office, and freedom of conscience.* In contrast to the Reformers, the Anabaptists emphasized the fallenness of Christendom* and the restoration of the NT church.

The strong emphasis on separation from the world was balanced by a burning missionary zeal which took the Anabaptists into the world. Unbounded by national and racial lines, they were the first to make the great commission the responsibility of every church member. This represented a break with the territorial principle and with Protestant and Catholic doctrine. Moreover, the church's relationship to society was informed by a two-kingdom theology in which the conflict between the church and the state* was seen to be much greater in principle than for the other Reformers. The Anabaptists were emphatic about the fallenness of humanity and its potential for redemption but not optimistic about changing the world system as such. Yet submission to governmental authority, ordered by God, was important, even though the state must not force the Christian community to compromise its allegiance to the way of the cross. For the most part Anabaptism was non-resistant in character. People who disagreed with the church should not be dealt with by the sword but by the process of church discipline governed by the way of Christ's suffering love. Thus, the non-resistance stance included more than a refusal to be involved in government, military service or war.* It applied to personal, social and economic relationships.

Such a way of life reflected the empowering of the Holy Spirit.* The Anabaptists exhibited a frequent sense of reliance on the Spirit. Clearly the doctrine of the Spirit was central in relation to the walk of faith.* Moreover, the Spirit made the Bible a living word of God which must be obeyed and practised in daily life. The spiritual understanding of the Scriptures* was strongly linked to the believing community where one heard the word and discerned its meaning and will. The message of the Spirit was given in the community of believers gathered around the word. At times, however, subjectivistic and spiritualistic tendencies did emerge.

In their interpretation of Scripture the Anabaptists had much in common with their 16th-century contemporaries. However, some basic differences existed, especially on the relationship of the New Testament to the Old, the degree to which Scripture was the *sole* authority, and the extent to which biblical interpretation was dependent on obedience to Christ. For the Anabaptists a large part of interpreting the Bible was imitating it. Theirs was a hermeneutic* of obedience.

The centrality of the transformed life of discipleship resulted in severe persecutions. For many, suffering the way of the cross was essential to this kind of discipleship and profoundly shaped their eschatology.* Suffering* became a key to understanding the role of the believer in history.* The kingdom comes and is consummated through suffering for Christ. They generally agreed that they were living in the last days, in the tribulation preceding the second coming. Although chiliastic tendencies existed (see Millennium*) and eschatology was central to many Anabaptists, there was no agreement regarding the specific time of the end and their own stance towards it.

See also: MENNONITE THEOLOGY; REFORMATION, RADICAL.

Bibliography

H. S. Bender, 'The Anabaptist Vision', *CH* 13 (1944), pp. 3–24; H. S. Bender *et al.* (eds.), *The Mennonite Encyclopedia*, vols. I-IV (Scottdale, PA, 1955–59); W. R. Estep, *The Anabaptist Story* (Grand Rapids, MI, 1975); R. Friedmann, *The Theology of Anabaptism* (Scottdale, PA, 1973); H. Goertz, 'History and Theology: A Major Problem of Anabaptist Research Today', *MQR* 53

(1979), pp. 177–188; W. Klassen (ed.), *Anabaptism in Outline* (Scottdale, PA, 1981); J. M. Stayer, W. O. Packull and K. Deppermann, 'From Monogenesis to Polygenesis: The Historical Discussion of Anabaptist Origins', *MQR* 49 (1975), pp. 83–121.

H.J.L.

ANALOGY. Argument by analogy reasons that if some principle obtains in one area it may well also obtain in some other, similar area. Thus, if complexity and regularity in a watch imply that it was consciously designed, perhaps complexity and regularity in the universe imply that it too was designed, by God. A celebrated theological use of this kind of analogy was the argument of Joseph Butler* that there is a likeness between the course of nature and the system described in revelation; both may therefore be believed to have the same author.

Analogical predication is a theory of the language* used to describe God. Human language arises from experience of finite, created things; surely, then, it cannot be used in its natural sense to describe an infinite creator. Yet it cannot be used *unnaturally* and still remain meaningful. The theory of Thomism* is that there is analogy between the meaning of words applied to the world and that of the same words when applied to God; and this in two ways. *Analogy of attribution* is found when, for instance, a climate is called 'healthy' as producing health in its inhabitants (to whom the word 'healthy' properly applies). Hence God may be called 'good' as the source of created goodness. But as this would equally justify calling God 'purple', this form of analogy is comparatively unimportant. *Analogy of proportionality* holds between corresponding qualities in two things of different kinds. Thus loyalty in a dog is neither identical with loyalty in humans nor wholly different; there is an analogy between the two. Similarly, the perfect justice, wisdom, *etc.* of God are neither identical with nor wholly different from the justice, wisdom, *etc.* we see around us, but are analogous to them: hence words like 'just' and 'wise' can be intelligibly applied to God, although his exact nature remains a mystery.

Objections to analogical predication are: 1. Does it not make reasoning about God impossible? If God's wisdom is mysteriously unlike human wisdom, may he not act in ways that in plain language are unwise? Analogists might answer that God's qualities differ from ours in being better, not worse (and quote 1 Cor. 1:25). 2. Is the theory not too closely tied to Thomist natural theology?* Historically the two have been associated, but there is no necessary link. 3. Perhaps most serious: is analogy really *needed*? The Bible, and Christian discourse generally, speak more of God's acts within the created world than of his inner being. Moreover, if, as some analogists hold, the difference between God's qualities and ours is that his are utterly free from the imperfections ours have, this can be understood without the aid of analogy. God remains greater than words can express; but where words can be used they are used naturally.

Bibliography

Thomas Aquinas, *Summa contra Gentiles*, I:32–34; J. Butler, *Analogy of Religion* (1736; often repr.), Introduction; A. Farrer, *Reflective Faith* (London, 1972); E. Mascall, *Existence and Analogy* (London, 1949); H. Palmer, *Analogy* (London, 1973); P. Sherry, 'Analogy Reviewed' and 'Analogy Today', *Philosophy* 51 (1976), pp. 337–345 and 431–446.

R.L.S.

ANAMNESIS, see EUCHARIST.

ANGELS. The term simply means 'messenger' (Heb. *mal'āk*, Gk. *angelos*) without any overtones of visual splendour. Where *God's* messenger is in view, there may be present credentials of the divine glory and majesty (Mt. 24:31; Lk. 2:9; Heb. 1:7 *etc.*), though this is not always the case (*cf.* Heb. 13:2). In general, the term 'Lord of hosts' points to the existence of angelic beings (*cf.* the parallelism of 'angels' and 'hosts' in Ps. 148:2), and the expression 'holy ones' may often be read in this way too, particularly in the OT.

That angels are regarded as part of creation is not in doubt (Ps. 148:2, 5; Col. 1:16), but Scripture accords to angelic beings a position of unusual authority over the created and historical order, including responsibility for children (Mt. 18:10), protection of God's people (Ps. 34:7), involvement in international affairs (Dan. 10:13; 10:20 – 11:10) and participation in the judgments of God (Rev. 15 – 16).

In keeping with such activity, a hierarchy of power may be detected among the angels, Michael being described as a prince and archangel with special authority (Dan. 10:13, 21; 12:1; Jude 9; Rev. 12:7). Moreover, the NT describes angels, in terms borrowed from the LXX, as 'powers' (*dynameis*), 'authorities' (*exousiai*), 'principalities' (*archai*) and 'rulers' (*archontes*).

Schleiermacher* and many others have posed the question of the *need* for angels. Several answers have been offered. The first is that the glory and majesty of God are given concrete expression by sheer numbers and power in angelic worship (Is. 6:3; Rev. 5:11). This is not because God needs any enhancement but so that man as worshipping creature, raised in Christ to the heavenly sphere, may enjoy a new participation in the heavenly praise (Eph. 1:3, 20; Heb. 12:22; Rev. 5:6–14). The second answer is that angels function as bearers of strength and sustenance to human creatures, being themselves sinless and in certain respects free from the limitations of the human constitution (Mt. 4:11; Mk. 1:13; Heb. 1:14). The third answer, more problematical, is that, by virtue of the infinite gap between creator and created humanity, the knowledge of God must always be *mediated* to mankind. The most obvious problem with this view is that the angels themselves are creatures, and, in any case, any hint of intermediate being has traditionally tended to erode the divine transcendence. This said, however, angels do indeed play a significant role in the mediation of revelation* (Lk. 1:30–33; Gal. 3:19; Heb. 2:2).

In Jude 6 some angels rebel, and in the NT generally personal evil beings accordingly take titles appropriate to the angels (Eph. 2:2; 6:12; probably Col. 2:14). Chief of these rebel spirits is the Devil* or Satan (Heb. 'accuser'), whose activity begins in legal oppression (Zc. 3:1; Jude 9; Rev. 12:10) but extends to a wider activity of harassment and temptation (1 Pet. 5:8).

Modern objections to a doctrine of angels, although often stemming from an irrational prejudice against anything mysterious, sometimes arise from the problem of fitting such beings into a world alleged to be explicable purely in terms of causes open to scientific examination. Some theologians would say angels *are* susceptible to this kind of investigation, but others refer the matter to the similar mystery of providence* in general.

In 2nd-century Christianity, attempts were made to describe both Christ and the Holy Spirit in angelic terms, but the New Testament picture of a Christ distinguished from, and infinitely superior to, all other powers prevailed (*cf.* Eph. 1:21–22; Col. 1:16; Heb. 1:4–5).

Bibliography

K. Barth, *CD*, III. 3; G. B. Caird, *Principalities and Powers* (London, 1956); W. Carr, *Angels and Principalities* (London, 1981).

R.K.

ANGLICANISM. This name is given to a pattern of Christianity which arose in England, Wales and Ireland under the influence of the 16th-century Reformation,* and was afterwards carried by emigrants and missionaries to the English or British possessions abroad, and to some extent beyond them. Its great architect was Thomas Cranmer (1489–1556), Archbishop of Canterbury from 1532 onwards, who owed much to the continental Reformers who preceded him (both Lutheran* and Swiss or Reformed*), but whose own scholarship and independence of mind gave the English Reformation its distinctive character (see Reformers, English*).

Like Luther, Cranmer worked on the relatively cautious principle of changing what (in the light of the Bible) needed changing, but not beginning afresh. He secured the authorization of the English Bible (itself the work of William Tyndale, *c.* 1494–1536 and Miles Coverdale, 1488–1568), he created the English liturgy of the *Book of Common Prayer* (a far-reaching revision of the Latin Sarum liturgy, in the vernacular), he drew up the Anglican confession* of faith (the Thirty-nine Articles, brought to their present form in 1571), he supported the break with the papacy* and the suppression of the monasteries (though the initiative in these matters was taken by Henry VIII and his ministers); but he allowed the Church of England to retain its identity, in that its membership, its places of worship and many of its patterns of life continued substantially unchanged. It remained liturgical in its worship,* parochial in its organization, episcopal in its oversight, paedo-baptist in its practice, and established in its relations with the state.* The description of Anglicanism as 'reformed Catholicism' is not therefore inappropriate, if rightly understood. Anglicanism remains 'Catholic',* *i.e.* traditional, in much of its practice, though reformed in its theology. This does not, however, make it unique in Christendom, as the Anglo-Catholic* school contends and as the Second Vatican Council* conceded (*Decree on Ecumenism* 13), for the same could be said of Lutheranism, though the 'Catholic' practices retained by Lutheranism are somewhat different.

The Thirty-nine Articles are mostly based on the Augsburg Confession, but the sacramental* articles are less Lutheran than Swiss, and the final eight articles, on matters of church order (see Church Government*) and church-state relations, are in various respects domestically English. Though historically Anglican clergy have had to subscribe to the Articles, and in many countries they still have to, the Articles have not influenced theological thought to the same degree as continental confessions* have done.

Cranmer's *Book of Common Prayer*, however, which includes the three creeds,* and expresses the same teaching as the Articles, though in a devotional manner, has had a greater influence than any continental liturgy, and, especially in its 1662 form, was until recently the most powerful unifying force in the Anglican world.

Since the 16th century, various schools of thought have risen among Anglicans – Puritan,* Laudian, Latitudinarian,* Evangelical,* Tractarian (Anglo-Catholic*), Liberal* – with greater or less loyalty to historical Anglican Protestantism.* The last three of these are still very prominent today, and lay their main stress, respectively, on Scripture,* tradition and reason (see Hooker*), all of which featured in the Anglican Reformation, though with Scripture supreme.

Anglican episcopacy was originally a domestic discipline, and did not exclude Protestants from abroad, in Presbyterian* orders, from being admitted to Anglican livings without re-ordination. In 1662, reacting against the abolition of episcopacy by Presbyterians and Congregationalists* during the Commonwealth, this permission was withdrawn, a decision which has since laid Anglicans open to the imputation of denying the validity of non-episcopal orders, though only the Tractarian school actually does so.

The Anglican Communion today is a worldwide fellowship of self-governing churches (mainly centred in the UK, Australasia, Africa and N. America), giving a primacy of honour, but not of jurisdiction, to the Archbishop of Canterbury. Only the Church of England is still an established church, so within England the Archbishop of Canterbury is himself subject to the supreme governor of the Church of England, the monarch, though during the colonial period Anglican archbishops and bishops abroad were similarly subject. The monarch now exercises her authority mainly through the prime minister.

Apart from this common bond of history and affection with Canterbury, which is given expression in the ten-yearly Lambeth Conference of bishops, it is becoming increasingly difficult to name factors which bind all the Anglican churches together. In 1888 the Lambeth Conference adopted a four-point statement, listing these factors as they then were, and since known as the Lambeth Quadrilateral. Its points were 1. the supremacy and sufficiency of the Scriptures; 2. the Apostles' Creed,* as the baptismal symbol (no longer so today) in many places, and the Nicene Creed as the sufficient statement of the Christian Faith; 3. the two dominical sacraments; 4. the historic episcopate. This already revealed the absurdity of excluding factors which were not *absolutely* universal, notably the Thirty-nine Articles (slightly revised in the USA), the Athanasian Creed (discarded in the USA) and the 1662 Prayer Book (revised in a few countries); but the recent adoption of revised liturgies not based upon the Prayer Book at all, and differing from country to country, has weakened the liturgical bond much more seriously. Furthermore, the ordination (see Ministry*) of women (see Feminist Theology*) to the presbyterate in a few countries but not the rest has put limits upon the mutual recognition of ministers. The Articles have also been downgraded in a number of countries, and discarded in one or two. Such developments strain even the bond with Canterbury, and it is essential today to stress the factors which *most* Anglican churches have in common, rather than all, if any cohesion and any distinctive Anglican ethos is to survive.

Bibliography

C. S. Carter, *The English Church and the Reformation* (London, 1912); *idem*, *The Anglican Via Media* (London, 1927); R. Hooker, *Of the Laws of Ecclesiastical Polity* (see Hooker*); S. C. Neill, *Anglicanism* (Harmondsworth, 1960); S. W. Sykes, *The Integrity of Anglicanism* (London, 1978); W. H. Griffith Thomas, *The Principles of Theology* (London, 1930); A. T. P. Williams, *The Anglican Tradition in the Life of England* (London, 1947).

R.T.B.

ANGLO-CATHOLIC THEOLOGY

stems chiefly from the insistence of the Oxford Movement (1833–45) that the Church of England was not a department of the state but a divine institution, a true branch or portion of the one holy, catholic and apostolic church of Christ. The implications of this rediscovery of the doctrine of the church* were worked out in a series of ninety *Tracts for the Times* (1833–41) written mainly by John Henry Newman,* E. B. Pusey (1800–82) and John Keble (1792–1886). These three Oxford dons also tried to make their fellow clergy aware of the rich theological tradition in which they stood, by translating a *Library of the Fathers*, beginning with Augustine's *Confessions* (1838). Such research into links with the patristic or medieval church persuaded some Tractarians, like Newman, to become Roman Catholics. Most were glad to work for the renewal of the Church of England, seeing it as the *via media* between Puritanism* and Rome.

Religion began to be taken more seriously. Private confession was reintroduced, fasting and the adoption of a rule of life were advocated. Theological colleges were founded, the monastic life was revived. Communities of men and women and slum priests like C. F. Lowder (1820–80) devoted themselves to the care of the under-privileged, fortified by frequent if not daily reception of Communion. Belief in the real presence of Christ in the sacrament, a doctrine stressed by Pusey, also prompted the adoption of vestments, candles and incense in worship.

Contemporary Evangelicals welcomed the Tractarians' stress on personal and corporate holiness (see Sanctification*) and shared their high view of Scripture* and the doctrines of the creeds,* but concentrated on points of disagreement, questioning the Anglo-Catholic understanding of the place of tradition, the role of bishops and the authority of the ordained ministry, the nature and efficacy of the sacraments and the place of ritual and ceremonial in worship (*cf.* P. Toon, *Evangelical Theology 1833–1856*, London, 1979). The result was party strife in the church, leading both groups to a polarization of attitudes whose visible expression and focus in public worship eventually made it necessary for bishops and parliament to attempt to outlaw excesses.

Although 'ritualism' or the revival of pre-Reformation practices like the wearing of vestments provoked much opposition in the 19th century, the Anglo-Catholic emphasis on worship and the centrality of the eucharist was later to bear fruit throughout the church in the Parish Communion movement (*cf.* A. G. Hebert, *Liturgy and Society*, London, 1935; *idem*, ed., *The Parish Communion*, London, 1937). Research into the practice of the early church (*cf.* Gregory Dix, *The Shape of the Liturgy*, London, 1945) influenced new services of Communion which were incorporated in due course in the Church of England's official *Alternative Service Book* (*ASB*), 1980, a significant development in a church that values doctrine implicit in liturgy as highly as any explicit statements based on creeds or Articles (*cf.* Doctrine Commission Report, *Believing in the Church*, London, 1981).

After the Oxford Movement, the publication of *Lux Mundi* (1889) and *Essays Catholic and Critical* (1926) marked a shift by some Anglo-Catholics towards the acceptance of modern biblical and historical criticism. Among the contributors to the latter volume were scholars of the stature and personal influence of E. C. Hoskyns (1884–1937), author, with F. N. Davey, of *The Riddle of the New Testament* (London, 1931) and translator of Barth's* *Romans;* K. E. Kirk (1886–1954), later bishop of Oxford, who adapted Roman Catholic moral theology* for Anglican use, *cf. The Vision of God* (London, 1931); L. S. Thornton (1884–1960), specialist in Christology and ecclesiology, *cf. The Incarnate Lord* (London, 1928), *The Common Life in the Body of Christ* (London, 1942); and the wide-ranging Leonard Hodgson (1889–1969), *cf. For Faith and Freedom*, 2 vols., (Oxford, 1956).

Thornton had recently contributed an essay

23

on the social implications of faith to *The Return of Christendom* (London, 1922), a precursor of the unique attempts by the Anglo-Catholic Summer School of Sociology (1925–) and the Christendom Group (1931–) to formulate a distinctively Anglican social ethic, spurred on by Bishop Frank Weston's reminder to the 1923 Anglo-Catholic Congress of the meaning of an incarnational religion: 'You cannot claim to worship Jesus in the Tabernacle, if you do not pity Jesus in the slum' (*cf.* John Oliver, *The Church and Social Order*, London, 1968).

Despite all this promise, the 1920s proved to be the high point of Anglo-Catholic influence in the parishes and in academic theology. Its subsequent decline is explained partly by a loss of identity and purpose following success in achieving many of its aims, and partly by a conservatism that largely failed to respond to post-war social change in Britain and to theological and liturgical developments in Roman Catholicism, particularly after Vatican II. On the other hand, hopes for reunion with Rome, going back at least as far as the abortive Malines Conversations (1921–25) initiated by Lord Halifax (1839–1934), have made it difficult for many Anglo-Catholics to support ecumenical progress in other directions or to favour the ordination of women to the priesthood.

What of the future? E. L. Mascall (b. 1905) has shown that it is possible to combine concern for church order and church union with the production of significant contributions to contemporary academic debate, *cf.*, *The Recovery of Unity* (London, 1958) and contributions to C. O. Buchanan *etc.*, *Growing into Union* (London, 1970) and *Man, Woman and Priesthood*, ed. P. Moore (London, 1978), alongside *The Secularisation of Christianity* (London, 1965), *The Openness of Being* (London, 1971) and *Theology and the Gospel of Christ* (London, ²1984). Kenneth Leech (b. 1939) and the Jubilee Group (1974/5–) follow more in the line of the Christendom Group in proposing a 'revolutionary orthodoxy' incorporating development of a theological critique of capitalism, *cf.*, K. Leech and R. Williams (eds.), *Essays Catholic and Radical* (London, 1983), K. Leech, *The Social God* (London, 1981), *True God* (London, 1985). Less radical assessments of Anglo-Catholicism past, present and future may be found in G. Rowell, *The Vision*

Glorious (Oxford, 1983), *idem*, ed., *Tradition Renewed: The Oxford Movement Conference Papers* (London, 1986), and in volumes of the *Faith and the Future* series, ed. D. Nicholls (Oxford, 1983). For a more general historical perspective see O. Chadwick, *The Victorian Church*, 2 vols. (London, ³1971, ²1972), and A. Hastings, *A History of English Christianity 1920–1985* (London, 1986).

P.N.H.

ANHYPOSTASIA, see Hypostasis.

ANIMAL RIGHTS, see Rights, Animal.

ANIMISM. A term introduced into the discussion about the origin and nature of religion by the anthropologist E. B. Tylor (1832–1917). He used it as a synonym for religion which he defined as 'the belief in Spiritual Beings'. This belief arose when primitive man, in attempting to explain phenomena such as sleep, death, dreams and visions, came to the conclusion that he possessed a detachable phantom or ghost soul. His primitive imagination then led him to attribute a similar soul to animals, plants and even inanimate objects.

According to Tylor, from this primitive reasoning, by means of general cultural influence, all forms of religion developed. As a positivist,* he also believed that animism or 'the spiritualistic philosophy', based as it was on a false process of reasoning, was destined to disappear before the flood of 'materialistic philosophy'. But, though very influential for half a century, the theory was eventually superseded since it was based on the false presupposition that so-called 'contemporary primitives' are 'survivals' of an actual primitive stage of human evolution. However, its influence is apparent in that, *e.g.*, the theories of primitive monotheism* of Lang (1844–1912) and Schmidt (1868–1954), the pre-animism of Marett (1866–1943) and the social theory of Durkheim* were all presented as alternatives to it. Despite the fact that the theory has been superseded the term can be usefully retained to describe a religion which is characterized by a belief in a multiplicity of spirits.

Bibliography

E. Durkheim, *The Elementary Forms of the*

Religious Life (London, 1915); E. E. Evans-Pritchard, *Theories of Primitive Religion* (Oxford, 1965); A. Lang, *The Making of Religion* (London, 1898); R. R. Marett, *The Threshold of Religion* (London, ²1914); W. Schmidt, *The Origin and Growth of Religion* (London, 1931); E. B. Tylor, *Primitive Culture* (London, 1871), and in *Mind* 2 (1877), pp. 141–156.

D.A.Hu.

ANOINTING. The practice of anointing, either with oil or with ointment (chrism), was widespread in antiquity, and had various purposes, religious and secular. In the OT, both priests and kings were consecrated in this way, and it is for this reason that English (British) monarchs, since Anglo-Saxon times, have been anointed during their coronation service. The Heb. title 'Messiah' (Gk. *christos*), meaning 'anointed one', also arose from the custom of anointing kings, since it was prophesied that the saviour would spring from the royal house of David.

In the OT, there is a link between anointing and the Spirit of God (1 Sa. 16:13; Is. 61:1, 3), and when in the NT Christians are spoken of as anointed, the meaning is sometimes simply that they have received the Holy Spirit (2 Cor. 1:21f.; 1 Jn. 2:20–27). In the 2nd century, however, the practice arose of literally anointing Christians at their baptism,* as either an alternative to laying hands on them or an addition to it, and these ceremonies, when separated from baptism, became the modes of confirmation.*

In the NT, literal anointing is spoken of as a Jewish custom, when one anoints the head of a guest, or anoints a body to prepare it for burial. As a Christian practice, it occurs in the context of healing* (Mk. 6:13; Jas. 5:14). It is noteworthy in the latter passage that 'the prayer of faith' is said to heal the sick, and not the anointing as such; so the promise of healing should be interpreted in the same way (and with the same qualifications) as the promises that God will answer prayer.

The anointing of the sick continued in the church for many centuries, but in the 9th-century West its purpose changed. From then on it was conferred simply for the benefit of the soul, after expectation of bodily recovery had been abandoned. Hence the so-called sacrament of extreme unction, which is one of the rites given in the Church of Rome to the dying.

Extreme unction was abolished in the churches of the Reformation. A short-lived attempt was made in England to restore the ancient anointing of the sick for their healing, in the 1549 Prayer Book. Other attempts are being made at the present time. It is quite widespread in churches and circles influenced by the Pentecostal* and charismatic movements.

Bibliography
D. S. Allister, *Sickness and Healing in the Church* (Oxford, 1981); L. L. Mitchell, *Baptismal Anointing* (London, 1966); F. W. Puller, *The Anointing of the Sick in Scripture and Tradition* (London, 1910).

R.T.B.

ANOMOEANS, see ARIANISM.

ANONYMOUS CHRISTIANITY. A theological concept developed by Karl Rahner* in order to explain the possibility of salvation without explicit Christian faith, which modern Roman Catholic theology has widely acknowledged. As Rahner expounds it, the idea follows from some of the most basic themes of his theology. He holds that every human person, in his pre-reflective experience, is orientated towards God, and that God gives himself in grace* to every human person, in the centre of his existence, as an offer which can be accepted or rejected. Thus God is always and everywhere present in human experience, and the possibility of a saving relationship with God is universal, corresponding to God's universal will for human salvation (see Universalism*). This universal revelation of God and the salvific experience of God which makes it possible are pre-reflective, implicit in human experience, before they are understood explicitly and conceptually. The religions of the world are more or less successful attempts to make this 'transcendental' experience of God explicit in reflective forms and social, historical embodiments. But salvation is possible not only within the non-Christian religions, but also for the atheist,* who does not thematize his transcendental experience in religious terms at all.

For Rahner, the specifically Christian revelation* of God is his 'categorical' revelation, *i.e.* his revelation of himself in explicit, historical forms. It is the explicit form of his universal, transcendental revelation. Consequently, the salvation which is universally available is essentially the same as salvation within the Christian church. Explicit Christian faith is the explicit form of the implicit faith which is possible without any knowledge of the Christian revelation. Those who are saved through such implicit faith, Rahner calls 'anonymous Christians'. They are *anonymous* Christians because they do not have explicit Christian faith, but they are anonymous *Christians*, because Rahner retains the doctrine that there is no salvation apart from Christ. Their implicit faith must be related to Christ.

How is this possible? Jesus Christ is the complete and definitive expression of God's self-communication to humanity and the human acceptance of this. He is therefore the supreme and unique fulfilment of that possibility of salvific relationship with God which is everywhere present in the human spirit. As such, he is the goal towards which the faith even of the anonymous Christian is implicitly orientated. Rahner is able to claim that the anonymous Christian is saved because of Jesus Christ.

Rahner's concept of anonymous Christianity has been very influential in Roman Catholic thought, but it has also been strongly criticized by some other Roman Catholic theologians. Hans Urs von Balthasar* charged Rahner with relativizing the biblical revelation of God. Hans Küng,* while agreeing that non-Christians can be saved, thinks that the idea of 'anonymous Christianity' is offensive to non-Christians and evades the real challenge of the world religions by pre-empting the dialogue before it has begun.

A full appraisal of Rahner's proposal would need to examine the understanding of transcendental experience and Christian salvation on which it rests. It is arguable that Rahner's whole transcendental approach to theology gives insufficient weight to the historical nature of all human experience, and therefore to the historical character of the knowledge of God available through Jesus Christ.

See also: CHRISTIANITY AND OTHER RELIGIONS.

Bibliography

K. Rahner, *Theological Investigations* (London, 1961–81), vol. V, ch. 6; vol. VI, ch. 23; vol. IX, ch. 9; vol. XII, ch. 9; vol. XVI, chs. 4, 13; vol. XVII, ch. 5; vol. XVIII, ch. 17; *idem*, *Foundations of Christian Faith* (London, 1978), pp. 311–321.

R.J.B.

ANSELM (*c.* 1033–1109). Born in Aosta in Italy, at the age of twenty-six Anselm became a Benedictine* monk, entering the abbey of Bec in Normandy. In 1063 he was made prior, in succession to Lanfranc (*c.* 1005–89), and fifteen years later abbot, a post he held for a further fifteen years (1078–93). He then again succeeded Lanfranc, as Archbishop of Canterbury, until his death in 1109. Anselm sought to uphold the pope's rights in England and to maintain the independence of the English church from the king. As a result, most of his time as archbishop was spent on the continent, in exile.

Anselm was the first truly great theologian of the medieval Western church and is seen by some as the founder of scholasticism.* He allowed philosophy a significant, though limited, role in his theology, following Augustine's* method of 'faith seeking understanding'. The content of the Christian faith is given by revelation,* not by philosophy. But the believing theologian can then seek, by the use of reason, to understand more fully that which he believes. Reason can thus show the rationality and inner coherence of the Christian faith (*cf.* Faith and Reason*).

This method Anselm pursued in his three major works. In the *Monologion* (1077), originally called *An Example of Meditation on the Grounds of Faith*, he offers a 'proof' for the existence of God (see Natural Theology*). The fact that we can discern degrees of goodness means that there is an absolute good, by which we measure it. This good is alone good of itself and is supremely good. Being supremely good it is also supremely great. There is therefore a supremely good and supremely great being, the highest of all existing beings – *i.e.* God. Anselm's argument was not original, Augustine having argued similarly. It depends for its force on the 'realist' assumption that the universal is more real than particular manifestations of it (see Nominalism*). Thus the (Platonic)* Idea of goodness is more real than the particular manifestation of it in the life of a good person. Anselm's apologetic would have had force in an age where Platonic realism was widely accepted, but carries little conviction today.

The following year Anselm broke new ground with the publication of his *Proslogion*, originally called *Faith Seeking Understanding*. Starting as a believer, he seeks to understand what he already believes. 'I am not seeking to understand in order to believe, but I believe in order to understand. For this too I believe: that unless I believe, I shall not understand.' In this work Anselm presents his famous ontological argument for the existence of God. God is defined as 'that, than which nothing greater can be conceived' or, to put it more simply, 'the greatest conceivable being'. This being must exist. Were he not to exist, he would be inferior to an identical being that did exist and thus would not be 'the greatest conceivable being'. Indeed the 'greatest conceivable being' exists so certainly that it cannot even be *conceived* not to exist. For the mind can conceive of a being which cannot be conceived not to exist and such a being is greater than a being which *can* be conceived not to exist. Therefore there is a 'greatest conceivable being' that cannot even be conceived not to exist. Anselm identifies this being with the Christian God.

Anselm has, with some justice, been accused of attempting to define God into existence. His approach represents the supreme confidence of the 11th-century West in the power of reason. Anselm considered that his argument should suffice to persuade even the 'fool' who denies God's existence (Ps. 14:1). But the validity of his argument was immediately questioned by a monk called Gaunilo, who wrote *On Behalf of the Fool*. The debate about the validity of the ontological argument continues to rage and shows no signs of abating.

Proslogion was of particular significance for one modern theologian: Karl Barth.* In his *Fides Quaerens Intellectum (Faith Seeking Understanding;* 1931), Barth analysed Anselm's method of 'faith seeking understanding' and found in it a precedent for his own approach to theology in the 20th century.

Anselm's most ambitious work was his *Cur Deus Homo (Why God Became Man)*, written in the 1090s. It is presented in the form of a dialogue between Anselm and Boso (one of his monks at Bec). Here Anselm, like the apologists* of the early church, faces the charge that it is unfitting and degrading for God to humble himself by becoming man and dying to save us. Anselm offers reasons why the incarnation* and cross are in fact both necessary and fitting (see Atonement*). But this does not mean that he is offering a natural theology,* building theology purely on the basis of reason. Here, as in the *Proslogion*, his method is one of 'faith seeking understanding'. Having believed the doctrines of the incarnation and the cross, he uses reason to understand why they are true. He suspends not faith itself, but the appeal to faith. But this does not mean that Anselm is a fideist, writing theology simply from the position of the believer and for believers. He does set out to convince the unbeliever, by arguing *remoto Christo*, as if we knew nothing about Christ. He starts, not with no presuppositions, but by assuming the existence of God as Trinity,* together with God's character, the nature of man and his sin against God. He then seeks to show, by necessary reasons, that given these presuppositions the incarnation and the cross are absolutely necessary, the only possible course of action open to God. Thus he seeks to show the unbeliever that the incarnation and the cross, far from being unfitting and degrading for God, are the only reasonable course of action open to him, granted a Christian view of God and man.

Anselm argues that sin, understood as a failure to render due obedience to God, dishonours him. God, as the upholder of justice (*cf.* Righteousness*) and law,* cannot simply forgive but must restore his lost honour. This can happen in one of only two ways: either a suitable satisfaction* is offered to God or he must restore his honour by punishing man. But the latter course is not open to God as man is needed to replace the fallen angels.* (This last point, taken from Augustine, does not carry much weight today, but there are other reasons why God cannot simply abandon the human race.) Therefore sinful man must restore God's honour by offering him a suitable satisfaction. But here God faces a dilemma. It is *man* who owes the satisfaction, but only *God* is able to pay it (which Anselm argues by showing the seriousness of sin). The need is for a God-man – hence the incarnation. As man, Christ owes God the obedience of a perfect life. But as a *perfect* man he need not die. His death earns him merit and serves as a suitable satisfaction for man's sins – hence the cross.

Anselm's case is impressive, but not without its weaknesses. He has been criticized on a number of grounds, some of which amount to blaming him for addressing his own particular context, where, for instance, talk of honour and satisfaction was familiar because of the penitential system in the church (see Penance*) and because of feudal concepts in society. He has with some justice been criticized for locating the salvific work of Christ exclusively in the cross, neglecting the life of Christ and his resurrection* and ascension.* But it must be remembered that his aim was precisely to give reasons why the *cross*, the great scandal to unbelievers, was necessary. Anselm also went beyond the usual Christian claim that the cross was necessary (*i.e.* God had to do *something*) to claim that it was *absolutely* necessary (*i.e.* God could not have done anything else). Here again he reflects the 11th-century confidence in the power of reason. But the attractiveness of Anselm's case is that it is very flexible. His basic case, suitably modified, makes a powerful argument today that the incarnation and cross are indeed fitting and reasonable.

Anselm's aim in his writings was to show how reasonable faith is, rather than to offer a strict proof of it. The beauty of the inner harmony of the Christian faith gives joy to the believer, who sees the accord of faith and reason. The unbeliever's objections (*e.g.* that it is degrading for God to have become man) are met, and he is pointed to the truth of the Christian message.

Bibliography

Works: in *PL* 158–9, and *Opera Omnia*, ed. F. S. Schmitt, 6 vols. (Edinburgh, 1946–61), ET J. Hopkins and H. Richardson, 4 vols. (London, 1974–76).

Studies: G. R. Evans, *Anselm and Talking about God* (Oxford, 1978); J. Hopkins, *A Companion to the Study of St Anselm* (Minneapolis, MN, 1972); J. McIntyre, *St Anselm and his Critics. A Re-Interpretation of the* Cur Deus Homo (Edinburgh and London, 1954); R. W. Southern, *Saint Anselm and his Biographer* (Cambridge, 1963; 21982).

A.N.S.L.

ANTHROPOLOGY. The question of the nature of man is one subject that we might expect to be able to consider independently, without reference to other elements of Christian doctrine, even without reference to faith. After all, we know what it is to be human because we are human; if we ourselves are not only the enquiring subject but also the actual object of enquiry then surely we must be qualified to formulate a valid anthropology. Yet this supposition is seriously flawed. There has always been a multitude of rival anthropologies to choose from, each expanding its own understanding according to the dogmas of its proponents' philosophical or religious stance. As in every other instance, what we believe about human nature is determined by what we believe about more fundamental issues.

The Bible's reference to the nature of humanity must be recognized as occurring within the overall context of our place within creation and our standing before God. Biblically the anthropological question cannot be answered without reference to this theological context of the doctrine of creation;* primarily human beings are creatures of God. We are not emanations emerging from the being of God himself, but a part of the total created order that is wholly distinct from God. Neither did the human race evolve as a product of an independent process of 'natural' selection and development. Rather humanity is portrayed biblically, as the special and direct creation of God.

Gn. 2:7 refers to God forming Adam* 'from the dust of the ground' and breathing 'into his nostrils the breath of life', so that man becomes a 'living being'. The word 'being' translates the Hebrew word *nepeš* which, though often translated by the Eng. word 'soul', ought not to be interpreted in the sense suggested by Hellenistic* thought (see Platonism;* Soul, Origin of*). It should rather be understood in its own context within the OT as indicative of men and women as living beings or persons in relationship to God and other people. The LXX translates this Heb. word *nepeš* with the Gk. word *psychē*, which explains the habit of interpreting this OT concept in the light of Gk. use of *psychē*. Yet it is surely more appropriate to understand the use of *psychē* (in both the LXX and the NT) in the light of the OT's use of *nepeš*. According to Gn. 2, any conception of the soul as a separate (and separable) part or division of our being would seem to be invalid. Similarly, the popular debate concerning whether human nature is a bipartite or tripartite being has the appearance of a rather ill-founded and unhelpful irrelevancy. The human person is a 'soul' by virtue of being a 'body' made alive by the 'breath' (or 'Spirit') of God.

Moreover, that Adam was made alive by the breath of God implies that his life as this 'soul' was never independent of the will of God and the Spirit of God (Gn. 6:3; Ec. 12:7; Mt. 10:28). The question of whether Adam was created mortal or immortal prior to the fall* may miss the point by following Plato in presupposing some form of immortality* that is independent of the will of God. Human life is never to be conceived of in terms of an independent immortality since that life is never independent of the will and Spirit of God. Prior to the fall, Adam was 'effectively immortal', in as much as he existed in an unbroken relationship with God in which his life was constantly maintained by the will of God and the Spirit of God. In consequence of his fall, death was pronounced as God's judgment upon Adam since the relationship which was the basis of his 'effective immortality' had been broken. It is this breach of spiritual relationship which constitutes the 'spiritual death' that characterizes the totality of human existence without Christ (Rom. 7:9; Eph. 2:1ff.).

On the same basis the biblical hope for life beyond death is expressed primarily in terms of the resurrection* of the body. Neither the references to the shadowy existence of Sheol, nor those passages which could be interpreted as implying some form of continued conscious existence prior to this final resurrection (see Intermediate State*), provide sufficient ground for maintaining the Gk. concept of an independent immortality of the soul. The gospels' testimony to the resurrection appearances of Jesus implies that the future resurrection body will exist as a physical phenomenon with physical continuity. Paul, however, refers to this resurrection body in 1 Cor. 15:44ff. as a 'spiritual body' (*sōma pneumatikon*) in contrast to a 'natural body' (*sōma psychikon*), thereby suggesting a degree of physical discontinuity as well as continuity. One practical consequence of this reference to physical discontinuity, together with the fact that the final resurrection is to be seen as a creative act of God and not merely a 'reconstitution', is the implication that no rigid dogmatic case

ought to be made for the practice of burial in contrast to cremation.

As in the case of the biblical words traditionally translated 'soul' (*nepeš*; *psychē*) the Heb. and Gk. words used to express physical, emotional and psychological being are an interpreter's minefield. The difficulty is compounded by the fact that a single Eng. word is often used to translate both a Heb. word and a Gk. word with apparently distinct meanings and references (*e.g.* both the Heb. *bāśār* and the Gk. *sarx* are usually translated 'flesh' though the words seem to have quite different connotations). However, the combined effect of such words is to portray the human person as the creature of God, existing before God as a thinking and deciding subject with emotional, physical and sexual needs and desires. Men and women are capable of self-expression through the creativity of music, art and human relationship but continually dependent upon the providence* of God for food, clothing and the breath of life itself.

To define the nature of men and women theologically as the creatures of God would be wholly inadequate in itself unless it were recognized that they occupy a unique place within creation. God's determination for mankind in creation is that we should reign: we are to 'fill the earth and subdue it', to 'rule over the fish of the sea and the birds of the air and over every living creature that moves on the ground' (Gn. 1:28). Yet just as we possess no life that is independent of the will and Spirit of God so we also possess no independent authority; mankind's authority within creation is to be the delegated authority of a steward;* we are accountable to God. In this sense Adam's fall can be interpreted not only as disobedience and rebellion but also as the grasping of moral autonomy and an independent authority. In this deluded claim for independence, the human race has fallen from its divinely determined destiny within creation. Through Adam's sin the ground is cursed and he can eat of it only through 'painful toil' (Gn. 3:17–19); creation itself has been 'subjected to frustration' (Rom. 8:20).

God's determination for mankind to rule is expressed in Psalm 8 in the form of a question: 'What is man?' (Ps. 8:4). Elsewhere in the OT the question is repeated in various forms (Jb. 7:17; 15:14; Ps. 144:3), but it is ultimately answered only in the NT with reference to

29

Christ; it is he who was 'made a little lower than the angels' and it is he who is 'now crowned with glory and honour because he suffered death' (Heb. 2:6–9). Ultimately the answer to the anthropological question 'What is man?' can be discerned only in Christ. Just as there can be no authentic knowledge of God independent of his self-revelation in Jesus Christ, so also there can be no authentic knowledge of human nature independent of this disclosure. Recent theological fashion begins with a definition of the humanity of Jesus and proceeds to a definition of his deity (*i.e.* Christology* from below). This mistakenly assumes the premise that an independently valid understanding of the nature of mankind is available as a Christological starting-point. In Jesus alone the Father's eternal will and purpose are both revealed and fulfilled; those who are chosen are chosen 'in him before the creation of the world...' (Eph. 1:4ff.). Moreover, only in the cross of Jesus are disclosed the depth, totality and consequences of humanity's fall from this eternal will and purpose of God. It is in this sense that Karl Barth* speaks of Jesus as the revelation both of the real man which we are and the true man which we are not. The person of Jesus Christ is alone the determinative source of a valid theological anthropology; the authentic goal and nature of human life is to be discerned primarily in him and only secondarily in us.

Men and women were originally created in the 'image of God'.* The precise identity of this 'image' has been a continuing issue of debate in the history of Christian thought and doctrine. Calvin* maintained that the true nature of this 'image' is revealed only in its renewal through Christ (*cf.* 2 Cor. 4:4; Col. 1:15). Furthermore, if God is in himself who he is in his revelation then the person and work of Christ are not only the revelation in time of the inner-relatedness of the Father, the Son and the Spirit in eternity, but also the revelation and the fulfilment of the eternal purpose of this triune God to elect men and women in covenant* relationship with himself by grace.

The theological question of anthropology has not been answered adequately until this divine determination for covenant relationship has been recognized. Perhaps the 'image of God' ought not to be thought of in static or individualistic terms but in the dynamic

terms of this relatedness; men and women are called in Christ to be the 'image' of the eternal inner-relatedness of the Trinity* (Jn. 17:21–23). Perhaps Barth is correct when he suggests that since man is created in the image of God as 'male and female' (Gn. 1:27) the covenant relationship between husband and wife may also be a reflection of this divine image (see Sexuality*). Certainly there can be no adequate doctrine of human nature without the recognition that we are created in the image of God as male and female; not in a false uniformity in which this created distinction is blurred, nor in the tension of opposition or inequality, nor in individualistic isolation, but in equality of status and complementarity and in the unity of relatedness (see Feminist Theology*).

To put it another way: there can be no adequate anthropology without reference to an adequate and thoroughly Trinitarian doctrine of the nature of God.

Bibliography

Karl Barth, *CD*, III. 2; Louis Berkhof, *Systematic Theology* (London, 1958); G. C. Berkouwer, *Man: The Image of God* (Grand Rapids, MI, 1962); Calvin, *Institutes*, I.xv; II.i-v; W. Eichrodt, *Man in the Old Testament* (ET, London, 1951); Bruce Milne, *Know the Truth: A Handbook of Christian Belief* (Leicester, 1982); H. W. Wolff, *The Anthropology of the Old Testament* (ET, Philadelphia, 1983).

J.E.C.

ANTHROPOMORPHISM refers to descriptions of God's* being, actions and emotions (more properly anthropopathism) in human terms. God is invisible, infinite and without a body, but human characteristics are frequently ascribed to God in order to communicate information about his nature or acts.

Illustrations abound in Scripture. Though God is without a body, his acts are said to be the result of 'his mighty arm' (Ex. 15:16). Though God is without gender, he is characterized in masculine (father, shepherd, king), and occasionally feminine (compassionate mother) terms. Besides an arm, God is pictured as having a face (Ps. 27:8), hand (Ps. 10:12; 88:5), finger (Dt. 9:10) and back (Ex. 33:23). God talks, walks, laughs, weeps; he is jealous, fickle, furious and caring.

Anthropomorphisms are poetic symbols or, more particularly, metaphors for divine attributes which would otherwise be indescribable. The Scriptures utilize anthropomorphic language, condescending to the limited abilities of men and women to understand God's nature and ways.

Danger enters when anthropomorphisms are taken literally rather than metaphorically, and people attribute a body to the invisible creator (e.g. the Audians of the 4th and 5th centuries). On the other hand, rejection of anthropomorphic language leads to scepticism and agnosticism,* since God cannot be otherwise discussed. Other misconceptions stem from the belief that biblical anthropomorphisms are an expression of a primitive religion or that biblical religion conceived of God in man's image (so Feuerbach*).

The Bible provides divine justification for anthropomorphic language. It is full of such language, though it recognizes the limitations of anthropomorphisms (Is. 40:18; 57:15; Jn. 1:8). The propriety of anthropomorphic language is supported further by the recognition that man (see Anthropology*) is made as the image* of God and that God himself took on human form in the person of Jesus Christ.

See also (for Bibliography too):
ACCOMMODATION; ANALOGY; RELIGIOUS
LANGUAGE.

T.L.

A NTICHRIST. The term (Gk. *antichristos*) is used in the Bible only in 1 Jn. 2:18, 22; 4:3; 2 Jn. 7. As used there, it probably indicates an opponent of Christ, rather than (as the Gk. *anti* could also imply) one who falsely claims to be the Christ. But many later interpreters have taken up the latter possibility and have seen the antichrist as a false Christ (*cf.* Mk. 13:22) as well as an opponent of Christ.

1 Jn. 2:18 indicates that the concept of antichrist, if not the word, was well known. Jewish apocalyptic* had developed the expectation of a final human embodiment of evil, a political ruler who would set himself up as divine and lead the pagan nations in a final assault on God's people. This figure was modelled especially on Daniel's descriptions of Antiochus Epiphanes, who set up the 'abomination of desolation' in the Temple

(Dn. 8:9–12, 23–25; 11:21–45; *cf.* Mk. 13:14). Jewish expectation sometimes also included the idea of a false prophet of the last days, who would perform miracles and deceive the nations (*cf.* Mk. 13:22).

NT writers shared the apocalyptic expectation of a crescendo of evil in the final period of history, leading to the final defeat of evil and the establishment of God's universal kingdom. They took up both types of antichrist figure – the king who claims divine worship and the false prophet who deceives – and interpreted them in various ways. In 2 Thes. 2:3–12, the 'man of lawlessness' is a figure still in the future, who will set himself in God's place and seduce the world into believing his lies. In Rev. 13 the two beasts represent respectively the political antichrist and the false prophet (*cf.* 16:13), and are used to highlight the anti-divine and anti-Christian character of the contemporary Roman Empire (*cf.* Rev. 17) and its cult of Caesar-worship. In the Epistles of John, the heretics who deny the reality of the incarnation are 'many antichrists' (1 Jn. 2:18), *i.e.* false prophets bent on deception. Other NT passages warn of the coming of false teachers in the church in the last days (Acts 20:30; 1 Tim. 4:1–3; 2 Pet. 2:1; Jude 18).

In the course of Christian history, the antichrist figures of biblical prophecy have been interpreted in three main ways. In the patristic and medieval periods, the idea of a future individual antichrist was popular, and a detailed account of his career was developed. This idea was rejected by the Protestant Reformers, and only became popular in Protestantism when a futurist interpretation of Revelation was revived in the 19th century. From time to time actual individuals, such as Napoleon III and Mussolini, have been identified as the antichrist, sometimes by means of interpretations of the number of the beast (Rev. 13:18).

Secondly, 16th-century Protestants developed the idea that the major biblical accounts of antichrist refer to a specific historical entity, but not to an individual man. Instead, they identified antichrist with an institutional succession of men over several centuries: the Roman papacy. This remained the dominant Protestant view until the 19th century.

Thirdly, antichrist has been understood more broadly as a principle of opposition to

Christ, which continually appears in history in the form of individuals and movements which set themselves against God and persecute or deceive his people. This view is compatible, of course, with the expectation of a final embodiment of the antichrist principle in the future.

Bibliography

R. Bauckham, *Tudor Apocalypse* (Appleford, 1978); W. Bousset, *The Antichrist Legend* (London, 1896); D. Brady, *The Contribution of British Writers between 1560 and 1830 to the Interpretation of Revelation 13.16–18* (Tübingen, 1983); R. K. Emmerson, *Antichrist in the Middle Ages* (Manchester, 1981); D. Ford, *The Abomination of Desolation in Biblical Eschatology* (Lanham, MD, 1979); C. Hill, *Antichrist in Seventeenth-Century England* (London, 1971).

R.J.B.

ANTINOMIANISM, see LAW AND GOSPEL.

ANTIOCHENE SCHOOL. The Antiochene School is in its Christology* generally opposed to the Alexandrian School,* but it is worth remembering that originally both schools reflected differing responses to the Arian* threat. Countering the Arian attribution of suffering to the divine Word, the Antiochenes insisted on a rigid separation between the two natures in Christ. It was the human nature which experienced suffering, whereas the divine nature remained untouched by this. Central to Antiochene theology was the great gulf between the immortality, incorruptibility and impassibility of God* and the mortality, corruptibility and passibility of humanity.

Diodore of Tarsus (*c.* 330–94), often regarded as the pioneer of this school, was content to use the Alexandrian terminology of the 'Word becoming flesh'. He departed, however, from the Alexandrian tradition when he challenged Apollinarius'* talk of one *hypostasis** (substance or person) in Christ. For Apollinarius this entailed a complete transfer of the properties (*communicatio idiomatum;* see Christology*) of the Word to the human side of Jesus' one nature; but for Diodore this inevitably involved the Word in suffering, and thereby compromised the divine nature. Diodore preferred to talk of two Sons

and two natures, and to deny any sort of transfer of properties. Thus it was only the human nature of Jesus which died on the cross, while the divine Word did not suffer. The denial of a transfer of properties remained the standard teaching of the Antiochene School.

It was Diodore's pupil, Theodore of Mopsuestia (*c.* 350–428) who first scrapped the Word-flesh framework in favour of the Word-man framework more commonly associated with the Antiochenes. He was motivated by a concern to do justice to Christ's human experiences. Since the weakness evident in these experiences could not be postulated of the divine nature, the divine Word must have assumed complete manhood, body and soul.

Theodore died shortly before the outbreak of the Nestorian* controversy, which focused on Nestorius, one of his pupils. Theodore may in some sense have paved the way for controversy since his talk of Christ's humanity as 'the man assumed' did lead in the hands of more extreme exponents to the suspicion of adoptionism.* So clear was Theodore's differentiation between the two natures that he could treat Christ's humanity almost as a separate person, as at Jn. 10:27–28, which he expounds as a conversation between Christ's two natures.

Theodore's opponents also pointed out that he failed to do justice to the interrelation of the two natures in Christ. He described this as a 'conjunction', a term which falls short of full union. He liked to illustrate this by the metaphor of indwelling. The human nature of Christ functions as a temple in which the Godhead dwells. But this indwelling, which is by God's own good pleasure, differs from God's indwelling in the prophets and other holy men by virtue of its permanence and completeness. Understandably, this theological construction was criticized as giving only the appearance of a union.

Though under fire in the Nestorian controversy, the Antiochene School was not completely identified with Nestorius, but produced more moderate exponents, of whom the monk-bishop, Theodoret of Cyrrhus (*c.* 393–458), was the most notable. In the aftermath of the Council* of Ephesus (431) they set forth a statement devoid of Nestorian excesses. In time this document, which became known as the Formulary of Reunion,

was accepted even by Cyril of Alexandria*
and brought fifteen years of relative peace in
the Eastern church.

At the beginning of the Nestorian controversy, Theodoret had objected to Cyril's talk
of a 'hypostatic' or natural union, because this
signified to him a fusion of the deity and the
humanity into a hybrid compound under the
influence of some physical law of mechanical
combination entirely opposed to any concept
of the voluntary, gracious act which characterized the incarnation.* At this stage in his
career Theodoret held that Christ had two
natures and two hypostases, but later he was
prepared to modify his terminology and
distinguish between his one hypostasis and his
two natures. In line with this, he saw orthodoxy as a middle path between the error of
dividing Christ into two persons and the
opposite error of confusing the two natures.

The Antiochenes held passionately by their
Christology in order to safeguard their
doctrine of salvation.* They would stress the
perfection and distinctness of Christ's
humanity because sin and death which had
been introduced into the world by a man
could only be undone in human nature. Again,
Christ had to demonstrate real moral progress
because sin was essentially an act of wilful
disobedience on the part of the soul and could
only be undone by absolute obedience to the
divine will. A divine initiative was required to
secure human salvation. God had to intervene
in human history by creating and uniting to
himself a new Man if man was to be re-established in obedience to God's will. After its
obedience on earth, Christ's human nature
was elevated to heaven by virtue of its
conjunction with the divine nature. By a
parallel process the believer, united to Christ
at baptism, is granted intimacy with the divine
nature – though it is never suggested that this
intimacy is on the same scale as that enjoyed
by Christ.

The moderate Antiochenes left their mark
on the Chalcedonian Definition (451; see also
Councils* and Creeds*), which for many
marked the dénouement of the Christological
controversies of the fifth century. Its key
phrase – one person 'made known in two
natures' – reflects the Antiochene concern to
preserve the integrity of the two natures in
Christ. But the corresponding stress on the
oneness of Christ represents a corrective to
the Antiochene tendency not to give sufficient

weight to the Word as the subject of the incarnation and to subordinate the concept of
person to that of nature.

The Antiochenes gave biblical exegesis
greater weight than systematic theology.
Commentaries on Scripture were written by
the leading members of the school, and the
greatest expositor of the early church, John
Chrysostom (c. 344/354–407), could be
reckoned among them. The Antiochenes
developed their own hermeneutical* principles in reaction to the unbridled allegoriz-
ation of the Alexandrians. The Antiochenes
insisted on the literal or historical interpretation, but were not averse to a further, spiritual sense provided this did not undermine
the historicity of the passage, and could form
some reasonably obvious parallel to the literal
sense. Insight (Gk. *theoria*) was the name they
gave to this additional sense. Diodore and
Theodore, the theorists of the school, were
also pioneers in a critical approach to the
canon of Scripture,* but their work on this
did not meet with much approval. Nor did it
significantly undermine the school's excellent
reputation in biblical exegesis.

Bibliography

A. Grillmeier, *Christ in Christian Tradition*,
vol. 1 (London, ²1975); R. V. Sellers, *Two
Ancient Christologies* (London, 1940); D. S.
Wallace-Hadrill, *Christian Antioch. A Study
of Eastern Christian Thought* (Cambridge,
1982).

G.A.K.

ANTI-SEMITISM, see HOLOCAUST;
JUDAISM AND CHRISTIANITY.

APARTHEID, see DUTCH REFORMED
THEOLOGY; RACE.

APOCALYPTIC. The term derives from
the word 'apocalypse' and primarily
describes a body of literature, the apocalypses.
It is also commonly used to refer to the ideas
characteristic of that literature, especially a
type of eschatology.* Thirdly, the term can
refer to a type of religious movement, which
produces apocalyptic literature and is motivated by apocalyptic eschatological expectations, but this use of the word is less helpful,
since apocalyptic literature has been written
and used by religious groups which are socio-
logically very diverse and in widely differing

circumstances. Probably the only valid generalization is that apocalyptic literature and eschatology tend to come into their own in periods of crisis.

As a genre of religious literature, in the Jewish-Christian tradition, apocalyptic originates in the late OT period and persists as a relatively continuous literary tradition, in both Judaism and Christianity, until the late Middle Ages. Many scholars identify parts of the OT prophetic books as 'proto-apocalyptic', because some features of the later apocalypses already appear in them, but the only true apocalypse in the OT canon is Daniel. Many other Jewish apocalypses were written in the great age of apocalyptic from the 2nd century BC to the 2nd century AD. From those centuries come the apocalypses of *1 Enoch, 2 Baruch, 4 Ezra* (known as *2 Esdras* in the English Apocrypha), *3 Baruch*, the *Apocalypse of Abraham*, and probably *2 Enoch* and the *Apocalypse of Zephaniah*.

As the term 'apocalypse' (Gk. *apokalypsis*, revelation) implies, the Jewish apocalypses contain revelations of heavenly mysteries, which may concern the nature of the cosmos, the contents of the heavens, the realms of the dead, the problems of suffering and theodicy,* the divine plan of history, and the eschatological future of the world and individuals. The recipient of revelation is usually a great figure of the biblical past, such as Enoch or Ezra, to whom the apocalypse is fictionally attributed. This device of pseudonymity can be seen as a way of claiming authority for revelatory works written in a period when prophetic revelation was believed to have ceased, but it may be better understood as a literary convention whereby the author claims to be an authoritative interpreter of the biblical revelation given in the past. The media of revelation in the apocalypses are usually dreams or visions, in which vivid symbolic imagery often features and is then interpreted by an angel.* Sometimes the revelation is conveyed in long discourses by an angel or in dialogues between the angel and the seer. Sometimes the seer is taken on a tour of the cosmos or the seven heavens, to view their contents. A vision of the heavenly throne-room is a prominent feature of many apocalypses.

Two main types of Jewish apocalypses can be distinguished. *Cosmological* apocalypses focus on the secrets of the cosmos and the heavens revealed in other-worldly journeys.

Historical-eschatological apocalypses (including Daniel) are concerned with God's purposes in history, often including reviews of history within a scheme of divinely ordained periods, and focusing on the coming end of the history of this age, usually thought to be imminent, when God will overcome the evil powers which oppress his people, eliminate all evil and suffering, and establish his universal kingdom for ever. The resurrection of the dead, the eternal judgment of the wicked, and the eternal blessedness of the righteous are major features of this apocalyptic eschatology. By assuring believers that, despite the apparent dominance of evil in the world, God is in control of history and is bringing it to a triumphant conclusion, this kind of apocalypse helped to sustain faith in times of crisis and persecution.

Jewish apocalyptic was an important feature of the context from which early Christianity emerged. The general features of apocalyptic eschatology, including the resurrection of the dead and the last judgment, are prominent in the NT writings, though significant modifications of the apocalyptic outlook can also be observed. In the first place, the early Christians believed that, with the events of the history of Jesus, his resurrection and the coming of the Spirit, eschatological fulfilment had already begun. Secondly, because this fulfilment was taking place through Jesus, Christian apocalyptic became focused on the figure of Jesus Christ. Apocalyptic in the NT is primarily a means of expressing the significance of Jesus for the future destiny of the world.

Besides the ideas of apocalyptic eschatology, some passages in the NT reflect the literary forms of apocalyptic, but there is only one true apocalypse in the NT canon: the book of Revelation, which belongs to the tradition of Jewish eschatological apocalypses. Among its novel, Christian features is the fact that the prophet John writes it in his own name, reflecting the resurgence of prophetic inspiration in the early church. Another early Christian apocalypse, the *Shepherd* of Hermas (see Apostolic Fathers*), is also written by a Christian prophet in his own name, but thereafter the writers of Christian apocalypses reverted to the practice of pseudonymity, writing under the names of OT figures or NT apostles.

The influence of Jewish apocalyptic on

Christianity was by no means channelled only through the OT and NT. All the Jewish apocalypses mentioned above, even those written after the rise of Christianity, were preserved by Christian scribes and were influential in the Christian churches. *4 Ezra* was treated as almost canonical for much of the Middle Ages. Many Christian apocalypses were written in the traditions of both types of Jewish apocalypse. Of the cosmological type, visionary descriptions of the torments of hell and the delights of paradise were especially popular in the patristic and medieval periods. The most influential of these was the *Apocalypse of Paul*, and the literary culmination of this tradition was Dante's *Divine Comedy*. Among apocalypses of the historical-eschatological type, the *Apocalypse of Thomas* exercised the greatest influence in the Middle Ages.

During the patristic and medieval periods, the tradition of apocalyptic thought and speculation in Christianity gradually shifted from the production of new apocalypses to commentary and systematic reflection on the apocalyptic parts of canonical Scripture, and this shift was virtually complete by the 16th century. In the late medieval period the scriptural interpretations of Joachim* of Fiore were the basis of widespread eschatological expectations, and in the period of the Reformation both Protestants and Catholics sought to understand the great religious crisis of their time in apocalyptic terms. From the 16th century down to the present a continuous Protestant tradition has found in the book of Revelation the key to the meaning of the events of the interpreter's own time and a basis for expecting the end of history in the near future. In England, the mid-17th century and the period of the French Revolution and the Napoleonic Wars were high points of apocalyptic expectation in this tradition. Millenarianism (see Millennium*) has been a prominent feature of this Protestant apocalyptic tradition. In many ways this tradition of interpreting Revelation was mistaken, as the continual failure of its predictions shows. Modern awareness of the literary conventions of ancient apocalyptic and of the extent to which the book of Revelation needs to be understood in the context of its own time can enable us to avoid some of the pitfalls of the apocalyptic interpretation of the past. But the tradition was right to find in biblical apocalyptic an assurance of God's purpose at work in history, even when evil seems to prevail, and the hope for the climactic achievement of God's purposes in the future, when Jesus Christ will come to judge the living and the dead.

Bibliography

R. Bauckham, *Tudor Apocalypse* (Appleford, 1978); J. J. Collins, *The Apocalyptic Imagination in Ancient Judaism* (New York, 1984); D. Hellholm (ed.), *Apocalypticism in the Mediterranean World and the Near East* (Tübingen, 1983); B. McGinn, *Visions of the End* (New York, 1979); *idem* (ed.), *Apocalyptic Spirituality* (London, 1979); C. Rowland, *The Open Heaven* (London, 1982).

R.J.B.

APOCRYPHA, see SCRIPTURE.

APOLLINARIANISM.

The heresy of the mingled natures of the one Christ, called Apollinarianism after Apollinarius, Bishop of Laodicea in Syria (361–90), was less infamous than others. Apollinarius, friend of Athanasius* and supporter of the *homoousion* (see Trinity*), wrote 'innumerable volumes on the holy Scriptures' (Jerome), and, on theological and apologetic subjects, 'filled the world with his books' (Basil). Most survive, however, only in fragments and quotations in other writers. Some appear under other names, *e.g.* a *Detailed Confession of Faith* attributed to Gregory Thaumaturgus; a sermon, *That Christ is One, On the Incarnation of the Word of God*, and a creed addressed to the emperor Jovian attributed to Athanasius; *On the Union of Body and Deity in Christ, On Faith and Incarnation*, and a letter to Dionysius of Rome attributed to Pope Julius I.

The context of the Apollinarian Christology* is that of the Alexandrian School* of Athanasius and Cyril,* which was strong in declaring for the deity of Christ and the union of the two natures in his incarnate person. From these presuppositions Apollinarius attacked the Antiochene* dualistic Christology. Throughout his concern was soteriological. A Christ less than totally divine cannot save. The death of a mere man has no redeeming efficacy. But if Christ is totally divine his human nature must somehow be 'taken up' into his divinity and so become a right object of worship. Salvation consists in man

35

partaking of Christ's apotheosized flesh in the eucharist.* By the deifying of the human element through union with the divine Logos, Christ was rendered morally unchangeable.

Negatively, therefore, Apollinarius rejects any mere juxtaposing of the two natures in Christ. To Jovian he writes, 'There are not two natures (in Christ), one to be worshipped and one not to be worshipped. There is one nature (*mia physis*) in the Word of God incarnate.' The Scriptures present Christ as one being, the embodiment of the one active principle, the divine Logos. Positively, he credited to Christ a 'new nature', with the result that in the constitution of his person he is 'a new creation and a marvellous mixture, God and man have constituted one flesh'. But how have the human and divine so coalesced into such an absolute oneness? A powerful motive in Apollinarius was to exempt Christ from the possibility of sinning. In current psychology the human mind was conceived as self-determining, being impelled by its own volition and so the seat of evil choices. Apollinarius thus eliminated this element from his structure of Christ's person. 'If with the Godhead which is itself mind, there was in Christ also a human mind, the first purpose of the incarnation which is the overthrow of sin is not accomplished in him' (*Apodeixis*, fragment, 74). Christ's person is then the 'co-mixture' of the Logos and 'abridged human nature': 'a mean between God and man, neither wholly man nor wholly God, but a combination of God and man' (*Syllogysmoi*, fragment, 113). The denudation of the human in the incarnation is counterbalanced from the divine end by a *kenosis* (see Kenoticism*). For the Logos who pervades all existence in his limitlessness must undergo self-limitation in human flesh.

Apollinarius was criticized by Gregory of Nyssa* for repudiating Christ's full human experiences of which the gospels and the epistle to the Hebrews give ample proof. The full salvation of man requires Christ's full identification with him in all the elements of his make-up. Apollinarianism was successively condemned by councils at Rome (377), Alexandria (378), Antioch (379) and finally at Constantinople (381).

Bibliography

J. N. D. Kelly, *Early Christian Doctrines* (London, ⁵1977); H. Lietzmann, *Apollinarius von Laodicea und seine Schule* (Tübingen, 1904); A. G. McGiffert, *A History of Christian Thought* (New York and London, 1932), vol. 1; Jaroslav Pelikan, *The Christian Tradition*, vol. 1: *The Emergence of the Catholic Tradition (100–600)* (Chicago, 1971); C. E. Raven, *Apollinarianism* (Cambridge, 1923).

H.D.McD.

APOLOGETICS.

The term apologetics derives from a Greek term, *apologia*, and was used for a defence that a person like Socrates might make of his views and actions. The apostle Peter tells every Christian to be ready to give a reason (*apologia*) for the hope that is in him (1 Pet. 3:15). Apologetics, then, is an activity of the Christian mind which attempts to show that the gospel message is true in what it affirms. An apologist is one who is prepared to defend the message against criticism and distortion, and to give evidences of its credibility.

Unfortunately, today the term apologetics has unpleasant connotations for many people. On a superficial level it sounds as if we are being asked to apologize for having faith. At a deeper level it may suggest an aggressive or opportunistic kind of person who resorts to fair means or foul in order to get people to accept his point of view. Such misunderstandings of apologetics are regrettable in view of the importance of the subject. A sound defence of the faith was important in the NT as it also is today.

The book of Acts presents the apostles engaging non-Christians in debates and arguments concerning the truth of the gospel (Acts 17:2–4; 19:8–10) and it is no exaggeration to say that most of the NT documents were written for specific apologetic reasons. They were written to commend the faith to one group or another, and to clear up questions that had arisen about the gospel.

Apologetic activities were vigorously pursued during the period of the early church and indeed throughout most of the church's history. In the beginning it was necessary both to define what the church believed in the face of heretical tendencies, and to offer an explication of its basis in rationality to enquirers and critics of different kinds. Since many of the apologists* were converts themselves – men such as Justin, Clement* and Augustine* – they knew what was needed to commend the faith to outsiders. Believers also needed to be strengthened against the impact of hostile criticisms. It would be true to say that apologetics stood proudly alongside dogmatics* as two indispensable responses to the challenges of the age. It cannot be otherwise in a period of missionary expansion.

Early apologetics were generally either political or religious. The political apologies were designed to win acceptance, as well as a measure of toleration and legitimacy for Christianity in society, while the religious apologies were intended to win converts from both Judaism and paganism. Of necessity, such writings had to be flexible and respond to specific issues just as they do today. Among the practitioners of the art of apologetics we may number some of the finest minds and personalities: Augustine, Anselm,* Thomas Aquinas,* Pascal,* Butler,* Newman* and C. S. Lewis.* Their work contains a great variety of approaches and styles of argument, but what characterizes it all is boldness and confidence in the truth of the biblical message and its relevance to human history and philosophy.

In the modern period, however, apologetics has suffered a severe setback. It encountered in the European Enlightenment* a spirit of scepticism towards theology and metaphysics and a wholesale assault upon Christian beliefs. The apologetic arguments of earlier centuries were subjected to withering critique by men like Hume,* and many came to feel that the whole of Christianity needed to be revised and reworked. Kant* declared that the human mind was incapable of knowledge beyond the phenomenal realm. In future, he said, theology would have to be content to function within the limits of reason and reduce its claims to knowledge. A gauntlet was thrown down in the path of apologetics. Religion can be practised in the realm of existence or morality, but it cannot be advanced, as previously, on supposedly rational grounds.

The Enlightenment created a severe crisis for Christianity. In its wake, religious liberalism* sought to operate within the limits Kant had indicated, accepting the implications which this would have for Christian thinking. This led to the kind of revisionism which is familiar from the work of Paul Tillich,* Rudolf Bultmann* and John A. T. Robinson.*

Even among classical Christians, the effect of the Enlightenment critique was clearly seen in a new hesitancy towards apologetics. In Kierkegaard* and Barth* one sees a kind of orthodoxy which does not rely upon apologetic arguments at all, but seeks to rest the claim of Christianity solely upon the faith-commitment.

But there are also signs of a resurgency of apologetic activity. The writings of C. S. Lewis and Francis A. Schaeffer* have helped to stimulate popular interest in defending the faith. Others who have contributed to this revival of apologetic activity at a more technical level include E. J. Carnell,* Basil Mitchell (b. 1917), A. Plantinga,* Richard Swinburne (b. 1934), Keith Ward (b. 1938) and C. Van Til.* Contemporary apologetics seems to be recovering from the Enlightenment shock, and is beginning to take up the challenge posed by a secular and pluralistic culture.

Bibliography

Colin Brown, *Philosophy and the Christian Faith* (London, 1969); *idem, Miracles and the Critical Mind* (Grand Rapids, MI, and Exeter, 1984); E. J. Carnell, *An Introduction to Christian Apologetics* (Grand Rapids, MI, 1952); Avery Dulles, *A History of Apologetics* (Philadelphia, 1971); Gordon R. Lewis, *Testing Christianity's Truth Claims, Approaches to Christian Apologetics* (Chicago, 1976); C. van Til, *The Defense of the Faith* (Philadelphia, 1955).

C.H.P.

APOLOGISTS. A small group of Greek authors of the 2nd century, who presented a defence of Christianity in the face of persecution, slander and intellectual attack (see Apologetics*). They sought to make Christianity understandable (and acceptable) to a Graeco-Roman or Jewish audience, to bridge the gap between this 'barbarian' religion and the culture of their day. Yet they contain important insights into the development of Christian theology. In all of them we find a 'high' view of the transcendence of God.* God is the 'uncreated, eternal, invisible, impassible, incomprehensible, and infinite, who can be apprehended by mind and reason alone, who is encompassed by light, beauty, spirit, and indescribable power, and who created, adorned, and now rules the universe' (Athenagoras, *Supplication* 10:1). They expose the immorality and irrationality of pagan religion and they defend the truth of the resurrection* of the flesh. Because they also differ in their theology, we shall deal with each one separately.

Aristides wrote his *Apology* either *c.* 125 or *c.* 140. Textual problems make it difficult to be sure about the details of his thought (the less reliable text has the more explicit theological statements). God is understood as the 'prime mover', who created all things because of man. Jesus Christ is spoken of as Son of God and (perhaps) as God, who was incarnate through a virgin, died and rose again, and was preached by the twelve apostles in all the world. Christians live an exemplary life in the knowledge of a judgment after death. These doctrines can all be found in the Scriptures of the Christians.

Justin Martyr, the most important of the apologists, wrote an *Apology* (I), some time after 151, to which he later added an *Appendix* (or *Apology* II). In his *Dialogue with Trypho* he seeks to persuade a Jew of the truth of Christianity. Unlike the other apologists, Justin focuses mainly on the nature and meaning of Christ. Christ was the Logos* who inspired the Greek philosophers and is present in all men as the *Logos spermatikos* (seminal reason or word; see Stoicism*). Through him, the best of the philosophers were able to grasp certain Christian truths (*e.g.* creation, the Trinity, final judgment, *etc.*). Those who lived according to the Logos, even before Christ, were Christians. In the OT theophanies* it was the Logos who was revealed, because the transcendent God could not thus speak to men. Though Justin uses the Trinitarian formula, his understanding of Christ is subordinationist (see Trinity*). The relation of the Son to the Father is compared to the relation of sunlight to the sun itself, but he also speaks of a fire kindled from a fire. At times the Logos and the Holy Spirit are apparently confused. Christ was incarnate for our salvation and healing, to teach us and to triumph over the demons (see Devil*) through the mystery of the cross. The demons were responsible for enslaving and deceiving men. They saw what was predicted in the OT about Christ and inspired the poets to say similar things about the Greek gods. They always instigate the persecution of just men. In order to be considered worthy of incorruption and of fellowship with God, it is necessary for men to believe these things and to do God's will.

The main evidence for Christianity consists in the fact that everything related to Christ's coming was foretold by the Hebrew prophets. Exegesis of the OT is important in the *Apology* and also in the *Dialogue*, where Justin argues that the Mosaic law has been abrogated, that the OT speaks of 'another besides God', who was manifest in the OT theophanies, and that the Christians are the true Israel. Justin is concerned to show the continuity between Greek philosophy and Christianity (see Philosophy and Theology;* Platonism*), as well as the continuity between the OT and the NT. Christ is the culmination and completion of all the partial knowledge of truth in Greek philosophy and he is the culmination of the history of Israel. He himself is Israel and because of him the church now bears the name of Israel.

Tatian, a disciple of Justin, wrote a *Discourse to the Greeks, c.* 160. He maintains the divinity of the Logos (understood as 'light from light'). He speculates on the nature of man and on the nature and activity of the demons. He emphasizes free will and the necessity to obey God.

Athenagoras wrote a *Supplication, c.* 177. The treatise *On the Resurrection*, traditionally ascribed to him, may be the work of a later author. Athenagoras says that Father, Son and Holy Spirit are united in power, yet distinguished in rank. The Spirit is understood as an effluence, like light from a fire. Goodness is so much a part of God that, without it, he could not exist. Evil* exists because of the fall of (some of) the angels,* who had been entrusted with the administration of the world. Evil is associated with matter. The exemplary life of the Christians is strongly emphasized. The instructions for the Christian life, as well as all other knowledge about God, are found in the writings of the prophets.

The work *On the Resurrection* argues for the resurrection on almost purely rational grounds, showing that God is both able and willing to raise the dead and that this corresponds to the purpose of man's creation. The soul is immortal.* Both the righteous and the wicked are raised.

Theophilus of Antioch wrote three books *To Autolycus* (after 180), in which he speaks of God, the Logos and Sophia (wisdom*) as a 'triad'. The Logos was first innate (*endiathetos*) in God and was made external (*prophorikos*) before creation. Sometimes the distinction between Logos and Sophia (understood as the Holy Spirit) is blurred. God may be apprehended through his works in the universe, which he created out of nothing. Man was made to know God, with the capacity both for mortality and for immortality. Through disobedience he became mortal. Terms like faith, repentance, forgiveness and regeneration are used and God is spoken of as healer. Yet man is to attain immortality primarily through obedience. All these doctrines may be found in the writings of the prophets, who were inspired by Sophia and whose authenticity is guaranteed by their antiquity and by the fact that their predictions have come true.

Bibliography

The Greek text of the Apologists may be found in E. J. Goodspeed, *Die ältesten Apologeten* (Göttingen, 1914); J. R. Harris, *The Apology of Aristides* (Cambridge, ²1893); J. C. Th. Otto, *Corpus Apologetarum Christianorum Saeculi Secundi* (Jena, 1847–72). English translations can be found in ANCL (repr. ANF); R. M. Grant (ed.), *Theophilus of Antioch: Ad Autolycum* (Oxford, 1970); C. C. Richardson (ed.), *The Early Christian Fathers* (Philadelphia, 1953); W. R. Schoedel (ed.), *Athenagoras: Legatio and De Resurrectione* (Oxford, 1972); A. Lukyn Williams (ed.), *Justin Martyr: The Dialogue with Trypho* (London, 1930).

T.G.D.

APOPHATIC THEOLOGY. The way

of *apophasis*, or negation, in contrast to the way of *cataphasis*, or affirmation, as the basis for knowing God. The idea that God cannot be understood in human categories of thought is very ancient, being implied, for example, in the second commandment. As a theological method however, apophatic theology traces its roots to the mysticism of Origen* and the Alexandrian School* generally. It is closely allied to Neoplatonism (see Platonism*), and reached its classical development in the 6th-century synthesis of the unknown philosopher-monk whose works circulate under the name of Dionysius the Areopagite (*cf.* Acts 17:34; see Pseudo-Dionysius the Areopagite*). Later, it was refined in the monastic tradition of the Eastern Orthodox church, where it is still prominent today.

Pseudo-Dionysius defined revelation,*

particularly the revelation of the divine names in Scripture, as an invitation to men to consider the knowledge of God. To say that God is good, or that he is truth, is not wrong, but it is bound by the limitations of our intellect, for which ideas of goodness and truth are ultimately finite. To know God, who is essentially infinite, the believer must escape from his finitude and ascend into heaven. This ascent occurs in progressive stages of transfiguration in the illumination of that uncreated light which shone on Mt. Tabor (*cf.* Mt. 17:2). It involves not only a knowledge of God, who dwells as non-being in a world beyond all conception, but of the celestial hierarchy of spiritual beings as well. Apophatic theology has a highly developed angelology,* and a spiritualized understanding of reality which is heavily reliant on an allegorical interpretation of the Bible.

Bibliography

V. Lossky, *The Mystical Theology of the Eastern Church* (Cambridge, 1957); J. Meyendorff, *St Gregory Palamas and Orthodox Spirituality* (New York, 1974).

G.L.B.

APOSTASY is a general falling away

from religion or a denial of the faith by those who once held it. Paul prophesied serious apostasy before the end of the age (2 Thes. 2:3; see also Antichrist*). Erstwhile nominal believers can obviously cease from appearing even to profess faith.* But can a regenerate* believer cease to believe and so be finally lost? All agree that he may lapse temporarily from full faith and then repent. Calvinists* hold that God's calling of the elect to faith prevents them from falling away; they point to texts which assert the eternal security of the believers: a faithful God will not allow any of his people to be overcome by unbelief and finally lost. Others point to the numerous warnings in the NT against the danger of apostasy and to specific references to apostate individuals. Calvinists insist that the warnings are hypothetical: their effect is to prevent people falling away (just as the sign 'Danger! Keep away from the edge!' prevents people from falling off a cliff). Those who fall away were never truly regenerate. The exegetical debate continues. While the Scriptures warn the deliberate sinner that he is in eternal danger, they also assure the worried believer that nothing can pluck him out of the Lord's hand.

Bibliography

G. C. Berkouwer, *Faith and Perseverance* (Grand Rapids, MI, 1958); D. A. Carson, *Divine Sovereignty and Human Responsibility* (London, 1981); I. H. Marshall, *Kept by the Power of God* (Minneapolis, MN, 1975).

I.H.Ma.

A POSTLE. A term used to describe members of a number of groups of people in the NT. 1. The twelve disciples called by Jesus to help him in his mission (Mt. 10:2). The number inevitably recalls the twelve tribes of Israel (*cf.* Mt. 19:28; Lk. 22:29–30) and suggests that the Twelve were the nucleus of a new Israel composed of those who accepted Jesus as Messiah; the future role assigned to them (judging the tribes of Israel) may simply be a way of saying that they will share in the future kingdom of God* while unbelieving Israel is cast out. 2. A wider group, including the Twelve, who had seen the risen Lord and received his command to be missionaries (1 Cor. 15:7; *cf.* 9:1). Luke tends to restrict the title to the Twelve (except in Acts 14:4, 14) as companions of the Lord and witnesses of his resurrection (Acts 1:21–22; 10:40–42), but Paul stresses their role as pioneer church-planters, whose credentials are the congregations they founded (1 Cor. 9:2). 3. In a broader sense some church workers or delegates were called 'apostles of the churches' (2 Cor. 8:23; Phil. 2:25). 4. Some people claimed falsely (in Paul's eyes) to be apostles and worked as missionaries in rivalry with him (2 Cor. 11:13).

The word 'apostle' could carry various connotations. If it is a translation of the Hebrew *šālîaḥ* it means a person who acts as the fully authoritative representative of somebody else. The sense of 'missionary' also comes over strongly. For Paul his sense of apostleship was of key importance in his self-understanding. An apostle was tantamount to a bond-servant of Jesus (note how Paul describes himself at the beginning of all his epistles when he is establishing his credentials). Apostleship is associated with founding churches and conveys authority over them in terms of imposing discipline and also in terms of receiving and transmitting authoritative revelation,* so that apostles, along with

prophets,* form the foundation of the church (Eph. 2:20; *cf.* 1 Cor. 12:28–29; 2 Pet. 3:2). Paul also stresses that it is the special destiny of the apostle to suffer and even to die so that his converts may live, and he explores the paradox of the humble position of the apostle despite his high calling (1 Cor. 4:9; 2 Cor. 4).

Since the apostles (except in the sense of delegates of the churches) were witnesses of the resurrection and formed the foundation of the church, it follows that their office was a first-generation phenomenon and incapable of repetition; they had no successors, and in principle there cannot be any. Yet the church can and must still be apostolic in the sense that it must live by their teaching, enshrined in the NT Scriptures, and must follow their example of suffering with their Lord. Some scholars have nevertheless argued that the church is 'apostolic' only if it has leaders (usually bishops) who have been consecrated by the laying on of hands in a physical chain extending back to the apostles. John Wesley* said what should have been the last word on the subject when he declared 'the *uninterrupted succession* I know to be a fable, which no man ever did or can prove.' Some non-episcopal groups have leaders who declare themselves to be apostles, but they too fail to recognize that apostleship is associated with being original witnesses of the resurrection.

Bibliography

C. K. Barrett, *The Signs of an Apostle* (London, 1970); J. A. Kirk, 'Apostleship since Rengstorf: Towards a Synthesis', *NTS* 21 (1974–75), pp. 249–264; K. H. Rengstorf, in *TDNT* I, pp. 407–447: W. Schmithals, *The Office of Apostle in the Early Church* (London, 1971).

I.H.Ma.

APOSTLES' CREED, see CREEDS.

A POSTOLIC FATHERS. A designation first used widely in the 16th century to refer to the earliest Christian writers not included in the NT canon (see Scripture*), but closest to them in time, ranging in date from 95 to about 150. This group is also distinguished from the so-called apologists,* who in the middle of the 2nd century began systematically to defend Christianity against the various objections and criticisms that confronted the church. The apostolic fathers are 'apostolic' only in the sense that they are orthodox – i.e. that they continue faithfully the teaching of the apostles.* There is beyond these general facts little that holds this very diverse group of writings together.

The collection consists of letters somewhat reminiscent of Paul's, namely, 1 Clement (to the church at Corinth) and the letter of Polycarp (to the Philippian church); the seven letters of Ignatius (of a more personal character); a Christian manual of conduct, the Didache ('teaching') of the Twelve Apostles; a sermon, 2 Clement; a treatise, known as the Epistle of Barnabas; a book of apocalyptic visions, the Shepherd of Hermas; the account of the Martyrdom of Polycarp; fragments of exegesis of sayings of Jesus by Papias; and sometimes also included, a letter to Diognetus (alternatively, and more appropriately, grouped with the apologists). In this group are three pseudonymous documents (2 Clement, Barnabas and the Didache) and among the authors are four bishops of the early church (Clement of Rome (fl. c. 96), Ignatius of Antioch (c. 35–c. 107), Polycarp of Smyrna (c. 69–c. 155) and Papias of Hierapolis (c. 60–130)).

The apostolic fathers were neither creative nor self-conscious and certainly not systematic in what they wrote. For the most part their writings, like the NT letters, are occasional and practical in character. When they address problems of doctrine it is particularly to save the church from strife and division, to rid it of inappropriate conduct and to call it to the experience of a settled authority (see Church Government*). The apostolic fathers find the solutions to the problems of their day in faithful dependence upon the tradition of the church as it had been handed down to them by the preceding generation, that of the apostles themselves (see Scripture and Tradition*). In this sense they admirably fulfil the mandates of the Pastoral Epistles of the NT, maintaining the tradition more than breaking new ground. It is mainly the practical orientation of these documents that is responsible for the mistaken impression that the doctrine of grace* was lost by the early 2nd century.

The appeal of Clement of Rome for the restoration of unity in the church at Corinth rests in large measure upon extensive quotation of the OT, apostolic tradition and even Stoic* thought. The readers are called to submit to the authority of bishops and elders (used interchangeably, as in the NT). The appeal is buttressed by a high Christology,* emphasis on the resurrection* of Christ and the atonement* by his blood.

Polycarp's epistle similarly consists largely of allusions to NT writings and Christian tradition. It too is concerned to exhort and instruct concerning the Christian life and appeals to the importance of submission to church leaders. Polycarp's Christology includes reference to Christ as the eternal high priest.

The letters of Ignatius emphasize the deity of Christ, explicitly referring to Jesus as God more than a dozen times. Ignatius argues for the importance of a threefold order of ministry* consisting of bishop, presbyters and deacons, and he is especially insistent on the importance of the absolute authority of the single bishop of each church. Only with submission to this kind of church order, argues Ignatius, could the church withstand the evils of that age. Ignatius also displayed a high regard for martyrdom.*

The Didache is primarily a manual of practical instruction for the church which includes such matters as pre-baptismal catechesis,* directions for worship and the administration of baptism* and the eucharist,* advice on the proper treatment of Christian missionaries,* and the role of bishops and deacons. The Epistle of Barnabas contains a very anti-Jewish perspective and argues Christianity's complete fulfilment of the OT, using a freely allegorical exegesis (see Hermeneutics*) reminiscent of Philo.* Another book, the Shepherd of Hermas, the longest document of the apostolic fathers by far, also contains little that is significant to the development* of the theology of the early church. It consists of a series of visions concerned with practical questions of righteousness* and forgiveness, and is preoccupied with the important 2nd-century problem of the possibility of repentance after post-baptismal sins (see Penance*).

The apostolic fathers show the early post-NT church grappling with the concrete problems of the day, using Scripture, the sayings of Jesus, and the tradition of the apostles in their attempt to consolidate the faith and practice of the church and to be faithful to what they had received. Herein lies their true contribution. And for this reason these writings are significant for the study of the emerging OT and NT canons as well as the early Christian understanding and use of Scripture. Without question, the apostolic fathers were influenced by the Hellenistic* environment in which they lived, yet because their perspective was dictated by Scripture and tradition it remains more Jewish than Greek.

Bibliography

E. J. Goodspeed, *The Apostolic Fathers. An American Translation* (New York, 1950); R. M. Grant (ed.), *The Apostolic Fathers. A New Translation and Commentary*, 6 vols. (New York, 1964–68), see especially vol. 1, *An Introduction*, by R. M. Grant; R. A. Kraft, 'Apostolic Fathers', *IDBS*, pp. 36–38 (for recent scholarship); K. Lake, *The Apostolic Fathers*, Loeb Classical Library, 2 vols. (London, 1912–13), Gk. text with ET; J. B. Lightfoot, *The Apostolic Fathers*, 5 vols. (London, 1885–90), Gk. text with ET (Clement, Ignatius, Polycarp).

D.A.Ha.

APOSTOLIC SUCCESSION, see
Ministry.

ARIANISM.

Arius (*c.* 250–*c.* 336), a presbyter in an urban parish in Alexandria,* was by 318 suspected of giving teaching contrary to that of his bishop, Alexander (d. 328). After due examination, this difference was adjudged fundamental and unbridgeable. Arius and his supporters were excommunicated, but by this time he had enlisted formidable backing among bishops outside Egypt, particularly Eusebius of Nicomedia (d. *c.* 342), the first prominent court bishop of the Constantinian era. The Arian controversy could not remain a purely Egyptian affair.

Arius' doctrine began from the absolute uniqueness and distinctness of God* – 'one God, alone ingenerate, alone everlasting, alone unbegun, alone true, alone having immortality, alone wise, alone good, alone sovereign'. This God could not possibly have communicated his essence to any other, for that would remove the great gulf between creator and creature, and would in effect be a reversion to polytheism.* But Arius' Supreme Being was God the Father, not the triune God (see Trinity*). The Son, by contrast, was a being created by the will and power of the Father. Hence he was not 'without beginning'. (Arius took particular exception to Bishop Alexander's assertion – 'always the Father, always the Son'.) Certainly Arius was prepared to treat the Son as a special creature in the sense that the Father created him first and for the specific function of undertaking the rest of the creation.* Indeed, the Son was created precisely because the created order could not bear the immediate hand of God. Thus Christ's major role for the Arians was as God's servant in the work of creation and (to a lesser extent) in revelation.*

Early in the controversy, some Arians even affirmed that, as a creature, Christ was liable to change and sin, but by his personal virtue he had in fact managed not to sin. Foreseeing Christ's successful resistance to temptation, God had accorded Christ special honour in advance. But through time the Arians preferred the simpler view that God had created in Christ an unalterable creature.

In order to embarrass their opponents, some Arians produced catenae of passages from the gospels illustrating the human development and weakness of Christ. They demanded how such experiences could be attributed to a divine figure. The Arians could adopt this approach because they found no place for a human soul in Christ. Few opponents of Arianism, however (apart from Eustathius of Antioch, *c.* 300–*c.* 377) were at first able to make much of this denial.

Arianism was a matter of fierce controversy when Constantine gained control of the eastern Roman Empire in 324. He promptly convened a council* at Nicaea which was designed, among other things, to settle the debate. The council failed, in that Arianism simply went underground for a period of thirty years. But the Creed of Nicaea did stand the test of time in its rebuttal of Arianism. Its key phrase – that Christ was of one substance (*homoousios*) with the Father – stood rigidly opposed to the Arian belief that the Son (or any other creature) was alien from the Father's substance.

Arianism enjoyed a resurgence in the 350s, and gained imperial patronage from *c.* 353–78. But in theological terms the impetus moved away from the ruling Arian group towards a more radical group, known as the Anomoeans or Eunomians. The latter differed both in doctrinal emphasis and in tactics from the Arianizing court bishops who were often content to keep their real sentiments hidden. By contrast, the Anomoeans, centred initially on Aetius (d. *c.* 370), a man who progressed no further than the diaconate, believed in open theological debate. Indeed, Aetius and his successor, Eunomius (d. *c.* 395), showed considerable logical agility in setting forth their doctrines.

They began from the idea that God was *per se* ingenerate essence. Whereas earlier Arians had described the Supreme Being uniquely as ingenerate, they did not believe this revealed God's essence. Indeed, Arius had shocked his opponents by asserting that the Father was incomprehensible even to his Son. The Eunomians, however, altered this. God's essence, they contended, could be known by anyone who thought through the logical implications of ingeneracy. This bold claim was based on the belief, which they derived from Scripture, that the correct name of anything revealed its essence. So commonplace had the ascription of ingeneracy to God become at this time that the Eunomians were able, on shaky grounds, to assume it as God's name. The Eunomians remained distinctive in their twin claims that they knew God's name and that name revealed his essence.

Their emphasis on ingeneracy was simply intended to drive a wedge between the Supreme Being, who alone was ingenerate, and the Son who was begotten. From this the Eunomians argued that the Son was unlike (*anomoios*) the Father in substance. Hence they were dubbed Anomoeans.

Arianism declined rapidly with the loss of the ruling Arian group's imperial patronage in 378 and with the Council of Constantinople of 381, which left Nicene orthodoxy dominant. Indeed, the creed* probably affirmed by this (the second ecumenical) council was not identical to that promulgated at Nicaea, but an extended version, which added points, mainly to safeguard the deity of the Holy Spirit.*

Early in the Arian controversy, little attention had been paid to the Spirit, but from *c.* 360 this changed. The new issue may have arisen because the Anomoeans clearly declared that the Spirit was simply next in rank of created beings after the Son, made to give illumination and sanctification.* The mainstream of the Nicene party wanted to place the Spirit alongside the Father and the Son since all three were mentioned together in the baptismal formula and the doxology. But some who were opposed to Arian teaching on the Son would not accord deity to the

Spirit. This group, called the Pneumatomachi (Spirit-fighters) by their opponents, complained of a lack of scriptural evidence for the Spirit's deity. In particular, they saw no warrant for another relationship than that of Father and Son within the Godhead. The Niceno-Constantinopolitan Creed rebutted the Pneumatomachi as well as all Arians. It did this simply by affirming divine titles like 'Lord' which are used of the Spirit in Scripture, and it dealt with the difficult question of the Spirit's mode of origin by declaring that 'he proceeds from the Father'.

Bibliography
R. C. Gregg and D. E. Groh, *Early Arianism: A View of Salvation* (London, 1981); J. N. D. Kelly, *Early Christian Creeds* (London, ³1972); *idem, Early Christian Doctrines* (London, ⁵1977); T. A. Kopecek, *A History of Neo-Arianism*, 2 vols. (Cambridge, MA, 1979); R. D. Williams, *Arius. Heresy and Tradition* (London, 1987).

G.A.K.

ARISTOTELIANISM. The philosophy of those who have used Aristotle's methods or doctrines in their own thought. In his science and philosophy Aristotle (384–322 BC) developed and systematized the extensive Greek learning before him, and as a result his writings have been a source of inspiration in many different times and places. He was the teacher of the Alexandrian Greeks, the Syrians, the Arabs and Jews in the 7th to 12th centuries, and of the Christian West in the 13th and following centuries. The influence of Aristotelian science ended with the rise of the modern empirical sciences. In physics and astronomy its influence waned much sooner than in biology where it lasted into the 19th century. Aristotle's ethics, politics and metaphysics remain a source to which philosophers turn even today.

While Plato* developed a philosophy which is orientated towards the spiritual world of Ideas and the divine, Aristotle, parting from his teacher, developed a philosophical system which focuses on the realm of nature* and the methods for studying nature. Penetrating analysis of the processes of thought are found in his logical works. His treatises on natural philosophy give an extraordinarily comprehensive account of the material universe. His ethical writings reveal the same insightful grasp of the life of the individual and of society. He is also the founder of the science of metaphysics,* though in this area a number of issues remain untreated or unresolved. The gaps in Aristotle's metaphysics also cause basic problems in the area of human psychology. In man both the spiritual and the material worlds are found; man's body belongs to the changing material world but his understanding transcends the corporeal and belongs to the eternal, incorruptible and divine. Endless debate followed concerning the relation of the understanding to the individual. Is there one intellectual soul for all men or does each person have a separate soul? How is this soul united to the body? What happens to it after death? Aristotle's followers have answered these and related questions in different ways.

The history of Aristotelianism has also been determined by the availability of Aristotle's writings. During his lifetime Aristotle was known for popular dialogues written in the Platonic style, but these have all been lost. The writings which we have were all works, often just notes, written for his school, the Lyceum. They were edited and published by Andronicus of Rhodes about 70 BC. In the 3rd century the Neoplatonist Porphyry (see Platonism*) wrote a commentary on the *Categories* which was translated into Latin by Boethius* in the 6th century. Although Boethius planned to translate all of Aristotle's works into Latin, he was executed before he completed this project. As a result only Aristotle's logical works were known in Western Europe until the 12th century, with the result that Abelard* and his contemporaries studied and debated about universals, but knew nothing of the rest of Aristotle's thought. However, his writings were translated into Syriac, Arabic and Hebrew and so were well known in the Islamic world, and eventually became known in the West first from Arabic translations and later in translations made directly from Greek texts. Since the 13th century Aristotle's writings have been accessible in Latin and Greek, and so their influence has depended on interest rather than accessibility.

Aristotle had a relatively limited influence on the church fathers. His empirical and scientific focus was not attractive to the predominately religious orientation of the time. For someone like Augustine* the Platonists* (Neoplatonists) incorporated everything that

was valuable from Aristotle in their own thought. In his *Confessions* Augustine records that he read Aristotle's *Categories* and understood it, but it did him little good because he still remained a materialist.

Aristotle's influence was felt in a more significant way in the 12th century. The discussion of the problem of universals (see Nominalism*) took place among theologians, and so Aristotle's logical methods were naturally applied to theological issues, such as the Trinity,* incarnation* and the like. The most influential contribution was made by Abelard* in his *Sic et Non* (*Yes and No*). In this work Abelard collected opinions of the fathers which seemed contradictory but when properly understood could often be harmonized. His dialectical method found its greatest development in the disputed questions and summas of theology of the 13th century.

Aristotle's influence reached its peak in the 13th and 14th centuries. In the early 1300s Aristotle's natural philosophy, psychology and metaphysics became available in the Latin West. The philosophers and theologians of the time recognized that it had a philosophical and scientific richness which far exceeded anything they had known, but it also became apparent that Aristotle held some positions which were contrary to the Christian faith. He maintained that the world was eternal and that there was only one intellectual soul for all men – at least this was the way Averroes,* his greatest commentator, interpreted him. In addition, for Aristotle philosophy or natural reason was presumed to be the only means to attain man's highest good, happiness. In spite of attempts to ban his writings, Aristotle was studied in the universities. In general, Augustinians* formed the conservative opposition which tried to limit the influence of Aristotle. The other extreme was found in certain arts masters who simply taught Aristotle's position without trying to evaluate it in the light of faith. They are known as Averroists. A middle ground was taken by Thomas Aquinas* who embraced Aristotle's thought whole-heartedly as a philosophy, but revised it as he found necessary. For him this philosophy became the basic tool for his theology; in his famous phrase, philosophy is the handmaid of theology. In almost every discussion – God's nature, the Trinity, the human soul, grace, faith, *etc.* – one finds Aquinas using distinctions developed by philosophers, especially Aristotle, to explain the meaning of faith.

By the latter part of the 13th century all of the university masters were Aristotelians in the sense that they were familiar with and employed Aristotelian concepts and methods. There was a variety of interpretations of Aristotle's texts, however, and so this Aristotelianism was never a unified movement. Rather Thomas Aquinas,* Duns Scotus* and William of Ockham,* to name just three, each had their own interpretation and resulting tradition.

Renaissance humanists* were the first to attack the Aristotelianism of scholasticism,* but for the most part they were ineffective. Their critiques of the bad style of the schoolmen were not complemented by a presentation of an equally comprehensive alternative explanation of reality, and so they were no more effective than literary critiques of professional journals would be today. In so far as the humanists were developing literary studies and a historical awareness in interpreting ancient texts they were going beyond what the Aristotelians had to offer, and this eventually influenced even the method of theology, as can be seen in Calvin* for example. In 17th-century Protestant scholasticism there is a return to a theological method which owes much to Aristotelian influences (see Ramus*).

When Aristotelian science was superseded, Aristotelianism as a comprehensive explanatory system was doomed. Many have concluded that because Aristotelian science has been superseded all of his thought is dated. Others, however, continue to find inspiration in Aristotle's writings. Austin Farrer,* Bernard Lonergan* and Karl Rahner* among others, are indebted both directly and indirectly to the thought of Aristotle. With historical studies and new translations of Aristotle continuing to appear, Aristotelianism appears to be guaranteed a continuing life.

Bibliography

J. Barnes, *Aristotle* (Oxford, 1982); E. Gilson, *History of Christian Philosophy in the Middle Ages* (London, 1955); N. Kretzmann *et al.* (eds.), *The Cambridge History of Later Medieval Philosophy* (Cambridge, 1982); R. P. McKeon, *Aristotelianism in Western Chris-*tianity (Chicago, 1939); W. D. Ross, *Aristotle* (London, ⁴1945).

A.V.

ARMINIANISM. Jacobus Arminius (1560–1609) was a Dutch theologian educated at Leiden, Basel and Geneva, at which latter place he studied under Beza.* Upon returning to the Netherlands, he served as pastor in Amsterdam before becoming professor at Leiden in 1603. He questioned some basic assumptions of Reformed theology,* arousing a bitter and vituperative controversy.

Central to Arminius' theology was his radical view of predestination.* He attacked the speculative supralapsarianism of Beza on the grounds of its lack of Christocentricity, Christ being not the foundation of election but only the subordinate cause of an already foreordained salvation, resulting in a split between the decree of election and the decree concerning salvation through the incarnate Christ. This Christocentric concern led Arminius to invert the order of election and grace.* For Reformed orthodoxy the historical manifestation of God's grace was dependent on election. For Arminius, election was subsequent to grace. God decrees to save all who repent, believe and persevere. Election is conditional on man's response, dependent on God's foreknowledge of his faith and perseverance.* The possibility of a true believer totally or finally falling from grace and perishing is not denied. Consequently, there could be no assurance* of ultimate salvation. Moreover, God gives sufficient grace so that man may believe on Christ if he will. His will* is free. He can believe or he can resist God's grace. Redemptive grace is universal not particular, sufficient not irresistible; man's will is free not bound and co-operates with God's grace rather than being vivified by it. Effectively, Arminius was saying that God does not choose anyone but instead foresees that some will choose him. This was a position with Pelagian* and Gk. patristic roots.

Arminius' views were developed by his followers in the five theses of the Remonstrant Articles (1610): 1. Predestination is conditional on a person's response, being grounded in God's foreknowledge; 2. Christ died for each and every person but only believers are saved; 3. a person is unable to believe and needs the grace of God; but 4. this grace is resistible; 5. whether all the regenerate will persevere requires further investigation. The resultant controversy assumed convulsive national importance, culminating in the Synod of Dort* (1618–19) which condemned the Remonstrant Articles and removed and exiled the Remonstrant ministers. To the Contra-Remonstrants it appeared that the followers of Arminius had adopted a Semi-Pelagian* view of grace, had destroyed the doctrine of assurance by questioning perseverance and, through their inversion of predestination, were introducing a conditional gospel which threatened the atonement* and justification.*

Some of the fears of the Contra-Remonstrants appear soon to have been fulfilled. Simon Episcopius (1583–1643), Remonstrant leader at Dort, a prominent figure behind the Remonstrant Articles and professor at Leiden, made further developments in his own theology. Reiterating a conditional doctrine of predestination, he held that only the Father had deity of himself, the Son and the Holy Spirit being subordinate not simply in terms of generation and spiration but also in essence (see Trinity*). His stress was on Christ as exemplar, with doctrine subordinated to ethics.

The commitment to universal atonement (see Atonement, Extent of*) led followers of Arminius to oppose the penal substitutionary view of the atonement held by Reformed orthodoxy whereby Christ actually paid the penalty of all the sins of all his people and thus made effective atonement. For Arminianism, since Christ was held to have suffered for everyone he could not have paid the penalty for their sins, since all are not saved. His death simply permits the Father to forgive all who repent and believe. It makes salvation possible but does not intrinsically atone for anyone in particular. In fact, the atoning death of Christ was not essential for salvation by virtue of God's own nature as both loving and righteous but was rather the means God chose to save us for prudential administrative reasons. Hugo Grotius,* an Arminian, was the first clearly to expound the governmental theory of the atonement.

Despite initial suppression in the Netherlands, Arminianism spread pervasively throughout the world, eventually permeating all Protestant churches. In particular, its growth was facilitated by the impact of John Wesley.* Wesleyan Arminianism allowed that depravity was total, affecting every facet of man's being, thus highlighting the need for grace. However, synergism (see Will*) was retained, for the work of Christ was related to all men, delivering all from the guilt of Adam's first sin and granting sufficient grace for repentance and faith, providing people 'improve' or appropriate it. Hence, the stress falls on human appropriation of grace. Additionally, the possibility of a true believer falling from grace was expressly accepted with the consequence that while one could have assurance of present salvation there could be no present assurance of ultimate salvation. The leading Wesleyan theologian, Richard Watson (1781–1833), in his *Theological Institutes* (1823) did not even include election in his table of contents, regarding it as a temporal act subsequent to the administration of the means of salvation.

In recent years, Arminianism has become intermingled with Baptist* and dispensationalist* ideas, particularly in its contact with American fundamentalism.* However, strictly speaking, it should be disentangled from such extraneous accretions so as to focus on its own intrinsic tenets: election based on foreknowledge, partial depravity, universal non-efficacious atonement, universal resistible grace, a voluntaristic view of faith, a Semi-Pelagian co-operation of a person with God's grace and the possibility of a true believer falling from grace with concomitant undermining of assurance.

Bibliography

J. Arminius, *Works*, 3 vols. (London, 1825, 1828, 1875).

C. Bangs, *Arminius* (Grand Rapids, MI, ²1985); A. H. W. Harrison, *Arminianism* (London, 1937); P. K. Jewett, *Election and Predestination* (Grand Rapids, MI, 1985); J. Owen, *Works* (repr. London, 1967), vol. 10; C. H. Pinnock (ed.), *Grace Unlimited* (Minneapolis, MN, 1975); P. Schaff, *The Creeds of Christendom* (New York, 1919 edn.); C. W. Williams, *John Wesley's Theology Today* (London, 1969).

R.W.A.L.

ART, see AESTHETICS.

A SCENSION AND HEAVENLY SESSION OF CHRIST. The Christian

doctrine of the ascension and heavenly session of Christ, though undoubtedly an important part of the NT witness (Lk. 24:51; Acts 1:9–11; Eph. 4:8), was little developed before the time of Augustine.* This was at least partly because until that time it was regarded as an integral part of Christology,* as both the Old Roman and the Nicene Creeds* bear witness.

Regarded as a separate doctrine, the ascension of Christ is significant for several reasons. First, it represents the culmination of the earthly ministry of Jesus. His death and resurrection could not have their full effect until he ascended to the presence of his Father, to whom he presented his finished work of atonement* (Heb. 4:14–15). The ascension is the moment when the manhood of Jesus is taken up to God and glorified, the final assurance and the first fruits of our eternal salvation.

The ascension is also important because it reminds us that the body of Christ is now no longer present within the time and space framework, but belongs to the Son of God in eternity. This has a significant bearing on the use of 'body of Christ' imagery to describe both the church* and the eucharist.* Augustine and the Reformers were both insistent that this had to be understood as a spiritual, not as a physical reality. For the Reformers in particular, this meant that the medieval doctrines of transubstantiation and the visible church as the body and bride of Christ could not possibly be true.

The ascension has also been interpreted in terms of man's glorification in the wake of the resurrection. At times this has been pressed to the point of denying the forty-day interlude between Christ's rising from the dead and his going up into heaven, the importance of which lies in the teaching ministry of Jesus to his disciples during that time. Some scholars have even argued that the transfiguration accounts in the gospels have been displaced from their supposed origin as ascension narratives. In fact, although there are superficial similarities between the two, the transfiguration more closely resembles a descent from heaven (as e.g. Moses and Elijah) than an ascent.

The heavenly session was not generally distinguished from the ascension before the Reformation, and it continues to be a characteristic mark of Calvinist* theology. It is important because it emphasizes Christ's entry into his kingly office,* and is distinguished for this reason in the ancient creeds. Christ's present reign is a reminder that his work on our behalf continues in the present. His victorious triumph assures us of the efficacy of his work of mediation,* and is particularly important for our understanding of the work of the Holy Spirit.* When the doctrine of heavenly session is eclipsed, the work of the Spirit can be detached from that of Christ, either by too high a doctrine of the visible church, or by a spirituality which virtually ignores the work of Christ altogether, or regards it as only the beginning of the church's life.

When that happens, the emphasis shifts from Christ's historical atonement to the power of God at work in the world today. The result of this is that many Christians believe that it is possible to draw on that power independently of the atonement, which is the true basis and content of Christ's mediation. The heavenly session reminds us that Christ's work is at once efficacious and complete, since the one who now sits on the throne is the Lamb who was slain on the cross of Calvary (Rev. 22:1, 3).

Bibliography

J. G. Davies, *He Ascended into Heaven* (London, 1958); W. J. Marrevee, *The Ascension of Christ in the Works of St Augustine* (Ottawa, 1967); W. Milligan, *The Ascension and Heavenly Priesthood of Our Lord* (London, 1892); H. B. Swete, *The Ascended Christ* (London, 1922); P. Toon, *The Ascension of Our Lord* (New York, 1984).

G.L.B.

ASCETICISM AND MONASTICISM. The word 'asceticism' derives from the Gk. *askēsis* (exercise), and refers to a system of spiritual discipline whose chief preoccupation is the renunciation of the world and the flesh as part of the great struggle against the devil. It has taken different forms, but the main tradition is characterized by the three principles of poverty, chastity and obedience. Poverty is the abandonment of the world's goods, chastity is the refusal of the pleasure of the flesh, and obedience is spiritual submission to the director or to a rule of life, whose purpose is to guide the soul on its upward journey into the presence of God.

Asceticism was practised in biblical times, and events like the temptations of Jesus in the wilderness (Mt. 4:1–11) were later regarded as models for Christians. The desert was the chosen place for the ascetic life, and by AD 250 there were hermits (*eremitae*, desert-dwellers) living in caves in Middle Egypt. From there the movement spread across the Mediterranean world, where it was popularized by Basil* of Caesarea and by Jerome.*

Despite considerable resistance among the laity and some of the clergy, ascetic practices soon became a standard mark of holiness. Pope Gregory the Great* began to impress an ascetic discipline on the clergy and church of Rome, which reached its peak in the decree of the First Lateran Council (1123), imposing celibacy on all clergy. This was rejected by the Reformers, but it remains a binding rule of discipline in the Roman Catholic Church.

Basil of Caesarea was partly responsible for the development of a coenobitic (*coenobium*, common life) form of asceticism, which became what we now call monasticism. The word 'monk' (*monachos*) means solitary, but it is now used almost exclusively of those who live in a community. Eastern monasticism remained highly individualistic and contemplative in its emphasis, but the Western or Latin variety quickly took on an important social and evangelistic dimension, even in Celtic Christianity, which was otherwise strongly influenced by the hermitic ideals of the East.

Basil's Rule was modified by Benedict of Nursia (see Benedict and the Benedictine Tradition*) who, together with his contemporary Cassiodorus, laid the foundations of medieval monasticism. Until the 12th century nearly all monks in the West were Benedictines, but the institutionalization of the monastic tradition had by that time led to a serious relaxation of the primitive ideals of poverty, chastity and obedience. A number of reforms were initiated, with the result that new monastic orders sprang up, most of which originated in France or Italy. The Cistercians, Dominicans,* Premonstratensians and Franciscans* all emerged as separate orders about this time.

The Crusades also had an effect on the monastic life, producing contemplative orders like the Carmelites, and military ones, like the Templars and the Knights of St John. In the later Middle Ages there was a revival of individualism in the monastic tradition, and wandering friars, some of whom followed the Rule of St Augustine* (Austin), made their appearance. There was also a growth of lay orders, especially in the Netherlands, which many scholars believe influenced the early Reformers.

Women's orders also played an important role in medieval monasticism, not least because they gave gifted women an opportunity to exercise authority and enjoy a freedom which the lay society of the Middle Ages did not permit them. There were even houses in which men and women lived side by side, though these tended to arouse suspicion and were eventually discontinued.

After the Black Death (1346–49) the depopulation of Western Europe was too great to support monasticism on a large scale, and the orders began to decline. By the time of the Reformation many monasteries were virtually empty, and their property was secularized with little resistance. At the same time, many of the leading Reformers, especially Martin Luther,* were monks who had left the cloister. They abandoned the traditional forms of monastic piety but sought to recover the underlying spiritual ideals in a way which was not ascetic.

Monasticism has never occupied a prominent role in Protestantism,* though there has been a certain revival of disciplined community life since about 1850, which has had an uneven success. In the Roman Catholic and Eastern Orthodox churches it continues much as it has always done, though the pressures of modern life have taken their toll, even in the most ancient and famous houses. Today there is a general shortage of new recruits, which will almost certainly mean that the traditional influence which monks and nuns have exercised will decrease still further in the foreseeable future.

Ascetics have been among the most fruitful spiritual and theological writers down the centuries, and at some periods, notably during the Middle Ages, the story of monastic spirituality* is almost identical with that of theology in general. In the Eastern Orthodox churches monks are to this day regarded as a privileged theological élite, and the ascetic experience is advocated as the highest form of theology, far above the attainments of the academic discipline which goes by that name.

This productive tradition however must be carefully distinguished from the theological principles of asceticism itself. These can be grouped under two main headings according to the type of monasticism practised. In terms of *individual spirituality*, asceticism demands a rigorous programme of self-discipline, particularly of the flesh, which it sees as the major impediment to communion with God. Mystical* experience plays a central role in this theology, and the ultimate aim is the beatific vision* of God. Prayer, some of it unceasing, is the chief task of the monk, together with related meditative practices. Western monks are usually expected to participate in a regulated pattern of communal worship, and to receive the sacraments as frequently as possible, but in Eastern monasticism there is a tendency to regard these things as outward signs which the true contemplative can leave behind in his ascent to the divine presence.

To the pattern of individual spirituality, Western monasticism adds the practice of *corporate spirituality* as well. The monastery is regarded as a window into the kingdom of heaven, a place in which the perfect life of the redeemed people of God can be lived as a foretaste of the parousia. Eastern monasticism also has a corporate aspect but it is much less developed, and its theology does not present the same radical separation from the world as its Western counterpart does.

Fundamental themes of monastic spirituality include the concept of spiritual warfare which the monk is called to wage against evil spirits which threaten him on all sides. Also of great importance is the allegorical interpretation of the Bible, with special emphasis on the Song of Solomon and the life of Moses, together with the Genesis account of the earlier patriarchs. This has come about because the monastic tradition regards the individual soul as the bride of Christ, and interprets Old Testament love poetry in this sense. The patriarchal period is attractive, partly because of its emphasis on desert life, which corresponds to the origins of monasticism, and partly because the typology of the Mosaic law appears to correspond to the spiritual experience of the individual Christian, on the ground that the law is spiritual.

It must of course be remembered that the diversity of monasticism has produced many variations on these basic themes, and that many writers from the tradition have done little or nothing to develop them, being concerned with other aspects of theology or even quite different disciplines.

Bibliography

D. Chitty, *The Desert a City* (London, 1966); C. H. Lawrence, *Medieval Monasticism* (London, 1984).

G.L.B.

ASIAN CHRISTIAN THEOLOGY.

Asian Christians share a common concern to relate their Christian faith to real life in various Asian contexts. Reflecting on the nature and content of theology, Asian theologians have come to believe that every form of theological production is culturally conditioned. As a result, on the one hand there has been a critical evaluation of traditional theology developed in the West and imported to Asia and, on the other, an enthusiastic pursuit of contextual theology that speaks to the actual questions people in Asia are asking today in the midst of changing social and political situations. Asian theology has started the growing process, already bearing fruits of different kinds. This article attempts to point out some observable trends and salient features of Asian theology, at the risk of over-generalizing a complex development.

From *c.* 1970 there has been a shift of emphasis in Asian theology from 'indigenization' to 'contextualization'.* The former tends to be 'past-orientated' and remains a static concept, with its stress on the relation of the gospel to traditional cultures;* the latter is 'future-orientated' and dynamic, concerned also with the gospel in relation to social change. On the whole, most evangelicals are slow in responding to this change, and have not really gone beyond the 'indigenization' stage.

Theology serves to articulate one's understanding of the eternal truth in terms of one's given locale and context. The Bible, being the foundation and the source, provides the content of any Christian theology. With the Christian gospel as the God-given answer to human problems, it is the task of indigenous theology to discover what the real questions are, in order that Asian theology may assume a systematic form dictated by the salient emphases of Asian culture. The issue involves gospel and culture, and centres on the presentation of the gospel in different contexts, such as Hindu,* Buddhist,* Islamic* and totalitarian contexts. In theology, this means that particular contexts help to decide what particular area of faith should receive special emphasis. In recent years, discussions on the relationship between evangelism* and social responsibility (see Missiology* and Society, Theology of*) have prompted evangelicals to face seriously some of the important issues in Asia (see Lausanne Covenant*). These include communism (see Marxism and Christianity*), poverty,* overpopulation, hunger, suffering,* war,* bribery and secularism.* However, evangelical theological works that deal with politics,* social ethics* and development with depth and insight are yet to be seen.

Bong Rin Ro categorizes Asian theologies into four models: syncretism,* accommodation, situational theology and biblically orientated theology. His analysis reflects a common evangelical caution against contemporary Asian theology: fear of syncretism and accommodation whereby the gospel is diluted and biblical truth compromised. The key issue in the whole argument of contextual theology, as he sees it, is 'whether the biblical and historical doctrines of the Christian Church can be preserved without compromise in the process of contextualization'. The strength of evangelical theology lies in its insistence on the uniqueness* of the Christian gospel, the revelatory* nature of biblical truth and the necessity of salvation.* Its weakness may be described as a self-imposed limitation which does not adequately appreciate the richness of Asian religions and cultures, or urgently recognize the gravity of the demonizing effects of social and political evils.

Theological reflection in ecumenical circles often takes a different point of departure. Ecumenical theologians have reacted against the merely conceptual, abstract and confessional nature of traditional theology. To them theology is more than an articulation of beliefs or a formulation of Christian doctrines (see Confessions* and Creeds*). Its task is rather to reflect on the contemporary situation in the light of the Christian faith. Therefore, the totality of life is the raw material of a living and confessing theology.

This approach to Asian theology, in terms of methodology and content, is very much determined by the context. Asian distinctives are used as a frame of reference in the theological task. These include plurality and diversity; colonial experience in the past; present

nation-building, modernization and the resurgence of traditional religions. Asian theology is committed to address such issues as social injustice, poverty, violation of human rights,* oppression and exploitation of the poor.

High on the Asian theological agenda is the theme of suffering. In Japan, Kazoh Kitamori (b. 1916) brings out the centrality of suffering in the gospel and the reality of human suffering. The divine and the human are thus joined together in suffering, through which one comes to realize the love of God. Choan-Seng Song (b. 1929) further develops this theme by emphasizing that God commits himself totally to the suffering of this world. His theology of the cross* depicts the crucified God (see Moltmann*) not so much as the God who vicariously suffers and dies *for* the world (see Atonement*) as the God who suffers and dies *with* the world. Vicariousness is in fact replaced by identification.

Concern for humanity and freedom* is another important theme. From South Korea we have *Minjung* theology, using a political concept (*minjung*) denoting people who are ruled and dominated (different from the Marxist proletariat which is defined socio-economically), and applying Christian themes of messianic kingdom* and resurrection* to interpret history* and give meaning to its vision. History is the process in which the *minjung* realize their own destiny to be free subjects through sufferings and struggles against oppressive powers. It may not be inaccurate to label this as a Korean version of liberation theology.*

What about the long history of Asian peoples and the significance of their cultures? In what ways can we perceive the work of God among them? C. S. Song suggests that the frontiers of Asian theology must move from the history of Israel and the history of Christianity in the West to the history of Asia, in order to gain insights into God's ways with the nations, and to discover what place history beyond the Jewish-Christian traditions plays in God's saving purposes in the world. Probing in such a direction may present a challenge to some and a problem to others.

The creative efforts and insights of ecumenical theologians offer contributions to Asian theology that cannot be ignored. Their strength lies in their relevance to contexts, openness to new ideas and boldness to search into the dark. Yet these may also turn out to be disastrous, if basic biblical foundations are forsaken in favour of other assumptions.

Bibliography

J. Elwood (ed.), *Asian Christian Theology* (Philadelphia, 1980), especially essays by Shoki Coe, Saphir Athyal and Emertio P. Nacpil; J. C. England (ed.), *Living Theology in Asia* (London, 1981); Kazoh Kitamori, *Theology of the Pain of God* (London, 1958); Bong Rin Ro, 'Contextualization: Asian Theology', in Bong Rin Ro and Ruth Eshenaur (eds.), *The Bible and Theology in Asian Contexts* (Taichung, Taiwan, 1984), pp. 68–75; Choan-Seng Song, *Third-Eye Theology. Theology in Formation in Asian Settings* (Maryknoll, NY, 1979); *idem*, 'New Frontiers of Theology in Asia', in D. T. Niles and T. K. Thomas (ed.), *Varieties of Witness* (Singapore, 1980); Kim Yong-Bok (ed.), *Minjung Theology* (Singapore, 1981).

W.W.C.

ASSURANCE. Historically, the question of whether certainty of ultimate salvation is possible in this life became a major issue at the time of the Reformation.* Earlier, while some, *e.g.* Augustine* and Duns Scotus,* had accepted the possibility, the overall consensus increasingly allowed only a conjectural knowledge of grace based on good works, since the medieval doctrine of penance* tied forgiveness to ecclesiastical authority. Correspondingly, the Council of Trent (see Reformation, Catholic Counter-*) anathematized all who taught that such assurance was possible apart from special revelation. The Reformers' assertion of the supremacy of Scripture* nullified the intermediary role of the ecclesiastical hierarchy. For Luther,* Zwingli,* Bucer* and Calvin,* assurance was a normative component of faith.* Calvin regarded saving faith as assurance of salvation (*Institutes*, III. ii. 7), since he grounded assurance on Christ (*e.g. ibid.* III. xxiv. 5). Later Calvinism* increasingly based assurance on sanctification,* making it dependent on one's state of piety. Consequently, it was no longer regarded as an indispensably constituent element of saving faith. Correspondingly, the Westminster Confession* of Faith (1647) separated saving faith and assurance into two non-contiguous chapters. Explanation for this change has been sought

in factors such as the extent of the atonement* and covenant* theology. Debate has also surrounded whether Calvin allowed sanctification to be a basis for assurance. Some (*e.g.* Niesel, Kendall) deny it, while others (*e.g.* Barth,* Berkouwer*) maintain that he did permit it, but in a strictly subordinate sense. Following the Enlightenment,* the absolutizing of time* occasioned by post-Kantian* dualism* has made questions of eternity problematic. Nevertheless, creative thinking with extensive implications for assurance has been undertaken, notably by Karl Barth and Jürgen Moltmann.*

To the extent that the OT concentrates on the acts of Yahweh it does not provide a detailed anatomy of faith and assurance. Nevertheless, the paradigmatic faith of Abraham is confidence in Yahweh and his covenant promise (Gn. 15:6), described by Paul as full assurance (Rom. 4:13–25). Despite overbearing struggles, many Psalms exhibit this same confidence (*e.g.* Pss. 22, 40 – 44, 46, 102, 130), although at times there is unrelieved gloom (Pss. 38, 88, 109). In the NT, redemptive history is fulfilled in Christ's death and resurrection, while Pentecost marks the presence of the future consummation in our present aeon. Consequently, the NT stresses the normative character of assurance, portraying Christian faith as joyful confidence in Jesus Christ. The closest thing to a definition of faith is Heb. 11:1, where it is seen as 'being sure of what we hope for', the context indicating obedient response to God's promise in certain expectation of its future realization. Even in suffering, readers of 1 Peter are directed to their secure inheritance for which they themselves are preserved by God (1 Pet. 1:3–5). Paul grounds assurance in the purpose of God, the saving work of Christ and the ministry of the Spirit, against which nothing can prevail (Rom. 8:12–39). 1 John insists repeatedly, 'we know'.

Theologically, assurance is grounded on the character of God and the finality of his revelation in Jesus Christ. Since Christ is consubstantial with the Father from eternity his word to us is a true expression of the eternal will of God. His incarnation is 'a pledge of our sonship' (Calvin, *Institutes*, II. xii. 3), since he has taken our nature into union with God. His death made effective atonement for our sins. His resurrection establishes our own exaltation with him. In union with Christ we are given to share in the communion of the life of God (Jn. 6:56–57; 17:21, 23; 2 Pet. 1:4). Moreover, the eternal purpose of God stands firm. He has pledged himself to preserve us (Jn. 6:37–40; 10:28–29; 17:12). The central covenant promise, 'I will . . . be your God, and you will be my people' (Lv. 26:11–12; Je. 32:38; Ezk. 37:27; Rev. 21:3) is God's affirmation of our salvation in Christ. It also displays the corporate nature of the gospel, for only in the church is assurance given, the Holy Spirit baptizing us into the body of Christ and enabling us to feed on him in the eucharist. Is sanctification a ground of assurance? Certainly, the work of the Holy Spirit in us attests the work of Christ in atonement and the work of the Father in election. However, introspection can lead to despair or to self-righteousness. While certainty is found only as God sanctifies us, the foundation of both is the finished work of Christ. With increased questioning of post-Renaissance individualism, we shall probably see the corporate dimension of assurance coming into sharper focus.

Bibliography

Karl Barth, *CD*, II.2, pp. 334–340; G. C. Berkouwer, *Divine Election* (Grand Rapids, MI, 1960); Calvin, *Institutes*, II. xii-xvii; III. ii. 1–43; III. xxiv. 5; R. T. Kendall, *Calvin and English Calvinism to 1649* (London, 1979); Jürgen Moltmann, *Theology of Hope* (London, 1967).

R.W.A.L.

ASTROLOGY, see OCCULT.

ATHANASIAN CREED, see CREEDS.

ATHANASIUS (*c.* 297–373). Few fathers of the church are more renowned than Athanasius. He was still very young when bitter persecution struck the church in Egypt and elsewhere. Formally educated in the catechetical school of Alexandria (see Alexandrian School*), his abilities and Christian devotion attracted the notice of Bishop Alexander. As a deacon he accompanied Alexander to Nicaea (see Councils*), and on Alexander's death was consecrated bishop. Forty-six years he served (seventeen of them spent in five exiles), much loved by his people but hated and persecuted by those with an Arianizing* bent. His writings reveal a great breadth of character – a rich devotion to the Word-become-man, an uncompromising, well-argued stance against the Arians, a great pastoral concern in his annual *Festal Letters*, and a profound interest in monasticism (see Asceticism*), evident in his *Life of Antony*.

Central to Athanasius' faith and theology was the incarnation* of the Word of God, climaxing in his death and resurrection.* Incarnation and atonement* were held inseparably together. Soteriology (see Salvation*) pervaded his whole thought, together with a living worship and acknowledgement of the triune God (see Trinity*). His *On the Incarnation*, dated 318 by some though considerably later by others, is a classic. Athanasius portrays the doctrine of creation* and man's place within it. Man has lost the life of God, entering into increasing decay, corruption and loss of the image* and knowledge of God. Only the original creator could restore, doing so by taking flesh, revealing himself and going to the cross, once a symbol of shame but now the trophy of victory, proclaimed in the resurrection.

In *Against the Arians* and other anti-Arian writings, Christian theology and epistemology* take a giant step forward. The issues, as Athanasius saw them, concerned the very life or death of the church. In taking an uncompromising stand against Arianism, Athanasius recognized that the heart of the Christian faith must be subjected to rigorous enquiry. His own earlier theological position also had to be reassessed, especially with his now clearer awareness, sharpened through the Arian controversy, of the principle: 'God is different in being from the world.' In everything, he argued, one must think of God in accordance with what God has actually done and revealed. God cannot be subjected to creaturely categories or limited by man's finite understanding. Rather a true theology must arise from a centre in God, governed and controlled by all he has done in creation, redemption* and revelation.* The connections in one's thought must reflect and arise out of the inner connections in God's action and being.

On the Incarnation had a strong cosmological flavour, with the main emphasis falling on the Word in his relation to the world. Despite its understanding of the Word as belonging fully to the Godhead and of creation as existing by grace, the very way in which the Word was seen evoked a perspective of the world rather than of the inner being of the triune God. This was simply the context of traditional theology. The Arian controversy forced Athanasius to think through the inner relations of Father and Word or Son, as well as their relation to the world. God exists eternally as Father, Son and Holy Spirit, quite independently of the created order, the persons of the Trinity being one in both substance (*homoousios*) and in action. Any dualism* excluding God from acting in his true being in his own world, such as was implicit in Arianism, was radically rejected.

In *Against the Arians* Athanasius developed further his sense of the wonderful harmony and order or created rationality within the world, a rationality not to be confused with, yet connected to and indicative of, God's rationality or Word. God is known, however, not through creation alone but primarily through Scripture,* and Athanasius evidences a profound grasp of Scripture and hermeneutics.*

Considerable differences lie between Athanasius' earlier and later thought in his understanding of the God-man. His soteriology was completely rethought and deepened. Prominent, as before, is the necessity for the sake of man's salvation, of the incarnation of the Word of God, and the inseparability of incarnation and atonement is reinforced. Reconciliation* occurs in the first place within Christ himself, between the God and the man, this being the ground for man's salvation, knowledge and receiving of the Spirit, for man is incorporated into Christ. The God and the man in Christ must be thought of according to their respective natures, never divorced yet not mixed either, with the centre of the Word-man being always the Word. The very awareness of the difference in being between God and man rests ultimately on the incarnation. In recent study of Athanasius, the question has been raised whether Athanasius was an early Apollinarian.* While many eminent theologians argue that he was, convincing reasons can be adduced to the contrary.

Concerning man's knowledge of God, in *Against the Arians* Athanasius moves again more in a Trinitarian perspective, the incarnation again being central. All knowledge of God as Father and creator occurs only in and through the Son, when the Son is known according to his nature. Man's knowledge of

God is always creaturely but not therefore false, for God has accommodated* himself to man's ways of knowing. Words used of God must be understood in the light of his being and nature, but certain words used of him, such as 'father' and 'son', apply properly only within the Trinity and only secondarily to mankind.

In his *Letters Concerning the Holy Spirit*, Athanasius, faced now with a denial of the Godhead of the Spirit, developed further his Trinitarian thought, integrating the Spirit much more fully into his theology. Whereas his previous references to the Spirit tended to the more formal, apart from *Against the Arians* III, where his mature understanding of the person and work of the Spirit is clearly emerging, in his *Letters Concerning the Holy Spirit* a rich understanding of God as Father, Son and Holy Spirit is evident, not only in intra-Trinitarian relations but also in relation to the world.

Much of Athanasius' theology can be summed up in the word *homoousion* – the Son is 'one substance' with the Father. The incarnate Son is the ground of all revelation and atonement. This word, though not occurring in Scripture, was for him a wonderful 'pointer' or 'precise declaration', possessing extraordinary illuminatory and explanatory power in bringing to light the whole work and being of the triune God. Athanasius' vigorous defence of it rested upon the fact that he was utterly convinced of its truth.

Bibliography

J. A. Dorner, *History of the Development of the Doctrine of the Person of Christ*, vol. I:2 (Edinburgh, 1862); G. Florovsky, 'The Concept of Creation in St. Athanasius', in *SP* 6 (1962), pp. 36–57; T. E. Pollard, *Johannine Christology and the Early Church* (Cambridge, 1970); A. Robertson, *St Athanasius* in *NPNF* 4 (1892); R. V. Sellers, *Two Ancient Christologies* (London, 1940); C. R. B. Shapland, *The Letters of Saint Athanasius Concerning the Holy Spirit* (London, 1951); T. F. Torrance, 'Athanasius: A Study in the Foundations of Classical Theology', in *Theology in Reconciliation* (London, 1975).

J.B.Wa.

ATHEISM is the view that holds that God* does not exist. The term is used conventionally to indicate lack of belief in the God of the Judaeo-Christian tradition.

Various arguments have been advanced for atheism, including arguments from the lack of evidence for God's existence, or from the manifest occurrence of certain phenomena (*e.g.* pain and suffering*) allegedly inconsistent with the existence of God. Alternatively atheism has been argued for on the grounds of logical simplicity and economy: in Lessing's* famous phrase it is alleged that there is no need for the hypothesis that God exists, since everything that exists can be explained in terms of scientific laws or human decisions. It is this naturalism which is characteristic of the atheism of modern humanism* and secularism* and which helped to provoke the 'death of God'* and 'religionless Christianity' (see Bonhoeffer*) debates of the 1960s. Such a view is in fact based upon a misunderstanding of the biblical concept and 'function' of God, who is declared to be, not the cause of such and such events (with the implication that there are other events of which God is *not* the cause), but the upholder of the whole universe.

Atheism, from its own standpoint, has had to account for the persistence of belief in the existence of God. It has done so by invoking either general human characteristics such as gullibility and sentimentalism, or more specific mechanisms. Thus Marx,* partly echoing Feuerbach,* maintained that belief in God is an element in human 'false consciousness', misbelief and misperception arising out of class-ridden social and economic circumstances. But even if this were true as an empirical hypothesis it would not be sufficient to show that God does not exist.

According to Paul in Rom. 1:18–32 creation bears witness to God's existence. His power and Godhead are 'clearly seen'. Whatever Paul means exactly by these phrases he is not to be taken as holding that atheism is a contradiction in terms, but rather that, at the practical level, all men live in such a way that acknowledges an objective physical universe, and objective moral rules, rendering them without excuse in refusing to acknowledge God. This leaves open the question of whether people sometimes label themselves 'atheist' in order to be able to distance themselves from awkward questions.

The emphasis of Scripture is much more upon what has been called 'practical atheism', the effective denial of God in human life. Thus Christ's parable of the man who planned to build bigger barns without reference to God (Lk. 12:16–21) and James' advice to Christians in commerce (Jas. 4:13–17) are typical warnings against practical atheism, the sin-born refusal of a person to acknowledge God in all his ways. Scripture also emphasizes the need to avoid thinking of God in the image of men, and of idolizing some aspect of or object in the created universe.

Bibliography
John Hick (ed.), *The Existence of God* (London, 1964); Hans Küng, *Does God Exist?* (London, 1980).

P.H.

ATONEMENT. The centrality of the atonement to Christianity has influenced our language, giving us the word 'crucial' which means literally 'pertaining to a cross'. When we say that anything is crucial we are saying that it is as central to that to which we apply it as the cross* is to Christianity. What Christ did on the cross is the heart of the Christian faith. The atonement is critical; it is the central doctrine of Christianity. That does not mean that other doctrines (*e.g.* the incarnation*) may be neglected. Each of the great Christian doctrines is important and has its place. But we must not minimize the centrality of the atonement.

The need for atonement arises from the universal sinfulness of mankind and our inability to deal with the problem posed by our sin.* That all are sinners is clear from specific expressions in Scripture (*e.g.* 1 Ki. 8:46; Ps. 14:3; Rom. 3:23), but perhaps more important is the whole thrust of the Bible. It is clear throughout Scripture that we do not measure up to the standards God lays down. Further, this is serious, for 'the wages of sin is death' (Rom. 6:23). The Bible makes it plain that sin excludes from the blessing of God (Is. 59:2; Hab. 1:13), and Jesus specifically said that blasphemy against the Holy Spirit can never be forgiven (Mk. 3:29). The sinner is in a desperate situation.

But God in his love and mercy has always made provision. The OT tells of a complicated system of sacrifices* which God gave Israel so that atonement might be made (Lv. 17:11). The killing of animals had no intrinsic worth that availed to do away with sin (Heb. 10:4).

The sacrifices availed because God chose that they should. It is the love of God, and not the blood of goats and calves, that puts sin away. And, of course, God looks for right dispositions in his worshippers, such as repentance* (1 Ki. 8:47; Ezk. 18:30–31).

New Testament teaching

The word 'atonement' is rare in the NT; it occurs once in AV (KJV), at Rom. 5:11, and not at all in many translations. But the idea is there throughout. God sent his Son to redeem (Gal. 4:4–5), and throughout the NT it is clear that it is what God has done in Christ that enables sinners to approach him and enter into his blessing now and in the hereafter.

Christ's atoning work is viewed from a number of angles. Thus sinners are slaves to their sin (Jn. 8:34), but Christ has set them free (Gal. 5:1). They were caught up in the sin of Adam: 'in Adam all die' (1 Cor. 15:22). But Christ died for our sins (1 Cor. 15:3) and the effects of Adam's sin have been nullified (Rom. 5:12–21). Sinners are subject to judgment, both a judgment in the here and now (Rom. 1:24, 26, 28) and a judgment at the end of the age (Rom. 2:16), but there is no condemnation for those who are in Christ (Rom. 8:1). We are captive to the law of sin (Rom. 7:23), while from another angle no-one will be justified by the works of the law (Rom. 3:20). But we are discharged from the law, dead to that which held us in bondage (Rom. 7:4). That the wrath* of God is exercised towards sinners is in much modern theology an industriously evaded doctrine, but it is plain in the NT (Lk. 3:7; Jn. 3:36; Rom. 1:18; 2:5; etc.). But there is also the clear teaching that Christ has turned that wrath away from sinners (1 Thes. 1:10; 5:9). This is the meaning of propitiation too (Rom. 3:25; 1 Jn. 2:2). Death is another tyrant (Rom. 6:23) from which Christ has freed us (Rom. 5:17; 1 Cor. 15:52–57). The flesh is evil (Gal. 5:19–21; Eph. 2:3), but it has been crucified in those who are Christ's (Gal. 5:24). There is a futility about much of life in this world, but Christians are delivered from it (Rom. 8:20–23); their lives are not in vain (1 Cor. 15:58; Phil. 2:16). The 'world'* is hostile to Christ (Jn. 7:7; 15:18), but he has overcome it (Jn. 16:33). The plight of sinners is many-sided, but view it how you will, Christ has saved his people by his atoning death.

The NT writers use a number of vivid word-pictures to bring out what Christ has done for us. Thus his work may be seen as a process of redemption* (Gal. 3:13), the payment of a ransom (Mk. 10:45), which points to the setting of sinners free from slavery or a death sentence. It is the offering of a sacrifice (Eph. 5:2), which must have been a vivid image to people accustomed to offering animals on altars in their worship. The frequent references to Christ's blood also point of course to the sacrifices. Sometimes there is a reference to a particular sacrifice, such as the Passover (1 Cor. 5:7), the sin offering (Rom. 8:3), or the Day of Atonement (Heb. 9:7, 11–12), but more usually it is left general. Christ is said to have borne the curse (Gal. 3:13), and to have died 'in the place of' sinners (Mk. 10:45). His work is seen as effecting justification* (Rom. 4:25), or as bringing in the new covenant* promised long before by Jeremiah (Lk. 22:20; Heb. 8). He can be said to have nailed to the cross 'the bond which stood against us with its legal demands' (Col. 2:14).

Especially important in some recent discussions is the Pauline concept of reconciliation. This is used in a small number of passages (Rom. 5:10–11; 2 Cor. 5:18–20; Eph. 2:16; Col. 1:20–22), but it is implicit in many others, for example, those that speak of peace being made between God and man. It is certainly an important concept and it is significant that Paul can see the death of Christ as doing away with the hostility that sin aroused and effecting a far-reaching reconciliation. This is a significant aspect of the atonement, though it should not be held in such a way as to minimize the variety of other ways of looking at it.

Historical theology

In the early church there was emphasis on the fact that Christ saves us, but few asked how he did so. Some early theologians, however, thought that sinners go to hell because they belong to Satan. In this situation God offered Christ to the evil one as a ransom in exchange for sinners. Satan eagerly accepted the offer realizing that he was getting far more than he was giving up, but when he got Christ down into hell he found that he could not hold him. On the third day Christ rose triumphant and Satan was left with neither his original prisoners nor the ransom price. Only a little thought was needed to see that on this view

God deceived Satan, but that did not worry the fathers. For them it simply showed that God was wiser than Satan, and they developed the theory with illustrations from catching fish and trapping mice. This bordered on the grotesque and the view faded in the light of better ways of looking at what Christ did. But in modern times G. Aulén* has revived the view, pointing out that, for all its absurdities, it enshrines an important truth, that in his death Christ won the victory over all the forces of evil. A place must surely be found for this in any adequate theory of atonement.

Anselm* worked out a theory of satisfaction.* He pointed out that a king is in a very different position from a private citizen. He may be ready to overlook an insult or an injury in his private capacity, but as supreme in the kingdom he cannot. Proper satisfaction must be rendered for all that harms the kingdom. Anselm saw God as a great king and he thought it was not proper for him to overlook any evil done in his kingdom. But sin against God is so serious that man is quite unable to provide the required satisfaction. That ought to be provided by one who is man and can be provided only by one who is God. Thus it was necessary for God to become man. This interesting theory is generally held to owe too much to the ideas current in Anselm's day. We no longer see medieval ideas about satisfaction as valid. And Anselm did not allow for the fact that a king may in fact exercise his prerogative of mercy without doing damage to his kingdom. But at least he took sin much more seriously than did his predecessors, and no-one can think about the atonement since his day without giving thought to just 'how heavy a weight sin is'.

The Reformers took over some of Anselm's views, but for his thought that sin outraged the majesty of God they substituted the idea that sin is a breaking of his law. The essence of the atonement, they thought, is that Christ took our penalty upon him. He stood in the place of sinners and since he bore their punishment it no longer falls on them. Opponents point out that this does not take account of the fact that, while penalties like fines may indeed be transferred, penalties like imprisonment or execution may not. Further, sin is not something that can be transferred from one person to another. Such criticisms have weight, but we must bear in mind that the Reformers were not thinking of an external, mechanical process. There is a twofold identification: Christ is one with the Father ('God was in Christ, reconciling the world unto himself', 2 Cor. 5:19, AV/KJV), and he is one with the sinners he saves (they are 'in Christ'). The view protects an important scriptural truth, that God saves in a way that is right. Due penalty is not overlooked in the process whereby Christ delivers us. Many modern views seem to boil down to the conviction that God is stronger than evil; in the end might is right. It is, of course, true that God is stronger than evil and this is a precious truth. But it is also true that God is concerned for what is right, even in the process whereby he saves people who are in the wrong.

Abelard* enunciated the subjective view of the atonement, a view that has been widely popular in modern times. The cross shows us how greatly God loves us and this causes us to respond with an answering love. We turn away from the sin that injured Christ so sorely and live new lives. There are various forms of the theory but they have in common that the essence of atonement is its effect on sinners. There is certainly truth in this. When we see what Christ has done in dying for us, we are moved to repentance and love and faith. But to say that this is all that happens is quite erroneous. It overlooks most of the scriptural evidence and leaves us in the uncertain position of being required to work out our own salvation by the way we respond to Christ's example.

There are other ways of looking at it. In modern times some have given emphasis to the concept of sacrifice, others draw attention to Jesus' abandonment by the Father (Mk. 15:34). But no theory has won universal acceptance and it is probable that none ever will. Christ's atoning work is so complex and our minds are so small. We cannot take it all in. We need the positive contributions of all the theories, for each draws attention to some aspect of what Christ has done for us. And though in the end we cannot understand it all, we can thankfully accept 'so great salvation'.

Bibliography

Anselm, *Cur Deus Homo*; G. Aulén, *Christus Victor* (London, 1931); D. M. Baillie, *God Was in Christ* (London, 1948); K. Barth, *CD*, IV. 1, *The Doctrine of Reconciliation*; J. Denney, *The Death of*

Christ (London, 1951); R. S. Franks, *The Work of Christ* (London, 1962); R. Martin, *Reconciliation* (Atlanta, GA, 1981); J. Moltmann, *The Crucified God* (London, 1974); L. Morris, *The Apostolic Preaching of the Cross* (London, ³1965); *idem, The Cross in the New Testament* (Grand Rapids, MI, 1965); J. R. W. Stott, *The Cross of Christ* (Leicester and Downers Grove, IL, 1986); V. Taylor, *The Atonement in New Testament Teaching* (London, 1940); F. M. Young, *Sacrifice and the Death of Christ* (London, 1975).

L.L.M.

ATONEMENT, EXTENT OF. For whom did Christ die? In the history of the church there have been two basic answers to that question. Most Christians have taught that Christ died for every human individual. Therefore the atonement* is universal in extent. Other Christians have held that Christ died only for the elect. Therefore the atonement is limited, definite or particular in extent.

Among those who hold that the atonement is universal in extent there are significant differences on the saving effect of the atonement. A small group, historically known as universalists,* teach that the saving effect of the atonement is as universal as the extent of the atonement. Therefore all humans are saved. Most, however, who hold that the atonement is universal in extent deny that it is universal in saving effect. These believe that Christ in his atonement intended to make salvation possible for all, but that the saving effect of the atonement is realized in the individual only when some condition is met (such as faith and/or obedience.) Roman Catholics, Eastern Orthodox, Lutherans, Arminians* and Amyraldians* hold this view. (Amyraldianism is a view that developed among some French Calvinists in the 17th century and which accepted the particularism of Calvinism except on the extent of the atonement.)

Those who hold that the atonement is limited or definite in extent teach that Christ died to save only those whom the Father had predestined to eternal life. Therefore the atoning work of Christ is applied in due time to all for whom it was accomplished. This view emerged clearly among the followers of Augustine* as a consequence of his teaching on sovereign, particular grace in salvation. Throughout the Middle Ages Augustinians*

like Prosper of Aquitaine, Thomas Bradwardine* and John Staupitz taught a limited atonement. Peter Lombard* in his *Sentences* offered a compromising, ambiguous position that Christ died sufficiently for all, but efficiently for the elect alone. In the 16th and 17th centuries the limited atonement was taught by the Roman Catholic Cornelius Jansen (see Augustinianism*) and by Calvinists. John Calvin* did not explicitly teach the doctrine, but it seems implicit in his work. His successors made it explicit and made it part of Reformed confessional orthodoxy in the Canons of Dort* and the Westminster Confession of Faith.

Defenders of a universal atonement appeal for scriptural support to Jn. 3:16; Rom. 5:18 and 1 Jn. 2:12. They argue their view is necessary to effective preaching so that each individual can be told, 'Christ died for you.'

Defenders of a limited atonement appeal for scriptural support to Mt. 1:21; 20:28 and Jn. 17:9. Texts that are apparently universal are explained as referring to all sorts and kinds of people in the world, rather than to every individual. They argue that only their view is theologically consistent with the character of the substitutionary atonement and with the harmony of the Trinity. If Christ truly bore all the wrath of God for all sin as a substitute for the sinner, then the extent of the atonement and the effect of the atonement must be the same. If the Father has elected some sinners to eternal life and if the Holy Spirit applies the saving work of Christ only to the elect, then Christ, in harmony with the purpose of the Father and the Spirit, died on the cross for the elect alone.

Bibliography

D. G. Bloesch, *Essentials of Evangelical Theology*, vol. 1 (San Francisco, 1978); R. H. Culpepper, *Interpreting the Atonement* (Grand Rapids, MI, 1966); W. R. Godfrey, 'Reformed Thought on the Extent of the Atonement to 1618', *WTJ* 37 (1974–75), pp. 133–171; P. Helm, 'The Logic of Limited Atonement', *SBET* 3:2 (1985), pp. 47–54; J. I. Packer, introd. to repr. of J. Owen, *The Death of Death in the Death of Christ* (London, 1959); J. B. Torrance, 'The Incarnation and "Limited Atonement",' *EQ* 55 (1983), pp. 83–94.

W.R.G.

AUGSBURG CONFESSION, see
CONFESSIONS OF FAITH.

AUGUSTINE (354–430). The greatest
theologian among the Latin fathers and
one of the greatest of all time. His influence
dominated medieval Christianity in the West
(where he became one of the four 'Doctors'
of the church) and provided the most
powerful non-biblical stimulus to the Reformation. For both Catholics and Protestants he
remains a major theological resource.

Life

He was born in Tagaste in Roman North
Africa (modern Souk Ahras in Algeria) to
Patricius, who only later became a Christian,
and the pious Monnica, who enrolled him as
a catechumen from infancy. His *Confessions*
(a kind of spiritual and intellectual autobiography) are the main source for tracing his
early development. During his education,
locally and at Carthage, his connection with
catholic Christianity became tenuous. He
excelled in literature and rhetoric but never
mastered Greek. His reading of Cicero's lost
Hortensius (373) kindled in him a consuming
love of divine wisdom (philosophy), for which
he turned to Manichaeism,* despairing of the
church's Scriptures. While teaching rhetoric in
Africa and at Rome (383) and Milan (384),
he remained a Manichaean adherent, despite
growing disenchantment with its intellectual
pretensions.

It was at Milan that he became a catholic
Christian. His conversion (386) and baptism
(Easter 387) resulted from the persistent
prayers of Monnica, the preaching of Bishop
Ambrose* (who showed him how to interpret
the Bible spiritually or allegorically and whose
eloquent wisdom deeply impressed him), the
Neoplatonic writings of Plotinus and
Porphyry (that finalized his release from the
shackles of Manichaeism), and the impact of
the ascetic* movement from the East. His
ideal was now the contemplative quest for
truth by the twin paths of reason and faith,
and this he pursued both in retreat before his
baptism and in ascetic community back at
Tagaste.

His writings from this period, partly
directed against Manichaeism, show how
profoundly Neoplatonism (see Platonism*)
had influenced him. Several are dialogues in
the Platonic mould. He confidently expected

that Platonic philosophy would unlock the
treasures of the faith of the catholic church
(*cf. True Religion*, 389–91). To vindicate the
roles of faith and authority in religion against
Manichaean objections, he argued that faith
must precede understanding (*cf.* Is. 7:9, LXX)
but that faith has its own grounds – which he
found in the moral and numerical achievements of the church world-wide (*cf. The
Usefulness of Believing*, 391–92). Against
Manichaean determinism, he insisted that
culpable sin proceeds only from the abuse of
free will* (*cf. Free Will*, 391–95). Against
Manichaean dualism* he stressed the goodness of creation* and adapted the Neoplatonic
approach to evil* by viewing it as the absence
of good, lacking substantial reality. His Christian Platonism entertained a high estimate of
man's moral and spiritual potential.

In 391 Augustine was press-ganged into the
church's ministry at Hippo (modern Annaba),
and was soon bishop of its catholic congregation (396), turning the bishop's house into
an ascetic seminary-cum-chapter. The needs
of the church increasingly determined his
theological output. He gave himself more
solidly to the study of Scripture, especially
Paul, under the stimulus of Tyconius (*fl. c.*
370–90), a nonconformist Donatist* from
whom Augustine learned at several significant
points. Exposure to pastoral realities also
steadily eroded his earlier more humanist optimism, encouraging a deeper awareness of
human frailty and perversity. One fruit of this
shift is the searching analysis of his own
sinfulness in the *Confessions* (397–401).
Another was *To Simplician, on Various Questions* (396), in which Rom. 9:10–29
convinced him of the basic interrelations
between election, grace, faith and free will
that he would later defend against the Pelagians.* Not until that subsequent controversy
did he realize that Rom. 7:7–25 must refer to
the Christian, not a person under law prior to
grace, as he argues in *To Simplician*.

At Hippo, Augustine continued to refute
Manichaean errors. In defending the OT
against their criticisms, he presented the most
substantial Christian case to date for the just
war (in *Against Faustus*, 397–98). But the
counter-church of Donatism now became his
main preoccupation, evoking important
contributions to Western doctrines of church*
and sacraments* (*cf.* especially *Against the
Letter of Parmenian*, 400; *Baptism, Against*

the Donatists, 400–401; *Against the Letters of Petilian*, 401–405; *The Unity of the Catholic Church*, 405). Augustine's teachings built on Tyconius and Optatus of Milevis (*fl. c.* 365–85), catholic Africa's sole prior critic of Donatism of any theological substance.

Donatism

To Donatism's exclusive claims Augustine opposed both the universality (or catholicity) of the church as foretold in Scripture and its mixed character, embracing both tares and wheat until the judgment. The quest for a pure community was doomed to failure (for only God knows who are his) and contrary to Scripture. The church's holiness is not that of its members but of Christ its head, to be realized only eschatologically. Augustine so emphasized the bond between Christ and his body that he could speak of them as 'one Christ loving himself', even 'one person' compacted by love or the Spirit (which Augustine closely identified – see below).

Since schism* is supremely an offence against love, schismatics are bereft of the Spirit of love. Although they profess the catholic faith and administer the catholic sacraments, these remain profitless to them until they enter the catholic fold which is the sole sphere of the Spirit. Reinforcing the 4th century's abandonment of the original African position (*cf.* Cyprian*), Augustine argued that schismatic or heretical sacraments are valid (but not regular), for their validity hinges not on the worthiness of the human minister but on Christ, who is the true minister of the sacraments. So Augustine could accept Donatists into the church without requiring their (re)baptism* or (re)ordination, but his distinction between sacramental validity (dependent on Christ) and profitability (dependent on the Spirit) was too subtle. It was the doctrine of the church itself that really needed development to accommodate orthodox schisms like Donatism. Augustine's artificial distinction helped to father the unfortunate notion of the indelible 'character' of sacraments irrespective of their relationship to the church community.

Augustine also provided a theological justification of the coercion of heretics and schismatics (*Epistle* 93, 408; *Epistle* 185, 417). Threats and sanctions were essentially corrective (and so could never include the death penalty), the special service to religion of Christians holding secular office. Augustine

originally assented to this policy for pragmatic reasons, but defended it by a dubious use of Scripture (including texts like Lk. 14:23), and in terms of how God dealt with recalcitrant humanity – by the harsh discipline of his 'benevolent severity'. In this context Augustine uttered his often misquoted dictum, 'Love, and do what you will', as a defence of paternal chastisement.

Pelagianism

Augustine's most influential legacy to Protestantism was his anti-Pelagian corpus (411–30). From the first of his many writings (*The Merits and Remission of Sins and Infant Baptism*, 411–12), he wove the Pelagians'* diverse emphases into a single heresy. The controversy unfolded in three stages: against Celestius and Pelagius (411–18; *The Spirit and the Letter, Nature and Grace, The Perfection of Human Righteousness, The Grace of Christ and Original Sin, Epistle* 194); against Julian (419–30; *Marriage and Concupiscence, Against Two Letters of the Pelagians, Against Julian, Unfinished Work against Julian*); and against the mis-named Semi-Pelagian* monks of Africa and Gaul (427–30; *Grace and Free Will, Correction and Grace, Epistle* 217, *The Predestination of the Saints, The Gift of Perseverance*).

The long conflict witnessed Augustine's construction of an ever more impregnable and forbidding theological fortress. Its building blocks included the following: an exalted view of the perfections of Adam and Eve, and hence of the disastrous consequences of the fall;* the insistence that, because all sinned 'in Adam' (on which Augustine appealed to Ambrosiaster's mistaken reading of Rom. 5:12), all are bound by the penalties for that sin – spiritual death, guilt and the diseased disordering of human nature; 'concupiscence', from which no sexual acts of fallen humanity are free (even within Christian marriage), as the locus of transmission of original sin from parents to children; the impossibility of even 'the beginning of faith' without the gift of prevenient grace* by whose power 'the will is prepared' to turn to God; the restriction of this grace to the baptized, so that infants dying unbaptized are condemned to hell, if perhaps to its milder reaches, and to the 'fixed number' of the elect, who receive it by God's sovereignly free mercy alone, with the rest of mankind left to their just deserts (Augustine rarely speaks of a divine predestination* to condemnation parallel to predestination to salvation); the denial that God 'will have all persons to be saved', and the disjunction of election and baptism, for not all the baptized belong to the elect; the infallibility of the eternal redemption* of the elect, in whom God's grace works irresistibly (but not coercively) and who receive the 'gift of perseverance'; and the conclusive appeal to the inscrutability of God's judgments when mere man dared to question them.

The church in both West and East repudiated basic Pelagian beliefs, but did not canonize the full scope of Augustine's refutation, either then or at the Second Council of Orange (529). Within Augustine's own thinking, undoubted development is identifiable at important points, especially on the nature and transmission of original sin* when compared with the voluntarist approach to sin of *Free Will* (391–95). Questions have often been raised (*e.g.* by Harnack*) whether the institutional doctrine of the church and baptism in the anti-Donatist writings can survive the heavy anti-Pelagian stress on the *certus numerus* of the elect. Dogmatically, one must fault the disjunction between the loving God who elects some and the just God who condemns the rest. But at its least controversial (*e.g.* in *The Spirit and the Letter*), Augustine's theology provides an exposition of the Pauline gospel unrivalled in the early church.

The Trinity

In his long labours on *The Trinity* (399–419), Augustine gave himself to faith's quest of understanding, free from the pressures of controversy. The result is a weighty exercise in dogmatic theology as well as a profoundly contemplative exploration. He takes with utmost seriousness the full equality of the three divine persons, who differ only in their mutual relations. He starts not with the Father as the fount of Godhead, but with God himself, whom he speaks of as 'essence' rather than 'substance' (to avoid implications derived from Aristotelian categories). He rejects any suggestion that the one essence of God and the three persons exist on different levels, and refers terms like person and *hypostasis* to the divine essence itself in its internal relations. The inseparability of the works of the Trinity leads him to suggest that some of

the OT theophanies* may have been of the Father or Spirit* rather than the Son.

As an alternative to 'proceeding' as the differentia of the Spirit (as 'begotten' was of the Son), Augustine contemplates the Spirit as 'gift' and 'love'. As the bond of communion between Father and Son, the Spirit is their mutual love as well as the gift that unites God's people. Augustine thus links Trinity and church. The Spirit is unambiguously the Spirit of both Father and Son, so that Augustine is a clear witness to the *filioque*.

Since the human person was made in the image* of the whole Trinity, Augustine sought in man's make-up patterns of relationship to aid understanding of the Trinitarian relations. With the help of Neoplatonic ideas, he found the most suggestive analogy in the self-relatedness of the mind or soul in memory (latent knowledge of itself), understanding (active apprehension of itself) and will or love (activating such self-knowledge). Closer still was the model of the mind remembering, knowing and loving God himself. As the image of God, the human being is called to become more godlike. Contemplating the images of the Trinity in man therefore serves to conform him to the divine image. Theology, worship and holiness have here a fruitful meeting-point.

City of God

The *City of God* also occupied Augustine over many years (413–26). It provides a wide-ranging crystallization of his thinking on history* and society.* Its dominant interest is in salvation-history,* based on the common Christian conception of the seven day-ages of the world. The church era is the sixth day, prior to the eternal sabbath. It is the millennium* of Revelation 20. Decisively abandoning the chiliasm (millenarianism) of earlier Christianity (which he had once held himself), Augustine views the whole period between incarnation and parousia as homogeneous. He rejects the Eusebian* theology of the Christian Roman Empire as a new stage in God's purposes. The *City of God* consistently plays down the significance of secular history, even of Rome under Christian rulers. Pagans and Christians alike had invested too much religious capital in it. The pilgrimage of the city of God on earth is ultimately independent of state or society. All human institutions are essentially ambiguous in Augustine's vision, so that the city of God can no more be identified *simpliciter* with the church than the devil's city with Rome, for only God knows the loves, of God or of self, that make us citizens of one or the other.

Augustine's notion of the role of government is minimalist; it exists to curb the excesses of sin, although Christian rulers have, as Christians, duties to promote the church. He is also very far from implying any kind of theocratic church power (as medieval theorists misunderstood him). Like a good Christian Platonist and biblical theologian, he projects solid reality beyond this world, to heaven and the future.

Bibliography

Most useful edition of works (in progress), *Bibliothèque Augustinienne* (Paris, 1947ff.); P. Brown, *Augustine of Hippo* (London, 1967), with chronological tables and details of works, on which see also B. Altaner, *Patrology* (New York, 1960); current literature is reviewed in *Revue des études augustiniennes*.

G. Bonner, *St. Augustine of Hippo* (London, ²1986); H. Chadwick, *Augustine* (Oxford, 1986); H. A. Deane, *The Political and Social Ideas of St. Augustine* (New York and London, 1963); G. R. Evans, *Augustine on Evil* (Cambridge, 1982); E. Gilson, *The Christian Philosophy of St. Augustine* (London, 1961); S. J. Grabowski, *The Church: An Introduction to the Theology of St. Augustine* (St. Louis, 1957); A. Harnack, *History of Dogma*, vol. 5 (London, 1898); R. A. Markus in *CHLGEMP*, pp. 341–419; idem, *Saeculum: History and Society in the Theology of St. Augustine* (Cambridge, 1970); J. B. Mozley, *A Treatise on the Augustinian Doctrine of Predestination* (London, ³1883); J. J. O'Meara, *The Young Augustine* (London, 1954); A. Pincherle, *La formazione teologica di Sant' Agostino* (Rome, 1947); E. TeSelle, *Augustine the Theologian* (New York, 1970); G. G. Willis, *St. Augustine and the Donatist Controversy* (London, 1950).

D.F.W.

AUGUSTINIANISM. The influence of Augustine has been so pervasive in Western Christianity that this survey can only be selective, concentrating chiefly on his (anti-Pelagian) 'doctrines of grace', to which Augustinianism as a theological system most commonly refers.

Critical reactions against Augustine's writings began in his lifetime with the Pelagians* and Semi-Pelagians.* The outcome of these controversies was the canonizing of the heart of Augustine's teaching in the 5th and 6th centuries. In 531 Pope Boniface II confirmed the decrees of the Second Council of Orange.

Legacy

Already Augustine enjoyed high esteem. Caesarius of Arles (d. 542) often seems little more than an adapter of Augustine, and other late fathers, like Gregory the Great* and Isidore of Seville (c. 560–636), treated him with deferential appreciation. Many digests and florilegia of his writings were produced, e.g. by Prosper of Aquitaine (d. 463), Eugippius, an abbot near Naples (d. 535), Bede (d. 735) and Florus of Lyons (d. c. 860). In the Carolingian renaissance, of which one inspiration was Augustine's charter for Christian education and culture, *On Christian Doctrine*, the homiliaries of Paul Deacon (d. c. 800) and others, and the biblical commentaries and theological compilations of Alcuin (d. 804), Walafrid Strabo (d. 849), Rabanus Maurus (d. 856) and many more made heavy use of Augustine.

In the 9th century Gottschalk* was a controversial exponent of Augustinianism, in particular of double predestination* and supralapsarianism. Among his opponents was the Neoplatonist Eriugena,* who owed much to another side of Augustine, while among his supporters was Ratramnus,* whose more spiritual view of the eucharist* was directed against the more 'realist' teaching of Paschasius Radbertus.* Both were able to appeal to Augustine – a regular feature of later eucharistic disputes.

Both Anselm,* the pioneer of the new scholastic* approach to theology, and Bernard,* one of its keenest critics, were indebted to Augustine. Augustine's correlation of faith and reason (see Faith and Reason*) appeared a ready-made justification for scholasticism, while Bernard's spirituality and his *Grace and Free Will* used him to quite different effect. Although scholasticism substituted Aristotle* for Plato* as the philosophical handmaid of theology, Augustine remained a dominant authority, not least in Peter Lombard* and

61

Thomas Aquinas,* but the schoolmen increasingly inclined towards explanations of the relation between human free will* and merit* and divine grace* that were in effect Semi-Pelagian.

The Franciscans* in particular accorded a prominent place to Augustine in their theological study. Bonaventura,* for example, was more of a Platonist than an Aristotelian, with a theory of illumination not unlike Augustine's. Duns Scotus* also picked up Augustinian motifs in his emphasis on God's freedom and on will and love.

Augustine's legacy was also acknowledged by the monastic movements named after the Rule of Augustine. (The Rule became influential only in the 11th century. The authenticity of its different versions is still disputed.) The Augustinian (Austin) Canons ('canons regular') were organized during the 11th-century Gregorian reform, not in a single order but in separate 'congregations'. Among these were the Victorines* at Paris who constituted a leading school of Augustinian thought and spirituality. The Windesheim congregation in the 14th and 15th centuries included the chief monastic representatives of the renewal movement known as the *Devotio Moderna*, whose ranks embraced Geert de Groote (1340–84), the founder of the Brethren of the Common Life, and Thomas à Kempis (see Spirituality*). Erasmus,* much influenced by those stirrings which fed into the Reformation* at several points, was also an Augustinian Canon for a time.

The Augustinian Hermits or Friars were formed as an order in the 13th century. They were originally hermitic but soon became mendicant. Gregory of Rimini,* a general of the order, was a thoroughly Augustinian theologian. Scholars debate the strength and significance of a renewed Augustinianism among the Augustinians in the pre-Reformation centuries. Later some of the Friars' congregations became Reformed (*i.e.* strict 'Observants' of the Rule), including the German one which Luther* joined at Erfurt in 1505. Its vicar-general was John Staupitz (1460/69–1529), Luther's predecessor as professor of the Bible at Wittenberg. He was an uncompromising exponent of Augustine's doctrine of election, with which he correlated a unilateral covenant* whereby God appointed Christ to be the mediator* of justification* for the elect. He stressed the praise of God, fostered by man's total dependence upon divine election and justification and by his assurance of the personal presence of the risen Christ. Staupitz's influence on Luther was significant at a critical time, pointing him to God's love in the cross, and interpreting his temptations as signs of God's election. Carlstadt (*c.* 1450–1541), Luther's colleague and radical critic, dedicated his commentary on Augustine's *The Spirit and the Letter* to Staupitz, although it was Luther who drove him to study Augustine afresh.

The Protestant Reformers

All the magisterial Reformers sat at Augustine's feet. They benefited from the Renaissance rediscovery of Christian antiquity. Several new editions of Augustine were printed, notably by Erasmus. The Reformation protest was directed against the prevalence in late medieval theology, for all its professed allegiance to Augustine, of one equivalent or other of Semi-Pelagianism. The nominalists,* such as William of Ockham* and Gabriel Biel,* taught that doing what was within one's natural power (*facere quod in se est*) merited the first infusion of grace from God (*meritum de congruo*). The Englishman Thomas Bradwardine* strongly opposed Ockham's Semi-Pelagianism with a somewhat extreme Augustinianism.

The Reformers highlighted different notes in Augustine. Calvin more thoroughly systematized his predestinarianism, while Luther was drawn to his grim portrayal of fallen humanity, probably going beyond Augustine's account of the bondage of the will. On some elements, such as free will and original sin, other Reformers too favoured divergent formulations, but the kernel of Augustinianism was everywhere the heart of the Protestant gospel.

Roman Catholicism

But Rome could not concede the Protestants' claims to be the true interpreters of Augustine. The two centuries after the Reformation were marked by controversies within Catholicism about the import of Augustine's teachings. In undiluted form they repeatedly raised the spectre of crypto-Protestantism infiltrating the fold. Michel Baius (de Bay, 1513–89) was a Louvain theologian who claimed to have read the anti-Pelagian works seventy times! In 1567 a papal bull condemned many propositions from his writings. He undoubtedly espoused a sharper version of Augustinianism than counter-reform Catholicism could tolerate. This became evident in the new Jesuit* Order's official adoption of Molinist opinions which were in substance Semi-Pelagian. Dominicans* who accused the Jesuits of Pelagianism were themselves accused of Calvinism. A papal ruling in 1607 allowed both main currents of teaching. Renewed controversy broke out a century later over Henri Noris (1631–1704), an Augustinian Hermit and author of a learned history of Pelagianism and defence of Augustinianism against Molinism. The outcome was another authorization of different systems of thought within the church. In practice the Jesuits' Semi-Pelagian Molinism widely prevailed.

1640 saw the publication of a posthumous work called *Augustinus* by Cornelius Jansen (1585–1638), a Dutchman who taught at Louvain. It sparked off a far more intense conflict, especially in France, where the Cistercian convent of Port-Royal, with two houses in and near Paris, became the headquarters of Jansenism, under the lead of St Cyran (Jean Duvergier de Hauranne, 1581–1643, the abbot of St Cyran), Antoine Arnauld (1612–94) and his sister Jacqueline Angélique (1591–1661), the abbess of Port-Royal. Support came from Dominicans, Pascal* and others sympathetic to a movement standing also for renewal of piety and devotion. The Jansenists' main target was Jesuit theology, especially Molinism. In 1653 Pope Innocent X condemned five propositions, allegedly extracted from Jansen's book, which affirmed that: God's commands cannot be fulfilled without grace; grace is irresistible; fallen man is free from coercion, not from necessity; the Semi-Pelagians' error was denial of the irresistibility of grace; it is Semi-Pelagian to say that Christ died for all mankind. Jansenists contested this presentation of Jansen's teaching, and dispute persisted. In 1713 a more comprehensive papal condemnation was given of a work by the French Oratorian, Pasquier Quesnel (1634–1719). Port-Royal was closed in 1709, but Dutch Jansenists formed an independent bishopric which has survived as part of the Old Catholic Church. This long controversy stimulated extensive study of Augustine and the Pelagian episodes. One fruit was the edition of his works, still the best complete one, by the Maurist

Benedictines (1679–1700). Jansenist sympathies had been observed among the Maurists.

Since the 18th century, Augustinian theology has been a less controversial subject for Catholics. Study of his works has continued to grow, with several periodicals and research centres, especially the Institut des Etudes Augustiniennes in Paris. In constructive theology other aspects of his thought have increasingly kindled keener interest than the anti-Pelagian corpus.

Protestantism

Within Protestantism, the legacy of (anti-Pelagian) Augustinianism has been largely subsumed within the Lutheran and Reformed traditions. Platonic dualism* has been held to be a major structural fault in Augustine's teaching by theologians in the Barthian* tradition, which also blames him for the Western preoccupation with anthropology rather than Christology. Reinhold Niebuhr's* 'Christian realism' was explicitly indebted to Augustine, and his *Nature and Destiny of Man* has been seen as a modern-day *City of God*.

Bibliography
N. J. Abercrombie, *The Origins of Jansenism* (Oxford, 1936); J. Cadier, 'S. Augustin et la Réforme', *Rech. august.* 1 (1958), pp. 357–371; L. Cristiani, 'Luther et S.Augustin', in *Augustinus Magister*, vol. 2 (Paris, 1954), pp. 1029–1035; H. de Lubac, *Augustinisme et théologie moderne* (Paris, 1963); A. Hamel, *Der Junge Luther und Augustin*, 2 vols. (Gütersloh, 1934–35); H. Marrou, *St. Augustine and His Influence Through the Ages* (London, 1957); H. A. Oberman, *Masters of the Reformation* (Cambridge, 1981), ch. 6, 'The Augustine Renaissance in the Later Middle Ages'; A. Sedgwick, *Jansenism in Seventeenth-Century France* (Charlottesville, VA, 1977); L. Smits, *S. Augustin dans l'oeuvre de Jean Calvin*, 2 vols. (Assen, 1957–58); D. C. Steinmetz, *Misericordia Dei: the Theology of Johannes von Staupitz in Its Late Medieval Setting* (Leiden, 1968); D. Trapp, 'Augustinian Theology of the Fourteenth Century', *Augustiniana* 6 (1956), pp. 146–274.

D.F.W.

AULÉN, GUSTAV (1879–1977). Professor of systematic theology in Lund and Bishop of Strängnäs in the Swedish Lutheran Church, Aulén was (with Nygren* and Wingren*) one of the foremost Scandinavian theologians of the modern era. A student of Nathan Söderblom (1866–1931) at Uppsala, his contributions to ecumenism and to the revival of Lutheran theology and church life in Sweden were many and various.

Much of his theological writing is characterized by a high appreciation of Luther's* dramatic presentation of the realities of sin, grace and redemption, and by a correspondingly low view of scholasticism,* whether medieval or Lutheran.

He is chiefly known for his short work on the atonement,* *Christus Victor*, which attempts to reinstate the so-called 'classic' view of the atonement. This interpretation, traced by Aulén in the NT, and also in Irenaeus* and Luther, envisages the cross as God's mighty act of triumph over powers of evil hostile to his will, and distinguishes itself from Latin ideas of satisfaction* and from 'subjective' or 'exemplarist' accounts. His work draws not only on some of the central preoccupations of Reformation theologies of the cross and of grace, but also on the techniques of 'motif-research' of which Anders Nygren is the chief exponent.

Aulén was also the author of a systematic theology, *The Faith of the Christian Church*, and of books on ecclesiology and sacramental theology. Towards the end of his life he published *Jesus in Contemporary Historical Research*, arguing forcefully against historical scepticism applied to the gospels. He was also a noted musician and composer.

Bibliography
Main works in ET: *Christus Victor* (London, 1931); *The Drama and the Symbols* (London, 1970); *Eucharist and Sacrifice* (Edinburgh, 1958); *The Faith of the Christian Church* (London, 1954); *Jesus in Contemporary Historical Research* (London, 1976); *Reformation and Catholicity* (Edinburgh, 1961).

J.B.We.

AUSCHWITZ, see HOLOCAUST.

AUTHORITY is 'that right or power to command action or compliance, or to determine belief or custom, expecting obedience from those under authority, and in turn giving responsible account for the claim to right or power' (B. Ramm).

The question of authority is the most fundamental issue which faces every theologian. According to R. Clyde Johnson, 'It is the previous question of theology, the question that has been answered if an answer is ventured to any other theological question.' The resolution of the problem forms the basis upon which every theological system is built. Its importance cannot be overestimated, for it is the means whereby worship, preaching, practice, discipline and organization are kept under the continuous scrutiny of the truth. The crucial role played by authority in matters theological is aptly expressed in P. T. Forsyth's assertion that, 'As soon as the problem of authority really lifts its head, all others fall to the rear . . . the principle of authority is ultimately the whole religious question.' Differing forms of authority produce contrasting systems of theology and religion, and invariably underlie most other theological differences. This is so even when the matter is not properly formulated or appreciated.

The question of authority is a complex one. It involves a multiplicity of objective and subjective criteria which must be correctly interrelated if an appropriate theological and spiritual equilibrium is to be established. Among the various elements involved in the discussion are the place and role of God (Father, Son and Holy Spirit), the Bible, tradition, the church (catholic and local), theological frameworks and systems, reason, conscience, will, emotion or feeling and faith. When analysed, every theological position will normally allocate, consciously or unconsciously, a place and role to each of these in its pattern of authoritative criteria. Differences arise as a result of the priority assigned to each criterion and the function allocated to it in contrasting systems. Just as a kaleidoscope has a set number of coloured pieces but produces a wide array of patterns, so differing theological systems emerge as the various elements in the spectrum of authority are allocated contrasting stations and functions. All the pieces or elements are present in every picture or system. The pictures are in marked contrast to each other because the constituent parts are interrelated in different ways in the various patterns.

A factor common to all classical theological standpoints is that God* himself is the *princi-*

pium essendi or first cause of theology, as of everything else. He is the foundation which underlies all theological activity; he is its beginning and its end. Similar agreement is evidenced in acceptance of the axiom that revelation* is the only cognitive source of theology. Differences emerge when attempts are made to determine the *principium cognoscendi* – the place or locus of revelation (see also Epistemology*). The revealed truth accessible by virtue of the source or sources of revelation constitutes the supreme authority in theology. Disagreement concerning sources makes it virtually impossible to agree concerning the corpus of truth and the ensuing doctrinal formulations.

At some stage or other in the history of Christianity each one of the loci mentioned above has been considered either the exclusive or the major source of authority. Comparatively little attention has been given to the relationship which exists between the supreme source and other loci involved in the pattern of authority. Among the positions which have been adopted historically are the following:

Sola Scriptura

The main features of this view were first stated formally during the Reformation* era. Basically, it asserts that Scripture* is the only source of all knowledge of supernatural theology. The creator has not left his creatures to hazard guesses at the truth concerning his person and will. He has revealed data concerning himself. Scripture is the written record of what God has spoken and still speaks to his people. In this view the Bible 'is a record and explanation of divine revelation which is both complete (sufficient) and comprehensible (perspicuous); that is to say, it contains all that the church needs to know in this world for its guidance in the way of salvation and service . . .' (J. I. Packer). The Bible is the inspired word of God; it is a true record of what God has to say to mankind.

This position is sometimes interpreted as though the Bible stood in splendid isolation *vis-à-vis* other criteria. This is not so. The Holy Spirit,* the divine agent who superintended the writing and compilation of holy writ, is the instrumental cause who enables believers to acknowledge it as the divine word and interpret it correctly. In the process of interpretation (see Hermeneutics*) the place

and function of other criteria such as tradition and reason are of vital importance.

But when all such qualifications are made, Scripture remains for biblical and evangelical Christianity the supreme teacher and arbiter in belief and practice. It is the judge of all claims advanced by any other authority.

Tradition

'Tradition' is an elastic term. It may refer to a body of extra-biblical material which is accepted as apostolic and of equal weight with Scripture. Or it may blend with the authority of the church and its historical pronouncements, although in this context the term 'church' is as problematical as 'tradition'. Whatever the connotation, efforts to establish the authority of tradition on a par with the Bible reflect misgivings about the clarity and sufficiency of Scripture (see Scripture and Tradition*). Tradition thus supplements deficiencies, throwing light on material which is either absent or, if present, not clear. Its authority, therefore, ultimately rests on an extra-biblical deposit which may be impossible to identify let alone systematize. The official voice of tradition, when viewed as an authority, is normally spoken of as the *magisterium* (Latin, 'teaching office') of the church. In Roman Catholic understanding, it is exercised through councils* of bishops or through the papacy,* or less precisely through the consensus of the church. Protestantism rejects the claim of an infallible *magisterium*, and regards all teachings of church and tradition as subject to the test of Scripture.

Subjective criteria

Since the Reformation there has been a shift of Copernican proportions from objective to subjective criteria. The supreme authority of Scripture has been consistently undermined, as reason, conscience,* feeling, experience and faith* have followed in the wake of tradition as oracles which, it is variously claimed, are able to pronounce with finality on the meaning and value of the Christian gospel. As with tradition the intention to *supplement* has frequently resulted in an act of *supersession*. An example of this is seen in Frederick Temple's essay in *Essays and Reviews* (1860). He writes, 'When conscience and the Bible appear to differ, the pious Christian immediately concludes that he has not really understood the Bible . . . [The Bible's] form is so

65

admirably adapted to our need, that it wins from us all the reverence of a supreme authority, and yet imposes on us no yoke of subjection. This it does by virtue of the principle of private judgment, which puts conscience between us and the Bible, making conscience the supreme interpreter, whom it may be a duty to enlighten, but whom it can never be a duty to disobey.' The supreme interpreter always has the final word.

Even when a pattern of authority is appropriately structured there are several matters which can nullify its effectiveness. Among these are:

Ignorance. Whatever the pattern we profess, the task of amassing knowledge and relating its numerous parts should ever keep us humble and mindful of Cromwell's appeal: 'I beseech you in the bowels of mercy, think it possible that you might be wrong.'

Illogicality. Much of the instruction contained in the letters of the NT was originally elicited from the apostles by a failure to grasp and apply the implications of grace (*e.g.* Rom. 5:20 – 6:23).

Inconsistency. Many theological systems supposedly subordinate to the teaching of Scripture assume, in practice, an authority superior to that of the word of God. This failing is observed among evangelicals too, when, contrary to the *sola Scriptura* principle, theological tradition determines convictions.

Ineffectiveness. Many profess adherence to the teaching of the word of God but in fact submit to some other standard. The confrontations between the apostle Peter and Ananias and Sapphira (Acts 5:1–10) and Paul and Peter (Gal. 2:11–14) furnish us with examples of this.

Bibliography

P. T. Forsyth, *The Principle of Authority* (London, 1952); C. F. H. Henry (ed.), *Revelation and the Bible* (Grand Rapids, MI, 1967); idem, *God, Revelation and Authority*, 6 vols. (Waco, TX, 1979–83); R. C. Johnson, *Authority in Protestant Theology* (Philadelphia, 1959); D. M. Lloyd-Jones, *Authority* (London, 1958); J. I. Packer, *Fundamentalism and the Word of God* (London, 1958); idem, *Freedom, Authority and Scripture* (Leicester, 1981); B. Ramm, *The Pattern of Religious Authority* (Grand Rapids, MI, 1959).

J.H.E.

AVERROISM. A branch of the Aristotelian* philosophical tradition inspired by the Arab philosopher Averroes (Latin for Ibn-Rushd, 1126–1198), the most influential commentator on the writings of Aristotle. Although Averroes was the greatest Islamic philosopher, his influence was felt primarily in the Latin West (he came from Cordoba in Spain), at the University of Paris in the 13th and early 14th centuries and at the universities of Bologna and Padua from the 13th to the middle of the 17th centuries. Recently this movement has been called 'radical or heterodox Aristotelianism'. This name is appropriate because the primary aim of its masters was to teach the philosophy of Aristotle. Their goal was not to follow Averroes, but simply to present Aristotle's thought. Most famous among these masters at the University of Paris are Siger of Brabant (*c.* 1235–*c.* 1282) and Boetius of Dacia (*fl.* mid-13th century). Among Italian Averroists the best known is Caesar Cremoninus (*c.* 1550–1631), who is supposed to have been the friend of Galileo who refused to look through a telescope because this might compel him to abandon Aristotelian astronomy.

There are three areas in which Aristotle's thought presented a direct challenge to Christian teaching. Aristotle asserted that the world is eternal and this is opposed to the doctrine of creation.* He also seems to have held that there is one immaterial soul for all men, and this calls into question the teaching of personal immortality* and the possibility of reward or punishment after death. Finally, he supposed that man can achieve perfection following reason alone, and this opposes the Christian teaching that faith is necessary for salvation. Because of these problems, the assimilation of Aristotle into the Christian West was difficult. Some wished to reject Aristotle entirely; others like Thomas Aquinas* used Aristotle but only after criticizing and modifying his thought. The Averroists tended to adopt Aristotle without reservation and so appeared to be maintaining teachings contrary to the faith. Averroism was opposed by Aquinas and others, and the Christian Averroists were condemned by the church in the 1270s.

For a long time the double-truth theory was attributed to Averroists. According to this theory a thesis could be true in philosophy and its contradictory thesis could be true for faith (see Duns Scotus*). For example, according to philosophy the world has existed eternally but according to faith the world has had a beginning. In fact, neither Siger nor any one else claims that such contradictory truths are compatible; rather, in cases where philosophy and faith are in conflict truth is always held to be on the side of faith. However, even while these masters say that truth is on the side of faith, they give the impression that they remain attached to the conclusions of philosophy. This gives the impression that they hold two contradictory propositions to be true, and indeed their opponents tried to attribute the double-truth thesis to them to show the untenability of their position.

In the Averroists' concern for reason there was not an interest in freedom of thought, as one might suppose, but rather an excessive regard for the philosophical tradition. Siger of Brabant states that to treat matters philosophically is to be concerned with determining the thought of the philosophers rather than discovering the truth. This same attachment to the philosophers, especially Aristotle, seems also to have dominated Cremoninus. Averroism was the most conservative and sterile form of Aristotelianism.

Bibliography

E. Gilson, *History of Christian Philosophy in the Middle Ages* (London, 1955); F. van Steenberghen, *Thomas Aquinas and Radical Aristotelianism* (Washington, DC, 1980).

A.V.

B

BAILLIE, DONALD MACPHERSON

(1887–1954), Scottish theologian. Born at Gairloch, Ross-shire, and educated at Edinburgh, Marburg and Heidelberg, he ministered at Bervie, Cupar and Kilmacolm before becoming professor of systematic theology at St Andrews in 1935. Dedicated ecumenist and brilliant scholar and writer, he travelled extensively in Europe and America. His academic reputation and saintliness of life brought many foreign students to study in St Andrews. His best-known publications are *God Was in Christ* and *The Theology of the Sacraments*.

The former was hailed generally as one of the greatest contributions to theological literature in recent times. In that volume he wrote: 'A toned-down Christology is absurd. It must be all or nothing – all or nothing on both the divine and the human side.' Baillie could communicate with candour, cogency and clarity. While theologically he was said to have occupied a reconciling position between the old liberalism and neo-orthodoxy,* a view perhaps confirmed by the warm support he gave to the Student Christian Movement, his own deeply evangelical upbringing and personal sensitivity ensured that more conservative students also found in him a wise counsellor and a friend.

Bibliography

God Was in Christ (London, 1948); *The Theology of the Sacraments* (London, 1957).

Biogr. essays in *The Theology of the Sacraments* by his brother John Baillie,* and in *To Whom Shall We Go?* (Edinburgh, 1955) by J. Dow; J. P. Carter, *The Christology of D. M. Baillie*, unpubl. dissert. (Edinburgh, 1969); articles on Christology in *SJT* 11 (1958), pp. 1–12 (J. H. Hick), pp. 265–270 (J. Baillie), 17 (1964), pp. 303–308 (J. L. M. Haire).

J.D.Do.

BAILLIE, JOHN (1886–1960), Scottish

churchman and theologian brother of Donald Baillie.* His life mirrored Presbyterian reunion in Scotland – son of a Free Church manse, student in the United Free Church's New College, Edinburgh, Moderator of the Church of Scotland's General Assembly (1943), as well as wider ecumenism – steward at the 1910 Edinburgh Conference, president of the WCC, signatory of the *Bishops Report* commending Anglican episcopacy to the Church of Scotland (1957). He was the distinguished helmsman of the Church's Commission for the Interpretation of God's Will in the Present Crisis, 1940–45 (*God's Will for Church and Nation*, 1946; *cf.* his *What is Christian Civilization?*, 1945).

Baillie taught philosophy in Edinburgh, and then theology in the USA and Canada 1919–34, before becoming professor of divinity at Edinburgh 1934–56, and latterly also dean of the faculty and principal of New College 1950–56. Perhaps at his best as an apologist (*cf. Invitation to Pilgrimage*, 1942), he has been called 'a mediating theologian' (W. L.

Power, *USQR* 24, 1968, pp. 47–68). A decided liberalism followed the undermining of his father's Calvinism. It earned Bonhoeffer's* critical judgment in New York, and is reflected in writings like *The Roots of Religion in the Human Soul* (1926). About 1930 he shifted towards a 'liberal neo-orthodoxy'* (*cf. And the Life Everlasting*, 1933; *Our Knowledge of God*, 1939), but subsequently a greater confidence in reason reasserted itself, as he predicted a strong reaction against Barthianism. *The Belief in Progress* (1950) was followed by *The Idea of Revelation in Recent Thought* (1956), an influential survey of anti-propositional positions, and his posthumous (undelivered) Gifford Lectures, *The Sense of the Presence of God* (1962). His best-known work was the frequently translated *A Diary of Private Prayer* (1936). Baillie combined a contemplative devotion with a humane Christian liberalism, which discriminated between competing theological tendencies.

Bibliography

Collected essays in *Christian Devotion* (London, 1962), with a memoir by I. M. Forrester; and *A Reasoned Faith* (1963). Unpublished papers in New College Library, Edinburgh.

Appreciations by D. S. Klinefelter, *SJT* 22 (1969), pp. 419–436; John A. Mackay, *ibid.* 9 (1956), pp. 225–235; T. F. Torrance, *Religion in Life* 30 (1961), pp. 329–333. P. B. O'Leary, *Revelation and Faith in Our Knowledge of God according to the Theology of John Baillie* (Rome, 1968).

D.F.W.

BALTHASAR, HANS URS VON (b. 1905). A leading Swiss Roman Catholic theologian and spiritual writer. After studies in philosophy and literature, he became a member of the Society of Jesus before founding a secular institute (the *Johannesgemeinschaft*) and engaging in wide-ranging literary and publishing activities. He has published voluminously, producing works of Christian theology and philosophy and interpretative studies in the history of culture and spirituality, as well as editing and translating the work of others.

His *magnum opus*, destined to become one of the classic pieces of 20th-century theological writing, is an unfinished multi-volume work in three parts, synthesizing theology, philosophy and literature in a massive study of the beautiful, the good and the true. The first part, *Herrlichkeit* (appearing in English as *The Glory of the Lord*), examines revelation from the vantage-point of theological aesthetics;* the second, *Theodramatik*, enquires into the nature of divine and human action; a third part, a treatment of 'theological logic', is as yet unwritten. The virtually unrestricted range of von Balthasar's knowledge and interests testifies to the catholicity* of his thought, which is directed by a vision of the universality of God's self-manifestation in Christ: here his debt to some of the fathers is evident. The breadth of his vision is intrinsically related, however, to a firm adherence to the particularity and uniqueness of Christ who is the form of God, the divine glory concentrated and focused in an unsurpassable way.

Von Balthasar's work is much influenced by that of Barth,* upon whom he has written with great perceptiveness and to whom he is particularly indebted for his vigorous Christocentrism (especially in constructing the doctrine of God on a Christological* base) and for an understanding of the theological task as directed by the givenness of revelation.* Von Balthasar's use of the category of 'beauty' to describe the nature of God in his self-manifestation to creation is a means of recovering a sense of the self-evidence, authority and necessity of revelation in a way closely similar to Barth's own understanding of God's self-manifestation as irreducible and needing no authentication beyond itself.

The gracious character of God's relation to man is a central preoccupation in his theology, and some of his emphases here owe much to the work of E. Przywara, whose account of analogy* laid greater stress on the distinction between God and the world than the 'Transcendental Thomism' later made famous by Karl Rahner.*

But perhaps most of all, von Balthasar's work has been deeply impressed by his close relationship with the mystic Adrienne von Speyr (1902–67). From her experiences he has developed a remarkable theology of Holy Saturday, in which Christ's descent into hell becomes a leading motif in Christology, soteriology and Trinitarian theology. As the ultimate act of self-emptying by the Son of God, Holy Saturday furnishes a theology of reconciliation as Christ's solidarity with the damned. It also provides the basis for a theology of the Trinitarian relations centred, like other contemporary Trinitarian theories, on Calvary.

Von Balthasar is increasingly recognized as a thinker who has made a potent restatement of some of the persistent themes of classical Christian theology, notably in the area of incarnational and Trinitarian doctrine. His interweaving of theological and cultural references, however, along with the integrative and speculative tone of much of his writing, may not commend him to strands of contemporary theology more concerned with the critical grounding and appraisal of Christian truth-claims and less confident about the objectivity of revelation.

Bibliography

Elucidations (London, 1965); *Engagement with God* (London, 1975); *The Glory of the Lord. A Theological Aesthetics* (Edinburgh, 1983–); *Love Alone. The Way of Revelation* (London, 1968); *Prayer* (London, 1971); *Theodramatik* (Einsiedeln, 1973–8).

M. Kehl and W. Löser (eds.), *A Von Balthasar Reader* (Edinburgh, 1983); J. K. Riches, 'The Theology of Hans Urs von Balthasar', *Th* 75 (1972), pp. 562–570, 647–655.

J.B.We.

BAMPTON LECTURES. An eminent series of eight 'lecture sermons' at Oxford endowed by John Bampton (1690–1751), canon of Salisbury. They began in 1780, annually, but became biennial from 1895. Bampton specified their purpose as 'to confirm and establish the Christian faith and to confute all heretics and schismatics – upon the divine authority of the holy Scriptures – upon the authority of the writings of the primitive fathers, as to the faith and practice of the primitive Church – upon the Divinity of our Lord and Saviour Jesus Christ – upon the Divinity of the Holy Ghost – upon the Articles of the Christian Faith, as comprehended in the Apostles' and Nicene Creeds'. The lectureship is confined to ordained Anglicans (and formerly only to MAs of Oxford and Cambridge). In 1952 the Sarum Lectureship was set up from the Bampton fund, alternating in years with the Bampton Lectures but open to non-Anglicans.

Celebrated lectures have included: R. D.

Hampden, *The Scholastic Philosophy Considered in its Relation to Christian Theology* (1832); H. L. Mansel, *The Limits of Religious Thought* (1858); J. B. Mozley, *Miracles* (1865); H. P. Liddon, *The Divinity of Our Lord and Saviour Jesus Christ* (1866); C. Bigg, *The Christian Platonists of Alexandria* (1886); W. Sanday, *Inspiration* (1893); N. P. Williams, *The Ideas of the Fall and of Original Sin* (1924); K. E. Kirk, *The Vision of God* (1928); G. L. Prestige, *Fathers and Heretics* (1940); T. G. Jalland, *The Church and the Papacy* (1942); H. E. W. Turner, *The Pattern of Christian Truth* (1954).

A Bampton fellowship was established in 1968. The Bampton Lectures in America began in 1950, and have included John Baillie,* *The Idea of Revelation in Recent Thought* (1954).

Bibliography

List to 1893 in J. F. Hurst, *Literature of Theology* (New York, 1896); summaries in J. Hunt, *Religious Thought in England in the Nineteenth Century* (London, 1896), pp. 292–332; lecturers in *The Historical Register of the University of Oxford* (1900), and *Supplements*.

D.F.W.

BAPTISM. In order to provide a unified treatment of baptism from its biblical roots to the present day, it is discussed here in two parts: the biblical theology of baptism, and reflection upon it in historical and systematic theology.

1. Biblical theology

Nature of the rite. Baptism as a washing in water with a spiritual significance had its roots in the OT and pre-Christian Judaism. The law prescribed bathing of persons deemed to be 'unclean' (see *e.g.* Lv. 14:8–9 and Lv. 15). Aaron and his sons were ceremonially washed at their ordination to the priesthood (Lv. 8:5–6). On the Day of Atonement Aaron had to bathe himself on entering the most holy place, and again on leaving it (Lv. 16:3–4); the person who released the scapegoat in the desert similarly had to bathe himself, as also he who burned his clothes (Lv. 16:26–28). Such ritual acts of washing led to a symbolic application in prayer for spiritual cleansing (*e.g.* Ps. 51:1–2, 7–10).

Shortly prior to the Christian era a kind of

baptismal movement took place in the Jordan valley, the most notable instance of which was the monastic community at Qumran (*cf*. Dead Sea Scrolls*). Originating among priests who rejected the temple worship as corrupt, its members emphasized the maintenance of ritual purity through daily baths, accompanied by repentance. It is possible that the baptism administered by John the Baptist was a radical modification of the Qumran practice. He preached 'a baptism of repentance for the forgiveness of sins' (Mk. 1:4) in preparation for the coming of the Messiah and his baptism of Spirit and fire (Mt. 3:11–12). Since his baptism was a conversion-baptism it was *once for all*, in distinction from the repeated washings of the Qumran community. Whether Jewish proselyte-baptism arose early enough to influence primitive Christian baptism is uncertain; it formed part of the initiation of Gentiles into Judaism, namely through circumcision, baptism and offering of sacrifice; since women had only to be baptized and offer sacrifice their baptism naturally assumed greater significance.

The submission of Jesus to John's baptism, intended to prepare sinners for the coming of the Messiah, is explicable only as a deliberate act of solidarity with sinful men and women. It was the initiation of the process whereby the saving sovereignty of God came among men, issuing in his ministry of kingdom-of-God word and deed, his death and resurrection and sending of the Holy Spirit. It is not surprising therefore that the missionary commission, given by the risen Lord, included a command to baptize (Mt. 28:18–20). The expression (baptize) 'in the name of' in a Semitic context signifies baptism 'with respect to', but especially denotes the baptism's basis and purpose, to enter into a relationship of belonging to God. Greek readers would understand the phrase very similarly, as meaning 'appropriation to the Father, Son and Holy Spirit with the use of this name' (W. Heitmüller, *Im Namen Jesu*, Göttingen, 1903, p. 121).

Meaning of the rite. In the apostolic teaching on baptism the rite primarily signifies *union with Christ:** 'All of you who were baptised into Christ have clothed yourselves with Christ' (Gal. 3:27). The language reflects the stripping off and putting on of clothes at baptism (*cf*. the use of the imagery in Col. 3:9–14); 'putting on' Christ denotes receiving

Christ, being in Christ, and so becoming one with him. In the Pauline instruction, since Christ is the crucified and risen Lord, baptism signifies *union with Christ in his redemptive* acts; it includes the thought of being laid alongside him in his tomb and one with him in his resurrection (Rom. 6:1–5; Col. 2:11–12), and so participating in the new creation initiated by his resurrection (2 Cor. 5:17) in anticipation of the resurrection* for the final kingdom (Col. 3:1–4). Baptism further signifies *union with Christ in his body, the church*, for to be 'in Christ' is to be one with all who are united to him (Gal. 3:26–28; 1 Cor. 12:12–13). And since union with Christ is inconceivable apart from the 'Spirit of Christ', baptism signifies *renewal by the Holy Spirit* (so already in Peter's Pentecostal proclamation, Acts 2:38, and in Paul's theology of the church, 1 Cor. 12:12–13). Baptism also signifies *entry into the kingdom* of God, for the salvation of Christ is none other than life under the saving sovereignty of God (*cf*. Mt. 12:28; Jn. 12:31–32; Rom. 14:17; Col. 1:13–14). Its connection with baptism is referred to in Jn. 3:5, where 'birth from above' (v. 3) is explained as birth 'of water and the Spirit'. This is best understood as alluding to the baptism of repentance, to which Nicodemus had declined to submit, and the outpouring of the Spirit which should come with the kingdom of God. In the gospel these two features become united through the redemption of Christ; baptism in the name of Jesus in repentance and faith, and the recreative action of the Spirit and entrance into the kingdom of God thus become one complex event. Finally baptism signifies *life in obedience to the rule of God*, as the main sentence in Rom. 6:4 indicates: 'We were . . . buried with him through baptism into death . . . in order that . . . we too may live a new life.' This is briefly illustrated in Col. 3:1–17 and worked out in detail in the catechetical instruction of the NT.

All this presupposes a fundamental assumption of the apostolic proclamation, that baptism is an embodiment of the gospel and of man's response to it (1 Pet. 3:21 illustrates it perfectly). Most Christians, however, have been baptized in infancy; how does their baptism relate to the apostolic exposition of baptism? The traditional belief that it applies without modification is questioned by many sacramental theologians. A theology of infant baptism will emphasize the initiatory function of the rite within the community of the Spirit, having respect both to the accomplished redemption of Christ and the goal of appropriation of that redemption by faith and consecration to the service of Christ. Whatever the age of the baptized, baptism signifies grace and call for lifelong growth in Christ with a view to the resurrection at the last day.

Bibliography

Baptism, Eucharist and Ministry (Geneva, 1982); M. Thurian (ed.), *Ecumenical Perspectives on Baptism, Eucharist and Ministry* (Geneva, 1983); M. Thurian and G. Wainwright (eds.), *Baptism and Eucharist, Ecumenical Convergence in Celebration* (Geneva, 1984).

K. Barth, *Baptism as the Foundation of the Christian Life*, CD, IV.4; G. R. Beasley-Murray, *Baptism in the New Testament* (London, 1963); D. Bridge and D. Phypers, *The Water that Divides* (Leicester, 1977); G. W. Bromiley, *Baptism and the Anglican Reformers* (London, 1953); N. Clark, *An Approach to the Theology of the Sacraments* (London, 1956); O. Cullmann, *Baptism in the New Testament* (London, 1951); W. F. Flemington, *The New Testament Doctrine of Baptism* (London, 1948); P. T. Forsyth, *The Church and the Sacraments* (London, ²1947); J. Jeremias, *Infant Baptism in the First Four Centuries* (London, 1960); P. K. Jewett, *Infant Baptism and the Covenant of Grace* (Grand Rapids, MI, 1978); G. W. H. Lampe, *The Seal of the Spirit* (London, ²1967); E. Schlink, *The Doctrine of Baptism* (St Louis, 1972); R. Schnackenburg, *Baptism in the Thought of St. Paul* (Oxford, 1964); G. Wainwright, *Christian Initiation* (London, 1969); R. E. O. White, *The Biblical Doctrine of Initiation* (London, 1960).

G.R.B.-M.

2. Historical and systematic theology

The earliest post-NT references come from the *Didache* (c. 100; see Apostolic Fathers*). Justin (see Apologists*) described baptism as a rebirth in water, and then as an 'enlightenment', a technical term for baptism by the fourth century.

Origen* saw in baptism the typological link between the OT, culminating in the baptism of Jesus by John, and the eschatological baptism inaugurating the new age. Baptism derived its meaning from the spiritual realities and, in imparting the grace of Christ, prefigured the final stage of baptism, the resurrection from the dead.

Tertullian* indicated the connection of the Holy Spirit with the water of baptism and thus prepared the ground for the blessing of the baptismal water. Amid third-century persecution, it was not surprising to discover martyrdom* described as baptism of blood which admitted the martyr directly into the church triumphant. He advocated the postponement of baptism until infants could make their own decision rather than jeopardize the spiritual future of their sponsors. The view of Tertullian, Cyprian* and others that schismatic baptism was invalid did not survive in the West beyond the third century, except in Donatism.*

Augustine* stressed the objective aspect of baptism, and because Christ is the real minister of baptism, the validity of the sacrament was not affected by its human agent. He was firmly convinced that baptism was indispensable for salvation. In his dispute with Pelagius* he justified the baptism of infants, developing the link between baptism and original sin.* He did not suggest that infants had faith, but that the faith of the church was of benefit to them, and this remains a classic position justifying infant baptism. By their baptism, infants were incorporated into the church, and thus shared in the faith of the church to which they belonged. The sponsors who answered on behalf of the infant did so not merely in their own right, nor simply as representatives of the infant, but as agents of the whole church, of which they were the instruments for the presentation of the infant for baptism.

However, for adult catechumens there was an insistence that very careful preparation was needed for baptism. By the fourth century, catechetical classes involved regular attendance at daily meetings during Lent, and lectures by Ambrose* of Milan, Cyril of Jerusalem (c. 315–86), John Chrysostom (c. 344/354–407), and Theodore of Mopsuestia (c. 350–428) remain available to us. Before these daily classes, exorcism* was a regular practice, and was a common element in the baptismal rite. The syllabi emphasized that in baptism the baptized shared Christ's redemption, death and resurrection by a tangible confession of faith, being conformed to the crucified and risen Lord. Thus baptism effected the rebirth of the baptized, clothed him in a new garment of immortality and bestowed an indissoluble seal upon him. Post-baptismal sin was taken extremely seriously, causing many people to follow the example of Constantine and postpone their baptism to their deathbeds (clinical baptism). A prerequisite of baptism was the renunciation of Satan and profession of faith in Christ, and these remain in many services in use today.

The scholastic* theologians described baptism as a sacrament of faith, a holy sign which grasped the whole work of redemption, representing the sanctification of the baptized through the passion of Christ, the grace of Christ, and its eschatological fulfilment. However, it was Christ who remained the master of his gifts, and he might choose to save a soul without the sacrament. Thomas Aquinas* taught that, although baptism removed the guilt of original sin, at any moment sin might be rekindled into flame. Peter Lombard,* however, taught that baptism weakened the desire to sin.

The Council of Trent crystallized pre-Reformation teaching, emphasizing the efficacy of infant baptism, but stressing the necessity for the adult candidate to approach baptism with sincerity. It reaffirmed that baptismal grace could be lost through serious sin.

While adopting much of the Roman Catholic baptismal theology, Luther* pointed out that the water of baptism was made a gracious water of life and a washing of regeneration by the intrinsic divine power of the word of God. Initially he made the effect of baptism dependent upon faith, but finally modified this position to emphasize the command of God as the justification for baptism.

The accessibility of Scripture brought about by the Reformation led to a number of Anabaptist* groups being formed who refused to allow their children to be baptized and re-emphasized believers' baptism, considering this the only baptism in the NT. Contact with one such group in Amsterdam in 1609 confirmed the view of baptism of John Smyth (1618–52) and Thomas Helwys (c. 1550–c. 1616), the first British Baptists.*

The Reformed* tradition emphasized the view that baptism was the sign of the new covenant,* and as such infants should be admitted to the new covenant as young as the Jewish child was admitted to the old covenant

by circumcision. Baptism strengthened faith, gave parents the assurance that their child was incorporated into the covenant and gave the child title to the covenant, even in an unconscious state, being a rich source of consolation as the child grew up.

Barth* introduced the subject of baptism into the realm of ecumenical debate, advocating the abandonment of infant baptism in favour of believers' baptism but with no rebaptism* meanwhile. Accepting the view of Christ as the primary minister of baptism, he stressed that the candidate was the 'second most important figure in the drama'. Christ's words and actions in baptism had a cognitive purpose, assuring the believer of his salvation and his pledge to the obedient service of the Lord. Because the nature, power and meaning of baptism are dependent on Christ, it cannot be made void by human inadequacy. Both NT exegesis and the sacrament required of the baptized a responsible willingness and readiness to receive the promise of grace directed towards him, and a pledge of allegiance concerning the grateful service demanded of him.

Vatican II (see Councils;* Roman Catholic Theology*) spent a considerable time on the matter of baptism and the restoration of the catechumenate, reaffirming that adult baptism was to be seen as the definitive rite of initiation, and seeking to restore it to its Easter setting. This restoration has been welcomed in the missionary churches but its full benefits have yet to be appreciated among the traditional churches.

The World Council of Churches Lima document (*Baptism, Eucharist, and Ministry*, Geneva, 1982) stated that baptism 'is a participation in the death and resurrection of Christ, a washing away of sin, a new birth, an enlightenment by Christ, a reclothing in Christ, a renewal by the Spirit, the experience of salvation from the flood, an exodus from bondage, and a liberation into a new humanity in which barriers of division are transcended'. It also spoke of baptism as 'a sign and seal of our common discipleship' and thus it becomes a basic bond of unity. Much recent thinking about baptism has seen it as the ordination of the whole people of God. Since the Christian's ministry is centred on the reconciling work of Christ, baptism is our commission to engage in that ministry.

Bibliography

K. Aland, *Did the Early Church Baptize Infants?* (London, 1963); R. F. G. Burnish, *The Meaning of Baptism* (London, 1985); J. D. C. Fisher, *Christian Initiation: Baptism in the Medieval West* (London, 1965); J. Jeremias, *Infant Baptism in the First Four Centuries* (London, 1959); Murphy Center for Liturgical Research, *Made, not Born* (Notre Dame, IN, 1976); B. Neunheuser, *Baptism and Confirmation* (Westminster, MD, 1964); H. M. Riley, *Christian Initiation* (Washington, 1974); E. C. Whitaker, *Documents of the Baptismal Liturgy* (London, 1960).

R.F.G.B.

BAPTISM IN THE SPIRIT is most helpfully treated under the following aspects:

Biblical

The New Testament proclaims the gift of the personal Holy Spirit* to indwell all believers (Acts 2:18; Rom. 8:9; Gal. 3:2) as the seal, guarantee, means and firstfruits (Rom. 8:23; 2 Cor. 1:22; Eph. 1:13–14) of their eternal life of fellowship with the Father and the Son (Jn. 17:3; 1 Jn. 1:3). The Spirit, now revealed as a distinct agent who speaks, shows, witnesses, helps, intercedes, and can be grieved and lied to (Jn. 16:13–15; Rom. 8:16, 26; Eph. 4:30; Acts 5:3), mediates the presence of Christ (Jn. 14:16–18; Eph. 3:16–17), unites us to him (Eph. 4:3–4), regenerates (Jn. 3:5, 8; 2 Cor. 3:6; Tit. 3:5), illuminates (1 Cor. 2:13–16; Eph. 1:17), and transforms us (2 Cor. 3:18; Gal. 5:22–23), testifies to our adoption, thus altering our self-knowledge (Rom. 8:16), sustains our praying (Gal. 4:6; Eph. 6:18; Jude 20), and gives to us all gifts for service (1 Cor. 12:4–11). His full new-covenant ministry, which presupposed Jesus' return to glory (Jn. 7:39, *cf.* 17:5; 20:22 is an acted prophecy), began at Pentecost (Acts 2), according to Jesus' pre-ascension promise of Spirit-baptism (Acts 1:5; 11:16) in fulfilment of John's prediction that the coming Lord would baptize with the Holy Spirit (Mk. 1:8; Mt. 3:11; Lk. 3:16; Jn. 1:33). Acts embodies expectations that the gift of the Spirit, signalized apparently by charismatic manifestations, would accompany the water-baptism of adult believers (2:38, *etc.*), and views non-accompaniment as anomalous (8:14–17, 19:1–6). The baptism-image shows that the gift is to be viewed as initiatory, one element in the total process whereby sinners consciously become new creatures in Christ, accepted and alive as limbs in his body (so when Paul uses the image, 1 Cor. 12:13); the Pentecost story shows the gift as animating, transforming, emboldening, and bringing ability and usefulness in ministry.

Historical

The idea that the apostolic experience of Acts 2 (*cf.* 4:31) is a paradigmatic model and a personal necessity for all Christians has appeared within pietistic Protestantism in various forms. 1. John Fletcher (1729–85), Wesley's* designated successor, and some later Reformed teachers too, spoke of repeatable baptisms of the Spirit, meaning intensifyings of assurance and enhanced enablings for holy living and powerful ministry. 2. Charles Finney,* D. L. Moody (1837–1899), R. A. Torrey (1856–1928), Andrew Murray,* A. B. Simpson (1844–1919) and others echoed this, but assimilated it in different ways to the Wesleyan idea of a single 'second-blessing' experience that lifts one's life to a permanently new level. 3. Pentecostals* and charismatics generally see Spirit-baptism in this Wesleyan way, relating it to the full reception or release of the Spirit in one's personal being, in assurance, emotional exuberance, glossolalia, inward liberty to speak for Christ, and the blossoming of all kinds of gifts for ministry, including (so it is often claimed) prophetic and healing gifts. Tongues are often made the touchstone of Spirit-baptism (see Gifts of the Spirit*).

Theological

1. Since 1 Cor. 12, which affirms that all were Spirit-baptized, assumes that not all spoke in tongues (v. 30), it is difficult to make glossolalia the touchstone. 2. Since the reason why the apostles had a two-stage Christian experience was that they became believers before the Spirit's full new-covenant ministry in this world began, and since they expected others to enjoy this ministry from conversion on (Acts 2:38; 5:32), it is difficult to make the two-stage experience a universal norm. 3. Since the essence of all Spirit-baptism experiences, so-called, appears to be an intensifying of assurance as the Spirit witnesses to God's love in adoption and the believer's security in that love, it is fittest to explain them

theologically in precisely those terms (Rom. 5:5; 8:15–17, 38–39, *cf.* Jn. 14:16–23). 4. Since experience of apostolic quality is rare and much to be desired, and the church today is weak for lack of it, it is right to ask God to lead us into it, by whatever name we call it and in whatever theology we express it. 1 Cor. 12:13; Acts 11:15–17, and John 1:33, with Acts 1:5; 2:4, 33, and 38 as background, yield together a definition of Spirit-baptism as entry, through the communion and commitment that faith generates, into the experienced reality of Christ's resurrection life: an entry that water-baptism both portrays and confirms (Rom. 6:2–11; Col. 2:11–13).

Bibliography

F. D. Bruner, *A Theology of the Holy Spirit* (Grand Rapids, MI, 1970); J. D. G. Dunn, *Baptism in the Holy Spirit* (London, 1970); T. M. Smail, *Reflected Glory* (London, 1976); J. I. Packer, *Keep in Step with the Spirit* (Old Tappan, NJ, and Leicester, 1984).

J.I.P.

BAPTISM OF CHRIST. The baptism of Jesus by John the Baptist in the Jordan river is recorded in the Synoptic Gospels (Mt. 3:13–17; Mk. 1:9–11; Lk. 3:21–22), and alluded to in Jn. 1:31–33. In all three Synoptic accounts the event involves the Holy Spirit descending upon Jesus like a dove, as well as a voice from heaven declaring approval of Jesus as 'my Son, whom I love'. An intimation of full Trinitarian involvement (Spirit-Father-Son) seems unmistakable.

The importance of this event in gospel history lies in its official or messianic significance. For Jesus to be baptized was not a merely personal or private matter. John's baptism was 'a baptism of repentance' (Mk. 1:4; Lk. 3:3), and personally Jesus had no need of such repentance; he was holy and sinless (*e.g.* Lk. 1:35). Rather, the baptism of Jesus is his 'coronation', the occasion of his official, public installation as Messiah. The approval pronounced by the heavenly voice is the good pleasure of messianic appointment. By submitting to John's baptism Jesus gives initial public expression to his messianic identity and calling and in so doing identifies himself with repentant sinners. By this act he shows specifically his solidarity with them in their sins, that as the Messiah he is to be their representative sin-bearer, 'the Lamb of God,

who takes away the sin of the world' (Jn. 1:29). Accordingly, the Father confirms his messianic identity and at the same time anoints him with the Holy Spirit. This anointing provides him with the spiritual endowment requisite for the messianic task lying before him (*cf.* Acts 10:38). This task all the Synoptics go on to describe as beginning with the temptation (Mt. 4:1–11; Mk. 1:12–13; Lk. 4:1–13), understood within the broader context of the Synoptics as opening the climactic, eschatological struggle between the kingdom of God* and the kingdom of Satan.

In each of the Synoptics the record of Jesus' baptism closely follows a summary description of the ministry of John the Baptist. Each description culminates in John's prophecy of impending messianic baptism with the Holy Spirit and fire. Mt. 3:12 and Lk. 3:17 make plain that this baptism will involve judgment, a judicial ordeal separating the repentant ('wheat') from the unrepentant ('chaff'). The inner connection between this prophecy and the baptism of Jesus is that the messianic Spirit-and-fire baptism will not take place immediately but is to be preceded and mediated by a period based on the Messiah's own baptism and on his own reception of the Spirit. For the prophesied messianic baptism to be a saving blessing and not a destructive judgment for the messianic community, the Messiah himself must first be endowed ('baptized') with the Spirit in order to bear away the wrath and condemnation their sins deserve (*cf.* Jn. 1:33; Heb. 9:14).

His baptism at the Jordan points the Messiah in the way he must go: the way of suffering, condemnation and death that ends on the cross, and the cross, his climactic exposure to God's fiery wrath on sin, is the ultimate 'baptism' he has 'to undergo' (Lk. 12:50; *cf.* Mk. 10:38–39; Lk. 22:42). Indeed, the entire earthly ministry of Jesus – from the Jordan to the cross and resurrection – may be seen as a species of 'baptism', a baptism-ordeal.

The baptism of Jesus, then, is not an event of merely passing interest; it marks an epochal juncture, not only in Jesus' ministry but in the whole history of salvation. It involves considerations that lie at the heart of the gospel. This does not mean, however, that Jesus was not the Messiah before his baptism or that only then did he become aware for the first time that he was the Messiah. The gospels teach plainly both that he was the Messiah from his birth, and that he was correspondingly self-aware (*cf.*, *e.g.*, Mt. 1:21; Lk. 1:31ff.; 2:21, 25–38, 49). At the same time, in view of his true humanity he had genuine need of endowment with the Holy Spirit for the new phase of sonship and messianic obedience inaugurated by his baptism and culminating on the cross.

Bibliography

J. D. G. Dunn, *Baptism in the Holy Spirit* (London, 1970); W. L. Lane, *The Gospel According to Mark* (Grand Rapids, MI, 1974); G. Smeaton, *The Doctrine of the Holy Spirit* (1882; London, 1958).

R.B.G.

BAPTIST THEOLOGY. Traditionally cautious about the possible misuse of doctrinal formularies, Baptists have none the less given verbal expression to their shared and distinctive theology in various confessions.* The (Calvinistic) Particular Baptist Confession of 1677 (a modified form of the more famous Westminster Confession of 1647 and the Savoy Declaration of Faith of 1658) and the (Arminian) General Baptist Orthodox Creed of 1678 are typical of the theological variety not only within 17th-century English Baptist life, but also of later periods and other countries. The denominational title was not self-chosen; like 'Quaker' and 'Methodist', 'Anabaptist'* was initially a term of popular abuse, which 17th-century Baptists specifically repudiated on historical and theological grounds. *Historically*, it tended to identify them with the stigma of Münster (1533–35), while *theologically* they claimed they were not 're-baptizers' in that they could not conscientiously recognize paedo-baptism as biblical, particularly if it were viewed as a sign of incorporation into state churches. Committed to the authority of Scripture for both doctrine and practice, the primary theological convictions of Baptists were ecclesiological and sacramental.

W. T. Whitley (1861–1947), a leading Baptist historian, maintained that 'their most distinctive feature is the doctrine of the Church'.* Treasuring their essential unity with the whole people of God (Lumpkin, p. 137, article 69), Baptists have nevertheless insisted on the essential autonomy of the local

congregation. Each 'gathered church' is composed of believers who confess their allegiance to Christ and value their right and freedom unitedly to discern his will for their life, work and witness. Asserting the priesthood of all believers,* the local church's members encourage a corporate ministry, and in addition appoint their own leaders (pastors, elders and/or deacons) who are themselves accountable to the local church's total membership which gathers periodically in a 'church meeting'. Historically, Baptists held this 'independent' strand of English dissenting ecclesiology in common with the Congregationalists.*

Their baptismal convictions insist that, like the Lord's Supper, this sacrament (or ordinance) is restricted to believers. Those who profess repentance towards God and personal faith in Christ's saving work choose to be baptized by immersion in water in the name of the Trinity. Although convinced that total immersion gives rich symbolic expression to the NT concept of the believer's identification with Christ in his death, burial and resurrection, Baptists have insisted that in baptism the proper subject (*i.e.* believer) rather than the most appropriate mode is the more important aspect of their distinctive witness. Suspicious of sacramentalism, most Baptists have until comparatively recently interpreted believers' baptism primarily in symbolic terms and as an individual act of personal witness. However, the past two decades have witnessed in many places an increasing desire to regard baptism as integral to the gospel (so that it becomes part of their proclamation of Christ), conversion (regarding it as the outward ratification of an inward turning to God) and church membership (so that baptism is viewed not solely in personal terms as 'into Christ' but also corporately as into his body, the church).

Bibliography

G. R. Beasley-Murray, *Baptism in the New Testament* (London, 1962); K. W. Clements (ed.), *Baptists in the Twentieth Century* (London, 1983); A Gilmore (ed.), *The Pattern of the Church* (London, 1963); W. L. Lumpkin, *Baptist Confessions of Faith* (Chicago, 1959); E. A. Payne, *The Baptist Union. A Short History* (London, 1958); *idem*, *The Fellowship of Believers* (London, 1952); H. Wheeler Robinson, *Baptist*

Principles (London, 1955); *idem, The Life and Thought of the Baptists* (London, 1927).

R.B.

BARCLAY, ROBERT, see QUAKER THEOLOGY.

BARCLAY, WILLIAM (1907–78), Scottish biblical scholar. Born in Wick, and educated at Glasgow and Marburg, he ministered on industrial Clydeside before his appointment in 1947 as lecturer in New Testament (professor from 1964) at Glasgow University. He combined classical scholarship with an ability to communicate with all classes, whether in shipyard, lecture-room, print, or through television. His *Daily Study Bible* (NT) series sold some 1.5 million copies, was translated into numerous languages including Burmese and Estonian, and brought him a further ministry through correspondence world-wide. Theologically he called himself a 'liberal evangelical'.* He claimed to be the only member of his divinity faculty who believed Matthew, Luke and John wrote the Gospels attributed to them. Nonetheless, he was a universalist,* reticent about the inspiration of Scripture,* critical of the doctrine of substitutionary atonement,* and given to views about the virgin birth* and miracles* which conservatives would find either heretical or imprecise. He once described Bultmann* as the most evangelical preacher he had ever heard because all his writings aimed at confronting the individual with Christ. In the context of marked decline in Church of Scotland membership he deplored the virtual disappearance of church discipline* and suggested a two-tier category of membership: those 'deeply attracted to Jesus Christ', and those prepared to make total commitment.

Bibliography

Testament of Faith (London, 1975), also published as *A Spiritual Autobiography* (Grand Rapids, MI, 1975).

R. D. Kernohan (ed.), *William Barclay: the Plain Uncommon Man* (London, 1980); J. Martin, *William Barclay* (Edinburgh, 1984); C. L. Rawlins, *William Barclay* (Grand Rapids, MI, and Exeter, 1984).

J.D.Do.

BARMEN DECLARATION. The Barmen Declaration (1934) comprised six articles issued by German Protestant representatives in opposition to the Nazi-supported 'German-Christian' movement. When it became increasingly clear that the latter was adding extreme nationalism and anti-Semitism to a theologically liberal stance, Martin Niemöller (1892–1984) and other pastors, including Dietrich Bonhoeffer,* organized the first synod of the Confessing Church at Barmen in the Ruhr. German-Christians had gained ascendancy in some regional churches and probably intimidated others, but to Barmen came representatives from Lutheran, Reformed and United churches. The declaration did not purport to be a comprehensive statement, but against contemporary deviations it stressed the headship and finality of Christ, and the pre-eminence of Scripture for belief and as the guide to practical action for Christians. There was pointed repudiation of the German-Christian subordination of Christ's church to the state. Written mainly by Karl Barth,* the Barmen Declaration was very much a document born out of political developments of the age, and pointed out the fatal fallacy of any compromise with National Socialism under Hitler.

Bibliography

Text in J. H. Leith, *Creeds of the Churches* (Richmond, VA, ²1973) and, with discussion, in W. Niesel, *Reformed Symbolics* (Edinburgh and London, 1962).

J.D.Do.

BARTH, KARL (1886–1968). The most significant theologian of the twentieth century. His multi-volume *Church Dogmatics* (*CD*) constitutes the weightiest contribution to Protestant theology since Schleiermacher.*

Life

Born into a Swiss theological family, Barth studied in Berne, Berlin, Tübingen and Marburg under some of the leading teachers of the day, notably Harnack* and Herrmann,* and after a brief period working for the journal *Die christliche Welt* (*The Christian World*) and as an assistant pastor in Geneva, he became a village pastor at Safenwil in the Aargau from 1911–21. Over the course of his ministry there Barth became increasingly dismayed with the resources of his liberal* theological education, and his gradual rediscovery of Scripture as revelation eventually led to his explosive commentary on Romans. From 1921–30 he taught in Göttingen and Münster, played a leading role in the co-called 'dialectical theology'* movement, and published very widely, including an abortive prolegomena volume *Christian Dogmatics*. After moving to Bonn, Barth began the *CD*, and became increasingly involved in opposition to Hitler, giving substantial theological weight to the Confessing Church, notably at the Barmen* Synod in 1934. This led to his dismissal, and appointment to a chair in his native Basel, where he remained for the rest of his career and retirement, and where the several volumes of the (finally unfinished) *CD* were written.

Decisive for an understanding of his earlier thought is his eventual rejection of the liberal heritage of his theological mentors. Along with his fellow-pastor, Eduard Thurneysen (1888–1974), Barth became increasingly dissatisfied with the historico-critical method as a way of handling Scripture. Combined with a reading of Kierkegaard,* Nietzsche,* Dostoevsky* and Franz Overbeck (1837–1905), Barth's rejection of liberal constructions of the Christian faith led to a renewed emphasis on the eschatological, supernatural element of Christianity. His refusal of any synthesis between the church and culture was given a further decisive twist under the influence of Christoph Blumhardt's (1842–1919) radical Christian socialism, and of thinkers such as Hermann Kütter (1863–1931) and Leonhard Ragaz (1868–1945). The fruits of these profound mutations in theological outlook are to be found in Barth's sermons and occasional writings during the First World War, but above all in *The Epistle to the Romans*.

Commentary on Romans

First published in 1919 and then completely rewritten for a second edition in 1922, the commentary is not so much an exegesis as a sustained and intense reflection on what Barth would later call 'the Godness of God'. Into the book Barth poured all his discontent with the synthesis of God and man which he found in the liberal religious ideal, and emphasized the radical disjunction between God and man in which God became man's interrogator, the

one who initiates a crisis in the continuity of human history. Both the content and the style of the book are at times apocalyptic,* and it attracted heavy criticism from the academic establishment. Nevertheless, Barth, now a professor, continued his assault on the heartlands of liberalism. He followed his work on Romans with expositions of 1 Corinthians 15 (1924) and of Philippians (1927), and in a famous published debate with Harnack in 1923 criticized the historico-critical method (which for Harnack was the expression of disciplined inquiry into objective truth) for its failure to treat Scripture as a revelation which disturbs. An early collection of essays, *The Word of God and the Word of Man*, develops Barth's hostility to human religion,* and similarly his published lectures from the 1920s demonstrate how radical was his confrontation with what he understood as the theology of subjectivity, as in his Göttingen lectures on Schleiermacher from 1923–4 and in the slightly later Münster lectures on ethics (1928–9).

Dogmatics

Towards the end of the 1920s Barth began serious work on dogmatics, and his *Christian Dogmatics in Outline* was published in 1927. Barth later came to see this volume as a halfway house between the writings of the earlier 1920s and the *CD*. Whilst more constructive than the earlier ground-clearing writings, it retained vestiges of liberal Protestant theological method, which Barth only finally corrected through intensive study of Anselm.* It was through his reading of Anselm, partly in debate with the philosopher Heinrich Scholz (1884–1956), that Barth left behind the 'dialectical theology' of his earlier period, and was able to expand a more solid basis for dogmatics than had been afforded either by the theologians of the religious consciousness or by his own eschatological and frequently aggressive rejection of their work. Barth's work on Anselm's theological procedure (which bore fruit as *Fides Quaerens Intellectum* [*Faith Seeking Understanding*] in 1931) enabled him to clarify the relationship between faith and rational inquiry in a more sophisticated way than the earlier debate with Harnack, and so furnished the methodological underpinnings for the *CD*. In particular, Barth came to envisage theology as an inquiry moulded by the object into which it inquires;

the theologian's task is not to establish the object of inquiry (by, for example, naturally-available 'proof' of God) but to be guided by the inherent rationality of the object itself. Theology presupposes an objective order of being, apprehended in the church's *Credo*, which alone provides the basis for rational discourse about God. Associated with this work on theological method* is Barth's polemical rejection of natural theology* in debate with an earlier fellow-traveller, Emil Brunner,* and a series of expositions of creeds and Reformation confessions.

In Bonn and then in Basel, in the midst of a host of controversial political and theological concerns, Barth began work on the *CD*. Originally delivered as lectures and then revised for publication, the *CD* is, for all its inner consistency, the record of a process of growth and change over thirty years: Barth is not simply mapping out a system. Perhaps the most remarkable feature of the work is Barth's ceaseless capacity for astonishment: at one level, the *CD* is the record of Barth's captivation by the sheer weight, beauty and variety of Christian truth.

The heart of the enterprise, both methodologically and substantively, is Christology.* For Barth, Christology is not simply one doctrine alongside others but the centre from which all other Christian doctrines radiate. Because of this, Barth's theological procedure takes a distinctive form: Christian doctrine is constructed by inference from the person of Jesus Christ, who is the locus of all truth about God and man. This leads not only to Barth's resolute realism and his hostility to all abstract metaphysical or anthropological foundations for theology, but also to his distinctive handling of analogy.* In effect, Barth reverses the usual direction of analogy: instead of moving by analogy from the known realities of creation towards knowledge of the divine, Barth moves from God in Christ as the fundamental given towards affirmations concerning creation and humanity. It is the profundity of Barth's exploration of this theocentricity which makes the *CD* one of the most important pieces of Protestant theology.

The *CD* as it stands comprises four volumes, on the doctrine of the word of God, the doctrine of God, the doctrine of creation, and an unfinished volume on the doctrine of reconciliation. A fifth volume on the doctrine of redemption was projected but never begun

before Barth's death. Each volume is subdivided into part-volumes, expounding and meditating on a series of theses, and includes a great wealth of detailed historical and exegetical discussion, as well as treatment of the ethical consequences of the main dogmatic discussion. Volume one weaves together the doctrines of revelation* and the Trinity, proposing that theology takes its rise from the self-positing of the divine subject. Revelation, as God's gracious self-repetition, creates the experience of faith in the church, and constitutes man as a recipient of God's word, which is God's self-disclosure. The theological task is that of the self-scrutiny of the church against its objective referent, from which theology receives its status as a science.

From the outset, Barth's consistent theological realism is evident: his starting-point, quite different either from his liberal heritage or from his contemporary existentialist* peers, is the given actuality of the self-revealing God. This surfaces in volume two in the discussion of the knowledge* of God, the capacity for which resides not in man's readiness for God but in God's readiness to share his own knowledge of himself with man: God's self-knowledge is graciously reduplicated in the receiver of revelation. Accordingly, Barth expounds a severely negative evaluation of natural theology and of what he understood to be traditional doctrines of analogy. The discussion of the being of God in volume two is one of the most important treatments of the theme since Calvin.* God's being is described as his being-in-act, that is to say, God is himself or becomes himself in the loving act of creating fellowship with man in Jesus Christ. In effect, Barth radically recasts the doctrine of God by making the person of Christ central for theology proper. God's absoluteness is therefore nothing other than his freedom for loving action. And similarly, the doctrine of election is a statement about God's choice to be himself in Jesus Christ, and so to choose mankind as his covenant partner, who is given the task of obedience to the divine command.

The reality of man as God's partner is treated at length in volume three. Barth refuses to handle the doctrine of creation* as a truth that is naturally available. Instead, he links creation to covenant:* man's creatureliness derives from his adoption into the covenant of God with mankind made actual in Jesus Christ, who is both electing God and elected man. Thus history and human being as such are what they are because of God's own assumption of historical, creaturely existence in the incarnation. Barth expounds the theme in particularly significant discussions of human temporality and human sin, again rigorously deploying the method of analogy from Christology, which comes to assume an increasingly large role in the argument.

When Barth turns to Christology in volume four, his style and thinking become increasingly concrete. At the time that Barth was working on volume four, he published an important essay on 'The Humanity of God', in which he corrected some of his earlier 'dialectical' thinking, and focused with even greater concentration on the man Jesus as the beginning and end of the ways of God with man. In this late stage of the growth of the CD, his writing becomes increasingly narrative in its handling of the Christological theme of abasement and exaltation. The ethical section of volume four, which was never finished (parts were published as a last fragment, CD IV.4, and parts as the posthumous The Christian Life) contains an increasingly realistic account of human ethical agency. This is expounded in Barth's handling of water-baptism, whose sacramental status Barth denies in order to affirm its proper character as a human act of obedient response. Volume four is the maturest expression of Barth's convictions about Jesus Christ the God-man, who furnishes a character-description of God and the origin of human participation in the covenant of God and creation. These writings also contain many suggestions for revision of aspects of his earlier theology, notably in their increasingly interactive account of the relationship of God and the natural order.

After retirement, Barth worked a little more on the CD, took a lively interest in the work of Vatican II, and published some smaller pieces, including his final lectures at Basel, Evangelical Theology. A full appraisal of his work would need to take note of his published sermons in Basel prison, Deliverance to the Captives and Call for God, his collections of essays such as Against the Stream and Theology and Church, and his reflections on past theologians and philosophers in Protestant Theology in the Nineteenth Century.

Interpretations

Barth's work substantially affected the course of Protestant theology in Europe and beyond; although Barth resisted pressure to become the centre of a school, his work has been interpreted and extended by many, notably H. Gollwitzer (b. 1908), O. Weber (1902–66) and E. Jüngel* in Germany, and T. F. Torrance* in Britain. Critical appraisal of Barth often focuses on his account of the relation of God to his creation, asking whether his method and his fundamental theological convictions lead him into offering only an ambiguous affirmation of the value and reality of the natural order. In terms of his account of the knowledge of God, Pannenberg,* for example, argues that Barth's confidence in the self-evidence of the object of theology leads him into a fideism which refuses to offer any sort of bridges between the knowledge of revelation and knowledge of the human world. Something of the same set of issues emerge in discussions of Barth's doctrine of man. Some critics suggest that by grounding the reality of man so completely in the humanity of God in Christ, Barth fails to give real weight to the natural order. Hence in his account of human freedom, sin and rejection of God, some find a lack of a real sense of man over against God. Or again, in the ethical sections of CD, particularly before volume four, he is interpreted as having so grounded man's agency in Christ that the impetus for human obedience is removed, and sanctification is not recognizable as a human process. Catholic theologians in particular sense an 'actualism' or 'occasionalism' in Barth's anthropology,* in that he does not appear to lay sufficient emphasis on the continuity of man as the recipient of divine grace. The effect of Barth's concentration on Christology upon his doctrine of the Trinity forms another area of discussion. By envisaging the Spirit as essentially the 'applicatory' or 'subjective' dimension of the work of Christ, Barth seems to lack a fully personalist account of the Spirit as a distinct divine agent. This is bound up with more general questions about the apparent 'modalism' (see Monarchianism*), in that his preference for the term 'mode of being' rather than 'person' suggests a high evaluation of the divine unity at the expense of a proper sense of plurality within God.

Many critiques of Barth are flawed by

treating his theology too systematically, without sensing the checks and balances within the corpus of his work. Barth's great strength perhaps above all was his ability to keep starting again. The several changes of course within his work were far from fickle; much more were they part of his restless reappraisal of his own thinking, and they bear witness to his ruthlessly interrogative and constantly fresh engagement with the matter of theology. Barth never settled down, and his readings of Scripture as well as of classical theologians from the past – Calvin and Schleiermacher above all – were constantly submitted to reappraisal and critique. Barth's work is not simply a persuasive restatement of the main lines of the Christian faith; it also constitutes one of the major critical responses to the Enlightenment,* with a significant place in the intellectual history of Europe.

Bibliography

Collected works: *Gesamtausgabe* (Zurich, 1971–). Academic writings: for a useful chronological bibliography see E. Busch, *Karl Barth* (London, 1976). Chief works: *The Christian Life* (Edinburgh, 1981); *CD*, I:1–IV:4; *Credo* (London, 1936); *Dogmatics in Outline* (London, 1949); *The Epistle to the Romans* (Oxford, 1935); *Ethics* (Edinburgh, 1981); *Evangelical Theology* (London, 1963); *Fides Quaerens Intellectum* (London, 1960); *The Humanity of God* (London, 1961); *The Knowledge of God and the Service of God* (London, 1938); *Prolegomena zur christlichen Dogmatik* (Munich, 1928); *Protestant Theology in the Nineteenth Century* (London, 1972); *The Resurrection of the Dead* (London, 1933); *Theology and Church* (London, 1962); *The Theology of Schleiermacher* (Edinburgh, 1982); *The Word of God and the Word of Man* (London, 1928).

See bibliography in M. Kwiran, *An Index of Literature on Barth, Bonhoeffer and Bultmann* (*Sonderheft* to *Theologische Zeitschrift*, 1977). See especially: H. U. von Balthasar, *The Theology of Karl Barth* (New York, 1971); G. C. Berkouwer, *The Triumph of Grace in the Theology of Karl Barth* (London and Grand Rapids, MI, 1956); G. W. Bromiley, *An Introduction to the Theology of Karl Barth* (Edinburgh, 1980); C. Brown, *Karl Barth and the Christian Message* (London, 1967); C. Gunton, *Becoming and Being* (Oxford, 1978); E. Jüngel, *Barth-Studien*

(Gütersloh, 1982); *idem, The Doctrine of the Trinity* (Edinburgh, 1976); *idem, Karl Barth: A Theological Legacy* (Edinburgh, 1987); H. Küng, *Justification* (London, 1964); K. Runia, *Karl Barth's Doctrine of Holy Scripture* (Grand Rapids, MI, 1962); S. W. Sykes (ed.), *Karl Barth* (Oxford, 1979); J. Thompson, *Christ in Perspective* (Edinburgh, 1978); T. F. Torrance, *Karl Barth* (London, 1962); R. E. Willis, *The Ethics of Karl Barth* (Leiden, 1971).

J.B.We.

BASIL OF CAESAREA (c. AD 329–379), also called Basil the Great, was the leading figure of the group of three Cappadocian fathers who championed Nicene orthodoxy against the Arians* in the later 4th century. Gregory of Nazianzus,* the second of the group, formed a close friendship with Basil while they were students in Athens. The third member of the group, Basil's younger brother, Gregory of Nyssa,* was educated at home. On returning to Cappadocia, Basil devoted himself to an ascetic* and devotional life and became a pioneer of coenobitic monasticism. He and Gregory of Nazianzus compiled an influential selection from the writings of Origen,* the *Philocalia*. Basil's intellectual and administrative gifts led to his election as metropolitan bishop of Caesarea, the Cappadocian capital, in 372. After the death of Athanasius* the following year, he was the chief pillar of orthodoxy in the East, defending the deity of the Son and Spirit against Arians and Pneumatomachi. He thus became the chief architect of the Cappadocian doctrine of the Trinity* which became definitive for East and West. He was also a noted liturgist.

Basil's two most important works are *Against Eunomius*, a reply to extreme Arianism, and *On the Holy Spirit*. Eunomius argued that since only creatures were begotten, the Son, being begotten, could not be God. Basil denies that 'unbegottenness' is an adequate definition of the essence of God, and defends the doctrine (inherited from Origen and Athanasius) of the eternal generation of the Son. The generation of creatures is physical and temporal. The generation of the Son is ineffable and eternal.

Basil's second main treatise, *On the Holy Spirit*, written to defend the glorifying of the Spirit in his doxology, must be set against the emergence of the so-called Macedonians and Pneumatomachi, who denied the deity of the Spirit. Basil clearly accepts the deity of the Spirit in his letters, but stops short in this treatise of declaring in so many words that the Spirit is God and consubstantial (*homoousion*) with the Father. This was politic, not giving his enemies an opportunity to dethrone him, and diplomatic. Without offending those hesitant to make an explicit confession of the Spirit's deity, he argued that the Spirit cannot be a creature (the only alternative to being creator) and is to be worshipped.

Here Basil makes his distinctive contribution to Trinitarian doctrine. Athanasius and the older Nicenes had defended the deity of the Son by insisting that he was consubstantial (*homoousios*) with, of the same essence or substance* (*ousia*) as, the Father. Basil made a distinction between *ousia* and *hypostasis** (which, confusingly, may also be literally translated as 'substance'), hitherto used interchangeably. He spoke of one *ousia* of God, but three *hypostaseis*, the *hypostasis* of the Father, the *hypostasis* of the Son, and the *hypostasis* of the Holy Spirit. This became the definitive doctrine of the Trinity in the East. Cappadocian doctrine greatly influenced the West through Ambrose,* although the West began from the oneness of God and spoke of three 'persons'.

Bibliography

Selected works in ET in *NPNF*, 2nd series, vol. 8, and in *FC* series.

H. von Campenhausen, *The Fathers of the Greek Church* (London, 1963); W. K. L. Clarke, *Basil the Great: A Study in Monasticism* (London, 1913); P. J. Fedwick, *The Church and the Charisma of Leadership in Basil of Caesarea* (Toronto, 1979); idem (ed.), *Basil of Caesarea: Christian, Humanist, Ascetic*, 2 vols. (Toronto, 1981); J. N. D. Kelly, *Early Christian Doctrines* (London, 51977); G. L. Prestige, *God in Patristic Thought* (London, 1952); idem, *St Basil the Great and Apollinaris of Laodicea* (London, 1956); I. P. Sheldon-Williams in *CHLGEMP*, pp. 432–438; E. Venables in *DCB* 1, pp. 282–297; J. W. C. Wand, *Doctors and Councils* (London, 1962).

T.A.N.

BAUR, F. C., see TÜBINGEN SCHOOL.

BAVINCK, HERMAN (1854–1921), Reformed* theologian. In 1882 he was appointed professor of dogmatic theology in the Reformed Seminary at Kampen, Netherlands. In 1902 he took the same chair in the Free University, Amsterdam, as the successor of Dr Abraham Kuyper* who had become prime minister. Bavinck was an outstanding theologian, deeply rooted in the Reformed tradition. Although he had a thorough knowledge and deep appreciation of post-Calvinian theology, he preferred to go back to Calvin himself. At the same time he wanted to develop Reformed theology in constant interaction with the theological and philosophical thinking of his own day. His major work is his four-volume *Reformed Dogmatics* (*Gereformeerde Dogmatiek*, 41928–30). Characteristic of his method is his firm foundation in biblical theology, his thorough grasp of historical theology and his synthetic approach. He always tried to incorporate all elements of truth which he found in other theological systems. Within Reformed theology itself, he tried to bring various strands of thought together in a new synthesis (*e.g.* infra- and supralapsarianism – see Predestination;* creationism and traducianism – see Soul, Origin of*). In the Netherlands his *Reformed Dogmatics* is still regarded as a standard work.

Bibliography

Works in ET: *The Doctrine of God*, vol. 2 of *Gereformeerde Dogmatiek* (Grand Rapids, MI, 1955); *Our Reasonable Faith*, a popularized version of *Gereformeerde Dogmatiek* (Grand Rapids, MI, 1956); *The Philosophy of Revelation* (Grand Rapids, MI, 1953).

E. P. Heideman, *The Relation of Revelation and Reason in E. Brunner and H. Bavinck* (Assen, 1959); C. Jaarsma, *The Educational Philosophy of H. Bavinck* (Grand Rapids, MI, 1935); B. Kruithof, *The Relation of Christianity and Culture in the Teaching of Herman Bavinck* (Edinburgh, 1955).

K.R.

BAVINCK, JOHAN HERMAN (1859–1964), Dutch missiologist.* A nephew of Herman Bavinck,* he studied theology in Amsterdam and Erlangen. His doctoral dissertation (1919) dealt with the medieval mystic Henry Suso (c. 1295–1366). He served as a minister in the Dutch East Indies and then in Holland at Heemstede, where he studied and wrote on psychology. On his return to the East Indies to Java, his knowledge of religious psychology and mysticism* enabled him to communicate the gospel effectively to Javanese mystics. In 1934 he published a book on the confrontation between the gospel and Eastern mysticism.

He spent over fifteen years as a missionary, including a few years teaching theology in Jokja, and in 1939 became the first professor of missiology in the Kampen seminary of the Reformed Churches of the Netherlands, and also professor extraordinary of missiology at the Free University of Amsterdam. From 1955 he combined the latter position with the chair of homiletics, liturgy and pastoralia at the Free University.

Although very well-versed in mysticism, psychology and the non-Christian religions, and hence sensitive to the demands of the missionary approach, Bavinck was an ardent opponent of syncretism* and compromise of the gospel. Salvation in Jesus Christ was quite different from the salvation offered by the (mystical) religions, he explained in a book on religious awareness and the Christian faith in 1949. His major work, translated as *An Introduction to the Science of Missions* (Philadelphia, 1960), emphasized both the missionary's call to share the life and culture of the community around him and the vast gap between the Christian faith and non-Christian religions. Superficial similarities when investigated become profound differences. One of his last books, on religions and world-views in 1961, stressed the uniqueness of the gospel over against attempts to harmonize the world's religions into a common front.

See also: CHRISTIANITY AND OTHER RELIGIONS.

Bibliography

Works in ET: *The Church between Temple and Mosque* (Grand Rapids, MI, 1966); *Faith and its Difficulties* (Grand Rapids, MI, 1959); *The Impact of Christianity on the Non-Christian World* (Grand Rapids, MI, 1948); *The Riddle of Life* (Grand Rapids, MI, 1958).

J. du Preez, 'Johan Herman Bavinck on the Relation between Divine Revelation and the Religions', *Missionalia* 13 (1985), pp. 111–120; J. Verkuyl, *Contemporary Missiology* (Grand Rapids, MI, 1978).

J.A.E.V.

BAXTER, RICHARD (1615–91), a leading Puritan* clergyman. In 1641–42 and 1647–61 (he was a Parliamentary army chaplain, 1642–47) he exercised at Kidderminster, Worcestershire, the most fruitful Puritan pastorate anywhere recorded, converting almost the whole town. Under Cromwell's church settlement (establishing Independency) he formed the interdenominational Worcestershire Association of pastors pledged to practise congregational evangelism by catechizing families and to maintain parochial church discipline, with member ministers as the informal consistory court. At the Restoration, Baxter was offered the bishopric of Hereford, but declined it. At the 1661 Savoy Conference he pleaded fruitlessly for the non-prelatical, synodical form of episcopacy devised by his deceased friend Archbishop Ussher (1581–1656), and for a Puritan revision of the Prayer Book. After the 1662 ejections he lived in the London area, an acknowledged leader among the ejected, and wrote constantly, becoming the most voluminous of all British theologians.

His output included three folios. *A Christian Directory* (1673) summarizes in a million words all Puritan 'practical', 'experimental', 'casuistical'* divinity (*i.e.* ethical and devotional teaching); *Catholick Theology* (1675), 'Plain, Pure, Peaceable: for the Pacification of the Dogmatical Word-Warriors', as the title proclaimed, embraces Calvinist, Arminian, Lutheran and Roman Catholic (Dominican and Jesuit) views about grace* in a *tour de force* of ecumenical accommodation; and *Methodus Theologiae Christianae* (1681) is a Ramist-style analysis of Christian truth in Latin, trichotomizing instead of dichotomizing as Ramus* and other Puritans did. Three more landmark books were *The Saints' Everlasting Rest* (1650), an 800–page classic that established Baxter as Puritanism's supreme devotional author; the passionate *Reformed Pastor* (1656; 'Reformed' means not just 'Calvinistic' but 'revived'), a volume which the Broad Church bishop Hensley Henson described in 1925 as 'the best manual of the clergyman's duty in the language'; and the electrifying *Call to the Unconverted* (1658), a pioneer evangelistic pocket-book that sold by tens of thousands. Also, Baxter's elaborate chronicle of his life and times, *Reliquiae Baxterianae* (1696), is a primary and trusted source for 17th-century church history.

Miscalled a Presbyterian, Baxter was a reluctant nonconformist who favoured monarchy, national churches, liturgy and episcopacy, and could accept the unsympathetically revised 1662 Prayer Book. But the 1662 Act of Uniformity required renunciation on oath of Puritan ideals of reformation as a condition of incumbency in the restored Church of England, and Baxter balked at that.

Baxter's gospel presents Christ's death as an act of universal redemption, penal and vicarious though not strictly substitutionary, in virtue of which God has made a new law offering amnesty to penitent breakers of the old law. As obedience to the new law, repentance and faith are one's personal saving righteousness, which effectual calling induces and preserving grace sustains. Called 'Neonomianism', this scheme is substantially Amyraldian,* with Arminian* 'new law' teaching added. Its obvious legalistic tendency, unrecognized by Baxter, was much criticized in his own day. Baxter also argued the reasonableness of Christianity on the basis of its coherence with natural theology,* a method that boomeranged by producing unitarianism* among his English Presbyterian followers after his death.

Bibliography

Practical Works, ed. W. Orme, 23 vols. (London, 1830).

C. F. Allison, *The Rise of Moralism* (London, 1966); W. M. Lamont, *Richard Baxter and the Millennium* (London, 1979); Hugh Martin, *Puritanism and Richard Baxter* (London, 1946); G. F. Nuttall, *Richard Baxter* (London, 1965); F. J. Powicke, *A Life of the Reverend Richard Baxter* (London, 1924); idem, *The Reverend Richard Baxter Under the Cross* (London, 1927).

J.I.P.

BECK, JOHANN TOBIAS (1804–78). German biblical theologian, who was a professor in Basel (1836–43) and Tübingen (1843–78). Often a lonely campaigner against rationalism and historical criticism, he was influenced by the pietism* of Württemberg,

although he was occasionally at variance with individual pietists. While identified with 'biblicism', he cannot be squeezed into any particular mould. Among his pupils were C. A. Auberlen (1824–64) and Martin Kähler.* A 'Society for the Promotion of Christian-theological Knowledge and Christian Life' took Beck to Basel to create a balance to the criticism of Wilhelm De Wette (1780–1849).

Beck demanded a 'pneumatic exegesis of Scripture'. Without faith it is impossible to arrive at 'an understanding with the spirit of Christianity'. The Bible is a unified system of teaching, 'the faithful image (*Abbild*) of the revelation of which it is the transmitted presentation'. We should be determined by neither the confessions of the church nor dogmatic presuppositions, but by Scripture alone.

The 'divine plan for the world' is expressed in the kingdom of God. The latter is already present but not yet visible. Only God can bring it to pass. Beck believed in the millennial* reign of Christ. Prophecy* is a fundamental pillar of the Bible.

Beck presses for 'moral separation' from the world, 'personal appropriation' of the truth, and 'moral purification'. Here sanctification* lives on as the central concern of pietism.

Bibliography

Major work: *Die Christliche Lehr-Wissenschaft nach den Biblischen Urkunden* ('Christian Science of Education according to the Biblical Sources', Stuttgart, 1841); in ET only: *Outlines of Biblical Psychology* (Edinburgh, 1877); *Outlines of Christian Doctrine* (Madras, 1879); *Pastoral Theology of the New Testament* (Edinburgh, 1885).

K. Barth, *Protestant Theology in the Nineteenth Century* (London, 1972), ch. 25; German life in B. Riggenbach, *Johann Tobias Beck* (Basel, 1888); H. M. Wolf in *TRE* 5, pp. 393–394.

G.M.

BEING. 'Being' or 'existence' is often held as the most general property of all reality. The study of being (ontology) was a key question in Greek philosophy. In considering the differences between being and not-being and being and becoming, Parmenides (515–450 BC) and Plato* described the realm of pure being as that of the unchanging, eternal, immutable, rational and one. Aristotle* was more interested in the various kinds of being and the variety of uses of the word 'is'. Modern philosophy has moved from the idealism* of Plato to Aristotle in analysing the different kinds of being. Problems over the being of fictional entities, abstract ideas and timeless objects led to distinguishing between the 'is' of predication, existence, classification and identity. In criticizing Anselm's* and Descartes'* forms of the ontological argument, which argues for the existence of God on the grounds of the reality of the concept of God, Hume,* Kant* and Bertrand Russell (1872–1970) denied that existence is a predicate, for it does not add to the description of something. W. O. V. Quine (b. 1908) has developed a view of ontological relativity which asks the question: 'To the existence of what kind of things does belief in a given theory commit us?' and answers that to be is to be the value of a variable.

Modern existentialism* has focused on the nature of being. Sartre has separated being *en soi* (the being of inanimate things) from being *pour soi* (the being of people). K. Jaspers separates *Dasein* (ordinary being) from *Existenz* (authentic being) and from Being (the transcending). Heidegger follows this closely with *Dasein*, *Ek-sistenz* and transcending Being. The existentialist is concerned to distinguish the being of things, from the self-conscious choosing being of humanity, from Being itself. This has influenced theology greatly and Tillich* typifies the impact in his description of God as being itself or as the ground of being. This looks like a return to the old Greek notion of the immutable, impassible, eternal One. It has been criticized by process* philosophy and theology which argue that becoming has precedence over being and that God is to be identified with the process of history and/or nature in the world. This God is pictured as being affected by the world and participating in its suffering.

In the Bible there is no attempt to argue for the existence of God. His being is assumed. He is the God who reveals himself and who and what he is. 'I am who I am' (Ex. 3:14). Nevertheless the being of the world and human being cannot be understood properly or explained without reference to God. God is the creator of the world and of humanity, and so the world and humanity bear the marks of their creator God. The events of history are to be understood in the light of God and his will for the world and humanity. Jesus reveals God's nature as love and says of himself, 'Anyone who has seen me has seen the Father' (Jn. 14:9). This account of God is not just of a concept, as Tillich argues, or merely identical with the world and history as process thinking suggests, but of the active, dynamic, creator, agent God of Abraham, Isaac and Jacob.

Bibliography

M. Heidegger, *Being and Time* (London, 1962); J. Macquarrie, *God-Talk* (London, 1967); E. L. Mascall, *He Who Is* (London, 1943); J. Sartre, *Being and Nothingness* (ET, London, 1969, 1976); W. O. V. Quine, *Ontological Relativity and Other Essays* (New York and London, 1969).

E.D.C.

BELGIC CONFESSION, see CONFESSIONS OF FAITH.

BELLARMINE, ROBERT (1542–1621). Roberto Francesco Romolo Bellarmino was born at Monte Pulciano, in Tuscany. His mother was the sister of the future pope, Marcellus II. In 1560 he joined the Jesuits* and in 1569 was sent to Louvain, to help in the struggle against a militant Protestantism.* The following year he became the first Jesuit professor of theology at Louvain University. He served there for six years before returning to Rome to become professor of controversial theology at the Collegium Romanum. From 1576 to 1588 he taught English and German missionary students at Rome. He went on to become spiritual director (1588), then rector (1592), of the college, provincial of the Jesuits' Neapolitan province (1594) and theologian to Pope Clement VIII (1597). In 1599 he was appointed a cardinal. He served for a time as Archbishop of Capua (1602–5) but was recalled to Rome for a wider ministry.

Bellarmine devoted himself to the controversy with Protestantism. He never met Protestant leaders personally, but took care to represent their positions fairly. He was prepared to acknowledge strengths as well as weaknesses in their theology. His aim was to answer Protestantism by reasoned argument, rather than abuse or naked appeal to authority. He devoted himself to the study of the Bible, the fathers and church history, to equip himself for his task. He was a formidable opponent and chairs of theology were founded in some Protestant universities for the purpose of refuting him. His lectures at the Collegium Romanum formed the basis of his greatest work, a three-volume *Disputations on Controversies about the Christian Faith against the Heretics of this Time* (1586–93). This was generally reckoned to be one of the best statements of Tridentine Roman Catholic theology.

Bellarmine became embroiled in some of the controversies of his time. His views of the papacy* caused him trouble. He took the papal side in a controversy with Venice over clerical immunities (1606–7). But in 1610, in refuting a work by W. Barclay of Aberdeen (1546–1608), which denied that the pope had any temporal (as opposed to spiritual) authority, Bellarmine denied that the pope has any *direct* temporal authority. Rulers receive their authority from God. The pope has only an *indirect* temporal jurisdiction. If a ruler prejudices the eternal salvation of his subjects, the pope may intervene, even to the extent of deposing the ruler and releasing his subjects from their obligation to obey him. This might appear to grant the pope considerable power, but it was not good enough for Pope Sixtus V. In 1590 he put the first volume of Bellarmine's *Controversies* (where the pope's direct temporal power is denied) on the Index of Forbidden Books.

Bellarmine was also involved in the early stages of the affair of Galileo, who was condemned for teaching that the earth rotates about the sun. The Inquisition declared in 1616 that it is the earth, not the sun, that is at the centre of the universe and that the sun moves round the earth. Bellarmine was entrusted with the task of communicating this to Galileo.

Bellarmine was also active in other ways. He was a member of the commission that produced the revised 'Sixto-Clementine' edition of the Vulgate in 1592. He wrote a Hebrew grammar and, late in life, a number of ascetic works. Soon after his death there were moves towards his canonization, but this was delayed until 1930, because of his views on papal authority.

See also: REFORMATION, CATHOLIC COUNTER-; ROMAN CATHOLIC THEOLOGY.

Bibliography

Collected editions of works published in Cologne (1617–21), Naples (1856–62), Paris (1870–74).

J. Brodrick, *The Life and Work of Blessed Robert Francis Cardinal Bellarmine, S. J. 1542–1621*, 2 vols. (1928; London, New York and Toronto, 1950).

A.N.S.L.

BENEDICT AND THE BENEDICTINE TRADITION. The pattern of monastic life set down by Benedict of Nursia (*c.* 480–*c.* 550) in the Rule for his community at Monte Cassino became in time the norm throughout Western monasticism, especially from *c.* 800. Monastic reforms regularly centred on a return to strict observance of the Rule, as in the widely influential Cluniac movement of the 10th–12th centuries. In the same era other orders, notably the Carthusians and the Cistercians, based themselves on Benedict's Rule while demanding a discipline of greater austerity. The Rule was therefore a text of extraordinary importance throughout the 'monastic centuries' of European Christianity.

Benedict made no provision for scholarly study as such. According to Gregory the Great,* he turned his back on higher education, taking up the ascetic life 'knowingly ignorant and wisely untaught' (*scienter nescius et sapienter indoctus*). Nevertheless, he was well-read in the great Latin fathers, and his monks spent up to four hours a day in *lectio divina*, the contemplative spiritual reading of the Scriptures and the fathers, especially monastic writers like Basil* and John Cassian (*c.* 360–435). The school (to teach youngsters vowed to the monastic life), the library and the scriptorium (where manuscripts were copied) became standard features of a Benedictine community. There developed a distinctive monastic culture, with its own style of theology, which has been brilliantly analysed by an eminent modern Cistercian scholar, Jean Leclercq (b. 1911), of the abbey of Clervaux in Luxemburg.

The theology of the Rule itself is unremarkable, except in its sensitive ordering of the ascetic life in community. Benedictine theology stood in deliberate continuity with patristic theology,* and derived both its literary forms and its content very largely from the fathers. (The Latin classics, which

85

were taught in the monastic schools in accordance with the educational programme of the *Institutions* of Cassiodorus (*c.* 485–*c.* 580), also provided some genres.) It was therefore orientated towards tradition. Taking the *auctoritas* of the Bible and the fathers as its basis represented, in theology, the humility so strongly inculcated by the Rule. As one writer put it, they merely gleaned after the great reapers – Augustine,* Jerome,* Gregory the Great* – had done their work. They approached the Bible in a spirit of meditation, and frequently interpreted it allegorically.

Not surprisingly, little creative originality is evident in the luminaries of the early Middle Ages, such as Bede (*c.* 673–735), who was first and foremost a biblical scholar, heavily dependent on the fathers in his commentaries and homilies. Benedictines were prominent in the Carolingian renaissance, but in theology their contribution lay chiefly in harvesting the biblical and doctrinal wisdom of the fathers, and applying it to contemporary needs. Writers like Alcuin from York (*c.* 735–804), Rhabanus Maurus of Fulda (*c.* 776–856) and Walafrid Strabo of Reichenau (*c.* 808–49) were enormously prolific, while others, like Paschasius Radbertus* and Ratramnus,* both monks at Corbie, engaged in controversies on the eucharist and predestination* that hinged on the true interpretation of the fathers.

Theology in the Benedictine tradition came to full flower in the 11th and 12th centuries, supremely in Bernard of Clairvaux.* Controversy with emergent scholasticism* depicted its distinctiveness in sharper colours. Theology for monks was determined by the goal of monastic life – the knowledge of God, and studied in relation to monastic experience, whose heart lay in worship and prayer. It preserved a respect for mystery, and distrusted too heavy an emphasis on the technique of dialectic.

At the same time, monastic-trained theologians like Anselm,* William of St Thierry (*c.* 1085–*c.* 1148) and Ailred of Rievaulx (1109–67), 'the English Bernard', fruitfully combined an ascetic orientation with more speculative methods. Anselm's disciple, Eadmer of Canterbury (*c.* 1055–1124), was a pioneer expositor of Mary's* immaculate conception, and other important teachers were the reformer Peter Damian (1007–72), Peter the Venerable (*c.* 1092–1156), abbot of Cluny,

and Rupert (*c.* 1070–1129), abbot of Deutz near Cologne.

In the later Middle Ages, the monasteries lost their pre-eminence as centres of Christian theological reflection. The emergence of the universities, the predominance of scholasticism, the success of new movements such as the Franciscans* and the Dominicans* and the appeal of humanism* all eclipsed the Benedictine tradition of theology. Later the Reformation and subsequent political upheavals drastically reduced the number of communities following the Rule.

For a century before the French Revolution, the houses of the congregation of St Maur (near Cluny), especially St Germain-des-Prés at Paris, accomplished monumental feats of scholarship, including a superb edition of Augustine (with a marvellous index) which exposed them to charges of Jansenism (see Augustinianism*). Jean Mabillon (1632–1707) edited Bernard's works, and Bernard de Montfaucon (1655–1741) those of Athanasius* and Chrysostom. Not all churchmen approved of such whole-hearted dedication to learning on the part of monks.

With the resurgence of Benedictine life in the 19th century, the Maurists' tradition of theological scholarship has also been revived. Important abbeys are found in Belgium at Maredsous (home of the *Revue bénédictine*) and Steenbrugge (where the *Corpus Christianorum* collections of the fathers and the medievals are edited), in Germany at Beuron and Maria Laach and in France at Solesmes. These last three have devoted themselves to the study and renewal of the liturgy, the core of Benedictine Christianity, which is called in the Rule 'the work of God' (*opus Dei*).

Bibliography

C. Butler, *Benedictine Monachism* (London, ²1924); L. J. Daly, *Benedictine Monasticism* (New York, 1965); D. H. Farmer (ed.), *Benedict's Disciples* (Leominster, 1980); D. Knowles, *The Benedictines* (London, 1929); J. Leclercq, *The Love of Learning and the Desire for God* (New York, 1961).

D.F.W.

B ENGEL, JOHANN ALBRECHT (1687–1752), German Lutheran, distinguished as a NT scholar. He was a pioneer of modern textual criticism (see

Biblical Criticism*), who produced an edition of the Gk. NT (1734) and formulated the canon 'The more difficult reading is to be preferred'. He is chiefly remembered for his *Gnomon Novi Testamenti* (1742), a delightful, sharply focused contextual commentary. John Wesley* wrote, 'I know of no commentator on the Bible to equal Bengel,' and he abridged the *Gnomon* (which here means something like 'pointer to') as the basis of his *Explanatory Notes upon the New Testament*. The *Gnomon* has been translated into English more than once (by A. R. Fausset, 5 vols., Edinburgh, 1857–58; C. T. Lewis and M. R. Vincent, 2 vols., Philadelphia, 1860–62), and it is still being reprinted.

Bengel was a Württemberg pietist,* 'who in his biblicism approximated to the attitude of orthodoxy and in his moralism to that of the Christian Enlightenment' (Barth). An heir of Johannes Cocceius (1603–69; see Covenant Theology*) as well as an opponent of the 'neology' of the Enlightenment,* he also espoused a prophetic chiliasm (see Millennium*) in an exposition of the Apocalypse (partial ET, London, 1757) and some chronological works which fixed the start of the millennium in 1836.

Bibliography

M. Brecht in *TRE* 5, pp. 583–589 (with bibliography); J. C. F. Burk, *A Memoir of the Life and Writings of John Albert Bengel* (London, 1837).

D.G.D.

BERDYAEV, NICOLAI, see RUSSIAN ORTHODOX THEOLOGY.

BERENGAR (*c.* 999–1088). Theologian, the last important opponent of transubstantiation before Wyclif.* He was rector of the schools of St Martin at Tours and archdeacon of Angers. In 1049 he addressed a letter to Lanfranc (*c.* 1005–89), then prior of Bec, and a firm upholder of the eucharistic* teaching of Paschasius Radbertus,* in which he declared himself a disciple of John Scotus Eriugena* (to whom he may also have attributed the treatise of Ratramnus*) and an opponent of Paschasius. As a result of these opinions, and his persistence in them, he was condemned at a series of synods and for a time excommunicated. He was also forced to make several recantations, including the notorious 'Ego Berengarius . . .' (1059), stating that the body and blood of Christ are 'perceptibly, and not only symbolically but truly, touched and broken by the hands of the priests and ground by the teeth of the faithful'. His chief work, *De Sacra Coena* (*On the Holy Supper*), written in reply to a treatise of Lanfranc about 1068–70, was lost until 1770. The positive teaching it gives is a form of symbolism,* though Berengar devotes much of the work to vindicating his own conduct and advancing logical objections to transubstantiation.

Bibliography

Critical edition of *De Sacra Coena* in W. H. Deekenkamp (ed.), *Kerkhistorische Studien* 2 (The Hague, 1941); N. Dimock, *The 'Ego Berengarius'* (London, 1895); A. J. Macdonald, *Berengar and the Reform of Sacramental Doctrine* (London, 1930).

R.T.B.

BERKELEY, GEORGE (1685–1753). Irish philosopher, bishop and apologist. Born in Kilkenny and educated at Trinity College, Dublin, he was ordained in the Anglican church in 1707, and from 1728 to 1731 was engaged in efforts to found a college in Bermuda for missionary work. From 1734 to his death he was Bishop of Cloyne.

Although his writings on the philosophy of science are also of interest, Berkeley is best known for the 'immaterialism' developed in his *Principles of Human Knowledge* and *Three Dialogues between Hylas and Philonous*. The colours, sounds and sensations ('ideas' in Berkeley's terminology) of which we are directly aware – these are real enough; so are the minds which perceive them. But there is no need to suppose any inert 'material substance' underlying ideas in some indefinable way yet unknowable except through them; indeed, such a concept is meaningless. Physical objects consist of 'ideas', and their *esse* is *percipi*, their existence consists in being perceived; a wholly unperceived object is impossible. Since, however, no-one doubts that objects exist when we ourselves do not perceive them, there must be another mind which is always aware of them all, the infinite mind of God. Furthermore, since 'ideas' do not cause one another, and there is no 'material substance' to cause them, their sources must be minds or spirits. (Scientific

87

laws express patterns of events among things, but do not explain their existence.) We ourselves cause some 'ideas', those of memory and imagination, but most have to be ascribed to another spirit – God.

In *Alciphron*, his only purely apologetic work, Berkeley added a further argument, not dependent on immaterialism, to the traditional argument from design (see Natural Theology*). The best indication of person-hood is language, that is, signs used to convey meaning but having no intrinsic connection with the thing signified. And this is precisely the relationship our visual experiences have to the things they inform us about: thus, small size and faintness indicate distance, although they neither entail nor resemble it. Visual impressions are thus analogous to human language, 'the universal language of the Author of nature', whereby he instructs and guides us, and proof of his reality and personhood.

Berkeley was a philosopher and apologist, not a theologian, and somewhat doubtful of the value of theology. 'The Christian religion', he said in a sermon, 'was calculated for the Bulk of Mankind, and therefore cannot consist in subtle and nice Notions.' Its mysteries were to be accepted in humility and faith, not measured by reason. But reason could defend them against atheist* or deist* critics, show the reasonableness of religion generally, and support the idea of revelation.

Bibliography

Works ed. by A. A. Luce and T. E. Jessup, 7 vols. (London, 1948–56); selections in *Principles of Human Knowledge* (London, 1962) and *Philosophical Works* (London, 1910).

A. A. Luce, *Life of George Berkeley* (London, 1949); E. A. Sillem, *George Berkeley and the Proofs for the Existence of God* (London, 1957); G. Warnock, *Berkeley* (Harmondsworth, 1953).

R.L.S.

BERKHOF, HENDRIKUS (b. 1914). Professor of systematic theology at the University of Leiden, and one of the most significant Reformed* dogmaticians of the 20th century. His work combines a thorough familiarity with and appreciation of the traditions of classical Reformed dogmatics* with a sensitivity towards developments in contemporary theology and philosophy. His

main work, *Christian Faith*, is one of the most persuasive attempts to write a systematic theology* in recent decades, not least because of its lively use of biblical criticism,* and because of its sympathetic but not uncritical relationship to classical orthodoxy. Berkhof has also written on the theology of history in *Christ the Meaning of History*, which contains valuable discussions of existentialist* and salvation-history treatments of the theme. His work on *The Doctrine of the Holy Spirit* is one of the best surveys of the territory by a contemporary Protestant theologian. Berkhof has also been much involved in ecumenical affairs.

Bibliography

Works in ET: *Christ and the Powers* (London, 1962); *Christ the Meaning of History* (London, 1966); *Christian Faith. An Introduction to the Study of the Faith* (Grand Rapids, MI, 1979, ²1986); *The Doctrine of the Holy Spirit* (London, 1964); *Well-founded Hope* (London, 1969).

J.B.We.

BERKHOF, LOUIS (1873–1957). Reformed* theologian, influential chiefly through the use in seminaries, colleges and churches of his frequently reprinted *Systematic Theology* (1941, first published in 1932 under the title *Reformed Dogmatics*).

Born in the Netherlands, Berkhof went to the USA in 1882. He graduated from the Christian Reformed Church's Calvin College and Seminary before taking further studies at Princeton Seminary (1902–4) under B. B. Warfield* and G. Vos.* From 1906–44 he served in various capacities at Calvin Seminary, including that of president from 1931.

Berkhof was heavily dependent on the Dutch Reformed tradition (and especially H. Bavinck*). The strength of his *magnum opus* lay in its presentation of that tradition in English dress and in a clear textbook format with up-dated discussions (*e.g.* of the earlier Barth*) rather than in any theological creativity.

Less well known is his earlier work which displayed considerable interest in the development of a coherent Reformed world-and-life-view (*e.g. The Church and Social Problems*, Grand Rapids, MI, 1913; *The Christian Laborer in the Industrial Struggle*, Grand

Rapids, MI, 1916). In 1920–21 he delivered the Stone Lectures at Princeton Seminary on 'The Kingdom of God in Modern Life and Thought' (published under that title in 1951). In the absence of a more adequate recent compendium of Reformed theology in English, his *Systematic Theology* has continued to enjoy widespread circulation.

Bibliography

James D. Bratt, *Dutch Calvinism in Modern America: A History of a Conservative Subculture* (Grand Rapids, MI, 1984); H. Zwaanstra, 'Louis Berkhof', in D. F. Wells (ed.), *Reformed Theology in America* (Grand Rapids, MI, 1985).

S.B.F.

BERKOUWER, GERRIT CORNELIS (b. 1903), Reformed* theologian. Having served as a part-time lecturer in the Free University of Amsterdam since 1940, he was in 1945 appointed to the chair of dogmatics,* a chair which had formerly been held by A. Kuyper,* H. Bavinck* and V. Hepp (1879–1950). Undoubtedly he felt attracted to the biblical-historical approach of Bavinck rather than to the more speculative approach of Kuyper and the strongly scholastic method of Hepp. His doctoral thesis of 1932 dealt with the relationship between faith* and revelation* in recent German theology. This relationship has held his attention throughout his entire theological career. In his early years there were two main foci of interest, the first being the theology of Karl Barth.* In his first major work *Karl Barth* (1936) he proved to be very critical. In his second major work (*The Triumph of Grace in the Theology of Karl Barth*, 1954; ET, Grand Rapids, MI, and London, 1956) he showed a more sympathetic understanding of Barth's intentions, although incisive criticism was by no means lacking.

Berkouwer's second focus of interest was Roman Catholic theology.* In his first major volume on Roman Catholic dogma, *Barthianisme en Katholicisme* (1940), criticism again prevailed. This was still true of the second (*Conflict with Rome*, 1948; ET, Philadelphia, 1958), although the general approach was more conciliatory. In 1961 he was invited to be an official observer at Vatican II. Since then he has published two other volumes on Catholic theology: *The Second Vatican Council and the New Theology* (Grand Rapids, 1965) and *Nabetrachting op het Concilie (Reflection after the Council*, Kampen, 1968), in which he offered a penetrating analysis of both the council and recent Catholic theological thinking.

Berkouwer's main achievement, however, is his series of *Studies in Dogmatics*, in which he treated several *loci* of dogmatics (Dutch ed., 18 volumes, most of which are available in ET, Grand Rapids, MI, 1952–75).

He has never written a formal introduction to theology (prolegomena), but it is quite evident that the guiding idea in all his theologizing is the correlation between faith and revelation (*cf.* the titles of his first *Studies in Dogmatics: Faith and Justification*, 1954, *Faith and Sanctification*, 1952, and *Faith and Perseverance*, 1958). God's revelation is never a communication of revealed truths, but it is God's coming in Jesus Christ to the sinner. This revelation can be accepted only in faith. No salvation without faith! Faith, however, is not a constitutive factor in the process of revelation but is totally dependent upon and directed towards its object: God's salvation in Christ. This correlation makes Berkouwer's theology strongly anti-speculative and anti-scholastic. All our theology has to be 'preachable'. Increasingly he also turned against all causal-deterministic ways of thinking (*cf.* his volume on *Divine Election*, 1960). The *sola Scriptura* of the Reformers has deeply appealed to him and increasingly determined his own theology. The question has been raised whether his correlation method and the return to the 'pre-scientific' *sola Scriptura–sola fide* approach of the Reformers (De Moor, pp. 46ff.) does not lead to a limitation of the possibilities of theology and to too easy a retreat to the notion of 'mystery'.

Bibliography

A Half Century of Theology (Grand Rapids, MI, 1977).

Alvin Baker, *A Critical Evaluation of G. C. Berkouwer's Doctrine of Election* (Dallas, 1976); Charles Millar Cameron, *The Problem of Polarization: An Approach Based on the Writings of G. C. Berkouwer* (PhD thesis, University of Glasgow, 1983); P. D. Collord, *The Problem of Authority for Dogmatics in G. C. Berkouwer* (PhD dissertation, University of Iowa, 1964); G. W. de Jong, *De Theologie van Dr. G. C. Berkouwer. Een Structurele Analyse* (Kampen, 1971); J. C. de Moor,

Towards a Biblically Theological Method. A Structural Analysis and a Further Elaboration of Dr. G. C. Berkouwer's Hermeneutic-dogmatic Method (Kampen, 1980); S. Meijers, *Objectiviteit en Existentialiteit* (Kampen, 1979), pp. 149–273; L. B. Smedes, 'G. C. Berkouwer', in P. E. Hughes (ed.), *Creative Minds in Contemporary Theology* (Grand Rapids, MI, 1966), pp. 63–97.

K.R.

BERLIN DECLARATION. The 'Berlin Declaration on Ecumenism' (BDE), entitled *Freedom and Fellowship in Christ* (1974), is a radical critique of the recent theological direction of the World Council of Churches (WCC). It also affirms the theological convictions on which its criticism is based, and calls for a return towards a biblically based concern for Christian unity.

It was produced by the same Theological Convention of Confessing Fellowships which issued the Frankfurt Declaration,* in co-operation with others all over the world who had responded positively to the Frankfurt Declaration. It was intended as a critical but constructive contribution to the forthcoming Fifth Assembly of the WCC which was to take place in 1975 in Nairobi under the theme 'Christ Frees and Unites'. The text was adopted at the first European Confession Congress in Berlin in May 1974, exactly forty years after the historic first Confessing Synod of the Evangelical Church in Germany which had issued the Barmen Declaration.* In 1975, prior to the Nairobi Assembly, a volume documenting the Declaration in detail (listed below) was presented to leaders of the WCC and the Lutheran World Federation as well as to the Vatican Secretariat on Christian Unity.

In twelve affirmations and refutations recent ecumenical* pronouncements on the Christological, soteriological and ecclesiological aspects of the Nairobi theme are analysed and condemned for their politicizing and syncretizing tendencies, while the authentic biblical content of these terms is expounded. The Declaration's call for a coming together of concerned Christian groups world-wide was partly fulfilled in the formation of the Lausanne* Movement for World Evangelization later the same year.

The BDE has been used as a model for similar declarations, *e.g.* the Seoul Declaration on Christian Missions (1975).

Bibliography
Hendrikus Berkhof, 'Berlin versus Geneva: Our Relationship with the "Evangelicals"', *Ecumenical Review* 28 (1976), pp. 80–86; Walter Künneth/Peter Beyerhaus (eds.), *Reich Gottes oder Weltgemeinschaft? Die Berliner Ökumene-Erklärung zur utopischen Vision des Weltkirchenrats* (Bad Liebenzell, 1975).

P.P.J.B.

BERNARD OF CLAIRVAUX (1090–1153). Bernard was born at Fontaines (near Dijon) of noble parents. At the age of twenty-one he entered the recently-founded abbey of Cîteaux, at that stage the only abbey of the new and strict Cistercian order. Three years later Bernard was appointed abbot of a new monastery, at Clairvaux. Under Bernard it grew rapidly and during his lifetime became parent to some seventy new Cistercian abbeys.

Bernard went to Cîteaux to flee the world, but in time he became one of the most active and widely-travelled leaders of the 12th-century church. During the 1130s he campaigned for Pope Innocent II against the rival pope, Anacletus. Eventually he secured Innocent's victory, which gained many favours for the Cistercians. Later he opposed the teaching of Peter Abelard,* securing his condemnation at the Council of Sens in 1140 and thereafter by the pope. His authority was further enhanced when one of his own monks, Bernard Paganelli, became Pope Eugenius III in 1145. In the next two years, at Eugenius' request, Bernard preached round Europe, raising support for the Second Crusade. This was launched in 1148 but failed dismally, a severe blow for Bernard. But his reputation was great enough to survive such a setback, and his popularity has never really waned.

Bernard has been called 'the last of the fathers'. He was the last great representative of the early medieval tradition of monastic theology.* He was a brilliant writer, earning himself the title 'mellifluous' (sweet as honey). He preached regularly and many of his sermons survive. Some are unpolished, probably much as originally preached. Others are in a highly polished literary form, designed for reading. These are mostly based on various Sundays and saints' days throughout the church year. Bernard corresponded widely and more than five hundred of his letters survive, ranging from the personal and devotional to the official and political. Some are virtually treatises, on baptism,* on the office of bishop and against the errors of Abelard.

Bernard wrote a number of treatises. Three of these are on monasticism: his *Apology* for the Cistercians against the Cluniacs, *Precept and Dispensation* on the correct interpretation of the Rule of St Benedict* and a treatise *In Praise of the New Knighthood* on the new order of Templars. He also wrote a biography of Archbishop Malachy of Armagh (1094–1148), who helped to bring the Irish church into line with Roman practices.

In his early years Bernard wrote a masterly treatise on *Grace and Freewill*. In this he relates the work of grace* and of the human will,* along Augustinian* lines. He argues that our good works are at the same time entirely the work of God's grace (thus leaving no room for boasting) and entirely the work of our freewill in that it is *we* who perform them (thus providing a basis for merit* and reward).

Towards the end of his life Bernard wrote on *Consideration* for his former disciple, Pope Eugenius III. Bernard urges him to find time for reflection or meditation in his busy life. He sees the pope as 'the unique vicar of Christ who presides not over a single people but over all' and has fullness of power. But he is equally emphatic in his opposition to papal tyranny (see Papacy*).

Bernard is best known as a spiritual writer. His book on *Loving God* has been called 'one of the most outstanding of all medieval books on mysticism'*. His *Steps of Humility and Pride* is based on the twelve steps of humility described in the Rule of St Benedict. But his best-known spiritual work is his eighty-six *Sermons on the Song of Solomon*, allegedly commenting on Song of Solomon 1:1 – 3:1, but in reality a treatise in sermonic form on the spiritual life of the monk.

Bibliography

Works in *PL* 182–185. Critical edition: J. Leclercq, H. Rochais, *et al.* (eds.), *Sancti Bernardi Opera*, 8 vols. (Rome, 1957–77). ET of works in the Cistercian Fathers series (Kalamazoo, MI, 1970ff.).

G. R. Evans, *The Mind of St Bernard of Clairvaux* (Oxford, 1983); E. Gilson, *The Mystical Theology of Saint Bernard* (London, 1940); J. Leclercq, *Bernard of Clairvaux and the Cistercian Spirit* (Kalamazoo, MI, 1976);

E. Vacandard, *Vie de Saint Bernard*, 2 vols. (Paris, 1895).

A.N.S.L.

BEZA, THEODORE (1519–1605). As Calvin's* successor Beza was the acknowledged champion of Genevan orthodoxy and chief spokesman for Reformed* Protestantism. In Geneva he served as moderator of the clergy (1564–80), rector of the Academy (1559–63) and professor of theology (1559–99). In addition, through generations of students, pastors, men and women of state and merchants who knew him personally and through correspondence, Beza's influence was felt in France, Britain, the Netherlands, Poland and Germany. It was principally through his writings, however, that Beza became established as the skilful polemicist and man of letters, indeed the authoritative guide for defining the doctrinal integrity of the Reformed faith. He wrote close to one hundred treatises, mostly polemical writings on the eucharist,* Christology,* and the church.* His *magnum opus*, the *Novum Testamentum*, was dedicated to Queen Elizabeth in 1565.

The interpretation of Beza's thought and his role in the development of Calvinism* has caused considerable controversy. His fidelity to Calvin was accepted by contemporaries, but by the middle of the 17th century Peter Heylyn (1600–62) in England and Amyraut* on the Continent found Beza responsible for hardening Calvin's theology. Such protests were largely ignored until Heinrich Heppe (1820–79) articulated this thesis in his 19th-century study of Beza's role in the development of the rational element in Calvinism. This challenge won few converts within 19th-century Calvinism which cherished the very rational coherence of the Calvinist system that Heppe deplored. By the middle of the 20th century the tide had turned in the historiography. By then Barth's* revolutionary theology had created a more favourable climate for a new interpretation of Calvin which celebrated the dynamic, Christological and biblical centre of his theology over against the more metaphysical* and systematic structure of the Calvinism attributed to Beza.

Certainly, one finds in Beza's writings a greater openness to Aristotelian* metaphysics* and dialectic, more reliance on patristic* authority and more insistence on systematic coherence: all of which served to re-shape Calvin's theology into a more tightly argued, logically unassailable body of truth. But this does not mean that he produced a rational synthesis based on a metaphysic of God's decree, or that there is a direct line from Beza to 17th-century Reformed scholasticism, as the German school of interpretation has insisted.

Evidence from recent studies calls for a revision of this thesis. Beza's education within French humanism* had a lasting impact on both the style and content of his theology. Using the literary models of Greek and Roman literature, humanism was drawn into the rhetorical and ethical style and concerns of the classics. Moreover, the logic and philosophy which Beza absorbed in Paris was a more broadly based Aristotelianism than the technical, impersonal and increasingly abstruse nature of medieval scholasticism.* It is this literary culture of French humanism which separates Beza from any easy identification with scholasticism and which binds him closely to the religious and biblical centre of his mentor's theology.

Bibliography

Many theological treatises in *Tractationes Theologicae*, 3 vols. (1570–82). Correspondence in *Correspondance de Théodore de Bèze* (Geneva, 1960–1983), vols. 1–11.

Studies: P. F. Geisendorf, *Théodore de Bèze* (Geneva, 1949); W. Kickel, *Vernunft und Offenbarung bei Theodor Beza* (Neukirchen-Vluyn, 1967); R. Letham, 'Theodore Beza: A Reassessment', *SJT* 40 (1987), pp. 25–40; T. Maruyama, *The Ecclesiology of Theodore Beza* (Geneva, 1978); J. Raitt, *The Eucharistic Theology of Theodore Beza* (Chambersburg, PA, 1972).

I.McP.

BIBLE TRANSLATION. From the beginning, the church's Gentile mission made it necessary to translate into Greek the sayings of Jesus spoken in Aramaic. There was a precedent for this in the Greek translation of the Old Testament, the Septuagint (LXX), on which most quotations in the New Testament are based. But Christians, more consistently than for example Jews or Muslims, have normally assumed that vernacular translations of the Scriptures were a necessary expression of the universality of their faith and witness.

Current Scripture translations are generally based on principles which are not radically different from those applied instinctively by the best older translators, but which have been clarified by the insights of modern linguistics.

The most fundamental of these, known as the principle of dynamic equivalence, is that translation should normally give priority to reproducing the meaning of the text, rather than its sounds or its grammatical structures. Exceptions to this rule are special translations, such as interlinear versions for students learning the biblical language, and where there are special sound effects in the original, such as plays on words. It should also be noted that meaning includes not only reference, but also such features as emphasis and emotion, equivalents for which are sought in translation.

Thus, meaning has priority, especially over grammar. A modern Bible translator will frequently, for example, translate a Greek abstract noun such as *metanoia* by 'to repent', if the text refers to an action more suitably expressed in the receptor (or target) language by a verb. Similarly, the order of words and clauses may be changed in translation, in order to convey the meaning more clearly, faithfully and naturally in the receptor language. Recognized procedures for the analysis of meaning, at every level from the individual word to the entire discourse, are applied by Bible translators in many parts of the world.

Languages spoken by large groups of people tend to operate at different levels or registers, from the highly literary to the colloquial. There is wide agreement that although literary translations of the Bible often serve a useful function, priority is best given to translations in common language, as used by the great majority of native speakers.

In English, the Good News Bible (Today's English Version) perhaps most consistently applies the principle of dynamic equivalence; it is also a common language translation. The New English Bible is a generally dynamic equivalent translation in literary language. Some other modern translations, such as the New International Version, make some use of the dynamic equivalence principle.

Modern Bible translations are thus designed to transfer, as precisely as possible, the meaning and content of the original text. They are quite different from so-called 'paraphrases' (a term not used in this sense by linguists), which tend to adapt or 'up-date' historical and cultural features of the original – so that, to take an extreme example, the cross may become an electric chair. This is no part of translation, which is an entirely linguistic process; it is also contrary to the nature of Christianity as a historical faith.

Where a modern reader has difficulty in understanding major cultural features of the biblical text, he may be aided by footnotes, glossaries, or other readers' helps, and on a larger scale by study Bibles or commentaries. Where, however, such cultural features are referred to incidentally, for example in similes, they may be adapted: for example 'white as snow' may become 'white as wool' in a language spoken in a tropical country.

Bibliography

John Beekman and John Callow, *Translating the Word of God* (Grand Rapids, MI, 1974); Mildred L. Larson, *Meaning-based Translation. A Guide to Cross-Language Equivalence* (Lanham, MD, 1984); E. A. Nida and C. R. Taber, *The Theory and Practice of Translation*, (Leiden, ²1974).

P.E.

BIBLICAL CRITICISM applies to the biblical writings a variety of techniques employed in the examination of many kinds of literature in order to ascertain their original wording, the nature of their composition, their sources, date, authorship and the like.

Textual criticism

Textual criticism is the discipline which endeavours to restore the original text of documents which have been exposed to the hazards of successive copying and recopying. When each individual copy had to be made separately by hand, before the invention of printing in Western Europe about 1450, scribal slips and alterations tended to be multiplied each time the process was repeated. Copies can be corrected by reference to the autograph, where that survives, but in most ancient literature (including all the biblical books) it has disappeared. The original text can then be reconstructed only by careful comparative study of surviving copies. Usually, but not invariably, earlier copies have suffered less from alterations than later ones. The scribal habits of individual copyists and schools of copyists must be studied; the main types of error must be identified and classified, a distinction being made between those that are due to imperfect reading of a master-copy and those that arise from imperfect hearing where the copying is done from dictation.

The biblical textual critic works not only on manuscripts of the OT and NT in the original languages but also on early versions in other languages (notably Syriac, Coptic and Latin; see Biblical Versions*) and biblical quotations in early authors.

In the OT the basis is the Masoretic text of the Hebrew Bible, given its final shape between the 7th and 11th centuries AD, but going back, so far as the consonantal text is concerned, to *c.* AD 100. Since the discovery of the Qumran manuscripts (see Dead Sea Scrolls*) in 1947 and the years following, evidence has become available for tracing the history of the Hebrew Bible back to a period a thousand years earlier than the final establishment of the Masoretic text. The main version which helps in the textual study of the OT is the Septuagint (LXX), the Greek translation made in Alexandria in the 3rd and 2nd centuries BC.

In the NT a number of early text-types can be discerned in the 4th and 5th centuries AD, but an increasing number of copies, mainly on papyrus, have come to light from the 3rd and even the 2nd century, antedating those text-types. NT textual study is being vigorously prosecuted, and even the latest standard critical editions are best recognized as interim reports.

The establishment of a reasonably reliable text is a necessary condition for further critical or exegetical study. At one time textual criticism was known as 'lower criticism' because it represented the lower courses in the edifice of biblical study.

Literary and historical criticism

Literary and historical criticism was at one time called 'higher criticism' because it presupposed the findings of 'lower' or textual criticism. Higher criticism was concerned with three issues: literary structure, date and authorship – but the term is now virtually obsolete.

Source criticism – the discernment of the oral or written sources on which a literary work has drawn – can be pursued with greater confidence when one or more written sources

93

of a work have survived alongside it. The author of Chronicles, for example, used Samuel and Kings among his sources, and a comparison of his work with those sources enables the student to reach fairly firm conclusions about his literary and historical method. In the NT Mark is commonly recognized as a major source of Matthew and Luke; since Mark has survived independently, it is easier to be certain about Matthew and Luke's use of it than about their use of other sources, such as the hypothetical 'Q' (the compilation of sayings of Jesus believed to underlie the non-Marcan material common to Matthew and Luke).

Where the sources have disappeared, their reconstruction must be largely speculative. It would, for example, be practically impossible to reconstitute our four separate gospels if they had disappeared, leaving extant only Tatian's *Diatessaron* – a continuous narrative (produced *c*. AD 170) weaving together material from all four, using John's record as a framework.

It is possible to discern points in Acts where the author begins to follow a new source, but there is no way of reconstructing the sources on which he draws, because he integrates them so skilfully into the flow of his narrative. The one exception is the travel diary, which is easily recognized because the pronoun 'we' is left unaltered, instead of being replaced by 'they'. The author leaves 'we' unaltered in order to indicate unobtrusively that he was present at the incidents recorded in this first-person style.

Again, where a document existed in more than one recension, it is the province of literary criticism to distinguish earlier from later recensions. This can be a hazardous proceeding in the absence of explicit evidence; occasionally, however, such evidence is provided. It is plain, for example, that the first edition of the oracles of Jeremiah, reproducing his spoken ministry over twenty-three years and written at his dictation by Baruch, existed in only one copy which was almost immediately destroyed by Jehoiakim. But it was quickly followed by a second, enlarged edition (Je. 36:1–32), and even that was not the final edition, for Jeremiah continued to prophesy for some seventeen more years. Two editions survive of the posthumous collection of his oracles (accompanied by some biographical and other historical material) – a longer one

in the Masoretic text and a shorter one in the LXX. Among the Qumran documents are some fragmentary Hebrew copies of both editions.

Historical criticism includes the relating of documents to their historical context. This involves the correlation of internal and external evidence. The dramatic date of a narrative (the date of the events which it records) should be distinguished from the date of its composition. Those scholars, for example, who find that the patriarchal narratives of Genesis are true to their dramatic date (because they reflect the cultural situation in which the patriarchs are represented as living) usually agree that the date of composition of Genesis is several centuries later than the patriarchal age.

In the historical criticism of the prophets* the element of genuine prediction must be treated seriously. A genuine prediction is earlier than the event predicted but not earlier than the events presupposed as background to the prediction. On this ground, for example, Nahum's prophecy is to be dated between the fall of Thebes (663 BC), to which it refers as a past event (Na. 3:8–10), and the fall of Nineveh (612 BC), to which it looks forward. A detailed study of the prophecy will help to date it more precisely within that half-century.

Two schools of biblical criticism in the 19th century owed their special influence to their combining of literary and historical criticism. Julius Wellhausen (1844–1918), building on his predecessors' literary criticism of the Pentateuch, found his basic principle in the history of the Israelite cultus, at first practised in a wide variety of local sanctuaries but finally centralized in a single sanctuary. Unfortunately much of his reconstruction of the cultic development had to be carried out in a historical vacuum, and as fresh discoveries filled it in, the defects in his reconstruction were exposed.

Two generations earlier, Ferdinand Christian Baur (1792–1860) and other members of the Tübingen school* reconstructed the history of the apostolic and sub-apostolic age by postulating a primitive antithesis between the interpretation of the gospel promoted by Peter and the church of Jerusalem and that represented by Paul and the Gentile mission. This antithesis gave way in the 2nd century to a synthesis presented in most of the NT writings, including in particular Acts and Ephesians – the synthesis which was perpetuated in the Catholic Church. The Tübingen school exaggerated the antithesis, underestimating Peter's positive role as a bridge-builder and unduly extending the time-scale required for the development which it envisaged. The final stage of this development was pushed back into the 1st century when Joseph Barber Lightfoot (1828–89) demonstrated the early 2nd-century date of the seven genuine letters of Ignatius (*The Apostolic Fathers*, pt. II, vol. 1, London, 1885, [2]1889).

Tradition and form criticism

Except when an author is relating, directly from personal knowledge, events that have taken place within his experience, or imparting teaching that is immediately his own, the earlier history of the material recorded is a subject for critical study. Since it has, by one means or another, been 'delivered' to him, its previous transmission must be examined. If it has been received in the form of written documents, source criticism will go some way in dealing with them. But if it has been delivered orally, it constitutes more particularly the subject-matter of tradition criticism. This can be applied in the OT to narratives, laws, poems and wisdom sayings which passed through a stage of oral transmission before being written down. In the NT it has been applied to the gospel material, although here the gap between the events and the extant documents which record them is very much smaller. Yet the gospel was preached before it was written, and it is helpful to study the stages of its oral presentation. The process is even more speculative than documentary source criticism. If appeal is made to the 'laws' of oral tradition, it must be remembered that these 'laws' are observed regularities and tendencies, and should not be applied where they do not fit.

One important aspect of tradition criticism is form criticism – the study of the 'forms' which the material took in the course of being handed down. In the OT this approach has proved fruitful in the study of the Psalms: they are classified according to their principal types, each type being related to its life-setting in communal worship or private devotion.

In the NT the form criticism of the gospels – the classification of their narratives and sayings according to their principal 'forms' – has been made the basis of an attempt to trace their history in the pre-literary stage. Despite exaggerated claims, form classification throws but little light on the historicity of any particular incident or utterance. With form classification has been linked the attempt to ascertain the life-setting of the various units of the gospel tradition. Here different life-settings must be distinguished – the life-setting in the ministry of Jesus, successive life-settings in the course of the tradition (what were the factors which dictated the preservation of certain incidents and sayings when others have been lost?), and the life-setting of the final literary work. When we reach this stage, tradition criticism makes way for redaction criticism. Thanks to tradition and form criticism, it becomes clear that, no matter how far back the investigation may be pressed, one never reaches a stratum where a totally non-supernatural Jesus is portrayed.

When applied to the NT epistles, form criticism of another kind may help the student to recognize a complete epistle as reproducing the form of a forensic argument according to contemporary rhetorical standards (*cf.* H. D. Betz, *Galatians*, Philadelphia, 1979), or to subject some recurring feature of epistolary style to minute comparative study (*cf.* P. Schubert, *Form and Function of the Pauline Thanksgivings*, Berlin, 1939).

Redaction criticism

Redaction criticism is complementary to tradition criticism: it studies the use which an author makes of the material at his disposal, whether received by tradition or otherwise. It has been particularly fruitful in the study of the gospels, because it recognizes the evangelists as true authors and not mere compilers. Matthew, for example, is revealed by his handling of the material to be interested in the church as a fellowship in which the teaching of Jesus is to be transmitted and observed from the resurrection to the final consummation. Mark writes not only to encourage Christians suffering for their faith to 'take up the cross' and follow Jesus but also to present Jesus as the Son of God: this is the 'messianic secret' which is divulged at the end of the passion narrative in the rending of the veil and the centurion's confession. Luke views the ministry of Jesus as the fulfilment of the mighty works and prophetic words in which God revealed himself in OT times and as being continued and spread abroad in the apostolic witness. John brings

95

out the permanent and universal validity of the essential gospel by introducing Jesus as the incarnation of the eternal Word of God, manifesting the divine glory to all who are capable of discerning it.

In the OT redaction criticism has heralded a new day by encouraging students to think of the Pentateuch, for example, as a literary unit and to study the author's purpose and message (*cf.* D. J. A. Clines, *The Theme of the Pentateuch*, Sheffield, 1978).

Canon criticism

Canon criticism takes up where redaction criticism leaves off; it has a more theological content. In it the critical enterprise is directed to the completed canon of Scripture,* to the individual books in the new context and inter-relationships which they acquire through inclusion in the canon, and to their canonical (*i.e.* their final) form. This emphasis on the canonical form contrasts with the attempt to establish the 'original' form which is the concern of certain other critical approaches. Canon criticism does not displace the other critical approaches, but endeavours to complement them and bring them to their proper goal.

Structuralism

Structuralism* studies the operation and interaction of signs within a structured system, controlled by an underlying 'code'. Many structuralists disclaim all interest in the original historical setting and purpose of a document: what concerns them is the final form of the text as a linguistic or semantic phenomenon. Its message is held to be true or relevant in its own terms, not in historical terms. Any process which enables the reader to view biblical texts in a fresh light has positive value, but a discipline which excludes any consideration of the author's intention is unlikely to be fruitful for biblical study.

Bibliography

C. E. Armerding, *The Old Testament and Criticism* (Grand Rapids, MI, 1983); R. S. Barbour, *Traditio-Historical Criticism of the Gospels* (London, 1972); J. Barr, *Holy Scripture: Canon, Authority, Criticism* (Oxford, 1983); J. Blenkinsopp, *Prophecy and Canon* (Notre Dame, IN, 1977); R. E. Brown, *The Critical Meaning of the Bible* (London, 1982); B. S. Childs, *Introduction to the Old Testa-*

ment as Scripture (London, 1979); *idem*, *The New Testament as Canon: An Introduction* (London, 1984); A. M. Johnson (ed.), *The New Testament and Structuralism* (Pittsburgh, 1979); J. Knox, *Criticism and Faith* (London, 1953); K. Koch, *The Growth of the Biblical Tradition* (ET, London, 1969); E. Krentz, *The Historical-Critical Method* (London, 1976); G. E. Ladd, *The New Testament and Criticism* (Grand Rapids, MI, 1967); B. M. Metzger, *The Text of the New Testament* (Oxford, ²1968); N. Perrin, *What is Redaction Criticism?* (London, 1970); E. B. Redlich, *Form Criticism* (London, 1939); J. A. Sanders, *Torah and Canon* (Philadelphia, 1972); E. Würthwein, *The Text of the Old Testament* (ET, Grand Rapids, MI, ²1979).

F.F.B.

BIBLICAL THEOLOGY. The term 'biblical theology' seems to have been used first in the mid-17th century, in deliberate contrast to scholastic* theology. It was intended to refer to a theology based on the Bible, as distinct from a theology which consisted largely of philosophical ideas and religious traditions.

Since then, 'biblical theology' has come to mean something rather different. According to the former meaning, biblical theology was dogmatic* theology based on or consistent with the Bible. The modern meaning refers to a historical study of the theology found in the Bible itself. Such biblical theology is in principle more objective because its purpose is to discover what theology is in the Bible, without necessarily prejudging the authority of that theology or relating it to a particular religious tradition. It can be done by a Protestant or a Catholic, a liberal or a conservative, a Jew or a Moslem, or even an atheist, and indeed all may co-operate in understanding the theology of the Bible, in spite of radically different perceptions of its authority and relevance today. For the Christian who recognizes the Bible as divine revelation it will certainly have an extremely practical relevance, as is expressed by Harrington (1973): 'Biblical theology . . . is really our searching through the Scriptures to find life — eternal life' (p.18).

A problem arises concerning the validity of using the word 'theology'* with reference to the content of the Bible. If 'theology' is understood to mean a systematic statement of the doctrine of God, then it is found only to a very limited degree in the Bible. In conventional usage, however, the word often has a much broader meaning and may include almost any reference to the nature of God and his activity. We should understand this broader meaning in the term 'biblical theology'.

The history of biblical theology

The Reformation. 'The story should begin as far back as the Reformation, when the theological exegesis of a Martin Luther and a John Calvin let the Scriptures come open and speak with a power and clarity that set new regenerative forces working not only in the church but in the whole of the Western world' (Smart, 1979, p. 49). Although the term 'biblical theology' was apparently not used at that time, it might well be said that it sums up the aims of the Reformers. One of their principles was *sola Scriptura*, 'Scripture alone', and their primary concern was to ascertain the theology of the Bible and ensure that it be the basis of Christian theology.

Johann Philipp Gabler (1753–1826). In the 17th century the term 'biblical theology' was used with reference to a reform of dogmatic* theology, as we have seen, but in 1787 Gabler proposed a new approach by making a clear distinction between the two. He defined biblical theology as a descriptive discipline in distinction from the constructive discipline of dogmatic theology: 'Biblical theology is historical in character and sets forth what the sacred writers thought about divine matters; dogmatic theology, on the contrary, is didactic in character, and teaches what a particular theologian philosophically and rationally decides about divine matters in accordance with his character, time, age, place, sect or school, and other similar influences' (quoted by Bright, 1967, p. 114).

Gabler himself never wrote a biblical theology, but the principle he laid down became the basis for all future work in the subject.

Historical criticism. During the 19th century, interest in biblical theology dwindled due to the rise of historical criticism. The majority of scholars were concerned to develop the historical-critical approach to the Bible, or to oppose it, and few were interested in the Bible as a theological book. A number of books published with titles such as 'OT

theology' or 'NT theology' were in fact substantially *histories* of biblical religion, not theologies. With some notable exceptions (*e.g.* Johann von Hofmann, 1810–77), the Reformers' theological approach to the Bible was replaced by a strictly historical one.

It was supposed that this was more objective and avoided religious bias. To some extent that was true, but the fundamental problem was that it was concerned only with the historical aspects of the Bible and ignored the equally important theological aspects. The result was a chasm between biblical scholars with their purely historical interest and ordinary Christians who were concerned about the practical theological meaning of the Bible. Students left universities and seminaries academically qualified but quite unprepared for ministry in the church.

The 'biblical theology movement'. The beginning of a revolution in biblical studies was marked by the publication in Germany of Barth's* commentary on Romans. It was followed in the 1930s by Walther Eichrodt's great *Theology of the Old Testament* (1933–39) and Wilhelm Vischer's programmatic work, *The Witness of the Old Testament to Christ* (1934). In the English-speaking world the writings of H. Wheeler Robinson (1872–1945; OT) and C. H. Dodd* (NT) were influential.

Many works on biblical theology were published in the period after World War II, in what has often been called the 'biblical theology movement'. A wide variety of prominent scholars have been named in connection with this, such as Rudolf Bultmann,* Oscar Cullmann (see Salvation-History*), Gerhard von Rad (1901–71), Joachim Jeremias (1900–79), Ernst Käsemann* and Martin Buber* in Germany; Gabriel Hebert (1886–1963), H. H. Rowley (1890–1969) and Alan Richardson* in Britain; and G. E. Wright (1909–74), Paul Minear (b. 1906), John Bright (b. 1908), James Smart and John McKenzie in North America. Childs summarized five major emphases of the movement: rediscovery of the theological dimension, unity of the whole Bible, revelation* of God in history, distinctiveness of the biblical mentality (Hebrew thought in contrast to Greek thought), and the contrast of the Bible to its environment.

Whether such a diverse collection of theologians and theologies can legitimately be called a 'movement' is debatable. Probably only the first of Childs' five emphases would be accepted by all the above-named scholars. There is no doubt, however, that a revival and development of biblical theology took place and had a revolutionary effect on biblical and theological study. A number of new journals appeared, such as *Interpretation* (1947), publishing significant articles on the Bible and theology. In Germany steady progress was made on Gerhard Kittel's (1888–1948) massive *Theological Dictionary of the New Testament* (1933–79; ET, 1964–76), and a major commentary series with a distinctively theological emphasis was launched in 1952 under the title *Biblical Commentary on the Old Testament*. The SCM Press began their long series of 'Studies in Biblical Theology' (1950) and not a few substantial works on Old Testament theology* and New Testament theology* were written.

Biblical theology today. Not surprisingly there were negative reactions to the 'biblical theology movement' from established biblical scholarship, and this was especially the case in North America. One of the most outspoken critics during the 1960s was James Barr (b. 1924), who showed that it was an over-simplification to contrast Hebrew and Greek thought and that revelation in history should not be over-emphasized in comparison with other forms of revelation. Childs (1970) went so far as to claim that the movement had collapsed. However, although some of its aspects have had to be modified, its most fundamental achievement holds good, that of demonstrating the theological dimension of the Bible.

Biblical theology has gradually come to be accepted as an essential part of biblical interpretation alongside linguistic, literary and historical study. This is visible in the increasing theological content in progressive volumes of the 'New Century Bible' and 'Anchor Bible', and a number of commentary series with a specific theological emphasis (*e.g.* the 'Old Testament Library', 'International Theological Commentary', 'Interpretation'). Since Vatican II (see Councils*), Roman Catholic scholarship has taken a new interest in biblical theology. In almost every denomination the conviction remains that theology can only be truly Christian if based on or at least related to the Bible.

The unity of the Bible

In practice biblical theology has generally been divided into OT theology and NT theology. Only a few works have attempted an account of biblical theology as a whole (*e.g.* Burrows 1946; Vos 1948) or considered specific themes in the context of the whole Bible (*e.g.* Rowley 1953; Bauer 1959; Bruce 1968). Biblical study in general remains split in two, with little contact between OT theology and NT theology in spite of the theoretical recognition by each of the other's importance. More recently the studies of Gese (1977), Terrien (1978) and Cronk (1980) have renewed the attempt to write a biblical theology, but still on a relatively small scale.

No doubt one reason for this is the magnitude of the task. With more and more information available and opinions to consider it is becoming increasingly difficult to write a theology of the whole OT or NT, let alone the whole Bible.

Another more fundamental reason is a lingering uncertainty about the relationship between the OT and the NT. Marcion's* dismissal of the OT as a Jewish book of no value to Christians is no longer advocated explicitly, but many Christians still have reservations and uncertainties about its use in the church. The theological basis of the relationship between the testaments has been expounded in many scholarly works, by means of concepts such as kingdom of God,* salvation-history,* promise and fulfilment, typology (see Hermeneutics*). It has been generally agreed that the relationship is a complex one, involving tension between continuity and discontinuity, unity and diversity. On the one hand the unity of the Bible has been reaffirmed, together with the vital importance of each of its constituent testaments. On the other hand there has been a deepening realization that the OT and NT are different in function and authority, and their theologies cannot simply be combined to create a 'biblical theology'. A major aim of the discipline of biblical theology is therefore to achieve an understanding of the Bible as a whole which gives full consideration to both its unity and its diversity.

The nature and content of biblical theology

Whatever criticisms may be made against

particular approaches to biblical theology, the essential principle has been established: the Bible is a theological book and cannot be properly interpreted without reference to its theology. This is not to deny that the Bible also contains literature and history or to justify any interpretation of the Bible which ignores them. The point is simply that the Bible contains a great deal of theology, in the broad sense of thought and teaching about God and his activity, and this theology is of fundamental importance for the Christian faith. It follows that biblical scholarship needs to give at least as much attention to biblical theology as to biblical history and literature.

The subject-matter of biblical theology is the Bible as a whole. This does not necessarily mean that the whole Bible must be studied at once, but that every individual text and theme should be understood in the context of the whole. We may study the theology of the Psalms or of Paul, the concept of suffering in Job or the Spirit in John, so long as it is recognized that such studies are concerned with only one aspect of the biblical witness and will need to be supplemented and complemented from other sources before they can truly be called 'biblical theology'.

Biblical theology plays a vital part in both biblical studies and dogmatic theology, and in fact bridges the two. Since its *purpose* is to establish the theology contained in and expressed by the Bible, it employs biblical exegesis which, by means of textual, literary and historical criticism, establishes the intention of specific texts. In turn it furnishes the materials with which dogmatic theology, aiming to establish the teaching of the church, must build. Taking as its *subject-matter* the Bible as a whole, biblical theology needs the work of biblical exegetes on individual Bible texts. It is also essential to dogmatic theology's task of relating dogma to the Bible, church tradition, philosophy, culture, *etc.*

It is important to appreciate the role of biblical theology as intermediary between exegesis and dogmatics. None of these disciplines can stand alone or be omitted. Without thorough exegesis biblical theology will be superficial. Without biblical theology the church is liable to approach the Bible as a collection of proof-texts, picking out those suited to its particular interests and ignoring the witness of the Bible as a whole. Without dogmatic theology the Bible will remain an ancient book of an alien culture, unrelated to the modern world. Too often biblical exegesis and dogmatic theology have been engaged in independently of each other and of biblical theology. Recently there has been a trend towards increasing co-operation among the three disciplines and this gives hope of a much better understanding of the Bible and its theology, and thereby of the Christian faith, in the years ahead.

Bibliography

Definition and history: B. S. Childs, *Biblical Theology in Crisis* (Philadelphia, 1970); G. Ebeling, 'The Meaning of Biblical Theology', *JTS* 6 (1955), pp. 210–225; W. J. Harrington, *The Path of Biblical Theology* (Dublin, 1973); G. F. Hasel in *Perspectives on Evangelical Theology*, eds. K. S. Kantzer and S. N. Gundry (Grand Rapids, MI, 1959), pp. 179–194; H.-J. Kraus, *Die Biblische Theologie* (Neukirchen, 1970); J. D. Smart, *The Past, Present and Future of Biblical Theology* (Philadelphia, 1979); G. E. Wright, *God Who Acts: Biblical Theology as Recital* (London, 1952).

Unity of the Bible: B. W. Anderson (ed.), *The Old Testament and Christian Faith* (London, 1964); D. L. Baker, *Two Testaments, One Bible* (Leicester, 1976); J. Barr, *Old and New in Interpretation* (London, 1966); J. Bright, *The Authority of the Old Testament* (Nashville, TN, 1967); C. Westerman (ed.), *Essays on Old Testament Interpretation* (London, 1963).

Biblical theologies: F. F. Bruce, *This is That: The New Testament Development of Some Old Testament Themes* (London, 1968); M. Burrows, *An Outline of Biblical Theology* (Philadelphia, 1946); G. Cronk, *The Message of the Bible* (New York, 1980); H. Gese, *Essays on Biblical Theology* (1977; ET, Minneapolis, MN, 1981); H. H. Rowley, *The Unity of the Bible* (London, 1953); S. Terrien, *The Elusive Presence: Toward a New Biblical Theology* (New York, 1978); G. Vos, *Biblical Theology* (Grand Rapids, MI, 1948).

Journals and reference works: BTB (1971–); HBT (1979–); Int see especially 25, (1971), pp. 3–23, 41–62, 78–94 (various contributors, on 25th anniversary of *Int*); 36 (1982), pp. 34–46 (W. E. Lemke, 'Revelation through History in Recent Biblical Theology'); *IDB*, see especially vol. 1, pp. 418–437.

D.L.B.

BIBLICAL VERSIONS, THEOLOGY OF.

The theological tendency of a Scripture translation is the product of a number of factors, some general and some more specific.

General factors include the convictions of the translators, first that translation is *necessary*, because the biblical message is not intended only for speakers of the original languages, and secondly, that translation is *possible*, because the essential is the meaning of the biblical message, not its grammatical form, and also because any natural language can in principle convey the meaning of that message. Christians have not always held these convictions with equal firmness, but it is difficult to translate the Bible without holding them to some extent. From these basic principles, Protestants have traditionally drawn a conclusion which is now increasingly accepted in other Christian traditions: Bible translations should be directly accessible to all members of a language community, that is, they should be available in common language, the language of the people.

Special factors may also influence the theological tendency of a translation. These may be difficult to assess, for various reasons. First, one must consider the translation as a whole, not just isolated texts. For example, the Good News Bible should not be condemned for not using 'virgin' in Lk. 1:27, since it does so in v. 34. Secondly, the translation itself is more important than external evidence of the theology of individual translators, especially when these work as members of a team. Thirdly, theological and linguistic conservatism should not be confused: the Living Bible is theologically conservative but linguistically liberal.

The history of Bible translation is marked by movement between two extremes: adapting the meaning of the text to fit the readers' situation, or retaining the grammatical structure of the original at the expense of the meaning. Both extremes are theologically superficial approaches to the message of Scripture.

The earliest versions of Scripture were probably the Aramaic oral translations of OT books, ancestors of the extant targums which are themselves marked by moralizing expansion, allegorical transposition, avoidance of the name of God, and anachronism. Some of these features are found to a lesser degree in the LXX Greek translation of the OT. Manu-scripts of this translation were influenced by the beliefs of Christian copyists, who tended to assimilate OT passages to the form in which they are quoted in the NT. The same tendency is seen in the later Syriac versions; by contrast, the earliest Syriac translations point to a situation in which the authority of the OT was greater than that of the (still emerging) NT.

In the West, the Old Latin translations were marked by over-literalness, but also by vivid and down-to-earth expressions. Jerome's* Vulgate, planned as a revision of existing Latin versions, benefited from his knowledge of Hebrew, and provided a firmer basis for dialogue with Jews. Paradoxically, by the 16th century, the Vulgate had become theologically influential as the Bible of the West.

Luther's* German translation used with profit the renaissance in Greek and Hebrew studies. Luther's translation was largely written in common language for ordinary people. It also sometimes made implicit information explicit (*e.g.* 'faith alone' in Gal. 2:16).

In modern times, discussion of Scripture translation tends to revolve around two main themes. The first is the degree to which so-called 'theological key words' should be retranslated, where traditional terms such as 'justification'* are no longer generally understood. The second, more directly theological, theme is that of the unity and internal consistency of the Bible in its various parts. Here the choice is between on the one hand a view of the Bible which tends to minimize differences, *e.g.* between OT and NT forms of the same text, or between gospel parallels, and on the other hand faithfulness to the meaning of individual texts, allowing each part of Scripture to speak with its own distinctive voice, the unity of the Bible emerging at a deeper level.

Bibliography

B. M. Metzger, *The Early Versions of the New Testament* (Oxford, 1977); F. Kenyon, *The Text of the Greek Bible* (London, 1975); C. Buzzetti, *La Parola Tradotta* (Brescia, 1973); W. Schwarz, *Principles and Problems of Biblical Translation* (Cambridge, 1955).

P.E.

BIEL, GABRIEL (*c.* 1415–95).

One of the last great scholastic* theologians. After a lengthy university career at Heidelberg (arts) and Erfurt and Cologne (theology), during which he was exposed to both the *via antiqua* ('old way') of Thomas Aquinas* and Albertus Magnus* at Cologne and the *via moderna* of Duns Scotus* and William of Ockham* at Erfurt, he became in middle life a pastor and preacher. He was cathedral preacher at Mainz, and from the 1460s onwards a leading figure in the Brethren of the Common Life, especially as the first provost of their new house at Butzbach. From 1479 he was provost at Urach in Württemberg, combining his responsibilities with the professorship of theology at the new university at Wittenberg from 1484 to *c.* 1490.

Biel was a true disciple of Ockham's nominalism,* but was able to be critical of all schools of thought. Though 'a faithful preserver of the impressively coherent structure of the Occamistic system' (Oberman), his teaching was more explicitly theological than Ockham's, demonstrating nominalism's potential for pastoral application (as did his friend and follower, the famous Strasburg preacher John Geiler of Kaysersberg, 1445–1510; see the study by E. J. Dempsey Douglass, *Justification in Late Medieval Preaching*, Leiden, 1966). Biel's thought is increasingly appreciated both for its thorough grounding in earlier medieval tradition and for its influence on Catholic responses to the Reformation. He was prominent among the nominalist writers with whom Luther's* early theology critically engaged.

Bibliography

H. A. Oberman, *Forerunners of the Reformation: The Shape of Late Medieval Thought*, (London, 1967); *idem, The Harvest of Medieval Theology: Gabriel Biel and Late Medieval Nominalism* (Grand Rapids, MI, ²1967).

D.F.W.

BIOETHICS is concerned with the interface between ethics and modern medical technology as it affects the control of human life. Reflecting recent technological advances, interest is focused particularly on procedures to control or induce fertilization and to inhibit the process of dying. Clusters of theological and ethical issues arise, relating to God's sovereignty, man's value and stewardship of creation's resources, God's will for marriage and parenting, and the nature of human life.

Some Christians believe that procreative technology in effect seeks to usurp *God's sovereign* role* in deciding who shall be born and when. Scripture is clear that God is involved in parenthood (Gn. 4:1, 25; Ps. 100:3), and equally clear about the disasters which may follow when childless couples become impatient (*cf.* Abram and Sarai, Gn. 16). Those who make new lives in laboratories, therefore, and treat babies as human products subject to the technician's quality control, breathe an ethical air which is alien to the Bible's.

In Roman Catholic moral theology,* this view is firmly anchored in the doctrine of natural law.* It is natural for pregnancy to follow intercourse, the argument goes, so it is contrary to nature* (and therefore wrong) both to prevent pregnancy by contraception and to enhance fertility by artificial insemination (AID) or *in vitro* fertilization (IVF).

Those who oppose these conclusions draw support from the biblical principle of *stewardship*.* God gave man and woman the responsibility for managing the rest of creation and its resources (Gn. 1:28). He also told them, in the context of an under-populated world, to 'be fruitful and increase in number'. Two things follow, it is suggested. In the first place, because it is God's will for married couples to procreate, it is a thoroughly right use of advanced medical technology to help sub-fertile men and women to have children. And secondly, it is equally right to regard contraceptive technology as God's gift to help men and women limit pregnancies in a world that has become overcrowded.

The Bible's creation teaching also lays down foundations for a Christian appreciation of *human value and dignity*. In particular, the making of man and woman in God's image* has long persuaded Christian ethicists that it is wrong to use persons as means.

This principle clearly relates to the practices of surrogacy (male or female) and embryo experimentation. The desire to be a parent is right, but not all possible means may rightly be used to gain that end. To employ a semen donor or a surrogate mother in a quest for parenthood is to demote that third party to the sub-human status of spermator or wombleaser. And to seek long-term benefits for humanity by experimenting on embryos is to use some human beings as helpless means to gain happiness for others.

At the other end of life, euthanasia that is

the human equivalent of putting a suffering animal to sleep is unacceptable. Also, more controversially, the extensive use of surgical techniques and ventilatory support systems to postpone the dying process becomes ethically highly questionable, especially if the patient is being kept alive only for utilitarian purposes. Vitalism (the conviction that physical life must be preserved at all costs) is fundamentally idolatrous from the viewpoint of Christian theology.

Serious questions are also asked about the practices of artificial insemination and *in vitro* fertilization in the light of Christian teaching on sex,* marriage and parenting.

Traditional Roman Catholicism opposes these practices because, like contraception, they drive an illegitimate wedge between the two main purposes of sexual intercourse in marriage. The encyclical *Humanae Vitae* (1968) summarizes the objection by drawing attention to 'the inseparable connexion, willed by God and unable to be broken by man on his own initiative, between the two meanings of the conjugal act: the unitive meaning and the procreative meaning' (12).

Most Protestant ethicists, while agreeing that the two ends of sex in marriage (the relational and the procreative) must never be divorced, apply the principle to marriage taken as a whole, and not to every act of intercourse within it. Some, however, go on to argue that AID and IVF (by donor) drive an unhelpful wedge of a different kind by separating unethically between biological and social parenting. Morally, a donor of egg or semen cannot simply walk away from the child he or she has helped to procreate.

As a third party, the surrogate father or mother may also pose an unintentional threat to the 'one flesh' nature of the marriage relationship itself. The charge of adultery is not appropriate (because there is no act of intercourse, no sense of sexual desire, and no intention of infidelity), but sperm and egg retain personal links with their donors in a way that blood and kidneys do not.

Most crucially of all, the whole area of bio-ethics raises the issue of *life's nature and meaning*. At one end of the spectrum, the sophistication of life-support systems and resuscitation procedures has led to a redefinition of death as the absence of brain-stem activity; while, at the other end, serious debate continues about the beginnings of human

personhood. Does life (with full human value) begin at fertilization? If so, all experimentation on embryos must be resisted on ethical grounds. But if, for example, the emergence of the 'primitive streak' (at fifteen days) is regarded as the earliest possible moment when we can say that a person is present, prior to this point such experiments become defensible along with the wastage of 'spare' embryos associated with IVF.

Many Christians believe that the Bible's references to life before birth (see Abortion*) commit them to protecting the developing embryo from the very beginning as a person with full human rights. The value of human life, they argue, is conferred by God from the moment of conception and does not depend on the development of, for example, the nervous system. Others find this biblical evidence equivocal, and prefer to speak of potentiality in the earliest stages of womb-life.

All, however, are agreed that the tendency of a technological culture to locate an individual's value in his or her function (what he or she can do, rather than who he or she is) is totally unacceptable, whether we are thinking about life's beginning or end. In Richard McCormick's words, 'this is a racism of the adult world profoundly at odds with the gospel'.

Bibliography

D. G. Jones, *Brave New People* (Leicester, 1984); *idem, Manufacturing Humans: The challenge of the new reproductive technologies* (Leicester, 1987); R. A. McCormick, *How Brave a New World?* (London, 1981); O. M. D. O'Donovan, *Begotten or Made?* (Oxford, 1984); P. Ramsey, *Ethics at the Edges of Life* (New Haven, 1979).

D.H.F.

BLACK CONSCIOUSNESS emerged in South Africa in the late 1960s and early 1970s among black African university students and quickly spread to other sections of the black population to become the most influential philosophy among the black African (especially young) people. It is largely, though not exclusively, the creation of the brilliant student leader Steve Biko (1946–1977), whose death while in police custody sent shockwaves around the world.

Analysing the socio-economic situation of the black African people under apartheid (see

Race*), Biko perceived that they suffered from a double-sided oppression. Externally they were the victims of a political and economic system which excluded them from power and denied them social and financial justice. Internally black people were conditioned to feel inferior to, and be afraid of, the whites. As articulated by Biko, black consciousness holds that the way to political freedom lies in overcoming the inward alienation which enslaves the blacks. Biko held that it was necessary first to bring about 'mental emancipation as a precondition to political emancipation'. But it is not an individualistic effort at self-improvement, for black consciousness 'is in essence the realisation by the black man of the need to rally together with his brothers around the cause of their oppression – the blackness of their skin – and to operate as a group in order to rid themselves of the shackles that bind them to perpetual servitude'.

Black consciousness deliberately rejects the integrationist aims of white political liberalism, because whites will always set the agenda to protect their own interests. In a society in which white racism is so entrenched, there 'can be only one valid antithesis, *i.e.* a solid black unity to counterbalance the scale. If South Africa is to be a land where black and white live together in harmony without fear of group exploitation, it is only when these two opposites have interplayed and produced a viable synthesis of ideas and a *modus vivendi*.'

Black consciousness is not a South African version of American Negro black power. Biko himself saw it as 'a sequel to the attainment of independence by so many African states within so short a time'. Nor, though it has important points of contact with it, is it to be confused with black theology.* Biko saw the latter as 'a situational interpretation of Christianity. It seeks to relate the present-day black man to God within the given context of the black man's suffering and his attempts to get out of it.' Black consciousness, on the other hand, is an ideology of psychological and political change which does not, in principle, require belief in God, though many of its advocates are professing Christians.

Viewed theologically, black consciousness can be seen as an assertion of the dignity of the black man who, no less than the white, is God's image-bearer. However, it would appear, by its emphasis on a present separation between black and white, to deny in practice the unity and catholicity of the church of Christ in whom black and white are one (Gal. 3:28) – not in a future, more just society but here and now, even in a country so sadly divided as South Africa is at present.

Bibliography
Steve Biko, *I Write What I Like*, a selection of his writings edited by Aelred Stubbs (London, 1979).

D.P.K.

BLACK THEOLOGY as a term is a product of North American black Christianity. Its origins lie in the response of black church leaders to the civil rights movement of the 1960s and especially to black power.

Its links with black power are affirmed by James H. Cone (b. 1938), the foremost advocate of black theology. Black theology is 'the religious counterpart of the more secular term Black Power . . . the religious explication of the need for black people to define the scope and meaning of black existence in a white racist society. While Black Power focuses on the political, social and economic condition of black people, Black Theology puts black identity in a theological context, showing that Black Power is not only *consistent* with the Gospel of Jesus Christ, but that it *is* the Gospel of Jesus Christ.'

Cone's statement of the nature of black theology is the most militant; more cautious positions are taken by J. Deotis Roberts (b. 1927), Major J. Jones (b. 1919) and Gayraud Wilmore (b. 1921). However, the link made by Cone between 'black identity' and 'the Gospel of Jesus Christ' points to a fundamental perception shared by all exponents of black theology, that though the term is relatively recent, its intentions and concerns lie deep in the experience of oppression on the grounds of race* that has characterized the lives of black people in the USA. Black theology, therefore, is inseparable from black history; it represents a stiffening of intellectual confidence in a people who have come to see their history as being theologically significant. Black theology is an attempt to articulate that significance within the black Christian community and beyond it.

Being thus the expression of a black religious and historical tradition, writings in black theology have a profoundly personal and experiential character. The designation 'black' is insisted upon not merely because black theology is produced by black people, but because it describes a particular outlook on the world; it emerges from a *black* reading of the Scriptures, from a *black* hearing of Jesus and a *black* apprehension of him as the liberator of *black* people, Jesus himself being the *black* Messiah. In other words, there is such a thing as a *black* spirituality, experienced in the black worshipping community and it is this which ultimately authenticates black theology.

The elevation of ethnicity, in this case, blackness, into a theological category has been one of the most controversial features of black theology. Some observers of black theology, including some black Christians, have wondered whether black theology could justly claim to be Christian.

The advocates of black theology have a ready response to the criticism. For James Cone, the fact that black people did not reject the gospel brought to them by their white oppressors suggests that 'Black people had a different perception of the gospel than Whites'. In the words of Gayraud Wilmore, the most eminent contemporary historian of black religion: 'Blacks have used Christianity not as it was delivered to them by segregated white churches, but as its truth was authenticated to them in the experience of suffering, to reinforce an ingrained religious temperament and to produce an indigenous religion oriented to freedom and human welfare.'

To designate the gospel *black* and call Jesus *black* is simply to articulate this sense of freedom of black people who find in the Jesus of the black gospel the liberation which was denied them by white Christianity. Salvation is by the same token black, and whites can be saved only by becoming black, that is, by entering into the black experience of oppression by whites in the context of which Jesus is encountered as liberator. As early as 1894 Henry McNeal Turner (1834–1915), a bishop in the African Methodist Episcopal Church in the USA, had declared that, in view of the racial discrimination practised by white Christians against black people, 'God is a Negro'.

Black theology thus becomes the theological and intellectual framework in which the white interpretation and application of the gospel, experienced by blacks as dehumanizing, are set aside in favour of new interpretations derived from the black apprehension of Jesus and the biblical God as liberating.

Black theology in the USA has therefore rightly been called a 'black theology of liberation', akin to theologies of liberation* in other parts of the world, notably Africa, Asia and Latin America.

Affinities with black theology in South Africa are obvious; the political, social and economic conditions of black people under the apartheid system in South Africa make it inevitable that North American black theology should have an appeal.

And yet South African black theology has developed its own insights which set it apart in some important respects (*cf.* Black Consciousness*). South African black theology has been strikingly lacking in any espousal of violent revolution and has drawn on the non-violent option of Martin Luther King Jr. (1929–68) more than North American black theology has done so far. Hence Allan Boesak (b. 1946), a leading exponent of South African black theology declares: 'Following the direction pointed out to us by Martin Luther King Jr. Black theology [in South Africa] takes Christian love* very seriously, opting for agape, which stands at the very centre of God's liberating actions for his people.' Similarly Manas Buthelezi (b. 1935) rejects 'the quest for a Black Theology purely in terms of the awakening of black nationalism or the consolidation of Black Power', regarding this as 'an indiscriminate alignment of Christian black awareness with an emotionally charged political concept'.

Consequently South African black theology interprets 'blackness' as a theological category in a quite different way. Allan Boesak validates black power in the South African context by equating 'blackness' with 'humanness': 'Black power is the legitimate expression of our humanness; it is black people at last resuming their responsibility as whole human beings . . . Blackness does not in the first place designate skin colour. It is a discovery, a state of mind, a conversion, an affirmation of being (which is power).' This makes 'blackness' equivalent also to Buthelezi's 'wholeness' which results from the realization that 'blackness, like whiteness, is a good natural facecream from God and not some cosmological curse'.

Here South African black theology echoes the concerns and affirmations of African Christian theology* in a way that North American black theology, lacking in the religio-cultural context of Africa, is unable to do. Allan Boesak is right to suggest that 'Black Theology cannot be easily divorced from African Theology', that they are not 'two separate theologies, but two aspects of the same theology, two dimensions of the same existential and theological experience'.

If black theology is to embrace increasingly the total black experience in black history, then a more profound and continuous dialogue between North American black theology and this twofold African theology will be needed.

Bibliography

Allan Boesak, *Farewell to Innocence: A Socio-Ethical Study on Black Theology and Black Power* (Kampen, 1976; Johannesburg and New York, 1977), also published as *Black Theology, Black Power* (London, 1978); James H. Cone, *Black Theology and Black Power* (New York, 1969); *idem*, *A Black Theology of Liberation* (Philadelphia, 1970); *idem*, *God of the Oppressed* (New York, 1975); Major J. Jones, *Black Awareness* (Nashville, 1971); Louise Kretzschmar, *The Voice of Black Theology in South Africa* (Johannesburg, 1986); John S. Mbiti, 'An African views American Black Theology' in *Worldview* 17 (August, 1974), pp. 41–44; Basil Moore (ed.), *Black Theology: the South African Voice* (London, 1973, several seminal studies in South African black theology); J. Deotis Roberts, *Liberation and Reconciliation: A Black Theology* (Philadelphia, 1971); Gayraud S. Wilmore, *Black Religion and Black Radicalism* (New York, 1973); Gayraud S. Wilmore and James H. Cone (eds.), *Black Theology: A Documentary History 1966–1979* (New York, 1979; important, contains an annotated bibliography).

K.Be.

BLASPHEMY connotes a word or deed that directs insolence to the character of God, Christian truth or sacred things. In its purest form blasphemy is 'a deliberate and direct attack upon the honor of God with intent to insult him' (*NCE* 2, p. 606). A violation of the third commandment (Ex. 20:7;

Dt. 5:11), blasphemy robs God of his majesty and holiness and thus is regarded by Scripture as a heinous sin.

In Scripture the greatest incidence of blasphemy is against God himself (Lv. 24:11–23; Is. 52:5; Ezk. 20:27; Rev. 13:6; 16:9, 11, 21). Others blasphemed are Christ (Acts 26:11) and the Holy Spirit (Mt. 12:24–32; Mk. 3:22–30; Lk. 12:10). 'The blasphemy against the Spirit' referred to in the above texts is no specific sin, such as denial of the Spirit's divinity, but that disposition of deliberate hostility to the power of God actualized through the third person of the Trinity which precludes a person's contrition and repentance (*cf.* 1 Jn. 5:16). Also blasphemed, as the Gk. text makes clear, are the word of God (Ps. 107:11; Is. 5:24), angels (Jude 8, 10), Christian teaching (1 Tim. 6:1) and Christian believers (Acts 13:45; 18:6; 1 Cor. 4:13).

Blasphemy is committed not only by slanderous words (Lv. 24:11, 15–16), but also by denying Christ (1 Tim. 1:13), the practice of idolatry (Ne. 9:18, 26), false teaching (1 Tim. 1:20), oppression of the saints (Is. 52:5), insulting the poor (Jas. 2:6–7) and profession without practice (Rom. 2:24; 2 Tim. 3:2).

Bibliography

H. W. Beyer, in *TDNT* I, pp. 621–615; G. D. Nokes, *A History of the Crime of Blasphemy* (London, 1928); H. Wāhrisch *et al.*, in *NIDNTT* III, pp. 340–347.

B.D.

BLOOD, see SACRIFICE.

BODY, see ANTHROPOLOGY.

BODY OF CHRIST, see CHURCH.

BOEHME, JACOB (1575–1624). German shoemaker and mystic of Görlitz who combined a concern for personal religious experience,* in reaction to Lutheran scholasticism, with speculation about the nature of God and his relation to creation.

Most of Boehme's writings from 1612 to 1622, prompted by mystical* experiences in 1600 and 1619, used language and ideas from his long study of Neoplatonism (see Platonism*), Jewish cabbalism and alchemy. Later writings, including the treatises collected in *The Way to Christ* (1624), were more clearly expressed in traditional Christian themes and images, but the thought remained complex and speculative. Boehme's writings were banned in his lifetime and subsequently generally ignored; although they strongly influenced *The Spirit of Love* (1752, 1754) and other later writings of William Law,* causing a rift between Law and John Wesley,* who described Boehme's writings as 'most sublime nonsense'.

While Boehme's ideas cannot be fitted into any system, his influence can be traced in pietism* and idealism.* The 'dazzling chaos' (Boutroux) of his thought also appealed to the imagination of artists and poets, including John Milton (1608–74), William Blake (1757–1827) and S. T. Coleridge.*

Bibliography
P. Erb (tr.), *Jacob Boehme: The Way to Christ* (London and New York, 1978); J. J. Stoudt, *Jacob Boehme: His Life and Thought* (New York, 1968).

P.N.H.

BOETHIUS (*c.* 480–524), statesman and Christian philosopher. Despite his noble Roman birth and senatorial rank, he gained real political power at the court of the Gothic ruler of Rome, Theodoric. His prominence, however, did not last. Accused of treasonable dealings with the emperor in Constantinople, he was imprisoned in Pavia, where he was eventually executed.

Boethius was a transitional figure between the classical and the medieval world. He laid the foundation of the *quadrivium* ('the four ways'), the standard introduction to serious study of philosophy (see also Philosophy and Theology*). More important, he was a major influence in the virtually universal acceptance by Western Christendom* of a marriage between Christian theology and the best of Greek philosophy, effectively Aristotle* and the Neoplatonists. Boethius' translation of and commentary on Porphyry's *Introduction* proved particularly influential in the medieval period.

Boethius also wrote on Christian doctrines, notably the Trinity and the person of Christ. But his most influential work has been *The Consolation of Philosophy*, written in prison as a vindication of the divine providence* behind the painful demise of his own political career. The work has been criticized because of its lack of explicit reference to Scripture and its reliance on logical reasoning. Indeed, Boethius actually identifies the 'highest good' of philosophers with the Christian God. But alongside this, deliberate parallels to the wisdom literature of the OT, particularly Ecclesiastes, must be recognized.

Bibliography
H. Chadwick, *Boethius: The Consolations of Music, Logic, Theology and Philosophy* (Oxford, 1981); M. Gibson (ed.), *Boethius: His Life, Writings and Influence* (Oxford, 1981); H. Liebeschütz in *CHLGEMP*, pp. 538–555.

G.A.K.

BONAVENTURA (1221–74). A scholastic* theologian, born in Tuscany, who became the greatest Franciscan* mystic* after St Francis himself. Earning the MA degree at Paris, he joined the order (1243) and studied under some of its most renowned scholars including Alexander of Hales (*c.* 1170–1245). In 1248 he began lecturing on the Scriptures and theology, but he was not formally received into the masters' guild at Paris until 1257 because of a dispute between the friars and the secular teachers. However, by that time he was no longer actively teaching because he had been elected minister-general of the Franciscans (1257) and had resigned his position so that he could spend time on his administrative duties. Despite many other responsibilities he continued to encourage Franciscan involvement in academic life. Although often absent on business for the order and the church, whenever possible he preached at the university on matters of philosophical and theological importance to the faculty and students. Declining the position of Archbishop of York (1265), he was persuaded to become Bishop of Albano (1273) and was also made a cardinal. He attended the Council of Lyons (1274) and contributed to an agreement to reunite the Western and Eastern churches.

Bonaventura was a mystic scholastic as distinct from other Franciscans who were scientific scholastics and the Dominicans* such as Thomas Aquinas* who were rational scholastics. His leadership of the Franciscans temporarily saved the order from division by achieving a compromise between the two opposing factions. His most original thought, expressed in books including *The Seven Jour-*

neys of Eternity and The Journey of the Mind to God, centres on mysticism and this caused him to be remembered as 'the Seraphic Doctor'. The works are profoundly influenced by Augustine* whom he regarded as a balance to the emphasis on Aristotle* and the Arabic commentaries which were so popular in his time.

The knowledge of God, according to Bonaventura, comes not through formulating propositions but by experience with him in the soul. Rational knowledge of God is actually impossible because he is different from humans in a qualitative sense. Information about the divine is hazy, equivocal and analogous. An understanding of God comes through a long and arduous struggle of the spirit rather than by means of a series of logical progressions. Preparation for an encounter with God requires separation from material concern. Then a person must look for God through shadows or reflections of the divine in things of the world. After one perceives God's presence in the world, he can see God through his own being. For example, the human will demonstrates his goodness and the intellect shows his truth. This leads to an appreciation of the grace and transcendence of God, but another leap of faith is required to accept the mystery of the Trinity. At this stage in the mystical quest, Bonaventura warns, a period of testing, monotony and spiritual fatigue often sets in; but then, like the light of dawn, comes the gift of the Spirit consisting of an experience of the ineffable joy of the divine presence.

Bonaventura influenced and foreshadowed the great period of mysticism during the 14th and 15th centuries, which produced such individuals as Meister Eckhart, John Tauler and Thomas à Kempis. The Augustinianism* and individual devotion that he emphasized helped to prepare the way for the Protestant Reformation.

Bibliography

E. Bettoni, Saint Bonaventure (Notre Dame, IN, 1964); J. G. Bougerol, Introduction to the Works of Bonaventure (New York, 1964); L. Costello, Saint Bonaventure (New York, London, etc., 1911); E. Gilson, The Philosophy of St Bonaventure (New York, 1965).

R.G.C.

BONHOEFFER, DIETRICH (1906–45).

Theologian and leader of the Confessing Church in Germany until his martyrdom* by the Nazis, Bonhoeffer remains one of the most provocative voices in contemporary Christianity, despite the fragmentary and occasional character of much of his writing.

Born into a leading German family and educated in Berlin, Tübingen and Rome, Bonhoeffer's earliest theological work, Sanctorum Communio, attempted to bridge the theology of revelation* and philosophical sociology by describing the way in which the transcendent is encountered in corporate life. This early work contains many seeds of his more famous later writings, as does another early study on the place of ontology in systematic theology, Act and Being.

A spell in New York at Union Theological Seminary led Bonhoeffer into a strong reaction against liberal theology* and confirmed his nascent attraction to Barth,* at that time beginning work on the Church Dogmatics. On his return to Germany Bonhoeffer taught in Berlin. His published lectures Creation and Fall (a highly charged interpretation of Gn. 1 – 3) and Christology are much under Barth's influence.

At the same time, Bonhoeffer became increasingly involved in the young ecumenical movement and in opposition to Hitler, and in the mid-1930s he emerged as a leader of the Confessing Church which refused any alliance between Christianity and Nazism. Until its enforced closure, he ran a seminary for the Confessing Church at Finkenwalde.

From this period of his work come some of his well-known writings on spirituality, notably Life Together and The Cost of Discipleship. Until his arrest in 1943, he was at work on his posthumously published Ethics. His prison writings, collected as Letters and Papers from Prison, became one of the most influential theological documents of the century, notably for their attempts to phrase questions about the relationship between Christianity and the apparatus of human religion.

Proponents of the so-called 'theology of secularity' sought an antecedent in Bonhoeffer, but generally missed the nuances of his work. Behind the Letters and Papers is not so much a confidence about human powers as Bonhoeffer's eventual departure from Barth's account of the relation of revelation to human history. It is this, rather than denials of the possibility of all objective language about God, which should provide the starting-point for appraisal of Bonhoeffer's fragmentary assertions about 'religionless Christianity' or man's 'coming of age'. In effect, Bonhoeffer seeks to correct Barth by reintroducing an emphasis on the relative autonomy of the natural order as the sphere of God's presence and action. In this way, Bonhoeffer moves towards a theological account of human responsibility, a theme which was to occupy Barth himself in his later years. Bonhoeffer's own biography, from which his theology is inseparable, shows a parallel growth into consciousness of responsibility for history. He lived through a critical phase of European political and intellectual history, and condenses many of its tragedies in his own life.

Bibliography

Works: Gesammelte Schriften, 6 vols. (Munich, 1958–74); *Sanctorum Communio* (London, 1963); *Act and Being* (London, 1962); *Christology* (London, 1978); *The Cost of Discipleship* (London, 1959); *Creation and Fall* (London, 1959); *Ethics* (London, 1978); *Letters and Papers from Prison* (London, ²1971); *Life Together* (London, 1954); *No Rusty Swords* (London, 1965); *True Patriotism* (London, 1973); *The Way to Freedom* (London, 1966).

Studies: E. Bethge, *Dietrich Bonhoeffer* (London, 1970); A. Dumas, *Dietrich Bonhoeffer, Theologian of Reality* (London, 1971); J. D. Godsey, *The Theology of Dietrich Bonhoeffer* (London, 1960); H. Ott, *Reality and Faith* (London, 1971); J. A. Phillips, *The Form of Christ in the World* (London, 1967); R. Gregor Smith (ed.), *World Come of Age* (London, 1967).

J.B.We.

BOOK OF CONCORD, see CONFESSIONS OF FAITH.

BOSTON, THOMAS (1676–1732). Church of Scotland minister and an accomplished theologian. Born in Duns, Berwickshire, he graduated MA from Edinburgh University and studied theology there for one term, later completing his course under presbyterial supervision. He was minister, successively, at Simprin and Ettrick in the Scottish Borders.

Boston published several books during his lifetime, the most famous being *Human Nature in its Fourfold State*, which later ranked alongside *Pilgrim's Progress* in its popularity among Scottish Christians. Boston's treatises on the covenant of works and the covenant of grace rival even Herman Witsius (1636–1708) and Johannes Cocceius (1603–69) in their cogent presentation of covenant* theology.

Boston was also an accomplished Hebraist and his *Tractatus Stigmologicus Hebraicus* on the divine inspiration of the Hebrew accents (published posthumously in Lat. in 1738) earned him high praise from Hebrew scholars all over the world, albeit that later scholarship has demonstrated its main thesis to be untenable.

Boston's name is best known through his involvement in the Marrow Controversy. In the early 18th century there was a legalistic strain in Scottish theology. This came to the surface in a dispute between the Presbytery of Auchterarder and a student whom they refused to license because of his understanding of the doctrine of repentance.* The Presbytery had asked the student to subscribe to the following proposition: 'I believe that it is not sound and orthodox to teach that we forsake sin in order to our coming to Christ'. The student refused and the General Assembly of 1717 supported him, censuring the Presbytery. Boston agreed with the intention of the so-called 'Auchterarder Creed', although he had some reservations about the precision of its formulation.

In the context of this dispute Boston began to recommend Edward Fisher's *The Marrow of Modern Divinity* (1645). It was a compilation of Reformed writing including passages from Luther,* Calvin* and English Puritan* divines, set in the form of a debate. Boston asserted that it had helped him to understand and preach the doctrines of grace. James Hog of Carnock republished the book in 1718.

At this stage the two schools of thought within the church became apparent. Principal James Hadow (c. 1670–1747) of St Mary's College, St Andrews, opposed the book, which was ultimately banned by the General Assembly. Boston and eleven others (the 'Marrow Men') made unsuccessful representations to have this ban lifted. Both sides claimed to represent the position of the church's subordinate standard, the Westminster Confession of Faith.

In retrospect we can say that Hadow and those who supported him were guilty of a legalistic perversion of covenant theology. They made repentance a condition of salvation and restricted the gospel offer in the mistaken belief that a universal offer required as its basis a universal redemption. Boston and the others represented covenant theology as a theology of grace.* As for Hadow's view that the *Marrow* and the Marrow Men were opposed to the Westminster Confession, it is significant that the 1645 edition of the *Marrow* appeared with a preface by Joseph Caryl (1602–73), who had been specifically appointed by the Westminster Assembly to 'revise and approve theological works for the press' (Beaton).

Boston later re-issued the *Marrow* with his own notes (in *Works*, vol. 7). This is the edition which is most significant for a proper understanding of the debate.

Bibliography
Memoirs, ed. G. H. Morrison (Edinburgh, 1899); *Works*, ed. S. McMillan, 12 vols. (Edinburgh, 1853).

D. Beaton, 'The "Marrow of Modern Divinity" and the Marrow Controversy', *Records of the Scottish Church History Society* 1 (1926), pp. 112–134.

A.T.B.McG.

BRADWARDINE, THOMAS (*c.* 1290–1349). Sometimes called 'Doctor profundus', Bradwardine was a member of Merton College, Oxford, and a student of mathematics and theology. He was chosen Archbishop of Canterbury a few weeks before he died of the Black Death.

Bradwardine's chief work, *De Causa Dei Contra Pelagium*, is a massive and profound metaphysical polemic against both the characteristic doctrines of Pelagianism* and the Pelagian temper. The work was edited in 1618 by Sir Henry Savile, with the help of William Twisse (1575–1646), who later became the prolocutor of the Westminster Assembly. In that work the Augustinian* (and biblical) themes of the bondage of the will,* predestination* and the need for prevenient grace* are developed with an unrivalled subtlety and precision (by one who had tasted the sweet-

ness of divine grace for himself), from a dominantly theocentric standpoint: that of a God who in timeless eternity unchangeably wills and controls all that comes to pass, without being the author of sin. The extent to which this represents a hardening of Augustine's position is a matter of continuing debate.

Bradwardine is regarded (with, for example, Wyclif*) as an important influence preparing the way for the Reformation,* and thus as an important element of continuity between the medieval church and the Lutheran* Reformation and its effects.

Bibliography
H. A. Oberman, *Archbishop Thomas Bradwardine* (Utrecht, 1965); G. Leff, *Bradwardine and the Pelagians* (Cambridge, 1957).

P.H.

BRITISH ISRAELITISM. This began in the middle of the 19th century and eventually centred in the British Israel World Federation, with its periodical *The National Message* and its Covenant Publishing Co. It never became a sect or separate church, but drew members from all denominations, provided that they declared their belief in 'the Lord Jesus Christ as the only Saviour of men'. A recent exception is its adoption by the Worldwide Church of God (Armstrongism).

British Israelitism is based on an application of prophecy which emphasizes the distinction between the Jews and those tribes of the northern kingdom of Israel who went into exile in 721 BC and who are not said to have returned. They are traced, *e.g.*, as Saxons (Isaac's sons) and Danes (Dan) across Europe to Britain, and thence as Manassites to America. Since Jeremiah says that Israel will always have a king of David's line (Je. 33:17), it is surmised that one of Zedekiah's daughters, taken to Egypt with Jeremiah (Je. 43:6–7), sailed to Ireland and married a king there. They became the ancestors of the British royal family. Thus biblical promises to Israel are given to Britain and America.

Others point out that the promise of the perpetual king and priest in Je. 33:17–18 follows immediately on the promise of Christ's coming, as in Lk. 1:32–33. In the NT the Christian church is Israel (Gal. 6:16; Heb. 8:8–13) and a nation (1 Pet. 2:9) which comprises all races (Col. 3:11). Conquest of enemies is lifted to a spiritual plane (Mt. 1:21;

Eph. 6:12. Note also the form of quotation of Am. 9:11–12 in Acts 15:16–18).

Bibliography
H. L. Goudge, *The British Israel Theory* (London, 1933); B. R. Wilson (ed.), *Patterns of Sectarianism* (London, 1967), pp. 345–376, by John Wilson.

J.S.W.

BRUNNER, EMIL (1889–1966). A Swiss Reformed theologian who was initially a pastor before becoming a professor of systematic and practical theology in Zurich from 1924 to 1955. He travelled widely, having a life-long interest in ecumenism and mission, and spent the concluding two years of his teaching career in Japan.

In reacting against Schleiermacher's* theology, and that of the liberal Protestant school, Brunner has been identified with Barth* and others as part of the neo-orthodox* movement, whose theology, couched in dialectical* terms, was influenced by Kierkegaard* and Buber.*

Brunner considered that the revelation* on which Christianity was based consisted of a person-to-person encounter. Thus God's revelation, occurring uniquely in the life, death and resurrection of Jesus, is only completed when the individual acknowledges that Jesus is Lord. Scripture* itself is not revelation, for it is not verbally inspired and infallible, but it may be the bridge used by the Spirit to bring a person to faith. Brunner admitted that there was historical uncertainty about the gospel events, but affirmed that the divine and human natures were united in Jesus Christ. Thus he embodies and accomplishes mediation between God and man; hence Brunner's Christology* is entitled *The Mediator* (London, 1934).

It was Brunner's conviction that belief in Christ necessitated universal revelation of God in creation, history and human conscience. This brought him into sharp conflict in 1934 with Barth, who completely rejected any notion of general revelation. (See Brunner's 'Nature and Grace' to which Barth replied with 'No!' Both are printed in *Natural Theology*, with an introduction by John Baillie,* London, 1946.) However, Brunner was not suggesting that general revelation offered the first reliable step into knowledge of God which special revelation completed.

Rather, fallen man retains something of the image of God* which enables him to perceive distorted truth about God. Special revelation brings this truth into focus, confirming what is right, and reforming what is wrong.

Brunner's major exposition of doctrine is to be found in his three-volume *Dogmatics* (London: vol. 1, 1949; vol. 2, 1952; vol. 3, 1962).

Brunner inherited from his family an interest in social issues which was kept alive by the questions arising from two world wars and the advance of Communism. Although man's revolt against God has led to despair and guilt, nevertheless the unbeliever is still related to and responsible to God. This theme, developed in *Man in Revolt* (London, 1939), lies behind his ethics found in *The Divine Imperative* (London, 1937). God gives man the opportunity to obey his command to love both God and man. Love for humanity is appropriately expressed as one recognizes the different orders of society: family; the community, understood economically, legally (the state) or culturally; and the church. Both books opposed the totalitarianism found in Hitler's National Socialism and in the Communist bloc on the grounds that they promoted the godless dehumanization of society and were to be identified with antichrist. Consequently both were banned in Hitler's Germany.

Brunner made a positive contribution to post-war reconstruction through his book *Justice and the Social Order* (London, 1945), which discussed both the principles and the practice of justice at different levels of society. That this dogmatic theologian also concerned himself with practical issues sprang from his conviction that dogmatics and ethics are inextricably linked both in the NT and in proclamation and in Christian experience.

Bibliography
C. W. Kegley (ed.), *The Theology of Emil Brunner* (New York, 1962).

C.A.B.

BUBER, MARTIN (1878–1965). Grandson of the famous Midrash scholar Solomon Buber, philosopher, theologian, Zionist and lover of the pietistic, messianic Hasidim. Buber's influence on Judaism and Christianity is enormous.

Jews will think of Buber in three areas:

1. *Hasidism*. This movement of ultra-orthodox and mystical Judaism was founded in the 18th century and had its base in Eastern Europe. Buber's youthful contact with Hasidic communities led, in his adult years, to his editing the *Tales of the Hasidim* and other works telling the legends and beliefs of the Hasidim. His love for Hasidic communities brought him to see the importance of community witness whereby the life of Israel should permeate the Gentile world. He noted the formative Jewish influence on Christianity, Islam and Marxism. He saw Israel as the 'gateway of the nations', fusing the spirit of the east and west in fruitful reciprocity.

2. *Zionism*. Buber became a Zionist at university and later edited the paper *Die Welt* (*The World*). During both World Wars he laboured tirelessly for Jews under German occupation. Having supported Jewish colonies in Palestine all his life, he migrated to Israel in 1938, where he was professor of social philosophy in Jerusalem. As a Zionist he advocated 'peace and brotherhood with the Arab people'.

3. *The Bible*. Buber dedicated himself to the translation of the Hebrew Scriptures into German for German-speaking Jews. Ironically his translation is now mainly used by Gentile Christians, the community for which it was intended having been largely exterminated. His biblical studies led also to a significant work on *The Kingship of God* as well as the books *Moses* and *The Prophetic Faith*.

Christians will know Buber best for his book *I and Thou* and for his work on dialogue. Both spring from the influence of existentialism* in the 1920s. Supported by Hasidic teaching that there is good in all things, Buber stressed the need for 'education', which unfolds what is in man, rather than 'propaganda'. He taught the need for an I-Thou relationship of love and appreciative understanding, not the proselytizing I-It confrontation which uses the other approach. But in his *Writings on the Dialogue Principle*, he also maintains that 'dialogue does not mean a mutual relativization of convictions, but the acceptance of the other as a person'.

The influence of Buber's I-Thou thought spread through Emil Brunner* to such 'Christian presence' thinkers as Max Warren (1904–77) and John V. Taylor (b. 1914). He has also played a formative part in the unfolding of Christian thought on dialogue and proselytiz-ation. But in this context it should be noted that Buber steadily upholds the calling of Israel to bring salvation to the nations.

Bibliography

I and Thou (New York, 1970); *On Judaism* (New York, 1967); *Tales of the Hasidim* (New York, 1947).

M. L. Diamond, *Martin Buber, Jewish Existentialist* (New York, 1968); M. Friedman, *Martin Buber: The Life of Dialogue* (Chicago, 1955).

M.F.G.

BUCER (BUTZER), MARTIN (1491–1551). Strasburg Reformer and a major source of the Reformed* tradition. A native of Sélestat in Alsace, Bucer became a Dominican* (1506), but Alsatian humanism* prepared him first for Erasmus* and then Luther,* who captivated him at the Heidelberg disputation in 1518. He left the cloister, was married in 1522 and excommunicated, and took refuge in Strasburg (1523), where he soon became the leader of reform.

Bucer was prominently involved in the Protestant Supper-strife (see Eucharist*). After supporting the approach of Zwingli* and Oecolampadius,* he formulated a mediating (South German) position from c. 1528, insisting that Luther and Zwingli were fighting merely about words. Strasburg did not at first subscribe to the Augsburg Confession (1530), submitting instead, in the interests of Protestant concord, the Tetrapolitan Confession. Eventually Bucer and Melanchthon* reached agreement on the eucharist in the Wittenberg Concord (1536). While unhappy with some Lutheran formulae, Bucer stressed that even unworthy believers (but not rank unbelievers) partake by faith of the true (real) presence of Christ's body and blood, presented and conveyed (*exhibere*) by and with the elements in a 'sacramental union'. Not all applauded Bucer's almost scholastic facility in formulating agreed statements. This applied also to his efforts with Melanchthon to negotiate doctrinal accord with Catholics in Germany c. 1540. Provisional agreement on justification was reached at Regensburg in 1541. In pursuit of consensus Bucer made much of the pure unity of the early church.

The strength of Bucer's theology lay in his ecclesiology. He was more deeply committed than Luther to the ordered life of a community renewed according to the biblical pattern and marked by mutual love and service in the Spirit. The civil authorities had, in his view, an important role in religious reform. His insistence on church discipline* reflected in part his responsiveness to some of the demands of Strasburg's numerous Radical Reformers (see Reformation, Radical*). On this and other issues (*e.g.* the four orders of ministry, the ordering of worship, congregational singing, education) Calvin* learned much at Strasburg (1538–41), and Bucer's vision of a reformed church and a Christian society found fuller realization in Geneva and elsewhere than proved possible in Strasburg.

So strong was Bucer's emphasis on spiritual renewal that he could acknowledge a twofold justification.* True faith, which he defined as a sure persuasion, was always 'active through love' (Gal. 5:6). He was more disposed than Luther and Calvin to speak of free will* in the unregenerate.

Bucer's last years (1548–51) were spent in exile, chiefly as regius professor in Cambridge. There he influenced the *Book of Common Prayer* (1552), and English Reformers* such as John Bradford (*c.* 1510–55), Matthew Parker (1504–75) and John Whitgift (*c.* 1530–1604). He produced for Edward VI a remarkable blueprint for a Christian England, *The Kingdom of Christ*, and, as one of the Reformation's ablest expositors, contributed to the shaping of the English exegetical tradition.

Bibliography

Collected edition of works in progress: in ET, selections in D. F. Wright, *Common Places of Martin Bucer* (Appleford, 1972), and *Kingdom of Christ* in W. Pauck, *Melanchthon and Bucer*, LCC 19 (London, 1970). H. Eells, *Martin Bucer* (New Haven, 1931); W. P. Stephens, *The Holy Spirit in the Theology of Martin Bucer* (London, 1970); W. Pauck, *The Heritage of the Reformation* (Oxford, ²1968).

D.F.W.

BUDDHISM AND CHRISTIANITY.
Siddhartha Gautama was born a prince in India during the 6th century BC. His father shrouded Siddhartha in comfort, preventing him from seeing human suffering. When Siddhartha grew to manhood, he saw diseased and elderly people, as well as corpses. After encountering a monk, he realized that life is full of pain. Disillusioned, he vowed to seek ultimate truth, forsook his luxuries, and became a wandering monk.

He practised austerity to achieve enlightenment. He learned, however, that neither present severity nor previous pleasures could give him inner peace. He decided to travel what is known in Buddhism as the Middle Way – a life devoid of both self-affliction and physical indulgence. While meditating under the bodhi-tree, he attained enlightenment and became a Buddha, the 'enlightened one'. From this experience he realized four important truths.

1. Life is full of sorrow. Every person is born, becomes old, and dies. Suffering marks an endless cycle of lives. Therefore, reincarnation (see Metempsychosis*) is a curse.

2. The origin of suffering is ignorance. People are ignorant of who they are and what life is. From ignorance proceeds desire for immaterial and material things. But there is neither eternal youth, nor ultimate power, nor absolute joy. All suffer because of ignorance.

3. A person can break this cycle of rebirths by realizing that the essence of all things, including the soul, is emptiness. The great doctrine of Buddhism is *anatta*, 'no soul'. This differs from the Hindu understanding of the soul. In Hinduism* union is sought between the Universal Soul (*Brahman*) and the individual soul (*Atman*) to bring about a oneness just as a raindrop becomes one with the ocean. In Buddhism, there is no soul. Rather, a consciousness is reborn and needs to be extinguished just as a candle flame is blown out. This consciousness is not a soul (as the Hindu or Christian would describe a soul) but it is the causal result of ignorance, and it is extinguished when one realizes the emptiness of its existence.

4. The path which leads to the cessation of suffering. This has eight steps: right views, right aspirations, right speech, right conduct, right mode of living (*i.e.* free from luxury), right effort, right awareness and right concentration. By walking the eightfold path, a person will eventually (after many successive reincarnations) receive enlightenment. Though the Buddhist doctrine of extinction may seem nihilistic to Christians, living a pure life to end a cycle of lives full of suffering is

understood to be idealistic rather than fatalistic.

Subsequent Buddhist schools responded to and interpreted the teachings of the Buddha differently. Two major philosophies soon emerged within Buddhism: Theravada and Mahayana Buddhism. The adherents of Mahayana, the Great Vehicle, referred to those Buddhists who held strictly to the letter of the Buddhist doctrine as followers of Hinayana Buddhism, the Little or Lesser Vehicle. The Hinayanists resented this term because it denoted an inferior method of Buddhism. Instead, they called their doctrine Theravada Buddhism, the doctrine of the Elders.

Theravada Buddhism contains major points of doctrine that differ from the beliefs of most Mahayana schools. Most significantly, the Theravadins revere the Buddha as a great ethical teacher, but not as a god as many of the Mahayanists do. Furthermore, their teachings are reserved for the Buddhist saints (*Arhats*) and not for the common people, another departure from many of the Mahayana schools that exalt those Buddhists who have attained to the role of saviours (*Bodhisattvas*).

Some Buddhist schools in the Mahayana branch of Buddhism have shifted the focus away from the doctrine of emptiness (*sunyata*) over the centuries. Instead, they concentrate on a Western Paradise, a place of bliss where faithful Buddhists sojourn until they achieve *parinirvana* – extinction. It is not that *sunyata* is removed from their philosophy, but rather that *parinirvana* is delayed in their spiritual odyssey in favour of a place which those Buddhists regard with solace and hope – that is, a Western Paradise.

Many Japanese-American Buddhists believe in Amida Buddha and follow the teachings of Shinran, the founder of Jodo-Shinshu, which fosters the belief in a Western paradise. Although many important Buddhist schools, such as Zen and Tibetan Buddhism, dismiss the Amidist doctrines, many Asians believe that faith in Amida Buddha's compassion will secure them a place in paradise.

Asian Buddhists of the Amida schools have also westernized their religion in North America and Europe. Buddhists in Asia might visit a temple or shrine any day of the week, but in the West they assemble on Sundays, conduct Sunday schools, and call their places of worship churches. Moreover, the architecture of their churches is similar to non-conformist buildings.

Meanwhile, Zen and Tibetan Buddhism not only retain the cultural features of Japan and Tibet but also emphasize spiritual techniques over a simple faith. Westerners, who have rejected what they regard as Christian doctrines and culture, gravitate toward the meditation schools of Buddhists because of those distinctions. Among Christians, it is chiefly Roman Catholics who have practised or advocated 'Christian Zen' or 'Zen Catholicism' – the result of grafting features of Zen Buddhism on to Christianity. The theory and practice of Zen meditation have been particularly attractive to Catholics keen to promote a renewal of mystical contemplation (*cf.* W. Johnston, *Christian Zen*, New York, 1971; A. Graham, *Zen Catholicism*, London, 1964). Others have identified points of connection between Zen *satori* (enlightenment) and Christian conversion, and between *koan* (a heuristic device, often in question and answer form) and Bible study (J. K. Kadowaki, *Zen and the Bible*, London, 1980). Even Buddhist economics have attracted Western Christian emulation (E. F. Schumacher, *Small is Beautiful*, London, 1973). Christian evangelism must consider the two types of Buddhists in the West: those who are mostly of Asian descent and who have inherited a faith in the compassion of the Amida Buddha; and those who are mostly of European descent and who have adopted a religion that emphasizes spiritual techniques of meditation. Nevertheless, a Christian can have dialogue with Buddhists in areas that are common to both.

The contrast between Christian teaching and Buddhist emerges in at least three areas:

1. Buddhist teaching denies the existence of soul. By contrast it is fundamental to biblical teaching that man *is* soul, or 'living being' (Gn. 2:7; see Anthropology*). His life must be defined in terms of his creation by God, his dependence on God, and his relationship to God. This is not destroyed by death, as Jesus indicates (Mt. 10:28).

2. The NT denies the doctrine of reincarnation. Men die but *once* and are judged on the basis of one life (Heb. 9:27). The Christian's hope is not the breaking of a cycle of rebirths, but eternal life with Christ (1 Thes. 5:9–10).

113

3. In biblical teaching, the origin of suffering* is not man's ignorance, but man's sinfulness. While Scripture warns against relating all individual suffering to individual sin, it does root the entrance into the world of evil and death in the fall. By contrast with Buddhist teaching, the gospel summons disciples to share in Christ's sufferings (Rom. 8:16–17), not to be detached from all suffering.

The Western church has spawned self-help workshops, seminars on self-improvement and success, and a focus on happiness and wealth, which confuse the message of the gospel to many Asians who see little difference between the affluence of the Western church and their own detachment from suffering. If Christians want to share the good news of Jesus Christ, they must enter into what he did, not into suffering for the sake of suffering, but into suffering for the sake of righteousness and truth, and for the sake of others. Jesus stood up for the oppressed, for the social outcasts, and was consequently rejected himself. What Jesus did – dying on the cross, suffering for others – is unique, but Christian materialism and self-centredness often mask his uniqueness.

When Jesus Christ is shared with Buddhists, his sacrifice as well as his resurrection must be emphasized and contrasted with the Buddhist teachings on detachment and emptiness. Others must see that Christians are willing to suffer for others, just as Jesus suffered for others. Such a testimony to cultural and Western Buddhists would be unique and powerful.

Bibliography

Edward Conze (ed.), *Buddhist Texts Through the Ages* (New York, 1954); H. G. Creel, *Chinese Thought from Confucius to Mao Tse-Tung* (New York, 1960); P. O. Ingram and F. J. Streng (eds.), *Buddhist-Christian Dialogue* (Honolulu, HI, 1986); David J. Kalupahana, *Buddhist Philosophy: A Historical Analysis* (Honolulu, 1976); Walpola Rahula, *What the Buddha Taught* (New York, 1974); Edward J. Thomas, *The Life of Buddha as Legend and History* (London, 1973); I. Yamamoto, *Beyond Buddhism: A Basic Introduction to the Buddhist Tradition* (Downers Grove, IL, 1982).

J.I.Y.

BULGAKOV, SERGEI, see RUSSIAN ORTHODOX THEOLOGY.

BULLINGER, JOHANN HEINRICH (1504–75). Born at Bremgarten, Switzerland, the son of the parish priest, Bullinger was educated at Emmerich, then Cologne, where he studied the fathers, felt the impact of Erasmus,* Luther* and Melanchthon,* and commenced a direct investigation of the NT. Back in Switzerland in 1522, he lived in Bremgarten, lectured at Kappel, and took courses at Zurich, where he supported Zwingli* and was elected a delegate to the Berne Disputation. Ordained in 1528, he ministered at Bremgarten, marrying a former nun in 1529.

The defeat at Kappel (1531) forced him into refuge at Zurich, and here, rejecting offers from Berne and Basel, he succeeded Zwingli as virtual leader of church life in both city and canton. He remained in this post until his death, exercising a quietly effective pastoral ministry, strengthening fellowship with other churches, and entertaining refugees, especially Anglican exiles under Mary, *e.g.* John Jewel (1522–71).

In addition to his regular duties Bullinger carried through an extensive literary programme; he himself collected his chief writings into ten volumes, but no full edition has yet been issued. Prominent among his works are commentaries, polemical treatises against the Anabaptists* and Lutherans, doctrinal writings on the eucharist* and Scripture, sermons on the Christian sacrifice and the Lord's Supper, a diary, and a history of the Reformation. Of special interest to Anglicans are the *Decades*, five books of ten sermons each on the heads of Christian doctrine which, by Archbishop Whitgift's order in 1586, became prescribed reading for the English clergy in an effort to meet Puritan protests against scholarly inadequacy.

More important, perhaps, than the academic labours were Bullinger's confessional contributions, which began in 1536 when, with Bucer* and Leo Jud (1482–1542), he drew up the First Helvetic Confession (see Confessions of Faith*) in a futile attempt to reach agreement with the Lutherans. Irenically disposed, Bullinger achieved greater ecumenical success in 1549, for in that year, after discussions with Calvin, the Consensus Tigurinus (Zurich Consensus), consisting of twenty-six articles on the sacraments, united Zurich and other German-speaking Swiss churches with Geneva and Neuchâtel. Bullinger's crowning confessional achievement came in 1566 when, at the request of the elector Palatine, he issued a statement of beliefs which, commonly known as the Second Helvetic Confession, found wide acceptance in Switzerland, France, Scotland, Hungary, Poland and the Netherlands as well as Germany.

Noteworthy among Bullinger's emphases in both his writings and his confessions are his commitment to the creeds,* his regard for the fathers, and his conviction that the Reformation was restoration, not innovation. In the tradition of Zwingli, creeds and fathers remain subordinate to the word of God in its threefold form as incarnate, spoken and written. The Spirit's role in the interpretation as well as the inspiration of Scripture receives attention, although not at the expense of scholarly, if prayerful, exegesis. Bullinger maintained Zwingli's position on the baptismal covenant* but added positive insights to the more negative eucharistic teaching. His presentation of election had an interesting Christological focus. He shared common Reformation views on such matters as justification,* atonement,* church* and papacy.* His position on adiaphora* and on church-state relations brought him into sympathy with early Elizabethan church leaders against their Puritan critics.

Bibliography

J. Wayne Baker, *Heinrich Bullinger and the Covenant* (Athens, OH, 1981); G. W. Bromiley, *Historical Theology* (Grand Rapids, MI, 1978); *idem* (ed.), *Zwingli and Bullinger* (London, 1953); T. Harding (ed.), *The Decades of Henry Bullinger*, 5 vols. (Cambridge, 1849–52); D. J. Keep, *Henry Bullinger and the Elizabethan Church*, unpub. dissert. (University of Sheffield, 1970); P. Schaff, *Creeds of Christendom*, vol. III (New York, 1919).

G.W.B.

BULTMANN, RUDOLF (1884–1976). NT scholar and theologian, influential most especially through his work on the existentialist* interpretation of the Christian faith. After studying at Tübingen, Berlin and Marburg, Bultmann taught at Breslau and from 1921 to 1951 was professor of NT at Marburg. His theology is expounded in his *Theology of the New Testament*, in a variety of studies of NT and theological issues, in his various collections of essays, and in his large-scale commentary on *The Gospel of John*.

Bultmann's basic proposals about existentialist interpretation were conceived early in his theological development, although the terminology of 'kerygma'* and 'myth'* did not emerge until late in the 1930s. For Bultmann, the interpretation of the NT involves 'demythologizing', *i.e.* a proper interpretation of the mythological language in which its kerygma or message about human existence is couched. 'Myth' is a flexible term in Bultmann's usage, but most commonly denotes 'objectifying' language. Such language projects reality 'out there', speaking of it as an object essentially unrelated to human self-understanding and existence. To 'demythologize' the biblical writings is not to eliminate their mythology while retaining some non-mythological material: such selectivity Bultmann criticized in the attempts of some 19th-century liberal theologians to disentangle Jesus' moral teaching from his eschatology, for example. Demythologizing is rather a process of interpreting mythology consistently, in terms of the understanding of human existence which it articulates. Thus, for example, to demythologize creation myths is not to repudiate them as untrue, but to interpret them as objectified expressions of man's understanding of himself as contingent.*

To some extent, demythologizing is an apologetic* exercise, seeking to distinguish between the Christian faith and an obsolete supernatural world-view in which it finds expression and which is no longer available to us. But philosophical and theological factors are more determinative upon Bultmann's programme than such considerations. Bultmann drew heavily on the work of his Marburg colleague Martin Heidegger (1899–1976; see Existentialism*), whose book *Being and Time* (1927) is one of the fundamental texts of German existentialism. Heidegger's analysis of human existence in that book was especially influential over the question of man as a subject within history,* whose selfhood is not the expression of a pre-given nature but rather created in historical acts of decision and choice. This sense of man as 'history' rather than 'nature', which surfaces in Bultmann's treatment of theological anthropology* in his *Theology of the New Testament*, was bound up with the further influence of the Marburg Neo-Kantian philosophy of Hermann Cohen (1842–1918) and Paul Natorp (1854–1924), with its radical dualism of 'fact' and 'value'. These philosophical influences are, however, absorbed within what is essentially a *theological* project. Behind the programme of demythologizing lies a tradition within 19th-century Lutheranism according to which knowledge of objective facts constitutes human 'works', that is, the attempt to secure the self against encounter with God by a codified account of the divine being and acts. In effect, demythologizing is for Bultmann the epistemological* equivalent of justification* by faith: both meritorious works and objectified knowledge of God are attempts to guarantee the self over against God. Here Bultmann owes a great deal to the turn-of-the-century Lutheran theologian Wilhelm Herrmann,* who laid emphasis on faith as encounter with God in the present rather than as mere assent to objective realities doctrinally described. From this perspective, it should be added, Bultmann's early attraction to the dialectical* theology of the early Barth* and Friedrich Gogarten (1887–1967) is readily comprehensible, in so far as he, like Barth in *The Epistle to the Romans* (1919), is rejecting any ground for human security against interruption by God.

This account of demythologizing or 'de-objectification' helps account for Bultmann's radical scepticism about the historicity of the NT records. Along with other early form-critics (see Biblical Criticism*) such as Martin Dibelius (1883–1947), Bultmann concluded in *The History of the Synoptic Tradition* (1921) that the gospels contain almost no authentic historical information about Jesus but rather material shaped and frequently created by the early Christian communities. Bultmann's theology can support such scepticism, however, precisely because objective historical facts simply constitute 'knowledge after the flesh'. Real knowledge of Christ is encounter with him in the word of the kerygma as one who summons man now to meaningful existence. Bultmann thus excises the 'Jesus of history' (see Historical Jesus*) from Christology;* historical interest in the

personality and deeds of Jesus both cannot and should not be satisfied, since it merely furnishes the occasion for human evasion of the claim of God by adhering to objective realities. Like Martin Kähler,* whose book *The So-Called Historical Jesus and the Historic, Biblical Christ* deeply influenced him, Bultmann envisages the concern of Christology to be the 'Christ of faith', Christ encountered in believing existence (or, as earlier Protestants would state it, in his *benefits*) rather than in abstract historical observation.

While Bultmann's influence on the course of 20th-century theology and biblical interpretation has been immense, subsequent critical scholarship has qualified much of his historical scepticism. Many pupils of Bultmann associated with the so-called 'New Quest of the Historical Jesus' (such as E. Käsemann,* E. Fuchs, 1903–83, and G. Ebeling*) have found a stronger historical anchor for the kerygma in the history of Jesus than Bultmann allowed; others have radically criticized his reading of the influence of Gnosticism* and Hellenism* on primitive Christianity.

In systematic theology and philosophy Bultmann acutely rephrased some fundamental questions concerning the relation of faith to history and the nature of divine presence and action in a way which remains fundamentally determinative for some contemporary theological reflection. Bultmann consistently attempted to construct a theology in which the question of God and the question of human existence would be inseparable. But because of his theological roots in Lutheranism and the influence of both dualist* and existentialist philosophy, he found acute difficulty in talking of God's transcendence and his action in history, since he always suspected such talk to be objectifying. Bultmann's theology is thought by many to lack any ontological reference in its interpretation of the Christian faith, and thus to be radically subjective, translating statements about God into statements about man. However, while this may be true of some followers of Bultmann such as H. Braun (b. 1903) and F. Buri (b. 1907), Bultmann himself always strove to retain the necessity of talking of God, if only paradoxically. 'The fact that God cannot be seen or apprehended apart from faith does not mean that he does not exist apart from faith' (*Jesus Christ and Mythology*, p. 72).

Along with his close contemporary, Karl Barth, Bultmann decisively reshaped the landscape of Protestant theology in Germany and beyond, and his work continues to set the terms of reference for some theological traditions.

Bibliography
Works: Essays (London, 1955); *Existence and Faith* (London, 1964); *Faith and Understanding* (London, 1969); *The Gospel of John* (Oxford, 1971); *History and Eschatology* (Edinburgh, 1957); *The History of the Synoptic Tradition* (London, 1963); *Jesus and the Word* (London, ²1958); *Jesus Christ and Mythology* (London, 1960); *Primitive Christianity* (London, 1960); *Theology of the New Testament*, 2 vols. (London, 1952, 1955).

Studies: H. W. Bartsch (ed.), *Kerygma and Myth*, 2 vols. (London 1962, 1964); G. Ebeling, *Theology and Proclamation* (London, 1966); R. A. Johnson, *The Origins of Demythologizing* (Leiden, 1974); C. W. Kegley (ed.), *The Theology of Rudolf Bultmann* (London, 1966); J. Macquarrie, *An Existentialist Theology* (London, 1955); *idem*, *The Scope of Demythologizing* (London, 1960); S. M. Ogden, *Christ without Myth* (London, 1962); H. P. Owen, *Revelation and Existence* (Cardiff, 1957); R. C. Roberts, *Rudolf Bultmann's Theology* (London, 1977); J. M. Robinson, *A New Quest of the Historical Jesus* (London, 1963); W. Schmithals, *An Introduction to the Theology of Rudolf Bultmann* (London, 1968); A. C. Thiselton, *The Two Horizons* (Exeter, 1980).

J.B.We.

BUNYAN, JOHN (1628–88). A Bedford pastor and author, Bunyan may well have been the most influential English religious figure of his time. Some twelve and a half years in Bedford's damp county jail awarded him the martyr's laurel. His courageous refusal to accept freedom in exchange for silence placed him in the lineage of the apostles. The opportunity to prove himself came after his conversion and call to the ministry as he joined a non-conformist church which was congregational in polity and Baptist in its ordinances.

Bunyan is completely Calvinistic* in his theology and is a prime exemplar of the Puritan* marriage of doctrine with life. He is concerned in his sermons and writings to present the truth experimentally (*i.e.* experientially). Bunyan as a Spirit-led theologian had the gift of interpreting evangelical truth to the masses. His many and varied writings and sermons purposefully applied Scripture to everyday living. His biblical and often earthy preaching was Christ-centred, powerful, practical and life-changing.

Bunyan's skill with the pen is surprising; though without formal education he produced some sixty-six works. These were widely circulated in cheap editions, few of which survived, for they were read until they disintegrated. Bunyan's very human spirit and allegorical style contributed to the popularity of his books. The volumes with the greatest appeal are *Grace Abounding to the Chief of Sinners* (1666), which recounts his conversion, and *Pilgrim's Progress* (1682), which describes spiritual warfare. It was not merely Bunyan's astounding allegorical expression which ensured his popularity, but rather his clear insight into mankind's desperate plight and God's redeeming, sovereign grace. For Bunyan justification, regeneration, mortification and sanctification are not theological pigeon-holes, but the substance of Christian experience.

We are impressed by Bunyan the preacher, pastor, evangelist and author but we are most moved by Bunyan the pilgrim, a man wrought upon by God, making his way to heaven's gate.

Bibliography
George Offor (ed.), *The Whole Works of John Bunyan*, 3 vols. (London, 1862); Roger Sharrock (ed.), *The Miscellaneous Works of John Bunyan* (Oxford, 1976– , to be completed in 17 vols.); *idem* (ed.), *Pilgrim's Progress* (Harmondsworth, 1965).

James F. Forrest and Richard L. Greaves, *John Bunyan: A Reference Guide* (Boston, 1982); Richard L. Greaves, *An Annotated Bibliography of John Bunyan Studies* (Pittsburgh, PA, 1972).

W.N.K.

BUSHNELL, HORACE (1802–76). After graduating from Yale University, he became a journalist and studied law before entering Yale Divinity School. In 1833 he became the Congregational minister of North Church, Hartford, Connecticut, where he served until ill-health led to his retirement in 1859. Drawing on the insights of German idealism* and the American Puritan* tradition, he became known as the father of American liberal theology* and of the social gospel* movement. During his ministry he had to battle with bitter opposition to his views as well as the threat of a trial for heresy.

In his writings he tried to develop a way of doing theology which would make dogma the servant of the spirit. In *Christian Nurture* (²1861) he expressed his belief that the child of Christian parents should be brought up in such a way as never to know a time when he was not a Christian. This represented a critique of the emphasis placed upon the conversion* experience by popular revivalism.* In *God in Christ* (1849), which proved to be highly controversial, he argued, from his own spiritual experience, that human language could not express absolute truth but must convey spiritual verities through the use of image, analogy* and paradox.* In such an understanding of the use of language he affirmed an instrumental view of the Trinity* and a moral view of the atonement* against the Unitarians* who believed that these doctrines were outdated on the one hand, and those who held a substitutionary view of Christ's crucifixion on the other. In *Nature and the Supernatural* (1858) he believed that these two elements constituted the one 'system of God' and appealed for a 'Christo-centric liberalism' with Jesus Christ as the centre and goal of history. In *The Vicarious Sacrifice* (2 vols., 1866) he expressed a developed view of the atonement: there is a cross in God before the wood is seen upon Calvary; hid in God's own virtue itself, struggling on heavily in burdened feeling through all the previous ages, and struggling as heavily now even in the throne of the worlds.

Bibliography

Selected Writings, ed. D. L. Smith (Chico, CA, 1984); *Selections*, ed. H. S. Smith (New York, 1965).

W. A. Johnson, *Nature and the Supernatural in the Theology of Horace Bushnell* (Lund, 1963); H. D. McDonald, *The Atonement of the Death of Christ* (Grand Rapids, MI, 1985); D. L. Smith, *Symbolism and Growth: The Religious Thought of Horace Bushnell* (Chico, CA, 1981); Claude Welch, *Protestant Thought in the Nineteenth Century* (New Haven and London, 1972).

I.D.B.

BUTLER, JOSEPH (1692–1752). Bishop Butler, 'the philosopher of Anglicanism', was outstanding in his century as a religious apologist* and moral philosopher. His *Analogy of Religion* constituted the most successful published refutation of deism.* In it, Butler argued that, granted that God is the author of nature, the veracity of Christian revealed religion attains a significant probability. This is because features are contained in it which are analogous to those found in natural religion, as we see when we properly interpret miracle,* prophecy* and messianic mediation. Rational probability provides an adequate ground for practical assent to Christianity.

Butler's moral philosophy (see Moral Theology*), contained mainly in his sermons, analyses the empirical actualities of human nature and psychology. It contains elements of intuitionism (where something is presented in moral experience as self-evidently right or true), utilitarianism (where moral obligation is directed or related to what produces happiness) and naturalism (where, in this case, behaviour in accordance with one's nature is morally advocated). Theologically, Butler ascribed importance to the role of conscience* in the moral sphere.

While the contemporary climate of discussion in the relevant areas is largely uncongenial to Butler's approach, Hume's* respect for him and the huge acclaim of the following century signal something of his stature as a religious thinker.

Bibliography

J. H. Bernard (ed.), *The Works of Bishop Butler*, 2 vols. (London, 1900); A. Duncan-Jones, *Butler's Moral Philosophy* (Harmondsworth, 1952); A. Jeffner, *Butler and Hume on Religion: a Comparative Analysis* (Stockholm, 1966); D. M. Mackinnon, *A Study in Ethical Theory* (London, 1957), ch. 5; E. C. Mossner, *Bishop Butler and the Age of Reason* (New York, 1936); T. Penelhum, *Butler* (London, 1985).

S.N.W.

C

CALENDAR, LITURGICAL. The Judaism from which Christianity sprang had an elaborate calendar of holy days: one weekly (the sabbath*), one monthly (the new moon), but most of them annual. The sabbath and the chief of the annual holy days (but not the new moon) are listed in Lv. 23 as 'holy convocations', days when the congregation was 'called together' for worship, not days when the priests alone were on duty. All of them are feasts except the Day of Atonement, which is a fast. Later in the OT the feast of Purim was added, and in the intertestamental period the feast of the Dedication (*cf.* Jn. 10:22) and other feasts and fasts were added.

For a time Jewish Christianity continued to practise, in some measure, the old observances along with Christian observances. However, Gentile Christians were from the outset exempted from literal obedience to the law, and at the council of Jerusalem (Acts 15) even the sabbath, which was reckoned the chief of the feasts, was excluded from the list of residual observances expected of Gentiles. With the destruction of the Temple in AD 70, and with the growing estrangement between Christian and non-Christian Jews as the 1st century progressed, Jewish Christians seem to have conformed more and more to Gentile Christianity, and to have continued the literal observance of the law only in sectarian groups (Ebionites, Nazaraeans). From then on, even in Palestine, the Christian calendar consisted only of Christian holy days.

The earliest Christian holy day was the Lord's Day, Sunday, which is attested in the NT and in the apostolic fathers,* and which, like the sabbath, is geared to the Jewish week. The next holy days that we know of are also weekly, the fasts on Wednesday and Friday enjoined in *Didache* 8 (*c.* 100), where they are deliberately set in opposition to the Jewish fasts on Monday and Thursday (*cf.* Lk. 18:12). The first annual festivals, significantly, are those which had Jewish models to follow, since they celebrated events which took place at two of the Jewish festivals: Easter* or Pascha (*i.e.* Passover) probably arose in the East at the beginning of the 2nd century, and Whitsun or Pentecost in the West at the end of it, making a fitting conclusion to the seven weeks of celebrations after Easter. Ascension Day, Epiphany and Christmas did not arise until the 4th century, the latter two being originally the Eastern and Western festival of the nativity (though the dates for the nativity on which they are held can be traced back to the year 200 or soon after). Trinity Sunday is peculiar to the West, and dates from the 10th century.

During the Middle Ages, the Christian year became increasingly complicated through the filling up of every day with festivals of saints,* sometimes legendary and more than one to a day. Another medieval development was festivals for medieval doctrines, such as All Souls (purgatory*) and Corpus Christi (transubstantiation; see Eucharist*). The Reformers, consequently, had to prune the Christian year drastically, but only in Scotland was it abolished, the Lord's Day alone being retained. There too, however, it was recognized that the existence of a sacred day was a way of acknowledging that all our time belongs to the Lord. The Christian year celebrates the course of the life, death and exaltation of Christ.

Bibliography
See Bibliographies for Easter and Saint.
R.T.B.

CALLING. Theologians, especially in the Reformed* tradition, have distinguished between general and effectual calling. *General calling* is a term applied to the universal offer of the gospel, made to all without distinction through the preaching of the word of God. As such, it meets with a wide variety of responses. *Effectual calling* is the event or process whereby people are brought into a state of salvation. Consequently, it is restricted in its scope. It is an act of God's grace and power by which he sovereignly unites us to Christ (1 Cor. 1:9; 2 Tim. 1:8–9). God the Father is the specific agent (Rom. 8:28–30; Gal. 1:15; Eph. 1:17–18; 1 Cor. 1:9; 2 Tim. 1:8–9), not only inviting but powerfully and graciously introducing us into his kingdom according to his eternal purpose in Christ, which can never be undone (Rom. 8:28–30, 11:29). Hence, effectual calling is a sovereign act of God and

119

can in no way be defined in terms of a person's response. It is the initial step in the application of redemption, on which faith,* justification,* adoption (see Sonship*), sanctification* and glorification are dependent (see Ordo Salutis*). It has a teleological orientation, being associated in the NT with God's ultimate purpose for his people of fellowship with Jesus Christ (1 Cor. 1:9), blessing (1 Pet. 3:9), liberty (Gal. 5:13), peace (1 Cor. 7:15), holiness (1 Thes. 4:17), eternal life (1 Tim. 6:12) and participation in God's kingdom and glory (1 Thes. 2:12).

However, general calling and effectual calling are not to be understood as two separate phenomena, but rather as one call viewed from differing perspectives. Effectual calling is grounded on the general call of the gospel, for the appeal by God to the human mind and conscience in the preaching of the word is the normal occasion for his calling of sinners to himself (1 Cor. 1:18 – 2:5, 1 Thes. 1:4–10, 2:13; Acts 16:13–14). While in the NT the overwhelming weight of discussion is placed on the effective drawing of men to Christ, consideration ought also to be given to the equally strong emphasis on the responsibility and privilege of proclaiming Christ to the world, in connection with which God's sovereign application of redemption is made.

In the early church, and again in the Reformation and post-Reformation periods, effectual calling tended to be identified with regeneration.* However, effectual calling relates more to the conscious life of men and women, whereas regeneration in its narrow sense occurs inwardly. Additionally, calling has a teleological orientation which regeneration, in the above sense, does not have.

Bibliography

H. Bavinck, *Our Reasonable Faith* (Grand Rapids, MI, 1977); L. Berkhof, *Systematic Theology* (London, 1958); L. Coenan, in *NIDNTT* I, pp. 271ff.; J. Murray, *Redemption Accomplished and Applied* (London, 1961).

R.W.A.L.

CALVIN, JOHN (1509–64), Reformation theologian. He was born at Noyon in Picardy, France. He spent much of his youth at school in Paris, being trained for the priesthood. His study of medieval scholastic theology was followed by a period of training for the legal profession which brought him into touch with the Christian humanism* current in France at the time, through teachers such as Lefèvre d'Étaples (1455–1529) and Guillaume Budé (1468–1540). He was greatly attracted by such learning and wrote, as his first work, a commentary on Seneca's *De Clementia*. He underwent, however, a 'sudden conversion,' the date of which is uncertain. The effect of this was to detach his mind from his former studies, as he became more committed to the study of Scripture and the Reformation* teaching. In 1536 he published in Basel the first edition of his *Institutes of the Christian Religion*. Thereafter, a short and unsuccessful ministry in Geneva was followed by an enriching experience of teaching and pastoral work in Strasburg from 1538 to 1541. Calvin then allowed himself to be recalled to Geneva. There he patiently worked and struggled for many years, seeking to put into practice his beliefs about the gospel, church and society.

When he began his theological work, the Reformation was entering an important second phase in its development. The word of God, under Luther* and others, had powerfully broken through the old forms which had for centuries restricted the Spirit and obscured the truth. The movement had inspired innumerable sermons, writings, conferences and controversies, and had brought about important changes in social and political life. People had been introduced to new experiences, ideals and hopes. The removal of old restraints, however, had given rise to wild speculations which threatened the dissolution of moral standards and social order.

In the midst of the confusion, Calvin took the lead in defining the new forms of Christian life and work, of church and community life, which under the newly discovered teaching of the Bible, and the power of the Spirit, were relevant to conditions in Europe in his day. Moreover he was able to help his contemporaries to attain a clarity of vision and an orderliness in theological thought and expression, which gave them a firmer grasp of the gospel in its fullness. At the same time, by the power of his preaching, the convincing clarity and simplicity of his teaching, and his practical ability and moral integrity which gave him finally an undisputed leadership in his community, he was conspicuously successful in achieving his aims in his own city-parish. His work in Geneva added greatly to the widespread fame which his writings had already brought him. His whole life-work, therefore, is an important and challenging illustration of how our theology, if it is healthy, should be related to our life-situation.

Calvin's theology is a theology of the word of God. He held that the revelation* given to us through Scripture* is the only reliable source of our knowledge of God. Though nature also reveals God, and all men and women have a natural instinct for religion, yet our human perversity prevents us from being able to profit from what nature presents to us. We must therefore turn to the witness to revelation given by God to his prophets and servants in the OT, and to the apostolic witness to Christ in the NT. The Scriptures themselves were inspired, and indeed 'dictated' by God. Their statements, stories and truths must be regarded as having infallible authority.

Calvin believed that there is a basic unity in the teaching of Scripture, and that the theologian must seek to clarify and give expression to this unity in the orderly setting out of its doctrines. As a theologian he sought to do justice to the whole content of the written word of God.

He also recognized, however, that Scripture was given to us by God not simply to present us today with truths and doctrines, but also to introduce us to the living revelation to which the written word bears witness. At the heart of this revelation which the apostles and prophets wrote about, there was for them a personal encounter with the Word of God himself, the second person of the Trinity. Even though they may have been the recipients of truths and doctrines, the biblical witnesses also knew themselves as men before God himself in personal love and majesty. Calvin believed that the theologian, in his approach to Scripture, must seek to find himself, and must regard himself, in this position too. He must therefore seek through the Scripture to be brought into communion and confrontation with the Lord himself, and in giving shape to his theology must take account of all the original events in and through which God revealed himself to his people. Calvin at times uses the language of mysticism to describe how faith enables us through the word and Spirit to grasp in vision much more than can be comprehended immediately by the understanding. In his approach to Scripture and his theological task, therefore, the prayerful quest for a fuller understanding of what he had already to some extent grasped, and for a closer communion with the living God, also played an important part.

Calvin did not therefore attempt to create a systematic theology* by subjecting the truths of Scripture to any controlling principles of human thought or logic. He tried rather to allow his thinking to be controlled by the whole word which God had spoken in Christ. The order in which he was able to cast his thought was an order which he found in the revelation which impressed itself upon his mind.

Calvin wrote commentaries on nearly all the books of the Bible. These had a vast circulation and are still of great use. He applied the methods of humanistic scholarship to the Bible to find out the exact meaning of the words of a text, and the circumstances of the history involved (see Hermeneutics*). His belief in the authority and integrity of the word made a critical approach to the text impossible. Though he allowed for a text to have various senses, he was sparing in his use of the allegorical method of interpretation. He believed that Christ was present to the people of God in the OT, though the revelation then given took different forms from that in the NT. He gave a lead in recognizing the use of typology as a clue to understanding the unity of the two testaments. His belief in this unity enabled him to interpret one text by the whole of Scripture. In his exegesis and theological work he always put himself into debt to other scholars. He was especially influenced by Augustine,* and he was a careful student of the Greek as well as of the Latin fathers. He gave final expression to his theology in the last edition of the *Institutes* in 1559 (French, 1560). The work is in four parts, following to some extent the order suggested by the Apostles' Creed: Book I, God the Creator; Book II, God the Redeemer; Book III, The Way we Receive the Grace of Christ; Book IV, The Church.

On the doctrine of God, Calvin avoids discussion of the hidden essence of God (*what God is*) and confines himself to the biblical teaching on the nature of God (*of what kind he is*). God himself proclaimed his 'eternity and self-existence' when he uttered his name,

'I am that I am'. Calvin's stress was always on the moral attributes or 'powers' of God. He finds such qualities adequately listed in two specific texts: Ex. 34:6–7 and Je. 9:24, which dwell especially on his mercy and justice. In his practice, too, in church and civil administration Calvin tried always to show that God was both 'a just God and a saviour', without one aspect of his goodness cancelling out the other. In discussing the doctrine of God, he does not mention the 'sovereignty* of God' which was not always (as some think) a dominating principle in his theology. For him, glory* was a special attribute of God, revealed everywhere in the world, shining out in all his redemptive works, but most fully displayed in the humiliation and love revealed in the cross. Calvin brings the Trinity* into the centre of his discussion on the nature of God, since revelation admits us into the heart of the mystery of the divine Being himself. Often in his theology Calvin reminds us that God has revealed himself fully in Christ, and that we must turn to no other source than the gospel for our knowledge of him.

When he discusses how God acts in providence,* we find ourselves often being spoken to pastorally (a characteristic of much of Calvin's theology). He assures us that God is always at work sustaining and guiding the whole of his creation, and directing the whole course of human history with gracious fatherly concern. The church and the Christian however are under especial care in the hands of God, as Christ was in the hands of God. We are never in the hands of 'fate' or 'chance'. Calvin's discussion of providence presents us with difficulty, however, when he suggests that by a decree of God from the remotest eternity, the plans and wills of people are so governed as to move exactly on the course which he has destined. When he discusses predestination* he traces the rejection of the non-elect back to this decree of God, which he describes in the Lat. word *horribile*, 'fearful, awesome'. It is at this point that many today would raise questions, and ask whether Calvin was himself being faithful to the central thrust of his own teaching on God, and whether he was doing justice to the freedom with which in the Bible God seems to act and react within developing situations. We have to remember that Calvin several times revised his *Institutes* as he wrote his commentaries, and did not regard his theology as having attained ultimate finality.

In his discussion of the person and work of Christ, Calvin repeated concisely and accurately the teaching of the church fathers and councils (see Christology*). He emphasized the mystery concealed in the person of the mediator, affirming that 'the Son of God descended from heaven in such a way that, without leaving heaven, he willed to be born in the virgin's womb, to go about the earth, to hang upon the cross; yet continuously filled the world even as he had done from the beginning'. Yet he so emphasized at times the limitations and frailty of Jesus' humanity that he was suspected by some of not believing in his divinity. He realized that we have to try to understand the person of Jesus in terms of the functions he fulfilled rather than in terms of the essence he concealed. He was the first theologian systematically to interpret Christ's work in terms of the threefold office* of prophet, priest and king. He stressed the penal element in Christ's sufferings on the cross, yet he also emphasized the value placed by God on his life-long obedience, both active and passive, and his sympathetic self-identification with us in our humanity. The incarnation created a 'holy brotherhood' between him and ourselves so that he might 'swallow up death and replace it with life, conquer sin and replace it with righteousness'.

Discussing how the fall* has affected humanity, originally made in the image of God,* Calvin will allow us to use the phrase 'total depravity' only in the sense that no aspect of man's original being or activity has been left unaffected by his sin. In all our dealings with others, we ourselves must still regard each person as being still in that image no matter how low he seems to have sunk. There are two spheres in which human life is set by God – the spiritual and the temporal. With regard to spiritual or heavenly matters mankind has been wholly deprived of all true knowledge and ability. With regard to temporal or earthly activities, the natural man still retains admirable qualities and abilities by which to conduct his manifold human affairs. Calvin admired, for example, the divine light which shone on the ancient heathen lawgivers in forming their legal codes, and he recognized that man has been endowed by God even in his fallen estate with brilliant gifts to adorn his existence, to allow him comfort, a measure of enjoyment and artistic self-expression in his earthly life. Calvin reminded his readers that in creation God has provided for our use not only the things that are necessary to sustain our life, but also many precious and beautiful things which are designed to give us pleasure and enjoyment. In Geneva one of his final achievements was to found an academy where the 'liberal arts and sciences' were taught by teachers trained in humanistic studies. Calvin was however concerned that the development and use of such arts and sciences should be in accordance with the law of God, and that they should be especially used in the service of the word of God and in the furtherance of a stable Christian community.

Calvin sought to continue and complete the work begun by Luther and other Reformers. He frequently re-echoed his predecessors' criticisms of Rome for denying the common man any place of personal security before a gracious God. Nine chapters of the *Institutes* were devoted to the doctrine of justification* by grace alone, and the Christian liberty this involved. Yet Calvin felt called upon by the situation prevailing around him to insist more firmly than had been already done on the importance of sanctification* or repentance,* and to define more clearly for his own day the new pattern of Christian living which alone could form a fitting and worthy response to God's grace and call in Christ. Therefore, in the final edition (1559) of his *Institutes*, he preceded his nine chapters on justification with nine on sanctification or repentance. He thus stressed the fact that there can be no forgiveness without repentance since both graces flow from our union* with Christ and neither can be prior to the other. He insisted that nothing which Christ suffered or did for us in his redeeming work is of any use if we are not united to him by faith, in order to receive personally from him the grace which he seeks to give us. He taught that this 'mystical union' between us and Christ is a work of the Holy Spirit.

The Christian must not only be united to Christ but must live in conformity to Christ in his death and resurrection. He listens to the imperative command of God: 'Be holy for I am holy', and to the call of the Lord to deny self, take up the cross and follow. Calvin attacks the root of human sin in self-love, and shows that self-denial can alone be the basis of outgoing love to all people. He urges the triumphal acceptance of every form of suffering to conform us to the image of Christ. Each of us gives obedient expression to our Christian faith as we pursue our earthly vocation.* We are meant to enjoy and use the earthly benefits which God often showers upon us as we pursue our path in life, yet even in such enjoyment we must remain detached, aspiring always towards the life to come, of which even now we enjoy some foretaste.

Calvin's desire to help the individual to live the Christian life with full assurance led him to give due place to the doctrine of predestination* in his discussion. He believed that no Christian could be finally victorious and confident unless he had some sense of his election to salvation. He believed that while Scripture taught this doctrine, it also pointed out that those who refused to believe must be predestined to damnation. Attacks on his writing on this matter forced him to defend himself in several treatises on the subject. We must not imagine, however, that this was the central doctrine in his theology. It is significant that next to his chapters on predestination in the *Institutes* Calvin places his magnificent chapter on prayer,* in which we are urged to exercise our free will in intercession before God and in seeking answers to the prayers we make.

A large section of the *Institutes* deals with the church* and its ministry.* Calvin was concerned that the form of ministry within the church, especially by the pastor, should reflect Christ's own ministry of utter humility, concern for each individual and faithfulness to the truth exercised in the power of the Spirit. He was concerned with instruction, discipline* and poor-relief. Therefore, along with the pastor in the ministry, he believed God had placed teachers or 'doctors' (experts in Scripture and theology), elders, and deacons. He found such offices indicated in Scripture, but he did not insist that every detail of the church's ordered life required explicit scriptural warrant. He admired the development of doctrine and liturgy during the first six centuries of the church's life and had no hesitation in reproducing features of this development. He believed that the 'bishop' of the NT and the early church corresponded to the pastor of a congregation in a truly reformed church. All ceremonies in the church must be simple and clearly intelligible and justifiable in the light of Scripture. He believed that the second commandment forbade not only the use of images* in worship, but also the invention of ceremonies merely to stimulate religious emotion. He encouraged congregational singing, but felt that musical instruments gave too uncertain a sound to be the accompaniment of rational worship.

Calvin followed Augustine in regarding a sacrament* as a visible sign of an invisible grace. Only baptism* and the Lord's Supper (see Eucharist*) were sacraments with dominical authority. He denounced the doctrine of transubstantiation and the idea that a sacrament was efficacious by virtue of its merely being performed as a ritual. He also rejected the view that the bread and wine were given by Christ as mere symbols representing his body and blood, meant simply to stimulate our memory, devotion and faith. The sacraments give what they represent, he insisted. We are not asked by the Lord merely to look, but to eat and drink. This is a sign that between him and us there is a life-giving union (in relation to which Calvin even uses the word 'substantial'). This union is given and created when the word is preached and responded to by faith; it is also increased and strengthened when the sacrament is received by faith. Calvin rejected current Lutheran explanations of this mystery of the efficacy of the sacrament. He often stated that the body of Christ, on which we feed, remains in heaven, and our souls are raised there by the wonderful power of the Spirit to feed upon him. Calvin insisted that a sacrament was inefficacious apart from the faith of the recipient. He justified the baptism of infants by his view of the unity of the old and new covenants,* and by urging that the efficacy of a sacrament need not be tied to the moment of its administration.

The relationship between church and state* was an acute issue in Calvin's lifetime. His struggle in Geneva involved him in a determined stand against attempts by the civil authority to interfere in matters relating to church discipline, which he felt should be entirely under the control of a specifically ecclesiastical court. He had a high view of the state, and stressed the duty of citizens to obey the law and to give honour to their rulers. He also stressed the duty of rulers to care, like shepherds, for each of their subjects. He advised obedience even to tyrants, and the

acceptance of unjust suffering rather than the resort to revolutionary* plotting. Yet he believed that a tyrant could be overthrown by the deliberate action of a justly constituted lower authority within a state, or by an 'avenger' from elsewhere raised up and elected by God.

Bibliography

Institutes, tr. F. L. Battles, ed. J. T. McNeill, 2 vols., London, 1961; *Commentaries* on the NT, tr. and ed. by D. W. Torrance and T. F. Torrance, 12 vols. (Edinburgh, 1959–72).

F. L. Battles (ed.), *The Piety of John Calvin* (Grand Rapids, MI, 1978); J. T. McNeill, *The History and Character of Calvinism* (New York, 1954); W. Niesel, *The Theology of Calvin* (London, 1956); T. H. L. Parker, *John Calvin* (London, 1975); H. Quistorp, *Calvin's Doctrine of the Last Things* (London, 1955); H. Y. Reyburn, *John Calvin: His Life, Letters and Work* (London, 1914); R. S. Wallace, *Calvin's Doctrine of the Word and Sacrament* (Edinburgh, 1953); idem, *Calvin's Doctrine of the Christian Life* (Edinburgh, 1957); F. Wendel, *Calvin: The Origins and Development of His Religious Thought* (London, 1963); E. D. Willis, *Calvin's Catholic Christology* (Leiden, 1966).

R.S.W.

CALVINISM, see REFORMED THEOLOGY.

CALVINISTIC METHODISM was the product of the 18th-century evangelical awakening in England and Wales. Its chief representatives were George Whitefield* and Daniel Rowland (1713–90). Its theology found expression in their sermons, in the prose and poetical works of William Williams of Pant-y-celyn (1717–91), and in the Confession of Faith which appeared in 1823 from the Welsh Calvinistic Methodists.

It can be described as theology for the heart, giving expression to a mainline Calvinism within an experimental and practical framework. It drew heavily and heartily on earlier Puritanism,* and yet shared unashamedly the individual pietism of contemporary (Arminian*) Methodism.* As such, it confessed a biblical authority for matters of faith and conduct, and a Trinitarian, Protestant* and evangelical* faith.

The distinctives of Calvinistic Methodism

lie in the prominence given to the Holy Spirit's* influences in man's salvation, and in the experimental ethos of its soul culture. Light and life, holiness and love, submission to the divine will and the realization of human dignity, were to be held in biblical balance. They were also to be enjoyed and nurtured in the disciplined context of warm but heart-searching fellowship or 'society' meetings.

In England, Calvinistic Methodism waned after the passing of Whitefield, but in Wales it remained vigorous for another century. It did so for two main reasons: able leadership from men like Thomas Charles ('of Bala', 1755–1814) and John Elias ('of Anglesey', 1774–1841), and repeated, powerful revivals. The Calvinistic passion for order later spilled over into church polity as well, determining for Welsh Calvinistic Methodism a place among the Presbyterian* family. Liberalism* and ecumenism* in the 20th century have contributed to the decline of Calvinistic Methodist theology.

Bibliography

E. Evans, *Daniel Rowland and the Great Evangelical Awakening in Wales* (Edinburgh, 1985); *idem, Howel Harris* (Cardiff, 1974); *idem*, 'The Confession of Faith of the Welsh Calvinistic Methodists', *Journal of the Hist. Soc. of the Presb. Church of Wales* 59 (1974), pp. 2–11; G. T. Hughes, *Williams Pantycelyn* (Cardiff, 1983); D. M. Lloyd-Jones, 'William Williams and Welsh Calvinistic Methodism', *The Manifold Grace of God* (The Puritan and Reformed Studies Conference) (London, 1968); W. Williams, *Welsh Calvinistic Methodism* (London, ²1884).

E.E.

CAMBRIDGE PLATONISTS. At the beginning of the 17th century, much Protestant theology was closely interwoven with Aristotelian* philosophy. Puritan* commitment to a reasoned faith and a liveable theology, English interest in the fathers and dissatisfaction with the aridity of theological systems led a group of scholars in Cambridge to restate theology in a Platonic* mode which emphasized the deification* of the believer.

While cherishing many previous insights, the Cambridge Platonists sought the fundamentals of authentic Christianity outside the Augustinian* tradition. Their reading of Plato, Plotinus and fathers such as Origen*

gave them new perspectives and optimism about the role of reason. 'Our reason is not confounded by our Religion, but awakened, excited, employed, directed and improved' (Benjamin Whichcote, 1609–83). Whichcote, Henry More (1614–87), Ralph Cudworth (1617–88) and John Smith (1618–52) were the leaders of this movement. They rejected the dominant Reformed* theology of the Church of England. At times they were accused of Socinianism* because of their critique of Protestant orthodoxy, their commitment to toleration,* their plea for essentials and their insistence on the inseparable connection between truth and holiness. They were not, however, interested in theological reductionism, but sought to ground faith securely in a more adequate metaphysic,* which safeguarded the heart of Christianity from the fanaticism of enthusiasts and the misunderstanding of materialist philosophers such as Thomas Hobbes (1588–1679). Their optimism about an alliance between revelation and reason was not uncritical. More was initially an admirer of Descartes,* but he saw Descartes less and less as an ally and had rejected him by 1671.

In books such as Cudworth's *The True Intellectual System of The Universe* (1678) they sought to uphold a spiritual account of reality against determinism* and materialism.* The complexity of their thought limited their influence to this field, but their theology of creation* provided the context for their account of Christ as the one who enlivened the divine seed within us and moulded us into the divine likeness. Their striking aphorisms were more easily remembered than their subtle and detailed arguments about the spiritual and rational.

While they gave an impressive account of the reality of the soul, they did not always do justice to human sinfulness and the insights of Protestant soteriology. They provided an important alternative to Puritan denigration of natural reason and virtue. The letters between Whichcote and Anthony Tuckney (1599–1670) brought out sharply the extent of the differences between Platonist and Puritan. The group's academic and religious stature provided important ingredients for the restatement of English theology after 1660, helping to create a more generous and tolerant spirit. Unfortunately some of their admirers lacked the depth of their mentors. The resulting latitudinarianism* could sometimes pass readily into deism.* Nevertheless, they shared the creative power of partnership between revelation and reason. Their emphasis on God's love and rationality provided a vital alternative to the doctrine of God in the Westminster Confession. They made lasting contributions to ethical reflection, as well as exploring contemporary philosophical and scientific issues with an authority and insight that is all too rare among theologians. Their style of writing often makes them difficult for modern readers, but they represent one of the high points of the English theological tradition.

Bibliography

G. R. Cragg, *The Cambridge Platonists* (Oxford, 1968); C. A. Patrides, *The Cambridge Platonists* (London, 1969); J. D. Roberts, *From Puritanism to Platonism in Seventeenth Century England* (The Hague, 1968).

I.B.

CAMPBELL, JOHN McLEOD (1800–72). A recent historian has suggested that Campbell is the outstanding name in Scottish theology during the last century (B. M. G. Reardon, *From Coleridge to Gore*, London, 1971, p. 404). The importance of Campbell derives from the fact that he departed significantly from the orthodoxy of his day and constructed a most novel view of the atonement.*

John McLeod Campbell was born at Kilninver near Oban, the son of a Church of Scotland minister. After study at Glasgow University and in the Divinity Hall at Edinburgh University, he was inducted into the parish of Row (Rhu) in 1825. From all accounts he was a faithful and well-loved pastor. It was not long, however, before he was plucked from relative obscurity and thrust into the ecclesiastical limelight. In 1830 he was arraigned for heresy, first by his presbytery and then by the General Assembly, accused of teaching that Jesus died to save the whole of mankind, and that assurance* of salvation belonged to the essence of saving faith. Both doctrines contradicted the teaching of the Westminster Confession of Faith, the Church's principal 'Subordinate Standard of Faith'. In 1831 the General Assembly voted by 119 to 6 to depose Campbell from the

ministry, a vote which he accepted without rancour. He spent the remainder of his ministry serving an Independent congregation in Glasgow.

Campbell is best remembered for his work *The Nature of the Atonement*, described by R. S. Franks as 'the most systematic and masterly book on the work of Christ produced by a British theologian in the nineteenth century' (*The Work of Christ*, London, 1962, p. 665). The acclaim accorded to Campbell's work led to the erstwhile heretic being praised as a theologian of renown, to the extent that in 1868 he was awarded an honorary doctorate by Glasgow University.

Campbell's novel theory was developed in response to his intense dissatisfaction with, and ultimate rejection of, the premises of Calvinistic theology. He believed that Calvinism's premise of the penal-substitutionary nature of Christ's atonement necessitated the conclusion that Christ died only for the elect (see Atonement, Extent of*). Campbell held that this view 'destroys the claim of the work of Christ to be what fully reveals and illustrates the great foundation of all religion that God is love' (*The Nature of the Atonement*, p. 65). Among the more important features of Campbell's new model of the atonement were: 1. The incarnation* and not the cross was regarded as the 'primary and highest fact in the history of God's relation to man'. 2. The penal-substitutionary model with its legal categories was displaced by a filial model, built upon personal categories. 3. The atonement was viewed as having a prospective as well as a retrospective element. 4. The atonement is made not by Christ suffering vicariously the wrath of God for sinners, but by Christ's perfect confession and repentance* of sin – an idea Campbell attributed to Jonathan Edwards,* who maintained that atonement for sin required 'either an equivalent punishment or an equivalent sorrow and repentance' (*The Nature of the Atonement*, p. 137).

Campbell's theory has been given prominence in the recent past most notably by Karl Barth,* T. F. Torrance* and J. B. Torrance (b. 1923). Their appreciation of his model of the atonement has done much to resurrect Campbell as a significant theologian. Despite this appreciation, however, Campbell's theory is beset with numerous difficulties. First, the cross and not the incarnation lies at the heart of the biblical view of the atonement.

Secondly, Campbell nowhere spells out *how* Christ's repentance avails for others, having rejected all notions of substitution* as unworthy. Robert Mackintosh* makes the observation that 'on the connection between Christ and mankind, Campbell's views seem peculiarly obscure' (*Historic Theories of Atonement*, London, 1920, p. 218). Critics of all schools have suggested that Campbell's theory, rather than superseding the traditional view of the atonement, substituted for it 'something very like absurdity. The idea of a confession made by a perfectly holy being, involving *all* the elements of a perfect repentance, *except* the personal consciousness of sin, is certainly absurd enough' (A. B. Bruce, *The Humiliation of Christ*, Edinburgh, 1881, p. 318).

Bibliography
The Nature of the Atonement (London, ⁴1959).

T. J. Crawford, *The Doctrine of Scripture Respecting the Atonement* (Edinburgh, 1871); J. Macquarrie, 'John McLeod Campbell, 1800–72', *ExpT* 83 (1972), pp. 263–268; G. M. Tuttle, *So Rich a Soil: John McLeod Campbell on Christian Atonement* (Edinburgh, 1986).

I.Ha.

CANON, see SCRIPTURE.

CANONIZATION, see SAINT.

CANON LAW. The Greek word *kanōn* means a rule, and canon law comprises the disciplinary regulations of the church. These began to be formulated in the early centuries by local and ecumenical councils,* and are distinct from the decisions which the ancient councils made on matters of belief. However, they are likewise expressions of an NT concern for order and moral discipline in the church. The common law of the Eastern church still consists essentially of the canons of the early councils (in which they include the so-called *Apostolic Canons*, appended to the 4th-century *Apostolic Constitutions*, and the numerous canons of the 692 Quinisext Council, not recognized in the West).

Influential individual bishops also issued decrees which became embodied in canon law, and this was especially the case with the decrees of popes, which continued to be added through the Middle Ages. The 9th-century *False Decretals* were also drawn upon. The 12th-century *Decretum* of Gratian of Bologna gained its fame as being a much-needed systematic and annotated arrangement of Western canon law, and was taken bodily into the official *Corpus* of Roman canon law. The *Corpus* has several times been revised, most recently in 1983.

Whether Roman canon law was binding in England during the Middle Ages has been disputed, perhaps wrongly, but since the Reformation the only parts considered by the courts to retain their force are those which have long been incorporated in the statute or common law of the realm and do not conflict with post-Reformation statute or custom. The Reformers proposed a new code of canon law entitled the *Reformation of the Ecclesiastical Laws* but, owing to the death of Edward VI, it was never enacted, though it was published by John Foxe in 1571. However, in 1603–4 a brief new code of canons was drawn up and approved by Convocation and received the royal assent. They became binding on the clergy of the Church of England (but not the laity, not having been submitted to Parliament). They were clearly Reformed in character, though with an anti-Puritan tendency, and remained in force until a fresh and less stringent code replaced them in 1969.

Bibliography
The Canons of the Church of England (London, 1969); *New Code of Canon Law* (London, 1983); Earl of Halsbury, *Ecclesiastical Law*, ed. R. P. Moore (London, ⁴1957); E. W. Kemp, *An Introduction to Canon Law in the Church of England* (London, 1957); R. C. Mortimer, *Western Canon Law* (London, 1953).

R.T.B.

CAPPADOCIAN FATHERS, see BASIL; GREGORY OF NAZIANZUS; GREGORY OF NYSSA; HISTORY OF THEOLOGY.

CARNELL, EDWARD JOHN (1919–67). An American evangelical apologist, theologian and president of Fuller Theological Seminary (1954–59), Carnell was a major figure in the mid-20th century development of an intelligent and articulate exposition of evangelicalism* in the USA. He was the author of books on Kierkegaard* (*The*

Burden of Søren Kierkegaard, Grand Rapids, MI, 1965) and on Reinhold Niebuhr* (*The Theology of Reinhold Niebuhr*, Grand Rapids, MI, 1951), and of three influential apologies.* In the first of these, *An Introduction to Christian Apologetics* (Grand Rapids, MI, 1948), Carnell proposes 'systematic consistency' (that is, 'obedience to the law of non-contradiction' and conformity with 'the totality of our experiences') as the test of truth. He attempts to show that the Christian world-view passes this test, while other religions and world-views cannot.

A Philosophy of the Christian Religion (Grand Rapids, MI, 1952) adds to the author's earlier work an apologetic based on values (axiologies). Carnell surveys 'a set of typical value options' for which an individual might live and die. In each case he gives reason why 'one must move on from the lower to the higher'. The 'lower immediacies' of material goods and pleasures, the 'higher immediacies' of the pursuit of knowledge, and the 'threshold options' of devotion to man and to sub-Christian gods, are all unable to provide ultimate satisfaction, which can only be found through faith in the person of Christ.

The argument of *Christian Commitment* (New York, 1957) is moral rather than axiological or rational. Carnell proposes 'a third way of knowing', in addition to knowledge by acquaintance and knowledge by inference. 'Knowledge by moral self-acceptance', or knowledge of truth as rectitude, is intimately involved in knowing persons, including oneself and God. But one cannot have this kind of knowledge without being 'morally transformed by the realities that already hold one'. Carnell's third apology is both an argument from 'the judicial sentiment' to God who is its source, and a call to humble ourselves in order to know the person of God.

Bibliography

M. Erickson, *The New Evangelical Theology* (Westwood, NJ, 1968); B. Ramm, *Types of Apologetic Systems* (Wheaton, IL, 1953); J. Sims, *Edward John Carnell – Defender of the Faith* (Washington, DC, 1979).

D.W.C.

CAROLINE DIVINES. During the first half of the 17th century there were three main parties in the English Church: the Puritans,* critical of the Elizabethan settlement and its spirituality as but half a reformation; the school of Richard Hooker,* appealing to the God-given principle of human reason as a guide to the Christian in 'things indifferent', and questioning the Puritan appeal to an exclusively biblical regulative authority; and what came eventually to be known as the 'High Church Party', led successively by Richard Bancroft (1544–1610) and William Laud (1573–1645), Archbishops of Canterbury. Among this group emerged a number of able moral and controversial theologians, most of whom held high office in the Church during the reigns of Charles I and Charles II. They were known collectively as the Caroline Divines, and included such churchmen as Jeremy Taylor (1613–67), Herbert Thorndike (1598–1672), Gilbert Sheldon (1598–1677) and Henry Hammond (1605–60).

Although they gave a high place in their theology to the authority of the Bible, their main theological inspiration was the writings of the fathers of the early church: probably no other group in English church history has been so skilled in patristics.* As a consequence, their spirituality reveals an openness to mystery and the more subliminal and less verbal aspects of relationship to God which was at odds with the Puritan preoccupation with the word. One practical effect of this was the 'beauty of holiness' programme conducted by Laud in the 1630s, restoring colour, music and beauty to the worship of the church. In this, as in other things, their instinct was to emphasize those features of the Church of England which reflected its continuity with the pre-Reformation church. They were, however, keen supporters of the Elizabethan settlement as a *via media* between the extremes of papacy and sectarianism, and had no hesitation in rejecting papal claims to supremacy. At the same time, however, they accepted (as others did not) that the Church of Rome was a genuine Christian church.

Their attitude towards other Protestant churches was more ambivalent. Increasingly they tended to question their right to be regarded as authentic churches unless they were episcopally ordered (see Ministry*). Indeed, they regarded the bishop as the *sine qua non* of the true church, and saw it as the peculiar glory of the Church of England that it had both bishops and a history of reformation. But in order to protect this insistence on episcopacy against the attacks of Puritans they forged an alliance with the monarch, thus attaching episcopacy as a theory to the doctrine of the divine right of kings which they did much to promote.

During the Interregnum the majority of the Caroline Divines went into exile with the King, and it was in this context that their apologia for the Church of England was finally formulated in dialogue with Catholic and Protestant critics, both of whom regarded the *via media* as an experiment that had failed. Not surprisingly, the sufferings of this time led to an intransigence towards the Puritan party once the Restoration had occurred. The few who remained in England seem to have adopted more irenic attitudes: Richard Baxter* deeply regretted the death of Henry Hammond, formerly canon of Christ Church, Oxford, in 1660, because of his known willingness to seek grounds for the comprehension of dissenters within the church.

Theologically the Caroline Divines were usually regarded as Arminian,* but this reflects more their antipathy to Puritanism than their views on salvation. They shared with the Puritans, however, the 17th-century preoccupation with the study of cases of conscience (see Casuistry*); Robert Sanderson (1587–1663), Bishop of Lincoln, was probably the leading English moral theologian* of the century. They were deeply committed to the *Book of Common Prayer*, and their corporate and private piety was focused on the Holy Communion. Their influence declined during the closing decades of the century, but was revived with the rise of the Oxford Movement in the 19th century (see Anglo-Catholic Theology*), which held them to be the authentic tradition of Anglicanism* after the Reformation.

Bibliography

R. S. Bosher, *The Making of the Restoration Settlement* (London, 1951); I. M. Green, *The Re-Establishment of the Church of England, 1660–1663* (Oxford, 1979); H. R. McAdoo, *The Structure of Caroline Moral Theology* (London and New York, 1949); J. Sears McGee, *The Godly Man in Stuart England* (New Haven, CT, 1976); P. E. Moore and F. L. Cross, *Anglicanism* (London, 1935); J. W. Packer, *The Transformation of Anglicanism, 1643–1660* (Manchester, 1969); N. Sykes, *From Sheldon to Secker* (Cambridge, 1959); H. R. Trevor-Roper, *Laud* (London, 1962).

D.D.S.

CASUISTRY. The application of moral principles and the determination of right and wrong in particular cases (Lat. *casus*) in light of the peculiar circumstances and situation. The need for casuistry arises because it is not possible to frame or express general moral rules relevant to every situation and case without exception. Casuistry seeks to make the general rule more specific, and apply it directly to the actual moral situation. This may be seen positively as making the law more specific and removing obscurity and doubt as to its application. In Puritanism* it accompanied a scrupulousness over 'cases of conscience'.* Unfortunately, however, casuistry in Christian history has been seen negatively as providing excuses and permitting exceptions where there ought to be none, particularly among Jesuits* in the 17th century. The term often suggests a debater able to justify even what is wrong by a process of reasoning based on exceptions. Casuistry thus bears some resemblance to 'situation' ethics.* Theologically, casuistry takes seriously the fallen nature of the world and of humankind and recognizes the complexity of moral decisions. Therefore, to cope with the ambiguity and finitude of human existence, people require moral guidance given in a detailed way.

Bibliography

J. C. Ford and G. Kelly, *Contemporary Moral Theology*, 2 vols. (Westminster, MD, 1958–63); K. E. Kirk, *Conscience and its Problems: An Introduction to Casuistry* (London, 1927); P. Lehmann, *Ethics in a Christian Context* (London, 1963).

E.D.C.

CATECHISMS. 'I must still read and study the Catechism daily,' declared Martin Luther,* in the Preface to his own Short Catechism (1529), 'yet I cannot master it as I wish, but must remain a child and pupil of the Catechism, and I do it gladly.' Luther's epochal Short and Long Catechisms were written in response to the spiritual ignorance which he discovered in Saxony. For him, a catechism was a clear statement, in question-and-answer form, of the essentials of the Christian faith, especially the Decalogue, the

Apostles' Creed,* the Lord's Prayer, and the sacraments.* This has become the chief meaning of the word, but it can also be used of teaching aids of different types (for example charts or books) and containing different subject-matter.

While in one sense Luther initiated a movement in catechesis which lasted until the present century, from another point of view his work was itself part of a far wider tradition. From the earliest days the church was concerned to instruct its converts and nurture its members. The focus and methods of instruction have changed from time to time. The careful initiation of the catechumenate characteristic of the earlier centuries, for example, gave way to the far more unstructured methods of the Middle Ages, largely as a result of the widespread practice of infant baptism. There remained, however, a concern that the ordinary Christian learn the basic truths of religion and piety, and, as their educational work began, the Protestant Reformers were able to draw upon an existing pattern of the instruction of children, however haphazardly it had been carried out. As Luther's words indicate, the catechism was not for children only, but was meant to form the basic doctrinal understanding of all Christians.

Luther's were not the first Lutheran* catechisms; nor were they the last. An immense multiplication of these teaching manuals occurred, in Germany and elsewhere, as pastors produced their own, often having them printed and distributed widely. In the Catholic Church, catechisms such as that of 1555 by the Jesuit* Peter Canisius (1521–97) were used widely for the laity, as was the catechism of the Council of Trent (1566) for priests. Such catechisms have continued to be used among Catholics to the present day. Of the thousands of Protestant catechisms composed in the 16th and 17th centuries, however, some deserve special mention.

Luther's Short Catechism is a masterpiece of its kind. Its pithy answers were intended to be learned by heart, but Luther was aware of the dangers of rote learning and insisted on comprehension. By adopting the order 'law, creed, prayer, sacraments', Luther was intentionally setting out the gospel as he taught it – the law* to reveal sin, faith* to provide the cure, and the Lord's Prayer to call for grace. Nonetheless, he clearly intended that the law

should guide the life of Christians as well. His division of the Apostles' Creed into three parts, corresponding with the work of the Trinity* in creation,* redemption* and sanctification,* gave his work a powerfully evangelical* orientation.

Reformed Christians were also quick to draw up catechisms. John Calvin's* Catechism of the Church of Geneva (1541) exercised a strong influence among churches of this persuasion. Calvin began with faith rather than the law, which he saw primarily as the rule of life for Christians. Distinctive Reformed* notes may be found in its treatment of Christ's descent into hell* and the Lord's Supper (cf. Eucharist*), as well as a pervasive emphasis on union with Christ.* Dean Alexander Nowell (c. 1507–1602), whose lengthy English catechism of 1563 relied heavily on Calvin, muted this teaching on union with Christ and reversed Calvin's order by treating the law first.

The most important of the early Reformed works, however, was the Heidelberg Catechism (1563), composed by Zacharias Ursinus (1534–83) and Caspar Olevianus (1536–87) for use in the Palatinate. Its sacramental theology is clearly Reformed, but it attempts on the whole to mediate between Lutheran and Reformed teaching. It is still in use today in Reformed Churches in the Dutch tradition (cf. Dutch Reformed Theology*), a tribute to its clarity, brevity and warm piety. The brilliantly conceived opening question, 'What is your only comfort in life and in death?' is matched by a profound answer which begins, 'That I, with body and soul, both in life and in death, am not my own, but belong to my faithful Saviour Jesus Christ . . .' The threefold shape, 'The Misery of Man', 'The Redemption of Man' and 'Thankfulness', likewise contributes to its attractiveness.

The Book of Common Prayer contains a brief specimen of an English catechism, but the most vigorous use of catechisms was to be found among the Puritans,* such as William Perkins (1558–1602). Perkins' The Foundation of Christian Religion is of interest because it provides an example of how teaching experience and theological concerns changed the form and content of the catechism. The Foundation was intended for use before the conventional catechism, in an attempt to make real the experience of the

Christian faith to the learner, that it may be 'in some measure felt in the heart'.

Perhaps the most famous of all Reformed catechisms, however, is the Shorter Catechism produced by the Westminster Assembly in 1648. Its influence, especially in Scotland, has been unparalleled. T. F. Torrance* calls it 'one of the greatest and most remarkable documents in the whole history of Christian theology'. The Catechism explains the law, the sacraments and the Lord's Prayer, but it abandons the creed in favour of an opening section which treats the subject of God, his decrees and covenants and sets out the story of redemption accomplished and applied. Its power arises from the logical progression of its thought and the brief but extraordinarily precise answers to the questions.

Instruction from catechisms was intended to occur at home, at school and at church. The well-taught congregation was thus thought to be equipped to benefit from sermons, since the catechism provided the doctrinal framework suitable to understand the exposition of passages of Scripture. The dialogical method attempted to create a perceptive response to divine truth and the catechisms attempted to structure the truth in an orderly way corresponding to the progress of the Christian life. As a form of teaching, however, they have largely fallen out of favour (although a new one is occasionally published and in some circles the practice of catechising has experienced a revival in recent years), and it is salutary to note G. Strauss's assessment that for all the efforts of the first generations of Lutherans the results were meagre and counter-productive. The question is now raised whether it is possible or desirable to organize the spiritual growth of an individual and whether the abstracting of creed, Decalogue and Lord's Prayer from the corpus of Christian truth was theologically justifiable. Whatever their faults, however, catechisms did attempt to teach basic doctrine and it is to the impoverishment of the church that nothing seems to have taken their place.

Bibliography

H. Bonar, *Catechisms of the Scottish Reformation* (London, 1866); D. Janz, *Three Reformation Catechisms: Catholic, Anabaptist, Lutheran* (New York, 1982); G. Strauss, *Luther's House of Learning* (Baltimore, MD, 1978); T. F. Torrance, *The School of Faith* (London, 1959); J. H. Westerhoff III and O. C. Edwards, Jr., *A Faithful Church* (Wilton, CT, 1981).

P.F.J.

CATHOLICITY is a 'note' (or mark) of the church* of God, along with unity, holiness and apostolicity. In the patristic* period catholicity pointed to the fact that the one church of God was a universal society, confessing one faith, with one baptism and engaged in God's mission in his world because it was united to Christ the Lord.

However, the fact of schism,* division and heresy* led to the need to have criteria to establish catholicity. The most famous and widely used test is that of Vincent of Lérins (d. before 450) who, in the early 5th century, provided a threefold test in what we now call the Vicentian Canon. It is: *Quod ubique, quod semper, quod ab omnibus creditum est* ('What has been believed everywhere, always and by all'). Those who take these criteria seriously have seen this as pointing to the sacred Scriptures, the ancient creeds,* the two sacraments* and the threefold ministry* as the necessary norms of catholicity. Others add the papacy* as the means whereby the norms are maintained. Taken in this way, this Canon excludes large parts of orthodox Protestantism* from the universal church of God. Thus, if the word 'catholicity' is to be useful it must bear another meaning.

One possibility is that it be used with a minimal meaning, merely pointing to the historical and existential fact that because Christ commanded the gospel to be preached throughout the whole created order, the church therefore became a universal society. Another, more productive, approach is to recall that 'catholic' points to wholeness (*kath' holou*, 'on the whole') and thus see catholicity as that into which God calls his church because he has already provided wholeness for his people in the Lord Jesus. This wholeness includes all that which Christ, in and by the Spirit, wants to share with, and pour into, his body, in terms of the fruit and gifts of the sanctifying and liberating Spirit. In this way of understanding, therefore, catholicity is experienced more or less now and is that towards which the people of God move in hope as pilgrims. It may be added that this approach accords with the first recorded use of 'catholic' in the literature of the church. In

131

c. 112 Ignatius of Antioch wrote to the church in Smyrna: 'Wherever Christ is, there is the catholic church'.

Bibliography
ET of Vincent's *Commonitorium*, in G. E. McCracken, *Early Medieval Theology* (*LCC* IX; London, 1957).

R. N. Flew and R. E. Davies (eds.), *The Catholicity of Protestantism* (London, 1950); A. Harnack, *History of Dogma*, vol. 2 (London, ²1896); D. T. Jenkins, *The Nature of Catholicity* (London, 1942); J. H. Maude in *ERE* 3, pp. 258–261; J. Pearson, *An Exposition of the Creed* (1659), ed. E. Walford (London, 1850).

P.T.

CELIBACY, see SEXUALITY.

CHALCEDON, CHALCEDONIAN DEFINITION, see CHRISTOLOGY; COUNCILS; CREEDS.

CHALMERS, THOMAS (1780–1847). A professor of divinity at Edinburgh from 1828 until his death, Chalmers was famous as a preacher, parish minister and leader of the evangelical* party in the Church of Scotland, and of the Free Church of Scotland after the Disruption of 1843. Although his reputation rests here, and his disdain for theological systems was well known if not well remembered, his influence on generations of Scottish students of theology was profound. He retained many of the finer values of the Moderate tradition which he had embraced prior to his conversion in 1811, and came to represent the evangelical tradition which finds its major concerns in the proclamation and application of the gospel, rather than in over-precise formulation of its content. The atonement* was central to the mission of the church in personal and social transformation, but he told his students not to preach predestination;* that was God's business, not theirs. The liberalization of Presbyterian adherence to the harsher aspects of the Westminster Confession of Faith which took place some thirty years after his death reflects many of the theological values of his preaching and lectures. His sermon 'The fullness and freeness of the gospel offer' summarizes in title and content his basic understanding of the Christian message. His *Theological Institutes* are volumes 7 and 8 of his *Posthumous Works*, 1847–49, and other relevant writings can be found in his *Works*, 1836–42.

Bibliography
S. J. Brown, *Thomas Chalmers and the Godly Commonwealth* (Oxford, 1982); A. C. Cheyne (ed.), *The Practical and the Pious: Essays on Thomas Chalmers (1780–1847)* (Edinburgh, 1985); S. Piggin and J. Roxborogh, *The St Andrews Seven* (Edinburgh, 1985).

W.J.R.

CHARISMATIC THEOLOGY, see BAPTISM IN THE SPIRIT; GIFTS OF THE SPIRIT; PENTECOSTALISM.

CHEMNITZ, MARTIN, see LUTHERANISM.

CHICAGO SCHOOL OF THEOLOGY. The leading proponent of theological modernism and the radical wing of the liberal* movement in American Protestantism, the Chicago school of theology is associated largely with the Divinity School of the University of Chicago during the half century from 1890 to 1940. Reaching its summit while Shailer Mathews (1863–1941) was dean (1908–33), other prominent members of the Chicago school included George Burman Foster (1858–1918), Shirley Jackson Case (1872–1947), Gerald Birney Smith (1868–1929), Edward Scribner Ames (1870–1958) and Henry Nelson Wieman (1884–1975). Incorporating a wide variety of perspectives, the Chicago modernists championed an empirical* and pragmatic approach to religion which stressed its functional values and betrayed an indebtedness to the philosophies of William James (1842–1910), John Dewey (1859–1952), George Herbert Mead (1863–1931), and Charles Peirce (1839–1914).

Chicago modernism celebrated the 'spirit of the age' in both its scientific and democratic dimensions. Theologically, this entailed a rejection of special revelation* as the basis for theological authority in favour of an appeal to experience as the criterion of truth in religion. However, their emphasis on experience was not in the Schleiermacheran* tradition of using personal religious experience,* but the more radical approach of securing scientific legitimacy for religion by appealing to experience in the public domain – that is, that which is accessible to and verifiable by all enquirers. A socio-historical method for studying religious phenomena as human behaviour, and not divine, was urged, since all theological traditions were thought to evolve with time. Thus an openness to radical questioning of theological forms, a willingness to experiment with new conceptions of God, and an affirmation of human ideals and values – with an accompanying drift toward humanism – all characterized the school.

Culturally, the Chicago modernists were also virtually apostles for a 'religion of democracy'. Exuding optimism about altruistic human nature and an evolutionary ascent that boded well for man's future, they combined and confounded Christianity and democracy. This liberal belief in an immanent and democratic deity was sorely tested by the new spirit of pessimism and cynicism emerging from Word War I and economic depression which followed it.

Bibliography

C. H. Arnold, *Near the Edge of Battle: A Short History of the Divinity School and the Chicago School of Theology 1866–1966* (Chicago, 1966); W. J. Hynes, *Shirley Jackson Case and the Chicago School: the Socio-Historical Method* (Chico, CA, 1981).

S.R.P.

CHRIST, JESUS, see CHRISTOLOGY; JESUS.

CHRISTENDOM. The term 'Christendom' has come to be particularly applied to that period of Christian history in which Christian religion was an integral and fundamental part of the social order. It has been more loosely used of the Christian world as a whole. On the narrower interpretation, to be a full member of society one also had to be a member of the church. The turning-point in Christian history which changed the relationship of the church to the state* from one of hostility or grudging acceptance to one of privilege and mutual affirmation, was the conversion of Constantine, *c.* 312 AD. The arrival of a Christian emperor in time changed the whole relationship of the church to the state. The possibility of a society which conformed to Christian values seemed to be

open to the whole of society and not just to the church within it. Thus in practice as well as in thought much more attention had to be given to the respective roles and relationships of the church and of the state as different aspects of the one Christian social order (see Society, Theology of*).

Medieval society is often considered to be the time of the full flowering of Christendom. The division of Christendom into the Western and Eastern traditions prevented the Christian parts of the world from being united in a single culture within one church. At the political end, the symbol of the Christian emperor following the tradition of Charlemagne (crowned by the pope on Christmas Day, 800) and at the church end the symbol of the pope as the vicar of Peter and of Christ, point to the hopes and aims of Christendom. The failure to resolve the battle for power between the papacy and the emperor and royalties of Europe, the attempt to destroy Islam through the Crusades, the flowering of classical non-Christian thought in the universities and the development of national political organization all sowed the seeds of the failure of the Christendom experience. Nevertheless, the Reformation in the 16th century did not destroy the notion of a uniform society of church and state. It undid the universal power of the papacy over the church in Western Europe, but in different ways theologians such as Luther,* Calvin* and Hooker* continued to believe in and work for a united form of Christian social order with complementary roles for church and state.

It has taken the combination of the Enlightenment,* secularization,* political revolution and reform, and the development of a pluralistic social order finally to destroy the reality of Christendom. Only the memories remain, in aspects of our culture and in folk religion.

There have been Christian thinkers who believed it right to seek to recover a Christian form of society in the 20th century. The Christendom movement which had some influence in England in the 1920s and 1930s, supported and enabled by men such as V. A. Demant (1893–1983) and Maurice B. Reckitt (1888–1980), was an example of such thought. T. S. Eliot, in his book *The Idea of a Christian Society* (1939), is a further

133

example of a thinker committed to a Christian form of social order.

Bibliography

S. L. Greenslade, *The Church and the Social Order* (London, 1948); M. B. Reckitt (ed.), *Prospect for Christendom* (London, 1945); *The Return of Christendom*, by a Group of Churchmen, introd. C. Gore (London, 1922). See also Bibliography for Society, Theology of.

J.W.G.

CHRISTIAN SCIENCE, see SECTS.

CHRISTIAN SOCIALISM. The Christian Socialist movement is usually thought to have begun in the 19th century. The interest of Christian thinkers and practitioners in the ideals of common ownership and of a universal society of human brotherhood is much older. It has often been said that the experiment in Acts 2:44–45 of holding all things in common is the first Christian socialist experiment. The commitment to such themes can be found in the early fathers and in the development of the monastic movement. Nevertheless the name 'Christian Socialist' came to be used in relation to 19th-century developments, many of which have their roots in the Church of England.

Robert Owen's (1771–1858) social experiments at New Lanark marked the first 19th-century attempt at a form of socialist organization. There were some clergy who took an interest in it. A few clergy were also to be found sympathizing with the Chartist movement in the 1840s. However, the beginnings of an organized movement of Christian leaders sympathetic to socialism came with the joining of J. M. F. Ludlow (1821–1911) with F. D. Maurice (1805–72). It was Ludlow's experience of socialism in Paris which provoked him to see the need for socialism to come under the influence of Christian thought. It was they, together with Charles Kingsley (1819–75) and Thomas Hughes (1822–96) for a time, who began to respond to the failure of the Chartist movement by experimenting in thought and action and who called their work 'Christian Socialism'.

F. D. Maurice stressed the universal character of the kingdom* of Christ. The Christian gospel reveals the true state of man.

The starting-point for Christian thought and the perspective from which we should view human life in the world is the kingship of Christ and the fact that God has both created and redeemed mankind in Christ. Maurice's theology is inclusive and universalist.* It was this fact of faith which Maurice brought to bear in his political interests in an age of social unrest as England moved into its industrial age and class-structured social order. Following the failure of the Chartist movement in 1848, Maurice and his friends sought to experiment in co-operative workshops, in the development of the Working Men's College and in journalism and tracts such as 'Politics for the People' and 'Tracts on Christian Socialism'.

The development of Christian Socialism took on a number of forms in the 19th century. In the 1870s a group of Anglo-Catholics* began to organize themselves and in 1877 formed the Guild of St Matthew. Stewart Headlam (1847–1924) was the founder priest of the guild. It was more radical and activist in kind than Maurice's group had been at an earlier stage. The Guild attacked social injustice wherever it found it and made many public statements as to what needed to be done. It pressed for action by Parliament on housing, education and working conditions. It produced the magazine *The Church Reformer*. Many dedicated Anglo-Catholic priests who worked hard in the slums of East and South London saw their commitment to the working classes as the proper expression of an incarnational understanding of Christian faith. Their commitment to action and radical reform was for them a direct consequence of a truly incarnational theology.

The Christian Social Union, founded in 1889, was much more respectable ('wishy-washy' was Headlam's judgment of it!). It was less concerned with direct action than with establishing social principles from Christian faith. It was more given to organizing study groups and encouraging writing. B. F. Westcott,* Bishop of Durham in the last years of the 19th century, was one of the most distinguished presidents of the Christian Social Union. His socialism, like that of Maurice, took its form from his conviction of our union and unity in Jesus Christ. 'Men are "one man" in Christ, sons of God and brethren' (quoted in A. R. Vidler, *F. D. Maurice and Company*, London, 1966, p. 26).

134

Westcott took a leading role in the settlement of the 1893 Durham miners' strike.

The influence of these movements on the church began to be felt towards the end of the 19th century. Diocesan conferences and church congresses began to pass resolutions on social issues – a mark of the growing feeling that the church had a duty to spell out some of the contemporary consequences for social order of the faith to which it was committed.

The Christian Socialist movement continues to this day. It could be said that movements such as the Jubilee Group have continued the tradition of the Guild of St Matthew. The Christian Socialist group and movement today maintain the belief that the proper contemporary political and social form of the gospel is to be found within socialist thought and practice.

Bibliography

T. Christensen, *Origin and History of Christian Socialism, 1848–54* (Aarhus, 1962); D. Hay, *A Christian Critique of Capitalism* (Bramcote, Nottingham, 1975); K. Leech, *The Social God* (London, 1981); F. D. Maurice, *The Kingdom of Christ* (1838; several editions); E. R. Norman, *The Victorian Christian Socialists* (Cambridge, 1987).

J.W.G.

CHRISTIANITY AND OTHER RELIGIONS. Christian faith confesses Jesus Christ to be the sole mediator between God and mankind (1 Tim. 2:5; *cf.* Jn. 14:6, Acts 4:12). This confession has traditionally implied the rejection of claims that a saving knowledge* of God may be found in non-Christian religions such as Hinduism* and Buddhism.* (Judaism* requires separate consideration, and so too to some extent does Islam,* given its original partial dependence on Judaism and Christianity.*) A forceful modern exponent of the radical discontinuity between the Christian faith and other faiths was Hendrik Kraemer.*

Such a denial of the presence of revelation* and salvation* in other religions has been widely revised or abandoned in recent decades, partly as a result of the indifferentism fostered by endemic theological liberalism and of the quest for universal harmony, leading perhaps even to a single world religion, pursued through inter-faith dialogue.

The change is clearly seen in the drastic reinterpretation in Roman Catholicism (which has so often evinced a genius for assimilation) of the dogmatic conviction, inherited from the fathers and starkly enunciated by Boniface VIII in the bull *Unam sanctam* (1302), that there is 'no salvation outside the church' (*extra ecclesiam nulla salus*). Vatican II (1962–65) declared that everlasting salvation was attainable by those who 'through no fault of their own do not know the gospel of Christ or His Church, yet sincerely seek God and, moved by grace, strive by their deeds to do His will as it is known to them through the dictates of conscience' (Dogmatic Constitution on the Church [*Lumen Gentium*] 2:16; *cf.* Declaration on the Relationship of the Church to Non-Christian Religions). In the light of the universality of God's providence and saving design, the Council affirmed that whatever is true and holy in other religions reflects 'a ray of that Truth which enlightens all men'.

Post-Vatican II Catholic theologians have argued that other religions are pre-Christian, not non-Christian, and ordained to find their fulfilment in Christ; that a fundamental life-decision made in faith and love in another religion under the influence of supernatural grace involves an implicit acceptance of the church; and that these other religions can be called the 'ordinary' way of salvation (the church being the 'extraordinary' way) for non-Christian humanity (*cf.* J. Neuner, ed., *Christian Revelation and World Religions*, London, 1967, for essays by Küng* and others; E. D. Piryns, 'Current Roman Catholic Views of Other Religions', *Missionalia* 13, 1985, pp. 55–62).

Such a reassessment depends in part on doctrines shared with other Christian traditions, especially general revelation (see Revelation*) and common grace (see Grace*). According to Scripture, God unceasingly reveals his being and general character to all mankind, in the ordering of creation, in providence and in the constitution of human nature (Rom. 1:19–20; 2:14–15; 14:17; Acts 17:26–28). By virtue of their very humanity, which is made in the image of God,* men and women are involved in a relationship to their creator. But this God-given *sensus divinitatis* ('awareness of God') is not a saving knowledge, for men and women have without exception perverted what they know of God into rebellious idolatry (Rom. 1:21–28). Nevertheless there remains in corrupt humanity an ineradicable *semen religionis* ('seed of religion'). Non-Christian religion is therefore a witness both to a universal divine self-communication to the human race, and to mankind's universal refusal to acknowledge the self-revealing God. As J. H. Bavinck* put it, 'God has had a great deal to do with [people] before their contact with the [Christian faith] . . . There is deep in the heart of man, even among those who live and believe in non-Christian religions, a very vague awareness that man plays a game with God and that man is always secretly busy escaping from him.' The divided being of fallen man manifests itself in his religions as in all else, in that 'he *simultaneously* seeks after God his Maker and flees from God his Judge'.

Some evangelical teachers claim that, without countenancing salvation by good (religious) works, the Bible justifies us in believing that the benefits of Christ's unique mediation may, by God's grace, be extended to some adherents of other religions. J. N. D. Anderson, for example, appealing to texts such as Acts 17:27 and (more questionably) 10:34–35, argues this for those who, while ignorant of Christ, come to a 'God-given sense of sin or need, and a self-abandonment to God's mercy.' If this is an acceptable interpretation of Scripture, such a genuine feeling after the true God, whether it is ascribed ultimately to the Spirit's inner stirring or the enlightenment of the Logos* (Jn. 1:9), cannot be wholly separated from its non-Christian religious matrix. In the light of Mt. 11:21–23, others have linked this way of thinking with God's so-called 'middle knowledge' of how such persons would have responded had the gospel been preached to them.

Early patristic reflection on the activity of the pre-incarnate Logos in Greek philosophy, engendering glimpses of true understanding about God, the world and the soul, preparatory to the full coming of the Logos in the flesh of Jesus (see Apologists*), has often prompted a parallel interpretation of the teachings of the great world religions. Yet the fathers never recognized more than distortions of truth in the philosphers, and if a Buddhist or Hindu, for example, is brought to an authentic desire for God, this happens as much despite his religion as because of it. The universal 'enlightening' by the Logos (Jn. 1:9)

is best interpreted of God's general revelation to all mankind in the context of creation (*cf.* Jn. 1:3–5). The whole thrust of John's prologue towards the affirmation of the once-for-all, historical incarnation* of the Logos argues against a saving presence of a non-incarnate Christ or Logos in other religions. There is no biblical warrant for speaking of Christ's being present but latent, hidden, 'incognito' or 'unknown' in other religions, or for discerning lesser or partial incarnations or Christophanies in persons other than Jesus of Nazareth.

Yet we are justified in recognizing at one and the same time both continuity and discontinuity between the quest for God in other faiths and the fullness and finality of the knowledge of God 'in the face of Jesus Christ'. Non-Christian religion, alike in its most debased and most elevated manifestations, always bears the dual impress of God's gracious revelation of himself to all mankind and mankind's universal exchange of the truth of God for a lie. So long as these twin biblical perspectives are maintained, there may be scope for legitimate differences in the way Christian theology balances or correlates them in its evaluation of other religions. The two perspectives are tellingly presented in Paul's address at Athens. Despite the universality of God's providential care and presence (Acts 17:24–28), the Athenians' religiosity suppressed the knowledge of the true God. Their abundant images and idols attested their ignorance of him (17:16, 22–23, 29–30), and even their awareness of that ignorance (17:23). Paul's message came to hearers whose refusal to know the living God had left its mark upon their religion.

Bibliography

J. N. D. Anderson, *Christianity and World Religions: The Challenge of Pluralism* (Leicester, 1984); G. H. Anderson and T. F. Stransky (eds.), *Christ's Lordship and Religious Pluralism* (Maryknoll, NY, 1981); J. H. Bavinck, 'Human Religion in God's Eyes: A Study of Romans 1:18–22', *Them* 2:2 (1964), pp. 16–23; Calvin, *Institutes* I; C. Davis, *Christ and the World Religions* (London, 1970); J. du Preez, 'Johan Herman Bavinck on the Relation between Divine Revelation and the Religions', *Missionalia* 13 (1985), pp. 111–120; L. Newbigin, *The Finality of Christ* (London, 1969); *idem*, *The*

Open Secret (London, 1978); S. C. Neill, *Crises of Belief* (London, 1983); O. C. Thomas (ed.), *Attitudes Towards Other Religions: Some Christian Interpretations* (London, 1969); W. A. Visser t' Hooft, *No Other Name: The Choice Between Syncretism and Christian Universalism* (London, 1963); articles in *Them* 9:2 (1984).

D.F.W.

CHRISTOLOGY, strictly speaking, the doctrine of Christ, his person and natures. In the past Christology has also included the work of Christ, now more usually treated separately as soteriology (*cf.* Atonement;* Salvation*).

The importance of Christology for Christianity is obvious, since without Jesus Christ, the religion named after him would never have emerged. Modern scholars debate the role of the historical Jesus* in the formation of Christianity, but there is no doubt that he occupies a place different from that given to the founders of other religions. Christianity *is* Jesus Christ in a way which is quite unique.

The NT picture of Jesus is one which has been hotly debated in modern times. Almost everyone agrees that he was at least an extraordinary prophet who attracted a considerable following, which made him appear dangerous to the Jewish authorities. They arrested him and had him crucified by the Romans, only to discover after a few days that his followers were preaching that he had risen from the dead. The significance of the resurrection,* or 'Easter-event', for Christianity is not disputed, but the historical facts are. Orthodox Christians of every church have always insisted that Jesus rose from the dead in historical fact, and this belief is a cornerstone of NT faith (1 Cor. 15:19). Paul himself claimed to have met the risen Christ on the Damascus Road, thereby joining his testimony to that of the apostles who had been his earthly disciples. Attempts to reduce this experience to a purely spiritual dimension do not correspond with the witness of the first Christians themselves.

Far more complicated than this however is the question of deciding how much of the NT witness about Jesus comes directly from him, and how much is the result of later ecclesiastical reflection. This has an important bearing on some of the traditional proof-texts for Christ's divinity, such as Peter's confession (Mt. 16:16), which many would like to claim is a later development. It is undoubtedly true that the gospels were written in the light of the resurrection; what point would they otherwise have had? But far from presenting a distortion in their portrait of Jesus, they provide an exposition of his real significance.

Another difficulty with NT Christology is its content, which apparently differs from that of later tradition. In particular, the gospels make frequent references to different titles borne by the Saviour-Messiah, some of which, *e.g.* Son of Man, are universally agreed to have been used by Jesus himself. These titles are not the basis of later dogmatic Christology, however, which has led some modern scholars to state that the NT presents a functional Christology within the framework of salvation-history* (*Heilsgeschichte*). The plausibility of this must be measured against the more ontological passages in the gospels, some of which, like Jn. 3, bear traces of a primitive origin and are unlikely to be later inventions. It seems at least logical to assume that who Jesus was would determine what he could do, so that ontology must inevitably precede salvation-history in theological terms.

The NT claims that Jesus, the son of David and inheritor of the kingly tradition of Israel, became the high priest and victim of the atoning sacrifice, made once for all upon the cross in order to save men from their sins. Only God had the authority to overturn the established order of Israelite society in this way, and establish a 'new way'. That this took place is consistent with the first Christians' claim that Jesus was God in human flesh, and this is in fact implicit in the frequent discussions of his authority which occur in the gospels.

Post-apostolic Christology developed at least partly in response to heresies of different kinds. There is some evidence that even in NT times there were those who believed that Jesus was a kind of angel, who had seemed to be a man on earth but who in fact was not truly human (*cf.* 1 Jn. 4:2–3). This heretical tendency is now called *docetism** (Gk. *dokein*, to seem). Many scholars believe that it was endemic among orthodox Christians as much as among the heretics. This however cannot be proved, and the assertion is not unconnected with a refusal on the part of the same scholars to admit that the first Christians believed that Jesus was ontologically God.

1. Classical Christology

The classical period of Christology began in the 4th century, in answer to the teaching of Arius.* Arius believed that Jesus Christ was a heavenly being, intermediate between God and man, but nevertheless a creature. He insisted that if Christ were not a creature it would have been impossible for him to suffer and die on our behalf, since God is both immortal and impassible. Arius was condemned at the Council* of Nicaea in 325, but his views lived on in various forms until at least the 8th century.

After Nicaea it became apparent that there were two main schools of thought in the church, centred on Alexandria* and Antioch* respectively. In doctrinal terms, Alexandria claims priority, and Antioch is best regarded as a reaction against what were believed to be Alexandria's excesses.

The Alexandrians stressed above all the unity of Christ. They believed that he was the divine hypostasis* (person) of the Son of God who had taken on human flesh for our redemption. The difficulty which they encountered lay in defining the nature of that flesh. The constant temptation was to argue that this term referred only to the physical body of Jesus, and did not include his soul. This was actually stated by Apollinarius,* a 4th-century disciple of Athanasius,* and it was condemned at the Second Ecumenical Council, held in Constantinople in 381. Apollinarianism was repudiated by the Alexandrian school, but never satisfactorily refuted. In the 5th century it became an article of faith in the Alexandrian tradition that the incarnate Christ had only one 'nature' (physis, used here almost in the sense of hypostasis), which by definition had to be divine. This brought the geniuneness of his humanity into question, and monophysitism* (as this teaching came to be called) was condemned at the Fourth Ecumenical Council (Chalcedon, 451).

The Antiochene school, in contrast, can trace its ancestry back to the 3rd-century heretic, Paul of Samosata (see Adoptionism*). He was condemned at Antioch in 268 for believing that Christ was a man whom God had adopted to be his Son. This belief was subsequently modified considerably, but its remains are apparent in the Christology of Theodore of Mopsuestia (d. 428) and Nestorius.* Both these men maintained that Christ was a conjunction (synapheia) of two distinct natures. Before the union, there had been the Son of God, with his divine nature, and a human embryo, with his human nature. The Son of God entered the human foetus at the moment of conception but did not mix with it in any way. God and man were linked in symmetrical union (rather like a pair of praying hands) in which the whole is greater than its parts. This whole is the person of Christ, the appearance of a union which could theoretically be dissolved without destroying either the Son of God or the man Jesus.

Nestorius was condemned in person at the Third Ecumenical Council (Ephesus, 431) and this condemnation was renewed at Chalcedon. The orthodox view was put by Leo,* bishop of Rome, in his Tome of 449. Leo said that Christ was a single person who in the incarnation had added a human nature to the divinity which he already possessed. The link between the human and the divine was to be sought in the divine person, not in the two natures. Leo's formula was an ingenious synthesis of Alexandrian and Antiochene emphases, but it was rejected by both as a compromise. However, the majority at Chalcedon subscribed to it, and it remains to this day the chief foundation of classical Christology. It was one of the main bases of Chalcedon's own Definition. This confessed 'the one and the same Christ, Son, Lord, only-begotten, to be acknowledged in two natures, without confusion, without change, without division, without separation, the distinction of the natures being in no way abolished because of the union, but rather the characteristic property of each one being preserved, and concurring into one person and one being'.

The period from 451 to 787 is often neglected by modern students, but it was of capital importance in elucidating the meaning of the Chalcedonian Definition. In particular, it was agreed that Christ had two wills (dyotheletism), not one (monotheletism), as the Byzantine emperor Heraclius (610–41) had maintained. It was also agreed that the human nature of Christ was hypostatized* in the Logos,* the Son of God. This explained how it was possible for the humanity of Christ to be complete without saying that he was a human person as well as divine one. Finally it was agreed that to see Christ in the flesh was to see God, and not just a man.

A constant problem for theologians of this

period was the witness of the gospels to the miracles and other extraordinary acts of Jesus. To many it seemed that his human flesh was divinized by the indwelling presence of the Logos, since otherwise he would not have been able to walk on water, nor would people have been cured simply by touching him. At other times however, he appeared to show signs of ignorance and weakness, which could not possibly be attributed to his divine nature. The dilemma was resolved by appealing to the principle of the transfer of properties (*communicatio idiomatum*). According to this theory, the humanity of Jesus borrowed divine attributes as and when required. As long as Christology was mainly concerned to explain how two natures of such different capacities could cohabit in a single individual, it was impossible to prevent the *communicatio idiomatum* from becoming total. The result was that Athanasius and others were reduced to saying that Jesus had pretended to be ignorant of the date of his return, for example, in order to convince his disciples that he was truly human!

The problem was eventually resolved by introducing the person of Christ as the agent of the incarnation in a way which made the divine nature dependent on the person, and not the other way round. Orthodox Christology thus believed in a divine person who manifested himself in and disposed of the capacities of two natures. On the cross the divine person suffered and died for us in his human nature, thereby neatly combining the sacrifice of God on our behalf with the doctrine of an impassible and immortal deity.

2. Modern Christology

After the close of the patristic period, there was little or no formal development of Christology (as distinct from soteriology) for centuries. Even the Reformers were content to accept their ancient inheritance, and John Calvin in particular stoutly defended the classical credal formulae as faithful representations of the teaching of Scripture (*Institutes* I.xiii). This judgment was repeated by his followers, and it has remained typical of Protestant orthodoxy to the present day.

Debate about the person and natures of Christ was resumed in the 18th century, under the impact of the Enlightenment.* A succession of thinkers, starting with Hermann Reimarus (1694–1768) and continuing to the time of the First World War, endeavoured to reconstruct the life of the 'historical Jesus'* on the assumption that claims to his divinity were a later development only marginally connected with his own life and teachings. Enlightenment Christology produced a Jesus who was essentially a prophetic moralist and religious reformer, crucified because his thinking was ahead of his time.

Albert Schweitzer* strongly criticized this picture of Jesus without returning to the earlier orthodox position. Schweitzer claimed that Jesus was really an apocalyptic figure whose teaching had been toned down, not exaggerated, by the NT writers. This created an added dimension to the debate about the historical Jesus, but did not fundamentally alter the underlying assumptions of Enlightenment thought.

Modern Christology is therefore divided into opposing camps using very different principles of theological method. The exponents of traditional 'Chalcedonian' Christology are said to hold a 'Christology from above', whilst those who begin from Enlightenment principles hold a 'Christology from below'. The former has often been caricatured as a form of docetism, which does not do justice to the human psychology of Jesus. In fact, however, exaggerated forms of Christology from above are more like monophysitism than like docetism, though there are few if any serious theologians writing today who can fairly be accused of this. Christology from below, on the other hand, not infrequently becomes a crude type of Nestorianism, or even adoptionism,* which leaves the non-specialist wondering whether there is anything distinctive about the life of Jesus at all.

Extreme exponents of the latter view have gained widespread publicity by using the word 'myth'* to describe the Christology of the NT. According to them, the framers of classical orthodoxy went wrong because they treated the NT myth(s) as historical fact, rather than as symbolical truth. But it must also be said that there are many scholars who reject this conclusion, even though they follow the method of Christology from below. Some, like P. T. Forsyth* and D. M. Baillie,* believe that the evidence we have for the historical Jesus adds up to credible proof for his divinity. Others, such as Oscar Cullmann (b. 1902; see Salvation-history*) and Ferdinand Hahn (b. 1926), have stressed the Christological titles which the NT applies to Jesus, and have claimed that the gospel writers were using originally mythical concepts to describe historical fact.

Still others, such as Martin Hengel (b. 1926) and Wolfhart Pannenberg,* have reasserted the fundamental historicity of the gospels, and have argued on that basis for the divinity of Christ. It is scholars of this type who come closest to the approach of traditional orthodoxy, which most of them are in fact concerned to uphold. The possibility that the two methods may eventually be harmonized to the benefit of the classical position has recently been greatly strengthened by the work of scholars such as I. H. Marshall (b. 1934), C. F. D. Moule (b. 1908) and J. Galot.

Bibliography

D. M. Baillie, *God was in Christ* (London, 1948); J. Galot, *Who is Christ?* (Rome, 1981); A. Grillmeier, *Christ in Christian Tradition*, vol. 1 (Atlanta, GA, and London, ²1975), vol. 2:1 (Oxford, 1987); A. T. Hanson, *The Image of the Invisible God* (London, 1982); I. H. Marshall, *The Origins of New Testament Christology* (Leicester, 1976); Alister E. McGrath, *The Making of Modern German Christology: From the Enlightenment to Pannenberg* (Oxford, 1986); C. F. D. Moule, *The Origin of Christology* (Cambridge, 1977); K. Runia, *The Present-day Christological Debate* (Leicester, 1984); J. Ziesler, *The Jesus Question* (London, 1980).

G.L.B.

CHURCH. The church is one of the most fundamental realities of the Christian faith. The doctrine of the church is often called ecclesiology.

1. Scripture

Scripture presents the church as the people of God, the community and body of Christ, and the fellowship of the Holy Spirit.

a. The people of God. Peter applies to the NT church terms used in the OT for the people of God (1 Pet. 2:9). The biblical word 'church' (Gk. *ekklēsia*, Heb. *qāhāl*) means 'assembly'. It describes the covenant-making assembly at Mount Sinai (Dt. 9:10, 10:4; LXX Dt. 4:10). Israel later assembled before God for covenant renewal (*e.g.* Dt. 29:1; Jos. 8:35; Ne. 5:13), and at the feasts (Lv. 23). The

prophets promised an ingathering to the feast of the Lord in the latter days (Is. 2:2; Zc. 14:16). Christ came to gather God's assembly (Mt. 9:36; 12:30; 16:18), announcing that the feast is prepared (Lk. 14:17). Christ fulfilled the feast of the Passover by his death and resurrection, and sent the Holy Spirit to the assembled disciples on the feast of Pentecost (Acts 2). As Christians assemble to worship, they gather not to Sinai, but to the heavenly Zion, the festival assembly of saints and angels, where Jesus is (Heb. 12:18–29). This heavenly assembly defines the church.

The church is also the dwelling of God. The symbolism of God's dwelling among his people in his tabernacle is fulfilled by Jesus Christ, first in the tabernacle of his flesh (Jn. 1:14; 2:19, 20), then in his Spirit. The church, like the Christian, is a temple of God (1 Cor. 3:16, 17; 6:19; 2 Cor. 6:16).

God's choosing of Israel to be his people flowed from his call of Abraham. It expressed the free love of God in calling Israel to sonship (Dt. 7:7, 8), and also God's purpose that in Abraham all nations would be blessed (Gn. 12:1–3). When Israel's covenant-breaking brought the judgment and exile, God promised to spare a remnant and to renew a remnant of the nations as well (Is. 19:24f.; 45:20; 66:18–23; Je. 48:47). The blessings of the new covenant could come only with the coming of God himself (Is. 40:3–11; Zp. 3:17–20; Zc. 12:8; Is. 59:17; Ezk. 34:11–16). His coming is one with the coming of the Messiah, the Lord and servant of the covenant (Ps. 110; Is. 9:6f.; 53).

b. The Messianic community. These promises are realized in the coming of Christ the Lord (Lk. 2:11) who shows his divine authority by his miracles, proclaims the coming of God's saving kingdom* with his own presence (Lk. 4:21; 11:20; 12:32), and triumphs over sin and Satan by his crucifixion and resurrection. To those who reject his claim, Jesus announces that the kingdom will be taken away from them and given to a new people of God (Mt. 21:43). He gathers his disciples as the remnant flock who will receive the kingdom (Lk. 12:32). Simon Peter, confessing Jesus to be the Christ, the Son of God, is declared to be the apostolic* rock upon whom Christ will build his church (Mt. 16:18). Peter shares the keys of the kingdom with the other disciples (Mt. 18:18), but it is Christ who builds his assembly as the new people of God.

His word is the law of the church (Heb. 1:1; 2:3, 4; Mt. 28:20; Jn. 14:26; 16:13, 14; 1 Cor. 14:37); his Spirit gives life to the church (Jn. 14:16–18; Rom. 8:9). As ruler of the universe and Lord of the church, he sends disciples to gather the nations (Mt. 28:19). His saving rule constitutes, governs, and protects the church as the community of the kingdom. In dispersion like the old Israel (1 Pet. 1:1), the new people of God are to respect the governments of their lands of residence (Je. 29:7; 1 Tim. 2:1, 2). The power of the sword, given by God to governments, is not to be exercised to bring in the kingdom of God, but only to maintain order while God's judgment is deferred and his kingdom of grace spreads (Jn. 18:36; Rom. 13:1–7).

c. The body of Christ. Paul describes the church as the body of Christ because of its union with Christ* (Eph 1:22–23). This is first a representative union. Christ, the last Adam,* is the head of a new humanity. When Christ died those who are 'in Christ' died with him. The body of Christ on the cross is therefore the body in which the church is united and redeemed (Eph. 2:16). The one loaf of the communion Supper symbolizes the union of the church with the broken body of the Lord. The church is also vitally united to Christ (Rom. 8:9–11; Jn. 14:16–18). Paul uses the body figure to describe the interdependence of Christians as members of Christ and of each other. Christ is united to his body, the church, as a husband to his wife. He is the head, not a part of the body, but, in a separate figure, as Lord over the body (Eph. 1:22, 23; *cf.* Col. 2:10; 1 Cor. 11:3; 12:21).

d. The fellowship of the Spirit. The coming of the Holy Spirit* at Pentecost fulfils the promise of the Father and of Christ (Jn. 14:18; Acts 1:4). The Spirit possesses the church in divine Lordship. As the Spirit of truth he completes the revelation of Scripture and illumines the church (Jn. 16:12–14). As the Spirit of witness, he leads the church in its mission (Acts 5:32; 13:2). As the Spirit of life, he liberates the church from sin, death, and the condemnation of the law (Rom. 5 – 8; Gal. 4; 2 Cor. 3:17). He creates a holy fellowship* in the bonds of love (Gal. 5:22). He provides a foretaste of glory as the Spirit of adoption, but fortifies the church for suffering (Rom. 8:14–17). The church also possesses the Spirit. The gifts* of the Spirit equip the church to praise God, nurture the saints, and witness to the world. The stewardship* of diverse gifts does not divide; it unites the church as a functioning organism.

2. Definition

a. Distinguishing the aspects of the church. How may this biblical teaching be applied? There are organizations that have falsely claimed to be the church as well as churches that have become apostate. It is necessary to distinguish the true church, and to understand its nature and ministry.

The church may be defined as God sees it, the so-called 'church invisible'. This is composed of all whose names are in the Lamb's book of life (Rev. 21:27). The 'church visible', on the other hand, is the church as we see it, the family of believers. This distinction guards against equating membership in the church visible with salvation, or, on the other hand, disregarding public identification with God's people.

The church may be defined as local, so that only the local church is the church proper and broader gatherings can be only associations of churches or of Christians. On the other hand, the church may be defined as universal, so that the local church is only a portion of the church, a part of the whole. Neither of these exclusive positions would appear to take account of the flexibility of NT use: the term is applied to house and city churches as well as to the whole people of God (1 Cor. 16:19; Col. 4:15,16).

The church may also be viewed as an *organism* in which every member functions and associates with other members, and also as an *organization* in which are exercised the various gifts of the Spirit.

b. Defining the attributes of the church. The Nicene Creed* confesses 'one holy catholic and apostolic church'. The apostolicity of the church refers to its foundation on apostolic teaching. The church is built on the foundation of the apostles* and prophets (Eph. 2:20), as recipients of revelation (Eph. 3:4, 5). Since the apostles were eye-witnesses of the resurrection (Acts 1:22) as well as communicators of the word of Christ (Jn. 14:26; 15:26; 16:13), their foundational office cannot be continued (1 Cor. 15:8), although their missionary task remains.

The holiness of the church fulfils the OT symbolism of ceremonial cleanness by a moral purity wrought of the Spirit (1 Cor. 6:14 –

141

7:10). Separation from unbelief and sin, together with dedication to the service of God in all of life, must mark the corporate life of the church. Love in the Spirit binds the saints to God and each other.

The NT church is catholic* or universal: it is not limited geographically as Israel was, and it joins in one fellowship people of every sort. The church cannot exclude from its membership any who credibly confess Christ. Sectarianism that limits church membership to any race, caste, or social class denies catholicity.

The church is the one family of God the Father (Eph. 4:6), it is one in the Lord Jesus Christ (Eph. 2:14, 16; 1 Cor. 10:17; Gal. 3:27; Jn. 17:20–26), and is one fellowship in the Spirit (Eph. 4:3; Acts 4:32). When denominational division threatened the Corinthian church, Paul cried, 'Is Christ divided? Was Paul crucified for you?' (1 Cor 1:13). The one body of Christ's sacrifice provides salvation in one fellowship (Eph. 4:3). Saints are joined by the unifying graces of the Spirit (Eph. 4:15, 31, 32; Col. 3:14). When the church is divided, it is injured and weakened, but not necessarily destroyed. The task of recovering scriptural unity requires a return to the apostolic foundation with zealous love.

c. The marks of the church as defined by the Protestant Reformation could not be found in outward unity with the papal see and its claim to apostolic succession, but must be drawn from biblical apostolicity. The pure preaching* of the word of God, the proper celebration of the sacraments,* and the faithful exercise of church discipline* distinguish the true church of Christ.

3. Ministry

The church worships God directly (1 Pet. 2:9; Heb. 12:28, 29; Rom. 15:5–12), ministers to the saints (Eph. 4:12–16) and to the world (Lk. 24:48; Acts 5:32; Phil. 2:14–18). The means of ministry* include: the ministry of the word; the ministry of order, by which Christian living is subjected to the law of love; and the ministry of mercy, manifesting the compassion of Christ. These means of ministry are common to all believers as they seek to fulfil their calling. Some members of Christ's body have gifts in one or more of these areas to an unusual degree. There are administrative gifts that require public recognition for their proper exercise. The NT there-

fore describes office in the church: apostles and prophets to lay the foundation and launch the mission (Eph. 2:20; 3:5); evangelists, pastors and teachers to proclaim the revealed word with authority (Eph. 4:11,); others with gifts for government to join them in ruling the church (Rom. 12:8; 1 Cor. 12:28; 1 Tim. 5:17); and deacons to administer the service of mercy (1 Tim. 3:8–13). Those who govern are given to the church by Christ to serve in his name, under his lordship. Church power is spiritual (2 Cor. 10:3–6), ministerial (1 Pet. 5:3; Mt. 20:25–28), and only declarative (Mk. 7:8; Rev. 21:18, 19). Yet it is authoritative (Mt. 16:19; 18:17–20; 10:14f.; Heb. 13:17).

4. Government and discipline

Patterns of church government* differ first because of differences regarding the normativity of NT patterns. Church polity developed from roots in Israel and the synagogue; some have concluded that this development was not completed in the apostolic age but that the metropolitan bishops of the early catholic church provide a model for hierarchical church government. Others assume that scriptural revelation regarding the order of the church is open-ended by divine intention, leaving it free to adopt a polity suited to its circumstances. The Reformed* tradition has held that the principles of church order and the specification of church offices are given in the NT. Since 'bishop' and 'elder' are interchangeable terms in the NT (Acts 20:17, 28), they describe one office. Teaching and ruling elders exercise government jointly in presbyteries (1 Tim. 4:14; Act 13:1; 15:23). According to Paul's apostolic authority, women are not to rule over men in the church family (1 Tim. 2:12–15). In the diaconal ministry of mercy, however, Paul commends the service of women (Rom. 16:1, 2). He recognizes a remunerated service of senior widows, and may describe the qualifications of women for diaconal office (1 Tim. 3:11).

The councils* of the church have been variously conceived: congregational* independency gives final authority to the autonomous local congregation, episcopacy provides for councils under the presidency of bishops or archbishops, presbyterianism* finds in the NT warrant for graded courts.

Discipline* in the church seeks the glory of God (2 Cor. 6:14 – 7:1), the purity of the church (1 Cor. 5:6; 11:27), and the reclaiming of the offender (1 Tim. 1:20; 2 Thes. 3:14; 1 Cor. 5:5). Faithful discipline will deter others from sin (1 Tim. 5:20) and avoid Christ's judgments (Rev. 2:14–25). Administrative discipline seeks to maintain good order in the church; judicial discipline is concerned with individual offences, whether private or public. Degrees of censure serve to rebuke and restore the guilty: admonition (Mt. 18:15–18; 1 Tim. 5:20), suspension from the Lord's table (1 Cor. 11:27; 2 Thes. 3:6–15), and excommunication (Mt. 18:17; Tit. 3:10; 1 Cor. 5:5, 11; Gal. 1:9). Loving fellowship provides the context for discipline that is more preventive than corrective.

See also: COMMUNION OF SAINTS; KOINONIA.

Bibliography
J. Bannerman, *The Church of Christ*, 2 vols. (Edinburgh, 1868); G. C. Berkouwer, *The Church* (Grand Rapids, MI, 1976); L. Cerfaux, *The Church in the Theology of St Paul* (New York, 1959); A. Dulles, *Models of the Church* (Garden City, NY, 1978); R. Newton Flew, *Jesus and his Church* (New York, 1938); J. A. Heyns, *The Church* (Pretoria, 1980); R. B. Kuiper, *The Glorious Body of Christ* (Grand Rapids, MI, n.d.); Hans Küng, *The Church* (New York, 1967); Paul Minear, *Images of the Church in the New Testament* (Philadelphia, 1950); L. Newbigin, *The Household of God* (London, 1957); Alan Stibbs, *God's Church* (London, 1959).

E.P.C.

CHURCH GOVERNMENT. It is debatable whether the NT presents us with one, final, uniform pattern of church* government to serve as a norm for all ages. There is certainly considerable development and modification between Pentecost and the Pastoral Epistles.

Initially, everything was in the hands of the apostles.* The first division of labour is that indicated in Acts 6:1–6, when the church appointed seven men, later assumed to be deacons, to relieve the apostles of routine administrative tasks. Later, elders (variously designated *presbyteroi, episkopoi, proistamenoi* and *hēgoumenoi*) were appointed (Acts 14:23; 20:17; 1 Tim. 3:1–7; Tit. 1:5–9; Heb. 13:7; 1 Pet. 5:1). These functioned alongside apostles and prophets* and more nebulous functionaries such as evangelists (Acts 21:8; Eph. 4:11; 2 Tim. 4:5) and deaconesses (Rom. 16:1).

It is perilous to try to work out a consistent polity on the basis of nomenclature alone. The terms are too imprecise and too fluid. For example, an apostle could describe himself as an elder (1 Pet. 5:1) and one of the Seven could be called an evangelist (Acts 21:8). Some elders preached, but not all did so (1 Tim. 5:17); and some (like Apollos) preached who were not elders at all (Acts 18:24–26).

What emerges from the NT is not a graduated list of office-bearers with precise designations and clearly defined functions, but clear evidence of three forms of ministry:* a ministry of tables (performed by apostles, deacons and some women); a ministry of oversight and pastoral care (performed by apostles, elders, bishops and pastors); and a ministry of the word (performed by apostles, prophets, evangelists, elders, deacons – and by some with no designation at all).

After the apostolic age, polity developed along three distinct lines.

1. Episcopacy
The essential claims of episcopacy are as follows:

a. By the middle of the 2nd century the threefold ministry of bishop, presbyter and deacon was firmly and widely established. This appears from such documents as the *Epistles* of Ignatius (*c.* 115) and of Polycarp (*c.* 70–155/160). Evidence is also drawn from the tacit assumptions of Christian writers at the close of the 2nd century: 'Episcopacy is so inseparably interwoven with all the traditions and beliefs of men like Irenaeus* and Tertullian* that they betray no knowledge of a time when it was not' (Lightfoot, *Philippians*, p. 227).

b. Traces of this threefold ministry are to be found in the NT itself. The instances usually cited are James, the Lord's brother, who had a special status in the church at Jerusalem; and Timothy and Titus, who appear to have had more than presbyterial authority as apostolic delegates.

c. These bishops had authority over the churches and presbyters of their areas. Charles Gore* even endorsed the view (which he ascribed to Ignatius) that presbyters bear the same relation to the bishop as the disciples did to Christ: they are 'like the circle of twelve round their Master' (*The Church and the Ministry*, p. 302).

d. Different views prevail as to the origins and development of episcopacy. According to Lightfoot (p. 227) 'the episcopate was created out of the presbytery'. Hatch (*The Organization of the Early Christian Churches*, p. 39) is one of the same opinion: 'The functions of the original plurality of co-ordinate officers came practically to pass into the hands of a single officer'. But Gore will have none of this. Presbyters never had the powers which belong to bishops: bishops are the successors of the apostles, not of presbyters. The only difference is that the authority of bishops is localized, whereas that of the apostles was universal. Gore even claims that the bishops are the successors of Christ himself: 'Each Church with its bishop and presbytery is like a little theocracy, in which the bishop represents the authority of God and is a fresh embodiment of that divine presence which was in the world when Christ moved about with His Apostles round Him' (p. 303). On this view, the episcopal bench is a permanent and official apostolate.

e. Opinions also differ as to whether episcopacy is of the essence of the church. Lightfoot saw it very much in terms of expediency. So did Hatch: 'The episcopate grew by the force of circumstances, in the order of Providence, to satisfy a felt need' (p. 99). But, again, Gore disagreed. Episcopacy is of divine right. It cannot be abandoned, and the churches which possess it cannot be asked to regard it as simply one of many permissible forms of church government (p. 348). The principle of the apostolic succession cannot be abandoned without treason to Christ (p. 349).

f. According to those who hold the apostolic-succession theory of episcopacy, only bishops have authority to ordain. Consequently, anyone admitted to office in a non-episcopal way does not have a valid ecclesiastical ministry. This means that Presbyterians* and Congregationalists* have violated a fundamental law of the church's life. They are mere organizations, not churches (Gore, p. 344).

2. Presbyterianism

The basic features of Presbyterianism were laid down by Calvin* (*Institutes* IV.iii–iv) and developed in 17th-century Scotland and England, largely by way of polemical interaction with episcopal Anglicanism.* Presbyterians assert:

a. That in the NT the words *presbyteros* and *episkopos* are synonymous and designate one and the same office. This is conceded by Lightfoot (p. 96) and even by Gore (p. 302). The only difference is that the designation *episkopos* is used only in Gentile churches.

b. The early Christian churches did not have to invent a new polity. They found one ready to hand, in the organization of the synagogues. The parallel between church and synagogue was a stock argument with early Presbyterians: 'Whatsoever kind of office-bearers the Jewish church had, such ought the Christian church to have also. But the Jewish church had elders of the people, who assisted in their ecclesiastical government, and were members of their ecclesiastical consistories; therefore, such ought the Christian church to have also' (George Gillespie, *Assertion of the Government of the Church of Scotland*, ch. 3). The later researches of Anglican scholars have served only to give added force to this argument. 'When the majority of the members of a Jewish community were convinced that Jesus was the Christ', writes Hatch, 'there was nothing to interrupt the current of their former common life. There was no need for secession, for schism, for a change in the organization. The old form of worship and the old modes of government could still go on' (p. 60).

c. The alleged traces of episcopacy in the NT are extremely nebulous. James' special position at Jerusalem was probably a reflection of his personal piety, force of character and close relationship to the Lord, rather than something inherent in his office. In any case, as Lightfoot points out (p. 197), he appears in Acts as a member of the presbytery. He might have been chief *of* the presbyters, but he was not chief *over* them. Nor does Lightfoot see much support for his own cause in the cases of Timothy and Titus: 'It is the conception of a later stage which represents Timothy as bishop of Ephesus and Titus as bishop of Crete. St Paul's own language implies that the position they held was temporary' (p. 199). Hence his conclusion: 'As late, therefore, as the year 70, no distinct signs of episcopal government have hitherto appeared in Gentile Christendom' (p. 201).

d. The situation in the sub-apostolic literature (see Apostolic Fathers*) is not as clear-cut as episcopalians claim. In the *Didache*, for example, *presbyteros* and *episkopos* are still synonymous; power (including the power to appoint bishops) resides in the congregation; and the basic pattern of ministry is still the twofold one of bishops and deacons. Moreover, the bishop had no diocesan powers. Instead, every congregation, however small, had its own bishop: 'When the episcopal system had established itself, there was a bishop wherever in later times there would have been a parish church' (Hatch, p. 79). The Ignatian *Epistles* confirm this. Nothing could be done without the bishop: not baptism, not the eucharist, not a marriage service, not an *agape*. This surely reflects not a *diocesan* but a *parochial* episcopacy. Besides, far from being an autocrat, the power of the bishop was severely limited by that of the congregation, which still appointed its own office-bearers, exercised discipline*, sent delegates to other churches and even directed bishops to go on missions. At this period, Ignatius himself being witness, the bishops are still closely related to the presbyters: 'Your honourable presbytery is attuned to the bishop, even as its string to a lyre' (*Ephesians* 4). As T. M. Lindsay points out, in the thought of Ignatius the ruling body of the church is a court in which the bishop sits as chairman surrounded by his council or session of elders: 'and the one is helpless without the other, for if the bishop is the lyre the elders are the chords, and both are needed to produce melody' (*The Church and the Ministry in the Early Centuries*, p. 197). Only in the 3rd century did what had been a relation of primacy become one of supremacy.

e. The main features of Presbyterianism are:

i. Presbyter and bishop are one.

ii. All presbyters/bishops are equal in authority.

iii. There should be a plurality of presbyters/bishops/pastors in every congregation. Together they form the local governing body (kirk session, in the influential Scottish tradition).

iv. Traditionally, Presbyterians have tried to maintain the theory of a twofold ministry of elders and deacons. An attempt is made to find a distinctive niche for the preacher by calling him a *teaching*, as distinct from a *ruling*, elder. But this leads only to artificiality. For example, a 'ruling' elder who becomes a 'teaching' elder has to undergo a second ordination. In practice, Presbyterianism operates with a three-fold ministry of preacher, elder and deacon. It may be difficult to fit this into the NT nomenclature but it harmonizes well with the basic contours of apostolic polity. What matters is not how the church designates its officers, but whether it fulfils the essential ministries of proclamation, pastoral care and compassion.

v. Elders are not merely representatives of the people, bound to implement their wishes. They are leaders, *hēgoumenoi*, called upon to rule (Heb. 13:7), to govern (1 Cor. 12:28), and to be *over* the church in the Lord (1 Thes. 5:12).

vi. Nevertheless, the people have what Hodge calls 'a substantive part in the government of the church' (*The Church and its Polity*, p. 119). This applies especially in the appointment of office-bearers and the exercise of discipline.

vii. Groups of local churches (provincial, national and even international) are to associate in presbyteries and synods (and, ideally, in ecumenical councils).

viii. The powers of presbyteries and synods are limited by the rights of local congregations. Their function is to exercise a general episcopacy, *i.e.* a ministry of creative oversight and review. In particular, they are to remedy local injustices, to ensure the maximum co-operation between local churches and to encourage the strong to help the weak.

ix. Decisions of presbyteries and synods are not merely advisory but authoritative, as were those of the council of Jerusalem (Acts 15:6–29).

3. Independency

The best exposition of independency is still R. W. Dale's classic, *Congregational Church Polity* (1885). An essentially independent policy is also set forth by John Owen, *The True Nature of a Gospel Church* (1689). With Presbyterianism, it rejects diocesan episcopacy. But it also denies the legitimacy of presbyteries and synods.

Independency has three essential principles:

a. The word 'church' in the NT refers either to the church universal (and invisible) or to particular local churches. It is never used of regional or national churches. 'There is no other sort of visible church organized but a particular church or congregation, where all

145

the members thereof do ordinarily meet together in one place' (Owen, p. 3).

b. The local church is independent of external control and must not be drawn into a larger organization under a central government. (In practice, however, the need for some kind of association is inescapable: witness the various unions, conventions, fellowships, *etc.* of Baptists, Congregationalists and others.)

c. Most independent churches have also been congregationalist, *i.e.* they are governed by the membership itself (practically, by the church-meeting). 'If all the members of a Christian Church are directly responsible to Christ for the maintenance of His authority in the Church, they must elect their own officers, regulate their own worship, determine what persons shall be received into their fellowship and what persons shall be excluded from it' (Dale, p. 69).

An increasing number of independent churches, however, are not congregational but are governed by a body of elders. These elders are elected by the people, but once elected they function as genuine leaders and overseers.

In the modern ecumenical* movement, especially since the Lausanne Faith and Order Conference in 1927, various attempts have been made to combine major elements of two, or all three, of these systems of church government.

See also: COLLEGIALITY AND CONCILIARITY; PAPACY.

Bibliography
J. Bannerman, *The Church of Christ*, 2 vols. (Edinburgh, 1868); R. W. Dale, *Congregational Church Polity* (London, 1885); G. Gillespie, *An Assertion of the Government of the Church of Scotland* (1641), repr. in *The Presbyterian's Armoury*, 3 vols. (Edinburgh, 1846); C. Gore, *The Church and the Ministry* (London, 1882); E. Hatch, *The Organisation of the Early Christian Churches* (London, 1909); C. Hodge, *The Church and its Polity* (London, 1879); J. B. Lightfoot, *The Christian Ministry*, a dissertation appended to his *Commentary on St. Paul's Epistle to the Philippians* (London, 1879); T. M. Lindsay, *The Church and the Ministry in the Early Centuries* (London, 1910); J. Owen, *The True Nature of a Gospel Church (Works*, vol. 16, London, 1868).

D.M.

CHURCH GROWTH. Founded by Donald A. McGavran (b. 1897), the Church Growth movement has become the most influential school of missionary thinking in the past thirty years. McGavran was born in India. His parents and grandparents had been missionaries, and to that same profession he committed his life. After three decades of mission service in India, he returned to the United States with deep convictions as to new directions which ought to be taken in missions. He founded the Institute of Church Growth in Eugene, Oregon, in 1961. A few years later this became part of the Fuller Theological Seminary, in Pasadena, California, with Donald McGavran serving as the first dean of the School of World Mission and Institute of Church Growth. This school is the indisputable leader of missionary thinking, writing and research in North America, and probably the world.

Notable missiologists associated with the Church Growth movement are Alan R. Tippett, anthropologist, Ralph Winter, mission historian and pioneer thinker in the recent Unreached People movement, C. Peter Wagner (b. 1930), mission strategist, J. Edwin Orr (1912–1987), student of great revivals, Arthur Glasser (b. 1914), mission theologian, and Charles H. Kraft (b. 1932), anthropologist and ethnologist. Eddie Gibbs (b. 1938), from Great Britain, recently joined the Pasadena school.

It is not easy to summarize the main ideas connected with the Church Growth movement, since they run in many directions, to theology and anthropology, sociology, linguistics, geography, economics, management principles, statistics and research. Alan Tippett has described the Church Growth movement as 'anthropologically based, indigenously focused, and biblically oriented.'

The major conceptual contributions of the Church Growth school of missiology* are the following: 1. The 'people-movement' concept, which is the idea that conversion to the Christian faith has a social [sociological] dimension which can and should be fostered by the missionary, so that at times a large part of a culturally homogeneous group will become Christian at the same time, making the change less disruptive of the social structures of the group.

2. The Church Growth movement interprets the great commission as primarily an

imperative to make disciples and build and multiply churches. McGavran reacted strongly against mission endeavours which did not result in the growth and multiplication of churches, nor make converts, disciples of Jesus Christ. Throughout the numerous writings of McGavran and his colleagues runs a note of urgency and passion for the discipling of the world's masses and the responsible 'folding' of new believers in visible churches.

3. The Church Growth approach to missions places strong emphasis on the use of the social sciences, research and analysis, as necessary tools for the carrying out of the missionary task.

Opposition to various emphases of the Church Growth movement has come from a number of sources. At the beginning, the criticism came from those who felt they had to defend mission endeavours which were not producing converts and multiplying churches. There has been continual opposition from sectors of the Christian community which feel that social concerns and justice issues are neglected by the Church Growth movement. Even some evangelicals have spoken out against the Church Growth school for what they see as a serious neglect of kingdom issues in missions. The loudest voices have been of those who opposed the so-called 'homogeneous unit' concept, which when elevated into a universal and normative principle of church growth leaves its proponents vulnerable to the charge of being concerned exclusively with numerical growth and of minimizing the social, ethical and cultural contexts in which evangelism takes place. Argentinian René Padilla has been a consistent critic of Church Growth missiology, saying that it represents North American 'culture Christianity' which is not the answer to Third World needs.

Bibliography

H. H. Conn (ed.), *Theological Perspectives on Church Growth* (Nutley, NJ, 1976); E. Gibbs, *I Believe in Church Growth* (London, ²1985); Charles H. Kraft, 'An Anthropological Apologetic for the Homogeneous Unit Principle in Missiology', *Occasional Bulletin of Missionary Research* 2:4 (1978), pp. 121–127; Donald A. McGavran, *Understanding Church Growth* (Grand Rapids, MI, 1970); C. René Padilla, 'Unity of the Church and the Homogeneous Unit Principle', *International Bulletin of Missionary Research* 6:1 (1982), pp. 23–31; Charles Van Engen, *The Growth of the True Church* (Amsterdam, 1981); Johannes Verkuyl, *Contemporary Missiology: An Introduction* (Grand Rapids, MI, 1978); C. Peter Wagner, *Our Kind of People* (Atlanta, GA, 1979).

R.S.G.

CIVIL RELIGION. The debate about 'civil religion' became a major academic issue in the late 1960s with the seminal article by sociologist Robert Bellah (b. 1927) entitled 'Civil Religion in America' (*Daedalus 96*, 1967, pp.1–21). Bellah's essay develops the argument of Jean-Jacques Rousseau (1712–78), who in *The Social Contract* (1762) discussed the role of civil religion in society. Rousseau argued that, by introducing a distinction between church and state based on the trans-national loyalty demanded by the God of the Bible, Christians actually undermine civil society. Bellah does not discuss Rousseau's obvious sympathy for pagan Rome, but concentrates instead on his outline of the essence of a civil religion. In Rousseau's views, belief in the existence of God, the life to come, the reward of virtue and the punishment of vice, and the rejection of religious intolerance, are all important for the smooth running of a state. All other religious beliefs may be held privately by individuals, but they must not be allowed to affect social duties or fundamental loyalty.

Bellah argues that the founding fathers of the United States shared a common outlook with Rousseau. He goes on to argue for the existence of an 'American civil religion' which is consciously or unconsciously appealed to by American leaders, especially presidents. To prove his point, Bellah analysed various presidential speeches from Washington's first inaugural in 1789 to Kennedy's in 1960. Behind these speeches Bellah found a strong affirmation of the purpose and destiny of America and a call for patriotic values based upon biblical imagery and archetypes.

Bellah's article sparked a lively and stimulating debate among theologians, philosophers, sociologists, and historians. Eventually, five types of religious activity were identified as civil religion. 1. Folk religion and American values, which seem to arise out of the actual lives of Americans. 2. A transcendent universal religion of the nation or religion of the republic. This view was propounded by Sidney Mead (*CH* 36, 1967, pp. 262–283) and assumes an essentially American prophetic faith. 3. A religious nationalism which glorifies American leaders and policies. Martin Marty (in Richey and Jones, pp. 139–157) argued that this type of religious response could be seen in the speeches of Richard Nixon which identified American policies with Nixon's own policies. 4. A generalized democratic faith which sees America as the pinnacle of democratic institutions and their highest expression in a providential history. 5. A Protestant civic piety which identifies American with Protestant moralism, individualism, activism, pragmatism and work ethic.

Against all of these views, various theologians have made major criticisms of an implicit idolatry. Herbert W. Richardson argued in his powerful essay 'Civil Religion in Theological Perspective' (in Richey and Jones, pp. 161–184) that the term civil religion 'unites two terms: the civil order and the religious order', and that this was an essentially unbiblical and anti-Christian position. He acknowledges that civil religion has had great influence in America but says it deserves strong condemnation from Christians. In Richardson's view, American civil religion is a growing force which is a corruption of the original ideals of American Puritans* and a potential threat to the future freedom of religion.

In addition to discussing civil religion in America, various authors have applied the theory to their own situation. Probably the most extensive discussion of civil religion outside America has taken place in South Africa. Here sociologists and theologians have debated the use of biblical imagery by Afrikaner nationalists in relation to apartheid (see Race*). T. Dunbar Moodie's *The Rise of Afrikanerdom* is an excellent example of the application of this perspective to South African history. Apart from helping Christians to understand how a state can manipulate religious symbols Moodie also helped to discredit the popular but false notion that apartheid was a natural historical development due to the influence of Calvinism.

Although there are many problems in identifying what exactly is meant by civil religion and how it operates in a society, the idea is a creative one which sensitizes Christians to the misuse of religious symbolism by secular groups. In the work of Bellah and Moodie the existence of a civil religion is found at the heart of political and social life in modern states. But this need not always be the case. In British history, groups like the British Israelites* represent an attempt to create a civil religion which would have legitimated British imperialism. Similarly, many observers find in the Unification Church or Moonies (see New Religions;* Sects*) elements of civil religion which glorifies South Korea and America (Thomas Robbins, 'The Last Civil Religion: Reverend Moon and the Unification Church', *Sociological Analysis* 37, 1976, pp. 111–125).

Among modern evangelicals the works of Francis Schaeffer* come close to propounding an evangelical civil religion as can be seen from books such as *How Should We Then Live?* (1976). In Schaeffer's case his intention is clearly to promote a biblical appreciation of history. But in practice, among theologically unsophisticated people, this theological history often translates into something completely different and quite unbiblical. It is the ease with which biblical ideas can become sources for an idolatrous glorification of the state which is, from a Christian perspective, the true danger of civil religion.

Bibliography

T. D. Moodie, *The Rise of Afrikanerdom: Power, Apartheid and the Afrikaner Civil Religion* (Berkeley, CA, 1975); R. E. Richey and D. G. Jones (eds.), *American Civil Religion* (New York, 1974).

I.He.

CLEMENT OF ALEXANDRIA (*c.* 150–*c.* 215). Christian philosopher, probably born in Athens, who succeeded his teacher Pantaenus as head of a Christian (catechetical?) school in Alexandria some time after 180. He left Alexandria around 202.

Apart from fragments preserved by various authors, his extant works consist of the *Protrepticus* (*Exhortation to the Greeks*), a polished work of Christian apologetics; the *Paedagogus* (*The Tutor*), a detailed guide for Christian life and conduct; the *Stromateis* (*Miscellanies*), a rich assortment of notes and outlines on a wide variety of topics, and *Quis*

Dives Salvetur?, an extended sermon on the rich young ruler in Mk. 10:17–31.

In many respects his thinking stands in the line of the Greek apologists,* but he represents a contrast to contemporary (Western) writers in his positive evaluation of Gk. philosophy, his speculative bent and his deliberate lack of system. Alexandria having been the home of Philonic* allegory (see Hermeneutics*) and various brands of Gnosticism,* it is necessary to note Clement's use of allegory (not yet systematized as it is by Origen*) and his description of the perfect Christian as a 'true Gnostic'.

Though he vigorously opposes Gnosticism, Clement apparently retains docetic* elements in his Christology,* by denying emotions and certain corporeal functions in the man Jesus. He frequently uses the Trinitarian formula, emphasizing the distinction between Father, Son (Logos*) and Holy Spirit and affirming the eternity of the Son's existence, without however coming to any clear definition of the nature of the Trinity.*

Before the incarnation, knowledge of God was given to the Jews through the law and to the Greeks through philosophy, which was inspired by the Logos, *i.e.* by Christ. The Logos became incarnate to impart knowledge and to serve as our model. Clement uses the language of atonement* and conquest of evil* with respect to Christ, but his main emphasis is on Christ as teacher. Though faith, understood as assent to the teaching of Christ, is sufficient for salvation, the true Gnostic moves beyond faith to knowledge, a full understanding of Christ's teaching, coupled with an exemplary mode of living (which corresponds closely to Platonic* and Stoic* ideals). This knowledge leads to perfect love and to a mystic* relationship with God, fully consummated only after death, when the believer becomes (like) God.

Salvation is obtained in relation to the church, and through baptism one is made a member of the church. In his arguments against the heretics, Clement emphasizes the antiquity and unity of the catholic church, the tradition handed down orally in the church from the apostles and the importance of interpreting the Scriptures (which for Clement included rather more than our present canon) in accordance with the 'rule of the church'.

Clement strongly affirms the freedom of the will* and the need for man to co-operate with God by accepting salvation. He apparently conceives of the possibility of repentance even after death.

Bibliography
Works in ET in *ANCL* and *ANF;* selections in G. W. Butterworth (ed.), *Clement of Alexandria* (*LCL*, London, 1919), and H. Chadwick and J. E. L. Oulton (eds.), *Alexandrian Christianity* (*LCC*, London, 1954); H. Chadwick, *Early Christian Thought and the Classical Tradition* (Oxford, 1966); S. R. C. Lilla, *Clement of Alexandria: A Study of Christian Platonism and Gnosticism* (Oxford, 1971); E. F. Osborn, *The Philosophy of Clement of Alexandria* (Cambridge, 1975).

T.G.D.

CLINICAL THEOLOGY is an approach to pastoral caring and healing developed by Dr Frank Lake (1904–82), who claimed to enable people with severe emotional problems to identify and relive the traumatic memories of birth and early life, in particular the first three months in the womb. He believed that such experiences were responsible for their suffering, and sought to bring them to an acceptance and understanding of these 'hurts' through courses and latterly 'primal integration workshops' which were conducted within groups in a context of prayer and specialist counselling. The theoretical basis and practice of Clinical Theology were presented in a voluminous textbook *Clinical Theology* (London, 1966), which included a wallet of charts and diagrams. A second book followed (*Tight Corners in Pastoral Counselling*, London, 1981) in which Dr Lake described the further development of his thinking and techniques.

The Clinical Theology Association under whose aegis Clinical Theology operates is composed of clergy, doctors and lay people. It was founded in 1958 and since 1962 has been based in Nottingham where there is a residential centre for teaching and healing. As a result of the early support of several Anglican bishops, several thousand Anglican clergy, along with others, have received training in Clinical Theology theory and practice through groups set up throughout the UK and abroad. They have followed a set two-year programme of training under the guidance of accredited tutors.

The movement has leant almost exclusively

upon the vision and teaching of Dr Lake. Having embarked upon psychiatric training in middle life, he sought to present an approach to specific pastoral situations which applied psychiatric insights to the suffering of mentally ill people, but within a Christian understanding of the person whose need is 'not self-realization but Christ-realization'. He drew close parallels between 'the agony of the human spirit as it endures ultimate injuries and the agonies of Christ in his crucifixion' (*Clinical Theology*, p. xvii). Lake himself was an evangelical and the theological basis of his approach reflected this. He acknowledged his debt to other Christians from many theological traditions, in particular to the mystics* whose experience and writings seemed to bridge theological and psychological approaches to suffering. Their language, full of metaphor and analogy, was often found in his writings – as when he spoke of the experience of the foetus in the first three months in the womb as being 'marinated in its mother's miseries' (*Tight Corners*, p. 141). While this has been helpful to many, to others there has seemed a confusion between analogy and fact. Also, the preoccupation with prenatal experiences suggested that spiritual development was actually determined by them.

Initially, Lake's psychiatry was based upon the psychoanalytic writings of Sigmund Freud (see Depth Psychology;* Psychology of Religion*) and Melanie Klein (1882–1960) in particular but also incorporated material from Ivan P. Pavlov (1849–1936). His own experiences in using the drug LSD to recover his patient's early life-experiences convinced him, in spite of much professional scepticism, that his patient's descriptions of prenatal experiences were true and factual. He later acknowledged his indebtedness to the new psychotherapies and saw affinities between his own insight and those of Arthur Janov (b. 1924) in Primal Therapy. All this reinforced his hypothesis that the first three months after conception were significant as the source of man's suffering, his personality disorders and psychosomatic stress which he described as the maternal foetal distress syndrome where a mother's 'distress, if that is her condition . . . invades the foetus in the form of a bitter, black flood' (*Tight Corners*, p. x).

It is still too soon after its founder and director's death to see in which direction Clinical Theology will develop. Perhaps its greatest contribution remains the challenge presented to others, in that it has forced Christians to look again at emotional suffering, and has demonstrated the inadequacies of many more traditional pastoral approaches. However, from a medical point of view, its theory and practice, although accepted by some doctors, are esoteric and unverified. Repeated challenges and criticisms remain unanswered in its literature, and the help which many have received may equally be attributed to group experience and the personal charisma of Dr Lake in addition to 'good honest listening' on the part of counsellors.

See also: PASTORAL THEOLOGY.

Bibliography

D. Atkinson and I. Williams, 'Frank Lake, Explorer in Pastoral Counselling', *Third Way* 5:9 (1982), pp. 25–28; M. G. Barker, 'Models of Pastoral Care' in M. A. Jeeves (ed.), *Behavioural Sciences* (Leicester, 1984), pp. 239–241; R. F. Hurding, *Roots and Shoots: A Guide to Counselling and Psychotherapy* (London, 1986); F. Lake, *Clinical Theology* (London, 1966), abridged version by Martin H. Yeomans (London, 1986); F. J. Roberts, 'Clinical Theology: an Assessment', *TSFB* 64 (1972), pp. 21–25.

M.G.B.

COCCEIUS, see COVENANT.

COLERIDGE, SAMUEL TAYLOR (1772–1834), one of the most important pioneering figures to appear on the English theological scene during the 19th century. Most probably the originator of the term 'existentialist',* he also scored a 'first' as a psychedelic theologian. The impact of his work permeated the entire religious spectrum in England during the last century. Among those influenced by him were such important figures as J. S. Mill (1806–73), Thomas Carlyle (1795–1881), J. C. Hare (1795–1855), J. H. Newman,* Thomas Arnold (1795–1842), James Martineau (1805–1900), Rowland Williams (1817–70), F. D. Maurice (1805–72; see Christian Socialism*) and F. J. A. Hort (1828–92).

In 1795 Coleridge married Sara Fricker but soon felt they were incompatible. Eventually, they agreed to separate. While suffering the torment of domestic tension he became addicted to opium. At about the same time he was making the acquaintance of the Wordsworths and emerging from his fascination with the determinism* which had captivated him at Cambridge University.

Opium introduced Coleridge to a vast uncharted spiritual domain. The appeal of the experience of the new dimension of existence was heightened by the sensation of freedom from the limitations of time and space. At such times reason was able to enjoy the unhindered realization of its potential in perceiving spiritual truth. The implications of these discoveries were, he considered, revolutionary. 'Need we wonder', he enquired, 'at Plato's opinions concerning the body, at least, need that man wonder whom a pernicious drug shall make capable of conceiving and bringing forth Thoughts, hidden in him before . . . is it not, that the dire poison for a delusive time has made the body . . . a fitter instrument for the all powerful soul?'

The nature of his religious experience* led him to insist, 'All revelation is *ab intra* [from within]'. The intellectually arid, law-court theology of the 18th-century apologist was a disservice to the cause of true religion. 'Evidences of Christianity,' he expostulates, 'I am weary of the word. Make a man feel his want of it . . . and you may safely trust it to its own Evidences.'

To safeguard religion from the assaults of the sceptic, Coleridge adopts Kant's* distinction between reason and the understanding, but adapts these concepts to suit his own purposes. In particular he insists that reason is able to 'behold' truth, and 'is the Source and substance of truths above sense'. The understanding has no jurisdiction over suprasensible knowledge. It cannot comprehend the essence of true religion. Its faltering attempts to articulate the truths of reality are, inevitably, incomplete and erroneous. History, theology, the natural and human sciences fall within the province of the understanding.

He held that as a historical document expressing 'ideas' or truths in human terms, the Bible contains much ineffectual and erroneous material. Those who adhere to the doctrine of the inspiration (by which he meant dictation) of Scripture* are branded as 'orthodox liars for God'. We discern the truth contained in Scripture by virtue of the fact that 'whatever finds me, bears witness for itself that it has proceeded from a Holy Spirit'.

In differing ways Coleridge appealed to and influenced theologians of every standpoint. Many of the questions he raised remain as burning issues today.

Bibliography

Works: ed. W. G. Shedd, 7 vols. (New York, 1953), especially: *Aids to Reflection* (1825); *On the Constitution of Church and State* (1820); *Confessions of an Inquiring Spirit* (1840).

Studies: J. R. Barth, *Coleridge and Christian Doctrine* (Cambridge, MA, 1969); T. McFarland, *Coleridge and the Pantheist Tradition* (Oxford, 1969); B. Willey, *Samuel Taylor Coleridge* (London, 1972).

J.H.E.

COLLEGIALITY AND CONCILIARITY.
These two concepts are concerned chiefly with the government* or ministry* of the church. Vatican II's Constitution on the Church (*Lumen Gentium*) spoke of the college of the apostles and of the college of bishops as successor to it (II:22–23). This was an attempt to redress the imbalance of Vatican I's exclusive concentration on the primacy of the bishop of Rome. The use of the concept of collegiality has not resolved the Roman problem of the relation between the papacy* and the rest of the bishops in governing the church, but it has encouraged regional episcopal conferences (virtually synods) and fostered more generally a co-operative, collegial spirit and style in church life.

The Faith and Order report, *Baptism, Eucharist and Ministry* (Geneva, 1982), set up the ideal of a collegial, as well as a personal (*i.e.* individual) and a communal, dimension of ministry at every geographical level. This pattern finds clear expression in Presbyterianism,* at the congregational level in the body of elders (including any ordained presbyters) and at broader levels in presbytery, synod and assembly.

In the Roman and Orthodox traditions, councils* comprise only bishops, so that collegiality and conciliarity inevitably overlap. But in so far as the latter is applicable to other churches, decision-making in synods, assemblies or conferences normally involves laity as well as ordained ministers, perhaps of different orders. 'Conciliar fellowship' as a way of describing the goal of church unity has been prominent in World Council of Churches

151

circles, especially since the Nairobi Assembly (1975). This speaks of a unity between churches that is publicly manifested when their representatives assemble for a council whose decisions will be authoritative for all the participating churches. Such conciliarity allows for the continuation of some diversity among the churches. 'Conciliar' is also used to denote a quality of life within each local church – one that integrates and co-ordinates rather than excludes the gifts of individual members.

Conciliarity is thus a more comprehensive ideal than collegiality, although their more generalized applications are closer to each other. They both bear comparison with the concepts of *sobornost** and *koinonia.**

Bibliography
Faith and Order: Louvain 1971 (Geneva, 1971); L. Vischer, 'After the Debate on Collegiality', *Ecumenical Review* 37 (1985), pp. 306–19.

D.F.W.

COMMON GRACE, see GRACE.

COMMON-SENSE PHILOSOPHY.

This is the name given to a number of anti-sceptical philosophical positions adopted in reply to Hume,* which stressed the philosophical importance of common-sense beliefs (for example, about the existence of the self, the external world, the past and other minds), and also to common sense as a method of settling philosophical disputes. More weakly, the appeal to common sense may be regarded as a dialectical move, placing the onus of proving scepticism on the sceptic. Common-sense philosophy received its most able expression and defence from the theological 'moderate' Thomas Reid (1710–96), but the basic tenets of the 'Scottish common-sense philosophy' were taken over by numerous evangelical theologians (particularly those influenced by Princeton* College and Seminary, probably through the influence of the Scot John Witherspoon, 1722–94), as providing both the epistemological* and ontological basis of their natural theology and their philosophical ethics. Common-sense philosophy withered under its own internal difficulties, particularly the vagueness of the criterion of common sense, but more especially under the impact of continental idealism.* It has enjoyed a revival in this century through the appeal to common sense by G. E. Moore (1873–1958) and to ordinary language by philosophers such as J. L. Austin (1911–60), and through the epistemology of R. M. Chisholm (b. 1916).

Bibliography
R. M. Chisholm, *Theory of Knowledge* (Eaglewood Cliffs, NJ, ²1977); J. McCosh, *The Scottish Philosophy* (London, 1875); G. E. Moore, *Philosophical Papers* (London, 1959); essays by N. Wolterstorff and P. Helm in H. Hart *et al.* (eds.), *Rationality in the Calvinian Tradition* (Lanham, MD, 1983), pp. 41–89.

P.H.

COMMUNICATIO IDIOMATUM, see CHRISTOLOGY.

COMMUNION OF SAINTS, a theological term meaning 'fellowship'* of believers' which is found in the classical creeds.* It was originally inserted in order to express the belief that the living and the dead were united in the body of a single church,* but it soon came to have a number of subsidiary meanings, according to how the terms 'saint' and 'communion' were defined.

In medieval theology, both Eastern and Western, a saint* was either a person whose name appeared in the Bible as that of a believer in Christ, a martyr, or a Christian whose earthly life had exhibited an outstanding degree of holiness. The fellowship of the saints came to mean their common confession of Christ, which the church formulated in its creeds and other confessional documents. In later medieval theology it was extended to the belief that it also meant a sharing in holy things, especially sacraments,* a meaning which could be substantiated on the basis of the Latin form *communio sanctorum*. This secondary meaning (which some have claimed to be the original meaning) has reappeared from time to time, but it has never displaced the primary meaning of 'fellowship', which has received a new importance in the light of modern ecumenical discussions.

In the Middle Ages it was believed that a Christian could enjoy the communion of saints only by remaining a member of the Roman or of one of the Eastern Churches. This view is still the official position of these churches, but it was rejected by the Protestant Reformers, who followed the NT and defined a saint as any true believer in Christ. It followed from this that not all members of the visible church were saints, and although mainline Protestantism accommodated itself to this discrepancy, there have always been sectarian groups who have seceded from the major denominations in the hope of founding a pure church, consisting exclusively of 'saints'.

At the present time, the doctrine of the communion of saints is generally interpreted according to the dimensions of both time and space. In time, it is taken to mean the fellowship of Christians in every age, past, present and future. In practical terms, this means that the church today has a duty to preserve the faith which it has inherited from the past, and to transmit it unimpaired to future generations. Roman Catholic Christians also maintain that it has a direct bearing on the church triumphant in heaven, and use the doctrine as a justification for praying to the dead, especially to the officially canonized 'saints'. Protestants vigorously reject this interpretation, because prayer may properly be offered only to God, because Jesus Christ, not the saints, is the one mediator between God and man (1 Tim. 2:5) and because the church triumphant has entered into eternal rest.

In space, it means that all true believers are united in fellowship, regardless of nationality, language or culture. Eastern Orthodox, Roman Catholics and some Protestants continue to regard confessional harmony and fellowship within the visible church as a necessary part of the communion of saints, though in practice all these bodies are obliged to make allowance for the existence of true believers outside their respective churches. In the present ecumenical climate, this allowance may be quite generous, as when Roman Catholics refer to other Christians as 'separated brethren' and not as schismatics or heretics, though it must be remembered that there has as yet been no change in the fundamental principle that communion with the see of Rome is an essential part of the fullness of the communion of saints.

Bibliography

P. D. Avis, *The Church in the Theology of the Reformers* (London, 1981); G. C. Berkouwer, *The Church* (London, 1976); O. C. Quick, *Doctrines of the Creed* (Welwyn, 1960).

G.L.B.

CONCILIARITY, see COLLEGIALITY.

CONCUPISCENCE, see AUGUSTINE; SIN.

CONFESSIONS OF FAITH. Confession has from the outset been constitutive of Christianity. The Jesus movement was distinguished from the rest of Judaism by its declared conviction that Jesus was Messiah. In various contexts in the developing life of the church, distinctive Christian beliefs were summarized in formulas of greater or lesser fixity in structure and wording (*cf.* 1 Tim. 3:16; O. Cullmann, *The Earliest Christian Confessions*, London, 1949). The martyrs* in particular made their confession before the world as they faced death (*cf.* 1 Tim. 6:12–13); the martyr-designate was a 'confessor'.

To serve the needs of the church there developed in the 2nd century the 'rule of faith' and later the creeds.* These may all be described as confessions of faith. So too may other statements such as the Chalcedonian Definition (see Christology*), technically not a creed, which begins, 'We all with one voice confess our Lord Jesus Christ.'

Normally, however, the phrase designates the formal presentations of belief produced mainly by Protestants in the church divisions of the Reformation, including writings not calling themselves 'confessions', such as the decrees and creed of the Council of Trent, the Heidelberg Catechism, the Thirty-nine Articles and the Canons of Dort.* Many of these confessions have remained authoritative doctrinal standards in their ecclesiastical traditions (hence 'confession' is also occasionally used with reference to such communions).

The survey given below restricts itself to the Reformation and post-Reformation confessions, but is still necessarily selective. But confessions continued to be formulated, such as the Methodist* Articles of Religion (Wesley's revision of the Thirty-nine Articles, adopted by American Methodists in 1784) and the Lambeth Quadrilateral (1888, stipulating the Anglican* essentials for church unity). Significant 20th-century examples are the Barmen Declaration* (1934), the

153

expanded but still very brief confessional basis of the World Council of Churches approved at New Delhi in 1961, the Lausanne Covenant* (1974), and the Confession of 1967 of the United Presbyterian Church in the USA. This last was included in the Church's *Book of Confessions* (1967), along with the Apostles' and Nicene Creeds, the Scots and Second Helvetic Confessions, the Heidelberg Catechism, the Westminster Confession and Shorter Catechism, and the Barmen Declaration (*cf.* E. A. Dowey, Jr., *A Commentary on the Confession of 1967 and an Introduction to the Book of Confessions*, Philadelphia, 1968). The ecumenical movement has produced many doctrinal formulations, including the widely-based *Baptism, Eucharist and Ministry* of 1982.

The contemporary pluralistic confusion in theology has not been conducive to the writing of new confessions. The *Book of Confessions* represents one solution to the churches' difficulties with their 16th or 17th-century confessional documents, which often speak disparagingly of the pope or inappropriately of the relation between church and civil power, as well as being offensive to theological liberalism. Another solution is relaxation of the terms in which office-bearers are required to subscribe to them. (The Church of Scotland requires acknowledgment of only the fundamental doctrines [unspecified] in the Westminster Confession, with liberty of opinion on issues not part of the [undefined] substance of the faith.) Or, again, churches have relegated confessions to the status of 'historic' statements of their faith.

In this debate, confessions are often compared to their disadvantage with the creeds, but the contrast is frequently overdrawn. Most confessions were certainly productions of dividing or divided churches, but so too was the Chalcedonian Definition. Both confessions and creeds were formed to exclude erroneous beliefs; both were historically conditioned by the heresies they refuted. The creeds' limitations (*e.g.* none mentions the Lord's Supper; they together contribute little on the atonement*) and obscurities (*cf.* 'descended into hell'* in the Apostles' Creed, to say nothing of the technical terms of Nicaea and Chalcedon) are far more obvious than those of the confessions, which are normally more balanced and thorough. If confessions are more controversial, creeds are more

minimal and have in practice lost more completely than confessions their originally basic function as touchstones of orthodoxy. This is, however, not true of the Apostles' Creed.

Conservative Christians may in response be found defending confessions undiscriminatingly, forgetting that for Protestants they (like creeds) can only be secondary to Scripture, and are subject to the judgment and revision of Scripture, as many of them explicitly state. Among some major traditions, *e.g.* the Baptist, churchmen have often refused subscription to any creed or confession; but claims to be 'Bible-only' Christians or churches ignore the quasi-confessional force of other forms, such as church constitutions, patterns of worship and practice, hymnaries and traditional schemas of biblical interpretation. In so far as most churches have found they cannot do without confessions in some form, the best defence of the Reformation confessions lies in their wider use in the teaching activities of the congregation.

Survey of confessions

References are to P. Schaff, *The Creeds of Christendom*, 3 vols. (New York, 1877ff., best ed. 1919); J. H. Leith, *Creeds of the Churches* (Richmond, VA, ³1982); A. C. Cochrane, *Reformed Confessions of the Sixteenth Century* (London, 1966).

Schleitheim Confession (1527), seven articles drafted by Michael Sattler (*c.* 1490–1527) and adopted by the Swiss Brethren, 'the free church of the Zwinglian Reformation'. They give a clear statement of the distinctive views of mainstream Anabaptists* on: baptism, discipline ('the ban'), the Lord's Supper, separation from the world, pastors, 'the sword' ('ordained of God outside the perfection of Christ'), and oaths (Leith).

Augsburg Confession (1530), the first major Protestant confession, a moderate account of Lutheran teachings compiled by Melanchthon* and presented to the imperial Diet (Parliament) of Augsburg. It retains an unrivalled status throughout Lutheranism.* In 1531 Melanchthon wrote an *Apology* for it in response to a Catholic *Confutation*. His subsequent revision of the Confession, softening in particular its assertion of Christ's real presence in the Supper, brought bitter controversy. It was the original, unaltered (*Invariata*), that was reaffirmed as the basic document of Lutheranism in the *Book of*

Concord (see below). It starts with the Trinity, condemns ancient heretics and Anabaptists and says nothing on predestination (Schaff; Leith; T. G. Tappert, *The Book of Concord*, Philadelphia, 1959).

Tetrapolitan Confession (1530), submitted to the same Diet by 'four cities' of South Germany led by Strasburg (hence largely Bucer's* work). It was unable to accept the Lutherans' Augsburg Confession on the Lord's Supper, on which, *inter alia*, it sought to mediate between Lutherans and Zwinglians* (Schaff; Cochrane).

First Helvetic (Swiss) Confession (1536), the first common confession of the Swiss Reformed cities, drawn up by Bullinger* and others, with help from Bucer* and Capito (1478–1541), still hoping to reconcile the Swiss and the Lutherans. It begins with Scripture, gives prominence to church ministry, and covers temporal government (whose supreme task is to promote true religion) and marriage (Schaff; Cochrane). It is also known as the Second Confession of Basel, where it was agreed. The First Confession of Basel (1534) was typical of earlier Swiss statements in having only local authority.

Genevan Confession (1536), produced by Calvin* and Farel* as part of the constitution of the city's newly reformed church. It was unique among the Reformation confessions in demanding subscription by all Geneva's citizens and residents – an impossibility, as events proved. Its twenty-one brief articles begin with Scripture as God's word, and include excommunication and the 'Christian vocation' of magistrates, but not predestination (Schaff; Cochrane).

Second Helvetic (Swiss) Confession (1566), a revision of Bullinger's personal confession, approved at Zurich by the Swiss Reformed cities now including Geneva (but not Basel). Although a short book, it has been widely translated and influential as perhaps the most mature of the Reformed confessions. It is marked throughout by a concern for continuity with the catholic orthodoxy of the early church, and by a practical, pastoral outlook. Article 1, on Scripture, declares that 'the preaching of the Word of God is the Word of God' (Schaff; Leith; Cochrane). The involvement of Geneva built on the Zurich Consensus (*Consensus Tigurinus*, 1549) on the Lord's Supper, between Calvin and Farel for Geneva and Bullinger for the more Zwinglian Swiss churches. The approach of the latter probably predominates in the Consensus.

Gallic (French) Confession (1559), adopted at the first national synod of the Reformed churches at Paris. It was a recasting into forty articles of a draft sent from Geneva, with some significant deviations from the latter. Article 2 declares that God reveals himself first in creation and 'secondly, and more clearly' in his word, which the Genevan draft placed alone as Article 1. It acknowledges the three creeds, without Calvin's reservations. The synod at La Rochelle in 1571 reaffirmed it after minor revisions (Schaff; Cochrane).

Scots Confession (1560), the first confession of the reformed Church of Scotland (superseded by the Westminster Confession in 1647), drawn up by John Knox* and five other Johns – Douglas, Row, Spottiswoode, Willock and Winram. It rings with a spontaneous and even disorderly vigour, reflecting the critical haste of its production. It draws on a wide range of Reformed sources, spanning Knox's experiences on the continent and in England. God and creation come first, but election appears between incarnation and the cross. 'Out of this Kirk there is neither life nor eternal felicity' – but 'this Kirk is invisible, known only to God'. The notes of the true church include discipline as well as the word and sacraments. Condemned is the notion that the sacraments are merely 'naked and bare signs'. This lively, combative confession has enjoyed considerable modern appreciation (Schaff; Cochrane; G. D. Henderson and J. Bulloch (eds.), *The Scots Confession* (modern English version), Edinburgh, 1960; K. Barth, *The Knowledge of God and the Service of God*, London, 1938).

Belgic Confession (1561), drawn up by Guido de Brès (1522–67) as an apologia for the persecuted Reformed of the Low Countries, finally becoming, at Dort* in 1619, one of the doctrinal standards of the Dutch Reformed Church (with the Heidelberg Catechism and the Canons of Dort). It closely follows the Gallic Confession, *e.g.* in its apologetic dissociation from 'Anabaptists', although its statement on natural revelation is more careful (Schaff; Cochrane).

Thirty-nine Articles (1563), the basic confession of the reformed Church of England (and hence of most other Anglican churches). Under Elizabeth I they were distilled from Cranmer's Forty-two Articles of 1553, with a

155

final change in 1571. Intended as an instrument of national religious unity, a *via media* between Rome and Anabaptism (not between Rome and Geneva), they reflect diverse continental influences – more Lutheran on predestination and in allowing beliefs and practices not contrary to Scripture, more Reformed on the sacraments. Their interpretation has been keenly disputed (*cf.* Newman's* *Tract 90*) (Schaff; Leith; W. H. Griffith Thomas, *Principles of Theology*, London, ⁵1956; O. O'Donovan, *On the Thirty Nine Articles*, Exeter, 1986).

Formula of Concord (1577), a long document which resolved Lutheran controversies between the 'Philippists', who followed the accommodating Melanchthon, and the 'Gnesio-Lutherans', the 'authentic' disciples of Luther himself. Compiled largely by James Andreae (1528–90), who also wrote an *Epitome*, and Martin Chemnitz (1522–86), its carefully balanced exposition had the effect of excluding rapprochement with the Calvinists, which the Melanchthonians hoped for. It was included in the Lutherans' *Book of Concord* (1580) together with: the three creeds; the Augsburg Confession and its *Apology;* Luther's *Smalcald Articles* and Melanchthon's *Treatise on the Power and Primacy of the Pope* (both 1537); and Luther's *Large* and *Small Catechisms*. This collection comprises all the generally accepted doctrinal standards of Lutheranism and is accepted by most Lutheran clergy at ordination (Tappert, *Book of Concord;* E. Schlink, The *Theology of the Lutheran Confessions*, Philadelphia, 1961).

An irenic response to the Formula of Concord was the *Harmony of the Confessions of Faith of the Orthodox and Reformed Churches* published at Geneva in 1581. Produced by Jean Salvart (d. 1585), Beza* and others, this harmony of fifteen Protestant confessions, including Augsburg, argued that Protestant unity was not to be despaired of, but it had little appeal beyond the Reformed constituency (Peter Hall, *The Harmony of Protestant Confessions of Faith*, London, 1842).

Westminster Confession (1646), a highly systematic exposition of Calvinist orthodoxy, of remarkable comprehensiveness, balance and precision, which was adopted by the Church of Scotland in 1647 and subsequently became the confession of most Presbyterian churches, and, with appropriate changes, of Congregationalists (and even Baptists) in

Britain and America. It was the work of the Westminster Assembly's largely Puritan* divines, commissioned to produce a confession to unite Scotland and England. It purveys a developed, so-called 'scholastic' Calvinism, reflecting the influence of Puritan covenant* theology and of the Irish Articles of 1615 (which were briefly adopted by the [Episcopal] Church of Ireland, despite saying nothing about the necessity of episcopal ordination and the three orders of ministry, being chiefly written by James Ussher, 1581–1656). Its more controversial features include double predestination (alongside free will* and contingent 'second causes'), the covenant of works with Adam, a Puritan doctrine of assurance and a sabbatarian view of Sunday. Even its critics recognize its solidity and majesty (Schaff; Leith; S. W. Carruthers (ed.), *The Westminster Confession of Faith . . . with Notes*, Manchester, 1937; B. B. Warfield, *The Westminster Assembly and Its Work*, New York, 1931; A. I. C. Heron (ed.), *The Westminster Confession in the Church Today*, Edinburgh, 1982).

Cambridge Platform (1648) and *Savoy Declaration* (1658) were the fundamental formularies of, respectively, American and English Congregationalism. In doctrine they essentially reproduced the Westminster Confession, with the changes needed to provide for a church polity of independent congregations (Schaff; Leith; W. Walker, *The Creeds and Platforms of Congregationalism*, New York, 1893).

London Baptist Confession (1677), known also as the Philadelphia Confession, similarly adapted Westminster Calvinism to Baptist polity and baptism. It was the most widely accepted of Calvinist Baptist confessions. The New Hampshire Confession (1833) was a milder statement of Baptist Calvinist faith.

Confession of Dositheus (1672), the most important Orthodox confession of modern times, defining Orthodox theology against Protestantism. Dositheus (1641–1707) was patriarch of Jerusalem and presided over the synod there which canonized this confession (Leith). Its specific 'Calvinist' target was Cyril Lucaris (1572–1638), the patriarch of Constantinople who was strongly attracted to Protestantism. His own Confession of Faith (Geneva, 1629; Schaff; G. A. Hadjiantoniou, *Protestant Patriarch*, Richmond, VA, 1961) is a thoroughly Calvinist interpretation of Orthodox doctrine.

Bibliography

W. A. Curtis, *A History of the Creeds and Confessions of Faith* (Edinburgh, 1911); E. Routley, *Creeds and Confessions* (London, 1962); C. Plantinga, Jr., *A Place to Stand: A Reformed Study of Creeds and Confessions* (Grand Rapids, MI, 1979).

D.F.W.

CONFIRMATION. The rite called 'confirmation' has become a 'rite in search of a theology'. It developed in the Western church from the separation of a secondary part of the 3rd-century baptismal rite from the actual (water) baptism,* and in the 5th century gained the Latin title 'confirmatio'. Whereas it appears to rest upon the apostolic precedent of a post-baptismal laying on* of hands (Acts 8:14–17; 19:1–7), in fact no direct continuity of usage can be traced to these occurrences, and, even if they do provide some precedent, it is doubtful whether they should be viewed as normative for Christian initiation in the way that water-baptism is. The gospels give no warrant for such a rite; the Acts of the Apostles has many instances of the use of water-baptism without a subsequent laying on of hands (so that these instances in fact appear as exceptions); the two instances themselves have very little in common with each other (and in particular the Acts 8 passage has the laying on of hands far apart in time from water-baptism, whereas the Acts 19 passage has it in immediate sequence); and the Pauline corpus (whether understood narrowly or broadly) has no mention of this rite, though much about water-baptism. The only further possible biblical evidence is the obscure reference in Heb. 6:2 (where *baptismōn* does not necessarily refer to 'baptisms' at all, and is not always translated as 'baptisms' in the English versions). In general, there is silence, and there is no theology of initiation (whether outward and sacramental, or inward and regenerative) which would correspond to such a ceremony. There is reference to water-baptism in some of the earliest post-apostolic authors, notably Ignatius of Antioch, the *Didache*, the *Shepherd* of Hermas (see Apostolic Fathers*), and Justin Martyr (see Apologists*). However, they too are silent about a post-baptismal laying on of hands or anointing.* The most primitive traceable practice, whether in the West or in the East, seems to have been simply water-baptism, for adults and probably for infants, and this led straight into participation in Communion.

A post-baptismal laying on of hands in initiation is first to be discovered in the West in the late 2nd century in Tertullian* and soon after in Hippolytus.* The East did not follow this until the second half of the 4th century, and then used anointing (the 'seal'), and still continues this practice to the present day (giving both water-baptism and the 'seal' even to infants in one single rite of initiation which leads them into Communion). In the West the complex rite of water-baptism (with or without anointing), laying on of hands, giving of the kiss of peace, and participation in Communion, held sway till around the 6th century, but afterwards broke into separate parts in most places. Augustine's* doctrine of original sin (see Sin*), and the necessity of baptism immediately subsequent upon birth where any chance of death existed, led to clinical baptism of infants in the Dark and Middle Ages. Confirmation (as it was called from the 5th century onwards) could not then take place at the same time (as it usually still required a bishop to give it), and the age of confirmation floated upwards in an unplanned way to suit the actual circumstances in which a bishop might be present to confirm. The title 'confirmatio' was used from the 5th century onwards of the detached episcopal laying on of hands. Thus the rite came, in process of time, to be interpreted not as initiatory, but (as its use declared it to be) 'confirmatory'. Thomas Aquinas* has it so far detached from baptismal initiation that he allows that ordination can proceed without the candidate having being confirmed!

Thus the Reformers inherited a pattern in which confirmation was given by anointing, and was viewed as a sacrament of strengthening or growth, for candidates at any age from infancy (though that was rare by the 16th century) to adulthood, though a mean age may have been between three and nine. The Reformers agreed that water-baptism was the sole sacramental initiation, and did not wish to add confirmation to the rite of baptism, which in general they still administered to infants. Instead they took the medieval pattern to its logical conclusion, raised

157

the age of confirmation to between thirteen and sixteen, required massive catechizing* to precede it, and used it as a rite for adult admission to Communion. In this they were assisted by some bogus early church history promulgated by Calvin,* and believed on his authority. In fact the new usage was unprecedented. What happened was that the outward sign reverted to the laying on of hands, which replaced 'the Bishop of Rome's buttering'. The Church of England *Book of Common Prayer* adopted exactly this discipline of Calvin's, and it has run to the present day. On the other hand Article XXV of 1563 (see Confessions*) added to the Edwardian Article a paragraph which said that confirmation is not to be counted as a sacrament of the gospel, as it arises from the corrupt following of the apostles, and has no visible sign or ceremony ordained of God. The *Book of Common Prayer* corresponded to this in that the prayer at the laying on of hands had no sacramental content or character ('Defend, O Lord, this thy servant with thy heavenly grace . . .'); and, when a section on the sacraments was added to the Anglican Catechism in 1604, even though it occurred within the confirmation service and was preparing candidates for confirmation, it asserted that there are but two sacraments of the gospel, and made no reference to confirmation whatsoever.

The 20th century has seen differing attempts to produce a satisfying theology, and to bring pastoral and liturgical practice into accord with it. Non-episcopal churches have followed Calvin's pattern. Anglicans have first flirted with the notion that water-plus-the laying-on-of-hands equals full initiation, and have attempted to 're-integrate' the 'disintegrated' parts of the primitive (*i.e.* Hippolytan) rite; but more latterly they have been ready to see water-baptism as full sacramental initiation, and have started to move towards child and even infant Communion on the basis of it. Roman Catholics have greatly widened the use of presbyteral confirmation (which has a long history in that church), and have sought in some places to associate it with first Communion. But thinness of the theological foundations in both Scripture, history and systematic theology, still generally leaves it a rite in search of a theology.

Bibliography

R. J. Bastian, *The Effects of Confirmation in Recent Catholic Thought* (Rome, 1962); C. Buchanan, *Anglican Confirmation* (Bramcote, Nottingham, 1986); G. Dix, *The Theology of Confirmation in Relation to Baptism* (London, 1946); J. D. G. Dunn, *Baptism in the Holy Spirit* (London, 1970); J. D. C. Fisher, *Confirmation Then and Now* (London, 1978); G. W. H. Lampe, *The Seal of the Spirit* (London, 1951); B. Neunhauser, *Baptism and Confirmation* (Freiburg, 1964); E. C. Whitaker, *Sacramental Initiation Complete in Baptism* (Bramcote, Nottingham, 1975).

C.O.B.

CONFUCIANISM AND CHRISTIANITY.

Confucianism has been the most significant philosophical system for centuries among the Chinese, Japanese and Korean peoples in providing ethical principles and contributing to the stability of society. While Mao Tse-tung (Mao Zedong) and other communist leaders in mainland China tried to exterminate Confucianism from Chinese society for hindering the cause of the communist revolution, Confucianism was strongly rejuvenated in recent years in Asia by the governments of the Republic of China (Taiwan) and Singapore in line with the resurgence of traditional values.

Confucianism is considered by the Chinese as a philosophy rather than a religion; but 'philosophy' is not here used in the normal sense of the word in the West. Confucianism is more than a philosophy, as it combines philosophy with life itself.

There are similarities between Confucianism and Christianity in their ethical* teaching and their concern for peace in family, society and nation. However, the methods of achieving peace and tranquillity in society are radically different in the two.

1. Confucius (551–479 BC) taught the golden rule and the moral perfection of the individual through harmony in five basic human relationships: between ruler and subject, husband and wife, parents and children, brother and sister, and brother/sister and friends. The ideal man in Confucianism is called Jün Tze (gentleman). He is not necessarily an aristocrat, but one who cultivates the moral characteristics of Jen (benevolence, love of others), Shiao (filial piety) and Li (sense of

propriety), and who keeps the five virtues of courtesy, magnanimity, good faith, diligence, and kindness. The ideal man knows how to cultivate himself, how to rule his family, and how to govern his nation properly. The chief objective of Confucianism is to establish peace and order in society through a strong moral basis with the help of rituals and music.

In Christianity, Jesus' Sermon on the Mount (Mt. 5 – 7) in the NT and the ten commandments (Ex. 20) in the OT similarly emphasize a moral and peaceful society. This may provide a starting-place for communication between Confucianism and Christianity.

2. In Confucianism, a man's chief concern should be the duties of the present life rather than what will happen after death. There is, therefore, an emphasis on the 'now' of this present world. When Confucius was asked how a man should serve the spirits of the dead, he replied, 'As you are not yet able to serve the living, how will you be able to serve the spirits of the dead?' (*Analect* XI.11). When he was asked about death, he said, 'As you know nothing yet about life, how can you know anything about death?' (*ibid.*) Death and life must be accepted with resignation as the result of natural law, and they are determined by the 'will of heaven' (Ming) rather than either fate or divine predestination.*

By contrast with biblical teaching on sin,* Confucianism considers wrongdoing as improper, inexpedient, and antisocial without any reference to man's direct responsibility to a higher being or God. Most important is human reformation. Scripture, on the other hand, presents a doctrine of salvation,* repentance,* and forgiveness of sins from God (see Guilt and Forgiveness*).

The Bible, in addition, gives due weight to both present and eternal existence, and stresses that man's earthly life possesses significance for him and God precisely in the light of his future existence (see Eschatology;* Judgment of God*).

There is also a radical difference between Confucianism and Christianity in the areas of epistemology* and methods of achieving human goals. The former starts with man and nature (humanism), the latter with the self-revelation of God (in a supernatural, theocentric and Christocentric outlook in life). Confucius was an agnostic and taught the basic goodness of human nature which man can cultivate for the betterment of mankind. For Confucius, man can achieve the peaceful society by his own ingenuity.

On the other hand, the Christian Bible teaches that man can do nothing apart from God and his grace,* and is totally dependent upon him for moral and spiritual life (Jn. 15:5). The question of whether man needs God for his moral and spiritual life distinguishes Christianity from Confucianism. Those in the West who deny supernatural elements in Christianity are attracted to Confucianism, while others in the Orient who see finitude and failure in humanism are open to Christianity.

Bibliography

Ching Feng, quarterly magazine produced by Tao Fong Shen Ecumenical Centre, New Territories, Hong Kong; Julia Ching, *Confucianism and Christianity* (Tokyo, 1977); Paul E. Kauffman, *Confucius, Mao and Christ* (Hong Kong, 1978); Bong Rin Ro (ed.), *Christian Alternatives to Ancestor Practices* (Taichung, Taiwan, 1985).

B.R.R.

CONGREGATIONALISM. The origins of Congregationalism may be traced back to England in the reign of Queen Elizabeth I (1558–1603). Her objective for the church was an enforced uniformity, but there were those who wanted to see the national church re-organized on presbyterian* (see also Church Government*) rather than episcopal lines. Others, however, repudiated the whole concept of a state church and favoured the 'gathered church' principle. These became known as 'Independents' and were the forerunners of the Congregationalists. They contended that the church* should consist only of those who had personally responded to the call of Christ, and who had covenanted with him and with one another to live together as his disciples.

A leading figure among the early Independents was Robert Browne (1553–1633), a Cambridge graduate who has been called the father of English separatism. In 1582 he published in Holland his famous *Treatise of Reformation without Tarrying for Anie* in which he set forth congregational principles. He asserted that 'the Church planted or gathered is a company or number of Christians or believers, which, by a willing covenant made with their God, are under the government of

God and Christ and keep his laws in one holy communion'. Such churches, he claimed, are subject to neither bishops nor magistrates. Ordination is not vested in elders, but is at the hands of the whole church.

In various areas, companies of men and women put Browne's teaching into practice. Rather than submit to ecclesiastical regimentation, many sought religious freedom in Holland. Some of these later crossed the Atlantic where churches of the congregational pattern became one of the formative influences in the New World. It was from John Robinson's (c. 1575–1625) church at Leiden that the 'Pilgrim Fathers' set off in 1620 in the *Mayflower*. Congregationalism became the recognized church order in Connecticut and Massachusetts and continued to be so until the first quarter of the 19th century. Meanwhile, in England the pattern of church life taught by Robert Browne spread with the formation of Congregational and Baptist* churches throughout the country, particularly in the later 17th century. Following the Act of Uniformity (1662), over 2,000 clergy opted for nonconformity rather than conform to the *Book of Common Prayer* and an episcopal order. The faith and beliefs of the Congregationalists were expressed in the Savoy Declaration of 1658, just as the Westminster Confession a few years earlier had expressed the Presbyterian* viewpoint.

During the following century there was less obvious growth in nonconformity, but two great Independents of this period call for mention – the hymnwriters Isaac Watts (1674–1748) and Philip Doddridge (1702–51). A number of Independent and Presbyterian churches at this time became virtually unitarian* in doctrine and dissenters lost much of their earlier zeal.

The Evangelical Revival, however, brought new life to the churches as a whole. In 1831 the Congregational Union was formed with the primary objective of 'promoting evangelical religion in connection with the Congregational denomination'. Insistence upon the independence of the local Christian community was never regarded as precluding a loose fellowship of independent local churches for purposes of mutual consultation and edification.

One of the great names in Congregationalism during the second half of the 19th century was that of R. W. Dale (1829–95).

He was one of a long line of distinguished ministers at the Carr's Lane Congregational Church in Birmingham. Dale combined moral fervour, intellectual power and intense religious conviction. He was the embodiment of nonconformity's interest in social and educational reforms. He maintained that Christian convictions either issued in political action or evaporated in pietistic sentimentality. He became a national figure and sat on the Royal Commission for Education. He was the ally and friend of leaders of the Liberal Party. It was said that in the city of Birmingham no major municipal decision would be taken before Dale's views had been canvassed. Dale found time to write a *History of Congregationalism* and was also instrumental in the founding of Mansfield College, Oxford (1886), the first principal of which, A. M. Fairbairn (1838–1912), was a significant mediator of German critical scholarship in Great Britain.

During the latter part of the 19th century the influence of biblical criticism was increasingly felt in Britain; Congregationalists and Presbyterians were, in many cases, only too ready to imbibe the teachings of 'liberal' theologians. 'Congregationalists drank more deeply of [them] than did any of the others. Congregationalism, freed by its new federation from the bondage of parochialism, and freed traditionally by its intellectual ethos from any risk of becoming mentally stagnant, offered enthusiastic hospitality to the new critical teachings on the Bible which came from Germany. There has always been a keen and energetic "modernist" movement in Congregationalism' (E. Routley, *The Story of Congregationalism*).

In Britain, Congregationalism took a decisive step in 1966 when local Congregational churches were invited to covenant together to form the Congregational Church. This step was later followed by the union of the Congregational Church with the Presbyterian Church of England leading to the formation of the United Reformed Church. With this new development Congregationalism, as traditionally understood, largely disappeared from the scene in England, but not in Ireland, Scotland and Wales, although it remains the basis of church order in Baptist churches as well as in a growing number of independent evangelical churches.

A group of Congregationalists, determined

to save historic independency, formed themselves into the Congregational Federation. Their quarrel with the scheme of union was not so much on theological grounds, but on the issue of the freedom of the local church to govern its own affairs under the direction of the Holy Spirit. The Federation believes strongly in the value of unity in diversity and deplores any tendency towards regimentation. A number of strongly evangelical Congregational churches did not enter the scheme of union, on the grounds that it was one further example of ecumenical compromise. They were critical of the scheme on the grounds of its theological ambiguity, as well as its abandonment of the principle of independency. They are linked together in an Evangelical Fellowship of Congregational Churches.

World-wide, Congregationalism has been closely involved with the ecumenical movement. This fact no doubt explains to some extent the underlying reasons for the various mergers which have taken place in different parts of the world between Congregational, Presbyterian and – in some cases – Methodist churches. The general trend in Congregationalism world-wide has been away from independency.

The congregational system of church government has often been wrongly described as democratic. Ideally the church is seen as being under the rule of Christ and the church meeting seeks to discern his will. It is hardly surprising that many Congregational churches have been relatively small in membership – a large congregation finds it harder to work out the principle of 'Christocracy' through the medium of the church meeting. In a Congregational church the members are empowered to elect their own church officers and to choose their own minister. Membership of the church is on profession of personal faith in Christ and new members are normally welcomed by being given the right hand of fellowship at a communion service.

Bibliography

R. W. Dale, *Manual of Congregational Principles* (London, 1884); D. Jenkins, *Congregationalism: A Restatement* (London, 1954); A. Peel, *A Brief History of English Congregationalism* (London, 1931); E. Routley, *The Story of Congregationalism* (London, 1961); W. Walker, *The Creeds and Platforms of Congregationalism* (New York, 1893).

G.W.K.

CONGRUISM, see MERIT.

CONSCIENCE has been variously understood as: an inner moral sense of right and wrong, the voice of God within, or the mind of human beings making moral judgments. Traditionally, there have been two elements to conscience. *Synderesis* (a corruption of Gk. *syneidēsis*) is humanity's consciousness of universally binding rules or principles of conduct. *Conscientia* is the ability to relate general rules to particular cases. 'Conscience', as we understand it, includes both.

Conscience is a universal capacity inbuilt in mankind by divine creation. Some see it as an element in the image of God.* Paul argues that everyone has moral awareness and describes even the Gentiles as having 'the requirements of the law written on their hearts, their consciences also bearing witness' (Rom. 2:15). Mankind, as distinct from the animals, has the capacity to distinguish right from wrong. This involves the mind, the emotions and the will, for conscience acts as both a judge and a guide.

Conscience is both retrospective and prospective. It judges actions done or omitted and brings feelings of guilt and the awareness of the need for repentance. It guides and directs before we act, so that we may act properly in good conscience.

While the OT has no specific reference to conscience, the notion underlies the law and prophets, and points to an awareness of right and wrong. In the NT, conscience is presented as an integral part of human personality. It is the internalizing of judgments and guidance from without.

Problems with conscience. The notion of conscience has been attacked at two levels. Freud and behaviourists (see Psychology of Religion*) have portrayed conscience simply as the interiorization of the norms of parents and society, and often as acting in a repressive way with a harmful overemphasis on guilt. For them conscience is nothing more than a social or psychological conditioning. This analysis fails to understand the scope of conscience in the Christian view and fastens on a narrow view of its origin. It then commits the 'genetic fallacy' – to explain the origin

161

does not explain the whole reality. However, conscience is subject to the fall* and is not an infallible guide. It may vary in its decisions, allow exceptions to general rules, and is not always clear in complex situations as to what is right. Historically, there have been over-sensitive consciences which have appeared obsessive and paralysed moral action. Nowadays the opposite extreme is the case. The NT shows that consciences may be weakened or deadened (1 Tim. 4:1–5; Eph. 4:19; Tit. 1:15). The Christian has a moral responsibility to educate and develop his or her conscience (Heb. 5:14; 9:9; 9:14; 10:2; 10:22; 2 Cor. 1:12). This involves directing the conscience to keep it in line with external moral norms. While the conscience is not to be disobeyed, it is not the sole guide to the moral life. It needs to be checked and tested in relation to the character of God as revealed in Christ, to be informed by Scripture as a whole and renewed by the Holy Spirit. Conscience then operates on the basis of God's grace and issues in love for others.

See also: CASUISTRY; PURITAN THEOLOGY.

Bibliography

J. C. Ford and G. Kelly, *Contemporary Moral Theology* (Westminster, MD, 1960); H. C. Hahn and C. Brown, *NIDNTT* I, pp. 348ff; K. E. Kirk, *Conscience and its Problems* (London, 1927); P. Lehmann, *Ethics in a Christian Context* (London, 1963); C. A. Pierce, *Conscience in the New Testament* (London, 1955).

E.D.C.

CONSERVATISM IN THEOLOGY, see LIBERALISM.

CONTEMPORARY THEOLOGICAL TRENDS.

Contemporary theology is characterized by such greatly divergent methods and proposals that any neat map of the territory is exceedingly difficult to draw. Partly this is because dominating models of an earlier generation (Barth,* Bultmann,* Tillich*) have receded but not been replaced; partly because much modern theology is pluralist, spanning different confessional and sometimes religious traditions; and partly because theology's conversation partners are no longer simply history, ethics and philosophy but also, for example, sociology, anthropology and political science.

Questions of method are to the forefront, and the last two decades have seen substantial work on such issues as theological pluralism, historical relativism* and the nature of change and continuity in theology (D. Tracy, N. Lash, D. Nineham), as well as some sophisticated work on patterns of theological procedure (D. Kelsey) and the ecclesial character of theology (E. Farley). Traditional areas of prolegomena and epistemology,* such as the relation of faith and reason* or the scope of natural theology,* continue to be debated (by, *e.g.*, W. Pannenberg* in German and K. Ward and R. Swinburne in English theology). There have been, however, a number of recent attempts to shift the ground of debate in this area from what some consider to be an excessively intellectualist approach towards enquiry into the roots of theology in worship* and the religious imagination.* Liturgical theologians* such as G. Wainwright (b. 1939) or R. Prenter (b. 1907) locate the basic datum of theology in the praise of God (see Doxology*), which is critically examined by the reflective theologian. There have been several attempts to affirm the heuristic function of the imagination (T. W. Jennings, J. Hartt, J. Coulson) and the cognitive significance of non-literal language, partly under the influence of hermeneutical* philosophers such as H. G. Gadamer and P. Ricoeur. Similarly, narrative theology* (explored by H. Frei, D. Ritschl, H. O. Jones, S. Hauerwas and others) has enquired into the function of stories and myths* in the articulation of truth in an attempt to break down the hegemony of positivist* epistemologies and recover confidence in the substance of Christianity.

Theology and social science increasingly interact in questions of the social context of Christian faith and theology and their role in the establishment and maintenance of social systems. 'Political'* or 'liberation'* theologians (G. Gutiérrez, J. Sobrino, J. L. Segundo, L. Boff, J. B. Metz,* J. Moltmann*) have sought to call into question characteristic assumptions about the primacy of theory and reinstated political action in identification with the poor and oppressed as the primary datum for theology. While it originated in the Third World, notably Latin America, the theology of liberation is now at the top of Western theological agendas also, through, for example, black* or feminist* theologies which seek to counter the ideological effects of much traditional theological reflection.

While there have been recent attempts to articulate a complete dogmatics* (K. Rahner,* H. Berkhof,* G. Ebeling*) or a large-scale defence of the Christian faith (H. Küng*), much contemporary work is exceedingly cautious about over-arching theological schemes, especially in Britain, where doctrinal criticism* has become a widespread approach. This style of critical appraisal of doctrine has been especially applied to Christology* (by M. F. Wiles and A. T. Hanson) and to the doctrine of the Trinity* (by G. W. H. Lampe, 1912–80, and J. P. Mackey), where there has been a rigorous testing of the viability of credal orthodoxy as a framework for contemporary theology. Others such as E. L. Mascall (b. 1905) or J. Galot have sought to reaffirm the tradition, or have looked for fresh categories apparently less reductionist than those of the doctrinal critics.

After a period of neglect, to some extent under the influence of Barth, the doctrine of creation* has begun to reappear in terms of the theology of nature* (G. S. Hendry) or a natural theology based either on dialogue with the human sciences (Pannenberg) or on a concept of the universal significance of Christ (Chr. Link, W. Krötke, E. Jüngel*). The doctrine of God has received a good deal of attention. Trinitarian theology has been thoroughly criticized but also thoroughly restated, notably in the work of K. Rahner but also by Moltmann, Jüngel and W. Kasper. Process theologians,* drawing upon the metaphysics of Whitehead and Hartshorne, have replaced language about divine being by language about divine becoming, since God is the supreme instance of the interactive process of reality (J. Cobb, L. Ford). Others more central to the Christian tradition have approached the doctrine of God via Christology, and particularly via the death of Christ (Moltmann, Jüngel, H. Urs von Balthasar*), and called into question attributes such as impassibility or immutability which, it is claimed, are not compatible with God's humanity in Christ. Out of this has grown a considerable theological and devotional literature on the suffering of God. The doctrine of the Spirit furnishes the basis for one of the most searching pieces of contemporary constructive theology, Lampe's *God as Spirit*; in Germany H. Mühlen and Moltmann have given greater prominence to pneumatology, especially in its manward aspects.

As for the most of the present century, sin and atonement have been little attended to beyond historical studies of past theories. Many contemporaries, particularly Lutherans, focus on the cross* as the revelation of the character and purposes of God to the neglect of its soteriological import. Again among Lutherans, the doctrine of justification* remains a fundamental article, particularly for the explication of theological doctrine about humanity. Apart from these areas, soteriology is chiefly discussed by liberation theologians and in dialogue with other religions – one of the heavy preoccupations of contemporary theology – with such leading theorists as J. Hick* and W. Cantwell Smith.

Attention to the social world of religious practice and belief by sociologists and philosophers has contributed to the widespread current revival of interest in ecclesiology (see Church*), which has also been stimulated by contemporary ecumenical* endeavour. Sacramental* and particularly eucharistic* theology has been furnished with a new conceptuality derived from phenomenology of signs (notably by E. Schillebeeckx*), and older confessional divides over question of eucharistic presence or sacrifice are vigorously debated. More generally, the functioning of Christianity as a religious system has been subjected to sophisticated theological analysis, e.g. by Farley and S. Sykes. In this context, the functioning of Scripture in regulating the life of the Christian community has been extensively examined.

Contemporary writing on eschatology* often focuses on theological interpretation of the meaning of human history,* especially in exploration of the theme of hope,* as in the earlier work of Pannenberg and Moltmann. Systematic and philosophical theologians have also devoted much attention to questions of personal survival and identity beyond death, and the intelligibility of language about life after death (H. D. Lewis, Hick, T. Penelhum).

Whilst there is much faddishness, the best recent theology is, compared with the radical theology of the 1960s, more methodologically sophisticated and more engaged in serious debate with the classical texts of the Christian tradition. While it remains fundamentally a critical exercise, with little sympathy for self-authenticating authorities, credal, ecclesial or scriptural, contemporary theology shows itself to be increasingly preoccupied with its constructive responsibilities.

Bibliography
A. Richardson and J. Bowden (eds.), *A New Dictionary of Christian Theology* (London, 1983) offers an excellent gauge of recent thinking. P. C. Hodgson and R. H. King (eds.), *Christian Theology* (London, 1983), is the best recent over-all survey. The journal *Concilium* is a useful index of current concerns, particularly since it is international. *ExpT* often carries survey articles of recent theological literature, especially from abroad.

J.B.We.

CONTEXTUALIZATION is a dynamic process of the church's reflection, in obedience to Christ and his mission in the world, on the interaction of the text as the word of God and the context as a specific human situation. It is essentially a missiological* concept. The interpreter or one engaged in this process may be part of the context or, as a cross-cultural communicator, represent a second context in a three-way process.

Contextualization is not a passing fad or a debatable option. It is essential to our understanding of God's self-revelation. The incarnation* is the ultimate paradigm* of the translation of text into context. Jesus Christ, the Word of God incarnate as a Jew, identified with a particular culture at a limited moment in history though transcending it. In his life and teaching he is the supreme model* of contextualization. His every command was *de facto* a command to contextualization, whether to love one's neighbour or to disciple the nations. The implication of this process is seen in the apostolic witness and the life of the New Testament church. The difference in theological emphasis and preaching method between Paul's address to the synagogue in Pisidian Antioch (Acts 13:16–41) and his address to the Areopagus in Athens (Acts 17:22–31) is but one notable illustration of the sociological and theological inevitability of contextualization. In the history of dogma the affirmations of the truths of God's revelation in Scripture have always involved a selection of themes and contextualized language in response to the particular theological and ethical issues confronting the church in that moment of history. The

creeds,* confessions* and statements of faith reflect this process.

With the rapid expansion of the Western missionary movement in the 19th century, missionary strategists Henry Venn (1725–97), Rufus Anderson (1796–1880) and others developed the concept of indigenization, whereby the unchanging gospel was transplanted into the static and generally 'primitive' cultures of non-Christian peoples. This movement was primarily concerned with indigenizing the forms of worship, social customs, church architecture and methods of evangelism. This emphasis is still valid as the current interest in cultural anthropology and the Church Growth* movement indicates. The failure to indigenize has resulted in the perpetuation of colonialism and the growth of a ghetto mentality among Christian communities. However, in recent years the adequacy of the indigenization principle has been seriously questioned. Since World War II, the rise of nationalism, the overthrow of Western colonialism, and the spread of political revolution leading to military dictatorship or socialist and Marxist governments have engulfed an increasing number of nations. The explosion of human knowledge, science and technology, and the spirit of materialism and secular humanism which have permeated all modern societies have resulted in a crisis of faith and a search beyond indigenous identity for truth and relevance.

The need to move from indigenization to contextualization has also been accelerated by issues raised by modern theologians and the global ministry of conciliar ecumenical* movements. These issues include: the situational hermeneutics* of R. Bultmann;* the call to the church in the midst of rapid social change to be action-orientated, made for example at the World Conference on Church and Society at Geneva (1966); the questioning of the distinction between salvation-history* and world history at the WCC Assembly at Uppsala (1968); the acceptance of the principle of humanization and universalism* in salvation at the WCC Commission on World Mission and Evangelism at Bangkok (1972); and the search for the unity of mankind at the WCC Assembly at Nairobi (1975). The focusing on issues of social reconciliation, humanization and liberation has led to a shift of priority from interpreting the text to reflection on suffering and oppression in particular contexts. Contextualization has become a way of doing politicized theology (see Political Theology*).

The origin of the term 'contextualization' is credited to Shoki Coe and Aharoan Sapsezian, directors of the Theological Education Fund of the WCC in their 1972 report, *Ministry and Context*. They suggested that the term 'contextualization' implies all that is involved in the term 'indigenization' but goes beyond it to take account of 'the process of secularity, technology and the struggle for human justice which characterised the historical moment of nations in the third world.'

Radical interpretations

Modern scholars and liberation* theologians in particular, have made extensive use of the concept of contextualization as part of a wider theological debate. They begin by rejecting the traditional view of divine revelation as inscripturated in the Bible, since the word of God cannot be equated with any particular form, whether Scripture or theological systems. They deny that the Bible contains propositional truths and argue that since all Scripture is culturally and historically conditioned, its message is relative and situational. Further, they hold that there is no truth outside of the action of concrete historical events of human struggle. There can be no epistemological split between thought and action, truth and practice. Thus all authentic theology must be participatory theology. Theological knowledge comes only from participation in action and reflection on praxis.* As a result radical theologians hold that the hermeneutical process does not begin with the exegesis of Scripture but with a prophetic 'reading of the times', discerning God's act of humanization and liberation in the general historical process and in particular situations. Gustavo Gutiérrez argues that theology is reflection on praxis in the light of faith. It is a dialectical movement between action and reflection. The hermeneutics of Scripture give place to the hermeneutics of history. Evangelical Latin American theologians René Padilla, Emilio Antonio Núñez and others, while recognizing the validity of the deep concerns raised by liberation theologians, argue that this way of doing theology leads to a truncated gospel, a secularized political theology and ultimately to the demise of the institutionalized church and of the centrality of evangelism.

Conservative interpretations

Evangelical scholars, missionaries, church and lay leaders have taken seriously the validity of the shift from indigenization to the enlarged agenda of contextualization. A beginning was made at the Lausanne* Congress on World Evangelization (1974) and followed up at the Gospel and Culture consultation in Bermuda (1978). Nevertheless, for many evangelicals the task of contextualization is restricted to the faithful and relevant communication of the unchanging message into the language and cultural thought forms of those to whom it is communicated. This concern takes seriously the issues of the cultural conditioning of the biblical message, the communicator's self-understanding and the receiving community's response to the message. In this way contextualization is understood in terms of 'dynamic equivalence', whereby the biblical message is seen to bring forth in the receiver a response equivalent to that which the biblical text produced in those to whom it was first addressed.

However, the task of contextualization calls for a more profound understanding of translating the gospel in its relationship to the contemporary historical situation. The time-honoured grammatico-historical method of biblical exegesis continues to be accepted as fundamental to authentic contextualization, giving clarity and understanding as to what the biblical writers said and meant in their own context. However, contextualization takes place only when the faithful exegesis of the text enters into a dialogical encounter with the issues of the human situation. This encounter will be both theological and ethical in which belief and action are interdependent. It takes place in dependence on the Holy Spirit who is the hermeneutic key to relating text and context.

The interpreter's critical reflection on his own cultural pre-understanding is an essential part of this three-way process. While drawing on the insight of Bultmann's hermeneutical circle, scholars such as Orlando Costas find an alternative symbol in a dialogical spiral that points to an eschatological goal. This dynamic process of critical reflection and interpretation takes place as the interpreter identifies by faith with the text of the Scripture and at the same time distances himself from it in study and reflection. At the same time the interpreter identifies with and distances himself also from the context. Authentic contextualization takes place when these horizons meet. In the dialogue between text and context the questions raised by the context are brought to the text for answers while the text in turn raises new questions that confront the context. For example, the context may focus on specific issues of violence while the text raises issues concerning sin and demonic power. Since the text is given and authoritative and the context relative and changing, the dialogical movement will always be from text to context. In this way the process of reflection differs sharply from that of the more radical views. However, while recognizing that there can be no absolute and final system of theology, the interpreter works in the confidence that the Spirit of God gives increasing clarity and assurance on the nature of the gospel and its relevance to every human situation.

Evangelicals recognize that valid contextualization takes place only where there is unreserved commitment to the path of discipleship. First and foremost, this calls for loyalty and commitment to Jesus Christ as Saviour and Lord of all of life, personal and social, and to his gospel. Evangelicals share with liberation theologians their commitment to the historic Jesus in his humility and suffering and his prophetic rebuke of hypocrisy and injustice. But they are equally committed to the Christ of faith – incarnate Son of God, crucified, risen from the dead and coming again at the end of time to consummate his kingdom. This commitment to Jesus Christ is within the Trinitarian framework of God the Father and God the Holy Spirit.

Furthermore, true contextualization demands commitment to the church* as the people of God. The church with its openness to God in worship and fellowship is also called to obedience in humble service, especially to the poor, and to proclaim to all people that salvation is in Jesus Christ alone. Contextualization takes place primarily within the sphere of the church and only secondly within the world. Reflection and interpretation are the work of the church. The priesthood of all believers and the work of the Holy Spirit in illuminating Scripture emphasizes that the church is the sphere in which contextualization takes place. It is not the prerogative of a professional theological élite alone but is open to all God's people. The church as the body of Christ with the Spirit-given diversity of gifts of ministry ensures that this dynamic process of contextualizing theology and practice takes place.

True contextualization warns against the dangers of syncretism* in theological beliefs, religious practices and ethical lifestyles, but it is not driven to inertia or to maintenance of the status quo by fear of this danger. A willingness to take risks and commitment to clear missiological goals enables the communicator to overcome this fear. The Holy Spirit as the divine Communicator is the pioneer and enabler in the fulfilment of this task.

In this dialogical relationship between the biblical text and the human context all forms of idolatrous beliefs and practices, whether religious or secular, are judged and stand condemned. The church is committed to their destruction. Though all of culture is tainted with sin it still reflects the truths and beauty of God's general revelation. Therefore that which is compatible with the law of God must be purified, transformed and put under the Lordship of Christ.

Contextualization culminates in the good news breaking into every situation, with the newness of redemption from sin, guilt and demonic power, liberation from human despair and social injustice and the actualization of faith, hope and love. Thus contextualization is a central task of the church in its mission in the world.

See also: CULTURE.

Bibliography

J. Miguez Bonino, *Doing Theology in a Revolutionary Situation* (Philadelphia, 1975); O. E. Costas, *The Church and its Mission* (Wheaton, IL, 1974); J. D. Douglas (ed.), *Let the Earth Hear His Voice* (Minneapolis, MN, 1975); B. C. E. Fleming, *Contextualization of Theology* (Pasadena, CA, 1980); D. J. Hesselgrave, *Theology and Mission* (Grand Rapids, MI, 1978); J. A. Kirk, *Theology and the Third World Church* (Exeter, 1983); C. H. Kraft, *Christianity in Culture* (Maryknoll, NY, 1979); L. J. Lutzbetak, *The Church and Cultures* (Pasadena, CA, 1976); I. H. Marshall (ed.), *New Testament Interpretation: Essays on Principles and Methods* (Exeter, 1977); B. J. Nicholls, *Contextualization: A Theology of Gospel and Culture*

(Exeter, 1979); Bong Rin Ro and R. Eshenaur, *The Bible and Theology in Asian Context* (Taichung, 1984); V. K. Samuel and C. Sugden (eds.), *Sharing Jesus in the Two-Thirds World* (Bangalore, 1983); J. Stott and R. T. Coote, *Gospel and Culture* (Pasadena, CA, 1979); J. Sobrino, *Christology at the Crossroads: A Latin American Approach* (Maryknoll, NY, 1978); TEF staff, *Ministry in Context* (London, 1972); A. C. Thiselton, *The Two Horizons* (Exeter, 1980).

B.J.N.

CONTINGENCY. All propositions are logically either contingent or necessary. They are logically contingent if their denial is consistent. States of affairs are causally either contingent or necessary. They are causally contingent if their existence depends on the existence of something else, causally necessary if not.

God's existence may be thought of as being causally necessary (he is uncaused) and even logically necessary (his non-existence is inconceivable), and these positions may be thought to have a scriptural basis (Ps. 90:2). Conversely, the universe may be thought of as causally and logically contingent, the expression of the free (*i.e.* unconstrained) goodness of God (Gn. 1). The contingency of the universe may seem to require an explanation, and this thought has been the basis of numerous 'cosmological' arguments for God's existence, most of them of dubious validity (see Natural Theology*). Anselm's* ontological argument, if cogent, would be a demonstration of God's logical necessity. Philosophers since Hume* and Kant* have claimed that all logically necessary truths are uninformative, and hence that 'God exists' is, at best, a contingent truth.

Thinkers of an existentialist* cast of mind have given prominence to the mystery of human contingency as an element in what is in their view the meaninglessness of human life. By contrast, the Bible gives the recognition of such contingency as one reason for awe, reverence, humility and thanksgiving (Pss. 90:12; 100).

Bibliography

D. R. Burrhill (ed.), *The Cosmological Arguments* (Garden City, NY, 1967); A. Plantinga, *The Nature of Necessity* (Oxford, 1974).

P.H.

CONTRACEPTION, see BIOETHICS.

CONVERSION. The term 'conversion' may be discussed in relation to a variety of disciplines, including biblical studies, history, theology, sociology and psychology. Its implications are wide-ranging, since conversion is a universal phenomenon which may be documented in non-religious as well as religious experience.* We shall be concerned with its significance in the Christian scheme.

In the NT the words used for this concept are *epistrephō* (which in the LXX regularly translates the Hebrew *šûb*, 'to turn back,' or 'return') and its cognates, especially *strephō*. The literal meaning of these two verbs is 'to turn,' in the sense of changing direction (*cf.* Jn. 21:20). From this usage derives the figurative and intransitive occurrence in the NT of 'turning' to denote (as in 1 Thes. 1:9) a decisive, God-ward reorientation.

In Christian theology conversion may be distinguished from spiritual rebirth, or regeneration.* Conversion is the act of turning from sin and self towards God through Jesus Christ, often as the result of some form of Christian proclamation. At a particular point in the process God, by grace,* regenerates the believer and gives that person eternal life (Rom. 6:23; 2 Cor. 5:17). According to NT teaching both actions are normally symbolized in baptism,* which expresses both the processes involved in conversion and the precise moment of regeneration. Regeneration and conversion therefore includes God's part *and* man's part. On the human side lies repentance* (or a change of mind) and saving faith* (Mk. 1:15), issuing in a new spiritual direction (Rom. 6:11). But the start of the conversion process is a response to God's work in Jesus Christ. Thus through a God-given faith articulated in baptism (Eph. 2:8; Col. 2:12), it becomes possible to receive forgiveness (Acts 2:38a), incorporation into Christ (Rom. 6:3–5), the gift of the Spirit (Acts 2:38b; *cf.* Jn. 3:5, 8), renewal (Tit. 3:5) and grace to live a new life (Rom. 6:4, 22).

Conversion is also related to the sanctification* of the Christian. It can be argued on the basis of NT linguistic evidence that conversion is *completed* by regeneration. Nevertheless baptismal incorporation, which acts as the focus of this two-way response between God and man, is linked in the NT to the demand for increasing holiness (1 Pet.

1:4–6). The converted Christian is called to *be* converted, and the reborn person who is baptized needs perpetually to live out the implications of that status. Moreover, while conversion is initially an individual experience, those who are converted belong to the community of the church, and are required to sustain their belief and exercise their service in a corporate context (*cf.* Acts 20:32). In this sense, conversion and renewal by the Spirit are life-long features of the Christian life.

The demand for personal conversion formed part of the apostolic preaching, and it has been a feature of some forms of evangelism ever since. But is conversion, in the sense of being 'twice born', essential to Christian commitment? There is, of course, no archetypal conversion 'experience' to which every believer must submit. But even if the process of turning to God may assume many forms, and be sudden or gradual in character, the NT evidence suggests that it is an indispensable foundation to Christian believing, and to all that should flow from that. We may conclude on this basis that 'preaching for conversion and rebirth,' so that those who are being saved may be added to the Christian community, is a crucial task in today's church.

Bibliography

J. Baillie, *Baptism and Conversion* (London, 1964); W. Barclay, *Turning to God* (London, 1963); G. Bertram, *TDNT* VII, pp. 714–729; W. James, *The Varieties of Religious Experience* (1902; ed. M. E. Marty, Harmondsworth, 1983); F. Laubach, J. Goetzmann and U. Becker, *NIDNTT* I, pp. 353–362; A. D. Nock, *Conversion* (Oxford, 1933); S. S. Smalley, 'Conversion in the New Testament', *Churchman* 78 (1964), pp. 193–210.

S.S.S.

COPTIC CHRISTIANITY. The Coptic Church is essentially the church centring on the ancient patriarchate of Alexandria,* the Egyptian Church (Arabic *qibt*, Ethiopic *qibs*, 'Egypt'). We may identify four groupings: the monophysite* Orthodox Copts; the Melchites ('Emperor's men'), adherents of the Chalcedonian position; the Eastern Catholic Copts, dating from 1741; and the Ethiopian Orthodox* Church, Coptic only in its historic links with Alexandria. The term Coptic Church is used properly only of the first of these four groups.

Although the Coptic Church is usually subsumed under the heading of the Eastern Orthodox churches it is, unlike them, monophysite. The distinction arose in the Christological* debates of the 5th century, which were brought to a focus at the Council of Chalcedon in AD 451. The conclusions of that Council are not accepted by the Coptic Church. The monophysite view is that there is only one (divine-human) nature in Christ. The Copts reject the extreme position of Eutyches (*c*. 378–454), but subscribe to the formula attributed to Cyril of Alexandria,* 'one nature of the incarnate Word'. Monophysitism is, in fact, peripheral to the theology of the Copts, and their initial acceptance of the monophysite view might be attributed primarily to national pride, injured by the deposing and banishment of their patriarch, Dioscorus (d. 454), at Chalcedon (451), as well as to traditional Egyptian religion which conditioned Egyptian thinking to divine-human unity, and to the influence of philosophy. The Coptic Church recognizes the formulations of the Councils* of Nicaea, Constantinople and Ephesus.

Three ranks of clergy are recognized: the diaconate, the priesthood and the episcopate, although in theory the laity are seen to act with the clergy in giving effect to liturgy and sacrament. The Coptic patriarch is a monk, reflecting the historic importance of monasticism,* which may be said to have originated in Egypt with Antony (*c*. 251–356) and Pachomius (*c*. 287–346). Monasticism, however, plays only a minor role in the contemporary Coptic Church.

Although no particular stress is laid on the number, seven sacraments* are recognized. Infant baptism is followed by anointing* with consecrated oil (chrism) and confirmation.* Communion is taken by the clergy in both kinds, but the laity more commonly take it in one kind only. Coptic doctrine concerning the divine presence in the two elements corresponds generally with what is conveyed in the Western term 'transubstantiation'. The three orders of priesthood are referred to above. Penance follows confession. Marriage is in theory indissoluble, although this view is modified by reference to a sacramental eternity for the relationship. Anointing of the sick is the seventh sacrament.

The Coptic liturgy is very rich, employing the Coptic language or Arabic. Lectionaries are widely used, as are *synaxaria*, lives of the saints, related to the church calendar. Fasting is widely practised. There is a strong evangelical element in the Coptic Church.

Bibliography

A. S. Atiya, *A History of Eastern Christianity* (London, 1968); K. Baus *et al.*, *The Imperial Church from Constantine to the Early Middle Ages* (London, 1980); W. H. C. Frend, *The Rise of the Monophysite Movement* (Cambridge, 1972; this includes a magnificent bibliography); P. Gregorius, W. H. Lazareth, and N. A. Nissiotis (eds.), *Does Chalcedon Divide or Unite?* (Geneva, 1981); O. F. A. Meinardus, *Christian Egypt, Faith and Life* (Cairo, 1970); K. Ware, *The Orthodox Way* (London, 1982).

F.P.C.

CORPORATE PERSONALITY. In Scripture and in human experience, self-awareness, moral and legal responsibility, blessing and trouble, reward and punishment are corporate as well as individual realities. Thus Israel and other nations can speak as 'I' as well as 'we' (Nu. 20 – 21); the fate of a family can be bound up together (Jos. 7); one generation can bear the consequences of earlier generations' sins (Mt. 23:35); a church can be addressed as a person invited to open its 'heart' to Christ (Rev. 3:20).

For a period in the mid-20th century, under the influence of the work of H. Wheeler Robinson (1872–1945), the OT version of this common phenomenon was given a rather mystical connotation by being described in terms of 'corporate personality' connected with a primitive way of experiencing reality that was different from our modern way. The theory was used to explain passages in the Psalms which alternate between 'I' and 'we', and the servant passages in Is. 40 – 55 with their changing identification of the servant. But it is now discredited, and such passages are better approached in other ways. There is no need for the hypothesis that OT or NT people's corporate or individual self-awareness was radically different from our own.

Bibliography

P. Joyce, 'The Individual and the Community' in J. Rogerson (ed.), *Beginning Old Testament Study* (London, 1983); J. R. Porter, 'The Legal Aspects of the Concept of "Corporate Personality" in the Old Testament', *VT* 15 (1965), pp. 361–380; H. W. Robinson, *Corporate Personality in Ancient Israel* (Philadelphia, [2]1980); J. Rogerson, 'The Hebrew Conception of Corporate Personality: a re-examination', *JTS* 21 (1970), pp. 1–16.

J.G.

COUNCILS. A church council is a gathering of all those members of the church who are responsible for guarding the deposit of the apostolic faith.

1. In Christian theology

Councils are summoned to settle disputes of interpretation, or to pass judgment on matters not found in Scripture,* and their decisions are regarded as binding if they are 'received' by the church* as being in accordance with Scripture and its traditional interpretation. A general or ecumenical or universal council is one for which universal 'reception' by the church is claimed.

This theory has a number of weaknesses, and is in fact understood in different ways. To begin with, there is disagreement as to who has the right to summon a council. According to Byzantine tradition, which is followed by the Church of England (Article VIII), only the secular authority has this power. The Roman Catholic Church, on the other hand, believes that it is the prerogative of the papacy.* Other churches do not define this right, but in practice it is conferred on representative synods or officials, who are elected by more or less democratic means.

It is not agreed who has the right to participate and vote in a council. The Eastern churches restrict both participation and voting to bishops. Rome allows wider participation, but also restricts voting to bishops, whereas Protestants* invariably believe that representatives of the whole church should take part and vote.

The authority* of councils is also a subject of debate. The Eastern church believes that councils are infallible because they are inspired by the Holy Spirit, who speaks not only in the unanimous voice of the bishops but also in the answering echo of the church, which must receive and find the proper application for the decisions taken. The practical difficulties with this are that dissenting bishops have had to be silenced or excommunicated in order to achieve unanimity, and that there have been notable instances of conciliar decisions which have subsequently been rejected by the church, largely on non-theological grounds.

The Roman position is that the pope is the ultimate arbiter and executor of conciliar decisions. No council is valid unless he has given it his approval. The difficulty with this is that the great councils of the early church were held without Roman approval or participation, at least in some cases, though Rome has always accepted them as authoritative. This position also creates a tension between papal monarchy and episcopal oligarchy, which is a standard feature of the life of the Roman Church and which remains unresolved.

Following the schism of 1378 which led to two rival popes, the theory of papal monarchy which had grown up in the Middle Ages was called into question by many churchmen. They wanted to see the church governed by councils which would meet in principle every five years. The membership of these councils would be chosen on a national basis, and their authority would be at least equal to that of the papacy, which would still retain its ancient primacy. The Conciliar movement, as this trend came to be called, reached its highest point at the Council of Constance (1414–18), where it was agreed to set up the appropriate conciliar machinery. A council of the new type actually met at Basel in 1431, but by that time the papacy had regained much of its former prestige, and slowly it strangled the Conciliar movement. First it disrupted proceedings at Basel, and then it transferred the council to Ferrara, where it could be more easily manipulated. By the time it ended, the papacy had regained complete control, and the Conciliar movement was effectively dead. However, memories of it survived, and were to be influential at the time of the Reformation, when various theologians were to propose its revival as an answer to the Protestant breakaway.

Protestants attach no infallible authority to councils, and recognize their decisions only in so far as they can be shown to be in accordance with Scripture. Indeed, for most Protestants, councils of the type described above no longer play any role in church life. There is no agreed machinery for calling an interde-nominational council, or for making its decisions binding on participants. The word has now come to be used mainly to describe interchurch organizations such as the World Council of Churches (see also Ecumenical Movement*), whose constitution explicitly eschews any interference in the internal life and doctrine of member churches.

See also: COLLEGIALITY AND CONCILIARITY.

Bibliography

B. Lambert, *Ecumenism: Theology and History* (London, 1967); P. Sherrard, *Church, Papacy and Schism* (London, 1978); G. Tavard, *Holy Writ or Holy Church: The Crisis of the Protestant Reformation* (New York, 1959); B. Tierney, *Foundations of the Conciliar Theory* (Cambridge, 1955).

G.L.B.

2. Survey of councils

What has been called the first council of the leaders of the church was held at Jerusalem in AD 48 or 49, in order to settle the dispute about the reception of Gentile converts into the covenant community (Acts 15). After that time, a number of local synods were held, at Antioch, Carthage and Alexandria, as well as Serdica (Sofia), Lyon and other places, to settle doctrinal disputes and heal schisms of different kinds. Some of their decisions have been preserved in church tradition and become authoritative in the wider Christian world. The most famous series of local synods were those held at Toledo between 400 and 694. Tradition records eighteen in all, and their canons are an invaluable source for the history and theology of the Spanish church during those centuries.

There is little doubt, however, that the most important church councils have been those which have received the title ecumenical, or universal. The Roman Catholic Church recognizes twenty-one of these, though other churches accept far fewer. Unlike the Roman Church, they have never given this title to an assembly consisting exclusively of members of their own church or communion.

The ecumenical councils may be conveniently grouped by historical period, with those which were held in ancient times having the greatest claim to universal recognition. The First Council of Nicaea (325) and the First Council of Constantinople (381) established the divinity of Christ and of the Holy

Spirit. They have been traditionally linked together by the so-called Nicene, or Niceno-Constantinopolitan, Creed (see Creeds*), which is supposed to have been composed in 381 on the basis of the Creed promulgated in 325. Modern scholars doubt this tradition, but there is no doubt that the Creed, the councils and their theology have been accepted by virtually all the major branches of the Christian church.

The third ecumenical council was held at Ephesus in 431. It was concerned with the Christological* issues raised by Nestorius,* who was eventually condemned, in circumstances which did the church little credit. The council was followed twenty years later by the fourth, held at Chalcedon in 451, which condemned the Christology of Eutyches (c. 378–454), a monk who had championed and misrepresented the Alexandrian tradition. The Council's famous Definition, perhaps the most significant Christological statement in the history of the Church, decreed that Jesus Christ was one divine person in two natures, one human and one divine. This eventually drove the Egyptian and Syrian Churches into schism, because they supported a doctrine of monophysitism,* according to which Christ had only one nature, which was divine.

The fifth council was the Second Council of Constantinople (553) which tried to heal the breach with the monophysites. It decreed that the human nature of Christ was not independent, but received its identity by being united with the divine person of the Son of God. This attempted compromise failed however, and the breach became permanent after the sixth council, the Third Council of Constantinople (680), which declared that Christ had two wills, a human and a divine, which the monophysites and some of their orthodox supporters had denied.

In 691–92 a synod was held in the palace of Trullum, in Constantinople, which endeavoured to complete the work of the fifth and sixth councils. For this reason it is known as the Quinisext (Fifth-Sixth) Council *in Trullo*. It established the canon law* of the Eastern Church, but it was rejected by Rome, whose traditions were somewhat different, especially in liturgical practice. As a result, this council is not included in the list of ecumenical councils.

The seventh ecumenical council was the Second Council of Nicaea (787), which was called to settle the iconoclastic controversy.*

List of ecumenical councils

Ancient councils

1.	Nicaea	325
2.	Constantinople I	381
3.	Ephesus	431
4.	Chalcedon	451
5.	Constantinople II	553
6.	Constantinople III	680
5–6.	*In Trullo***	692
7.	Nicaea II	787
8.	Constantinople IV*	870
	Constantinople IV**	880

Medieval councils

9.	Lateran I*	1123
10.	Lateran II*	1139
11.	Lateran III*	1179
12.	Lateran IV*	1215
13.	Lyons I*	1245
14.	Lyons II*	1274
15.	Vienne*	1311–12
16.	Constance	1414–18
17.	Florence*	1438–45
18.	Lateran V	1512–17

Modern councils

19.	Trent*	1545–63
20.	Vatican I*	1869–70
21.	Vatican II*	1962–65

* Not recognized by the Eastern Churches
** Not recognized by the Western Church(es)

It authorized the veneration of icons on the ground that it was possible to portray the divine person of Christ after the incarnation. This decision was rejected at the Council of Frankfurt (794) and it has never affected the practice of the Western Church, although it was later accepted by Rome. The Protestant Reformers all rejected it, but in the Eastern Church it has come to occupy an important place as the last of the officially recognized ecumenical councils.

The eighth council, recognized as such only by the West, is the subject of dispute even today. Roman canonists have traditionally claimed that it was the council held at Constantinople in 870. This council condemned and deposed the Patriarch of Constantinople, Photius (c. 820–c. 895) who had broken with Rome over the double procession of the Holy Spirit (the *Filioque* clause in the Nicene Creed) and the evangelization of Bulgaria. However, Photius was rehabiliated at another council of Constantinople, held in 880, and Rome apparently approved of this decision at the time. Modern scholars believe that the canonists of the 11th century preferred to make the earlier council ecumenical, because by that time the two churches were in schism and it suited the Roman canonists' case to argue that the Eastern Church had been condemned in the person of Photius. In the modern ecumenical climate, research by Roman Catholic scholars has altered our understanding of events, and it is at least possible that both Rome and the Eastern Churches may one day be able to declare the council of 880 to have been the eighth ecumenical council.

The next series of councils are the ten which were convened by the Western Church during the Middle Ages. None of these is recognized today by the East, and their status among Protestants is undetermined. The first four were held at the Lateran Palace, the pope's official residence in Rome, and are of importance largely because they mark successive stages in the rise of papal* power in the medieval church. At the first of these, in 1123, the church condemned lay investiture, which meant the practice of rulers in effect appointing the higher clergy in their realms. It also enjoined the monastic practice of celibacy on all clergy. The second council inveighed against false popes (1139), and the third against the Albigensian* heretics, who were fomenting rebellion in the south of France (1179). The Fourth Lateran Council (1215) asserted the unique primacy of the Roman see over all Christendom, and it is usually held to represent the high point of papal power in the Middle Ages. It also officially defined the dogma of transubstantiation.

Later medieval councils pursued similar themes, but the circumstances and locations in which they were summoned indicate a waning of papal power. The First Council of Lyons (1245) attacked the Holy Roman Emperor, Frederick II (1194–1250), but he paid little attention, and the pope was obliged to turn to France for support. The Second Council of Lyons (1274) attempted to heal the breach with the Eastern Church. The Byzantine Emperor Michael VIII (1259–82)

agreed to accept papal authority of a limited kind in return for aid against the Turks and the Normans (in Sicily), but help was not forthcoming, his own subjects repudiated him, and the union lapsed after his death. The Council of Vienne (1311–12) was called in order to dissolve the Crusading Order of the Knights Templar, on the ground that they were indulging in magical practices.

The Council of Constance (1414–18) was called to heal the papal schism which had broken out in 1378 and had resulted in the existence of three rival popes. The council resolved the schism, and also condemned Jan Hus* to be burned at the stake for heresy. It decided to weaken the papacy by decreeing that the church would thenceforth be governed by synods meeting at five-yearly intervals. The scheme was not put into effect until 1429, when a council met at Basel, without papal support or participation. The popes were determined to crush this Conciliar movement, and the opportunity to do so came in 1438, when the Byzantine Emperor John VIII (1425–48) offered church union to the West in exchange for support against the Turks. The pope called a council of his own which met at Ferrara, only to be moved to Florence after a few months, because of an outbreak of plague. Eventually it was moved to Rome, where it was finally wound up in 1445. The Council of Florence, as it is most generally known, promulgated union with the different Eastern churches, including the Nestorians and monophysites, but these unions were forced, were dependent on aid against the Turks (which materialized, but did not succeed) and were concerned chiefly to back papal claims against the Council of Basel, which gradually petered out as its members withdrew their support and turned back to Rome. In the East, church union was not even proclaimed openly until 1452, and it was immediately repudiated when Constantinople fell to the Turks the following year. Nevertheless, the Council's decrees remain the basis of the so-called Eastern Rite Catholic Churches ('Uniates'), who are Eastern in ritual but owe allegiance to Rome.

The last medieval council was the Fifth Lateran Council (1512–17), which tried to introduce some modest reforms into the church, but was overtaken by events in Germany which led to the Reformation.

Since the Reformation,* the Roman Catholic Church has held three councils, to which it has given the name ecumenical, even though no other church recognizes them. The first and most important of these was the Council of Trent, which met in three distinct stages between 1545 and 1563. After initial attempts to include at least some Protestants, the Council's attitude hardened and became extremely hostile to them. Trent spent its time defining and regulating Roman doctrines and practices which the Reformers had attacked, and it did so in a way which polarized the church and drove Rome into a Counter-Reformation which characterized it until the 20th century (see Reformation, Catholic Counter-*). It produced a very influential catechism,* and the Tridentine Mass, authorized as the official Roman canon from 1570 until 1970, which enshrined the doctrines of transubstantiation and eucharistic sacrifice in a way which came to be regarded as typically Catholic. The abandonment of this Mass after 1970 even caused some conservative Catholics to accuse the church of having sold out to Protestantism.

The First Vatican Council (1869–70) completed the work of Trent by defining the infallibility of the pope when making official (ex cathedra) statements in matters of faith and morals. The Second Vatican Council (1962–65) has been widely interpreted as a reaction against the Counter-Reformation spirit of Trent and Vatican I, although it did not repudiate any of their decisions. Vatican II adopted some of the Reformers' principles, such as the use of the vernacular in worship, and many radical Catholics have since appealed to it as justification for their avant-garde and occasionally heterodox ideas. It is undoubtedly true that the Roman Church is more open to outside influences than it was before Vatican II, though the long-term effects of this are still unclear. Rome is now committed to ecumenical dialogue in a way in which it was not previously, and it must be wondered whether the pope will ever again summon an ecumenical council without the active participation of other churches. On the other hand, it is far from certain whether the Eastern Orthodox or the Protestant churches would be prepared to attend a council under papal chairmanship, something which never happened in the undivided church of the early centuries.

Bibliography

The Seven Ecumenical Councils (texts), in *NPNF* series 2, vol. 14; W. H. Abbott (ed.), *The Documents of Vatican II* (New York, 1966); C. J. Hefele, *A History of the Christian Councils*, 5 vols. (Edinburgh, 1883–96); P. Hughes, *The Church in Crisis: A History of the Twenty Great Councils* (London, 1961); H. Jedin, *Ecumenical Councils of the Catholic Church* (Freiburg, 1960); H. J. Margull (ed.), *The Councils of the Church: History and Analysis* (Philadelphia, 1966); R. V. Sellers, *The Council of Chalcedon* (London, 1961).

G.L.B.

COUNTER-REFORMATION, see Reformation, Catholic Counter-; Roman Catholic Theology.

COVENANT. A concept of fundamental importance in Scripture and in the history of theology.

1. In the Bible

a. The Old Testament. The Hebrew idiom for establishing a covenant is 'to cut a covenant'. This is because a covenant is made by sacrifice (*e.g.* Gn. 15:7–21; Ps. 50:5).

The covenants are started with God's declaration, 'I will establish my covenant' (*e.g.* Gn. 6:18; Ex. 6:4–5). In this sense, the covenant is one-sided and reflects the unconditional character of election. God promises to be ever faithful to his covenant (*e.g.* Lv. 26:44–45; Dt. 4:31).

The essence of God's covenant is captured in the summary promise, 'I will be your God, and you shall be my people' (*e.g.* Gn. 17:7; Ex. 6:7; 2 Cor. 6:16–18; Rev. 21:2–3).

While the covenant is unilateral in establishment, it is mutual or two-sided in accomplishment. This accents the importance of personal sanctification* and perseverance.* God commands his people to keep the covenant through love and obedience (*e.g.* Dt. 7:9, 12; 1 Ki. 8:23). The law and the entire worship system of Israel were related to the covenant (Ex. 24:7–8; 31:16; 34:28). Both spiritual and material blessings and curses fall on Israel from God according to their obedience (Ex. 19:5; Lv. 26:1–13; Dt. 29:9) or disobedience to the covenant (Lv. 26:14–39; Dt. 29:18–28).

Although there are several covenants in the OT, they are considered as one covenant by the OT itself (Ex. 2:24; 6:4–5; Lv. 26:42; 2 Ki. 13:23; 1 Ch. 16:16–17; Ps. 105:9–10). God's covenants include the successive generations of the person with whom he joins himself in covenant. This is true in the cases of Adam (Gn. 1:27–28; 3:15; Ho. 6:7; Rom. 5:12–18; 1 Cor. 15:22), Noah (Gn. 6:18, 9:9), Abraham (Gn. 17:7), Moses (Ex. 20:4–6, 8–12; 31:16), Aaron (Lv. 24:8–9), Phinehas (Nu. 25:13), David (2 Ch. 13:5; 21:7; Je. 33:19–22) and the people of the new covenant (Is. 59:21).

Israel's history reveals that the gracious covenant of God is violated by their infidelity (e.g. Jdg. 2:20; Ps. 55:20). Even God 'breaks' his covenant because of a generation's rejection of the covenant (Is. 33:8; Je. 14:21; Ezk. 16:59; Zc. 11:10). Israel on occasion reclaims the covenant's privileges with the maturation of a new generation by renewing their covenant vows (Dt. 5:2–3; Jos. 24:25–27). In the case of apostasy, Israel re-enters covenant fellowship by repentance (2 Ki. 11:17; 23:3; 2 Ch. 15:12; 29:10; 34:31; Ezr. 10:3; Ne. 9:38).

The OT holds out the hope of a coming era when a new covenant will be granted by God to his wayward people (Is. 55:3; 59:21; 61:8; Je. 31:31–40; 32:40; 50:5; Ezk. 20:37; 34:25; 37:26; Ho. 2:18). This time is described as a reign of the Messiah in universal righteousness (Is. 42:6; 49:8; Mal. 3:1) joined with the regeneration of the Holy Spirit (Isa. 59:21; Ezk. 36:24–38; Joel 2:28–29.)

b. The New Testament. The distinction between the old and new covenants comes from the Scriptures themselves (Je. 31:31–32; 2 Cor. 3:3–6, 14; Heb. 8:8–9, 13; 9:15). Both are the same in substance in that they contain God's promise that he will be the God of his chosen people (2 Cor. 6:16–18; Heb. 8:10; Rev. 21:2–3) by redeeming them in Christ (e.g. Jn. 8:56; Rom. 9:3–5; 1 Cor. 10:1–4). Yet, the new covenant is superior to the old covenant (Heb. 7:20–22, 28; 8:6). Hence the covenants differ in the way they are administered by God (Gal. 3:23–25; 4:1–7). In this latter sense, it can properly be said that the new covenant displaces the old covenant (Heb. 8:13; 10:9).

The great events in the life of Jesus are related to the covenants of the OT: his birth (Lk. 1:72–75), his kingdom and resurrection (Acts 2:30), the Lord's Supper (Ex. 24:8; Mt. 26:28; 1 Cor. 11:25) and the cross (Heb. 9:15–22; 12:24; 13:20). He is the mediator of the new covenant (Heb. 9:15; 12:24) and the source of all the new covenant's blessings (1 Cor. 1:30; Eph. 2:11–22; Heb. 13:20–21).

The new era in no way diminishes God's demand for a covenant-keeping people (Mt. 5:17–20). Hence, the new covenant itself promises the ability to keep the covenant as one of its greatest benefits (2 Cor. 3:3–6; Heb. 8:10; 10:16; 13:20–21). The chief benefits of the new covenant are justification* and sanctification (Heb. 8:10–12; 10:15–18; 13:20–21). The curses associated with violating the new covenant are more severe than those of the old (Heb. 10:28–29).

Israel* received God's covenant blessings in the OT, while the Gentiles were strangers from the covenant (Eph. 2:12). Having rejected the Messiah, however, their covenant position has become an empty claim. They are people of only the letter of the OT law, while the Christian church has the Spirit that turns the law of God into the freedom of serving Christ (Gal. 4:21–31; 2 Cor. 3:6, 17–18). But there is hope for a future conversion of Israel, because of God's covenant promises made to Israel (Acts 3:25; Rom. 9:4; 11:27–29).

Covenant theologians (with the exception of some Calvinistic Baptists) have argued firstly that the children of Christians are no less in the covenant than the children of the old covenant (Is. 59:21; Lk. 18:15–17; Acts 2:39; 16:31; 1 Cor. 7:14; Eph. 6:4; 1 Tim. 3:4–5; 2 Tim. 3:15; Tit. 1:6). Secondly, they have contended that the application of baptism as the sign of the new covenant parallels the OT covenants, each of which included children: Noah (1 Pet. 3:20–21), Abraham (Col. 2:11–12), Moses (1 Cor. 10:1–4). Since children of believers are in the new covenant, and believers are in the Abrahamic covenant which gave the sign of the covenant to the children of believers (Gal. 3:29), many Christians believe that baptism, as one of the signs of the new covenant, ought to be administered to believers' children.

2. In the history of Christian theology

a. The ancient church. No systematic use of the covenant emerged during this period. Irenaeus* used the idea to defend his premillennialism, because of the land promises of the OT covenants. Chrysostom (c. 344/354–407) spoke of the sacraments of the church as covenants. Augustine* defined a covenant as an agreement between two parties.

b. The medieval church. The medieval period saw the development of three important ideas associated with the covenant.

i. With the arrival of papal absolutism in the 11th and following centuries, political thinkers within the church developed the idea of a baptismal covenant of the Christian with the pope. Failure to obey the pope resulted in breach of covenant which entitled the pope to resist the power of even a king, and to teach his subjects to do the same. Here one sees covenant-breaking as a ground for resisting political authority.

ii. Sacramental theologians began to speak of the saving properties of the mass's re-sacrifice of Christ as a covenant of God.

iii. The most important form of covenant thought is associated with Gabriel Biel.* He helped develop the idea of a covenant of merit,* whereby God justified a man for doing his best. This covenant was summarized as, 'to the ones who do their best, God does not deny grace.' This doctrine of justification by works in God's covenant of merit was held at first by Luther,* but with his rediscovery of justification by faith in 1517, he became an earnest opponent of medieval covenant theology.

c. The Reformation. With the advent of the Reformation, and the re-emphasis upon Scripture's authority, the covenant became extremely important for theology. However, Luther's law/gospel distinction was a direct result of his repudiation of the medieval form of covenant. Consequently, he made very little use of the covenant idea in his writings.

Zwingli* began to emphasize the covenant with Abraham in Gn. 17 as a model for the relationship of the Christian with God. This was prior to the debates with the Anabaptists (1525), who denied the validity of infant baptism. Hence it is clear that the Reformers did not confiscate the idea of the covenant from the Anabaptists as is frequently argued. Only as a result of these debates, however, did Zwingli make the covenant the main argument for the Reformed understanding of infant baptism. In 1534, Bullinger* wrote the first treatise in church history on the covenant entitled *Of The One and Eternal Testament or Covenant of God.* Bullinger argued that the whole of Scripture must be seen in light of the Abrahamic covenant in which God graciously offers himself to man, and in turn, demands that man 'walk before him and be blameless.'

Calvin* is in many ways the forerunner of Reformed federal theology. Calvin makes extensive use of the covenant idea in his *Institutes* (1559) and other writings in the following areas: the unity of the OT and NT, the mutuality and conditionality of the covenant, the benefits of salvation, the Christian life (law, prayer, repentance, assurance), predestination (predestination explains why the covenant works as it does), the reformation of the church (the Roman Church has broken the covenant, and therefore may be and must be resisted), the sacraments. One can also observe an elementary form of the covenant of works in his writings.

As a result of the work of two students of Calvin, the ideas of a pre-fall covenant of works and a pre-temporal covenant of redemption developed. In 1562, Zacharias Ursinus (1534–83) spoke of a pre-fall covenant of law between God and Adam in the garden that demanded perfect obedience with the promise of life and threatened disobedience with the penalty of death. In 1585, Caspar Olevianus (1536–87) presented the idea of a pre-temporal covenant between God the Father and God the Son for the salvation of man. These ideas coupled with the covenant of grace resulted in the federal theology of men such as Johannes Cocceius (1603–69). The covenants of works and grace received credal status in the Westminster Confession and Catechisms (1643–49)

d. Later developments in covenant theology. It is obvious at this point that Cocceius is not the *inventor* of covenant theology. He is important for the history of the covenant theology because of his desire to develop theology from the vantage point of the history of the covenant. Theologians of his day used the logical arrangement that is still found in many systematic theologies. Instead, he developed his theology as a history of how God graciously abrogated the covenant of works and its curse upon fallen humanity by bringing him eternal life. In as much as he was an acknowledged infralapsarian, he did not develop his covenant views to blunt predestination as has often been claimed.

Several theological controversies among Reformed theologians revolved around the covenant in later years. These include: i. political resistance to tyranny as in Samuel Rutherford's* *Lex Rex* (1644); ii. the claim of Arminius* and his followers to a conditional election paralleling a conditional covenant; iii. the denial of a pre-fall covenant of works by certain schools of Reformed theology; iv. the denial by the school of Saumur, led by Moses Amyraut,* that the Mosaic covenant was to be included in the covenant of grace; v. the covenant as a central point in the New England Puritans' discussions concerning legalism and antinomianism; as well as, vi. their famous 'half-way covenant' that allowed non-professing adults who had been baptised as infants to bring their infants to be baptized.

Covenant theology has continued to be an important aspect of modern Reformed theological discussion. Federal theology, especially in its 17th-century developments, has come in for sharp criticism in respect of, *e.g.*, the covenant of works and an allegedly contractual colouring, largely from theologians in the Barthian tradition (*cf.* J. B. Torrance in *SJT* 23, 1970, pp. 51–76, and 34, 1981, pp. 225–43). Discussion remains confused, partly because of linguistic imprecision.

Bibliography

J. W. Baker, *Heinrich Bullinger and the Covenant: the Other Reformed Tradition* (Athens, OH, 1980); L. D. Bierma, *The Covenant Theology of Caspar Olevian* (PhD dissertation; Duke University, 1980); J. W. Cottrell, *Covenant and Baptism in the Theology of Huldreich Zwingli* (PhD dissertation; Princeton Theological Seminary, 1971); E. M. Eenigenburg, 'The Place of the Covenant in Calvin's Thinking', *RR* 10 (1957), pp. 1–22; K. Hagen, 'From Testament to Covenant in the Early Sixteenth Century', *SCJ* 3 (1972), pp. 1–20; A. A. Hoekema, 'The Covenant of Grace in Calvin's Teaching', *CTJ* 2 (1967), pp. 133–161; P. A. Lillback, 'Calvin's Covenantal Response to the Anabaptist View of Baptism', *CC* 1 (1982), pp. 185–232; *idem*, *The Binding of God: Calvin's Role in the Development of Covenant Theology* (PhD dissertation; Westminster Theological Seminary, 1985); *idem*, 'Ursinus' Development of the Covenant of Creation: A Debt to Melanchthon or Calvin?', *WTJ* 43 (1981), pp. 247–288; C. S. McCoy, *The Covenant Theology of Johannes Cocceius* (PhD dissertation; Yale University,

1956); J. Murray, 'Covenant Theology' in *EC*, vol. III; E. A. Pope, *New England Calvinism and the Disruption of the Presbyterian Church* (PhD dissertation; Brown University, 1963); S. Preus, *From Shadow to Promise* (Cambridge, MA, 1969); L. B. Schenck, *The Presbyterian Doctrine of Children in the Covenant* (New Haven, CT, 1940); D. A. Stoute, *The Origins and Early Development of the Reformed Idea of Covenant* (PhD dissertation; Cambridge, 1979); G. Vos, 'The Doctrine of the Covenant in Reformed Theology' in R. B. Gaffin, Jr. (ed.), *Redemptive History and Biblical Interpretation* (Phillipsburg, NJ, 1980), pp. 234–267.

P.A.L.

COVENANTERS, Scottish Presbyterians* who from 1638 resisted attempts by Stuart monarchs to impose and maintain an episcopal system of church government.* Previously uneasy about the modified episcopacy established under James VI (d. 1625), the country became increasingly alarmed when Charles I not only made friendly overtures to Rome, but imposed upon the Scottish Church a Book of Canons (1636) and a liturgy (1637) without the endorsement of General Assembly or Parliament. These documents demanded explicit acknowledgment of the royal supremacy, transferred full power to the bishops, and threatened excommunication on those who rejected episcopacy.

When the king ignored their protests, Scots leaders prepared a legal bond of association known as the National Covenant (1638). After repeating a 1581 Confession condemning Roman Catholic errors, including 'tyrannous laws made . . . against our Christian liberty', the Covenant detailed those Acts of Parliament which had established the Reformed faith and church government, and subscribers bound themselves to defend the Presbyterian religion and 'the King's majesty . . . in the preservation of the foresaid true religion'.

Charles prevaricated, Archbishop Laud (1573–1645) was unmoved; so a General Assembly met in Glasgow to reject Erastian tendencies (see State*) and royalist pretensions by proclaiming Christ as the only head of the church. The Scottish bishops were deposed, offending ecclesiastical legislation condemned, and the notorious Court of High Commission abolished. The king, who was embroiled also in conflict with the English Parliament, lost the battle of Newburn against the Covenanting forces, and was forced to yield to Scottish demands. The Glasgow Assembly was given legal validity, and the Kirk with dubious wisdom asked the Privy Council to require all Scots to sign the Covenant. Thus the Covenanters took upon themselves the power they had denied to the crown, but more blame attaches to a king who had obtusely converted a protest against episcopacy into a rebellion against himself.

Basic to the Covenanting position was the firm opposition of the Reformed Church of Scotland to two principles: the authority of the civil power in spiritual matters, and the prelatic superiority of one minister over others. Among the early Covenanters who guided the Kirk in its return to Presbyterianism were Alexander Henderson (1583–1646), George Gillespie (1613–49) and Samuel Rutherford,* all of whom had a prominent part in the Westminster Assembly. Henderson, meanwhile, was the chief drafter of the Solemn League and Covenant, a religious alliance between the Scots and the English parliamentary party, though one essentially forced on the latter by political expediency.

Soon after the Restoration of 1660, Charles II had two leading Covenanters executed: the Marquis of Argyle and James Guthrie, minister of Stirling. Episcopacy was reimposed upon the land and church government vested in the Crown. Covenanter-ministers were ejected from their parishes, the process helped by a dissolute court, a Scottish Council of profligate nobles, and military leaders who carried out a policy of savage repression. Latterly known as 'the killing times', the persecution of Covenanters continued until James VII fled in 1688 and the Revolution Settlement vindicated the rebels and re-established Presbyterianism.

Cameronian or Reformed Presbyterian churches maintain a Covenanting succession, on both sides of the Atlantic.

Bibliography

J. D. Douglas, *Light in the North: The Story of the Scottish Covenanters* (Exeter, 1964); J. K. Hewison, *The Covenanters*, 2 vols. (Glasgow, ²1913); A. Smellie, *Men of the Covenant* (1908; repr. London, 1975); E. Whitley, *The Two Kingdoms* (Edinburgh, 1977).

J.D.Do.

CRANMER, THOMAS, see
REFORMERS, ENGLISH.

CREATION. 'In the beginning God created the heavens and the earth'. Creation is usually attributed in the Bible to the Father, but in the OT the Holy Spirit is mentioned as involved (*e.g.* Gn. 1:2), and in the NT Jesus Christ is spoken of also as both the agent and the goal of creation: 'All things were created by him and for him' (Col. 1:16). Creation is the sovereign act of the triune God who was 'before the foundation of the world'.

The fact of God's sovereign creation *ex nihilo* ('out of nothing') is the clearest biblical teaching. There is no eternal matter or eternal evil spirit. The sun is a mere creature, not a god. Gn. 1:1 includes the whole of reality, including time,* as God's creation. This key truth has far wider importance than is always realized. It is necessary first, however, to clear out of the way some debates which have tended to obscure the main uses of this doctrine in the Bible.

The time-scale of creation

Augustine was one of the early theologians who suggested that the time-scale of Gn. 1 might be very long. Before the rise of evolutionary theory, geologists were proposing a great age for the earth on scientific grounds. Christian responses will depend on the literary form of Gn. 1, on which devout Christians have held very different views. If that chapter is something like modern history, then creation took place in six-times-twenty-four hours, not so long ago. But the meaning of the word 'day' is not absolutely certain – especially before the existence of the sun and moon. Even if Gn. 2 and 3 are 'history', Gn. 1 seems to have a different literary form. If Gn. 1 is not 'history' but a more symbolic account, then the time-scale is an open question.

Creation and process

The words used for 'created' and 'made' in Gn. 1 cannot be pressed. *Bārā'*, which is used in vv.1, 21, 27, is also used for instance in Ps. 104:30 and other places for a 'natural' or historical process. Indeed there is no clear distinction in the Bible between creation by a process and creation without process. There is, therefore, in principle no conflict between the truth of God's sovereign creation and the idea that that may include the sort of processes we could describe in science. Both are equally God's sovereign action.

Evolution

Charles Darwin's *Origin of Species* (1859) brought to public attention the idea that species are not rigid and unchangeable entities but have come to their present state by a long process of 'descent with modification' from at most a few original types. For this process the word 'evolution' is now a dangerously ambiguous shorthand. Darwin's theories have been modified with time, but the present 'neo-Darwinian' view held by most scientists in the relevant fields is that new varieties, leading to new species, which in time have developed into new genera, new types of animals and plants and even new phyla, have arisen by descent with modification from probably one first ancestor. This can be called 'macro-evolution'.

The mechanism proposed is natural (or human, artificial) selection based on naturally arising heritable variations. The word 'chance' is often introduced here, but it is really no more than the scientist's way of describing the fact that we have practically no knowledge of how these variations arise and cannot predict them.

Even the most vigorous anti-evolutionists agree that very small-scale changes of this kind do arise, and do so by this sort of mechanism. This can be called 'micro-evolution'. God has brought into being organisms that are not rigid, but can adapt to changes in the environment and so survive. That is a marvellous and intricate aspect of God's world as we have it.

The disputes arise as to, first, whether macro-evolution has taken place, and secondly, whether these mechanisms could be the scientific explanation for such large-scale changes. Thirdly, it is argued by some that natural selection, which is evidently part of God's world now, could not have been part of an unfallen world because such mechanisms could in their view not be described as 'very good'. If Gn. 1 is more symbolic than modern history and there is a possible great age for the earth, then at least the first two of these

questions are open questions – unless there is other biblical evidence that can be brought to bear. The third question is speculative and we have little clear biblical evidence to go on. All scientific theories, both evolutionary and 'special creation', have their problems. These questions are in continual debate (see bibliography).

The so-called evolutionary philosophies which constitute a large section of 20th-century naturalism are a different matter. Their claims to be derived in some way from science are exceedingly weak. They are philosophical views that have no logical derivation from views of how God chose to create his world – let alone of why he did so. Biological evolution does not necessarily lead to 'evolutionism' though many non-Christians have tried to make it do so. This, in turn, has led many Christians to oppose all that goes under the name of evolution.

The biblical doctrine of creation

The Bible, however, apart perhaps from Gn. 1, places its emphasis not on the method or time-scale of creation, but on the very wide-ranging implications of this great truth. These are applied frequently to worship (*e.g.* many Psalms), obedience to God, faith in his ability to rule history, and our understanding of ethics, *etc.* The Bible emphasizes the spiritual uniqueness of man in the image of God* and his stewardship* over nature* (*e.g.* Ps. 8), but at the same time it stresses his creatureliness and the folly and wickedness of ignoring our creator and his instructions. The created order is God's and we are mere stewards of it, a truth which controls our views of the environment and the use of animals.

The doctrine of creation has stood against various forms of naturalism and pantheism* which are again becoming popular in the late 20th century. 'Nature' or even 'Mother Nature' (with capital letters) are becoming substitute concepts for God in the popular mind. Humanity's right and duty to subdue the earth is questioned by those who think of animals (see Rights, Animal*) as our brothers (viewing man as *only* an animal). Belief in the unique created value of every individual has far-reaching consequences for education and politics as against those who think of the human being in lesser terms as either a mere animal, an economic unit, or a lump of protoplasm.

Today it is frequently claimed that ethics* have no objective basis. By contrast, Christians believe that God's commands are the commands of our loving creator who always knows best, 'It is he that made us, not we ourselves.' Therefore to flout his commands is to suffer at best impoverishment and at worst partial judgment in this life for going against the way we are made to live. Christians believe that there are moral absolutes because the world is a created world and not infinitely plastic. They also believe that there is such a thing as truth because God has created and maintained this world in faithfulness. This was a major factor in the rise of modern science. The frequent calls in the Psalms and elsewhere to wonder and astonishment at God's creation are a stimulus to science and should be shared even more readily by scientists than most others.

The doctrine of creation is a necessary background to many other doctrines, yet on its own it can be intimidating. To our astonishment, however, God the creator has revealed himself in Christ as our loving heavenly Father and even as our saviour. Though creation is a foundational truth, it is not the crown of the Christian faith.

Bibliography

H. Blocher, *In the Beginning* (Leicester, 1984); E. Brunner, *Dogmatics*, vol. 2: *The Christian Doctrine of Creation and Redemption* (London, 1952); D. C. Burke (ed.), *Creation and Evolution* (Leicester, 1985); K. Heim, *The World: Its Creation and Consummation* (Edinburgh, 1962); R. Hooykaas, *Religion and the Rise of Modern Science* (Edinburgh, 1972); K. L. McKay, 'Creation', in *NBD*; F. A. Schaeffer, *Genesis in Space and Time* (London, 1972); A. N. Triton, *Whose World?* (London, 1970).

O.R.B.

CREEDS. A creed (from the Lat. *credo*, 'I believe') is an authoritative statement of the main articles of the Christian faith to which believers are expected to assent. Broadly speaking, biblical religion has always been credal. Biblical and post-biblical Judaism confessed Yahweh's absolute unity and uniqueness by the *Shema*': 'Hear, O Israel: the Lord our God, the Lord is one' (Dt. 6:4). The genesis of the church's symbols (as creeds have been called from early times) resides in proto-credal statements of faith and worship embedded in the NT (see Confessions of Faith*). With the confession, 'Jesus is Lord' (Rom. 10:9; 1 Cor. 12:3) early Christians acknowledged that the Nazarene was to be spoken of in the same terms as Yahweh of the OT. The text interpolated at Acts 8:37, 'I believe that Jesus Christ is the Son of God,' represents a primitive Christian baptismal affirmation. Other NT credal formulas affirm Christ's incarnation, saving death and glorious resurrection (Rom. 1:3–4; 1 Cor. 15:3–4; 1 Jn. 4:2). The great Christological passage Phil. 2:6–11 may have been sung at early Christian baptismal services. 1 Cor. 8:6 affirms the unity of God and the co-ordination of the Father with Jesus Christ. Finally in the NT a Trinitarian confessional pattern emerged (Mt. 28:19; 2 Cor. 13:14; see Trinity*), which became the paradigm for later credal formularies.

The apostolic fathers* reflect what J. N. D. Kelly calls 'quasi-credal scraps', and the apologists* a growing corpus of teaching that distils the essence of the Christian faith. What scholars refer to as the Old Roman creed (c. 140, Harnack) was an expanded Trinitarian baptismal formula: 'I believe in God the Father Almighty and in Christ Jesus his Son, our Lord, and in the Holy Spirit, the holy Church, and the resurrection of the flesh.' In the writings of Irenaeus,* Clement of Alexandria,* Tertullian* and Hippolytus* is found the 'rule of faith', or 'the tradition', which was an informal corpus of teaching provided to catechumens. The so-called Apostles' Creed, while not apostolic in authorship, is nevertheless apostolic in content. Its present form (8th century) represents a lengthy development from simpler Trinitarian baptismal formulas, particularly the Old Roman creed. The Apostles' Creed indirectly refuted various heresies (*e.g.* Ebionites, Marcion,* Gnostics,* docetists*) and was widely used in the West for instruction and worship. 'The Creed of creeds' (P. Schaff), it contains the fundamental articles of the Christian faith necessary to salvation.

The Creed of Nicaea (325), which was probably based on earlier creeds from Jerusalem and Antioch, was drafted to refute the Arian* claim that the Son was the highest creation of God and thus essentially different from the Father. The Nicene Creed as we know it today represents in effect an enlargement of the teaching of the Creed of 325, probably approved by the Council of Constantinople (381). It affirms the unity of God, insists that Christ was 'begotten from the Father before all time', and declares that Christ is 'of the same essence (*homoousios*) as the Father'. Thus the Son is God in every respect. The Creed also upheld the divinity of the Holy Spirit* and his procession from the Father. In the West the phrase 'who proceeds from the Father' was later altered to read, 'from the Father and the Son'. This so-called *Filioque* clause, that affirms the double procession of the Spirit, followed the teaching of Hilary,* Ambrose,* Jerome* and Augustine* and appears in the Athanasian Creed, but was rejected by the Eastern Church. It became the major doctrinal issue in the schism between East and West that came to a head in 1054.

The Athanasian Creed, or *Quicunque vult* (from the opening words of the Latin text), was written by an unknown author in the Augustinian* tradition in Southern Gaul about the mid-5th century. It contains a clear and concise statement of the Trinity and the incarnation* of Christ, both of which must be believed for salvation. Concerning the Trinity, the Creed affirms that 'the Father is God, the Son is God, and the Holy Spirit is God; and yet there are not three Gods but one God'. The articles on Christ uphold his eternal generation from the substance of the Father, his complete deity and complete humanity, his death for sins, resurrection, ascension, second coming and final judgment. The East never recognized the Athanasian Creed.

The Chalcedonian Definition was prepared by over 500 Greek bishops at the Council of Chalcedon in 451. In response to erroneous interpretations of the person of Christ advanced by Apollinarius,* Nestorius* and Eutyches (see Monophysitism*), the Definition states that Jesus Christ is perfectly God and perfectly man, that he is consubstantial with God as to his divinity, and with mankind as to his humanity. Moreover, humanity and deity are joined in the God-man 'without confusion, without change, without division, without separation'. Chalcedon represents the definitive statement, albeit in Greek ontological language, of how Jesus Christ was God and man at the same time.

Creeds have served a variety of functions in the church. Initially elemental creeds were used in a *baptismal** context. By responding to questions or reciting certain formulas which later became fixed, the baptismal candidate made confession of faith in Christ. Moreover, creeds were used for *catechetical** purposes, *i.e.* for instructing new Christians in the essentials of the faith. The creeds (especially the 'rule of faith') were also employed for *confessional* purposes, that is, to refute and expose the heretical teachings of the docetists, Gnostics, Monarchians,* Arians and others. And finally, the creeds served a *liturgical** purpose as they were recited at various places in the worship services of the churches.

As for the authority of the creeds, the Eastern Orthodox churches ascribe authority to the decrees of the seven ecumenical councils,* from the First Council of Nicaea (325) to the second at Nicaea (787). The Eastern churches have not accepted the Western doctrinal creeds and reject the *Filioque* addition to the Nicene Creed. Rome, on the other hand, claims infallibility for all the pronouncements of the magisterium. Traditionally the Apostles', Nicene and Athanasian creeds were known as 'the three symbols'. According to Rome the ancient credal formulas contain truths revealed by God and thus authoritative for all time. The Protestant Reformers accepted the Apostles' Creed and the decrees of the first four councils by virtue of their agreement with Scripture, the only rule of faith and practice. Luther* said of the Apostles' Creed: 'Christian truth could not possibly be put into a shorter and clearer statement' (*LW* 37, p. 360). Calvin* said of the formulas of the ecumenical councils: 'I venerate them from my heart, and would have all of them held in due honour' (*Institutes* IV.ix.1). The main branches of Protestantism value the four creeds discussed above as faithfully embodying the teachings of Scripture. Beginning with A. von Harnack* critical scholarship has attacked the classical creeds for their reliance upon an alleged alien Greek philosophical system and an outmoded cosmology. Thus Protestants such as Tillich,* Bultmann* and J. A. T. Robinson* claim that the ancient creeds possess little cash value in the modern world. Even Roman Catholics such as H. Küng* and the Dutch compilers of the *New Catechism* (1966) claim that the creeds are human statements formulated in cultural contexts foreign to our own and are thus beset with serious limitations and even errors.

Orthodox Protestantism views each of the above-mentioned creeds as a *norma normata*, *i.e.* as a rule that is ruled by the final authority of the word of God. In general terms, the creeds expound 'what has always been believed, everywhere, and by everyone' (Vincentian Canon; see Catholicity*). But ultimately even the best human formularies must be ruled by the infallible word of God. In sum, by virtue of their general agreement with Scripture, the orthodox creeds provide a valuable summary of universal Christian beliefs, refute teachings alien to the word of God, and are serviceable in Christian instruction and worship.

See also: CONFESSIONS; COUNCILS.

Bibliography

P. T. Fuhrmann, *Introduction to the Great Creeds of the Church* (Philadelphia, 1960); J. N. D. Kelly, *Early Christian Creeds* (London: ³1972); *idem*, *The Athanasian Creed* (London, 1964); J. H. Leith, *Creeds of the Churches* (Richmond, VA, ³1982); P. Schaff, *The Creeds of Christendom*, 3 vols. (New York, 1877ff., best ed. 1919).

B.D.

CREMER, HERMANN (1834–1903).
A Lutheran biblical scholar and theologian with a very wide influence on conservative Protestant* thought in Germany in the latter part of the 19th century. Born into a family deeply influenced by the pietist* movement, he moved away from that spirituality towards a more biblicist orientation, especially in his mature years as a professor at Greifswald from 1870. A determined and forceful personality, and a thinker of exceptional cogency, Cremer became a stout opponent of what he regarded as the destructive legacy of the Enlightenment,* rejecting the alliance with human culture* which he found among many contemporary Protestants. Besides his work on the language of the NT (which bore fruit in his *Biblico-Theological Lexicon of New Testament Greek*, ET, Edinburgh, 1878, widely used in both Germany and Britain at the end of the 19th century), he is remembered particularly for his work on the doctrine of justification,* where he urged a strong doctrine of human sin* and a forensic account of the work of Christ. Cremer was a leading figure in church politics, and deeply influential on pupils and colleagues (notably the biblical and doctrinal theologian Adolf Schlatter*), as much by his character as by his theology. Towards the end of his life he became a noted opponent of Harnack,* then at the height of his influence in German intellectual life.

Bibliography

H. Beintker in *TRE* 8, pp. 230–236 (with German bibliography); G. Friedrich in *TDNT* X, pp. 640–650 (on his *Lexicon*); W. Koepp in *RGG* 1, cols. 1881–2.

J.B.We.

CROSS, THEOLOGY OF THE. The
term *theologia crucis* was first used by Martin Luther* to describe his Reformation theology in its early period. It refers not simply to the *doctrine* of the cross, in which the cross is seen as the focal point of Christ's work of salvation (see Atonement*), but to an understanding of the whole of theology as theology of the cross, in that the cross is seen as the focal point of God's revelation of himself and therefore as the foundation and centre of all truly Christian theology. In the theology of the cross, the cross becomes a methodological key to the whole of theology. In Luther's epigram: *Crux probat omnia* ('the cross is the criterion of all things': *Weimarer Ausgabe* 5, p. 179). Hence Luther could claim that 'the cross alone is our theology' (p. 176), a claim which recalls Paul's words (1 Cor. 2:2) in a passage which was of fundamental significance for Luther's concept of a theology of the cross (1 Cor. 1 – 2).

In the *Heidelberg Theses* (1518) Luther contrasted his *theologia crucis* with the theology of glory (*theologia gloriae*), a term which sums up his objections to late medieval scholastic* theology. The two terms represent two approaches to the knowledge of God:* the theologian of glory perceives the glory of God – his power, wisdom and goodness, manifest in the works of creation; while the theologian of the cross perceives God hidden in the suffering and humiliation of the cross. Luther does not deny that there is a natural knowledge of God to be had from the created world (see Natural Theology*), but in the soteriological context in which he insists that *our* knowledge of God must belong, it is useless. Indeed, it can be worse than useless, because the sinner distorts it to create an idol who supports his own attempts at self-justification by moral and intellectual achievement. But in God's revelation of himself in the cross, God shatters human preconceptions of divinity and human illusions about how God may be known. In the cross God is not revealed in the power and glory which natural reason can recognize as divine, but in the very opposite of divinity, in human disgrace, poverty, suffering and death, in what seem to us weakness and foolishness. Paradoxically, therefore, Luther says that God is hidden in this revelation (see Hidden and Revealed God*), because he is not here immediately recognizable as God, but can be perceived only by faith. To recognize God in the crucified Christ is to realize that God is not truly knowable by those who pride themselves on their progress towards divine wisdom and goodness, but can only be known at the point where human wisdom is silenced and human ethical achievements are worthless.

Finally, it is important for Luther's concept of the theology of the cross that the humiliation and suffering of Christ, in which God hides his revelation, correspond to the humiliation and suffering of the sinner, for whom God conceals his real work (*opus proprium*) of salvation behind his strange work (*opus alienum*) of humiliation, which furthers it. Only the humbled sinner, struck down by the experience Luther calls *Anfechtung* ('spiritual conflict') can know the God who for his justification underwent the humiliation and condemnation of the cross. Hence Luther, in a famous sentence, insisted on the experiential basis of the theology of the cross, against any purely speculative theology: 'Living, or rather dying and being damned make a theologian, not understanding, reading or speculating' (*Weimarer Ausgabe* 5, p. 163).

The central and critical role of the cross in Christian theology has rarely been perceived as clearly as it was by Luther, but in modern times theologians as diverse as K. Barth*, K. Rahner*, J. Moltmann*, and E. Jüngel* have attempted to do justice to it, and in some respects have pressed it further than Luther. In particular, they and others have sought to revise our (and the theological tradition's) preconceptions of God in the light of the cross. Barth, for example, insists that it is in the humiliation of the cross that Christ's divinity is most fully revealed. In the humanity, lowliness and suffering of the cross,

the true God truly expresses his divine nature, which is his freedom to love humanity in this way, by contrast with all the false gods who cannot do so. A strong tradition of English theology in this century, as well as other theologians such as the Japanese Lutheran K. Kitamori (b. 1916), have argued that the cross is not taken seriously until a doctrine of God's suffering love replaces the traditional notion of divine impassibility.

Probably the two most notable recent attempts to develop a theology of the cross are Moltmann's (in *The Crucified God*) and Jüngel's (in *God as the Mystery of the World*). Moltmann, whose treatment owes much to Luther, aims to recover 'the profane horror and godlessness of the cross' from behind its religious interpretations. Jesus' godforsaken death is to be understood as the loving solidarity of the incarnate Son of God with godless and godforsaken men and women. Here, as in Luther, God is revealed in his opposite – in abandonment by God – because he is love which identifies with what is alien. But the implications of this revelation of God in the cross Moltmann wishes to pursue as far as 'a revolution in the concept of God,' rejecting all notions of God not derived from the cross. The death of Jesus, as death, not *of* God, but *in* God, as an event between God and God, in which God abandons God to death, makes it necessary to conceive of God in terms of a Trinitarian history. The cross is the event of God's love in which the Son suffers abandonment by the Father, the Father suffers the death of the Son, and the Holy Spirit is the powerful love which spans the gulf between Father and Son and so reaches godforsaken humanity. Thus Moltmann finds a consistent *theologia crucis* to require both a Trinitarian doctrine of God and a doctrine of divine passibility, and further claims that such a *theologia crucis* thereby opens a way through the impasse of both metaphysical theism* and atheism* in the face of the problem of suffering.* Rather similarly, Jüngel makes the cross the starting-point for a Trinitarian understanding of God which transcends the modern dispute between metaphysical theism and atheism.

Bibliography

E. Jüngel, *God as the Mystery of the World* (Edinburgh, 1983); A. E. McGrath, *Luther's Theology of the Cross* (Oxford, 1985); J.

Moltmann, *The Crucified God* (London, 1974); W. von Loewenich, *Luther's Theology of the Cross* (Belfast, 1976).

R.J.B.

CULLMANN, OSCAR, see SALVATION-HISTORY.

CULTS, see NEW RELIGIONS; SECTS.

CULTURE is a term that is not easily definable. However, if it is taken to mean the way of thinking and behaviour shared by a substantial social grouping which gives them identity in relation to others, then it is obvious that all persons participate in one culture or another.

Culture's effect on theology can be said to consist in the fact that 'no one can escape sharing in the mentality and intellectual climate of his own culture' (John Macquarrie, *Principles of Christian Theology*, London, 1966, p. 12). However, it is doubtful whether this fact has been sufficiently recognized at all times. In the 20th century, the question of culture has been raised with acuteness as Christianity has become more than ever before a world faith. Part of the impact of the emergence of sizeable Christian communities in areas of the world other than Western Europe and North America has been the recognition that the theological traditions of Western Christianity are culturally determined and therefore not universally normative.

One of the remarkable developments in this connection has taken place among evangelical Christians. The Lausanne Covenant* (1974), an important statement of evangelical commitments on a wide range of issues, declares that 'because man is God's creature, some of his culture is rich in beauty and goodness. Because he is fallen, all of it is tainted with sin and some of it is demonic' (para. 10). The Willowbank (Bermuda) Consultation (1978), convened to study the interrelationships of gospel and culture, reaffirmed this view. The Willowbank Report affirms quite clearly, 'No theological statement is culture-free. Therefore all theological formulations must be judged by the teaching of the Bible itself which stands above them all. Their value must be judged by their faithfulness to it as well as by the relevance with which they apply its message to their own culture' (para. 5 (b)).

This is not to deny that the Bible itself was given in particular culturally conditioned contexts.

Thus, while evangelicals maintain their traditional insistence on the reality of an abiding, divine revelation* given in Jesus Christ and in the Scriptures of the OT and NT, they also recognize that theology, as the human intellectual effort to express in human language the apprehension of this revelation, shares in the limitations of human culture itself.

This relativization* of *all* human cultures may be said to have opened the way for the generally positive acceptance among evangelicals of the principle of contextualization,* the process whereby an attempt is made to reformulate the Christian message within another language and culture in ways which answer to the twin concerns to be faithful to the divine revelation and relevant to the particular culture. The incarnation* is taken as a fitting model of such a theological enterprise, in that it demonstrates the possibility of the divine identification with the human and the culturally particular without loss of identity. On this analogy, the quest for indigenous, culturally relevant theologies, therefore, need not be at the expense of the integrity of the one gospel which should inform them all.

Such considerations show that the issues raised for any theology of culture remain as complex as ever. In *Christ and Culture*, Richard Niebuhr* distinguished five different, yet overlapping attitudes to human culture that have found expression in the history of Christian thought on this question. He described them respectively as 'Christ against culture', 'the Christ of culture', 'Christ above culture' (or rather, Christ and culture in synthesis), 'Christ and culture in paradox'* and 'Christ as the transformer of culture'. Apart from the first attitude which emphasizes a radical opposition between the revelation in Christ and the achievements of human culture, all the others indicate in varying degrees a positive estimation of culture.

As we have noted, theology itself is a culturally determined and therefore provisional enterprise. Thus a theology of culture implies a continual revision of the church's and the theologian's perception of the polarities of Christ and culture in the light of the supreme significance of the death and resurrection of Christ for the destiny of the world and all human achievement (Eph. 1:9–10). This also means that there can be no final solution to the question of culture before the *eschaton*, and that no theological formulation of the relation of 'the mind of Christ' in the church to forms of culture can be without a measure of tension.

Bibliography

C. H. Kraft, *Christianity in Culture* (New York, 1979); H. Richard Niebuhr, *Christ and Culture* (New York, 1951); J. R. W. Stott and R. Coote (eds.), *Down to Earth – Studies in Christianity and Culture* (Grand Rapids, MI, 1980); P. Tillich, *Theology of Culture* (New York, 1959); *The Willowbank Report – Gospel and Culture* (Lausanne Occasional Papers, 2; Wheaton, IL, 1978), also printed in *Explaining the Gospel in Today's World*, (London, 1978).

K.Be.

CYPRIAN (*c.* 200–58). Latin church father, and Bishop of Carthage from about 249 until his death, Cyprian was a pagan who was converted to Christianity in middle age and quickly rose to the office of bishop. He was well educated and a gifted speaker, able to unite and inspire a church which was undergoing severe persecution. Cyprian himself fled to safety in 250, but this left him ill-prepared to deal with the rigorist element in the church, which demanded that no concessions be made to backsliders. Cyprian disagreed, and began to preoccupy himself with the underlying issues of church order which had surfaced during the controversy.

His writings are less voluminous than those of Augustine* and less varied than those of Tertullian,* but they are an important source for our knowledge of the period and its problems. Cyprian's lasting importance for theology lies in his 'high' view of the church,* which he developed to counter the schismatic* tendencies which were latent in North Africa. He held an advanced theory of apostolic succession, and was insistent in demanding that his rights as a bishop be respected, ceding his authority to no-one, not even to the bishop of Rome (see Church Government;* Ministry*). He was also determined to insist that outside the church there is no salvation (*extra ecclesiam nulla salus*), and he presided over the Council of Carthage (256), which

expressly decreed that schismatic and heretical baptisms* were invalid (see Rebaptism*). This decision was repudiated by Rome, and is not held today, but it was typical of the rigorous outlook of the North African Church. Cyprian is an important witness to infant baptism, whose necessity he linked to original sin, and to the application of priestly and sacrifical terms to the ministry and sacraments of the church.

Cyprian might have been forced, ironically, into schism with Rome had it not been for a renewed outbreak of persecution, which claimed his life, and perhaps that of the Bishop of Rome as well. After his death, Cyprian became the patron saint of the North African church, and the authority to whom later rigorists and schismatics, notably the Donatists,* would appeal.

Bibliography

P. Hinchliff, *Cyprian of Carthage* (London, 1974); G. S. M. Walker, *The Churchmanship of St Cyprian* (London, 1968).

G.L.B.

CYRIL OF ALEXANDRIA (375–444). Born and raised in Alexandria, Cyril succeeded his uncle Theophilus (*fl.* 385–412) as bishop of the city in 412. His early career (412–28) was dedicated to the exposition of the Scriptures and the refutation of heretics and unbelievers. The second period of his episcopate, 428–33, more intense and fruitful than any other, was marked by his opposition to Nestorius.* Cyril's stand, strengthened by his alliance with the Church of Rome, led to the summoning of the Council of Ephesus (431) which ended with Nestorius' condemnation. The last period of Cyril's life, 433–44, was reasonably peaceful, though he had to explain his teaching to critics from both the Alexandrian* and the Antiochene* sides.

Cyril was a prolific writer who wrote in Attic Greek and had an extensive knowledge of the classics, the Scriptures and the fathers, especially Athanasius* and the Cappadocians. His many commentaries demonstrate his biblical orientation. He employed the typological and historical methods of interpretation which are most clearly set out in his writings, *On Worship in Spirit and in Truth* and the *Glaphyra on the Pentateuch*. Cyril's anti-heretical dogmatic works are numerous, the most substantial being: *Thesaurus on the Holy and Consubstantial Trinity, Dialogues on the Holy and Consubstantial Trinity*, and *Five Books of Negation against Nestorius' Blasphemies*. In the last-named he argues for a true and personal (*kath'hypostasin*) union of the divine Logos/Son with the flesh born from Mary, against Nestorius' Christology based on a conjunction between the divine Logos and the man born from Mary. Cyril also argues for two births of one and the same (divine) Son, one (divine) in eternity and one (human) in time, whereas Nestorius' argument implies two sons, one divine and one human, who are conjoined in Christ.

Cyril also wrote many homilies, and about seventy of his letters are extant. Some of these played a central role in the conflict with Nestorius (see T. H. Bindley, rev. by F. W. Green, *The Oecumenical Documents of the Faith*, London, 1950, and L. R. Wickham, *Cyril of Alexandria: Select Letters*, Oxford, 1983).

Cyril is one of the most distinguished theologians of the early church, recognized by his contemporaries and his successors in the East (Chalcedonian Orthodox and anti-Chalcedonian monophysites*) and in the West (Roman Catholics and Protestants). He is the first father to establish firmly the patristic* argument, which appeals to the earlier fathers of the church for the right understanding of the apostolic preaching and the gospel of Christ.

Following Athanasius and the Cappadocians, Cyril accepted the Nicene *homoousios*, the three *hypostaseis** of the Father, the Son and Holy Spirit and the unity of the divine *ousia* (see Substance*) seen in the three *hypostaseis* and expressed in their common will and activity. He is not as original in the content of his triadology as in the presentation of it, and he is not so much interested in the 'essential Trinity'* as in the 'economic', because of his soteriological interest which he inherited from Athanasius. As far as the essential Trinity is concerned, Cyril emphasizes both the coinherence of the three *hypostaseis* or persons and the primacy of the Father from whom the Son is born and the Spirit proceeds. But Cyril does speak of the procession of the Spirit from both the Father and the Son, not, however, with reference to the *hypostasis* of the Spirit, but with reference to the common essence of the Spirit with the Father and the Son.

Christology* is the key to Cyril's theology and the topic to which his contribution became decisive for the early church and subsequent generations. His terminology initially presented certain problems, because it was flexible and equivocal, but his thought was clear and helped to clarify and eventually settle problems relating to linguistic formulations. He followed Athanasius' principle that theological disputations were not about terms but about the meaning embedded in them. This is why Cyril could use the term *physis* (nature) as equivalent to both *hypostasis* or person and *ousia*, and so speak of 'one nature of God the Word incarnate' and 'one person of God the Word in (from) two natures'. Thus it is unfair to argue that he changed his mind in Christology from a monophysite to a dyophysite standpoint. Cyril has been unfairly accused of Apollinarianism* both by his Nestorian opponents and by modern patristic scholars who wish to stress the humanity (or, specifically, the psychology) of Christ almost independently of the Logos/Son of God. Equally unfair is the modernist charge that Cyril's Christology is only a Christology 'from above'. The doctrine of the two births of Christ does not imply the either/or of the schema 'from below' and 'from above', but brings the two together in the mystery of Immanuel, his kenosis,* his economy, his hypostatic union of two natures, his communication of idioms (properties) and, above all, in his virgin mother who is true *theotokos* (see Mary*).

Cyril understands salvation* in terms of both participation in and imitation of the human nature in relation to the divine nature, objectively in Christ and subjectively appropriated by human beings through the Holy Spirit who acts in and through the sacraments (for his eucharistic doctrine see Ezra Gebremedhin, *Life-Giving Blessing*, Uppsala, 1977). The objective aspect of salvation in Christ is particularly stressed in his doctrine of justification of grace developed in a masterly way in his evangelical interpretation of the law in *On Worship in Spirit and in Truth*.

Cyril's theological legacy has been influential in all Christian contexts in the East and in the West. A contemporary positive reassessment of this legacy would prove especially beneficial for the current ecumenical dialogue, since it affirms the basic dogmatic perceptions of classical Christianity.

Bibliography

Works listed in *CPG* III, nos. 5200–5438, and, with secondary literature, in J. Quasten, *Patrology*, vol. 3 (Utrecht, 1960), pp.116–142.

Selected recent studies: A. M. Bermejo, *The Indwelling of the Holy Spirit according to St Cyril of Alexandria* (Oña, Spain, 1963); essays on Cyril's Christology by J. N. Karmiris, J. S. Romanides, V. C. Samuel, in *Does Chalcedon Divide or Unite?* (Geneva, 1981); C. Dratsellas, *Questions of the Soteriological Teaching of the Greek Fathers with Special Reference to St Cyril of Alexandria* (dissertation, Edinburgh, 1967), in *Theologia* 38 (1967), pp. 579–608, 39 (1968), pp. 192–230, 394–424, 621–643; A. Grillmeier, *Christ in Christian Tradition*, vol. 1 (London, ²1975); F. J. Houdek, *Contemplation in the Life and Works of St Cyril of Alexandria* (unpublished dissertation, University of California, Los Angeles, 1979); A. Kerrigan, *Cyril of Alexandria, Interpreter of the Old Testament* (Rome, 1952); T. F. Torrance, *Theology in Reconciliation* (London, 1975).

G.D.D.

D

DABNEY, ROBERT LEWIS (1820–98). A leading Southern Presbyterian theologian, educator, author and social critic, who taught for many years at Union Theological Seminary, Richmond, VA. Dabney firmly adhered to the conservative Calvinist 'Old School' tradition of American Presbyterianism. His popular text book, *Lectures in Systematic and Polemic Theology* (²1878; repr. Edinburgh, 1985), owes much to the writings of Calvin,* the British Puritans,* and especially the Westminster Confession of Faith. His approach to the philosophical and theological currents of his day is influenced by Scottish common-sense* realism.

Dabney's exposition of such topics as the decrees of God (see Predestination*), sovereignty* and responsibility, the imputation of sin,* and eschatology* is marked by the same

non-speculative sobriety of statement found in the Westminster Standards. He gave much attention to anthropology,* particularly human psychology and the proper organization of social institutions. He endeavoured throughout to base his theology on the clear meaning of relevant texts of Scripture.

See also: Princeton Theology.

Bibliography

Discussions, 4 vols. (1890–97), repr. as *Discussions: Evangelical and Theological*, 2 vols. (London, 1967), *Discussions: Philosophical* and *Discussions: Secular* (Harrisonburg, VA, 1980 and 1979); *The Practical Philosophy* (1897; repr. Harrisonburg, VA, 1984).

T. C. Johnson, *The Life and Letters of Robert Lewis Dabney* (1903; repr. Edinburgh, 1977); D. F. Kelly, 'Robert Lewis Dabney', in D. F. Wells (ed.), *Reformed Theology in America* (Grand Rapids, MI, 1985); M. H. Smith, *Studies in Southern Presbyterian Theology* (Jackson, MO, 1962).

D.F.K.

DALE, R. W., see Congregationalism.

DARBY, JOHN NELSON (1800–82), a founding father of the Brethren movement, formative influence on modern forms of dispensationalism,* and influential exponent of premillenialism (see Millennium*). While serving as curate in the Church of Ireland at Calary, Co. Wicklow, he became disillusioned with the establishment, associated with those of separatist tendency in the late 1820s and developed distinctive views, particularly on the 'ruin of the church' as a structured body. He taught the duty of believers to gather for unstructured worship associated with 'breaking bread', to preach the gospel to unbelievers, and to lead lives of sacrificial devotion to Christ in expectation of his second coming (which would be preceded by the 'secret rapture' of believers).

In 1845 Darby broke with B. W. Newton (1807–99) of Plymouth and in 1848–9 with George Müller (1805–98) and Henry Craik (1805–66) of Bristol, leading to permanent division between those Brethren who followed him ('Exclusives') and those who did not ('Open'). Despite their turgid style, his voluminous writings on controversial, expository, doctrinal, apologetic and devotional themes have attracted both readers and popularizers (notably C. H. Mackintosh, 1820–96). His Bible translations in German, French and English reflect serious scholarship. Darby travelled extensively in Western Europe and, later, in North America, the West Indies and New Zealand. Though his ecclesiology has had little influence beyond the Exclusive Brethren, his eschatology* has attracted much support, particularly in North America.

Bibliography
W. Kelly (ed.), *Collected Writings of J. N. Darby*, 34 vols. (London, 1867–1900; repr. Winschoten, Holland, 1971); F. R. Coad, *A History of the Brethren Movement* (London, 1968); H. H. Rowdon, *The Origins of the Brethren 1825–1850* (London, 1967); W. G. Turner, *John Nelson Darby* (rev. ed., London, 1944).

H.H.R.

DARWINISM, see CREATION.

DEAD SEA SCROLLS. The name 'Dead Sea Scrolls' is the popular designation of a collection of manuscripts discovered between 1947 and 1956 in the neighbourhood of the Wadi Qumran, north-west of the Dead Sea, in Palestine, and dated palaeographically to the two or three centuries preceding AD 70. They apparently belonged to the library of a Jewish religious community. This community was most probably one branch of the widespread Essene order. The building complex called Khirbet Qumran, on a terrace overlooking the Dead Sea, was excavated in 1951–56; it evidently formed the headquarters of the community from *c.* 130 BC to *c.* 37 BC and again from *c.* 4 BC to AD 68.

Most of the manuscripts are very fragmentary. When completed, they amounted to some 500 documents. Of these 100 are biblical texts; all the books of the Hebrew Bible except Esther are represented. The others include biblical commentaries, apocrypha and pseudepigrapha, liturgical and calendrical texts, prescriptions for community life, apocalyptic treatises, *etc.* The biblical fragments present us with valuable evidence for the history of the text of Hebrew Scriptures, 1,000 years earlier than the production of the Masoretic text.

The community withdrew from Jewish public life, mainly because of the Hasmonaean family's acceptance of the high-priesthood (153 BC), which it believed was reserved by divine decree to the house of Zadok. The Hasmonaean usurpation of the sacred office, it was held, conveyed defilement to the temple and its services. The community therefore took no part in these, but consecrated itself as a living temple to God, the lay members constituting the holy place and the priests the holy of holies. During the current emergency (the 'epoch of Belial') they contented themselves with offering up the spiritual sacrifices of prayerful and obedient lives.

The members were 'volunteers for holiness'. They were admitted only after rigorous screening and probation, but once they were fully initiated they were subject to an ascetic* regime. Their interpretation and application of the law of Moses were stricter than those of the Pharisees, whom indeed they despised as preferring 'smooth' interpretations (*cf.* Is. 30:10).

They looked forward to the dawn of a new age when they, as the elect of God, would be his agents in the destruction of the ungodly and the restoration of acceptable worship in a purified temple, served by a worthy priesthood. The new age would be inaugurated by the rise of the Davidic Messiah, accompanied by an anointed priest (who would be head of state) and a prophet (the prophet like Moses of Dt. 18:15–19), who would declare unerringly the mind of God.

The advent of the new age, constantly expected by the community from its first beginnings, was steadily postponed. The Teacher of Righteousness, the first organizer of the community, led his followers to the Judaean desert to 'prepare the way for the Lord' (Is. 40:3), and taught them to read their eschatological role in the Scriptures, rightly interpreted. He neither claimed nor was claimed to be the Messiah; when he died (*c.* 100 BC), the messianic age lay in the future, as it still did when the community ceased about AD 68.

After the Jewish revolt of AD 66 the community perhaps made common cause with the Zealots; it was dispersed two years later when Roman soldiers destroyed the Qumran settlement.

Bibliography
G. Vermes, *The Dead Sea Scrolls in English* (Harmondsworth, ²1975); *idem, The Dead*

Sea Scrolls: Qumran in Perspective (London, ²1982).

F.F.B.

DEATH. In biblical usage the word has four main senses. *Physical death* generally denotes the irreversible cessation of bodily functions (2 Sa. 14:14; Rom. 6:23; Heb. 9:27) but occasionally the gradual weakening of physical powers (2 Cor. 4:12, 16). *Spiritual death* describes man's natural alienation from God, his lack of responsiveness to God, or his hostility to God, because of sin (Gn. 2:17; Mt. 8:22; Jn. 5:24–25; 8:21, 24; Rom. 6:23; Eph. 2:1; Jas. 5:20; Jude 12; Rev. 3:1). The 'second death' refers to the permanent separation from God that is the destiny of the unrighteous (Mt. 10:28; Rev. 2:11; 20:6, 14–15; 21:8). *Death to sin* involves the suspension of all relations with sin that results from being alive to God through dying and rising with Christ (Rom. 6:4, 6, 11).

By divine decree, physical and spiritual death is the consequence and penalty of sin (Ezk. 18:4, 20; Rom. 5:12; 6:23; 7:13; Eph. 2:1, 5) and is the common lot of mankind because all have sinned (Jos. 23:14; 1 Ki. 2:2; Ec. 9:5; Rom. 5:12; Heb. 9:27). Man and woman were not created unable to die but were created able not to die, although after the fall death became a universal biological necessity. God takes no pleasure in death (even of the wicked, Ezk. 18:23), yet premature death may be the result of the divine displeasure (Ps. 55:23; 1 Cor. 11:29–30).

So pervasive and devastating is the influence of death that the NT can depict death as a realm where the devil reigns (Heb. 2:14; Rev. 1:18; 20:13), as a warrior bent on destruction (Acts 2:24; 1 Cor. 15:26; Rev. 6:8; 20:14), or as a domineering ruler (Rom. 5:14, 17). But by his death and resurrection Christ robbed death of its power (Rom. 6:9; 14:9; Col. 1:18; 2 Tim. 1:10) and emancipated its captives (Rom. 8:2, 38–39; 1 Cor. 3:21–22; Heb. 2:14–15; Rev. 1:18), and through his second advent it will be finally destroyed (1 Cor. 15:23–26, 54–55; Rev. 20:14; 21:4).

Christians view physical death as a destructive force, because through it the bodily tent is permanently dismantled (2 Cor. 5:1) or stripped off (2 Pet. 1:14) and all links with the securities of earthly existence are severed (2 Sa. 12:23); there is a loss of physical corporeality and corporateness. Yet positively death may be seen as God's reclaiming of the breath of life (Ps. 104:29; Ec. 12:7), as resting from one's labours (Rev. 14:13), as the surrender of the spirit into divine hands (Lk. 23:46; Acts 7:59), or as the believer's departure from this life (Lk. 2:29; 2 Tim. 4:6; 2 Pet. 1:15) to the immediate presence of the Lord (2 Cor. 5:8; Phil. 1:23; contrast with this Ps. 6:5; 88:5), where the believer enjoys an enriched form of the intimate fellowship with Christ enjoyed on earth. Through resurrection the believer becomes immortal (Lk. 20:35–36; Jn. 11:25–26; 1 Cor. 15:52–54). That is, he or she becomes immune from any type of decay or death through a direct sharing in the life of God who alone is inherently immortal (1 Tim. 6:16). The Christian's attitude to physical death is therefore ambivalent; it should be neither welcomed nor feared.

The imminent advent of death or uncertainty about the time of death ought to prompt repentance* and preparation to meet God (2 Ki. 20:1; Lk. 12:16–20), for death terminates all opportunity to repent (Heb. 9:27).

The Roman Catholic and Eastern Orthodox churches teach that after death those who have died in fellowship with the church but who lack Christian perfection enter an intermediate period of suffering in purgatory that 'purges' them of venial sins and fits them for an eternal life of heavenly bliss with God (2 Macc. 12:39–45). Luther,* on the other hand, taught that at death all remaining traces of original depravity are eradicated from the believer's soul; death marks the final purgation of the soul.

See also: IMMORTALITY; INTERMEDIATE STATE; RESURRECTION, GENERAL.

Bibliography

L. R. Bailey, Sr. (ed.), *Biblical Perspectives on Death* (Philadelphia, 1979); L. O. Mills (ed.), *Perspectives on Death* (Nashville, TN, 1969); L. Morris, *The Wages of Sin. An Examination of the New Testament Teaching on Death* (London, 1954); J. Pelikan, *The Shape of Death. Life, Death, and Immortality in the Early Fathers* (London, 1962); K. Rahner, *On the Theology of Death* (London, 1972).

M.J.H.

DEATH-OF-GOD THEOLOGY. In the mid-1960s, counter-cultural radicalism was echoed in theology as a few thinkers adopted Nietzsche's* slogan, 'God is dead.' Thomas J. J. Altizer (b. 1927) argued that God had become fully human in Christ, so as to lose his divine attributes and therefore his divine existence (a sort of extreme kenoticism*). William Hamilton (b. 1924), with less claim to theological profundity, said that modern people were no longer able to believe in God, and the church ought therefore to seek to do without him as well. Paul van Buren (b. 1924) followed linguistic philosophers in arguing that the concept of God was 'cognitively meaningless', since God's existence and nature were not verifiable or falsifiable by the methods of science (cf. Logical Positivism*).

The death-of-God theology was a minor movement (though it brought great notoriety, briefly, to its authors), but an instructive one: because it underscored the bankruptcy of the liberalism* and the weakness of the neo-orthodoxy* dominating 20th-century theology. Altizer's extreme kenoticism had roots in Barth,* and Hamilton's talk about modern man recalls Bultmann.* Tillich* taught that one may find God by passionately embracing unbelief. (Bonhoeffer's* 'religionless Christianity' also influenced the movement, perhaps by the authors' misuse of Bonhoeffer.) If we agree (with liberalism and neo-orthodoxy) that God is too transcendent to be described in words, or too immanent for his acts and words to be distinguished from those of nature and man, then what do we have but a dead, or non-existent God?

Bibliography

T. J. J. Altizer, The Gospel of Christian Atheism (Philadelphia, 1966); idem and W. Hamilton, Radical Theology and the Death of God (New York, 1966); J. Ice and J. Carey, (eds.), The Death of God Debate (Philadelphia, 1967); J. Montgomery, The 'Is God Dead?' Controversy (Grand Rapids, MI, 1966); idem and T. J. J. Altizer, The Altizer-Montgomery Dialogue (Chicago, IL, 1967); C. Van Til, Is God Dead? (Philadelphia, 1966).

J.M.F.

DECREES, see PREDESTINATION.

DEIFICATION. In Gk. theōsis, in Church Slavonic obozhenie, deification is a teaching associated mainly with the Orthodox churches of the East. It may be compared with Western teaching about the sanctification* of the believer, though it has peculiar characteristics of its own which give it its distinctive flavour.

Deification is based on the statement in Gn. 1:26, that man and woman are created in the image* and likeness of God. The Gk. fathers understood this to mean that at the fall humanity lost the likeness but retained the image, so that the Christian life is best conceived as the restoration of the lost likeness to those who have been redeemed in Christ. This is a work of the Holy Spirit, who communicates to us the energies of God himself, so that we may become partakers of the divine nature (2 Pet. 1:4). The energies of God radiate from his essence and share its nature; but it must be understood that the deified person retains his personal identity and is not absorbed into the essence of God, which remains for ever hidden from his eyes.

In practice, the Orthodox spiritual masters have tended to focus on these attributes of God* which in Protestant theology are called 'communicable', so that there is a certain similarity between evangelical and Orthodox beliefs at this point. However, the Eastern churches have never defined the attributes of God in the way that the Western churches have done, so that it is impossible to equate the two doctrines exactly. This becomes particularly obvious when Protestant and Orthodox views of the image of God are compared; the standard Western view, that the image has been corrupted and even lost, finds no echo in Eastern theology, which is generally optimistic in its assessment of our fallen state, though without going so far as to deny the necessity of grace for salvation.

Deification corresponds most closely to the Western understanding of the imitation* of Christ. In Orthodox theology, the Holy Spirit who proceeds from the Father rests on the Son and becomes his energies. We who are called to the imitation of Christ are likewise called to manifest the energies of the Holy Spirit, who, by adopting us as sons of God, makes accessible to us the spiritual power which belongs to Christ. In this way we can fulfil what is seen as the biblical vision, that those redeemed by Christ will be like gods (cf. e.g. Ps. 82:6).

See also: VISION OF GOD.

Bibliography

V. Lossky, *The Vision of God* (New York, 1963); *idem, The Mystical Theology of the Eastern Church* (Cambridge, 1957); D. Staniloae, 'The Basis of Our Deification and Adoption', in L. Vischer (ed.), *Spirit of God, Spirit of Christ* (Geneva, 1981); T. Ware, *The Orthodox Church* (London, 1964).

G.L.B.

DEISM is the name given to a movement which started late in the 17th century and persisted long into the next, with its programme for replacing traditional by rational religion. It is popularly regarded as belief in a remote creator, uninvolved in the world whose mechanism he devised; but this does not readily serve as a defining or even essential characteristic of the movement. Deism is hard to define, and deists are sometimes hard to identify. Broadly, deism stands for the abolition of dogma founded on alleged revelation* and promulgated by an authoritarian priesthood such that the principle of rational scrutiny is quashed and its results disavowed. Constructively, deists often sought to promote a natural religion, universally bestowed on humanity by an impartial and benevolent God, its action in conformity with the unchanging moral law. Assault on the principle of revelation in history* (if it proclaims more than what reason can, or does, know independently) and on the claim that it occurred (if founded on belief in miracles,* prophecies* or inerrant Scripture*) was meant to vindicate reason over against superstition. Deists, Dryden remarked, are 'rationalists with a heart-hunger for religion'. Prominent representatives included: in England, John Toland (1670–1722), Anthony Collins (1676–1729) and Matthew Tindal (1655–1733); on the continent, Hermann Reimarus (1694–1768) and Voltaire;* and in America, Thomas Paine (1737–1809).

Deism has seldom been regarded as of high intellectual calibre; its representatives were commonly outmatched at the level of pure debate. Arguably, however, they drew forth from their opposition a defence that would ultimately prove unable to sustain orthodox claims, in the form of concessions (for example) to reason and natural religion. At the least, deism demonstrates what forces were at work in the 18th century to undermine classical Christianity. Its perception of God exhibits the revulsion felt at what was perceived to be the primitive deity of the OT and the arbitrary deity of historically particular revelation; its understanding of man indicates the confidence of the day in the sufficiency of rational morality for life and salvation. Its view of nature* illustrates how the stable harmonies in which Newton* had apparently enfolded the world could call forth a non-Christocentric worship of God; its assessment of the clergy shows how the structure of socio-ecclesiastical power revolted a free-thinking fraternity, sick of aggressive dogmatism masquerading as the prime Christian virtue. In the midst of this, the biblical scheme of fall and redemption was dismissed and its literary presentation regarded as crude, corrupt and variously flawed. Scripture was discredited as the sole, sufficient or necessary foundation of religion.

Deism has long been regarded as a spent force and a non-combatant in 20th-century theological battles. Yet it could earmark a set of ideas, such as those involved in the divine perfection or the morality of rational discrimination in religion, which had great potential for overthrowing the traditional scheme. Meeting the thrust if not the actual particulars of the deists' arguments may still promote fruitful reflection on the nature of Christianity.

Bibliography

G. R. Cragg, *Reason and Authority in the Eighteenth Century* (Cambridge 1964); J. Redwood, *Reason, Ridicule and Religion: the Age of Enlightenment in England, 1660–1750* (London, 1976); L. Stephen, *English Thought in the Eighteenth Century*, vol. 1 (London, 1962); R. E. Sullivan, *John Toland and the Deist Controversy: a Study in Adaptations* (Cambridge, MA, 1982).

S.N.W.

DEITY OF CHRIST, see CHRISTOLOGY.

DEMYTHOLOGIZING, see MYTH.

DENNEY, JAMES (1856–1917), Scottish theologian. He was born in Paisley, educated at Glasgow University and Free Church College, and became Minister of East Free Church, Broughty Ferry (1886–97), before being appointed first to the chair of systematic theology (1897), then NT language, literature and theology (1900), finally principal of the United Free Church College, Glasgow.

Denney's voluminous literary output and correspondence reveals a man of great spiritual stature, of whom H. R. Mackintosh* said, 'I have never known his equal for making the New Testament intelligible as the record and deposit of an overwhelming experience of redemption.'

Passionate scholarship wedded to a burning conviction about the power of the gospel were hallmarks of a theological position centred on the atonement.* W. Robertson Nicoll (1851–1923) maintains that his wife 'led him into a more pronounced evangelical creed', inducing him to read Spurgeon,* whom he came to admire greatly, and who was instrumental in constraining him to proclaim the atoning death of Christ as the heart of the gospel. The cross became for him the centre of all Christian theology and the heart of all true preaching. He was influenced in some measure, however, by the critical theological spirit of his age: his attitude to matters such as the inspiration and authority of Scripture* (cf. his Studies in Theology), and confessional* subscription, which he proposed should be abandoned in favour of a simple confession of faith in God through Jesus Christ (cf. Jesus and the Gospel), became matters of debate, as did his Trinitarian position and his eschatology.

Bibliography

J. R. Taylor, God Loves Like That – The Theology of James Denney (London, 1962), contains complete bibliography.

J.P.

DEPRAVITY, see SIN.

DEPTH PSYCHOLOGY is a broad generic term for any system of psychology which posits and uses the notion of 'the unconscious'. Such psychology is often termed dynamic psychology, and is contrasted with behavioural or experimental psychology (where the existence and utility of the term 'unconscious' is denied), and sometimes with humanistic or third-force psychology (which attempts to steer a middle course between depth psychology and experimental psychology). Of the schools of depth psychology by far the most important are psychoanalysis,

deriving from the work of Freud, and analytic psychology associated with Jung (see Psychology of Religion*). For an introduction to the range of these various psychologies see Roger Hurding, Roots and Shoots: a Guide to Counselling and Psychotherapy (London, 1986).

Most of the key elements in depth psychology can be found in Freud's work on dream interpretation, and in the other early studies that arose from his self-analysis. In his words: 'I believe that a large part of the mythological view of the world, which extends a long way into most modern religions, is nothing but psychology projected into the external world. The obscure recognition . . . of psychical factors and relations in the unconscious is mirrored . . . in the construction of a supernatural reality, which is destined to be changed back once more by science into the psychology of the unconscious. One could venture to explain in this way the myths of paradise and the fall of man, of God, of good and evil, of immortality, and so on, and to transform metaphysics into metapsychology' (The Psychopathology of Everyday Life, 1901, repr. Harmondsworth, 1975, pp. 321–322). Freud consequently saw religion as an enemy to be taken seriously.

In contrast, Jung, though in no sense orthodox theologically, saw religion as a noble attempt to explore transcendence: 'my attitude to all religion is . . . a positive one. In their symbolism I recognize those figures which I have met with in dreams and fantasies of my patients. In their moral teachings I see efforts that are the same as or similar to those made by my patients when, guided by their own insight or inspiration, they seek the right way to deal with the forces of psychic life. Ceremonial ritual, initiation rites, and ascetic practices, in all their forms and variations, interest me profoundly as so many techniques for bringing about a proper relation to [psychic] forces' ('Freud and Jung: Contrasts', Freud and Psychoanalysis, 1929, Collected Works, vol. 4, Princeton, NJ, 1985, p. 337).

The impact of depth psychology may be considered under three headings.

1. As a psychology of religion*

Different perceptions of depth psychology's critique of religious psychology were reflected in some of the early apologetically inclined theological responses (cf. the differences in tone between F. R. Barry's *Christianity and Psychology*, London, 1923, and David Yellowlees' *Psychology, Defence of the Faith*, London, 1930, from the Student Christian Movement, and J. C. M. Conn's more aggressive *The Menace of the New Psychology*, London, 1939, from the Inter-Varsity Fellowship). From the 1920s onwards an extensive literature has explored the relationship between Christianity and depth psychology (*e.g.* L. W. Grensted's 1930 Bampton Lectures, *Psychology and God: A Study of the Implications of Recent Psychology for Religious Belief and Practice*, London, 1931). This tradition continues. For comprehensive modern statements of this tradition see W. W. Meissner's *Psychoanalysis and Religious Experience* (New Haven, NJ, and London, 1984) and David Wulff's essay 'Psychological Approaches' (in *Contemporary Approaches to the Study of Religion*, vol. 2: *The Social Sciences*, ed. F. Whaling, Berlin, 1985, pp. 21–88).

2. As a psychotherapeutic system

Many of the attempts to explore the relationship between depth psychology and theology have had a primarily pastoral concern. Leslie Weatherhead's classic study *Psychology, Religion and Healing* (London, 1951) and Albert Outler's *Psychotherapy and the Christian Message* (New York, 1954) illustrate this sort of response to depth psychology. Even studies as theoretically inclined and expansive as R. S. Lee's *Freud and Christianity* (Harmondsworth, 1948), or Victor White's *God and the Unconscious* (London, 1952), or more recently, Christopher Bryant's *Depth Psychology and Religious Belief* (Mirfield, W. Yorks., 1972) and *Jung and the Christian Way* (London, 1983) have strong pastoral or therapeutic undercurrents. This tradition spans the theological spectrum, from the Catholic wing (*e.g.* Jack Dominian, *Cycles of Affirmation*, London, 1975); through the Episcopal perspective (*e.g.* Morton Kelsey, *Christo-Psychology*, New York, 1982, and *Christianity as Psychology: The Healing Power of the Christian Message*, Minneapolis, MN, 1986); to a broadly evangelical position in the writings of Gary Collins (*e.g. Christian Counselling*, Waco, TX, 1980) and Paul Tournier (*e.g. Guilt and Grace*, London, 1962). The degree of assimilation of depth psychology's assumptions within any of these

traditions varies from whole-hearted acceptance to cautious tolerance.

Philosopher Ernest Gellner, commenting on the tendencies inherent in such syntheses between Christianity and psychotherapy, makes the following trenchant observations: '[There is] a guild of professionals whose duties include pastoral care for people in distress – especially, perhaps, people in moral, emotional distress . . . But they are organized in the name of a system of beliefs surviving from pre-scientific and pre-industrial society, which virtually no-one (including members of the guild itself, and its teaching prelates) takes very seriously. . . . Hence pastoral attention by members of this guild has virtually no efficacy. Ironically, if they wish to have any charisma, they add something like psychotherapy to their equipment, and in any case eagerly imitate its style and stance. In fact, there is a well-organized system of "religious counselling" which blends the old faith with the new depth therapy. It squares the circle. . . .' *The Psychoanalytic Movement* (London, 1985).

Another tradition, which perhaps had its efflorescence in the 1960s, has attempted to marry depth psychology with Zen Buddhism.* Its roots may be found in the work of Jung and of Erich Fromm (*Psychoanalysis and Religion*, New Haven, NJ, and London, 1950). Works that reflect this essentially syncretistic* perspective are D. T. Suzuki *et al.*, *Zen Buddhism and Psychoanalysis* (New York, 1960) and Alan Watts, *Psychotherapy East and West* (London, 1960).

3. As a general theory of human activity

This is where Freud himself thought that his contribution was most profound. He used to liken his achievements to those of Copernicus in ousting the earth from the centre of creation, and Darwin in ousting man from the pinnacle of creation. Many studies have explored the theological implications of psychoanalysis particularly within liberal Protestantism, *e.g.* by Tillich* and Reinhold Niebuhr.* Tillich affirmed: 'Theology has received tremendous gifts from. . . . psychoanalysis, gifts not dreamed of fifty years or even thirty years ago. Analysts themselves do not need to know that they have given to theology these great things. But theologians should know it' (*Theology of Culture*, Oxford, 1959). This literature has been superbly chronicled by Peter Homans in *Theology after Freud: An Interpretive Inquiry* (Indianapolis, IN, and New York, 1970). He ultimately opts for a position within the Jungian tradition. Homans is particularly important too for his analysis of the theological implications of some of the more significant reinterpretations of psychoanalysis. Similarly, Wolfhart Pannenberg's* *Anthropology in Theological Perspective* (Philadelphia, 1985) engages in creative dialogue both classical psychoanalysis and some of the rich modern variant traditions. Of those traditions, perhaps the most important theologically is that emanating from the work of Paul Ricoeur whose *Freud and Philosophy: An Essay on Interpretation* (New Haven, NJ, and London, 1970) is a key text in the development of modern theories of hermeneutics.*

Interpretation of psychoanalysis within the Catholic tradition has continued most notably in Hans Küng's* *Freud and the Problem of God* (New Haven, NJ, and London, 1979), and in his monumental *Does God Exist? An Answer For Today* (London, 1980). He attempts an over-all evaluation of the psychoanalytical perspective. The philosopher Adolf Grünbaum has recently attempted a similar comprehensive assessment in *The Foundations of Psychoanalysis: A Philosophical Critique* (Berkeley, CA, and London, 1984) and in his Gifford Lectures. Works such as these which explore the philosophical and sociological impact of psychoanalysis on culture are essential for attaining an adequate *theological* perspective on depth psychology. In Gellner's words: 'The crucial strategic position occupied by Freudianism in the social and intellectual history of mankind, makes it possible for us to learn a vast amount from it about, on the one hand, the general anatomy of belief-systems and, on the other, the special conditions prevalent in our age' (*op. cit.*, p. 204).

Bibliography

P. Gay, *A Godless Jew: Freud, Atheism and the Making of Psychoanalysis* (London and Cincinnati, 1987); J. N. Isbister, *Freud: An Introduction to his Life and Work* (Oxford, 1985); P. Rieff, *The Triumph of the Therapeutic: The Uses of Faith after Freud* (London, 1966).

J.N.I.

DESCARTES, RENÉ (1596–1650), a Frenchman who worked largely in Holland, often termed the father of modern philosophy. In a bid to reconstruct the foundations of human knowledge, he inaugurated a method of intellectual enquiry whose procedure and results have commanded the attention of generations of successors.

In the Reformation era the problem of validating claims to knowledge was acutely raised: differing religious convictions, scientific enquiry and the recovery of classical scepticism were all contributory factors. Descartes set about methodically doubting* all and any received certainties in order to discover the criterion and content of indubitable truth. This led him, by arguments that can be both described and assessed in different ways, to formulate the principle: *cogito, ergo sum* – 'I think, therefore I am.' The very act of doubting one's own existence constitutes a demonstration of that existence, for only an existing self can think or doubt. Once Descartes attained this, he established successively the existence of God and of the external world (*cf.* Natural Theology*). The former is proved in more ways than one: the idea of a perfect being, implied in the knowledge of one's own imperfection, cannot come from a source other than such a being. Again: as the idea of a triangle contains the equality of its three angles to two right angles, so the idea of a perfect being contains the real existence of God. Further, if (as we can conclude) God is benevolent and not deceitful, we must infer that the world we perceive really exists, for God's goodness guarantees the correspondence here between what appears and what is the case. Scepticism has been vanquished.

Theologically, important consequences followed from another set of convictions, those pertaining to the relation of mind and body. Descartes was a dualist,* holding that a human being is composed of these two substantially distinct entities (mind, or soul, and body) characterized respectively by thought and extension. Moreover, it is the immaterial soul, not the corporeal body, that constitutes the person. This conviction, quite apart from Descartes' attempts to expound and defend it, has come in for heavy criticism especially in the philosophy of our century (see Anthropology*). But some Christian philosophers such as H. D. Lewis (b. 1910) hold that a form of 'Cartesian dualism' is indispensable to Christian belief, including belief in life after death. In theology and ethics, in different ways, this issue is a vital one.

Descartes was more than a philosopher; he was a mathematician of distinction, using algebraic notation to describe spatial relations in his 'analytic geometry', and was also a keen scientist. His continental successors, pre-eminently Spinoza* and Leibniz,* have been labelled, along with Descartes, 'rationalists', to draw attention to the role of the mind apart from the senses in possessing and acquiring knowledge.

Bibliography

J. Cottingham, R. Stoothoff and D. Murdoch, *The Philosophical Writings of Descartes* (Cambridge, 1985); E. M. Curley, *Descartes Against the Skeptics* (Oxford, 1978); A. Kenny, *Descartes: a Study of his Philosophy* (New York, 1968); B. Williams, *Descartes: the Project of Pure Enquiry* (Harmondsworth, 1978).

S.N.W.

DESCENT INTO HELL. The term derives from the clause in the Apostles' Creed* (also included in the Athanasian Creed): Christ 'descended into hell' (*descendit ad inferna*). 'Hell' here refers not to the hell of eternal punishment (Gehenna), but to the realm of the dead, the underworld (OT Sheol, NT Hades). Hence modern translations of the Creed read 'he descended to the dead'.

That Christ in his human soul departed at death to the place of the dead, until his resurrection, is stated in the NT (Acts 2:31; Rom. 10:7; Eph. 4:9) and amounts to saying that he really died. According to one interpretation of 1 Pet. 3:19; 4:6, he preached the gospel to those who had died before his coming, in order to make salvation available to them. But it should be noted that this interpretation, first attested in Clement of Alexandria,* was rejected by Augustine* and many medieval exegetes, and was not until modern times a major exegetical basis for the doctrine of the descent. Although it is an interpretation which is still vigorously defended by some (*e.g.* E. Schillebeeckx,* *Christ: The Christian Experience in the Modern World*, London, 1980, pp. 229–234), many modern exegetes take 3:19 to refer to Christ's ascension, during which he proclaimed his victory to the rebel-lious angels imprisoned in the lower heavens, while 4:6 refers to Christians who died after the gospel was preached to them (see W. J. Dalton, *Christ's Proclamation to the Spirits*, Rome, 1965).

That Christ's descent effected the transference of OT believers from Hades to heaven has been thought to be implied by Mt. 27:52; Heb. 12:23. This notion is certainly found in the earliest post-apostolic writings (Ignatius, *Ascension of Isaiah*) along with Christ's preaching of the gospel to the dead (Hermas, *Gospel of Peter*, Justin Martyr, Irenaeus*). This was the normal understanding of the descent in the patristic period. Although the Alexandrian* fathers included the pagan dead among those whom Christ delivered from Hades, the prevailing view, which became the orthodox medieval view, was that only believers of the pre-Christian period were recipients and beneficiaries of Christ's preaching in Hades.

Alongside the theme of the preaching to the dead, another motif which was associated with the descent from a very early period (*Odes of Solomon, Ascension of Isaiah*, Hippolytus*) was Christ's victory over the infernal powers in order to liberate the souls they kept imprisoned in Hades. The earliest credal reference to the descent (in the 'Dated Creed' of Sirmium, 359) clearly alludes to this theme, and it would have been in the minds of those who recited the words, 'he descended into hell', when this clause appeared in some Western creeds from the 5th century and eventually in our Apostles' Creed. Christ's triumph over the devil and death in his descent was vividly narrated in the *Gospel of Nicodemus*, which became very popular in the medieval West, and it was graphically portrayed in medieval art. Although this theme of 'the harrowing of hell' strictly referred only to the salvation of pre-Christian believers, it represented symbolically Christ's liberation of all believers from death and the powers of evil. It dramatized the *Christus victor* theme in atonement* theology for the ordinary medieval Christian.

Luther* continued to make pedagogic use of the idea of the harrowing of hell, and it became Lutheran doctrine in the *Formula of Concord*. But Calvin* (*Institutes* II.xvi.10) interpreted the clause in the Creed as a reference to Christ's vicarious endurance of the torments of hell on the cross, and this became a common Reformed view.

In the 19th century, the descent into hell and an appropriate interpretation of 1 Pet. 3:19 became part of the relatively novel idea of opportunities of salvation after death for all who had no opportunity in this life, and even of a hope for universal* salvation based on 'extended probation' after death (the classic treatment is E. H. Plumptre, *The Spirits in Prison*, London, 1885). Among contemporary theologians who take the descent to symbolize the possibility of salvation through Christ for those who have not heard the gospel in this life are Schillebeeckx (*loc.cit.*) and W. Pannenberg (*The Apostles' Creed*, London, 1972, pp. 90–95).

Bibliography
F. Loofs, *ERE* IV, pp. 654–663; J. A. Mac-Culloch, *The Harrowing of Hell* (Edinburgh, 1930).

R.J.B.

DETERMINISM. Most discussions of determinism are bedevilled by confusion between several different uses of the term.

1. In *science* it stands strictly for the hypothesis that the form of every physical event is determined uniquely by the conjunction of events preceding it. Science attempts to discover the pattern of interdependence and express it in 'laws'. Note that this hypothesis does *not* necessarily imply that all events are *predictable-by-us*, nor even that they are *predictable-for-us* (see below). It is also consistent with (but distinct from) the biblical theistic doctrine that every physical event depends on God for its coming into being (Col. 1:16–17; Heb. 1:3).

In physics, Heisenberg's 'Uncertainty Principle' (1927) asserts that *observable* data can never suffice for exact predictions of physical events; but (despite common assertions to the contrary) it does not logically deny strict determinism.

2. *Theological* determinism is the doctrine that the form of all events is determined according to 'the determinate counsel and foreknowledge of God' (Acts 2:23, AV (KJV)). This neither depends on nor implies scientific determinism: it could apply even in a world that was scientifically indeterminate.

3. In *philosophy* determinism often stands for the doctrine that the future of human beings is inevitable-for-them, so that freedom of choice is illusory. This doctrine is often thought to follow from scientific determinism, and Heisenberg's principle has been invoked as a defence against it; but 'compatibilists' (including the writer) consider both these moves to be mistaken. A future event E may be physically determinate without being inevitable-for-an-agent-A, if its form *depends* (among other things) upon *what A thinks or decides about it.*

Suppose, for example, that the physical states of A's brain reflect what A thinks and believes, so that no change can take place in what A believes without a corresponding change in his brain-state (as assumed in mechanistic brain science). It follows that no completely detailed specification of the immediate future of A's brain can claim to be equally accurate regardless of what A thinks of it, for (*ex hypothesi*) it must *change* according to what A thinks of it! In other words, no completely determinate specification of A's future exists, even unknown to A, which A would be correct to believe, and mistaken to disbelieve, if only he knew it. What does exist is a range of options, any one of which will be realized, if, and only if, A opts for it, and none of which is inevitable-for-A. This is a rational basis for holding A responsible for the outcome, whether or not it was predictable-for-others. There is here a principle of relativity: what others might be correct to believe about A's future is not what A would be correct to believe.

Notice that the question here is *not* what A would do if offered a prediction. The question is whether A's future is inevitable-for-A, in the sense of having one, and only one, determinate specification (unknown to A) with an unconditional *logical claim* to A's assent. The argument shows that no such specification can exist.

This disproof of 'philosophical determinism' requires us neither to assume nor to deny determinism in either its scientific or theological senses.

Bibliography
G. Dworkin (ed.), *Determinism, Freewill, and Moral Responsibility* (London, 1970); D. M. MacKay, *Human Science and Human Dignity* (London, 1979), pp. 50–55; G. Watson (ed.), *Freewill* (London, 1982).

D.M.MacK.

DEVELOPMENT OF DOCTRINE.
We possess, on the one hand, the Bible as a collection of books written over many centuries, and, on the other, a continually increasing number of doctrinal statements produced by individuals and groups over the centuries (see Confessions* and Creeds*). Development of doctrine may refer to the relation of the Bible's later teaching to its earlier teaching (e.g. that of the doctrine of the resurrection* of the body to the concept of a shadowy existence in Sheol). However, the expression is more often used with reference to 1. the relation of the doctrine/theology produced within the church of post-apostolic times to that contained within the books of the Bible (e.g. the dogma of the Trinity* as found in the Athanasian Creed to the doctrinal statements about Father, Son and Holy Spirit* in the books of the NT); and 2. the relation of a dogma* or precise doctrinal statement which appeared late in the history of the church, to earlier expressions of the same basic teaching (e.g. the doctrine of justification* as taught by Luther* to that taught by Augustine* of Hippo).

Given that there is a difference – which may be in emphasis, arrangement of words, contextualization,* language, aim or purpose – between the teaching that appears in the Bible and the church's doctrinal statements allegedly based on the original scriptural information, the question arises: How best can this difference be explained? What kind of models* help us to understand the (often subtle) changes? There is the further question: What are the primary factors in a given situation which lead to the formulation of a doctrine for the first time, or to the more precise formulation of a doctrine already confessed within the church; and what models give helpful insight into these processes?

Before the middle of the 19th century, the word 'development' was not used to refer to these processes within history and human thought. Roman Catholic apologists emphasized the immutability of doctrine, that one doctrine had been preserved unchanged from the apostolic teaching recorded in the Bible in the teaching of the (Roman, Western) Church throughout the centuries: verbal changes were not of the essence of the matter; the concept had always been the same. In response, Protestants* emphasized the corruption of doctrine – especially after the patristic* period through the medieval era – and saw their own doctrinal emphases and insights as recovery of the pristine, original teaching of the apostles and the early fathers.

However, it was J. H. Newman* in his important work, An Essay on the Development of Doctrine (1845), who insisted on the very fact of development as a new model replacing the models of immutability and corruption. He knew that there was a real difference between biblical data and statements from the church, as well as between earlier and later pronouncements from the church. He suggested models based on the way in which an idea enters the mind, grows and develops before it is expressed as a clear concept. However, Newman still needed the existence of the papacy* to guarantee that the development of doctrine within the mind of the church was the one approved by God. Thus, since Newman's work, it has become customary to talk about the problem of the development of doctrine. Though some Protestants still think that their doctrinal statements are direct modern-day equivalents of biblical data, most scholars are very much aware that an account has to be offered of the formulation of new doctrines and dogmas, as well as of the relationship between these as they exist within the continuing church. It is probably true to say that while Roman Catholics have been much more absorbed with the problem of development this century, Protestants have been more absorbed with the problem of hermeneutics* – how to interpret the Bible today. Of course these are related, and both exercises are necessary.

Bibliography
O. Chadwick, From Bossuet to Newman (Cambridge, ²1987); R. P. C. Hanson, The Continuity of Christian Doctrine (New York, 1981); N. Lash, Newman on Development (London, 1975); P. Toon, The Development of Doctrine in the Church (Grand Rapids, MI, 1978).

P.T.

DEVIL AND DEMONS.
In Christian theology the idea of a devil has its origins in the OT notion of an 'adversary' (Heb. śāṭān): as people opposing each other (2 Sa. 19:22), as God using people to oppose someone (1 Ki. 11:14), or as a supernatural agent sent by God (Nu. 22:22). The OT has

few references to creatures that have been taken to be demons. The satyrs/'hairy ones' (Lv. 17:7; 2 Ch. 11:15; Is. 13:21; 34:14); the *šēḏîm* (Dt. 32:17; Ps. 106:37); the horse-leech or vampire (Pr. 30:15); Azazel (Lv. 16:8, 10, 26; *cf.* Ethiopic Enoch 10:8) and Lilith (RSV = night hag, Is. 34:14), an Akkadian demon thought to be found in desolate places with the unclean owl and kite, may all have been understood to be demons. Protection from them was sought (Ps. 91) but Is. 6:2 and 6 show that these beings (*śerāphîm*) could also perform positive functions for God (see Angels*). There is also the belief in the OT that the evil spirits are under Yahweh's control (1 Sa. 16:14–23). Only in a few places did the LXX use the word 'demon' – often as a description of the heathen gods: *i.e.* Dt. 32:17; Pss. 91:6; 96:5; 106:37; Is. 13:21; 34:14; 65:3, 11. Probably under Persian influence *Satan* appears as man's accuser in the heavenly court (Jb. 1 – 2). There is speculation on the origin of demons (Jubilees 4:22; Ethiopic Enoch 6f.) and Satan becomes the chief of an army of demons over against God and his angels (1 QS 3:19ff.).

Outside soteriology, the NT writers are little interested in demonology. They believed demons were Satan's minions (Mk. 3:22); inhabited water (Mt. 8:32) as well as waterless places (Mt. 12:43); were potential objects of worship (1 Cor. 10:20–21; 1 Tim. 4:1; Rev. 9:20); could speak through those they possessed (Mk. 1:34); could also possess animals (Mk. 5:12); could cause suffering (Mt. 12:22–24; Mk. 1:21–28; 5:1–20; 7:24–30; 9:14–29) and grant superhuman strength (Mk. 5:3–5); could deceive Christians (1 Jn. 4:1, 3, 6); and needed to be withstood by Christians (Eph. 6:12). Paul sometimes uses the phrase 'principalities and powers' to describe evil spiritual beings which oppose God and, potentially, are able to separate the Christian from God (Rom. 8:38–39; 1 Cor. 15:24; Col. 2:8–15). Paul also associates idols with demons (1 Cor. 10:20–22). Jesus saw his ministry, particularly of exorcism,* as the first of a two-stage defeat of Satan (Mt. 12:22–30; *cf.* Lk. 10:18). In Paul and Johannine theology, the cross was the focus of the defeat (Col. 2:15; Jn. 12:31). Jesus believed that the final defeat would be at the end of the age (Mt. 13:24–30), a view shared by early Christians (Rev. 20).

In the patristic period, speculation abounded. Ethiopic Enoch was particularly influential. In thinking that demons, who also became the gods of the pagan world, were the sons of the fallen angels and human women in Gn. 6, the *Clementine Homilies* were widely representative of the thought of the period. Origen* did not accept either the influence of Ethiopic Enoch or that the heavenly powers fell because of envy (*cf.* Wisdom 2:24). He equated Lucifer (Is. 14:12–15) with Satan who, with the powers, revolted and fell from heaven because of pride. Augustine* followed Origen, but not in thinking that the devil could be reconciled to God. Over against Anselm,* Abelard* believed that the atonement* had nothing to do with the devil.

Thomas Aquinas* held that the devil, who is the cause of all sin, was once probably the very highest angel who, through pride, fell immediately after creation, seducing those who followed him to become his subjects.

Calvin* refuted those 'who babble of devils as nothing else than evil emotions' by pointing to texts where the reality of Satan and the devils is assured. The devil was an angel whose malice came as a result of his revolt and fall. The little Scripture tells us is to arouse us 'to take precaution against their stratagems' (*Institutes* I.xiv.13–19). 19th-century theologians expressed little interest in demonology. For example, Schleiermacher* questioned the conception of a fall among good angels and said that Jesus did not associate the devil with the plan of salvation; rather, Jesus and his disciples drew their demonology from the common life of the period rather than from Scripture, so that the conception of Satan is not a permanent element in Christian doctrine. In contemporary theological enquiry Bultmann* still sums up the prevailing view: 'It is impossible to use electric light and the wireless and to avail ourselves of modern medical and surgical discoveries, and at the same time to believe in the New Testament world of daemons and spirits' ('The New Testament and Mythology', in H. W. Bartsch, ed., *Kerygma and Myth*, vol. 1, London, 1953, p. 5). E. L. Mascall, in, *e.g.* *The Christian Universe* (London, 1966), represents a significant minority of theologians who believe that there are, in our human situation and experience, signals and dimensions of evil and sickness that are best accounted for by accepting the existence of some form of evil agency legitimately characterized 'devil' and 'demons'.

Bibliography

O. Böcher, *Dämonenfurcht und Dämonenabwehr* (Stuttgärt, 1970); S. Eitrem, *Some Notes on the Demonology in the NT* (Oslo, ²1966); W. Foerster in *TDNT* II, pp. 1–20; H. Kaupel, *Die Dämonen in Alten Testament* (Minneapolis, MN, 1930); E. Langton, *Essentials of Demonology* (London, 1949); J. B. Russell, *The Devil: Perceptions of Evil from Antiquity to Primitive Christianity* (Ithaca, NY, 1977); *idem, Satan: the Early Christian Tradition* (Ithaca, NY, 1981); H. Schlier, *Principalities and Powers in the New Testament* (Freiburg, 1961).

G.H.T.

DIALECTICAL THEOLOGY developed as a reaction to liberal Protestantism, and to the rationalism which has led scholars to suppose that discourse about God could be achieved in logical propositional sentences. It was heralded by Karl Barth's* commentary on Romans (*Der Römerbrief*, 1919). Developed in collaboration between Barth, E. Brunner,* R. Bultmann* and Friedrich Gogarten (1887–1967) it is closely associated with neo-orthodoxy,* for its leading proponents can be classified under either head.

Dialectical theology owes more to S. Kierkegaard* than it does to G. W. F. Hegel,* and it should not be confused with Hegel's rational, philosophical dialectic, where thesis and antithesis lead into synthesis. Kierkegaard's dialectic was existential,* for it began with the individual facing the opportunities of existence. Dialectical theology learned from Kierkegaard to affirm the infinite qualitative distinction between God and humanity; between eternity and time, infinite and finite. It is these opposites which dialectical theologians claim have come together in an absolutely paradoxical* way in Jesus Christ. There is no higher synthesis of the two sides, for the two poles remain in creative tension.

This dialectic is echoed in human encounter with Christ today: bound by time, we can nevertheless encounter the historical Jesus in each present moment by faith. Moreover the encounter with Jesus is now, as then, one of both judgment and mercy. The same event or parable precipitates both faith and rejection.

In Jesus may be seen both God's *No* to human self-reliance or sin, and his *Yes* to man's faith and acceptance of divine grace. Consequently this is sometimes called the 'theology of crisis'. Knowledge of God depends on personal encounter; divine subject relating to human subject. This brings recognition that God is so much beyond anything known ordinarily that we are forced to talk about him in ways that seem contradictory. It seems as if there is dialectic in God himself, in his way of relating to the world, and therefore necessarily in our way of talking about him.

These new ideas spread rapidly in Germany and Switzerland, being published in the journal *Zwischen den Zeiten* (*Between the Times*) which was initiated by Barth, Gogarten and Eduard Thurneysen (1888–1974). Begun in 1922 when it seemed that these theologians were of one mind, early contributors included Bultmann and Brunner. But it ceased in autumn 1933 when it was clear that Barth and Gogarten had developed their theologies in such different ways that it could no longer be sustained.

Friedrich Gogarten was a German Lutheran, a pastor who later taught at Jena and Göttingen. Inspired by Luther,* he held so strongly to the principle of justification* by faith that he concluded that Christians were free to live in the world without trying to justify themselves by good works: an emphasis on secularization* which later became influential. Secondly, Gogarten, influenced by existentialism* and defending Bultmann's programme of demythologizing (see Myth*), rejected attempts to deal with history as if it were objective facts. He considered that faith should focus on the saving purposes of Jesus' activities *for us*, since historical certainty might be had when one encountered Christ through the kerygma* or preaching.

These two views led to the third affirmation that man is 'able to envisage history only from the point of view of his own responsibility for it' (F. Gogarten, *Demythologizing and History*, London, 1955, p. 19). Gogarten considered it was necessary to develop secular ethics based on the 'orders of creation'. It was this last anthropocentric or subjective tendency, along with his willingness to co-operate with the pro-Nazi German Christian church, which finally led Barth to break with him.

Dialectical thinking continued to be a major

feature of the theologies of each of its major proponents, but whereas Barth and Brunner emphasized the objective pole of God's given revelation, Bultmann and Gogarten stressed its subjective apprehension. Other differences showed that early consensus about what to reject did not lead to later agreement about what to affirm.

Bibliography
A. I. C. Heron, *A Century of Protestant Theology* (Guildford, 1980); J. Macquarrie, *Twentieth-Century Religious Thought* (London, 1963); S. P. Schilling, *Contemporary Continental Theologians* (London, 1966); J. D. Smart, *The Divided Mind of Modern Theology* (Philadelphia, 1967).
C.A.B.

DIDYMUS, see Alexandrian School.

DILTHEY, WILHELM (1833–1911). Professor of philosophy at Basel from 1866, Kiel from 1868, Breslau from 1871 and Berlin from 1882 until his death. At the beginning of his university career he studied theology with the intention of entering the ministry, but, realizing that he could not accept the traditional doctrines of the Christian faith, soon abandoned this course. Henceforth his labours were devoted to philosophical, psychological and sociological studies, in which he developed a relativistic* approach and methodology to the *Geisteswissenschaften* (cultural or human sciences) in contrast to the *Naturwissenschaften* (natural sciences). In Dilthey's methodology there is no place for the supernatural;* knowledge of life comes from understanding the mental processes and world-views (*Weltanschauungen*) of human beings, and seeing these as part of the ongoing flow of universal history.

In theological circles, Dilthey is best known for his biography of Schleiermacher* (1870), but his greatest importance lies in his development of a philosophy of history* in which – over against the biblical understanding of history – God has no place. This scheme of history in turn provided a basis for the phenomenology* of Edmund Husserl (1859–1938), the historicism of R. G. Collingwood (1889–1943), and the existentialism* of Martin Heidegger (1889–1976), which was to influence Bultmann.* Although Dilthey lies outside the main stream of theological scholarship, his approach to the philosophy of history was to influence the whole course of 20th-century historical methodology, not only in the philosophical field, but also in the theological.

Bibliography
I. N. Bulhof, *Wilhelm Dilthey* (The Hague, 1980); H. A. Hodges, *The Philosophy of Wilhelm Dilthey* (London, 1952); H. P. Rickmann, *Wilhelm Dilthey* (London, 1979).
H.H.

DIODORE OF TARSUS, see Antiochene School.

DIONYSIUS OF ALEXANDRIA, see Alexandrian School.

DIONYSIUS THE AREOPAGITE, see Pseudo-Dionysius the Areopagite.

DISCIPLINE. For 16th-century Reformed churchmen, discipline was one of the essential activities of the church. For Calvin* it was a *mark* of the true church:* 'Those who think that the church can stand for long without this bond of discipline are mistaken; unless by chance we can afford to omit that support which the Lord foresaw would be necessary for us' (*Institutes* IV.xii.4). It was essential because based on the word of God. Discipline is as necessary as the ligaments in the human body, or as discipline in a family. These who join themselves to a church thereby submit themselves to its discipline.

Discipline is already implicit in preaching.* People are called not only to forgiveness, but to holiness of life; and towards this end the word is to be applied to individual members. Without personal counselling and admonition, preaching is 'throwing words into the air' (Calvin). Church order demands the care of souls, a *positive* discipline to prevent offences, only secondarily to abolish any that have arisen. Private teaching is the first foundation of discipline.

Such admonition is not given solely by ministers of the word, but is the right and duty of every member of the church (Mt. 18:15–20). Naturally, 'pastors and presbyters, beyond all others, should be vigilant in the discharge of this duty . . . the doctrine then obtains its full authority, and produces its due effect' (*Institutes* IV.xii.10). The church has the responsibility of guiding its members and helping them to progress in sanctification.* So preaching, pastoral work and discipline, when properly understood, are seen to be closely linked and mutually interacting. It is an unfortunate mistake to think of discipline as purely negative and repressive. It should be primarily pedagogic.

Martin Bucer's* great treatise *Von der Waren Seelsorge* (*On the True Care of Souls*, 1538) was the first work on pastoral theology* in the Reformed* churches. In this book, the exercise of discipline is inextricably linked with the pastoral office and also with the elders' task of caring for souls. Richard Baxter's* careful pastoral work in Kidderminster owed much to Bucer.

When offences are not prevented by the constant application of the word, then the other, negative, parts of discipline must be employed, *e.g.* censures and finally excommunication. Public faults, however, are to be rebuked publicly (1 Tim. 5:20; Gal. 2:11, 14). Discipline, no matter how carefully applied, will never result in an entirely pure church. Tares will always be mixed with the wheat in the field.

Discipline is *ecclesiastical* discipline. Paul, though an apostle, does not excommunicate as an individual, but participates with the church in a common authority (1 Cor. 5:4), exercised through [properly] elected representatives. The ultimate aim is to regain the offender for the fellowship. Behind discipline lies love, not harshness, even less Pharisaism.

Such a power is part of the use of the keys (Mt. 18:17–18), 'binding' being equivalent to exclusion. Upon repentance, the offender is 'loosed'. Ecclesiastical tyranny is avoided by the loving purpose and by the heartfelt prayer for God's guidance and authority (Mt. 18:19–20).

The dynamic behind the restoration of discipline must be the honour of Christ, his name being dishonoured by unworthiness in his body, the church. Laxity allowed will only spread (1 Cor. 5:6). True discipline is an expression of Christian concern, and encourages a real distinction between the church and the world.

Discipline has traditionally been exercised in connection with the sacraments:* the 'unworthy' (1 Cor. 11:27) should not take the Lord's Supper, and, if infant baptism* is practised, it should be limited to the infants of at least one believing parent. There are contemporary problems in connection with marriage and re-marriage after divorce, and in the choice and scrutiny of accredited church leaders.

See also: PENANCE.

Bibliography

J.-D. Benoît, *Calvin, directeur d'âmes* (Strasburg, 1947); *Calvin: Theological Treatises*, ed. J. K. S. Reid (London, 1954); R. N. Caswell, 'Calvin's View of Ecclesiastical Discipline', in G. E. Duffield (ed.), *John Calvin* (Appleford, 1966), pp. 210–226; I. M. Clark, *A History of Church Discipline in Scotland* (Aberdeen, 1929); N. Marshall, *The Penitential Discipline of the Primitive Church* (1714; repr. Oxford, 1844); F. Wendel, *Calvin* (London, 1963).

R.N.C.

DISCIPLING, see SHEPHERDING MOVEMENT.

DISPENSATIONAL THEOLOGY. Dispensationalism rests on the view that God's dealings with men have proceeded through 'well-defined time-periods' (Chafer), *i.e.* 'dispensations', in each of which God reveals a particular purpose to be accomplished in that period, to which men respond in faith or unbelief. Dispensationalists deny that they teach more than one way of salvation, admitting only that the *content* of faith varies according to the revelation given in each dispensation. Scriptural support is derived from passages which distinguish between, *e.g.*, past ages (*e.g.* Eph. 3:5; Col. 1:26), the present age (*e.g.* Rom. 12:2; Gal. 1:4) and the age to come (Eph. 2:7; Heb. 6:5), and especially the use of *aiōnas* in Heb. 1:2 and 11:3. Dispensationalists differ in identification of the dispensations, but it is fairly general to distinguish those of innocency (Adam before the fall), conscience (Adam to Noah), promise (Abraham to Moses), Mosaic law (Moses to Christ), grace (Pentecost to the rapture) and the millennium.* The sharp distinction drawn between Israel* and the church (except during the dispensation of grace) is crucial. The systematization of modern dispensational theology owes much to J. N. Darby* and the Scofield Reference

Bible (1909, by the American Congregationalist, Cyrus I. Scofield, 1843–1921).

The basic hermeneutical* principle is literal interpretation, which does not rule out symbols, figures of speech and typology, but does insist that, throughout, 'the reality of the literal meaning of the terms involved' is determinative (Ryrie, *Dispensationalism Today*, p. 87). Consequently, the promises of an earthly kingdom given to Israel as a nation must be fulfilled literally in a future, millennial kingdom (on the analogy of the literal fulfilment of the messianic promises relating to Jesus). Dispensationalists accept that believing Jews – as individuals – find their place in the church during the dispensation of grace, but the promises made to the natural seed of Abraham await the premillennial return of Christ with his church for their fulfilment. Then will be initiated the dispensation during which the material blessings promised to Israel will be bestowed – and will be characteristic, though not to the exclusion of the spiritual dimension.

Some details are in dispute among dispensationalists. These include the number and designations of the dispensations and the point at which the dispensation of grace began. The most extreme view is that of E. W. Bullinger (1837–1913) who commenced the church age with the ministry of Paul after Acts 28:28, held that Paul's prison epistles are the only Scriptures addressed *primarily* to the church, and denied that water baptism and the Lord's Supper are for this age. There is less disagreement over the *terminus ad quem* of the dispensation of grace, though some believe the rapture of the church (which marks its termination) will not take place until the end (a few say the middle) of the great tribulation.

See also: ESCHATOLOGY.

Bibliography
L. S. Chafer, *Systematic Theology*, 8 vols. (Dallas, TX, 1947); A. H. Ehlert, 'A Bibliography of Dispensationalism', *BS*, *passim* (1944–46); C. C. Ryrie, *Dispensationalism Today* (Chicago, 1965); E. Sauer, *From Eternity to Eternity* (Exeter, 1954); J. F. Walvoord, *The Millennial Kingdom* (Findlay, OH, 1959).

H.H.R.

DIVORCE, see SEXUALITY.

DOCETISM is the view that the body of Christ was not real but only seeming (Gk. *dokein*, 'to seem'), and so either the sufferings were only apparent, or else the redeemer who could not suffer was separate from the man in whom he appeared. The premise of this syllogism was a tendency in the church from the beginning; the conclusion was a theory of most of the Gnostic* sects of the 2nd century and the Manichees* of the 4th. John's reference to the 'flesh' and 'blood' (1 Jn. 4:2; 5:6) suggests that the view appeared early and is given apostolic repudiation. Even among the more orthodox of the early fathers docetic ideas are voiced. Irenaeus,* for example, speaks of Christ's body as 'a shade of the glory of God covering him', although he elsewhere asserts that his body is 'nothing seeming'. Statements with similar docetic flavour could be adduced from Athanasius'* *On the Incarnation of the Word of God*. Of the Alexandrians, in Clement* and Origen,* for whom the Logos* indwelt, and in some way even permeated, the body of the man Jesus, the tendency towards docetism is marked. Later Christological heresies deriving from the School of Alexandria,* *i.e.*, Apollinarianism,* Eutychianism and monophysitism,* tend towards doceticsm. For them God appears almost in masquerade, in the appearance of a human body. The view was condemned specifically and by implication by the great ecumenical councils* of the church.

The docetists among the Gnostics and Manichees denied explicitly the reality of Christ's human body. The view was the logical consequence of their assumption of the inherent evil of matter. If matter is evil, and Christ was pure, then Christ's body must have been merely phantasmal. The origin of such docetism was not biblical but pagan, with Alexandria as its chief seat. The theological counterpart of the acceptance of docetism is the denial of a real incarnation* of God the Son, of atonement* through his death, and his bodily resurrection.* Docetism met its strongest opposition from Ignatius (d. *c.* 115) who condemned docetic views then prevalent in Asia Minor: 'Jesus Christ was of the race of David, the child of Mary, who was truly born and ate and drank, was truly persecuted under Pontius Pilate.' Ignatius uses the term 'truly', or, perhaps better translated, 'genuinely' (*alēthōs*), as a sort of watchword against docetism. Tertullian* was foremost in repudiating Gnostic docetism: 'Let us examine our Lord's bodily substance, for about his spiritual nature we are all agreed (*certum est*). It is the flesh that is in question. Its verity and quality are the points in dispute.' He proceeds to establish that Christ's was 'a thoroughly human condition'. The Antiochene School* with its emphasis on the humanity of Christ was strongly anti-docetic, as is the modern stress on Christ as not merely representative manhood but himself *a* man. But modern theology by divorcing the Christ of faith from the Jesus of history (see Christology;* Historical Jesus*) is in danger of initiating a new form of docetism.

Bibliography
A. Grillmeier, *Christ in Christian Tradition*, vol. 1 (London, ²1975).

H.D.McD.

DOCTRINAL CRITICISM is the appraisal of the truth and adequacy of doctrinal statements. The term owes its currency in British theology to a programmatic essay by G. F. Woods (1907–66), setting out the task of the doctrinal critic as that of subjecting doctrinal statements to the same kind of critical scrutiny brought to bear upon the biblical writings by biblical criticism.* As well as analysing the capacity of human symbols to articulate the transcendent, the critic assesses doctrines in the light of the historical setting in which they were formulated and in the light of contemporary understandings of reality. Woods's suggestions have been extensively developed and applied in the work of Maurice Wiles (b. 1923), notably in the area of Christology. While doctrinal criticism has contributed much to the renewed interest in systematic theology of recent years, it inherits a changed perspective on the authority and self-evidence of revelation* which stems from the Enlightenment,* according to which no contingent* statement or system may be accorded a position of privileged immunity from critical examination.

See also: CONTEMPORARY THEOLOGICAL TRENDS.

Bibliography
B. L. Hebblethwaite, *The Problems of Theology* (Cambridge, 1980); *idem, Th* 70 (1967), pp. 402–405; M. F. Wiles (ed.), *Explorations in Theology*, vol. 4 (London,

1979); *idem, Working Papers in Doctrine* (London, 1976); G. F. Woods, 'Doctrinal Criticism' in F. G. Healey (ed.), *Prospect for Theology* (London, 1966).

J.B.We.

DODD, CHARLES HAROLD (1884–1973) was probably the leading 20th-century British NT scholar. He showed that Jesus taught that the kingdom of God* was already present during his ministry. Dodd tried to understand his teaching, especially his parables, on the assumption that he did not expect any future apocalyptic events; later he modified this position. Dodd's recognition of 'realized' eschatology* was a necessary reaction to the 'futurist' eschatology of A. Schweitzer* and others. Dodd also gave a profound analysis of the use of Jewish ideas in a Hellenistic* framework in John's Gospel, and analysed its historical contents to show that it contained valuable historical traditions independent of the other written gospels. Dodd emphasized the combination of historical facts plus interpretation in revelation.* He was thus at the opposite end of the theological spectrum from R. Bultmann,* and he showed that it was possible and legitimate to write about the historical Jesus.* Dodd also showed how a basic pattern of preaching (kerygma*) lay at the root of NT theology,* and how this theology was developed from a study of various 'fields' of OT Scriptures. Despite some 'liberal' elements in his interpretation of Scripture, he made a positive and lasting contribution to NT scholarship.

Bibliography
F. F. Bruce, 'C. H. Dodd', in P. E. Hughes (ed.), *Creative Minds in Contemporary Theology* (Grand Rapids, MI, 1966), pp. 239–269; F. W. Dillistone, *C. H. Dodd. Interpreter of the New Testament* (Grand Rapids, MI, 1977).

I.H.Ma.

DOGMA This Gk. word was used in the pre-Christian world of public ordinances, judicial decisions or statements of principle in philosophy or science. In the LXX, it is used of government decrees in Est. 3:9; Dn. 2:13; 6:8. In the NT, the judgments of the law are so referred to in Eph. 2:15 and Col.

2:14 and the decisions of the Council of Jerusalem in Acts 16:4.

In the Christian church 'dogma' became teaching which was considered authoritative. Throughout the first three centuries, the Lat. and Gk. writers were inclined to call everything related to faith 'dogma'. Chrysostom used the word specifically for those truths revealed by Christ and above reason. Thomas Aquinas* and the scholastics* did not often use the term and preferred to speak of the articles of faith.

From the Reformation onwards, the word came to designate those articles of faith which the church officially formulated as the truth which had been revealed. It reflected therefore a common recognition by the Reformed and Roman churches that dogmatic formulation is an activity of the church, often arising out of theological controversy or the need to clarify the faith to be embraced.

The Reformed milieu

In the debate over the nature of authority, the Reformed understanding of dogma reflected its anchorage of authority in Scripture rather than in the church. The response of the church to doctrinal controversy was seen to be *materially* based upon Scripture. *Formally* dogma bears the marks of the intellectual and cultural ethos in which it is formulated. It is not infallible, but nevertheless provides grounds for unity and stability within the church catholic.

Pietism* challenged the *formal* dimension of dogma in perceiving it as perpetuating an arid and intellectual scholasticism, far removed from the experience of God in the life of the believer. The Enlightenment* increasingly undermined the classic *material* substance of dogma, by challenging the church's identification of the word of God with Scripture. A new understanding of dogma and how it develops emerged. This is found in the writings of Schleiermacher,* Ritschl* and specifically in Harnack's* *History of Dogma*. Here the focus is upon the religious and ethical experience of the Christian community in which divine revelation is authenticated. Dogma is the articulation by and for that community of their perception of the revelation of God.

The return to orthodoxy spearheaded by Emil Brunner* and Karl Barth* in post-war Germany sought to purge the Reformed faith of 17th-century scholasticism while preserving the ground of dogma in the revelation of God in Jesus Christ. Dogma was seen as the articulation of the church's understanding of this revelation as the Holy Spirit bears witness to Christ in the Scriptures. Unlike their immediate liberal* predecessors or existential* successors, the neo-orthodox school did not view dogma as an attempt to understand and express human experience of God, but as the necessary and scientific response to 'the light of the knowledge of the glory of God in the face of Jesus Christ'. The *modus operandi* for dogmatic formulation has its roots in the nature of God and his revelation and not in the nature of man and his religious awareness. What is then the role of Scripture? It remains, in this framework, the source of the material content of dogma, but only in so far as its equation with the Word is indirect, for the Word of God is the revelation itself, *i.e.*, Jesus Christ.

Dogma is essentially a corollary of orthodoxy. The increasing pluralism within Reformed confessional churches and their inability to function with objective criteria of authority* have produced a growing ambivalence to the articulation of dogma. Only in pragmatic areas of morality do the Reformed churches appear to speak with authority.

The Catholic stance

The Roman Catholic Church has sought to affirm its understanding of dogma under the same pressures as that of the Reformed community. The traditional view in the Catholic Church is that dogma is truth revealed by God in Scripture and/or tradition and formulated by and for the church against error. Such truth is irrevocable, unchangeable and infallible. Dogma, therefore, does not add to what has been revealed but merely defines and declares it.

Although not denying this view of dogma, since the 19th century many Catholic theologians have queried the static and scholastic manner in which the church is perceived to have stated dogma. Newman* argued for a dynamic process of dogmatic development* in the church. Truth was implanted like seeds in the mind of the church and organically developed, so that latent truth became under the focus of controversy a full-grown dogma explicitly approved by the church.

A further stage in Catholic reflection is the

awareness that there is a continual process of uncovering the meaning of what is expressed in dogma. Apart from truth transcending human thought and requiring analogical language to communicate, it was increasingly recognized that church pronouncements are the product of their age and reflect the cultural, philosophical and linguistic norms of the period. Most Catholic theologians would want to argue that the reality expressed will remain unchanged and unchanging, and that dogmas have an objective content whose meaning is valid for all ages. Nevertheless, *the form* of expression can be subject to revision.

Three further convictions have affected the contemporary Catholic stance. First, revelation is not the divine communication of abstract truths which dogma would put into propositions. Second, all truth is organically inter-related and finds its central focus in Jesus Christ. Third, revealed truth is self-authenticating in that it demands an existential response. Karl Rahner* argues that dogma is deduced from revelation, which is a 'saving event' wherein 'the incarnate Word' communicates the reality of God himself. Dogmas are not therefore merely statements about God but are 'exhibitive' words with a 'sacramental' nature; *i.e.* 'what [a dogma] states actually occurs and is posited by its existence'. Dogma, therefore, when rightly affirmed and personally assimilated is 'life'. This view he would wish to incorporate within the traditional twofold distinction between *the formal* (expressed by the church explicitly and definitively as a revealed truth) and *the material* (belonging to Christian revelation as it is found in the word of God addressed to us in Scripture and/or tradition).

Neo-orthodoxy* in the Reformed and Roman Catholic churches continues to grapple with how to draw from revelation truths which are organically interdependent, whose logic stretches traditional models to breaking-point, and yet when articulated in dogmatic form may receive the allegiance of the faithful.

Ecumenism* and social and economic realities are in practical terms the two most powerful influences upon the major Christian traditions in their revaluation of dogma. Today ecumenical dialogue has heightened the awareness of the influence of Western/Greco-Roman thought forms upon dogmatic formulations which, in the eyes of cultures more akin to the world of the OT and NT, are a distortion of the revelation with unsettling moral and spiritual ramifications. The socio-economic conditions to which the gospel is to speak expose the bourgeois nature of the churches' historic dogmatic statements and their failure to emphasize those aspects of the revelation which hold together creation* and redemption* in cosmic deliverance.

See also: CONTEXTUALIZATION; LIBERATION THEOLOGY; POLITICAL THEOLOGY; SYSTEMATIC THEOLOGY.

Bibliography

K. Barth, CD I:1; E. Brunner, *The Christian Doctrine of God* (*Dogmatics*, vol. 1; London, 1949); A. Harnack, *History of Dogma*, vol. 1 (London, 1894); A. Lecerf, *An Introduction to Reformed Dogmatics* (London, 1949); J. Orr, *The Progress of Dogma* (London, ³1908); W. Pannenberg, *Basic Questions in Theology*, vol. 1 (London, 1970), pp. 182–210 ('What is a Dogmatic Statement?'); O. Weber, *Foundations of Dogmatics*, vol. 1 (Grand Rapids, MI, 1981).

T.W.J.M.

DOMINIC AND THE DOMINICANS.

The Dominicans, officially known as the Order of Friars Preachers (O.P.) and more popularly called the Black Friars, are one of the four great mendicant orders of the Roman Catholic Church. The founder of the order, Dominico (Dominic) de Guzman (1170–1221), was a Spaniard whose early career began in Castile. Educated at the University of Palencia, which was later moved to Salamanca, he became a member of the religious community attached to the cathedral at Osma. Because of his impressive ability he was sent to Southern France to help convert the Albigensian* heretics. Dominic came to believe that the only way to reach them was with evangelical preaching accompanied by a life-style of apostolic poverty. To accomplish this task he set out on preaching missions in market-places and roadsides, living in poverty so extreme that he wore no shoes or sandals and begged for his food. At first his policy met with little success and his mission was forced to end when Pope Innocent III (1198–1216) began to use force against the heretics in 1208.

Inspired by this vision of a group of preachers who would win heretics and heathen by preaching the word and living a simple life, Dominic attracted a group of followers (1214). He prepared them for their task by careful instruction and by sharing his dream of a learned preaching order of mendicant friars. Despite the rather impressive nature of the group they were denied recognition by the Fourth Lateran Council* (1215), but later Pope Honorius III (1216) sanctioned their mission, and in 1220 their rule, adopted from the Augustinians* with added requirements of preaching and apostolic living, was confirmed. Dominic spent the remainder of his life travelling in Italy, France and Spain organizing his order. He was canonized in 1234. A man of intelligence, courage and zeal, he was also an extremely effective administrator.

From its inception the order has accepted from its founder its synthesis of an active ministry with a spiritual life. The members live in community, observe diet and fast rules, and conduct liturgical rites, but, according to their constitution, time is to be given for study and preaching. Dominicans are governed by a relatively democratic order. However, a balance is maintained between the elected representative bodies, or chapters, and strong but elected superiors. In contrast to other orders of its time, the Dominicans were not a collection of autonomous houses but were an army of preachers organized in provinces under a master general and prepared to go wherever they were needed. This organization has served as a model for many monastic movements, organized after the Dominicans took form.

From the beginning they insisted that no-one should preach without three years of theological training. Within forty years of the founding of the order their scholars were teaching at Oxford, Paris, Bologna and Cologne. Dominican intellectual activity led to the founding of several universities, where they emphasized the teaching of languages including Greek, Hebrew and Arabic, in addition to the more standard curriculum of scriptural studies and theology. Some of the great masters of medieval thought, led by Thomas Aquinas* and Albertus Magnus,* were Dominicans who sought to harmonize faith and reason* in a series of massive volumes (see Scholasticism*). They lived at a time when Muslim scholars had made the works of Aristotle* available for the first time

to medieval Europeans. These books, which presented a complete explanation of reality without any reference to the Christian God, challenged the academic mind of the 13th century. After a period of conflict and uncertainty, the thought of Thomas, bringing the Aristotelian and Christian systems together, was accepted as the basis for Roman Catholic theology.*

The academic pursuits of the Dominicans did not divert them from their mission to combat heresy and convert the heathen. They continued to work among the Albigensians and extended their efforts to include the Jews and Moors in Spain. Their evangelistic efforts led them to preach to the heathen in Eastern Europe and in Asia. When the Inquisition was established, Dominicans were assigned to help carry it out because of their dedication to the church and orthodoxy. They entered the new world as the first and most energetic missionaries under the Spanish and Portuguese explorers.

The Dominican order has experienced periods of achievement and of decline. During the 14th and 15th centuries discipline relaxed as Europe suffered from plague, warfare and division in the church. However, the 16th century witnessed a period of Thomistic renewal under leaders such as Francisco de Vitoria (c. 1485–1546) and Thomas de Vio Cajetan (1469–1534; see Luther*). During this period Dominican studies were revised to meet the challenge of humanism* and Protestantism.* At the Council of Trent (1545–63), attended by many Dominicans, Thomistic theology was made the basis for the dogmatic decisions. With some modern revisions, it still remains basic to much of Roman Catholic thought. Despite this recognition, there were forces at work that undermined the order. The rise of new groups such as the Jesuits* and the loss of much of Eastern Europe to Western control began to push the Dominicans into the background. The 18th-century Enlightenment* also dampened enthusiasm, weakened discipline and made recruiting difficult.

The order continues into modern times standing firmly for orthodoxy and opposing novelty in theology. Paradoxically many Dominicans have been active in the reform movement that resulted from Vatican II, including theological reform (e.g. E. Schillebeeckx*). They have also led in the worker-priest movement, spoken decisively for the

205

Third World and made extensive use of the fields of radio, television, films and the stage in their preaching ministry.

Bibliography
R. F. Bennett, *The Early Dominicans: Studies in Thirteenth-Century Dominican History* (Cambridge, 1937); W. R. Bonniwell, *A History of the Dominican Liturgy* (New York, 1944); A. T. Drane, *The History of St Dominic, Founder of the Friars Preachers* (London, 1891); W. A. Hinnebusch, *The History of the Dominican Order* (Staten Island, NY, 1966); B. Jarrett, *Life of St Dominic (1170–1221)* (London, 1924); *idem, The English Dominicans* (London, 1921); P. F. Mandonnet, *St Dominic and His Work* (St Louis, MO, 1944); *idem,* in *DTC* 6 (1920), cols. 863–924; M. H. Vicaire, *Saint Dominic and His Times* (London, 1964).

R.G.C.

DONATISM, a schism* which broke out in North Africa *c.* 313 and persisted until after the Muslim conquest in 698. Donatism is so called because its leading spirit was a man named Donatus, whom the schismatics elected as Bishop of Carthage in 313, shortly after the outbreak of controversy.

The origins of the schism were bound up with personal rivalries at Carthage, and later took on social and political implications in that the Donatists drew much of their support from the less-Romanized Berber tribespeople of the country. Yet the main and enduring cause was religious and theological. The Donatists were rigorous in their support of the spiritual rewards of martyrdom,* and it was the lax policy of the church at Carthage towards *traditores, i.e.* those who had 'handed over' their copies of the Scriptures to be burned during the Great Persecution of 303, which caused the bad feeling and led to schism. The election as bishop in 312 of Caecilian, who seemed unenthusiastic about the martyrs, and his consecration by a suspected *traditor*, caused a scandal among the rigorists and led to separation. Donatists regarded themselves as the true church,* and claimed Cyprian's* authority in rebaptizing* Catholics.

In the 4th century Donatism possessed gifted teachers in Parmenian (against whom Augustine* later wrote) and Tyconius (*fl. c.* 370–90), a layman who was a somewhat nonconformist Donatist and exercised a major influence on Augustine (who incorporated the essence of his *Book of Rules*, the first Latin Christian treatise on hermeneutics,* into his *Christian Instruction*) and on Western interpretations of the Apocalypse of John. Tyconius taught that the church was truly universal, a 'bipartite' mixture of the 'cities' of God and devil. His Paulinism also influenced Augustine.

It is sometimes said that the Donatists were against the links which the emperor, Constantine, was beginning to forge between church and state* at the moment the schism erupted, but the fact that they were prepared to appeal to the emperor for support argues against this conclusion. Donatist opposition to the Roman authorities stemmed from the attempts of the latter to persecute them. These attempts started in 317 and continued intermittently thereafter. A conference held at Carthage in 411 tried to reintegrate the Donatists into the Catholic Church, with some success. Augustine wrote against them, and justified their forcible coercion, and by the time he died Donatism was a declining force. Its remnants may have partly merged with the Catholic Church during the Vandal occupation of North Africa (439–533) and the final phase of Roman rule (533–698).

Bibliography
W. H. C. Frend, *The Donatist Church* (Oxford, 1952).

G.L.B.

DOOYEWEERD, HERMAN (1894–1977), Dutch Christian jurist and philosopher, at the time of his death professor emeritus at the Free University of Amsterdam and editor-in-chief of *Philosophia Reformata*, the scholarly journal of the Association for Calvinistic Philosophy. He was the founder, together with his colleague D. H. Th. Vollenhoven (1892–1978) and others, of the Christian philosophy now called the 'philosophy of the Cosmonomic Idea'.

Dooyeweerd was born into a family that had a strong attachment to the movement in the Netherlands which was headed by the Dutch theologian, journalist and statesman Abraham Kuyper.*

Dooyeweerd approached philosophy by way of investigating his own field of jurisprudence, penetrating to its foundations, which, he said, could be understood only in terms of a radically Christian world-and-life view. The great turning-point of his thought came when he discovered that all thinking, and indeed all of life, has a religious root. He began to examine the foundations of jurisprudence and statecraft as adjunct director of the Abraham Kuyper Foundation in the Hague (1922–26). After assuming his professorship at the Free University in 1926, he worked out his principles more broadly and in greater detail and published in 1935–6 his *magnum opus*, the three-volumed *Philosophy of the Law-Idea* (or *Cosmonomic Idea*). The appearance of this seminal work marked the beginning of a new philosophy, which sought to base itself on the teachings of the Scriptures and to participate in the reformation of all of life in the name of Jesus Christ.

In all science and philosophy, Dooyeweerd argued, thought is guided by a threefold idea: that of the coherence (how things hang together), the deeper unity (where and how things come to a single focus), and the origin of all things (how, in this focusing, they manifest their dependence on the creator-God, who has expressed and continues to express his will in his law, *i.e.* in the created order that holds for the entire cosmos). Dooyeweerd attempted throughout to demonstrate that thought, by its very nature, is dependent on underlying presuppositions, and ultimately on basic religious motives. He argued, furthermore, that science and philosophy can perform their respective tasks successfully only on a sound Christian foundation. Thus he entered, along with other reformational thinkers, into a critique of systems of thought that attempt to build on non-Christian foundations or seek to combine Christian and non-Christian (apostate) motifs.

Because of the intrinsic relation of thought and religion, Dooyeweerd's critique is fundamentally a critique of theoretical thought itself, a theme that assumed greater prominence as his career progressed. Dooyeweerd's philosophy has also made many positive contributions to other disciplines; for instance, in its examination of the foundations of jurisprudence, in its development of a theory of individuality structures as a foundation, *e.g.*, of a Christian sociology,* and in settling forth a new theory of the intertwining (*enkapsis*) of such individuality structures in

man's body, as a foundation for a Christian anthropology.*

Closely associated with Dooyeweerd's name are those of the other original representatives, broadly speaking, of this philosophy, who, following the lead of Abraham Kuyper, have attempted to reform scholarship in the name of Christ: D. H. Th. Vollenhoven (history of philosophy); H. G. Stoker (b. 1899; psychology); and C. Van Til* (apologetics).

Bibliography

A New Critique of Theoretical Thought, 4 vols. (Philadelphia, 1953–58); *In the Twilight of Western Thought* (Philadelphia, 1960); *Roots of Western Culture: Pagan, Secular, and Christian Options*, tr. John Kraay (Toronto, 1979); *Transcendental Problems of Philosophic Thought: An Inquiry into the Transcendental Condition of Philosophy* (Grand Rapids, MI, 1948).

V. Brümmer, *Transcendental Criticism and Christian Philosophy* (Franeker, 1961); L. Kalsbeek, *Contours of a Christian Philosophy* (Toronto, 1975); C. T. McIntire (ed.), *The Legacy of Herman Dooyeweerd: Reflections on Critical Philosophy in the Christian Tradition* (Lanham, MD, and Toronto, 1986).

R.D.K.

DORT, SYNOD OF. This was a gathering of representatives of the international Reformed* community intended to resolve certain doctrinal difficulties which had arisen in the Netherlands at the beginning of the 17th century. The synod was held in 1618–19 by the invitation of the government of the Netherlands. There were sixty-two representatives of the Dutch provinces and twenty-four foreign delegates.

Very considerable dissension had arisen in the Netherlands at the beginning of the century concerning the understanding of divine sovereignty.* This centred for a period in the teaching of Arminius* but continued unabated after his death. In 1610 a document known as the Remonstrance was issued by those who were restless with traditional Calvinist doctrine. It affirmed: 1. God's election is grounded in his foresight of faith* and perseverance,* and his reprobation in the foresight of unbelief; 2. The intent of the redemptive work of Christ was the salvation of all human beings but forgiveness is actually given only to those who believe; 3. Fallen humanity is incapable of any good and specifically of saving faith, except by the intervention of the Holy Spirit;* 4. While grace* is necessary for all good, it is not irresistible; 5. The question of perseverance must be more carefully studied from Scripture* before any firm conclusion can be reached.

A number of conferences, notably at The Hague (1611) and at Delft (1613), did not resolve the questions. Resolution was therefore sought in a large gathering in which not only the Dutch churches but the international Reformed community would be represented. The issues were considered in the order of the Remonstrance, with the understanding that the third and fourth points were considered jointly. In the deliberations the Remonstrants did not have a part; they were viewed as accused of heresy and subject to trial rather than as members of the synodical party. The conclusions of the synod were set out in what are known as the Canons of Dort, consisting of four chapters with a number of articles and a rejection of errors. The chapters relate respectively to sovereign predestination,* definite atonement,* radical depravity (see Sin*) and effectual grace, and the perseverance of God with the saints. It is from this document that the articulation of five-point Calvinism has arisen.

In spite of certain differences among the delegates, particularly concerning the second point, there was a general approval of the Canons. They were worded at times in such a way as to accommodate certain differences of emphasis. In particular the rejection of errors has often been thought to embody a very harsh repudiation of Arminianism. The Canons, complete with rejection of errors, were approved as a formulation of the faith of the Reformed Church of the Netherlands, and ministers were required to subscribe to them. This requirement was not maintained seriously in later times, but it still functions in the Netherlands and in churches of Dutch extraction in South Africa and the United States. In 1620 at the National Synod of Alais, French Reformed pastors were similarly enjoined to subscribe to the Canons.

Those who oppose the conclusions of Dort are almost unanimous in thinking that the synod was unduly harsh with the Arminian leaders and their views and that the Canons embody a scholastic form of doctrine which

is foreign to the Scriptures. Those who approve of them ordinarily judge that the Reformed consensus on these difficult topics was expressed in a proper and balanced manner, and that a grievous deviation was thus warded off for at least a century in Reformed thinking. The subsequent history of the Arminians in the Netherlands, and the direction of Arminian bodies since that time, tend to confirm this opinion in the minds of traditional Calvinists, although some feel that if Arminian leaders had been treated more amicably at Dort and later, they might not have so quickly moved into positions which were in stark opposition to Reformed orthodoxy.

Bibliography
P. Schaff, *Creeds of Christendom* (New York, 1919 ed.). A modern translation is found in the *Acta* of the 1985 Synod of the Christian Reformed Church.

P. Y. DeJong, *Crisis in the Reformed Churches* (Grand Rapids, MI, 1968); W. R. Godfrey, *Tensions within International Calvinism: The Debate on the Atonement at the Synod of Dort, 1618–1619* (PhD dissertation, Stanford, 1974); *idem* and J. L. Boyd III (eds.), *Through Christ's Word* (Phillipsburg, NJ, 1985), pp. 121–148; J. I. Packer, 'Arminianisms', *The Manifold Grace of God* (Puritan and Reformed Studies Conference Papers, London, 1968); T. Scott, *The Articles of the Synod of Dort* (Utica, 1831).

R.N.

DOUBT. It is a popular misconception that doubt is tantamount to unbelief. In fact, although doubt may lead to unbelief it may equally produce a firmer faith.* The Gk. words for doubt in the NT have the root meaning of divided judgment (being in two minds about a matter) or lack of resources, helplessness. They are sometimes translated in terms of being perplexed, at a loss or unsure (*e.g.* Jn. 13:22; Acts 2:12; 10:17).

In a Christian sense doubt is being in two minds about God or his word. It takes many forms. It may have its source in the agonizing questions thrown up by the apparent contradiction between God's word and human experience (*cf.* Suffering;* Theodicy*). Frequently this form of doubt is to be found in the OT when expressions of bewilderment lead to much surer faith. Such doubters need support. Doubt may also imply a desire to know more. Since Descartes,* learning through radical questioning has been an important and accepted method of making progress in understanding. An example of this may be found in Thomas (Jn. 14:5; 20:25). Here doubt is genuinely provisional and open to instruction.

Doubt may stem from a lack of faith as in Mt. 14:31; 28:17 and Mk. 9:24. The doubter would like to believe but cannot quite bring himself to trust God's word unequivocally. Such weak faith needs encouragement to become stronger.

But doubt may also be culpable. It may have its origin in moral obstinacy or intellectual scepticism. The earliest example of this is the insubordinate questioning of God's word by the serpent in Gn. 3:1. In form it may vary from an unwillingness to be convinced by evidence (Mt. 12:38–42; Mk. 6:6), through an inability to interpret the evidence due to wilful immorality (2 Thes. 2:10–12) to outright rejection of the evidence (Jas. 2:19). Such doubts are already expressions of unbelief.

Pastorally, Scripture commands us to 'be merciful to those who doubt' (Jude 22) and indicates that doubters can be saved from slipping into apostasy.* In general the doubter should not be condemned, but gently encouraged and patiently instructed. More specifically, doubt is not simply a 'spiritual' issue but involves intellectual, emotional, moral and experiential dimensions as well. Care should be taken to discover the particular form of doubt and its cause before applying a remedy.

Guinness argues that some doubts arise because of defective spiritual birth, e.g. through ingratitude, an inadequate view of God, weak foundations or malformed commitment, while others relate to problems of continuing faith, e.g. a lack of growth, unruly emotions or lack of confidence.

Christian maturity aims to overcome doubt and produce settled faith. Jesus teaches that certain faith is essential for answered prayer (Mt. 21:21; Mk. 11:23). James develops the same point more widely to stress the dangers of doubt and to advocate mature stability (Jas. 1:5–8).

Bibliography
R. Davidson, *The Courage to Doubt* (London, 1983); O. Guinness, *Doubt: Faith in Two Minds* (Berkhamsted, 1976); B. Gärtner in *NIDNTT* I, pp. 503–505.

D.J.T.

DOSTOEVSKY, FYODOR MIKHAILOVICH (1821–81), Russian novelist. Brought up in a pious Russian Orthodox home, as a young man Dostoevsky went through a period of serious doubt. Exile in Siberia (1849–59) helped him to reaffirm his commitment to Christian principles, as embodied in the traditions and spirituality of the Russian church, and to develop a sense of the 'messianic destiny' of the Russian people. As a novelist Dostoevsky gave expression in different ways to concepts such as the tremendous power of evil, the dangers of Roman Catholicism and socialism (which Dostoevsky tended to equate with each other), of individualism, indeed of any philosophy which did not give God his rightful place, and recognize the salvific value of suffering.*

Dostoevsky was not, however, a systematic thinker. He did not write works of philosophy and theology, still less novels about abstract ideas. As a brilliant, creative writer, he has left us a series of unforgettable characters motivated by many different kinds of ideas and passions, some of which were those of the author himself. Undoubtedly the most powerful exposition of ideas occurs in the 'Legend of the Grand Inquisitor' (*The Brothers Karamazov*, Book 5, ch. 5), of which Dostoevsky makes Ivan Karamazov the author. Dostoevsky aimed to portray the bankruptcy and pernicious influence of the philosophy of Ivan Karamazov/the Grand Inquisitor which led to man's putting himself in the place of God. This, Dostoevsky felt, was the heresy both of Roman Catholicism, whose 'Grand Inquisitor' condemns Christ for rejecting the three temptations in the wilderness, and also of socialism.

Bibliography
A. B. Gibson, *The Religion of Dostoevsky* (London, 1973).

M.D.

DOXOLOGY is the offering of worship to God in 'wonder, love and praise', exalting him, glorifying him and proclaiming his greatness in 'humble adoration'. 'In doxology the believer . . . simply worships

God . . . "for thine is the kingdom, the power and the glory for ever and ever" ' (E. Schlink). Theology can make no real progress without the spirit of worship. Doctrine and doxology belong together. Worship divorced from sound doctrine degenerates into superficial emotionalism. Doctrine divorced from true worship lapses into barren intellectualism. Theology must take seriously the NT imperative to 'be transformed by the renewing of your mind' if its work is to be offered to God as 'spiritual worship', grounded in 'God's mercy' (Rom. 12:1–2). A truly doxological theology will give due emphasis to both 'the Scripture' and 'the power of God' (Mt. 22:29). It will emphasize both knowledge of the Scriptures and enlightenment by the Holy Spirit. The authority of Scripture is essential if the contemporary interest in doxology is to amount to more than theology giving an account of man's experience of worship. The power of the Holy Spirit is essential if theology is to 'sing like a hymn, not read like a telephone book' (C. Pinnock).

Doxology is not merely one theme among other theological themes. Rather, it is the spirit in which theology is to pursue all of its work. As the holy Scriptures are studied in dependence on the Holy Spirit, theology will increasingly enter into the doxological spirit of the God-breathed Scriptures. The Holy Spirit enables the believing reader to enter deeply into the doxological affirmation concerning Jesus Christ: 'My Lord and my God!' (Jn. 20:28). Through the word and the Spirit, the theologian learns to ask his questions concerning God and man doxologically (Mi. 7:18; Ps. 8:4). He learns both the warm personal devotion which calls God 'my Rock and my Redeemer' (Ps. 19:14) and the cosmic doxology, 'O Lord, our Lord, how majestic is your name in all the earth!' (Ps. 8:1, 9). Seeing the whole of life in the light of the soul-reviving 'law of the Lord' (Ps. 19:7), he worships the God who is both great and near. 'The Hallelujah resounds to the God who is not far away, but very close at hand' (G. C. Berkouwer). Since God is near as well as great, doxology cannot be a super-spirituality with little practical relevance. The believer who says the doxology must also pray, 'your will be done on earth as it is in heaven' (Mt. 6:10). Doxology must be set within the context both of practical Christian living and caring service, and of 'prayer and the ministry of the word'

(Acts 6:1–4). It may not be detached from the discipline of intercessory prayer: 'Doxology without petitionary prayer does not remain true doxology' (Schlink). The common contrast, 'more worship, less preaching', must not be permitted to obscure the vital connection between the clarity of proclamation and true worship (1 Cor. 14:24–25). In doxology, there can be no question of 'competition between God's praise and man's need' (Berkouwer).

A doxological theology, written in 'the language of worship' (A. W. Tozer), seeks to 'join the language of the heart to the words of the intellect' (E. P. Heideman). The endeavour to 'marry the spirit of enquiry with that of devotion' (A. P. F. Sell) aims at emphasizing 'the praise of God in worship, doctrine and life' (G. Wainwright). The nature of 'doxological theology' is well-expressed by Berkouwer's emphasis (characteristic of his approach in his *Studies in Dogmatics*) that 'in doctrine a song of praise sounds forth'. Indeed all theology should exemplify the principle that 'the work of theology must be climaxed . . . with a doxology to the God of grace' (L. B. Smedes).

See also: LITURGICAL THEOLOGY.

Bibliography

G. C. Berkouwer, *Studies in Dogmatics*, 14 vols. (Grand Rapids, MI, 1952–75); E. P. Heideman, *Our Song of Hope* (Grand Rapids, MI, 1975); E. Schlink, *The Coming Christ and the Coming Church* (Edinburgh, 1967); A. P. F. Sell, *God our Father* (Edinburgh, 1980); L. B. Smedes, 'G. C. Berkouwer' in P. E. Hughes (ed.), *Creative Minds in Contemporary Theology* (Grand Rapids, MI, 1969); A. W. Tozer, *The Knowledge of the Holy* (London, 1965); G. Wainwright, *Doxology* (London, 1980).

C.M.C.

DUALISM. A dualism exists when there are two substances, or powers, or modes, neither of which is reducible to the other. Dualism is to be distinguished from monism,* according to which there is only one substance, power or mode. In philosophical argument, the advantages of accounting for the diversity of human experience by positing a dualism (for example, a dualism of the mind and the body as two irreducible types of substance) must be weighed against the problems of how the two sorts of substance are to be related (*e.g.*, how can a non-physical mind causally influence a physical body, and *vice versa?*).

In Christian theology it is possible to discern at least four different contexts in which it seems necessary to affirm or deny some form of dualism.

1. *God and the creation.* It would be a profound mistake to identify God with his creation,* in either metaphysical pantheistic* or mystical* fashion. God is distinct from his creation; he is its ground and (unlike in deism*) its sustaining cause, being both transcendent beyond it and immanent within it. How God acts as this sustaining cause gives rise to profound difficulties, *e.g.*, over the relation between divine and human action. These are best dealt with by indicating what God's relation to the creation does *not* imply, *e.g.* that God is the author of sin.

2. *The mind and the body.* While Scripture indicates that human beings are unities (see Anthropology*), and that the body is not related to the soul or mind as a person is to the car he is driving, nevertheless it is hard to avoid some version of dualism in the face of the biblical teaching that a person survives the death of his body (2 Cor. 5:1–10). For if such survival takes place, what survives must be non-physical, the Paul who longed to be 'with Christ' (Phil. 1:23; see Intermediate State*). The monisms of both materialism* and idealism* seem to be ruled out by these data.

3. *Moral and physical evil.* Attempts are made to account for moral and physical evil* by positing two principles, one of good and the other evil, locked together in conflict. Christian theology rejects such a dualism, characteristic of, *e.g.*, Zoroastrianism,* and accounts for such evils by a voluntary (and in the Augustinian* tradition God-ordained) human fall.* Evils occur either by God's permission, as in the story of Job, or by God's own agency, as in the stories of the punishment of the cities of the plain. And sin and evil are conquered by the work of Christ (1 Cor. 15:52–57).

4. *Revelation and reason.* The source of the saving knowledge of Christ is divine revelation, while the knowledge that, for example, London is the capital of the UK, is not from revelation but from reason and sense experience. It is characteristic of theological rationalism to suppose that Scripture is a republi-cation of truths otherwise discernible by reason, and of some forms of 'positivism of revelation' to suppose that all knowledge is ultimately derivable from Scripture. Both alike are to be resisted, and a dualism of revelation and reason, with all its attendant problems, is to be retained.

Bibliography

R. Descartes, *Meditations of the First Philosophy* (1641; many reprints); T. S. L. Sprigge, *Theories of Existence* (Harmondsworth, 1984).

P.H.

DUNS SCOTUS, JOHN (1255/6–1308). Born in Scotland, at Maxton-on-Tweed or Duns, Duns Scotus was accepted for the Franciscan* order at the age of fifteen. In 1291 he was ordained priest, having studied theology, probably at Oxford and at Paris, where he also studied between 1294 and 1297. By 1302 he was teaching at Paris, having already taught at Oxford and Cambridge. But the following year he was forced to leave Paris and return to Oxford. In 1304 he returned to Paris, to resume his teaching. But again his stay was brief; in 1307 he was transferred to Cologne, where he taught at the Franciscan House of Studies until his premature death.

Because Duns died young, he never wrote a *Summa Theologica.* He wrote two commentaries on Peter Lombard's* *Sentences*, of which the *Opus Oxoniense* (*Oxford Work*), a synthesis of his various sets of lectures on the *Sentences*, is his most important work, outlining his thought as a whole. Unfortunately he did not live to revise it fully and this task was continued by his disciples. The modern critical edition seeks to restore it to the form in which Duns himself left it. Duns's second most important work, and probably his last, is his *Quaestiones Quodlibetales* (*Various Questions*). This is clearer and more methodical than his earlier works and so provides a valuable supplement to the *Opus Oxoniense.* Duns's writings are not easy to read, due partly to his style and partly to the fact that he died before he could present his thought in a definitive form. Their difficulty earned him the title 'Subtle Doctor'. The 16th-century humanists and Reformers were less polite and coined the word 'dunce' from his name.

As a Franciscan, Duns followed in the Augustinian* tradition of Bonaventura.* He attacked the rival Aristotelian* tradition, especially the teaching of Thomas Aquinas.* But Duns was not an uncritical supporter of the Franciscan tradition. He revised it in the light of Aristotelian philosophy, rejecting Bonaventura's theory of divine illumination, for instance.

Thomas believed in the primacy of reason and knowledge over the will.* The will follows what reason presents to it as the highest good. God's will can therefore be explained by the use of reason. Duns by contrast stressed the primacy of the will. Reason shows the will what is possible, but the will is free to choose whichever option it wants to. The freedom of the will means that it does not simply follow whatever reason dictates.

Two major implications follow from this. Duns stressed the freedom of God. Things are the way that they are, not because reason requires it, but because God freely chose it. But God's will is not arbitrary or beyond all constraint. He cannot contradict himself, for instance. One aspect of God's freedom lies in his predestination.* First he predestines Peter (representing the elect) to eternal glory. Secondly he decides to give Peter the means to this end – grace. Thirdly he permits both Peter and Judas (representing the reprobate) to sin. Finally Peter is saved by God's grace, while Judas is justly rejected because he perseveres in sin.

Duns's stress on the freedom of God means that the role of reason and philosophy is necessarily limited. While earlier apologists, such as Anselm,* had sought to demonstrate rationally that the incarnation and the cross *had* to happen, Duns held that they happened because God *chose* that they should. This emphasized God's freedom, but also limited the possibility of showing such doctrines to be reasonable. In his stress on God's freedom, Duns went so far as to suggest that the Son would have become incarnate even had man not sinned, thus making the incarnation a free choice on God's part, not a necessity imposed upon him by man's sin. Duns believed that reason and philosophy could prove God's existence and some of his attributes. But much that Thomas believed to be demonstrable by reason (God's goodness, justice, mercy, predestination) Duns held to be known only

by revelation. Such doctrines are accepted by faith alone, not proved by reason. But Duns agreed with Thomas that the truths of theology are never *contrary* to reason.

Duns is famous as the first major advocate of the doctrine of Mary's* immaculate conception. The predominant view at this time was that Mary had been freed from sin *after* her conception, but before her birth. Duns was the one who began to turn the tide, and he did this in a way that was remarkable for one with so little confidence in the power of reason to tell us about God. He argued that it is more perfect to preserve someone from original sin than to liberate them from it. Jesus Christ, as the perfect redeemer, must have redeemed someone in the most perfect way possible – and who more fittingly than his mother? By presenting Mary's immaculate conception as the most perfect form of redemption, Duns defused the major objection to the doctrine: that it would mean that Mary did not need redemption. He himself claimed no more for the immaculate conception than its *probability*. But he argued that if there are a number of options, all of which are consistent with the teaching of Scripture and the church, that one is to be chosen which ascribes the most glory to Mary. This principle, in addition to his argument for the immaculate conception, is of great value to those who wish to further the growth of Mariology, and Duns has been duly rewarded with the title 'Marian Doctor'.

See also: FAITH AND REASON.

Bibliography
Critical edition: C. Balic (ed.), *Opera Omnia* (Vatican City, 1950ff.).

E. Bettoni, *Duns Scotus: The Basic Principles of his Philosophy* (Washington, DC, 1961); J. K. Ryan and B. M. Bonansea (eds.), *John Duns Scotus 1265–1965* (Washington, DC, 1965).

A.N.S.L.

DURKHEIM, EMILE (1858–1917), French sociologist in the positivist* tradition, generally regarded, with Max Weber,* as a founder of modern sociological* theory. His most significant work on religion was *The Elementary Forms of the Religious Life* (1912). He argued that one of the basic characteristics of religion is the classification of all things into two categories, the sacred and the profane. 'Beliefs, myths, dogmas and legends are . . . representations which express the nature of sacred things' (*The Elementary Forms*, p. 37). These representations are also collective since they arise from human experience in society. The primal type of a 'collective representation' is the totem which is 'at once the symbol of the god and of the society' which means that 'the god and the society are only one' (p. 206). The symbols are created as a result of collective emotion, which means that Durkheim, who was influenced in this by W. Robertson Smith (1846–94), emphasized the primacy of ritual over myth* in the formation of religious traditions. Durkheim's views had some direct, if ephemeral, influence on biblical studies through the work of scholars such as A. Lods (1867–1948) and C. A. H. Guignebert (1867–1939), but he is more significant as the fountainhead of the sociological way of viewing religion in terms of its function, which has become a part of contemporary thought and with which contemporary theology has to come to terms.

Bibliography
The Elementary Forms of the Religious Life, tr. J. W. Swain (London, 1915); G. Baum, 'Definitions of Religion in Sociology' in *What is Religion?*, ed. M. Eliade and D. Tracy (*Concilium* 136, 1980), pp. 25–32; S. Lukes, *Emile Durkheim* (Harmondsworth, 1973); J. Macquarrie, *Twentieth-Century Religious Thought* (London, 1963); W. S. F. Pickering, *Durkheim's Sociology of Religion: Themes and Theories* (London, 1984); K. H. Wolff (ed.), *Emile Durkheim 1858–1917* (Columbus, OH, 1960).

D.A.Hu.

DUTCH REFORMED THEOLOGY. As the epithet 'Dutch' implies, Dutch Reformed theology had its origins in the Reformation* in the Netherlands. The early Dutch settlers, who came to the refreshment post established at the most southern point of Africa to supply ships on their trade route to the East, transplanted the Dutch Reformed Church from Dutch soil to African soil. For almost two centuries this theology developed in close contact with and along similar lines to Reformed* theology in Holland. The three earliest Christian ecumenical confessions (*i.e.* the Apostles', the Nicene and the Athanasian creeds) together with three Protestant confessions* of faith (*viz.* the Belgic Confession, the Heidelberg Catechism and the Canons of Dort*) formed its confessional basis. It is still mandatory for at least twelve sermons on the Heidelberg Catechism to be preached annually in all congregations of the Dutch Reformed Church, and a summary of the Catechism is still used in preparing catechumens for church membership.

When Britain finally took over the Dutch colony at the Cape in 1806, Presbyterian ministers from Scotland were imported to serve the Dutch Reformed Church with the intention of influencing the White inhabitants. This, in turn, introduced a strong evangelical-Puritan* type of Scottish Presbyterian theology, directed more at Scripture and its direct implications for the personal life of the individual, into the more confession-orientated Dutch Reformed theology, which tended to centre upon the teaching of the church and its way of existence. Under Andrew Murray,* in particular, this influence increased and spread, eventually turning Dutch Reformed theology into a strong evangelical, Puritan and conservative type of Reformed theology.

After the Anglo-Boer War early in the 20th century, the Dutch Reformed Church in the northern provinces (the Orange Free State and the Transvaal) identified strongly with the downtrodden Boers (Afrikaner people). Consequently Dutch Reformed theology became more people-orientated, which may be interpreted as a form of indigenization. Dutch Reformed theology gradually became deeply embedded in the newly awakened and growing nationalism of the white Afrikaans-speaking (Afrikaner) section of the South African population and subsequently developed in isolation from the rest of the country.

In the early 1930s the Dutch Reformed Church in South Africa experienced a severe theological crisis when a professor at the theological seminary for the training of ministers was accused of heresy concerning the divine/human nature of Christ. As a result of this controversy, most of the theological students started to go to the Free University of Amsterdam instead of the University of Utrecht, where the majority had previously studied. The Free University of Amsterdam was considered to be more orthodox in its theological teaching. It was started by Abraham Kuyper,* who represented a strong

213

confessional type of Reformed theology. The university stressed the confessional aspect of Reformed theology rather than the existing evangelical/Puritan types.

One aspect of confessional Reformed theology in particular, which developed strongly in the late 1930s, was the emphasis on the pluriformity in creation as stressed by Abraham Kuyper. This emphasis in Dutch Reformed theology eventually supplied the main motivation and justification for apartheid – the separation of races* in South Africa. Kuyper had strongly emphasized the variety in the created order. He insisted that because God loved this variety it must be preserved. This element in his theological thinking had a profound influence on some professors of theology in Holland, and it also found fertile ground in which to grow in South Africa. Variety was seen also to apply to people, and was given biblical sanction, it was believed, in the division of people at Babel and by Paul's words in Acts 17:26. The essence of pluriformity was that God created mankind as pluriform as the rest of creation. Therefore each race has a God-given responsibility to maintain its identity.

Another aspect of Dutch Reformed theology which should be mentioned is that it developed *in* Africa but in total isolation *from* Africa. The separation between Westerners and Africans (whites and blacks) caused this theology to remain almost purely Western with very little African influence. Dutch Reformed theology thus lost relevance for the African context in which it developed. A multiracial education in Reformed theology may eventually turn Dutch Reformed theology into African Reformed theology, which will certainly contribute significantly towards the Christianization of the African context (see Contextualization*).

Bibliography

L. Cawood, *The Churches and Race Relations in South Africa* (Johannesburg, 1964); J. W. De Gruchy, *The Church Struggle in South Africa* (Cape Town, 1979); W. A. Landman, *A Plea for Understanding: a Reply to the Reformed Church in America* (Cape Town, 1968); *Reply of the Dutch Reformed Church to the Report of the General Synod of Haarlem, 1973–1975, in Connection with the 'Programme to Combat Racism'* (Cape Town and Pretoria, 1976); J. M. Sales, *The Planting of the Churches in South Africa* (Grand Rapids, MI, 1971); J. H. P. Serfontein, *Apartheid, Change and the N. G. Kerk* (Johannesburg, 1982).

N.J.S.

DYOTHELITISM, see CHRISTOLOGY.

E

EASTER (in Gk. *pascha*, which also means Passover). The earliest and greatest annual festival of the Christian calendar.* On the basis of the evidence quoted by Eusebius (*EH* 4.24.1–8), its existence can certainly be traced back to the time of Anicetus and Polycarp (*c.* 155) and probably to the time of the birth of Polycrates (*c.* 125). The reference in *Epistle of the Apostles* 15 may also date from *c.* 125. It is likely that the festival arose at Antioch *c.* 110, out of the weekly commemoration of Christ's resurrection on Sunday, the intention being to give special prominence to that Sunday which fell nearest to the actual season of the resurrection, *i.e.* the Sunday next after the Jewish Passover on 14 Nisan.

In the 2nd century, the small province of Asia observed Easter on 14 Nisan itself, whereas virtually the whole of the Christian world outside observed it on the Sunday following, and this has given rise to an alternative explanation of the origin of Easter. It has been supposed, notably by B. Lohse, that the practice of the province of Asia was the original Christian practice, and was a continuation of the observance of the Passover itself by Jewish Christians in NT times. However, it is very hard to understand why Jewish-Christian practice should have been preserved in Asia (a largely Gentile area, evangelized by the author of Col. 2:16–17 and Gal. 4:9–11) but not in Palestine or Syria (where there were more Jews than anywhere else, and where Jewish Christianity had its centre). So it is better to see the practice of Asia as presupposing the existence of Easter Sunday, and as an attempt to achieve greater precision than the rest of the Christian world, by transferring Easter from the Sunday after the Passover to the Passover itself. There is no evidence, incidentally, for the hypothesis that the church of

Asia was celebrating Christ's death and the rest of the church his resurrection. The ancient Easter day celebrated both events (the separate Good Friday first appears in the 4th century).

The practice of Asia gave rise to an internal controversy between Melito and Claudius Apollinaris (c. 150–60) and to the world-wide Quartodeciman ('about the fourteenth') controversy (c. 190) in which the non-Asian view prevailed. Up to this point, all Christians dated Easter by following the decision made each year by the Jews about the Passover, which was still being fixed by observation; so they kept Easter either on the Sunday following the Jewish festival or (in Asia) on the actual Jewish festival day. However, since this dependence aroused Jewish mockery, in the 3rd century Christians began to fix Easter independently, by astronomical calculation. The problem they faced was to reconcile the Jewish lunar year with the standard solar year of the Roman Empire. For this purpose the Roman church used a doubled 8–year cycle, and later an 84–year cycle, while the Alexandrian church used the Metonic cycle of 19 years, which was the most accurate of the three, and ultimately prevailed everywhere. In the meantime, however, the second great Easter controversy arose, between those who had begun to fix Easter astronomically, and those who continued to be guided by Jewish practice, and to hold it on the Sunday after the Passover. This controversy (often confused with the Quartodeciman, causing Quartodecimanism to be thought more lasting and widespread than it was) was resolved in principle by the Council of Nicaea in 325, the decision being in favour of the new method. The dissidents this time were not the church of Asia but the churches of Syria, Cilicia and Mesopotamia.

The subsequent Easter controversies arose from the different methods of calculating Easter. The 7th-century controversy over the Celtic Easter was due to the Celtic churches having retained the 84–year cycle after Rome had abandoned it. The controversy extending from the 16th century to our own day over the Julian and Gregorian calendars is due to the slight but accumulating inaccuracy in the Roman solar year, as established by Julius Caesar. By 1582 this had become significant enough for Pope Gregory XIII to have it corrected, but churches out of communion with Rome were naturally slow in adopting his reform. It was not adopted in England until 1752, when new Easter tables were introduced into the *Book of Common Prayer*; many of the Eastern churches have still not adopted it. Since Easter is a movable festival, related to the moon, it coincides in the Julian and Gregorian calendars about once every three years; but the fixed festivals, such as Christmas, now fall thirteen days later in the Julian calendar than in the Gregorian. The modern secular concept of a *fixed* Easter, which would mean abandoning the Jewish lunar year altogether, has met with some degree of favour in the Western churches but none in the Eastern, where the only interest is in an *agreed* Easter.

Already in the 2nd century the Easter celebrations were being continued over the following seven weeks, and a preparatory period of one or more days of fasting (the ultimate source of the later Lent) was also being added. The uniquely early origin of Easter, the scale of its celebrations, and the heat with which its date was debated, all bear witness to the unrivalled importance of Christ's death and resurrection (the actual fulfilment of the ancient *pascha*) in primitive Christian thinking.

Bibliography

R. T. Beckwith, 'The Origin of the Festivals Easter and Whitsun', *SL* 13 (1979), pp. 1–20; J. G. Davies, *Holy Week* (London, 1963); A. A. McArthur, *The Evolution of the Christian Year* (London, 1953); T. Talley, 'Liturgical Times in the Ancient Church: the State of Research', *SL* 14 (1982), pp. 34–51.

R.T.B.

EASTERN ORTHODOX THEOLOGY. The theology of the churches in communion with the patriarchate of Constantinople (Istanbul). These include the national churches of Greece, Cyprus, Bulgaria, Romania, Serbia, Russia and Georgia, as well as the ancient patriarchates of Antioch, Jerusalem and Damascus. There are smaller Orthodox churches in a number of other countries, notably the USA, Britain and France, though these are composed mainly of immigrants and expatriates from Orthodox countries.

History

The historical development of Eastern Orthodox theology can be conveniently divided into five main stages. The first of these is the *pre-Chalcedonian period* (to 451). During this time the foundation of later Orthodoxy was laid in the writings of the Greek fathers, of whom the most notable are Athanasius,* John Chrysostom (*c.* 344/354–407), Cyril of Alexandria* and the 'Three Hierarchs', known in the West as the Cappadocian Fathers. These are Basil the Great,* of Caesarea, Gregory the Theologian, of Nazianzus,* and Basil's brother, Gregory of Nyssa.* These men, most of whom were virtually contemporaries, expounded the theology of the first ecumenical council, held at Nicaea in 325, and ensured that their interpretation would carry the day at the Second (Constantinople, 381) and Third (Ephesus, 431). The main influence came from the Alexandrian* school of theology, which strongly emphasized the unity of the divine Christ, both before and after his incarnation.* There was also a great development of Trinitarian* theology, largely thanks to Basil of Caesarea. The period ends with the fourth ecumenical council, held at Chalcedon in 451. There the doctrine of Christ as one divine person in two natures, one human and one divine, was upheld (see Christology*), in spite of the objections of the Alexandrians (who favoured a doctrine of one nature in Christ), and the Nestorians* (who regarded the person as the result, not the cause, of the incarnation). After Chalcedon these groups split off to become the Nestorian Church, now a very small body of 50,000 members, and the Monophysite* Church, known in Egypt as Coptic* and in Syria as Jacobite (after its 6th-century leader, Jacob Baradaeus). These churches still flourish, both in their countries of origin and in areas where they have spread, notably Ethiopia* (Coptic) and South India (Jacobite).

The next phase was the *early Byzantine period* (451–843). This was dominated by Christological controversy, first against the Monophysites, and then against the iconoclasts.* The fifth ecumenical council (Constantinople, 553) tried to reconcile the churches of Egypt and Syria, but without success, and the attempt was formally abandoned at the sixth council (Constantinople, 680). The seventh and, in Orthodox eyes, last ecumenical council (Nicaea, 787) condemned the iconoclasts. The leading theologians of this period were Leontius of Byzantium (see Hypostasis*) and his namesake Leontius of Jerusalem (both 6th century), Maximus the Confessor* and John of Damascus.* They gave Orthodox Christology a shape which reflects a deep and sophisticated appropriation of the dogmatic pronouncements of the Council of Chalcedon. The period is also notable for the development of Orthodox spirituality, especially the veneration of icons, the great liturgies, and the canonical regulations which govern the church's life. These were codified at the so-called Quinisext Council, or Synod *in Trullo*, held at Constantinople in 691–92. The canons regulated such practices as clerical marriage, and the use of leavened bread in the eucharist, which were rejected by the Western church. Many of the visible differences between Orthodoxy and Roman Catholicism can be traced to the canons of this council.

The third stage may be called the *late Byzantine period* (843–1452). During this time, Orthodoxy engaged in increasingly bitter polemic against Western theology and, as a counterweight to it, developed tendencies which were latent in the Eastern tradition. The main cause of dispute was the *Filioque* clause, added to the Nicene Creed in the 6th century in Spain, and adopted officially at Rome *c.* 1014. The addition raised the question of papal authority in matters of doctrine, as well as the theological issue of the double procession of the Holy Spirit.* Photius, Patriarch of Constantinople from 858–67 and again from 880–86, led the opposition to the *Filioque* clause, and his views are still repeated by Orthodox theologians today. On a more positive note, the period also witnessed a remarkable spiritual revival, which bore fruit first in the conversion of the Slavs (850–1000) and then in the practice of devotional meditation. The great names whose counsels are still followed by Orthodox monks today are Symeon the New Theologian (949–1022) and Gregory Palamas (*c.* 1296–1359). The latter championed a monastic movement known as Hesychasm,* which practised a system of spiritual exercises not unlike yoga. This was bitterly resisted by Westernizing influences at Constantinople, but was declared to be orthodox in 1351. The Westernizers, who had been gaining in strength since the abortive union of the churches at the Council of Lyons in 1274, were now put on the defensive. A second union was promulgated at the Council of Florence in 1439, but it was never popular and was abandoned after Constantinople fell to the Turks in 1453.

Ironically it was during the period of *Turkish domination* (1453–1821) that Western influence reached its peak in the Orthodox world. After the Reformation, all parties courted the Eastern churches, who were able to send many of their students to be educated in the West. This did not win Orthodoxy either to Rome or to the Protestant cause, but it made Orthodox theologians much more Western in their theological method and interests. In the 17th century, the Patriarch successively of Alexandria and Constantinople, Cyril Lucaris (1572–1638), composed a Calvinistic confession* of faith, which was published at Geneva in 1629. This provoked a Catholicizing reaction, which can be seen in the Confessions of Peter Mogila (1596–1646) and Dositheus of Jerusalem (1641–1707). Both these confessions are now regarded as more faithful to Orthodoxy than that of Lucaris, but many modern Orthodox reject them because they reflect a theological method which is foreign to the Eastern tradition.

The *modern period* (1821 to the present) is characterized chiefly by a recovery of the monastic traditions of Byzantine Orthodoxy and by the struggle of the church against persecution from both communism and Islam. During the 19th century, the established theological tradition of both Greece and Russia was almost completely subservient to German liberal Protestantism, and this trend has continued to some extent up to the present time. There developed an Orthodox dogmatic theology modelled on the West, as can be seen in the works of Chrestos Androutsos (1869–1937), J. Karmiris (b. 1904) and P. N. Trembelas (1886–1977; *Dogmatique de l'église orthodoxe catholique*, 3 vols., Chevetogne, 1966–68). An almost heretical mysticism* characterizes the leading Russian* theologians of the period, notably Alexis Khomiakov (1804–60) and Sergei Bulgakov (1871–1944). These trends have produced a reaction, however, which is now very powerful. Beginning in the 18th century, with the edition of patristic texts known as the *Philokalia*, monastic ideas began to revive in the Orthodox world. These have borne fruit in the 20th-century revival of neo-Byzantinism, associated with the work of the Russians, Vladimir Lossky (1903–58) and John Meyendorff (b. 1926) and with the Romanian theologian Dumitru Staniloae (b. 1903). At the present time, Orthodoxy is torn between liberal and conservative tendencies, with the latter appearing to be gaining the upper hand.

Characteristics

Orthodox theology differs from both Roman and Protestant teaching in a number of important respects. In general terms, it relies more on the philosophical base of Neoplatonism (see Platonism*), which the West in the main abandoned in the 13th century. It has a strongly mystical flavour, and fights shy of dogmatic definition as much as it can. Its authority is derived from 'tradition', which includes both the Scriptures, decisions of the councils,* especially the Nicene Creed,* and the Greek fathers. The Latin fathers before the 11th century are honoured as part of this tradition as well, but in practice they are ignored. Also important are the testimony of the liturgies, which have not changed for over a thousand years, and the veneration of icons, which is much more 'theological' in tone than any comparable devotion in the West.

The Orthodox doctrine of the Trinity* is superficially the same as the Western one, with the exception of the *Filioque* clause, but in conception it is very different. The Orthodox put the primary stress on the persons of the Godhead, and tend to regard the Father as the hypostatization* of the divine essence. He is the unique fountainhead of Deity (*pēgē tēs theotētos*), which explains why the Orthodox cannot accept that the Holy Spirit derives his being from the Son as well as from the Father. They also place great emphasis on the energies of God, a concept which is strange to Western minds. The Holy Spirit, for example, is said to proceed from the Father but to rest on the Son, whose energy he becomes. The concept is analogous to the Catholic notion of grace, though the Orthodox insist that they do not see the divine energy as a substance which can be infused into the believer.

This naturally affects their doctrine of sanctification, and their sacramental theology. Orthodox believe in baptismal regeneration, and administer chrismation (confirmation)

217

and Holy Communion to the newly baptized, including infants. They believe that the Holy Spirit descends on the elements of bread and wine by liturgical invocation (*epiclēsis*; see Eucharist*), but resist Roman Catholic ideas of transubstantiation. The believer is called to a life of deification,* which means transfiguration into the image and likeness of God. The supreme manifestation of this can be found in the ecstasy of the contemplative life, which occupies a much more important place in Orthodox spirituality than it does in Roman Catholicism.

By Western standards, Orthodoxy has a weak doctrine of sin* and atonement.* Sin is regarded as the effect of death and finitude, not as its cause. Salvation therefore tends to be seen primarily in terms of freedom from death, not as a release from guilt. In modern times this soteriology has made a great impact on Western theologians who for various reasons have recoiled from the Reformed doctrine of the atonement, and its influence can be seen in recent liturgical revisions.

Since 1961, Orthodox churches have participated in the World Council of Churches, which has forced them to take an interest in other kinds of theology. They have established very friendly relations with the non-Chalcedonian churches of the East, and have made some moves in the direction of Rome and the Protestant churches as well. On the whole, however, they remain by far the most closed of the major branches of Christendom. At the WCC their influence has mostly been exercised in favour of a more theological approach, and against political involvement. Today creative Orthodox thinking is more vital than at any time since the 14th century, and it offers itself as a conservative challenge to Western Christendom. There are a number of signs that its influence may be growing, and it is certain to become a major force in ecumenical circles in the future.

Bibliography

V. Lossky, *The Mystical Theology of the Eastern Church* (Cambridge, 1957); G. A. Maloney, *A History of Orthodox Theology since 1453* (Belmont, MA, 1976); J. Meyendorff, *Byzantine Theology* (London, 1974); T. Ware, *The Orthodox Church* (London, 1963).

G.L.B.

EBELING, GERHARD (b. 1912), German theologian. Ebeling studied theology at Marburg under Bultmann,* at Zurich with Brunner* and at Berlin. After a time as a colleague of Bonhoeffer* in the theological seminary at Finkenwald (1936–37), he took charge of a provisional congregation of the Confessing Church in Berlin. In 1946 he became Professor of Church History in Tübingen, moving to Systematic Theology in 1954. Two years later he transferred to Zurich to the chair of Systematic Theology, History of Theology and Symbolics. Here he founded the Institute of Hermeneutics (1962), finally retiring, as Professor of Fundamental Theology and Hermeneutics, in 1979.

Ebeling's theological thought shows him to be indebted equally to Luther* and Schleiermacher.* His unusually wide-ranging (historical, exegetical, dogmatic) monographs all concentrate on the attempt to interpret the relationship between God, man and the world as a continuum of living reality, to be experienced, understood and articulated by faith. His *Dogmatik des christlichen Glaubens* (*Dogmatics of the Christian Faith*, 3 vols., Tübingen, 1979) offers the Bultmann school's first substantial, systematic conspectus. In it Ebeling not only inculcates the basic and essential theological differentiations (*e.g.* between God and the world, visible and eternal life, political and evangelical use of biblical teaching), but also, with noteworthy impressiveness, makes us conscious that the proof of all Christian theology is prayer.

Bibliography

Many works in ET, including: *God and Word* (Philadelphia, 1967); *Introduction to a Theological Theory of Language* (London, 1973); *Luther: An Introduction to His Thought* (London, 1970); *Word and Faith* (London, 1963); *The Word of God and Tradition* (London, 1968).

Ebeling is one of the editors of the Weimar edition of Luther's works (*Weimarer Ausgabe*) and of a complete edition of Schleiermacher.

S. P. Schilling, *Contemporary Continental Theologians* (London, 1966), ch. 6.

R.E.F.

ECCLESIOLOGY, see Church.

ECKHART, see Mystical Theology.

ECOLOGY, see NATURE, THEOLOGY OF.

E CUMENICAL MOVEMENT. Theological discussion has featured prominently in the quest for church unity which has loomed large in 20th-century Christianity. After the stimulus of the Edinburgh Missionary Conference (1910), the concern to confront divisive issues of doctrine, polity and practice gave birth to the Faith and Order movement, of which the leading midwife was the American Episcopalian, Bishop Charles H. Brent (1862–1929). After a preliminary meeting at Geneva in 1920, the first world conference on Faith and Order convened at Lausanne in 1927. Whereas Edinburgh was a gathering of missionary societies, Lausanne was formally an inter-church assembly, with some 90 churches represented but not including the Roman and the Russian Orthodox Churches and most of the evangelical churches. The next milestone was the second Faith and Order conference at Edinburgh in 1937, when representatives of 123 churches met under the presidency of William Temple (1881–1944), Archbishop of Canterbury. Both of these conferences discussed ministry and sacraments among other central themes.

The Edinburgh assembly endorsed a proposal for a World Council of Churches, which came into being, after delay occasioned by World War II, at Amsterdam in 1948. The Faith and Order Commission became one of the main agencies of the WCC, reporting to its plenary assemblies at Evanston, Illinois (1954), New Delhi (1961), Uppsala (1968), Nairobi (1975) and Vancouver (1983). Membership multiplied from 147 churches at Amsterdam to 301 at Vancouver. At New Delhi the Russian Orthodox and the first Pentecostal churches joined the Council. Since New Delhi, official Roman Catholic observers have played an increasingly full part in WCC affairs, not least in Faith and Order, in the more open atmosphere fostered by Vatican II (1962–5). International Faith and Order conferences have continued to be held, notably at Lund (1952) and Montreal (1963). A meeting at Lima in 1982 finalized the important consensus on *Baptism, Eucharist and Ministry* (Geneva, 1982), as part of a programme to reach an agreed presentation of the apostolic faith for today. This report represents the restoration of Faith and Order to a central place in WCC concerns, after their virtual eclipse, in the period of the Uppsala assembly, by its preoccupation with economic, political and social issues.

Ecumenism is, of course, not restricted to the WCC. In recent years, bilateral conversations have been taking place between major traditions at a world level, the best-known being the Anglican-Roman Catholic International Commission (*ARCIC: The Final Report*, London, 1982; *ARCIC II: Salvation and the Church*, London, 1987 – on justification). Others have included Anglican and Reformed (*God's Reign and Our Unity*, London and Edinburgh, 1984) and Baptist and Reformed (*Baptists and Reformed in Dialogue*, Geneva, 1984). For yet others see H. Meyer and L. Vischer, *Growth in Agreement: Reports and Agreed Statements of Ecumenical Conversations on a World Level* (Ramsey, NJ, and Geneva, 1984).

The WCC's original basis declared it to be 'a fellowship of churches which accept our Lord Jesus Christ as God and Saviour'. This limited (and easily criticized) confession was enlarged at New Delhi to read 'a fellowship of churches which confess the Lord Jesus Christ as God and Saviour according to the Scriptures, and therefore seek to fulfil together their common calling to the glory of the one God, Father, Son and Holy Spirit'.

Because of the variety of participant traditions, with their differing confessional standpoints, especially on where authority lies in matters of faith, ecumenical theological agreement has often seemed to require formulations capable of being understood in different, if not irreconcilable, senses. At the same time, the study of theology has become, in the second half of the 20th century, increasingly an ecumenical activity, with co-operation and interaction between scholars of different traditions so commonplace that confessional distinctives have steadily diminished. Ecumenical engagement has made churches more self-critical and more aware of the non-theological factors that have helped to shape their own inherited positions. The Montreal conference produced a useful clarification of the relation beween tradition (in different senses) and Scripture (P. C. Rodger and L. Vischer, eds., *The Fourth World Conference on Faith and Order*, London, 1964).

219

Ministerial order has proved an intractable problem. Lausanne affirmed, and Edinburgh endorsed, an influential declaration that episcopal, presbyteral and congregational elements must all feature in a reunited church, but this conclusion was reached without regard to biblical or theological criteria (and indeed, without regard to its feasibility. Cf. the critique of Ian Henderson, *Power Without Glory: A Study in Ecumenical Politics*, London, 1967). The adoption of episcopacy (see Church Government*) remains the most crucial change expected of non-episcopal churches, but the case for it tends to rest less and less on concepts of apostolic succession (see Ministry*) and 'the historic episcopate', and more and more on pragmatic grounds. While this trend mitigates the offensiveness of episcopacy, its advocacy makes it answerable at the bar of pragmatic reason, as well as to biblical and historical theology. Nevertheless, the measure of clarification attainable in ecumenical debate is evident in ARCIC's recognition that 'the New Testament contains no explicit record of a transmission of Peter's leadership; nor is the transmission of apostolic authority in general very clear' (*The Final Report*, p. 83).

Evangelical churchmen have repeatedly criticized ecumenical theology on several grounds: the imprecision of its language (*e.g.* in *Baptism, Eucharist and Ministry*, where many indicative statements express ideals or aspirations rather than realities); its abuse of biblical terms and concepts (starkly exemplified in Uppsala's use of 'Behold, I make all things new', Rev. 21:5, but frequently seen in the use of 'peace', 'salvation', 'life', *etc.*); its quest for consensus rather than truth, made inevitable by taking the churches' standpoints rather than the Bible as its basis (evident on baptism, with the tendency to accommodate both infant and believers' baptism as 'equivalent alternatives' within one church, rather than persist with the question whether infant baptism is biblical and primitive); the subtle pervasiveness of universalist* assumptions, tending to embrace other faiths in the pursuit of world community and so soft-pedal evangelism as liable to interfere with inter-religious dialogue (although *Mission and Evangelism: An Ecumenical Affirmation*, 1982, has been widely welcomed by evangelicals); political one-sidedness, with Marxist social analysis to the fore and the neglect of personal, as distinct from social, ethics; the justification of violent revolution* in some forms of liberation theology;* and excessive deference to feminism.*

At the Vancouver assembly, evangelical opinion was divided, although those opposed to continued evangelical participation were in the minority. Others noted that the influence of the Orthodox, now the largest confessional grouping in the WCC, made for greater attention to conservative biblical and theological beliefs. (It has also intensified the 'sacramentalizing' of approaches to baptism and the Lord's Supper.) An alternative, or complementary, evangelical ecumenism, born out of co-operation in evangelism, produced a significant manifesto in the Lausanne Covenant* of 1974. It has been followed by various international evangelical consultations which have made their own contribution to ecumenical theological debate, on issues such as the nature of salvation and the mission of the church.

See also: BERLIN DECLARATION; FRANKFURT DECLARATION.

Bibliography
G. K. A. Bell (ed.), *Documents on Christian Unity*, 4 vols. (Oxford, 1924–58); J. D. Douglas (ed.), *Evangelicals and Unity* (Appleford, 1964); E. Flesseman-van Leer (ed.), *The Bible: its Authority and Interpretation in the Ecumenical Movement* (Geneva, 1980), and see articles on this theme by R. T. Beckwith in *Churchman* 89 (1975), pp. 213–224, and P. G. Schrotenboer in *CTJ* 12 (1977), pp. 144–163; D. Gillies, *Revolt from the Church* (Belfast, 1980); H. T. Hoekstra, *Evangelism in Eclipse. World Mission and the World Council of Churches* (Exeter, 1979); D. A. McGavran (ed.), *The Conciliar-Evangelical Debate: the Crucial Documents 1964–1976* (Pasadena, CA, 1977); R. Rouse and S. C. Neill, *A History of the Ecumenical Movement:* vol. 1, *1517–1948* (London, ²1967), vol. 2, *The Ecumenical Advance 1948–68*, by H. E. Fey (London, 1970); A. J. van der Bent, *Major Studies and Themes in the Ecumenical Movement* (Geneva, 1981); L. Vischer (ed.), *A Documentary History of the Faith and Order Movement 1927–1963* (St Louis, MO, 1963).

D.F.W.

EDWARDS, JONATHAN (1703–58), American theologian and philosopher. Edwards was reared in a Christian home and culture, studying at Yale University. The first period of his ministry (in the Congregational Church, Northampton, MA, 1727–33) was a time of relative obscurity, followed by great popularity and success (1734–47), which ended with rejection (1750) and virtual burial in a little Indian outpost (Stockbridge, 1751–57) where he did his greatest work (*Freedom of the Will*; *Original Sin*; *End of Creation*; *True Virtue*). He was called to the presidency of the then nascent Princeton College shortly before his death.

According to Edwards' thought, 'nothing is more certain, than that there *must* be an unmade and unlimited being' (*The Insufficiency of Reason as a Substitute for Revelation*). *On Being* maintained that eternal being alone can be thought, and *Freedom of the Will* that 'we first prove *a posteriori* . . . there must be an eternal cause . . . and prove many of his perfections *a priori*'. In spite of this, apart from biblical revelation, man is 'naturally blind in the things of religion' (Sermon on Ps. 94:8f.). This is partly because of the complexity of metaphysical questions and mainly because of the noetic influence of sin. The Bible evidences its own inspiration by its shining 'bright with the amiable simplicity of truth' (*Observations on Scripture*), as well as in the external certification by its authors' God-enabled powers (*The Miracles of Jesus Not Counterfeited*).

By natural reason and Scripture God reveals his purpose in creating the world for his glory and therein the blessedness of his people (*End of Creation*), which consists in their disinterested benevolence toward his being-in-general (*Religious Affections; True Virtue*). Adam was first created upright but fell into temptation (not calling on the efficient grace available to him) and brought the race which was 'constituted' one with him into ruin (*Original Sin*). Through the covenanted work of the God-man (*On Satisfaction*), God redeems the elect (*Efficacious Grace*), leaving the non-elect to their inexcusable unbelief and judgment (*The Justice of God in the Damnation of Sinners*).

This work of Christ is brought to the elect usually through the preaching in which the Spirit arouses previously 'sottish' people (*Sinners in the Hands of an Angry God*) to 'seek' (*Pressing Into the Kingdom*; *Ruth's Resolution*). Of the many called few are the chosen. Only those who give a credible profession of faith and life are rightly admitted to and remain in the membership of the church* and are entitled to her sacraments* (*Qualifications for Communion*), others being barred or excommunicated (*The Nature and End of Excommunication*).

A general awakening that was occurring in the American colonies made Edwards believe the 'latter day' millennium* was dawning (*Thoughts on Revival*) which would be followed by the general judgment, conflagration, eternal hell and heaven (*The Portion of the Wicked*; *The Portion of the Righteous*). The awakening under Edwards, in addition to its immediate effects, had considerable power in preparing established churches for disestablishment after the American Revolution and, according to some scholars, in bringing about the Revolution itself. B. B. Warfield* thought that Edwards' defence of Calvinism had delayed the Arminian* conquest of New England for a hundred years.

Edwards is still regarded today as perhaps America's profoundest theological and philosophical mind. His *Works* are currently being edited for the Yale University Press (ed. P. Miller, New Haven, CT, 1957–).

See also: NEW ENGLAND THEOLOGY.

Bibliography

Works: many editions, *e.g.*, 2 vols. (Edinburgh, 1974–75); *cf.* H. T. Johnson, *The Printed Writings of Jonathan Edwards, 1703–1758: A Bibliography* (Princeton, NJ, 1940).

Best comprehensive study, O. E. Winslow, *Jonathan Edwards, 1703–1758: A Biography* (New York, 1940); C. Cherry, *The Theology of Jonathan Edwards. A Reappraisal* (New York, 1966); D. J. Elwood, *The Philosophical Theology of Jonathan Edwards* (New York, 1961); I. H. Murray, *Jonathan Edwards. A New Biography* (Edinburgh, 1987).

J.H.G.

ELECTION, see PREDESTINATION.

ELLUL, JACQUES (b. 1912). Historian, social scientist and lay theologian, Ellul was born in Bordeaux, France, and worked as a professor at the Institute of Political Studies in the university there. In his youth he was converted to the Christian faith, and he has been an active lay-preacher in the French Reformed Church.

His prolific writings fall into five categories:

1. *History.* He wrote an extensive history of institutions. 2. *Sociology.* In *The Technological Society*, his most important study, he examines the influence of 'modern technique' on all spheres of society as well on the human mind. Technique is considered an independent factor which functions in accordance with its own rules and which is developing into the 'technical system'. 3. *Social criticism.* He has proved himself to be a debunker of many a modern commonplace. For instance, he questions whether modern man has ever come of age and whether modern society has really become secular. In his view modern man is subject to the requirements of technique and believes his future and well-being are dependent on it, as if it were 'God himself'. 4. *Biblical studies.* Some remarkable commentaries deserve attention (Jonah, 2 Kings, Apocalypse). His (biblical) study on *The Meaning of the City* is fundamental to an understanding of his theological thinking. The city stands for civilization and is the outcome of the efforts of men to build a world without the living God, which includes systems of religion, of morals, of defence, of insurance, *etc.* Man is now doomed to live in this city, which is judged by God. However, the Christian knows that God has promised a transformation of the works of men. The end of history is marked not just by the terror of Babylon, but also by the coming of the New Jerusalem. 5. *Ethics.* These are based on 'the meaning of the city'. In his ethical works he attempts to escape the dangers of idealism, of moralism or of planning a sound society which can only lead to a well-ordered system which controls everything and everybody. What is left is the individual person, who is encouraged to be realistic about the situation he is in, determined by technical and political necessities, who is also encouraged to accept his responsibilities and to continue to hope for the impossible: true dialogue, righteousness, peace, freedom, love.

In this theological thinking, the influence of Karl Barth* is noticeable. Characteristic of his work is the dialectical tension between biblical revelation and modern technical consciousness. Also characteristic is his insistence on the importance of personal freedom and of the dialogue between God and the human person, which is continually obstructed by human systems.

Bibliography

The Technological Society (New York, 1964); *The Meaning of the City* (Grand Rapids, MI, 1970); *The Politics of God and the Politics of Man* (Grand Rapids, MI, 1972); *The Ethics of Freedom* (Grand Rapids, MI, 1976).

C. G. Christians and J. M. van Hook, *Jacques Ellul, Interpretive Essays* (Champaigne, IL, 1981); J. M. Hanks, assisted by R. Asal, *Jacques Ellul: A Comprehensive Bibliography* (Greenwich, CT, and London, 1984); B. Kristensen, 'Jacques Ellul', *CG* 29:4 (1976), pp. 106–110.

B.K.

EMPIRICISM is the view that the source of all knowledge is sense-experience. It is based on the common perception that our senses provide us with knowledge. Its roots stem from the ancient Greeks, but it flourished as a reaction to rationalism and its belief that reason was the basis of certain knowledge. In contrast, John Locke,* Bishop Berkeley* and David Hume* argued that all knowledge was based on the senses. This response was part of that critique of scepticism which operates by finding a source of absolutely certain knowledge. Hume divided what we know into matters of fact and relations of ideas. The realm of the *relation of ideas* is that of logic and mathematics. The truths of mathematics and logic are true by definition, necessary (*i.e.* they could not be false) and are known *a priori*. These truths are not part of the real world. In contrast, *matters of fact* stem from ordinary sense experience. They are contingently true – they could be otherwise. They are known only by direct experience and *a posteriori*. They give genuine knowledge of the way the world is, and may be used to check what is said and claimed on the basis of experience. Common sense claims that we have ideas and concepts as well as sense-experience. Hume argued that these ideas or concepts either are relations of ideas, or can be analysed into having sensations or reflecting on them. For Hume, impressions were the actual content of the mind in the moment of perception. Ideas were less vivid copies of impressions, which could be amalgamated into complex ideas by the imagination. In the end, however, empiricism claims that there is nothing in the mind which was not previously in the sense.

Modern empiricism

Empiricism provides an answer to the sceptic and a unified source of all knowledge. This has developed in two ways. The search for certainty has led to the analysis of experience into irreducible, infallible units of experience called sense-data. These are the raw basics of our experience (e.g. a reddish blur) about which we cannot be mistaken. This approach highlights the problems of the reality of the external world and of the self. Logical* positivism has turned empiricism into a search for meaning based on ostensive definition, which sees knowledge as like learning a language, in which we give a name and point out an object so that no other understanding is possible. Verifiability has been the other basis for meaning, in which a statement is meaningful if, and only if, it can be verified by sense-experience. This was modified and even became a 'Principle of Falsifiability', which based knowledge on the failure to disprove. Empiricism is still based on verification* by sense-experience, using the methods of the empirical and inductive sciences as a solution to scepticism. It has created doubt about the truth and validity of religious statements and doctrines, based on a narrow view of experience being reducible to sense experience alone.

Bibliography

A. J. Ayer, *The Problem of Knowledge* (Harmondsworth, 1971); D. Hume, *An Inquiry Concerning Human Understanding*, ed. L. A. Selby-Bigge (Oxford, ³1975); H. Morick (ed.), *Challenges to Empiricism* (Belmont, CA, 1972).

E.D.C.

ENHYPOSTASIA, see HYPOSTASIS.

ENLIGHTENMENT, THE. Between the close of the 17th and the 18th centuries, the intellectual history of Europe and America underwent such signal development that the whole age has been named after it. This is the era of Enlightenment. The Enlightenment varied from nation to nation; it took moderate or radical forms; one may speak of a 'High' or a 'Low' Enlightenment; and it also developed, rather than existing unchanged. These and other considerations suggest that to identify a single 'Enlightenment' is, perhaps insuperably, difficult. Nor can its nature be properly grasped if treated as a purely intellectual or literary phenomenon. For example, demographic studies, such as those revealing the facts about decline in infant mortality in some nations where there was Enlightenment, show the vital social context of themes such as 'progress'.* Whatever the contours or conclusions of future studies, however, to understand and to evaluate 'modernity' we need to go back to the Enlightenment.

In their religious thought, prominent Enlightenment thinkers were markedly hostile to traditional Christianity. The Reformation* and its aftermath witnessed the dissipation, not demise, of dogma,* as alternative interpretations of Christianity claimed its authentic inheritance and condemned each other as well as unbelief. Bloodshed and persecution accompanied this, so that Enlightenment thinkers attacked the consequences as well as content of traditional dogma. Negatively, they rejected the principle of the rule of dogma, and, with it, a range of ideas both formal (such as revelation,* where it provided exclusive, necessary knowledge) and material (such as the accepted doctrine of original sin*). Positively, they sought the rule of reason, and with it the adumbration of new formal ideas (such as the nature of morality) and material ones (such as the relation of God to physical nature). Kant* defined Enlightenment as the spirit's determination to exercise its intellectual faculties in unfettered integrity – 'Dare to know.' He who did so had some claim to be called an 'enlightened' thinker.

But if the term 'reason' is used to pick out a typical Enlightenment attitude, it requires cautious treatment. Comprehensive metaphysical constructions, based on rational deductions, could be criticized in the name of practical philosophy. Cold analytic reason, conceived as the instrument of universal understanding, could be censured in the name of passionate sensibility. If the Enlightenment is the age of reason, reason must be understood either as the alternative to dogma or in terms of broad intellectual autonomy. Nor did Enlightenment thinkers abandon religion or revelation. Atheistic materialism could develop in France certainly, but it had its anti-Christian critics (such as Voltaire*). Revelation might be deprived of sole religious authority, of the right to impart anything not

223

knowable by reason or of the ability even to provide significant incentive for the religious life; yet it could be domesticated (as in German neology) rather than eliminated.

It is hard to account for the forces behind Enlightenment thought without offering, in this case, a theological interpretation. The rise of modern science was a major factor: Newton,* sometimes almost deified in the 18th century, had impelled the search for scientific explanation that would lead to interpreting the physical world in terms of physical law. The growth of historical criticism was significant: while the Enlightenment is often regarded as deficient in real historical understanding, it could distinguish between its own and the biblical world. Yet Newton found no quarrel with Christianity at points where his later admirers did, and antiquity as such was not alien to the Enlightenment thinkers, as the prestige of the ancient Roman world revealed. Unless one suspects that the logic of scientific method – whether in physics or in history – is hostile to faith, one may look for a broader context, in which scientific explanation could develop into the rival, rather than the complement, of religious explanation; and in which historical criticism could develop into the opponent, rather than exponent, of Christian doctrine. This is neither to commend Newtonian science, nor to accept the operative principles of early historical criticism – but neither is it to hold them intrinsically responsible for what followed.

This broader context is surely supplied by the explicit or implicit sense of human autonomy. Indeed, in any comprehensive account, this must be related to political and economic change and policy. But, in the present perspective, 'autonomy' has both a relative and an absolute meaning. It was *relative* to the Christian claims about man. It was *absolute* in its willingness in principle to dispense with external, even divine, authority if that was where its logic led. Christianity opposes autonomy on grounds of creation, fall and redemption. The Enlightenment could relegate the Creator to a remote caretaker or irrelevant possibility, deny the incapacity of human nature to attain heaven by its own created resources and affirm that the moral life, conducted in good faith, if not complete knowledge, fulfils the basic purpose of existence. If God is finally disposed of, as he dramatically was in the 19th century, it is

because he is not needed; if he is not needed, it is not because he is simply intellectually disposed of, but because the heart is satisfied – or satisfied to look – elsewhere. In such matters, the will, as well as the intellect, is at work.

This brief summary cannot avoid, any more than can other generalizations, misrepresenting the Enlightenment in some of its aspects. It is also no more disinterestedly neutral than any other fundamental interpretation. But, in a truistic or profounder sense, autonomy is compatible with the phenomenon of Enlightenment thought in its flow or formulations. Hume,* Edward Gibbon (1737–94), Voltaire, Jean Jacques Rousseau (1712–78), Christian Wolff (1679–1754), Lessing,* Giovanni Battista Vico (1668–1744), Thomas Jefferson (1743–1826) – these represent a cultural and intellectual range in the Enlightenment. There may be others more significant; for the question of who is significant, and why, will continue to be debated, as will the significance of the Enlightenment itself, if it is to be retained as a viable concept. To reject or accept the 'Enlightenment' overall seems futile. If calamitous consequences flow from the adoption of some of its axioms, note that there were calamitous aspects to the preceding history of Christianity. Karl Popper (b. 1902) remarked that the urge to improve the lot of our fellows is both 'admirable and dangerous' and was rooted in the 'longing of uncounted, unknown men to free themselves and their minds from the tutelage of authority and prejudice'. By considering what is here claimed or assumed about the motives of the 'Enlightened', we grasp and estimate the nature and significance of the enterprise.

See also: FRANKFURT SCHOOL.

Bibliography

E. Cassirer, *The Philosophy of the Enlightenment* (Princeton, NJ, 1951); P. Gay, *The Enlightenment: an Interpretation*, 2 vols. (London, 1970); N. Hampson, *The Enlightenment* (Harmondsworth, 1968); M. Jacob, *The Radical Enlightenment: Pantheists, Freemasons and Republicans* (London, 1981); R. Porter and M. Teich (eds.), *The Enlightenment in National Context* (Cambridge, 1981).

S.N.W.

EPICLESIS, see EUCHARIST.

EPISCOPACY, see MINISTRY.

EPISCOPIUS, see ARMINIANISM.

EPISTEMOLOGY, from the Gk. word for knowledge or science (*epistēmē*). Epistemology is the study of the nature and basis of experience, belief and knowledge. It asks what we know and how we know it. It is concerned to differentiate knowledge from feeling sure or believing. It asks how we justify claims to know, whether we can be wrong about what we know, if we can know only if it makes sense that we can also *not* know, and whether we know that we know something. There are many areas of difficulty in knowledge: *e.g.* knowing the self, the past, the future, universal facts, scientific laws and the facts of philosophy, aesthetics, morality, religion, logic and mathematics. Various modern philosophers have introduced distinctions to help analyse the nature of knowing. Bertrand Russell (1872–1970) distinguishes knowledge by acquaintance, which is direct and immediate, from knowledge by description, which is indirect. Gilbert Ryle (1900–76) distinguishes knowing how to do things, from knowing that such and such is the case.

Rationalism and empiricism

Descartes* sought absolute certainty in knowledge. He stressed that reason alone provided the route to absolute certainty. This rationalist emphasis was countered by the empiricism* of Locke,* Berkeley* and Hume,* who argued that certainty was to be found through the senses alone. These key strands in philosophy share in a common debate over the origin of knowledge, are aware of the problems of universals and abstract ideas, use rational and scientific approaches, and engage in a search for certainty. Both are responses to the sceptical challenge to knowledge. The sceptic queries the reliability of knowledge, and argues that it is always possible to doubt. Rationalism and empiricism are attempts to cure doubt. Kant* offered a bridge between the senses and reason with his stress on the synthetic *a priori* categories of understanding which make knowledge possible. Knowledge of these categories was not derived from experience, yet was a condition of the comprehensibility of experience. His synthetic *a priori* claims have been much disputed. Recent philos-

ophers have argued variously. G. E. Moore (1873–1958) and Wittgenstein* have set aside the issues of doubt and analysed knowledge in terms of meaning through linguistic usage. Ordinary language and common sense have little problem with philosophical doubt and offer a simple solution to it. Polanyi* has stressed the personal nature of knowing and its tacit dimension in which we know more than we can say. The logical* positivists have taken empiricism along the road of verification* and falsification as means for testing knowledge and truth claims, often using sense data as the ultimate source of certainty. A. J. Ayer (b. 1910) offers an analysis of knowledge in terms of its being justified true belief. The key issues in epistemology seem to concern: the role of justification and its nature; ways of setting aside, or coping with, doubt,* and whether the sceptic's position makes any sense; the nature of what is known (whether it be in terms of ideas or what is real); an adequate theory of truth* (whether in terms of coherence or correspondence with reality); and the relationship between objectivity and subjectivity, in terms of whether we can know something totally objectively and to what extent subjectivity intrudes or is seen to be problematic.

Epistemology in theology

Traditionally, the distinction between belief and knowledge has taken the form of faith* and reason in theology. Biblical writers do not seem hesitant about making claims that God is known and that Christianity is not simply a question of faith, but also one of knowledge. Anselm* argues that faith seeks understanding while others similarly assert that we believe in order that we may understand. Theologians express the various sources of knowledge in religion in terms of revelation* and experience. Revelation is usually divided into special and general. Special revelation includes the incarnation, the resurrection and the miracles, where God reveals himself in a 'special' way to particular people. General revelation is open to all and is usually seen in terms of natural theology.* This looks to the nature of the world and the nature of humanity as revealing something of the nature of God. He may be known by deducing his nature from the world or humanity. Religious experience* seems to offer a direct knowledge of God as seen in the call of the prophets and the many direct experiences of God and Christ as recounted in Scripture. Distinctive religious experiences, or simply interpreting the world or events in one's life or in the world's life as God's activity, have allowed personal claims to know God directly.

These knowledge-claims have been criticized by philosophers, especially logical positivists, because of the absence of the kind of proof required by theories of verification and falsification. Theologians have responded in various ways. Some argue that religious experience is self-authenticating. Others argue that the positivist view of experience is too narrowly defined in terms of sense-experience. Religious experience has been interpreted as a disclosure model or situation parallel to scientific discoveries (see Ramsey, Ian*). John Hick* offers eschatological verification as the ground of knowing God. Others have argued that reason does not offer absolute knowledge in any realm and that belief is the best that any area of study and life can offer. Thus Christian presuppositions are no worse or better off than any other set of presuppositions.

If we follow the biblical balance between faith and knowledge, it is crucial to deal with questions of truth and justification whenever claims of knowledge and belief are made. Both sets of claims require evidence and support and the theologian must not shrink from seeking the best evidence and offering the strongest justification for knowledge and belief-claims. Nevertheless, we must recognize the limits of reason and when there are unreasonable and inappropriate demands for proof and justification. This may be demonstrated by showing that nothing would count as satisfying these demands. Christians need to reflect on what would count against knowledge and belief in God. Biblical Christianity does not claim immunity from criticism nor assume automatic acceptance by its hearers; it offers good reasons for the hope that is within us.

Bibliography

A. J. Ayer, *The Problem of Knowledge* (Harmondsworth, 1956); S. T. Davis, *Faith, Skepticism and Evidence: An Essay in Religious Epistemology* (Cranbury, NJ, 1978); D. W. Hamlyn, *Theory of Knowledge* (London, 1971); J. Hick, *Faith and Knowledge* (London, 1966); T. Penelhum, *Problems of Religious Knowledge* (London, 1971); D. L. Wolfe, *Epistemology* (Leicester, 1982).

E.D.C.

ERASMUS, DESIDERIUS (c. 1469–1536). The most renowned scholar of his time, Erasmus of Rotterdam was a complex and cosmopolitan Christian humanist.* Although courted by universities, popes, kings and an emperor, this frail intellectual carefully protected his independence. His consuming passion for piety and unity was best served, he felt, through the power of his pen.

Overcoming the stigma of an illegitimate birth, Erasmus was raised in a clerical world of monastic schools and rules. Although ordained in 1492, the young priest sought a release from his Augustinian* order to pursue university studies in Paris. He was steeped in classical literature and became a consummate Latinist.

A visit to England in 1499 proved to be a turning-point when he was both captivated and challenged by an Oxford lecturer, John Colet (c. 1466–1519), the future dean of St Paul's Cathedral, who fired his imagination with the ideals of Christian humanism and specifically the importance of a return to the normal sense of the biblical text. Such a goal, the two agreed, would best be realized through a working knowledge of the original languages of the Bible.

The next years were given to travel and research, especially the study of Greek grammar. Inspired by the chance discovery of an obscure manuscript by Lorenzo Valla (1407–1457) which criticized the accuracy of the Latin Vulgate, Erasmus gave himself to the production of a new Latin NT based on a critical Greek NT. In 1516 this *New Instrument*, as he titled the first edition, was published. Its influence was immense. With one book, Erasmus put the Greek NT within reach of preachers and scholars.

As his fame grew, Erasmus began to direct his influence against various abuses in the Roman Catholic Church. The satirical *In Praise of Folly* blasted away at the foibles of contemporary monasticism. He stood squarely against the misuse of indulgences, and when Luther* delineated his Ninety-five Theses, Erasmus gave his support. As Luther became more strident, however, the irenic Erasmus began to distance himself from the controversial Reformer. Correspondence between the two churchmen became increasingly bitter. Goaded by Rome to strike out at the Lutheran heresy, Erasmus wrote a treatise *On the Freedom of the Will* in 1524, which took Luther to task on the thorny issue of predestination* and human freedom. The differences between the two men, however, were by no means solely theological. Erasmus sincerely wanted reform, but not at the expense of unity. The humanist defended Luther's freedom to criticize abuses, but he could never condone an ecclesiastical rebellion against authority.

Despite the fact that the Reformers faulted Erasmus for vacillation and timidity, and various popes put a number of his works on the *Index* of forbidden books, the influence of Erasmus was enormous. Protestants and Catholics alike quoted and cited him freely on matters of biblical and theological interpretation. Calvin's *Institutes* are more indebted to him than appears on the surface. His *Paraphrases on the New Testament*, which were translated into many languages, had a sustained popular influence. His editing of the collected writings of major early church fathers was probably his most important contribution next to the 1516 NT.

Erasmian studies have burgeoned in the 20th century. Several biographical works have been published as well as major new editions of his works and letters.

Bibliography

R. A. B. Mynors *et al.* (eds.), *The Correspondence of Erasmus* (Toronto, 1974– , being part of complete new ET of J. K. McConica *et. al.* (eds.), *The Collected Works of Erasmus*); E. G. Rupp *et al.* (eds.), *Luther and Erasmus: Free Will and Salvation* (LCC 17; London, 1969); *Opera Omnia*, ed. C. Reedijk *et al.* (Amsterdam, 1969–).

R. H. Bainton, *Erasmus of Christendom* (New York, 1969); J. Huizinga, *Erasmus of Rotterdam* (New York, 1952).

N.P.F.

ERASTIANISM, see STATE.

ERIUGENA, JOHN SCOTUS (*c.* 810–*c.* 877), philosophical theologian of Christian Neoplatonism (see Platonism*). Reared in Ireland (as both 'Scotus' and 'Eriugena' tautologically indicate), John became the most original thinker of the Carolingian renaissance, spending over 30 years from *c.* 840 as the leading light of Charles the Bald's palace academy near Laon in Gaul. Late in life he may have taught in England.

John's knowledge of Greek (rare in the West at the time and probably acquired in Ireland) equipped him to Latinize the thought of Greek Christian Neoplatonism. As well as works by Gregory of Nyssa* and Maximus the Confessor,* he translated and commented on the influential corpus of Pseudo-Dionysius.* He was also indebted to Boethius'* interpretation of Aristotelian* logic; his dialectical style has earned him the title 'the first scholastic'.*

His most important work *Periphyseon* or *The Division of Nature* (*c.* 862) was condemned in the 13th century. Its apparent fusion of biblical teaching and Neoplatonism (for he viewed both reason and revelation* as manifestations of divine wisdom, and virtually equated philosophy and religion) verged on pantheism.* All creation proceeds outward from God as source, by 'division' or 'progress', and by a circular motion of 'resolution' or 'regress' returns to him as goal. John's thought bears the typical marks of Neoplatonism: a preference for apophatic* or negative theology, a poetic, almost mystical ardour and intensity, a hierarchical scale of being, the deification* of all creatures, and the 'restoration of all things' proposed by Origen.* Nature and grace could scarcely be separated in John's system.

He opposed Gottschalk* on predestination. Appealing to Augustine's* early anti-Manichaean works, he advanced what seemed a Pelagian* appreciation of mankind's moral abilities, and denied that Augustine taught double predestination. No credible version of predestination or election survived in John's thought, any more than did eternal punishment or hell.

In the eucharistic* controversy associated with Paschasius Radbertus* and Ratramnus,* Eriugena taught a refined symbolist interpretation of the sacrament. Christ is offered and eaten 'not dentally but mentally' (*mente non dente*). In his vision of reality, all visible and corporeal things signified something incorporeal and intelligible.

Recent Irish scholarship has rediscovered John as the greatest Irish philosopher (except perhaps for Berkeley*). He has been too often depicted as a lonely outpost of Greek thought in the medieval West. Yet he worked among a colourful community of scholars, and must not be detached from the tradition that derives from Augustine.* He posed in an acute form the perennial question of the relation between faith and reason.*

Bibliography

Most works in *PL* 122; for list see I. P. Sheldon-Williams in *JEH* 10 (1960), pp. 198–224; *Periphyseon*, ed. and tr. Sheldon-Williams (Dublin, 1968ff.).

H. Bett, *Johannes Scotus Erigena* (Cambridge, 1925); *CHLGEMP*, pp. 518–533 (Sheldon-Williams), 576–586 (H. Liebeschütz); J. J. O'Meara, *Eriugena* (Cork, 1969); J. Pelikan, *The Growth of Medieval Theology (600–1300)* (*The Christian Tradition*, vol. 3; Chicago and London, 1978), pp. 95–105.

D.F.W.

EROS, see LOVE.

ERSKINE, THOMAS (of Linlathen) (1788–1870), outstanding Scottish lay theologian, who combined the roles of leisurely laird and theological author and correspondent. Denominationally uncommitted, Erskine travelled theologically from an initial Calvinism, through Irvingism,* to a final though far from easygoing universalism.* His first book, *Remarks on the Internal Evidence for the Truth of Revealed Religion* (1820), argued that Christianity's truth was demonstrated by its correspondence with man's moral needs. It was well received by the orthodox world. His *Unconditional Freeness of the Gospel* (1828), however, provoked bitter criticism for its advocacy of universal atonement. In 1828 Erskine met John McLeod Campbell,* and enthusiastically supported him during his trial and deposition from the Church of Scotland. They became lifelong friends. Campbell's mature Christology is seminally present in Erskine's *Brazen Serpent* (1831). Erskine also encountered Edward Irving at this period, and adopted his views on premillennialism, Christ's humanity and the gifts* of the Spirit. *The Doctrine of Election* (1837) concluded Erskine's breach with Calvinism.

Erskine's thought shows increasing preoccupation with conscience* as the criterion of truth. He regarded God as a universal Father who is educating all men into a filial relationship with himself, and in later years saw the ultimate salvation of all as the essential gospel. Always a deeply pious and charming man, Erskine's writings and personal influence contributed notably to the liberalizing of 19th-century British theology.

Bibliography

Other writings by Erskine include *An Essay on Faith* (1822); *The Gifts of the Spirit* (1830); *The Spiritual Order* (1871).

For his life and thought, see W. Hanna, *Letters of Thomas Erskine*, 2 vols. (Edinburgh, 1877); J. S. Candlish in *British and Foreign Evangelical Review* 22 (1873), pp. 105–128; H. F. Henderson, *Erskine of Linlathen* (Edinburgh, 1899); N. R. Needham, *Thomas Erskine of Linlathen, His Life and Theology 1788–1837* (unpublished PhD thesis, University of Edinburgh, 1987).

N.R.N.

ESCHATOLOGY, from Gk. *eschatos*, 'last'; the term refers to 'the doctrine of the last things'.

1. Development of the doctrine

In contrast with cyclical views of history,* which hold that the universe is locked into a cycle of endless repetition, special divine revelation* led the Hebrews to see history as moving towards a future goal. Although earlier OT prophets looked for God to bring judgment and salvation within history, there eventually developed the hope of a final resolution of history, whereby God would banish evil and establish a permanent age of salvation, peace and righteousness. This perspective, often envisaging salvation in a transcendent world, was characteristic of apocalyptic.*

Jesus* took over prophetic and apocalyptic* thought-forms, but with a crucial difference: in his ministry the longed-for time of salvation had dawned, the kingdom* of God had drawn near (Mk. 1:15). His possession of the Spirit, his miracles and his exorcisms were evidence of this (Mt. 11:2–6; 12:28). Yet the kingdom had not fully come, for, despite the real blessings of God experienced with a new immediacy, evil, death and the ambiguities of life remained. The complete realization of the kingdom lay in the future, at the coming of the Son of Man (Mk. 13:26). The distinctive feature of NT eschatology, found especially in Paul, is thus a tension between what is *already* known and experienced (because Christ has come), and what is *not yet* experienced (because Christ is still to come).

After the NT period, attention gradually came to be focused less on the eagerly awaited coming of Christ and more on the individual's prospects after death. In the Middle Ages and the periods of the Reformation* and scholasticism* the doctrine of the last things – death, the second coming of Christ, resurrection of the dead, judgment, heaven and hell – reached its classic expression. This approach tended to 'lull us comfortably to sleep by adding at the conclusion of Christian Dogmatics a short and perfectly harmless chapter entitled – "Eschatology" ' (K. Barth, *The Epistle to the Romans*, London, 1933, p. 500).

But the rise of biblical criticism* provoked a series of rude awakenings. It was argued, for example, that predictions in the gospels of approaching woes and the end of the world (*e.g.* Mk. 13) derived not from Jesus but from the apocalyptic atmosphere of the early church. Hence liberal Protestants such as A. Ritschl* could understand the kingdom of God as 'the association of mankind through the reciprocal moral action of its members'. Such a bland combination of Jesus' message with the 19th-century myth of progress* was shattered by the claim of J. Weiss (1863–1914) and A. Schweitzer* that Jesus' message was thoroughly eschatological and could not be made congenial to modern thought-forms. Schweitzer argued that Jesus believed himself to be Messiah-designate; when his sending out of the Twelve failed to produce the eschatological kingdom, he offered himself in death so that God would grant the new age. In believing that the final kingdom would arrive soon after his death, Jesus was mistaken (*The Quest of the Historical Jesus*, London, 1981, ch. 19).

Much 20th-century NT scholarship has been reaction to Schweitzer. R. Bultmann* agreed that Jesus proclaimed an imminent apocalyptic kingdom, but attempted to make it meaningful to modern man by 'demythologizing' the message (see Myth*): Jesus is not 'coming again' at a future date but 'comes to me' demanding decision. C. H. Dodd's* earlier work propounded an unmodified 'realized eschatology': the heart of Jesus' message was that the kingdom of God was already realized in his ministry. A more balanced synthesis is achieved by scholars such as O. Cullmann (b. 1902) (see Salvation-history*), R. H. Fuller (b. 1915) and G. E. Ladd (1911–82), who have argued that present and future references in Jesus' message of the kingdom must be held in tension. The kingdom promised in the OT was *inaugurated* at the coming of Jesus, but awaits its consummation. (The phrase 'inaugurated exchatology' comes from J. A. T. Robinson,* though his viewpoint is closer to Dodd's.) In the 1970s and 1980s NT scholars have debated vigorously whether Jesus used the term 'Son of Man' to refer to his own future coming and vindication.

On a broader front, discussion of life after death has had to come to terms with questions about whether life beyond death is philosophically conceivable (*e.g.* P. Badham, *Christian Beliefs about Life after Death*, London, 1976), and whether eternal life is for all mankind or only for some (the question of universalism*). A notable attempt to build a (universalist) theology of eternal life on the insights of Eastern religions as well as of Christianity is John Hick,* *Death and Eternal Life* (Collins, 1976).

Political theology* and liberation theology* have used eschatological categories to argue for Christian action in the light of the future towards which God call us. (For survey of historical development see P. Hebblethwaite, *The Christian Hope*, London, 1984.)

2. The kingdom and the coming of Christ

Key features of a Christian eschatology may be summarized as follows. Jesus, in inaugurating God's kingdom, has revealed God's intentions for the world. These include forgiveness of sins (Lk. 7:48–50), the conquest of evil, suffering and death (Mt. 12:28–29; Lk. 4:18–21; Mt. 11:5; Jn. 11), the bringing of a new order of things which overturns common assumptions about power in society and the value of people (Lk. 6:20ff.; 13:30). But while there is real evidence of the kingdom's power at work in individual lives and in the creation of a community embodying such goals and values, the kingdom's coming remains incomplete. We await a final day when God's intentions revealed in Jesus will be triumphantly fulfilled.

This 'final day' is commonly called in the NT the *parousia* of Christ (1 Cor. 15:23; 1 Thes. 4:15). The word means 'presence' or 'arrival', and was used of visits of gods and rulers. This parousia may be called the 'second coming' of Jesus (*cf.* Heb. 9:28), and may be described as 'personal', since it is the revelation and vindication of Jesus of Nazareth (Acts 1:11). Eschatology concerns a person, not merely an event. But it is inappropriate to think of the parousia simply as the physical arrival of a person or as 'a historical event in the future', because the parousia not only marks the end of our present historical order but will itself be beyond history, introducing a new order discontinuous with the present course of history.

Twentieth-century scholarship has been much concerned with the problem of the delay of the parousia: since the early church's expectation of an imminent parousia was not fulfilled, is not the whole notion discredited? In fact the problem has been exaggerated. There are few clear references to it in the NT (2 Pet. 3:1–10; Jn. 21:22–23). Passages about 'signs of the times' (*e.g.* Mk. 13) were not intended to enable the calculation of an eschatological timetable but to warn of conflicts to be expected throughout history until the parousia. Alongside passages suggesting imminence (e.g. Mk. 9:1; 13:30; Rom. 13:11–12) are others which declare that the date of the end is unknown (Mk. 13:32; Acts 1:7). Passages suggesting imminence indicate a *theological* rather than chronological relationship between present and future. They indicate the certainty, not the timing, of God's completion of what he has begun. (For related issues, see Millennium,* Sects.*)

NT writers are in fact less concerned with the timing and manner of Christ's coming than with its purpose.

3. Immortality and eternal life

Christ will come to welcome his people into his presence. They will be resurrected and transformed to be 'with the Lord for ever' (1 Thes. 4:13–18; 1 Cor. 15:35–57). In the biblical view (unlike Platonism*), man (or his soul) is not naturally immortal. Immortality* belongs to God alone (1 Tim. 6:16), though it is bestowed on believers as a gift (1 Cor. 15:42, 50–54). Perhaps to emphasize that the destiny of believers is an act of God's grace rather than a natural attribute of mankind, the NT speaks less of immortality, more of resurrection* and eternal life.

But because Christ's first coming has already inaugurated his kingdom, eternal life is experienced by the believer during the present life (Jn. 3:36; 5:24; 1 Jn. 5:13; 2 Cor. 4:7–18). Since eternal life means 'the life of the age to come', it implies not only everlastingness but a quality of life derived from relationship with Christ (Rom. 6:23; Jn. 17:3). Thus the perfect life of God's ultimate kingdom is the consummation of the life 'in Christ' experienced now (Col. 3:1–4; Jn. 6:54). Although death marks a discontinuity between this life and the next, eternal life guarantees a continuity of relationship to Christ even through death.

4. Judgment, heaven and hell

The distinction between those who possess eternal life and those who do not will be ratified at the final judgment.* Believers will enter into God's presence. The traditional language of 'going to heaven' is not so securely based on Scripture as is usually supposed. The ultimate 'destination' of God's people is a transformed universe, 'a new heaven and a new earth' (Rev. 21:1). While history runs its course, heaven is where God is (Mt. 6:9), where Christ is ascended (Heb. 4:14), and therefore by implication where believers go at death, since they are 'with Christ' (Lk. 23:43; Phil. 1:23). But there is ambiguity in Scripture and Christian tradition about the relationship between a Christian's destiny at death and at the final judgment and resurrection (see Intermediate State*). Some argue that between death and resurrection a believer is in heaven with Christ in disembodied form. (This perhaps is the meaning of 2 Cor. 5:1–8.) Here (as elsewhere) Scripture seems to describe what is beyond our experience in terms of the limitations of our experience of temporal distinctions (*e.g.* Rev. 6:10). At death, however, a person passes outside the limitations of time. From his (and God's) perspective there may be no consciousness of a 'between'; he may pass through death into resurrection in God's presence with all his people. In that ultimate kingdom God guarantees freedom from death, suffering, fear and sin (Rev. 21:4). For the rest, evocative pictures must suffice: it is a banquet (Mt. 8:11), a wedding feast (Rev. 19:9), a secure city, filled with worship and loving activity (Heb. 11:10; 12:22–24).

'Hell', the final destiny of those rejected at the judgment, translates Gk. *Gehenna*, derived from Heb. *Gêhinnōm*, the valley outside Jerusalem which became a symbol of condemnation because child sacrifices had been offered there (2 Chr. 28:3; 33:6). The gospels' picture of Gehenna as a place of darkness and unquenchable fire (Mk. 9:43; Mt. 8:12) symbolizes the utter destruction and negativity involved in exclusion from God's presence. That exclusion from God's presence is the real significance of hell is clear in Jesus' teaching (Mt. 7:23; 10:32f.) and in Paul, who does not mention Gehenna but whose images of 'destruction', 'death' and 'corruption' refer to separation from God, the source of all true life. Whether this involves eternal conscious torment (the traditional Christian view) or cessation of existence (as taught by advocates of 'conditional immortality') is a matter of ongoing debate.

Heaven and hell do not have equal status in the purpose of God. The kingdom has always been God's goal for his people (Mt. 25:34); hell was 'prepared for the devil and his angels' (Mt. 25:43), and if people go there it is because they have rejected their true destiny.

5. Christ our hope

The distinctive feature of Christian eschatology is its Christ-centredness. Christ's second coming marks the completion of his work begun in Bethlehem and at Calvary. The resurrection of believers depends on the resurrection of Jesus (1 Cor. 15:20–22). Christian hope is not mere wish-fulfilment, because it looks for fulfilment of a plan already in operation. The kingdom of God is not mere compensation for present miseries, but rather the full experience of blessings already experienced in part through the Spirit, 'who is a deposit guaranteeing our inheritance' (Eph. 1:14).

Eschatology concerns the vindication of God's purposes for all creation. It calls people not so much to contemplate their individual destinies, as to allow the perspective of hope* to influence the whole of life.

Bibliography

In addition to works already cited: G. C. Berkouwer, *The Return of Christ* (Grand Rapids, MI, 1972); E. Brunner, *Eternal Hope* (London, 1954); R. Bultmann, *History and Eschatology* (Edinburgh, 1957); O. Cullmann, *Salvation in History* (London,

1967); C. H. Dodd, *The Parables of the Kingdom* (London, 1936); R. H. Fuller, *The Mission and Achievement of Jesus* (London, 1954); M. J. Harris, *Raised Immortal* (London, 1983); A. A. Hoekema, *The Bible and the Future* (Grand Rapids, MI, and Exeter, 1979); H. Küng, *Eternal Life?* (London, 1984); G. E. Ladd, *The Presence of the Future* (Grand Rapids, MI, 1974); N. Perrin, *The Kingdom of God in the Teaching of Jesus* (London, 1963); W. Strawson, *Jesus and the Future Life* (London, 1970); H. Thielicke, *The Evangelical Faith*, vol. 3 (Grand Rapids, MI, 1982); S. H. Travis, *Christian Hope and the Future of Man* (Leicester, 1980).

S.H.T.

ESSENCE OF CHRISTIANITY. Although association with Feuerbach's* *The Essence of Christianity* (1841) and Harnack's* *What is Christianity?* (1900) has suggested that the subject is of interest only to historians of 19th-century thought, or one whose pursuit inevitably leads to abstract generalizations or reduction of living religion to sociological or ethical principles, these are not necessary conclusions. In fact the issue is a central one of permanent and even increasing contemporary significance, in at least five areas.

Definitions of the essential features of Christianity, which include religious experience,* worship* and ethics,* as well as doctrine, are: 1. offered in varying degrees by all creeds,* confessions* of faith and catechisms,* both ancient and modern; 2. the basis of ecumenical* discussions promoting re-union of the churches (*cf.* H.-G. Link, ed., *Apostolic Faith Today*, Faith and Order Paper 124, Geneva, 1985); 3. necessary for undertaking intra-religious dialogue; 4. entailed in every attempt at the contextualization* or cross-cultural communication of the gospel, which is a particularly sensitive issue for the Roman Catholic Church in different parts of the world (*cf. Concilium* 135, 1980; 171, 1984, R. J. Schreiter, *Constructing Local Theologies*, London, 1985); and 5. the implicit or explicit basis of every work of systematic theology* or apologetics.*

Looking at the breadth and implications of the subject in this way makes it clear that there is a distinction to be made between understandings of the essence of Christianity

231

that seek to reduce it to one or more key ideas, and those that attempt to do full justice to its complex elements. In this respect there are important differences between the approaches taken by Feuerbach and Harnack and those adopted by contemporaries such as Schleiermacher* or Newman* (*cf.* S. Sykes, *The Identity of Christianity*, London, 1984).

The constant tendency of a search for an 'essence' to de-historicize Christianity (*cf.* N. Lash, *Theology on Dover Beach*, London, 1979) has to be resisted both by careful consideration of its components – religious experience, worship, ethics and doctrine – and by due regard for the unity and diversity of their manifestation from earliest times (*cf.* J. D. G. Dunn, *Unity and Diversity in the New Testament*, London, 1977; G. E. Gunton, *Yesterday and Today; A Study of Continuities in Christology*, London, 1983).

The question of 'essence' thus turns out to be closely related to the question of the development* of doctrine. It may thus be useful to consider the arguments of Newman's celebrated *Essay on the Development of Doctrine* (1845, ³1878). Whether or not his understanding of the church's role in interpreting the mystery of revelation is felt to be completely satisfactory, two of Newman's conclusions are worth noting. The first is that Christian truth may be organized around one idea, in his case the incarnation,* providing it does not exclude another aspect of revelation. The second is that ultimately revelation is a mystery that cannot be systematized or exhausted in words, a timely reminder that knowledge of God comes through the response of the whole person.

P.N.H.

ETERNAL LIFE, see ESCHATOLOGY.

ETERNITY, see TIME AND ETERNITY.

ETHICS. All ethics is to do with human conduct. The special concern of Christian ethics is to relate an understanding of God to the conduct of men and women and, more specifically, to explore the response to God which Jesus Christ requires and makes possible.

This article will focus on the distinctive features of Christian ethics as seen from the standpoint of biblical theology. (For a broader perspective, see Moral Theology.*)

God first

The Bible's ethical teaching is essentially God-centred: 'The power of the good rests entirely on the One who is good. Of moral behaviour for the sake of an abstract good, there is none' (W. Eichrodt, *Theology of the Old Testament*, vol. 2, London, 1967, p. 316). This theocentric basis means that doctrine is inseparable from ethics in Scripture. The two are related as foundation to building. Thus the ethical demands of the Decalogue are deliberately based on redemption, and Jesus' moral teaching in the Sermon on the Mount is presented as a series of deductions from religious premises (*cf.* Mt. 5:43–48).

If we want to discover the nature of goodness, the Bible directs us to God's own person. He alone is good, according to Jesus (Mk. 10:18). When the Lord promised Moses, 'I will cause all my goodness to pass in front of you' (Ex. 33:19), Moses was rewarded with a specially revealed insight into the Lord's character (Ex. 34:6–7).

Hence the fundamental ethical demand in Scripture is to imitate God. The repeated OT command from the Lord, 'Be holy, because I am holy' (*e.g.* Lv. 11:44–45) is matched by Jesus' instruction to his disciples that they should aim to reflect their heavenly Father's moral perfection (Mt. 5:48; *cf.* Lk. 6:36). Indeed, the NT goes further by calling Christians to imitate Christ as well. It is as we 'live a life of love, just as Christ loved us' that we will become 'imitators of God' (Eph. 5:1–2).

Love* (*agapē*) sums up the character of God (1 Jn. 4:8). It follows, then, that the most important of God's ethical commands is that people should reflect his *agapē* in their lives (Mk. 12:28–31). And again, they will do this as they copy the love of Jesus for them (Jn. 15:9, 12).

The NT expounds the meaning of *agapē* with enormous care (see especially 1 Cor. 13). It is a love which reaches beyond family, friendship and nation (Lk. 10:25–37). It embraces the undeserving and the unresponsive (*cf.* Col. 1:21–22). And it does not look for returns (Lk. 6:32–35; 14:12–14).

Some scholars take Jesus' stress on love as the NT's point of departure from the OT's law ethic. This, however, is to misunderstand the relationship between law* and love in both testaments.

The OT law is set within the context of

the covenant.* It expresses God's love for his people, and the psalmists (in particular) extol law-keeping as a powerful means of expressing his people's love for them (Pss. 19:7–11; 119: 33–36, 72). Jesus, too, saw no clash between love and law within the parameters of God-centred ethic (Jn. 15:10; cf. 1 Jn. 2:3–6). He blended an affirmation of law with an insistence that law-keeping must be warmed and motivated by love (Mt. 5:17–20).

The presence of so much law in the Bible does, in fact, bear its own witness to the theocentric foundation on which Christian ethics is built. If knowledge of right and wrong is not so much an object of philosophical enquiry as an acceptance of divine revelation,* it is only to be expected that imperatives will be prominent among the indicatives in the Bible. And if discovering what is right is the same as discerning God's will, the absence of arguments in support of his revealed demands is hardly surprising.

Creation

The Bible's account of creation* sets out some significant theological truths about mankind which determine Christian ethical principles. Paramount among them is the assertion that both man and woman were made in God's image* (Gn. 1:27). This carries implications for the value of human life which are fundamental in forming Christian attitudes to abortion,* euthanasia and medical experimentation (see also Bioethics*); as well as fuelling Christian anger when distinctions of race,* class or gender are used to exploit any individual or group (cf. Acts 17:26; Gal. 3:28).

Because God's character defines goodness, creation in his image also implies an innate ethical knowledge on the part of all men and women. People who have no knowledge of special revelation 'show that the requirements of the [i.e. God's] law are written on their hearts' by the activity of their consciences* (Rom. 2:14–15).

The doctrine of creation provides directions for social as well as personal ethics (a distinction which the Bible never in fact draws). And further ethical principles emerge from the relationship of mankind to the rest of creation, according to the maker's design set out in Gn.

The institution of marriage is especially prominent. The account of woman's creation (Gn. 2:18–24) is made the basis for the NT's insistence on the ideal of an exclusive, permanent relationship as the only ethically correct context for sexual* union (Mt. 19:3–6; cf. Eph. 5:28–31). Thus intercourse with a prostitute is a 'sin against the body', because 'the body is not meant for sexual immorality' (1 Cor. 6:13–18). Homosexual practice is ruled out on similar grounds; it is 'unnatural' for two people of the same sex to express their affection for one another genitally (Rom. 1:25–27).

Government is another God-given institution which man must not ignore (see State*). It may be morally legitimate to resist individual governing authorities on specific occasions (cf. Dn. 3:14–18; Acts 16:35–39), but the principle of being governed is fundamental to human life as the creator has designed it (Rom. 13:1–7).

As far as mankind's attitude to nature is concerned, the keyword biblically is 'management'. The creator put man and woman in charge of the rest of creation, with instructions to manage its resources (Gn. 1:26–29; cf. Ps. 8:3–8). Hence the Christian's twofold ethical concern – to conserve (because wastage is bad management) and to develop (because it is part of managerial responsibility to use resources imaginatively; cf. Lk. 19:12–26; see Stewardship*).

This call to manage provides the starting-point for a positive attitude in Scripture towards work.* Theologically, working is a vital part of what it means to be human – an assertion which fortifies Christian opposition to unemployment, though wage-earning is itself too narrow a definition of work to satisfy the Bible's creation ethic.

God himself is frequently described as a worker (cf. Is. 45:9; Ps. 19:1), so the implicit summons to imitate him is a major feature of the biblical approach to work. And the implicit becomes explicit when the Decalogue codifies the creator's example in maintaining a proper balance between work and leisure (Gn. 2:2–3; Ex. 20:9–1)

Sin

While the doctrine of creation sets out theocentric ideals, it is the doctrine of sin* which provides the most powerful analysis of life as we know it today. Specifically, man's and woman's rebellion against God resulted in the blurring of ethical knowledge, the weakening of the will* to do right, the breaking up of basic relationships and the complicating of moral judgments.

Sin distorts the guidance of conscience, which is corrupted and anaesthetized by repeated acts of disobedience (Tit. 1:15; 1 Tim. 4:2). Man's and woman's knowledge of right and wrong has therefore become blurred. One person's conscience may lead him to do something wrong with the most enthusiastic zeal (Acts 26:9), while another may experience guilt feelings which are totally unjustified (1 Jn. 3:19–20).

There are certainly times when conscience praises or blames in full harmony with God's will (*cf.* Rom. 2:15). But even on those occasions – when the right course of action is crystal-clear – the power to do it is often absent. Sin weakens the will (Rom. 7:15–23) and even twists the special knowledge of right and wrong which God's law provides into a keener desire to do the latter (Rom. 7:8–9). This accounts for the presence of a strong penal element in biblical ethics, not least in Jesus' teaching (*cf.* Mk. 9:41–48). People who are too weak-willed to do what is right out of love for God and others must be deterred from doing wrong, by fear of punishment.*

Social relationships are also victims of sin's destructive power. The biblical passage which records sin's arrival also spells out its consequences for the relationships between man and woman. They see each other as sex objects, not persons, so nudity becomes a matter of embarrassment and fear (Gn. 3:7–10; contrast 2:25). Ties of love and loyalty snap as man tries to justify his failure (Gn. 3:12–13). And woman's experience of childbirth is spoiled (Gn. 3:16).

Working relationships are broken by selfishness too. Seller cheats buyer and employer cheats employee (Dt. 25:13–16; Jas. 5:4). The same is true on the international scene, as wars are fought for narrow nationalistic ends. This provides the backcloth for the OT prophets' denunciation of discrimination and for their fervent proclamation of the Lord's justice. His love will express itself, they thunder, in the vindication of the oppressed (*e.g.* Mal. 3:5).

In a sin-soaked world, ethical issues become extraordinarily complex. Situations arise where every possible line of action is less than ideal. The Bible accepts and reflects this dilemma by advocating the choice of the lesser evil. So divorce, though always bad (*cf.* Mal. 2:16), may sometimes be right (Mt. 19:9; 1 Cor. 7:12–15). And even killing a human being who bears God's image becomes justified in extreme circumstances (*e.g.* Gn. 9:6).

Redemption

Against this sombre background, God's redeeming intervention provides an escape route from moral despair. Ethically, the Bible's doctrine of redemption* makes four special contributions: 1. It recalls fallen men and women to know God and follow his example. 2. It provides a stimulus to do right and avoid wrong. 3. It sets goals for moral living. 4. It points to a source of supernatural power to strengthen the failing human will.

The OT's covenant law contains many specific appeals to God's character and actions, in support of ethical demands. So the law's command to treat slaves* generously is backed by a reminder of the generous way God dealt with Hebrew slaves in Egypt; and businessmen are told not to cheat their customers, bearing in mind that it was the God of justice who vindicated their oppressed ancestors (Dt. 15:12–15; Lv. 19:35–36).

Such reminders of God's love and justice also provided a powerful stimulus to behave well. As God's covenant partners, men and women were invited to respond gratefully to their redeemer's undeserved love (*cf.* Lv. 22:31–33). And the NT reinforces this tug on the conscience by reminding believers that Christ is constantly at their side and that the Holy Spirit lives within them. So Christian children are encouraged to obey their parents because 'this pleases the Lord', and Christian slaves find fresh motivation to serve 'as working for the Lord, not for men' (Col. 3:20, 23). There is a similar incentive to avoid sexual immorality, because the body 'is a temple of the Holy Spirit, who is in you' (1 Cor. 6:18–20).

Christ's teaching about the kingdom* of God added a sense of urgency. Because the coming of the kingdom is imminent (and because it carries the promise – or threat – of judgment*), there is a powerful stimulus to live life the way God wants you to live it *now* (Mk. 1:15). The selfish person who plans for a leisurely, comfortable retirement may be in for a shock meeting with his king and judge sooner than he thinks (*cf.* Lk. 12:16–21).

The inauguration of the kingdom also

provides Christians with social ethical goals. Although the full manifestation of the king's rule awaits the king's own sudden, decisive intervention, there is a sense in which kingdom values permeate the world now (*cf.* Mt. 13:31–33). Because Christ's work is complete, the kingdom is already established. Christians are therefore called to live out its values and witness to its new relationships, knowing that this will sometimes involve conflict and challenge (*cf.* Lk. 4:18–19).

Such a call would have a hollow ring if Christians were powerless to heed it. But here the NT makes probably its most important contribution. Because the kingdom is a present reality, the king's power is available to those who put themselves under his rule. The indwelling Holy Spirit produces his fruit in the believer's life (Gal. 5:22–23). 'It is God who works in you', explains Paul, 'to will and to act according to his good purpose' (Phil. 2:13).

There is no automatic triumphalism in this aspect of the Bible's teaching, but there is a clear promise of potential. Biblical ethics does not stop at setting out creation principles and at analysing the effects of sin. It points believers to redemptive power that can transform their lives and life-styles.

Bibliography

D. Cook, *The Moral Maze* (London, 1983); A. F. Holmes, *Ethics* (Leicester, 1984); O. O'Donovan, *Resurrection and Moral Order – An Outline for Evangelical Ethics* (Leicester, 1986); H. Thielicke, *Theological Ethics*, 2 vols. (London, 1968); C. J. H. Wright, *Living as the People of God* (Leicester, 1983).

D.H.F.

ETHIOPIAN ORTHODOX THEO-LOGY.

The principal classical texts currently recognized, in addition to the Scriptures, as sources for the theology of the Ethiopian Orthodox Church are the Ethiopic Liturgy (pre-anaphora with fourteen anaphoras) and the work *Haymanotä abäw* ('The Faith of the Fathers', a collection of excerpts on the Trinity* and Christology*).

The Ethiopian Orthodox Church is heir to a rich theological tradition which cannot be described briefly. A full account would need to note what is more central to the tradition, and what is more peripheral; it would describe the historical doctrinal disputes with other churches, and within the Ethiopian Orthodox Church itself, which led to the production of theological literature; it would review the actual shifts which have taken place in the main-line Ethiopian Orthodox Church tradition; and it would portray the close integration of belief and practice in the daily life of the faithful.

The creeds* accepted by the Ethiopian Orthodox Church are those contained in the Ethiopic Liturgy, namely the 'Creed of the Apostles' (not the Western 'Apostles' Creed'), and the Niceno-Constantinopolitan creed (without the *Filioque*).

A framework which is commonly used for expositions of Ethiopian Orthodox theology is that of the 'five pillars of mystery', namely the doctrines of the Trinity, the incarnation, baptism, the eucharist, and the resurrection of the dead. Not infrequently, texts of the 'five pillars' are preceded by accounts of creation, and Ethiopian preaching of the gospel often follows this pattern – 'Adam was created, then fell, and Christ came to set him free.'

Modern Ethiopian theological statements also commonly contain an account of the 'seven sacraments'* – baptism, post-baptismal anointing, eucharist, repentance, orders, marriage, unction – but such systematization is less evident in the classical texts, and may have arisen in response to Roman Catholic teaching.

Further study of specific Ethiopian theological positions must take account of the actual language in which these are expressed. A bald statement such as that the Ethiopian Orthodox Church 'teaches transubstantiation' or 'honours icons' is misleading, as such ideas are differently conceived in Ethiopia, or at least have sets of associations different from those of Western theology.

The principal issue dividing the Ethiopian Orthodox Church from most other churches has been Christological, namely that it does not accept the Chalcedonian Definition, and specifically rejects the phrase 'in two natures'. The Ethiopian position has been termed 'monophysite'* or 'non-Chalcedonian', but the preferred description is 'Oriental Orthodox Christology'; the oriental orthodox churches are the Coptic* Church of Egypt, the Ethiopian Orthodox Church, the Syrian Orthodox Church of Antioch, the Orthodox Syrian Church of India, and the Armenian Orthodox Church.

See also: EASTERN ORTHODOX THEOLOGY

Bibliography

D. Crummey, *Priests and Politicians* (Oxford, 1972), esp. ch. 2, with further bibliography; M. Daoud (tr.), *The Liturgy of the Ethiopian Church* (Addis Ababa, 1954); S. H. Sellassie (ed.), *The Church of Ethiopia: A Panorama of History and Spiritual Life* (Addis Ababa, 1970); E. Ullendorff, *The Ethiopians: An Introduction to Country and People* (London, 1960), esp. ch. 5.

R.W.C.

EUCHARIST (Gk., meaning 'thanksgiving') is an early patristic name (found in the *Didache*, Ignatius, *etc.*) for the Lord's Supper or Holy Communion. It is derived from the thanksgivings or graces which, from the Last Supper onwards, have been part of the sacramental action.

The Last Supper, at which the sacrament* was instituted, was a larger meal, probably the Passover meal, with which the week of Unleavened Bread commenced, though many have argued (from Jn. 18:28 especially) that it must have taken place one or more days earlier. Since it was held inside the city (despite the crowds), continued into the night, was eaten reclining, and included wine and an interpretation of the elements, it had many of the distinctive features of a Passover meal, and the first three of these features are in John's account also. At all events, the occasion was the Passover season.

For a time, the eucharist continued to be part of a larger meal, called the *agapē* (*i.e.* love, meaning 'love-feast'; Jude 12) and provided by the wealthier Christians for the benefit of the poorer (*cf.* 1 Cor. 11: 20–22), which may help to account for the custom of holding the sacrament weekly not annually (Acts 20:7 onwards). Strictly, the eucharist was *two* parts of the larger meal – the action round the bread 'while they were eating', and the action round the cup 'after supper' – but when in the early 2nd century the agape and eucharist were separated, the two parts of the eucharist came together and the two thanksgivings were amalgamated. Hence the single thanksgiving or consecration prayer of the ancient Christian liturgies.

'Consecration' means 'setting apart as holy', and there is a long-standing disagreement between the Western and Eastern churches over what it is that consecrates the sacrament, *i.e.* makes it more than an ordinary meal. The Eastern church says it is the *epiclēsis*, *i.e.* the invocation or calling down of the Holy Spirit* upon the elements, which from the time of Hippolytus* was included in most ancient consecration prayers; the Western church says it is our Lord's words of institution, similarly included; and many modern liturgiologists have added a third proposal, the thanksgiving. However, the only new thing which Christ instituted was his interpretation of the elements, *i.e.* his words of institution; for the thanksgivings, breaking of the bread and distributing of the elements took place at any formal Jewish meal, as the rabbinical literature shows. There were, indeed, interpretative words at the Passover meal, but they interpreted the elements in relation to the deliverance of the exodus, not in relation to the new deliverance through Christ's death. All that our Lord instituted needs to be performed, but the distinctive thing is his new interpretative words, so the Western view has most to be said for it; though the way that the words of institution came to be used, as a formula of transubstantiation not of interpretation, is another matter.

The sacramental actions are interpreted because they are symbolic.* When interpreted and understood, they evoke faith,* just like the ministry of the word (see Preaching*) and through faith Christians feed spiritually upon Christ (Jn. 6). There is therefore a reality behind the symbolism, as the early fathers never ceased stressing; but in time their emphatic language began to be interpreted as identifying the symbol with the reality symbolized. Paschasius Radbertus* is usually regarded as the first propounder of transubstantiation, or the change of the substance of the bread and wine into the substance of Christ's body and blood. This was defined as a dogma* of the (Western) church by the Fourth Lateran Council* (1215), and was given a subtle philosophical explanation by Thomas Aquinas,* according to which it takes place in such a way that Christ's body and blood are never in fact separated from each other, or from his soul and divinity (concomitance). At the Reformation,* Luther* substituted an alternative view, also discussed in medieval philosophy, which has come to be known as consubstantiation. According to this view,

Christ's body and blood are present 'with, in and under' the bread and wine, instead of replacing them. The Swiss and other Reformers, however, firmly distinguished the symbol from the reality symbolized, a difference which led to the painful 'Supper strife' among the Reformers, in which Zwingli* and Luther were opposed, while Bucer,* Calvin* and others took a mediating position.

At times, Zwingli even denied that the sacraments were means of grace; a position which, Hooker* was later to declare, constituted one of the deepest divides in Christendom. In his happier utterances, however, Zwingli fully agrees with the other Reformers that the sacraments are means of grace, in which Christ is offered to men, to be received by repentance and faith or rejected by impenitence and unbelief. The offer is objective, and is in no way created by our faith, for where there is no faith or no repentance it brings judgment, as 1 Cor. 11 says. This teaching is sometimes called receptionism, because it holds that Christ is truly received, though without any change (except of use) in the elements; and it is linked with virtualism, which holds that the virtue or benefit of his sacrifice on the cross is also received.

The other great controversy about the eucharist which came to a head at the Reformation concerns the sacrifice* of the mass, or eucharistic sacrifice. Here the Reformers were united not only against Roman teaching but among themselves. At the Last Supper, Christ used sacrificial language, but he used it about his coming death. The sacrament which he was instituting was not an *offering* of his body and blood, but a feast upon his body and blood, which were to be offered at the cross. He then looked forward towards the cross, just as the church was ever afterwards to look back towards it, and it was at the cross that the offering took place. The Passover meal, similarly, was not an offering of the Passover lamb, but a feast upon the lamb which had already been offered in the Temple court.

At a very early period, however, the language of offering started to be used in relation to the eucharist, not just in relation to the cross. We find this in the *Didache*, Justin Martyr (see also Apologists*), Irenaeus,* Hippolytus,* *etc*. At first, what is offered is thanksgiving, or the elements for use in the sacrament, but by the 4th century the language has been transferred to the body and blood of Christ which the elements signify. Along with the doctrine of transubstantiation, therefore, the idea developed that the transubstantiated elements were offered to God, and that in this way the sacrifice offered at the cross was repeated, or (since such language was in direct contradiction to Heb. 7:27; 9:25–28; 10:10, 12, 14, 18) was 'made present again'.

The eucharistic sacrifice was first defined as a dogma of the (Western) church by the Council* of Trent in 1562: 'In this divine sacrifice which is celebrated in the mass, that same Christ is contained and sacrificed in an unbloody manner, who once offered himself in a bloody manner on the altar of the cross . . . The victim is one and the same, the same now offering by the ministry of priests, who then offered himself on the cross, the manner alone of offering being different . . . If anyone says that the sacrifice of the mass is only a sacrifice of praise and thanksgiving . . . but not a propitiatory sacrifice . . . let him be anathema.'

In the last hundred years or so, strenuous efforts have been made both by Roman Catholic* and by Anglo-Catholic* theologians to restate the Tridentine teaching without basically departing from it. Some have tried to avoid the objection of the once-for-all character of Christ's sacrifice by transferring attention from his death to his heavenly intercession (V. Thalhofer, S. C. Gayford, F. C. N. Hicks). Others have tried to avoid the same objection by claiming that the acts of the divine Word are timeless, or that the sacramental world is a world of its own, in which what was historically a once-for-all event can be made present again without being repeated (O. Casel, A. Vonier, E. Masure, G. Dix, E. Mascall). Some have contended that the Last Supper was part of the offering of Christ's sacrifice, so the eucharist is also (M. de la Taille, W. Spens). Most commonly, it has been argued that when Christians offer themselves to God, Christ is offering himself, since the church is Christ's mystical body (E. Mersch, Dix, Mascall, *etc*.). The last of these arguments is least obviously at variance with the Epistle to the Hebrews, but the self-offering of Christians is by no means confined to the eucharist; and even if it is theologically correct to say that Christ offers himself in our self-offering, this does not make it an atoning self-offering, as his self-offering on the cross was; so the consideration, though true, is irrelevant.

Much play has also been made with the term *anamnēsis*. This is the Gk. noun used in our Lord's command 'Do this in remembrance of me' (Lk. 22:19; 1 Cor. 11:24–25) and normally means a 'remembering' or 're-minding'. In later liturgical usage, it de-notes the commemorative offering regularly included as part of pre-Reformation conse-cration prayers, but the important question is: What did Christ mean by it at the Last Supper? It has been argued that he meant a reminding of God, not of men, possibly with sacrificial overtones; but the question about who is being reminded is always dependent on the context. Here the Passover background indicates a remembering by men (Ex. 12:14; 13:3, 9; Dt. 16:3), as Paul's paraphrase of the term by *katangellō* (proclaim), an ordinary word for preaching to men, in 1 Cor. 11:25–26, also indicates. Recently, it has been commonly asserted that the term has really nothing to do with reminding or remem-bering, and speaks of making something in the past present again today. This is the way the term is used in recent ecumenical reports, such as those of the Anglican-Roman Catholic International Commission and the Lima Faith and Order conference (*Baptism, Eucharist and Ministry*, Geneva, 1982). This is, however, an obvious piece of wishful thinking, unsupported by either etymology or usage. The real sense of the term in the Jewish Gk. of our Lord's day is shown by Philo, *De Congressu* 39–44.

Bibliography

A. Barclay, *The Protestant Doctrine of the Lord's Supper* (Glasgow, 1927); R. Bruce, *The Mystery of the Lord's Supper* (1590–91; ed. T. F. Torrance, London, 1958); N. Dimock, *The Doctrine of the Lord's Supper* (London, 1910); D. Gregg, *Anamnesis in the Eucharist* (Bramcote, Notts., 1976); J. Jeremias, *The Eucharistic Words of Jesus* (London, 1966); A. J. Macdonald (ed.), *The Evangelical Doctrine of Holy Communion* (Cambridge, 1930); J. I. Packer (ed.), *Eucharistic Sacrifice* (London, 1962); J. B. Segal, *The Hebrew Passover from the Earliest Times to AD 70* (London, 1963); G. Wainwright, *Eucharist and Eschatology* (London, ²1978).

R.T.B.

EUNOMIANS, see ARIANISM.

EUSEBIUS OF CAESAREA (*c.* 265–*c.* 339). Eusebius is chiefly famous for his *Ecclesiastical History* (definitive edition *c.* 325) but theologically for pronouncements upon the Trinity* at the time of the Arian* controversy. He adopted the strains in Origen's* teaching which most leant towards a subordinationism, being imbued, like Origen, with a sense of God's unique self-existence as the author of all things. While insisting that the Son or Logos* existed before all the ages and all times, he nevertheless denied that the Son was coeternal with God, and he associated his generation with the Father's will. The focus of unity between Father and Son rested with a shared glory. Not surprisingly Eusebius was embarrassed by the *homoousios* formula of Nicaea, probably because it recalled the spectre of Paul of Samo-sata (see Adoptionism*). The Holy Spirit* fared even worse at his hands, being described as a 'third' rank and power and, as Origen said, 'one of the things which have come into existence through the Son'.

Eusebius was radical but not as radical as Arius himself, though possibly drawn by the fear of Sabellianism (see Monarchianism*) into the circle of Arian influence. Those who were not Arians (but could not be counted among the more moderate opponents of Athanasius*) readily identified with his views.

The other strand of Origenism in Eusebius was his approach to Christology.* He continued the tradition of emphasizing the pre-incarnation mediatorial* function of the Word but pressed the centrality of the Word in incarnation* even further, so that the human soul was eclipsed altogether. Thus in some measure he anticipated the develop-ments which led up to Apollinarianism.*

Perhaps Eusebius' greatest influence derived from his role as the apologist of the 'Constan-tinian revolution'. His theology of the Chris-tian empire and the Christian emperor, correl-ating them with the kingdom of God and the Logos, laid down the main lines of Byzantine thought for centuries to come, but had less impact on the West.

Bibliography

J. N. D. Kelly, *Early Christian Creeds* (London, ³1972); *idem*, *Early Christian Doctrines* (London, ⁵1977); C. Luibhéid,

Eusebius of Caesarea and the Arian Crisis (Dublin, 1981); D. S. Wallace-Hadrill, *Eusebius of Caesarea* (London, 1960).

R.K.

EUTHANASIA, see BIOETHICS.

EUTYCHES, see MONOPHYSITISM.

EVANGELICAL THEOLOGY. Contemporary evangelical theology has long and deep roots. Some consider that it was primarily formed by reaction to theological liberalism,* and while it is no doubt true that this conflict has frequently introduced a certain complexion to evangelical theology, its basic substance is drawn from the heritage of orthodox Christian theological formation. Evangelical theology in essence stands in the great Christian theological tradition.

Evangelical theology goes back to the creeds* of the first centuries of the Christian era, in which the early church sought to correlate the teaching of Scripture, penetrate its meaning and defend it. In concert with the thought of this period, evangelical theology affirms that: the Bible is the truthful revelation of God and through it the life-giving voice of God speaks; God is the almighty creator and we are his dependent creation; God has entered history redemptively in the incarnation of Jesus Christ; God's nature exists in Trinitarian expression; Jesus Christ is fully divine and fully human, the power and judgment of sin is a reality for all humanity; God graciously takes the initiative in coming to us savingly in Jesus Christ and by the Holy Spirit; Jesus Christ is building his church; and the consummation of history will be expressed in the second advent of Jesus Christ, the general resurrection, the final judgment, heaven and hell.

Evangelical theology also has strong links with the early medieval church. It draws heavily upon the satisfaction* view of the atonement* enunciated by Anselm* of Canterbury and shares the concomitant stress upon the passion of Jesus Christ expressed by no-one more fully than Bernard of Clairvaux.*

Evangelical theology has particular ties with the distinctives of the Protestant* Reformation.* It is deeply committed to the centrality of the Bible (see Scripture*), to its power by the Holy Spirit with special reference to preaching,* to its final authority* in all matters of doctrine and life, and to the necessity of interpreting it as naturally as possible and disseminating it widely in the vernacular. It is equally committed to justification* by faith in which acceptance with God is received by trusting his loving self-disclosure and not by any human accomplishment. It also readily confesses that the church* is composed of all believers who have thus been incorporated by the Holy Spirit, and who have direct, personal and constant access to their heavenly Father.

The Reformation expressed itself in various institutional structures, frequently the result of nationalistic impulse, and in these entities many of the diversities within evangelical theology arose. There were differences in understanding the nature of the sacraments,* the place of the divine decrees in relation to personal salvation (see Predestination*), the time of the millennium,* the form of church government,* the precise nature of biblical inspiration, the way to arrive at Christian assurance* and the relation of the church to culture* and the state* — most of which would be considered by evangelicals today as matters of somewhat secondary importance.

Evangelical theology is also deeply indebted to the series of evangelical awakenings which began about the middle of the 18th century. Here the tendency was to reaffirm the theology of the great and received tradition, and to lay special emphasis on the theology of the Christian life. The nature of saving faith, or conversion,* was continually to the fore, as was the consciousness of the love of God in Christ and the change of disposition which accompanied it, although there might be differences about the instantaneousness of conversion. The means and possibilities of sanctification* were also emphasized, while once again there could be some disagreement over timing and possible achievement. The theology of corporate spiritual life was also stressed, assigning special consideration to the renewing of the church, the evangelizing* of the world and the improving of society.

By the third decade of the 19th century there is evidence that evangelical theology was about to break out of its preoccupation with the theology of the Christian life, and through serious exegetical work and reflective thought once again make the orthodox theological heritage a vibrant option as had been done in the early Middle Ages and at the Reformation. Unfortunately for evangelical theology it was hit just at this time with the full force of theological liberalism,* which combined the older Enlightenment* rationalism with the post-Kantian stress on the human consciousness as the bridge to the knowledge of God – which was singularly appealing to a Romantic* age. Amid such a scene, evangelical theology tended to move either into enervating accommodation with the new views or retreat into a ghetto, defending the received deposit and shooting at almost anything that moved. While such 'confessionalists' did yeoman service in upholding the essentials of orthodox theology, they frequently did so in a way that dismissed much of their contemporary world of thought out of hand, played down the distinctive evangelical emphases on the theology of the Christian life, and gave the impression that the final formulation of all theology was imbedded in the confessions* of the Reformation period.

One glimmer of what evangelical theology might have been was the Dutch school that emerged later in the century around Abraham Kuyper.* Their genius was able to affirm the orthodox tradition, have a profound sense of the importance of a theology of the Christian life in all its ramifications, and at the same time be sensitive to many of the issues and approaches being raised by the world in which they lived.

In the late 19th century, as the pressure of theological liberalism continued to intensify and evangelicalism weakened, an even more defensive evangelical theology arose in the form of fundamentalism.* Its key bulwark was an extreme millenarianism which affirmed that the church and society were hurtling into irremediable ruin. Christianity had nothing to say to the issues of the 'now'; it was all in the 'not yet'.

From the middle of the 20th century, a revitalization has been taking place within evangelical theology. British scholars have contributed a serious and scholarly exegetical approach; Americans have been hard at work in areas of systematic theology* and its adjunct disciplines such as apologetics* and ethics;* the Dutch and the Mennonites* have been developing theologies of social action from significantly diverse starting-points, and the Pentecostal*/charismatic movement has

been enunciating a theology of the Holy Spirit which insists that God is powerfully and miraculously present through the church to minister to the needs of mankind (see Baptism in the Spirit;* Gifts of the Spirit*).

Finally, it should be emphasized that evangelical theology is what might be termed a spiritual theology. It has a way of doing theology which is again part of the great theological tradition. It is 'live' orthodoxy. The Bible is not only central to the theological enterprise, but it is meditated upon and prayed over as well as studied. The goal of theological work is not so much to know theology as to know God; the temptations of academic pride must be mortified, theology must be done within a community of love and out of love for others, and in the awareness that the return of Jesus Christ and the day of accounting is near. Thus the whole of the evangelical theological enterprise is for the glory of God.

Bibliography

D. G. Bloesch, *The Evangelical Renaissance* (Grand Rapids, MI, 1973); idem, *the Future of Evangelical Christianity: A Call for Unity Amid Diversity* (New York, 1983); G. W. Bromiley, *Historical Theology: An Introduction* (Grand Rapids, MI, 1978); E. J. Carnell, *The Case for Biblical Christianity* (Grand Rapids, MI, 1968); C. F. H. Henry (ed.), *Christian Faith and Modern Theology* (New York, 1964); E. Jay, *The Religion of the Heart: Anglican Evangelicalism and the Nineteenth-Century Novel* (Oxford, 1979); G. M. Marsden, *Fundamentalism and American Culture: The Shaping of Twentieth Century Evangelicalism 1870–1925* (New York, 1980); Mark A. Noll, *Between Faith and Criticism: Evangelicals, Scholarship, and the Bible in America* (San Francisco, CA, 1987); B. L. Ramm, *The Evangelical Heritage* (Waco, TX, 1973); idem, *After Fundamentalism: The Future of Evangelical Theology* (San Francisco, CA, 1985); E. R. Sandeen, *The Roots of Fundamentalism: British and American Millenarianism 1800–1930* (Chicago, 1970); J. D. Woodbridge et al., *The Gospel in America: Themes in the Story of America's Evangelicals* (Grand Rapids, MI, 1979).

I.S.R.

EVANGELISM, THEOLOGY OF. The theology of evangelism must be derived from the original setting in which the word was used. The Gk. verb *euangelizesthai* means 'to announce good news', and is found 52 times in the NT. The noun *euangelion* means 'good news', and occurs 72 times, mostly in Paul. The noun *euangelistēs*, meaning 'evangelist', appears only three times (Acts 21:8; Eph. 4:11; 2 Tim. 4:5).

Evangelism, then, is 'to share or announce the good news'; and as such it is not to be defined in terms of particular methods. Methods may vary widely, provided only that their style matches the message to be proclaimed (2 Cor. 2:17; 4:2, 5). Nor should evangelism be defined in terms of successful results. The NT shows that wherever the good news is proclaimed some will respond with repentance and faith, while others will be indifferent and still others reject it (*e.g.* Acts 17:32–34; 2 Cor. 4:3–4).

Recent debates have concerned the scope of the good news. All would agree that the central message is salvation* in Jesus Christ (Acts 8:35; Rom. 1:1, 3); but differences occur over what is crucial and what is peripheral to the explanation of his salvation. Traditionally, evangelism was addressed to individuals, and exclusively concerned the forgiveness of sin. However, the gospels set evangelism in the context of the inauguration of the kingdom of God* (*e.g.* Mk. 1:14–15; Lk. 4:18–19), and so some have argued that the social dimensions of the gospel are integral. The result is that some emphasize God's concern to create a new community; while others argue that there cannot be a strong divorce between evangelism, in a narrow sense, and social action. Yet others, for similar reasons, have argued that the proclamation of the good news of Jesus should not merely be verbal, but must be accompanied by supernatural signs and wonders as a demonstration of God's power and a sign of Satan's defeat (Mk. 16:15–18; Acts 2:22, 43; 4:30; 5:12; 6:8; 14:3; 1 Cor. 4:20).

The theology of evangelism also addresses itself to the motives for evangelism. Among the primary motives identified in the Bible, we find a concern for God's glory; obedience to Christ's commission (Mt. 28:19–20); gratitude for God's grace, and a concern for the fate of the unbeliever.

The Lausanne* Congress on World Evangelization (1974) aptly agreed the statement: 'To evangelize is to spread the good news that Jesus Christ died for our sins and was raised from the dead according to the Scriptures, and that as the reigning Lord he now offers the forgiveness of sins and the liberating gift of the Spirit to all who repent and believe. Our Christian presence in the world is indispensable to evangelism, and so is every kind of dialogue whose purpose is to listen sensitively in order to understand. But evangelism itself is the proclamation of the historical, biblical Christ as Savior and Lord, with a view to persuading people to come to him personally and so be reconciled to God. In issuing the Gospel invitation we have no liberty to conceal the cost of discipleship. Jesus calls all who would follow him to deny themselves, take up their cross, and identify themselves with his new community. The results of evangelism include obedience to Christ, incorporation into his church and responsible service in the world.'

See also: CONTEXTUALIZATION; MISSIOLOGY.

Bibliography
J. D. Douglas (ed.), *Let the Earth Hear His Voice* (Minneapolis, MN, 1975); M. Green, *Evangelism in the Early Church* (London, 1970); J. I. Packer, *Evangelism and the Sovereignty of God* (London, 1961); J. R. W. Stott, *Christian Mission in the Modern World* (London, 1975); D. Watson, *I Believe in Evangelism* (London, 1976).

D.J.T.

EVIL. The apparent contradiction in the coexistence of evil and a good God* is perhaps the commonest charge levelled by critics against theism.* A number of philosophical systems have tried to resolve this dilemma by offering a different view of either the nature of evil or the nature of God. Some forms of pantheism* claim that evil is not real, or at least, 'less than real'. One form of dualism* contends that evil is eternal, like its perpetual war with the good. Those who try to settle the issue by their definition of God assert that God is either not all-good, or not all-powerful, or both (*e.g.* panentheism*). The classical theist, however, cannot resolve the problem of evil by denying or limiting either the reality of evil or the goodness and power of God.

The nature of evil

One of the difficulties faced by the theistic explanation of the problem of evil is that, according to theism, God is the author of everything. Therefore if evil is something, it follows that God is its author. While theists do not reject the first premise, they challenge the premise that evil is some*thing*. The reality of evil does not necessarily imply that it is a substance or a thing. Evil could be a real privation or lack of some good thing (as Augustine* maintained). Accordingly, evil could exist in a good thing as an imperfection in it, like a hole in a piece of wood. Hence, it does not follow that God is the author of something evil.

The origin of evil

Yet, if God is the perfect author of all things, everything he makes has to be perfect. How, then, can his creatures (*e.g.* Adam* the perfect man) be the origin of evil? Classical theists agree that God is the perfect Creator.* In fact, one of the perfect things God created was *free* creatures.

Without free choice, neither good nor evil could be chosen. Hence, if man is ever to choose the good, he must have the freedom to choose evil as well. Therefore, since free will* is the cause of evil, imperfection (evil) can arise from the perfect (not directly, but indirectly, through freedom). In other words, whereas God created the *fact* of freedom, man performs the *acts* of freedom. God made evil possible; creatures make it actual.

The persistence of evil

In the 17th century, Pierre Bayle (1647–1706) formulated the following argument: If God were all-good, he would destroy evil. If God were all-powerful, he could destroy evil. But evil is not destroyed. Hence, there is no such God.

The first theistic objection to Bayle is that evil cannot be 'destroyed' without the destruction of freedom. Love, for example, is impossible without freedom. The same is true of other moral goods such as mercy, kindness, and compassion. And so, contrary to Bayle's argument, to destroy freedom would not be the greatest good, for it would destroy the greatest goods.

However, theists insist that evil will be defeated without the destruction of free choice. If God is all-powerful, he can defeat evil. If God is all-good, he will defeat evil. Thus, since evil is not *yet* defeated, the very nature of the all-powerful, all-good theistic God is the guarantee that evil will eventually be defeated.

The purpose of evil

Even with the explanation based on free will and its role in the presence of evil, what of those who apparently had no choice in the suffering* they endured? It seems that there is no good purpose in much suffering. An all-good being (God) must have a good purpose for everything. Hence, it is argued that there cannot be an all-good God.

However, it is logical to assume that, since God's mind is infinite and man's mind is finite, man will never fully comprehend the divine intellect. So even if *we* do not know God's purpose, he may still have a good purpose for evil. Moreover, we do know some good purposes for evil: to warn us of greater evil; to keep us from self-destruction; to help bring about greater goods; and to defeat evil. If a finite mind can discover some good purposes for evil, surely an infinite good and wise God has a good purpose for all suffering. The crucifixion of Jesus may be said to bear this out.

The avoidability of evil

Some critics have argued that they can propose morally more attractive options for the present world that an all-knowing God supposedly made. If God is omniscient, then he knew evil would occur when he created the world. God had several other non-evil possibilities, such as: 1. not to create anything; 2. not to create anything free; 3. to create free creatures that would not sin; 4. to create free creatures who would sin, but would all be saved in the end.

Briefly, all of these alternatives are poor substitutes for the real thing. Option 1 wrongly implies that nothing is better than something. Every comparison assumes a point of similarity. But how can one compare non-being with being? Option 2 makes the same error, since it wrongly assumes that a non-free world can be compared to a free one. But a non-moral world has nothing morally in common with a moral one.

And while option 3 is logically possible, it may be that it is actually unachievable and morally less desirable. To put it another way, option 3 may be workable on a blackboard, but not in real life. It is possible that options 3 and 4 would never come about freely. But God cannot force freedom, for coercing a free choice is a contradiction in terms. Moreover, option 3 may also be morally less desirable. The possibility and reality of evil provide occasions where the highest virtues can be achieved. Without trials, patience cannot be produced (*cf*. Job). Without the fear of real evil, courage could not be realized.

In short, the classical theist does not have to claim that this world is 'the best of all possible worlds'. Surely this world could be morally better than it is with one fewer rape or murder. However, this world may be the best possible *way* to the best possible world, *i.e.* where moral creatures are given the maximal moral good in accordance with their free choice, including the moral good of mercy for the repentant and the moral good of just punishment for the impenitent.

Bibliography

Augustine, *The Nature of the Good*, in *LCC* vol. 6, *Augustine: Earlier Writings*, tr. J. H. S. Burleigh (London, 1953); S. T. Davis (ed.), *Encountering Evil: Live Options on Theodicy* (Atlanta, GA, 1986); A. Farrer, *Love Almighty and Ills Unlimited* (Garden City, NY, 1961, and London, 1972); N. Geisler, *The Roots of Evil* (Grand Rapids, MI, 1981); G. Leibniz, *Theodicy* (London, 1951); C. S. Lewis, *The Problem of Pain* (London, 1940); J. Wenham, *The Enigma of Evil* (Grand Rapids, MI, and Leicester, 1985).

N.L.G. and J.Y.A.

EXCOMMUNICATION, see DISCIPLINE.

EXISTENTIALISM covers a wide range of themes and authors, Christian, Jewish to atheistic; from Kierkegaard,* K. Jaspers, (1883–1969), J. P. Sartre (1905–80) and M. Heidegger (1889–1976) to A. Camus (1913–60), G. Marcel (1889–1973) and S. Weil (1909–43). It finds its expression in and through drama, literature, poetry, art, music, psychoanalysis and philosophy. The variety of authors is bound together by the refusal to belong to any school of thought or philosophy, the denial of the adequacy of any and every system and set of beliefs, and dissatis-faction with traditional philosophy as superficial and remote from real life. Essentially existentialism is a revolt against rationalism, with its stress on reason alone, for its failure to progress beyond the obvious, its lack of engagement with people, and its ignoring of their real needs. Existentialism revolts against romanticism* on the grounds of its self-deceptive escape from the horrors of life in the here and now, and its unjustifiable optimism about people.

Given the existentialist rejection of systems, the main common thread lies in the themes on which the existentialist expresses his view obliquely. Existentialism is to be experienced directly rather than taught.

Main themes

*1. Anxiety (*Angst*), dread and death.* Existentialist thinking is intended to appeal to the whole personality of a person. It involves one's whole life. One thinks existentially when matters of life and death are at stake. These fundamental realities and our experience of them evoke overwhelming feelings of anxiety, dread and ontological wonderment – amazement at being. The experience of suffering and the meaninglessness of life cause such feelings.

2. Being and existence. Existentialism is concerned with the nature of being and non-being. These realities always evade our concepts and cannot be reduced to neat formulae. Sartre distinguishes the being of objects, which is being *en soi*. This is being which rests in itself and is present, at hand, for humanity to use or abuse. In contrast, human being is being *pour soi*. It is self-awareness, and the capacity to shape other beings and one's own being. For Heidegger, being is understood through an analysis of time. Temporality is basic to the very constitution of existence in terms of past, present and future. This he calls 'care'. Past, present and future are paralleled by facticity, fallenness (forfeiture) and possibility. Humanity is possibility, because it stands before an open future in which it is always in process and incomplete. Humanity is facticity, because its past in terms of heredity, environment and previous experience inevitably shapes what we are and may become. Humanity is 'fallen' in its tendency to shrink from responsibility to the past and the future by hiding in the present. Humanity is faced with a choice in existence. Unauthentic existence lacks will

243

(irresoluteness), lives in the present, the past or the future, and refuses to acknowledge facticity and possibility. Authentic existence is resolute and makes choices in the present in light of the past and open to the future. The authentic self is a unitary, stable, and relatively abiding structure, in which the polarities of existence are held in balance and its potentialities are brought to fulfilment.

3. *Intentionality*. Existentialism focuses on the inner experiences of will, emotions, beliefs, imagination and intention. These are understood by examination of the individual consciousness. The key to understanding all knowledge is the study of internal phenomena, rather than the external behaviour which appears to follow such states.

4. *Absurdity*. The existentialist believes that there is no meaning in any one thing, or in everything put together. The world is absurd and pointless. To be human is to choose in the light of the absurdity of the world.

5. *Choice and the individual*. Choice is the centre of human existence. Self-conscious being is being which chooses. We are what we choose. We make ourselves by our choices. Not to choose is itself a choice. Choices have no rational basis or purpose, so it does not matter *what* we choose, only *that* we choose. Thus in drama, literature and poetry the existentialist often focuses on impossible choices, especially of the moral variety, and the human necessity to choose in the face of absurdity. The individual agent is the one who has to choose, for the crowd is a lie and offers an escape from responsibility. Individual responsibility for one's own existence is necessary.

Impact on theology

Existentialism, through Heidegger, has influenced and formed existential theology especially in the work of Barth,* Bultmann,* Tillich* and Macquarrie.* This approach stresses the existential moment in hermeneutics* and preaching, in which humanity is summoned to respond to the call of God to live an authentic life. Jesus is the perfect example of an authentic existence. The nature of being, as outlined by existentialism, has led Tillich to interpret God as the 'ground of our being' rather than as a being at all. This affects both theological epistemology* and ontology (see Being*). Existentialist philosophy asks the

fundamental human questions of existence. Theology's task is to provide the answers.

Other writers such as Marcel and Weil have adopted an existential approach to theology in contrast to a clinically abstract theology. For them, theology is participative and incarnational, emphasizing the ontological weight of human experience. The key is dialogue and communication as an individual (the 'I') with the eternal 'Thou'. This leads to faith and assurance.

Critical reflections

Positively, the existentialist reminds us that true religion must be individual, involved with the real needs of people, and lived out authentically. The existentialist paints an accurate picture of life without God. It is no accident that many find in existentialism the roots of the 'Death of God'* theology. Negatively, the philosophy is self-contradictory in its basic statement that 'everything is meaningless'. It isolates the will from the whole personality, the individual from the community, and the inner life from the outer life. It concentrates on the exceptional and unusual and gives too little systematic understanding of the nature of being itself. In theological terms, the danger is of a loss of objectivity and any genuine understanding of God and of an amalgamation of a philosophy which is at root anthropocentric and atheistic with an approach to theology which is too individualistic and experience-oriented, and allows modern culture to operate a critical function as a standard by which to judge biblical and theological understandings and expressions.

Bibliography

J. Macquarrie, *An Existentialist Theology* (London, 1955); *idem*, *Existentialism* (London, 1972); D. E. Roberts, *Existentialism and Religious Belief* (New York, 1957); J.-P. Sartre, *Existentialism and Humanism* (ET, London, 1948); M. Warnock, *Existentialism* (London, 1970).

E.D.C.

EX OPERE OPERATO, see Sacrament.

EXORCISM. Babylonian and Egyptian texts indicate that the practice of expelling evil spiritual beings from people (and places) is very ancient. The oldest exorcism story is in 1 Sa. 16 – 19. Eastern influence in

Palestine brought an increase in the belief that demons (see Devil*) could control people, so that by the time of Jesus exorcism was relatively common.

The gospel traditions and the use of Jesus' name by other exorcists show that Jesus was considered a particularly successful exorcist against whom the demons sought to defend themselves (Mk. 1:24). His ministry of exorcism was distinctive, in that he used no mechanical aids or proofs; nor was prayer part of his technique; nor did he call upon any outside power-authority (though cf. Mt. 12:28; Lk. 11:20). Rather, in saying 'I cast out . . .' Jesus deliberately drew attention to himself and his own resources in his ability to expel demons. Not surprisingly, responses to Jesus' exorcisms are described as fear and amazement (Mk. 1:27; 5:14–15). Some said that he was demon-possessed (Mk. 3:20–27). The interpretation that his exorcisms showed that he was the Messiah probably reflects the faith of Christians for there is little or no pre-Christian evidence that the Messiah was expected to be an exorcist. Jesus was the first to make the specific connection between exorcism and the first stage of the defeat of the devil.* The charge that Jesus exorcized by magic is also late (cf. Eusebius, EH 4.3.2; Origen, Against Celsus 1.6, 68–71).

The disciples shared Jesus' ministry of exorcism (Lk. 9:1–6) and it was an important part of the ministry of the apostolic church, except in the Johannine community. In Jn. it is the cross which functions as the focus of the complete defeat of the evil ruler of this world (12:31; 14:30; 16:11), which becomes existential as Jesus draws all men to himself (12:32). Paul was reluctantly involved in exorcism (Acts 16:16–18). Matthew plays down exorcism, probably because his church suffered from the exploits of false prophets whose activities included exorcism (7:15–23; 24:11, 24). Mark and Luke emphasize exorcism in the church's ministry (Mk. 6:7–13; 9:14–29; Lk. 10:17–20) and show that early Christians like other exorcists use the name of a power-authority, viz. Jesus (Mk. 9:38–41; Lk. 10:17; Acts 16:18; 19:13). The early Christians believed they were successful as exorcists not because of what they said or did, but because, by simple commands, the demons were confronted and defeated by Jesus. Prayer was required in difficult cases (Mk. 9:28–29).

The charismatic understanding of the authority to exorcise demons using the name of Jesus continued for some time in the post-apostolic period. Apart from the central use of the name of Jesus, the practice of exorcism soon began to vary. In places a 'history' of Jesus (Origen, Against Celsus 1.6; 3.24) was used as well as the 'name'. The breath of the exorcist, touch, and the sign of the cross were also used. Exorcism was commonly an element of the baptismal rite, and the Clementine Recognitions state that baptism frees a person from an unclean spirit. A letter from Cornelius of Rome to Fabius of Antioch in 252 shows that in the West 'exorcist' had become one of the four minor orders of clergy. By the 6th century the exorcist on appointment received a book of formulae containing prayers and adjurations.

Until 1969 exorcism was part of the rite of infant baptism in the Roman Catholic Church and it is still retained in adult baptism. With the bishop's permission only priests may perform an exorcism. Luther's revised Order of Baptism (1526) omitted the exsufflation and reduced the exorcisms from three to one (J. D. C. Fisher, Christian Initiation: The Reformation Period, London, 1970, pp. 6–16, 23–25). Outside baptism, he advised prayer rather than exorcism. The first Book of Common Prayer (1549) contained a rite for pre-baptismal exorcism, but since 1552 it has contained no provision for exorcism. Canon 72 (1604) of the Church of England forbids the priest without episcopal licence 'by fasting and prayer to cast out any devil or devils'. Today, for some, a changed view of the world means that little or even nothing can be attributed to the activity of demons. Rather, the proper way to cast out evil is by repentance, faith, prayer and the sacraments (cf. Don Cupitt, Explorations in Theology, vol. 6 (London, 1979), pp. 50–51). Despite hesitations among theologians and church hierarchies the practice of exorcism has increased in recent years in almost all denominations in response to pastoral needs.

See also: DEVIL AND DEMONS.

Bibliography

O. Böcher et al., 'Exorzismus', TRE 10 (1982), pp. 747–761: T. K. Oesterreich, Possession, Demoniacal and Other (London, 1930); J. Richards, But Deliver Us From Evil: An Introduction to the Demonic Dimension *in Pastoral Care* (New York, 1974); G. H. Twelftree, *Christ Triumphant* (London, 1984).

G.H.T.

EXPIATION, see ATONEMENT; SACRIFICE.

EXTREME UNCTION, see ANOINTING.

F

FAIRBAIRN, A. M., see CONGREGATIONALISM.

FAITH. Faith is a word that has a poor press in the 20th century. Many regard it as simple-mindedness and as an expression of an uncritical spirit inappropriate to men and women 'come of age'. By contrast, the Scriptures seem to regard faith as a stepping forward, not into darkness but into the light which God has given.

Faith, of course, must be understood in a number of ways. It may refer to dogma* which is believed (in this sense the expression 'the faith' comes to mind) or it may refer to trust in a person, which is essentially relational in character.

Faith is a quality highly prized in Scripture. Heb. 11:6 sums this up by saying that 'without faith it is impossible to please God'. The Reformers recovered from Scripture, notably from Paul's letters, the doctrine of justification* by faith alone (*sola fide;* Rom. 4:5; 9:30; Gal. 3:2). At times, evangelical theology has been in danger of making faith a 'work' in itself. However, the Reformation tradition at its best has seen that believers are justified and saved by God's grace operating through faith. Faith has been essential, for example, to justification, but it is not so much in strict terms that we are saved *by* it: rather we are not saved without it.

In Scripture faith is both an attitude of spirit which we freely exercise, and the gift of God. Eph. 2:8 lays stress on the gift aspect. Yet, throughout the NT, people are exhorted to believe or trust or have faith (*e.g.* Jn. 14:1; Acts 16:31). The relationship between our freedom to repent and to believe in Christ, on the one hand, and the giving of repentance and faith, on the other, has been a matter of contention among Christians since the days of Augustine* in the 5th century. Both Scripture and the church traditions (Catholic and Protestant) appear to say that faith is mysteriously both a divine gift and an uncoerced human activity.

A common traditional distinction is that between *assensus*, assent, and *fiducia*, trust. While trust in God and in his Son, Jesus Christ, is of paramount importance in Scripture and in Christian experience, clearly *what* we believe is also of considerable practical importance. What we believe tends to determine our attitudes and behaviour. Moreover, Heb. 11:6 recognizes that before a person comes to God he must believe in the reality of God, and further believe that he will reward those who seek him diligently.

As emphases differ in laying stress either on the human or divine character of faith in justification and salvation, so some theologians lay more stress on the human factors leading to conviction about God and Christ, while others suggest that such conviction is wholly or primarily the result of a unique operation of the Holy Spirit in human hearts.

Assensus has often been associated in traditional natural theology* with intellectual assent to general truths about God and providence, which are at least consistent with reason, though perhaps not established by it. It has also been associated with belief in truths made available to us through the Scriptures or through the authority of the church. It has been urged that it is consistent with reason to rest upon the authority of the Scriptures and/or that of the church: accordingly, we accept the detailed truths made available to us thereby, such as the doctrine of the Trinity or of salvation. This accords the way in which people commonly accept today the truths made known to us on the authority of the scientific establishment, such as the age of the earth or the chemical composition of the stars.

Another strain of Christian theology, associated in the early church with Tertullian,* and in modern centuries with the names of Calvin,* Kierkegaard* and Barth,* lays greater stress upon the inability of the natural person to receive truth about God, and upon the work of the Holy Spirit in supernaturally imparting such knowledge. Karl Barth is doubtless the most extreme exponent of this emphasis, but Reformation and post-Reformation theologians have tended to stress this also.

The options are not simply between discovering at least some basic truths about God by reason, and discovering them through the supernatural revelation of truth witnessed to in the Scriptures. Liberal theologians, influenced by 19th-century idealist* philosophy, have made much of faith (whether in God or in Christ) as a matter of judgment. Liberals have not intended to deny divine influence in leading us to truth, but they have been resistant to seeing revelation of divine truth as operating in some special way that is unrelated to the way in which we apprehend truths about the world. Apprehension of the truths of theology, it is held, must be of the same order as the apprehension of all truth.

In Scripture, and in the historical Christian tradition, faith always points beyond itself to that which is believed in, or to the one in whom we believe. Just as in justification faith is necessary but has the value of a link, relating us to the source of our salvation, so in the grasp of the truths of Christian theology the emphasis falls upon the givenness of that truth in its objective reality. Faith is only the means by which we apprehend.

Behind all faith in Scripture and in the mainstream of the Christian tradition (especially in its more evangelical understanding) lies the reality of God and his Christ. At the level of intellectual grasp of truth this has an affinity with that understanding of the world of nature which sees it as objectively 'being there' and being available for our understanding. Our knowledge is not so much a relative man-centred view, in which these truths hold good for us but which may not inhere in reality beyond us. Our knowledge is, rather, a penetration into reality, creaturely or divine, which exists beyond our perceiving spirits.

In experiential Christian faith we also get into difficulty when we become more concerned about the character of our faith than about the one to whom faith should be directed, namely, Jesus Christ. When this happens assurance* of salvation is weakened.

Faith in its various forms is central to the Christian life. Paul's understanding is that genuine relational faith is expressed in ethical behaviour, while James sees it as intimately coupled with its expression in good works.

'Faith without deeds is dead' (Jas. 2:26). Faith has a bearing on the intellect, the heart and will, and on behaviour patterns.

Bibliography

H. Berkhof, *Christian Faith* (Grand Rapids, MI, ²1986); G. Ebeling, *The Nature of Faith* (London, 1961); J. Hick, *Faith and Knowledge* (London, 1974); B. Milne, *Know the Truth* (Leicester, 1982); K. Runia, *I Believe in God* (London, 1963); T. F. Torrance, *God and Rationality* (London, 1971).

G.W.M.

FAITH AND ORDER, see ECUMENICAL MOVEMENT.

FAITH AND REASON. Because conceptions of both faith and reason have varied so widely in the Christian church, there is no one answer to the question of the relationship between the two. However, a few broad patterns may be distinguished.

If by 'reason' is meant the faculty of *reasoning* – drawing deductive and inductive conclusions from data – there is a broad measure of agreement within the Christian church that faith (whether understood as 'the faith' or as the act of faith) is compatible with reason; indeed it requires reason both in order to understand what is believed, and to articulate what is believed in an orderly, coherent and systematic way. Christians have recognized such logical influences on the very surface of the Bible (*e.g.* Mt. 12:26; Lk. 6:39) and in the outworking of the mysteries of the faith in creeds* and confessional formulae (*e.g.* the Nicene Creed). This attitude of reason to (the) faith has found classic expression in the words of the Westminster Confession, that 'the whole counsel of God, concerning all things necessary for his own glory, man's salvation, faith and life, is either expressly set down in Scripture, or by good and necessary consequence may be deduced from Scripture' (I.vi). Even Luther,* who was capable of making very uncomplimentary remarks about philosophers such as Aristotle, did not shrink from writing a first-rate work of systematic theology, *De Servo Arbitrio* (*On the Bondage of the Will*; 1525).

In both the medieval period and in the Enlightenment* (as well as less dominantly in other periods), 'reason' came to mean not only the faculty of reasoning from data but also the ability to certify certain data as 'reasonable'. This has operated, destructively, in rationalist attacks upon the Christian gospel from outside the church. But also, from within the church, it has operated in three discernibly different ways. 1. In the classical medieval position, and in all forms of natural* or rational theology since then, reason is said to provide a stock of initial propositions or data 'evident to the senses' or acceptable to all rational people, from which certain theological conclusions can be deduced which act as the *praeambula fidei*. Not that all Christians are capable of making the requisite inferences; but they can all be assured that such inferences are possible. Weaker senses of 'reasonable' also operated in anti-deist* writers such as Joseph Butler* and William Paley,* and those influenced by them. The religious and theological danger of this approach, quite apart from the success or otherwise of the 'proofs' of God's existence, lies in its abstract rationalism.

2. It was a characteristic position of the 18th-century Enlightenment that, in Kant's* words, religion should be confined 'within the limits of reason alone'. What this meant, in practice, was the excision of all supernatural references from Scripture, or the adopting of a hermeneutic* which effectively 'naturalized' them by regarding Scripture as a re-telling of the truths of reason in figurative and emblematic form for popular consumption, and (in the case of Kant and his immediate followers) the distilling of the pure essence of religion in terms of individual ethics (Kant), sentiment and pious affection (Schleiermacher*) or social engagement (through the implementation of the ethics of Jesus; Ritschl*). It is of the utmost importance to recognize that such appeals to 'reason' and 'logic' are not neutral and objective, as they may appear to be, but incorporate substantive ontological, epistemological* and sometimes moral positions.

3. 'Reason' has been appealed to in order to set up a barrier against the incursion of what has been regarded as mystical or enthusiastic excess. Thus John Locke,* writing against the background of what he regarded as the sectarian chaos of 17th-century England, could write: 'If anything shall be thought *revelation* which is contrary to the plain principles of reason and the evident knowledge the mind has of its own clear and distinct ideas, their reason must be hearkened

to, as to a matter within its province' (*Essay* IV.xviii.8). Locke himself is somewhat equivocal in the way in which he employs this criterion, employing it not only in order to assert that no credible revelation can be unintelligible gibberish, but also to assert a more substantive control of what may count as revelation.

There has been a fairly definite correlation, and perhaps a logical connection, between views of the place of reason in articulating, reconstructing or delimiting the faith, and views of faith.* In the medieval church, and in much present-day Roman Catholic theology, faith is primarily, if not exclusively, assent to the basic doctrines of 'the faith'. The credibility of these doctrines is attested by the church's authority which is in turn based upon an appreciation of the rational arguments for God's existence, divine revelation, and the church as the infallible teaching authority. Faith is thus assent (sometimes explicit, often implicit) to those propositions certified by the church.

At the other extreme, faith is seen by many, particularly those influenced by existentialism* from Søren Kierkegaard* onwards (some would find antecedents in Luther* and Pascal,* probably mistakenly), as a leap in the dark. It is an act of trust in God which goes beyond the evidence, and in some cases goes against the evidence. (This distrust of reason has sometimes been called 'fideism'.) It is clear that it would be difficult to hold such a view along with an acceptance of natural theology. But it would be a mistake to suppose that because faith requires no reasons, no reasons can be given for this view of faith.

In classical Protestantism, faith is trust in Christ for salvation, the Christ to whom the Scriptures exclusively bear witness. Though some have ventured to attempt to authenticate the Scriptures as the divine revelation by reason, appealing to certain of its unique features to do so, in general in Protestantism the Scriptures have been regarded as self-authenticating. God, by his Spirit, bears testimony to his people to the divine and saving character of his word not by investing that word with a set of private, Gnostic meanings, but by bearing testimony in the mind and conscience of the regenerate, in a dynamic, ongoing fashion, to the divine authority of Scripture. Faith in Christ is thus of a piece with faith in the trustworthiness of the Scriptures, which reveal and testify to Christ. It is not the 'reason' alone to which the Scriptures appeal but the whole person in the context of the fellowship of the church.

See also: EPISTEMOLOGY; PHILOSOPHICAL THEOLOGY; PHILOSOPHY AND THEOLOGY; PHILOSOPHY OF RELIGION.

Bibliography
G. H. Clark, Religion, Reason and Revelation (Nutley, NJ, 1961); P. Helm, The Varieties of Belief (London, 1973); J. Hick, Faith and Knowledge (London, 1967); C. Michalson, The Rationality of Faith (London, 1964).

P.H.

FALL. The post-Enlightenment* primacy of rationalism and idealism,* together with the rise of biblical criticism* and the development of evolutionary theory (see Creation*), have provided the context and impetus for a rigorous questioning of the doctrine of the fall and the concepts of original sin* and original righteousness.* Was there ever a state of original righteousness? Was there ever a time when nature was not 'red in tooth and claw'? Was there ever an historical Adam* and, if there was, how can the sin of one man affect the whole of humanity? Such questions have inevitably led to symbolic interpretations of the narrative of Gn. 3 which view it as a mythical account of the condition of all mankind and the nature of human sin.

Yet while the account is clearly capable of such symbolic and existentialist* interpretations, the apparently historical elements of the narrative ought not to be arbitrarily ignored or avoided. The fall may be that in which all of mankind are personally involved and thus the story of all mankind, but it is primarily presented in the narrative as the experience of one particular man whose history has come to affect the history of mankind as the truth concerning the whole human race. Moreover, it is not merely humanity that is affected by Adam's fall. The narrative also refers to God cursing the ground as a consequence of Adam's sin. Paul speaks of the whole created order as being 'subjected to frustration' in the hope of being 'liberated from its bondage to decay' (Rom. 8:20–21). Such references appear to signify a 'cosmic fall' as the consequence of the sin and fall of this one man.

While the narrative of Gn. 3 relates the event of Adam's fall and its consequences, there is no biblical account of a *doctrine* of the fall of mankind (in the sense of a clear statement of the relationship between the sin and guilt of Adam and the sin and guilt of all mankind) apart from Rom. 5:12–21 (and by implication 1 Cor. 15:21–22). The OT never refers to either the origin or transmission of sin and guilt (but *cf.* hints such as Ps. 51:5). Similarly, neither in rabbinic nor in Jewish apocalyptic literature is there reference to anything recognizably similar to the Christian doctrine of the fall. Sin and evil are variously attributed to Satan (or demonic beings) or a 'spirit of evil' within man (as distinct from a 'spirit of good'). The implication here (as in the gospels) is that man is himself accountable for the sin he commits and responsible for living according to the one 'spirit' as opposed to the other. Even in the gospels, there is no explicit reference to either the origin or the transmission of sin.

Although the early church fathers refer to Adam's fall, they generally retain a strong emphasis upon individual human responsibility. Not until Augustine* do we find an extended attempt to define clearly a doctrine of the fall in terms of the connection between the sin and guilt of Adam and the sin and guilt of all humanity. Augustine understood the corruption of human nature to be primarily 'concupiscence' (*i.e.* lust; especially sexual lust). He thought of original sin as inherited sin, the fallen nature of Adam transmitted biologically through sexual procreation from fathers to their children. Moreover, since all were germinally present in Adam, all actually participated in Adam's sin.

This understanding was rejected by Pelagius* who argued that men and women were born in the state of Adam prior to his fall, and were therefore free both from Adam's guilt and the pollution of Adam's sin; though they now had the example of Adam's and others' sin before them. Pelagius' account is clearly inadequate, since it considers sin as the outcome of individual acts rather than as a state of separation from God from which we need to be liberated in order to choose what is good (Rom. 7:14–25). Moreover, as Calvin* was to indicate, since the righteousness of

Christ does not benefit us merely as an example to be followed, the same must surely be true of Adam's sin.

Augustine's interpretation was largely confirmed at the Council of Orange (529). Despite modification by Anselm* and moderation by Thomas Aquinas* it remained generally that of the church throughout the Middle Ages. This understanding of concupiscence and inherited sin was obviously influential in the development of monastic asceticism* and Mariology (see Mary*).

While the Reformers generally (with the notable exception of Zwingli*) reaffirmed Augustine, his account of the transmission of sin and guilt is modified by Calvin. In the first place Calvin understood the text of Rom. 5:12 differently. Augustine interpreted the verse to mean that all men and women were themselves included in the particular sin of Adam, and therefore were included in his guilt and subject to the condemnation of death. Calvin argued that it was rather because all received depravity from Adam that all were guilty and under the dominion of death: all have sinned because all are 'imbued with natural corruption'. Moreover, though Calvin refers to 'a hereditary depravity and corruption of our nature' (*Institutes* II.i.8) he considers the relationship between Adam's sin and the sin of all to be a result of an ordinance of God, rather than primarily a matter of biological heredity; original sin is the outcome of a judgment of God upon mankind, imputing Adam's sin to all, just as Christ's righteousness is now imputed to all believers. Beza,* Calvin's successor at Geneva, expressed this representative understanding of the inclusion of all mankind in the fall by referring to Adam as the 'federal representative' of all; it is in this representative manner that all are included in Adam's sin, an inclusion confirmed by the individual sinful acts that all men and women commit.

The conception of original sin as 'inherited sin' is totally abandoned in the writings of Karl Barth.* Barth interprets the narrative of Gn. 2 – 3 as 'saga' or 'story' (*praehistorisch Geschichtswirklichkeit*; *i.e. Urgeschichte*), not just the truth about every person but the story and truth that are determinative for everyone. His Christ-centred concentration tends to a 'supralapsarian' interpretation of creation, whereby man is seen as created and immediately fallen (Barth makes much of the lack of

any time sequence in Gn. 2 – 3). Hence there is no state of original righteousness (other than that of Christ himself) and man is not 'on probation', but rather his fall is inevitable and immediate. Nor is he originally immortal: his effective immortality* was dependent upon his continuation in relationship with God; death was 'hidden' from Adam but now confronts everyone in the form of judgment.

Perhaps the most helpful aspect of Barth's contribution (and Calvin's) is the determination to argue from Christ to Adam rather than from Adam to Christ. It is only from the perspective of our inclusion in the righteousness of Christ and its consequences in terms of justification and sanctification that we can comprehend the reality of our inclusion in the sin of Adam with its consequences of guilt, death and total depravity. Our inclusion in Adam may be 'chronologically' prior to our inclusion in Christ, but noetically the roles are reversed. (This may explain the absence of a doctrine of the fall prior to Rom. 5.) Given this Christological framework, however, the fall of Adam must be seen as determinative for us (for all mankind, irrespective of the extent of 'inclusion in Christ'), and not just the truth about us; since the death and resurrection of Christ are determinative for us, as the basis for being the truth of our experience.

The other fundamental question raised by the doctrine of the fall concerns that *from* which Adam fell and that *to* which he fell, a question involving the various interpretations of the phrase 'the image of God'.* Whether a person sins because of 'the bondage of the will' (so Luther and the Reformers) or because he lacks a 'supernatural endowment' of the grace of God (so Aquinas) cannot be dismissed as an irrelevant academic debate. If human reason has been left unaffected by Adam's fall then human reason can be appealed to without qualification. But if it has been 'depraved' as a consequence of Adam's sin, then such an appeal has the appearance of a 'blind alley': 'The man without the Spirit does not accept the things that come from the Spirit of God, for they are foolishness to him, and he cannot understand them, because they are spiritually discerned' (1 Cor. 2:14).

Bibliography

Barth, *CD*, IV.1., pp. 358ff.; G. C. Berkouwer, *Sin* (Grand Rapids, MI, 1971); Calvin, *Institutes*, II.i-ix; M. Luther, *The Bondage of the Will* (1525; trans. J. I. Packer and O. R. Johnston, Cambridge, 1957); D. B. Milne, *Know the Truth: A Handbook of Christian Belief* (Leicester, 1982); J. Murray, *The Imputation of Adam's Sin* (Grand Rapids, MI, 1959); H. Rondet, *Original Sin: The Patristic and Theological Background* (Shannon, 1972); N. P. Williams, *The Ideas of the Fall and of Original Sin* (London, 1929).

J.E.C.

FAMILY. The OT family is a wider circle than the typical two-generation nuclear family of parents and children characteristic of contemporary Western society. It consists of those who share a common blood and common dwelling-place. It also includes servants, resident aliens (*gērîm*) and stateless persons, widows and orphans, who live under the protection of the head of the family, as well as his wife (or wives and concubines if he is a polygamist) and children (see Gn. 7:1, 7; 46:8–26).

Though from the first the divine intention was that marriage (see Sexuality*) should be monogamous (Gn. 2:21–24), the OT furnishes plenty of evidence of the practice of polygamy and concubinage (*e.g.* 2 Sa. 5:13; 1 Ki. 11:3). Yet it would seem that monogamy, not polygamy, though not practised by her kings, was the common form of marriage in Israel. Samuel and Kings do not record a single instance of polygamy among commoners except that of Samuel's father. Polygamy, it would seem, was allowed by God for the same reason as divorce, namely as a temporary concession to human weakness and sinfulness before the coming of Christ (on this point see J. Murray, *Principles of Conduct*, London, 1957, pp. 14–19). The NT leaves no room for it, for otherwise Paul's parallel between the mystical union of Christ and his church and the union of man and wife 'in the Lord' would be altogether inappropriate (Eph. 5:24–33).

The Israelite family is patriarchal, as the term 'house of one's father' (*bêth 'āb*) indicates. Genealogies are always given in the father's line, and women are mentioned only infrequently. Throughout the Bible, the husband as the head of the family is responsible for the godly ordering of family life. This includes the tender care of his wife (Eph. 5:28–29; 1 Pet. 3:7), providing for his family (1 Tim. 5:8), and instructing, encouraging and

disciplining his children in the ways of godliness (Dt. 6:4–7; Eph. 6:4; Col. 3:21). The God-given authority of parents over the family is to be respected and accepted by their children (Ex. 20:12; Eph. 6:2).

In the OT the husband exercises an almost priestly function. Before the formal establishment of the Levitical priesthood he was responsible for offering sacrifices to God on behalf of himself and his family (Gn. 8:20; 12:7–8; 22:2–9). At the Passover, which is observed in the home, the priestly duty of prayer is assigned to the father and he is expected to be able to explain the significance of the meal to his children (Ex. 12:24–27). The weekly sabbath is likewise observed in families, all of whose members share in the day of rest (Ex. 29:9–11; Dt. 5:13–15).

Within the family the covenant* faithfulness of God to his people is to be mirrored in the conjugal fidelity of husband and wife (Pr. 5:18ff.). In the love and care he bestows upon his children the father is to provide a model, albeit imperfect, of the fatherly love and care of God himself. According to Eph. 3:14–15 every family (Gk. *patria*) implies a father (*patēr*), 'so behind them all stands the universal fatherhood of God whence the whole scheme of ordered relationships is derived' (D. W. B. Robinson, *NBD*, p. 372). And the warmth of a mother's love as she comforts her children mirrors God's tender love for his people (Is. 66:13).

In the light of the biblical data it is possible to frame a theological understanding of the family. First, it is evident that the family unit is a basic part of the structure of creation.* From the beginning it is God's purpose that mankind should increase by families, not as isolated individuals. As it is not good for Adam to be alone because he is created for community, so God also sets the lonely in families (Ps. 68:6). From this perspective childlessness (Is. 54:1; *cf.* 1 Sa. 1:10–11), widowhood (La. 1:1) and orphanhood (La. 5:3) may be bitter experiences which involve a desolating loss of community.

Secondly, the family lies at the centre of God's covenant purpose. God promises Abraham that in him all the families of the earth shall be blessed (Gn. 12:3; the Heb. word means an extended family or clan). The family is thus a theological as well as a biological and social structure. Under the Abrahamic covenant the sign of circumcision is administered to every male child within the context of the family (Gn. 17:11–14). He who lacks this sign is to be cut off from his people (v. 14). This means that it is through membership in a covenant family that the child is related to the covenant people Israel.

The relationship of the Christian family to the visible church* continues to be disputed. The Reformed* tradition regards infants as related to the church through their birth-connection with believing parents (Westminster Confession, XXV.ii). However, the status of the children of believing parents is variously understood by Reformed theologians. Charles Hodge* is representative of the majority in holding that the ground of baptism is the presumed regeneration of infants, whereas R. L. Dabney* and J. H. Thornwell* argued that children of Christian parents are to be regarded as unconverted covenant children until such a time as they are brought to faith in Christ. Other disputes arose over the rightness of baptizing adopted children and slaves.

Those who define the visible church as consisting of professed believers tend to relate the family to the church only in terms of the privileges bestowed upon the children of believing parents. However, their privileges do not mean that such children are to be regarded as Christians. Rather they are to be urged to improve their privileges by giving themselves to the Saviour.

The responsibility which is laid upon parents to bring up their children in 'the training and instruction of the Lord' (Eph. 6:4) is seen within both the Roman Catholic and Reformed theological traditions as demanding the setting up of Christian schools. There is however this difference, that Roman Catholic schools are church schools whereas the Reformed emphasis falls upon parent-teacher controlled schools. The latter are seen as necessitated by the place given in Scripture to the family, even more than the church, as the fundamental means of Christian nurture and education.

The nuclear family is variously viewed by contemporary writers as repressive (many Marxist and feminist authors); an instrument of social control, subversive of state or religious authority; a frequent source of psychological disorders; and potentially idolatrous. Many in the West, regarding it as in a state of crisis, seek alternative forms of community such as revived extended families or communes.

Bibliography

R. de Vaux, *Ancient Israel* (London, 1961); J. Gladwin, *Happy Families* (Bramcote, Nottingham, 1981); M. Gordon (ed.), *The Nuclear Family in Crisis: The Search for an Alternative* (New York and London, 1972); A. Greeley (ed.), *The Family in Crisis or in Transition: A Sociological and Theological Perspective* (New York, 1979); John Paul II, *Familiaris Consortio: The Christian Family in the Modern World* (London, 1981); O. R. Johnston, *Who Needs the Family? A Survey and a Christian Assessment* (London, 1979); D. Kingdon, *Children of Abraham: A Reformed Baptist View of Baptism, the Covenant, and Children* (Worthing and Haywards Heath, 1973); L. B. Schenk, *The Presbyterian Doctrine of Children in the Covenant* (New Haven, CN, 1940); M. Schluter and R. Clements, *Reactivating the Extended Family*, Jubilee Centre Papers, no. 1 (Cambridge, 1986); L. Segal (ed.), *What is to be Done about the Family?* (Harmondsworth, 1983) for a radical feminist perspective; J. A. Walter, *A Long Way from Home: A Sociological Exploration of Contemporary Idolatry* (Exeter, 1980).

D.P.K.

FAREL, WILLIAM (1489–1565), was born in Gap, France. He matriculated at the University of Paris (1509) and came under the influence of Jacques Lefèvre who directed Farel to the Scriptures, especially Paul's doctrine of justification* by faith. After persistent struggle, Farel experienced an evangelical breakthrough in 1516. In 1520 he followed Lefèvre to Meaux to preach reform in the French church. His banishment from France in 1522 caused him to itinerate among the Swiss cantons while engaged in debate against Roman theology.

During this period he composed his *Sommaire* (1525), a pocket-sized manual presenting a theology for the laity based heavily on Scripture. Along with forensic justification, Farel stressed a doctrine of the Christian life with a strong emphasis on obedience to the law through good works and ardent devotion. Expositions of the Lord's Prayer and the Apostles' Creed (neither extant), and a liturgy, completed a trilogy of writings explaining the 'new' theology.

Farel's fame lies in securing a hearing for Protestantism in Geneva, from 1532 to 1535. His forceful charge to young Calvin to remain in Geneva is memorable. Later, from 1541 to 1565, he devoted himself to preaching in Neuchâtel, where he faced intense opposition. Those struggles among 'the lost sheep' portray a tireless evangelist with compassion for the common man.

Bibliography

R. Hower, *William Farel, Theologian of the Common Man, and the Genesis of Protestant Prayer* (unpublished ThD thesis, Westminster Theological Seminary, Philadelphia, 1983); D. H. McVicar, *William Farel, Reformer of the Swiss Romand: His Life, His Writings, and His Theology* (unpublished ThD thesis, Union Seminary, New York, 1954); S. E. Ozment, *The Reformation in the Cities* (New Haven, CT, 1975); B. Thompson, *Liturgies of the Western Church* (Cleveland and New York, 1962), pp. 216–218.

R.G.H.

FARRER, AUSTIN MARSDEN
(1904–68). A graduate in 'Greats' (classics and philosophy) and theology, chaplain of St Edmund Hall, 1931–35, and of Trinity College, 1935–60, and warden of Keble 1960–68, Farrer was a brilliant Christian thinker of quintessential Oxford type.

His prolific writings on philosophy, theology, and NT exegesis show an independent, lucid, agile, argumentative and articulate mind, fastidiously whimsical, witty in the matter of a metaphysical poet, Newmanesque in sensitivity, incantatory in expression, and committed to a rational credal orthodoxy. He embodied a devotionally robust Anglican catholicism comparable to that of his peers, Kenneth Kirk (1886–1954), E. L. Mascall (b. 1905), and C. S. Lewis.* He is difficult to read, for his informality of style, alternately musing and leaping, gives an appearance of waywardness to his tightest arguments.

His philosophical theology (*Finite and Infinite*, 1943; *The Freedom of the Will*, 1957; *Love Almighty and Ills Unlimited*, 1961; *Faith and Speculation*, 1964) has roots in both the substance-philosophy of medieval scholasticism* and the modern metaphysics* of action and clarification, based on linguistic

usage (see Religious Language*). His exegesis of Matthew, Mark, and Revelation is heavily (some would say, fantastically) typological. In *The Glass of Vision*, 1948, he argued for images* rather than sentences as bearers of God's revealed truth.

Bibliography

C. C. Conti (ed.), *Reflective Faith: Essays in Philosophical Theology* (London, 1972); P. Curtis, *A Hawk Among Sparrows: A Biography of Austin Farrer* (London, 1985); J. C. Eaton, *The Logic of Theism: Analysis of the Thought of Austin Farrer* (Lanham, MD, 1983); J. C. Eaton and A. Loades (ed.), *For God and Clarity. New Essays in Honor of Austin Farrer* (Pittsburgh, PA, 1983).

J.I.P.

FATHERHOOD OF GOD. The
character of God as Father is revealed preeminently in the teaching of Jesus recorded in the gospels. It is here for the first time that we see God as the Father of the believer and not simply of the nation, and that revelation arises out of the inner life of Jesus himself.

Our Lord's use of the intimate Aramaic address *Abba*, so significant that it is preserved in our Gk. gospels (Mk. 14:36) and (as a term used by believers) elsewhere in the NT (Rom. 8:15; Gal. 4:6), breaks decisively with the remote and highly formal modes of divine address employed by the Jews of his day. While some interpreters have overstressed the informality of the term (as equivalent to 'Daddy'), it was apparently the name a respectful son would have given his father in every stage of life (so, better, 'Papa', with its connotation of affectionate respect). The gospel witness that Jesus used *Abba* of God in public personal prayer, and his invitation to his disciples to call God Father also ('Our Father . . .'), have led some to see this as the single most important feature of his teaching.

The pattern of that teaching, with its move from his own experience of God to that of the disciples, is also the pattern for our understanding. The basis of the divine fatherhood of all believers is his fatherhood of Christ, the elder brother. There is an analogical* relation between God's fatherhood and Christ's sonship, on the one hand, and God's fatherhood and our sonship* on the other. The believer's knowledge of God as Father is the corollary of his adoption as son. What is the

253

significance of the employment of this mode of address? A familial intimacy is immediately introduced into the divine-human relationship, in which the merely formal – as also the merely fearful – can have no place. But the implications go much further. The concern of God for the individual believer is that of a father for his child. If man leaves Eden under a curse, it is to a father's smile that the prodigal returns. The entire conduct of religion is set in a most distinctive context by the entry of father-and-son terminology. It is important to note that this is not intended simply as illustration, in the way in which God is spoken of as a shepherd or a servant's master. The ground of this description, as of the relationship which it describes, lies in the Godhead itself, in the eternally subsisting relations between the Father and the eternal Son in the Trinity* of Father, Son and Holy Spirit.

This doctrine has been the occasion of more than one controversy. A different concept of divine fatherhood gained wide currency as a hallmark of the theological liberalism* of the early years of this century, in which it extended not only to believers but to all mankind, nullifying by implication the distinction between the church and the world and denying the need for the gospel (cf. Harnack,* What is Christianity?). The sense in which God can be described as the Father of all (i.e. as creator – a common usage in the early fathers, and probably the original meaning in the Apostles' Creed) is fundamentally distinct from his redemptive fatherhood of the church. The rise of feminist* thinking within the Christian church has inevitably led to calls for God to be addressed as 'Mother' or 'Parent' as well as, or instead of, Father. This is the result of a series of misunderstandings. According to the biblical revelation this address to God is a gracious privilege announced by God himself, not some human theory about him which is open to revision. Moreover, the character of God revealed in Scripture is not simply masculine, for the biblical images are of one who cares, pities, cherishes and protects, not of a chauvinistic deity. And it is his love that is supremely evident in our invitation to call him our Father.

Bibliography
P. T. Forsyth, *God the Holy Father* (London, 1897); J. Jeremias, *The Prayers of Jesus* (London, 1967).

N.M.deS.C.

FATHERS, see PATRISTIC THEOLOGY.

FEDERAL THEOLOGY, see COVENANT.

FELLOWSHIP. Linguistic research by H. Seesemann, A. Raymond George and others confirms that the meaning of the group of words deriving from the Gk. root *koin-* (whether in adjectival, verbal, or substantival form), and variously translated in the Eng. versions of the NT as 'fellowship' (12 times), 'communication' (once), 'contribution' (once), 'communion' (4 times) is either 'having a share in', *i.e.* 'participating in', or 'giving a share'. A whole series of adjectival usages in different contexts (Mt. 23:30; Lk. 5:10; Rom. 1:5; 11:17; 1 Cor. 9:23; 10:18; 2 Cor. 1:7; Phil. 1:7; Eph. 3:2, 8; 1 Pet. 5:1; 2 Pet. 1:4; Rev. 1:9) makes the meaning of 'sharing in' certain. This serves to dispel any doubt as to the interpretation of the word *koinōnia* where alternative translations and meanings might be possible, as for example in 1 Cor. 1:9, where 'called into the fellowship of his Son, Jesus Christ' (RSV) could be taken as referring to the Corinthians' calling to the family of God, but in fact means their calling to share fellowship with his Son Jesus Christ. This is also the meaning of such references as 1 Cor. 10:16; 2 Cor. 8:4; 13:14; Phil. 2:1; 3:10, and extends to the references in 1 Jn. 1:3, 6, 7, of which Brooke, in his *ICC* commentary, says the word 'is always used of active participation, where the result depends on the co-operation of the receiver as well as on the action of the giver'. Outside the NT, *koinōnia* is used to mean friendship, partnership or marriage, and also sharing with gods in a common meal.

The second meaning of the word, 'giving a share', is found in Rom. 12:13; 15:26; 2 Cor. 9:13; Gal. 6:6; Phil. 4:14–15; 1 Tim. 6:18; Phm. 6. This meaning is a necessary logical implication of the former. To share or participate in the blessings of grace will inevitably lead to a desire and determination to 'pass on' and to share these blessings with others (*cf.* the logical connection between Ps. 68:18, 'you *received* gifts from men' and the Pauline use of this in Eph. 4:8, '*gave* gifts to men'). This expresses itself in different ways, as the above references show, and *koinōnia* can take on 'a concrete form as a generosity which clothes itself in practical action, and is so applied to the collection for the saints of the Jerusalem church in their poverty-stricken condition' (R. P. Martin).

In the light of the above, it is beyond question that the use of the word 'fellowship' to describe the 'company of believers' is a misunderstanding of the NT use of *koinōnia*. C. A. Anderson Scott's view that *koinōnia* is a translation of the Heb. *ḥᵃbûrâ* meaning a religious society or association, has been disputed by the majority of scholars. However, the idea contained in the phrase '*the fellowship*' may be held to be implicit in the word, since mutual participation does involve mutual association. But the idea of the church as a fellowship can have validity only in terms of *what* it participates *in, i.e.* the life of God, in Christ, by the Holy Spirit.

See also: KOINONIA.

Bibliography

A. R. George, *Communion with God in the New Testament* (London, 1953); R. P. Martin, 'Communion', in *NBD;* H. Sessemann, *Der Begriff KOINONIA im Neuen Testament* (Giessen, 1933).

J.P.

FEMINIST THEOLOGY is an increasingly significant feature of theological reflection today.

Feminist studies

The rise of the women's liberation movement from the mid–20th century helped to create a feminist critical consciousness. That consciousness, interacting with the Bible and Christian theological traditions, has called for a new investigation of past paradigms,* and a new agenda of study.

This agenda increasingly focuses on hermeneutical* questions. How do we interpret what is seen as the male orientation of the Bible? Is the experience of women more than merely a corrective for the Christian context? Is it not also a starting-point and a norm? In what sense can liberationist feminism serve as part of a biblical hermeneutic?

1. The rejectionist (or post-Christian) model* of studies sees the Bible as promoting an oppressive patriarchal structure and rejects it as not authoritative. Some reject the whole Judaeo-Christian tradition as hopelessly male-oriented. The most radical wings of this approach call for the restoration of the religion of witchcraft or are attracted to a nature mysticism based exclusively on women's consciousness.

2. The loyalist (or evangelical) model is in many ways the opposite of the rejectionist. Refusing to discredit the whole testimony of the Bible, it finds no radically oppressive sexism in its message. But the model divides in its approach to the biblical material. One form of the model accepts the traditional argument for order through hierarchy. Woman's place in God's created order is said to be fulfilled in her role of submission and dependence in church and family (and, add some, society). At the same time, it insists that such a divine pattern of leadership as an ordained male prerogative, adhered to with love, does not diminish the true freedom and dignity of women.

The other loyalist model argues that the full biblical data calls for an egalitarianism and mutual submission. It fears the collapse of the hierarchical framework into a form of female subordinationism.

3. The reformist (or liberation) model shares with the rejectionist a deep consciousness of alleged patriarchal chauvinism in the Bible and Christian history, and a desire to overcome it. But its commitment to a perception of human liberation as the central message of the Bible keeps it from a wholesale discarding of the Christian tradition. Some concentrate their work on exegetical study, 'reading between the lines' of the so-called chauvinist texts to bring to light the positive role of women in the biblical sources. Others struggle with what they see as 'unusable' male bias in the Scripture and search for a 'usable' hermeneutic of liberation in the prophetic tradition. In texts not dealing specifically with women, they find a call to create a just society free from any kind of social, economic or sexist oppression.

The most radical wing of this model calls for a more far-reaching feminist 'hermeneutic of suspicion'. It begins with an acknowledgement that the Bible has been written, translated, canonized and interpreted by males. Under the control of this hermeneutic, the canon of the faith itself has become male-centred. Through thoroughgoing theological and exegetical reconstruction, women must enter again the centre stage that they occupied in early Christian history.

A hermeneutic of feminism

Patriarchalism is clearly the orientation of the OT. The preponderance of biblical images for the Father-God are masculine. The slant of cultic legislation is male-oriented. The period of uncleanness for giving birth to a son was seven days, for a daughter fourteen (Lv. 12:1–5). A Hebrew daughter sold into slavery could not go free 'as menservants do' (Ex. 21:7). A man might divorce his wife if he found 'something indecent about her' (Dt. 24:1–4), but nowhere is there mention of women divorcing their husbands. A compensation gift, the *mōhar*, was given to the family of the bride to seal the marriage covenant and bind the two families together ('bride-price' in the NIV, Gn. 34:12; Ex. 22:17; 1 Sa. 18:25, but better rendered 'marriage present', RSV, or 'dowry', AV).

At the same time, this patriarchalism does not descend to chauvinistic androcentrism. Even the masculine images of God in the OT are set forth only as anthropomorphisms.* Unlike the deities of the ancient Near East, God is a spirit and not to be depicted as either male or female. In fact, feminine imagery, though not common, is also used to describe Jehovah. The Lord is nursing mother (Is. 49:15), midwife (Ps. 22:9–10), female homemaker (Ps. 123:2), and helpmate to humankind as Eve was to Adam (Ex. 18:4; Dt. 33:26; Ps. 121:1–2).

In the same way, patriarchalism was also transcended in the OT legislation. Both father and mother are deserving of honour (Ex. 20:12). The woman was to share in the sabbath rest (Ex. 20:8), to benefit from the reading of the Law (Dt. 31:9–13). Both adulterer and adulteress are to be put to death (Lv. 20:10). Food taboos are mandatory for both sexes (Lv. 11).

OT legislation was also sensitive to the dangers of abuse of power.* And much of that concern for justice on behalf of the oppressed is also aware of the woman as a unique object of chauvinist oppression. The husband could divorce his wife, but she was protected by a letter of repudiation; its intention was to guard her dignity from any easy abuse of the permission. Widows (Ex. 22:22–24), women taken captive in war (Dt. 21:10–14), and virgins seduced (Ex. 22:16–17), all offer samples of that sensitivity for justice and compassion towards those marginalized by a sinful and cruel society (Ex. 22:21–27).

In the OT description of women in Hebrew society and worship, there are obvious similarities to the cultural practices of the ancient Near East. And yet these are constantly balanced by legislation and history that point forward to a fuller, more liberating place for women in the redemptive plan of God. Traditional social roles for women are overturned. Children are not the special province of women (Pr. 1:8; 6:20). The ideal wife works outside as well as in the home (Pr. 31:10ff.). Though it was not usual, women held every office in Hebrew society except that of the priesthood; prophetess (2 Ki. 22:14; Ne. 6:14), judge (Jdg. 4:4), 'the wise' (Jdg. 5:28–29; 2 Sa. 14:2; 20:16), even ruler (2 Ki. 11:3). Unlike other religions of the ancient Near East, there were no priestesses. But it has been suggested this was to avoid the dangers of the fertility cults and sacred prostitution.

How do we reconcile what seem contradictory, or at least discontinuous, traditions within these biblical materials? Rejectionist and reformist theologies answer by either denying altogether any egalitarian emphasis (rejectionist) or seeing this strain as 'counter-cultural' to the dominant focus (reformist). Neither recognizes the integrity of biblical revelation, and therefore each rejects in some way or other any patriarchal tradition found in the Bible. Such a radical process is not necessary if our thinking is controlled by hermeneutics structured by biblical theology, the history of special revelation.

1. The entire biblical message, including that about women, revolves, not around patriarchalism or egalitarianism, but around God's covenant,* his redemptive dealings with humanity and the creation. The closest thing to a biblical definition of who we are, man or woman, is our creation as 'image of God'* (Gn. 1:27). This 'definition' revolves around our common calling, in unity with one another and the creation, to serve God in obligation to him and to one another. This calling is beyond both feminism and patriarchalism, to life in covenant.

2. The Bible contains the record of the progressive unfolding of God's will for

humanity. Its message develops progressively, and always the goal of the development is the consummation of all things, the restoration of creation to what it was intended to be. Man's and woman's covenant partnership is to be perfectly fulfilled in the final renewal of God's original purpose (Gal. 3:28).

3. Revelation is progressive because God reveals his covenant, redemptive purposes to men and women in divine accommodation* to the cultural patterns in existence at the time when he gives his word. Those patterns sometimes existed in violation of God's explicit teaching, *e.g.* polygamous marriages, flagrant male chauvinism. So the Lord allows polygamy, even laying down rules for its regulation (Dt. 21:15–17). He permits divorce because of the hardness of our cultural hearts (Mt. 19:8), in spite of his divine intent for lasting monogamy (Gn. 2:24–25; Mk. 10:4–9). Even in the NT, the pattern continues. Culturally perceived improprieties prompt Paul to warn against married women appearing in a worship service with hair uncovered (1 Cor. 11:4–7), or 'speaking in church' (1 Cor. 14:34–35). Our liberty in Christ must not be curtailed, but always it must be exercised with a view to possible cultural misunderstandings by 'outsiders' (1 Cor. 11:5, 13–14).

4. This accommodation is always accompanied by a divine eschatological polemic against the culture, pointing to Christ as the transformer, the re-possessor of our social settings. So, when God calls us not to covet our neighbour's ox or ass or wife (Ex. 20:17), it is not to be seen as an affirmation of women as an object of male property in a chauvinist culture; it is to provide a defence of her integrity and worth within such a culture. Even within the old order, there is an 'intrusion ethic,' an intrusion into the present of the final order to be brought by Christ. Divorce, though permitted in the old order, is thus abolished by Christ in the new day of the kingdom of God (Mt. 5:32; 19:9). In the new age of the Spirit, daughters as well as sons, servants both women and men, will be filled by the Spirit and be participants in the prophethood of all believers (Acts 2:16–18). Over against those forms of Judaistic chauvinism of the 1st century that prohibited women from being legal witnesses in law courts or studying the law of God, women will testify before men of the resurrection of

Christ (Lk. 24:1–10), and be exhorted by Paul to 'learn in quietness' (1 Tim. 2:11). Mary will be commended for staying out of the kitchen (a culturally defined role responsibility) and 'listening to what he said' (Lk. 10:38–42). Women's liberty in Christ must always keep far enough ahead of a particular time and culture to continue being called 'liberation', and yet not so far ahead that it does not continue to touch and alter that context in the light of the consummation design.

God's covenant intention for woman

Redemption's purpose is the restoration of creation to what it was intended to be. Thus salvation can be described as 'the new creation' (2 Cor. 5:17), Jesus 'the last Adam' (1 Cor. 15:45), and Christians, those who now bear in Christ the (re)created image of God (Eph. 4:24).

Given this flashback intention of salvation to creation, the description of woman in Gn. 1 – 2 takes on new significance. In sharp contrast to the male chauvinism of the ancient Near East where the woman was the property of man and always his inferior, in Gn. she, with man, is 'image of God,' called in regal partnership to subdue and rule the creation (Gn. 1:28). Not a subordinate slave, she is a 'helper suitable for him' (Gn. 2:18), the complementing counterpart. Like man, woman alone is created from existing matter (Gn. 2:22). Adam, put to sleep by God, does not participate in her creation as someone inferior to man. Unlike the animals, she is endowed with those unique qualities that complement the man (Gn. 2:19–20). As 'bone of his bone and flesh of his flesh' (Gn. 2:23), woman bears the closest of kin sociality to man (Gn. 29:14; Jdg. 9:2; 2 Sa. 5:1; 19:12–13). They are 'one flesh' (Gn. 2:24). As 'the glory of man' (1 Cor. 11:7), woman must pray and prophesy in public worship with covered head. Her glory (worth, importance, honour) is so bright it will distract from the glory of God. The covering of the hair is not a sign of subservience but of authority (1 Cor. 11:10).

The effect of sin upon covenant mutuality

Before the fall into sin, man and woman lived in covenant mutuality and solidarity before God. In partnership they rebel against God and rend that harmony with Adam blaming his wife and God (Gn. 3:12) and the woman blaming the serpent (Gn. 3:13). God's judgment now fits the crime, as always (Rom. 1:24, 26, 28); sin becomes its own reward. Solidarity is to be replaced by struggle, tyranny and the desire for domination by one partner over the other (Gn. 3:16b). The battle of the sexes is begun, the woman's desire to control the husband, the man's to master her (*cf.* Gn. 4:7b). Mutuality turns to superiority and inferiority.

This sexual power struggle had developed into theological heresy by NT times. Forms of Gnosticism* spoke of systems of intermediate beings who bridged the gap between God and man. Some spoke of women as these intermediaries and of Eve as the bringer of both light and life, the mediatrix who brought divine enlightenment to mankind. Some even embellished the Gn. accounts and sometimes gave Eve a prior existence in which she consorted with the celestial beings.

Paul's prohibition against women teachers in 1 Tim. 2:11–15 probably had such groups in mind. The heretics had led astray 'weak-willed women' (2 Tim. 3:6), even forbidding marriage (1 Tim. 4:3). In opposing them, Paul reminds the whole church, not just women, of the sole mediatorship of Christ (1 Tim. 2:5–9). Adam, he continues, was created first rather than Eve; and Eve, far from being an instrument of light, was deluded (1 Tim. 2:13–14). No-one, he argues, has a privileged position with God on the basis of gender.

The restoration of covenant mutuality in Christ

In Christ the curse on marriage is lifted and complementarity restored (1 Cor. 11:11). The husband's role of headship (1 Cor. 11:3; Eph. 5:23) and the wife's role of submission are reaffirmed but radically altered. Submission becomes a mutual calling (Eph. 5:21), transforming male headship from authoritative control to responsible care. Its paradigm is now modelled after the self-sacrificial death of Jesus for the church (Eph. 5:25–33); and its purpose is not to crush but to liberate. Submission on the part of the wife is transformed from servility and subordination to respect (Eph. 5:33) voluntarily given, and to 'the unfading beauty of a gentle and quiet spirit' (1 Pet. 3:4). In traditional patriarchy, the husband was a despot and the wife a virtual slave. In Christ-centred covenant

mutuality, each complements the other in their transformed roles.

Bibliography

D. G. Bloesch, *Is the Bible Sexist?* (Westchester, IL, 1982); A. Carr, 'Is a Christian Feminist Theology Possible?' *TS* 43 (1982), pp. 279–297; H. Conn, 'Evangelical Feminism . . .', *WTJ* 46 (1984), pp. 104–124; S. B. Clark, *Man and Woman in Christ* (Ann Arbor, MI, 1980); M. Evans, *Woman in the Bible* (Downers Grove, IL, and Exeter, 1983); E. Fiorenza, *In Memory of Her* (Westchester, IL, 1984); S. Foh, *Women and the Word of God* (Phillipsburg, NJ, 1979); J. Hurley, *Man and Woman in Biblical Perspective* (Leicester, 1981); P. Jewett, *Man as Male and Female* (Grand Rapids, MI, 1975); R. and C. C. Kroeger, 'May Women Teach? Heresy in the Pastoral Epistles', *Reformed Journal* 30:10 (Oct. 1980), pp. 14–18; A. Mickelsen, *Women, Authority and the Bible* (Downers Grove, IL, 1986); L. Russell (ed.), *Feminist Interpretation of the Bible* (Philadelphia, 1985); L. Scanzoni and N. Hardesty, *All We're Meant to Be* (Waco, TX, 1974); P. Trible, *God and the Rhetoric of Sexuality* (Philadelphia, 1978); B. Witherington III, *Women in the Ministry of Jesus* (London, 1984).

H.M.C.

FEUERBACH, LUDWIG ANDREAS (1804–72) was the best-known 19th-century proponent of the view that religion* arises as a projection of human aspirations. After study with Hegel* in Berlin (and several years as a convinced Hegelian), Feuerbach underwent a philosophical conversion. The result appeared first in *The Essence of Christianity* (1841) and then in a series of works which explicated both his anti-Hegelianism and his distinctive convictions about religion. Feuerbach's arguments rested upon a post-Kantian conception of reality. That is, since we cannot know the world *in itself*, our minds contribute to our conception of what actually exists. Feuerbach also drew on Schleiermacher's* assertion that religion consists in an inner conviction, or sense, of absolute dependence. Feuerbach, however, differed from Kant* and Schleiermacher, who were theists.* He insisted that if these thinkers are correct, they demonstrate that all our supposed knowledge of God is merely an enlargement of ideas about ourselves and human experience.

'God', Feuerbach wrote in 1841, 'is himself the realized wish of the heart, the wish exalted to the certainty of its fulfilment . . . the secret of theology is nothing else than anthropology – the knowledge of God nothing else than a knowledge of man!' (*Essence of Christianity*, pp. 121, 207). Thus, when humans talk about their God or religion, they do nothing more than abstract and externalize their own experience. Feuerbach claimed the support of Luther,* since Luther had emphasized the way in which God expressed his divinity in human qualities through the incarnation. Feuerbach also went further to make a general statement about the basis of reality. Against Hegel, who postulated ideas or intelligence as the foundation, Feuerbach contended that 'Nature, Matter, cannot be explained as a result of intelligence; on the contrary, it is the basis of intelligence . . . Consciousness develops itself only out of nature' (*Essence of Christianity*, p. 87). Feuerbach felt that the atheism* which resulted from his views was not a message of despair, but a testimony to the nobility of humanity. If humans could project such an ennobling and altruistic faith as Christianity, this spoke very well indeed for the quality of humanity itself.

Feuerbach's ideas had a significant influence on Karl Marx* and Friedrich Engels who drew from him the belief that the material realm is the basis for all ideology. For Marx, Feuerbach established true materialism and true science by demonstrating that human social experience establishes our conception of humankind. Yet Marx also criticized Feuerbach for not breaking cleanly enough with Hegel. The key for Marx was not idealized humanity, but people in their concrete social and economic relationships. Feuerbach's influence can also be seen in Sigmund Freud's treatment of religion as an 'illusion' (see Depth Psychology;* Psychology of Religion*), and in Martin Buber's* concentration upon inter-human relationships as the source of knowledge and ethics.

The mark of Feuerbach has been especially great on 20th-century theology. Radical thinkers such as John A. T. Robinson* concede that 'in a real sense Feuerbach was right in wanting to translate "theology" into "anthropology" ' (*Honest to God*, London, 1963, p. 50). Other theologians have contended against Feuerbach. Chief among these is Karl Barth* whose insistence upon God's transcendence is, among other things, an effort to repudiate Feuerbach. When Barth denies the value of natural theology,* and when he contends that Christianity is not a religion, he is responding to Feuerbach's description of faith as mere human projection. The seriousness of Barth's response to Feuerbach suggests that while the latter's human-centred atheism is important for understanding 19th-century German philosophical history, it is even more important as a continuing challenge to those who believe in divine revelation,* the supernatural* and the otherness of God.

Bibliography

The Essence of Christianity, tr. G. Eliot (New York, 1957); *The Essence of Faith According to Luther* (ET, New York, 1967).

K. Barth, *Protestant Thought From Rousseau to Ritschl* (ET, New York, 1959); M. Buber, 'What is Man?' in *Between Man and Man*, tr. R. G. Smith (Boston, 1955); K. Marx, 'Theses on Feuerbach' (1845), in *Marx and Engels on Religion* (ET, New York, 1964); E. Schmidt, 'Ludwig Feuerbachs Lehre von der Religion', *Neue Zeitschrift für systematische Theologie und Religionsphilosophie* 8 (1966), pp. 1–35.

M.A.N.

FIDEISM, see FAITH AND REASON; PHILOSOPHICAL THEOLOGY; PHILOSOPHY OF RELIGION.

FILARET (PHILARET), DROZDOV (1782–1867), Russian Orthodox* theologian and churchman. Filaret was a monk who, after teaching biblical studies, theology and philosophy at St Petersburg, became archbishop (1821) and metropolitan (1826) of Moscow. Through his lectures and sermons, and his *Christian Catechism of the Orthodox Catholic Eastern Graeco-Russian Church* (1823), he exercised a wide influence on 19th-century Russian theology. Having assimilated Protestant elements in his youth (especially from the works of Feofan Prokopovich, 1681–1736), he exemplified an intense biblicism (which led to attempts to purge his *Catechism* of its 'Lutheranism'). He keenly supported Bible Society work, dissented from declarations that Western Christians were heretics, and reflected the abandonment of the scholastic* style in theology in favour of the patristic.* He was enormously influential in

259

affairs of church and state, despite the restrictive rule of Nicholas I (1825–55), which he survived long enough to become the honoured author of the 1861 manifesto emancipating Russia's peasants from serfdom.

Bibliography
ET of *Catechism* in P. Schaff, *The Creeds of Christendom*, vol. 2 (New York, 1877), pp. 445–542; G. Florovsky, *Ways of Russian Theology*, pt. 1 (*Collected Works*, vol. 5: Belmont, MA, 1979).

D.F.W.

FILIOQUE, see CREEDS; EASTERN ORTHODOX THEOLOGY; HOLY SPIRIT; TRINITY.

FINNEY, CHARLES GRANDISON (1792–1875). For Finney, the 'father of modern revivalism', the doing of theology was always an eminently practical matter. Whether serving as itinerant evangelist, pastor, professor of theology or college president, his fundamental goal remained the same: to secure the conversion* of sinners and to set them to work in preparing the way for the coming millennial* kingdom.

Finney was trained as a lawyer, but after his dramatic conversion in 1821 sought ordination in the Presbyterian Church and began his labours as a missionary to the settlers of upstate New York. Using such 'new measures' as the anxious seat, protracted meetings and allowing women to pray in public, a series of revivals* soon began to sweep across that region with such frequency that it came to be known as the 'Burned-over District.' Although Finney was involved in promoting revivals throughout his lifetime, even travelling to England for that purpose (1849–50, 1859–60), the period 1824–32 remained the highwater mark of his revival career.

When illness began to curtail his travels, he became pastor of the Chatham Street Chapel in New York. He subsequently held pastorates at the Broadway Tabernacle of New York (1836–37) and the First Congregational Church of Oberlin, Ohio (1837–72). In 1835 he became professor of theology at the newly formed Oberlin Collegiate Institute in Ohio (now Oberlin College). He later served as president of Oberlin College (1851–66).

Theologically, Finney is best described as a New School Calvinist (see New Haven Theology*). His preaching and teaching, always pointed and dramatic, stressed the moral government of God, human ability to repent and create new hearts, the perfectibility of human nature and society, and the need for Christians to apply their faith to daily living. For Finney, this included the investment of one's time and energy in establishing the millennial kingdom of God on earth by winning converts and involving oneself in social reform (including anti-slavery, temperance and the like).

Throughout his lifetime, Finney produced a variety of books, sermon collections and articles. Among the more important were his *Lectures on Revivals of Religion* (1835; repr., ed. W. G. McLoughlin, Cambridge, MA, 1960), a kind of manual on how to lead revivals; his *Lectures on Systematic Theology* (Oberlin, 1846), reflecting his special brand of 'Arminianized* Calvinism,' and his *Memoirs* (1876), recounting his involvement in the great revivals of the earlier 19th century.

Bibliography
W. G. McLoughlin, Jr., *Modern Revivalism: Charles Grandison Finney to Billy Graham* (New York, 1959); G. M. Rosell, 'Charles G. Finney: His Place in the Stream of Evangelicalism', in L. I. Sweet (ed.), *The Evangelical Tradition in America* (Macon, GA, 1984); G. F. Wright, *Charles Grandison Finney* (Boston and New York, 1891).

G.M.R.

FLACIUS, MATTHIAS, see LUTHERANISM.

FORGIVENESS, see GUILT AND FORGIVENESS.

FORMULA OF CONCORD, see CONFESSIONS OF FAITH; LUTHERANISM.

FORSYTH, PETER TAYLOR (1848–1921), Scottish theologian. Born in Aberdeen where he later graduated, Forsyth studied under Ritschl* at Göttingen and briefly at New College, London, where he eventually returned as principal (1901–21). He served in four English Congregational pastorates, and in the early 1880s underwent a costly theological change in which he rejected his earlier humanistic ideas, yet retained the tools of liberal higher criticism.

Gratefully confessing that he had been turned 'from a lover of God to an object of grace', his emphases in some respects anticipated (but did not influence) Barth.*

Forsyth sought by a passionate concentration on God's holiness to divert his optimistic contemporaries from their sentimentalized portraiture of the divine Fatherhood, writing trenchantly about sin* as humanity's arrogant and persistent assault on God. His atonement* teaching takes the form of a strongly ethicized interpretation of the penal view. The cross is God's own self-imposed act of redemption in which Christ 'felt the weight of God's wrath in full'. His extensive, occasionally repetitious and obscure writings are in a finely polished, highly epigrammatic style with arresting illustrations and frequent use of paradox. They have enjoyed considerable popularity since World War II.

Bibliography

R. McA. Brown, *P. T. Forsyth: Prophet for Today* (Philadelphia, 1952); A. M. Hunter, *P. T. Forsyth: per Crucem ad Lucem* (London, 1974); D. G. Miller, B. Barr and R. S. Paul, *P. T. Forsyth: The Man, the Preachers' Theologian, Prophet for the 20th Century* (Pittsburgh, PA, 1981); J. H. Rodgers, *The Theology of P. T. Forsyth: The Cross of Christ and the Revelation of God* (London, 1965).

R.B.

FOX, GEORGE, see QUAKER THEOLOGY.

FRANCIS AND THE FRANCISCAN TRADITION. The founder of the Order of Friars Minor (the Franciscans), Francis of Assisi (1182–1226), is one of the most admired figures of Christendom. Reared in an atmosphere of luxury, parties and polite society, during his youth he dreamed of a career of military glory and composed love poetry in the style of the Provençal troubadors. Francis' father (Pietro Bernardoni) believed that his son should become a knight or a merchant, but in his early twenties Francis experienced a religious conversion* which was expressed in a number of dramatic ways. One of them involved the distribution of some family goods for religious purposes. By 1209 he began to live in 'apostolic' poverty* and wandered the countryside

clothed in a ragged cloak and a robe belt from a scarecrow – hence the distinctive dress of the Franciscans. He attracted followers to the life-style of poverty, love and brotherhood that he taught and exemplified. They begged from the rich and ministered to the sick and the poor while they preached the gospel to the outcasts of medieval society.

In 1210 Pope Innocent III allowed Francis to organize a religious order, the Little Brothers, based upon poverty and service to others. A second order was founded in 1212 when an influential woman named Clare was commissioned by Francis to perform many of the same activities as the brothers. Thus was formed the order for women called the Poor Clares. In addition to his activities among Christians, Francis was concerned with missionary activity and went to Syria (1212), Morocco (1213–14), and Egypt (1219) to evangelize the Muslims. Illness and other misfortunes prevented much success in these endeavours.

Because of the rapid growth of the Order and the need for organization beyond the few simple rules formulated by Francis, a new set of regulations was approved by Pope Honorius III in 1223. A cardinal was named protector of the group but this displeased Francis who became less involved in the order. He spent the remainder of his life in solitude, prayer and writing. It was during this period that he produced the 'Canticle to the Sun', his *Admonitions* and his *Testament*. In 1224 he allegedly received the stigmata, a series of wounds on his body similar to those inflicted on Jesus as he was crucified. He was canonized (see Saint*) by Gregory IX in 1228.

Of all the achievements of Francis the one which may be of greatest interest today is the respect he showed for God's creation. His enthusiastic, sacred outlook on the world led him to view everything as a living comrade. Many sources report his sermons to the birds which included the charming line: 'My brother birds, much ought you to praise your Creator and to love him ...'

Despite his personal example, it was probably inevitable that the Order founded on the principles of simplicity, poverty and service could not adhere to them once it became a successful movement. The Franciscans developed into one of the leading 13th-century orders of friars that sought to meet the spiritual needs caused by rapid urban growth and the spread of heresy. Unlike earlier groups of monks, the friars lived among the people ministering the gospel as well as providing social services to the needy. The problem was that such large-scale enterprises needed financing and organization. All such businesslike activities were discouraged by Francis who left a will asking that the vow of poverty should not be changed among his followers. Only four years after his death Pope Gregory IX declared that the will was not binding, thus permitting the Order to hold property. A conflict arose between the Spirituals or Fraticelli who insisted on keeping the founder's request and those who accepted the new approach. The main body of the Franciscans, the Conventuals, agreed with the changes. During the latter half of the 13th century, tension between the two groups eased under the leadership of Bonaventura,* who maintained a balanced approach between structure and spirit. As an outstanding intellect he represented the increasing role of scholarship within the Order which began working in the new urban universities.

As the Franciscans increased their material wealth Europe entered a difficult time during the 14th and 15th centuries, experiencing plague, warfare and papal division. The Order declined during these years but a reform movement, the Observants, developed in its ranks. They wished to re-establish a strict rule and were granted ecclesiastical recognition in 1415. The new group was opposed by the more moderate Franciscans represented by the Conventuals. In 1517 Leo X officially separated the Order into two independent branches: the Friars Minor of the Regular Observants and the Friars Minor Conventuals. Further discord among the Observants led them to divide into several factions including the Capuchins, the Discalced (Shoeless) and the Recollects. Increasing division caused Leo XIII (1897) to unite all the Observants except the Capuchins.

Despite the admonition of Francis that the Christian faith 'consists not in working miracles . . . nor in learning and knowledge of all things; nor in eloquence to convert the world,' his followers have been heavily involved in theological scholarship, preaching and missions and even in politics. During the medieval period all branches of scholasticism* were influenced by Franciscan contributions. Because the order is so diverse it included those, such as Duns Scotus* and William of Ockham,* who undermined the theological system of Thomas Aquinas* through Aristotelian* logic; while others followed Bonaventura and emphasized the role of meditation and prayer in Christian thought; and a third group supported the outlook of Robert Grosseteste (c. 1175–1253) and Roger Bacon (c. 1214–92) and insisted on the centrality of observation in arriving at truth. However, all groups of Franciscans were agreed in opposing the synthesis of faith and reason* elaborated by Thomas Aquinas.

The Franciscans have also been active in preaching the gospel. Their missionary journeys took them to China as early as 1294 and they accompanied the Portuguese and Spaniards on their pioneering journeys to India and America. Currently, Franciscans are found working in every mission field of the world.

Many popular devotional practices of the Roman Catholic church have been encouraged by Franciscan influence. Among the better-known of these are devotion to the Christmas Crib, the Sacred Heart, and the Precious Blood, and the Stations of the Cross.

Today, the Franciscans are divided into three major branches; the Observants, the Conventuals, and the Capuchins. The largest of these is the Observants (21,000 members in 1985). They revised their constitution after Vatican II (1962–65) and have defined the Order's goal as that of a movement which continually reinterprets the gospel in the light of current problems. Many of these friars look on their role as that of the conscience of the church. Such an attitude has led individuals including Leonardo Boff (b. 1938), a Brazilian theological professor, to apply Marxist* ideas to the problem of the poor. The support that his liberation theology* has received has caused conflict between the Order and the Vatican. Other Franciscan groups have remained more conservative and continue to apply the teachings of their leading medieval scholars such as Bonaventura to contemporary issues.

The Franciscans have contributed in an important way both to Catholicism and to Christendom in general. Their work in evangelizing the new towns of the Middle Ages, developing Christian scholarship and serving in a variety of missionary and social ministries, has helped to make faith in Christ a living reality.

Bibliography

L. Boff, *Church: Charism and Power* (New York, 1985); *idem, St Francis: A Model for Human Liberation* (London, 1985); I. Brady (ed. and tr.), *The Marrow of the Gospel: A Study of the Rule of St Francis of Assisi* (Chicago, IL, 1958); L. Cunningham (ed.), *Brother Francis: An Anthology of Writings by and about S. Francis of Assisi* (New York, 1972); O. Englebert, *Saint Francis of Assisi* (Chicago, 1966); E. H. Gilson, *History of Christian Philosophy in the Middle Ages* (New York, 1955); M. A. Habig, *St Francis of Assisi: Writings and Early Biographies* (Chicago, IL, 1973); H. Holzapfel, *The History of the Franciscan Order* (Teutopolis, IL, 1948); A. George Little, *A Guide to Franciscan Studies* (London and New York, 1920); P. Sabatier, *Life of St Francis of Assisi* (New York, 1917).

R.G.C.

FRANKFURT DECLARATION. The Frankfurt Declaration on the Fundamental Crisis of Christian Mission (1970) reaffirms the basic elements of biblical mission over against their distortions in contemporary missiological* thinking, particularly in the ecumenical movement* since the integration of the former International Missionary Council with the World Council of Churches in New Delhi in 1961. The Declaration was promulgated by a gathering of German theologians who had joined the struggle of the confession movement 'No Other Gospel' to counteract the effects of radical biblical criticism* on the life of the church. The Declaration was occasioned by the unhappiness of many evangelical mission leaders and theologians about Section II, 'Renewal in Mission', of the Fourth Assembly of the WCC in Uppsala, 1968, and might be considered as a German equivalent to the Wheaton Declaration* (1966). Both stand in the tradition of modern confessional statements of which the Barmen Declaration* of the Confessing Church in Germany in 1934 is the most outstanding example.

In fact, the form of the Frankfurt Declaration is modelled on the Barmen Declaration. Its seven affirmations, each one introduced by a biblical key-text, restate the classical understanding of mission and condemn opposing modern theological concepts. The 'Seven Indispensable Basic Elements of Mission' are intended to safeguard: 1. the sole authority of the Bible over against situational hermeneutics;* 2. the primacy of doxology* over against humanization as the goal of mission; 3. biblical Christology over against an anonymous Christ-presence in human history; 4. the significance of personal faith in salvation over against universalism;* 5. the spiritual nature of the church over against a merely functional understanding of it; 6. the uniqueness of the gospel over against other religions; 7. the reality of Christ's second coming for the eschatological orientation of mission over against an ideology of progress* or revolution.*

The original purpose of the Declaration was not a call for separation from the WCC's Commission of World Mission and Evangelism, but a call to it to return to its former biblical tradition, seen most clearly in the pronouncements of the World Missionary Conferences of Whitby (1947) and Willingen (1952). This call went largely unheeded. Rather, the actual effect of the Frankfurt Declaration was to stir up an intense debate, not only in Germany but all over the world. In Germany it contributed to the split between the conciliar organization of mission societies and the 'working fellowship of evangelical missions' which became final after the Bangkok World Missionary Conference of 1973. The basic concerns of the Declaration influenced the Lausanne Covenant* in 1974.

Bibliography

CT XIV:19 (June 19, 1970), pp. 3–6; P. Beyerhaus, *Missions: Which Way?* (Grand Rapids, MI, 1971); *idem, Shaken Foundations* (Grand Rapids, MI, 1972).

P.P.J.B.

FRANKFURT SCHOOL. Founded in 1923 as the Institute for Social Research, the School's influence may be dated from Max Horkheimer's directorship in 1930. Its members left Germany under the Third Reich, settling in New York, but returned to Germany after World War II as the only surviving institution from the Weimar Republic.

In the earlier generation of scholars, key figures are Max Horkheimer (1895–1973), Theodor Adorno (1903–69) and Herbert Marcuse (1898–1979). The leader of the younger generation is Jürgen Habermas (b. 1929). An eschatological character in the

School's thought reflects the influence of Hegel* and Marx,* but the Jewish background of many of the members is a distinct and conscious influence. The major theme in their work is critique of the Enlightenment,* both its philosophy and its impact on 'mass-culture'. Closely linked with this is their analysis of Nazism.

The School has consistently attacked the positivism* central to the Enlightenment theory of knowledge, and with it the view that nature* should be made subject to human control, and that this subjection/domination should become the chief purpose of knowledge; that 'whatever does not conform to the rule of computation and utility is suspect' (Adorno and Horkheimer, *Dialectic of Enlightenment*, 1944, repr. London, 1979, p. 6). A world dominated by technology is the material realization of the Enlightenment goal.

Positivism and technology are linked by a popular view of physical science as both the model form of knowledge and the bringer of material benefit to the world. In this way they legitimate one another. The result is that 'the fully enlightened world radiates disaster triumphant' (*ibid.*, p. 3); for man, 'existent social practice, which forms the individual's life down to its least details, is inhuman, and this inhumanity affects everything that goes on in society' (Horkheimer, 'Traditional and Critical Theory', 1937, in P. Connerton, ed., *Critical Sociology*, Harmondsworth, 1976, p. 220).

The Frankfurt School's anthropology has, therefore, a dialectical character; in this inhuman world, 'critical thought has a concept of man as in conflict with himself' until inhumanity is overcome. There are parallels here and elsewhere with the thought of Jacques Ellul.*

A right view of reality is imperative; central to it is a refusal of the Kantian* distinction between subject and object. 'Social reality' is not 'extrinsic' to the individual. The critical thinker rejects analyses of the world which cut him off from 'the experience of the blindly dominating totality and the driving desire that it should ultimately become something else' (Adorno, *et al.*, *The Positivist Dispute in German Sociology*, London, 1976, p. 14). 'Totality' here has more than rhetorical significance: 'totality is what is most real' (p.

12), but it is also illusory (it hides the fact that a really human world would be different).

Public debate, even in a democracy, is seen as deformed. Habermas' primary concern is to criticize forms of rationality which lead to such distorted discourse (drawing on insights from psychoanalysis as well as from classical philosophy), and to construct a theory of 'communicative action' in which a genuinely consensual generalized ethics can develop. Theory-building in this sense is a salvific activity; 'theory is the telos, not the vehicle' (*ibid.*, p. 113).

Bibliography

P. Connerton, *The Tragedy of Enlightenment* (Cambridge, 1980); J. Habermas, *Knowledge and Human Interests* (London, 1978); D. Held, *Introduction to Critical Theory* (London, 1980); M. Jay, *The Dialectical Imagination* (London, 1973); H. Marcuse, *From Luther to Popper* (London, 1972).

H.W.S.

FREEDOM, CHRISTIAN. Jesus was sent, he said, 'to proclaim freedom for the prisoners' (Lk. 4:18, quoting Is. 61:1). Humanity is subject to various kinds of bondage; freedom involves liberation from bondage. Christian freedom differs from political or civil liberty; it can be enjoyed by slaves or the subjects of despotic regimes. Jesus refused to become a leader of enthusiastic freedom-fighters bent on resisting their Roman oppressors (Jn. 6:15). Paul encourages Christian slaves to recognize themselves as the Lord's freedmen and freedwomen (1 Cor. 7:22). The freedom for which 'Christ has set us free' (Gal. 5:1) is presented by Paul as freedom from sin* and freedom from law.*

Sin is viewed as a slave-owner, whose slaves can be liberated only by death or by becoming the property of another. Christians have been liberated through 'dying' in Christ's death and being raised with him to live as God's willing servants. Sin is viewed as a jailor, refusing to release his prisoners. But Christ has invaded the prison-house and released them.

For Paul, freedom from law was as essential to salvation as freedom from sin. Sin uses the law as a means of inciting people to disobey God, so that they incur the death-sentence passed on the law-breaker (Rom. 7:11). Liberation from this sentence implies freedom from sin and law alike. Law, for its part, is viewed as the slave-attendant who accompanied the freeborn boy and disciplined him until he came of age (Gal. 3:24). With their acceptance of the gospel, the people of God have come of age spiritually and have no further need of a custodian: they enjoy freedom from law. This freedom from law is not antinomianism (see Law and Gospel*): they are empowered to do 'the will of God from the heart' (Eph. 6:6) instead of trying to achieve conformity to an external code. It is in those who 'walk not according to the flesh but according to the Spirit' that the law's righteous requirements are fulfilled (Rom. 8:4, RSV).

The service of God and of one's fellows is not incompatible with Christian freedom; it is in God's service that perfect freedom consists. 'Though I am free and belong to no man,' says Paul, 'I make myself a slave to everyone, to win as many as possible. . . . I have become all things to all men so that by all possible means I might save some. I do all this for the sake of the gospel . . .' (1 Cor. 9:19, 22–23). 'A Christian is a most free lord of all, subject to none. A Christian is a most dutiful servant of all, subject to all' (Martin Luther, *The Liberty of a Christian*).

Christian freedom is subject only to the self-imposed constraint of Christian charity. No-one may dictate what Christians must do in indifferent matters such as food or the observance of special days (see Adiaphora*); it is for them to restrict their freedom voluntarily if its exercise may harm the spiritual life of others. Plainly, true spiritual freedom will not lead Christians into courses of action which enslave them, nor can it encourage practices which are generally unhelpful and not conducive to the healthy upbuilding of the whole believing community.

Freedom from law is not freedom to sin: that would be exchanging one bondage for another. If legalism is one enemy of freedom, licence is another.

'Where the Spirit of the Lord is, there is freedom' (2 Cor. 3:17). This freedom is consummated at the resurrection, when 'creation itself will be liberated from its bondage to decay and brought into the glorious freedom of the children of God' (Rom. 8:21).

Bibliography

E. Käsemann, *Jesus Means Freedom* (ET,

London, 1969); P. Richardson, *Paul's Ethic of Freedom* (Philadelphia, 1979); C. Spicq, *Charité et liberté selon le Nouveau Testament* (Paris, 1964); W. C. van Unnik, 'The Christian's Freedom of Speech in the New Testament', *BJRL* 44, 1961–62, pp. 466–488.

F.F.B.

FREEDOM OF WILL, see WILL.

FREE WILL, see WILL.

FUNDAMENTAL THEOLOGY is one of the most problematic and creative areas of Christian theology. An established discipline in Roman Catholic theology,* fundamental theology is being increasingly recognized as a useful demarcation of a vital area of Protestant* theology too. Latest trends point to an attempt to explore the possibilities of an ecumenical* fundamental theology that is politically aware and socially self-critical.

Traditionally, fundamental theology examined the presuppositions of the Christian faith – the existence of God,* the reality of revelation* and man's capacity to receive it (the sensitive area of the relation of revelation and reason; see Faith and Reason*) – in a systematic way as a *prolegomenon* to the study of dogma.* But the fundamentals were already given, rather than proposed as hypotheses to be established. At its best, this approach could be seen as 'faith seeking understanding' (see Anselm*); at its crudest, it could appear to be an attempt to prove revelation, a purely formal way of handling the most basic questions of theology.

The current conception of fundamental theology stems from Rahner's* reassessment of the discipline and the encouragement this derived from Vatican II's Constitution on the Church in the Modern World (see Councils*). This approach is the beneficiary of the old discipline of apologetics.* It is motivated by a concern to commend the faith to the world and to establish its credentials in the light of modern thought, but it seeks to do this by a critical presentation of the whole self-expression of the Christian faith, rather than by an artificial abstraction from the contents of Christian doctrine (see Systematic Theology*). Rahner set out to reconstruct fundamental theology in union with dogmatic theology so as to impart to the whole enterprise of Christian theology an open and apologetic character that responds to the questions raised by man's subjectivity in the modern world.

Fundamental theology is in a vulnerable position as it mediates between Christian doctrine and other relevant disciplines. But it is a theological, not a pre-theological discipline, since it is conducted from the standpoint of faith. Here it is distinct from both philosophy of religion* (see also Philosophical Theology;* Philosophy and Theology*), which does not require faith,* and apologetics proper* which, though obviously conducted from the standpoint of faith, does not presuppose faith in its audience.

A new departure in Roman Catholic fundamental theology has been initiated by J. B. Metz,* who, though in sympathy with Rahner's approach, regards it as naively theoretical – neither acutely aware of its ideological determinants nor committed to the struggle against oppression at the level of praxis.* (See also Political Theology.*) Metz proposes a practical fundamental theology structured by the three practical hermeneutical* categories of narrative, memory and solidarity, in relation to which the standard themes and problems of fundamental theology – the actuality, character and credibility of revelation, and the subjects, conditions and consequences of its reception – would be interpreted.

In Protestant theology, the discipline of fundamental theology owes its momentum to G. Ebeling,* for whom it is concerned with the question of the truth* of theology through a process of verification* and self-criticism in an integrated dialogue not only with other theological disciplines, but with all relevant sources of information and insight. This is of course conspicuously and intentionally lacking from Barth's* CD, but has been substantially achieved in Tillich's* Systematic Theology.

Some degree of coherence can be imposed on this varied scene if fundamental theology is understood as analogous to the philosophy of science or of history, in other words as a theological epistemology* or as the discipline of theological method comprising the sources, scope, aims and rationality of theology in dialogue with the whole range of theological studies. Such a fundamental theology would have a public aspect and serve an apologetic

function as the meeting-point of Christian doctrine and other relevant disciplines.

Bibliography
P. Avis, *The Methods of Modern Theology* (Basingstoke, 1986); G. Ebeling, *The Study of Theology* (London, 1979); H. Fries, 'Fundamental Theology', *SM* II, pp. 368–372; R. Latourelle, 'A New Image of Fundamental Theology', in R. Latourelle and G. O'Collins (eds.), *Problems and Perspectives of Fundamental Theology* (Ramsey, NJ, 1982), pp. 37–58; J. B. Metz, *Faith in History and Society: Towards a Practical Fundamental Theology* (London, 1980), together with P. Avis, *SJT* 35 (1982), pp. 529–540; K. Rahner, *Foundations of Christian Faith: An Introduction to the Idea of Christianity* (London, 1978).

P.D.L.A.

FUNDAMENTALISM developed its distinctive characteristics primarily in North America, and has had its widest influence in the USA where revivalist evangelicalism* has been the dominant religious heritage. Although it has many missionary exports and also many parallels in anti-modernist Protestant movements in other countries, we can best understand its distinguishing features by looking at the prototypical and widely influential American developments.

The word 'fundamentalism' originated in the USA in 1920 as the designation that editor Curtis Lee Laws (1868–1946) used for his anti-modernist party in the Northern Baptist Convention. The term was soon used to describe a broad coalition of evangelical Protestants who fought militantly against modernist* (*i.e.* liberal) theology and against some features of secularization* of modern culture. This remains the most accurate way to use the word. Essential to being a fundamentalist is that one be 1. an evangelical Protestant; 2. an anti-modernist, meaning that one subscribes to the fundamentals of traditional supernaturalistic biblical Christianity; and 3. militant in this anti-modernism or in opposition to certain aspects of secularization. A fundamentalist, then, is a militantly anti-modernist evangelical.

The picture is complicated by a number of other broader and narrower usages. Sometimes the word is used generically to designate any religious anti-modernist, hence 'Islamic fundamentalists'. Or opponents of Protestant fundamentalism may use the term loosely to describe almost any of the features, especially the more extravagant or anti-intellectual ones, of evangelical revivalism, such as those especially common in the American South. Such usage invites confusion of fundamentalism with revivalism generally and with several closely related movements with revivalist roots. For instance, the holiness movement,* which arose in the second half of the 19th century, was distinguished especially by emphasis on experiences of outpourings of the Holy Spirit leading to lives of sinless perfection.* Pentecostalism,* arising in the early 20th century, was marked by stress on receiving spectacular spiritual powers. Fundamentalist anti-modernist militancy was sometimes also adopted by these groups, so that they often become fundamentalistic. Nonetheless, these movements tended to remain distinct and ecclesiastically separate. All three, however, were related by common origins to the broader and still more diverse heritage of 19th-century American revivalism and many of their traits commonly called 'fundamentalist' are more accurately called 'revivalist'.

Still another broad use of 'fundamentalism' is that common in British parlance. There, 'fundamentalism' often refers to any evangelical conservatism that has a high view of the Bible and its fundamental claims. For instance, J. I. Packer defended fundamentalism in this sense in his *'Fundamentalism' and the Word of God* (London, 1958), and James Barr in *Fundamentalism* (London, 1977) conflates most of the branches of conservative evangelicalism in his attack on the movement.

In America, on the other hand, 'fundamentalism', when used carefully, has come to refer to the more narrow phenomenon of the main groups of militantly anti-modernist white evangelicals. (American black evangelicals are often revivalist in style, fundamental in doctrine, and anti-modern in ethics; but they do not typically call themselves 'fundamentalists'.)

The characteristics of the distinctively 'fundamentalist' movement can be seen best from its history. As Ernest R. Sandeen has shown in his important study, *The Roots of Fundamentalism: British and American Millenarianism, 1800–1930* (Chicago, 1970), one major source of fundamentalism was the premillennial prophecy movement originating from the work of J. N. Darby* and others. Although in England this movement produced primarily the Plymouth Brethren who left the traditional churches, in the United States its main expressions in the late 19th century were within major northern denominations, such as the Presbyterian and the Baptist. Dispensationalism* was the distinctive feature of this movement and became almost canonized in the notes of C. I. Scofield's famous *Reference Bible* (New York, 1909). Many American dispensationalists also adopted the moderate holiness teachings fostered by England's Keswick Convention.

Dispensationalism, which predicted the ruin of the church in this epoch, encouraged militancy against the rise of aggressive theological modernism in the early 20th century. In the USA, especially, where modernism was strong, dispensationalists found many allies who wished to defend the fundamentals of the faith against modernism. Among the northern Presbyterians, conservatism was strong, bolstered by the intellectual leadership at Princeton Theological Seminary (see Princeton Theology*). Conservative Presbyterians first developed the strategy of defending lists of fundamental doctrines. Dispensationalists also organized the publication, from 1909 to 1915, of *The Fundamentals*, defending traditional doctrines. Many fundamentalist groups had lists of 'fundamental' doctrines, though no one list was ever standard. The commonest points were the inerrancy of Scripture* (see Infallibility and Inerrancy*), the deity of Christ, his virgin birth,* the substitutionary atonement,* Christ's resurrection,* and his second coming.

During the 1920s fundamentalists fought hard against modernist gains in the major northern Presbyterian and Baptist denominations. Smaller fundamentalist controversies occurred in other denominations, and parallel splits between conservatives and liberals took place in a number of churches in the United States and Canada. Meanwhile, fundamentalists took on a cultural as well as an ecclesiastical dimension as they attacked aspects of moral erosion after World War I. The campaign led by William Jennings Bryan (1860–1925) to keep evolution from being taught in American public schools was the chief expression of such concern. The spread of evolutionary teaching was seen as undermining the authority of the Bible in American life and as fostering moral relativism. Marxism, Romanism, alcohol, tobacco, dancing, card-playing and theatre attendance were other major targets for fundamentalist attacks. Amid these conflicts, fundamentalism grew as a coalition of anti-modernist Protestants from many traditions, throughout the USA, north and south, other English-speaking countries, and their missionary outposts. At the centre of the coalition were American dispensation-alists, whose fundamentalism was least tempered by other traditions.

By the 1930s fundamentalism was beginning to take a distinctive ecclesiastical expression. Increasingly the most militant fundamentalists felt that they should separate from groups which contained modernists, and form independent congregations or denominations. Most such fundamentalists became Baptist and were dispensationalist. Separatism was becoming a test of true faith.

What had been the broader militant anti-modernist coalition of the 1920s thus began to split by the 1940s. One major group in America softened its militancy and tried to retain contact with mainline denominations. Led by spokespersons such as Harold John Ockenga (b. 1905), Carl F. H. Henry,* and Edward J. Carnell,* they at first called themselves 'neo-evangelicals' and by the later 1950s simply 'evangelicals'. Their associations with Billy Graham (b. 1918) signalled the growth of this inclusivist wing of 'evangelical' ex-fundamentalists. Meanwhile, militant separatists, such as John R. Rice (1895–1980), Bob Jones (1883–1968), and Carl McIntire (b. 1906) claimed they were the only true fundamentalists. After 1960 'fundamentalism' in America could be used to distinguish this separatist sub-group from the broader 'evangelicalism', which included ex-fundamentalists and Bible-believing Christians from many traditions.

Separatist fundamentalism continued to grow, although it probably never constituted more than 10% of America's estimated forty to fifty million 'evangelicals' in the 1970s and 1980s. By the 1980s, especially with the rise of Baptist fundamentalist Jerry Falwell's (b. 1933) Moral Majority, the political concerns of fundamentalists to preserve traditionalist Christian mores in American public life had become prominent again, as they had been in the 1920s. Fundamentalist politics now also included strong support for the state of Israel,* important to dispensational prophetic interpretation.

Bibliography

G. W. Dollar, *A History of Fundamentalism in America* (Greenville, SC, 1973); G. M. Marsden, *Fundamentalism and American Culture: the Shaping of Twentieth-Century Evangelicalism, 1870–1925* (New York, 1980); C. A. Russell, *Voices of American Fundamentalism: Seven Biographical Studies* (Philadelphia, 1976).

G.M.M.

G

GALLICANISM, see PAPACY.

GENERAL REVELATION, see REVELATION.

GENERATION, ETERNAL, see TRINITY.

GIFFORD LECTURES, the lectureships endowed at the ancient Scottish universities (Aberdeen, Edinburgh, Glasgow, St Andrews) by the will of Lord Adam Gifford (1820–87), an eminent judge. A follower of Spinoza,* Gifford wished to promote 'the study of natural theology,* in the widest sense of that term, in other words, the knowledge of God', to be pursued as 'a strictly natural science, the greatest of all possible sciences . . . that of Infinite Being, without reference to or reliance upon any supposed special exceptional or so-called miraculous revelation. I wish it studied just as astronomy or chemistry is.'

Starting in 1888, the lectures have featured the most distinguished religious thinkers within and beyond the English-speaking world, and have been issued in numerous significant publications. Lecturers have included: John Baillie,* Barth* (who justified his series as an exposition of 'a totally different theology' without whose challenge natural theology loses its vitality), Brunner,* Bultmann,* Christopher Dawson, John Dewey, A. S. Eddington (*The Nature of the*

Physical World), Austin Farrer,* J. G. Frazer, Gilson,* J. S. Haldane, W. C. Heisenberg, W. R. Inge, W. Jaeger, William James (*The Varieties of Religious Experience*), John MacMurray, G. Marcel, E. L. Mascall, Moltmann,* F. Max Müller, Reinhold Niebuhr,* Polanyi,* A. E. Taylor (*The Faith of a Moralist*), William Temple,* Tillich,* Arnold Toynbee, C. C. J. Webb, and A. N. Whitehead (*Process and Reality*).

Such a selection illustrates how generously the founder's terms have been interpreted.

Bibliography
B. E. Jones (ed.), *Earnest Enquirers After Truth: A Gifford Anthology* (London, 1970), with a full list to date; S. L. Jaki, *Lord Gifford and His Lectures. A Centenary Retrospect* (Edinburgh, 1986).

D.F.W.

GIFTS OF THE SPIRIT.

These are to be distinguished from the gift of the Spirit promised by Jesus.

The gift, the gifts and the fruit of the Holy Spirit

The Holy Spirit* was received by the church from Pentecost onwards, as the Spirit of Christ present to fill and empower his people (Acts 1:4–5, 8; 2:1ff.). The Spirit himself is distinct from the various particular gifts or manifestations of his presence and ministry granted to (and through) different individual Christians. These gifts, which are an equipment for particular forms of service, are also to be distinguished from the 'fruit' or (as later theologians put it) the 'graces' of the Holy Spirit, which are qualities of Christian character (Gal. 5:22–23). The gift of the Holy Spirit himself is for *all* believers under the new covenant* (unlike the OT), and all his fruit or graces are needed in the life of every Christian. But although the Holy Spirit can manifest any of his gifts through anyone who has received him (as he chooses, and where people are open to his working), he does not give all the gifts to one person, but rather gives differing gifts to different people. The NT words used stress their nature as God's free gift, proceeding from his grace, and as manifestations of the Holy Spirit working as the Spirit of Jesus Christ in his people.

Gifts for the body of Christ

While several NT writers mention various spiritual gifts, it is Paul who provides a controlling framework to illuminate their purpose and operation, by his description of the church* as the body of Christ, comparing the functions of its different gifted members with those of the parts of the human body (1 Cor. 12; Rom. 12:3ff.; Eph. 4:11–16). The main points of this analogy are that Christ continues to manifest his life, ministry and word in the world through the church as his body on earth; that he gifts its members by his Spirit who indwells it; that the members' gifts and resultant functions differ from one another; that the gifts are given for the good of the body, not for one's self; that a gift's spectacular prominence or lack of it is no guide to its importance; that gifts must be used under the Lord's direction, and controlled by love; and that their use must be overseen and tested by those over the congregation or with mature spiritual discernment.

Types of gifts – and Pentecostalism

The NT contains several lists of different kinds of gifts (*e.g.* in Acts 2; Rom. 12; 1 Cor. 12; Eph. 4; 1 Pet. 4) and other references to them (*e.g.* in Lk., Heb., *etc.*). Twentieth-century Pentecostalism,* in both its earlier (eventually denominational) and later (charismatic or renewal movement) phases, has focused attention especially on the gifts treated in 1 Cor. 12 and 14, believing that the church had seriously neglected some or all of these gifts. The earlier Pentecostalism produced in the mainline denominations a strong reaction against such unaccustomed manifestations, which effectively forced them to form their own separate churches. In the later charismatic renewal (post–1950) this has only partially happened. The earlier Pentecostals connected the gifts with a 'baptism in the Spirit'* subsequent to conversion, but the later movement has varied on this point.

Historically, the classic Reformed view has been that the 1 Cor. 12 group of gifts died out, either with the apostles or with the completion of the NT canon (Calvin, John Owen, Jonathan Edwards, Warfield). The degree of NT support for this position is a matter of debate. In the judgment of charismatic writers and many others today it lacks an adequate basis in the NT. Some of those

269

who do not find this cessationist position biblically demonstrable explain the spasmodic and uneven appearance of the gifts in church history by reference solely to the sovereign choice of the Holy Spirit (1 Cor. 12:11; Heb. 2:3–4 and the history of redemption in the OT). Others (including Pentecostal/charismatic writers) ascribe the absence of these gifts in the past life of the church to a failure to desire, pray for and expect God's working in these ways (appealing, for example, to 1 Cor. 12:31; 14:1, 5, 13, 19, *etc.*). This article takes the view that some combination of these two viewpoints provides the most reliable explanation.

Against some Pentecostal teachings, it should be noted that no one spiritual gift or manifestation (such as tongue-speaking) is to be regarded as the universal, invariable and exclusive sign that a person has received the Holy Spirit, although in Acts the Spirit's coming is evidenced on several occasions by the presence of some gift or gifts in the recipients. Also, there are other lists of gifts besides 1 Cor. 12. There is no good reason for concentrating exclusively on any one list to the neglect of others. In any case, the NT lists do not seem to be exhaustive catalogues, but rather representative examples. There is no universal agreement as to what all the gifts listed actually refer to, some seeing, for example, 'a word of wisdom/knowledge' as revelation and others as gifts of counsel and teaching. Among the various gifts of speech, revelation, power, or pastoral organization and care, some involve inborn or learned abilities or aptitudes, sanctified and possibly heightened by the Holy Spirit, while others are more clearly supernormal endowments *ab initio* following a Christian's reception of the Spirit.

Institutional office and/or charismatic ministries

In principle, the full range of the gifts and ministries of Christ by his Spirit is intended for all the churches, just as every Christian should be filled with the Spirit and open to his working. In God's plan there should never be two groups of Christians or churches – 'charismatic' and 'non-charismatic'. The latter would be an anomalous contradiction in NT terms. However, the history of OT Israel and the NT church down the centuries illustrates copiously the tension between two aspects in

the life of God's people, the institutional and the charismatic. The OT records both priestly/prophetic and judges/monarchy tensions, and not long after the NT a settled ministry of bishops/presbyters and deacons is found alongside itinerant prophets, *etc*. The institutionalizing tendency of the church catholic has often been in tension with revivalist and charismatic characters and movements (both heretical and orthodox) from at least 2nd-century Montanism* onwards. This must be a creative, not a destructive, tension, for the church needs both order and openness to the Holy Spirit's charismatic ministry and gifts, as he often raises up people or groups to meet the needs of a particular time or place.

Testing the gifts and regulating their use

Both OT and NT stress the need to test spiritual gifts, by their conformity to Scripture, their consistency, and whether they exalt the Lord (Dt. 13:1–5; 18:21–22; Mt. 7:15–20; 1 Cor. 12:1–3; 14:29; 1 Thes. 5:19–22; 1 Jn. 4:1–6). Such 'testing' is necessary due to the presence of evil demonic spiritual powers at work in the world seeking to mislead the church, spirits of antichrist, obviously rife in idolatry and occultism.* These produce counterfeit, devilish reproductions of the gifts of the Holy Spirit, such as false teaching, false prophecy, lying visions, false tongue-speaking and interpretation, occult 'spiritual' healing powers, lying signs and wonders, *etc*. The church needs to guard against the twin dangers of either letting in false (demonically inspired) gifts, with disastrous results, or rejecting the true and good gifts of God along with the false and evil. There is no greater need than a discerning, weighing or testing of spiritual gifts, to guard the church from both these fatal errors. In the congregation, its worship and ministry, Scripture demands that the use of gifts be also properly regulated and overseen, but not quenched or forbidden (1 Cor. 14 and 1 Thes. 5:19–21). Freedom for the Spirit to work and good order *are* compatible, and the balance between them must be kept right.

Bibliography

A. Bittlinger, *Gifts and Graces* (London, 1967; *idem, Gifts and Ministries* (London, 1974); N. Bloch-Hoell, *The Pentecostal Movement* (London, 1964); D. Gee, *Concerning Spiritual Gifts* (Springfield, MO,

1947); J. Owen, *Works*, ed. W. H. Goold, vol. IV (Edinburgh, 1852), pp. 420–520; J. I. Packer, *Keep in Step with the Spirit* (Leicester, 1984).

J.P.B.

GILL, JOHN, see HYPER-CALVINISM.

GILSON, ETIENNE (1884–1978), Thomist* historical philosopher. He taught medieval philosophy in France, chiefly at the Sorbonne (1921–32) and the Collège de France (1932–51), and then at the Pontifical Institute of Medieval Studies in Toronto, which he had directed since its inception in 1929. Resident again in France from 1959, he wrote prolifically until his death, producing over a hundred books and articles after his seventy-fifth birthday.

Gilson was early influenced by H. Bergson (1859–1941), the French philosopher and champion of 'intuition' and creative evolution. From studies of Descartes* he moved to the medieval era, with monographs on Bonaventura* (1924), Augustine* (1928; ET, *The Christian Philosophy of St Augustine*, London, 1961), and Bernard* (London, 1934). His Gifford Lectures of 1930–31 were translated as *The Spirit of Medieval Philosophy* (1936).

Gilson always presented himself as a *Christian* philosopher, refusing to modernize Thomism as though its essence could be independent of theology. Among the different scholastic* syntheses of medieval Christian philosophy, the Thomist was for him, as for his ally Jacques Maritain (1882–1973), the best creative basis for interpreting modern culture. He defended teleology for both philosophy and biology, and called himself a dogmatist, while insisting that unchanging dogma* requires ever-fresh expression.

A man of public life, honoured by the French resistance and at one time a senator in the government, he enjoyed universal recognition as perhaps the most distinguished historian of medieval philosophy.

Bibliography
A. C. Pegis, *A Gilson Reader* (New York, 1957); L. K. Shook, *Etienne Gilson* (1984), and M. McGrath, *Etienne Gilson. A Bibliography* (1982), both in *The Etienne Gilson Series* (Toronto).

D.F.W.

GLORY OF GOD, THE, fundamental characteristic of God to which believers respond by giving him glory.

Biblical
'Glory' in Heb. is *kābôd*, from a root signifying 'weight' (a fact which Paul seems to remember in 2 Cor. 4:17); in Gk. (LXX and NT) the word is *doxa*, which originally meant an opinion. In both testaments the word means 1. excellence and praiseworthiness set forth in display (glory *shown*); then 2. honour and adoration expressed in response to this display (glory *given*). In his acts of creation, providence and grace, God shows his glory, 'glorifying' himself (Is. 44:23; Jn. 12:28; 13:31–32), his Son (Jn. 13:31–32; 17:5; Acts 3:13; *cf.* 1 Pet. 1:21) and his servants (Rom. 8:17–18, 30; 2 Cor. 3:18). Seeing this, his worshippers give him glory, 'glorifying' him by praise, thanks, obedience and acceptance of providentially ordered suffering for his sake (Jn. 17:4; 21:19; Rom. 4:20; 15:6, 9; 1 Cor. 6:20; 10:31; 1 Pet. 4:12–16).

Glory as seen in people takes the form of wealth, position and power (Gn. 31:1; 45:13; Is. 8:7). The glory that God shows, however, is the reality of his active presence, linked with the quality of his acts themselves. In OT times this 'glory' took the physical form of light (lightning, Ps. 29:3; the brightness of theophany,* Ezk. 1:27–28; the bright cloud that led Israel through the wilderness, locating itself in the tabernacle, Ex. 40:34–38, and appearing later in the Temple, 2 Chr. 7:1–3; *cf.* Ezk. 8:4; 9:3; 43:2); so too in the annunciation to the shepherds and Paul's conversion (Lk. 2:9; Acts 7:55). God made Moses realize, however, that the essence of his glory is his holiness and goodness (Ex. 33:18 – 34:8; *cf.* Is. 6:1–5; Jn. 12:41), and in the NT 'glory' is regularly linked with God's display of power, wisdom and love in the death, resurrection, enthronement and mediatorial ministry of Jesus Christ (Jn. 12:23; 13:31–32; Rom. 6:4; 2 Cor. 3:7–11; 4:6; Eph. 1:6, 12, 14, 17–18; Phil. 4:19), whose glory as the Son in action both embodies and reflects the glory of the Father (Jn. 1:14; Heb. 1:3).

The giving of glory to God in worship is called *doxology*.* The psalms are full of it. Formal doxologies appear in Rom. 9:5; 11:36; 16:25–27; Eph. 3:20–21; Phil. 4:20; 1 Tim. 1:17; 6:16; 1 Pet. 4:11; 2 Pet. 3:18; Jude 24–25; Rev. 1:6; 5:13.

Theological

All serious Christian thinkers acknowledge that glorifying God is at once man's divine calling and his highest joy, both here and hereafter. Reformed* theology goes beyond other views, however, in emphasizing these three truths. 1. God's goal in all that he does is his glory, in the sense of a. displaying his moral excellence to his creatures and b. evoking their praise for what they see and for the benefit it brings them (*cf.* Eph. 1:3). 2. Man's goal in all his actions must be God's glory in the sense of doxology by word and deed. 3. God so made us that we find the duty of doxology to be our supreme delight, and in that way the furthering of our own highest good. This coinciding of duty with interest and devotion with fulfilment was classically formulated in the first answer of the Westminster Shorter Catechism: 'Man's chief end is to glorify God, and to enjoy him for ever.'

Bibliography

S. Aalen, *NIDNTT* II, pp. 44ff.; A. M. Ramsey, *The Glory of God and the Transfiguration of Christ* (London, 1949).

J.I.P.

GNOSTICISM. The Gnostics were followers of a variety of religious movements which stressed salvation through *gnōsis* (Gk.) or 'knowledge', above all of one's origins. Cosmological dualism* was an essential feature of Gnosticism – an opposition between the spiritual world and the evil, material world. Gnosticism was attacked in the writings of the church fathers (2nd–4th centuries; see Patristic Theology*), who regarded the various Gnostic groups as heretical* perversions of Christianity. Many modern scholars believe that Gnosticism was a religious phenomenon which was in some cases independent of Christianity. There is as yet no consensus as to when and how it originated, but a context in heterodox or fringe Judaism has the support of several scholars.

Patristic sources

Until the 19th century, we were entirely dependent upon the descriptions of the Gnostics found in the church fathers. In some cases the patristic sources preserved extracts of the Gnostic writings, but for the most part they were polemical in nature. Our most important sources include Justin Martyr (see Apologists*), Irenaeus,* Hippolytus,* Tertullian,* Clement of Alexandria,* Origen* and Epiphanius of Salamis in Cyprus (*c.* 315–403). Especially valuable is Irenaeus' account, which has been mostly preserved only in a Lat. translation, *Adversus Haereses* (*Against Heresies*). Clement and Origen were in many ways sympathetic to the Gnostic emphases. Though Epiphanius had some firsthand contact with Gnostics in Egypt, his *Panarion* ('Medicine Box'), while comprehensive, is not very reliable.

Some of the observations of the fathers, especially Irenaeus, have been confirmed by the discovery of original Gnostic documents from Nag Hammadi (see below). On the other hand, we have nothing as yet from the Gnostic sources themselves which corresponds to the patristic description of the licentious wing of Gnosticism.

Gnostic leaders

The church fathers are unanimous in regarding Simon of Samaria as the first Gnostic, though our earliest source, Acts 8, describes him only as one who practised sorcery (*mageia*, *cf.* Eng. 'magician'). According to the later sources, Simon claimed to be divine, and taught that his companion, a former prostitute, was the reincarnated Helen of Troy. The *Apophasis Megale* attributed to Simon by Hippolytus was a later philosophical exposition attached to his name.

Simon was followed by a fellow Samaritan, Menander, who taught at Antioch in Syria towards the end of the 1st century. He claimed that those who believed in him would not die. His claims were nullified when he himself died. Also teaching in Antioch at the beginning of the 2nd century was Saturninus (Satornilos), who held that the 'incorporeal' Christ was the redeemer. That is, he held a docetic* view of Christ which denied the incarnation* (*cf.* 1 Jn. 4:2–3).

Teaching in Asia Minor in the early 2nd century was Cerinthus, who held that Jesus was but a man upon whom Christ descended as a dove. As Christ could not suffer, he departed from Jesus before the crucifixion. Another early Gnostic teacher was Basilides in Egypt, to whom have been attributed both a dualistic system (by Irenaeus) and a monistic* system (by Hippolytus).

An important though atypical Gnostic was

Marcion* of Pontus. He contrasted the God of the OT with the God of the NT. Marcion drew up the first canon or 'list' of NT books (see Scripure*), including a truncated Gospel of Luke and ten Pauline letters. Marcion's docetic teachings were sharply rebuked by Tertullian.

The most famous Gnostic teacher was Valentinus, who came from Alexandria to Rome in 140. He taught that there was a series of divine emanations, including the First Ogdoad (four pairs), and he divided mankind into three classes: *hylics*, or unbelievers immersed in nature and the flesh; *psychics*, or common Christians who lived by faith; and *pneumatics*, or the spiritual Gnostics. The later Valentinians divided into Italian and Oriental schools over the question of whether Jesus had a psychic or pneumatic body. The many outstanding Valentinian teachers included Ptolemaeus, Heracleon, Theodotus and Marcus. The earliest known commentary on a NT book is Heracleon's on the Gospel of John.

Coptic Gnostic sources

In the 19th century the contents of two Coptic Gnostic codices were published: the Codex Askewianus containing the *Pistis Sophia*, and the Codex Brucianus containing the *Books of Jeu* – both relatively late Gnostic compositions. A third work, the Codex Berolinensis, though acquired in the 19th century, was not published until 1955. It contains a *Gospel of Mary* (Magdalene), a *Sophia of Jesus, Acts of Peter*, and an *Apocryphon of John* – a work mentioned by Irenaeus.

In 1945 a cache of eleven Coptic codices and fragments of two others was found by a peasant near Nag Hammadi in Upper Egypt. The first translation of a tractate, that of *The Gospel of Truth*, appeared in 1956. After various vicissitudes, an English translation of the fifty-one treatises appeared in 1977 largely through the efforts of James Robinson. A considerable body of original Gnostic writings is now for the first time available to scholars.

The Nag Hammadi library, as this important collection has come to be called, contains a variety of texts: non-Gnostic, non-Christian Gnostic, and Christian Gnostic. The most famous example of the latter is *The Gospel of Thomas*, an apocryphal gospel, probably composed *c.* AD 140 in Syria, which contains over a hundred purported sayings of Jesus. Scholars who believe that Gnosticism was a pre-Christian phenomenon have cited especially *The Apocalypse of Adam* and *The Paraphrase of Shem* as non-Christian Gnostic works. Some have claimed that *The Trimorphic Protennoia* gives us the prototype for the prologue of the Gospel of John.

Mandaean sources

The Mandaean communities in southern Iraq and south-western Iran are today the sole surviving remnants of Gnosticism. Their texts, though known only through late manuscripts, were used by the history-of-religions* scholars and Bultmann* to reconstruct an alleged pre-Christian Gnosticism. In addition to the manuscripts there are earlier magic bowl texts (AD 600) and some magical lead amulets which may date from as early as the 3rd century AD. There is no firm evidence to date the origins of the Mandaeans earlier than the 2nd century AD.

Gnostic teachings

Because they had no central authority or canon of Scriptures, the Gnostics taught a bewildering variety of views. Central and essential to clearly Gnostic systems was a dualism, which set over against each other the transcendent God and an ignorant and presumptuous demiurge (see Platonism*), often a caricature of the OT Yahweh. In some systems the creation* of the world resulted from the fall* of Sophia (Wisdom). In every case the material creation was viewed as evil.

Sparks of divinity, however, have been encapsulated in the bodies of certain pneumatic or spiritual individuals. The pneumatics, however, are ignorant of their celestial origins. God sends down to them a redeemer, often a docetic Christ, who brings them salvation in the form of a secret *gnōsis*. This is most often communicated by Christ after his resurrection. Most Gnostics held that Christ was not truly incarnated nor could he truly suffer on the cross.

Thus awakened, the Gnostics escape from the prison of their bodies at death and traverse the planetary spheres of hostile demons to be reunited with God. There is, of course, no resurrection of the body.

Since salvation is not dependent upon faith or works but upon the knowledge of one's true nature, some Gnostics indulged deliberately in licentious behaviour. Carpocrates, for example, urged his followers to sin, and his son Epiphanes taught that promiscuity was God's law.

Most Gnostics, however, took a radically ascetic* attitude towards sex* and marriage, deeming the creation of woman the source of evil, and the procreation of children but the multiplication of souls in bondage to the powers of darkness. They looked forward to the time when females would be transformed into males, as in Eden prior to the creation of woman.

We know very little about the cult and the community of the Gnostics. As a general rule they interpreted rites such as baptism* and eucharist* as spiritual symbols of *gnōsis*. Women were prominent in many of their sects.

Gnosticism and the NT

Despite the lack of Gnostic texts prior to Christianity, many scholars (*e.g.* J. M. Robinson, K. Rudolph) have assumed a pre-Christian origin of Gnosticism. They also believe that they can detect references to Gnosticism in the NT, especially in the writings of John* and Paul.*

Bultmann explained the Gospel of John as the revision of an originally Gnostic document which contained traditions similar to those of the Mandaeans. Following R. Reitzenstein (1861–1931), he also held that the NT was dependent on a pre-Christian Gnostic myth of a 'redeemed' redeemer. But such a myth is found only in Manichaeism,* a late form of Gnosticism. Most scholars are today convinced that such a redeemer myth is a post-Christian development patterned after the person of Christ.

At best, one may see the development of a rudimentary Gnosticism at the end of the 1st century AD. It is anachronistic to read back into the NT period the fully developed Gnosticism of the 2nd century AD.

Bibliography

F. Borsch, *The Christian and Gnostic Son of Man* (London, 1970); J. Doresse, *The Secret Books of the Egyptian Gnostics* (London, 1960); R. M. Grant, *Gnosticism and Early Christianity* (New York, ²1966); H. Jonas, *The Gnostic Religion* (Boston, MA, ²1963); B. Layton (ed.), *The Rediscovery of Gnosticism*, 2 vols. (Leiden, 1980–81); A. Logan and A. Wedderburn (eds.), *The New Testa-*

274

ment and Gnosis (Edinburgh, 1983); E. Pagels, *The Gnostic Gospels* (London, 1979); P. Perkins, *The Gnostic Dialogue* (New York, 1980); J. M. Robinson (ed.), *The Nag Hammadi Library in English* (New York, 1977); K. Rudolph, *Gnosis* (New York, 1983); R. McL. Wilson, *Gnosis and the New Testament* (Philadelphia, 1968); E. Yamauchi, *Pre-Christian Gnosticism* (Grand Rapids, MI, ²1983).

E.M.Y.

GOD, the object, as revealed in Scripture, of the church's confession, worship and service.

1. The identity of God

The Christian view of God comes from the biblical revelation,* in which mankind's maker appears as mankind's redeemer, unchangeably and unchallengeably sovereign in creation,* providence* and grace.* Since he is not open to direct observation, a meaningful account of him can only be given by indicating at each point his relation to ourselves and the world we know. Scripture does this, setting an example that this article will follow.

a. The names of God. In mainstream Christian usage, 'God' (capital 'G') functions as a proper noun; that is, it is a personal name, belonging to one being only, which draws into itself all the thoughts that the biblical names and descriptions of God express.

The main names of God in the OT, all proclaiming aspects of his nature and his link with mankind, are these:

i. *El, Eloah, Elohim* (Eng. 'God', following *ho theos* in LXX), *El Elyon* ('God most high'). These names convey the thought of a transcendent being, superhumanly strong, and with inexhaustible life in himself, one on whom everything that is not himself depends.

ii. *Adonay* ('Lord'; *kyrios* in LXX). This means one who rules over everything external to him.

iii. *Yahweh* ('the LORD' in AV(KJV), RV, RSV, NIV, following *ho kyrios* in LXX), *Yahweh Sebaoth* ('Lord of [heavenly, angelic] hosts'). 'Yahweh' is God's personal name for himself, by which his people were to invoke him as the Lord who had taken them into covenant* with himself in order to do them good. When God first stated this name to Moses at the burning bush, he explained it as meaning 'I am what I am', or perhaps most accurately 'I will be what I will be'. This was a declaration of independent, self-determining existence (Ex. 3:14–15). Later God 'proclaimed' – that is, expounded – 'the name of the LORD' as follows: 'The LORD, the LORD, a God merciful and gracious, slow to anger, and abounding in steadfast love and faithfulness, keeping steadfast love for thousands, forgiving iniquity and transgression and sin, but who will by no means clear the guilty, visiting the iniquity of the fathers upon the children and the children's children, to the third and fourth generation' (Ex. 34:6–7, RSV). Thus in sum 'Yahweh' carries the thought of a marvellously kind and patient, though also awesomely stern, commitment to the covenant people as the path chosen by the self-sustaining, self-renewing being whom the theophany* of the burning bush depicted.

The NT identifies the God who is Father of Jesus Christ and of Christians through Christ as the God of the OT, the only God there is (cf. 1 Cor. 8:5–6), and it sees the Christian salvation as the fulfilment of God's OT promises. Thus it rules out in advance all dualisms* that oppose the God, or the idea of God, which the OT sets forth, to the redeemer-God seen in and described by Jesus. 'Father'* appears as the invocation of God that Jesus, who himself prayed to God as Father, prescribed for his disciples (cf. Mt. 6:9; 1 Pet. 1:17); 'Lord', used as in LXX to imply deity as well as dominion, becomes the regular term for characterizing, confessing and invoking the risen and enthroned Christ (Acts 2:36; 10:36; Rom. 10:9–13; 1 Cor. 8:6; 2 Cor. 12:8–10; Rev. 22:20; etc.); and the 'name' (singular) into which disciples of Jesus are to be baptized, as a sign of God's committed salvific relationship to them and their responsive commitment to him, is the tripersonal name of three distinguishable though evidently inseparable agents, 'the Father, the Son, and the Holy Spirit' (Mt. 28:19). This is God's 'Christian name', as Barth happily put it.

b. The concept of theism. Views of God of the Judaeo-Christian type are called theism* to offset them from deism* and pantheism,* and monotheism* to offset them from polytheism.* Deism, first formulated in the 17th century, sees the cosmos as a closed system with its maker outside it and so denies God's direct providential control of events and his miraculous creative intrusions into the ongoing life of the physical world-order. Pan-

theism, which goes back to pre-Christian Eastern religion, recognizes no creator-creature distinction, but sees everything, good and evil included, as a direct form or expression of God; so that as William Temple* said, God minus the universe equals nought. (For theism, by contrast, God minus the universe equals God.) Polytheism, the constant form of the ancient near-Eastern and Graeco-Roman paganism which Scripture denounces, posits many supernatural beings limited by each other, none of whom is omnicompetent, so that worship must be spread and allegiance divided among them all, since we cannot know whose help we may need next. The biblical idea of God is thus diminished by deism, dissolved by pantheism, and debased by polytheism. Creation and control of the cosmos, and a beneficent disposition to rational creatures within it, are the essential tenets of theism in all its forms.

c. Trinitarianism. Distinctive to Christian theism is the belief that the personal creator is as truly three as he is one. Within the complex unity of his being, three personal centres of rational awareness eternally coinhere, interpenetrate, relate in mutual love, and cooperate in all divine actions. God is not only *he* but also *they* – Father, Son and Spirit, coequal and coeternal in power and glory though functioning in a set pattern whereby the Son obeys the Father and the Spirit subserves both. All statements about God in general or about the Father, the Son or the Holy Spirit in particular, should be 'cashed' in Trinitarian terms, if something of their meaning is not to be lost. This form of belief, argued by Athanasius* and the Cappadocian Fathers and stated in the Nicene-Constantinopolitan Creed in the 4th century, and analysed in the so-called Athanasian Creed of the 5th–6th century (see Creeds*), reflects the conviction that Jesus' recorded teaching and attitudes with regard to the Father and the Spirit (cf. Jn. 14 – 16), and the pervasive triadic thought-forms whereby the NT regularly presents salvation as the joint work of the three persons together (cf., e.g., Rom. 3; 1 Cor. 12:3–6; 2 Cor. 13:14; Eph. 1; 2 Thes. 2:13–14; 1 Pet. 1:2; Rev. 1:4–5), actually reveal God rather than obscuring him. Being unique, the Trinity is to us a mystery, that is, a matter of incomprehensible fact, and rationalistic thinkers and sects have often attacked the doctrine of God's tripersonality on that account. But the implications of the NT material are too clear to be denied.

d. The language of belief. Human language is all that we have for worshipping, confessing and discussing God, and it is adequate; but it has to be systematically adapted for the purpose. Scripture itself unobtrusively exhibits this adaptation, for it regularly presents God as the super-person who made mankind in his image (see Image of God*) and whose life, thoughts, attitudes and actions are basically comparable to our own, though they contrast with ours in being free both from the limitations of our creaturely finiteness and from the moral flaws that are part and parcel of our fallenness. The Bible's narrative and descriptive language about God is thus used in a sense analogous to, though never quite identical with, the sense that the words would carry if used of humans, and the language of theology must self-consciously follow the Bible at this point. The ontological basis for this rule of thought and speech is what Thomas Aquinas* called *the analogy of being* that exists between God and ourselves, *i.e.* the qualified similarity between his existence as creator and ours as creatures (see Analogy*).

When Christianity moved out of Palestine into the wider Greek-speaking world, Christian spokesmen borrowed words from Hellenistic culture. Platonic,* Aristotelian* and Stoic* thinkers saw the world as shaped somehow by a principle, in some sense divine, that was immaterial, impassive, immobile, immutable and timeless. Apologists* and theologians took over this vocabulary to express the transcendence of God and the difference between him and man. Arguably these impersonal static Greek terms were a poor fit by biblical standards, but those who have used them from the 2nd to the 20th century have never let them obscure the fact that God is personal, active and very much alive.

2. The being of God

The 'attributes' of God – that is, the qualities that may truly be ascribed to him – concern either his way of existing as compared with ours, or his moral character as shown by his words and deeds. The main points in historic Bible-based, time-tested Christian theism with regard to the way in which God exists are these:

a. God is self-existent, self-sufficient and *self-sustaining.* God does not have it in him, either in purpose or in power, to stop existing; he exists *necessarily*, with no need of help and support from us (*cf.* Acts 17:23–25). This is his *aseity*, the quality of having life in and from himself.

b. God is simple (that is, totally integrated), *perfect and immutable.* These words affirm that he is wholly and entirely involved in everything that he is and does, and that his nature, goals, plans and ways of acting do not change, either for the better (being perfect, he cannot become better) or for the worse. His immutability is not the changelessness of an eternally frozen pose, but the moral consistency that holds him to his own principles of action and leads him to deal differently with those who change their own behaviour towards him (*cf.* Ps. 18:24–27).

c. God is infinite, bodiless (a spirit), *omnipresent, omniscient, and eternal.* These words affirm that God is not bound by any of the limitations of space or time that apply to us, his creatures, in our present body-anchored existence. He is always present everywhere, though invisibly and imperceptibly, and is at every moment cognizant of all that ever was, is, or shall be. Individual theists have denied that God knows the future, but this imposes on him an unbiblical limitation and is thus eccentric.

d. God is purposeful, all-powerful, and sovereign in relation to his world. He has a plan for the history of the universe, and in executing it he governs and controls all created realities. Without violating the nature of things, and without at any stage infringing upon human free agency, God acts in, with and through his creatures so as to do everything that he wishes to do exactly as he wishes to do it. By this overruling action, despite human disobedience and Satanic obstruction, he achieves his pre-set goals. Some question the reality of the eternal decree (that is, decision) whereby God has foreordained everything that comes to pass, but this also imposes an unbiblical limitation on such texts as Eph. 1:11, and it too must be judged eccentric.

e. God is both transcendent over, and immanent in, his world. These 19th-century words express the thought that on the one hand God is distinct from his world, does not need it, and exceeds the grasp of any created intelligence that is found in it (a truth sometimes expressed by speaking of the *mystery* and *incomprehensibility* of God); while on the other hand he permeates the world in sustaining creative power, shaping and steering it in a way that keeps it on its planned course. Process theology* jettisons transcendence and so stresses the immanence of God and his struggling involvement in the supposedly evolving cosmos that he himself becomes finite and evolving too; but this is yet another unbiblical oddity.

f. God is impassible. This means, not that God is impassive and unfeeling (a frequent misunderstanding), but that no created beings can inflict pain, suffering and distress on him at their own will. In so far as God enters into suffering and grief (which Scripture's many anthropopathisms, plus the fact of the cross, show that he does), it is by his own deliberate decision; he is never his creatures' hapless victim. The Christian mainstream has construed impassibility as meaning not that God is a stranger to joy and delight, but rather that his joy is permanent, clouded by no involuntary pain.

3. The character of God

Character is personal moral nature revealed in action. In God's dealings with mankind his character is fully displayed, supremely in the incarnate Son: God is Jesus-like, for Jesus is God in the flesh. Concerning God's character the key statements appear to be these:

a. God is holy love. The essence of all love is giving prompted by goodwill, with joy in the recipient's benefit. The statement, 'God is love' (*agapē*, 1 Jn. 4:8) is explained in context as meaning that God gave his Son as a sacrifice to quench his wrath* against human sins and so bring believers life. *Agapē* is the regular NT word for love that gives even to the unlovely and undeserving. Behind the statement, however, must be held to lie the Johannine conviction that love is the abiding quality of inter-Trinitarian relations (*cf.* Jn. 5:20; 14:31). Both internally and externally, therefore, giving in order to make the recipient great must be understood as the moral shape of the Triune God's life.

But God is also 'the holy one' (some 50 references), and holiness (purity, hatred of moral evil, and inner compulsion to show judicial anger against it) always qualifies the divine love. The need for retributive judgment* on our sins through Christ's cross ('the measure and the pledge of love', *cf.* Jn. 3:16; Rom. 5:8), as a basis for the free gift of justification* and forgiveness (see Guilt and Forgiveness*), is rooted in this fact, and so is the requirement of holiness in the justified (Rom. 6; 2 Cor. 6:14 – 7:1; 1 Thes. 4:3–7; Heb. 12:14; 1 Pet. 1:15–16).

b. God is moral perfection. God's revealed ways with mankind render him not only awesome but also adorable by reason of his truthfulness, faithfulness, grace, mercy, loving-kindness, patience, constancy, wisdom, justice, goodness, and generosity – all of which find exercise as functions of his love to believers, as well as in his sustained dominion over a rebel world which he governs with both goodness and severity. For the display of these glorious qualities God is worthy of endless praise, and right-minded study of God's moral character will always end in doxology.*

Bibliography
K. Barth, *CD*, I.1, II.1, 2; H. Bavinck, *The Doctrine of God* (Grand Rapids, MI, 1952); L. Berkhof, *Systematic Theology* (Grand Rapids, MI, 1949); E. Brunner, *Dogmatics*, vol. I: *The Christian Doctrine of God* (London, 1949); E. J. Fortman, *The Triune God* (London, 1972); C. F. H. Henry, *God, Revelation and Authority*, vols. V, VI (Waco, TX, 1982, 1983); C. Hodge, *Systematic Theology*, vol. I (Grand Rapids, MI, 1960); E. Kleinknecht, G. Quell, E. Stauffer, K. G. Kuhn, *TDNT* III, pp. 65–123; E. L. Mascall, *Existence and Analogy* (London, 1949); H. P. Owen, *Concepts of Deity* (New York, 1971); *idem*, *Christian Theism* (Edinburgh, 1984); J. I. Packer, *Knowing God* (London, 1973); *idem*, 'Theism for Our Time', in P. T. O'Brien and D. G. Peterson (eds.), *God Who is Rich in Mercy* (Homebush West, NSW, 1986); G. L. Prestige, *God in Patristic Thought* (London, 1936); J. Schneider and C. Brown, *NIDNTT* II, pp. 66–84; A. E. Taylor, 'Theism', *ERE* XII, pp. 261–287; A. Wainwright, *The Trinity in the New Testament* (London, 1962).

J.I.P.

GOGARTEN, FRIEDRICH, see DIALECTICAL THEOLOGY.

GOODWIN, THOMAS, see PURITAN THEOLOGY.

GOOD WORKS, see Sanctification.

GORE, CHARLES (1853–1932), Anglo-Catholic leader and scholar, and Bishop of Worcester (1902–5), Birmingham (1905–11), and Oxford (1911–19). Scion of an aristocratic family, Gore was educated at Harrow where his early 'Catholic' spirituality was nurtured by, among others, B. F. Westcott.* An outstanding undergraduate at Balliol, Oxford, he was elected fellow of Trinity College in 1875. As vice-principal of the newly-founded theological college at Cuddesdon (1880–83), and as first Principal Librarian of the new Anglo-Catholic* study centre in Oxford, Pusey House (1884–93), Gore exerted a personal and spiritual influence comparable to that of J. H. Newman.* These early years were also Gore's most significant theologically, as he controversially sought to imbue traditional Tractarianism with the modern spirit of a critical scripturalism in his quest for an effective popular dogmatic. His *The Ministry of the Christian Church* (1888, new ed. 1919) is, however, a spirited conservative defence of High Church views of the historical origins of episcopacy. His liberal catholicism came to fruition in his contribution to, and editorship of, the controversial volume of Oxford essays by like-minded scholars, *Lux Mundi: A Series of Studies in the Religion of the Incarnation* (1889). Traditional Tractarians were further discomfited by Gore's Bampton Lectures* *The Incarnation of the Son of God* (1891), which not only contained a Greek patristic reaffirmation of the dogmatic centrality of the incarnation, but also claimed that Christ's full earthly humanity involved a voluntary self-emptying (kenosis*) of his divine knowledge and a resultant human ignorance.

No narrow-minded academic aristocrat, Gore was passionately concerned for social justice and for a credible grass-roots manifestation of Christian thought and life: hence, his lifelong involvement with the Oxford Mission to Calcutta and the Christian Socialist Union,* and and his civic involvement and support of the Workers Educational Association when Bishop of Birmingham (1905–11). Gore wedded an Anglo-Catholic apologetic to this concern for Christian social action. His *Dissertations* (1895), *The Body of Christ* (1905), *Christ and Society* (1928), and exposition of the *Sermon on the Mount* (1896),

reveal a Catholic sacramental dogmatic accompanying his call for Christian service in church and world. Despite successful episcopal labours, Gore became increasingly isolated, vigorously and unpopularly denouncing a progressive Anglo-Catholicism which commended liturgical supplementation (*e.g.* reservation of the eucharist) and credal laxity. He devoted his last years in London to teaching and writing, notably in defence of the Christian faith (*cf.* his dogmatic trilogy *Belief in God*, 1922, *Belief in Christ*, 1922, *The Holy Spirit and the Church*, 1924) and of his Anglo-Catholic position (*e.g.* his critique, *The Anglo-Catholic Movement Today*, 1925).

Bibliography
J. Carpenter, *Gore, A Study in Liberal Catholic Thought* (London, 1960); W. R. Inge, in *Edinburgh Review* 207 (1908), pp. 79–104; G. L. Prestige, *The Life of Charles Gore: A Great Englishman* (London, 1935); A. R. Vidler, 'Charles Gore and Liberal Catholicism' in *Essays in Liberality* (London, 1957); A. T. P. Williams in *DNB (1931–1940)*, pp. 349–353.

C.D.H.

GOSPEL. The NT use of Gk. *euangelion*, 'joyful tidings', 'good news', has an OT background in Is. 40 – 66, where the LXX verb *euangelizomai*, 'bring good news', is used of the declaration of Jerusalem's deliverance from bondage (Is. 40:9; 52:7) and also of a wider announcement of liberation for the oppressed (Is. 61:1, 2). This last passage provided the text of Jesus' inaugural preaching at Nazareth: he gave notice that it had been fulfilled as he spoke (Lk. 4:17–21). Jesus' message was otherwise described as the gospel of the kingdom of God.* Its contents are set out in his parables, where the Father's loving bestowal of mercy and free forgiveness on the undeserving and the outcasts is presented with vividness and warmth.

With Jesus' death and resurrection a new phase of the gospel begins. The preacher becomes the preached one: his followers, whom he commissioned to preach the gospel after his departure, proclaimed him as the one in whom the Father's pardoning grace had drawn near. 'The gospel of God... concerning his Son' (Rom. 1:1–3) tells how, in the coming and redemptive work of Christ,

God has fulfilled his ancient promise of blessing for all nations.

For the first generation after Christ's ascension the gospel was exclusively a spoken message; the earliest written record of the gospel appeared in the 60s.

Only one saving message is attested by the NT. The 'gospel to the circumcision' preached by Peter and his colleagues did not differ in content from the 'gospel to the uncircumcised' entrusted to Paul (Gal. 2:7), though the form of presentation might vary according to the audience. Paul's testimony is, 'Whether therefore it was I or they [Peter and his colleagues], so we preach, and so you believed' (1 Cor. 15:11).

The basic elements in the message were these: 1. the prophecies have been fulfilled and the new age inaugurated by the coming of Christ; 2. he was born into the family of David; 3. he died according to the Scriptures, to deliver his people from this evil age; 4. he was buried, and raised again the third day, according to the Scriptures; 5. he is exalted at God's right hand as Son of God, Lord of living and dead; 6. he will come again to judge the world and consummate his saving work.

Bibliography

C. H. Dodd, *The Apostolic Preaching and its Development* (London, 1936); J. Munck, *Paul and the Salvation of Mankind* (ET, London, 1959).

F.F.B.

GOTTSCHALK (*c.* 803–69), Benedictine* theologian, poet and monk who caused an argument over predestination* that agitated the church in France and Germany during the Carolingian era. His father, Berno, a Saxon noble, placed him in the monastery at Fulda; but when he came of age he asked to be released from his vows. This request was granted by the Synod of Mainz (829), but Louis I the Pious, on an appeal from the abbot of Gottschalk's monastery, Rabanus Maurus, reversed the decision. Gottschalk was then moved to the monastery at Orbais where he began an intensive study of the work of Augustine.* Becoming a priest, he visited Rome and later served as a missionary in the Balkans. His constant emphasis upon double predestination led to his condemnation at the synods of Mainz (848) and Quiercy (849 and 853). He was dismissed from the priesthood, beaten until he almost died and imprisoned for life at the monastery of Hautvillers.

His view of predestination included the belief that God foreordains those he wishes to heaven or to hell, that one can have absolute certainty of salvation or damnation, that God does not will that all shall be saved, that Christ died only for the elect, and that no-one can exercise free will* for the doing of good works but only for performing evil acts. Several theologians wrote in support of his views including Ratramnus,* Prudentius of Troyes (d. 861) and Remigius of Lyons (d. 875). When three opponents of Gottschalk's teaching, including Hincmar of Reims (c. 806–82), sent letters to Remigius to justify the harsh treatment he had received, Remigius responded in the name of the Church of Lyons with a *Reply to the Three Letters* which criticized the treatment given to the monk, clarified the issues and partially supported Gottschalk's position.

The lively debate over predestination demonstrates that the issues raised in the earlier Pelagian* controversy had not been settled. They were to surface again at the time of the Protestant* Reformation and in more recent times as a result of the Wesleyan* movement. These discussions, accompanied by a certain amount of rancour, continue to divide evangelicalism in modern times. There was little new ground broken in the 9th-century phase of the argument and neither party prevailed, nor was any compromise reached. Some of Gottschalk's fellow monks tried to free him by appealing to the pope, but this attempt failed. He remained in prison unreconciled to his ecclesiastical superiors. The resentment he felt because of the severe treatment he had received probably led to the mental illness he experienced before his death. A man of great literary talent, he left several thoughtful poems that rank with the finest literature produced by the Carolingian Renaissance.

Bibliography

G. W. Bromiley, *Historical Theology* (Grand Rapids, MI, 1978); J. Jolivet, *Godescalc d'Orbais et la Trinité* (Paris, 1958); J. Pelikan, *The Growth of Medieval Theology (600–1300)* (*The Christian Tradition*, vol. 3; Chicago, 1978); K. Vielhaber, *Gottschalk der Sachse* (Bonn, 1956).

R.G.C.

GRACE. The biblical words translated 'grace' are *ḥēn* (Heb.) and *charis* (Gk.). Neither word carries the usual sense of the English word 'grace' implying a personal virtue. They indicate rather an objective relation of undeserved favour by a superior to an inferior, which, in the case of divine grace towards mankind, accompanies the ideas of covenant* and election (see Predestination*). This favour to the individual as both creature and sinner results, however, in a transformed life through an effective calling* (Gal. 1:15) and the production of faith* and repentance* (Eph. 2:8–9; 2 Tim. 2:25). The subjective effects of grace may sometimes seem to make God's grace an independent virtue, a 'thing' possessed by the believer (Acts 4:33; 11:23; 13:43; Rom. 5:21), but attention to context reminds us that these are rather references to the operations of the Spirit of grace (Heb. 10:29). Theories that the Gk. idea of *charis* as an independent potency is present in NT usage are quite unproven. Ultimately NT grace comes in a person, Jesus Christ, and is bound up with him (Jn. 1:14, 16–17; Rom. 5:21; 1 Cor. 1:4, *etc.*).

The very sense of the word implies the freedom of grace. It is wholly unmerited, not evoked by the creature's disposition (*e.g.* Eph. 2:1–10; Tit. 3:3–7). As early as the 2nd century, however, the priority of grace over human response was obscured by an interest in redemption as a new revelation and law and a channelling of grace through clerical ministrations, while the doctrine of the Holy Spirit was neglected. In some measure Irenaeus* and Tertullian* recovered the place of the Spirit as the unique source of all grace in its transforming effects, but Tertullian's feeling for concrete realism and legal terminology threatened even further to turn grace into an impersonal 'substance'.

It was Augustine* who spoke once more of the priority of grace, especially in his doctrine of predestination.* In opposition to the contention of Pelagius* that each individual, untrammelled by any burden of inherited sin, was essentially free for moral choice, Augustine* etched out starkly the radical and enslaving character of sin and grounded salvation in 'prevenient' grace which alone facilitates repentance and faith. Yet for Augustine there was also a grace subsequent to faith which made the renewed will the agent of God's own loving acts towards others.

The pre-scholastic and scholastic* periods made many refinements in the concept of grace, leading in particular to the distinction of 'actual' grace (grace actualized in concrete acts) and 'habitual' grace (grace as the fundamental principle of a new nature), and the distinction between 'uncreated' grace (the gift of God himself which underlies all other kinds of grace in salvation) and 'created' grace (the effect or impact of uncreated grace upon the individual's own 'nature' or disposition). By the time of the Reformation,* however, grace was widely thought of as an independent virtue by means of which the sinner could produce acts commending himself to God's favour having once received it from God as gift.

Under the preaching of the Reformers, a revival of the primacy of grace occurred, together with a conviction of its basic sense of divine favour. Luther* renewed Augustine's evaluation of human sinfulness and so emphasized justification* as to obscure any real process of sanctification* or consolidating state of grace. Grace was, for Luther, manifested in the irregular surges of faith against the temptation to legalism and self-sufficiency. For Calvin,* however, a new state of sanctification or regeneration* inseparably accompanied justification by faith.

Calvin also formulated a doctrine of grace at work in the world at large, and distinguished between the grace of Christ, by which one became and remained a Christian, and a 'general' or 'common' grace to which may be attributed the restraint of gross sin. This also accounted for religious aspiration, decent behaviour, social brotherliness and the achievements of art and science. 'Special' grace was a special capacity, virtue or endowment. This sympathetic view complements but does not modify Calvin's agreement with Luther and Augustine on human helplessness in sin, at least with regard to acceptance with God.

Later Arminian* theologians rejected the distinction between common grace and the grace in salvation, seeing only a single divine grace held out to every person. They were unable, however, to dispose of the NT references to predestination and election or to explain satisfactorily the many distinctions of human response and privilege before the one grace. More recently some Calvinist theologians in America have jettisoned altogether Calvin's doctrine of common grace, believing that to the non-elect even God's kindness in the gospel intensifies the severity of the sinner's rejection by God. In general, this view has not convinced most in the Calvinist tradition.

Since the Reformation, controversy has continued on the way grace reaches Christians through the sacraments* and on the relation of grace to law.* On the latter, some have opted for Luther's view of the law as merely an ever-present power directing to grace, while others have adopted Calvin's 'third use' of the law as an active element in Christian sanctification. The OT dispensation appears to some as a 'legal' (or even legalistic) parenthesis and to others as a preparatory period of law bearing us to the coming grace in Christ and partially anticipating it, or as a phase of one covenant of grace centring ultimately on Jesus Christ.

The primacy of grace in Christian thought has reached into the 20th century in the massive work of both Karl Barth* and Karl Rahner,* each of whom, in his own way, returns to the idea that in grace God essentially gives himself.

Bibliography

K. Barth, CD, passim but especially II.1, pp. 351–368; J. Calvin, Institutes; J. Daane, The Freedom of God (Grand Rapids, MI, 1973); C. Mœller and G. Philips, The Theology of Grace and the Oecumenical Movement (London, 1961); J. Pohle, Grace Actual and Habitual (London, 1919); K. Rahner, Theological Investigations, vol. I (London, 1965); T. F. Torrance, The Doctrine of Grace in the Apostolic Fathers (Edinburgh, 1948); C. Van Til, Common Grace and the Gospel (Philadelphia, 1974); P. S. Watson, The Concept of Grace (London, 1959).

R.K.

GRATIAN, see CANON LAW.

GREGORY OF NAZIANZUS (c. 329–90), also known as Gregory the Theologian, was one of the three great Cappadocian Fathers (with Basil* and Gregory of Nyssa*). He formed a close friendship with Basil, later the leading figure of the group, while they were students in Athens. After his return to Cappadocia, Gregory reluctantly submitted to be ordained a presbyter to help his aged father, the Bishop of Nazianzus. A sermon preached subsequently (Oration II) is a seminal work of pastoral theology.* Later Gregory was consecrated bishop against his will to help Basil, by then the metropolitan Bishop of Caesarea, in an ecclesiastical power struggle. After Basil's death, he was called to lead the tiny remnant of orthodox Christians in Constantinople, capital of the Eastern Roman Empire. Gregory's outstanding oratory and the accession of the emperor Theodosius I led to the triumph of orthodoxy over Arianism.* After becoming Bishop of Constantinople and briefly presiding at the Council* of Constantinople (381), Gregory resigned and retired thankfully to Cappadocia.

Gregory's theology is to be found in his sermons, letters and poems. The five Theological Orations, preached in Constantinople in 380, contain his classic exposition of the doctrine of the Trinity.* After emphasizing the purification necessary for the theologian and the incomprehensibility of God,* he expounds the doctrine of the Trinity in terms of relationships within the Godhead. The Father is the begetter and emitter, the Son is the begotten and the Holy Spirit is the emission. The begetting of the Son and the procession of the Spirit are beyond time, so that all three are coeternal. While the Father may be greater than the Son in the sense that he is the cause, he is not greater by nature, for the two are of the same nature. The names, Father and Son, make known to us an intimate relation within the Godhead.

On this basis, Gregory strongly defends the deity of the Holy Spirit.* The Spirit must be either a creature or God, and only the latter alternative can give coherence to Christian doctrine. The Spirit, however, is neither begotten nor unbegotten, but the one who proceeds (to ekporeuton). The distinction of the three is thus preserved in the one nature. Gregory unequivocally proclaims what Basil had expressed so guardedly, that the Spirit is God and consubstantial with the Father.

Gregory's main contribution to the development of Christology* was in his opposition to Apollinarius.* He argued that the whole of human nature which fell in Adam must be united to the Son, body, soul and mind, 'for the unassumed is the unhealed'.

Bibliography

ET of selected works by C. G. Browne and J. E. Swallow in *NPNF*, second series, vol. 7 (1894; repr. Grand Rapids, MI, 1974); *cf.* also E. R. Hardy and C. C. Richardson, *Christology of the Later Fathers* (*LCC* 3, London, 1954).

A. Benoit, *Saint Grégoire de Nazianze* (1876; repr. Hildesheim, 1973); J. L. González, *A History of Christian Thought*, vol. 1 (Nashville, TN, 1970); J. N. D. Kelly, *Early Christian Doctrines* (London, ⁵1977); J. Plagnieux, *Saint Grégoire de Nazianze Théologien* (Paris, 1951); R. R. Ruether, *Gregory of Nazianzus. Rhetor and Philosopher* (Oxford, 1969); I. P. Sheldon-Williams in *CHLGEMP*, pp. 438–447; J. H. Srawley in *ERE* III, pp. 212–217; J. W. C. Wand, *Doctors and Councils* (London, 1962); H. H. Watkins in *DCB* II, pp. 741–761.

T.A.N.

GREGORY OF NYSSA (*c.* 335–95),

the youngest of the three Cappadocian Fathers (together with his elder brother Basil of Caesarea,* and their friend Gregory of Nazianzus*). In the late 4th century, he helped to bring about the victory of Nicene orthodoxy over Arianism* and give definitive shape to the doctrine of the Trinity.* Gregory lacked the university education of the other two, but became like them a teacher of rhetoric and surpassed them as a speculative thinker. He was created Bishop of Nyssa in 372 by Basil to assist him in an ecclesiastical power struggle. After Basil's death, Gregory was one of the leading figures at the Council* of Constantinople in 381.

Gregory's contribution to the Cappadocian doctrine of the Trinity is most succinctly expressed in his short treatise, *That We Should Not Think of Saying There Are Three Gods*. The Cappadocians had balanced the emphasis of Athanasius* and the older Nicenes on the unity and common *ousia* (substance*) of the Trinity with an emphasis on the distinctiveness of the three *hypostaseis* (persons). But this could lead to the danger of tritheism,* especially if the analogy of three men sharing the same substance of humanity is used. But Gregory argues that we ought not to speak of three gods sharing the same substance of deity (or Godhead), because it is actually inaccurate and misleading to speak of three men when the 'man' (*i.e.* the human

nature) in them is one and the same. Furthermore, the analogy falls short in that three men may pursue activities separately, whereas in God, each act towards the created world is common to all three, having its origin in the Father, proceeding through the Son and being perfected by the Spirit. Gregory's dogmatic works also include an important treatise *Against Eunomius* and a treatise against Apollinarius.*

A fuller account of Christian doctrine is given in the *Catechetical Oration*, written to help the instruction of converts. Here the influence of Neoplatonism (see Platonism*) and of Origen* is evident in his interpretation of the Christian doctrines of creation,* humanity (particularly sexuality*) and evil.*

Gregory is more faithful to the orthodox tradition than Origen, yet he clearly teaches universalism,* a redemption and restoration of the whole creation (including the devil). Those not purified in this life will be purified by fire after death. Gregory's originality is seen particularly in his doctrine of the atonement* and of the eucharist.* He explains the atonement in terms of the paying of the ransom (the life of Christ) to Satan (see Redemption*), who took it 'like a greedy fish' swallowing 'bait', not realizing that the Godhead was concealed within the flesh 'like a fishhook'. This grotesque imagery, together with any idea of a ransom being paid to the devil, has generally been rejected by the church. The merits of Gregory's theory lay in its objective and cosmic view of the atonement and in the way in which he linked it to the divine attributes of goodness, power, justice and wisdom. His doctrine of the eucharist arises from his understanding of the physical aspect of salvation in the resurrection* of the body. He taught that salvation* was communicated to the body through the eucharist. The bread and wine became the elements of the body of Christ through the words of consecration so that as we receive them our bodies share in divine immortality.

Gregory is also noted for his influential mystical* writings in which he traces three stages in the ascent of the soul from *apatheia*, freedom from passion, through *gnōsis*, mystical knowledge in which the senses are left behind, to *theōria*, the highest stage of contemplation in which (since a created soul cannot see God) one passes into the limitless ascent into the divine darkness.

Bibliography

ET of selected works by W. Moore and H. A. Wilson in *NPNF*, second series, vol. 5 (1890; repr. Grand Rapids, MI, 1976); cf. also E. R. Hardy and C. C. Richardson, *Christology of the Later Fathers* (*LCC* 3, London, 1954).

G. W. Bromiley, *Historical Theology, An Introduction* (Edinburgh, 1978); A. S. Dunstone, *The Atonement in Gregory of Nyssa* (London, 1964); *idem*, 'The Meaning of Grace in the Writings of Gregory of Nyssa', *SJT* 15 (1962), pp. 235–244; J. L. González, *A History of Christian Thought*, vol. 1 (Nashville, TN, 1970); J. N. D. Kelly, *Early Christian Doctrines* (London, ⁵1977); I. P. Sheldon-Williams in *CHLGEMP*, pp. 447–456; J. H. Srawley in *ERE* III, pp. 212–217; E. Venables in *DCB* II, pp. 761–768.

T.A.N.

GREGORY OF RIMINI (*c.* 1300–58).

Gregory was born at Rimini in Italy. Having become an Augustinian friar he proceeded to study and then to lecture in theology. From 1341 to 1351 he taught at Paris. In 1351 he returned to the Augustinian house at Rimini, becoming in 1356 and 1357 vicar general and prior general of the order. His most important surviving work is a commentary on the first two books of Peter Lombard's* *Sentences*.

Gregory's theology has been described as an Augustinian* response to the questions of the 14th century. He accepted, with his contemporaries, the separation of faith and reason,* revealed truth and natural knowledge. He emphasized the limits of reason and the inscrutability of God's ways. He based theology on God's revelation,* allowing little scope for a natural theology.* He was a philosophical nominalist.* Thus far Gregory was in accord with the dominant and radically untraditional Ockhamist school (see William of Ockham*). But Gregory's theology was more traditional than theirs, a return to the teaching of Augustine. Together with his contemporary Bradwardine,* he opposed the current Semi-Pelagianism.* He stressed the sovereignty of God and our total dependence upon grace for salvation. Fallen humanity can do no good without God's grace. Election is God's sovereign and unmerited choice of us. Gregory followed Augustine in teaching that those who die unbaptized in infancy are condemned to hell, for which he earned the title '*tortor infantium*'. But a fairer assessment of his theology as a whole is found in the more traditional title, '*doctor authenticus*'.

Bibliography

G. Leff, *Gregory of Rimini* (Manchester, 1961).

A.N.S.L.

GREGORY PALAMAS, see EASTERN ORTHODOX THEOLOGY; HESYCHASM.

GREGORY THE GREAT (*c.* 540–603).

Gregory renounced a secular career as prefect of Rome in order to become a monk following the Benedictine* rule (see Asceticism and Monasticism*). Out of the proceeds of his own estates he founded monasteries in Sicily and Italy. Even as pope, an office he held from 590, he retained a monk's garb and lived with his clergy under a strict rule. His most influential work was his *Pastoral Rule*, which had a decidedly monastic tone.

Gregory's papacy* fell during chaos and internal strife for Italy. In a power vacuum Gregory took various initiatives, appointing governors to Italian cities and providing materials for the war against the Lombards. Thus he effectively extended the temporal power of the papacy.

Though Gregory asserted the sovereign authority of the apostolic see, whenever he suspected heresy or uncanonical procedure, he preferred not to interfere with the authority of other bishops. He abhorred the title 'ecumenical patriarch' adopted by the Patriarch of Constantinople as uncanonical and arrogant. In reaction he adopted for himself the humble title of 'the servant of all the servants of God'.

Gregory combined a learned Augustinianism* with various traits of popular piety. He published *Dialogues* full of accounts of bizarre prodigies and visions of Italian saints, which he credulously accepted. He gave the doctrine of purgatory* an important extension when he made it a dogma that souls in purgatory would be released by the sacrifice of the mass. Again, though not himself approving the worship of images,* he allowed them a place in the worship of the illiterate.

Gregory also played an active role in the expansion of the church. His initiative behind the mission of Augustine of Canterbury to England is well known, but he also took steps to strengthen the church in Spain, Gaul and North Italy.

Bibliography

F. H. Dudden, *Gregory the Great*, 2 vols. (London, 1905); G. R. Evans, *The Thought of Gregory the Great* (Cambridge, 1986).

G.A.K.

GROTIUS, HUGO (1583–1645), Huig de Groot, Dutch jurist, publicist, statesman and theologian. Precocious in study and attainment, Grotius imbibed rational humanism from both his family and his studies at Leiden University which he entered in 1595. After being granted the degree of LL.D by the University of Orleans, he practised as a lawyer in Holland, and held important public offices.

In 1610 the followers of Arminius* published a Remonstrance stating the five points on which they departed from strict Calvinism (see Reformed Theology*). The debate was, however, complicated by its being embroiled in questions as to the relative powers of the Dutch Provinces and central authority. Grotius, of the Arminian persuasion, strove for peace and urged moderation in *Ordinum Pietas* (1613). He also drafted the Resolution for Peace (1614) by which the States-General forbade preaching on controverted doctrines, and commended toleration. Politically the dispute was dealt with by a coup, Maurits of Nassau, Prince of Orange and leader of the Calvinists, seizing major cities in 1618. Jan van Oldenbarnevelt, the leader of the Arminians and supporter of provincial autonomy, was executed for treason, and Grotius was imprisoned for life. The Synod of Dort* (1619) asserted the five points of Calvinism against the Remonstrance of the Arminians.

In 1621 Grotius escaped and settled in Paris. He returned briefly to Holland in 1631, retiring thereafter to Germany. From 1635 to 1645 he was Swedish ambassador to Paris. He died at Rostock as a result of shipwreck off Danzig.

Grotius had a literary reputation, his early drama *Adamus exul* (1601) influencing Milton's *Paradise Lost*. In law his *Mare Liberum* (1609) first expounded the freedom of the high seas, and his works in civil law are still used. His *De Iure Praedae* (1604, but published 1868) foreshadowed *De Iure Belli ac Pacis* (1625), a seminal work of modern international law, in the course of which Grotius indicated that the principles of natural law* might be based as much on reason and social order as on revelation, and be valid even if there were no God – a hint which others took much further.

In theology Grotius moved to a creedless position, moderation and toleration* being paramount. His *De Veritate Religionis Christianae* (1627) stated the common core of Christianity irrespective of denomination and theology, and recommended trust in God and the following of Christ's teaching. It was translated for missionary purposes into Arabic, Persian, Chinese and other languages. Other works, such as the *Via ad Pacem Ecclesiasticam* and the *Votum pro Pace Ecclesiastica* (both 1642) were attempts to promote reunion and peace. However, these were rejected by many as sacrificing too much of the Protestant and Reformed cause. His *Annotationes in Vetus et Novum Testamentum* (1642) rely on philology, science and history to explicate the texts commented on in a way unusual at a time when received doctrines of inspiration would have excluded such methods.

His *Defensio fidei catholicae de satisfactione Christi adversus Faustum Socinum Senensem* (1617, ²1636), an attack on Socinianism* of doubtful effect, contains what has become known as the governmental or rectoral theory of the atonement,* which derives from, but is tangential to, penal theories of the atonement. Coloured by then developing notions of the role of the sovereign, the theory anticipates some modern views. God's pardon of sinners is within his absolute unfettered discretion, the death of Christ being accepted by him as ruler or governor, not as creditor or offended party. As ruler God's interest is in the good government of the world. The death of Christ illustrates the punishment which sin may attract and therefore serves good government by acting as a deterrent. It also forms a contrast with the mercy shown through God's forgiveness of sinners, thus bringing home to mankind the depths of that mercy.

Bibliography

ET of *De Iure Belli ac Pacis* by F. W. Kelsey

(London and Washington, DC, 1923–8; repr. New York, 1964); E. Dumbauld, *The Life and Legal Writings of Hugo Grotius* (Norman, OK, 1969); W. S. M. Knight, *The Life and Works of Hugo Grotius* (London, 1925; repr. New York and London, 1962); R. W. Lee, 'Hugo Grotius', *Proceedings of the British Academy* 16 (1930), pp. 3–61; J. ter Meulen, *Concise Bibliography of Hugo Grotius* (Leiden, 1925); *idem* and P. J. J. Diermanse, *Bibliographie des écrits imprimés de Hugo Grotius* (The Hague, 1950).

F.L.

GUILT AND FORGIVENESS. Guilt is the state of one who has committed a sin or a crime. Sometimes it is defined in terms of penalty – the state of someone who is liable to punishment – but this is inadequate. Even if the penalty is deferred or even cancelled, the offender remains a guilty person, for guilt concerns the unalterable past. In Scripture, mankind is viewed as guilty because of the evil we have done and cannot now undo.

Guilt and a sense of guilt are not the same thing. It is clearly possible to be guilty without 'feeling' guilty. It is also possible to have an ill-proportioned or morbid sense of guilt. It is important to deal with such a 'guilt-complex', but we must not make the mistake of thinking that alleviating the condition of the individual's mind disposes of guilt itself. They are not the same.

Scripture portrays humanity as created by God to advance his good purposes. We are accountable to God and called to be obedient to his commands. But 'all have sinned and fall short of the glory of God' (Rom. 3:23), and thus incur guilt. James brings out the seriousness of this by saying that 'whoever keeps the whole law but fails in one point has become guilty of all of it' (Jas. 2:10); to break even one law means to become a law-breaker. None is guiltless.

Such guilt may, according to Jesus, be eternal (Mk. 3:29). Its seriousness should never be underestimated. Guilty sinners face eternal death (Rom. 6:23).

The central emphasis in the NT is on the wonder of forgiveness. In this sense, none of the NT writers dwells on guilt. It is forgiveness and not sin that is at the centre of their interest.

In Scripture, salvation from guilt means more than salvation from the power of evil.

Much effort today is concentrated on freeing people from the power of evil, so that they can live better lives. This is an important part of the gospel. But, wonderful though it is, this deliverance is not deliverance from guilt. We are responsible for the evil that we have done, and salvation in Christ means deliverance from guilt as well as power over evil.

Divine forgiveness means more than pardon. The pardoned criminal is still a guilty person. Everybody knows that he committed the sin for which he has received his pardon. It is the punishment, not the guilt that is gone. But Christ's forgiveness also means that the sin is gone. The sinner has been cleansed as well as pardoned. Sinners were dead in their trespasses but God has made them alive together with Christ, 'having forgiven us all our trespasses' (Col. 2:13). Our sins are forgiven for Christ's sake (Eph. 4:32; 1 Jn. 2:12).

It is a most important part of the Christian message to proclaim the forgiveness of sins. In the history of the Christian church this element of the gospel has been seen as so significant that it has been taken into our worship. We confess our sins and are assured of forgiveness in Christ. Absolution of this kind has been an important part of worship. The view that a 'priest' in the church of God has the power to grant forgiveness in the name of God and the right to decide whether it is to be given or refused is based on a wrong reading of Jn. 20:22–23. That passage speaks of the church as a whole, not its individual ministers; and it speaks of sinners in the plural. It is saying that the Spirit-filled church is able to assert authoritatively which groups of sinners have their sins forgiven and which do not. It confers no powers on individual Christians, be they 'priests' or laymen. Forgiveness is a gift conferred by God in Christ, but in the NT there is no power of absolution conferred on Christian ministers. Remission of sins is a divine prerogative.

Bibliography
E. M. B. Green, *The Meaning of Salvation* (London, 1965); T. McComiskey, *NIDNTT* II, pp. 137–145; V. Taylor, *Forgiveness and Reconciliation* (London, ²1946).

L.L.M.

H

HALLESBY, OLE (1879–1961), Norwegian evangelical theologian. He lost his evangelical convictions through the influence of liberalism* at the University of Oslo, but was converted shortly before graduation (1903). He was called to be a preacher of the 'Inner Mission' within the Church of Norway (Lutheran), and his preaching resulted in widespread spiritual revival.

In 1909 he received his PhD from Erlangen and became a professor of systematic theology at the Free Faculty of Theology in Oslo, recently founded (1907) in reaction against the liberalism dominant in the state university.

From 1919 Hallesby took a clear stand in preaching, teaching and writing for the biblical faith against liberal ideas that denied the truth of the Apostles' Creed. He advised evangelicals not to cooperate with liberal theologians and pastors. Though he strongly emphasized the need for conversion and vital Christian experience, Hallesby remained a firm Lutheran, laying strong emphasis upon the teaching of the confessions of the Lutheran Church in Norway. In this respect he is typical of many of the leaders of the 'free' organizations within that church. He initiated the establishment of a variety of institutions sponsored by such voluntary societies.

During the Second World War, Hallesby was a member of the Christian Council that resisted Nazi control of the church. For this reason he was imprisoned together with other Christian leaders in Norway.

The author of textbooks on dogmatics and ethics, Hallesby is best known outside Norway for his works on *Prayer* (ET, London, 1948) and *Why I Am a Christian* (ET, London, 1950).

N.Y.

HARNACK, ADOLF (1851–1930). Harnack (created von Harnack in 1914), church historian, was the son of the Lutheran theologian Theodosius Harnack. After studying at the universities of Dorpat (where his father held a chair) and Leipzig, he taught at the universities of Leipzig (1874–79), Giessen (1879–86), Marburg (1886–89) and Berlin (1889–1921). From 1905 to 1921 he was director of the Prussian State Library; in 1910 he became president of the Kaiser Wilhelm Gesellschaft for the promotion of learning and science. With Emil Schürer he founded the *Theologische Literaturzeitung* in 1876, and in 1882 he became founding editor, with Oscar von Gebhardt, of the series *Texte und Untersuchungen zur Geschichte der altchristlichen Literatur*. His literary output continued without intermission from his collaboration with von Gebhardt and Theodor von Zahn in an edition of the apostolic fathers (1876–78) to his final study of *1 Clement* (1929).

In theology he was generally a Ritschlian.* With the publication of his popular series of lectures *What is Christianity?* (1900; ET, 1901) he came to be viewed as the spokesman of liberal* Protestantism. He perceived the essence* of Christianity to lie in the fatherhood of God, the infinite worth of the individual soul, the higher righteousness and the commandment of love. This work, by stimulating Alfred Loisy to write *L'Evangile et l'église* (1908), indirectly precipitated the modernist crisis in the Roman Church (see Modernism, Catholic*). Another modernist, George Tyrrell, observed that 'the Christ that Harnack sees, looking back through nineteen centuries of Catholic darkness, is only the reflection of a Liberal Protestant face, seen at the bottom of a dark well' (*Christianity at the Crossroads*, London, 1909, p. 44).

Jesus' simple message, Harnack believed, had been distorted and corrupted by Catholicism, resulting from the alien intrusion of Greek metaphysics.* This belief was elaborated in his study of the Apostles' Creed (*Das apostolische Glaubensbekenntnis*, 1892) and in his multi-volume *History of Dogma* (1886–90, ⁶1922; ET, 1894–99).

His work in early church history is of abiding value. One of his greatest works was his study of Marcion* (1921, ²1924), a heretic with whose outlook (especially on the OT) he felt considerable sympathy. Also worthy of honourable mention are his *Geschichte der altchristlichen Literatur bis Eusebius*, 3 vols. (1893–1904), *The Mission and Expansion of Christianity* (1902, ⁴1924; ET, 1904–5); *The Constitution and Law of the Church* (1910; ET, 1910), and *Die Briefsammlung des Apostels Paulus* (1926).

In his monographs on NT criticism he reached increasingly conservative conclusions. In his *Sayings of Jesus* (1907; ET, 1908) he reconstructed the text of Q (the source presumably underlying the non-Marcan material common to Matthew and Luke) and argued that it was 'a document of the highest antiquity', reflecting in places 'the memory of an apostolic listener' and presenting a reliable portrait of Jesus. *Luke the Physician* (1906; ET, 1907) argued that Luke and Acts were composed by one man, an associate of Paul, and in particular that this man was the author of the 'we' narratives of Acts. Further evidence on this last point was adduced in *The Acts of the Apostles* (1908; ET, 1909), which also investigated the sources underlying the earlier chapters. In *The Date of the Acts and of the Synoptic Gospels* (1911; ET, 1911) he dated Luke-Acts (and *a fortiori* Mark) not later than AD 64 and Matthew shortly after AD 70.

Bibliography

G. D. Henderson, *ExpT* 41 (1929–30), pp. 487–491; W. Pauck, *Harnack and Troeltsch: Two Historical Theologians* (New York, 1968); Agnes von Zahn-Harnack, *Adolf von Harnack* (Berlin, ²1951).

F.F.B.

HARTSHORNE, CHARLES, see PROCESS THEOLOGY.

HEALING, the restoration of a sick person to health.

Health

The word 'health' comes from the Old Eng. root *hal* which means 'whole' and from which the words 'wholeness' and 'holiness' are also derived. Health is defined by the World Health Organization as 'a state of complete physical, mental and social well-being and not merely the absence of disease and infirmity'. To this definition we must add the dimension of spiritual well-being which arises from a right relationship to God. This complete well-being of man in all aspects of his being was God's original purpose for man.

Health in the OT is described by Heb. *šālôm*, usually translated 'peace', but by derivation meaning 'soundness' or 'well-being'. It occurs 250 times in the OT. Health as the well-being of the whole man is illustrated by the lives of the patriarchs (esp. Abraham), and

described by psalmist and prophet (esp. Is. and Je.). There is a vital connection between man's health and his ethical and spiritual obedience (Ex. 15:26; Dt. 28:58–61). Health in the OT consists of wholeness and holiness. The NT presupposes the OT teaching about health and has more to say about healing. When Jesus speaks about health, he speaks of blessedness (*makarios*, Mt. 5:3–11), life (*zōē*, Jn. 10:10) and being whole (*hygiēs*, Jn. 5:6). In the gospels the verb *sōzō*, save, is used equally for the healing of the body and the saving of the soul (Lk. 7:50; 9:24).

In the Christian understanding, health is the complete well-being of a person who is in a right relationship to God, to himself, to his fellows and to his environment.

Sickness

Sickness is the opposite of health and is denoted in Scripture by words which denote the weakness it produces – Heb. *ḥolî*, Gk. *astheneia*. Human sickness is the result of the sin and rebellion against God which produced the fall. There would be no sickness in the world if there were no sin. Not all sickness, however, is due to personal sin, as we see from the book of Job and Jn. 9:3. The presence of sickness in the world is testimony to God's requirement from us of obedience, to human solidarity in sin and susceptibility to infection and disease, and to the parasitism, corruption and decay which at present exist in our fallen world (Rom. 8:18–25). Nevertheless, God can use sickness and suffering to his glory and as a means of grace to men and women (Jb. 42:1–6; 2 Cor. 12:1–10).

Healing

The word 'healing' is uncommon in medicine and in Scripture. In ordinary usage today it is applied to the non-medical treatment of disease, often spoken of as faith, divine or spiritual healing. This usage is based on a fragmented view of the human person in which the doctor looks after the body and the church looks after the soul. If we adopt the scriptural view of a person as a whole being, then healing includes the whole person and all means of healing, whether medical or non-medical, physical or spiritual. All healing is of God whether provided through creation,* providence* or redemption.* He created the body and the mind with limited powers of self-healing, and placed healing agents in our environment. Healing on the basis of creation is that practised by the health care professions today, but it has no answer to the problems of sin,* guilt* and death.* For the complete restoration of human well-being, healing on the basis of redemption is required. This is provided by God through the ministry and work of his Son Jesus Christ. Healing on the basis of redemption brings forgiveness of sin, reconciliation* with God, renewal of all human relationships and the promise of complete wholeness when our perishable earthly body will be exchanged for an imperishable resurrection body (1 Cor. 15:52–53).

In the gospels, the work of physicians on the basis of creation is recognized (Mk. 2:17; Lk. 4:23), but much more is said about miraculous healing and healing on the basis of redemption. Jesus did not come primarily to heal our bodies (cf. Jn. 5:1–9 where he healed only one out of a multitude), but to make people whole. In the epistles we read of no miraculous healings, but of four sick people who were not healed in the sense of having their disease immediately removed. These were Paul (2 Cor. 12:7–9), Epaphroditus (Phil. 2:25–27), Timothy (1 Tim. 5:23) and Trophimus (2 Tim. 4:20). We do read, however, of gifts of healing (1 Cor. 12) and the involvement of church elders and members in healing (Jas. 5:14–16).

The gifts of healing were given by the Holy Spirit to certain individuals in the church for the benefit of the whole (1 Cor. 12:7, 9, 28). They are distinguished from the gift of working miracles (vv. 10, 28–30). They are mentioned only in 1 Cor. Their nature is not clear, whether they are supernatural enhancements of natural gifts already possessed, or entirely new supernatural gifts. Some believe that these gifts still continue in the church, while others deny this (see Gifts of the Spirit*). The modern charismatic movement lays great stress on their continuation and possession, as did Pentecostalism* before it.

In Jas. 5:14–16 the sick man is to call the elders who are to visit him, pray over him and anoint him with oil. This latter instruction may be interpreted ritually or medically. The verb used for anointing* (aleiphō) suggests a medical interpretation, otherwise the verb chriō would have been used. James is saying that the elders should pray over him and carry out the prescribed medical treatment in the name of the Lord. Healing on the basis of

redemption is to be combined with healing on the basis of creation.

The ministry of healing of the church

The phrase 'the ministry of healing' was first used as the title of a booklet by the Rev. A. J. Gordon DD of Boston, MA (1836–95) in 1881. It is now commonly used to describe the church's involvement in healing which has continued from the early centuries of its history. This involvement has been a comprehensive one. It has included medical healing on the basis of creation as when the church founded hospitals (from the 4th century AD), provided hospices and grew medicinal plants in the herb gardens of monasteries. Since the rise of an organized medical profession, the church has continued this ministry through the work of Christian doctors and nurses, and medical missionaries. In a similar way, the church has complemented medical care with physical and spiritual care, through prayer and the laying on of hands,* and sometimes with anointing with oil. There is now a renewed interest in this part of the church's ministry which is complementary to medical healing, and which, with medical healing, ministers to the well-being and needs of the whole person.

Bibliography

J. P. Baker, *Salvation and Wholeness* (London, 1973); V. Edmunds and C. G. Scorer, *Some Thoughts on Faith Healing* (London, ³1979); M. T. Kelsey, *Healing and Christianity in Ancient Thought and Modern Times* (London, 1973); F. MacNutt, *Healing* (Notre Dame, IN, 1974); M. Maddocks, *The Christian Healing Ministry* (London, 1981); J. C. Peddie, *The Forgotten Talent* (London, 1966); D. Trapnell, 'Health, Disease and Healing', in *NBD*, pp. 457–465; B. B. Warfield, *Counterfeit Miracles* (1918), repr. as *Miracles: Yesterday and Today* (Grand Rapids, MI, 1965); J. Wilkinson, *Health and Healing. Studies in NT Principles and Practice* (Edinburgh, 1980).

J.W.

HEAVEN, see Eschatology.

HEGEL, GEORG WILHELM FRIEDRICH (1770–1831), generally regarded as the greatest German philosopher of the first half of the 19th century. He was born at Stuttgart in the province of Württemberg in southern Germany and studied theology at Tübingen. For some years he taught at Jena and in Bavaria; then, in 1818, he was appointed professor of philosophy at Berlin, where he remained until his death from cholera in 1831.

Moving on from the moral rationalism of Kant,* and viewing all reality as cosmic reason (Spirit, Idea, Truth or God – the terms were more or less synonymous) realizing itself in specific processes, he taught an idealism* which encompassed everything and operated by a dialectical* process in which the infinite becomes finite and the finite becomes the infinite.

To understand Hegel's theology it is essential to understand his concept of God. Hegel's God is an absolute, eternal and dynamic Idea, a process of thought consisting of three stages or moments. In the first moment God is infinite Spirit, not a static unity but a thinking process which must come to self-consciousness. To this end the Spirit, in the second moment, descends ('dirempts' itself) into finite forms of social expression – art, literature, religion, science, *etc.* – where it becomes conscious of itself as part of the Absolute Spirit to which it is impelled to return from its 'diremption'. In the third moment this separation is abolished and the Spirit returns to itself, being reconciled to itself within its own unity as the Absolute Spirit. This threefold process of being (thesis), descent into finite forms (antithesis), and reconciliation (synthesis) lies at the basis of all Hegel's thought, including his theology.

For Hegel, life is not static, but ever-evolving through this dialectical evolution of the Infinite Spirit. God, therefore, is not to be thought of as personal, but as a process. The Absolute Spirit is the identity of God with humanity, the unity of the infinite with the finite. In Jesus this unity was manifested to the human race in concrete form. Hegel distinguished the three separate moments in this process as follows. The historical moment is the viewing of Jesus as a historical figure, although who or what Jesus was is regarded by Hegel as a purely historical problem of no decisive importance. The second moment, the moment of faith, sees Jesus as the divine Son of God. The third moment is the *real* or *actual* moment, the crystallizing out of what Jesus *actually* was, namely, the unity of infinite and

finite, of divine and human, which in essence for Hegel means that Jesus was the man who first perceived and embodied the reality of this unity.

Hegel's interpretation of the Christian faith thus dissolved away the traditional understanding of Jesus as the Son of the God who was and is a person, the designer and creator of the universe. Although Hegel's Absolute Spirit functioning triadically might appear similar to the traditional Christian understanding of the triune God revealing himself in history, in reality the two concepts are poles apart. For Hegel, Christian beliefs were little more than primitive conceptions and presentiments of reality which needed to be interpreted and reformulated in terms of his own system.

During the first part of the 19th century, Hegel's ideas penetrated German theology through the influence of such theologians as P. K. Marheineke (1780–1846), from 1811 professor of theology at Berlin, who promoted the Hegelian philosophy for more than thirty years. Strauss'* *Life of Jesus* (1835–36) was written while he was an ardent Hegelian, as were F. C. Baur's dogmatic works dating from the late 1830s and early 1840s. Following in Strauss' footsteps came Bruno Bauer (1809–82) and Ludwig Feuerbach* with even more virulent and radical attacks on the Christian faith and the historicity of the NT. Traditional orthodoxy in general, however, was largely untouched by these attacks, and the Hegelian philosophy influenced only the more avant-garde theologians, for the orthodox regarded Strauss and Baur as unbelievers, and looked upon Bruno Bauer and Feuerbach as rank atheists. Moreover, during the 1840s most of the Hegelians abandoned Hegel's metaphysical ideas and drifted into the atheism of Feuerbach, who declared that God – whether the Christian God or the Absolute Spirit – was merely a projection of the human mind.

See also: TÜBINGEN SCHOOL.

Bibliography

W. J. Brazill, *The Young Hegelians* (London, 1970); D. McLellan, *The Young Hegelians and Karl Marx* (London and Toronto, 1959); J. E. Toews, *Hegelianism* (Cambridge, 1980); J. Yerkes, *The Christology of Hegel* (Albany, NY, 1983).

H.H.

HEIDEGGER, MARTIN, see EXISTENTIALISM.

HEIDELBERG CATECHISM, see CATECHISMS.

HEIM, KARL (1874–1958). A Protestant systematic theologian, Heim taught at Tübingen. His theological development was strongly influenced by pietism,* especially by its evangelistic emphases. His major theological legacy is a six-volume work of apologetics, *Der evangelische Glaube und das Denken der Gegenwart* (*The Protestant Faith and Contemporary Thought*) (Tübingen, 1931–52), translated into English in a variety of volumes.

Heim attempts to mediate between Protestant theology and modern world-views, notably those he finds presupposed in natural science, and tries to develop a critical role for Christian theology in the contemporary world. His work was for a time influential on teachers and pastors in Germany, and he remains one of the few German theologians to address himself seriously to natural science.

Bibliography

Christian Faith and Natural Science (ET, London, 1953); *God Transcendent* (ET, London, 1935); *Jesus the Lord* (ET, Edinburgh, 1959); *Jesus the World's Perfecter* (ET, Edinburgh, 1959); *Spirit and Truth* (ET, London, 1935); *The Transformation of the Scientific World-View* (ET, London, 1953).

I. Haolmstrand, *Karl Heim on Philosophy, Science and the Transcendence of God* (Stockholm, 1980); C. Michalson, 'Karl Heim' in D. G. Peerman and M. E. Marty (eds.), *A Handbook of Christian Theologians* (Nashville, TN, ²1984).

J.B.W.

HELL, see ESCHATOLOGY.

HELLENIZATION OF CHRISTIANITY, the penetration into Christianity of beliefs and practices which originated in the pre-Christian or non-Christian culture of ancient Greece. Generally speaking, this is now regarded as a positive development by most Roman Catholic and Orthodox theologians, whereas most Protestants tend to think of it as a corruption of the faith.

The facts of Hellenization, beyond the superficial level, are almost impossible to document with any degree of certainty. The NT was written in Greek, but this followed the established practice and style of Hellenized Judaism and was not a Christian innovation. There is much debate as to whether the apostolic interpretation of the OT was seriously affected by Greek ideas or not. At one time it was widely believed that Jn. 1:1–14 reflected a Middle Platonic *logos** doctrine, possibly mediated through Philo of Alexandria,* but this has been strongly challenged by modern scholarship, which tends to emphasize John's Hebraic roots.

Matters are more complex when we turn to the post-apostolic period. Christianity spread in the Hellenized Roman Empire more than it did elsewhere, and this certainly left its mark. Justin Martyr thought that Socrates and Plato were Christians before Christ, and the belief that Platonism* was a kind of Gentile OT, preparing the Greeks for the coming of Christ, later became widespread. There were a number of syncretistic sects, now known collectively as 'Gnostic',* which tried to merge pagan and Christian ideas in different ways. Perhaps the most significant development along these lines was the widespread adoption of the allegorical method of interpretation (used earlier by Jewish writers such as Philo), to overcome difficulties which Greek minds felt in the literal text of Scripture. By using this method, Origen* and others were able to harmonize Christianity with late Middle (and later Neo-) Platonism, much to the detriment of the former.

How far Hellenizing tendencies were responsible for the development of Christian doctrine is a matter of considerable controversy. Conservatives generally argue that the creeds* and other doctrinal statements were a reaction against the influence of Hellenism, which after the 4th century became a term of abuse, even among the Greeks (who subsequently called themselves *Rōmaioi* rather than *Hellēnes*). Liberals, however, argue that dogma* is itself a philosophical concept. According to them, a non-Hellenized Christianity would have been much more pluralistic in its theology, and would probably not have insisted that Jesus Christ was God incarnate. Some of them even regard Islam as a Semitic reaction against Hellenized Christianity, though that is certainly an oversimplification of what was a very complex development.

Bibliography

J. Daniélou, *Gospel Message and Hellenistic Culture* (London and Philadelphia, 1973); E. Hatch, *The Influence of Greek Ideas on Christianity* (New York, 1888); M. Hengel, *Judaism and Hellenism*, 2 vols. (London, 1974); R. H. Nash, *Christianity and the Hellenistic World* (Grand Rapids, MI, n.d.).

G.L.B.

HELVETIC CONFESSIONS, see CONFESSIONS OF FAITH.

HENOTHEISM, see MONOTHEISM.

HENRY, CARL F. H. (b. 1913). Protestant theologian, widely recognized as an intellectual spokesman for evangelical Christianity. Converted in 1933 as a New York journalist, Henry studied at Wheaton College (MA), Northern Baptist Theological Seminary (BD, ThD) and Boston University (PhD). He taught theology at Northern Baptist (1940–47) and at Fuller Theological Seminary (1947–56), prior to becoming founding editor (1956–68) of the influential *Christianity Today* magazine. Always an understanding encourager and adviser of younger Christian writers, Henry from 1968 devoted himself to research and writing. He was chairman of the World Congress on Evangelism (Berlin, 1966), and has presided over the Evangelical Theological Society (1967–70) and the American Theological Society (1980–81).

Among his numerous books are *The Uneasy Conscience of Modern Fundamentalism* (1948), which spurred conservative Protestants in America out of cultural isolation into social engagement; and *Christian Personal Ethics* (1957), now a standard textbook. His *magnum opus* is *God, Revelation and Authority* (Waco, TX, 1976–82), the six volumes of which are also available in Korean and Mandarin. Henry was a founder of the Institute for Advanced Christian Studies which produces literature directed at secular university students. As lecturer-at-large for World Vision International from 1974, he gained a global ministry of teaching, lecturing and preaching.

Bibliography

Confessions of a Theologian (Waco, TX, 1986).

G. Fackre, 'Carl F. H. Henry', in D. G. Peerman and M. E. Marty (eds.), *A Handbook of Christian Theologians* (Nashville, TN, ²1984); Bob E. Patterson, *Carl F. H. Henry* (Waco, TX, 1984).

J.D.Do.

HERBERT OF CHERBURY (*c.* 1583–1648). Edward, first Baron of Cherbury, brother of the poet, George, made his reputation as a philosopher, historian, diplomat and adventurer. He has been styled 'the father of deism*' but his system differs significantly from much later deist thought and the extent of his influence upon it is debatable.

In his foundational work, *De Veritate (On the Truth)*, he sought to refute the sceptical denial of the possibility of knowledge, by adumbrating an original method of discovering the truth. His theory of universal 'Common Notions' provided the grounds for cognitive certainty and produced a scheme of rational religion when extended into that sphere. The five 'Common Religious Notions' are: 1. there is a supreme God; 2. he ought to be worshipped; 3. virtue and piety constitute the main elements of such worship; 4. sin must be expiated by repentance; 5. there are future rewards and punishments.* Herbert passionately advocated a form both of religious tolerance and of religious liberation for the laity. To the extent that he assimilated religious to general epistemology* and maintained that the practice of natural religion can lead to eternal blessedness, Herbert heralded an approach to religion that became broadly characteristic of much 17th- and 18th-century British and European thought.

Bibliography

M. H. Carré (tr. and ed.), *De Veritate* (Bristol, 1937).

R. D. Bedford, *The Defence of Truth: Herbert of Cherbury and the Seventeenth Century* (Manchester, 1979); R. H. Popkin, *The History of Scepticism from Erasmus to Spinoza* (Berkeley, CA, 1979).

S.N.W.

HERESY connotes doctrinal deviation from the fundamental truths taught by

Scripture and the orthodox Christian church, and active propagation of the same. The primary Gk. word *hairesis*, which appears nine times in the NT, fundamentally meant a school of thought or sect: so the sect of the Sadducees (Acts 5:17), the Pharisees (15:5; 26:5), the Nazarenes, *i.e.* the Christians (24:5; 28:22). In Acts 24:14, Paul substituted 'way' (*hodos*) for 'sect' (*hairesis*) when referring to the Christian movement, probably because *hairesis*, even then, possessed a negative connotation. *Hairesis*, secondly, developed the meaning of schism or faction that developed within the church due to a strong party spirit or lack of love (1 Cor. 11:19; Gal. 5:20). Paul's use of the adjective *hairetikos* in Tit. 3:10 suggests that a heretic is a person who is divisive or factious. The shade of meaning that came to predominate in Christian usage is that of false theological doctrine. Thus 2 Pet. 2:1 refers to the 'destructive heresies' of certain false teachers who denied the person and work of Christ.

The writings of the church fathers contain numerous warnings against heretical teaching. Ignatius (d. 98/117) compared heresy with the working of lethal drugs (*Trall.* 6:1–2) and the attacks of wild beasts and rabid dogs (*Eph.* 7:1). Irenaeus* wrote the treatise *Against Heresies* to refute the various Gnostic* errors in the 2nd-century world. He urged Christians 'to avoid every heretical, godless and impious doctrine' (*Against Heresies* III. 6.4). Clement of Alexandria* insisted that heresies spring from self-conceit, vanity and the deliberate mishandling of Scripture (*Strom.* VII.15). Tertullian* claimed that 'the philosophers are the fathers of the heretics' (*Against Hermogenes* 8). Cyprian* added: 'Satan invented heresies and schisms with which to overthrow the faith, to corrupt the truth and to divide unity' (*Unity of the Church* 3).

In a sense, the history of the church is the history of heresies. In the 2nd century, Gnosticism* and Marcionism* perverted the orthodox doctrine of God. Later, various forms of modalism (see Monarchianism*) and Arianism* corrupted the doctrine of Christ. Apollinarianism,* Nestorianism* and monophysitism* dealt inadequately with the two natures of Christ. At the time of the Reformation, Socinianism* denied the Trinity and the efficacy of Christ's atoning work, as did later Unitarianism.* In modern times neo-Protestantism has denied the personality of God, the substitutionary atonement of Christ, and the divine inspiration of the Scriptures.

The early church defended itself against heretical teaching by appealing to 'the rule of faith' or 'the rule of truth', which were brief summaries of essential Christian truths (see Creeds*). Irenaeus lamented that heretics follow neither Scripture nor the tradition that originates from the apostles and was preserved in the churches through the succession of elders (*Against Heresies* III.2). Tertullian added that 'to know nothing in opposition to the rule of faith is to know all things' (*Prescription of Heretics* 7). The fluid 'rule of faith' gave way to more precise instruments for refuting heresies and defining faith, namely, credal formulations such as the Apostles' Creed, the Nicene Creed, the Definition of Chalcedon and the Athanasian Creed (see Councils,* Creeds*). From the time of the Reformation, Protestant bodies have distinguished truth from heresy in numerous confessional* statements such as the Formula of Concord, the Thirty-nine Articles, and the Westminster Confession.

Walter Bauer (1877–1960), in his book *Orthodoxy and Heresy in Earliest Christianity* (1934), advanced the radical thesis that the Roman church rewrote the history of the early church, making its interpretation of primitive Christianity the 'orthodox' view and depicting other early Christian teachers as 'heretical' and immoral. According to Bauer, forms of Christianity that came to be understood as 'heretical' were prior to and more widespread than the so-called 'orthodox' teaching. Thus, many Christian movements in the early church commonly viewed as heterodox are said to constitute authentic primitive expressions of the religion of Jesus.

Canon H. E. W. Turner rejected Bauer's thesis in his book, *The Pattern of Christian Truth* (1954). While allowing for certain flexibility in early Christian teaching, Turner argues that primitive Christianity universally held to three kinds of 'fixed elements': 1. crucial 'religious facts', such as the creator God and the divine Christ as the historical redeemer; 2. the centrality of biblical revelation; and 3. the creed and the rule of faith. 'Christians lived Trinitarianly before the evolution of Nicene orthodoxy' (p. 28).

Most evangelical authorities agree that the data of early church history and theology show that orthodoxy was earlier and more widespread than Bauer allowed. Indeed, the teachings of Jesus and the apostles were summed up at an early date in the 'rule of faith' and the writings of the apostolic fathers. The orthodox faith was attacked by heretical opponents (Gnostic sects, Marcion, Arius, *etc.*), but the latter were opposed by the apostles and early church fathers in both the East and West. Evangelical authorities likewise agree that Bauer's account of the triumph of Roman 'orthodoxy' falls short of credibility.

Given the modern bias against timeless, propositional truths and the belief that faith is a matter of lived experience, the notion of heresy has been substantially diluted in non-Evangelical Christianity. For example, Karl Rahner,* working from the ethical view of truth as a lived reality, views heresy as the failure to attain authentic existence at the point where God meets a person. Rather than the repudiation of particular doctrines, heresy embraces subjective attitudes, such as spiritual indifference and a critical spirit. Primary responsibility for this 'latent heresy' lies with the individual Christian rather than the magisterium. Yet the NT expresses serious concern for 'false doctrines' (1 Tim. 1:3; 6:3) and places the highest priority on maintaining 'the pattern of sound teaching' (2 Tim. 1:13; *cf.* 1 Tim. 6:3). Scripture urges Christians to be alert to doctrinal deception (Mt. 24:4) and to avoid heresy by carefully guarding the pure content of the gospel (1 Cor. 11:2; Gal. 1:8).

Bibliography

W. Bauer, *Orthodoxy and Heresy in Earliest Christianity* (Philadelphia, 1971; London, 1972); J. D. G. Dunn, *Unity and Diversity in the New Testament: An Inquiry into the Character of Earliest Christianity* (Philadelphia, 1977); G. L. Prestige, *Fathers and Heretics* (London, 1977); K. Rahner, *On Heresy* (New York, 1964); H. E. W. Turner, *The Pattern of Christian Truth: A Study in the Relations Between Orthodoxy and Heresy in the Early Church* (London, 1954).

B.D.

HERMENEUTICS, term derived from the Gk. verb 'interpret' (*hermēneuō*).

Definition and scope

Hermeneutics may be defined briefly as the theory of interpretation. Traditionally and until very recently it has been taken to mean the study of rules or principles for the interpretation of particular texts. But this definition is too narrow. First, hermeneutics concerns not only the interpretation of texts, but the interpretation and understanding of any act of communication, whether written or oral, verbal or non-verbal (such as symbols or symbolic acts). Biblical hermeneutics is a specific area which concerns the interpretation, understanding, and appropriation of biblical texts. Second, theorists are no longer content to speak of rules for the interpretation of texts, as if to imply that understanding can be generated merely by the mechanical application of purely scientific principles. Hermeneutics raises prior and more fundamental questions about the very nature of language, meaning, communication and understanding.

The subject thus involves an examination of the whole interpretative process. This raises issues in the philosophy of language, theories of meaning, literary theory, and semiotics (theory of signs), as well as, in biblical hermeneutics, those which also arise in biblical studies and in Christian theology. The subject is no longer seen as a supplementary tool for ensuring 'correct' interpretation, but as a profound reflection on the very basis and purpose of interpretation and of how we decide what would count in the first place as a 'correct' interpretation. Indeed, whether we should speak of an interpretation as 'correct', 'productive', 'valid' or 'responsible' remains still a hermeneutical question. The first step is to enquire into the conditions under which any kind of interpretation is possible or appropriate to certain given purposes of reading, writing or understanding.

Main issues in the history of traditional biblical hermeneutics

The period of the Bible itself. The term 'hermeneutics' appeared probably for the first time as the description for a subject-area in J. C. Dannhauer's *Hermeneutica Sacra* (Strasburg, 1654). But reflection about interpretation and interpretative processes began long before this in the ancient world. Interpretation begins within the Bible itself, whenever earlier traditions or writings are reviewed from the standpoint of later ones. Jesus interprets his death in accordance with the OT Scriptures, and interprets the OT in accordance with his own work (Lk. 24:25–27; Gk. *diermēneusen*, 'interpreted'). He interprets Is. 61:1–2 in terms of his present ministry (Lk. 4:21). Some scholars see a parallel between this kind of 'fulfilment' in the NT and the so-called *pēsher* interpretations in the Dead Sea Scrolls,* which interpret certain OT passages in terms of the present or imminent experience of the Qumran community. Present applications of earlier texts is a persistent concern in hermeneutics. The term *midrash* more broadly denotes 'interpretation' in rabbinic Judaism. Rabbi Hillel is credited with the formulation of seven 'rules' (*middōth*) of interpretation, although their value is strictly limited. For the most part they concern the drawing of logical inferences and comparisons.

Allegorical interpretation and typology. The theory and practice of allegorical interpretation goes back to pre-Christian times. Many Stoic* philosophers respected Homer as a classic text, but were embarrassed by the crudities and absurdities of stories about the gods and goddesses of ancient polytheistic Greek religion. Some interpreters in the Stoic and Platonic* tradition reduced this tension by reinterpreting the personages and activities of these gods and goddesses as human qualities or elements of nature. Stories about Apollo, Hera and Poseidon could thus be read as accounts of interactions between sun, air and water. Plato spoke of a 'meaning below' (*hyponoia*) the surface of the text, and many 1st-century writers describe this as *allegoria*. From Greek thought, this method of reading a text found its way into Jewish circles. Philo* wrote as a Jew seeking to commend Jewish faith to educated Greeks and Romans. He used allegorical interpretation as a device for re-reading passages in the early chapters of Genesis which he found embarrassingly anthropomorphic,* or passages in Leviticus which described the minutiae of animal sacrifice. Thus the method was established in Jewish and Greek circles before its growth within the Christian church.

Allegorical interpretation has had an ambivalent status in Christian tradition. Origen* argued that Paul himself provides precedent for allegorical interpretation in his identification of the wilderness rock with Christ in 1 Cor. 10:1–4. There has always been controversy about whether this passage and Gal. 4:22–26 constitute genuine examples of allegorical interpretation. Much depends on definition and questions about Paul's purpose. Many draw a firm distinction between allegory, which depends on a correspondence between *ideas*, and typology, which depends on a correspondence between *events*. Some argue that Paul uses typology but not allegory. However, while it is true that events are given whereas ideas are entertained, criteria for the typological interpretation of such events remain problematic.

Clement of Rome (*c*. AD 96) provides a very early example of Christian allegorical interpretation. Commenting on Jos. 2:18, he observes that the Israelite spies gave Rahab a sign 'that she should hang out a scarlet thread from her house, foreshowing that all who achieve and hope in God shall have deliverance through the blood of the Lord' (*1 Clem.* 12:7). Clement of Alexandria,* a century later, argued that the interpreter should expect to find hidden meanings in the biblical writings, because the mystery of the gospel transcended the meaning of any particular passage. Origen argued that the interpreter should begin with the plain or grammatical meaning, but should then 'rise from the letter to the spirit'. He saw the outward events or outward grammar of a text as like the human body: what gave it *soul* was *moral* application, and what gave it *spirit* was the frame of reference informed by *spiritual* perception. In spite of his attempt to acknowledge, at least in theory, the importance of the letter, or of the grammatico-historical meaning of a text, his own use of allegorical interpretation moved too far in the direction of those Gnostic* opponents who also ransacked the Bible for esoteric or 'secret' meanings. By way of response and reaction, the fathers of Antioch,* especially Theodore of Mopsuestia (350–428) and John Chrysostom (344/354–407), opposed the allegorical excesses of Alexandria,* and insisted on the priority of linguistic considerations.

Multiple meaning and the perspicuity of Scripture. In the medieval period Origen's threefold sense was developed into four. The basic meaning of a passage (the so-called 'literal' or letter-sense) was expanded by considering its place in the context of salvation (the allegorical or typological sense). An interpreter might then draw out its significance for practical conduct (the moral sense), and finally consider its relation to the culmination of God's purposes in eternity (the anagogical sense). From the standpoint of religion, this might yield edifying results. But often the primary meaning of a text became buried and lost under layers of pious tradition. The Reformers were concerned to show that the Bible could stand on its own feet, and could actually speak as judge of the validity of church traditions. Neither Luther* nor Calvin* belittled the importance of history and tradition. But Luther insisted that the primary or grammatical meaning of the Bible was clear (*claritas Scripturae*) rather than obscure, while Calvin urged that the meaning of a passage was one (*simplex*) rather than many. In no way did they intend to imply that hermeneutics was unnecessary. Quite the reverse was the case. As against Erasmus,* Luther argued that biblical knowledge was sufficiently accessible to yield productive results when all the appropriate tools of language and literature were applied. Calvin's 'one' meaning was that which could be recovered by historical, linguistic and contextual enquiry. Neither term must be taken out of the context of the Reformation debate in such a way as to devalue the need for hermeneutics.

The status of the OT. Following the example of Jesus and the earliest Christian communities, Christian tradition has always affirmed the authoritative status of the OT. In the 2nd century, Marcion* attempted to devalue the OT on the basis of a Pauline contrast between gospel and law. But Christians repudiated his work. The main resultant hermeneutical problem has been simultaneously to respect the integrity of the OT writings in their own right, and also to acknowledge their relationship of fulfilment to the NT, and their decisive witness to Christ (see Biblical Theology*).

The role of historical criticism. In the 17th century Baruch Spinoza* argued the importance of asking questions about the authorship, date, occasion and purpose of particular biblical writings. A hundred years later J. S. Semler (1725–88) went further, and argued that purely historical questions should be asked without reference to doctrine or theology. But historical-critical enquiry need not, and indeed should not, exclude theological considerations. Hermeneutical theory calls for broader, not narrower, horizons of interpretation, and a positivist or reductionist perspective conflicts with the interpretative openness which hermeneutics invites. However, by the very same token this openness also includes a recognition of the importance of historical method and the concrete contributions of rigorously critical historical enquiry (see Biblical Criticism*).

Modern and recent perspectives and approaches

Romanticist hermeneutics. With the work of Friedrich Schleiermacher* a new era in hermeneutics began. In the Romanticist* tradition, the goal of the interpreter is to reach 'behind' the text to the mind of its author, and ultimately to the creative experience which called the text into being. The text is seen as an objectification, or objective residue, of this creative human experience. Following G. A. F. Ast (1778–1841) and F. A. Wolf (1759–1824), Schleiermacher saw the circular nature of hermeneutical enquiry. The interpreter has to undertake a creative leap into a provisional understanding of what the text is about, *i.e.* to grasp its meaning as a whole. But this depends on an understanding of its parts, *i.e.* of its component words and phrases. However, what the words and phrases mean depends equally on their context within the meaning of the text as a whole. Hence there remains a circular interplay between grasping the parts and grasping the whole. This is one aspect of the hermeneutical circle. Similarly, interpretation entails both linguistic and psychological processes. At the linguistic level, the scientific considerations of grammar and vocabulary have a part to play. But at a deeper level, the interpreter must seek to enter into psychological rapport with the author. An essential hermeneutical bridge is that of 'lived experience' (*Erlebnis*).

Wilhelm Dilthey* developed Schleiermacher's approach with particular reference to the problem of historical understanding. The aim of the interpreter is 'to re-discover the "you" in "me"'. In other words, the life-experience of the interpreter provides a point of contact, or of 'pre-understanding', with which to approach a text. Dilthey admitted that this method stands in contrast with that of the physical or natural sciences. But historical understanding and the interpretation of texts born out of human history cannot be equated with any purely scientific enterprise. What counts as objectivity is not the same in each case. Natural science turns on 'knowledge'; interpreting the utterances of persons turns on 'understanding' (*Verstehen*). Understanding is never entirely value-free, for both author and interpreter are historical persons whose horizons are shaped by their place in history.

The best-known and most important representative of the Romanticist hermeneutical tradition in our century is Emilio Betti (1890–1968). Betti sees hermeneutics as vital to the well-being of society. The recognition that all interpretation is open to correction and revision should, he argues, promote greater tolerance between persons. Like Schleiermacher, he sees interpretation as essentially a tracing back of the process of composition, in which we move back from the text to the experience which produced it.

Existential* and phenomenological hermeneutics. The impossibility of beginning enquiry other than from within *given* horizons was the starting-point for Martin Heidegger's (1889–1976) earlier thought. A particular person, Heidegger urged, will interpret what he or she sees in terms of the purposes and practical standpoints around which his or her life is already organized. Pre-understanding becomes, therefore, a major hermeneutical issue. In theology, Rudolf Bultmann* shared some, but not all, of Heidegger's perspectives. Bultmann believed that the biblical writings only apparently or secondarily presented generalizing and descriptive statements about God and man. Their primary purpose, he urged, was the existential or practical function of calling persons to appropriate attitudes and responses of will. For example, the utterance, 'God will judge the world' is to be interpreted less as a statement about a future event than as a call to responsibility before God in the present moment. The affirmation 'Jesus is Lord' represents not so much a statement about Christ's cosmic status as a confession that Christ directs and controls my own life (see Myth*).

Ontological hermeneutics. A closely related but different tradition in hermeneutical theory refuses to reduce questions of meaning and truth to individual experience in the way suggested in existentialist hermeneutics. Heidegger, in his later writings, and more especially his pupil Hans-Georg Gadamer (b. 1900), seek to relate language and meaning to the disclosure of truth in a way which transcends and calls attention to the reality of the 'world' projected and mediated by a work of art. In theology Ernst Fuchs (1903–83) pays attention to the narrative 'world' of the parable. The reader enters such a world and is grasped *by* it. The hermeneutical focus is not now upon the interpreter actively scrutinizing the text as object, but on the text actively addressing and scrutinizing the interpreter. The text must translate us, before we can translate the text. Hermeneutics, for Gadamer and Fuchs, is not a matter of simply using the right method. Their approach is sometimes known as the 'new' hermeneutic.

Socio-critical hermeneutics. Among the social sciences, hermeneutical explorations also began with Dilthey, and called attention especially to the role of 'interest' in interpreting texts. Interests shape what seems to count as a 'natural' interpretation within the framework of a tradition of social assumptions and practices. The interpretations of biblical texts about slavery, women or the poor, provide examples in recent liberation theologies* and feminist hermeneutics (see Feminist Theology*). Neo-Marxist social theory and the work of J. Habermas (b. 1929) are often pressed into the service of this approach. Many Latin American liberation theologians call for a second reading of the Bible which is undertaken within the context of present social struggles, or present praxis. Juan Luis Segundo (b. 1925), for example, speaks of the need not so much to demythologize but to 'de-ideologize' in interpretation. The hermeneutics of traditional Western scholarship are largely rejected as intellectualist and incapable of sufficient ideological suspicion.

Biblical hermeneutics and the problem of unity and diversity. The recent revival of interest in biblical hermeneutics has received added impetus from two major trends in biblical studies, namely redaction criticism and canon criticism (see Biblical Criticism*). 1. Whereas the so-called biblical theology* or salvation-history* movements of the 1940s had emphasized the unity of the biblical writings, increasing attention has been paid since the mid–1950s to distinctive theological emphases and concerns represented by individual authors or editors within the Bible. Redaction criticism, in other words, called attention to a range of emphases within the biblical writings. 2. At the same time, these different emphases belong together to a single canon of Scripture. Their coexistence and interaction shape their canonical meaning. Concern for this level of meaning, currently known as canon criticism, is associated especially with the name of Brevard Childs (b. 1923). Contemporary biblical hermeneutics thus wrestles with two sides of a single problem. Paul and James, for example, must be interpreted each on his own terms. Each speaks to a particular pastoral and historical situation on faith and works. But their distinctive emphases within the canon must not be reduced or flattened out in the interests of superficial harmonization; nor should one be eclipsed by treating the other as the key to the whole gospel message. How the interpreter can best avoid these pitfalls and yet do full justice both to biblical unity and diversity remains a major focus of contemporary biblical hermeneutics.

Other hermeneutical approaches. It is impossible to list in a short article the full range of hermeneutical approaches at present under exploration. In his earlier works Paul Ricoeur (b. 1913) explores the role of suspicion in interpretation, not on the basis of Marx,* but taking as his point of departure Freud's work on our capacity for self-deception in the interpretation of dreams, symbols and language (see Depth Psychology;* Psychology of Religion*). In his later work Ricoeur examines metaphor and theories of signs (semiotics). Increasing attention is being paid in literary and biblical hermeneutics to the active role of the reader in creating meaning (reader-response hermeneutics). Alongside the more usual notion of hermeneutics as the process of understanding (related to the theory of knowledge), other models are brought into play, such as that of textual action or the reading process. All this is not merely the result of academic fashion. It represents a widespread recognition over several different disciplines of the fundamental and far-reaching nature of hermeneutical questions. Biblical interpretation can never outgrow the work of the biblical specialist. But neither can biblical hermeneutics ever again be isolated from these broader yet fundamental interdisciplinary questions.

Bibliography

J. Bleicher, *Contemporary Hermeneutics* (London, 1980); D. A. Carson (ed.), *Biblical Interpretation and the Church* (Exeter, 1984); D. A. Carson and J. D. Woodbridge (eds.), *Hermeneutics, Authority and Canon* (Grand Rapids, MI, and Leicester, 1986); R. W. Funk, *Language, Hermeneutics and Word of God* (New York, 1966); H.-G. Gadamer, *Truth and Method* (ET, London, 1975); R. M. Grant and D. Tracy, *A Short History of the Interpretation of the Bible* (Philadelphia, 1984); I. H. Marshall (ed.), *New Testament Interpretation* (Exeter, 1977); E. V. McKnight, *Meaning in Texts* (Philadelphia, 1978); R. Palmer, *Hermeneutics* (Evanston, IL, 1969); P. Ricoeur, *Interpretation Theory* (Fort Worth, TX, 1976); idem, *Hermeneutics and the Human Sciences* (London, 1981); J. D. Smart, *The Interpretation of Scripture* (London, 1961); P. Stuhlmacher, *Historical Criticism and Theological Interpretation of Scripture* (Philadelphia, 1977); A. C. Thiselton, *The Two Horizons* (Exeter, 1980); C. Walhout, A. C. Thiselton, and R. Lundin, *The Responsibility of Hermeneutics* (Exeter, 1985).

A.C.T.

HERRMANN, WILHELM (1846–1922) grew up under pietist* influences, but during his theological studies embraced the up-and-coming theology of Albrecht Ritschl* and became his foremost disciple. After a period as a lecturer at Halle, he was appointed professor of theology at Marburg in 1879, where he remained to the end of his life. His most famous work is *The Communion of the Christian with God* (1886; ET, 1971), which deals with the doctrine of God and the Christian's relationship with him.

'God' for Herrmann is not the traditional three-in-one of orthodox Christianity, but rather 'the personal vitality and power of goodness'. Jesus is not the Son of God in the sense traditionally understood by the church, but rather a man in whose exemplary character the power of God, *i.e.* the power of the highest good, was revealed. For Herrmann there are no supernatural miracles. Jesus demonstrated that the highest good is a life of love. It is the beauty of Jesus' life that reveals God.

In contrast to the scepticism of the 'Did Jesus live?' movement, Herrmann maintained that the evangelists' portrayal of Jesus is completely independent of historical reality;

even if Jesus had never existed, the portrait of him would still remain permanently valid for its purpose. He therefore discounted the results of the higher-critical investigation of the Bible as in no way requiring amendment of the picture of Jesus contained in the gospels. In Herrmann's opinion, the portrait would stand for all time as a model of how we should live, even if it were completely devoid of historicity. Christianity did not need a historical apologetic.

Bibliography

R. T. Voekel, *The Shape of the Theological Task* (Philadelphia, 1968).

H.H.

HESYCHASM (*i.e.* quietism, from Gk. *hesychia* = quietness), though generally regarded as a theological movement in 14th-century Byzantium stemming from a particular type of Christian spirituality, finds its beginnings in the early development of anchoritic asceticism.* In the beginning it was a matter of practice, but from the 4th century onwards, with the rise of great figures like Basil the Great,* Evagrius Ponticus (346–99), Macarius,* Pseudo-Dionysius the Areopagite,* Maximus the Confessor,* John Climacus (*c.* 570–649) and Symeon the New Theologian (see Eastern Orthodox Theology*), ascetic hesychasm was given a theoretical or theological basis. The 4th-century hesychast was one who attempted to be totally freed from visible realities, through mastery over passions and acquisition of virtues, illumination of the mind by contemplation and prayer of the mind (or heart), so that he might arrive at quietness in God or vision* of God.

From the 6th century onwards 'monologic' prayer, consisting in the rhythmic repetition of one sentence, phrase or word, usually the name of the Lord Jesus Christ, became the means of attaining divine *hesychia*. In the 7th century St Catherine's Monastery at Sinai became the centre of a type of hesychasm epitomized in *The Ladder* of John Climacus (tr. C. Luibhèid, London, 1982). In the second half of the 10th century Symeon the New Theologian gave hesychasm a new impulse by linking it with a purely Christocentric vision of the 'divine light' (*cf. Symeon the New Theologian: The Discourses*, tr. C. J. de Catanzaro, London, 1980, and G. A. Maloney, *The Mystic of Fire and Light: St*

Symeon the New Theologian, Denville, NJ, 1975). Growing out of this, a psychological technique of prayer was developed. The central element was the ceaseless repetition in solitude of 'Lord Jesus Christ, have mercy on me a sinner', to which the posture of the body and the manner of breathing could be added as secondary elements. The end of it all was the vision of the 'uncreated light' of God.

In the 14th century both the vision of the 'divine light' and especially the method used for its attainment became the subjects of bitter controversy. Opposition to hesychasm was led by Barlaam of Calabria (*c.* 1290–1350) and George Akindynos (*c.* 1300–49). The 'uncreated' light of the hesychasts was held to imply ditheism. Gregory of Palamas (1296–1359) was the greatest apologist of hesychasm, putting forward the distinction between God's essence (*ousia*) and energies, linking the latter with the uncreated divine light and arguing that God, who is invisible, unapproachable and incommunicable in his essence, becomes visible, approachable and communicable in his energies.

After intense conflict, a decisive synod of 1351 endorsed Gregory's distinction, and also the principles, 1. that the energies are uncreated, 2. that God is not composite, 3. that the word 'divine' can be attributed not only to the essence, but also to the energies of God, and 4. that men do not participate in the essence, but in the energies and grace of God. Henceforth Barlaam and Akindynos would be regarded as heretics, and Palamas as the mouthpiece of orthodoxy. Yet disputes over hesychasm continued, especially as a result of Lat. influence from the West. Hesychasm lives on in the Orthodox East, especially on Mt Athos.

Bibliography

Gregory Palamas: The Triads, tr. N. Gendle (London, 1983).

L. Clucas, *The Hesychast Controversy in Byzantium in the Fourteenth Century*, unpublished dissertation, UCLA, 2 vols. (Los Angeles, CA, 1975); J. Meyendorff, *Byzantine Hesychasm* (London, 1974); *idem, St Gregory Palamas and Orthodox Spirituality* (New York, 1974); *idem, A Study of Gregory Palamas* (London, 1962); G. C. Papademetriou, *Introduction to St Gregory Palamas* (New York, 1973).

G.D.D.

HICK, JOHN HARWOOD (b. 1922), philosopher of religion and radical theologian. He was educated in Edinburgh, Oxford and Cambridge, and was formerly a minister of the United Reformed Church in Britain and H. G. Wood Professor of Theology in Birmingham, but now teaches in Claremont, California.

Hick's earlier works were concerned with central traditional issues in the philosophy of religion* (cf. *Philosophy of Religion*, Englewood Cliffs, NJ, ³1983; *Faith and Knowledge: A Modern Introduction to the Problem of Religious Knowledge*, New York, 1957; and essays on the existence of God, *etc.*). His most significant book in this field is *Evil and the God of Love* (London, ³1985), which prefers a so-called Irenaean* to an Augustinian* approach to the problem of evil,* and also appeals to an eschatological resolution that will be unveiled only at the end.

Hick's attention then turned to questions about the uniqueness* of Jesus as the incarnate Son of God in the context of the other world-religions (cf. *God and the Universe of Faiths*, London, 1973). He argues for the reduction of the 'high' Christology of the Nicene Creed and the Chalcedonian Definition of the Faith (cf. Hick, ed., *The Myth of God Incarnate*, London, 1977). It can be established that there has been a historical development in Hick's Christology* from an earlier orthodoxy to the later rejection of it. This is due to his assumptions that: no special revelation of God is possible; unconditional universal* salvation is certain (cf. *Death and Eternal Life*, London, ²1985); and all world-religions are equal in their theological aspirations and claims. Hick has argued that the traditional arguments for the uniqueness of Jesus Christ are invalid, regressive, and even harmful to the harmonious co-existence of people of different faiths which is the need of the hour. He therefore pleads for a return from a Christocentric to a theocentric theology, with all the great religious systems alike providing access to the 'ultimate reality' of God.

See also: CHRISTIANITY AND OTHER RELIGIONS.

Bibliography
C.-R. Brakenheim, *How Philosophy Shapes Theories of Religion . . .* (Lund, 1975) – with special reference to Hick; N. Jason, *A Critical Examination of the Christology of John Hick, with Special Reference to the Continuing Significance of the 'Definitio Fidei' of the Council of Chalcedon, AD 451* (unpublished dissertation, University of Sheffield, 1978); T. R. Mathis, *Against John Hick: An Examination of His Philosophy and Religion* (Lanham, MD, 1985).

N.J.

HIDDEN AND REVEALED GOD. A concept particularly associated with the theology of Martin Luther* and Karl Barth.*

Meaning of terms

To speak of God as revealing himself is to imply that God is a hidden God: the *Deus revelatus* still remains a *Deus velatus*. Moses, Jacob, Job, the psalmists and prophets are all aware of the 'hiddenness' of God, even in his act of revealing himself. Clement,* Origen,* Chrysostom (*c.* 344/354–407), Augustine,* doctors, mystics, schoolmen were all conscious of the unknowability of God, and Luther intensely so. Modern, secularized humanity may have lost its earlier awareness of the mystery of God, that divine holiness which transcends all human experiences, aesthetic, intellectual and moral. Nevertheless, the mystery of God remains, as well as the question, 'How do I know him?'

In the Bible revelation* is disclosure of truth about God by the agency of God, as distinct from man's discovery of truth as he investigates his secular experience. In the NT it is expressed as God's disclosure in his Messiah in judgment and salvation, an event already effected in the advent of Jesus, though still to come on the last day.

The OT left unresolved the problem of how the God of Israel can be 'squared with' the history of Israel. The NT sharpened this poignantly in the disclosure of the work of God who, in showing his righteousness and mercy, yet suffered on the cross. The revelation of God cannot simply be read off from history or human experience. The crucial question still remains: How can the hidden God be revealed to me? How shall I find a gracious God?

The hidden God revealed in Christ

No theologian has tackled the problem of God as hidden and revealed more penetratingly than Luther. Luther argued that knowledge of God was twofold: 1. *General*, that there is a God, that he created heaven and earth, that he is righteous, and that he punishes the wicked. This knowledge was open to all mankind; 2. *Particular* or 'proper', that God loves us and seeks our salvation. This was revealed only in Christ.

Luther did not share the scholastic* view of Thomas Aquinas,* or even of Duns Scotus* and William of Ockham,* that the general knowledge of God attained by inference, and that reason was the foundation on which the proper knowledge of God revealed in Christ could be erected. He argued biblically that no man can see God and live. We cannot say what God is like in himself, but only what he does for us. In any dealings with man God has to wear a 'mask' (*larva*), and these 'masks' describe the way God meets man in his concrete existence, *i.e.* through the ordinances he established, and through the human beings he had created doing God's work in their appointed roles.

This had an exact parallel in the incarnation. Just as we do not infer God's existence, nature and attributes from his masks or veils but recognize that God comes to meet us in them, so is it none other than God who comes to us and meets us in Christ. God gives no gifts less than himself. This was the supreme revelation wherein the hidden God is revealed: 'He who has seen me has seen the Father' (Jn. 14:9); 'No man comes to the Father but by me' (Jn. 14:6). We see by, and in, faith alone. Similarly, the faculty of reason, though of divine origin, cannot of itself find God or the road to salvation.

In a striking passage in the Heidelberg Disputation (1518), referring to God's 'face' and God's 'back' (Ex. 33:23), Luther argued against the 'theology of glory' of the schoolmen in favour of the 'theology of the cross'.* God's 'back' means his humanity, his weakness, his foolishness (1 Cor. 1:21, 25; *cf.* Is. 45:15), *i.e.* the incarnation. God is always revealed 'under a contrary form'; weakness is strength, foolishness is wisdom, death is life. In this simple truth of the gospel lies the divine secret, the disclosure supreme. We must stoop to learn about God from God as revealed in Christ, and not from our own understanding.

Deliverance by faith

The problems of election and predestination,*

of suffering* and the wrath* of God remain, but they are delivered by faith out of our minds into the hands of God where they belong: they now appear as solutions, not problems. Luther never speculated on these problems, for he never faltered in faith: it is faith alone and only faith which fortifies and safeguards a soul from doubt, speculation, despair. In those memorable words, *Wer glaubt, der hat* (if you believe, you already possess), he argued that sufficient truth for man had been revealed in Christ, and only the believing heart which had grasped (or rather had been grasped by) the theology of the cross could see this. Even then, God is more deeply hidden in Christ crucified than he is in creation or in history. Power in weakness, glory in suffering, life in death, all show how hidden he is. This paradox of the cross and of God working in 'contrary form', reveal him as hidden, and leave him open to faith only. Election and predestination Luther experienced as God's love, without whose prior move he would have known nothing and been lost. Even in the wrath of God is hidden God's love, for wrath is but the annihilating reaction of the love of God to man's sin and disobedience: it disguises God's care and concern to redeem man. Similarly, in weakness, fear and suffering: all we need to know is that grace is sufficient, strength is made perfect in weakness.

When Barth (as Luther before him) argued that we can know God only in Christ, he meant that it is only in a faith-experience of Christ that a person becomes open to revelation: the problems of wrath, predestination, suffering, the painful hiddenness of God, are all transmuted into an experience of the love, the care and the mercy of God. All experiences of life, evil and good, now become the raw material of the good life in which the believer experiences God's loving care in all things. In this experience of Christ, the hidden God becomes the revealed God.

Bibliography

J. Atkinson, *Luther's Early Theological Works*, LCC 16 (London, 1962); J. Dillenberger, *God Hidden and Revealed* (Philadelphia, 1953); B. A. Gerrish, 'To the Unknown God: Luther and Calvin on the Hiddenness of God', *JR* 53, 1973, pp. 263–292.

J.A.

HIGHER-LIFE THEOLOGY. A pattern of Christian holiness teaching popularized by the American Presbyterian minister, William Edward Boardman (1810–86), in his *Higher Christian Life* (1859). Boardman's book, which sold over 100,000 copies on both sides of the Atlantic, asserted that the experience of sanctification* is a distinct work of grace, clearly separable from justification,* if not in theory, then certainly in practice (see Holiness Movement*). He insisted that it is not to be confused with Wesleyan perfectionism* (Boardman's *bête noire*), and that it has been enjoyed throughout the centuries by outstanding Christians such as Luther,* Baxter,* Jonathan Edwards* and (surprisingly, in view of his aversion to Wesley's* teaching), some early Methodist people such as Hester Ann Rogers (1756–94) and William Carvosso (1750–1835). The book's immediate popularity released Boardman for an itinerant convention ministry during which he met, and was later joined by, Robert Pearsall Smith (1827–98) and Hanna Whitall Smith (1832–1911), a couple who were to give his teaching wider popularity throughout Britain.

Emphasizing sanctification as a crisis experienced by faith, Boardman accepted neither the Wesleyan nor Reformed* doctrine of holiness, believing that Wesley claimed too much whilst the Puritans* and Reformers did not expect enough. Robert Pearsall Smith endeavoured further to meet the demand for popular holiness literature by writing *Holiness Through Faith* (1870). His wife, Hanna, added to the partnership some further concepts from her Quaker* background (particularly stillness and guidance), and this unusual fusion of Wesleyanism and Quakerism, expounded in her book, *The Christian's Secret of a Happy Life* (1875), was to become one of the most remarkable features of late 19th-century holiness teaching, combining the idea of a dramatic crisis with the 'rest of faith' ('Let go and let God').

The Boardman and Pearsall Smith message came to be presented in England at holiness conventions held at Broadlands (1874), Oxford (1874), Brighton (1875) and Keswick (1875). In its infancy the movement was in danger of concentrating on subjective experiences rather than objective teaching; some of its earlier addresses were more in the nature of extemporaneous talks and testimonies than

carefully prepared expositions of Scripture. Over successive decades the teaching of the annual interdenominational Keswick Convention, held each July, gradually changed. Throughout its history the Convention Council has refrained from formulating a closely defined theology of sanctification, leaving its speakers free to expound and apply the various facets of scriptural teaching concerning personal and practical holiness. While recognizing that for some Christians the appropriation of their unique resources in Christ may find its focus in a particular moment of crisis, the Convention has given greater prominence to central biblical themes such as promised deliverance from known sin, continual cleansing by and identification with Christ, the practical implications of his Lordship and the perpetual filling of the Holy Spirit* (see Baptism in the Spirit*), equipping Christians for service in the world. A strong missionary and evangelistic concern has been present from its earliest days and is integral to the Convention's main message.

Bibliography

S. Barabas, *So Great Salvation: The History and Message of the Keswick Convention* (London, 1952); J. B. Figgis, *Keswick From Within* (London, 1914); C. F. Harford (ed.), *The Keswick Convention* (London, 1907); W. B. Sloan, *These Sixty Years: The Story of the Keswick Convention* (London, 1935); J. C. Pollock, *The Keswick Story* (London, 1964); H. F. Stevenson (ed.), *Keswick's Authentic Voice* (London, 1959); *idem* (ed.), *Keswick's Triumphant Voice* (London, 1963); B. B. Warfield, *Perfectionism*, 2 vols. (New York, 1931); *The Keswick Week* (London, 1892 onwards).

R.B.

HILARY OF POITIERS (*c.* 315–67). Hilary was born of a pagan, noble family. Like Augustine* after him, he found pagan philosophy a useful preliminary to the Christian gospel. Shortly after his conversion he was made Bishop of Poitiers. Subsequent resistance to Arianizing* trends within the Gallic church led to a term of banishment in Asia Minor.

During his exile Hilary gained firsthand experience of Eastern theology, and was particularly influenced by the Origenism* of men like Basil of Ancyra (*fl.* 340–60). His work *On the Synods* dates from this period. It was an attempt to reconcile fellow Westerners to the different theological approach of the anti-Arians in the East.

His exile was also the occasion for his *On the Trinity*, the outstanding Latin theological treatise of the Arian controversy. Hilary added little to the orthodox view on the relationship of the Father and the Son or on the role of the Holy Spirit; but he did make an original contribution in Christology,* for he saw the most effective counter to Arian insistence on the human weakness of Christ in the postulation of three distinct stages in Christ's existence.

In the first stage, Christ was pre-existent as the Son of God, united with his Father in a mutual indwelling. At the incarnation (the second stage) he was born as a man without in any way ceasing to be God. Nevertheless, since Christ appeared in the form of a servant for man's benefit, effectively a breach was created within the Godhead. The human nature which Christ assumed was separated by an infinite distance from God the Father, though it was indissolubly linked to the divinity of God the Son. It was the latter's task to raise the human nature to the level of the divine – a task accomplished at his resurrection and ascension. In the third stage Christ was restored to that glory which he shared with his Father before the incarnation. Believers, therefore, might hope that they too would share in the glory to which Christ had elevated human nature.

The key to Hilary's soteriology is the deification* of humanity, which God had purposed from the beginning. Its achievement had merely been complicated, not first inspired, by sin. Hilary has a clear concept of the two natures in the incarnate Christ, as well as of the unity of his person. His treatment, however, of the events of Christ's life falls into docetism.* He argued that Christ possessed a unique sort of body – a heavenly body, because its owner, who had come down from heaven and was on earth, was still in heaven. This body might fulfil all the functions of a human body and go through suffering, but it did so only by special condescension, and even then it did not really feel pain. According to its own nature, the body was free of human needs, and evinced the sort of power shown in the miracles and in the transfiguration. In effect, he had reached the polar opposite

position from the Arians on the incarnate Christ. For him the miraculous displays of power were the rule, not the exception, for Christ's human body.

Bibliography

Select works in ET in *NPNF;* P. Galtier, *Saint Hilaire de Poitiers* (Paris, 1960); G. M. Newlands, *Hilary of Poitiers: a Study in Theological Method* (Berne, 1978).

G.A.K.

HINDUISM AND CHRISTIANITY.

Frederic Spiegelberg has commented that, 'As we study the religions of the modern world we immediately become aware of one outstanding phenomenon – that the Occident and the Orient are apt to conceive the basic concepts of which the human race is capable in diametrically opposed ways' (*Living Religions of the World*, London, 1957, p. viii).

Superficial acquaintance may convey a different opinion, but it remains an indisputable fact that Hinduism and its derivatives, Buddhism,* Jainism and Sikhism, stand in diametrical divergence from Christianity on every major doctrine of faith and practice. A brief survey of Hindu teachings basic to the understanding of human destiny and salvation will amply demonstrate the truth of this statement.

Scripture

Hindu theology places a high premium on the Vedas as the revealed scriptures, rooted in the divine omniscience and 'received' by sages in deep transcendental meditation. The Vedas are referred to with reverence, and at first sight appear to have the same claim to authority as the Bible does in Christianity. Yet in spite of the insistence on the divine origin of the Vedas, another doctrine completely alters the nature of scriptural authority. This is well stated later in the *Gita*, probably the most popular scripture in present-day Hinduism: 'As is a pool of water in a place flooded with water, so are all the Vedas to a person who has attained Enlightenment' (2:46), *i.e.*, once the seeker has attained *Moksha* or 'the Enlightened Consciousness' or 'Nirvana' or 'God-realization' (all of which signify salvation* in Hinduism), even the revealed scriptures no longer have a claim on him. In effect, this doctrine elevates the subjective experience of God-realization beyond the claim of the objective word of scripture. As a consequence, probably not even a handful of Hindus have ever read the entire Vedas. Aspirants prefer to bypass the close study of scripture in pursuit of experience in meditative practice (see Religious Experience*). In this hazardous retreat into the subjective world of private experience, each individual is supreme and above authority.

God

There is no conception of God in Hinduism similar to the Christian doctrine of a sovereign God* who created the universe and governs it in the exercise of his omnipotent power (see Sovereignty;* Creation;* Providence*). In Hinduism, God is utterly beyond form and definition; he is the totally Other, unknowable and unknown. A distant omniscience in the heavenlies, he is also immanent in the universe, so that everything in nature is shot through with the divine. It is for this reason that the worship and propitiation of the forces of nature, or even of great men, comes so easily to Hindus.

Incarnation

Hindus have a doctrine of incarnation. The unknowable Divine becomes incarnate in flesh and blood during times of world crisis, and dwells among men in order to restore righteousness. But by contrast with the finality of Christ's incarnation, in Hinduism incarnation is a process and is recurrent whenever the world is threatened by upheaval. The concept of a God of love, especially the sacrificial love that is inherent in the Christian gospel, is foreign to the Hindu understanding of the divine.

Humanity and its destiny

In Hinduism, the human person is a perfectible being. It is freely admitted that he is imperfect and prone to evil, but the cause of this is nothing inherent in his nature but ignorance (*Avidya*). This ignorance is his absence of understanding of his true divine nature. He is essentially a spiritual being with the divine spark as his core. If this were truly realized and made manifest, his radiant spiritual nature would shine forth. The highway that leads to this state is spiritual practice, especially silence, meditation, intense self-abnegation and the chastening of one's gross carnal nature. Thus man is the architect of his own salvation and needs no mediator,* still less a saviour or redeemer. Hinduism is *par excellence* a blueprint for auto-salvation. The individual achieves his own deliverance from the knot of human bondage into the liberty of God-realized people of spirit.

Karma and reincarnation

These twin doctrines are characteristic of all oriental mysticism,* especially in the Indo-Aryan world. The law of Karma is simply the law of causality applied rigorously in the moral and conceptual realm as well as the physical. 'As a man thinketh, so is he' is an example of this law as it works in the realm of thought and moral intent. The law of rebirth or reincarnation (see Metempsychosis*) is the safety-valve in Hinduism. If a seeker fails to realize his destiny of God-consciousness in this life, he can always lay the foundations of a second chance to labour for his salvation in another incarnation. Probation does not exhaust itself in one life; there is always a second opportunity for those who cannot face the rigours of the discipline prescribed for the spiritual athlete who sets himself single-mindedly to break through the coils of his earthly bondage. Divine grace is operative only at the fringes of the process, almost at the end of the human effort.

Hindu-Christian dialogue

It is an essential Hindu doctrine that all religions are pathways to God and that no religion can justifiably make any claim to exclusiveness (see Christianity and Other Religions;* Uniqueness of Christ*). Any religion that insists on being the only true one is unwarrantedly restrictive and narrow, in the light of the all-embracing amplitude of the divine will. Here Christ and Hinduism emerge in clear conflict (*cf.* Jn. 14:6).

However attractive Hinduism may appear superficially, especially with its techniques of meditation and spiritual practice, it needs to be clearly stated that its 'Achilles' heel', its most grievous flaw, is its total failure to address itself meaningfully to the cold, hard, inescapable fact of sin. Sin, by which we mean that alienation of humanity from God which leads to alienation from his fellows and, above all, from himself, is the great harasser of mankind. Unless this is dealt with by the divinely appointed method, namely, reconciliation by repentance and self-surrender through faith in the Lord Jesus and his redemption, anyone who gives himself to meditation and spiritual discipline, however sincerely, is playing a dangerously losing game.

These profound differences between Hindu and Christian beliefs have not deterred writers and teachers from both traditions attempting to identify and build on points of contact between the two. Reforming Hindus such as Sri Aurobindo (1872–1950) have drawn on the Bible and Christian teaching to correct what they have seen as the weaknesses of Hinduism. Christians such as Raimundo Panikkar (b. 1918) have urged the use of Hindu concepts to commend Christianity to Hindus. Panikkar's book, *The Unknown Christ of Hinduism* (London, ²1980), finds common ground in the humanity shared by Hindu and Christian and brought to true focus in the incarnation – for Hindus have not found it impossible to regard Jesus as an incarnation of deity. But other Indian Christian theologians (*e.g.* S. Kulandran, *Grace. A Comparative Study of the Doctrine in Christianity and Hinduism*, London, 1964) continue to view the two faiths as incompatible, and the approach of Panikkar as verging on syncretism.*

Bibliography

S. Nirved-Ananda, *Hinduism at a Glance* (Calcutta, 1957); S. Radhakrishnan, *The Hindu View of Life* (London, 1960); D. S. Sarma, *Hinduism Through the Ages* (Bombay, 1967); H. E. W. Slade, *Schools of Oriental Meditation* (London, 1973); H. Smith, *The Religions of Man* (New York, 1957); R. Tagore, *The Religion of Man* (London, 1966).

P.M.K.

HIPPOLYTUS (*c.* 170–*c.* 236). Hippolytus came to Rome from the Eastern Mediterranean, perhaps Egypt, and was the last major ecclesiastical writer in Greek at Rome. A presbyter and then counter-bishop in the church at Rome, he was exiled (*c.* 235) under Emperor Maximin to Sardinia, where he died.

The facts of his life are obscure, and the authorship of some works attributed to him is disputed. His major work, *Refutation of all Heresies (Philosophumena)*, attempts to trace the origin of Gnostic* systems and other erroneous teachings to Greek philosophies. He was indebted to Irenaeus* for much of his information on heresies (as he was for much of his theology), but he had access to other sources. His *Commentary on Daniel* is the earliest surviving orthodox commentary; it placed the return of Christ at 500 years after his birth and so sought to quiet anxiety about the end. Similar eschatological concerns are found in *On Christ and Antichrist*. The *Apostolic Tradition* is important for liturgical practices and theology, especially with reference to baptism, eucharist, ordination and the love feast. Recovery of its text is difficult because it survives mainly in later (expanded) versions. *Against Noetus* opposes the modalism (see Monarchianism*) of Noetus of Smyrna, active at the end of the 2nd century.

Hippolytus led his followers into schism shortly after Callistus was elected Bishop of Rome in 217. The two men were personal rivals: Hippolytus was educated and came from cultured circles; Callistus was a former slave whose practical abilities had made him a leading deacon. The two men clashed on church discipline:* which sinners could be reconciled to the church and on what terms, and what would be the church's attitude in fellowship on social and moral questions. Callistus favoured taking a forgiving and moderate approach, willing to reconcile those guilty of sexual sins and to recognize marriages not sanctioned by Roman law. Since the church* is a saving society, it should be inclusive in membership. Hippolytus favoured keeping serious sinners under discipline until their deathbed, leaving forgiveness in the hands of God. He wanted a church of the pure. The two men also represented rival Christologies.* Callistus emphasized the oneness of God, trying to walk a middle way between the modalism of Sabellius and what he called the ditheism of Hippolytus. The latter developed his doctrine of Christ from the Logos* Christology of the Apologists* and from Irenaeus. The Logos, immanent in God, is eternal, but came forth to have a separate existence in connection with creation and separate personality in the incarnation, when he became fully Son of God.

Hippolytus and Pontianus, Callistus' second successor, were exiled at the same time. They apparently became reconciled, for the two parties reunited and commemorated both men as martyrs. A statue of Hippolytus has been found containing a list of his writings and tables which he prepared for determining the date of Easter.*

Bibliography

G. Dix, *The Treatise on the Apostolic Tradition of St Hippolytus of Rome* (London, ²1968); J. H. I. von Döllinger, *Hippolytus and Callistus* (Edinburgh, 1876); D. G. Dunbar, 'The Delay of the Parousia in Hippolytus', *VC* 37 (1983), pp. 313–327; J. M. Hanssens, *La Liturgie d'Hippolyte (Orientalia Christiana Analecta* 155, Rome, ²1965); J. B. Lightfoot, *The Apostolic Fathers*, part 1, vol. 2 (London, 1890), pp. 317–477; P. Nautin, *Hippolyte et Josipe: Contribution à l'histoire de la littérature chrétienne du troisième siècle* (Paris, 1947); D. L. Powell, 'The Schism of Hippolytus', *SP* 12 (1975), pp. 449–456; J. E. Stam, 'Charismatic Theology in the "Apostolic Tradition" of Hippolytus', in G. F. Hawthorne (ed.), *Current Issues in Biblical and Patristic Interpretation* (Grand Rapids, MI, 1975); C. Wordsworth, *St Hippolytus and the Church of Rome* (London, ²1880).

E.F.

HISTORICAL JESUS, QUEST FOR.
This phrase achieved currency as the title of Albert Schweitzer's* famous survey of attempts to write the life of Jesus,* originally published under the (German) title *From Reimarus to Wrede*. In it he summarized all the main 'lives of Jesus' published from the end of the 18th century to the beginning of the 20th.

Granted that our sources for the life of Jesus (for all essential purposes, the four gospels) present somewhat different accounts of him, historians must necessarily ask what really happened. They must test whether the evangelists were reliable historians, and which accounts are to be followed in the case of differences. Previously it had been assumed for the most part that, since the gospels were part of Scripture, they were reliable accounts and that the differences between them were only apparent and could be dealt with by harmonization. The 19th-century scholars insisted that they could not be bound by the untested assumption that the gospels relate reliable history, or by the assumption that the teaching of systematic theology and dogmatics about Jesus is to be accepted without question. Rather, Jesus must be subjected to historical enquiry just like any other historical

figure. In practice, many of the 'questers' were sceptical concerning the reality of the miraculous,* or insisted that in a historical work there could be no place for the miraculous, and therefore they tried in one way or another to explain the accounts in the gospels on the assumption that the 'real' Jesus was in no way a supernatural* figure. Thus from the start the 'quest' described by Schweitzer was based on the assumption that the gospels were unreliable and that the historical Jesus was an ordinary person round whose memory legends had developed. The quest led to detailed critical examination of the gospels, as for the first time they were studied like any other ancient documents and placed in their historical setting. But the general picture produced of Jesus was that of the so-called 'liberal' Jesus, an inoffensive ordinary man who was an effective teacher of somewhat trite religious truths. The last figure discussed by Schweitzer was Wilhelm Wrede (1859–1906), who argued that the gospels were never intended to be historical works, but were theologically motivated and coloured throughout; this made it doubtful whether much reliable information about Jesus could be extracted from them. This position was reinforced by such scholars as Rudolf Bultmann* who used form-criticism (see Biblical Criticism*) to demolish the value of the oral traditions incorporated in the gospels and finished up by declaring that the historical Jesus is inaccessible to the historian; all that we possess of historical worth is a handful of his sayings. This work marked the zenith of historical scepticism.

It fell to an American scholar, James M. Robinson (b. 1924), to coin the slogan 'A New Quest of the Historical Jesus' and thereby to create something of a myth (in the popular sense of the term). Robinson argued that there could be no going back on the conclusions of Bultmann, and that no methods to rescue something from the wreck could work. Nevertheless, he saw the possibility of progress in a new kind of historical approach which would interrogate the gospels to find out something about the 'selfhood' of Jesus through determining his understanding of his existence. It may be doubted whether Robinson was accurately describing what the scholars whom he labelled as the 'new questers' thought they were doing. E. Käsemann,* who generally gets the credit for inaugurating the so-called 'new quest', had the boldness to disagree with Bultmann from within the 'school' of Bultmann's disciples, and he claimed that there was more history (though not very much more!) in the gospels than Bultmann had allowed. The only real significance in this was that for the first time a scholar infected by Bultmannism was showing signs of antibodies developing in his system. Outside the circle there had always been scholars who believed, on sound historical grounds, that the gospels contained reliable information – and rightly so, despite the sweeping indictment of their methods by J. M. Robinson. Within Germany we should mention Joachim Jeremias (1900–79), 'the most significant New Testament scholar of the last generation' (as Martin Hengel, b. 1926, called him) and at least spare a thought for K. Bornhäuser (1868–1947), Bultmann's contemporary at Marburg. And outside it there is the great British trio of C. H. Dodd,* T. W. Manson (1893–1958) and Vincent Taylor (1887–1968), and many others.

There are, of course, still scholars who adopt the extreme sceptical position (such as W. Schmithals and S. Schulz who deserve a place in any roll of dishonour), and it would be false optimism to suggest that the gospels are now generally accepted as historical works. It is certainly true that we cannot reconstruct from the gospels – the materials are too fragmentary for the purpose – a modern biography of Jesus in which there would be a full coverage of the events in his life in chronological order with some account of his psychological development. It is not possible to prove the historicity of many events recorded in the gospels. We cannot be sure that the evangelists were in fact trying to tell the story 'just as it happened' in every detail – the differences which they display over against one another show that they allowed themselves a good deal of editorial freedom; we should not fault them for what they were *not* trying to do, but should recognize that they were being inspired to write *gospels*, works that present the historical Jesus in his theological significance. But, when all this is said, it can be affirmed with confidence that the traditions recorded in the gospels rest on a historically reliable basis; it is the task of the gospel critic and historian to analyse the material and to work out at each point

what this historical basis is. Thus the quest for the historical Jesus is an on-going quest.

Bibliography

R. Bultmann, *The History of the Synoptic Tradition* (Oxford, ²1968); *idem, Jesus and the Word* (London, 1934); W. G. Kümmel, *The New Testament: The History of the Investigation of its Problems* (London, 1973); I. H. Marshall, *I Believe in the Historical Jesus* (London, 1977); S. Neill, *The Interpretation of the New Testament 1861–1961* (Oxford, 1964); J. M. Robinson, *A New Quest of the Historical Jesus* (London, 1959); A. Schweitzer, *The Quest of the Historical Jesus* (London, ³1954).

I.H.Ma.

HISTORICAL THEOLOGY is the study of the history of Christian doctrine. Over the centuries there has always been some study of the theology of past ages, but historical theology first became an established discipline in its own right during the last century. With the rise of the historical-critical method or the scientific approach to history,* the history of Christian doctrine became a field for study. While earlier generations had looked into the past for evidence of an unchanging core of Christian truth, historical theology draws attention to the changes in beliefs over the years. Historical theology also points to the influence on theology of the philosophical and social climate of the day, showing that all theology is, intentionally or otherwise, contextualized.

Two major 19th-century pioneers of historical theology were J. H. Newman* on the Roman Catholic side and A. von Harnack* on the Protestant side. Newman saw that the phenomenon of changing beliefs challenged the claim that Roman Catholic belief is always the same (*semper eadem*). He met this challenge with his concept of the development* of doctrine. Harnack saw the change in terms of the progressive Hellenization* of doctrine, a process which he traced back as far as the apostle Paul.*

Historical theology is often accused of being a relativizing* discipline. This is true in that it draws attention to the inescapably human and historical character of all our theology. As such, it points us to the need constantly to address today's problems in the light of God's word and not to absolutize the theological systems of the past.

Bibliography

J. Pelikan, *Historical Theology* (New York and London, 1971).

A.N.S.L.

HISTORY, in the sense of the historical process, is recognized by Christians as the sphere of earthly existence where God has dealings with humanity. Although the whole chain of world events, past, present and future, was rarely, if ever, described as 'history' before the late 18th century, discussion of its significance has formed part of theology down the ages. In the Bible there are ample materials for constructing an understanding of history, even if (as has been much debated) it contains little elaboration of a theology of history as such. In the OT God is presented as an agent in the historical process. Supremely in the exodus from Egypt, but also in many other events, God displays his power (*e.g.* Ps. 136). By contrast with the nature deities of surrounding nations, God reveals* himself primarily in history. In the NT God takes a decisive part in human affairs through Christ, his purposes begin to unfold through the church and it is promised that history will come to an end with Christ's return for judgment.* So the chief biblical convictions about history are that 1. God has been shaping the overall course of the historical process from the beginning in creation;* 2. he intervenes in particular events, usually in judgment or mercy; and 3. he will bring his plans to a triumphant conclusion in the last things. By contrast with the cyclical view of history, widespread in ancient and oriental civilization, that events regularly recur on the seasonal pattern of nature, Christians have therefore held a linear view of history as a process moving towards a climax predetermined by God. His control they have described as providence;* the future climax is the ground for their hope.*

Different Christian estimates of the future have frequently been based on beliefs about the millennium.* In particular, if the bliss of the millennium was to be expected before the end of history, hope could be intensified into an ebullient optimism. By the 4th century, such millenarianism was fading before an 'imperial theology' holding that the Roman Empire was earning God's favour by adopting the Christian faith. Voiced most eloquently by Eusebius,* the first great historian of the church, the imperial theology, together with millenarianism, was sharply challenged by Augustine.* In *The City of God* he propounded a magisterial theology of history according to which the welfare of the community of believers in every age does not depend on temporal power and the millennium is identified with the present history of the church. Augustine's periodization of time into seven epochs was to haunt the medieval Christian imagination. It was not until the rise of Joachimism* in the 13th century that Augustine's framework was significantly modified. The teaching of Joachim that history is approaching a new age of the Spirit freed from ecclesiastical forms was to inspire a range of groups including many associated with the Radical Reformation.* Nevertheless, Augustine remained the main influence over the classical Reformers at the same time as cyclical motifs drawn from ancient literature were re-injected into Christian thought by the Renaissance. The last Augustinian* theology of history, the *Discourse on Universal History* (1681) by Bishop J. B. Bossuet (1627–1704), was to be ridiculed for its parochialism by Voltaire.* The Enlightenment* generated its own view of history, a secularization* of the Christian understanding, in the idea of progress.* Philosophies of history, however, were most in vogue in the Romantic* era, when the scheme of Hegel* was but the most elaborate. From the same soil sprang the German tradition of historicism, according to which each society produces its own distinctive values in the course of its history. The tradition could incline, as it did in the hands of F. C. Baur of the Tübingen School,* to discount the possibility of miracle* in history. It eventually led, in the thought of Troeltsch,* to the belief that, without God, all values are relative.

With Troeltsch we enter the lively 20th-century debates on the relation of faith* to history. Perhaps the chief stimulus has been the existentialist* claim of Bultmann* that history is irrelevant to faith, a claim to which the new phase of the quest for the historical Jesus* was a response. Another source has been interest in Hegel, the chief influence over both the contention of Pannenberg* that all history is revelatory and the critique of

307

traditional Catholicism in Gustavo Gutiérrez and some other exponents of liberation theology.* Biblical studies, specially in Gerhard von Rad (1901–71) and Oscar Cullmann, have drawn attention to the centrality of 'salvation-history'.* And Moltmann* has argued that eschatology* is the key to understanding history as well as theology. Meanwhile others have tried to state a Christian understanding of history for our time. Nicolas Berdyaev from an Eastern Orthodox standpoint (see Russian Orthodox Theology*), Herman Dooyeweerd* from a Dutch Reformed standpoint and Eric Voegelin (b. 1901) from a Lutheran standpoint have wrestled with the issue. Most influential, however, have been Reinhold Niebuhr,* with his rejection of the idea of progress, and Sir Herbert Butterfield (1900–79), a Methodist historian whose *Christianity and History* (1949) discerns God at work in the past. Looming behind these studies is the central question for any Christian philosophy of history, the problem of suffering,* which is perhaps treated most tellingly by P. T. Forsyth* in his wartime work, *The Justification of God* (1916).

Bibliography
D. W. Bebbington, *Patterns in History* (Leicester, 1979); D. P. Fuller, *Easter Faith and History* (London, 1968); V. A. Harvey, *The Historian and the Believer* (London, 1967); C. T. McIntire (ed.), *God, History and Historians: Modern Christian Views of History* (New York, 1977).

D.W.Be.

HISTORY-OF-RELIGIONS SCHOOL, the English translation of the German phrase, *Religionsgeschichtliche Schule*. It designates a group of scholars who in the late 19th and early 20th century attempted to understand the religious developments of the OT, the NT, and the early church by relating them to the context of other religious movements. Inspired by positivist* principles, these scholars used historical and philological approaches to explain the origin of biblical religion.

The Old Testament

Hermann Gunkel's *Schöpfung und Chaos in Urzeit und Endzeit* (*Creation and Chaos at the Beginning and End of Time*, Göttingen,

1895) derived much of the OT's themes of creation and chaos from Babylonian mythology. As opposed to Julius Wellhausen (1844–1918), Gunkel (1862–1932) placed this derivation not in the exilic period but in the 2nd millennium BC. Hugo Gressmann (1877–1927) in *Der Ursprung der israelitisch-jüdischen Eschatologie* (*The Origin of Israelite-Jewish Eschatology*, Göttingen, 1905) attempted to demonstrate the antiquity of the mythological themes found in the prophets. Rudolf Kittel's (1853–1929) *Geschichte des Volkes Israel* (*History of the People of Israel*, rev. edn., Gotha, 1912) maintained that Moses had taught not a monotheism but an 'ethical monolatry'.

The New Testament

Wilhelm Heitmüller (1869–1926) in 1903 argued that Paul's understanding of the eucharist* was not derived from the original teachings of Jesus but from the Hellenistic world. Wilhelm Bousset (1865–1920) examined the early church as a Hellenistic-Jewish phenomenon. His greatest work, *Kyrios Christos* (1913; ET 1970), set forth the thesis that it was the Gentile Christians in the context of their worship who first addressed Christ as *Kyrios* ('Lord') in place of the title 'the Son of Man', which derived from Jewish eschatology. Some of the Christians who had been members of the mystery cults thus reinterpreted Christ as their new 'mystery god'.

In his work, *Hauptprobleme der Gnosis* (*The Main Problems of Gnosticism*, 1907), Bousset explained Gnostic teachings as the result of a transformation of older oriental Hellenistic philosophy. He held it self-evident that Gnosticism* existed prior to Christianity.

Richard Reitzenstein (1861–1931) was a philologist who studied the role of mysticism in Hellenism. His *Poimandres* (1904; repr. Darmstadt, 1966) suggested that the Hermetic tractate Poimandres was the source of Johannine thought. He also used late Mandaean (see Gnosticism*) texts to reconstruct the background of Christian baptism (*Die Vorgeschichte der christlichen Taufe* (*The Prehistory of Christian Baptism*, 1924; repr. Darmstadt, 1967).

In his most famous book, *Die hellenistischen Mysterienreligionen* (*The Hellenistic Mystery Religions*, Stuttgart, 1910; ET 1978), Reitzenstein argued that Paul was profoundly influenced by Hellenistic religious traditions such as the mystery religions and Gnosticism. In fact, he went so far as to call Paul the greatest of all the Gnostics.

In his work, *Das iranische Erlösungsmysterium* (*Iranian Mystery Religion*, 1921), Reitzenstein used recently discovered documents from Turkestan to recover the alleged Iranian roots of a pre-Christian Gnosticism – without realizing at the time that these were Manichaean* texts. Later he maintained that Manichaeism must have preserved some very ancient Iranian Gnostic traditions.

Appraisal

The views of such scholars as Reitzenstein and Bousset had a great impact upon Rudolf Bultmann,* one of the leading NT scholars of this century. Despite the enormous impact of the writings of Bousset and Reitzenstein in Europe, their writings were not translated into English in their lifetimes.

The use by the history-of-religions scholars of late and unrelated sources to explain Paul's religion or to reconstruct a hypothetical pre-Christian Gnosticism has been severely criticized. In Earle Ellis' trenchant phrase, 'There is a tendency to convert parallels into influences and influences into sources' (*Paul and His Recent Interpreters*, Grand Rapids, MI, 1961, p. 29).

Bibliography

W. Bousset, *Kyrios Christos* (ET, Nashville, TN, 1970); H. F. Hahn, *The Old Testament in Modern Research* (rev. ed.; Philadelphia, 1966), ch. III, 'The Religio-Historical School and the Old Testament'; R. Reitzenstein, *Hellenistic Mystery-Religions* (ET, Pittsburgh, PA, 1978); E. M. Yamauchi, *Pre-Christian Gnosticism* (Grand Rapids, MI, ²1983).

E.M.Y.

HISTORY OF THEOLOGY. As that which is said about God, theology is given by God himself through Scripture.* But this primary, authoritative theology evinces a human response in the form of theological study and formulation, *i.e.* the exposition of the primary theology, reflection upon it, and its presentation and application. Hence theological thought and practice arise which call for constant review, evaluation and correction in the light of the biblical norm. In this process four historical groupings may be discerned:

the patristic, medieval, Reformed, and modern.

Patristic*

The reference here is to the period of theological study which began with the apostolic fathers, reached a climax with the great age of Trinitarian* and Christological* formulation, and ended with the decline of Rome.

After fragmentary efforts, converted philosophers took the first considered theological steps as in the form of apologies* (*cf.* Justin) they tried to present the gospel to rulers and the educated classes. Contacts with pagan thought carried the dangers of Gnosticism* and speculation which even Clement* and Origen* in Alexandria did not wholly avoid as they pursued similar goals in a catechetical setting. The teaching office exercised by Irenaeus,* Tertullian* and Hippolytus* proved to be a more stabilizing if no less formative influence. Supported by the formulation of the canon and the appeal to the historical ministry and tradition, their work gave early shape to the church's thinking in Christology and soteriology.

Preoccupation followed with the problems posed by the basic confession of Jesus as Lord. Every conceivable deviation and overemphasis emerged during the long debate, as theologians adjusted their inherited metaphysical vocabulary (*e.g.* such terms as nature, person and substance) to the biblical data. Out of the strife and confusion the church eventually forged the Nicene and Chalcedonian statements in a process in which conciliar discussion played a vital theological part. To the related debates we owe some of the best of patristic theology contributed by such bishop- or presbyter-theologians as Athanasius,* the Cappadocians, Cyril of Alexandra* and Cyril of Jerusalem (*c.* 315–86), and Jerome,* whether in a pastoral, polemical, confessional or catechetical context.

At the same time the Pelagian* and Donatist* controversies testify to the anthropological* and ecclesiological concerns of the church even in the thick of Christological debate. These issues enabled Augustine* in particular to develop both a strong doctrine of original sin* and electing grace* on the one side and a more rigid doctrine of the church and sacraments* on the other. The Pelagian episode also heralded the emergence of monasticism* as a context of theological reflection; this was an important development in view of the later role of the monasteries in preserving Scripture and caring for theological education. Behind other issues lay always the central question of the atonement,* which might be presented in different forms, especially that of a ransom, but which gave urgency to what might otherwise seem to be abstruse debates. After all, it was because of his mediating work that Christ's deity needed to be asserted against the Arians,* his unity against the Nestorians,* and his humanity against the Apollinarians* and Eutychians (see Monophysitism*). The Bible, which supplied the primary data, formed a permanent centre of interest in the various forms of textual study, translation, exposition and catechetical and homiletical application. Of particular significance was the distinction between the allegorical exposition of Alexandria* (cf. Origen*) and the more natural exegesis of Antioch* (see Hermeneutics*).

In view of its range and variety, the patristic age resists facile generalization. It produced outstanding figures who used the tools available to do theology of lasting worth. In general it remained faithful to Scripture, which it prized highly and studied with great assiduity. It established for all succeeding generations essential biblical doctrines even if it couched them in what is often an alien vocabulary. Yet philosophical and ascetic* influences militated against the more authentic biblical understanding which in the main was best preserved in pastoral, confessional and catechetical circles. In particular much of patristic theology lay exposed to the dangers of rationalistic and dualistic* intrusion. Even pastoral and catechetical theology, while better preserving the basic Christian deposit, opened the door to subversion in the forms of a new legalism and ecclesiasticism. In such ways the patristic age prepared the ground for the growth of many evils in later thought and practice.

Medieval

The patristic era ended with Gregory the Great* in the West and John of Damascus* in the East. A comparatively less influential period followed in which orthodoxy hardened in the East, the barbarians created a need for new beginnings in the West, and schism separated the two, the Filioque forming a narrow point of doctrinal division. During the confused age of readjustment in the West the monasteries and cathedral schools played a vital part by copying manuscripts, training the clergy and producing fine scholars like Bede (c. 673–735) and Alcuin (c. 735–804). The predestinarian debate flared up briefly with Gottschalk,* and Radbertus* and Ratramnus* at Corbie engaged in a discussion of the eucharistic* presence which would be renewed more fiercely between Berengar* and Lanfranc (c. 1005–89) in the 11th century and re-emerge in the Reformation period (e.g. in Edwardian and Marian England).

The more developed medieval period saw the initiative pass from the monastic and cathedral schools to the newly forming universities with teaching faculties devoted specifically to theological study and courses leading to recognized qualifications in divinity. Anselm,* it is true, came from a monastic setting at Bec with his fresh attempt at faith seeking understanding in such matters as the existence of God and the rationale of the incarnation and atonement. But Abelard* with his questing rationalism belonged to the heady formative period of the new learning of the schools. The rediscovery of Greek philosophy gave urgency at this time to the whole question of faith and reason.* Later nominalists* like William of Ockham* tended to magnify the role of faith in submission to the divine sovereignty. Thomas Aquinas,* however, took the middle ground which would finally have so potent an influence. He admitted that philosophy can give some knowledge of God, and made liberal use of its resources. Yet he still attributed the true content of Christian knowledge to revelation apprehended in faith.

Scholasticism* absorbed rather than crushed the older forms of theological study, drawing much of its strength from the monastic orders, the newly founded Dominicans* and Franciscans,* and the support of the hierarchy as well as the secular authorities. Its superiority of method and organization ensured its success both practically and in its application to the whole range of theological problems. Its contribution was not wholly beneficial, for, in concert with official promulgations such as those of the Fourth Lateran Council in 1215, it helped to establish various perverted ideas, e.g. purgatory,* penance,* infused grace, implicit faith, transubstantiation, and the eucharistic sacrifice. Nevertheless its valuable aspects include the transmission of historic doctrines and seminal thinking on the atonement, whether in the form of Anselm's satisfaction* theory, Abelard's subjective approach, the Christological orientation of Bernard of Clairvaux,* or the balanced presentation of Thomas Aquinas. It sensed the need for a biblical commitment, as may be seen in the extensive commentaries, the use of proof texts, and the more direct appeal of Wyclif* and Hus.* Allegorical exegesis plagued much of the biblical work, but natural exegesis had its champions, and Aquinas drew careful limits for the allegorical method. Scholasticism also preserved the doctrines of grace, even if at times in a more rationalistic, semi-Pelagian,* or exaggeratedly sacramentalistic form. It maintained a good spirit of enquiry which only in the later stages could degenerate into tediously formal quibbling. These virtues do much to offset the problems which ultimately jeopardized the scholastic enterprise, and which included, at the practical level, the enhancement of theological education for the few at the expense of the many, and the resultant decline in theological knowledge at the common level of priest and people.

Reformed

By the 15th century scholasticism, although retaining its subtlety, had lost constructive force. But new influences were either infiltrating older universities (e.g. Cambridge) or inspiring the founding of new ones (e.g. Wittenberg). Recovery of the biblical languages, more direct exegesis, publishing of the fathers and the development of printing combined to produce a shift in theological curriculum and a reorientation to the simplified piety of Erasmus* or the deeper biblical theology of Luther.* For all the differences between the Lutherans, the Reformed, and even the Radicals* on the fringe, their biblically centred theology has enough homogeneity to justify the title of 'Reformed'.

Primarily it was a biblical theology* in the direct sense. Philosophy might hover in the background but did not form the basis or framework. The exposition of the original Scriptures as the supreme rule of faith came first on the agenda. To think or talk about God one must be taught by God. Study of the text, sustained by prayer and illumined by the Spirit, must inform and correct all reflection.

Reason had a role only as orientated to the Bible and put to biblical use. Commentaries based on the natural sense served as the basis rather than the crown of theological study in the work of Luther, Calvin* and Bullinger.* The biblical focus of Reformed theology* quickly enabled it to expose false methodology, to dethrone competing authority, and to correct doctrinal and practical aberration.

Being biblical, Reformed theology recaptured essential evangelical verities. It was Christological, not just in the sense of retaining established dogmas, but in that of finding in Christ alone the ground of acceptance. Luther, Zwingli,* Calvin and the Radicals shared the perception of Christ himself as the basis, centre and theme of the message. It was a theology of faith in Christ as our only wisdom and righteousness. Going to Christ in faith, it became a theology of gospel, if not without some dialectic of law (see Law and Gospel*). Luther recovered an understanding of justification,* Calvin finely related it to sanctification,* and all Reformers stressed the impotence of sinners and God's omnipotence in electing grace and reconciliation. If the ministry and sacraments also received due weight as the means of grace, they did so only in the context of the supreme ministry of the Spirit. Yet they did so also in practical application. Here was theology that reformed the schools but did not remain in them. It flowed over into the pulpit and from the pulpit to Christian life, transforming piety by the elimination of masses, pilgrimages, relics and the like, and fashioning conduct appropriate to the freedom and power of the gospel as these were now opened up by the translation and exposition of Scripture.

The Reformers did not enjoy the infallibility they denied to others. They came under contemporary influences, made mistakes, squabbled over important and less important matters, missed essential truths and overemphasized others. Yet they revitalized theological study by doing theology's proper work, giving it a true basis, achieving a happy blend of academic, spiritual and practical power, promoting the normativity of Scripture, and accepting the need to submit all faith and practice to its scrutiny.

Modern

Unfortunately much of the West, as well as the East, resisted the Reformed correction, although not without initiating some significant reforms. The modern period has consequently seen two separate if interacting forces, each with its own tensions, and each coming into increasing contact with the East.

As regards Roman Catholicism, theology continued in the schools, within the orders, and in the new seminaries. Much of it took a polemical turn (*cf.* Bellarmine*). The renewed Augustinianism* of Jansenism brought an abortive attempt at reconstruction in the 17th century, and missionary enterprise opened up debate about the relationship between Christianity and culture. Liberalism* encountered stern resistance in the 19th and early 20th centuries. Ultramontanism (see Papacy*), with a stress on the church and its teaching office, resulted in the infallibility decree of 1870, and resurgent Mariology brought the decrees of Mary's* immaculate conception (1854) and bodily assumption (1950). Rejuvenated biblical study culminated in Vatican II (1962–65) with its practical reforms, redefinitions, and relativizing of traditional formulations. The drawing of Roman Catholics into ecumenical discussion formed part of this more hopeful trend.

In the non-Roman sphere, the university theologians of the 17th century fashioned Reformed and Lutheran orthodoxies in mutual debate and in response to Roman Catholics, Radicals and Arminians.* The Carolines* in England developed their own *via media*, while the Puritans* added a practical concern, combined with the Scots to bring confessional theology to a climax at the Westminster Assembly, and made perhaps the most significant contribution to American theology in Jonathan Edwards.* With the 18th century, which brought further university expansion, stress on biblical study took a more rationalistic and empiricist* turn. This provoked questioning of Scripture but brought immense gains in knowledge of its human context. The various movements of liberal Protestantism tried to fill the resultant gap with natural religion (the deists*), subjective experientialism (Schleiermacher*), moralism (Ritschl*), and the social gospel* (Walter Rauschenbusch, 1861–1918). Yet countermovements also developed in the concern for holiness,* the Princetonian* stress on biblical inerrancy (Hodge* and Warfield*), the attempted integration of liberal Catholi-

cism (Gore*), and the new biblical and Christological concentration of Barth.*

The 20th century has had both a negative and a positive side. Liberalism, dominant in older schools, has dissolved in successive movements, *e.g.* Bultmann's* demythologizing, death-of-God* theology, liberation* teaching, and the attenuated Roman Catholicism of Küng.* Yet biblical, historical and hermeneutical theology has enjoyed healthy growth, Barth's work has revived dogmatic interest, ecumenical dialogue has been a fruitful mode of theological study, and through seminaries, publications, and individual scholars Evangelicalism* has begun to make a significant contribution to theological teaching, literature, thought and dissemination.

Throughout the modern period theology has suffered either from over-rigid formulation or from the intrusion of alien forces. Nevertheless it has experienced unparalleled expansion of biblical knowledge, continuing witness to the biblical norm and reconstructions comparable to those of any age for force and grandeur. If the situation is ambivalent, theological study, vigorously pursued in many forms, holds the promise of results genuinely informed by Scripture and faithful, under the Spirit, to God's revelation of himself and his reconciling work in Christ.

Bibliography

G. W. Bromiley, *Historical Theology* (Grand Rapids, MI, 1978); H. Cunliffe-Jones (ed.), *History of Christian Doctrine* (Edinburgh, 1978); A. Harnack, *History of Dogma*, 7 vols. (London, 1894–99); P. Hodgson and R. H. King (eds.), *Christian Theology* (Philadelphia, 1982); P. Schaff, *Creeds of Christendom*, 3 vols. (New York, 1877).

G.W.B.

HODGE, CHARLES (1797–1878) was the best-known proponent of the conservative Calvinistic theology that came from the Presbyterian seminary in Princeton,* New Jersey, from its founding in 1812 to its reorganization in 1929. Hodge arrived from his native Philadelphia in 1812 to study at Princeton College, where he was converted during a period of revival. He then entered the seminary and soon became a devoted student and close friend of Archibald Alexander (1772–1851), the professor of theology.

Hodge became professor of oriental and biblical literature at Princeton in 1822; in 1840 he was transferred to the chair of exegetical and didactic theology, a position which was augmented by the professorship of polemic theology at Alexander's death in 1851. Well before then, however, Hodge had proven his mettle as a forceful voice for conservative Reformed* theology against a wide variety of alternatives. Especially in the pages of the *Princeton Review*, which he edited for nearly fifty years, Hodge was a lion in controversy. His adversaries ranged across the theological spectrum – from Schleiermacher* and other Romantic* theologians of inward subjectivity, through representatives of the Oxford Movement (see Anglo-Catholic Theology*) and 19th-century conservative Roman Catholicism, to Americans such as Charles G. Finney,* Horace Bushnell,* John W. Nevin (1803–86) and Philip Schaff (1819–93) of Mercersburg,* and Nathaniel W. Taylor (1786–1858) and Edwards Amasa Park (1808–1900) from New England.* Hodge's point of view was consistent. He contended for 16th- and 17th-century understandings of Calvinism. He proclaimed the dangers of unchecked religious experience, whether in the form of sophisticated European Romanticism* or frontier American revivalism. He championed scientific method, understood in terms of Francis Bacon's empiricism,* as the proper way to organize the infallible* teachings of Scripture. But what most troubled him were positions which undercut high Calvinistic convictions about divine sovereignty in salvation* or which valued too highly the moral capacities of unregenerate human nature. Hodge could sometimes appear overly rationalistic in these polemics, and he occasionally misread his opponents to their disadvantage; but by and large, he conducted his polemics on a very high plane. After Hodge's death, the Lutheran theologian C. P. Krauth said that 'next to having Hodge on one's side is the pleasure of having him as an antagonist' (A. A. Hodge, *Life of Charles Hodge*, p. 616).

Although Hodge exerted his greatest efforts in the defence of Calvinism, his interests ranged very widely. He was the author of major commentaries on Romans, Ephesians, and 1 and 2 Corinthians. He wrote frequently on Presbyterian ecclesiastical affairs. He penned numerous expositions of Christian teaching for laymen, of which *The Way of Life* (1841) was perhaps the most notable in its limpid prose and affective power. He wrote a not inconsiderable objection to Darwin's apparent assault on the idea of design (*What is Darwinism?*, 1874). He often commented cogently on public affairs, taking generally conservative positions on social issues. His lifetime's classroom instruction was summed up when he published his *Systematic Theology* in 1872, a work which like many of his other writings remains in print and in use to this day.

It has been noted that Hodge's *Systematic Theology* and some of his polemical essays play down the role of the Holy Spirit and the noncognitive dimensions of the faith. In other writings, however, like his commentaries and works for the laity, these aspects of Christian experience receive much fuller consideration. Hodge probably did not integrate the various aspects of his thought as carefully as one could wish. But his work remains the most effective 19th-century American presentation of Calvinism. It is wide-ranging in its concerns, spiritually sensitive in its insights, and thought-provoking in its defence of Reformed distinctives.

Bibliography

Systematic Theology, 3 vols. (New York, 1872–3); *Essays and Reviews: Selections from the Princeton Review* (New York, 1857).

W. S. Barker, 'The Social Views of Charles Hodge (1797–1878): A Study in 19th-century Calvinism and Conservatism', *Presbyterion. Covenant Seminary Review* 1 (1975), pp. 1–22; A. A. Hodge, *The Life of Charles Hodge* (New York, 1880); J. O. Nelson, 'Charles Hodge (1797–1878): Nestor of Orthodoxy', in Willard Thorp (ed.), *The Lives of Eighteen from Princeton* (Princeton, NJ, 1946); D. F. Wells, 'Charles Hodge', in *idem* (ed.), *Reformed Theology in America* (Grand Rapids, MI, 1985); *idem*, 'The Stout and Persistent "Theology" of Charles Hodge', *CT* XVIII:23 (30 Aug. 1974), pp. 10–15.

M.A.N.

HODGSON, L., see Anglo-Catholic Theology.

HOLINESS, see God; Holiness Movement; Sanctification.

HOLINESS MOVEMENT.

The Protestant holiness movement stemmed from John Wesley.* Wesley claimed that God raised up Methodism* to spread 'scriptural holiness', and taught that God roots all sin* out of Christian hearts in this life, so that motivationally Christians become all love. 'Christian perfection',* 'perfect love', 'entire sanctification',* and in the 19th century 'the second blessing' and 'holiness' simply, were names given to this posited work of grace. It was held to be wrought instantaneously in response to earnest seeking, and to be attested immediately by the inner witness of the Holy Spirit.* Pursuing this blessing, and keeping it when found, calls for intense effort in the form of self-renouncing devotion to God and immersion in all good works. Christians will advance spiritually after being sanctified, as they did before, but with an altered experience, since their hearts are now ablaze with love to God and man, and nothing else. Unwise, inept and misconceived action can still occur, but motivationally the sanctified are sinless. Wesley's doctrine blended classic mystical* lore about Christ purging the heart, with pietism's* stress on the affective element in spiritual experience and the Reformation* emphasis on assured* faith* as the sole means of salvation* throughout.

When mainstream Methodist commitment to this teaching cooled, the 'holiness movement' emerged, reaching its peak between 1850 and 1950. It sought to restore the centrality and recover the power of the 'second blessing' and the enriched discipleship to which it leads. Theologically, the movement took three forms.

Wesleyan holiness

Denominational offshoots from mainstream Methodism (e.g. the Church of the Nazarene; the Salvation Army*), some educational institutions (e.g. Asbury College and Seminary, Kentucky) and some individual teachers (e.g. Oswald Chambers, 1874–1917; A. Paget Wilkes, 1871–1934), have upheld Wesley's doctrine essentially unchanged, equating holiness with the transformed inner life as such rather than with any consequent manifestation of moral wisdom and rectitude.

Keswick holiness

This name signifies the teaching first institutionalized at the week-long (now two-week) Keswick Convention in England, founded in 1875 (see Higher-Life Theology*). It represents a fourfold modification under Reformed influence of the Wesleyan position, thus: 1. The 'second blessing', while increasing one's love and transforming one's life, does not eradicate one's sin. 2. The blessing itself is essentially a matter of being filled with the Spirit for the ongoing battle with inward corruption. 3. A single decisive act of trustful self-surrender brings the blessing automatically: one may 'take it by faith', whether one feels it or not. 4. In the moral battle one must not strive against one's sinful impulses directly ('in one's own strength') or defeat will follow. Instead, one must prayerfully remit them to Christ to counteract, looking to him in trustful and expectant passivity. Slogans like 'let go and let God', 'stop trying and start trusting', pinpoint this imperative. Exponents of some or all of this have included Phoebe Palmer (1807–84), W. E. Boardman (1810–86), Robert Pearsall Smith (1827–98) and Hanna Whitall Smith (1832–1911), Evan H. Hopkins (1837–1919), H. C. G. Moule (1841–1920), F. B. Meyer (1847–1929) and Andrew Murray.*

Pentecostal holiness

Pentecostalism,* historically a mutation of Wesleyan holiness teaching, equates the 'second blessing' with the apostles' baptism-of-Spirit* recorded in Acts 2, links it with glossolalia (see Gifts of the Spirit*) as its ordinary evidence, and in practice conceives of holiness as an exuberant style of life and worship, linked with rigorous separation from the ways of the world.

While undoubtedly deepening devotion in a materialistic era, the holiness movement has frequently spawned disfigurements – élitism, legalism, quietism, cultural negativism, anti-intellectualism, self-deception, fanaticism, moral insensitivity and unrealism, among others – which its exponents have not always noticed. The Augustinian* holiness teaching of Lutheran* and Reformed* theology, which declines to parcel out salvation into a 'first' and 'second' blessing, is arguably truer and healthier.

Bibliography

S. Barabas, *So Great Salvation* (on Keswick) (London, 1946); M. E. Dieter, *The Holiness*

Revival of the Nineteenth Century (Metichan, NJ, 1980); H. Lindström, *Wesley and Sanctification* (London, 1946); J. I. Packer, *Keep in Step with the Spirit* (Old Tappan, NJ, and Leicester, 1984); V. Synan, *The Holiness-Pentecostal Movement in the United States* (Grand Rapids, MI, 1971).

J.I.P.

HOLL, KARL (1866–1926), professor of church history, Tübingen 1901–6, Berlin 1906–26; distinguished German church historian. His *Habilitationsschrift* was on Greek monasticism (1896), followed by works on John of Damascus* (1897), and Amphilochius of Iconium (*c.* 340–95) in 1904. He later assumed the editorship of the 'Berlin Corpus' of the Greek fathers (*Griechische Christliche Schriftsteller*), and in this series published his renowned three-volume edition of Epiphanius (*c.* 315–403) (1915–33). During these years of intensive research on the Greek fathers he also worked on Luther,* as well as Calvin* and the Enthusiasts (see Reformation, Radical*). These years culminated in his epoch-making *Gesammelte Aufsätze* (*Collected Essays*; vol. 1, 1921, ⁷1948; vols. 2–3, 1928, ²1932). It was his immense knowledge of patristics which, reinforced with his unique grasp of Luther, gave both originality and independence to his judgments as well as an interest in systematic theology.* He was no party man, for his interests were wide, covering Russian as well as English church history: this breadth of outlook gave him a balanced and informed mind. He reacted against certain emphases of Lutheran orthodoxy, notably the forensic view of justification* (as formulated by Melanchthon* rather than Luther). More than any other single person it was he who was responsible for the Luther renaissance of the 1920s.

His contribution lies first in that he made the sole basis of his thought the exact historical and philological study of sources. Secondly, he related Luther to the whole spiritual and historical development of the West, thereby making Luther of intense contemporary significance. Thirdly, he showed Luther's to be a theocentric religion based on man's relation to God, a theology of conscience.

Bibliography
W. Bodenstein, *Die Theologie Karl Holls* (Berlin, 1968); A. Jülicher and E. Wolf, *RGG* III, cols. 431–433; W. Pauck, introd. to ET of Holl's *The Cultural Significance of the Reformation* (New York, 1959); J. Wallmann, *TRE* XV, pp. 514–518.

J.A.

HOLOCAUST. Derived from the LXX Gk. for a wholly burned offering (*e.g.* Lv. 6:23), and originally used figuratively of wholesale sacrifice, according to Yehuda Bauer the term came into use in the English language between 1957 and 1959 to describe what happened to European Jews under the Nazi regime, when 6,000,000 were murdered in the death camps in a concerted attempt at genocide. The name of one of these, Auschwitz, is often used as a symbol of the total horror of Hitler's 'Final Solution'.

The Holocaust has rightly prompted deep and agonized reflection by both Jewish and Christian theologians. Many have felt that it is, as Roy Eckardt put it, 'uniquely unique'. There is general agreement among these theologians that the Holocaust marks such a break in human history* that history can no longer be understood as linear or continuous, much less as an evolution from lower to higher forms of civilization. 'When facing *that* event, history becomes interruption' (Elizabeth Schussler Fiorenza and David Tracy (eds.), *The Holocaust as Event of Interruption*, p. xi). Thus the Jewish theologian Arthur A. Cohen applies Rudolf Otto's* term *tremendum* to the Holocaust to emphasize both its vastness and its terror.

The events of the Holocaust raise the question 'Where was God?' For Richard Rubenstein, 'After Auschwitz it is impossible to believe in God.' Arthur Cohen, however, argues that the omnipotent God of traditional theology no longer exists. It is necessary to construct a new doctrine of God which faces the evil of the death camps realistically. Jürgen Moltmann* sees the issue of theodicy* differently. In his view, to theologize after the Holocaust would prove a futile exercise. God was in Auschwitz participating in the suffering of the victims because he is the crucified God, not the impassible God of traditional theology. Moltmann's answer to the question has itself raised questions. As John Pawlikowski has observed, 'There has to be some question

315

about the propriety of combining the theology of the Cross with the Auschwitz experience in view of the significant Christian complicity in the Nazi effort' (*ibid.*, p. 47). Furthermore the cross is the voluntary act of the Son of God, whereas the victims of death camps did not voluntarily surrender their lives.

Reflection upon the anti-Semitism (see Judaism and Christianity*) which inspired the Holocaust has brought some scholars to argue that it is to be found not only in much traditional Christian theology but also in the NT. Thus Mark's presentation of the Pharisees, John's description of the enemies of Christ as 'the Jews' and Paul's remarks in 1 Thes. 2:14–16 are alleged to be anti-Semitic, or at least anti-Judaistic. Building on this view of such elements in the NT, Rosemary Ruether sees anti-Judaism as 'the left hand of Christology'. The absolutist claims of NT Christology* constitute a basis from which anti-Semitism can develop, so the tendency is to reinterpret them and to call for the abandonment of all attempts to convert Jews to the Christian faith. The agenda for Christological reflection after the Holocaust is spelt out by Louise Schottroff: 'With regard to the present, from a theological point of view, this means that it is not enough to foster an awareness of actual anti-Judaism in the NT and later Christian theology; it is irresponsible simply to quote NT passages without providing them with a hermeneutics* which reflects their social milieu. Such a hermeneutics must take account of the present reality of Christianity and Judaism and of their shared history' ('Anti-Judaism in the New Testament', *ibid.*, p. 58).

Yet however horrific the Holocaust, it is difficult to see how a reduced Christology and a moratorium on the evangelizing of Jewish people can be reconciled with the fundamental assertions of the NT that Jesus is the Messiah who fulfils the expectation of the OT and that the gospel is 'the power of God for the salvation of everyone who believes: first for the Jew, then for the Gentile' (Rom. 1:16).

See also: EVIL; JUDAISM AND CHRISTIANITY; SUFFERING; THEODICY.

Bibliography

Y. Bauer, *The Holocaust in Historical Perspective* (Seattle, WA, 1980); A. A. Cohen, *The Tremendum* (New York, 1981); E. Schussler Fiorenza and D. Tracy (eds.), *The Holocaust as Event of Interruption* (*Concilium*, 175; Edinburgh, 1984); A. H. Friedlander, *The Death Camps and Theology within the Jewish-Christian Dialogue* (London, 1985).

D.P.K.

HOLY SPIRIT – often considered by systematic theologians under the heading of pneumatology (see below).

Biblical

In the OT the spirit (*rûaḥ*) of Yahweh is God's power in action. Yahweh's spirit is God himself present and at work, as are his 'hand' and his 'arm'. The Spirit's distinct personhood can, and according to the NT should, be read into the OT, but cannot be read out of it. A term for both breath blown out and wind blowing (wind is viewed as God's breath, Is. 40:7; Ezk. 37:9), *rûaḥ* has vivid and awesome associations when used of God's energy let loose. It is so used in nearly 100 of its nearly 400 OT appearances. Yahweh's spirit is said to 1. shape creation, animate animals and mankind, and direct nature and history (Gn. 1:2, 2:7; Jb. 33:4; Pss. 33:6, 104:29–30; Is. 34:16); 2. reveal God's messages to his spokesmen (Nu. 24:2; 2 Sa. 23:2; 2 Chr. 12:18, 15:1; Ne. 9:30; Jb. 32:8; Is. 61:1–4; Ezk. 2:2; 11:24; 37:1; Mi. 3:8; Zc. 7:12); 3. teach by these revelations the way to be faithful and fruitful (Ne 9:20; Ps. 143:10; Is. 48:16; 63:10–14); 4. elicit faith, repentance, obedience, righteousness, docility, praise, and prayer (Ps. 51:10–12; Is. 11:2; 44:3; Ezk. 11:19; 36:25–27; 37:14; 39:29; Joel 2:28–29; Zc. 12:10); 5. equip for strong, wise and effective leadership (Gn. 41:38; Nu. 11:16–29; Dt. 34:9; Jdg. 3:10; 6:34; 11:29; 13:25; 14:19; 15:14; 1 Sa. 10:10; 11:6; 16:13; 2 Ki. 2:9–15; Is. 11:1–5; 42:1–4); and 6. give skill and application for creative work (Ex. 31:1–11; Hg. 2:5; Zc. 4:6). Revealing and enabling are the activities mainly stressed.

In the NT, as in the LXX, spirit is *pneuma*, a word with similar associations to *rûaḥ*, and the Holy Spirit poured out by Christ at Pentecost (Jn. 1:33; Acts 2:33) is identified with the OT spirit of God (Acts 2:16–21; 4:25; 7:51; 28:25; 1 Pet. 1:11; 2 Pet. 1:19–21). But now he appears as a person distinct from the Father and the Son, with a ministry of his own. Over and above his previous functions, he is now given to the church as 'another (*i.e.*

a second) Paraclete' (Jn. 14:16), taking over Jesus' role as counsellor, helper, strengthener, supporter, adviser, advocate, ally (for the Gk. *paracletos* means all of these). Like the Father and the Son, he acts as only a person can do – he hears, speaks, convinces, testifies, shows, leads, guides, teaches, prompts speech, commands, forbids, desires, helps, intercedes with groans (Jn. 14:26; 15:26; 16:7–15; Acts 2:4; 8:29; 13:2; 16:6–7; 21:11; Rom. 8:14, 16; 26–27; Gal. 4:6; 5:17–18; Heb. 3:7; 10:15; 1 Pet. 1:11; Rev. 2:7, *etc.*). Again like the Father and the Son, he can be personally insulted (blasphemed, Mt. 12:31–32; lied to, Acts 5:3; resisted, Acts 7:51; grieved by sin, Eph. 4:30). The 'name' (singular, meaning revealed reality) of the one God now takes the form of three divine persons together, Father, Son and Holy Spirit (Mt. 28:19; *cf.* the 'triadic' accounts of God's activity, Jn. 14:16 – 16:15; Rom. 8; 1 Cor. 12:4–6; 2 Cor. 13:14; Eph. 1:3–14; 2:18; 3:14–19; 4:4–6; 2 Thes. 2:13–14; 1 Pet. 1:2; Rev. 1:4–5). Tripersonal thinking about God surfaces in the NT constantly (see Trinity*).

John reports Jesus as saying that the Spirit's second-paraclete task is to mediate knowledge of, and union and communion with, the physically withdrawn, ascended, and glorified saviour (see Jn. 14:15–26; 16:14). Less explicitly Christocentric statements about the Spirit elsewhere in the NT should be understood as rooted in this understanding, which is the tap-root of apostolic spirituality from first to last. Only after Jesus' return to glory (*cf.* Jn. 17:5) could the Spirit's paraclete ministry start (Jn. 7:37–39; 20:22 is clearly acted prophecy): Pentecost morning was when it actually began. In this ministry the Spirit 1. *reveals* Jesus' reality and the truth about him, first by reminding and further instructing the apostles (Jn. 14:26; 16:13; Eph. 3:2–6; 1 Tim. 4:1) and then by so enlightening others that they receive the apostolic witness with understanding, confess the divine Lordship of the man Jesus, and experience his life-changing power through faith (Jn. 16:8–11; Acts 10:44–48; 1 Cor. 2:14–16; 12:3; 2 Cor. 3:4 – 4:6; Eph. 1:17–20; 3:14–19; 1 Jn. 2:20, 27; 4:1–3; 5:6–12); 2. *unites* believers to Christ in regenerative, life-giving co-resurrection, so that they become sharers in his kingdom (*cf.* Rom. 14:17) and members (living limbs) in the body of which he is head (Jn. 3:5–8; Rom. 6:3–11 with 7:4–6; 8:9–

11; 1 Cor. 6:17–19; 12:12–13; Gal. 3:14 with 26–29; Eph. 2:1–10 with 4:3–16; Tit. 3:4–7); 3. *assures* believers that they are children and heirs of God (see Sonship*), both through the direct witness of immediate inward certainty and by the indirect testimony of implanted filial instincts and dispositions, from which the reality of the new life may safely be inferred (Rom. 8:12–17; 2 Cor. 1:22; Gal. 4:6; Eph. 1:13; 1 Jn. 3:24; 4:13; 5:7); 4. *mediates fellowship** with the Father and the Son of a kind that is already heaven's life begun, and is thus, as a first instalment, a guarantee of the fullness of heaven's life to come (Rom. 5:5; 8:23; 2 Cor. 5:5; Eph 1:14; 2:18; 4:30; 1 Jn. 1:3 with 3:1–10, 24); 5. *transforms* believers progressively through prayer and conflict with sin into Christ's moral and spiritual likeness (2 Cor. 3:18; Gal. 5:16–25; Jude 20–21); 6. *gives gifts** – that is, witnessing and serving abilities – for expressing Christ in the believing community that is his body, so building it up (Rom. 12:3–13; 1 Cor. 12; Eph. 4:7–16; 1 Pet. 4:10–11), and for evangelistic proclamation in the world, so extending the church (Acts 4:8, 31, 9:31; Eph. 6:18–20); 7. *prays effectively* in and for believers in Christ who feel unable to pray properly for themselves (Rom. 8:26–27); 8. *prompts missionary action* to make Christ known (Acts 8:29; 13:2; 16:6–10), and *pastoral decision* for consolidating Christ's church (Acts 15:28). Ecstatic exuberances (tongues and prophecy), if from the Spirit, can be brought under control for the edifying of the body (1 Cor. 14:26–33), and 'religious' urges that misrepresent, displace, or dishonour Christ, or that downgrade his apostles and the authority that they had from him, are thereby shown not to be from the Spirit (1 Cor. 12:3; 1 Jn. 4:1–6). Since the Spirit is Christ's agent, doing his will, what the Spirit does in Christians Christ himself may be said to do (indwell, Col. 1:27, *cf.* Jn. 15:4–5; give life, Col. 3:4; sanctify, Eph. 5:26; *etc.*). This Christocentric focus of the Spirit's paraclete ministry is consistently sustained in NT thought.

Theological

Christian thought about the Spirit has been intermittent and patchy. In the West, Augustine's* habit of ascribing potency to internal grace rather than to the Holy Spirit, and the medieval substitution of the institutional church and its sacraments for the Spirit and the word as bringing salvation, blocked serious pneumatology for centuries. Only Eastern Orthodoxy,* with its rigorous Trinitarian formalism, and Evangelicalism out of Reformed,* Methodist* and pietist* stables, with its experiential-ethical emphasis, have ever made much of the theme. The main areas explored have been these:

1. The Spirit and the Godhead. After rejecting the Montanist* idea of a present era of the Spirit following the two past eras of the Father and of the Son respectively, patristic theology* paid little attention to the Spirit till the late 4th century, when his coequality and coeternity with the Father and the Son were affirmed against various opponents (Tropici, Pneumatomachians, 'Macedonians'), and the Constantinopolitan Nicene Creed (381) called him 'the Lord, the Lifegiver, who proceeds from the Father, who with the Father and the Son is worshipped and glorified, who spoke through the prophets' (see Creeds*). The question whether the Spirit 'proceeds' (that is, in his own being, as distinct from his mission to mankind, about which Jn. 14:16, 26; 16:7 leave no doubt) from the Son as well as the Father then divided the West from the East. The addition of *Filioque* ('and from the Son') to the Nicene Creed in 589 by the Western Council of Toledo has always seemed to the Eastern church both heretical and schismatic. It is natural to suppose that the double sending of the Spirit reflects, and so reveals, a double procession in the divine life-pattern, but Scripture speaks only of the former, leaving the latter totally opaque to us in fact, however much it is argued over.

2. The Spirit and the word. Challenging Rome's equation of tradition with true biblical interpretation and Anabaptist* claims to be Spirit-led apart from and in disregard of Scripture, the Reformers maintained that Scripture and Spirit are inseparably conjoined. *Sola Scriptura* (by Scripture alone) was a Reformation* watchword; the intrinsic clarity and sufficiency of Scripture* for saving knowledge and faithful service of God were affirmed, and new inward revelations were denied. But without the Spirit who inspired the biblical word authenticating and interpreting it and enlightening sin-blinded hearts so that they receive it, the word will not be understood. Calvin* spoke of the internal, secret witness of the Spirit doing what

external evidence in apologetic arguments could not do, that is, sealing on our hearts (= making us unable to doubt) the divine quality of all Scripture and in particular the biblical promise of mercy in Christ; and he further held that through the word opened up audibly in preaching and made visible in the Lord's Supper the Spirit effects life-giving direct communion between the living Christ and those who believe.

3. The Spirit and salvation. The Reformers and Puritans,* with Augustine, emphasized fallen man's bondage to sin and consequent need of the Spirit's prevenient grace in effectual calling* to renew his heart and bring him to that personal faith without which no preaching or sacrament could save him. Puritan, pietist and Methodist teachers developed out of this a deeply experiential concept of conversion* (or, new birth) involving conviction of sin, faith as a cry for help, total repentance and consecration, and the Spirit's initial gift of assurance.* With this, Puritan pastoral theologians such as John Owen expanded Calvin's concept of progress in godliness through self-denial, cross-bearing, restraint as a lifestyle, hope, prayer, and single-eyed obedience into a profound analysis of sanctification as an ongoing pilgrimage and battle in which by 'God's free grace . . . we are renewed in the whole man after the image of God, and are enabled more and more to die unto sin, and live unto righteousness' (Westminster Shorter Catechism, q. 35). Behind this language lies the thought of the sovereign Spirit stirring Christians to will and act in God-pleasing obedience (Phil. 2:12–13), and of prayerful Christian activism in which much is attempted for God in the knowledge that without Christ nothing significant can be achieved (Jn. 15:5).

Into this scheme John Wesley* inserted a second work of grace wrought by the Spirit (new birth being the first). This second work eradicates sinful desire entirely and leaves 'perfect love' to God and man as henceforth the only motive in the heart. All Evangelicals expect this change at death, but Wesley was urging that if sought in faith it can be enjoyed earlier. Its effect, according to him, was not strictly sinless perfection,* since it secured only perfect motivation, nor faultless performance, but even so Reformed Evangelicals have judged his notion an unreality and those who profess the 'clean heart' somewhat self-deceived.

From Wesley's 'second-blessing' doctrine have stemmed a variety of 'two-step' accounts of the Christian life, in which 'Spirit-baptism' (see Baptism in the Spirit*) or 'Spirit-filling' for holiness (see Holiness Movement*), or for power in service, or for spiritual gifts with or without glossolalia, is the transition-point from lower-level to higher-level Christian advance. Distinct from these ideas was the belief of some Puritans (*e.g.* Thomas Goodwin, Thomas Brooks) that the Spirit will on occasion vouchsafe to Christians an overwhelmingly intense direct assurance of God's love. They based their view on an unlikely exegesis of Eph. 1:13 which saw the Spirit as God's sealer rather than his seal and posited a time interval between believing and being sealed; but a good case can be made for their contention from Eph. 3:14–19 with Rom. 8:15–16 and Jn. 14:18–23, and it is arguable that it is this element of Christian experience, misunderstood, that the many testimonies produced to confirm the several 'second-blessing' doctrines actually reflect.

4. The Spirit and the church. Though organization is needed for its self-expression, the church* is essentially not an organization but an organism, the Spirit-baptized body of Christ (1 Cor. 12:13), the new-created humanity in which the risen life of Christ (Col. 3:3) is realized through worship in the Spirit (Eph. 2:18; Phil. 3:3; Heb. 12:22–24), shared through ministry* in the Spirit (1 Cor. 12; 2 Cor. 13:14), and shown forth through 'good works' and evangelism in the power of the Spirit (Rom. 15:18–19; Eph. 2:4–10; 1 Thes. 1:5–6; Tit. 3:4–7). Each local gathering is a microcosmic outcrop of this one universal believing community, and as Christ's agent the Holy Spirit acts as Lord in it, designating and equipping particular individuals for particular stated ministries (Acts 13:1–2; 2 Tim. 1:6–7; *cf.* 1 Tim. 4:14) and enabling every member of the body to render service that furthers corporate growth into Christlike maturity (Eph. 4:11–16). Episcopal, presbyterian and congregational polities all aim to implement these principles, though only in this century has the 'every-member ministry' aspect been widely emphasized. Contemporary Pentecostal* movements, which emphasize it, also claim a renewal of the spectacular gifts* that once authenticated the

apostles' personal ministry (Heb. 2:3–4), *i.e.* tongues with interpretation, miracle-working, supernatural healing,* prophecy embodying new revelations: this is debatable, though God's power to renew these manifestations, should he so will, remains. The great spiritual vitality in the church that the outpouring of the Spirit at and after Pentecost produced recurs in measure at times of revival,* when the renewing ministry of the Spirit is sought and found (Lk. 11:13). Mission, meaning gospel proclamation linked with all forms of service, is empowered by the Spirit (Jn. 20:22), and is every Christian's business; Christ's commission in Jn. 20:22–23; Mt. 28:19–20; Acts 1:8 was given to the apostles as representing the whole church.

Bibliography

H. Boer, *Pentecost and Missions* (Grand Rapids, MI, 1961); F. D. Bruner, *A Theology of the Holy Spirit* (Grand Rapids, MI, 1970); J. Calvin, *Institutes* I.vii, ix, III.i, ii, vi-ix, IV.xvi, xvii; J. D. G. Dunn, *Baptism in the Holy Spirit* (London, 1970); *idem, Jesus and the Spirit* (London, 1975); D. Ewert, *The Holy Spirit in the New Testament* (Scottdale, PA, 1983); M. Green, *I Believe in the Holy Spirit* (London, 1975); A. I. C. Heron, *The Holy Spirit* (Philadelphia, 1983); A. Kuyper, *The Work of the Holy Spirit* (Grand Rapids, MI, 1946); H. Lindström, *Wesley and Sanctification* (London, 1946); John Owen, *Works*, ed. W. H. Goold, vols. II, III, IV, VI, VII (repr. Edinburgh, 1965); J. I. Packer, *Keep in Step With the Spirit* (Old Tappan, NJ, and Leicester, 1984); T. A. Smail, *Reflected Glory* (London, 1975); W. B. Sprague, *Lectures on Revivals of Religion* (London, 1959); W. H. Griffith Thomas, *The Holy Spirit of God* (London, 1913).

J.I.P.

HOMOOUSIOS, see ARIANISM, ATHANASIUS; CREEDS; TRINITY.

HOMOSEXUALITY, see SEXUALITY.

HOOKER, RICHARD (*c.* 1553–1600), Anglican* theologian and apologist. Apart from his famous controversy with the Puritan* Walter Travers (*c.* 1548–1635) at the Temple Church in 1586, Hooker's life was uneventful (Fellow of Corpus Christi College, Oxford, 1577–84, master of the Temple, 1585–91, and rural incumbencies), but his later years were devoted to the writing of his masterpiece, *Of the Laws of Ecclesiastical Polity*, of which Books I–IV were published in 1593 and Book V in 1597. The remaining books, which Hooker apparently failed to put into final form, were published after his death (VI and VIII, 1648, VII, 1662). The authenticity of these last three books, once discredited because their views on monarchy and episcopacy were not those of the later 17th-century Church of England, has been vindicated by modern scholarship. Hooker's aim in the *Polity* was to defend the Elizabethan Church of England against Puritan criticisms of its polity, ceremonies and liturgy.

Like most Anglican theologians of his day, Hooker was at first preoccupied with apologetic against Rome, and only after his controversy with Travers did he make the defence of the Elizabethan ecclesiastical establishment against the Puritans his major concern. Although his Puritan critics, including Travers, regarded him as dangerously sympathetic to the Church of Rome, and traditional interpretation of Hooker has praised his ecumenical outlook, in fact his attitude to Roman Catholicism was only a little more generous than that of most of his Protestant contemporaries. His allegiance to the royal supremacy (the monarch's role as governor of the Church of England) and the doctrine of separate national churches, and his firm conviction that justification* by faith alone is essential to true Christianity, made him view the Roman Catholic doctrines of the papacy* and justification as extremely serious errors. However, without surrendering a fundamentally Protestant* position, Hooker's very independent theological development produced, in the *Polity*, a theology less influenced by continental Reformed theology and more influenced by the fathers and, especially, the medieval scholastics,* than that of any of his Anglican contemporaries.

Hooker's approach to anti-Puritan apologetic in the *Polity* differed from that of other Elizabethan apologists, who debated detailed differences over polity and liturgy* on the basis of a common Calvinist* theological position. Hooker's method was to produce a broad theological structure on which to base his defence of the details of the ecclesiastical establishment. By broadening the whole

discussion and setting the immediate issues of the controversy in the context of a comprehensive theological structure of his own creation, Hooker produced a work of controversy which was also an enduring contribution to the English theological tradition. His theology is not at all representative of the 'Anglican' theology of his day, but later became a major influence on the emergence of a distinctively Anglican theological tradition.

In opposition to what he saw as the Puritans' unbalanced reliance on Scripture alone as a sufficient guide in all religious and ecclesiastical matters, Hooker went back to the scholastic (especially Thomist*) synthesis of reason and revelation,* with its appropriation of both the Aristotelian* and Platonic* philosophical traditions (see Faith and Reason*). On this basis, Hooker created a vision of the universe ordered by reason expressed in law.* All reality is or should be governed by a harmonious structure of rational law, which extends from the eternal law of God's own being, through the natural laws of creation and human reason, and the positive divine law revealed in Scripture, to the human positive laws of church and state. As all being, in its various levels, derives from God, so all law, in its various levels, derives from the rational law of God's being. Thus both Scripture and human reason, expressed in antiquity, tradition and political authority based in implicit consent, belong within a universal and hierarchical rational order. The stress is on harmony rather than conflict, so that reason in the form of tradition and authority may be expected to complement and interpret revelation.

From this structure the profound conservatism of Hooker's thought follows, making his work a massively uncritical defence of the status quo in church and state. An organic, hierarchical, law-governed concept of the universe supports an organic, hierarchical, law-governed concept of human society. The rational nature of hierarchy, law and tradition provides the rational basis for the necessity of obedience to the established order. The harmony of revelation and reason supports the integral harmony of church and state, as coextensive aspects of the one Christian society.

In his defence of the Anglican liturgy against the Puritans, Hooker extols the value of beauty and order in external ceremonies and signs, plays down the necessity for preaching, and gives a central role to the sacraments. Within a general context of the harmony of nature and grace (see Natural Theology*), Hooker's theology is incarnational and sacramental. The sacraments* effect our participation in Christ who is humanity's participation in God.

Hooker had little influence in his lifetime, but during the 17th century, with the growth of an Anglican theology which distanced itself from Calvinism, he attained his position as the Anglican apologist *par excellence.* Especially this was the case after the Restoration (1660), when, with the aid of Izaac Walton's tendentious and unreliable biography, the Restoration bishops promoted Hooker's theology as the quintessence of Anglicanism, while at the same time creating an image of Hooker more in line with the principles of the Restoration Church of England than the historical Hooker was.

To the influence of Hooker, traditional Anglican theology owes much of its reasonable moderation, its sense of the harmony of Scripture and tradition,* faith and reason, grace and nature, church and state, its boast of representing the golden mean between Roman and Protestant extremes, and its social and political conservatism.

Bibliography
Of the Laws of Ecclesiastical Polity, 4 vols. (Folger Library edition, Cambridge, MA, 1977–82); *The Works of Mr Richard Hooker*, ed. J. Keble, 7th ed. rev. by R. W. Church and F. Paget, 3 vols. (Oxford, 1888).

R. Bauckham, 'Hooker, Travers and the Church of Rome in the 1580s', *JEH* 29 (1978), pp. 37–50; W. Speed Hill (ed.), *Studies in Richard Hooker* (Cleveland, OH, 1972); O. Loyer, *L'Anglicanisme de Richard Hooker*, 2 vols. (Lille, 1979).

R.J.B.

HOPE. 'Hope' has two main senses in theology. It can define either the *object* of hope, namely Christ and all that his final coming implies (see Eschatology*), or the *attitude* of hoping. This article deals with the latter.

To hope means to look forward expectantly for God's future activity. The ground of hope is God's past activity in Jesus Christ, who points the way to God's purposes for his creation. Thus the believer looks forward to the resurrection* of God's people and the arrival of God's kingdom,* confident because Jesus has inaugurated the kingdom and has been raised from death. In worship he prays, 'Your kingdom come', and celebrates the Lord's Supper in anticipation of the heavenly banquet, because he looks back to Christ's death and resurrection which open the way to the kingdom (1 Cor. 11:26). In community with others, he experiences the Spirit as a foretaste of the eschatological kingdom (2 Cor. 1:22). Because he expects to be like Christ in the end, he seeks to be like Christ now (1 Jn. 3:2–3). Because he longs for 'a better country' (Heb. 11:13–16), he adopts the attitude of a pilgrim.

But as long as he lives in hope rather than in the fullness of the kingdom, he walks by faith* rather than by sight (2 Cor. 5:7). His life is marked more by suffering* than by triumph (1 Cor. 4:8–13; 2 Cor. 4:7–18).

The Christian is liberated from fear about his own future in order to care about the fear and struggles of others. Hope is not a merely private matter, for the scope of God's kingdom is universal. Hence the broader, socio-political dimension of hope has become prominent in modern theology. The debate has been stimulated by recognition that eschatology is at the heart of Jesus' message, by philosophical interest in the phenomenon of hope as a human experience (*e.g.* Ernst Bloch, *The Principle of Hope*, 3 vols., Oxford, 1986), by the challenge of Marxism* and the cries of oppressed groups (see J. B. Metz,* J. Moltmann,* W. Pannenberg,* Liberation Theology,* Political Theology*).

An eschatological perspective, unlike cyclical views of history,* expects *new* things to happen, and therefore allows the possibility of progress* within history. The future kingdom of God, characterized by justice, peace, community and love, provides the guidelines and motivation for Christian social action (see Missiology,* Righteousness,* Social Ethics*). For if those values are God's ultimate will for human society, they must also be his will for societies now. In committing itself both to the proclamation of the gospel* and to the socio-political struggle for justice and liberation,* the church is 'like an arrow sent out into the world to point to the future' (Moltmann, *Theology of Hope*, p. 328).

But a Christian's hope is not utopian. He expects progress but not the perfection* which will only come by God's own act at the final coming of Christ. He can cope with human failure without despair, because he trusts 'the God of hope' (Rom. 15:13) whose kingdom is surely coming.

Bibliography
C. E. Braaten, *Christ and Counter-Christ* (Philadelphia, 1972); E. Hoffmann, *NIDNTT* II, pp. 238–246; J. Moltmann, *Theology of Hope* (London, 1967); S. H. Travis, *I Believe in the Second Coming of Jesus* (London, 1982).

S.H.T.

HUMANISM emerged as an intellectual movement that developed along with the Renaissance, that rebirth of classical culture which characterized Western Europe in the 15th and 16th centuries. This was a dynamic transitional period of dramatic discoveries, new art forms and critical evaluation of long-held dogmas. In a strict sense humanism began as a reaction to the traditional academic curriculum of the scholastic* period. At its heart was a basic confidence in the power of human intellectual and cultural achievement. Specifically, humanists advocated a new approach to education which was modelled on the form and content of the languages, history, rhetoric, philosophy, poetry and ethics of Graeco-Roman civilization. The rallying cry of these visionaries was *ad fontes*, *i.e.* a return to the sources. By recovering these foundations, the humanists envisaged a cultural, intellectual and sociopolitical revitalization of Europe.

In Italy, where the movement began, the emphasis of humanism was on the pagan classics. Francesco Petrarch (c. 1304–74), and Lorenzo Valla (c. 1406–57), two early humanist luminaries, devoted their energies to the development of literary criticism and its application to newly discovered classical manuscripts. A generation after Valla, Marsilio Ficino (1433–99) and Giovanni Pico della Mirandola (d. 1463–94) sought to harmonize secular philosophy with Christianity.

In northern Europe in the 16th century, an amalgam of evangelical piety and classical scholarship produced a Christian or biblical humanism. As the sources of wisdom were to be found in the words of Greek and Roman philosophers, so the Christian humanist sought the purest truth in a return to the sources of the faith, the Scriptures. These scholars wanted to discard the layers of scholastic interpretation which had accumulated for 400 years, and return to the essence of Christianity. As Erasmus,* the 'prince of humanists', expressed it, theology must be called back to 'the sources and to ancient simplicity'. Two primary foci emerged in achieving this goal: 1. the need for a working knowledge of the biblical languages; and 2. the availability of accurate texts of both testaments.

In their exposition of Scripture, the Christian humanists drew upon the newly developed classical resources of pagan literature and Jewish Hebrew studies. Enchanted by the newly invented process of printing with movable type, many humanists became publishers, such as Robert Estienne (1503–59) and his son Henry (1531–98) and John Froben (c. 1460–1527), whose presses in Paris, Geneva and Basel printed thousands of biblical and secular texts. Others, like Erasmus, edited the works of the early church fathers.

In England, John Colet (c. 1466–1519) greatly promoted a grammatico-historical approach to biblical interpretation. In France, Jacques Lefèvre D'Etaples (c. 1455–1536) published a Latin commentary on the epistles of St Paul and a French translation of the NT. Johannes Reuchlin (1455–1522), a German humanist, pioneered Christian Hebraic studies with his *Rudiments of Hebrew* (1506).

In recent times the term 'humanism' has been loosely applied to any system of thought or philosophy which centres on human achievement, sometimes to the exclusion of any divine reality. Historically, however, there was a definite link between humanism and the Reformation.* Many leading Reformers, including Calvin,* Thomas Cranmer (1489–1556), Melanchthon* and Zwingli,* had humanist training and inclination.

Bibliography
E. H. Harbison, *The Christian Scholar in the Age of the Reformation* (New York, 1956); A. Hyma, *Renaissance to Reformation* (Grand Rapids, MI, 1951); L. Spitz, *The Religious Renaissance of German Humanism* (Cambridge, MA, 1963).

N.P.F.

HUMAN RIGHTS, see RIGHTS, HUMAN.

HUME, DAVID (1711–76). Such is Hume's influence on philosophy in the English-speaking world of our century that he has been described as the founder of modern philosophy of religion.* He himself, in his general philosophy, can be regarded as a radical descendant of Locke,* using and developing the latter's emphasis on the role of sense-experience (see Empiricism*) in knowledge to achieve epistemological* scepticism. Whatever the merits of such a characterization, Hume announced distinctive and independent theses which are still lively – for example, on the mistaken ascription of moral judgments to reason rather than feeling, and on the error of supposing that observation or inference establishes causal connections as matters of empirical fact.

Two aspects of Hume's religious thought have commanded special attention. 1. In the celebrated Book X of the *Enquiry Concerning Human Understanding* (1748) he challenged the reasonableness of belief in miracles.* The probability of their having occurred is less than the probability of false report; therefore one cannot claim a rational basis for belief in them. Hume's definition of miracle, its relation to the laws of nature and his asseverations concerning scientific impossibility tempt one to conclude that he disallowed miracles even in principle. But, especially in the context of the entire *Enquiry*, this verdict has no safe warrant. Investigating the regulative grounds of assent to particular claims suffices to show that miracles cannot constitute the foundation of a credible religion.

2. In the posthumously published *Dialogues Concerning Natural Religion* (1779), Hume challenged the validity of an argument from the world considered as an order to the existence of the one God of traditional Christianity. Not only does the argument fail, but it cannot remotely succeed in demonstrating God's moral attributes as traditionally described. Hume's classic discussion deals with a number of perennially significant issues in philosophical theology,* such as the problem of evil* and the coherence of theism.* However, in the context of the 18th century, demolishing the argument from 'design' in itself constituted a major threat to the grounds of theistic belief.

Some have maintained that Hume, in freeing Christianity from false dependence on ill-conceived ideas of 'rationality', has rendered a service to faith. But certainly there is little direct comfort for the religious believer to be found in his work. He may not have been an atheist, but his whole enterprise jeopardized traditional ways of speaking of or believing in God without providing a positive alternative obviously compatible with Christianity. His tribe, embodying both his spirit and his argumentation, lives on.

Bibliography
Dialogues Concerning Natural Religion, ed. N. K. Smith (Edinburgh, 1947).

R. M. Burns, *The Great Debate About Miracles: from Joseph Glanvill to David Hume* (London, 1981); A. Flew, *Hume's Philosophy of Belief* (London, 1961); J. C. A. Gaskin, *Hume's Philosophy of Religion* (London, 1978); N. K. Smith, *The Philosophy of David Hume* (London, 1941).

S.N.W.

HUS, JOHN (1372/3–1415). Czech reformer and martyr, Hus was a preacher of rare power as well as a scholar and theologian. He held it as a basic truth that Scripture possesses unique authority as the 'law of God'. At the same time he considered the tradition of the church, especially the teaching of the early fathers up to Augustine,* to be a source of doctrine, but with the proviso that it too was subject to the superior authority of the Bible. The same proviso applied to the declarations of church leaders at all times. Even laymen were entitled to challenge such declarations if they were inconsistent with Scripture. For this reason he firmly believed that the Bible should be made available in translation to the public.

This was the basis of his sharp criticism of the abuses of power and wealth by the church in his own day. It was these views, especially as expressed in his impressive book, *De ecclesia (The Church*, 1413) that led to his condemnation and death at the hands of the Council of Constance in 1415. The church in the real sense of the word is the whole company of the elect. This is the mystical body of Christ, whose only head is Jesus Christ. The pope cannot be head of the church in this sense. As an earthly institution, however, the Roman Church is a mixed company, since the 'foreknown' – the non-elect – belong to it. Office in the church does not of itself place anyone among the elect. This Augustinian understanding of the nature of the church implied that even the pope himself as well as the cardinals might belong to the 'foreknown' rather than the elect. Indeed, the stark contrast between the extravagant lives of these men and the poverty of Christ raised deep suspicions about their spiritual status.

The true church is wider than the communion of the Roman Church, and includes all those in the world who confess with Peter that Christ is the Son of the living God. This faith is the rock upon which the true church is founded. Hus understood faith in the Catholic sense as 'faith formed by love accompanied by the virtue of perseverance'.

If the pope emulates Christ's virtuous life, he is Christ's vicar. But his authority is spiritual not civil. It is unfitting that any priest should exercise coercive power and so Hus drew the conclusion that there is no justification for using violence to uproot heresy.

Hus accepted that there were seven sacraments, but called for a firmer emphasis on their spiritual character. Thus, with regard to penance,* he insisted that God alone can forgive sin and that the priest has authority only to declare God's forgiveness in absolution. He adhered to the doctrine of transubstantiation in the eucharist* but insisted that Christ's body is not present in a material way in the elements; it is a sacramental presence.

It is incorrect to think of Hus's teaching as a mere echo of Wyclif's.* He revered his predecessor but was a discriminating user of his books. Hus was a moderate Catholic reformer but is rightly admired by Protestants because in his attitude to biblical authority, his passion for reform and insistence upon Christ's Lordship over the church, he paved the way for the spiritual enlightenment that culminated in the Protestant Reformation.

Bibliography

D. S. Schaff, tr., *John Hus' De Ecclesia* (New York, 1915); D. S. Schaff, *John Huss* (London, 1915); M. Spinka, *John Hus* (Princeton, NJ, 1968).

R.T.J.

HYPER-CALVINISM, an exaggerated or imbalanced type of Reformed theology,* associated with Strict and Particular Baptists of English origin and with Dutch-American Reformed groups. Originating in the 18th century before the Evangelical revival, it has always been the theology of a minority, which today is extremely small. Here are two definitions:

1. It is a system of theology framed to exalt the honour and glory of God and does so by acutely minimizing the moral and spiritual responsibility of sinners. It puts excessive emphasis on acts belonging to God's immanent being (*cf.* Hidden and Revealed God*) – the immanent acts of God – eternal justification, eternal adoption and the eternal covenant of grace. It makes no meaningful distinction between the secret and revealed will of God, thereby deducing the duty of sinners from the secret decrees of God. It emphasizes irresistible grace to such an extent that there appears to be no real need to evangelize; furthermore, Christ may be offered only to the elect (from P. Toon, *The Emergence of Hyper-Calvinism in English Nonconformity, 1689–1765*, London, 1967).

2. It is that school of supralapsarian 'five-point' Calvinism which so stresses the sovereignty of God by over-emphasizing the secret over the revealed will of God and eternity over time, that it minimizes the responsibility of sinners, notably with respect to the denial of the use of the word 'offer' in relation to the preaching of the gospel; thus it undermines the universal duty of sinners to believe savingly in the Lord Jesus with the assurance that Christ actually died for them; and it encourages introspection in the search to know whether or not one is elect (from the unpublished PhD thesis of C. D. Daniel, *Hyper-Calvinism and John Gill*, University of Edinburgh, 1983).

The greatest theologian of this school of thought is John Gill (1697–1771), whose theology is summarized in his *A Body of Doctrinal Divinity* and *A Body of Practical Divinity*, which have been reprinted several times. The most prominent recent theologian is the Dutch-American, Herman Hoeksema, in his *Reformed Dogmatics* (Grand Rapids, MI, 1966). However, the fact that these and similar books present hyper-Calvinism is only obvious to those who are fully acquainted with authentic Calvinism and orthodox Reformed theology.

Bibliography

D. Engelsma, *Hyper-Cavinism and the Call of the Gospel* (Grand Rapids, MI, 1980).

P.T.

HYPOSTASIS, a Gk. noun (plural *hypostaseis*) which became the standard designation in Eastern theology of a 'person' of the divine Trinity. Its nearest Lat. equivalent was *persona*.

Hypostasis had a wide range of non-technical meanings (*cf.* its NT occurrences in 2 Cor. 9:4; 11:17; Heb. 1:3; 3:14; 11:1), but in philosophy and theology it denoted 'being, substantial reality', with reference either to the stuff or substance of which a thing consisted (*cf.* Heb. 1:3) or to its particularity. Against Monarchianism,* Origen* insisted that Father, Son and Spirit were eternally distinct *hypostaseis*. Until the later 4th century (*e.g.* in the Creed of Nicaea of 325), *hypostasis* was used almost interchangeably with *ousia* (see Substance*), but Basil* and his fellow-Cappadocians vindicated its appropriateness to designate the three objective presentations of God, while restricting *ousia* to the single Godhead. This differentiation broadly corresponded to Lat. theology's one *substantia* and three *personae* – which bred confusion, since *substantia* was the etymological equivalent of *hypostasis*, not of *ousia*.

The difference between *hypostasis* and *ousia* is subtle, for both speak of single entities or beings. *Ousia* has more reference to internal essence or nature (God in respect of his God-ness), while *hypostasis* more to the objective, concrete individuality of the three 'persons' (to which a closer Lat. counterpart would be *subsistentia*).

In Christology,* the Council of Chalcedon (451) distinguished between the one *hypostasis* of Christ's incarnate being and the two *physeis*, 'natures' (divine and human), which were united in what Alexandrian* theologians called 'the hypostatic union'. (They had earlier used *physis* almost in the sense of *hypostasis*, for the single being of Christ.) After Chalcedon, debate continued on the integrity of Christ's human nature – whether it lacked a personal centre or focus and was strictly 'non-personal' (*anhypostatos*), as theologians in the mould of Cyril of Alexandria* taught. (Some Antiochene* divines liked to ascribe a *hypostasis* to the human nature.) The one *hypostasis* affirmed by Chalcedon was normally interpreted as that of the divine Word.

A resolution of the difficulty was provided by Leontius of Byzantium (d. *c.* 543), whose life remains obscure, although he was probably a Palestinian monk who spent several years at Constantinople. He wrote against both Nestorians* and Monophysites,* using Aristotelian* categories in a new way in the service of Christological definition. According to the traditional interpretation, his basically Cyrilline teaching declared that Christ's humanity, although *anhypostatos*, was *enhypostatos*, 'in-personal, intrahypostatic', *i.e.* had its personal subsistence in the person of the Logos, while still preserving, as Chalcedon affirmed, its own characteristic properties. God incarnate thus encompassed within himself the perfection of human nature. This notion of *enhypostasia* (a form not found until much later; *enhypostatos* had not earlier been used by Neoplatonists) was developed by Maximus the Confessor* and John of Damascus.*

A recent reinterpretation by D. B. Evans (*Leontius of Byzantium: an Origenist Christology*, Washington, 1970) claims that for Leontius both divine and human natures were enhypostatized, in the *hypostasis* of Jesus Christ which was not that of the Logos. This view (which makes him an Origenist in Christology, indebted to Evagrius Ponticus (346–99), a pioneer writer on monastic spirituality) has found some acceptance (*e.g.* J. Meyendorff, *Christ in Eastern Christian Thought*, New York, ²1975) but much resistance (*e.g.* J. J. Lynch in *TS* 36, 1975, pp. 455–471, and B. Daley in *JTS* n.s. 27, 1976, pp. 333–369).

Bibliography

J. N. D. Kelly, *Early Christian Doctrines* (London, ⁵1977); G. L. Prestige, *God in Patristic Thought* (London, 1959); H. M. Relton, *A Study in Christology* (London, 1917); M. Richard, *Opera Minora*, vol. II (Turnhout and Louvain, 1977), chapters on *hypostasis* and on Leontius.

D.F.W.

I

ICONOCLASTIC CONTROVERSIES.
A series of debates about the place of images* (Gk. *eikones*, icons) in worship which took place in Byzantium between 726 and 843. The first controversy began when the emperor, Leo III (717–41), issued a decree ordering the destruction of pictures in churches (726). His motives may have been partly religious, though they were certainly very mixed, and there is no evidence that the Islamic prohibition of image-worship had any effect on his thinking. Leo's policy was continued by his son Constantine V (741–75), and by Leo IV (775–80), but after Leo's death it was gradually reversed by his widow Irene, acting in the name of her son, Constantine VI (780–97). At the Seventh Ecumenical Council,* held at Nicaea in 787, iconoclasm (*i.e.* the destruction of icons) was condemned and outlawed.

The Council's decisions were strongly supported by the papacy, which had never approved of iconoclasm, but they were rejected by the Frankish Church at the Council of Frankfurt in 794. In 815, during the reign of Leo V (813–20), there was a renewed outbreak of what was now a heresy, which was not finally overcome until 842. The restoration of the images was formally proclaimed at the so-called Triumph of Orthodoxy, on 11 March 843, the first Sunday in Lent. Since that time, this Sunday has been specially commemorated in the Eastern church.

Iconoclasm had great social and political implications, but it was fundamentally a theological controversy. The iconoclasts appealed to the second commandment, and to passages like Jn. 4:24, as evidence to support their belief in a purely spiritual worship of God. Their opponents, the so-called iconodules (Gk. *douleia*, service), accused the iconoclasts of denying the reality of the incarnation.* The great exponent of this view was John of Damascus,* who made the classical distinction between worship paid to God (*latreia*), honour paid to the saints (*douleia*), and veneration given to created objects (*proskynēsis*).

John argued that man was the image of God* (Gn. 1:26), that Christ was the image of the invisible God (Col. 1:15) and that the Christian's destiny was to be re-formed in the image of God's Son (Rom. 8:29). Those who had met Jesus in the flesh had seen God, whether they had recognized that fact or not. To say otherwise was to fall into the heresy of Arius,* who had denied the divinity of Christ.

In the second period of iconoclasm, John's mantle was taken up by a monk of Constantinople, Theodore the Studite (759–826). Theodore argued that an icon was a true representation of the *hypostasis** (*i.e.* person) of its subject, but that it had a different nature (*ousia*; see Substance*). An icon of Christ was thus able to bring the believer into direct contact with his person, but it was not an idol.

Theodore also championed the compulsory veneration of icons, claiming that they were a necessary part of Christian worship. This became the teaching of the Eastern church after 842, but it has never really caught on in the West, even in those churches which use images in worship. It should be noted, however, that the Eastern church does not tolerate statuary in worship, on the grounds that it is idolatrous. This is because the third dimension, which in an icon is believed to be the transcendent divine reality, is contained by statuary within the finite realm.

Bibliography

A. Bryer and J. Herrin (eds.), *Iconoclasm* (Oxford, 1977); E. J. Martin, *A History of the Iconoclastic Controversy* (London, 1930; New York, 1978); L. Ouspensky, *The Theology of the Icon* (London, 1977).

G.L.B.

IDEALISM. As a metaphysical doctrine, idealism is the view that all that really exists are minds and their ideas. Though it is possible to have secular versions of idealism (*e.g.* phenomenalism), its most notable exponent, George Berkeley,* advanced a theistic version, a chief reason for which was to combat the allegedly atheistic consequences of John Locke's* doctrine of material substance, the view that the objects of the external world were substances possessing sets of primary and secondary qualities. If it is allowed that a thought is a mental image, it is possible to give a plausible idealist version of Christian theology, as Berkeley shows and Jonathan Edwards* and others appear to have held, but this can scarcely be regarded as the most natural view. For though God's decree or thought that *x* shall exist or happen, is a necessary and sufficient condition of *x* existing or happening, it does not follow that *x* is itself only an idea in God's mind.

In the philosophies of Kant* and Hegel* idealism is a consequence of Kant's 'Copernican revolution' – his view that the knowing mind contributes to the character of what is known. According to Hegel, reality develops historically in dialectical fashion towards the absolute idea, and the distinction between the knowing subject and a known object is a convenient and conventional one rather than one which corresponds to reality as it is.

The influence of transcendental or absolute idealism upon Christian theology is chiefly through versions of post-Kantian idealism. Denying, with Kant, any possibility of knowing God through either reason or revelation, idealism came to understand the Christian faith in immanent and largely ethical terms. The Christian gospel is not the proclamation of redemption from sin by the self-offering of the God-man but a way of life consisting in observing the ethical teachings of Jesus of Nazareth in an effort to bring about the kingdom of God on earth. This outlook is characteristic of the theology of, *e.g.*, Albrecht Ritschl.*

Idealism became influential in England and the English-speaking world through the writings of S. T. Coleridge* and F. D. Maurice (see Christian Socialism*) in England and the Cairds (Edward, 1835–1908, and his brother John, 1820–98) in Scotland, and is one important source of theological liberalism in Protestantism.

Kant gave prominence to the so-called moral proof of God's existence, but for him morality is severed from divine command, and stress is laid on human autonomy in devising and endorsing the moral law. Put in terms of Christian theology, in Kant's philosophy the creature assumes some of the roles of the creator, giving the world its character, and legislating the moral law.

In a less technical sense 'idealism' concerns the holding and propagating of *ideals*, as opposed to *ideas*. While holding out perfect conformity to the will of God, or to the imitation of Christ,* as ideals, Christian theology has typically cautioned against the thought that such ideals are attained or attainable in this life, regarding this as perfectionism,* which fails to take the effect of indwelling sin, even in the regenerate, with sufficient seriousness.

Bibliography
A. C. Ewing, *Idealism: A Critical Survey* (London, 1969); B. M. G. Reardon, *From Coleridge to Gore* (London, 1971); W. H. Walsh, *Hegelian Ethics* (London, 1969).

P.H.

IDOLATRY, see IMAGES.

IGNATIUS OF LOYOLA (1491–1556) was the founder of the Society of Jesus (Jesuits*). He was a Spaniard. Following his conversion from a military career to a determination to be a soldier of Christ, Ignatius went into retreat at Manresa (1522–23) and his meditations and mystical experiences at that time formed the basis for his *Spiritual Exercises*, which were complete by 1535 and became the major instrument in forming Jesuit spirituality* thereafter. It is in the *Exercises* that Ignatius' spiritual theology comes to clearest expression.

The *Exercises* provide instructions for a month of intensive, supervised retreat, with the object especially of discovering and committing oneself to God's particular will for one's life, or of renewing such a commitment. Following the fundamental meditations on the Kingdom of Christ and the Two Standards, in which the exercitant receives the call of Christ the King to enlist in his service in the battle against Satan, the *Exercises* focus on contemplation of the gospel history of Jesus, through which the exercitant encounters the living Christ and commits himself to discipleship following Christ's way of service to God and victory through the cross. Ignatius' spirituality is primarily one of service through love, in which, out of his realization of Christ's love for him, the Christian always asks, 'What *more* can I do for Christ?'

See also: REFORMATION, CATHOLIC COUNTER-.

Bibliography
H. Rahner, *Ignatius the Theologian* (London, 1968).

R.J.B.

IMAGE OF GOD.

IMAGE OF GOD. Man was created 'in' (= 'as'; the Heb. particle is the *beth essentiae*) the image (*ṣelem*) and likeness (*dᵉmût*) of God (Gn. 1:26–27). 'Image' suggests the idea of a statue or plastic representation (Eichrodt). 'Likeness' qualifies 'image' in two ways: 1. limitation – man is not identical to God; and 2. amplification – man is actually a reflection of God himself, and is to live as his created analogy. Either expression is therefore used to denote the total concept (Gn. 5:1; Jas. 3:9). The theological tradition, probably adumbrated in Irenaeus,* which sharply distinguishes between the two ideas, has no basis in the biblical text.

Specific references to man as the image or likeness of God are infrequent in Scripture (Gn. 1:26–27; 5:1–3; 9:6; 1 Cor. 11:7; Jas. 3:9 of the creation of man; 2 Cor. 4:4; Col. 1:15, *cf.* Heb. 1:3 of Christ; Rom. 8:29; 1 Cor. 15:49; 2 Cor. 3:10; Eph. 4:22–24; Phil. 3:21; Col. 3:10 of the Christian being restored in Christ. But the allegation (*e.g.* by Hermann Gunkel, 1862–1932) that the *imago Dei* plays a far more significant role in systematic theology than in biblical thought must be questioned. While statistically the phrase is infrequent, the interpretation of man which it enshrines is all-pervasive (*cf.* with the above Ps. 8; Rom. 1:18ff.; Phil. 2:5–11).

Interpretations of the image of God

A wide variety of interpretations of the *imago Dei* appears in the history of theology. Among the most noteworthy are:

1. The view of the so-called Anthropomorphites (or Audiani, 4th century) that man is physically the image of God, who is also, therefore, physically embodied. While treating seriously the plastic connotation in 'image', such a view does serious injustice to the anthropomorphic nature of biblical language about God. God is invisible, therefore immaterial.

Nonetheless, creation as a whole gives 'visibility' to the invisible God (Rom. 1:19–20). In this sense, Reformed theologians have argued that even physically man reflects what God is morally, spiritually, invisibly. Calvin* asserts that even in man's body 'some sparks' of God's image glow (*Institutes* I.xv.3; *cf.* also H. Bavinck*).

2. A second approach takes God's being in Trinity* as the prototype, and therefore looks for *vestigia Trinitatis* in man (*cf.* Gn. 1:26,

'Let *us* . . .'). Augustine* says, 'We must find in the soul of man the image of the Creator which is immortally planted in its immortality' (*De Trinitate* 14:4). He identified the 'footsteps' (*vestigia*) in the trinity of man's memory, intelligence and will.

Such a view has several attractions in addition to its Trinitarian foundation. It is consistent with the biblical assumption that the image is not utterly destroyed by the fall (Gn. 9:6; Jas. 3:9). Its weakness lies in the element of dualism inherent in its formulation (the image is located in the rational 'soul'), and its location of the image 'in' man, when Scripture suggests that man *as such* is the divine image.

3. Image has been defined in terms of man's dominion (*cf.* the connection between image and dominion in Gn. 1:26–28). This seems to fit well with other biblical statements (*e.g.* man being said to be God's image in Gn. 9:6 in the 'new creation' context of man's dominion in Gn. 9:1–3; the reflection of man as God's image in the dominion context of Ps. 8; Christ as the New Man, the true *imago Dei* crowned with glory and honour awaiting the consummation of his dominion in Heb. 2:5–9). Its weakness is that in the exegesis of Gn. 1:26 given in 1:27–28, dominion is a *function* of man as God's image, rather than a *definition* of the image itself.

4. The image has been defined in ethical and cognitive terms. God is holy and righteous. Man made in his image is so as well. Calvin, in particular, argued for this position *via* the hermeneutical principle that what was restored by grace (in re-creation) was what was marred by sin (in the fall). Thus, from Eph. 4:24 and Col. 3:10 he read off not only the nature of regeneration, but 'also what is the image of God which Moses speaks of; that is, the rectitude and integrity of the whole soul' (*Commentary*, on Col. 3:10; *cf. Institutes* I.xv.4). The image of God, therefore, consisting of holiness, righteousness and knowledge of the truth is dynamic rather than static in nature.

Reformed theology* recognized that more than this was required in order to express fully the biblical teaching (*cf.* Calvin's belief that not even the body is excluded from the idea of the divine image). Consequently, the image was thought of in a 'broad' and 'narrow' sense. The former denoted man as such, the latter focused on man's faith-relationship with God which was destroyed by the fall.

5. More recently, attention has focused on the societal nature of the image. Thus Brunner* argued that the divine 'us' and 'our' of Gn. 1:26 is reflected in man as the 'them' of Gn. 1:27. The image of God is not the possession of the isolated individual but of man-in-community expressing his 'existence-for-love' by actual 'existence-in-love' (*Dogmatics*, vol. 2, p. 64). Barth* developed this idea in characteristically Christocentric fashion: the image of God is reflected in man-and-woman created as the sign of the hope of the coming Son of Man who is himself the image of God. In the last analysis, for Barth, Christ alone is the image of God. (To suggest that man *in himself* could be, would be to establish in man the 'point of contact' which Barth so strenuously rejected.) While the *imago Dei* has profound relevance for man-and-woman (see below), Barth's teaching suggests that the Bible's 'Last Adam', Jesus Christ, is, in fact, the 'First Adam' (which Barth in fact affirms). Barth's Christocentrism ultimately undermines the historicity of the creation narrative and the significance of the flow of redemptive history.

The image of God in biblical theology

Recent Ancient Near Eastern studies help to throw light on the original significance of the biblical phrase. An image might be either a statue, representing the one imaged, or perhaps the king, adopted as the son of a god. The image expressed the 'presence' of an absent lord in the sphere of his own dominion. In that context the 'image' was to his context what the 'god' was to the entire sphere of his lordship. This suggests that it is man *as man* (not some element in his constitution) which constitutes the divine image.

In a biblical theology, Gn. 1:26–28 may therefore stress certain features of the biblical view of man:

1. Man in his entirety is the viceroy of the earth. He is to be to the earth what Yahweh is to the entire universe. His life is to be a microcosm of the macrocosm of divine life.

2. As such man is the 'son' of the Great King (*cf.* Lk. 3:28). Man is made for filial fellowship with the divine and intended to express the family-likeness in righteousness, holiness and integrity.

3. All men and women (not only kings, or occasionally also priests) are thus created. The doctrine of the image of God is the foundation for human dignity and for the biblical ethic (*cf.* Calvin's use of this idea, *Institutes* III.vii.6).

The image of God in systematic theology

Consequently, the doctrine of the image of God forms the theological groundwork for the Christian's understanding of and response to: ecological concerns (man's dominion is a stewardship* regulated by the sabbath principle given to man as image, *cf.* Gn. 2:1–3; Lv. 23 – 26); humanitarian concerns (all men are viewed in terms of the image of God); sexual* concerns (Scripture radically emphasizes the dignity of women, in that, uniquely, it sees both men and women as made to be royal children of the heavenly Father-King); evangelistic and apologetic concerns (man can never escape from the 'point-of-contact' of his own existence as the image of God, however marred and distorted; further, he is always to be approached in the totality of his humanity); eschatological concerns (in view is the restoration of the whole man, physically as well as spiritually, to the image of God's glory; *cf.* 1 Cor. 15:47–49; 2 Cor. 3:18; Phil. 3:21).

See also: ANTHROPOLOGY.

Bibliography

K. Barth, *CD* III.1, pp. 183–206; G. C. Berkouwer, *Man: The Image of God* (Grand Rapids, MI, 1957); D. Cairns, *The Image of God in Man* (London, 1953); D. J. Clines, 'The Image of God in Man', *TynB* 19 (1968), pp. 53–103; A. A. Hoekema, *Created in God's Image* (Grand Rapids, MI, 1986); M. G. Kline, *Images of the Spirit* (Grand Rapids, MI, 1980); H. D. McDonald, *The Christian View of Man* (London and Westchester, IL, 1981); J. Orr, *God's Image in Man* (London, 1906).

S.B.F.

IMAGES. An image (Lat. *imago;* Gk. *eikōn*) is a likeness of someone or something, most often in another medium, as a statue is a likeness of a great personage, *e.g.* in marble. An image represents and symbolizes, but it is more; it is the similitude of something, reflecting or mirroring it. Man is created in the image of God;* he was made to reflect or mirror the divine nature, but in a creaturely way. The high Christological passage of Col. 1:15–20 declares that Christ is the image of the invisible God, without suggesting that he is anyone less than God himself, although in truly human form. Nevertheless, as God's image, Christ manifests and represents God, reflecting his nature. As Christ said, 'Anyone who has seen me has seen the Father' (Jn. 14:9).

In the Bible and the history of the Christian church, 'image' is closely associated with 'idol' and 'idolatry'. The Ephesians worshipped the goddess Diana, whose image was supposed to have fallen from heaven. The preaching of the gospel, with its message that God is not like anything formed by human contrivance, threatened this worship and provoked a violent reaction from the artisans (who made their living from carving images of Diana) and from the Ephesian populace, who were whipped up into a frenzy in defence of their false worship (Acts 19:23–41). The second commandment clearly forbids idolatry: 'You shall not make for yourself an idol . . . You shall not bow down to them or worship them . . .' (Ex. 20:4–5). We see this commandment more clearly if we examine it in its extended or, better, its root meaning. According to biblical revelation, understanding God and man depends on a proper understanding of the relation of the creator to the creature. God, the creator, is not to be confused with anything that is created. Significantly, the commandment prohibiting idolatry follows upon that prohibiting having any other gods before God's face. Giving anything the worship and service that belong to God alone is idolatry; it is, in effect, serving the creature rather than the creator (Rom. 1:23, 25). Furthermore, God is invisible. He is discerned only through his conscious self-revelation. God is also exalted and holy. He is not to be approached in a commonplace way. Disregarding these truths easily leads to a distortion of true religion in magic, which seeks to gain control over and manipulate divine power. The invisible God is present everywhere in his creation;* nevertheless, he is tangible and approachable only in the ways that he has himself established. 'No-one has ever seen God, but God the only [Son], who is at the Father's side, has made him known' (Jn. 1:18).

Some, e.g. Lutherans and Anglicans, believe that they can avoid imaging God himself while using images of creaturely beings in worship.

Appeal is made particularly to the implications of the visible incarnation* of God in Christ. Thus, in contrast to the complete prohibition of images, as in the Reformed tradition, there has been the use of fully rounded figures of bas-relief icons. A distinction has been made between the worship that is due to God alone and the reverence that may be given to images. In responding to this, one must remember that the invisible God and his power are tangible only as he himself has established. He has given us the only mediator, Christ Jesus* (see Atonement;* Christology*), and the memorials of the sacraments.* Worshippers, made in the image of God, should not seek to capture God or his power in images; rather, they should seek to serve God according to his own revelation of his will in Christ Jesus, thus bringing to expression the image of God within them.

See also: ICONOCLASTIC CONTROVERSIES; IMAGE OF GOD.

Bibliography

O. Barfield, *Saving the Appearance: A Study of Idolatry* (London, 1957); E. Bevan, *Holy Images* (London, 1940); J. Gutmann (ed.), *The Image and the Word: Confrontations in Judaism, Christianity and Islam* (Missoula, MT, 1977); L. Ouspensky, *The Theology of the Icon* (London, 1977).

R.D.K.

IMAGINATION IN THEOLOGY. Imagination has been an orphan in Western philosophy and theology. Plato* disqualified all image-making activity (*eikasia*) as intrinsically deceptive: imaging always pictures what is not really there. Aristotle* credited human imagination (*phantasia*) with the power to remember patterns of sense-images, and believed such memory helped the intellect construct general concepts like 'bravery'.

Early in its history the church debated whether images* had a proper place in worship. Pope Gregory the Great* approved, but Emperor Leo III said not so (edict of AD 726); and Leo's son, Emperor Constantine V (who ruled 741–75), was a vigorous iconoclast,* 'image-breaker', because he believed images in the churches had become idols. The Second Council* of Nicaea (AD 787) settled the dispute with the dogma that only God deserves worship (*latreia*), but images may be venerated (*proskynēsis*) as aids in devotion and in teaching the confessions of the church.

To this day there is confusion about images, icons and idols. *Images* are retinal or remembered pictures of which one is conscious. *Icons* are images legitimated in Eastern Orthodoxy as means of God's grace, like sacraments. *Idols* are images which are no longer channels of praise or worship; they have become makeshift no-gods, like relics, which usurp the attention due only to the Lord.

In his *Critique of Judgment* (1790) Kant* distinguished from the normal imagination which reproduces images for our cognitive activity a productive imaging power which transcends natural affairs and creates aesthetic* ideas. Kant's 'aesthetic ideas' do not provide knowledge, but are good, he believed, for ennobling humanity. Romantic* Idealists* like Coleridge* and Schelling (1775–1854) came to idolize such a transcendental (secondary) imagination as the supreme organ of human knowledge.

Current theologians from various traditions have been tempted to follow the Romantic lead on imagination in order to fight old-style, rationalistic dogmatics. Mennonite Gordon D. Kaufman (*The Theological Imagination*, Philadelphia, 1981) and Roman Catholic David Tracy (*The Analogical Imagination*, New York, 1981), as well as Paul Ricoeur (b. 1913; *The Rule of Metaphor*, Toronto, 1977), believe that human imagination provides a more supple context than strict analysis in which to discuss God and to imagine truly what God wants done today. Imagination then tends to become a gnostic solvent of orthodoxy.

A biblically Christian conception of imagination will distinguish imagining from perceptual error, from imaging and from being an oracle of truth. Imaginative human activity is quite distinct from sensing or thinking but is also a bona fide activity interrelated with all human functioning. Imagining is a gift of God with which humans make-believe things. With imagining ability one pretends and acts 'as if' this is that (*e.g.* God is a rock, Is. 17:10; Christ is a bridegroom, Mt. 25:1–13). Human imagination is the source of metaphorical knowledge and the playfulness so important to anyone's style of life. Imagination is meant to be an elementary, important, residual moment in everything God's adopted children

do. Imagination becomes a curse only if it becomes an exercise in vanity.

Bibliography

M. W. Bundy, *The Theory of Imagination in Classical and Medieval Thought* (Champaign, IL, 1927); J. Coulson, *Religion and Imagination* (Oxford, 1981); R. L. Hart, *Unfinished Man and the Imagination* (Freiburg, 1968); G. D. Kaufman, *The Theological Imagination* (Philadelphia, 1981); J. McIntyre, *Faith, Theology and Imagination* (Edinburgh, 1987); J. P. Mackey (ed.), *Religious Imagination* (Edinburgh, 1986); P. Ricoeur, *The Rule of Metaphor* (Toronto, 1977); C. Seerveld, 'Imaginativity', *FP* 3 (1986–87); D. Tracy, *The Analogical Imagination* (New York, 1981).

C.S.

IMITATION OF CHRIST. The
expression of this ideal of Christian discipleship has varied widely, and its meaning, possibility and validity have often been questioned. Yet whenever discipleship has been taken seriously the ideal has re-emerged, prompting re-examination of its biblical foundation.

The imitation of Christ is implied throughout the gospels and more explicitly taught in the epistles (*cf.* 1 Cor. 11:1; Phil. 2:5; Heb. 12:1–3; 1 Pet. 2:21; 1 Jn. 2:6; 4:7–11). In Christian thought after the NT the theme can be traced from the apostolic fathers* onwards. Sometimes, as with Francis* of Assisi, it appears in literal form; more usually it features in devotion to the humanity of Christ in mystical theology.* It continued in Catholicism after Teresa of Avila (1515–82) as a theme of 17th-century French spirituality and inspired several later reformers and idealists, including Charles de Foucauld (1858–1916) and his heirs, the Little Brothers and Little Sisters of Jesus.

The work of this title normally ascribed to Thomas à Kempis (*i.e.* from Kempen; *c.* 1380–1471) has had enormous appeal. Thomas was reared in the reforming piety of the Brethren of the Common Life, and spent his life in an Augustinian house near Zwolle. The title applies in fact only to the first chapter. The book as a whole is a guide to spiritual communion with God.

In Protestantism Luther's* difficulties with the doctrine have obscured Calvin's* acceptance of it. Luther did not find in the distinctions made in medieval spirituality between active and passive imitations of Christ a proper reflection of biblical teaching on grace* and union with Christ.* Declaring, 'It is not imitation that makes sons, but sonship that makes imitators,' Luther preferred to speak of conformity to Christ. He also emphasized individual Christian vocation* against ideals of any fixed pattern of imitation such as the monastic* life or the literal excesses of the Radical Reformation.*

Despite Luther's influence the ideal surfaced again whenever people like William Law* or Kierkegaard* recalled believers to serious discipleship. Interpretation of the imitation of Christ in 20th-century Protestant theology may be described as the combining of a partial assimilation of Kierkegaard and a reaction against Schleiermacher* and his successors for appearing to stress Christ the example at the expense of Christ the redeemer. This has produced either 1. significant yet unfinished movements towards a fresh understanding (Bonhoeffer*); 2. qualified approval (Barth*); or 3. rejection (Bultmann*).

Much recent NT exegesis has tended to play down imitation of Christ, resolutely interpreting 'imitation' as 'following' and 'obedience' alone (cf. W. Michaelis, 'mimeomai', TDNT IV, pp. 659–674). It may however be asked how much such interpretation has been affected by agnosticism about the historical Jesus or presuppositions about the existential* nature of faith. In Bultmann's case these clearly involve an emphasis on the words rather than the actions of Jesus and a tendency to see Jesus' connection with the believer solely in terms of isolated individual responses to commands. This not only eliminates practice of the virtues in imitation of Christ, it also leaves almost no content to the idea of Christian character, a position unknown in traditional moral theology.* Removal of imitation of Christ from ethics* or its confinement to mystical theology or individual spirituality* is also challenged by contemporary liberation theology.* This maintains that the imitation and following of Jesus should take its place in systematic theology as a source of knowledge in Christology,* for 'It is the real following of Jesus that enables one to understand the reality of Jesus' (J. Sobrino).

Bibliography

W. Bauder, 'Disciple', NIDNTT I, pp. 490–492; M. Griffiths, The Example of Jesus (London, 1985); J. M. Gustafson, Christ and the Moral Life (New York, 1968); E. Malatesta (ed.), Imitating Christ (Wheathampstead, 1974); E. J. Tinsley, The Imitation of God in Christ (London, 1960); R. E. O. White, Biblical Ethics (Exeter, 1979).

P.N.H.

IMMANENCE, see GOD.

IMMORTALITY.

The OT lacks a distinct term for immortality, although Pr. 12:28 has the coinage 'not-death' ('al-māwet): literally, 'In the way of righteousness is (eternal) life; the treading of her path is not-death (= immortality)'. On the relatively few occasions that the OT does express positive hope regarding the hereafter (e.g. Jb. 19:26; Ps. 17:15; 49:15; 73:24; Is. 26:19; 53:10–12; Dn. 12:2, 13), it is couched in terms that imply resurrection,* not immortality.

Three Gk. terms express the idea of immortality in the NT: athanasia, 'deathlessness' (as in 1 Cor. 15:53–54); aphtharsia, 'incorruptibility' (Rom. 2:7); aphthartos, 'incorruptible' (1 Pet. 1:4). Immortality denotes immunity from any kind of decay and death (the negative aspect), that comes from having or sharing the eternal divine life (the positive aspect).

1 Tim 6:16 unequivocally asserts that God alone has immortality (cf. Rom. 1:23; 1 Tim. 1:17). Because he has within himself inexhaustible springs of life and energy (Ps. 36:9; Jn. 5:26; 1 Tim. 6:13), decay and death are foreign to his experience. He is never-dying because he is ever-living (Je. 10:10). But God's immortality implies his inviolable holiness as well as his perpetual life. Just as man is mortal as a sinner (Rom. 5:12), God is immortal as the holy One (1 Tim. 6:16). When Jesus rose from the dead (Rom. 6:9; Rev. 1:18), his immortality was being regained, not first attained.

From the Genesis account it seems that man was not created either immortal or mortal (see Gn. 2:17; 3:22), but with the possibility of becoming either, depending on his responsiveness to God. He was created for immortality rather than with immortality. Such a view coheres with 1 Tim. 6:16. God is inherently immortal, but man is derivatively immortal, receiving immortality as a gracious divine gift (Rom. 2:7). Potentially immortal by nature, man becomes immortal through grace. Thus Paul describes immortality as a future acquisition (1 Cor. 15:52–54), not a present possession, and as a privilege reserved for the righteous (Rom. 2:6–7, 10; 1 Cor. 15:23, 42, 52–54), not the inalienable right of all mankind or a property of the human soul.

Immortality is closely related to eternal life and resurrection. Eternal life is the positive aspect of immortality (that is, sharing the divine life), while immortality is the future aspect of eternal life. Resurrection, or a resurrection transformation in the case of believers alive at the second advent of Christ (1 Cor. 15:51–54), is the means of gaining immortality (Lk. 20:35–36; Acts 13:34–35; 1 Cor. 15:42), while immortality guarantees that the glorious resurrection state is permanent.

Therefore, given Paul's clear teaching that immortality is a divine gift that will be acquired only by the righteous and only through a future resurrection or resurrection transformation, we must conclude that Scripture teaches 'conditional immortality'. It is conditional in the sense that after their resurrection there will be immunity from bodily and spiritual death only for those 'in Christ', but not in the sense that only believers live for ever, unbelievers being annihilated. NT warnings of the eternal consequences of rejecting Christ (Mt. 25:46; 2 Thes. 1:9) make it clear that the first Christians rejected both universalism* and annihilationism.

Plato* argued for the immortality of the soul in its rational or divine function, while Aristotle* reserved divinity and eternality for 'active intellect', the highest operation of the soul. Under Plato's influence the Christian church has always affirmed 'the immortality of the soul' in the sense that the soul of every person has, by divine fiat, an immortal subsistence (for example, the Westminster Confession of Faith XXXII). Although the concept embodied in this phrase is certainly biblical, the expression itself is not found in Scripture, where the terms 'immortal' and 'immortality' are used of believers' future resurrection bodies (1 Cor. 15:52–54), never of their present earthly 'souls', and there is the danger that the human soul be thought of as intrinsically immortal, contrary to 1 Tim. 6:16. According to Scripture, what is immortal is the resurrected believer, and the creator-creature relationship (including both believer and unbeliever).

Christian theologians have defended the soul's immortality (in a Platonic sense of immortal subsistence) on several grounds: 1. being immaterial and indivisible by nature, the soul is independent of the body and indestructible; 2. only a future life can bring to the necessary fruition the capacities and endowments of human nature and can rectify present inequalities and injustices; 3. the instinctive, universal and persistent belief of mankind that there is life after death argues for its reality.

See also: DEATH; ESCHATOLOGY; INTERMEDIATE STATE; RESURRECTION, GENERAL; RESURRECTION OF CHRIST.

Bibliography

J. Baillie, *And the Life Everlasting* (Oxford, 1934); H. C. C. Cavallin, *Life After Death*, part 1 (Lund, 1974); K. Hanhart, *The Intermediate State in the New Testament* (Groningen, 1966); M. J. Harris, *Raised Immortal* (London, 1983); J. H. Leckie, *The World to Come and Final Destiny* (Edinburgh, 1918); C. H. Moore, *Ancient Beliefs in the Immortality of the Soul* (Oxford, 1931); G. W. E. Nickelsburg, Jr., *Resurrection, Immortality and Eternal Life in Intertestamental Judaism* (Oxford, 1972).

M.J.H.

IMPASSIBILITY, see GOD.

INCARNATION. That the gospel writers saw Jesus as thoroughly human is obvious. He is portrayed as a 1st-century Jew undergoing the whole range of physical and emotional experiences common to man. He was born and underwent the normal process of growth and development from infancy to adulthood (Lk. 2:52). He is viewed as the son of David (Mt. 1:6; Lk. 2:4; 3:31) and the son of Adam (Lk. 3:38). He calls himself a man (Jn. 8:40) and speaks of his body and its impending dissolution (Mt. 26:26, 28), continuing to emphasize its reality after his resurrection* (Lk. 24:36–37). He is described as experiencing a full range of human experiences: compassion (Mt. 9:36), love for friends (Jn. 11:35–36), surprise (Mt. 8:10; Mk. 6:6), prayer (Mt. 14:23), agony (Lk. 22:44), thirst (Jn. 19:28), weariness (Jn. 4:6), sleep (Mt. 8:24) and, ultimately, death (Jn. 19:30, *etc.*).

As man, he is seen as limited in his knowledge, needing to learn and develop (Mk. 13:32; Acts 1:7; Heb. 5:8). Public opinion considered him to be a prophet, an outstanding religious teacher certainly, but no more than that. Apart from his sinlessness,* about which the NT writers have no question (Jn. 8:46; 2 Cor. 5:21; Heb. 4:15; 7:26–27; 1 Pet. 1:19; 2:22–23; 1 Jn. 3:5), his identity and solidarity with us is absolute and unqualified.

Yet it became evident to the disciples that Jesus was more than simply a man. His miracles displayed a personal authority over creation (*e.g.* Mt. 8:23–27; 14:22–23 and par.). He claimed the right to forgive sins (*e.g.* Mt. 9:2–8; Mk 2:3–12; Lk. 5:18–26). He pointed to an equality and reciprocity in his relationship with God, calling him Father and himself Son (Mt. 11:25–27; Jn. 5:19–23; 10:14–30; 14:1ff). The resurrection vindicated his claims. Thereafter the NT writers, especially Paul, felt able to employ the title *kyrios*, used of God in ninety-five per cent of its occurrences in the LXX, in reference to Jesus as an index of his status. Thus, in Phil. 2:5–11 Jesus of Nazareth is exalted by God and given the supreme name of *kyrios*, in allusion to Is. 45:23 where Yahweh is the subject (*cf.* also Rom. 10:13; 14:11; 1 Cor. 1:31; 2 Thes. 1:8–9). Correspondingly, a doctrine of pre-existence emerges whereby Jesus Christ is regarded as the creator of the universe as well as saviour of his church (Col. 1:16–17; Heb. 1:1ff., Jn. 1:1–5, 1 Cor. 8:6), and as possessing equality with God (Phil. 2:5–6), having been sent into the world by the Father (Rom. 8:3; Gal. 4:4). He is also the eschatological Son of Man who will come to judge the world (Mt. 25:31–46; *cf.* Jn. 5:27–30; Acts 17:31; 2 Cor. 5:10; 2 Thes. 1:7–10). Consequently, it is hardly surprising that on a number of occasions he is addressed in worship as the subject of a doxology (Rom. 9:5; 2 Pet. 3:18; Rev. 1:5b–6; probably 2 Tim. 4:18), or in a prayer (Acts 7:59–60; 1 Cor. 16:22; 1 Thes. 3:11–12; 2 Thes. 3:5, 16; Rev. 22:20).

The resulting question of Christology* dominated the agenda of the church for centuries. In essence, the problem was to have a twofold dimension. First, how did Christ's equality and identity with God relate to the strict monotheism* of the OT (the problem of the Trinity*)? Secondly, how was the man Jesus of Nazareth simultaneously God and yet one (the problem of the incarnation)? Whatever the parameters and configurations of later debate, these issues emerged from the biblical writings themselves. The salvation promised in the OT was something only God himself could fulfil. The prophets had looked forward to the day when Yahweh was to come in person for the deliverance of his people and the establishment of his kingdom (Is. 11:12; 31:1ff.; Ps. 33:16–17; Ho. 5:13ff.; *cf.* Is. 11:1–10; 25:9–12; 45:16–17; Je. 14:8; Mi. 7:7; Hab. 3:18). Yet it was to be the seed of the woman that would bruise the serpent's head (Gn. 3:15), since only man could ultimately atone for the sin of man. (As many of the fathers were to claim, 'whatever is not assumed cannot be healed'.) The broad background of the doctrine of the incarnation can thus be discerned in principle, if only faintly, in the OT. The crucial covenant promise, 'I will be your God, you shall be my people' would find its most complete fulfilment only in the incarnate Christ.

Hence, the underlying thrust of the biblical witness concerns a movement by God towards man. The Father sends the Son. The Word became flesh. God was in Christ. At root, to save us God came not in his full glory as God but rather as man; as a baby crying in his mother's arms, requiring feeding and changing, and as a condemned criminal on a cross. He hid his glory, he limited himself. Remaining one with and equal to God he took the form of a slave. By becoming one with us, he was able to share our sorrows, bear our burdens, atone for our sins and unite us to God.

See also: KENOTICISM.

Bibliography

Historical: A. Grillmeier, *Christ in Christian Tradition*, vol. 1 (Atlanta, GA, and London, ²1975), vol. 2:1 (Oxford, 1987); J. N. D. Kelly, *Early Christian Doctrines* (London, ⁵1977); J. Pelikan, *The Christian Tradition*, vol. 1 (Chicago, 1971).

Biblical: J. D. G. Dunn, *Christology in the Making* (Philadelphia and London, 1980); M. Hengel, *The Son of God* (London, 1976); S. Kim, *The Origin of Paul's Gospel* (Grand Rapids, MI, 1982); C. F. D. Moule, *The Origin of Christology* (Cambridge, 1977).

Dogmatic: D. M. Baillie, *God Was in Christ* (London and New York, 1948); G. C. Berkouwer, *The Person of Christ* (Grand Rapids,

MI, 1954); A. B. Bruce, *The Humiliation of Christ* (Edinburgh, 1881); C. E. Gunton, *Yesterday and Today* (Grand Rapids, MI, and London, 1983); K. Runia, *The Present-day Christological Debate* (Leicester, 1984); T. F. Torrance, *Space, Time and Incarnation* (Grand Rapids, MI, and London, 1969); D. F. Wells, *The Person of Christ* (Westchester, IL, 1984; Basingstoke, 1985).

R.W.A.L.

INDIAN CHRISTIAN THEOLOGY.
There are three major strands in Indian Christian theology.

1. The dominant strand for many centuries was the reflection of converts from the upper castes of Hinduism,* principally Brahmins. There are no clear landmarks. The early churches in India, which claim to date their existence from the apostle Thomas, were in the Orthodox tradition. They broadly followed the theology of the Eastern Orthodox* churches and made some points in the debates with Rome. But being set in Indian soil made little or no difference to them. They were upper caste in membership and the church was treated as one of the higher castes. This tradition still continues.

In the 17th century the Jesuit Robert De Nobili (1577–1656) attempted in theory and practice to relate the Christian faith to the practice of the Indian caste system. He did not so much reflect theologically on Christianity and the caste system as attempt to come to terms with socio-religious realities.

Christian involvement in India from Western countries between 1600 and 1900 at first developed a largely negative attitude to Indian religions. The concern of Christian theology was to point out the errors and supposed irrationality of Hindu religions.

At the same time Orientalists from the West helped spark a renewal in Hinduism. Hindu leaders sought to encourage the best in their own religion, and some, such as Vivekananda (1862–1902), responded to the impact of Christian mission in India by taking Christ seriously as the revealer of God.

Christian leaders who were all personal converts from the Brahmin upper castes responded to this movement of renewal and reform in Hinduism. This marked the birth of Indian Christian theology. These upper-caste converts were also shaped by the liberal tradition in Western Christianity, which had responded to the Enlightenment* challenge that a supernatural God could not exist by locating God solely in the individual's inner experience. It identified Christianity with personal religious experience.* Indian Christian theologians then searched for parallels in Hindu religious experience in seeking the most adequate terms to express Christian faith. Proponents of this method were Ram Mohan Roy (1772–1833), Brahmabandhab Upadhyaya (1861–1907) and P. Chenchiah (1886–1959).

2. A second major stream related Christian faith to the process of nation-building, in order to identify the role Christians should play in pre-independent and post-independent India. India became independent in 1947. Some leading Indian Christian theologians addressed the social and economic realities that confronted the new state. P. D. Devanandan (1901–62), M. M. Thomas (b. 1916), K. M. George and J. R. Chandran took the lead. They urged Christian commitment to nation-building, and to the ecumenical movement as a pledge and sign of Christian commitment to the unity of mankind. Christians could hardly argue for a united India if their own ranks were rent with division.

Evangelical Christians were slow to respond to these issues. But in the 1970s the formation of the Evangelical Fellowship of India's Committee on Relief and its involvement in both relief and development projects stimulated increasing theological work on the biblical basis of social involvement. Documents like the Madras Declaration on Evangelical Social Action reflect this.

3. A third stream is only now beginning to emerge, in Indian Christian reflection from the context of the poor and the outcast. In previous centuries no theology has been done by converts from the lower castes of Hinduism and from poor people. This is especially striking since over ninety per cent of India's Christians come from this background. The Roman Catholic theologian Sebastian Kappen, though not from this background, has sought to identify with them.

A number of key issues have occupied Indian Christian theologians in the period since 1947. One major issue was how far Christianity was continuous with the experience and even the revelation of other religions. H. Kraemer* insisted that Christianity was totally discontinuous, but M. M. Thomas responded by speaking of a Christ-centred syncretism.* He pointed out that in every society Christianity took over and endorsed some aspects of the life and experience of society in order to communicate its meaning. By its very nature Christianity was syncretistic. The issue was whether this syncretism was centred on Christ. According to Thomas an important way of harnessing all religions for the task of nation-building was the specific focus of humanization. He saw the Christian faith as providing a definite force for humanization and as a dynamic in dialogue with the vertical foci of other faiths pushing them in the direction of new horizontal relationships in concern for humanity.

J. N. Farquhar (1861–1929) had posited Christianity as the crown of Hinduism. Post-independence reflection did not accept this judgment. The most dominant thought came through Raimundo Panikkar (b. 1918) and M. M. Thomas who spoke of the hidden Jesus in Hinduism which found expression in Hindu compassion and justice. S. M. Samartha focused on religious experience* as a way of relating to other religions. He regarded dialogue as a method not of evangelism but of relating in an open-ended pilgrimage where experience of different religions influences pilgrims in their search for truth and true religious experience.

A second major issue was how to witness to the uniqueness* of Christ in an atmosphere of religious universalism and philosophical pluralism. Hinduism finds everything in Christ prefigured in its own religious experience. So how could unique claims be made of Christ? Furthermore, Hinduism, while open to receive insights from all religions, is fundamentally centred on personal experience. It is therefore impossible to make objective judgments, since everyone's religious experience is equally valid. In this context how could someone claim that the experience of salvation through Christ is uniquely valid without appearing arrogant and thus undermining their very claim by their pride?

A third issue is whether it is proper to use Hindu categories to describe Christian faith. In Hindu mythology many gods appeared on earth as men, as *avatars*. Could the incarnation of Jesus be described in these terms? Could Hindu religious language be used for Christian realities without compromising Christian truth?

A fourth issue concerns the socio-economic context of India. How does the gospel contribute to building a united nation out of many fragmented groups? This issue was addressed at the time of independence when the Christians declined an offer by the government to have a certain number of parliamentary seats reserved for Christians elected by Christian constituencies. Their reason was that the Christian goal was not to be one sect among many, but to contribute in every group to the unity of the whole.

In the socio-economic sphere the church is also grappling with how to be a prophetic voice on behalf of the poor. Sixty per cent of India's population live below the poverty line. Should the church work with structures of the establishment, whether government agencies or business interests, to secure its own institutions which were founded to serve the poor but increasingly serve the rich? Or should the church work with action groups in the grass roots of society? Should the church encourage people to discover their identity as the creatures of God with equal rights to the earth's resources by the process of welfare provision or through political protest?

Important thinking has been done in this area by Roman Catholic theologians of the Jesuit Order. The Indian Social Institute, John Desrochers (*Jesus the Liberator*, Bangalore, 1976), Sebastian Kappen (*Jesus and Freedom*, Maryknoll, NY, 1978), Desmond D'Alreo and Stanley Lourduswamy have contributed important perspectives which share much in common with liberation theology* from Latin America.

A fifth issue concerns the relationship between the church's role in the socio-economic spheres and its concern to challenge people to accept Christ. What is the true biblical relationship between social responsibility and evangelism? This issue specially focuses on whether the church should require people to renounce caste on becoming Christian or allow caste-churches to emerge.

A sixth issue is how to express Christian worship and communication in appropriate cultural forms (see Contextualization*). Can Hindu patterns of architecture, dance, worship and prayer express Christian devotion and worship, or does the fact that Hindu spirituality excludes the poorest people make it totally inappropriate? Would an outcaste person feel at home in Hinduized Christian worship? While Western forms of church practice may appear foreign in the Indian context, for many the only alternative to Hindu practices which completely excluded them has been a total break. Such people are now discovering that the Western practices themselves compromise biblical priorities in some aspects and are looking for new models. Important work is being done in this area by the Roman Catholic D.S. Amalorpavadass of the National Biblical Catechetical and Liturgical Centre in Bangalore, and by the Christian Arts and Communication Services in Madras.

In summary, the responses of Indian Christians to the Hindu religious reality have been described in a number of ways: 1. the cosmic Christ includes all the various pluralities of religious experience; 2. Christianity takes shape within a pluralistic environment and so becomes a Christ-centred syncretism; 3. Christ is the unknown force for justice within Hinduism; 4. Christ is the goal of the religious quest of Hinduism; 5. Hinduism is related to Christianity as its OT Scriptures; 6. Christianity is totally discontinuous with Hinduism; 7. the Hindu context produces a particular form of Christian, an Indian Christian; 8. Hinduism must be addressed with the question of the poor and marginalized as the question about religion which Jesus validated.

See also: CHRISTIANITY AND OTHER RELIGIONS; UNIQUENESS OF CHRIST.

Bibliography
R. Boyd, *Indian Christian Theology* (Madras, 1969); V. Samuel and C. Sugden, *The Gospel among our Hindu Neighbours* (Bangalore, 1983); G. Shiri, *Christian Social Witness* (Madras, 1983); M. M. Thomas, *The Acknowledged Christ of the Indian Renaissance* (Madras, 1969); idem, *Man and the Universe of Faiths* (Madras, 1975); *Tr* 2:2 (1985) – issue on Caste and the Church.

C.M.N.S. and V.K.S.

INDULGENCES, see MERIT.

INFALLIBILITY AND INERRANCY OF THE BIBLE.
These words are used by evangelicals to explicate biblical authority. Infallibility signifies the full trustworthiness of a guide that is not deceived and does not deceive. The Westminster Confession (1647) spoke of the Bible's 'infallible truth', the Belgic Confession (1561) called it an 'infallible' rule (see Confessions*), and Wyclif* (1380) named it the 'infallible rule of truth'. Inerrancy signifies the total truthfulness of a source of information that contains no mistakes; the word is 19th-century, but the belief it expresses is as old as Christianity. Clement of Rome (90–100) held that in 'the Holy Scriptures which are given through the Holy Spirit . . . nothing iniquitous or falsified is written', and Augustine* declared: 'I believe most firmly that none of these (canonical) authors has erred in any respect of writing.' Christian belief in the normative authority of Scripture rested from the start on confidence that all Scripture is God's true teaching through the human writers.

When Enlightenment scepticism challenged the trustworthiness of biblical history and theology, new interpretative procedures were devised to midwife God's authority out of material now viewed as uneven and unreliable human tradition. Today only conservatives in Protestantism,* Roman Catholicism* and Orthodoxy (see Eastern Orthodox Theology*) base their faith in biblical authority on acceptance of all Scripture as true, and Protestants see Catholics and Orthodox as imposing misinterpretations on the text at key points. But conservatives unite to deprecate post-Enlightenment* interpretation which, rating the text as less than God's infallible and inerrant instruction, is regularly selective, picking a canon within the canon; impressionistic, disregarding much data when generalizing about the Bible's main thrusts; relativistic-reductionist, diminishing biblical teaching to fit supposedly definitive perceptions drawn from secular culture; and existential-illuminist, constantly drawing from the text challenges that historical exegesis does not warrant while ignoring some that it does. But subjective interpretation of this kind is unavoidable when assertion of biblical authority is wedded to denial of biblical infallibility.

Theologically, as conservatives see it, the authority* of Scripture means its actual functioning as the means of people coming to know God through seeing the sequence of his self-disclosing words and deeds from Eden to the life, death, resurrection and reign of Jesus Christ, and through being taught to respond to this redemptive revelation with belief, worship and obedience. So the less reliability is ascribed to Scripture the less precise becomes its authority, the more pluralistic becomes Christian theology, the smudgier becomes the believer's vision of Christ and the less certain his faith, and the more problematical becomes the wisdom of God as communicator. Denying biblical infallibility thus exchanges manageable problems in the text for unmanageable perplexities in theology and spiritual life.

The warrant for affirming biblical authority as resting on biblical infallibility is the testimony of biblical writers to this principle, and especially the recorded teaching of Jesus. Unquestioning submission to his Bible (our OT) as the creator's word (*cf.* Mt. 19:4–5) which he had come to fulfil (Mt. 5:17, 18–19; 4:1–11; 26:53–56; Lk. 22:37; *cf.* Jn. 10:35) shaped his ministry, leading him to crucifixion in the confidence that resurrection would follow as predicted (Lk. 18:31–33) – as it did (*cf.* Lk. 24:25–27, 46–47). Similar submission to Scripture is required of Jesus' disciples – to the OT plus the NT, the God-given truth of which is guaranteed by apostolic inspiration, just as prophetic inspiration guaranteed the divine truth of the OT (*cf.* Je. 1:6–9; 2 Pet. 1:19–21).

For two millennia the church has celebrated Scripture as the written, life-transforming word of God, which is just the testimony that NT teaching on the Holy Spirit's witness – that is, his presence to convince sin-darkened minds of the divine authority of Christ and the message concerning him – would lead us to expect. Biblical infallibility as undergirding biblical authority is a matter of catholic conviction as well as of dominical instruction.

In this century, evangelical scholars such as James Orr,* Herman Ridderbos (b. 1909) and G. C. Berkouwer,* along with others feeling pressure from biblical criticism, have urged that since biblical infallibility focuses on salvific guidance (showing God in Christ and the path of devotion) historical, geographical and scientific details might be substantially false without infallibility being lost (see Liberal Evangelicalism;* Science and Theology*). But other evangelicals, who recognize the culturally conditioned particularity of biblical teaching and the legitimacy of critical enquiries and are exegetically as accomplished as the first group, censure this proposal as the thin end of a wedge. (What dare one jettison as not mattering theologically? And how, once

one starts, can one avoid eventually treating points of biblical theology and ethics* as faulty?) They urge that full inerrancy must be maintained if infallibility is not to be a nose of wax; that to treat factual statements proceeding from the God of truth as untrue is deeply irreverent; and that only an absolutely trustworthy Bible can serve as a basis for restoring rationality to our radically irrational world. Discussion continues.

Some evangelicals who affirm that Scripture is infallible, never misinforming or misleading us, will not call it inerrant because they think that word tainted by association. They see it as committing its users to: 1. rationalistic apologetics* that seek to base trust in the Bible on proof of its truth rather than on divine testimony to it; 2. a docetic* view of Scripture that obscures its humanity; 3. unscholarly exegesis that lacks semantic soundness and historical precision; 4. unplausible harmonizing, and unscientific guesswork about textual corruption where inconsistencies seem to appear; 5. a theology preoccupied with peripheral details and thus distracted from Christ, who is the Bible's focal centre. Such fears are understandable since professed inerrantists have lapsed in all these ways, especially in North America, and inerrantist scholars today have to disclaim all these pitfalls.

As there is a rationalistic inerrantism that bases belief of the Bible on proving it true, so there is a relativistic non-inerrantism that, by the light of logic, secular learning and critical know-how, claims to find in Scripture errors that do not really matter. Both are theologically objectionable, though both present themselves as sound and orthodox; but each errs by making human reason the arbiter of divine realities. However successfully faith in Scripture is shown to be reasonable and unbelief of it unreasonable, the warrant for actually and habitually believing it remains, objectively, the teaching of Christ and his apostles about its nature and place and, subjectively, the conviction of its divine authority that the Holy Spirit induces. On this twofold basis all Christians should commit themselves comprehensively in advance to trust and submit to all biblical teaching about Christ, salvation, life, world history, and every other topic that the text deals with, and labour constantly to fulfil that commitment as through Spirit-prospered study their grasp of

Scripture grows. It matters less what words they use to articulate the authority of the Bible than that they live under it in this way.

See also: SCRIPTURE.

Bibliography

G. C. Berkouwer, Holy Scripture, tr. and ed. J. B. Rogers (Grand Rapids, MI, 1975); D. A. Carson and J. D. Woodbridge (eds.), Scripture and Truth (Leicester, 1983); idem, Hermeneutics, Authority and Canon (Grand Rapids, MI, and Leicester, 1986); P. D. Feinberg, 'The Meaning of Inerrancy', in N. L. Geisler (ed.), Inerrancy (Grand Rapids, MI, 1979); J. D. Hannah (ed.), Inerrancy and the Church (Chicago, 1984); C. F. H. Henry, God, Revelation and Authority, IV (Waco, TX, 1979); A. Kuyper, Principles of Sacred Theology (Grand Rapids, MI, 1954); C. H. Pinnock, 'Limited Inerrancy: A Critical Appraisal and Constructive Alternative', in John Warwick Montgomery (ed.), God's Inerrant Word: An International Symposium on the Trustworthiness of Scripture (Minneapolis, MN, 1973); idem, The Scripture Principle (San Francisco, CA, 1984); J. B. Rogers and D. K. McKim, The Authority and Interpretation of the Bible. An Historical Approach (San Francisco, CA, 1979); J. D. Woodbridge, Biblical Authority, A Critique of the Rogers/McKim Proposal (Grand Rapids, MI, 1982); E. J. Young, Thy Word is Truth (London, 1963).

J.I.P.

INFALLIBILITY, PAPAL, see PAPACY.

INFANT BAPTISM, see BAPTISM.

INFRALAPSARIANISM, see PREDESTINATION.

INSPIRATION, see SCRIPTURE.

INTERCESSION OF CHRIST, see OFFICES OF CHRIST.

INTERMEDIATE STATE. This expression is not found in the Bible but traditionally refers to the condition of mankind between death and resurrection.* For unbelievers it is a state of anguish and torment in Hades (Lk. 16:23–25, 28; 2 Pet. 2:9) as they await resurrection – and final judgment (Jn. 5:28–29). Since divine judgment is based on an evaluation solely of one's life on earth (Rom. 2:6; 2 Cor. 5:10; 1 Pet. 1:17), the intermediate state affords no second chance to repent and embrace the gospel. For the believer it is a period during which his bodiless soul, in conscious communion with Christ, awaits the receipt of the resurrection body. Alternatively, if believers receive their spiritual bodies at death, there is no hiatus of disembodiment between death and the second advent, and the intermediate state denotes more generally the interval between death and the consummation of all things. In either case the state is both temporary and imperfect (Rev. 6:9–11). The focus of the NT is not on the penultimate, interim state of the believer but on his final destiny, viz. the resurrection state of immortality.*

Although departed believers are no longer active in or conscious of the contemporary earthly world of time and space (cf. Is. 63:16), they are fully alert to their new environment, for they are not only 'resting' from their labours in joyful satisfaction (Heb. 4:10; Rev. 14:13) and safe in God's hands (Lk. 23:46; cf. Acts 7:59), but are (literally) 'in the presence of Christ' (Phil. 1:23; cf. 2 Cor. 5:8), 'live for God's glory' (Lk. 20:38) and 'live spiritually, as God does' (1 Pet. 4:6).

Throughout church history some Christians have held that between death and resurrection the believer's disembodied spirit or 'inner man' is in a state of sleep in Christ's presence (psychopannychism, the doctrine of 'soul sleep'; thus, recently, O. Cullmann, Immortality of the Soul or Resurrection of the Dead?, London, 1958, pp. 48–57). There are several objections to this view.

1. The verb koimasthai, used by Paul nine times and always in reference to the death of Christians, generally means 'fall asleep'. Only in reference to physical sleep need the verb mean 'be asleep'. Christians who die 'fall asleep', in that they cease to have any active relation to the present world. If this common euphemism for the act of dying has any further implications, it is that a resurrection 'awakening' is certain, not that the intermediate state is one of unconsciousness or suspended animation.

2. Immediately after death the Christian is 'with' the Lord (meta, Lk. 23:43; pros, 2 Cor. 5:8; syn, Phil. 1:23), which refers to active inter-personal communion, not impassive spatial juxtaposition.

3. Paul prefers (2 Cor. 5:8) or desires (Phil.

1:23) to depart and be in Christ's presence. He would hardly have viewed unconscious rest with Christ in heaven as 'far better' than conscious communion with Christ on earth.

4. Lk. 16:19–31 suggests that in the intermediate state there is (at least) awareness of circumstance (vv. 23–24), memory of the past (vv. 27–28) and rational thought (v. 30; *cf.* Rev. 6:9–11).

The doctrine of purgatory,* advocated by the Roman Catholic and Greek Orthodox churches, affirms that during the period between death and resurrection the souls of believers who died in a state of ecclesiastical grace but without Christian perfection experience penal and purifying suffering of varying degrees and duration to atone for venial sins and to prepare them for heaven. Claiming to be based on such NT passages as Lk. 12:59; 1 Cor. 3:15; 5:5 and Jude 23, this view ignores the immediacy of the believer's transition at death from residence in the body to residence with the Lord (Lk. 23:43; 2 Cor. 5:6–8; Phil. 1:23) and the blessedness of the departed believer's state (Rev. 14:13), and undermines the sufficiency of Christ's single sacrifice to atone for all sins completely and for ever (Heb 1:3; 9:26; 10:12).

See also: ANTHROPOLOGY; DEATH; PURGATORY; RESURRECTION, GENERAL.

Bibliography

K. Hanhart, *The Intermediate State in the New Testament* (Franeker, 1966); M. J. Harris, *Raised Immortal* (London, 1983); P. Hoffmann, *Die Toten in Christus* (Münster, 1969); P. H. Menoud, *Le Sort des Trépassés* (Neuchâtel, 1966).

M.J.H.

INTERPRETATION, see HERMENEUTICS.

INVOCATION, see EUCHARIST; SAINT.

IRENAEUS (*c.* 130–*c.* 200). A vigorous anti-heretical writer devoted to the biblical faith, Irenaeus, whose lifetime connected the sub-apostolic church to the old Catholic church, was a pivotal figure in the development of Christian theology. Coming from Asia Minor, where he heard Polycarp of Smyrna teach, and becoming a presbyter and then bishop at Lyons, he united Asian and Western theological traditions. Maintaining contacts with Rome, he attempted to mediate in the paschal (see Easter*) and Montanist* controversies in order to preserve the unity of the church, which was so important to his theology.

Irenaeus' *Demonstration of the Apostolic Preaching* elaborates catechetical instruction according to biblical history as the saving plan of God. Following a literal history of the mighty acts of God – beginning with creation and continuing through the events of Genesis, the Mosaic covenant, the taking of the promised land, the sending of the prophets, the coming of Christ, the sending of the apostles, and the general resurrection – the work treats the spiritual sense of Scripture in which OT prophecies are presented as testimonies to Christ's pre-existence, his divine and human nature, his virgin birth, miracles, passion, resurrection and calling a new people through the apostles.

The chief fame of Irenaeus rests on his *Against Heresies*. The first two books expound various Gnostic* systems and offer rational arguments against them. Books 3–5 undertake the refutation of Gnostic teachings from the apostolic writings and words of the Lord. Although primarily a theologian, Irenaeus was knowledgeable about philosophy and employed rhetorical devices in structuring his treatise.

One can interpret Irenaeus as a 'biblical theologian' for his emphasis on Scripture, creation, redemption and resurrection; or one can interpret him as a theologian of the developing Catholic tradition for his arguments from tradition, apostolic succession (see Ministry*), the importance of Rome, and Mary* as the new Eve. Since Scripture and tradition* had the same content for Irenaeus (*i.e.* the gospel), biblical theology* is the substance of his thought. The 'Catholic' elements appear primarily as polemical arguments against the Gnostics and Marcion.* Likewise, the doctrines he emphasizes are those challenged by heretics.

Irenaeus argued for the unity of Scripture as the historical revelation of 'one and the same God' who had initiated different covenants with human beings. Thus the OT is in harmony with the NT, although the law of Moses is now superseded by the gospel of Christ. The historical pattern of revelation was the prophets, Christ and the apostles; but the essential content throughout was Christ.

Whereas the Gnostics interpreted the Bible according to their mythical views of reality, Irenaeus defended the interpretation of the Bible according to the 'canon (rule) of truth'. This consisted of summaries of the apostolic preaching as representing the proper content of Scripture. He argued that the correct understanding of apostolic teaching was preserved in the churches which went back to apostolic times and had personal acquaintance with the apostles (*cf*. E. Molland in *JEH* 1, 1950, pp. 12–28). Contrary to Gnostic claims to a secret tradition handed down from the apostles, Irenaeus insisted that the apostles would have appointed as bishops and presbyters those to whom they would have revealed any secrets. The succession in doctrine and life was transmitted from one holder of the teaching chair in each church to the next (not from ordainer to ordained). The consistency of the teaching in the churches of Irenaeus' day with the apostles' teaching was assured by its public character. Its correctness was further guaranteed by its agreement in each locality.

Irenaeus contributed to the explanation of the Trinity* the image of God's Word and Wisdom (Christ and the Holy Spirit) as the 'two hands of God'. The image expressed God's direct action in creation and revelation. The one God created all things out of nothing. God's providence exists alongside human free will. Adam was created as a child and so was easily deceived into sin.

The fully divine Son of God became Son of Man for human salvation. The incarnation through the virgin birth involved his assuming real flesh and retracing the steps of humanity in order to bring humanity to perfection in himself (recapitulation). His contact with every circumstance of human experience sanctified all ages and conditions of life. Christ's perfect obedience reversed the effects of the first Adam's disobedience, the blood of his death bringing forgiveness of sins and his resurrection a triumph over death, and so the devil was defeated.

Baptism brings regeneration and the gift of the Holy Spirit. The addition of the Holy Spirit to the human person, consisting of body and soul, restores the likeness of God lost in the first transgression. Salvation is progressively realized, a process to be completed only in the end-time. As the Spirit becomes accustomed to dwell in the flesh, so the person grows in the fullness of salvation, leading to communion with God and participation in immortality. The availability of grace to all, and the human freedom to respond to grace were important to his argument against Gnosticism.

The human creature in its wholeness, including the flesh, is saved. Thus Irenaeus' eschatology includes an earthly kingdom of the Lord at his second coming, a renewed material world and a literal resurrection of the flesh. The millennial* kingdom is the last stage of preparation for the ultimate perfection of the vision of God.*

The eucharistic* elements of bread and wine, by receiving the invocation of God, come to consist of two realities, one earthly and one heavenly. The human bodies nourished by the body and blood of the Christ become capable of the resurrection and eternal life.

The church* contains the deposit of truth, and in the church the Holy Spirit is found. The presbyters, including bishops, when they succeed to their teaching chairs, receive the apostolic teaching (the deposit of truth) to transmit to others. The church at Rome, as founded by Peter and Paul, was especially important to Irenaeus as preserving the apostolic tradition (see Papacy*). In a passage which has been given many interpretations (*Against Heresies* III.3.2) Irenaeus seems to say that all must agree with the church at Rome. Rome was a model of sound doctrine, and the agreement must be primarily with that sound doctrine preserved at Rome and secondarily with the church there as exemplary of the apostolic teaching (*cf*. J. F. McCue in *TS* 25, 1964, pp. 161–196).

Bibliography

A. Benoit, *Saint Irénée: Introduction à l'étude de sa théologie* (Paris, 1960); R. Berthouzoz, *Liberté et grâce suivant la théologie d'Irénée de Lyon* (Paris, 1980); D. Farkasfalvy, 'Theology of Scripture in Irenaeus', *RBén* 78 (1968), pp. 319–333; R. M. Grant, 'Irenaeus and Hellenistic Culture', *HTR* 42 (1949), pp. 41–51; J. Lawson, *The Biblical Theology of Saint Irenaeus* (London, 1948); J. T. Nielsen, *Adam and Christ in the Theology of Irenaeus of Lyons* (Assen, 1968); W. R. Schoedel, 'Theological Method in Irenaeus', *JTS* 35 (1984), pp. 31–49; J. P. Smith, *St Irenaeus: Proof of the Apostolic Preaching* (London, 1952); G. Vallee,

'Theological and Non-Theological Motives in Irenaeus's Refutation of the Gnostics' in E. P. Sanders (ed.), *Jewish and Christian Self-Definition*, vol. 1 (Philadelphia, 1980), pp. 174–185; G.Wingren, *Man and the Incarnation: A Study in the Biblical Theology of Irenaeus* (Philadelphia, 1959).

E.F.

IRVING, EDWARD (1792–1834), was born at Haddington, and after graduating from Edinburgh University in 1809, spent the next ten years teaching at Haddington and at Kirkcaldy. While at Kirkcaldy he became firm friends with Thomas Carlyle (1795–1881), who had also come there to teach. In 1815 Irving was licensed to preach in the Church of Scotland, and in 1819 he became assistant in Glasgow to Thomas Chalmers,* the leading Scottish evangelical of the day.

Irving was a man of considerable gifts, and when the opportunity came to become minister of the Caledonian Church in London he readily accepted. He soon became the most heralded preacher of his day, and many of the great names of London society flocked to hear him. His popularity was such that a new and more spacious building had to be built to accommodate the vast congregation. By this time, 1827, he had married Isabella Martin, despite his attraction to Jane Welsh, who was later to marry Carlyle.

Partly due to the influence of Coleridge,* whom he had come to admire, Irving became increasingly prophetic and apocalyptic in his preaching. Chalmers for one began to fear 'lest his prophecies and the excessive length and weariness of his services may not unship him altogether'. When Irving came to Scotland in 1828 to lecture on the coming of Christ, Chalmers thought him incoherent and 'woeful'.

Two events thrust Irving even more into the ecclesiastical limelight. From about 1828 he began to maintain the sinful nature of Christ's flesh (*cf.* too Campbell, J. Mcleod*). In his preaching and in his published writings he argued that the sinlessness* and incorruption of Christ's flesh was due not to 'its proper nature' but to the indwelling of the Holy Spirit. Such teaching exposed him to the charge of heresy, and in 1833 he was deprived of his ministerial status by the presbytery of Annan. The uproar over his views on the humanity of Christ was more than matched by that over his teaching that the 'Pentecostal gifts' (see Gifts of the Spirit*) had been restored to the church. He had been greatly influenced by one of his assistants, A. J. Scott (1805–66), who convinced him that the supernatural gifts the church had possessed in apostolic times would be restored to it. In 1831, one of Irving's church members spoke in tongues. The trustees of the church pleaded with Irving to stop the tongues-speaking. When he refused, they appealed to the presbytery of London, and he found himself locked out of the church. Undeterred, he developed his doctrine of the baptism* in the Holy Spirit, 'whose standing sign, if we err not', he maintained, 'is the speaking with tongues'. His followers reconstituted themselves as the '(Holy) Catholic Apostolic Church', and he was appointed the 'Angel' of the church. He soon became somewhat dominated by those in the church who possessed the 'gifts', as he himself never spoke in tongues. His health rapidly declined, and he died in Glasgow in December 1834.

Irving is best known for his teaching on the Pentecostal gifts (although his views on Christ's sinful humanity have attracted increasing interest of late). Two recent commentators have described him as 'the first Reformed Pentecostal theologian', and 'the forerunner of the charismatic movement'. Gordon Strachan's sympathetic study of Irving's theology accuses Irving's critics of tackling him at the purely psychological level. He argues that the manifestations of the gifts in his church 'were occasioned not by the overflow of powerful religious feeling but by faithful response to the systematic study and preaching of the Word of God'. Strachan is perhaps too generous to Irving's method of preaching, but the whole story cannot be dismissed as 'a curious instance of religious delusion'.

Bibliography

A. Dallimore, *The Life of Edward Irving* (Edinburgh, 1983); M. O. W. Oliphant, *The Life of Edward Irving* (London, 1862); C. G. Strachan, *The Pentecostal Theology of Edward Irving* (London, 1973); B. B. Warfield, *Counterfeit Miracles* (1918; Grand Rapids, MI, 1972); H. C. Whitley, *Blinded Eagle. An Introduction to the Life and Teaching of Edward Irving* (London, 1955).

I.Ha.

ISLAM AND CHRISTIANITY. Islam alone among the great world religions (apart from Judaism) has had continuous and wide-ranging contact with Christianity throughout its history. Arabia, the cradle of Islam, was surrounded by Christian countries and civilizations. On the one hand were Syria, Egypt and Palestine (all part of the Eastern Roman Empire), and on the other, Ethiopia and her colonies (such as the Yemen). Muhammad (c. 570–632), the founding Prophet of Islam, had early contact with both groups. Within Arabia too there were Arab Christian tribes and settled communities with which Muslims had regular contact.

The Qur'an addresses itself to Christians. While recognizing particular qualities such as humility (5:85) and a degree of commonality (2:136; 29:46), it criticizes certain basic Christian beliefs including the divine sonship of Jesus Christ* (see Christology*) and the doctrine of the Trinity.* It is, however, possible that at least certain Qur'anic criticisms are based on misunderstandings of the Christian position. On the Christian side apologists of the stature of John of Damascus* and later Timothy of Baghdad (8th–9th centuries AD) engaged theologically with Islam. By this time Islam had established its hegemony over nearly the whole of the Middle East and Christians there (along with Jews and others) became a subject people. As such they were divided into *Millats* (or communities) which corresponded to the different Christian sects (Melkite, Jacobite or Nestorian*). Such communities retained a certain amount of autonomy and are still the basis for the social and political organization of Christians in the Middle East today. Christians in the Middle East have always been a cultured and learned community and they have made a tremendously significant contribution towards the development of classical Islamic civilization. Christians transmitted classical Hellenistic learning (particularly science, medicine and philosophy) to the Muslim Arabs. This learning was then brought to Western Europe through Muslim Spain (see further: R. Walzer, *Greek into Arabic*, Oxford, 1962; D. L. E. O'Leary, *How Greek Science Passed to the Arabs*, London, 1949).

The Crusades brought Islam into prolonged and painful contact with Western Christendom and many of the images of Christianity in the Muslim mind date from this period. Even during this period, however, there were Western Christians such as Raymond Lull* and Francis* of Assisi who advocated a peaceful approach to Islam.

The colonial period and the advent of the Western missionary movement have brought increased Christian-Muslim contact and, even more significant, the establishment of new churches in Muslim lands for the first time since the rise of Islam. Although Christians are a small minority over-all in the Muslim world, they are a significant minority and often make a contribution out of all proportion to their number.

Doctrinal issues which remain outstanding between Islam and Christianity include the following four theological points.

1. *The Islamic rejection of the doctrine of original sin.** Muslims generally believe that human beings are born innocent but weak. Their weakness generally leads them to sin, though prophets are believed to be sinless throughout their lives. Although most human beings are regarded as able to sin, there is no general belief in the human disposition to sin. Some traditions about the Prophet of Islam, however, record his teaching that all children (with the exception of Jesus and Mary) have been touched by the devil at birth (see further: A. J. Wenswick, *The Muslim Creed*, London, 1965, p. 137).

2. *The rejection of the doctrine of the atonement.** Although atonement is rejected in the Qur'an (6:164) the Prophet is widely regarded as an intercessor who turns away divine wrath. Also, there are hints in the Qur'an that the Prophet was aware of the notion of substitutionary sacrifice (37:107). Orthodox Muslims usually hold that the Qur'an denies the death of Christ, teaching that he was raised bodily to heaven at the time of his arrest. The Qur'anic evidence is more ambiguous, however, and there seems to be mention of Christ's death, physical resurrection and ascension into heaven (3:54–44; 4:157f.; 19:33; *etc.*). It is difficult to say what content the Qur'an actually gives to these references to events in the life of Jesus.

3. *The integrity of the Christian Scriptures.* Muslims often claim that the Jews and the Christians have altered their Scriptures and that this accounts for the disagreement between the Bible and the Qur'an, but some commentators hold only that Jews and Christians have falsified the true interpretation of

343

the text. The question of the reliability of the Scriptures is thus raised at an early point in Christian-Muslim encounter.

4. *The nature and authenticity of Muhammad's religious experience.* This is also a controversial area. Whatever is said of it, however, it has to be acknowledged that he is the founder of a major civilization which has had a profound impact on the history of our world.

In the socio-political area outstanding issues are the applicability of Shar'iah (Islamic law) to non-Muslims, the relation of the human rights movement to societies where the Shar'iah penal laws are being enforced, and the rights of women in Islamic societies. An interesting area for further discussion is the relation between the rights of religious minorities in Western countries and those of such minorities in Islamic lands. The nature and scope of social and economic justice are also subjects which are often discussed in Muslim-Christian dialogue.

Muslims believe that they have a serious obligation to conduct Da'wah (invitation) to Islam. It is important for Christians to explain that they too have an obligation to share the good news of Jesus Christ, his person, work and teaching, with everyone including Muslims. In the work of commending the gospel to Muslims, the Christian apologist to Islam needs to call upon a wide spectrum of theological scholarship. He needs to take account of critical research on Scripture as his Muslim interlocutor is quite likely to be aware of it; he needs to express the doctrines of the Trinity, the incarnation and the atonement in ways which are both faithful to Scripture and Christian tradition as well as comprehensible to a Muslim; he needs to be aware of contemporary social issues and the distinctive Christian response to them as well as the whole range of responses which may be found in the Muslim world. It is only by taking the Muslim and his situation seriously that we shall be able to commend the gospel effectively.

Bibliography

A. S. Atiya, *A History of Eastern Christianity* (London, 1968); R. Bell, *The Origin of Islam in its Christian Environment* (London, 1926); D. Brown and G. Huelin, *Christianity and Islam Series*, 5 vols. (London, 1967–68); K. Cragg, *Muhammad and the Christian: A Question of Response* (London, 1984); W. Young, *Patriarch, Shah and Caliph* (Rawalpindi, 1974); M. J. Nazir-Ali, *Islam: A Christian Perspective* (Exeter, 1983).

M.J.N.-A.

ISRAEL. Israel's coming into being has to be seen against the background of the opening chapters of Scripture. God's purposes for the world are frustrated by humanity's rebellion, and the world sits under his curse instead of his blessing. He begins again by reaffirming his creation promises to a particular family who in time become 'Israel'. Israel is thus that people through whom God's purpose to bless the world is to be fulfilled; this significance of Israel is reaffirmed at various points in the OT (*e.g.* Is. 2:1–4), and is the theological context in which the OT's preoccupation with the destiny of Israel has to be seen, even where the focus seems to be on Israel for her own sake.

As this story of Israel unfolds, various facets of what it means to be the people of God emerge. In the patriarchal period, she is a family, brought into existence by God's sovereignty, power and grace; a people on the way, living between promise and fulfilment; a brotherhood in which conflict is overcome by reconciliation. From Moses to the judges, she is a theocratic* nation, directly led by him, committed to a life of detailed obedience to his will, with human leadership structures not allowed to obscure his kingship; she experiences and in her life testifies to the blessing that comes to the people that is dependent on nothing but God's promises. From Saul to the exile she is an institutional state, rejecting the kingship of Yahweh for human kingship, yet continuing to prove the grace of God, now as the one who condescends to carve out for his people an alternative way if she will not have his highest one; she is open to learn from the world as well as to attract the world, but easily finds that the style of the nations becomes the style of the people of God. With the exile, she becomes an afflicted remnant, her waywardness proving that God's ultimate purpose cannot be fulfilled even through her, yet her affliction also becoming the context of the insight that God can turn the affliction that comes from confronting the world into the means of bridging the gulf between the world and God. After the relative disappointment of the return from exile, she has to be a people that lives in the present dedicated to the praise of God for what he has done in the past, yet also to hope in him for what he is yet to do in the future.

When Jesus* comes, it is to restore and renew Israel, but he is rejected as Messiah. He declares that Israel has forfeited her place as the people of God. God will exercise his capacity to raise up new children for Abraham from the nations (Mt. 21:33 – 22:10). Paul speaks in similar terms (Phil. 3:2–3; 1 Thes. 2:14b–16). The early Christians thus see themselves as heirs of Israel's position as God's people (Phil. 3:3; 1 Pet. 2:9–10).

It might seem that the NT is thereby declaring that God has cast off Israel as such. Yet within OT times prophets have already spoken as radically as if Israel was now cast off (Is. 5:1–7 lies behind Mt. 21:33–44; see also Am. 9:7); yet this was evidently not a final rejection. Furthermore, other NT material presents another perspective. The matter is most systematically treated in Rom. 9 – 11. Here Paul assumes that, though the bulk of contemporary Israel have forfeited their place in Israel, God has not cast off Israel herself. How could he do so without being unfaithful to himself (11:29)? On the contrary, God will restore her; she will come to faith in Jesus as Messiah. 'All Israel will be saved' (11:26; as is the case each time 'Israel' appears in these chapters, the reference must be to Israel herself, not to the church). The rejection that comes through Israel's response to Jesus and to the preaching of the gospel is only a rejection of that generation, such as had happened in OT times. It has a place within God's purpose, to turn attention to preaching to the Gentiles, who share with Jews (they do not replace them) in the blessings of the gospel in the context of membership of the renewed Israel. In keeping with his teaching in Rom. 9 – 11, Paul prays for God's mercy on 'the Israel of God' in Gal. 6:16 (cf. AV(KJV), NEB, GNB; it is less likely that here 'the Israel of God' is a term for the church [so RSV, NIV] – the church is not elsewhere described as 'Israel' or 'the new Israel' in the NT).

In contemporary discussion, the question of the theological significance of Israel arises in two further contexts. The first is that of the theological significance of Judaism.* In the context of Jewish-Christian dialogue, some Christians, repenting of the history of Christian attitudes to the Jews as wholly cast off by God for crucifying the Messiah, have explored the possibility of Judaism and Christianity being alternative ways of salvation, both being the result of covenant* relationships entered into by God with different groups. This is difficult to reconcile with Paul's handling of the issue in Rom. 9 – 11. God's faithfulness to Israel on the basis of the commitment he made to her under the old covenant does not mean that the new covenant need not apply to her. The argument of Rom. 9 – 11 works the opposite way: it is that commitment which guarantees that the new covenant also belongs to her and that she will come to Jesus to find the forgiveness that she, like the Gentile world, needs.

The second is the question of the theological significance of the return of some Jews to Palestine and of the establishment of the modern state of Israel. It is hard not to see this return as a sign of God's further fulfilment of his promises to Israel. Yet this affirmation needs to avoid implying that the Arab peoples (many of them Christians) are outside God's direct concern, avoid forgetting that it is the worldwide Jewish people, not just those Jews who live in Palestine, who constitute the 'physical' Israel, and avoid inferring that Christians (perhaps salving their consciences for attitudes to Jews in the past) should offer unequivocal support for the policies of the modern state of Israel, which arguably has no particular theological significance.

See also: JERUSALEM.

Bibliography

K. Barth, CD II. 2, pp. 195–305; C. E. B. Cranfield, *The Epistle to the Romans*, vol. 2 (Edinburgh, 1979); J. Goldingay, 'The Christian Church and Israel', *Theological Renewal* 23 (1983), pp. 4–19; idem, *Theological Diversity and the Authority of the Old Testament* (Grand Rapids, MI, 1987); P. Richardson, *Israel in the Apostolic Church* (London, 1969); D. W. Torrance (ed.), *The Witness of the Jews to God* (Edinburgh, 1982).

J.G.

J

JANSENISM, see AUGUSTINIANISM.

JASPERS, KARL, see EXISTENTIALISM.

JEROME (*c.* 347–420) was baptized as a young man into the church at Rome. He retained a lifelong attachment to the Roman church, though he spent his last years in the East.

Early on, Jerome attempted to lead a solitary, monastic life in the desert, but found the isolation uncongenial. He remained, however, a keen exponent of the ideals of virginity and a modified asceticism.* Through this and his reputation as a biblical scholar Jerome won the admiration of a group of pious aristocratic Roman women to whom he acted as teacher and counsellor.

Jerome's greatest achievement lay in biblical translation. A vigorous advocate of reference to the original languages, he completely revamped current Latin translations. The fruit of this work was the Vulgate. Jerome's attempts, however, to restrict the OT canon to what was written in Hebrew (see Scripture*) met with no response until the Reformation.*

Alongside this, Jerome embarked on a series of commentaries, particularly on OT prophets. These contain invaluable comments on philological and topographical matters, but rarely give much theological insight. Nor did Jerome contribute significantly to contemporary theological debates, to which he invariably brought an acrimonious taste. His anti-Origenism seems to have been determined more by personal circumstances than by considered theological reflection, since in his early days he had greatly admired Origen's* vast scholarship. A similar verdict applies to Jerome's anti-Pelagianism,* for Jerome does not reveal much understanding of the theological issues at stake.

Bibliography

J. N. D. Kelly, *Jerome* (London, 1975).

G.A.K.

JESUIT THEOLOGY. Among the 'Rules for Thinking with the Church' which Ignatius Loyola,* the founder of the Jesuits, added to his *Spiritual Exercises* after encountering Protestantism at Paris, is the injunction 'to praise both positive and scholastic* theology'. 'The positive doctors' such as Augustine,* Jerome* and Gregory the Great* promote the love and service of God, and 'the scholastic

doctors' such as Thomas Aquinas,* Bonaventura* and Peter Lombard* 'define and explain for our times the things necessary for eternal salvation, and refute and expose all errors and fallacies'. Ignatius' *Constitutions* (finalized 1550–51) name Aristotle* as the Jesuits' authority in philosophy and Thomas in scholastic doctrine. Their adoption of Thomas, confirmed by the order's *Ratio Studiorum (Scheme of Study)* in 1598, helped to make him Catholicism's dominant theologian, displacing Peter Lombard. On certain topics Thomas' opinions were declared to be not binding. In particular, the minority (Scotist*) belief in Mary's* immaculate conception was espoused by the Jesuits, who subsequently proved ardent Mariologists. The early generals of the order, especially Claudius Aquaviva (1543–1615), were concerned to ensure 'solidity and uniformity of doctrine' in its varied teaching activities.

Although Ignatius had declared that 'the scholastic doctors, being of more recent date, . . . have a clearer understanding of the Holy Scripture and of the teachings of the positive and holy doctors', the Jesuits' polemical engagement with Protestantism* and later Jansenism (see Augustinianism*) demanded increasing attention to the branches of 'positive' theology, especially the Bible, the fathers and church history. The Dutchman Peter Canisius (1521–97) produced a widely used *Catechism (Summa Doctrinae Christianae,* 1554) and worked tirelessly against Protestantism in Germany and beyond, but the prolific and learned Bellarmine* was the Jesuits' supreme anti-Protestant controversialist. They had powerful centres of study at Louvain, Paris (Collège de Clermont), Cologne, Ingolstadt, Würzburg, Vienna, Prague, Alcala, Valladolid, Cracow and elsewhere, and their ranks included a remarkable number of weighty theologians and scholars, such as Francisco de Toledo (1532–96, scholastic), Jakob Gretser (1562–1625, historical-patristic controversialist), Peter de Fonseca (1528–99, 'the Portuguese Aristotle'), and Leonhard Lessius (1554–1623, dogmatic and moral theologian).

Ignatius' 'Rules' had warned against detracting from free will and good works by speaking too much of predestination and faith. From 1613, by a decree of Aquaviva, the Jesuits' official teaching on grace* became what was known as 'Molinism', from the Spaniard Luis de Molina (1535–1600). His *Concordia . . .* (*Harmony of Free Will with the Gifts of Grace*, 1588) taught that the efficacy of grace lay not 'intrinsically' in the gift itself but in the divinely foreknown co-operation with it of human free will. Efficacious grace, distinguished from sufficient grace, was defined as the grace to which a person consents. Francisco de Suarez (1548–1617), perhaps the greatest of Jesuit theologians, spoke of this as 'congruism'. God bestows *gratia congrua*, *i.e.* grace 'congruent' with its profitable use by the recipients, which is foreknown by God's special knowledge (*scientia media*). This obviously anti-Protestant position provoked a sharp dispute with the Dominicans,* who were more faithful Thomists in following Augustine on the primacy of (irresistible) grace. A special congregation at Rome (*De Auxiliis*, 1597–1607) ended with toleration of both viewpoints, but subsequently the Jesuit one has more generally prevailed in the Roman church.

In the mid-17th century the Jansenists accused the Jesuits of Pelagianism* and Semi-Pelagianism.* Jesuits were to the fore in the campaigns against Jansenism. The French patristic experts, Denis Petau (Petavius, 1583–1652) and Jean Garnier (1612–81), contested Jansenist interpretations of Augustine and the Pelagian movements. About a century earlier the teaching of Michel Baius of Louvain (1513–89) represented in effect an anticipation of Jansenism, and was condemned by Jesuits like Bellarmine and Lessius.

Jansenists also criticized the Jesuits' zeal for papal* supremacy, which went back to Ignatius himself. Two of his original associates, Diego Lainez (1512–65) and Alonzo Salmeron (1515–85), contributed effectively to the Council of Trent as (anti-conciliarist) 'theologians of the pope'. Canisius was also active at Trent. Lainez insisted that bishops possessed their power of jurisdiction immediately from the pope, not from Christ. Later Jesuits were forceful in preparing for the definition of papal infallibility at Vatican I (1870). They were essentially ultramontane and anti-Gallican theologians. Early Jesuits also accorded to the pope an 'extraordinary and indirect' power in the temporal realm. This belief was an element in the justification of lawful rebellion and tyrannicide advanced by Juan de Mariana (1536–1623), Bellarmine, Suarez and other Jesuits (along lines similar to contemporary Calvinists). Such political theology brought damaging accusations of sedition upon Jesuits in England and France in particular.

Jesuits also developed ascetic* theology and spirituality, based on Ignatius' *Spiritual Exercises*. In India and the Far East Jesuit missionary pioneers like Matteo Ricci (1552–1610) and Robert de Nobili (1577–1656) were adventurous in the theology as well as the practice of mission. Jesuit moral theology* has given too great a place to casuistry,* and has earned the order a degree of notoriety. Its stress on 'responsibility' meant that one could not culpably sin without knowledge of what one was doing, and hence 'good faith' was always a valid excuse. Its 'probabilism', developed by Suarez and others and condemned by the Jansenists as 'laxism', in effect removed a moral obligation as soon as any serious doubt arose on informed and conscientious reflection. It was based on the principle that, in any doubtful case, it was lawful to follow a merely probable course of action contrary to the established norm, even if a more probable opinion favoured the norm itself. The system was subject to extended controversy in Catholic moral theology.

The golden age of the Society of Jesus was its first century, when it was a major factor in the reinvigoration of post-Reformation Catholicism (see Reformation, Catholic Counter-*). Although a prey to controversies, and suppressed by Rome from 1773 to 1814, it remained a bastion of scholastic orthodoxy and fidelity to the papacy. As recently as 1916 the general of the order promulgated an instruction *On Increasing Devotion to the Teaching of St Thomas in the Society*. Although a few years earlier George Tyrrell (1861–1909) had been expelled from the order for his Catholic modernism,* it was not until Teilhard de Chardin* and Vatican II that the traditional image of Jesuit theology markedly changed. Jesuits remain at the centre of Catholic theological endeavour, with their own universities, *e.g.* the Gregorian at Rome, and numerous periodical publications, but their ranks have included some of Catholicism's most controversial, as well as most important, modern theologians – Lonergan,* Rahner,* the Dutchman Piet Schoonenberg (b. 1911), the Latin American liberation* theologian Juan Luis Segundo (b. 1925), Josef Jungmann (1889–1975), theologian of liturgy Henri de Lubac (b. 1896) and Jean Daniélou (1905–1974). With few exceptions (*e.g.* Jean Galot) Jesuit theologians can no longer be characterized as defenders of traditional orthodoxy.

Bibliography

X. le Bachelet *et al.*, in *DTC* 8 (1924–25), cols. 1012–1108; J. de Guibert, *The Jesuits. Their Spiritual Doctrine and Practice* (Chicago, 1964); D. Mitchell, *The Jesuits. A History* (London, 1980).

D.F.W.

JESUS. Who is Jesus? How much can be reliably discovered about him? What is the significance of his ministry in 1st-century Palestine? Such are the questions posed by contemporary NT scholarship.

Modern questions about Jesus

Questions about Jesus have been central to, and symptomatic of, most major movements in the theology of the last three centuries. The rationalism of the Enlightenment,* for all its obvious faults, did at least press these questions in an ultimately useful way, forcing the church to take seriously its own confession that in Jesus God had not merely addressed the world but had actually entered it. This movement produced the so-called 'Quest for the historical Jesus',* chronicled and criticized by Schweitzer,* who offered by contrast an apocalyptic* Jesus, firmly anchored in 1st-century Judaism (as it was then perceived), often strikingly dissimilar to the religious needs and expectations of the early 20th century.

A different kind of criticism had already been made by Kähler,* who argued (1892) that the search for the 'historical Jesus' was based on a mistake and was theologically worthless. This position was developed in different ways by Barth* and Bultmann,* the latter of whom stoutly denied even the possibility, let alone the significance, of knowing anything about the 'personality' of Jesus, the category with which Schweitzer had tried to make the 1st-century Jesus relevant to subsequent ages. What the church needed was the 'Christ of faith', the living Lord known in the present. The so-called 'New Quest' initiated by Käsemann* as an antidote to the

potential docetism* of Bultmann's position modified the latter's scepticism to only a limited degree.

Since the mid-1970s, however, a distinct new movement, a third 'quest', has begun, taking the Jewish background and the actual historical task far more seriously than most of its predecessors: it can be seen in the (very different) books of B. F. Meyer, Geza Vermes, A. E. Harvey, M. Borg and E. P. Sanders. A feature of modern study of Jesus has been a renewed awareness of the importance of the subject for contemporary Jewish-Christian relationships, and many Jewish writers have attempted to 'reclaim' Jesus as a good Jew misinterpreted by his subsequent followers. As yet few major questions are settled in this new wave of study, but the way in which the problems are being posed is potentially fruitful, despite the Kähler-like scepticism which still greets any historical work on Jesus whose theological usefulness to the church is not immediately apparent.

Within current scholarship, then, there is still wide divergence over the amount of information available to us about Jesus. This state of affairs has the merit of drawing attention to the fact that most reconstructions include or exclude material not for 'objective' reasons, nor because of particular views of the source-criticism of the gospels, but because of the historian's over-all hypothesis. It is becoming clear that the old liberal disjunction of facts and values, of 'event' and 'interpretation', and ultimately of history* and theology, is unsatisfactory. All reporting of the past involves selection, and hence interpretation: three people were crucified on Good Friday, and even to say 'Jesus died' selects Jesus' death as the significant one. To say 'Jesus died for us' is not to move from event to interpretation but to claim that the event has, in itself, a particular significance. The fact that such language permeates the gospels does not therefore invalidate them as historical sources: it merely means that they must be read with uncommon sensitivity.

Jesus in his historical context

1. Any attempt to reconstruct the history (in the fullest sense) of Jesus must begin with the Jewish context (see also Paul*). Modern study of 1st-century Judaism has revealed a much more varied picture than used to be supposed by those who simply painted Judaism, and the

Pharisees in particular, in dark shades to offset the jewel of the gospel. Three features of 1st-century Judaism stand out: a. belief in the one creator God who had entered into covenant* with Israel; b. hope that this God would step into history to establish his covenant by vindicating Israel against her enemies (a recurring metaphor for this vindication was the resurrection* of God's people); and c. the determination to hasten this day by remaining loyal to the covenantal obligations enshrined in the law (Torah). Debates within Judaism tended to focus on the precise way in which the hope would be fulfilled or on the precise details of covenantal obligation.

For many Jews, hope crystallized in the expectation of a Messiah (i.e. an 'anointed' king from David's family) who would spearhead God's deliverance of his people. For virtually all, the temple was the focus of the national life and hope: more than merely the place of prayer or sacrifice, it was the symbol of God's presence with his people, the sign that he had not forgotten them. Temple and Messiah went together in the Jewish mind: the original temple had been built by David's son (Solomon), and the coming Son of David would restore the temple to its full, and promised, glory.

Jesus, then, was born into a people whose national aspirations were all the stronger for being constantly trampled upon by the callous Roman government and equally constantly whipped up by would-be revolutionary leaders. It was a time when almost all Jews of any description looked for God to inaugurate his kingdom, his sovereign rule, and so to vindicate their cause in fulfilment of his ancient promise.

2. Jesus' message consisted in the announcement that the time of fulfilment had now dawned. The kingdom of God,* long awaited, was now at hand. He saw himself, and was seen by his contemporaries, as a prophet, bringing God's word to his people. But a good part of his ministry was devoted to explaining, in word, symbol and deed, that, although the nation's aspirations were now at last being met, the fulfilment was not at all as had been expected. Many of the parables are designed to answer the objection (prevalent in modern, as in ancient, Judaism): if the kingdom of God is really here, why is the world still going on as it is? Jesus' answer is that the kingdom is present like leaven in dough; like a seed

growing secretly; like a wedding invitation which ends up with the wrong people coming to the party. His ministry puts into effect the warning of John the Baptist (Mt. 3:9): 'Do not think you can say to yourselves, "We have Abraham as our father." I tell you that out of these stones God can raise up children for Abraham.'

Thus Jesus called Israel to repent of her nationalist ambition and follow him in a new vision of God's purpose for Israel. Resistance to Rome was to be replaced by love and prayer for the enemy. Israel's plight was radically redefined: sin, not Rome, was the real enemy. Jesus' exorcisms* point to God's healing of his sick Israel, and they consequently belong with the controversy stories (e.g. Mk. 2:1 – 3:6) as part of his lifelong battle with the forces of evil which came to a climax on the cross (cf. Mt. 4:1–11; 8:28–34; 12:22–32; 27:39–44). His healings of the blind, lame, deaf and dumb, and his calling of the outcasts and poor to enjoy fellowship with himself, all of which hinge on faith as the appropriate response to Jesus, indicate his reconstitution of the people of God (Lk. 13:16; 19:9–10). For those with eyes to see, the 'resurrection', i.e. the remaking of Israel, has already begun (Lk. 15:1–2, 24, 32; 16:19–31).

3. Alongside Jesus' announcement of the (paradoxical) inauguration of God's kingdom we find a constant warning: If the nation refuses to turn from its collision course with God's purposes, the inevitable result will be terrible national devastation. Jesus couches these warnings in the standard language of apocalyptic* prophecy. Just as Jeremiah had prophesied that the 'Day of the Lord' would consist not in the salvation of Jerusalem from Babylon but in her destruction at Babylon's hands, so Jesus warns that the coming of the kingdom will mean, within a generation, destruction for the nation, the city and the temple that have turned their back on the true purposes for which they had been called and chosen (e.g. Lk. 13:1–9, 22–30, 34–35). These warnings come to a head in the great discourse (Mt. 24; Mk. 13; Lk. 21) in which the imminent destruction of Jerusalem and the temple is predicted.

4. In both these elements of Jesus' ministry we find a. a constant, albeit veiled, self-reference, and b. the seeds of that conflict with

349

the Jewish establishment which led to Jesus' death. Thus:

a. In Jesus' welcome of sinners and outcasts, and in his preaching of the good news of the kingdom to the poor, there is the constant implication that to be welcomed by Jesus was to be welcomed by the God of Israel into membership in his true people. The calling of the twelve disciples makes the same point, signifying the renewal of the twelve tribes, with Jesus not as *primus inter pares* but as the one who calls this renewed Israel into being. He apparently draws the nation's destiny on to himself, fulfilling in himself the call of Israel to imitate God in the holiness of mercy, not of separation from the world (Lk. 6:27–36), and summoning others to find their true vocation in following him. The title 'Son of Man' which he apparently used as his favourite self-designation could have been heard as meaning simply 'I' or 'somebody like me', but it also carried the implication of the apocalyptic picture in Dn. 7, in which the suffering Israel is seen as the human figure at present in subjugation to the 'beasts' (*i.e.* the foreign nations) and who is then vindicated by God. There is good evidence that this figure, Israel's representative, was already by the time of Jesus regarded by some as messianic. Thus it is no surprise to find Jesus regarded as Messiah during his lifetime: the title did not, by itself, imply more than 'Israel's anointed representative, through whom God is redeeming his people', although Jesus was engaged in filling this title, too, with fresh meaning. So, too, in Jesus' warnings to the nation the constant repetition of 'within a generation' indicates that the imminent destruction of Jerusalem would come inevitably on the generation that had rejected *him*: over and above any ideas of specially inspired knowledge, Jesus knew himself to be God's final word to his people, rejection of which would mean swift judgment (*cf.* Lk. 23:31).

b. Jesus' acting out of his announcement of the kingdom met with strong opposition from various groups, particularly from the Pharisees with whom, in other respects, Jesus had much in common. His radical attacks on scrupulous observance of the sabbath and the *kosher* laws (cleanliness, purity, dietary regulations) were aimed not so much at 'legalism' as at the key symbols of Jewish nationalism. They can thus be directly correlated with such actions as the welcome to quisling tax-collec-

tors. Jesus, like Elijah and Jeremiah, was regarded as a traitor to the national cause. At the same time there is good evidence to support the verdict of the gospel writers that the national aristocracy (the Sadducees, who held power as puppets of the Romans) would be alarmed at someone who, regarded as a prophet and herald of the kingdom of God, might fan nationalist sentiment (however far that was from Jesus' intention).

5. All these elements in Jesus' ministry come together in the events which, in the synoptic gospels at least, cluster together in the last week of his ministry. He enters Jerusalem in apparently deliberate fulfilment of messianic prophecy. He acts out in symbolic form God's judgment on the temple which has become the focal point of spurious national ambition. He engages in controversy with Pharisees and Sadducees, pointing to their impending final rejection of him as the climax of Israel's renunciation of God's call (Lk. 20:9–19) and hinting that the Messiah might be more than a mere nationalist leader (Lk. 20:41–44). He makes his final predictions of God's impending judgment on the nation (in characteristically apocalyptic language, often misread as referring to the end of the entire world). He celebrates the Passover with his disciples, investing the occasion with new meaning by pointing forward to his own death, not backward to the exodus, as the true redemption of God's people. After betrayal by one of the twelve, he is tried on a charge which, like everything else in his life and work, defies separation into 'religious' and 'political' elements: his words against the temple, his claims to Messiahship, were re-emphasized in his final answer to the high priest (Mk. 14:62), claiming that Israel's destiny, and her long-awaited vindication by God after suffering, was about to be fulfilled in him and, apparently, him alone. He would carry out Israel's task: and, having pronounced Israel's impending judgment in the form of the wrath of Rome which would turn out to be the wrath of God, he would go ahead of her and take that judgment on himself, drinking the cup of God's wrath so that his people might not drink it (Mk. 14:36; 10:45, etc.).

In his crucifixion, therefore, Jesus identified fully (if paradoxically) with the aspirations of his people, dying as 'the king of the Jews', the representative of the people of God, accomplishing for Israel (and hence the world) what neither the world nor Israel could accomplish for themselves. To the question 'Why did Jesus die?' there are traditionally two sorts of answers: the theological ('He died for our sins'), and the historical ('He died because he fell foul of the authorities'). These two answers turn out to be two ways of saying the same thing. In Israel's final national crisis the evil of the world, ranged against God's people, and the evil within God's people themselves, came to a head and, as a matter of history, put Jesus to death. As the story of the exodus is the story of how God redeemed Israel, so the story of the cross is the story of how God redeemed the world through Israel in person, in Jesus, the Messiah.

6. It is within this story, not superimposed upon it from outside, that we can trace the beginnings of that doctrine of incarnation* which had already become common property in the early church by the time of Paul (see Phil. 2:5–11). The task to which Jesus knew himself to be called, and to which he was obedient, was a task which, in OT terms, could be done only by God himself (Is. 59:15–19; 63:7–9; Ezk. 34:7–16). Conscious of a vocation appropriate for Israel's God himself, the human Jesus conducted his life in confident faith and obedience, making implicit and explicit claims which, if not true, would be blasphemous. He spoke and acted with an underived authority. It is in this light that we can understand the phrase 'son of God', in the OT a title for Israel and for the Messiah, which becomes in the NT the vehicle of a further truth which includes but transcends both. And the God who can be seen active in the ministry and especially the death of Jesus is precisely Israel's God, the God of covenant love and faithfulness. The love which apparently contracted uncleanness in contact with the sick and the sinners, but which turned out to be life-giving, is fully unveiled on the cross as God himself takes on the role of the king of the Jews, leading the people of God in triumph against their true enemy.

7. The resurrection (see Resurrection of Christ*) is thus God's demonstration that the claims made during the ministry, which reached their climax on the cross, were true. 'We had hoped', said the disciples on the road to Emmaus, 'that he was the one who was going to redeem Israel' (Lk. 24:21), with the implication 'but we were wrong: he was cruci-fied'. The resurrection demonstrates that they had been right all along, and that the cross, so far from being the failure of Jesus' messianic mission, was its crowning achievement.

In the light of Jewish expectation a non-physical resurrection would be a contradiction in terms. At the same time, the Jews expected the resurrection of all the righteous dead at the end of time, not that of one man within continuing human history, so that Jesus' resurrection took its place within the over-all remoulding of the current expectation of God's kingdom. That which had been glimpsed in his ministry (a renewed world order, and a renewed people of God which all were summoned to join) had been brought to actualization. It was left to Jesus' followers, empowered by his Spirit, to implement his achievement by means of world-wide mission, exploring its implications in worship and theological reflection.

Bibliography

E. Bammel and C. F. D. Moule (eds.), *Jesus and the Politics of His Day* (Cambridge, 1984); M. Borg, *Conflict, Holiness and Politics in the Teachings of Jesus* (New York and Toronto, 1984); J. W. Bowker, *Jesus and the Pharisees* (Cambridge, 1973); G. B. Caird, *Jesus and the Jewish Nation* (London, 1965); A. E. Harvey, *Jesus and the Constraints of History* (London, 1982); B. F. Meyer, *The Aims of Jesus* (London, 1979); J. M. Robinson, *A New Quest of the Historical Jesus* (London, 1959); E. P. Sanders, *Jesus and Judaism* (London, 1985); E. Schillebeeckx, *Jesus: An Experiment in Christology* (ET, London, 1979); A. Schweitzer, *The Quest of the Historical Jesus* (ET, London, 1954); G. Vermes, *Jesus the Jew* (London, 1973).

N.T.W.

JOACHIMISM. Joachim of Fiore (*c.* 1135–1202) developed an elaborate and very influential theological interpretation of history* and the future, which he expressed both in exegetical writings and in symbolic pictures (*figurae*). He understood the development of history in terms of the activity of the Trinity (in history) so that history reflects the Trinitarian relationships. As the Spirit proceeds from the Father and the Son, so an age (*status*) of the Spirit will develop out of the OT age of the Father and the NT age of the Son. Among many other ways of thinking of this third age of the Spirit, Joachim identified it with the millennium* of Revelation. Unlike some of his radical followers, he did not hold that the NT gospel of Christ would be superseded in the age of the Spirit, but that the full spiritual meaning of both testaments would be realized in this period of peace and contemplation before the end of history. Joachim's thought constituted a revolution in medieval eschatology:* for the first time in medieval Christianity he made it possible to envisage progress of a theologically significant kind within the future history of this world. If the subtlety of his theology was lost on many of his followers, the potent expectation of a third age of the Spirit inspired many people in the late medieval period (especially the Spiritual Franciscans), in the 16th century (both Catholics and Protestants), and even down to modern times.

Bibliography

M. Reeves, *Joachim of Fiore and the Prophetic Future* (London, 1976); *idem, The Influence of Prophecy in the Later Middle Ages* (London, 1969); D. C. West (ed.), *Joachim of Fiore in Christian Thought* (New York, 1975); A. Williams (ed.), *Prophecy and Millenarianism* (London, 1980).

R.J.B.

JOHANNINE THEOLOGY. The NT documents which bear the name of 'John' – the gospel, the letters, the book of Revelation – need to be taken together in any consideration of Johannine theology. That theology is most fully developed in the Gospel of John, and this article will therefore give prominence to the teaching of the fourth evangelist, without ignoring either the Johannine epistles or the Apocalypse.

The Johannine corpus

The problem of authorship – which 'John', if any, wrote the literature to which this name is attached – is an important one. But more crucial is the nature of the *tradition* which underlies the Johannine corpus, and the possibility that this tradition may have been directly associated with and interpreted by a living church community, gathered in some sense around the apostle John.

The presumption here is that John the apostle may be identified with 'the beloved disciple' (Jn. 13:23, *etc.*), that he handed on to a group of followers his version of the historical Jesus tradition, and that they in turn developed this in the light of John's distinctive theological understanding. The first written Johannine work to have emerged from this group may have been the Revelation, perhaps written by the apostle himself. Then followed the gospel, written by Johannine Christians and addressed to a community of Jewish and Hellenistic believers located in Ephesus. The members of this circle seem to have been divided in their estimate of the person of Christ: some regarding him as less than divine, and others viewing him as only apparently human (*cf.* Docetism*). This accounts for John's balanced Christology:* Jesus is both one with God and one with man. As time went on, and heterodox opinions within the community polarized, leading Johannine 'elders' wrote 1, 2 and 3 John. This was an attempt to recall the membership to the fundamentals of Christian faith and practice; although, despite the stress on love and unity in the letters as well as the Gospel of John, the disintegration of the Johannine community which may be traced in both seems finally to have taken place (see 3 John, especially vv. 9–10).

Johannine theology

John's account of salvation* moves consistently on two levels at once: the earthly and the heavenly. In the gospel this account is presented as a drama in two main acts, with a prologue (Jn. 1) and an epilogue (Jn. 21). The first act of the drama (Jn. 2 – 12) deals with the revelation of the Word (*cf.* Logos*) of God to the world. By means of signs and associated discourses, punctuated with 'I am' sayings, Jesus reveals the glory* of God to a widening circle of Jews, Samaritans and Greeks (representing the Gentiles). For those with eyes to see and ears to hear, the identity of Jesus* as the Christ is plain. The second act of the gospel (Jn. 13 – 20) unfolds the theme of the glorification of the Word for the world. John's passion narrative moves the drama to its climax in the exaltation of the Christ, and the confession of Thomas that the risen Jesus is 'Lord and God' (20:28). On the basis of Christ's revelation and glorification the fourth evangelist can appeal to his readers to exercise a life-giving faith* in Jesus as Messiah and Son of God (Jn. 20:31). On this ground also the disciples, beginning with Peter and the beloved disciple himself, are commissioned and enabled to follow Jesus, to tend the flock of Christ and to inaugurate the church's mission* to the world (Jn. 21:1–25).

The heart of John's theology, as we have already seen, is *Christological*. The chief figure in the Johannine drama is Jesus himself, one in nature with humanity (Jn. 16:28a), and in some sense one in being with the Father (Jn. 16:28b; *cf.* 14:28; 10:30). This perception, which moves far beyond the synoptic portrait of Jesus, forms the basis of John's understanding of salvation, normally described by him as 'eternal life' (Jn. 3:16, 36; see Eschatology*). The abundant life which God gives to the believer is mediated through his Son, incarnate, crucified and exalted (Jn. 10:10; *cf.* 12:32). Coming from God, and returning to him, Jesus can be the way to the Father* (Jn. 13:3; 14:6).

John thus sees God as acting through the material, supremely in the incarnation,* in order to communicate the spiritual (Jn. 1:14; 1 Jn. 1:1–2; Rev. 1:17–18). This theological viewpoint is not confined to John's gospel. The Johannine literature in general regards the setting of God's salvific activity as one in which earth and heaven, time* and eternity, have been conjoined. On this foundation eternal life can become a reality in the present, as the worlds 'above and below' intersect (Jn. 1:51; *cf.* 1 Jn. 4:16–17; Rev. 3:14–15; hence also the dual nature, both physical and spiritual, of the seven 'signs' in the fourth gospel).

John's basic theological approach may be termed 'sacramental'; for John is less interested in the sacraments* of baptism* and eucharist* as such, than in the sacramental quality of life in Christ. Such an approach determines the characteristic Johannine teaching about *God*,* as both transcendent and immanent (*cf.* Jn. 4:23–24; 3:16; 1 Jn. 1:5; 4:9–14; Rev. 4:2–11; 5:6–10); about the *world*,* as both loved by God and opposed to him (*cf.* Jn. 3:17–19; 17:15–16; 1 Jn. 2:15–17; 4:14; Rev. 11:15; 14:8; *cf.* 21:1–2); and about *mankind*, as both committed to the light and drawn to the darkness (*cf.* Jn. 12:35–36; 1 Jn. 1:7; 2:8–11; 3:14; Rev. 18:21–24).

A similar tension, between that which is 'from above' and 'from below' (*cf.* Jn. 8:23), is noticeable in other major areas of Johannine theology. For example, John's presentation of the *death of Jesus* tells us less about the sacrifice* offered on the cross than about the divine glory which it exhibits and conveys, through which believers may be delivered from the Satan (Jn. 13:31–32; 1 Jn. 3:8; Rev. 12:10–11). The Johannine doctrine of the *church*,* equally, makes it clear that the faithful can share the life of heaven while at the same time experiencing the realities of existence in this world (Jn. 17:6–19; 1 Jn. 4:17; Rev. 2 – 3). Built into this ecclesiology is a further dynamic, for John views the church in both corporate and individual terms (hence the balanced images which are used in the gospel to describe the Christ-Christian relationship: notably Jesus as the 'vine', and his followers as the branches; Jn. 15:1–11). Life in the Christian church, on earth and in eternity, is experienced both by a community and by single members of a group which is universal in membership and potential scope (*cf.* Jn. 21:1–9; 1 Jn. 2:1–3; Rev. 7).

John's *eschatology*,* which emerges in all parts of his theological outlook, is also bipolar in character. For him, the 'end' is yet to come; but for the disciples of Jesus, both before and after the resurrection, it has already occurred. Indeed, the tension between what is 'now', and what is 'not yet', is fundamentally Johannine. For him 'eternal life now' is a reality, and not a paradox (*cf.* Jn. 5:25; 2 Jn. 8–9; Rev. 22; despite the apocalyptic* character of the Revelation, that work has much to say about the *present* tense of salvation).

The 'two-level' tensions in John's theology are more apparent than real; for the resolution is to be found in Christ himself. By bringing together supremely the material and spiritual dimensions, he makes possible life at every level, the saving knowledge of God and the exercise of a life of faith through the Spirit (Jn. 16:7–11; 17:3; 1 Jn. 2:12–14; Rev. 2:7).

According to John, it is the Spirit-Paraclete (identified in the farewell discourse, Jn. 14 – 16, as the *alter ego* of Jesus) who empowers the individual and the Christian community to abide fruitfully in Christ, while journeying on in the light as children of God (Jn. 15:1–8; 1 Jn. 4:12–13; Rev. 3:1–3); to worship* truthfully; to serve others sacrificially for Christ's sake; and to bring the good news of Jesus to the world (Jn. 4:19–26; 20:21–22; 1 Jn. 3:11–18; *cf.* 2 Jn. 5–6; Rev. 22:17). John's theology of the apostolic gospel is thus relevant to the ongoing life of the church in every age.

Bibliography

R. E. Brown, *The Gospel According to John*, 2 vols. (London, 1971); idem, *The Community of the Beloved Disciple* (London, 1979); G. B. Caird, *A Commentary on the Revelation of St John the Divine* (London, 1966); C. H. Dodd, *The Interpretation of the Fourth Gospel* (Cambridge, 1953); E. S. Fiorenza, *The Book of Revelation: Justice and Judgment* (London, 1985); G. Goldsworthy, *The Gospel in Revelation* (Exeter, 1984); E. C. Hoskyns (ed. F. N. Davey), *The Fourth Gospel* (London, ²1947); E. Malatesta, *Interiority and Covenant* (Rome, 1978); S. S. Smalley, *John: Evangelist and Interpreter* (Exeter, 1983); idem, 'Johannine Spirituality', in G. S. Wakefield (ed.), *A Dictionary of Christian Spirituality* (London, 1983), pp. 230–232; idem, *1, 2, 3 John* (Waco, TX, 1984); J. R. W. Stott, *The Epistles of John* (London, 1964).

S.S.S.

JOHN OF DAMASCUS (*c.* 652–*c.* 750). Born and raised in Damascus in an eminent Christian family called Mansur, John at first assumed high civil office, but later (after the eruption of Emperor Leo Isaurian's iconoclastic* policy) joined his adopted brother Cosmas as a monk at the monastery of St Saba near Jerusalem. He was ordained to the priesthood and devoted the rest of his life to writing books and composing church hymns for which he has become most famous. Some of these hymns are used in English today, *e.g.* 'Come ye faithful, raise the strain' and 'The day of resurrection! Earth, tell it out abroad'. John defended the use of icons and as a result was personally condemned by the iconoclastic Synod of 754. He died at a very advanced age, most probably some time before the Seventh Ecumenical Synod (Nicaea II, 787), which reinstated him in the church and acknowledged his contribution. Later generations called him Chrysorroas, 'gold-pouring', because of his erudition and his inspiring hymns.

It was at St Saba, where one can still see his cell, that John wrote most of his works, using material from earlier authors but arranging it in a superbly methodical and original way. They were translated into various languages and utilized by many authors (*e.g.* Peter Abelard* and Thomas Aquinas* in the West and practically all systematic theo-

logians in the East). The Greek *Life* divides them into four categories, the 'melodic hymns', the 'panegyric orations', the 'sacred Bible and divinely inspired tablet' (*i.e.* his most important systematic/dogmatic work, *The Fountain of Knowledge*) and the 'treatises on the icons'. Modern patrologists divide them into exegetical, dogmatic, antiheretical, polemical, ethical, homiletical, hagiographical and poetical.

As a theologian John of Damascus was a traditionalist who wanted to follow the Scriptures and the accredited fathers, because he saw both as inspired by the Holy Spirit. He was interested in particular theological questions and issues, but he was supremely a systematician* who wanted to supply a comprehensive *summa* of theological knowledge. Thus he covered almost all theological topics both broadly and in detail. He made use of philosophy in an eclectic manner, making a clear distinction between true (psychical) and false (demonic) philosophical knowledge and holding that philosophy was related to theology as a servant was related to a queen. He held that God is transcendent in his being and immanent in his grace, *i.e.* his creative and redeeming acts through which are revealed respectively the divine attributes (eternity, immutability, majesty, *etc.*) and the divine persons (the three *hypostaseis** of the Father, the Son and the Holy Spirit). Following the doctrine of the Greek fathers and especially of the Cappadocians (see Basil of Caesarea,* Gregory of Nazianzus,* Gregory of Nyssa*), he always began with the Trinity* and moved to the unity of the Godhead which he expounded in terms of communion (*koinōnia*), while always retaining the priority of the Father who begets the Son and projects (*ekporeuein*) the Holy Spirit.* The world, consisting of spiritual and material creatures without any dualism* (anti-Manichaean*), is contingent and destined to last in order to reveal God's plans, especially through the activities of angels* and men. Yet a free fall* (he decisively opposed Muslim predestination*) from goodness into evil led to the frustration of this destiny and caused slavery and death. Some angels have been turned into demons and human beings have fallen into sin,* which is not only a loss of God's grace, of life and understanding, but also subjection to corruption and death through procreation. The solution to these problems is given in

Christ the Saviour. For John of Damascus, Christ is in his person not a deified man but an 'inhominated' God, consisting of two natures, the divine and the human, resembling every human being in consisting of two parts, one immaterial and another material, but differing from them in not forming 'another out of the two' but remaining 'one in the two'. In this John followed both Chalcedonian orthodoxy and post-Chalcedonian clarifications, especially Leontius of Byzantium's doctrine of *enhypostasia* (see Hypostasis*) and Maximus the Confessor's* and the Sixth Ecumenical Synod's 'two natural energies and wills' which remain distinct though harmonized, whereby he exposed both errors, the Nestorian* and the Monophysite* (see Christology*). Christ's saving work comprises his teaching, his life and his sacrifice on the cross with its outcome in his resurrection, ascension and final parousia, which become gifts offered to and ends to be freely attained to by believers through the reception of the sacraments and the response of personal faith and works respectively.

For John of Damascus, Christian works were summed up in the Christian ascetic* ideal of the renunciation of 'the world'. Closely connected with this emphasis on Christian works was the doctrine of the final judgment which is to follow after the general bodily resurrection of all human beings (forcefully asserted in his work *Against the Manichaeans*) as well as the memorial services and prayers for the dead which were of particular benefit for the living. John regarded the Virgin Mary* and the saints* as living epistles of the saving truth of Christ ('friends of Christ' and 'children of God'), with whom they were to be honoured and exalted but not worshipped. This point became clearer in his defences of the use of icons, whereby he affirmed, not only that 'the veneration of honour given to the icon goes to the prototype', but also that there was a crucial distinction between veneration of honour given to the icons (*proskynēsis*, *timē*) and true worship (*latreia*) offered only to the Trinity. But as with his doctrine of Mary and the saints so also with his doctrine of icons, John had Christ as his focus and aimed at expounding the appropriation of Christ's gift of salvation by human beings. This was probably why, like most of the Eastern fathers, he did not develop any explicit doctrine of the church.

Bibliography
Works in ET: NPNF, vol. ix; M. H. Allies, *St John Damascene on Holy Images followed by Three Sermons on the Assumption* (London and Philadelphia, 1898); D. Anderson, *St John of Damascus, On the Divine Images* (New York, 1980); F. C. Chase, *St John of Damascus' Writings* in FC 37.

Studies in English: D. Ainslee, *John of Damascus* (London, ³1903); B. Altaner, *Patrology* (Freiburg, 1960), pp. 635–640; P. M. Baur, *The Theology of St John Damascene's 'De Fide Orthodoxa'* (Washington, DC, 1951); F. Cayré, *Manual of Patrology and History of Theology* (Paris, Tournai, Rome, 1940), pp. 326–339; A. Fortescue, 'John of Damascus' in *The Greek Fathers* (London, 1908), pp. 202–248; J. H. Lupton, *John of Damascus* (London, 1882); V. A. Michell, *The Mariology of St John Damascene* (Kirkwood, MO, 1930); D. J. Sahas, *John of Damascus on Islam* (Leiden, 1972).

G.D.D.

JOHN OF THE CROSS, see Mystical Theology.

JOY is an essential ingredient of all true Christianity as it was a conspicuous feature of Hebrew religion at its best. The reading of a new edition of the law led to great rejoicing at the time of Ezra, who summed up the scene by saying: 'The joy of the Lord is your strength' (Ne. 8:10). The book of Psalms rings with the joy of worship, especially that associated with the great Jewish festivals in the temple at Jerusalem.

The NT is 'the most buoyant, exhilarating and joyful book in the world' (J. Denney, *Studies in Theology*, London, 1895, p. 171). It contains a variety of words for joy which occur a total of 326 times. For example, there is exultant joy (*agalliasis* – *e.g.* Acts 2:46); optimism is the mood of faith (*euthymein*, to take heart – Acts 27:22, 25); Paul can exult in God on account of the death of Christ (*kauchasthai*, to boast – Rom. 5:11); and in the Beatitudes Jesus pronounces happy those who display certain characteristics (*makarios*, blessed – Mt. 5:3–11; Lk. 6:20–22). The most common root for joy in the NT, however, is that which expresses inward joy (*chara*, joy; *chairein*, to rejoice). This occurs 146 times out of the total of 326 instances. The message of the whole of the NT is good news of great joy for all people (Lk. 2:10).

Every NT writer has something to say about joy in one or more of its varieties. Luke's Gospel is, *par excellence*, the gospel of joy, while Paul's letter to the Philippians, written though it was from prison, is the letter of joy. In the Johannine literature, fullness of joy is stressed (see, *e.g.*, Jn. 17:13; 1 Jn. 1:4). 1 Peter teaches about joy in suffering (1 Pet. 3:14; 4:13–14). The joy of practical religion is shown in the letter of James (*e.g.* Jas. 1:25). The joy of the redeemed is found in Revelation (*e.g.* Rev. 22:14).

The basis of Christian joy lies in the main theological doctrines of the faith: the Fatherhood of God* and the forgiveness of sins, the incarnation,* the atonement,* the resurrection of Christ* and the doctrine of the Holy Spirit.* Christians rejoice because God is their heavenly Father who forgives the penitent, because God sent his Son into the world for the salvation of all who have faith (Jn. 3:16), because Jesus Christ not only died but was raised again from the dead and because joy is one of the ninefold fruits of the Spirit (Gal. 5:22). Such are the firm theological foundations of Christian joy.

Joy finds expression in a new attitude to life as a whole and in revitalized worship. This latter aspect has come to the fore in recent years especially through the charismatic movement. Every Sunday is a celebration of the resurrection of Christ and as such should have about it the joy of Easter. Yet joy is not confined to the first day of the week. It affects the daily life and work of the Christian. The whole of life is to be spent in joyful service of Jesus Christ.

Bibliography

J. Moltmann, *Theology and Joy* (London, 1973); W. G. Morrice, *We Joy in God* (London, 1977); *idem*, *Joy in the New Testament* (Exeter, 1984).

W.G.M.

JUDAISM AND CHRISTIANITY. The primary problem of the largely Jewish early church was not its attitude to Jewish religious backgrounds, but rather the question of Gentiles becoming believers in the God of Israel and in the Jewish Messiah. Must Gentiles become as Jews in order to become followers of Jesus? Must Gentiles follow the law* of Moses and so be circumcised? In this context the NT church and particularly Paul, the apostle to the Gentiles, affirm that justification* comes through faith rather than the Jewish law. As may be observed in Romans (*e.g.* Rom. 3:28–31) and Galatians (*e.g.* Gal. 3:10–14, 23–29), the context of justification through faith demonstrates the universality of the Christian way of salvation.* The Jewish law is not necessary for salvation. But in the NT there is no suggestion that Jews should no longer follow the law as believers in Jesus. Both Jesus and the apostles claim that they do not negate the law. In Acts 21 Paul shows the accusation to be false that he teaches believing Jews 'to forsake Moses . . . not to circumcise their children or observe the customs' (Acts 21:21). He therefore observes ritual temple purification, including the shaving of the head and the presentation of offerings (Acts 21:24, 26). Yet such observance was not felt to be obligatory, as even Peter's example shows (Gal. 2:14).

But the NT church did face the problem that the Jewish authorities largely rejected Jesus as Messiah. The gospels (particularly John) and Acts frequently refer to 'the Jews' refusing the Lord and stirring up opposition. While this seems to be true of the majority of Jews, we need to note that John himself was Jewish and that many priests and leading Jews were also converted. Nevertheless, the seeds of the coming rift between synagogue and church are evident in the NT. After the destruction of the temple, the Jewish authorities became increasingly strong in their anti-Christian position, while the church retaliated as soon as it gained power under Constantine in the 4th century. Church councils* began to issue anti-Semitic statements and judgments. It thus became more and more difficult for truly Jewish believers to maintain their Christian faith and still remain culturally Jewish. To follow *kashrut* (the Jewish law) and remain in the largely Gentile church became impossible.

Anti-Semitism became a normal part of Christian life. The Jews were accused of deicide and it was commonly maintained that Jews stood under the curse of God. As recorded in the Jewish Matthew's Gospel, the Jewish people had said, 'His blood be on us and on our children!' (Mt. 27:25). Christians assumed therefore that this curse of God should apply to all future generations of Jews.

As Christians gained power in the Roman Empire, Jews lost civil liberties. Christian preachers were permitted to enter synagogues at will and to preach the Christian faith. Persecution broke out from time to time and Jews today particularly remember enforced baptisms and 'conversions', the Crusades, the horrors of the Inquisition, the anti-Semitic writings of Luther,* Russian pogroms and the 'final solution' of Hitler's extermination policy when a third of the total Jewish population in the world was destroyed. As a result, words like Christ, Christian, church, crusade or campaign are associated by most Jews with hatred and are not generally used by Jews who believe in Jesus as Messiah.

While the NT church faced the issue of whether Gentiles must become as Jews, today the question is reversed. Must believing Jews forsake the law of Moses, join Gentile churches and worship with alien forms? Some Jewish believers have responded by forming 'messianic synagogues' in America, 'messianic assemblies' in Israel and 'messianic fellowships' in Britain and elsewhere. In seeking to establish churches with Jewish forms, questions arise about relations with Gentiles and existing Gentile churches, attitudes to the Jewish *kashrut* laws, what synagogue forms to continue, the use of Hebrew and the development of leadership patterns which fit the Jewish background. Despite the dangers of a weakened Christology and of isolationism, Jews feel the importance of a clear Jewish identity in the Christian church.

The church today faces several controversies with regard to Jewish evangelism.*

1. Is conversion* necessary? Some Christians affirm a two-covenant* approach to the Jewish question. While the new covenant in Jesus Christ is the way of salvation for Gentiles, God's ordained way for Jews continues to be the old covenant. This inevitably raises the issue of the meaning of Jesus' fulfilment of the OT – *e.g.* the emphasis in John's Gospel that Jesus fulfils all in the OT (*cf.* R. E. Brown's Anchor Bible commentary).

2. Is there discontinuity as well as continuity in Jewish conversion? Judaism affirms belief in the Torah, the word and law of God. Rabbinic and talmudic studies are considered to be 'oral Torah' revealed by God to Moses and then developed in succeeding centuries. If Judaism were indeed purely founded on the rock of God's revelation in the OT, then the Christian faith in Jesus as Messiah would be only continuous with it. If, however, we see rabbinic and talmudic studies as man-made additions to God's Torah, then human fallibility and error form an essential part of modern Judaism and discontinuity requires repentance and new birth.

3. Do Christians have the right to evangelize Jews? The history of Christian persecution of Jews has made some Gentile Christians feel that they cannot go beyond friendship to Jews. Emphasis is placed on a form of dialogue which makes no attempt to bring the other to conversion. Many believe, however, that this denies the biblical mandate for mission with a loving and humble desire for Jews to share the fullness of life in Jesus Christ.

4. What is the future for Jews? Christians are divided in their opinions concerning the state of Israel.* Is the 1948 establishment of the state of Israel a fulfilment of prophecy? Or is Jesus Christ the fulfilment of all in the OT? Is the church in some way the 'new Israel'? Is God interested only in the people or also in the land of Israel? All Christians are at least agreed that God is the sovereign Lord of history and therefore the return of the Jews to the land of Israel must be in his sovereign purposes.

The debate about the future of the Jews centres on Rom. 9 – 11. Paul seems clear that the Gentiles have the opportunity to receive the gospel in obedience because of the disobedience of the Jews. And the faith of the Gentiles will provoke the Jews to jealousy so that they too will be regrafted into their own olive tree. If the Jews' disobedience brings rich blessing to Gentiles, Paul asks what the Jews' 'full inclusion' will mean for the world. Thus he foresees the day when 'the fullness of the Gentiles' will come in and when 'all Israel' will be saved. Whatever this may mean in detail, we can at least expect a considerable turning both of Jews and Gentiles to the faith of Jesus Christ.

See also: HOLOCAUST; ISRAEL; JERUSALEM.

Bibliography

L. Baeck, *Judaism and Christianity* (New York, 1970); G. Hedenquist (ed.), *The Church and the Jewish People* (London, 1954); J. Jocz, *The Jewish People and Jesus Christ* (London, 1949); idem, *The Jewish People and Jesus Christ after Auschwitz* (Grand Rapids, MI, 1981); C. Klein,

Anti-Judaism in Christian Theology (London, 1978); P. Lapide and J. Moltmann, *Jewish Monotheism and Christian Trinitarian Doctrine* (Philadelphia, 1981); J. Parkes, *The Conflict of the Church and the Synagogue* (London, 1934); M. H. Tamenbaum, M. Wilson, J. Rudin (eds.), *Evangelicals and Jews in Conversation* (Grand Rapids, MI, 1978); 'Christian Witness to the Jewish People', *Lausanne Occasional Papers* 7 (Wheaton, IL, 1980).

M.F.G.

JUDGMENT OF GOD. The belief that God passes judgment on the lives of his human creatures is important for Christianity, as it is for most of the world's religious traditions (see, e.g., S. G. F. Brandon, *The Judgment of the Dead*, London, 1967). In the OT divine judgment commonly takes the form of earthly blessing (*e.g.* harvest, national security) for obedience to God's commands, and punishment (*e.g.* plague, earthquake, exile) for disobedience. But the NT presupposes the belief, developed in apocalyptic* literature, in a great assize at the end of history. A doctrine of judgment based on the NT would include the following elements:

1. All people will be judged, both 'the living and the dead' (Acts 10:42), both Christian and non-Christian (Rom. 14:10–12). This future judgment is associated with Christ's final coming (Mk. 8:38; 1 Cor. 4:5; 2 Thes. 1:5–10; and see Eschatology*).

2. Judgment will be 'according to works' (Mt. 16:27; Rom. 2:6; Rev. 22:12). This does not conflict with justification* by grace through faith. Although justification is a gift of God's free grace, it involves the obligation to work out our new status in practice. Thus, at the final judgment, a person's works will be the evidence of whether a living faith is present in him or not. It is not a question of earning salvation by good works: works are the evidence of the reality of the faith through which we are saved.

3. The final judgment will be a moment of division between those who are revealed truly to belong to Christ and those who do not. It will not be arbitrarily imposed from on high. Rather, the verdict of the final judgment will underline and make known the self-judgment which men and women have chosen during the present life. There is a real sense in which, by the choices people make, by the way they respond when confronted by Christ and his

gospel, they bring judgment on themselves. This idea of a present self-judgment is prominent in John's Gospel (*e.g.* 3:19–20) but is not peculiar to him (Mt. 10:32–33; Rom. 1:18–32).

4. Salvation and condemnation are best understood in terms of relationship or non-relationship to God. The criterion by which people's destinies will be determined is a double one – their failure to worship and serve the God revealed in the created order (Rom. 1:18–20), and their attitude to Christ – their relationship to him, of which their deeds give evidence (Jn. 3:36). The destinies themselves consist in being either in God's presence or excluded from that presence (*cf.* 2 Thes. 1:8–10).

In modern times the image of the great assize has for many people lost the power which it held throughout much of the church's history. But it serves to safeguard important truths: judgment is serious, just, inescapable. It is judgment under the searching gaze of holy love, judgment by Christ himself.

Recent discussion has considered whether divine judgment can be perceived in the events of history (see D. Bebbington, *Patterns in History*, Leicester, 1979); on what basis God may judge those who have not heard the gospel; and whether the possibility of eternal condemnation is consistent with his love (see Universalism*).

Bibliography

J. A. Baird, *The Justice of God in the Teaching of Jesus* (London, 1963); J. P. Martin, *The Last Judgment* (Edinburgh, 1963); L. Morris, *The Biblical Doctrine of Judgment* (London, 1960); S. H. Travis, *Christ and the Judgment of God* (London, 1986). See also Bibliography for Eschatology.*

S.H.T.

JÜNGEL, EBERHARD (b. 1934), professor of systematic theology at the University of Tübingen, and a leading contemporary Protestant theologian. He has published widely on the NT, historical and dogmatic theology, and philosophy of religion. His work is deeply influenced by Ernst Fuchs' (1903–83) theories of language and by Barth's* rigorous Christocentrism. Three main areas of theological concern can be identified. 1. Jüngel expounds an incarnational and Trinitarian understanding of God, rooted in God's humble self-identification with the crucified Christ. Much of his work is preoccupied with the theological and ontological implications of Calvary. 2. He uses the motif of justification to develop an anthropology* emphasizing man as receptive and relational rather than self-realizing. 3. He has recently tried to rephrase natural theology* as a theology of the natural, that is, as an exploration of the universal implications of God's particular self-revelation. All three themes contribute to a theology whose intention is to give an account of the proper distinction between the human God and his human creation. Jüngel has also published perceptive studies of Barth, essays on analogy, metaphor and ontology, and a book on death.

Bibliography

Death (ET, Edinburgh, 1975); *The Doctrine of the Trinity* (ET, Edinburgh, 1976); *God as the Mystery of the World* (ET, Edinburgh, 1983).

G. Wainwright, *ExpT* 92 (1981), pp. 131–135; J. B. Webster, *Evangel* 2:2 (1984), pp. 4–6; *idem, Eberhard Jüngel: An Introduction to his Theology* (Cambridge, 1986).

J.B.We.

JUSTICE, see RIGHTEOUSNESS.

JUSTIFICATION denotes, primarily, that action in the lawcourt whereby a judge upholds the case of one party in dispute before him (in the Hebrew lawcourt, where the image originates, all cases consist of an accuser and a defendant, there being no public prosecutor). Having heard the case, the judge finds in favour of one party, and thereby 'justifies' him: if he finds for the defendant, this action has the force of 'acquittal'. The person justified is described as 'just', 'righteous' (on the terminology, see Righteousness*), not as a description of moral character but as a statement of his status before the court (which will, ideally, be matched by character, but that is not the point).

Since this lawcourt imagery is used in Scripture to elucidate God's dealings with Israel,* his covenant* people, 'justification' comes to denote God's action in restoring the fortunes of Israel after she has been oppressed: it is as though Israel, or a faithful individual within Israel, is the innocent defendant in a trial (see

Pss. 43:1; 135:14; Is. 50:8; Lk. 18:7), whose cause will be upheld by the righteous covenant God. As Israel's troubles increase in the period after the exile, it becomes increasingly clear that what is needed is a final day of judgment, when God will right all wrongs, and vindicate his people, once and for all. This notion, which is closely correlated with the hope of resurrection* (God's vindication of Israel after her suffering) is staunchly upheld in the NT.

At the same time, in the NT Israel's expectation is radically redefined. In his welcome for outcasts and sinners, Jesus enacts God's vindication of (apparently) the wrong group in Israel – the poor, the humble. 'This man [the tax-collector], rather than the other [the Pharisee], went home justified before God' (Lk. 18:14). In continuity with his paradoxical ministry, Jesus goes to the cross apparently condemned by God. The resurrection,* however, is quickly seen by the disciples as God's 'vindication' or 'justification' of Jesus (*e.g.* Acts 3:14–15, 26; 1 Tim. 3:16). God has finally acted, within history, to identify his covenant people, and it turns out that Jesus, 'the king of the Jews', has alone represented that people.

Justification in Paul and James

Although, therefore, the *doctrine* of justification is discussed quite rarely in the NT, the *fact* of it is everywhere apparent. God has redefined his covenant people around Jesus. The entire Christian mission is built on this foundation. It is left to Paul, however, to articulate this conviction fully and draw out its implications: and he does so at the appropriate point, *i.e.* when the question of the identity of the covenant people is raised (Rom. 3:21 – 4:25; 9:30 – 10:13; Gal. *passim;* Phil. 3:2–11). Five points need to be observed here.

1. The question of justification is a matter of *covenant membership*. The underlying question in (for instance) Gal. 3 and 4 is: Who are the true children of Abraham? Paul's answer is that membership belongs to all who believe in the gospel of Jesus, whatever their racial or moral background.

2. The *basis* of this verdict is *the representative death and resurrection of Jesus* himself. In view of universal sin, God can only be in covenant with human beings if that sin is dealt with, and this has been achieved by God himself in the death of his Son (Rom. 3:24–26; 5:8–9). Jesus takes on himself the curse

which would have prevented God's promised blessing finding fulfilment (Gal. 3:10–14). The resurrection is God's declaration that Jesus, and hence his people, are in the right before God (Rom. 4:24–25).

3. The verdict issued in the present on the basis of faith (Rom. 3:21–26) *correctly anticipates the verdict to be issued in the final judgment* on the basis of the total life (Rom. 2:1–16, on which see Cranfield, *Romans*, vol. 1, pp. 151–153). This future 'verdict' is in fact, seen from another angle, simply resurrection itself (Phil. 3:9–11). The logic of this 'eschatological' perspective is explained as follows: faith is itself the sign of God's life-giving work, by his Spirit (1 Cor. 12:3), and what God has begun he will complete (Phil. 1:6).

4. Justification thus *establishes the church as a new entity*, the renewed Israel, now qualitatively distinct from Jew and Greek alike, transcending racial and social barriers (Gal. 3:28). The sharp edge of this point, for Paul, was the conviction not only that pagan converts to Christianity did not need to become Jews in order fully to belong to God's people, but also that the attempt to do so was in itself a renunciation of the gospel, implying that Christ's achievement was insufficient or even unnecessary (Gal. 2:21; 5:4–6). At the same time, Paul warns pagan converts against the opposite mistake, that of imagining Jews to be now cut off without hope – the mirror image of the characteristic Jewish mistake, and one which some post-Reformation theology has not always avoided (Rom. 11:13–24).

5. 'Justification by faith' is thus a shorthand for 'justification by grace through faith', and in Paul's thought at least *has nothing to do with a suspicious attitude towards good behaviour*. On the contrary: Paul expects his converts to live in the manner appropriate for members of the covenant (Rom. 6, *etc.*), and this is in fact necessary if faith is not to appear a sham (2 Cor. 13:5). His polemic against 'works of the law' is not directed against those who attempted to *earn* covenant membership through keeping the Jewish law (such people do not seem to have existed in the 1st century) but against those who sought to *demonstrate* their membership in the covenant through obeying the Jewish law. Against these people Paul argues a. that the law cannot in fact be kept perfectly – it merely shows up sin; and b. that this attempt would reduce the covenant to a single race, those who possess the Jewish law, whereas God desires a world-wide family (Rom. 3:27–31; Gal. 3:15–22). This means that Jas. 2:14–26 is not in conflict with Paul, but expresses the same truth from a different perspective. The 'faith' which is insufficient is bare Jewish monotheism (Jas. 2:19); and Abraham's faith, through which God declared him within the covenant in Gn. 15 (Jas. 2:23), was simply 'fulfilled' in the later incident of Gn. 22 (Jas. 2:21).

New developments

With the disappearance of Paul's particular polemical situation, it was likely that the doctrine of justification would be reapplied in new ways, and this happened with its development as the over-all view of how one becomes a Christian – a much wider notion than the very precise NT usage. Allied to the medieval view of God's righteousness as *iustitia distributiva* (see Righteousness*), this encouraged a belief in good works as the means by which one earns merit or favour with God. In reacting against this, Luther* never totally avoided the risk of making faith a substitute for works, and hence itself a meritorious performance on man's part. His failure to note the Jewish, covenantal and eschatological content of Paul's doctrine led to exegetical difficulties (*e.g.* the meaning of Rom. 2 and Rom. 9 – 11) and theological problems (the danger of a dualistic rejection of the law, and the difficulty of providing a thorough foundation for ethics) which have beset subsequent Protestantism. In particular, popular Protestantism has often more or less elided the distinction between justification and regeneration,* using 'justification by faith' as a slogan for a romantic* or existentialist* view of Christianity, rightly criticized by Roman Catholics. Roman Catholic views of justification have continued to be influenced by Augustine,* who saw it as God's action in *making* people righteous, through pouring into their hearts love towards himself. This stress on the actual change which God effects in the sinner has continued into modern Roman Catholic theology. The result of this is significantly to broaden the reference of the word, to include far more than Paul (or the Reformers) intended.

Current debates

Current debates about 'justification' have

tended to raise much wider issues than the specific concerns of Paul, and modern ecumenical agreement on the subject (cf. Küng*), while welcome in its own right, does not always do justice to the nuances of biblical teaching. Thus, for instance, for Paul it is not the doctrine of justification that is 'the power of God for salvation' (Rom. 1:16), but the gospel of Jesus Christ. As Hooker* noted, it is perfectly possible to be saved by believing in Jesus Christ without ever having heard of justification by faith. What that doctrine provides is the assurance that, though Christian obedience is still imperfect, the believer is already a full member of God's people. It establishes, in consequence, the basis and motive for love (and true obedience) towards God. The teaching of present justification is thus a central means whereby the fruits of the Spirit – love, joy, peace and the rest – may be produced.

Bibliography

J. Buchanan, *The Doctrine of Justification* (repr. London, 1961); C. E. B. Cranfield, *A Critical and Exegetical Commentary on the Epistle to the Romans*, 2 vols. (Edinburgh, 1975, 1979); Richard Hooker, Sermon on Justification (1612), in *Works*, ed. I. Walton (London, 1822, *etc.*); H. Küng, *Justification: The Doctrine of Karl Barth and a Catholic Reflection* (London, 1964); A. E. McGrath, *Iustitia Dei: A History of the Christian Doctrine of Justification*, 2 vols. (Cambridge, 1986); G. Reid (ed.), *The Great Acquittal* (London, 1980); J. Reumann, *'Righteousness' in the New Testament: 'Justification' in the United States Lutheran-Roman Catholic Dialogue*, with responses by J. A. Fitzmyer and J. D. Quinn (Philadelphia, 1982); H. N. Ridderbos, *Paul: An Outline of His Theology* (ET, Grand Rapids, MI, 1975).

N.T.W.

JUSTIN MARTYR, see Apologists.

KÄHLER, MARTIN (1835–1912), German Protestant theologian. He studied law at the University of Königsberg

and theology at the universities of Heidelberg, Tübingen, and Halle. Following a brief time at Bonn (1864–67), he served as professor of systematic theology and NT exegesis at Halle (from 1879). His *magnum opus* was a 3-volume work on Christian Doctrine (*Die Wissenschaft der christlichen Lehre*, 1883–87), but the work for which he is remembered today is a small booklet entitled *The So-called Historical Jesus and the Historic Biblical Christ* (tr. with introd., C. E. Braaten, Philadelphia, 1964; *Der sogenannte historische Jesus und der geschichtliche, biblische Christus*, 1896), in which he rejected the terms of reference of the liberal 'quest of the historical Jesus'* with its implied separation of faith from history, of the Jesus who lived from the church's kerygma concerning him. The attempt to get behind the data of the gospels to the 'real Jesus', he argued, is futile. He raised critical, dogmatic and apologetic objections to the work of the liberal 'questers'. Their critical basis was flawed by their assumption that the gospels give us the material necessary to construct a coherent, developmental life of Jesus; they were never intended to give us this. Theologically, they mistakenly presupposed that Jesus was a mere man like themselves. And, apologetically, they made the faith of the ordinary Christian believer the captive of the latest results of scholarly opinion, rather than allowing him direct access to the object of his faith, the historic Jesus portrayed in the gospels and proclaimed by the apostles. The united confession of the early church that 'Jesus is Lord' was no mere theological construction but was firmly rooted in history.

Bibliography

C. E. Braaten, 'Martin Kähler on the Historic, Biblical Christ', in Braaten and R. A. Harrisville (eds.), *The Historical Jesus and the Kerygmatic Christ* (Nashville, TN, 1964), pp. 79–105; Braaten and Harrisville (eds.), *Kerygma and History* (Nashville, TN, 1962).

W.W.G.

KANT, IMMANUEL (1724–1804). For many years professor of logic and metaphysics at the University of Königsberg, East Prussia, he is seen now as a seminal figure of the Enlightenment* period. His immense influence on the whole range of human enquiry, including theology, stems out of his distinctive understanding of the nature of human knowledge and belief.

The background to Kant's thinking here was the development of two philosophical traditions: British empiricism* and Continental rationalism. The former, in its understanding of the nature of human belief, placed a primary emphasis on experience. The latter stressed the importance of innate principles and ideas within the human mind. Kant at once unites, and stands at the climax of, both traditions. Thus he affirms the importance of sense-organ experience in human knowledge. But Kant also argues that the human mind is not a wholly passive receptor of these sense experiences. On the contrary, the mind is constantly active in organizing and classifying the *raw materials* of experience. In this way the human mind imposes *on* experience its own distinctive categories and concepts. (These 'Forms of Intuition' or 'Pure Ideas' are what Kant terms the synthetic *a priori* dimension of human understanding.) Here, however, an obvious question arises: If we are constantly imposing our own ideas and categories on the world of experience, is this not a source of distortion and prejudice? We may constantly wear red-tinted spectacles. If so, then everything without exception will appear to be red. But this does not mean that the whole of reality is actually red.

It is, in effect, Kant's response to this problem which constitutes his most important contribution to philosophy. Kant maintains that we cannot know *things in themselves:* all knowledge is from a certain perspective and through a particular mode of understanding. But he also argues that, whilst the human mind does impose its own forms of understanding on the world, nevertheless, the world must be of a certain character in order to *receive* these forms of understanding.

An example here is his teaching about causality. The Scottish philosopher, David Hume,* had argued that sense-experience could, by itself, never furnish us with the idea of causal connection but only that of constant conjunction. (For example, we never, have a genuine sense-experience of the actual causal relationship between the hot stove and the boiling water. All we ever experience is the constant conjunction or co-existence of these two events.) So where does the idea of causality come from? Hume's answer had been that the mind is psychologically (a-rationally)

predisposed to make the step from constant conjunction to causal connection. But, he provocatively urges, the fact that human beings happen to have these particular psychological tendencies does not mean that the material world is actually of a certain character. This is the basis of Hume's scepticism.

Kant's philosophy of knowledge is best understood by reference to the way in which it departs from Hume's at this crucial point. For Kant's fundamental position is this: Our actual experience of nature (and in particular the orderliness, regularity and consistency which characterizes this experience) must entail a world to which causal laws are applicable. Only a certain sort of a world would be able to *receive* our causal pre-understandings. An order of reality characterized by natural anarchy and unqualified random chance could never *conform to* our fundamental categories of cause and effect. There is philosophical disagreement as to just how much Kant has established here. Nevertheless, the departure from Hume is clear. For Kant, the idea of causation is established as an authentic part of rational human judgment because it is a belief – alongside other fundamental beliefs about the material world – which expresses the *conditions of the possibility of experience.*

But if for Kant this philosophical approach establishes the possibility of a distinctive *knowledge* of the material world, it also confirms our inability to *know* anything beyond it: to know of God, the soul or life beyond death. This is the case since, for Kant, there is no theological proposition whose truth is necessary in order to explain the character of the experiences which we actually have. (In saying this Kant had already dispelled, to his own satisfaction, the traditional proofs of God's existence. See Natural Theology.*) For Kant, the essential problem with religious knowledge is not a shortage of raw data (as a detective might despair of a lack of clues). Rather it is that the infinite God must forever elude our pre-understandings. He is beyond our limited conceptual apparatus, and thus we cannot in any substantial sense know him. The categories through which we apprehend the world of sense-experience are simply inappropriate for the infinite, the non-conditioned, the eternal metaphysical. And thus in religion, demonstrative *reason* must give way to *practical faith*.

The implications for theology here were obviously immense. If God is, in the strictest sense, unknowable, then the proper object and study for theology is not God but man's religious states and sentiments and their individual and communal expressions. Theology becomes anthropocentric. (Witness, for example, the direct impact of Kant's thinking on Schleiermacher's* theology.) Similarly, within such anthropocentricism, the Scriptures will be seen as a descriptive record of human religious experience, but as having no authority beyond this.

What then is practical faith? And is it wholly divorced from reason? While, for Kant, human beliefs about God, transcendence, human free-will, the soul and immortality are not within the scope of demonstrative reason, they are *practical presuppositions* of the moral life. Kant does not (contrary to what is sometimes stated) argue here that God is the only possible source of moral judgments – of an objective morality. Rather he argues that to be committed to the moral life is to make the practical presupposition of a beneficent being of sufficient power to unite full virtue and happiness (that is, to bring about the *summum bonum*), and also of a future state in which the soul will enjoy this union.

The idea (anticipated by Hume) that our minds are constantly imposing their own pre-understandings on to the successive items of experience is today part of common intellectual currency. Thus, for example, it is an idea which is central within the present debates about biblical interpretation (*cf.* Hermeneutics*). It is also, to cite just two further examples, a key concept in the sociology of knowledge and in much of our thinking about personal relationships. It is also a conception which, not least through the writings of the later Wittgenstein,* continues to play a significant part in formal philosophy. All of this testifies to the considerable historical importance of Kant's contribution to human thought. As a figure of the Enlightenment, his self-sufficient reliance on human understanding and reason separates him sharply from the most fundamental principles of Protestantism. But it would be unwise to underestimate his influence on the modern mind.

Bibliography
A Critique of Pure Reason, tr. N. Kemp Smith (London, 1929); *Critique of Practical Reason*, tr. T. K. Abbott (London, ⁶1909).
S. Körner, *Kant* (Harmondsworth, 1955); D. J. O'Connor (ed.), *A Critical History of Western Philosophy* (New York, 1964).

M.D.G.

KÄSEMANN, ERNST (b. 1906). A student of Bultmann,* Käsemann was professor of NT successively in Mainz, Göttingen and Tübingen, and was also identified with the German Confessing Church during the Third Reich. His main achievements have been significant and necessary modifications in the dominant Bultmannian hypothesis.

1. He initiated the so-called 'new quest of the historical Jesus', pointing out that to have the 'Christ of faith' without historical anchorage led to potential docetism.* He still insisted, however, on the importance of demythologizing (see Myth*) the gospels as the necessary corollary of justification* by faith* alone. (Faith must not be based on history, according to the Bultmannian school, lest it turn into a 'work': see 4. below.)

2. He argued that apocalyptic,* not Gnosticism,* was the 'mother of early Christianity', *i.e.* that Christianity, including Paul's* theology, was essentially Jewish in origin.

3. He argued that 'the righteousness of God' was not, as in Bultmann (and, so he claimed, in Luther), a status or attribute given by God to people, but God's own 'salvation-creating power'.

4. He understood Paul's theology as revolving around the 'justification of the ungodly' as opposed to an immanent process of developing salvation-history* (which he saw, embryonically, in Luke).

He was active in World Council of Churches circles, speaking on ecclesiology and the political implications of the gospel (see his *Jesus Means Freedom*). In 1977 he left the Lutheran church to become a Methodist following a dispute over student protest in Tübingen. Alongside shorter works on Hebrews and John, his *magnum opus* is the commentary on Romans (1973: ET, London and Grand Rapids, MI, 1980), for which he prepared with three volumes of essays on NT theology, particularly that of Paul. A collection of essays in his honour was published in

1976 under the title *Rechtfertigung* ('Justification'), edited by J. Friedrich *et al.* (Tübingen).

Bibliography

R. Morgan, *The Nature of New Testament Theology* (London, 1973), pp. 52–65; N. T. Wright, 'A New Tübingen School? E. Käsemann and His Commentary on Romans', *Them* 7 (1982), pp. 6–16.

N.T.W.

KENOTICISM, from the Gk. *kenōsis*, meaning (self-)'emptying' (used in Phil. 2:6–7), refers to a number of related Christological theories concerning the status of the divine in the incarnate Christ. While the term is found in a number of patristic writers and formed a key point of controversy between the Lutheran theological faculties of Tübingen and Giessen in the 17th century, kenoticism is usually associated with a group of German theologians in the mid-19th century: G. Thomassius (1802–75), F. H. R. von Frank (1827–94) and W. F. Gess (1819–91) and a group of British theologians in the late 19th and early 20th centuries: Charles Gore,* H. R. Mackintosh,* Frank Weston (1871–1924), P. T. Forsyth* and O. C. Quick (1885–1944).

The German kenoticists took the idea of self-emptying beyond its usual bounds of voluntary self-restraint of the divine nature by the God-man (the position of the Giessen faculty). Instead they believed that the divine Logos* limited itself in the act of incarnation.* The actual theories varied. Thomassius separated the metaphysical attributes, omnipotence, omnipresence and omniscience, from the moral attributes, love and holiness. The Logos gave up the former while retaining the latter. Other German kenoticists (Frank and Gess), however, took more radical positions, which stripped Jesus of any of the attributes of divinity and called into question the use of the term 'incarnation'.

The British kenoticists had a more positive orientation. Although often accused of developing kenoticism simply as a means of accommodating the results of biblical criticism by admitting the possibility of human ignorance in Jesus, it would be more true to say that British kenoticists, under the impact of a more historical reading of the gospels, came to the conclusion that traditional Christologies did not do justice to Jesus' human life. Thus, it was the gospel records of the human and limited consciousness of Jesus that the British kenoticists asserted over the strongly docetic* dogmatic tradition. Among the individual kenoticists the actual manner in which the divine self-emptying was believed to have occurred varied, but in general the emphasis was on the gracious character of the divine condescension and not on the precise metaphysical explanation of the act.

The current status of kenoticism is difficult to assess. On the one hand, although kenoticism is not a popular way of expressing the nature of the incarnation among conservative Christians, it should be noted that many of the major themes of the British kenoticists have been incorporated into modern evangelical Christologies. The reality of Jesus' temptations, his single (as opposed to double) consciousness, and the depth of pathos of the cry of dereliction from the cross are universally affirmed today. In the 19th century these were often considered part of the kenoticists' heretical innovations. On the other hand, modern evangelicalism is justifiably sceptical of any metaphysical speculation concerning the process of incarnation and sees the use of kenotic language as almost always inviting such speculation.

Bibliography

P. Dawe, *The Form of a Servant: A Historical Analysis of the Kenotic Motif* (Philadelphia, 1963); P. T. Forsyth, *The Person and Place of Christ* (London, 1909); O. C. Quick, *Doctrines of the Creed* (London, 1938).

B.E.F.

KERYGMA, KERYGMATIC THEOLOGY. The Gk. word *kērygma* is usually translated 'proclamation', 'preaching' or 'announcement' and, outside of the NT, it was used generally of a public notice proclaimed by a herald whereby that which was announced became effective by the act of announcing it.

The usage of the word within the NT makes no distinction between the act of proclamation and the content of that proclamation, though C. H. Dodd* and others have tried to trace a single core of content in the gospel* proclamation of the primitive church as recorded in the sermons and letters of the NT. Though one may presume a unanimity among the writers of the NT concerning the essential elements of the gospel message there is little evidence of any fixed or definitive 'creed'* to which the proclamation of the primitive church invariably conformed. In this sense, the content of the kerygma as recorded in the NT must be discerned from each specific context of proclamation.

However, the word kerygma has acquired a more specific philosophical and technical significance in modern theology through its usage by Rudolf Bultmann.* Bultmann suggests that the writing of the NT documents occurred within the context of the proclamation of the primitive church and therefore the documents themselves are kerygmatic in character. He then argues that it is both inappropriate and futile to probe behind this kerygma of the primitive church as recorded in the NT documents in order to discern the underlying historical data. The attempt to legitimize the kerygma in historical terms is considered by Bultmann to be symptomatic of a lack of faith;* the quest to discover the 'historical Jesus'* behind the 'Christ of faith' must be dismissed as invalid. Bultmann then considers that, since the kerygma of the NT is expressed in the terms of a primitive worldview, this kerygma must be demythologized (see Myth*) and reinterpreted in the terms of an existentialist* philosophy. This stretching of the term kerygma and the resultant wedge that is driven between the 'Jesus of history' and the 'Christ of faith' is both unhelpful and misleading. It is hard to avoid the conclusion that through this process of demythologization and an existentialist reinterpretation of the kerygma Bultmann has arrived at a 'different gospel' (Gal. 1:6).

Bultmann's hermeneutic developed from the seed-bed of dialectical theology* which is sometimes itself referred to as kerygmatic theology and which was characteristic of the early writings of Karl Barth.* In reaction to the liberalism* of 19th-century German theology, Barth proclaimed the radical discontinuity between God and man. The authentic subject of theology is not man and his religion but God and his Word: the Word that demands obedience; the Word that authenticates itself; the Word that does not therefore require historical legitimization. Though Barth in his *Church Dogmatics* continues to reject any authentication of God's Word by means of historical criticism, he avoids the dualism implicit in Bultmann's distinction between the 'Jesus of history' and the 'Christ of faith' and also rejects Bultmann's process of demythologization: the resurrection* of Jesus Christ is a real event of space and time, albeit an event which will not yield to the scrutiny of positivistic historical science.

Bibliography

H. W. Bartsch (ed.), *Kerygma and Myth*, 2 vols. (London, 1953, 1962); Rudolf Bultmann, *Theology of the New Testament*, 2 vols. (London, 1952, 1955); C. H. Dodd, *The Apostolic Preaching and its Developments* (London, 1936); Van A. Harvey, *The Historian and the Believer* (London, 1967).

J.E.C.

KIERKEGAARD, SØREN AABYE (1813–55). In philosophical terms Kierkegaard can be seen as the father-figure of existentialism.* He consciously opposed Hegel's* philosophy, stressing by contrast the role of individual decision and active engagement with truth within the confines of concrete, finite existence. Truth must be true 'for me'. In religious terms, he saw the purpose of his writings as that of showing what it meant to be a Christian. This was very different from being a 'name-Christian' in the Danish state church of his day. In theological terms he rejected an over-intellectualist notion of faith* and reflected extensively on the role of ethical decision and a stage of faith which might be said to transcend it.

Kierkegaard was born and educated in Copenhagen. Three sets of events or relationships have special importance for an understanding of his writings.

1. He grew up under the shadow of a dominating father who was himself plagued by a sense of guilt. Mikaël, the father, believed that his own act in childhood of cursing God could never be forgiven. He exacted high standards of academic success from Søren, who tried his best to please his father in this dismal atmosphere of duty, anxiety and guilt. But Søren was deeply shocked when he discovered that his father was not the morally upright man he had assumed him to be. His authority-figure collapsed and now he sought to discover what it meant to live as and for himself. For a period he experienced moral decline, but self-discovery led on further to an experience of repentance and faith.

365

2. Kierkegaard resumed his studies, and had begun pastoral ministry in the Lutheran Church when he fell deeply in love with Regine Olsen. But as soon as they became engaged he was filled with a sense of utter unworthiness. He felt compelled to withdraw both from the engagement and from the life of a Lutheran pastor. He interpreted his 'sacrifice' of Regine in terms of the divine call to Abraham to sacrifice Isaac. For Abraham to slay the son of promise was on one level paradoxical and a suspension of the ethical. Nevertheless God's call took precedence over the seemingly rational and ethical. For him, the broken engagement was the way of authentic discipleship in all its loneliness and contradiction of convention.

3. Kierkegaard now lived a withdrawn life. He began to write prodigiously, producing more than twenty books in the twelve remaining years before his premature death. A third event, however, contributed even further to his distress. He attacked the low standards of a satirical paper *The Corsair*, and the paper responded by making Kierkegaard effectively the object of public ridicule. Its devastating caricature made him the laughing-stock of Denmark. He interpreted this as the price for authentic Christian obedience, and set this in contrast to the easygoing pseudo-faith of 'name-Christians' in the Danish church.

Individualism

Kierkegaard's life seemed to turn on a radical contrast between authentic individual first-hand faith and the inauthentic acceptance of second-hand values. Kierkegaard saw this contrast in religious terms. He writes: 'The most ruinous evasion of all is to be hidden in the crowd in an attempt to evade God's supervision . . . in an attempt to get away from hearing God's voice as an individual' (*Purity of Heart is to Will One Thing*, London, ²1961, p. 163). Each one, he continues, 'shall render account to God as an individual'. In modern secular existentialism* this principle has become a largely negative one, as it is traced through Nietzsche* to Camus and Sartre. Authentic existence is seen in the terms of throwing off the conventions of Western bourgeois society and its predetermined expected roles. But Kierkegaard's criticisms were directed towards a second-hand claim to Christian faith. 'Christianity has been

abolished by *expansion* – by these millions of name-Christians . . .' (*Attack upon 'Christendom'*, London, 1944, p. 237). The notion of a 'Christian' state, for example, is 'shrewdly calculated to make God so confused in his head by all these millions that He cannot discover that He has been hoaxed, that there is not one single Christian' (*ibid.*, p. 127). In the venture of faith the individual stands alone before God. Kierkegaard chose for his own epitaph only the words 'That Individual'. He paid a price for his individualism. In his isolation from the church, his faith was always shot through with agonizing doubt, though he saw this as a mark of its authenticity.

Participation and subjectivity

It is impossible simply to acquire truth passively from others, because the appropriation of truth involves active engagement with truth on the part of the individual human subject. It is crucial to Kierkegaard's position that 'everyone who has a result merely as such does not possess it; for he has not the way' (*The Concept of Irony*, London, 1966, p. 340). Actively to become engaged in decision, struggle and response is what Kierkegaard calls 'the task of becoming subjective'. Subjectivity, in his use of the term, does *not* mean the arbitrary elevation of personal opinion over the claims of objective evidence. He defines subjectivity as 'being sharpened into an "I" rather than being dulled into a third person' (*Journals*, London and Princeton, NJ, 1938, p. 533). 'The objective accent falls on WHAT is said; the subjective accent on HOW it is said . . . Thus subjectivity becomes the truth' (*Concluding Unscientific Postscript*, Princeton, NJ, 1941, p. 181).

Finitude and indirect communication

Kierkegaard ironically called Hegel's philosophy 'the System'. He attacked Hegel for claiming, in effect, that reality can be viewed 'eternally, divinely, theocentrically', when in fact the philosopher is 'only a poor existing human being not competent to contemplate the eternal either eternally or divinely or theocentrically' (*ibid.*, p. 190). Kierkegaard would not have followed secular existentialists in effectively reducing truth to a matter of 'viewpoints'. But he insisted that the communication of truth proceeds indirectly or dialectically. Truth is not to be presented on a plate, as if it can be reduced to the dimensions of a single package. In his earlier writings Kierkegaard wrote under pseudonyms, leaving the reader to judge between competing perspectives in such a way that truth was perceived through struggle, engagement and decision. Truth cannot be 'surveyed' from a comfortable armchair, situated somewhere beyond or above the confines of human finitude. 'Truth becomes untruth in this or that person's mouth' (*ibid*. p. 181).

Bibliography

Works: In addition to those mentioned above: *Either/Or*, 2 vols. (London, 1944); *Fear and Trembling* (London, 1954); *Philosophical Fragments* (Princeton, NJ, and New York, 1936); *The Point of View* (London and New York, 1939); *Christian Discourses* (London and New York, 1939); *The Last Years: Journals 1853–55* (London, 1965); *A Kierkegaard Anthology*, ed. R. Brettall (New York, 1946). Complete ET in progress (Princeton, NJ, 1978–).

Critical studies include: E. J. Carnell, *The Burden of Søren Kierkegaard* (Grand Rapids, MI, 1965); H. Diem, *Kierkegaard's Dialectic of Existence* (Edinburgh, 1959); L. Dupré, *Kierkegaard as Theologian* (ET, London, 1963); W. Lowrie, *Kierkegaard* (London and New York, 1938); idem, *A Short Life of Kierkegaard* (Princeton, NJ, 1942); D. G. M. Patrick, *Pascal and Kierkegaard* (London, 1947).

A.C.T.

KINGDOM OF GOD, one of the principal themes of Scripture, along with the covenant,* which is the constitution or polity of the kingdom.

1. The phrase 'the kingdom of God' does not occur in the OT. But the notions of God as king and of his kingly rule are pervasive. There are various dimensions to this kingship. As the maker and sustainer of all that exists, he is 'the great King over all the earth' (Ps. 47:2), and 'his kingdom rules over all' (Ps. 103:19); his kingly control equally encompasses past, present and future ('Your kingdom is an everlasting kingdom, and your dominion endures through all generations', Ps. 145:13; see Providence,* Sovereignty of God*).

Along with this general and eternal kingship, God is the king of his covenant people, Israel.* In a particular, exclusive sense, not true of any other nation, he is 'Jacob's King' (Is. 41:21). Accordingly, Israel, the 'holy nation', is 'a kingdom of priests' (Ex. 19:6). This covenantal kingship, in turn, gives rise to the hope which is at the heart of the prophetic expectation of the entire OT. In the midst of national decline and even exile, the prophets announce the time when God will manifest himself as king, when in a climactic and unprecedented fashion, 'the Sovereign LORD comes with power, and his arm rules for him' (Is. 40:10), and when for Zion the proclamation at last holds true in the eschatological sense: 'Your God reigns' (Is. 52:7; *cf*. Dn. 2:44; 7:14, 27). This great future, realized through the ministry of the Messiah (*e.g.* Is. 11, 49), will mean salvation and blessing, not only for Israel but for all the nations (*e.g.* Is. 2:1–4; 49:7; Mi. 4.1–5); it is the fulfilment of the primal covenantal promise made to Abraham: 'and all peoples on earth will be blessed through you' (Gn. 12:3).

2. In contrast to the OT, the phrase 'the kingdom of God' or 'the kingdom of heaven' occurs frequently in the NT, especially in the synoptic gospels where it is the central theme in the proclamation of Jesus. Apparently the expression was taken over by him, and before him, by John the Baptist (Mt. 3:2), from contemporary Judaism. They give it, however, a sense radically at odds with the legalistic and nationalistic conceptions that permeate the great variety of apocalyptic and rabbinic materials. There is no difference in reference between 'the kingdom of God' and 'the kingdom of heaven' (*cf*. Mt. 4:17 with Mk. 1:15; Mt. 13:11 with Mk. 4:11 and Lk. 8:10). Mt. almost always uses the latter (in distinction from Mk. and Lk. who never do), probably in view of the Jewish background of his audience for whom 'heaven' was a reverent circumlocution for the divine name. Also the Gk. word *basileia*, conventionally translated 'kingdom', can have the dynamic meaning of 'rule', 'reign', 'kingship', as well as the concrete meaning of 'realm', 'territory governed by a king', 'kingdom'. Although the one meaning plainly suggests the other, the dynamic sense fits best, *e.g.* in key pronouncements like Mt 4:17; 12:28; Lk. 17:21; *cf*. Jn. 18:36.

The kingdom proclaimed by Jesus is not an ideal moral order (see Idealism;* Liberalism, German*). Nor is it more or less equivalent with divine sovereignty. Rather it answers to the great OT expectation. What Jesus announces is the realization of Israel's hope, the fulfilment of the covenant promises made to the fathers; the new and final order at the end of history has arrived at last with Jesus. In this sense his kingdom-preaching is eschatological;* it has a profound historical thrust. This is made plain by the summary statement of his ministry from its outset in Galilee (Mk. 1:15; *cf.* Mt. 3:2; 4:17): the gospel-call to repentance and faith is not a timeless, self-evident summons but is grounded in the situation defined jointly by what has finally taken place ('the time has come') and what is still impending ('the kingdom of God is near').

It is important to grasp the temporal pattern of Jesus' teaching. The kingdom is *future*. a. In the *distant* future, faithful Jews and Gentiles will gather for the great kingdom-banquet at the same time that unbelieving Jews (as well as all other unbelievers) are excluded, that is, at the time of final judgment* (Mt. 8:11, 12; *cf.* the references to 'weeping and gnashing of teeth' in the kingdom parables of Mt. 13:39–42, 49–50). Similarly, the kingdom inherited by the 'sheep' is concomitant with the destruction of the 'goats' and subsequent to the coming of the Son of Man and the angels for final judgment (Mt. 25:31–34, 41). b. However, 'some who are standing here will not taste death before they see the kingdom of God' (Lk. 9:27; *cf.* Mt. 16:28; Mk. 9:1; Mt. 10:23). Here the kingdom lies in the *immediate* future (*cf.* Mt. 4:17; Mk. 1:15), and is best understood as arriving in the death and exaltation of Jesus (including Pentecost; note how the Transfiguration, which directly follows this imminence statement in all three synoptic gospels, is essentially a preview of Christ's resurrection glory, see especially Mt. 17:9; Mk. 9:9).

Most striking, however, is Jesus' announcement that the kingdom is *present*. The disciples are blessed, just in distinction from those most prominent under the old covenant, because they have been granted an experiential knowledge of 'the secrets of the kingdom' as a present reality (Mt. 13:11, 16–17). The 'least' one presently in the kingdom is greater in this respect than John the Baptist (Mt. 11:11; *cf.* vv. 12–13). The healing of the demon-possessed man (Mt. 12:22–28) is evidence, not of Satan's kingdom-power (v. 26), but that 'the kingdom of God has come

upon you' (v. 28; *cf.* Lk. 11:20). This emphatic passage highlights a. the redemptive character of the kingdom; its programme is shaped negatively by its opposition to the rule of Satan, and b. the eschatological power of the Holy Spirit, as the dynamic of the kingdom.

These present and future aspects cohere not as two or more kingdoms but as the one, eschatological kingdom arriving in successive stages or instalments. Concretely, these stages are distinguished by the critical junctures in the work of Christ, resulting in a basic three-stage structure: a. the period of Jesus' earthly ministry, b. the period from his exaltation to his return (the time of the church), and c. the period beyond his return. Plainly this is not a matter of some preformed eschatological schema, from which Jesus is detachable. Rather the kingdom and its coming is thoroughly *messianic*, shaped by the unique demands of Christ's work. Truly he is *autobasileia* ('the kingdom in person').

3. In the rest of the NT, in contrast to the teaching of Jesus, explicit references to the kingdom are relatively infrequent. Stated globally, Jesus preached the kingdom, the apostles preached Jesus as the Christ. Sometimes this has been seen as evidence of a fundamental conflict: Paul and others have presumably turned the religion *of* Jesus into an essentially alien religion *about* Jesus. In fact, however, apostolic proclamation 'does nothing but explain the eschatological reality which in Christ's teaching is called the kingdom' (H. Ridderbos, *When the Time Had Fully Come*, Grand Rapids, MI, 1955, pp. 48–49). Because his death and resurrection, anticipated by Jesus himself as a decisive turning-point in the coming of the kingdom (see above, *cf.* Mt. 16:21; Mk. 9:31; Lk. 18:31–34; 24:7), had in fact taken place, it was inevitable that apostolic preaching and teaching focus on these climactic (kingdom) events (*e.g.* Acts 2:14–36; 17:2–3; 1 Cor. 15:3–4; 1 Pet. 1:10–12), and make use of themes (*e.g.* reconciliation, righteousness, the Holy Spirit) that bring out their significance. In fact, in the few references in Paul, for example, the kingdom, as for Jesus, is the great eschatological reality which is both future (1 Cor 6:9–10; Gal. 5:21; Eph. 5:5) and present (Rom. 14:17; 1 Cor. 4:20; Col. 1:13). For Paul, 'to proclaim . . . the whole

will of God' is to 'have gone about preaching the kingdom' (Acts 20:27, 25).

4. Much debated is the relationship between the kingdom and the church.* In distinction from the one extreme which *identifies* them (notably Roman Catholicism) and the other which views the kingdom as *currently postponed*, during the church-age, until the return of Christ (characteristically, at least, 'Dispensationalist theology'*), the church in fact manifests the kingdom without being identified with it under all circumstances. The church alone has been entrusted with 'the keys of the kingdom' (Mt. 16:18, 19), as it alone has been commissioned to preach 'the gospel of the kingdom' (Mt. 24:14). The church and only the church is made up of the citizens of the kingdom, those who by repentance and faith submit to the redemptive lordship of Christ. But the scope of his eschatological rule, the extent of his realm, is nothing less than the entire creation; all things are subject to him (*cf., e.g.,* Mt. 28:18; 1 Cor. 15:27; Heb. 2:8). Paul has captured the requisite balance: the exalted Christ is 'head over everything for the church' (Eph. 1:22).

5. Traditional theology did not grasp the eschatological presence of the kingdom announced by Jesus. In effect, it distinguished two kingdoms: one manifested through the church and the present spread of the gospel; and an entirely future, eschatological kingdom, associated with Christ's return (*cf., e.g.,* the distinction in answer 102 of The Westminster Shorter Catechism between the present 'kingdom of grace' and the future 'kingdom of glory'). Liberal theology of the late 19th and early 20th centuries, in keeping with its conception of Jesus as an inculcator of neo-Kantian ethics, viewed the kingdom of God in exclusively ethical terms as an ideal moral order. With the emergence, around the turn of the century, of the history-of-religions school* with its comparative approach, the Liberal view was felt to be an unbearable modernization. Instead, the self-understanding and message of Jesus were explained against the background of eschatological expectations within Judaism at that time. Specifically, Jesus proclaimed the imminent end of the world and arrival of the kingdom in violent, apocalyptic upheaval, with himself as its Messiah designate. This view ('consistent eschatology', *e.g.* J. Weiss (1863–1914), A. Schweitzer*) involved a one-sided,

exclusive stress on the future element in Jesus' kingdom proclamation that eliminated all present references. Eventually it prompted, in reaction, an equally one-sided emphasis on the undeniable present element that sought to explain away all future references ('realized eschatology', *e.g.* C. H. Dodd*). By mid-century critical scholarship had reached a consensus that the kingdom proclaimed by Jesus is an eschatological reality that is both present and future (the view already advanced at the turn of the century by G. Vos*). Debate, however, continues over how this eschatological structure is normative and can be made relevant for contemporary Christianity (the more conservative pole of the hermeneutical spectrum represented, *e.g.*, by O. Cullmann, see Salvation-history;* the more radical pole, *e.g.*, by R. Bultmann*).

Bibliography

G. R. Beasley-Murray, *Jesus and the Kingdom of God* (Exeter, 1986); O. Cullmann, *Salvation In History* (New York, 1967); W. G. Kümmel, *Promise and Fulfillment* (London, 1957); G. E. Ladd, *A Theology of the New Testament* (Grand Rapids, MI, 1974); H. Ridderbos, *The Coming of the Kingdom* (Philadelphia, 1962); G. Vos, *The Kingdom and the Church* (Philadelphia, 1903; 1972).

R.B.G.

KIRK, KENNETH E., see ANGLO-CATHOLIC THEOLOGY.

K NOWLEDGE OF GOD. The question whether and to what extent God can be known has been vigorously debated in both philosophy and theology. Philosophers quite often arrived at an agnostic* position (Kant,* Fichte, Comte, Spencer and others), while some assumed an atheistic* position (Feuerbach,* Marx,* Freud and others).

In theology the possibility for man to know God has hardly ever been doubted or denied. Rather, the questions that concerned theologians were the extent to which God can be known and how man can come to a true knowledge of God.

As to the *extent* of the knowledge of God, the view generally held was that God, although he can be known, remains incomprehensible, not only as to his innermost being but also in his revelation* itself. This incomprehensibility of God is due to our human limitations on the one hand, and to the nature of revelation on the other. The orthodox position is well stated by H. Bavinck:* 'God's revelation in creation and redemption fails to reveal him adequately. He cannot fully impart himself to creatures, inasmuch as in that case the latter must needs be God. Accordingly adequate knowledge of God does not exist. There is no name that makes known to us his being. No concept fully embraces him. No description does justice to him. That which is hidden behind the curtain of revelation is entirely unknowable' (*The Doctrine of God*, p. 21; *cf.* Jb. 11:7; Is. 40:28; Rom. 11:33–34). The inadequacy of all our knowledge of God does not mean, however, that this knowledge is not true or trustworthy. Christian theology has always maintained that God's revelation imparts a knowledge that is both reliable and true. From the nature of the case it follows that this knowledge is always analogical* in character. God reveals himself always 'indirectly', that is, by means of something belonging to the creation. All our knowledge is only 'by means of and in a mirror' (*cf.* 1 Cor. 13:12). It is therefore only a likeness of that perfect knowledge God has in himself. But because it is the likeness of that perfect knowledge it is real, dependable and true.

As to the *way* by which man comes to the knowledge of God, there is first of all the question whether there is an *innate* knowledge of God. Although under the influence of Platonic* thought some theologians came very close to such an idea, Christian theology in general has rejected it, even though it quite often did speak of the *cognitio Dei insita* (the innate knowledge of God). H. Bavinck describes it as follows: 'It indicates that man possesses both the "capacity, aptitude, power, ability" and the "inclination, tendency, disposition" to obtain some definite, certain, and indubitable knowledge of God; a knowledge gained in the normal course of development and in the environment in which God caused him to see the light, and arrived at in a natural way; *i.e.* "without scholarly argumentation and reasoning" ' (*op. cit.*, p. 58). Still, it is a confusing term, since it suggests that man is born with this knowledge. Even John Calvin* is not altogether clear at this point. In his *Institutes* he speaks of the 'sense of divinity', which God has engraved upon human minds

(I.iii.1), and of the 'seed of religion', which has been divinely planted in all (I.iv.1), before he speaks of revelation in the rest of the created order (I.v.1ff.).

It is generally agreed in Christian theology that *all* human knowledge of God is the fruit of God's own self-revelation. If God had not revealed himself, no-one would know anything at all about God. In this sense all human knowledge of God is acquired knowledge (*cognitio Dei acquisita*). This knowledge, however, is of two kinds, since God's self-revelation occurs in two ways. There is God's *general* self-revelation in creation, history and man himself, and there is God's *special* self-revelation in the history of salvation, which started immediately after the fall, was continued in the history of the patriarchs and of Israel, and found its culmination in the history of Jesus Christ and of the Spirit in the early church. This special revelation now comes to us in and through Scripture.

In the history of Christian theology this distinction of a twofold revelation has led to the idea of a twofold knowledge of God: *natural* and *revealed* theology. Especially in medieval theology and subsequently in Roman Catholic theology the idea of natural theology* has played a major part. According to Thomas Aquinas* it is possible to obtain some strictly scientific knowledge of God, for instance, concerning his existence and some of his attributes. This teaching became official church dogma when the First Vatican Council (1870) stated that God 'may be certainly known by the natural light of human reason, by means of created things' (note the word 'certainly'!). Such truths among things divine which of themselves are not beyond human reason can be known by everyone 'with facility, with firm assurance, and with no admixture of error'. It is no wonder that the so-called proofs of God's existence were always very prominent in Roman Catholic theology.

In our century Karl Barth* has strongly opposed every idea of natural theology, not only in its Roman Catholic and liberal forms but also in the way it was advocated by Emil Brunner.* For Barth there was no revelation apart from God's self-revelation in Jesus Christ. It is simply impossible for man to know God, the world and himself as they really are, apart from Christ. This means that Barth rejected not only natural theology but also the very idea of a general revelation in nature and history. Later on, in *CD* IV.3, Barth slightly modified his position in that, within the framework of the doctrine of the prophetic office of Christ, he granted that in the history of the world there may be lesser 'lights' that in a worldly fashion reflect '*the Light of the world*'.

Protestant theology, in both its Lutheran* and Reformed* forms, has commonly accepted the reality of a general self-revelation of God, while at the same time rejecting the idea of natural theology. Although general revelation is a fact, it is not a separate source of theology. The only starting-point for the Christian theologian is Scripture, which tells him who God is in Jesus Christ and also what God has revealed about himself in nature and history and man. Using the 'spectacles' of Scripture (Calvin), the believing theologian then also recognizes this self-revelation of the God and Father of Jesus Christ in the world around him. But it never becomes a separate source for the knowledge of God. Scripture remains the only source of all our *theo*-logy.

Bibliography

K. Barth, *CD, passim;* H. Bavinck, *The Doctrine of God* (Grand Rapids, MI, 1955); L. Berkhof, *Systematic Theology* (Grand Rapids, MI, 1953); G. C. Berkouwer, *General Revelation* (Grand Rapids, MI, 1955); E. Brunner and K. Barth, *Natural Theology* (London, 1946); G. H. Clark, *Religion, Reason and Revelation* (Nutley, NJ, 1961); E. A. Dowey, *The Knowledge of God in Calvin's Theology* (New York, 1952); H. Küng, *Does God Exist?* (London, 1980); T. H. L. Parker, *Calvin's Doctrine of the Knowledge of God,* (Grand Rapids, MI, 1959); B. Ramm, *Special Revelation and the Word of God* (Grand Rapids, MI, 1961).

K.R.

KNOX, JOHN (*c.* 1514–72). The principal theologian and architect of the Reformed Kirk of Scotland, Knox was born at Haddington and educated at St Andrews University, possibly under John Major (1467–1550), an advocate of scholasticism* and conciliarism. Following his ordination in 1536, Knox held minor posts as a notary and a tutor. Shortly after his conversion to Protestantism he came under the influence of George Wishart (*c.* 1513–46), from whom he learned an amalgam of Lutheran* and Reformed* ideas, including the views of Martin Bucer* on the Lord's Supper (see Eucharist*). Knox's conception of his calling as a prophet also dates from this period. While supporting a group of Protestant rebels in the castle at St Andrews, he was captured by the French and enslaved on a French ship. During his imprisonment he prepared a summary of the compendium of Lutheran thought by Henry Balnaves (d. 1579). Thus by 1549, when he was released and returned to England, Knox's theology was characterized by its eclectic fusion of the principles of Lutheran and Reformed thought, particularly with respect to the doctrines of justification* and the Lord's Supper.

In England Knox's preaching at Berwick, near the Scottish border, attracted so many Scots that the government became nervous. He accepted an invitation to preach to Edward VI's court but declined an offer to become Bishop of Rochester. During the revision of the first *Book of Common Prayer*, he was instrumental in the inclusion of the 'Black Rubric,' which stipulated that kneeling during Communion did not imply transubstantiation. When the Catholic Mary Tudor became queen in 1553, Knox struggled with his conscience over the duty of martyrdom before deciding he should flee the country. His years of exile were spent at Frankfurt, where he lost a battle to continue reforming the second *Book of Common Prayer*, and Geneva, where he was influenced by John Calvin.* At Geneva he wrote a series of tracts on political disobedience to idolatrous rulers, particularly the well-known *First Blast of the Trumpet Against the Monstrous Regiment of Women*, which generally denied the right of females to rule, excepting only those rare individuals such as the Hebrews' Deborah who had a divine calling. In these political tracts he developed the revolutionary view that common people had the right to overthrow a tyrannical and idolatrous sovereign (see Revolution, Theology of*). During his exile he also wrote a lengthy and tendentious defence of the Calvinist doctrine of predestination* against the work of an unknown Anabaptist.

Knox's exile was interrupted in 1555–56 by a return to Catholic Scotland, where he was fortunate to escape a charge of heresy. A group of Protestant lords invited him to return in 1559, and his preaching and leadership in the ensuing year was a major factor in the success of the Scottish Reformation. With a select group of colleagues, he helped draft the Scots Confession of Faith (1560), a classic of Reformed Protestantism (see Confessions*), and the *Book of Discipline*, with its pattern for church government and an ambitious blueprint for educational reform. After Mary Stuart returned to Scotland in 1561, Knox confronted her in three emotion-charged interviews in which he uncompromisingly condemned idolatry. His years in Scotland were characterized by major theological controversies with Catholics, the first with Ninian Winzet (c. 1518–92) over ordination and the second with Quintin Kennedy (1520–64) over the mass. Knox's greatest achievement in these years was the writing of his *History of the Reformation of Religion within the Realm of Scotland* (ed. W. C. Dickenson, 2 vols., Edinburgh, 1949). The triumph of Protestantism in Scotland was assured when Mary Stuart abdicated in 1567 and Knox preached the coronation sermon for her infant son, James VI.

Bibliography

Works, 6 vols., ed. D. Laing (Edinburgh, 1846–52); *John Knox: Political Writings*, ed. M. Breslaw (Cranbury, NJ, 1986).

R. L. Greaves, *Theology and Revolution in the Scottish Reformation: Studies in the Thought of John Knox* (Grand Rapids, MI, 1980); R. G. Kyle, *The Mind of John Knox* (Lawrence, KS, 1984); W. S. Reid, *Trumpeter of God* (New York, 1974); J. Ridley, *John Knox* (Oxford, 1968).

R.L.G.

KOINONIA. This English transliteration of the NT Greek term often translated 'fellowship'* is in common use in ecumenical* theology, particularly in discussions involving Roman Catholics and Anglicans. It is presented as the key concept underlying the Agreed Statements of the Anglican-Roman Catholic International Commission on the eucharist, ministry and ordination, and authority in the church (*The Final Report*, London, 1982). Its meaning is near to 'communion', a relation between individual Christians or Christian communities resulting from their common participation in one and the same reality. 'Koinonia with one

another is entailed by our koinonia with God in Christ.' It has thus become the controlling model for understanding the nature of the church,* which is not the case in the NT. Its currency, often with a somewhat fluid meaning, attests the prevalence of the notion of the church as 'mystery' over more institutional or social approaches to the church. A somewhat comparable concept in Eastern Orthodoxy is *sobornost.**

Bibliography

B. C. Butler, *The Church and Unity* (London, 1979); A. Dulles, *Models of the Church* (Garden City, NY, 1974).

D.F.W.

KRAEMER, HENDRIK (1888–1965). A Dutch layman who deeply influenced international missionary thinking in the period 1930–60. After the early death of his father and mother he was sent to a diaconal orphanage. There he began to study the Bible and, at the age of fifteen, went through a deep spiritual experience which led him to the Christian faith and into the Christian church. He first received a training as a missionary, but then went on to study Indonesian languages and in 1922 was sent to Indonesia in the service of the Dutch Bible Society. Here he obtained a wide and deep knowledge of Javanese mysticism and Indonesian Islam. He greatly assisted the Indonesian churches in their struggle for independence.

In 1928 he attended the International Missionary Conference at Jerusalem and participated in the discussion about the relationship between the Christian faith and other world religions. At the invitation of the International Missionary Council he wrote as a study guide for the Third World Missionary Conference held at Tambaram, India, in 1938, *The Christian Message in a non-Christian World* (London, 1938). In a way this was a reply to the report *Re-thinking Missions* of the Laymen's Foreign Mission Inquiry (1932), which asserted that the aim of missions is 'to seek with people of other lands a true knowledge and love of God, expressing in life and word what we have learned through Jesus Christ'. In his own book Kraemer strongly emphasized the radical discontinuity between 'biblical realism' and non-Christian religious experience.* Acknowledging that our Christian *religion** also stands under the judgment of God, he maintained that the Christian *revelation** is incomparable and absolutely *sui generis*, because it is 'the record of God's self-disclosing and re-creating revelation in Jesus Christ . . . giving the divine answer to this demonic and guilty disharmony of man and the world'. He did not deny the reality of 'general revelation', but for him this revelation did not lead to true religion, but was itself an object of faith, because it could be discovered only in the light of the 'special revelation' in Christ. Co-operation with non-Christian religions and a combined search for further truth, therefore, would mean a betrayal of the word of God.

In 1937 Kraemer was appointed professor of the science of religion at Leiden. During World War II he was imprisoned as a hostage by the Germans. After the war he was very active in the reorganization of the Netherlands Reformed Church. Largely due to his influence the new church order mentioned missions as an essential element of the life and work of the church. From 1948 to 1958 he served as the first director of the Ecumenical Institute at Bossey, near Geneva.

Kraemer was one of the most influential missionary and ecumenical thinkers of this century. Other important books of his published in English are: *Religion and the Christian Faith* (London, 1956); *The Communication of the Christian Faith* (Philadelphia, 1956); *A Theology of the Laity* (London and Philadelphia, 1956); *World Cultures and World Religions: The Coming Dialogue* (London, 1958).

See also: CHRISTIANITY AND OTHER RELIGIONS; MISSIOLOGY.

Bibliography

C. F. Hallencreutz, *Kraemer towards Tambaram. A Study in Hendrik Kraemer's Missionary Approach* (Uppsala, 1966); idem, *New Approaches to Men of Other Faiths*, WCC Research Pamphlet no. 18 (Geneva, 1970), for Kraemer after Tambaram; A. Th. van Leeuwen, *Hendrik Kraemer, Dienaar der Wereldkerk* (Amsterdam, 1959).

K.R.

KÜNG, HANS (b. 1928). A Swiss Roman Catholic theologian, who has taught at Tübingen since 1960. Küng's theological work has been dominated by three main concerns: apologetics, ecumenism, and reform in the Roman Catholic Church. He sees his most important task as a theologian to be that of using all the resources of modern theology to present the Christian gospel as a credible and relevant message for the modern world. Especially in his *On Being a Christian*, which he called 'a kind of small "Summa" of the Christian faith', but which for all its theological weight was aimed at and achieved a very wide readership, Küng expounded a Christianity centred on the historical Jesus as its distinguishing feature, and a Christian faith compatible with modern critical rationality and the aspirations and achievements of modern humanism. Jesus is presented as the true man who makes it possible for modern men and women to live in a genuinely human way. Further works on the existence of God and life after death have continued Küng's apologetic work.

His ecumenical concerns go back to his first book, in which he attempted the *tour de force* of reconciling the Protestant and Roman Catholic doctrines of justification* by comparing the teachings of the Council of Trent (see Councils;* Roman Catholic Theology*) and Karl Barth* on this classic point of denominational division. His ecclesiological studies also demonstrate a strong ecumenical concern, and in general it could be said that Küng's theological approach results in an ecumenical, rather than specifically Roman Catholic, theology. It belongs to the 'evangelical Catholicity' or 'Catholic evangelicity' which is obligated to the whole church but brings everything to the 'evangelical' test of the gospel, which is Jesus himself as the criterion of Christian faith.

Since the point in the Second Vatican Council (see Councils;* Roman Catholic Theology*) when it seemed to Küng that the progressive direction initiated by Pope John XXIII was being frustrated by the reactionary authoritarianism in the church, he has seen himself in the role of 'his Holiness's loyal opposition'. His reforming critique of the church is based on the twin principles of the normative priority of the historical Jesus and the NT gospel over all subsequent developments of the tradition, and the need to be open to the critical rationality and liberal attitudes of the modern world. These principles characterize much recent progressive Roman Catholic theology, but Küng's radical, often polemical and provocative application of them makes him virtually a Protestant in conservative eyes. Criticism of his theology focused on his Christology,* since in *On Being a Christian* he interpreted the ontological Christology of incarnational dogma in purely functional terms, and on his explicit denial of the dogma of ecclesiastical (not only papal*) infallibility. In the latter case, his deliberate rejection of the teaching of Vatican I and Vatican II and his demand for frank recognition that the church has unequivocally erred in doctrinal statements in the past constitute a radical break with the principles and method of traditional Roman Catholic theology.* Protracted investigations of his work by the Congregation for the Doctrine of Faith led in 1979 to the Vatican's withdrawal of his canonical mission, *i.e.* his authorization to teach as a Catholic theologian.

Bibliography

The Church (London, 1967); *Does God Exist?* (London, 1980); *Eternal Life?* (London, 1984); *Infallible?* (London, 1971); *Justification* (London, 1965); *On Being A Christian* (London, 1977).

H. Häring and K.-J. Kuschel (eds.), *Hans Küng: His Work and His Way* (London, 1979); C. M. LaCugna, *The Theological Methodology of Hans Küng* (Chico, CA, 1982); R. Nowell, *A Passion for Truth* (London, 1981).

R.J.B.

KUYPER, ABRAHAM (1837–1920). The son of a Dutch Reformed Church minister, Kuyper was born in Massluis, the Netherlands. At the University of Leiden he distinguished himself as a brilliant student and strong advocate of liberalism. During his first pastorate, in the small fishing village of Beesd, Kuyper experienced an evangelical conversion after reading the English novel *The Heir of Redclyffe* by Charlotte Yonge. Influenced by the simple, Calvinist piety of his parishioners, he renewed his study of theology to become the leader of the Dutch neo-Calvinist movement.

Kuyper wrote hundreds of books and articles, the majority of which have never been translated into English, on topics as diverse as art, politics, literature, philosophy and social issues. In all of these he sought to develop a consistent Christian world-and-life-view. He founded two newspapers, the weekly religious magazine *De Heraut* ('The Herald') and the daily newspaper *De Standaard* ('The Standard').

In 1874 he entered the Dutch parliament as a representative for the newly founded Anti-Revolutionary party which, following the lead of Groen van Prinsterer (1801–76), was opposed to the principles expressed by the French Revolution and political liberalism. He became prime minister in 1900 but lost office in 1905 largely because of his controversial handling of the bitter railway strike of 1902. From 1908 to shortly before his death in 1920 he was a member of the Dutch Second Chamber of parliament and continued to edit *De Standaard*.

Kuyper was active in the 'Christian school struggle' and fought for state aid for private Christian schools. He founded the Free University of Amsterdam in 1880 and led a successful secession from the State Church to found the independent Gereformeerde Kerk (Reformed Church) in 1886.

Theologically, Kuyper developed Calvin's* teachings about common grace* to provide a basis for Christian social action. He also placed great emphasis on the importance of the kingdom of God,* an idea he seems to have picked up from F. D. Maurice (1805–72; see Christian Socialism*). His greatest contribution is in his development of the notion of 'sphere-sovereignty' which is similar to Michael Novak's and Peter Berger's (b. 1929) idea of 'mediating structures' as a basis for the development of religious, social and political pluralism. To Kuyper's work many contemporary Christian movements can be traced. Probably the best-known evangelical to be influenced by Kuyper is Francis Schaeffer* whose work has helped popularize some of Kuyper's ideas with, amongst others, the so-called 'Moral Majority' in America. However, left-wing Christian activists have also been influenced by Kuyper, and in North America there is a growing interest in his work.

See also: DUTCH REFORMED THEOLOGY.

Bibliography

Lectures on Calvinism (Grand Rapids, MI, 1898); *Principles of Sacred Theology* (Grand Rapids, MI, 1898); *The Work of the Holy Spirit* (Grand Rapids, MI, 1900).

P. Kasteel, *Abraham Kuyper* (Louvain,

1938; in Dutch); F. Vandenberg, *Abraham Kuyper* (Grand Rapids, MI, 1960).

I.He.

L

LAITY. This is the conventional designation of church members who are not clergy (ordained). The Gk. *laos*, 'people', is used in the NT of Israel* (Mt. 2:6; Acts 7:34; Heb. 11:25 – reflecting a characteristic LXX usage) and the church* (Tit. 2:14; Heb. 4:9; Rev. 18:4). 1 Pet. 2:9–10 ('You are ... a royal priesthood ... a *laos* for God's possession ... now you are God's *laos*') shows that both 'laity' and 'priesthood' should be used only of the whole church. (In early Christian writings *laos* often denotes the church as 'the new people' or as God's people gathered for worship.) 'Laity' has enjoyed greatest theological acceptance where a restricted 'priesthood' has operated. In other traditions it is used, if at all, non-theologically, by custom or convenience. (*Cf.* 'members' in 'members and minister(s)', often implying separate categories. In some denominations ministers are *not* members of their congregations.)

Laos could mean 'the populace, masses', in distinction from leaders or experts (Lk. 20:19; Acts 6:12; *cf.* Eng. 'layman' contrasted with doctor, scientist, *etc.*), and so the people of Israel apart from the priests (Heb. 5:3; 7:27). From this usage the adjective *laikos* entered Christian literature, first in *1 Clement*, which distinguishes 'the lay person' from the high priest, priests and Levites (40:5; *laikos* never occurs in the LXX, but occasionally in other Gk. versions of the OT, meaning 'common, ordinary'). Clement is talking about Judaism, *not* the church, but from *c.* 200 (Tertullian,* Hippolytus*) 'lay' became common to designate non-clergy, as the obverse of regarding bishops and presbyters as priests.

For much of church history the laity have had little scope, especially in worship and church government, although most centuries have produced outstanding exceptions. Early monasticism was in part a lay protest against increasing clerical monopolization, and anticlericalism was common in medieval dissent (*cf.* Waldensians*). The early Reformation had a strongly anticlerical thrust. Luther,* followed by all the Reformers, overthrew the deep-seated medieval dichotomy between religious (therefore superior, *i.e.* monks and clergy) and secular (therefore inferior) by his doctrines of the priesthood* of all believers and the callings of all Christians (see Vocation*), but the ordained/non-ordained distinction survived or resurfaced in all the Reformation churches.

The ecumenical movement* claims the credit for 'the rediscovery of the laity', *i.e.* of the church as God's people (not a hierarchy or institution). 'Never in church history, since its initial period, has the role and responsibility of the laity in Church and world been a matter of so basic, systematic, comprehensive and intensive discussion', implying 'a new examination and general reshaping of all ecclesiologies which we have had for centuries' (H. Kraemer*). The earlier missionary expansion deserves credit also. The biblical theology* movement has been influential, as have secularization* and the disintegration of Christendom and advances in general education. Emphasis is now laid on the role of lay Christians in society – 'the laity as the dispersion of the Church' (Kraemer). Roman Catholics talk of 'the lay apostolate'.

For all its convenience, 'laity' remains without theological substance, for ministers* belong to the *laos* of God. They neither constitute an order apart from it nor differ from other members except in function.

Bibliography
H. Kraemer, *A Theology of the Laity* (London, 1958); *idem*, *Laici in Ecclesia: An Ecumenical Bibliography* (Geneva, 1961); S. C. Neill and H.-R. Weber (eds.), *The Layman in Christian History* (London, 1963); H. Strathmann in *TDNT* IV, pp. 29–57.

D.F.W.

LAMBETH QUADRILATERAL, see ANGLICANISM.

LATITUDINARIANISM. This term describes the attitudes and opinions of those in the English church of the late 17th and 18th centuries who sought a pattern of religious belief and experience free from what were perceived as the opposing extremes of Puritan* fanaticism and High Church extremism. As the name suggests, it was characterized by breadth and variety, but its most salient features were the appeal to reason as authoritative in religious questions, the pursuit of toleration* and irenicism in theological and ecclesiastical debate, and a deep-seated horror of 'enthusiasm'. The movement marks the emergence of that tendency to liberal and pluralistic opinions which is so characteristic of the broad middle ground within the Church of England (cf. Anglicanism*).

The origins of Latitudinarianism can be traced back to Richard Hooker's* appeal to the light of reason as a supplementary authority to the Bible, which was taken up in the early 17th century by divines such as William Chillingworth (1602–44). The original Latitudinarians were a group including Chillingworth who were associated with Lord Falkland at Great Tew in Oxfordshire during the 1630s. The term was also applied to the Cambridge Platonists* of the Interregnum because of their breadth of sympathy and rejection of the personal animosities which characterized Puritan controversial theology. However, the term is most commonly used today of a wide group of leading churchmen of the late 17th century, many of whom were disciples of the Cambridge Platonists, but who neglected their mysticism* and emphasis on religious experience* in favour of their appeal to reason as 'the candle of the Lord' in the soul. And even in this respect the Latitudinarians were less than completely faithful to their mentors, for where the Platonists saw reason as a divine light permeating the whole personality, they tended to identify it with common sense. As a result, by comparison, they appear worthy, but pedestrian and pragmatic.

The background to the emergence of Latitudinarianism was the low level of personal morality characteristic of Restoration court circles, and the rise of natural science in the intellectual world. In this context its adherents appealed to reason as a defence against what they saw as the unbridled 'enthusiasm' of the dissenting sects. As the counterpart of the new natural science they emphasized natural theology* and the ability of the rational mind to grasp the fundamentals of religion without recourse to revelation,* and this led to a tendency to formulate the faith in minimal terms. For them the basic religious motivation was the hope of immortality, and on this foundation they erected a utilitarian appeal to moral behaviour, commending religion for its advantages, as in John Tillotson's (1630–94) sermon *The Wisdom of Being Religious* (London, 1664). They were opponents of all kinds of superstition and of the dogmatism which had characterized the Calvinist theology of the preceding age. Theological complexity was regarded with suspicion as a plot by divines to keep simple people from perceiving the truth, and they cultivated a preaching and writing style of dispassionate simplicity. Their preaching lacked the drama of the Puritan pulpit, but appealed to an age that had grown weary of religious controversy. Pastoral care was a high priority though its substance was of a piece with their whole approach. They knew something of the inwardness of religion, though they rejected the public expression of emotion. Like the Platonists before them, they passed on to succeeding generations less than all that they were, and their evacuation of *feeling* from religion was an important contribution to that emotional starvation which made the Evangelical Awakening of the mid-18th century so cathartic an experience for so many.

Bibliography

G. R. Cragg, *From Puritanism to the Age of Reason* (Cambridge, 1950); idem, *Reason and Authority in the Eighteenth Century* (Cambridge, 1964); N. Sykes, *From Sheldon to Secker* (Cambridge, 1959); B. Willey, *The Eighteenth Century Background* (Harmondsworth, 1972).

D.D.S.

LAUSANNE COVENANT. In July 1974 an International Congress on World Evangelization, convened under the leadership of the evangelist Dr Billy Graham (b. 1918), was held at Lausanne, Switzerland. At the end, the vast majority of the 2,700 participants put their name to a document called the Lausanne Covenant.

The Covenant is a statement of intent concerning the unfinished task of evangelization.* It consists of 15 paragraphs affirming God's purpose to create a special people for himself, Jesus Christ as the world's only saviour, the nature and urgency of evangelism, Christian social responsibility, evangelism across cultures, human rights* (particularly religious freedom), the Holy Spirit in evangelism and the hope of Christ's return. Its evangelical thrust is underlined in a paragraph on the authority and power of the Bible.

The document was originally drawn up from statements in the main speakers' papers and revised in the light of the participants' contributions, especially those from a Third World perspective. The title 'covenant', rather than 'declaration', is meant to emphasize commitment to the task of world evangelization.

The Covenant's significance lies in the breadth of its vision of the church's missionary task, its courage in handling controversial issues, its ability to combine different evangelical traditions and its subsequent extensive reception by the evangelical constituency world-wide as a fresh theological charter, expressing basic convictions about the church's multiple task in a changing world.

Bibliography

J. D. Douglas (ed.), *Let the Earth Hear His Voice* (Minneapolis, MN, 1975) – Congress papers; C. R. Padilla (ed.), *The New Face of Evangelicalism* (London, 1976); J. Stott, *The Lausanne Covenant – An Exposition and Commentary* (Minneapolis, MN, 1975).

J.A.K.

LAW. The term 'law' is used in a variety of contexts and senses: for example, laws of physics, laws of nature and laws of hygiene, and laws which form part of a legal system. The primary distinction here is between laws which are basically descriptive (and which, if it transpires that they do not fit the facts, are *ipso facto* modified) and laws which are prescriptive (and so demand a conformity which may not always be forthcoming). It is primarily with prescriptive laws that this article is concerned.

No society of human beings has ever been able to dispense with laws which regulate how they should behave. In an autocracy these ultimately rest on the fiat of some monarch or dictator; in an oligarchy on the authority of a ruling clique, whether this is an aristocracy of social status, intellectual superiority or military might – or, indeed, a plutocracy of wealth; whereas in a democracy they should always represent the will of the community as a whole, whether this is determined by means

of a referendum or, more often, by the decision of duly appointed representatives. But in most societies a considerable part of their law consists of customs which have come to have the force of law: that is, customs which could be enforced by a court or at least form the basis of litigation. Such is 'positive' law.

It is a common phenomenon, however, for societies to regard part of their law as having been divinely revealed to some prophet, priest or king. It is therefore held to be especially sacrosanct, and to be enforceable, ultimately, at the bar and by the sanctions of divine power. Such is 'divine' law.

Frequently, again, the claim is made that certain principles of law are inherent in the very nature of things, and that they can be discerned by rational creatures in the light of reason. Such is 'natural' law, which can often be distinguished from 'divine' law only by the fact that the latter depends on special revelation,* while the former represents principles which, in theory at least, all intelligent and right-minded persons can perceive for themselves. But the distinction sometimes goes further than this, as may be seen in the fact that the strictest school of Muslim jurists held that it is impossible for man to distinguish good from evil apart from divine revelation. Not only so, but in their view an act is good only because God has commended it, or evil solely because he has prohibited it. Nor has he commanded the good because it is intrinsically good, or forbidden the evil because it is inherently evil. So had he reversed his decree, what is now regarded as virtue would have become vice, and vice would have been virtue. Other Muslim jurists were less extreme and held that God commanded the good because it was by nature good, and forbade evil because it was essentially evil; and that man could *sometimes* distinguish virtue from vice by the light of reason. There is a clear link here with the medieval Christian schoolmen (see Scholasticism*) since some of them, like Thomas Aquinas,* insisted that the divine law proceeded from God's mind and wisdom, while others, like Duns Scotus,* traced it to God's will and decree.

Ancient Israel was virtually a theocracy* in which 'divine' law was almost synonymous with morality. As in Islam, there was little, therefore, to distinguish law from morality, since both law and morality rested essentially on divine revelation. Yet the basic distinction must always have prevailed: that some precepts and injunctions can be enforced by human courts, while others cannot. The Torah (lit. 'instruction'; commonly translated 'law' in the OT) could, and did, command a man to love his neighbour; but no human courts could do more than penalize actions or words which injured him.

Then, in the fullness of time, Jesus came, not 'to abolish the Law or the Prophets ... but to fulfil them' (Mt. 5:17). It was to his person, work and teaching that they had both pointed, and they found in him their perfect fulfilment. He fulfilled the Decalogue in his life of perfect obedience and reinterpreted it in his authoritative teaching, since its precepts are basically as immutable as the lawgiver whose character they reflect. He fulfilled the sacrificial law when he 'offered for all time one sacrifice for sins', and thereby 'set aside' the OT law in this respect, since 'by one sacrifice he has made perfect for ever those who are being made holy' (Heb. 10:9–14). He also set aside the laws of ceremonial defilement by his teaching that what really defiles a man, and erects a barrier between him and a holy God, is the moral corruption of his heart rather than the ceremonial uncleanness of his body (cf. Mk. 7:1–23). As for the judicial law of the OT, this had accomplished its purpose (cf. Mt. 5:18) when 'the kingdom of God' was 'taken away' from Israel as a nation and 'given to a people who will produce its fruit' (Mt. 21:43).

Drawn as they are from 'every nation, tribe, people and language' (Rev. 7:9), Christians are today subject to the criminal and civil law of the human governments to which they owe allegiance (1 Pet. 2:13–17). It is when 'positive law' cuts right across the moral law of God that Christians are called to 'obey God rather than men' (Acts 5:29; cf. 4:19), and only when the authorities of the state in which they live act wholly contrary to the mandate God has given them that Christians cease to owe them the respect and obedience they can otherwise rightly claim (Rom. 13:1–7).

The NT also recognizes the concept of 'natural' law in the sense that when those who do not know God's revealed law 'do by nature things required by [that] law, they are a law for themselves ... since they show that the requirements of [that] law are written on their hearts, their consciences also bearing witness, and their thoughts now accusing, now even defending them' (Rom. 2:14–15). This is why the apostle declared that 'The wrath of God is being revealed from heaven' against the wickedness of those who 'suppress the truth' which they in fact know – and are therefore 'without excuse' (Rom. 1:18–20). Only so could he refer to an intelligible distinction between 'natural' and 'unnatural' sexual* relations (Rom. 1:26–27) and then, after a comprehensive list of sins, conclude that: 'Although they know God's righteous decree that those who do such things deserve death, they not only continue to do these very things but also approve of those who practise them' (Rom. 1:32).

It is chiefly Roman Catholic* theologians who have attempted to develop the doctrine of 'natural' law as a detailed system which goes far beyond this biblical basis. Perhaps the most controversial point today is the official Roman Catholic teaching that contraception, except by total abstention from intercourse (whether permanently or in between somewhat dubious 'safe' periods), is 'intrinsically immoral'. The argument is that the primary purpose of marital intercourse, in natural law, is the procreation of children, rather than the mutual expression and renewal of conjugal love. All admit that the latter is right and proper even when there is little, or no, prospect of procreation; but papal teaching insists that no 'artificial' means of contraception can ever be right, whatever may be the cost (whether personal or in terms of the marriage relationship). To attribute this dogma to 'natural' law, when the overwhelming majority of men and women cannot, in conscience, regard a responsible use of all such means of contraception as 'intrinsically immoral', seems to undermine the very basis of the doctrine – a view shared by some theologians, and vast numbers of laymen, in the Roman Church.

See also: BIOETHICS; ETHICS; LAW AND GOSPEL; LOVE; MORAL THEOLOGY.

Bibliography

J. N. D. Anderson, Morality, Law and Grace (Leicester, 1972); idem, God's Law and God's Love (London, 1980); B. N. Kaye and G. J. Wenham (eds.), Law, Morality and the Bible (Leicester, 1978); E. F. Kevan, The Grace of Law (London, 1964); O. O'Donovan, Resurrection and Moral Order:

An Outline for Evangelical Ethics (Leicester, 1986); *Contraception and Holiness: the Catholic Predicament*, a symposium introduced by Archbishop Thomas D. Roberts (London, 1965).

J.N.D.A.

LAW AND GOSPEL. The law* expresses God's holy will for the life and behaviour of mankind. The gospel* is the good news of reconciliation with God accomplished by Jesus Christ. Throughout the history of the church, law and gospel have been variously related to one another.

In the Middle Ages there was a tendency to identify law with gospel. The gospel was at times called the new law. For many, keeping the law was an essential element in becoming reconciled to God.

Luther* and the Protestant Reformation saw the relation of law and gospel quite differently. There were differences of emphasis and expression within classic Protestantism* on the relation of law and gospel, but there was an underlying basic conceptual agreement. For Protestants the law was understood as the way to life given to Adam. After the fall* the law could no longer function as the way to life for corrupted and sinful mankind because it could not keep the law perfectly. So the law – good and spiritual in itself – stood to condemn humanity. Men and women needed another way to life that could deliver from the guilt of sin. That way was provided in Jesus Christ. The gospel is the good news that Jesus, the sinless one, kept the law in the place of his people and died to bear the curse for their sin, and that his saving work is received by faith* alone, not by obedience. The gospel, then, is life through Christ who justifies* believers by forgiving their sin and imputing his righteousness to them.

As the Reformers reflected on the law they came to see three uses for it. First, the law serves as a guide to society* in promoting civic righteousness. Secondly, the law convicts sinners and drives them to Christ. Thirdly, the law directs Christians in holy living.

For Lutheran theology* the distinction between the law and the gospel became a key organizing principle. The law produces repentance and the gospel leads to faith. On the third use of the law Luther taught that a holy life arises spontaneously from the heart of a believer, but that the law does help the Christian recognize and confront the sin* that remains in him.

In Reformed theology* the law-gospel distinction is foundational but is often implicit rather than explicit. In Reformed orthodoxy a key manifestation of the law-gospel distinction is in the distinction between the covenant of works and the covenant of grace (see Covenant*). On the third use of the law Reformed theology teaches that the believer needs the law to direct him in holy living.

Historically both Lutherans and Reformed have had trouble maintaining the proper balance between law and gospel. Imbalance produces either antinomianism on the one hand or legalism and moralism on the other.

Antinomianism so stresses Christian freedom* from the condemnation of the law that it underemphasizes the need of the believer to confess sins daily and to pursue sanctification* earnestly. It may fail to teach that sanctification inevitably follows justification. Roman Catholics in effect charged the Reformation with antinomianism in claiming that the doctrine of justification by faith alone would lead to moral laxity.

As early as the 1530s Luther expressed concern that one of his followers, Johann Agricola (*c.* 1494–1566), had become antinomian. Luther criticized Agricola for not stressing adequately the moral responsibility of Christians. In the 17th century several English Calvinists such as Tobias Crisp (1600–43) were charged with antinomianism. In the first three centuries of Protestantism the number of antinomians was very small, yet among 17th-century English Protestants there were very exaggerated fears of it.

The much greater danger historically facing the Reformation balance of law and gospel has been moralism and legalism. Moralists or neonomians so stress Christian responsibility that obedience becomes more than the fruit or evidence of faith. Rather obedience comes to be seen as a constituent element of justifying faith. Legalism inevitably undermines Christian assurance* and joy* and tends to create a self-centred, excessively introspective piety – remarkably like medieval piety. (C. F. Allison traces the development of neonomianism in England in his excellent book, *The Rise of Moralism*, London, 1966.)

Moralism became so pervasive in Reformed churches in the 18th century that several

379

strong reactions occurred. In Scotland the Marrow men, Thomas Boston,* the Erskine brothers, Ebenezer (1680–1754) and Ralph (1685–1752), and others, confronted the dominant moralism in the Church of Scotland and were roughly treated. In America the Great Awakening led by the preaching of George Whitefield* more successfully challenged the moralism of the churches.

In the 19th century the dispensationalism* of J. N. Darby* was another effort to avoid moralism. Law was identified as the way of salvation in the Mosaic dispensation whereas the gospel of grace was the way of salvation in the NT dispensation. The actual effect of dispensationalism has been to move in the direction of antinomianism, especially with the development of the distinction between Christ as Saviour and Christ as Lord. This distinction is not only theoretically antinomian but has in fact led to and justified moral laxity in Christian circles.

Another influential stage in the effort to balance law and gospel came in the work of Karl Barth.* Barth wrote of 'gospel and law', arguing a basic unity between the two. He agreed with the Roman Catholic Hans Küng* that the Reformers had set law and gospel too much in opposition. Barth's amalgam of gospel and law led him to agree with Küng that justification was both by the imputation of Christ's righteousness and by an infusion of his righteousness resulting in moral transformation. Barth's position self-consciously rejects the Reformation balance and moves in the direction of moralism. Yet his position has affected evangelical theologians such as Daniel Fuller (b. 1925).

The church today needs to understand afresh the biblically balanced teaching on law and gospel taught by the 16th-century Reformers in their confessions* and theologies. Such an understanding is foundational to balanced Christian living.

Bibliography

W. Andersen, *Law and Gospel. A Study in Biblical Theology* (London, 1961); K. Barth, *God, Grace and Gospel* (Edinburgh, 1959); C. H. Dodd, *Gospel and Law* (Cambridge, 1951); G. Ebeling, *Word and Faith* (London, 1963); H.-H. Esser, in *NIDNTT* II, pp. 438–56; W. Gutbrod, in *TDNT* IV, pp. 1059–91; E. F. Kevan, *The Grace of Law: A Study in Puritan Theology* (London, 1964); T. M. McDonough, *The Law and the Gospel in Luther* (Oxford, 1963); H. Thielicke, *The Evangelical Faith*, vols. 2–3 (Grand Rapids, MI, 1978, 1982); idem, *Theological Ethics*, vol. 1 (London, 1968); O. Weber, *Foundations of Dogmatics*, vol. 2 (Grand Rapids, MI, 1983).

W.R.G.

LAW, WILLIAM (1686–1761), Anglican writer and mystic. His best-known work, *A Serious Call to a Devout and Holy Life* (1728), possibly second only to Bunyan's *Pilgrim's Progress* (1678) in its enduring impact upon the Protestant conscience, was greatly admired by John Wesley.* But the latter was troubled when, around 1734, Law turned from classical mystical theology* to the works of Boehme.* The break in their relationship (1738) was made public in 1756 by an open letter from Wesley criticizing the theology of Law's *Spirit of Prayer* (1749, 1750) and *Spirit of Love* (1752, 1754).

Wesley felt that the influence of Boehme had led Law to a denial of God's omnipotence and justice, and to faulty understandings of justification, new birth, the presence of Christ in every person, inward prayer, and hell as a state of soul.

Though he wrote a number of spirited pamphlets supporting the Anglican position on issues of the day, Law did not publicly defend his mystical views. From 1740, when he returned to his birthplace, Kings's Cliffe, Northamptonshire, Law lived quietly as chaplain to a household community of three: himself, his aunt Hester Gibbon and a rich widow named Mrs Hutcheson. They lived on a small proportion of their large joint income, devoting themselves to the principles of *A Serious Call*: prayer, relief of the poor and the running of schools and almshouses.

Bibliography

Many editions of *A Serious Call*, *e.g.* with *Spirit of Love* (London, 1979); *Spirit of Prayer, Spirit of Love* (Cambridge, 1969).

A. K. Walker, *William Law: His Life and Thought* (London, 1973).

P.N.H.

LAYING ON OF HANDS. The laying of hands on people has its roots in the OT. It has been practised by the Christian church from the first, generally with prayer,

and is included amongst the 'foundations' of Christian belief in Heb. 6:2. The basic ideas associated with it are identification, and the imparting of something (blessing, power, authority, etc.). The OT worshipper laid his hands on the sacrificial* animal to be killed as a sin-offering, and the high priest did it on the second goat on the day of atonement, confessing the people's sins over it (Lv. 1:4; 16:21). Otherwise, the main uses and occasions of this rite which continue to the present day are: 1. to invoke or pronounce a blessing, as Jacob in Gn. 48:8–20 and Jesus in Mt. 19:13–15; 2. usually with prayer, to signify and convey healing* to those in need of it (Mk. 5:23; 6:5; Lk. 13:13; Acts 28:8); 3. in connection with the gift and reception of the Holy Spirit, usually at the time of baptism,* although not universally (cf. Dt. 34:9; Acts 8:14–19; 19:6; 2 Tim. 1:6); 4. ordaining, or setting apart, people for a particular ministry or office in the church, e.g. OT Levites (Nu. 8:10), Joshua as leader (Nu. 27:18–23), Christian elders and missionaries (Acts 6:5–6; 13:3; 1 Tim. 1:18; 4:14).

The church has continued these uses down the centuries, some churches regularly linking it with baptism, some with unction (anointing*) of the sick and some with confirmation.* The latter rite is variously seen as the conferring/reception of the gift of the Holy Spirit, admission to communion, or entry into full adult church membership for those baptized in childhood. (Other churches, especially those not practising infant baptism, do not have confirmation at all.) Many in episcopal churches attach importance to the continuous succession of ordinations of ministers down the centuries by prayer with the laying on of hands, stretching back in an unbroken line to Christ and the apostles (see Ministry*). The concept may be valuable, as it strengthens the sense of historical continuity for many, but it lacks both conclusive historical proof and NT evidence of its being necessary to true church order.

Bibliography

J. Coppens, L'imposition des mains et les rites connexes dans le NT et dans l'église ancienne (Paris, 1925); G. W. H. Lampe, The Seal of the Spirit (London, 1951); I. H. Marshall in IBD, pp. 889–890; J. K. Parratt in ExpT 80 (1968–69), pp. 210–214; H. G. Schütz in NIDNTT II, pp. 150–153; H. B. Swete in HDB 2, pp. 84–85.

J.P.B.

LEIBNIZ, GOTTFRIED VON (1646–1716). German mathematician and philosopher, According to Leibniz, the full definition of any thing involves describing all things from its unique stand-point; each thing is an independent 'monad' 'mirroring' the rest. The highest monad, and creator of all others, is God.

Leibniz produced classical versions of the arguments for the existence of God (adding one of his own from the 'pre-established harmony' needed to ensure that the monads mirror one another accurately; see Natural Theology*), and a famous rebuttal of anti-theistic arguments from evil,* holding that this is the best of all possible worlds, at least in being the best possible sequence of events moving towards perfection, even if it is not perfect yet; evil elements in it are essential ingredients in the whole. He was the first to use the word 'theodicy'.*

Leibniz was also the promoter of unsuccessful schemes for reunion between Catholic and Protestant churches, and between Calvinists and Lutherans. Later he drifted towards a more purely 'natural' religion, and declined the assistance of any minister at his deathbed.

Bibliography

Only some works are available in English. There are selections by G. Montgomery (La Salle, IL, 1977) and by M. Morris and G. Parkinson (London, 1973).

S. Brown, Leibniz (Brighton, 1984); B. Russell, Critical Exposition of the Philosophy of Leibniz (London, 21937); R. Saw, Leibniz (Harmondsworth, 1954).

R.L.S.

LEO THE GREAT. Leo, who held the office of pope from 440 to 461, magnified the papacy* in various ways. Not only did he see himself as the successor to Peter, but he believed that Peter actually spoke through all he preached or wrote. Hence he expected all his statements as pope to be accepted without question. On the political front he obtained from the emperor Valentinian III (425–55) effective jurisdiction over the Western Empire. If any bishop resisted papal authority, the pope could now resort to secular authority. Leo also added the decretals of his predecessors to Western canon law* of which he became the effective guardian.

Leo enhanced his political standing by his achievements in negotiation with Rome's enemies, the Huns and the Vandals. Again, he boosted the city of Rome's own Christian tradition by claiming Peter and Paul as its patrons in succession to Romulus and Remus.

Leo made a significant contribution to the Eastern Christological* controversies of his time. Shortly before the 'Robber Council' of Ephesus in 449 Leo came out decisively against Eutyches (see Monophysitism*) and wrote a *Tome* to Bishop Flavian of Constantinople (d. 449) to confirm him in his stance against Eutyches. Leo hoped that the promulgation of his own doctrine would render a general council unnecessary, but it was not to be. At Ephesus Leo's *Tome* was not even read, and the supporters of Eutyches held the day. Leo immediately pressed for the decisions of this council to be overthrown. Circumstances following the death of Theodosius II (in 450) favoured this. A new general council* was held at Chalcedon in 451, where the *Tome* was acclaimed among other documents as an orthodox statement.

The *Tome* was designed to refute Eutyches, whom Leo understood to be denying that it was real human flesh which Christ derived from Mary.* Leo, by contrast, held that Christ had to assume true human nature if he was to restore to humanity by his divine power that which it had once lost through sin. It was equally vital that Christ should have lost nothing of his divinity. In the one person of Jesus Christ each of the two natures retained its own natural properties unimpaired, and yet they always acted in concert with one another. Not surprisingly, this aspect of the *Tome* raised misgivings at Chalcedon among Illyrian and Palestinian bishops, who thought Leo was guilty of the Nestorian* error of dividing the natures and seeing in Christ two persons. This undoubted ambiguity in the *Tome* may be explained by its immediate purpose – to answer Eutyches. Elsewhere Leo disowned Nestorianism, which he interpreted as a form of adoptionism.* Thus Leo would stress the indivisible connection which was achieved when the two natures came together in Jesus Christ. But the fact remains that Leo did not explain the unity of

Christ's person as well as he did the manifestation of the two natures in the life of the incarnate Christ.

Bibliography

T. G. Jalland, *The Life and Times of St Leo the Great* (London, 1941); J. N. D. Kelly, *Early Christian Doctrines* (London, ⁵1977).

G.A.K.

LEGALISM, see LAW AND GOSPEL.

LEONTIUS OF BYZANTIUM, see HYPOSTASIS.

LESSING, GOTTHOLD EPHRAIM (1729–81). A pioneer in modern German drama, Lessing was one of the most elusive and seminal religious thinkers of his age. Even in its essentials, his thought has been interpreted in widely varied and incompatible ways. Lessing apparently sought to adopt a theological stance that avoided the deadlocked rationalism and orthodoxy of his day, but he can be regarded either as crypto-rationalist or as providing an alternative non-rationalist position to that held by the orthodox. There are at least two reasons for these, and other, discrepant verdicts. First, Lessing was a subtle author whose real views, it has been maintained, defy easy access. Secondly, he did not obviously correlate his main ideas coherently and gave no comprehensive, systematic account of them. One may therefore put it in terms which he himself applied to religion: it is the spirit of Lessing's enterprise, not the letter of his writing, that guides us best in the interpretation of his thought.

Such thought gains its unity, in part, from its preoccupation with a set of questions, namely, those that cluster around the issue of religious truth and how it is apprehended. In particular, Lessing propounded several theses on the general relation of religion and history of which the following are among the most significant. 1. The Bible, including its historical record, is open to critical investigation. Lessing momentously published the *Wolfenbüttel Fragments* of H. S. Reimarus' (1694–1768) work between 1774 and 1778 and vindicated at least the critical principle adopted by the latter in his attack on the orthodox approach to the Bible. 2. True religion antedates its literary expression and furnishes us with a spiritual criterion for assessing the force of the 'letter'. Hence it is not the historical account that actually authorizes our religious beliefs. 3. Historical testimony is technically 'uncertain' in the sense that, at its most reliable, it cannot warrant our absolute conviction. Its credibility therefore does not establish its religious authority. 4. Historical truths are, logically, of a different order from 'necessary truths of reason'. The former are contingent (an event, for example, might not have happened); the latter are necessary (their contradictories cannot be supposed). 5. History is process, and the communication or apprehension of religious truth can vary with its change. Revelation can be conceived as the education of the human race so that eventually it may be possible to comprehend the truths of morality and religion without recourse to earlier, partial, ways of apprehension.

Certainly, such theses may be described differently, related in different ways and supplemented with others of note. Furthermore, their abstract statement fails to capture the fluid, suggestive, thrusting style of their author. Lessing appears to have deemed orthodoxy totally unrealistic in its religious foundations and rationalism quite ineffective by its failure to break new ground. It is hard to chart with precision the direct or indirect influence of Lessing's thought, but the various ways in which he organized the issue of faith and history continue to command attention. When Lessing wrote that the endeavour to find truth is preferable to its possession in itself, it may reveal much of the man and his thought: in the spirit of this, one is perhaps more intellectually indebted to him for his attempts than his accomplishments.

Bibliography

H. E. Allison, *Lessing and the Enlightenment* (Ann Arbor, MI, 1966); K. Barth, *Protestant Theology in the Nineteenth Century* (London, 1972); H. Chadwick (ed.), *Lessing's Theological Writings* (London, 1956); L. P. Wessell, *G. E. Lessing's Theology: a Reinterpretation* (The Hague, 1977).

S.N.W.

LEWIS, CLIVE STAPLES (1898–1963). Born in Belfast, Lewis took a triple First at Oxford, and after a short time teaching philosophy became Fellow of Magdalen College and University Lecturer in English. He had abandoned Christian belief in adolescence, but was converted to theism* in 1929 and to Christianity two years later. For an account of his life up to conversion see his *Surprised by Joy* (London, 1955). He was for many years the centre of a group of friends, the 'Inklings', which included the writer and lay theologian Charles Williams* and J. R. R. Tolkien (1892–1973), author of *The Lord of the Rings*. From 1954 he was Professor of Medieval and Renaissance English at Cambridge.

Lewis was a prolific writer, whose specifically Christian writings fall mainly into three classes. His *fiction* includes a series of three 'science fantasy' novels (*Out of the Silent Planet, Perelandra* – later retitled *Voyage to Venus* – and *That Hideous Strength*), a retelling of the myth of Psyche (*Till We Have Faces*) and his seven 'Narnia' books for children. In them Christian themes are introduced unmistakably and yet naturally; Lewis hoped that by setting them in new contexts he could help readers see them as they were, not spoilt by 'stained-glass and Sunday school associations'.

Avowedly *apologetic* works include the broadcast talks collected in *Mere Christianity*, the studies *The Problem of Pain* and *Miracles*, and the allegorical *Pilgrim's Regress*. Here Lewis sought, without limiting himself to any one philosophical or theological position, to defend the common ground of traditional Christian orthodoxy, blending logical argument with insight into the workings of the human mind (especially the conscience*) and leading on to the transformed world-view that follows conversion.

Of his writings on the *Christian life*, the best known is *The Screwtape Letters* (from a senior devil to a novice tempter, advising on traps for the patient's soul). *Letters to Malcolm*, closer to theology proper than most of his work, deals with problems raised by prayer.* *The Four Loves* analyses in turn affection, friendship, eros and charity and the part they play in natural and Christian lives. *Reflections on the Psalms* is not a commentary but an exploration of Christian use of the psalter.

Lewis was probably the best-known apologist of his day, and his popularity continues. His works are characterized by his command of lucid and enjoyable English, enough philosophy to make his arguments coherent and persuasive without becoming technical, and his ability to lead his reader from the everyday, even the humorous, to hints of glory. His appeal was chiefly to the imagination and the intelligence; but though he seldom went very deep (except perhaps in *A Grief Observed*, written after his wife died), the fact that there *were* depths beyond was always made clear.

Bibliography
H. Carpenter, *The Inklings* (London, 1978); J. Gibb (ed.), *Light on C. S. Lewis* (London, 1965) (essays by friends and pupils); R. L. Green and W. Hooper, *C. S. Lewis* (London, 1974); W. H. Lewis (brother) (ed.), *Letters of C. S. Lewis* (London, 1966); C. Walsh, *The Literary Legacy of C. S. Lewis* (San Diego, CA, 1979).

R.L.S.

LIBERAL EVANGELICALISM. The Evangelical party in the Church of England was strong by 1880. The Free Church of Scotland and the main Protestant churches in Ireland and North America were large and their theological training was still almost entirely orthodox. The Student Christian Movement (SCM), which was developing strongly in the student world, and the Keswick Convention (see Higher Life Theology*) were a constant influence in all denominations, and at that stage could be described as firmly evangelical* and somewhat pietist.* Missionary enthusiasm ran high and many students as well as others were offering for the mission field.

By 1900, however, change was evident, largely as a result of the introduction of rationalistic theology in the theological colleges and faculties. What was called the 'modern' view of the Bible began to prevail. This amounted to a loss of confidence in the reliability of Scripture* as the final authority in matters of faith and conduct. Many of the leaders of evangelical thought and of evangelical movements such as the Church Missionary Society (CMS) and SCM were deeply influenced, while retaining features of evangelical life and devotion, apart from their doctrine of the Bible. But they gradually changed their emphases. By 1910 there was a clear division between the more conservative and the more liberal evangelical leaders. By

the 1920s many evangelicals preferred to be thought of as 'liberal evangelicals'.

In 1922 the CMS in Britain was split and most of the conservative element left to found the Bible Churchmen's Missionary Society. In 1928 the Inter-Varsity Fellowship (now Universities and Colleges Christian Fellowship) was created, bringing together those who had left the SCM in a steady trickle since 1910. An almost identical split took place in several other countries. In Britain the Anglican Evangelical Group Movement with its Cromer Convention (an alternative to Keswick) continued for a while; but with its collapse and the dramatic decline of the SCM, *c.* 1940–60, liberal evangelicalism was largely replaced by a frank theological liberalism. This had few orthodox elements remaining and its leaders moved towards a bolder denial of traditional Christian beliefs. In the late 1970s and early 1980s a new kind of (as yet unorganized) liberal evangelicalism emerged. But few people would now like the title 'liberal evangelical', though their position might be similar to that of those who used it in the 1920s.

Bibliography
O. R. Barclay, *Whatever Happened to the Jesus Lane Lot?* (Leicester, 1977); R. Rouse, *The World Student Christian Federation* (London, 1948); V. F. Storr (ed.), *Liberal Evangelicalism. An Interpretation* (London, 1922); *idem, Freedom and Tradition: A Study of Liberal Evangelicalism* (London, 1940); T. Tatlow, *The Story of the Student Christian Movement of Great Britain and Ireland* (London, 1933).

O.R.B.

LIBERALISM AND CONSERVATISM IN THEOLOGY. 'Liberal' as a self-commending description, implying readiness to welcome new ideas and freedom from the restraints of obscurantist traditionalism and irrational bigotry, has been adopted at various times over the past 150 years by 1. French Roman Catholics who favoured political democracy and church reform; 2. Anglican Broad Churchmen who desired some doctrinal loosening-up; and 3. Protestants world-wide who held post-Enlightenment* views stemming from Schleiermacher* and Ritschl* in theology, Kant* and Hegel* in philosophy, and Strauss* and Julius Wellhausen (1844–1918) in biblical study.

'Liberalism' ordinarily signifies the thought-pattern found in the second and third groups. Developed by academic theologians who were very much men of their own time and critical of pre-Enlightenment thinking, liberalism has everywhere displayed most if not all of the following features:

1. A purpose of adapting the substance of faith, however conceived, to current natural-istic and anthropocentric viewpoints, aban-doning traditional dogmas when necessary.

2. A sceptical view of historic Christian supernaturalism;* an unwillingness to treat anything as certain just because the Bible or the church affirm it; a positivist* penchant for making 'objective', 'scientific', anti-miracu-lous assessments of biblical and ecclesiastical teaching; and bold readiness to elevate the culturally moulded opinions of latter-day scholars above the received tradition.

3. A view of the Bible as a fallible human record of religious thought and experience rather than a divine revelation* of truth and reality; doubts, more or less extensive, about the historical facts on which Bible writers base Christianity; insistence that the churches should be undogmatic in temper, tolerating a plurality of theologies, and seeing personal and social ethics as their main concern; and a belief that seeking society's renewal rather than evangelizing individuals is the primary Christian task.

4. An immanentist, sub-Trinitarian idea of God as working chiefly in cultural develop-ments, philosophical, sociological, moral and aesthetic; a non-incarnational Christology* that conceives of Jesus as a religious pioneer and model, a man supremely full of God, rather than as a divine saviour; and an optimistic, evolutionary world-view (cf. Progress*) that understands God's plan as perfecting an immature race rather than redeeming a fallen one.

5. An optimistic view of cultured humanity's power to perceive God by reflecting on its experience, and to formulate a true natural theology;* a belief that all religions rest on a common perception of God, and differ only in details and emphases according to where each stands on the evol-utionary ladder; and a hostility towards any exclusive claims for the Christian faith (cf. Christianity and Other Religions*).

6. A denial that the fall* of a primitive pair brought guilt,* pollution and spiritual impotence upon our race, in favour of a vision of mankind moving spiritually upward; a denial of penal-substitutionary views of the atonement,* and of Christ's imputed right-eousness as the ground of justification,* in favour of moral-influence and representative-trailblazer accounts of Christ's death for us, and thoughts of God forgiving on the ground that penitence makes us forgivable; and a denial of Christ's personal return, in favour of the hope that universal moral progress will establish the kingdom of God* on earth.

Liberalism dominated European Protestan-tism for half a century till the First World War shattered its optimism and the lead passed to the existentialist* biblicism of the neo-orthodox genius Karl Barth.* In the English-speaking world, reconstructed forms of liber-alism, often at odds with each other, still make sure of the running in academic theology.

'Conservatism', when used, signifies a rejec-tion of the liberal outlook as a provincial aber-ration, neither objective nor scientific nor rational in any significant sense, and with this a conservationist purpose of handing on the doctrines and disciplines of historic Chris-tianity intact and undiluted. There are conservative Protestants, Anglo-Catholics and Roman Catholics; there are conservative biblical scholars and theologians, congre-gations and denominations, para-church agencies and teaching institutions. There is a conservative Christian literature and a conservative missiology, in which evangelism comes first. Conservatism in this sense implies no particular political stance or eschatological expectation, though the contrary is often alleged. Self-styled fundamentalism* is a mili-tant form of conservatism. Protestant conservatism has gained great strength during the past forty years, though it is still a minority position in the older Protestant churches.

See also: EVANGELICAL THEOLOGY; LIBERALISM, GERMAN.

Bibliography

D. G. Bloesch, *Essentials of Evangelical Theology*, 2 vols. (San Francisco, 1978); R. J. Coleman, *Issues of Theological Conflict: Evangelicals and Liberals* (Grand Rapids, 1980); J. D. Douglas (ed.), *Let the Earth Hear His Voice: International Congress on World*

Evangelization (Minneapolis, 1975); G. M. Marsden, *Fundamentalism and American Culture* (New York, 1980); J. I. Packer, *'Fundamentalism' and the Word of God* (London, 1958); B. Reardon, *Liberal Protestantism* (London, 1968).

J.I.P.

LIBERALISM, GERMAN. The roots of 19th-century German liberalism are mainly to be found in the 18th-century Enlightenment,* the French Revolution, and the romanticism* and idealism* of the turn of the century. The philosophical and political ideas generated during this period permeated both secular and ecclesiastical thinking, producing a growing reaction against traditional institutions and beliefs.

Within the circle of theological liberalism one must distinguish between liberalism of doctrine and liberalism in biblical scholarship. The former was an undermining or denial of the traditional doctrines of the Christian faith, while the latter challenged the authenticity, historicity and divine inspiration of the Bible. These two forms of liberalism were generally connected in varying degree, yet one might hold one without necessarily holding the other.

In the realm of Christian doctrine German liberalism may be traced back to Kant* and Lessing,* but above all to Schleiermacher,* who drastically reinterpreted the fundamental doctrines of Christianity from an anthropocentric viewpoint. For Schleiermacher there was no transcendent, self-disclosing God in the traditional sense; man's own feelings constituted his ground of reality, with Jesus as the man in whom these feelings of God-consciousness attained their highest perfection.

The first serious challenge to the authenticity of the NT writings was Strauss's* *Life of Jesus* in 1835. With this book Strauss proclaimed that the supernatural* elements of the gospel history were unhistorical 'myth'.* In this same year appeared Peter von Bohlen's (1796–1840) commentary on Genesis and Wilhelm Vatke's (1806–82) *Biblischen Theologie*, both of which demonstrated that Strauss's non-supernatural approach could also be applied to the OT. These works evoked a flood of literature dealing with the Bible and its reliability. In the forefront came the Tübingen School* which from a non-

supernatural theological and historical perspective examined the history of the early church and determined the dating and authorship of each book according to its own particular 'tendency'. The gospels were all pronounced to be productions of the 2nd century, and apart from Romans, 1 and 2 Corinthians, Galatians and Revelation, no book was authentic.

In the realm of the OT came the documentary theory in which the Pentateuch was divided up into at least four different sources or documents, all thought to have originated at different times several centuries after Moses. This hypothesis was fully developed by Karl Heinrich Graf (1815–69), Abraham Kuenen (1828–91) and Julius Wellhausen (1844–1918), who brought it to its dominant position at the end of the 19th century.

Implicitly underlying the whole critical investigation of the Bible was the idealistic philosophy which developed from the Enlightenment in the second half of the 18th century and culminated in the writings of J. G. Herder (1744–1803), Hegel,* J. G. Fichte (1762–1814), F. W. J. von Schelling (1775–1854) and J. W. von Goethe (1749–1832). God was conceived as an Absolute Spirit manifested in many different forms and ways, but chiefly as immanent in nature and revealed in history and humanity. This revelation* was thought of as a general revelation throughout history in all peoples and cultures, and not as special and miraculous revelation to one particular nation, *i.e.* Israel. Thus the Jewish religion was regarded simply as one natural religion among others, its myths and folklore parallel to that of other primitive cultures, with its development from simple beginnings to a complex priestly cultus following a pattern which could be traced more or less clearly in the history and culture of every nation. And just as the Tübingen school had fitted the NT books into Baur's historical perspective, so the OT scholars fitted the literature of Israel into this evolutionary scheme of religion, determining the date and provenance of every part and section according to how its 'tendency' best fitted into the predetermined historical and religious framework.

Following Strauss's *Life of Jesus* came a host of other works of the same genre, each advocating the author's own interpretation of Jesus' life – G. H. A. von Ewald's (1803–75) rationalistic portrayal (1855), K. T. Keim's

(1825–78) tedious three-volume account (1867–72), Strauss's *New Life of Jesus* (1864), and J. E. Renan's (1823–92) sentimental embellishment (1863) – to name only the most widely read. By the 1880s these and a host of lesser works were being eagerly translated into English. In Great Britain it was primarily this scholarship which was regarded as liberal. Only in the 1880s and 1890s did liberalism come to possess the narrower sense originating with the Ritschlian* theology.

In the 1880s the Ritschlian school became the dominant influence in the realm of dogmatics, and it was the liberalism of this school which largely determined non-orthodox theology until the First World War. For Ritschl the kingdom of God* was an ethical and moral kingdom which would develop and grow to maturity, with Jesus as the great example for humanity to follow. Sin was not the radical evil of the will, but rather ignorance which could be corrected by moral upbringing and education. For Ritschl's pupil W. Herrmann,* the portrait of Jesus contained in the gospels provided man with the example to which he himself should aspire. For A. Harnack,* Jesus himself did not even belong in the gospel: 'Not the Son, but the Father only, belongs in the gospel, as Jesus proclaimed it.' For others Jesus was merely a great moral teacher who taught a purely ethical kingdom of goodness, kindness, tolerance, and love for one's neighbour. His death was regarded not as an atonement for sin – that was a relic of primitive Judaism – but as a wonderful example of moral fortitude and resolution. Above all, liberalism desired an *un*dogmatic form of Christianity, free from the constricting trammels of the traditional doctrines and creeds, while still retaining an outward vestige which might pass for orthodoxy.

Such was the essence of German liberalism at the turn of the 19th century. There were other movements which denied the authenticity of the Scriptures, such as the history-of-religions school,* but these were not necessarily identified with the doctrinal liberalism of the Ritschlians. For the orthodox, however, who regarded all non-orthodox literature as liberal, unbelieving or atheistic, fine distinctions between these various viewpoints were not of great significance.

Two main causes led to the decline of theological liberalism in Germany. The first was the onslaught of the rationalists during the decade preceding the First World War. Led by Albert Kalthoff (1850–1906) and Arthur Drews (1865–1935), who argued that Jesus had never lived, the rationalists regarded the liberal view of Jesus as a compromise between the supernatural Jesus of orthodoxy and their own rationalistic explanations. Either one or the other, but not half and half! Thus ensued a long and acrimonious controversy in which many flaws in the liberal viewpoint were exposed.

The second cause was the First World War itself, which shattered the liberal idea of a civilization growing upwards in goodness and perfection. It became evident that the world was not getting better. The evil which was laid bare struck a mortal blow against the old liberal idea that evil was only ignorance which might be corrected by education. After the war came Karl Barth* who radically opposed the pre-war liberal theology, and proclaimed that the God of the Bible must not be confused with human ideas about God. Yet while it is true that doctrinal liberalism received a severe check, liberalism in biblical scholarship continued unabated in the demythologization (see Myth*) programmes of the Bultmannians.* It was only the old liberalism of the Ritschlians that received its demise, for liberalism's underlying unbelief in the veracity of the Bible simply adopted new guises.

Bibliography

A. I. C. Heron, *A Century of Protestant Theology* (Guildford and London, 1980); H. R. Mackintosh, *Types of Modern Theology: Schleiermacher to Barth* (London, 1937); B. M. G. Reardon, *Liberal Protestantism* (London, 1968); C. Welch, *Protestant Thought in the Nineteenth Century*, vol. 1: *1799–1870* (New Haven, CT, and London, 1972).

H.H.

LIBERATION THEOLOGY. The diffuse movement we monolithically call liberation theology was born in Latin America in the late 1960s. Still largely Roman Catholic in orientation, it differs from previous systematic expressions of the faith: it seeks to interpret the Christian faith from the perspective of the poor and the oppressed.

Anglo-Saxon theologies struggle with issues of faith and post-Enlightenment* scepticism, defending the supernatural* in a natural world. They ask, 'Where is the God of truth in a world of science* and technology?' Liberation theologies struggle with issues of faith and post-colonial deprivation, searching for hope in a world of poverty.* They ask, 'Where is the God of righteousness* in a world of injustice?'

In the language of Gustavo Gutiérrez (b. 1928), 'The starting point of liberation theology is commitment to the poor, the "non-person". Its ideas come from the victim.' The two Brazilian priests, Leonardo (b. 1938) and Clodovis Boff, speak of it as a kind of 'chemical reaction': faith + oppression → liberation theology.

Especially since the 1970s, these same concerns of liberation theology have created a new interest in it outside its original Latin American setting. Black theologies* such as those of James Cone (b. 1938) in the USA, concerned over racist oppression, have begun to interact with its formulations. Some Afrikaners see its influence in the anti-apartheid direction of black theology in South Africa (*cf*. African Christian Theology*). A brand of liberation theology has emerged in the war-torn struggles of Northern Ireland. In socio-political settings of deprivation and oppression, its message is receiving increased attention.

Sources and development

1. The most basic source of liberation theology is the experience of poverty, destitution and repression in a region which Christendom has dominated for centuries. Liberation theologians perceive this suffering as against the will of God. It constitutes a moral imperative for the Christian conscience. Says Gutiérrez, 'We are on the side of the poor, not because they are good but because they are poor.'

What should be our Christian response to outrage against it, to guilt at allowing it to continue? Says the Catholic priest Juan Luis Segundo (b. 1925) of Uruguay, 'Do not forget that we live at the same time in one of the most Christian lands and in one of the most inhuman ones.'

2. Some of the theological roots of liberation theology can be traced to Europe's political theology* and to Jürgen Moltmann's* theology of hope. From the work of J. B. Metz,* liberation theologians see the need to underscore the political dimensions of faith, and for a perception of the church as an institution of social criticism. Moltmann's emphasis on the political character of eschatology,* and on hope* as having a liberating function in history, sounds very reminiscent of many of the themes of Gutiérrez. From Dietrich Bonhoeffer* comes the call to redefine religion* in a secular context, and support for the rejection of any church-world dualism.*

But to speak of liberation theology as 'made in Germany' says too much. European discussions, charge the liberation theologians, lack concreteness; their reflections are theoretical abstractions, ideologically neutral, neglecting the miserable, unjust present for some 'Christianity of the future'.

3. The deepest theological roots remain in the growing interest of the Roman Catholic Church* in dialogue with the world. Vatican II (1962–65) opened the door to a renewed look at socio-economic conditions in the world. To a Latin American priesthood increasingly involved with the poor, it signalled the opportunity for a new examination of past answers (communism and socialism) formerly suspect to the church. These signals were explored and amplified at the Medellín Conference of Latin American bishops (CELAM) in 1968.

The papacy of John Paul II (1978–) has been considerably more conservative towards liberation theology. At the Puebla Conference of Bishops (1979), he warned that those 'who sup with Marxism should use a long spoon'. A series of theological skirmishes with the Vatican curia has continued. These were highlighted in the 1984 interrogation of liberation theologian Leonardo Boff, and the issuing of the famous *Instructions* of the Sacred Congregation for the Doctrine of the Faith, specifically addressed to the excesses of liberation theology.

A more nuanced position now seems to be emerging. In 1986, the Vatican issued a new *Instruction on Christian Freedom and Liberation*. The document recognizes several forms of liberation theology while underlining the church's determination to identify with the poor and oppressed. It also suggests that there are conditions of repression which may require the use of arms to bring about social justice, and it places a higher priority on the principle of concern for the common good than on the acquisition of private property. Behind the emerging 'both/and' posture of the Vatican may lie the continued conflict in Latin America between those supporting the traditional teachings of the church and those endorsing liberation theology.

4. A major cause of the Vatican's conflict with liberation theology has been the continuing use of Marxism* by liberation theologians. It was not, however, Marxism as a philosophy or a holistic plan of political action that was adapted for use. It was Marxism as an instrument of social analysis; the focus was on the economic system as a key factor in oppression and the class struggle as the battleground for that oppression. In recent years, say some observers, there may be a lessening of even that use. The opposition of the Vatican to Marxist categories of hermeneutics* is undoubtedly a factor.

This may be one of those cases where it is dangerous to see liberation theology as a monolithic whole. The Mexican scholar, José Miranda, may still be right when he says, 'We are all riding on Marx's shoulders.' But it also appears true that there are growing differences between theologians on exactly what the role of Marxism should be.

Differences are being perceived elsewhere too. Samuel Escobar (b. 1934), an evangelical critic based in Peru, distinguishes three types of liberation theology – the pastoral one of Gutiérrez; the academic emphases of Hugo Assmann and Segundo; and a populist style which uses the language of liberation theology but remains old-style Catholicism.

More recently, Juan Luis Segundo speaks of 'at least two theologies of liberation coexisting now in Latin America' (1985). 1. In the early stage, liberation theology was born in the universities, among the middle classes. By the 1970s, its champions were increasingly the common people. The major symbol of this change is the growth of the Base Ecclesial Communities. These are small, grass-roots, lay groups of the poor or the ordinary people, meeting to pray, conduct Bible studies and wrestle concretely with social and political obligations in their settings. 2. The earlier writings of liberation theologians were those of the 'systemizing intellectuals' who spoke *to* the poor and ignorant. Now some of those same theologians (*e.g.* Gustavo Gutiérrez) see their role as 'interpreters' who speak *with* and *for* the poor and socially deprived. Even the

style and tone of writing sound more like the street and less like the study. 3. In the early stage, especially among those theologians who came from Europe, liberation theology took a violent swing away from 'popular Catholicism' as non-Christian. Church officials, striving to keep the masses in the church, reacted strongly to this criticism. Liberation theology shifted to a more positive stance.

Theological method

1. Orientation: the liberation of the oppressed. Liberation theology argues that theology must start with 'the view from below', with the sufferings of the excluded and oppressed. It is a theological commitment to the poor; the poor are seen not as the objects of gospel pity but as the artisans of a new humanity – shapers, not shaped. Sobrino comments, 'The poor are the authentic *theological source* for understanding Christian truth and practice'.

2. Domain: the concrete social situation as context. The mission of the church, says liberation theology, is to be defined in terms of history and historical struggles for liberation. Any theological model that locates the meaning and purpose of history* outside the concreteness of the historical 'now' is idealistic.

In the past, theology answered philosophical questions: How can we believe in the unchangeable God in a world of flux? Now theology is called on to answer questions of social analysis, politics and economics: How can we believe in God in a society that crushes the poor and marginalizes their humanity? Our hermeneutical tool for understanding the Bible becomes a 'preferential option for the poor'.

*3. Method: reflection on praxis.** Theology is to be done, contends liberation theology, not just learned. How is this possible? Gutiérrez replies, by seeing theology 'as critical reflection on historical praxis'. Theology follows praxis as the second stage.

In the first stage, praxis, we commit ourselves to the renovation of society on behalf of and alongside the oppressed poor. Praxis is more than experience apart from theory, application following principle. It is a term borrowed from Marx and oriented to a Marxist analysis of society. It describes the two-way traffic that is always going on between action and reflection – a dialectical engagement with the world in transforming action. It is the precondition of knowledge, in which people seek not merely to understand the world but to change it. Through praxis, people enter into their socio-historical destiny.

Exegetical and doctrinal directions

1. Liberation theology seeks to approach biblical study from the perspective of the oppressed. Early exegetical efforts concentrated on the OT, especially the exodus narrative. The biblical account served basically not as canon but as a model,* a paradigm* of that concern for the plight of the poor.

More recent studies are expanding their biblical interests. In the face of a long and protracted battle against social injustice, some have begun to reflect on the significance of the exile. The NT concept of the kingdom of God* has received much more attention. In connection with these studies, a growing body of material is appearing on the work of Christ and his identification with the poor and oppressed. There is no sign that this expansion of the exegetical agenda signals any departure from the paradigm model used by liberation theology to link the Bible with Latin America today. But it does indicate that liberation theology has become more serious about sharpening its hermeneutical tools.

2. It would be a misunderstanding to reduce liberation theology's academic agenda to the area of Christian social ethics. Theology's classic themes are receiving increasing attention. Major works have appeared, on Christology* and ecclesiology (see Church*) in particular. All are undergoing revision in the light of liberation theology's pivotal question: what is the meaning and significance of this theme, or this truth, for the oppressed of our continent?

Leonardo Boff, for example, summarizes the main themes of liberation theology with regard to the person and work of Christ. He sees three emerging emphases: 1. an underlining of the incarnation* and, more particularly, the social condition of the human Jesus:* that of a poor person, a labourer, who preferred the poor, surrounded himself with them, and identified with them; 2. an emphasis on Jesus' message of the kingdom of God as 'integral liberation – spiritual, yes, but material as well (liberation from hunger, grief, contempt, and so on), within history and beyond history'; 3. a concentration on

Jesus' redemptive death as that of 'the victim of a plot laid by the mighty of his time'.

Some preliminary assessments

To the Anglo-Saxon, liberation theology may appear to be an easy target for criticism. We offer the following warnings, then, as questions, aware of our own impotence and of the danger of quick generalizations.

1. Does liberation theology ultimately pay adequate attention to the vertical, Godward, dimension of salvation*? In its legitimate protest against the spiritualization of the biblical theme of poverty, has liberation theology lost itself in the socio-economic dimension that also needs underlining? To say that 'God is on the side of the oppressed' does not mean that 'the oppressed are on the side of God'.

2. In its necessary protest against a reduction of sin* to the merely private, has liberation theology left us with too shallow a view of sin? Are some of the richest pictures of sin in the Bible blurred in liberation theology? Sin provokes the wrath* of God; it is slavery to Satan (see Devil*); it is a state of spiritual death;* it is a disease of the whole person and of the whole of society. It is, in short, a state of corruption so profound that the elimination of poverty, oppression, racism, sexism, classism and capitalism cannot alter the human condition of sinfulness in any radical way.

3. Is liberation theology in danger of unconsciously falling into a view of atonement* by moral influence only? What is the gospel prior to the end of the class conflict? Is it only a goad to action, a goal to be achieved? Is there a real presence of the gospel before the arrival of the consummated kingdom? Is this why liberation theology has been charged with Pelagianism?* What keeps the call for socio-political-economic liberation from slipping into a crypto-salvation by socio-economic works?

4. Does the Marxist ideology of the class-struggle really serve as an adequate understanding of oppression? Is its pessimistic idealism ultimately any less distorted than an optimistic idealism that makes an ideology out of economic growth and individual initiative as the only way out of poverty and injustice? Liberation theology's protection of the autonomous principle of the class-struggle as inviolate, a Marxist universal 'given', remains

a messianic-like ethic without a messianic commitment.

5. How will liberation theology guarantee that the Scriptures will control the praxis or 'first-stage' level of theology? The action-reflection process of praxis is structured by the Marxist 'pre-understanding' of social clash; this appears to be an irrevocable 'given' in understanding the very nature of praxis. But is this not an unguarded ideology that merits the same Christian critique offered to any other form of human autonomy? Marxism, even as merely a tool of social reflection, builds on a metaphysical view of humanity shaped by Enlightenment human posturing. Liberation theology restricts God to the 'second stage' of the hermeneutical circle. And in doing so it opens up to the danger of docetizing* God to a secondary role in the 'post-commitment' process.

On the other hand, liberation theologies offer theology new opportunities for self-examination, challenges to new lines of obedience that cannot be ignored. Included in the emerging agenda must be questions such as the following:

1. How can academic theology escape the sterility of a reflection abstracted from the concrete social and political problems of the poor? How is theology to be oriented to the practice of justice and compassion towards the marginalized?

2. How can we recognize that all theological reflection takes place in a social context (see Contextualization*) and still avoid reducing universal 'givens' to mere features of one particular situation? How do we develop a humble method of doing theology, recognizing our own limitations and avoiding inhibiting other cultures and societies in their own theological reflection?

3. How can we develop a better method of hermeneutics that will take more seriously the socio-cultural setting of the Bible and the interpreter's blindness to his or her own set of socio-cultural presuppositions?

4. Does our distinction between principle and application hinder us from linking the transforming power of the gospel and the transformation of society and its structures? Does our understanding of the hermeneutical process still leave us with a gap between action and reflection that silently models a Christian commitment only to the *status quo?*

5. In what sense may we speak biblically of commitment to the poor? What effect should that commitment have on our theology and how we do it, on our understanding of the relation of Jesus and his church to the poor? Is there a 'hidden agenda' in our theological formulations that has helped to make the world-wide church more comfortable with the middle and upper classes than with the poor?

See also: AFRICAN CHRISTIAN THEOLOGY; AFRICAN INDEPENDENT CHURCHES; BLACK THEOLOGY; MISSIOLOGY.

Bibliography

L. and C. Boff, *Liberation Theology: From Confrontation to Dialogue* (New York, 1986); R. McA. Brown, *Theology in a New Key* (Philadelphia, 1978); H. M. Conn, 'Theologies of Liberation', *Tensions in Contemporary Theology*, eds. S. N. Gundry and A. F. Johnson (Grand Rapids, MI, ²1986); M. Cook, 'Jesus from the Other Side of History: Christology in Latin America', *TS* 44 (1983), pp. 258–287; G. Gutiérrez, *A Theology of Liberation* (Maryknoll, NY, 1973); idem, *We Drink From Our Own Wells* (Maryknoll, NY, 1984); S. Jordan, 'Bibliography: Latin American Liberation Theology since 1976', *MC* 28 (1986), pp. 32–39; J. Kirk, *Liberation Theology: An Evangelical View from the Third World* (London, 1979); D. A. Lane (ed.), *Liberation Theology: An Irish Dialogue* (Dublin, 1977); J. Miguez Bonino, *Doing Theology in a Revolutionary Situation* (Philadelphia, 1975); A. Neely, 'Liberation Theology in Latin America: Antecedents and Autochthony', *Missiology* 6 (1978), pp. 343–370; E. A. Núñez, *Liberation Theology* (Chicago, 1985); J. L. Segundo, *The Liberation of Theology* (Maryknoll, NY, 1976); idem, 'The Shift within Latin American Theology', *JTSA* 52 (1985), pp. 17–29; idem, *Theology and the Church: A Response to Cardinal Ratzinger and a Warning to the Whole Church* (London, 1986); J. Sobrino, *Christology at the Crossroads* (Maryknoll, NY, 1978); J. E. Weir, 'Liberation Theology Comes of Age', *ExpT* 98 (1986), pp. 3–9.

H.M.C.

LIMBUS. In Roman Catholic theology this word (Lat. *limbus*, 'border, hem, edge') denotes the region on the border of hell thought to be inhabited by those who do not experience the pangs of hell or the joys of heaven (or purgatory.*). On this view *limbus* (*cf.* Eng. 'limbo') is the abode of two categories of the dead. 1. Those who on earth never gained the use of reason and were not baptized, whether infants (*limbus infantium*, 'the limbo of infants') or the mentally incompetent. Although they were innocent of personal guilt,* their original sin had not been removed by baptism.* According to Pope Innocent III (1160–1216), the punishment of original sin is deprivation of the beatific vision of God.* Some writers maintain that such infants are in some way conscious of their permanent exclusion from eternal beatitude, others believe that they are unaware of this loss or are in a state of natural happiness such as Adam enjoyed before the fall.* 2. OT saints prior to their liberation by Christ on his 'descent into hell'* and their ascent into heaven (see Eschatology*) (*limbus patrum*, 'the limbo of the fathers', sometimes referred to as *sinus Abrahae*, 'Abraham's bosom', based on Lk. 16:22).

Bibliography
P. Gumpel, 'Limbo', *SM* III, p. 319.

M.J.H.

LITURGICAL THEOLOGY. Although the concept has probably always existed in liturgical churches (those which use settled forms of corporate worship,* including settled forms of the spoken texts), liturgical theology has only recently attracted wider interest, owing to the growing interest in liturgy itself. It is an attempt to provide a theological interpretation of traditional forms of liturgy, not merely a devotional or historical interpretation. More specialized than the theology of worship in general (which includes non-liturgical worship), it also follows a different method. It begins not from the Bible, tracing the development (good and bad) of biblical principles in historical practice, but from historical practice, examining how, and how far, this can be understood in terms of biblical principles. Such, at least, would be a reformed approach to liturgical theology. Writers of a traditionalist standpoint, on the other hand, tend to see the principles of liturgical practice as self-evident and self-justifying, while those of a liberal standpoint tend to interpret and test liturgical practice by the principles of reason and sociology, rather than by those of the Bible.

The Anabaptist* view that Christian worship should as far as possible reproduce NT practice unchanged, allows no validity to the historical development of worship, and therefore none to liturgical theology. The Lutheran,* Anglican* and (to some extent) Calvinist (see Reformed Theology*) approach is different, however, taking history seriously and making allowance for changed conditions, but seeking fully to implement biblical principles in the context of those changed conditions. On this view, the development (*e.g.*) of daily services, services for marriage and burial, particular texts for these services and others, and a calendar* of annual festivals, is not invalidated merely by showing that they did not exist in biblical times, but only by showing that they do not accord with biblical principles.

Jewish synagogue practice of the 1st century, in which our Lord and his disciples shared, appears to have included many features which neither go back to the OT nor are mentioned in the NT. It is this pattern of worship which was refashioned but not abolished by the impact of the gospel,* and evolved into historic Christian practice. Its origins, therefore, are good, and, just as it is the true task of liturgical revision to reform it by the teaching of the Bible, so it is the task of liturgical theology to interpret it by the teaching of the Bible, in order that it may be understood and used in the most edifying way.

See also: Doxology.

Bibliography
J. J. von Allmen, *Worship: Its Theology and Practice* (ET, London 1965); A. Schmemann, *Introduction to Liturgical Theology* (ET, London 1966); G. Wainwright, *Doxology: a Systematic Theology* (London, 1980).

R.T.B.

LITURGY, see Liturgical Theology; Worship, Theology of.

LLOYD-JONES, DAVID MARTYN (1899–1981). Although born in Wales, Lloyd-Jones completed his education at Marylebone Grammar School and St Bartholomew's Hospital, London. A distinguished career as a physician lay before him when, after severe inner struggle, he committed himself to the Christian ministry in 1926. Following a notable pastorate at Aberavon (1927–38), he was called as colleague and then successor to G. Campbell Morgan (1863–1945) at Westminster Chapel, London. He played an early leadership role in the Inter-Varsity Fellowship and was also involved in the founding of such new evangelical agencies as the Evangelical Library, the London Bible College and the International Fellowship of Evangelical Students.

While he gave much time to helping students, ministers and missionaries, the pulpit was Lloyd-Jones' most important work. By authoritative exposition and application of the Scriptures he sought to restore the true nature of preaching,* rejecting the prevalent opinion that scientific knowledge had outmoded commitment to the inerrancy of Scripture (see also Infallibility*). He saw faith in the word of God and dependence upon the Holy Spirit as the foremost needs in contemporary Christianity, and regarded human unbelief as moral rather than intellectual (see his *Truth Unchanged, Unchanging*, London, 1951). He reintroduced consecutive expository preaching with subsequent publications on *The Sermon on the Mount* (London, 1959–60), *Ephesians* (Edinburgh, 1974–82), *II Peter* (Edinburgh, 1983), and *Romans* (London and Edinburgh, 1970–). But the majority of his preaching was evangelistic as he itinerated constantly for over fifty years (including Europe and the United States in summer vacations). Thoroughly committed to Calvinistic Methodism,* Lloyd-Jones' ministry did not harmonize with the prevailing religious ethos in Wales or England, and while constantly helping many evangelical agencies, his convictions on the importance of Reformed theology* kept him from any full identification. He was, however, closely involved with a new doctrinal awakening commenced through the IVF, the Puritan Conferences and the Banner of Truth Trust (subsequently to be his principal publisher).

In his later years, faced with a general decline of Christianity in England, Lloyd-Jones called for the priority of evangelical unity above denominational loyalties. He did not propose a new denomination but urged the importance of the true unity of churches (which he hoped to see expressed in the British Evangelical Council) and warned that evangelical neutrality to the ecumenical movement* was contributing to the spread of low views on saving faith.

Resigning from Westminster Chapel in 1968, he remained active in preaching and in the preparation of sermons for publication until shortly before his death. By his preaching and books he profoundly influenced the whole English-speaking world, as one who stood in the tradition of the Reformers and Puritans, Whitefield,* Edwards* and Spurgeon.* Emil Brunner* once described him as 'the greatest preacher in Christendom today.'

Bibliography
With the works above, *Preaching and Preachers* (London, 1971), gives invaluable insight into his views of the ministry. For biography see: C. Catherwood, *Five Evangelical Leaders* (London, 1984); idem (ed.), *Chosen by God* (Crowborough, 1986); B. Lloyd-Jones, *Memories of Sandfields* (Edinburgh, 1983); I. H. Murray, *D. Martyn Lloyd-Jones: The First Forty Years, 1899–1939* (Edinburgh, 1982); J. Peters, *Martyn Lloyd-Jones: Preacher* (Exeter, 1986).

I.H.Mu.

LOCKE, JOHN (1632–1704). The first of the great British empiricist* philosophers, Locke held that knowledge derives from experience alone, seeking on this basis to do justice to common sense and science. In politics, his insistence that government depends on consent and his advocacy of constitutional checks and balances were notably influential during the American Revolution.

His *Essay Concerning Human Understanding* (1690) allowed for religious knowledge through both reason and revelation.* *The Reasonableness of Christianity* (1695) defended revelation: it is guaranteed by Christ's miracles* and fulfilment of prophecy,* and is needed both because salvation by works is impossible and because reason has not in fact disclosed the full truth about God or our duties. The faith God accepts in place of complete legal righteousness is belief that Jesus is Messiah; more elaborate beliefs are unnecessary, and were not preached by Jesus or his apostles. (The epistles were written to believers, who already knew all that was necessary to salvation.) Locke's stress on reason, and his minimal doctrinal element, helped the growth of deism* – which was certainly not his intention. He also influenced more orthodox theologians such as Jonathan Edwards.*

Bibliography
Essay often repr.; abridged and ed. A. D. Woozley (London, 1964); *Reasonableness*, abridged and ed. I. Ramsey (London, 1958); *Two Treatises of Government* (London, 1975).

R. I. Aaron, *John Locke* (Oxford, ²1955).

R.L.S.

LOGIC IN THEOLOGY.

Logic is the study of the conditions of valid inference and the methods of proof. In its broadest sense it concerns the structures and principles of reasoning and sound argument. Logic is relevant to every area of life where argument is used. Its methods distinguish between correct and incorrect reasoning, good and bad arguments. Logicians are interested in the *form* of the argument rather than the content, so there is no requirement that a logically valid argument be based on true premises. If the premises are false, the argument may still be valid. In examining the relation between the premises of an argument and its conclusion there are two main forms of inference. Deduction implies a necessary relation, so that acceptance of the premises means accepting the conclusion. Induction implies only a probability in the relation between premises and conclusion. Deductive logic rests on the principle of non-contradiction and is concerned with validity rather than truth. Inductive logic is more concerned with the standards of reasoning used in empirical and scientific reasoning, where what is reasonable or probable is not based on avoiding contradiction.

If logic is concerned with form, then it is neutral and simply a tool to enable proper argument to take place. Varieties of logical systems and notations seem, however, to suggest some assumptions about the nature of reality and need to be examined on that basis.

Theologians use arguments in the discussion and presentation of the Christian faith. Accordingly it is crucial that they understand and use logical means properly, to avoid contradictions and to present the truth of what is claimed by valid argumentation. Medieval theologians used various deductive and inductive arguments of the ontological and cosmological variety to prove the existence of God (see Natural Theology*). They argued deductively that, from an acceptance of the concept of God as 'that than which nothing greater can be conceived', God must necessarily exist, for to exist is more perfect than not to exist. This led to a philosophical debate over the nature of existence, necessity, perfections, concepts and their relation to reality. Cosmological arguments argued inductively from features of our experience of the world such as motion, causation, being, values or purpose to a source of these things, which was called God. The critique of these arguments centred on the relationship between each premise in the argument and its claimed relationship to the conclusion. It was argued that these arguments made an illicit leap from experience of this world to a transcendent realm.

Modern theology has revitalized the proofs of God's existence, but uses logical argument more to defend theology from philosophical attacks. These attacks stress the contradictions in theology, whether in the nature of God or in our talk about God, Christ, the Spirit and other doctrines. The task of the Christian theologian is to clarify the nature of the premises, the validity of the conclusions and the truth of the claims made by Christians using both deductive and inductive reasoning.

Bibliography
E. J. Lemmon, *Beginning Logic* (London, 1965); S. E. Toulmin, *The Uses of Argument* (Cambridge, 1958); N. Wolterstorff, *Reason within the Bounds of Religion* (Grand Rapids, MI, 1984).

E.D.C.

LOGICAL POSITIVISM.

There are two main sources of logical positivism. The first is David Hume* and empiricist* philosophy with its emphasis on sense experience leading to certainty about matters of fact, which it contrasted to relations of ideas which told nothing about the real world. The second is Auguste Comte (1798–1857), who coined the word 'positivism'* to cover six features of things: being real, useful, certain, precise, organic and relative. His desire was to apply a scientific attitude not only to science but also to human affairs. These came together in the Vienna Circle of the 1920s and 1930s whose main members were M. Schlick (1882–1936), R. Carnap (1891–1970), O. Neurath (1882–1945), F. Waismann (1896–1959), with Wittgenstein* and K. Popper (b. 1902) on the fringe, and C. G. Hempel (b. 1905) and A. J. Ayer (b. 1910) as allies. The general aim was to develop and systematize empiricism using tools and concepts derived from logic and mathematics, especially from the early works of Wittgenstein and Bertrand Russell (1872–1970).

The approach was highly critical of theology and metaphysics* as meaningless. Their statements were either nonsense or interpreted like those of ethics and aesthetics as expressing feelings, attitudes or matters of taste. The Vienna Circle focused on the nature of meaning and developed the 'verification* principle'. This stated that a statement or proposition was meaningful only if it were verifiable by sense experience. Thus for a statement to have a truth value it must be known what would count for or against it in terms of sense experience. If it could not be tested by sense experience, it was dismissed as meaningless. The positivist, following the empiricist, divided knowledge into either 1. relations of ideas which were tautologies, like the truths of mathematics and logic, and were true by definition but uninformative, or 2. matters of fact which were known only by sense experience. Theology and metaphysics were neither and their statements were therefore meaningless. The positivists ran into problems over the status of the principle of verifiability and whether the aim was verification in principle or practice, in a strong or weak sense. Popper turned to falsifiability as a better test for scientific laws, while Carnap and Ayer tended to stress testability or confirmability. Much of their debate was over attempts to preserve the notion of verification, but this tended to lose ground in view of the struggle over the exclusion of scientific laws and historical propositions. Logical positivism stressed the underlying unity of science and the strong belief that reality could be fully expressed by translation into statements about physical objects or sense experience and that this would ultimately have the form of logic or mathematics. The role of philosophy was not to establish philosophical doctrines, but to elucidate meaning or call attention to the lack of meaning. With the failure of the strict notion of verification, there tended to be a drift towards less dogmatic forms of linguistic and conceptual analysis (see Religious Language*). Nevertheless, the themes of meaning, verification, anti-metaphysics and unified science have continued to exercise a powerful influence on modern philosophy, and provided a major challenge to religion and theology through the work of Ayer and A. Flew (b. 1923).

Bibliography

A. J. Ayer, *Language, Truth and Logic* (London, ²1946); *idem* (ed.), *Logical Positivism* (London, 1959); R. B. Braithwaite, *An Empiricist's View of the Nature of Religious Belief* (Cambridge, 1955).

Critiques: H. D. Lewis (ed.), *Clarity is not Enough. Essays in Criticism of Linguistic Philosophy* (London, 1963); E. L. Mascall, *Words and Images* (London, 1957); I. T. Ramsey (ed.), *Christian Ethics and Contemporary Philosophy* (London, 1966).

E.D.C.

LOGOS. The Gk. term *logos* can indicate either discourse or reason. It is important because Christ is understood as the Logos, 1. in the prologue of John (1:1–18) and 2. in the early fathers. The two cases need to be considered separately.

1. In Gk. philosophy the concept is first found in Heraclitus (5th century BC) of the Logos as the unifying, rational principle holding together a world in perpetual flux. For the Stoics* (*c.* 300 BC onwards), the Logos was the active, unifying principle of the universe and the source of all existing things, through the *logoi spermatikoi*, the seeds from which things come into being. The Logos was also the natural law* in accord with which people had to live. In the Hellenistic Judaism of Philo,* the term Logos denoted the instrument by which the world was created and represented a bridge between a transcendent God and the material world.

From the OT perspective, the concept evoked God's word that called creation into being (Gn. 1:1–3; Ps. 33:6, 9), the revelatory word that came to the prophets (Je. 1:4, 11; 2:1) and was preached by them (Je. 2:4; 7:2), the word as equivalent to the law (Ps. 119:9, 105) and the word as God's agent of salvation (Ps. 107:20), or of judgment (Je. 23:29; Ho. 6:5), that would accomplish its purpose (Is. 55:11). It probably also contained echoes of the concept of Wisdom* in Pr. 8:22–31.

Though this background is important, John breaks decisively with the Gk. concepts and goes well beyond the OT perspective by affirming the personal pre-existence and the incarnation* of the Logos. His interest lies not in any metaphysical concept of Logos, but rather in the identification of Christ as the divine Logos, by whom the world was made, who was the light of men and yet rejected, who became flesh to enable people to become children of God.

2. In post-NT writings the Logos-concept of John's prologue was important in the early formulations of the relation of Christ to the Godhead (see Christology;* Trinity*). Using the Gk. concepts mentioned above and the modified Stoicism of Middle Platonism,* the Apologists* sought to maintain both monotheism* and the divinity of Christ. Christ was understood to have been the 'immanent' reason (logos endiathetos) of the Father, who came forth (logos prophorikos, the uttered word) before creation, being generated then, although already existent in the Father, and became man in the incarnation.*

The Logos was understood 1. as revealer and interpreter of the invisible, transcendent Father, 2. as the rational principle in God, related to man's reason (to Justin Martyr and Clement of Alexandria* he was the inspirer of the best of Gk. philosophy), and 3. the (expression of the) will of the Father, thus maintaining the unity of word and deed seen in the OT understanding of God's word.

While this perspective avoided the extremes of modalism (cf. Monarchianism*) subordinationism (see Trinity*) and adoptionism,* the idea of 'dating' the Son's generation in time created difficulties. Also, the (Philonic) concept of the Logos as the intermediary between a transcendental God and the material world (e.g. in Justin Martyr) led easily to some form of subordinationism. Later Trinitarian theology developed along different lines, but retained the term Logos as a title of Christ.

Bibliography

A. Debrunner et al., in TDNT IV, pp. 71–136; G. Fries et al., in NIDNTT III, pp. 1081–1117; J. N. D. Kelly, Early Christian Doctrines (London, ⁵1977); G. E. Ladd, A Theology of the New Testament (Grand Rapids, MI, 1974); G. L. Prestige, God in Patristic Thought (London, 1952).

T.G.D.

LOISY, A. F., see MODERNISM, CATHOLIC.

LOMBARD, PETER (c. 1100–59). Peter Lombard was born in the Novara region of Lombardy. He studied at Bologna, Reims and Paris universities. From c. 1140 he taught at Paris. In 1158 he became bishop of Paris, where he died the following year.

Twenty of Peter's sermons survive, together with commentaries on the psalms and on Paul's letters, the latter written between 1139 and 1142. But he is remembered primarily for his Four Books of Sentences (Sententiarum Libri Quatuor). They cover the Trinity, providence and evil (Book I), creation, sin and grace (Book II), incarnation, redemption, virtues and commandments (Book III), sacraments and the four last things (Book IV). In this work Peter discusses various theological questions and resolves them by reference to the Bible, the fathers (especially Augustine*) and other later authorities. He quotes extracts (sententiae, 'sentences', meaning maxims or opinions) and uses reason, dialectic and logic* to arbitrate between them. In this he was following the methods of the canon lawyers* (such as Gratian) which had been applied to theology by Peter Abelard.* But while Abelard had run foul of authority, Lombard was to meet with general approval. Bernard of Clairvaux,* who had hounded Abelard, commended Lombard. While Lombard used Abelard's methods, he combined them with a respect for authority uncharacteristic of Abelard. His aim was not to introduce new ideas but simply to decide the truth on the basis of the established authorities.

In one area Peter did break new ground – in the theology of the sacraments.* He was probably the first to give what is now the standard Roman Catholic list of seven sacraments. The concept of seven sacraments met with rapid approval, seven being the perfect number. But not all agreed with Peter as to which seven rites should be included in the number. In due course Peter's list prevailed and it was defined as orthodoxy by the Council of Florence in 1439. Peter's limitation of the number of sacraments to seven was based on the distinction between a sacrament proper, supposed to have been instituted by Jesus Christ himself, and other less important rites, called sacramentals. Peter also argued that a sacrament is not simply a 'visible sign of an invisible grace' (Augustine), but also the effective cause of that grace. Here again, Peter's view prevailed.

Peter's theology did not meet with immediate acceptance. At first the orthodoxy of his teaching on the doctrines of the Trinity and the person of Christ was questioned, by Joachim* of Fiore (c. 1135–1202) among others. But at the Fourth Lateran Council in 1215 Lombard was fully vindicated and this encouraged the use of his *Sentences*. They became the standard theological textbook until the time of the Reformation and beyond. For centuries, writing a commentary on Lombard's *Sentences* was a standard part of the preparation for a doctorate in theology. Not inappropriately, Peter came to be known as the 'Master of the Sentences'.

Bibliography

Works in *PL* 191–192; *Libri IV Sententiarum*, 2 vols. (Quaracchi, ²1916). Selections in ET in E. R. Fairweather, *A Scholastic Miscellany: Anselm to Ockham* (LCC 10; London, 1956), and R. McKeon, *Selections From Medieval Philosophers*, 2 vols. (New York, 1929–30).

P. Delhaye, *Pierre Lombard: sa vie, ses oeuvres, sa morale* (Montreal and Paris, 1961); J. de Ghellinck, 'Pierre Lombard' in *DTC* 12, cols. 1941–2019; E. F. Rogers, *Peter Lombard and the Sacramental System* (New York, 1917).

A.N.S.L.

LONERGAN, BERNARD (1904–85),
Canadian Jesuit* theologian. After teaching in Canada (1940–53), Lonergan was professor of theology at the Gregorian University in Rome until his retirement in 1965, after which he lived in North America. His life work has been the study of intellectual enquiry in general and theological method* in particular. In his early works on specific Christian doctrines he was beginning to develop his method, and his work on Thomas Aquinas* also prepared the way for his own study of method. In *Insight* (1957; London, ³1983) he studied the structure of human understanding in all fields of knowledge, and then, especially in *Method in Theology* (London, 1972), he applied his thinking to theological method.

Lonergan pursues a 'transcendental method' of reflecting on the activity of knowing, an enquiry into enquiry. This reveals a basic cognitional structure common to all human knowing in all areas of knowledge. There are three operations (experience, understanding and judgment) involved in all knowledge, and a fourth (decision) in which we decide to act on what we know. The activity of knowing can thus be summed up in Lonergan's four 'transcendental precepts': be attentive, be intelligent, be reasonable, be responsible. Through the transcendental method of reflecting on this dynamic structure of all knowing, there takes place a heightening of consciousness and a move to interiority, 'a personal appropriation of one's own rational self-consciousness', which Lonergan calls intellectual conversion.

In a very complex discussion, *Insight* moves from cognitive analysis through epistemology* to metaphysics* and a kind of natural theology.* The three steps involved in knowing take one beyond naive realism and idealism* to the kind of critical realism which is implied in the combination of the three steps. Knowledge is objective knowledge of reality, and reality is intelligible. Humanity's unrestricted desire to know intelligible reality points towards God.

In his work on theological method, Lonergan takes up his scheme of mental operations, but also divides the theological task into eight 'functional specialties'. These are not the usual subject specializations of theology (OT studies, patristics, *etc.*), but 'distinct and separate stages in a single process from the data to ultimate results'. There is a sequence of specialties in two phases. Those of the first phase (research, interpretation, history, dialectic) are concerned with understanding religion in the past: assimilating and assessing the tradition. Those of the second phase (foundations, doctrines, systematics, communications) are concerned with contemporary appropriation, interpretation and communication. All four levels of mental operation (experience, understanding, judgment, decision) operate in each specialty, but in each they operate to achieve the end proper to one level. Thus (in the first phase) research corresponds to experience, interpretation to understanding, history to judgment, and dialectic to decision.

Of special interest is the transition from the first phase to the second, through dialectic and foundations. Dialectic sorts out and clarifies the fundamental conflicts which arise in and from the religious tradition, and which can only be decided or overcome on the basis of a fundamental intellectual, moral or religious outlook. Such an outlook results from conversion (intellectual, moral or religious) and is expressed in the fifth specialty, foundations. Thus whereas the specialties of the first phase do not presuppose conversion, those of the second do. A personal appropriation of the tradition is required for its contemporary mediation.

In delineating this series of interdependent stages in a single process of theological work, Lonergan aims to unify the whole area of theological endeavour and to provide 'a framework for collaborative creativity'. His method as such is not confessional,* but ecumenical,* in that it provides a methodological framework for the study and assessment of all religious traditions, but in a properly theological, not merely phenomenological,* way. Lonergan has found enthusiastic disciples, but the results of his method remain to be seen.

Bibliography

Collection (London, 1968); *A Second Collection* (London, 1974).

P. Corcoran (ed.), *Looking at Lonergan's Method* (London, 1975); H. A. Meynell, *An Introduction to the Philosophy of Bernard Lonergan* (London, 1976); M. C. O'Callaghan, *Unity in Theology: Lonergan's Framework for Theology in its New Context* (Lanham, MD, 1983); D. Tracy, *The Achievement of Bernard Lonergan* (Freiburg, 1970).

R.J.B.

LORD, see CHRISTOLOGY; GOD; JESUS.

LORD'S DAY, see SABBATH.

LORD'S SUPPER, see EUCHARIST.

LOVE. Christ summarized our whole duty as to love God with our whole being, and our neighbour as ourself (Mt. 22:34–40). But what is love?

The various 'loves'

In the OT the commonest Heb. word for 'love,' *'āhēb*, has as wide connotations as the Eng. word, but in Gk. several words were used to describe different types and facets of love. *Storgē* meant 'natural affection' (as between a mother and child), *philia* the affec-

tion of friends and kindred spirits (or a liking for something), and *erōs* the attraction of desire, especially in sexual love (although it also had a higher philosophical reference at times). But *agapē* was the relatively uncommon Gk. noun used by both LXX and the NT to describe the self-giving love of God* revealed in Jesus Christ* (see Grace*), which is the motivating power and pattern of Christian living. All these four 'loves' in common denote at one and the same time an inner state of feeling or disposition of the heart, plus an attitude of mind or way of thinking, and also a way of behaving, acting or reacting, towards the object(s) of love.

Agapē and erōs

Beyond that, however, *agapē*, in the sense of Godlike love, is clearly distinguished from the rest. The first three are all natural, even to fallen* man, whereas Godlike *agapē*-love is not. All four are essentially God-given, but sin* in fallen humanity has badly distorted the first three, and effectively banishes *agapē* until the grace of the Holy Spirit of Christ begins to recreate it in regeneration,* and renews a person progressively in God's image.* (*Erōs* had become so badly debased into lust in the Graeco-Roman world that the NT avoids its use altogether.) Further, whereas *philia* can be used of sub-personal objects, *agapē* is used only of fully interpersonal relationships (human and/or divine) in Scripture.

A. Nygren* (in *Agape and Eros*) charged Augustine* and others with confusing *agapē* and *erōs* in relation to divine love, and especially human love for God, and ending up with a hybrid of both – *caritas* ('charity') – based more on attraction and desire than on the unselfish outgoing love of God awakening a like response in the heart. Although Nygren's warning against such confusion is important, it is questionable whether Nygren has been quite fair to Augustine.* Certainly some of the language of the psalms, for instance, supports the idea of spiritual attraction and desire drawing the believer's heart after God; but clearly the attempt to ground love for God (as Augustine sometimes appears to do) in a proper love for one's self and one's own highest good is fraught with the danger of misunderstanding. Much more dangerous is the excessive use of physical and sexual imagery by some of the medieval mystics* in describing the believing soul's relation to Christ (largely based on an excessive and wrong allegorizing of the Song of Songs).

Agapē, that love in men and women which images divine grace, needs to permeate, inform, direct and control all the other 'loves' and all the Christian's relationships with others. Indeed, the other loves will only be healed, to function truly and be held and enjoyed in proper proportion, when *agapē* is in control. This can be seen in Paul's application of its controlling principles to the specific relationships of life in Eph. 5:21 – 6:9 and Col. 3: 12 – 4:1. Such love is not only to control relationships in the family and the workplace, but especially in church members' relations to one another (1 Jn. 4:7 – 5:3), and also to those in need and even enemies (Lk. 10:25–37; 6:27–36).

A unique and distinctive love

Agapē, as Godlike love, stands in total contrast to all pagan ideas of love in a fallen world. While they are manipulative, because largely self-centred and working for self-interest, self-gratification and self-protection, *agapē* is completely unselfish. It is based neither on a felt need in the loving person nor on a desire called forth by some attractive feature(s) in the one loved; it is not afraid to make itself vulnerable, and it does not seek to get its own way by covert ruses and psychological 'games'. It rather proceeds from a heart of love and is directed to the other person to bless him or her and to seek that person's highest good (*cf.* 1 Cor. 13:4–7). Its source is God, and its pattern and inspiration are Jesus Christ (1 Jn. 4:7–19). It values other persons as worthy ends in themselves, and does not merely use them as a means to an end. Whether in relation to God or man, however, its keynote is not merely emotion, but devotion, shown in commitment and measured by self-giving, practical action and sacrifice (Jn. 14:1, 24; 15:12–14). By such love, the most essential and abiding quality in human life, Christians are to be recognized (1 Cor. 13; Jn. 13:34–35).

Love and law

The proper relating of love to the law* of God is one of the hallmarks of a balanced theology and Christian life (see Law and Gospel*). Two equal and opposite dangers have to be avoided. Legalism effectively ousts love as the dynamic of the gospel and the Christian life (and so banishes the joy* from religion), by reducing both to obedience or conformity to a set of external commands or rules, after the manner of the scribes and Pharisees in the gospels. Its opposite, antinomianism, misconstrues both Paul's teaching about our having 'died to the law' and Augustine's famous, often misquoted, dictum, 'Love [God], and do as you will.' Its adherents tell the Christian to forget about law altogether, and leave behind every command but love – a course which has usually degenerated in practice into immoral licence, rather than promoted true Christian liberty (*i.e.* freedom* from sin to serve God and our fellows). The gospel of God's grace in Jesus Christ frees the Christian from both these erroneous tendencies. First, no-one can earn salvation* by legal good works, but only receive it as the free gift of God's love in Christ (Rom. 3:19–28; Eph. 2:8–9). Secondly, the Holy Spirit* comes to dwell within Christians and writes God's law in their hearts in letters of love (Heb. 10:16; 2 Cor. 3:1–6). Thirdly, people's rebellious hearts, convicted of sin through the commandments, are transformed by God's love and begin to see the law as good, the expression of God's loving will for human life and blessing and a framework for loving relationships. Hence they begin to delight inwardly in them (Rom. 7:7 – 8:8; 13:8–10; Jas. 2:8–13). Fourthly, while not despising, but rather respecting, the letter of God's commands in the law, the Christian is taught by Christ to look beyond the letter to the intention and spirit behind them, and to seek to apply those underlying principles of total love for God and others in every situation (Mt. 22:34–40; 23:23–24). But the whole basis of his or her life (its security, motivation, dynamic and pattern) is not law, but grace – God's *agapē* 'poured out . . . into our hearts by the Holy Spirit' (Rom. 5:5) – which sets people free to fulfil his will in the obedience of faith (Rom. 5:5–8; 6:14; 7:6; Gal. 5:1, 13–25).

See also: LOVE OF GOD.

Bibliography

J. N. D. Anderson, *Law, Morality and Grace* (London, 1972); M. C. D'Arcy, *The Mind and Heart of Love* (London, 1945); D. Day Williams, *The Spirit and the Forms of Love* (London, 1968); D. Guthrie, *New Testament Theology* (Leicester, 1981); E. W. Hirst,

Studies in Christian Love (London, 1944); C. S. Lewis, *The Four Loves* (London, 1960); J. Moffat, *Love in the New Testament* (London, 1929); L. Morris, *Testaments of Love* (Grand Rapids, MI, 1981); A. Nygren, *Agape and Eros*, 3 vols. (ET, London, 1932–39); O. O'Donovan, *The Problem of Self-Love in St Augustine* (New Haven and London, 1980); C. Spicq, *Agape in the New Testament* (ET, St Louis and London, 1963).

J.P.B.

LOVE OF GOD. Since God is both light (1 Jn. 1:5) and love (1 Jn. 4:8), his love is not viewed in Scripture apart from his holiness.

God is holy love

God's self-revelation, culminating in Jesus Christ, shows his inner character as essentially holy love (1 Jn. 4:7–8). Love and holiness combine so perfectly in him as to be at once gentle and patient yet firm and strong. This love finds eternal expression within God, in the relations of the Father, Son and Holy Spirit (Jn. 17:5, 22–26), and therefore it does not depend upon a relationship with the creatures, although reaching out to them (Ps. 50:12ff.). The OT and NT use several pictures from human relationships to illustrate God's love for humanity – for sinners, and for his own people or children: the pictures of friendship, parent and child, courtship and marriage, and of compassionate care for those in need (Jn. 15:13–15; Lk. 15:11–32; Ezk. 16; Lk. 11:5–8). In fact all these have their source in God himself (Eph. 3:14–15). Human love, unlike God's, is often marred and distorted by sin, and therefore care must be taken in interpreting this human imagery.

A unique love

So unique and distinctive is God's love in a fallen world, that the Bible regularly uses a relatively uncommon Gk. word to describe it (*agapē*; see Love*). God's love is eternal, constant and ultimately invincible by the power of hatred and evil from devils or men. It is seen in his gracious dealings with the whole of creation (Ps. 145:9), but most clearly in his saving of sinners and his dealings with his people. God's love is sovereign, free and gracious, electing to confer his grace and blessings on the basis of his own character, desire and purpose, not on the basis of any superior merit on the part of those who are loved (Dt. 7:6–9; Eph. 2:8–9; Rom. 3:20–28; 9:6–24). God's love is constantly reaching out to rebellious mankind: he forgives and accepts sinners into his kingdom. His love awaits, expects and elicits a response of trust and love in human hearts (Jn. 3:16–21).

Love supremely revealed in Jesus Christ

The extent and depth of divine love is seen most clearly in Jesus* – his birth, life, ministry, passion and gift of the Holy Spirit.* The self-emptying of the creator to take human nature at Bethlehem; the ministry and care of Jesus towards the despised, the outcast and the neglected; his parables of the Father's love and care; his deliberate humbling of himself to endure the ignominy, shame and agony of his sin-bearing death and passion on behalf of those who rejected him; all these declare with one voice the amazing love of God (Phil. 2:5–8; Lk. 5:27–32; 7:36–50; 15; 1 Pet. 2:22–24). The characteristic activity of this love is committed self-giving, and its measure is self-sacrifice. His resurrection showed the invincibility of such holy love, and the promised gift of the Holy Spirit transforms it from an outward demonstration into an inner reality of deep assurance and life-changing power, by which he renews men and women progressively into his own image (Rom. 8:9–30).

The motive, dynamic and pattern of Christian life

God's love shown to people in Christ and received inwardly through the Spirit is the ultimate and unshakeable security of the Christian (Rom. 8:31–39), and it constitutes the motivation, the dynamic and the pattern of Christian living and relationships both with God himself and with one's fellow men and women. Christians are called to treat others with the same love, forgiveness and compassion which they themselves have received from God in Christ (Mt. 5:43–48; 18:21–35; Eph. 4:32 – 5:2; 1 Jn. 4:7 – 5:3; Gal. 6:10; 1 Pet. 2:19–25; 3:8–9). The most distinctive feature of Godlike love in human life is its ability and desire to love, not only those naturally attractive, congenial, like-minded or friendly to us, but also the unlovely and the despised, those whom others will not love (Lk. 6:27–38; 14:12–14). Such love is not merely a feeling or desire in the heart, but an inner disposition and constant attitude of mind, and also a way of treating people by word and deed, putting their interests before one's own (1 Cor. 13:4–7; Mt. 7:12; Phil. 2:4).

Bibliography
See Bibliographies for God; Love.

J.P.B.

LULL, RAYMOND (*c.* 1232–1316). Lull's father participated in the armada which delivered Majorca from the Muslim Moors. The young Raymond grew up with influential contacts, allowing considerable travel and contact with Moors. A series of visions of Christ turned him from a dissolute life to an assurance of sins forgiven and a total dedication to mission among Muslims. His aim was threefold: 1. to write books on apologetics,* particularly for Muslims; 2. to inspire popes, prelates and princes to found colleges for the study of Christian sciences and Arabic; 3. to give his life as a martyr among Muslims.

1. Lull broke the medieval tradition by writing not only in Latin, but also in his native Catalan and in Arabic. He was prolific, producing some 290 books of which about 240 still survive. He loved religious allegories with apologetic aims. *The Book of the Gentiles and the Three Wise Men* and *Blanquerna* typify this. But he also wrote the semi-autobiographical *The Book of Contemplation* in seven volumes in Arabic and some more directly apologetic works – *e.g. The Great Art* for which he was examined at Paris University in 1287 and awarded the title Master. In *The Great Art* he seeks to supply incontrovertible answers to questions of theology (particularly the doctrines of the Trinity* and the incarnation*) metaphysics and natural science. Thus Aristotelian* philosophy and scholastic* theology are fused – as also in Thomas Aquinas,* Al Ghazzali (the formative Muslim theologian, 1059–1111) and the Jewish Maimonides (1135–1204).

Lull travelled widely and frequently to share his vision of training colleges with popes, prelates and princes. Frequently, however, his visits coincided with events which prevented these leaders giving attention to his aims. He persuaded King James of Majorca to establish such a college in Miramar with thirteen friars, but to Lull's grief it lasted only sixteen years. Then in 1285 Pope Honorius IV was persuaded to set up a school of Arabic and other languages in Paris. Lull himself not only spent nine years after his conversion in concentrated study of Arabic and Latin, but also then lectured in the University of Montpellier and worked in Paris, where he combated the heresies of the Averroists.* Lull's struggle with Islam-related Averroism was motivated by the hope that the heretics might then preach the pure Christian truth to Muslims. Lull's concern for pure doctrine always had a missionary purpose.

3. Lull engaged in three major missionary journeys to North Africa in 1291, 1307 and 1313. His pattern was to challenge leading Muslims to debate, with the pretext that he would become a Muslim if persuaded. He also did evangelistic preaching in market places and streets. Like the apostle Paul he experienced shipwreck, preaching to visitors in prison and mob violence. (Only on his third journey at the ripe age of eighty did he see people converted, both leading Moors in Tunis and simpler folk in villages.) Finally he was stoned in the streets of Bugia and died virtually a martyr.

See also: ISLAM AND CHRISTIANITY.

Bibliography
E. A. Peers, *The Fool of Love: The Life of Ramon Lull* (London, ²1948); F. A. Yates, *Lull and Bruno* (London, 1982); S. M. Zwemer, *Raymond Lull, First Missionary to the Moslems* (New York and London, 1902).

M.F.G.

LUTHER, MARTIN (1483–1546). Luther' ancestry was rugged, independent farming stock of Saxony. He was brought up in a home characterized by two features: deep religion and dignified poverty. He carried these marks to the grave, for all his life he sought a true religion, and he died penniless.

Educated at the cathedral school at Magdeburg and the grammar school at Eisenach, he entered the already old and famous University of Erfurt (1501–5) at his father's expense. Owing to some distressing experience of death, he turned away from the secular employment intended for him, to seek the life of a religious. He entered the prestigious monastery of the Augustinian* Hermits in Erfurt (1505). Ordained priest in 1507, the brilliant young Luther was selected by his superiors to lecture in the new University of

Wittenberg in 1508. In 1510 he was sent to Rome on monastic business, an experience which opened his eyes to the corruption of the curia as well as to the general failure of the church to fulfil the mission intended by God. In 1511 he became Doctor of Theology, and was recalled to Wittenberg as professor of biblical studies, holding this post till his death. In 1511 he was made vicar of his order and prior of eleven monasteries.

Luther had entered the monastery to find peace with God, but the closer experience of God which he sought turned out to be a torment and desperate struggle, even a worse alienation. To understand this struggle, and how Luther was delivered into the glorious liberty of the sons of God, is to understand Luther's intense evangelical theology, as well as his significance for the Reformation* and for posterity.

During those early years of intense spiritual struggle he was making a deep study of the Bible, and, as monk/professor, lectured on Genesis (1512), Psalms (1513), Romans (1515), and Galatians (1516). It has been traditional to think of his making a dramatic breakthrough into evangelical theology, but a close reading of the evidence, from the early monastic sermon at Leitzkau in 1512, shows Luther's mind and spirit, captured by the biblical, evangelical theology, discovering stage by stage the authentic, evangelical, Christian experience.

Clear though Luther's evangelical theology is in his earlier expositions, it first emerges at a controversial level in the *Disputation against Scholastic Theology* (1517). Here he challenged philosophy (Duns Scotus* and Biel*) in favour of theology (Augustinian*). He attacked the Aristotelianism* of the schoolmen (see Scholasticism*) as inimical both to the NT doctrine of grace* and to Christian ethics.* He expounded the distinction between law* and gospel.* This *Disputation* could be claimed to be the beginning of the Reformation, though it was the later Ninety-five Theses of 1517 against the sale of indulgences (see Merit;* Penance*) which actually sparked off the movement. This second series of theses spread like wildfire: within a fortnight they had overrun Germany, within a month, Europe.

In April 1518 Luther attended the triennial chapter of his fellow Augustinians at Heidelberg. He set aside the peripheral, controversial issues of indulgences and penance, and handled the great central theological themes: God's righteousness* and man's righteousness; law and gospel (see Law and Gospel*); sin,* grace, free will* and faith;* justification* by works and justification in Christ; the theology of the cross.* Unable to extradite him, the pope summoned Luther to Augsburg to be corrected and disciplined by the Dominican* Cardinal Cajetan (1469–1534). After an abortive meeting, he faced the redoubtable John Eck (1486–1543) at Leipzig in 1519, for a week-long disputation on Luther's theology, when he denied the primacy of the papacy* and the infallibility of general councils.* Luther was now virtually at the head of the Reformation movement.

The year 1520 marked the decisive break with medieval Catholicism, with the publication of the three definitive 'Reformation treatises'. The first was the *Appeal* to the laity,* when he invited the German princes to take the reform of the church into their own hands, and to abolish the tributes to Rome, the celibacy of the clergy, masses for the dead, pilgrimages, religious orders, and other Catholic practices and institutions. He then appealed to the clergy in his *On the Babylonian Captivity of the Church* wherein he set forth positively a NT sacramental* theology and communion in both kinds, and negatively, rejected transubstantiation and the sacrifice of the mass with the theology as well as the abuses which went with them (see Eucharist,* Sacraments*). In the third, *The Freedom of a Christian Man*, a fine, spiritual non-controversial work, he expounded justification by grace as distinct from justification by works. By the bull *Exsurge, Domine* (15 June 1520), Luther's theses were censured as heretical; his books were ordered to be burnt; and he himself was given sixty days to recant. Luther publicly burnt the bull, not his books (15 December 1520), along with some obsolete tomes of canon law,* and was duly excommunicated by the bull *Decet Romanum* (3 January 1521).

Summoned before the emperor at the Diet of Worms (1521), he again refused to recant, arguing that his books were sound, and that, unless he could be convinced by Scripture* and sound reason, he would not recant. Luther was put under the ban of the Empire, and, on the way home under the imperial safe-conduct, was whisked off to the Wartburg, where he was secretly kept under close custody.

What exactly was the nature of Luther's protest, and why did such a scholarly and religious protest result in excommunication and, further, split Christendom from top to bottom?

Luther's protest did not initially arise from criticism of Catholic doctrine, for he was a deeply committed Catholic believer. Neither was it a mere criticism of abuses as such, for he knew that abuses creep into every kind of human institution. It arose rather from the nature of his religious experience.* In the monastery Luther had pursued with devoted diligence all the ways a monk was taught to find God: the mystic* path of confession, devotion and prayer; the intellectual path of reason; the practical discipline of good works. Luther went through the darkest agony of despair when he found that the more diligently he pursued the well-trodden paths of spiritual growth, the further God seemed distanced from him, and even hostile towards him.

It was at this moment that the simple foundational truth of Christianity burst into his darkness: he was not to think of God as remote and far off, for it was he in his self-centredness who was far off. God had come all the way in Christ to find him, and continued to come to the penitent and believing heart. Luther rediscovered the original gospel – the truth of Eph. 2:8. As he expressed it, 'The door of paradise was flung open to me, and I entered.'

This discovery meant the unqualified centrality of Christ, the proclamation of the original gospel message, and the restoration of biblical, evangelical thinking. Here lay the source of Luther's Reformation theology, as he felt driven by God to re-form what had been de-formed. He said that he was led on as a horse is led by a man: 'I simply say that true Christianity had ceased to exist among those who should have preserved it – the bishops and scholars.'

He rediscovered the authority* and finality of Christ; his was a Christological corrective. He corrected the distortions of medieval theology and the superstitions of medieval practice in the interests of a full NT Christology, based on the incarnational* theology of John* and the theology of redemption* of Paul.* He set Christ and his work in the centre rather than humanity and its works. He put the common man on his theological feet by restoring the doctrine of the priesthood* of all believers. This emphasis modified the mysterious power and authority of the priesthood, and by removing the priest's mediatorial,* almost magical, powers, knocked the bottom out of the prevailing Catholic system and cultus. The threat of purgatory* with its mitigation by indulgences for money, inimical to the truth of the gospel, was challenged by the biblical message of unmerited forgiveness through faith in Christ alone. The mass and transubstantiation were replaced by the NT reality of communion. The cult of Mary* and the saints,* of pilgrimages and wonder-working images,* fell away as superstitious and otiose ecclesiastical bric-a-brac. The papal claims to universal secular authority, even to doctrinal infallibility, were seen as the claims of a worldly prince, not of a vicar of Christ. The doctrine of salvation in Christ alone meant justification by faith alone through the grace of Christ alone. Luther saw this as the central message of the entire Bible, OT and NT alike, and this was to him the word of God, the sole and sufficient theological authority.

Locked away in the Wartburg, Luther translated the entire NT in a matter of weeks into fine German, powerful and warm: he not only made it the dominant influence in German religion, but creatively shaped the modern German language. Owing to radical and fanatical elements taking over the Reformation in Wittenberg in his absence (see Reformation, Radical*), Luther returned in 1522 to stabilize university and church life there.

Back at Wittenberg, Luther faced all the problems consequent on reformation, generated by fanatics, Catholics, humanists,* and exponents of a socially radical gospel. In addition to the fanatics, he had to deal with the more responsible Catholic resistance, represented by Latomus (1521) and Henry VIII (1522), as well as John Cochlaeus (1479–1552), Thomas Murner (1475–1537), Eck and others. The radical attack culminated in the tragic Peasants' War of 1525. Though deeply sensitive to the justice of the peasants' cause, all his life Luther had opposed civil rebellion as the worst evil that can befall society, and resisted the peasants' revolt, not only for this reason, but because it made the disastrous identification of social rebellion with the cause of evangelical theology.

The Reformation suffered a wound in the Peasants' War from which it never recovered. It was this movement of destructive rebellion and tumult which alienated the scholars and humanists,* and turned the gentle Erasmus* against the Reformation, though, with the humanists, he had hitherto supported it. Erasmus chose to attack Luther's Augustinian theology of the unfree will,* in reply to which Luther wrote his finest book, *The Bondage of the Will* (1525) – finest in that it offers a learned, theological defence of biblical, evangelical theology, by showing the bondage of the natural man to himself and his own interests, and the freedom* wherewith Christ sets him free.

Now confined to Saxony, Luther strengthened local church life by drawing up a reformed *Mass* (1523), and, under popular demand, the *German Mass* (1526). He wrote books for pastors on the parochial ministry, collections of sermons, a litany, an ordinal, a baptism service, and about twenty-four fine biblical hymns, with music. 1529 brought the division within Protestantism on the doctrine of the eucharistic presence, though in that same year the Diet of Speier secured the right of princes to organize national churches. Luther produced two magnificent catechisms* that same year: the Great Catechism as a basis for pastors to teach, the Short Catechism for everyman. He also produced an immense corpus of theological works, commentaries and sermons, and, with others, completed the translation of the whole Bible.

It was Christendom's greatest mistake when she rejected the monk of Wittenberg, a fact admitted today by most Catholic scholars. Luther was to say to his students towards the end of his life, 'I have taught you Christ, purely, simply and without adulteration.' This statement sums up his entire life. In 1546, some thirty years after he had nailed his Ninety-five Theses to the door of the Castle Church in Wittenberg, he was buried within its walls, where his mortal remains still lie. We could not sum up Luther's life's work in words better than his own: 'I simply taught, preached, wrote God's Word: I did nothing ... The Word did it all.'

See also: HIDDEN AND REVEALED GOD; LUTHERANISM; VOCATION.

Bibliography

Sources: best edition of works is *Weimarer Ausgabe*, ed. J. C. F. Knaake and others (Weimar, 1883–); best collected translation, *Luther's Works*, 55 vols. (St Louis and Philadelphia, 1955–).

Biographies: J. Atkinson, *Martin Luther and the Birth of Protestantism* (Basingstoke, ²1982); R. Bainton, *Here I Stand* (New York, 1950); H. Bornkamm, *Luther in Mid-Career; 1521–1530* (Philadelphia, 1983); M. Brecht, *Martin Luther* (Stuttgart, 1983); W. von Loewenich, *Martin Luther* (Munich, 1982); J. Mackinnon, *Luther and the Reformation*, 4 vols. (London, 1925–30); J. M. Todd, *Luther* (London, 1982).

Theology: T. Harnack, *Luthers Theologie*, 2 vols. (Erlangen, 1862–86); J. Köstlin, *The Theology of Luther*, 2 vols. (1863; ET, Philadelphia, 1897); H. H. Kramm, *The Theology of Martin Luther* (London, 1947); W. von Loewenich, *Luther's Theology of the Cross* (Belfast, 1976); E. G. Rupp, *The Righteousness of God* (London, 1953); P. S. Watson, *Let God be God* (London, 1947).

J.A.

LUTHERANISM AND LUTHERAN THEOLOGY.

The Lutheran Reformation was pre-eminently a theological movement. Its overriding goal was not to change political or social structures (although it had a profound effect upon the political, social and academic life of Western Europe), but was deeply religious and evangelical. The burden of all Luther's* theological activity and output was to find a gracious God and to lead other sinners to him for salvation.* His significant contributions in liturgy, catechetics* and hymnody, even his deep concern for social justice and order, all served and contributed to this great soteriological goal.

There are three sources for an understanding of the nature and structure of Lutheranism. First, the Lutheran confessions comprised in the Book of Concord (see Confessions*); second, the writings of Luther; third, the writings of other Lutheran Reformers, notably Philip Melanchthon,* Matthias Flacius (1520–75) and Martin Chemnitz (1522–86).

Although the Book of Concord (to which virtually all Lutheran ministers have subscribed to this day) is normative for Lutheran theology, the Lutheran confessions do not vary on any significant point from the theology of Luther himself. Melanchthon made no substantial contribution beyond what Luther had already articulated, and the Augsburg Confession (1530), written by him, is the primary symbol of the Lutheran church and a brilliant exposition of Lutheran theology. Flacius, one of the fathers of the study of church history and of hermeneutics,* effectively defended Lutheran doctrine and practice against all detractors. Chemnitz was the principal writer of the Formula of Concord (1577), written to settle doctrinal disputes which had arisen among Lutherans after Luther's death, chiefly between the so-called Gnesio-Lutherans ('authentic Lutherans', *i.e.* followers of Luther) and the Philippists (*i.e.* followers of Melanchthon), who were more concerned to secure some rapprochement with the Calvinists. The Formula of Concord, the last of the Lutheran confessions, although it does not differ from the theology of Luther or the earlier Lutheran symbols,* clarifies, reformulates and defends the earlier theology on a number of important articles of faith such as original sin* and the bondage of the human will,* justification,* law and gospel,* the Lord's Supper, the person of Christ (see Christology*) and predestination.* Chemnitz also presented the entire Lutheran theology in a massive book on dogmatics, and his defence of Lutheran theology against the Council of Trent (see Councils;* Reformation, Catholic Counter-;* Roman Catholic Theology*) established him as the 'second Martin' without whose theological labours the work of the first Martin might have been less fruitful.

On the fundamental articles of the Trinity,* the person of Christ, creation* and Christ's vicarious atonement,* Lutheran theology consciously follows the great Eastern and Western creeds* and fathers of the early church (see Patristic Theology*). Luther and later Lutheran theology deliberately constructed their confessions and dogmatic disquisitions according to a Trinitarian scheme and pattern of thought. The distinctive contribution of Lutheran theology in the history of Christian theology is in two areas: the authority* of God's word (see Scripture*) in the church, and soteriology.

The theology of the word

The sacred Scriptures are the very word of God, and as such carry with them the authority and truthfulness of God himself. Against the authority of the papacy,* church councils,* reason (see Faith and Reason*) and experience, even religious experience,* Lutheran theology teaches that Scripture alone (*sola Scriptura*) is the source of all theology and the rule and norm for judging all teachers and teachings in the church.

The divine Scriptures and the word proclaimed on the basis of Scripture have a soteriological purpose and to this end are inherently powerful, both to condemn and destroy (law) and to comfort, create faith and save (gospel). Just as the law is God's own means of judging and condemning sinners, the gospel word, which is the cognitive message of salvation through the atoning work of Christ, is his means of salvation and grace. The word of gospel (which includes the 'visible word' of baptism* and eucharist*) actually creates and sustains the church, which is the community of all believers everywhere. Or, more precisely, the Holy Spirit* works always and only through these means of grace to call, build, comfort and save his church. The doctrine of the real presence of Christ's body and blood in the communion bolsters this function of the sacrament as means of grace, for by his body and blood Christ procured forgiveness of sins for all. Furthermore, the gospel and all its articles, that is, the doctrine drawn from Scripture, is the Spirit's means to reform the church and to unite it against all schism.* For church unity and external fellowship* unity in biblical doctrine is necessary.

The theology of the cross

According to Lutheran theology the chief article of the Christian faith centres in the person and work of Christ, in his substitutionary* atonement. It is this saving, redemptive* work of Christ, often called his obedience* (in living and dying in the place of all sinful mankind), which constitutes not merely the cause but also the basis for God's loving and gracious justification, or acquittal, of the sinner. Furthermore, the vicarious obedience of Christ constitutes the very form and essence of the righteousness* which becomes the sinner's through faith. In other words, in justification (God's effective forensic act of forgiveness and acquittal for Christ's sake), God reckons to the sinner the very righteousness

405

which Christ acquired by his perfect obedience to God's law and his atoning death.

The article of justification through faith, so central in Lutheran theology, builds upon Luther's theology of the cross.* Through faith alone (sola fide), as through an instrument, the sinner receives and appropriates to himself all the benefits Christ has acquired for the world – Christ's righteousness, God's forgiveness, peace and reconciliation with God and eternal life. Thus the article of justification, or rather, the reality of the sinner's justification through faith, offers abundant comfort and certain assurance* to troubled Christians. As the theology of the word affords the Christian certainty of his doctrine and confession, the theology of the cross affords the Christian certainty of God's grace and of his own personal salvation.

The faith through which a sinner is justified is wrought by the Holy Spirit through the gospel word and sacraments.* Only the Spirit and the word are the causes of faith in Christ. Sinful man, depraved and dead in sin, contributes nothing by his own will* or interests or best efforts or works towards his justification, conversion, or salvation. Salvation and everything pertaining to it are by God's grace alone (sola gratia). Good works, the Christian life and all principles of personal and social ethics,* for which God's law epitomized in Scripture is the norm, issue from the finished atonement which is both the power and the motive for them. God is pleased with the Christian's faith not because faith is a virtue, but for Christ's sake, because Christ is the object of the faith; he is pleased with the Christian's life, not because of the nobility or value of his works, but again for Christ's sake, because the believing sinner stands and lives before God in the imputed righteousness of Christ. Even the Christian's worship* pleases God, not because of its intensity or sincerity or outward form, but for Christ's sake. The highest worship of God is to believe in Christ. Thus, the entire Christian life flows from the theology of the cross, and all the articles of faith proceed from this central article of faith of the Christian.

Bibliography

P. Althaus, The Theology of Martin Luther (Philadelphia, 1966); W. Elert, Structure of Lutheranism (St Louis, MO, 1962); A. Koeberle, Quest for Holiness (New York, 1936); F.

Pieper, Christian Dogmatics, vol. 2 (St Louis, MO, 1951); H. Sasse, Here We Stand (New York, 1938).

R.D.P.

M

MACARIUS (PSEUDO-). This Greek ascetic* teacher was active in Asia Minor or Syria-Mesopotamia between c. 380 and 430. Many of his homilies and letters have been ascribed to Macarius of Egypt (c. 300–c. 390) (wrongly) or Symeon of Mesopotamia (perhaps his true name), and so he is sometimes referred to as Macarius-Symeon. The scope and significance of his corpus, clarified only in recent years, remain the subject of keen research.

Macarius had links with the Messalians, ascetic extremists who stressed prayer to the virtual exclusion of outward religion and were inclined to denigrate matter (like Manichaeans*). The movement was condemned in the Eastern church in the late 4th and early 5th centuries. But Macarius was also related to the more central tradition of ascetic and mystical* theology stimulated by Origen* and notably exemplified in Gregory of Nyssa,* one of whose works was dependent on Macarius' Great Letter on the monastic life (or perhaps vice-versa; scholars disagree). The Fifty Spiritual Homilies have been much admired in the West, not least by John Wesley,* who translated several of them. Macarius inculcated an interiorized quest for Christian perfection, freedom from all earthly passions, and mystical enlightenment.

Bibliography

Macarius' works are listed in CPG nos. 2410–2427; collected edition begun by V. Desprez, Pseudo-Macaire, oeuvres spirituelles, vol. 1 (SC 275– , 1980–); Fifty Spiritual Homilies, tr. A. J. Mason (London, 1921).

W. Jaeger, Two Rediscovered Works of Ancient Christian Literature: Gregory of Nyssa and Macarius (Leiden, 1954); V. Desprez in DSp 10, cols. 20–43.

D.F.W.

MACDONALD, GEORGE (1824–1905).

Born in Huntly in rural Aberdeenshire, the son of a bleacher. He was to write nearly thirty novels, several books of sermons, a number of abiding fantasies for adults and children, short stories and poetry. His childhood is captured in his semi-autobiographical *Ranald Bannerman's Boyhood* (1871). Like C. S. Lewis* and J. R. R. Tolkien (1892–1973) in our own time, MacDonald was a scholar as well as a story-teller. He entered Aberdeen University in 1840, and had a scientific training. Much later he was for a time professor of literature at Bedford College, London. After a short spell in the Congregational ministry, he found freer rein in the precarious life of a writer and lecturer. His broad theology allowed him to approve of both C. H. Spurgeon* and F. D. Maurice (see Christian Socialism*). It is, however, for his theology of the imagination,* and its outworkings in his writings, that he is memorable. His psychological grasp of the unconscious laws upon which the human making of meaning is based predates Freud and Jung (see Depth Psychology;* Psychology of Religion*). His sense that all imaginative meaning originates with the Christian creator became the foundation of C. S. Lewis's thinking and imagining. Two seminal essays, 'The Imagination: Its Functions and its Culture' (1867) and 'The Fantastic Imagination' (before 1882), remarkably foreshadow Tolkien's famous essay 'On Fairy Stories' (1947), the gist of which persuaded C. S. Lewis of the truth of Christianity on a windy night in 1931. Writes MacDonald, 'One difference between God's work and man's is, that, while God's work cannot mean more than he meant, man's must mean more than he meant.'

Bibliography

R. N. Hein, *The Harmony Within: The Spiritual Vision of George MacDonald* (Grand Rapids, MI, 1982); C. S. Lewis (ed.), *George MacDonald: An Anthology* (London, 1946); G. MacDonald, *George MacDonald and His Wife* (London, 1924); K. Triggs, *The Stars and the Stillness: A Portrait of George MacDonald* (Cambridge, 1986).

C.P.D.

MACHEN, JOHN GRESHAM (1881–1937),

the last major advocate of the Princeton theology.* He was a NT scholar, apologist and popular theologian who by training and disposition was cut out for a life of scholarship, but who as a result of a tumultuous ecclesiastical conflict became a creator of new institutions to carry on conservative Presbyterian Calvinism in America. Machen came from a well-to-do family in Baltimore, MD, and studied at Johns Hopkins University, Princeton Seminary (under B. B. Warfield*), Princeton University and in Germany. From 1906 to 1929 he taught NT at Princeton Theological Seminary. When his appointment to a chair of theology was denied at the same time as the governing structure of the seminary was changed in favour of 'inclusive' Presbyterianism, Machen left Princeton to found Westminster Theological Seminary in Philadelphia. Shortly thereafter, in an effort to certify the orthodoxy of missionaries, he helped establish a missions board independent of the Presbyterian General Assembly. This move led to Machen and several other conservative leaders being ousted from the large Northern Presbyterian Church. As a result the Orthodox Presbyterian Church was formed to maintain a 'true Presbyterian' witness in the United States. Machen, who never married, was a careful scholar, a tireless organizer, and most of all a personal inspiration to many others, especially young ministers, who were troubled about the theological drift of American Presbyterianism.

Machen's best-known scholarly efforts were books defending traditional understandings of NT topics. His *Origin of Paul's Religion* (London, 1921) provided a careful rebuttal of the fashionable belief that Paul* had propounded a gospel heavily indebted to Gk. philosophy and strikingly at odds with the simple teachings of Jesus. His study *The Virgin Birth* (London, ²1932) carefully sifted through biblical, historical and philosophical scholarship to conclude that no valid reasons existed for questioning the church's belief in the supernatural conception of Jesus (see Virgin Birth*). In these and similar works Machen displayed the type of thorough orthodox scholarship that had marked Old Princeton since its founding in 1812 but which had become a rare commodity in the heated days of the fundamentalist-modernist controversy (see Fundamentalism*).

Machen's popular works presented logical and intelligent arguments for traditional Christian faith. Among these his *Christianity* and Liberalism (Grand Rapids, MI, 1923) has rightly received the most attention. Here Machen examined theological liberalism* with respect to beliefs about God and humanity, the Bible, Christ, salvation and the church. His conclusion was that 'the chief modern rival of Christianity is "liberalism." An examination of the teachings of liberalism in comparison with those of Christianity will show that at every point the two movements are in direct opposition' (Christianity and Liberalism, p. 53). The argumentation in this volume is careful, yet compelling. The critic Walter Lippman, who was no friend to any variety of Christianity, called it a 'cool and stringent defense of orthodox Protestantism' (Preface to Morals, New York, 1929, p. 32).

With Machen's premature death on 1 January 1937, American conservative Presbyterians lost more than just an important leader. He had been at once a model of scholarship and a rallying point for consistently Reformed churchmen. Friendly critics have suggested that his thought was perhaps too closely tied to intellectual conventions of the 19th century and that he was overprone to independence. But critics and supporters alike have acknowledged the integrity of his work and the influence of his life.

Bibliography

G. M. Marsden, 'J. Gresham Machen, History, and Truth', WTJ 42 (1979), pp. 157–175; W. S. Reid, 'J. Gresham Machen', in D. F. Wells (ed.), Reformed Theology in America (Grand Rapids, MI, 1985); C. Allyn Russell, 'J. Gresham Machen: Scholarly Fundamentalist', in Voices of American Fundamentalism (Philadelphia, 1976); N. B. Stonehouse, J. Gresham Machen: A Biographical Memoir (Grand Rapids, MI, 1954).

M.A.N.

MACKAY, DONALD M. (1922–1987). An internationally-known neuroscientist who was Granada Research Professor of Communication and Neuroscience at the University of Keele (1960–82), where he led an interdisciplinary research team on the organization of the brain. All his work, both in this area, and in his more philosophical reflections on the human person, and on science and faith, were motivated by a strong Christian faith. He was reared in the strong Reformed* faith of the Free Church of Scotland.

Theologically MacKay's work is important for two bold metaphysical theses which he developed with great thoroughness and tenacity. MacKay insisted that science* and religion stand in a logically complementary relationship. Science expresses the physically measurable and testable aspects of created reality. The findings of science are not exhaustive – MacKay was a fervent anti-reductionist – but are complemented by other levels of significant description, among which is that of the Christian religion. Thus the description of an event as 'confession of sin' is not a rival to the description of the same event in terms of physical changes in the brain, but complements it. Both science and Christian theology make claims which are objectively true or false, and the Christian faith has nothing to fear from scientific enquiry. Both science and faith progress, in different ways, in a humble, listening and enquiring attitude to the data.

The roots of MacKay's approach to science and religion lay in his view about the relation between the brain and the mind, and in his Augustinian* emphasis upon the divine timeless upholding of all things. God is not active in the 'gaps' of our present understanding, nor does he interfere with the working of otherwise immutable physical laws.

MacKay also gave prolonged and intense effort to defending the view that free choices are logically indeterminate (see Determinism;* Will*). For the chooser there is no future specification of any of his free actions which it would be correct for him now to believe, even though such specifications can, in principle, exist for another human observer, and do exist in the mind of God.

These views were expounded in two books Science, Chance and Providence (Oxford, 1978) and The Clockwork Image (London, 1974) and in numerous articles and reviews. MacKay was Gifford* Lecturer in 1986.

P.H.

MACKINNON, DONALD M. (b. 1913), held chairs in moral philosophy at Aberdeen and latterly in philosophy of religion at Cambridge until 1978. His work represents a powerful and consistent rejection of idealism* in philosophy and theology in favour of a realism given its distinctive shape by the doctrines of the person of Christ and the atonement.* His main concerns lie in the overlapping areas of theology, metaphysics and moral philosophy. MacKinnon has been especially concerned to explore the ontological and metaphysical* implications of Christian beliefs about the person and work of Christ, and it is here that his restless and interrogative analysis is at its best. His ethical work is much preoccupied with offering a realist account of the nature and significance of human action and moral freedom, especially as this determines the character of human political action. He has also written perceptively on the history of philosophy (notably on Kant* and Butler*), on Marxist-Leninism,* and on sacramental and dogmatic theology. Much of his best work is highly complex and allusive, approaching issues tangentially through particular historical incidents or texts. Partly because of this, and partly because his preferred form is the suggestive essay rather than the systematic treatise, his work has not received the attention which it deserves.

Bibliography
Borderlands of Theology and Other Essays, eds. G. W. Roberts and D. E. Smucker (London, 1968); *Christian Faith and Communist Faith*, ed. MacKinnon (London, 1953); *Explorations in Theology*, vol. 5, ed. MacKinnon (London, 1979); *Making Moral Decisions*, ed. MacKinnon (London, 1969); *The Problem of Metaphysics* (London, 1974) – Gifford Lectures 1965–66; *A Study in Ethical Theory* (London, 1957).
B. Hebblethwaite, S. Sutherland (eds.), *The Philosophical Frontiers of Christian Theology: Essays Presented to D. M. MacKinnon* (Cambridge, 1982); P. G. Wignall, 'D. M. MacKinnon: An Introduction to his Early Theological Writings', *New Studies in Theology* 1, 1980, pp. 75–94.

J.B.We.

MACKINTOSH, HUGH ROSS (1870–1936), Scottish theologian. Born in Paisley and educated at Edinburgh and in Germany, he ministered in Tayport and Aberdeen before appointment in 1904 to the chair of systematic theology in New College, Edinburgh, which post he held until his death. His early experience on the continent gave him a continuing interest in 19th-century

German Protestant writers whose work he sought to publicize in Scotland, particularly by his participation in translating Schleiermacher* and Ritschl.* As with a later Scottish scholar, William Barclay,* he would accept the classification of 'liberal evangelical'.* The two were alike in recommending their students to have a number of non-religious interests. Mackintosh rejected the view that saw propitiatory or punitive features in the atonement.* His works, which have proved more durable than those of other early 20th-century scholars, include *The Doctrine of the Person of Jesus Christ* (Edinburgh, 1912), *The Christian Experience of Forgiveness* (London, 1927) and *Types of Modern Theology* (London, 1937), which latter presents developments from Schleiermacher to Barth.*

Bibliography
J. W. Leitch, *A Theology of Transition: H. R. Mackintosh as an Approach to Barth* (London, 1952) – with bibliography; T. F. Torrance, 'H. R. Mackintosh: Theologian of the Cross', *SBET* 5:2 (1988).

J.D.Do.

MACQUARRIE, JOHN (b. 1919) taught in Glasgow, New York and latterly in Oxford, and is one of the best-known English theologians of the present day, having published very widely in the areas of Christian doctrine and philosophy of religion. Much of his writing shows the influence of a variety of thinkers in the existentialist* tradition. His earlier books *An Existentialist Theology* (London, 1955) and *The Scope of Demythologizing* (London, 1960) are particularly concerned with the resources to be found in Bultmann's* theology, though they do not counsel uncritical acceptance. His much-used textbook *Principles of Christian Theology* (London, 1966, ²1977) draws heavily on Tillich's* thought, among others, in its reinterpretations of central Christian doctrines. He is also well known for his history of *Twentieth Century Religious Thought* (London, 1963), and for a variety of other books on such topics as ethics,* spirituality,* theological language and Christian eschatology. Macquarrie's more recent work is to be found in two large treatises on the Christian doctrines of God and man, *In Search of Deity* (London, 1984) and *In Search of Humanity* (London, 1982). Best read as essays in natural theology,* these volumes are particularly good examples of the range of theological and philosophical reference, both historical and contemporary, which his work commands.

See also: MYTH.

Bibliography

Christian Hope (London, 1978); *Existentialism* (Harmondsworth, 1973); *God and Secularity* (London, 1968); *God-Talk* (London, 1967); *Paths in Spirituality* (London, 1972); *Studies in Christian Existentialism* (London, 1966).

J.B.We.

MAN, see ANTHROPOLOGY; FEMINIST THEOLOGY.

MANICHAEISM. Once regarded as a Christianized form of Zoroastrianism,* Manichaeism is now generally accepted as one of the last and most complete manifestations of Gnosticism.* It was founded by the Syro-Persian Mani (AD 216–76) who was brought up in a Jewish-Christian sect in south Babylonia and subsequently rebelled against it. The Manichaean *gnōsis* embodies a complex cosmic drama which centres on a primordial battle between the originating principles of Light and Darkness. An initial invasion of Light by Darkness led to a counter-attack by Light which was designed to fail, tricking the powers of Darkness into swallowing particles of Light. The universe was then created to redeem and purify this captive light and to punish and imprison the archons of Darkness. Through their concupiscence some of this defiled Light escaped from the archons' bodies and became plant life. They also brought forth mankind through a series of horrific acts involving abortion, incest and cannibalism; this resulted in the imprisonment of Light-particles, the soul, in a body which is utterly evil and corrupt. The soul could, however, be awakened by *gnōsis* and be made aware of its divine origins.

Jesus in Manichaeism is one of a series of Gnostic saviours and his historical manifestation was purely docetic.* The individual details of the Manichaean cosmic drama are derived mainly from Jewish and Christian apocrypha and from the cosmogonic teaching of the Edessan philosopher Bardaisan (154–222). Mani was also heavily influenced by Marcion,* from whom he acquired a strong 'Pauline' antinomianism and claimed the title of 'Apostle of Jesus Christ'.

The Manichaean sect was extremely hierarchical, and was divided into elect and hearers; the former were priests who had to observe sexual abstinence and strict food taboos including vegetarianism so that they could enable the liberation of the Light-particles trapped in the plants. The hearers, the lay followers, had to attend to the needs of the elect, and were not bound by the same rigid rules. Easily organized into small units, the religion was able to spread swiftly and to survive persecution.

A combination of missionary zeal and persecution by Sassanian authorities resulted in the religion being diffused in the Roman Empire and the lands east of the River Oxus. It was particularly well established in Roman Africa where it passed itself off as a more perfect form of Christianity, including the young Augustine* among those who were captivated by its 'higher criticism' of the Jewish and Christian Scriptures. The dualism* of Manichaeism was later seen by church authorities in the Middle Ages as having been inherited by heretical movements such as the Paulicians, the Bogomils, the Paterenes and the Cathars (see Albigenses*). In the East, the religion gradually expanded along the Silk Road and eventually reached China where it was outlawed. After the 9th century, however, the religion became strongly established in Central Asia. Later the sect went underground in China and survived as a secret religion in the south until the 16th century.

The Manichaean canon consists of a corpus of seven works by Mani, none of which has survived in a complete form. Besides a large body of polemical writings on the sect by the church fathers, our knowledge has been greatly increased by the discovery of genuine Manichaean writings from Turfan, Dunhuang (both in China), Medinet Medi (Egypt) and Theveste (north Africa). More recently a small papyrus codex from Egypt, belonging to the papyrus collection of the University of Cologne, containing a hagiographical version of the life of the founder (the *Cologne Mani Codex*), has been successfully restored and edited. It shows beyond doubt that the sect had its origins in the fringe of Judaeo-Christianity and not in Iranian religions.

Bibliography

Sources: A. Adam (ed.), *Texte Zum Manichäismus* (Berlin, ²1969); A. Böhlig and J. P. Asmussen (eds.), *Die Gnosis*, vol. 3: *Der Manichäismus* (Zurich and Munich, 1980); R. Cameron and A. J. Dewey (eds.), *The Cologne Mani Codex* (Missoula, MT, 1979).

Studies: F. Decret, *Mani et la tradition manichéenne* (Paris, 1974); H. J. Klimkeit, *Manichaean Art and Calligraphy* (Leiden, 1982); S. N. C. Lieu, *Manichaeism in the Later Roman Empire and Medieval China. A Historical Survey* (Manchester, 1985); H.-Ch. Puech, *Le Manichéisme, son fondateur, sa doctrine* (Paris, 1949); idem, *Sur le Manichéisme et autres essais* (Paris, 1979); M. Tardieu, *Le Manichéisme* (Paris, 1983).

S.N.L.

MARCELLUS OF ANCYRA (d. *c.* 374),

bishop of Ancyra in Galatia. He first became prominent as a supporter of Athanasius* and the Nicene term *homoousios* (the Son being 'of one substance' with the Father). From this perspective he attacked the teaching of Arius'* supporters Asterius (d. *c.* 341), Eusebius of Nicomedia (d. *c.* 342) and Eusebius of Caesarea,* but in so doing exaggerated the oneness of the Father and the Son before and after the incarnation. Eusebius of Caesarea responded with his *Contra Marcellum* and *De ecclesiastica theologia*, charging Marcellus with Sabellianism* (see Monarchianism*). Marcellus was accordingly condemned by a synod of Constantinople (336). In exile in Rome he gained the support of Pope Julius I, and with the arrival of Athanasius (339) he was cleared of 'the falsehood of Sabellius, the malice of Paul of Samosata, and the blasphemies of Montanus' (Rome, 341; Sardica, 343). He was, however, again removed from his see by the emperor Constantius (347) and died in exile, his teaching being repudiated by Basil* and condemned by the Council of Constantinople (381).

Marcellus's ideas *On the Subjection of the Son* are preserved by Eusebius and in his own letter to Julius. According to Basil, he taught that only to the incarnate Logos* is the title 'Son' properly applied. By the return or contraction of the Son to the pre-incarnate state his temporary separate existence came to an end. 'He returned again to him whence he came forth and had no existence before his coming forth, nor hypostasis* after his return' (Basil, *Letter* 69). It was to counter Marcellus' teaching that the phrase 'whose kingdom shall have no end' was included in the Nicene Creed. Marcellus regarded the flesh of the incarnate Logos as itself the image of God and thus developed a stark Logos-man Christology* in opposition to the Logos-flesh Christology of the Arians.

Bibliography

A. Grillmeier, *Christ in Christian Tradition*, vol. 1 (Atlanta, GA, and London, ²1975); T. E. Pollard, *Johannine Christology and the Early Church* (Cambridge, 1970), ch. 8; idem in J. Fontaine and C. Kannengiesser (eds.), *Epektasis. Mélanges Patristiques ... Jean Daniélou* (Paris, 1972), pp. 187–196.

H.D.McD.

MARCION (*c.* 80 – *c.* 160)

was reared in Sinope of Pontus, where his father was reported to have been a bishop and himself a wealthy ship-builder. He was active as a teacher in Asia Minor, perhaps as early as the opening decades of the 2nd century, before going to Rome. The rejection of his teaching by the leaders of the main Christian centres led him to set up a rival church which in a few years was nearly as widespread as the great church.

Marcion is best known for his work on the text and canon of the Bible (see Scripture*). He rejected the OT as a Christian book and collected the earliest known Christian canon, composed of an abbreviated version of Luke's Gospel and ten edited Pauline epistles (lacking the Pastorals). He presented his theological views in the *Antitheses*, in which he set forth contradictions between the OT and the NT. His works do not survive, so his positions must be reconstructed from the refutations made by his opponents, the fullest of which is Tertullian's* five books *Against Marcion*.

Marcion was convinced that Paul* was the only true apostle and that the original twelve, by 'Judaizing', became false apostles. Galatians was placed first in his collection of Paul's letters. The opening words of the *Antitheses*, 'O wealth of riches! rapture, power, amazement! seeing that there can be nothing to say about it, or to imagine about it, or to compare to it!' express his wonder before the Pauline gospel of grace. From Paul, Marcion deduced an exaggerated contrast between law and gospel.* In agreement with his contemporary Aquila of Pontus he practised a literal interpretation of Scripture, rejecting all allegory (see Hermeneutics*). Marcion went far beyond Paul in concluding that there are two Gods: the God of the OT, the creator, who is a God of law and justice and who predicted the Jewish Messiah; and the previously unknown God of the NT, the Father of Jesus Christ, who is a God of mercy and salvation.

Jesus Christ revealed the Father in the 15th year of the emperor Tiberius, for Marcion omitted the birth narratives from the gospel. Jesus' death purchased human salvation, and Jesus raised his own soul from the grave. Marcion advocated asceticism:* the avoidance of sex frustrates the creator God. Marcion administered baptism only to the unmarried or abstinent before the end of life. Water was substituted for wine in the Lord's Supper. To the charge of antinomianism in the absence of law he responded with 'God forbid'.

The church fathers objected to Marcion's separation of salvation from creation* and of the church from its OT heritage. Marcion's challenge accelerated the church's recognition of a NT canon and sharpened its emphasis on certain doctrines in the rule of faith (see Creeds*). Marcion shared in common with Gnosticism* such things as the idea of the unknown God, a negative view of the created world and a depreciation of the OT; but he differed in his lack of speculative, mythological interest, rejection of allegory, emphasis on faith rather than 'knowledge', and concern to establish a church.

Bibliography

B. Aland, 'Marcion. Versuch einer neuen Interpretation', *ZTK* 70 (1973), pp. 420–427; A. Amann in *DTC* 9, cols. 2009–2032; D. Balás in *Texts and Testaments: Critical Essays on the Bible and Early Church Fathers*, ed. W. Eugene March (San Antonio, TX, 1980), pp. 95–108; G. Bardy in *DBS* 5, cols. 862–877; E. C. Blackman, *Marcion and his Influence* (London, 1948); E. Evans, *Tertullian: Adversus Marcionem*, 2 vols. (Oxford, 1972); A. Harnack, *Marcion: Das Evangelium vom fremden Gott* (*TU* 45, Leipzig, ²1924; repr. 1960); R. J. Hoffmann, *Marcion: On the Restitution of Christianity* (Chico, CA, 1984); J. Knox, *Marcion and the New Testament: An Essay on the Early History of the Canon* (Chicago, 1942); G. Ory, *Marcion* (Paris, 1980); R. S. Wilson, *Marcion: A Study of a Second-Century Heretic* (1933; repr. New York, 1980).

E.F.

MARRIAGE, see SEXUALITY.

MARROW CONTROVERSY, see BOSTON, THOMAS.

MARTYRDOM. The word 'martyr' derives from the Gk. *martys*, 'witness'. In Christian usage the term soon acquired (at least as early as *Martyrdom of Polycarp* (see Apostolic Fathers*) and perhaps in Rev. 2:13; *cf.* Acts 22:20) the meaning 'blood-witness', the person who was killed because of testimony to Jesus. Although the persecutions of Christians before Decius (AD 250) were sporadic and local, they were a possibility with which all Christians had to live. The martyrs were the heroes of the church.

A considerable literature of martyrdom was produced in the early church: 1. acts of the martyrs, accounts of the trial (not transcripts of the court proceedings but often based on them), of which the earliest is the *Acts of Justin* and his Companions (c. 165); 2. passions, freer accounts of the last days and death of the martyr (the earliest of the authentic passions is *Martyrdom of Polycarp*, not long after his death in *c.* 156); 3. exhortations to martyrdom, represented by the treatises of Tertullian* and Origen;* 4. panegyrics on the anniversary of the martyr's death for the edification of the faithful, many of which are found in the sermons of the church fathers; 5. later legendary embellishments and inventions.

Extraordinary privileges were ascribed to the martyrs. They were assured of the presence of Christ and the Holy Spirit to give them endurance, visions, and words to speak. Martyrdom brought a forgiveness of sins. The martyr went immediately to heaven and not to an intermediate state* to await the resurrection.

The high evaluation of martyrs was the presupposition for the development of the cult of the martyrs, which was widespread in the 3rd century. Special regard for the remains ('relics') of the deceased was shown from earliest times. The funerary meals and annual commemorations of the deceased were assimilated to the eucharist.* Since the martyrs were already in the presence of God, they were invoked as intercessors on behalf of the living. The cult of the martyrs was fully developed by the late 4th century, promoted by the annual festivals, erection of memorial buildings, and discovery of relics previously forgotten or unknown (see also Saints*).

The importance of martyrdom was emphasized by the theological concepts used to interpret it. Since the martyr in death was conformed to the passion of Jesus and won a victory over Satan, he was considered the perfect Christian who brought the eschatological gifts to realization in himself. The martyr drank the cup of Jesus and shared the 'blood-baptism' of suffering (cf. Imitation of Christ*) The Christian was not to force martyrdom, for one had to be chosen for this grace by God.

During the 'peace of the church' from Constantine (d. 337) onwards martyrdom was spiritualized as the ascetic* sacrifice of monks and service of bishops. Throughout Christian history opposition to the faith has brought recurring experience of martyrdom.

Bibliography

T. Baumeister, *Die Anfänge der Theologie des Martyriums* (Münster, 1980); N. Brox, *Zeuge und Märtyrer: Untersuchungen zur frühchristlichen Zeugnis-Terminologie* (Munich, 1961); H. von Campenhausen, *Die Idee des Martyriums in der alten Kirche* (Göttingen, ²1964); H. Delehaye, *Les passions des martyrs et les genres littéraires* (Brussels, 1921); idem, *Les origines du culte des martyrs* (Brussels, ²1933); W. H. C. Frend, *Martyrdom and Persecution in the Early Church* (Oxford, 1965); H. Musurillo, *The Acts of the Christian Martyrs* (Oxford, 1972); D. W. Riddle, *The Martyrs: A Study in Social Control* (Chicago, 1931); W. C. Weinrich, *Spirit and Martyrdom* (Washington, 1981).

E.F.

MARXISM AND CHRISTIANITY.
Someone who approvingly quotes Prometheus in his doctoral thesis, as Karl Marx (1818–83) did, saying, 'In a word, I hate all gods', is making his position crystal clear. Yet the themes for which he has become famous the world over, when translated into the concern of 'justice for the oppressed', strike strongly Christian chords.

This apparent paradox lies at the root of all efforts to consider the relation of Marxism to Christianity. For Marx, while he was scathing in his denunciation of the established church (not only for colluding with exploitation but also for spawning its own inadequate 'Christian socialism'*), also recognized that religion* could be 'the heart of a heartless world'. It could bring genuine consolation to sufferers. Yet his criticism of religion focuses mainly on its alleged superfluity. Do away with the wretched conditions which evoke religious response, he thought, and religion will wither through disuse.

Those social conditions which he analysed with such thoroughness (above all in *Das Kapital*, 1867), are known as capitalism (see Weber, Max*). His complaint was that exploitation is built into the capitalist system of production, because labour is bound to sell its power to capital on the market, but then has no say over what is produced, how it is produced or where the profit goes. The class associated with the ownership or control of capital makes profit, Marx said, at the expense of the class which thus has 'nothing to lose but its chains'. Marx devoted his life to explaining the mechanisms by which this happens, and why capitalism will eventually collapse through its own internal contradictions, permitting a proletarian revolution.

Relations between Marxism and Christianity have been strained from the start. Marx was a 'post-Christian humanist', in that he rejected his Jewish-Lutheran heritage with a proclamation of human independence of God and religion. In practice, however, his 'Marxist' followers extended their hostility well beyond the level of philosophical critique. In countries which have gone through revolution, or have been colonized by the Soviet Union, religion is scarcely tolerated. Christianity in particular is taken to be a vehicle of reaction and of an unsocial other-worldliness. Its adherents are subject to varying degrees of antagonism from demotion at work to psychiatric incarceration.

During the 1960s, however, the period of 'cold war' between East and West, one tension-reducing effort emerged which came to be known as the 'Christian-Marxist dialogue'. Motifs from the writings of the 'young Marx' were rediscovered (especially 'alienation'*), and their common ancestry in Christianity formed the basis of discussion. While some Christians were brought face-to-face with some temporarily forgotten social demands of faith, some communist-country participants found authentic Marxist tools with which to criticize their dogmatic and repressive regimes. Although sporadic attempts were made (mainly in the USA) to continue the dialogue, the Soviet invasion of Czechoslovakia (1968) symbolically marked its demise.

In a sense, however, the dialogue was relocated in Latin America, in the liberation theology* of the 1970s. For once again Marxian themes – alienation, exploitation, praxis* – were explored for their commonality with Christian concerns. But this time the background was political action in situations of oppression and poverty rather than mere intellectual debate. The urgent question became how far Christians could join hands with Marxists in the struggle against domination, using the same forms of class analysis and cultivating the same hopes of revolution.*

Such questions are still confronted today. The persistence of capitalism (not to mention its origins, in which some claim Christian parentage) means that Marx's agenda still appears relevant. For class difference still divides capitalist societies, producing asymmetries of power* and resources. And the capitalist system still depends upon this imbalance for its very existence. Christian concerns with justice (see Righteousness*) and equity sit uneasily with capitalism, particularly in its more naked forms. At the very least, these facts should spur attempts to make a Christian critique of capitalism.

But it must also be said that Marxism appears to have few tools for understanding contemporary phenomena such as nationalism, or other social divisions which cut across 'class' – those based on gender and ethnic background (see Black Consciousness;* Black Theology;* Feminist Theology*). So even if some item of Marxian analysis is found to have qualified application within Christian social thinking, this does not mean that Marxism (as a whole 'package') and Christianity are compatible, or even complementary, in any strong sense.

For at the world-view level there exists a fundamental clash between the two belief-systems. However much Marxism rightly challenges the church to praxis (in the Johannine* sense of 'doing truth'*), or to make a systematic critique of the political and economic *status quo*, it fails to produce either a convincing account of the root cause and cure of human alienations, or a satisfactory guide to how human life ought properly to be lived. Marxism decisively places human beings instead of God at the centre of the universe, thus rendering all its insights vulnerable to the futility of life 'under the sun'.

In considering the relations between Marxism and Christianity, then, both the basic divergences and the invaluable insights have to be borne in mind. But not only these. Marxism is now a many-headed hydra. Philosophically, deep rifts divide 'humanist' Marxists (who stress intentional human action within the class struggle) and 'scientific' Marxists (who claim that their beliefs are capable of empirical demonstration and tend to emphasize social structure over against human action). Practically, major variations exist between dogmatic and ossified *Marxist-Leninism*, the conservative ideology of 'communist' countries, *revolutionary Marxism* in Latin America or Africa (see Revolution, Theology of*), dedicated to the overthrow of neo-colonial and elitist regimes, and what one might call *critical Marxism*, usually associated with trade-union or left-wing intellectual activity, in Europe and North America.

Christianity continues to face the threat of Marxism as an alternative belief-system, and as an ideology which binds two-thirds of the world's population. It is a threat because it will not recognize that more than altered environments are required to overcome alienation and that we live 'not by bread alone', and because in practice the dignity and destiny of the person are subsumed under that of the state. Simultaneously, Christianity has to face the challenge of Marxism; the challenge to global concern (see Missiology*), to identify the causes and resist the realities of poverty* and injustice, and to practise what is proclaimed in every sphere of human life.

Bibliography

K. Bockmühl, The Challenge of Marxism (Leicester, 1979); J. A. Kirk, Theology Encounters Revolution (Leicester, 1980); D. Lyon, Karl Marx – A Christian Appreciation of his Life and Thought (Tring, 1979); M. Machovec, A Marxist Looks at Jesus

(London, 1976); J. Miguez Bonino, *Christians and Marxists: the Mutual Challenge to Revolution* (London, 1975).

D.L.

MARY. The Roman Catholic doctrine of Mary is a classic example of the gradual development* of doctrine. From the 19th century the development has accelerated, stimulated by alleged appearances of Mary at Lourdes, Fatima and elsewhere. Some Catholics were hoping that the Second Vatican Council (1962–65; see Councils*) would further the process by proclaiming Mary 'Co-Redemptrix' (Co-Redeemer with Christ), but others felt that the greater need was to curb the excesses of popular piety. The first group wanted a separate document on Mary, but by a tiny majority the Council voted instead to devote to her a chapter of the Dogmatic Constitution on the Church. The decision to view Mary as a *member* of the church was itself a significant moderating step. But the document reaffirms all of the traditional Marian doctrines, albeit with certain qualifications. The aim was 'carefully and equally [to] avoid the falsity of exaggeration on the one hand, and the excess of narrow-mindedness on the other' (67). (Here and hereafter numbers in brackets refer to the sections of ch. 8 of the Constitution.)

The Eastern Orthodox view of Mary is similar, with two main qualifications. The Orthodox are hesitant about the doctrine of Mary's immaculate conception and incline towards rejecting it. They also object in principle to the Roman Catholic elevation of these beliefs and practices to the status of dogmas.*

Theotokos (53, 61, 66)

In Luke 1:43 Mary is called 'the mother of my Lord'. In the early Alexandrian tradition this was made more explicit by the term *theotokos* ('one who gave birth to God', traditionally translated 'mother of God'). The initial concern was Christological,* not Mariological, to affirm the deity of Christ and the reality of the incarnation. At the Council of Antioch in 325 the term was used to state the deity of Christ, in opposition to Arius.* In the next century Nestorius* attacked the term (preferring *Christotokos*). As a consequence, *theotokos* was affirmed by the Council of Ephesus in 431 as a safeguard against adoptionism.* Thus far the concern was Christo-

logical, although Nestorius did, in a sermon, warn his hearers to 'beware lest you make the Virgin a goddess'. This warning was timely in that the cult of Mary burgeoned during the Middle Ages. She came to be seen as Queen of Heaven, a title that enjoys no favour in Scripture (Je. 7:18; 44:17–19, 25). She was increasingly venerated with a worship (*hyperdoulia*, Gk. *hyperdouleia*) above that offered to other saints (*doulia*, Gk. *douleia*) but below that offered to God (*latreia*).

Mediatrix (60–62)

In the Middle Ages the practice grew of praying to saints.* Mary became especially popular. There was a tendency to see Jesus Christ as stern and unapproachable and so the faithful were directed to Mary as a sympathetic figure who could mediate* between the believer and Christ. This view of Mary as mediatrix was forcefully stated in 1891 by Pope Leo XIII in an encyclical: 'Nothing is bestowed on us except through Mary, as God himself wills. Therefore as no-one can draw near to the supreme Father except through the Son, so also one can scarcely draw near to the Son except through his mother.' The Second Vatican Council reaffirms Mary's role as mediatrix, but states that it should be so understood as 'neither [to] take away from nor [to] add anything to the dignity and efficacy of Christ the one mediator' (62; *cf.* 60, where 1 Tim. 2:5–6 is quoted).

Immaculate conception (59)

By the beginning of the Middle Ages it had come to be believed that Mary had lived without sin.* But *when* had she been delivered from sin? Anselm* held that she was *born* with original sin (*Cur Deus Homo?* 2:16). Bernard of Clairvaux* held that she was *conceived* with original sin but purified before birth (*Ep.* 174). This view was also held by Thomas Aquinas* and the Dominican* school. It was Duns Scotus* who popularized the idea that Mary was conceived without original sin. This new idea did not meet with universal acceptance and Pope Sixtus IV in 1485 and the Council of Trent* (see Councils,* Roman Catholic Theology*) in 1546 both left the matter undecided. But eventually Duns Scotus' view prevailed and in 1854 Pope Pius IX proclaimed it a dogma in his bull *Ineffabilis Deus*: 'We declare, pronounce and define that the most blessed Virgin Mary, at the first instant of her conception was preserved immaculate from all stain of original sin, by the singular grace and privilege of the omnipotent God, in virtue of the merits of Jesus Christ, the saviour of mankind, and that this doctrine was revealed by God and therefore must be believed firmly and constantly by all the faithful.'

This doctrine was proclaimed on the basis of the unanimity of the *contemporary* church. There was no scriptural basis for it. It was asserted that this doctrine had always been held in the church as a revealed doctrine. But this is not so much an appeal to tradition (which does not support the doctrine) as the triumph of dogma over tradition. The definition of the immaculate conception is rightly seen as a 'trial run' for the doctrine of papal infallibility, to be defined sixteen years later at the First Vatican Council.

Assumption (59)

In the 4th century there arose the legend that Mary had been assumed into heaven, like Enoch and Elijah in the OT. During the early Middle Ages it came to be generally believed. From the 7th century there was pressure for its definition as a dogma and this finally took place in 1950. Pope Pius XII defined it in his apostolic constitution, *Munificentissimus Deus:* 'Since [Jesus Christ] was able to do [Mary] so great an honour as to keep her safe from the corruption of the tomb, we must believe that he actually did so . . . The majestic mother of God . . . finally achieved, as the supreme crown of her privileges, that she should be preserved immune from the corruption of the tomb and, like her Son before her, having conquered death should be carried up, in body and soul, to the celestial glory of heaven, there to reign as Queen at the right hand of her Son, the immortal king of the ages.'

Again, the basis for the definition is said to be its theological suitability and the consensus of the *contemporary* Roman Catholic Church. It should be noted that the doctrine concerns more than an (alleged) episode in Mary's personal history. It is the basis for belief in her as Queen of Heaven and as mediatrix.

Co-Redemptrix

Some had hoped that Mary would be proclaimed 'Co-Redemptrix' at Vatican II, but

this did not happen. But while the *term* was avoided, the *concept* is clearly stated. Mary plays a (subsidiary) role in Christ's work of redemption. The incarnation could not occur without Mary's permission or 'fiat' (Lk. 1:38). Mary 'gave life to the world' (53); 'Death through Eve, life through Mary' (56). She suffered grievously with Christ at the cross and 'lovingly consented to the immolation of this Victim which she herself had brought forth' (58). She 'was united with [Christ] in suffering as he died on the cross' and co-operated 'in the Saviour's work of restoring supernatural life to souls' (61).

Mother of the church (53f., 61f.)

At Vatican II Mary is seen both as 'a preeminent and altogether singular member of the church' and as the mother of all Christians (53). While the Constitution does not actually refer to her as 'mother of the church', Pope Paul VI used the title in promulgating the document in 1964.

Protestants as a whole reject these doctrines. While the virgin birth* is scriptural and while *theotokos* can be seen as an affirmation of the biblical doctrine of the incarnation, the other Marian doctrines are seen as a classic example of the *bad* development of doctrine, of the way in which unscriptural if not pagan devotional practices can become dogmas. They can be seen as a striking proof of the need to test all doctrine by Scripture* and of the dangers of making ecclesiastical tradition infallible.

See also: SCRIPTURE AND TRADITION.

Bibliography

D. Attwater, *A Dictionary of Mary* (London, New York and Toronto, 1956); H. Graef, *Mary: A History of Doctrine and Devotion*, 2 vols. (London and New York, 1963 and 1965); G. Miegge, *The Virgin Mary* (London, 1955); P. F. Palmer, *Mary in the Documents of the Church* (London, 1953); M. Warner, *Alone of All Her Sex. The Myth and Cult of the Virgin Mary* (London, 1976).
A.N.S.L.

MASCALL, ERIC, see ANGLO-CATHOLIC THEOLOGY; THOMISM.

MATERIALISM, the doctrine that whatever exists is either physical matter, or depends upon physical matter.

Thus stated, the doctrine is vague enough to have had numerous expressions from the materialism of Democritus (*c.* 460–*c.* 370 BC) and Epicureanism, in which everything is reducible to the movements of atoms, to the mechanical materialism of Thomas Hobbes (1588–1679) and the physicalism both of logical positivism* and the dialectical materialism of Karl Marx.* Besides being a philosophical position with definite ontological explanations (the denial of the existence of minds or spirits), materialism may also be regarded as a research programme and research methodology with no such implications.

Materialism is opposed both by forms of mind-body dualism* (*e.g.* that of Descartes*) and by a more general anti-reductionism, which warns that although the universe has a materialistic aspect it is invalid to conclude that it is 'nothing but' matter. At first glance the biblical stress on humanity as part of the creation* may seem hospitable to a wholly material creation, but the biblical doctrine of personal continuity after bodily death (2 Cor. 5:1–10) appears to rule this out (see Immortality;* Intermediate State*).

'Materialism' may also refer to an ethical outlook which regards the only worth-while pursuit to be that of wealth and sensual gratification, but there is no logical connection between the philosophical doctrine of materialism and this ethical stance.

Bibliography

J. R. Smythies (ed.), *Brain and Mind* (London, 1965).

P.H.

MAURICE, F. D., see CHRISTIAN SOCIALISM.

MAXIMUS (*c.* 580–662), called 'the Confessor' because he suffered for his teachings, was the most creative theologian of his age and the principal architect of Byzantine theology.

Aristocratic by birth, Maximus held high office in Byzantium before becoming a monk *c.* 614 (later abbot) at Chrysopolis across the Bosphorus. He defied emperor Heraclius' policy of conciliating the monophysites* to secure unity against the Persians. He fled their invasion (626) and made his way to Alexandria and westwards to Africa, where from *c.* 640 he triumphantly spearheaded the resistance to monothelitism (see Christology*), first in a disputation at Carthage (645), then in African synods and finally at Rome in the Lateran Council of 649. Although he was forcibly repatriated to Byzantium (653), he refused to yield and after mutilation died in exile. The condemnation of monothelitism by the (sixth ecumenical) Council of Constantinople (680–1) sealed his stand, and he was soon widely revered.

Maximus had studied Aristotle* alongside Plato* at Byzantium. In over ninety works he developed the basic teachings of the Cappadocians and Pseudo-Dionysius* with the aid of Aristotelian categories, giving their mysticism a more rational framework and their Christian Platonism a more dynamic thrust with his concepts of the goal-directed 'movement' and 'energy' natural to all things. His paraphrases and citation of Dionysius were important in establishing the latter's eminent orthodoxy in East and West.

For Maximus the incarnation was the centre of history, and mankind the pivot of creation. Through incorporation into the divine Logos, human beings were capable of deification* ('while remaining in his soul and body entirely man by nature, he becomes in his soul and body entirely God by grace') and hence of mediating creation's return to pristine harmony and perfection. There was a strong cosmic dimension to Maximus' theology, *e.g.* in his interpretation of the crucifixion and resurrection and in his mystical liturgical theology. Maximus favoured, like Origen* and Gregory of Nyssa,* 'the restoration of all things' (see Universalism*), but not its open propagation.

Maximus' soteriology was grounded in post-Chalcedonian Christology, in which the defence, against the monothelites, of two wills, divine and human, in Christ was fundamental. In him alone did the 'physical' will of human nature conform fully to the purposeful 'gnomic' will directed by the 'person' (*hypostasis**) of the Logos, thus excluding all error and sin. In hypostatic union with the Logos (here Maximus built on the doctrine of *enhypostasia* – see Hypostasis*), Christ's humanity was both deified and enabled to fulfil its truly human 'natural movement'. All who enjoy communion with him have access to deification, being freed from the delinquency of their own personal 'gnomic' will

417

and restored to the divine image. Their goal is union with God through love. In the vision of God* only his energies, not his essence, could be known – a distinction that anticipated Gregory of Palamas (see Eastern Orthodox Theology*).

Maximus' Christology, anthropology* and mystical theology* provided a lasting terminological and conceptual foundation for Byzantine thought and spirituality. It was basic to John of Damascus'* exposition of *The Orthodox Faith*.

Bibliography

H. Urs von Balthasar, *Liturgie cosmique: Maxime le Confesseur* (Paris, 1947); J. Meyendorff, *Byzantine Theology* (New York, [2]1979); J. Pelikan, *The Spirit of Eastern Christendom (600–1700)* (Chicago, 1974); P. Sherwood, *An Annotated Date-List of the Works of Maximus the Confessor* (Rome, 1952); L. Thunberg, *Microcosm and Mediator: The Theological Anthropology of Maximus the Confessor* (Lund, 1965).

D.F.W.

MEDIATION. Literally, the function or condition of coming between two parties for the purpose of encounter, transaction or reconciliation. In Christian thought it pertains both (legitimately) to Christ's supreme interposition between God and man, and (illegitimately) to the active ministry of other heavenly or earthly intermediaries.

The principle of mediation is common to any of the world's religions, as various religious mediators (*e.g.* priests, medicinemen, rain-makers, sorcerers) interpose with supernatural or natural powers between a transcendent order (and often an offended deity) and a terrestrial realm (and offending earthly party). The OT describes a multiplicity of 'mediations' and mediators, *e.g.* the patriarchs (Gn. 18:22–32), Moses (Ex. 3:10), judges, prophets, kings (*e.g.* 2 Sa. 6:14–18), and Levitical priests. Fundamentally, a twofold pattern of mediation exists: the prophetic (manward), in which an appointed agent reveals, proclaims, and interprets God's will to people; and the priestly (Godward), in which God is approached, reconciled, and besought on man's behalf by an appointed representative. This pattern of mediation is consummated in Christ. He is both the consummation of antecedent mediation and the redefinition of mediation.

The Christian faith centres on the person and work of Christ as mediator. The NT presents Christ's unique mediatorship directly and indirectly. He is directly declared to be 'the one mediator (*mesitēs*) between God and men' (1 Tim. 2:5), and the mediator of a new and better covenant (Heb. 8:6; 9:15; 12:24). He is indirectly portrayed, in his person and work, as the unique intermediary, the principle of cosmic unity (Col. 1:16–20), who in himself not only fulfils a 'prophetic' ministry of revelation, proclamation and interpretation of God's will (*cf.* Mt. 11:27; Jn. 1:18; 14:6; Acts 2:36; 3:13; 4:10; 2 Cor. 4:6; Rev. 19:13), but also a 'priestly' ministry of approach, reconciliation of sinful man to God by sacrifice, perpetual intercession and heavenly blessing (*cf.* Lk. 22:19; Jn. 17:9; Rom. 3:24f.; 5:5f.; 6:23; 2 Cor. 5:19; Heb. 1:2; 2:17; 7:25; 9:14–15). The NT portrays Christ's mediation as both an active function (as the agent of salvation) and a static condition (uniting in himself God and man, heaven and earth). Both strands have at times come to the fore in subsequent Christian reflection.

Patristic and scholastic* thought emphasized Christ's static mediation as the God-man as the basis or prerequisite of his active mediation of salvation though his death, resurrection and exaltation, while Thomas Aquinas,* somewhat artificially, located Christ's mediation in his taking of perfect manhood, which distinguished him both from God and sinful humanity. The Protestant Reformers reaffirmed Christ's active salvific mediatory work, and Reformed theology* expounded Christ's person and work as mediator in terms of his threefold 'office' as prophet, priest, and king (see Offices of Christ*). In addition, against medieval Roman Catholic sacerdotalism, the Reformers affirmed the uniqueness,* finality and permanence of Christ's mediation. Protestant tradition has subsequently consistently repudiated both an official human priestly caste, with the power to forgive sin (in absolution) and to offer sacrifice* (in the eucharist*), and additional heavenly intermediaries (*e.g.* Mary* and the saints*), stressing rather the perfection of Christ's atoning sacrifice and continual intercession, and the priestly prerogative of access for all believers in Christ (see Ministry;* Priesthood of Believers*). Though in Vatican II (1962–65) Roman Catholicism explicitly reaffirms Christ as 'the one Mediator', its adherence to a human derivative priesthood, co-operative with Christ, the great High Priest, to representative intermediaries (*cf.* the saints) and to Mary as Mediatrix, or Auxiliatrix, with him, continues to sound to many Protestant ears as compromising scriptural teaching and unnecessarily adding to Christ's consummation of mediation.

Bibliography

L. Berkhof, *Systematic Theology* (London, 1969); E. Brunner, *The Mediator* (London, 1934); Calvin, *Institutes* II.xii-xv; A. Oepke in *TDNT* IV, pp. 598–624.

C.D.H.

MELANCHTHON, PHILIP (1497–1560).

Born in Bretten, a grand-nephew of the humanist Johannes Reuchlin (1455–1522), Melanchthon was a child prodigy and became a Protestant Reformer. His scholarly output started when he was only seventeen and was admired by Erasmus* as early as 1515. At this stage he was a humanist.* In 1518 he came to Wittenberg to be professor of Greek. He quickly absorbed Reformation theology and this, together with his brilliance both as a scholar and as a teacher, ensured that he was much admired by Luther.* In 1521 he produced the first edition of his *Loci Communes* (*Commonplaces*) which developed throughout his life as a Lutheran dogmatic textbook.

Melanchthon was more a scholar than a man of action and displayed weaknesses when faced with situations of conflict. When he was confronted by the demands of Carlstadt (*c.* 1480–1541) and the Zwickau prophets (see Reformation, Radical*) for a very radical and rapid reform of Wittenberg in 1521–22, he proved incapable of providing the strong leadership that was necessary. Despite this, supported by Luther, he exercised an important influence on the Colloquy of Marburg (1529) and drew up the Augsburg Confession (1530) (see Confessions of Faith*) and the accompanying *Apology* (1531). The Augsburg documents were highly significant for the Reformation, and Melanchthon's temperament and skills were well suited to their irenic objectives. These skills were again

demonstrated at the Colloquy of Regensburg (1541) when Melanchthon and Bucer* and Catholic representatives including John Eck (1486–1543) and Gaspar Contarini (1483–1542) reached agreement on justification* without being able to persuade their respective sides of its appropriateness. Typically Melanchthon signed the Schmalkaldic Articles (1537) with the proviso that if the pope would allow the gospel he would concede him superiority over the bishops.

Throughout Luther's life Melanchthon declined to involve himself as fully in theology as Luther desired. He never, for example, took his doctorate in theology. He was, however, an independent thinker. On the eucharist* he leaned towards Calvin,* on predestination* and free will* more towards Erasmus and on justification towards a more forensic view than that of Luther. When Luther died (1546), Melanchthon was his natural successor. He could not quite cope with the task. He compromised with the Catholics after the Protestant defeat in 1548 by accepting the Leipzig Interim which in effect allowed Protestant theology but required Roman Catholic ritual. This degree of compromise undermined his authority and, for the remainder of his life, he was involved in a series of conflicts within Lutheranism; with Andreas Osiander (1498–1565) over justification, with Nicholas von Amsdorf (1483–1565) over predestination and with a variety of Lutherans over the Lord's Supper. He died praying for deliverance from the 'fury of the theologians'. He was very widely learned and retained his humanistic interests. He was a most significant educational reformer, making an important contribution to university and school education in Germany.

Assessments of Melanchthon vary. He can be interpreted as a figure somewhat alien to the true direction of the Reformation. However, in an age which recoils, as Melanchthon did, from some of Luther's most vehement polemic, Melanchthon stands as a rational, moderate, ecumenical figure more able than Luther to find *rapprochement* and to look for a middle way.

Bibliography

ET of *Loci Communes* (1521) in W. Pauck, *Melanchthon and Bucer*, LCC 19 (London, 1969); C. L. Manschreck (tr.), *Melanchthon* on *Christian Doctrine: Loci Communes 1555* (Oxford, 1965).

K. Aland, *Four Reformers: Luther, Melanchthon, Calvin, Zwingli* (Minneapolis, 1979); F. Hildebrandt, *Melanchthon: Alien or Ally?* (Cambridge, 1946); C. L. Manschreck, *Melanchthon, the Quiet Reformer* (New York, 1968); D. C. Steinmetz, *Reformers in the Wings* (Philadelphia, 1971); R. Stupperich, *Melanchthon* (ET, London, 1966).

C.P.W.

MENNONITE THEOLOGY. The roots of Mennonite theology are to be found in 16th-century Dutch, German and Swiss Anabaptism.* Menno Simons, Pilgram Marpeck (*c.* 1495–1556), Conrad Grebel (*c.* 1498–1526) and others provided the theological inspiration for the movement which later took the name Mennonite from its major Dutch leader, Menno Simons (1496–1561). Historically the Mennonite tradition has assumed the substance, if not always the authority, of the early Christian creeds.* Confessionally – in statements of faith, doctrinal writings, catechisms,* sermons, hymns, devotional literature and worship – it has stressed scriptural themes often omitted in the historic creeds and confessions,* especially Christ's way of suffering love, the life of Christian discipleship* and obedience, and the nature of the believers' church* as separated from the world. Moreover, it has also affirmed the triune understanding of God, the substitutionary atoning death and exemplary nature of Christ's life, sin as a voluntary act of disobedience, human accountability for faithfulness in the Christian life, the return of Christ and the primacy of Scripture for all theological reflection.

The doctrine of the church is the most central theme in Mennonite theology. Its hallmarks are regeneration,* holy living, believers' baptism, the Lord's Supper, footwashing, church discipline,* nonconformity, integrity, non-resistance, religious liberty and the separation of church and state.*

In the course of its migrations, in both Europe and the Americas, the Mennonite movement came under the influence of pietism.* The effects were frequently beneficial and revitalizing, especially in regard to mission and to the personal dimensions of salvation. The experience-oriented pietism, however, also tended to erode Mennonite theological distinctives pertaining to Christian discipleship and ethics.

Mennonites sympathized with the fundamentalist* struggle against modernism but did not formally join those ranks, even though certain sectors were strongly influenced by it. In general, Mennonite theology has been conservative and evangelical.* Liberal theology* has not had a great impact on Mennonite thought in North America and most other continents, although common ethical interests are more evident in recent times. During the 19th and 20th centuries, however, most of the Dutch and many of the North German Mennonites turned towards liberalism. Their assimilation into mainstream European culture also meant the abandonment of many traditional doctrinal positions. Some theological renewal has taken place since World War II. Today, Mennonite theology in northern Europe is more ecumenical in its interests.

The development of the Mennonite theological tradition can be characterized by the struggle for greater confessional unity (17th and 18th centuries), the quest for religious and cultural stability (18th to early 20th centuries) and, more recently, a search for theological identity (20th century). Since World War II, Mennonite theology and ethics have explored their 16th-century roots in the Radical Reformation.* This 'recovery of the Anabaptist vision' has sought to recapture the biblical-ethical emphasis in discipleship, ecclesiology and non-resistance, the challenge of social responsibility and the nature of Mennonite theological identity as it relates to Mennonite ethnocentrism, cultural pluralism, contemporary evangelicalism and historic Anabaptism.

Representing the free-church tradition, Mennonite faith and life have contributed to an understanding of the church as a covenant community of faithful believers. Its greatest internal challenge today is the quest for theological identity and the integration of its ecclesiology with the changing relationship of the church to society.

See also: ANABAPTIST THEOLOGY; REFORMATION, RADICAL.

Bibliography

H. S. Bender *et al.* (eds.), *The Mennonite Encyclopedia*, vols. I-IV (Scottdale, PA, 1955–1959); C. J. Dyck (ed.), *An Introduc-*

tion to Mennonite History (Scottdale, PA, 1967); H. J. Loewen, One Lord, One Faith, One Hope and One God: Mennonite Confessions of Faith in North America – An Introduction (Newton, KS, 1985).

H.J.L.

MERCERSBURG THEOLOGY.

A movement named after the small town in central Pennsylvania where in the 19th century the theological school of the German Reformed Church was located. From 1844, under the direction of John W. Nevin (1803–86), formerly an Old School Presbyterian theologian (see Princeton Theology*), and Philip Schaff (1819–93), a young historian from Germany, the school attempted to provide a classical Calvinist alternative to what it perceived to be the decline of American New England and Princeton Calvinism (see Edwards, Jonathan;* New England Theology;* New Haven Theology;* Reformed Theology*) into 'Puritan' revivalist subjectivism. Emphasis was placed on the ecumenical Christological* theology of the ancient church (see Creeds*), the significance of the institutional church* with its sacraments,* ministry* and catechetical method, and the organic development of that church throughout history.

Its theological thrust may be regarded as the American counterpart of English Anglo-Catholicism* and German high-church Lutheranism* in the same period, reflecting the philosophical shift from the subjectivism of Kant* and Schleiermacher* to historical and corporate expressions of reality in Hegel* and Ritschl,* which in Germany must be seen against the background of evangelical pietism.*

In much evangelical piety, the reality of personal salvation had made denominational, confessional* and particularly sacramental concerns substantially irrelevant. Heaven will be populated with representatives from all confessions, it was said. The important issue was not baptism* or church membership, but whether one had made a personal commitment to Christ. While awakenings divided denominations, their adherents regarded them as unifying true believers. Nevertheless, within the American context, the multiplicity of denominations seemed to conflict with the unity experienced in the awakenings (see Revival*).

Resolutions to this tension were varied. Princeton theologians ordinarily considered Calvinism as the most consistent expression of awakening theology. Methodists* and others expressed themselves similarly. Others thought it necessary to repudiate all existing denominations and 'restore' the primitive church, now possible in a time of 'latter-day' blessing (as in the Church of Christ, the Adventists and the Latter Day Saints; see Sects*).

Mercersburg's response was to see the Reformed church as the embodiment of the Protestant and ecumenical church. This was seen not as sectarian, but rather as an expression of a developing church with its roots in history. This led to the repudiation of the innovative conversion experience in favour of catechetical instruction (Nevin's Anxious Bench), and to an emphasis on the real presence of Christ in the Lord's Supper (see Eucharist*) in the place of revivalist subjectivism. (American Calvinism's view of the Supper had to some extent weakened into naive Zwinglianism,* and Nevin's understanding of the Reformed sacramental heritage was more accurate than that of Charles Hodge.*) Renewed interest in Reformed liturgy and the nature of the ministerial office was also characteristic. Following the lead of German research into Calvinism, Mercersburg concluded that a Melanchthonian* lack of interest in the divine decrees and rejection of reprobation (see Predestination*) was more typical of Calvinism than the New England and Princeton direction. Perhaps that was encouraged by the way it considered Puritanism* to have misused election.

While Mercersburg produced helpful insights and correctives in a confusing period in American church history, it did not provide lasting direction. Its ecumenical stance was seen to be too sympathetic towards Roman Catholicism, and it failed to give substantial leadership in the emerging arena of biblical authority (see Fundamentalism;* Scripture*). Nevertheless, questions about the value of confessions and sacraments in a pluriform American evangelical community are still present, and Mercersburg's answers may still be studied with profit.

Bibliography

J. H. Nichols, Romanticism in American

Theology (Chicago, 1961); *idem* (ed.), *The Mercersburg Theology* (New York, 1966).

D.C.D.

MERIT is that which in a good action qualifies the doer for reward. In a superficial sense the theological idea of merit arises from the many passages of Scripture which promise reward for obedience and punishment (or demerit) for disobedience (*e.g.* Dt. 5:28–33; Mt. 5:3–12). Paul affirms that God 'will give to each person according to what he has done' (Rom. 2:6). The apostle goes on to teach, however, that the rebellion of man precludes the possibility of relating to God on the basis of merit. Reliance on the principle of reward is fatal, for 'the wages of sin is death'; eternal life comes from 'the gift of God . . . in Christ Jesus our Lord' (Rom. 6:23). Jesus* refused to accord merit to obedience, advising his disciples to say, 'We are unworthy servants; we have only done our duty' (Lk. 17:10). In parables he proclaimed God's grace without prejudicing his justice (Mt. 20:1–16; Lk. 15:11–32). The gospel blesses through forgiveness, not desert (Mt. 18:21–35); only thus is it good news for the ungodly. Both Jesus and Paul* attacked the merit theology of their own day, and thereby established that God chose his people by grace* without any prior goodness on their part (*cf.* Dt. 7:7–8). Where Scripture speaks of rewards for service, it does so for those already saved and thus expresses the fatherly righteousness* of the God who chastises and blesses his children and who is himself their chief reward (*e.g.* Heb. 12:4–11).

While later theology accepted Augustine's* view that meritorious acts arise from God's grace in us, the necessity of human co-operation was also insisted upon. Discussions in medieval theology distinguished between *congruent* and *condign* merit. Congruent merit was understood to reflect God's generous character as he rewards the acts of those who do not meet the strict conditions for merit. Condign merit is a matter of strict justice towards those in a state of grace in which God is bound to reward the doer of a good work. It was held, too, that there were deeds which went beyond what God normally required of a person (works of super-erogation), and that the excess merits so earned by the saints could be added to the church's 'treasury of merits', which could be applied for the benefit of other less worthy Christians through indulgences. In this way the punishment of sin could be remitted. The Protestant Reformers strongly repudiated these ideas, asserting that perfect obedience to God was demanded of all and could earn no extra merit, and that the gospel itself was the only 'treasury of merit'. Justification* was understood to be the declaration of God's forgiveness, independent even of the good works brought forth by grace, and based on the merits of Jesus Christ alone. The Council of Trent (session VI:16) clarified the Catholic position without changing its essence, arguing that good works merit eternal life. Recent study by Catholic and Protestant scholars questions whether 'merit' is an adequate word to describe the scriptural treatment of good works, and has laid stress on God's grace in justification. None the less, Catholics have retained their conviction that the 'treasury of the church' includes the value of the prayers and good works of the saints by which they contribute to 'the salvation of their brothers in the unity of the mystical Body', a view which Protestants reject as compromising the sole sufficiency of Christ.

Bibliography

Calvin, *Institutes*, III. xv-xviii; D. A. Carson, *Divine Sovereignty and Human Responsibility* (London, 1981); H. G. Anderson *et al.* (eds.), *Justification by Faith* (*Lutherans and Catholics in Dialogue* VII; Minneapolis, MN, 1985).

P.F.J.

METAPHYSICS may be defined as the attempt to work out the most basic structure of reality, not by observation and experiment, as in science, but by systematic and critical thought, seeking to analyse, test and connect such concepts as 'cause', 'quality', 'matter', 'mind' and 'event'. Metaphysicians may simply try to describe the form taken by our normal thought about the world when set out systematically; or, more often, to revise and improve on this, and, it may be, to demonstrate a reality behind the appearances. In the former class might be found such thinkers as Aristotle,* Locke,* and perhaps Thomas Aquinas*, in addition to some contemporaries such as Sir Peter Strawson (b. 1919); in the latter class, Plato,* Spinoza,* Leibniz,* Berkeley* and Hume.* Most metaphysicians have of course included elements of both these approaches; and some might hold, with R. G. Collingwood (1889–1943), that as the presuppositions of our thought vary over the years, even the first kind of metaphysics needs constant revision.

Metaphysicians have at times made spectacular claims: to show, for instance, that time is an illusion; that the whole of existence forms a single unity, all else being at best only partially real; that mind and matter are both constructed out of a more basic 'neutral stuff'; or, more relevantly to the Christian, that reason can prove or disprove the existence of God or of the human soul. The frequent conflict between these claims, and the failure of metaphysicians to convince one another, have cast some suspicion on the whole enterprise. Indeed, a number of philosophers have thought that metaphysics may be in principle impossible, except perhaps in our first sense, the description rather than the revision of our normal thought. Thus Kant* argued that the 'categories' which made science (and experience generally) possible, such as unity, limitation, substance and cause, are not part of reality in itself, but only conditions of our experiencing of it. They cannot therefore be used to go beyond that which we experience, to argue, for example, that the world is or is not limited in extent or duration, or that it was or was not created and caused by a God. More recently, the logical positivism* of the 1920s and 1930s argued that metaphysical claims had no real meaning at all. Since they did not provide any way for us to test whether they were true or false, how could they be said to assert anything? To the Christian believer, this was a more disturbing criticism than Kant's; for he had left it possible (and indeed himself believed) that the reality of God might be known by faith, though not proved by reason, whereas it was now argued that all metaphysical propositions, including those which Christians would wish to make, were totally meaningless and asserted nothing at all that could even be believed in faith.

Accordingly, some philosophers have seen metaphysics not as a system of factual assertions but as a way of seeing and interpreting the world; while others have retained some metaphysical arguments as analyses of our concepts, while abandoning hope of any all-inclusive system. A number, however, remained obstinate. They could reply that as

they were seeking the necessary structure of *any* world, it was absurd to demand that particular features of the world prove or disprove the reality of this structure; and that if it was legitimate to analyse concepts like time or cause, it was also legitimate to see whether, for instance, there were contradictions in the idea of time, or whether belief in causes should entail belief in a first cause, God.

Some metaphysical systems, such as those of Hegel* or Spinoza, were explicitly offered as substitutes for (and improvements on) traditional religious beliefs. Others, such as those of Thomas Aquinas, Descartes* or Leibniz, while avowedly Christian, claimed that human reasoning was able to prove such religious truths as the reality and goodness of God, and so seemed, to some, to depreciate revelation* (see Natural Theology*). Accordingly, some theologians have wished to repudiate metaphysics altogether. And clearly there is no need for Christians to construct a metaphysical system, or accept an existing one. But many Christian concepts and beliefs involve metaphysical assertions, even when they are not argued for by metaphysical methods: the ideas of creation,* miracle,* spirit, revelation, grace* and, above all, of God,* all carry implications about the structure of reality, and may well need metaphysics, not for their discovery, but for explanation and defence. It seems a mistake therefore for the theologian to reject metaphysics completely. The truth of Christianity surely implies that some metaphysical systems (*e.g.* atheist* or materialist* ones) are false, and this suggests that some system – perhaps known only to God – is true; unless, indeed, with a few extreme radicals, we abandon the idea of supernatural truths and reduce Christianity to a way of life (while repudiating much of the beliefs and teaching of the Christ who founded that way). Whether in fact reason (with or without the aid of God's revelation given to us) is adequate to work out the fundamental nature of reality can only be found out in practice.

See also: FAITH AND REASON; PHILOSOPHY OF RELIGION.

Bibliography

A. J. Ayer, *The Central Questions of Philosophy* (London, 1973); B. Blanshard, *Reason and Analysis* (London, 1962); C. D. Broad,

'Critical and Speculative Philosophy', in J. H. Muirhead (ed.), *Contemporary British Philosophy* (London, 1924); R. G. Collingwood, *An Essay on Metaphysics* (London, 1940); I. Kant, *Prolegomena to any Future Metaphysics* (ET, Manchester, 1957); J. McTaggart, 'Introduction to the Study of Philosophy', in his *Philosophical Studies* (London, 1934); D. F. Pears (ed.), *The Nature of Metaphysics* (London, 1957); W. H. Walsh, *Metaphysics* (London 1963).

R.L.S.

METEMPSYCHOSIS is (the belief in) the 'transmigration of souls', *i.e.* that human or animal souls pass through more than one bodily existence in this world. In some forms the reincarnation of human souls is restricted to human bodies, but in others may extend to animals (and hence its advocates are often also vegetarians). The purpose of metempsychosis is often presented as progressive purification or evolutionary development, which is not infrequently related to the view that the soul's entry into bodily life is in some sense a punitive confinement, *e.g.* following a pre-existent or pre-cosmic fall.

Reincarnation is widely believed in Eastern religions such as Buddhism* and Hinduism,* and was taught by influential Gk. traditions, especially Pythagoreanism, Platonism* and Neoplatonism. From such sources it was adopted by many Gnostics* (and hence by Manichaeans* and their later counterparts, the Cathari or Albigenses*). It was consequently much discussed by the early church fathers, normally with unqualified hostility, although they sometimes observed, for apologetic reasons, that it bore a partial similarity to the Christian belief in the resurrection of the body (*cf.* Tertullian,* *Resurrection of the Flesh* and *The Soul*), as too did the Stoic* doctrine of a cyclical succession of worlds.

Whether Clement of Alexandria* and Origen* espoused metempsychosis remains a matter of debate. Origen undoubtedly accepted the eternal pre-existence of souls (see Soul, Origin of*), but may well have envisaged only a single bodily 'incarnation' (at least in this world). He certainly resisted any fatalist kind of reincarnation. If he did entertain it, he would have exploited it, like the soul's pre-existence, apologetically, to help explain some of life's apparent injustices and inequalities.

In later centuries, metempsychosis has found occasional advocates, *e.g.* among the Neoplatonists of the Italian Renaissance, in Lessing,* among spiritualists and theosophists, such as Emanuel Swedenborg (1688–1772; see Sects*) and Annie Besant (1847–1933), as well as among a few Christian thinkers of a liberal cast of mind.

The theory not only lacks biblical support but is also incompatible with central doctrines such as the resurrection* of the body. It is also dependent on the notion, now largely abandoned by Christian theology, of the soul as a substance or essence different from the body (see Anthropology*).

Bibliography

Q. Howe, Jr., *Reincarnation for the Christian* (Philadelphia, 1974); G. MacGregor, *Reincarnation as a Christian Hope* (London, 1982).

Critique: M. Albrecht, *Reincarnation: A Christian Appraisal* (Downers Grove, IL, 1982); R. A. Morey, *Reincarnation and Christianity* (Minneapolis, MN, 1980).

D.F.W.

METHOD, THEOLOGICAL. The concept of theology* has nowadays two placings, related but distinct.

1. In the educational world of universities and seminaries theology is a generic description of a group of interconnected studies that feed Christian minds: exegesis, analysis and synthesis of biblical teachings; the history of Christian thought, action and experience; dogmatics, ethics, apologetics and liturgics; missiology, spirituality and pastoralia; along with comparative religion and religious sociology, when explored with a Christian focus.

2. In the church's life of worship, witness and service, theology signifies: a. ordered reflection, analytical and critical, thematic and systematic, descriptive, interpretative, or normative, on the content and expression of distinctive Christian belief, plus b. explorations of other things – arts, sciences, human problems, philosophical questions – by the light of those beliefs ('the comprehension of all knowledge, directed to its true end,' as Locke* put it about 1698).

Questions of method arise in relation to both 1. and 2., and there have been and are notorious tensions between the educational demand that method be unprejudiced, open-minded and scientific – in a word, *rational* –

and the churchly requirement that method be faithful and obedient, confessional and doxological – in a word, *religious*. However, believers who define 'unprejudiced', 'openminded' and 'scientific' as meaning 'determined by the object of study itself' rather than 'shaped by the anti-Christian positivism* of some natural and historical scientists', and who go on to recognize that the central object of study is in fact the living creator, self-revealed in Scripture as triune personal Subject, have already in principle overcome this tension, so far as it affects themselves. The present article deals with method in relation to 2. specifically.

The question of method covers, first, the way theologians proceed in criticism and construction and, secondly, the way they justify their procedure. Historically, there have been three main methods, the first two recognizing given absolutes and so setting limits to the range of acceptable opinion, the third making it impossible to set such limits and so producing uncontrollable relativistic pluralism. They are as follows.

Method one identifies the revealed word of God with the testimony of the biblical writers to God's works, will and ways, evaluates all actual beliefs, practices and proposals by this standard, and 'theologizes' – *i.e.* constructs accounts of reality and gives answers to questions about it – by directly formulating and applying biblical teaching. Justification for this procedure is found in 1. the status of all canonical Scripture,* whatever its literary character, as essentially divine instruction, and 2. the incompetence of our fallen, perverse, culture-bound human minds to think true thoughts about God apart from the corrective and directive guidance of the Holy Spirit,* who teaches us the meaning for ourselves of the Scriptures which he originally inspired, now authenticates, and constantly interprets to the church. This method, exemplified and inculcated for substance by the apostles, was partly lost in the patristic and medieval periods, was recovered at the Reformation,* and has characterized scholastic and conservative Protestantism and pietistic* evangelicalism* ever since (see Hermeneutics*).

Method two inserts into the frame of method one the notion of the historic institutional church infallibly identifying and interpreting the Scriptures. This method makes the tradition of ecclesiastical orthodoxy, as such, into the immediate object of belief for the faithful, and on basic issues exempts it from biblical challenge and correction; all that is permitted is the amplification and reformulation of it in the light of Scripture, and that is by no means the same thing. The justification offered is that 1. Scripture is intrinsically unclear and 2. Christ promised to indwell, uphold and preserve his church through the Holy Spirit, thus guaranteeing the permanent trustworthiness of all its essential agreed teaching. This method, with variations of detail, marks patristic,* medieval, Roman Catholic,* Eastern Orthodox,* and Anglo-Catholic theology.* For it, Scripture is in tradition and vice versa (see Scripture and Tradition*).

Broad assumptions in both methods are: 1. The biblical revelation of God is *rational* and hence *intelligible*. Anthropomorphic* scriptural speech about God is actually analogical,* expressing qualified similarities between our thinking, speaking and acting, and the personal existence of the creator whose image we bear. Since God, though not wholly like us, is not wholly different from us, we can really if not perfectly understand what he tells us in Scripture about himself. 2. The teaching of the canonical Scriptures, proceeding as it does from a single divine mind, is substantially *true* and *coherent*. 3. God, the infinite, personal, self-sustaining creator, still works *supernaturally* within the world that he upholds. 4. God's gracious work of supernaturally saving sinners, so securing a covenant people and showing forth his kingdom in and through Jesus Christ, is the substantive centre of biblical doctrine, and God-wrought Christlikeness as a lifestyle for the new community is the substantive centre of biblical ethics. 5. The church's tradition, expressed in creed, hymns, liturgies, literature and behaviour-patterns, flows largely if not wholly from the Spirit's interpreting of Scripture, and is thus an important (method two says decisive) guide to what the Bible means. Both methods prompt opposition to any undermining or eroding of these Bible-based assumptions.

Method three views Scripture not as absolute divine truth, at least not totally so, but as in essence a product of human imagination, experience, research and reflection that at every point was coloured and confined by

425

the culture out of which it came. Revelation is then seen as the self-authenticating personal perception of the divine (with some imperative claim, though not necessarily with any cognitive content) that Scripture becomes instrumental in triggering off or crystallizing out in a person's own situation. Since these perceptions are themselves culturally relative, unending theological pluralism is inevitable. Considerations invoked to justify this approach are: 1. Intense critical study of the Bible as human literature has made it impossible to regard it as more than this. 2. Philosophy since Kant* has been hostile to ideas of theistic supernaturalism and definitive verbal revelation. 3. We are culturally too remote from the biblical writers for it to be either proper or possible for us to identify with their thoughts. This method has for a century and a half produced liberal,* modernist,* radical and revisionist theologies in both Protestantism and Roman Catholicism, all shaped in practice, more or less explicitly, by trends in secular philosophy, psychology, economic theory, sociology and natural science, to which biblical affirmations are made relative.

Testing of theories by appeal to evidence, to prior certainties and to implications, is a formally parallel process on all three methods, but agreement as to what evidence is relevant, what are the fixed points of certainty, and what implications are acceptable, is often lacking.

Bibliography

M. J. Erickson (ed.), *The Living God*, part 1 (Grand Rapids, MI, 1973); C. F. H. Henry, *God, Revelation and Authority*, vol. 1 (Waco, TX, 1976); B. Lonergan, *Method in Theology* (New York, 1972); J. W. Montgomery, *The Suicide of Christian Theology* (Minneapolis, MN, 1970).

J.I.P.

METHODISM. Although the designation Methodist was at first attached to all supporters of the 18th-century evangelical awakening in England, it was eventually reserved for John Wesley's* adherents who, shortly after his death, left the established church to form a separate denomination. Methodism began as a religious society within the Anglican Communion and it was Wesley's intention that it should remain as such. But his own insistence that sacrosanct parish boundaries should yield to the demands of itinerant evangelism, and later the ordination of ministers for work in North America as well as in Scotland, together with the licensing of preaching-places under the Toleration Act, made secession virtually inevitable.

In the official deed of 1932 authorizing the reunited Methodist Church in Great Britain, reference is made to the doctrines of the evangelical* faith which Methodism has held from the beginning and still holds. These are based on the divine revelation recorded in the Scriptures,* which is recognized as the supreme rule of faith and practice, and are contained in Wesley's *Notes on the New Testament* and his standard sermons.

In its origins Wesleyan theology was shaped by Methodism's involvement in mission and focused on the doctrine of salvation.* Other aspects of Christian belief were viewed from this perspective. Stress was laid on the sovereignty* of God, although not in isolation from other divine attributes or to the removal of human responsibility. The deity of Christ was upheld in face of Arian* and Socinian* tendencies (see Christology*). Human inability to achieve one's own salvation was strongly asserted. The atonement* was seen as a distinctive feature of the authentic gospel as over against the deists,* and as accomplished for all even if not accepted by all. Justification* by faith was central and determinative, leading to the transformation effected by the new birth (see Regeneration*). The work of the Holy Spirit* in bringing assurance* and producing holiness (see Sanctification*) was appreciated in an age when this dimension was in danger of being overlooked. A firm commitment to the ethics of grace represented a necessary corrective. The overall stance of Wesleyan theology is that of an evangelical Arminianism* infused with the warmth and power of the Holy Spirit, as M. B. Wynkoop has shown. Although it echoed Arminius in its resistance to theological determinism, however, the Wesleyan approach was unsympathetic to contemporary English Arminianism with its Pelagian* and unitarian* associations.

In the later stages of the controversy with Calvinists (see Whitefield*) over predestination, the leading Methodist spokesman was John William Fletcher (1729–85), whose five *Checks to Antinomianism* (1771–75) reflected Wesley's views and were endorsed by him.

Fletcher maintained the principle of evangelical liberty while at the same time safeguarding the divine initiative and control in the area of salvation. He feared lest an unbalanced account of sovereign election might open the door to moral anarchy – hence the title of his publications. Elsewhere Fletcher amplified Wesley's teaching on entire sanctification by underlining its relationship to Pentecost and interpreting it as an instantaneous occurrence. The terms 'baptism'* and 'fullness' of the Spirit were both applied to the experience (see also Holiness Movement;* Perfection*).

On a broader canvas, Wesley's theology was developed by the noted biblical scholar Adam Clarke (c. 1760–1832), who reiterated Wesley's emphasis on the authority and sufficiency of Scripture as revealing God's being and purpose. He anticipated more recent trends by recognizing that the task of biblical theology involves the attempt to recover the original significance of the text and to demonstrate its contemporary relevance.

The first outline of systematic theology in the Wesleyan tradition was prepared by Richard Watson (1781–1833) in his *Theological Institutes* (1823–24). He saw himself as a defender of the evangelical faith against deist and unitarian assailants. He also contended both with Pelagian and developed Calvinist views – a lengthy section dealt with the extent of the atonement.* Watson did not quote Wesley with any frequency but was nevertheless faithful to his outlook. He stressed the deductive use of Scripture, which he regarded as inerrant, although he appealed also to the Protestant Reformers as well as to orthodox English theologians.

Wesleyan theology, however, found its classic expression in the *Compendium* (1875–76) of William Burt Pope (1822–1903). By this time Methodism had largely liberated itself from sectarian shackles and was claiming its place in the universal church. While defending and expounding Wesleyan emphases, Pope insisted that in essence Methodist theology was scriptural, catholic* and orthodox in terms of a continuing evangelical tradition. This he traced from the early church to Wesley himself. He viewed the Arminianism of Wesleyan theology as its divergence only from the more extreme forms of Calvinism. Pope's *Compendium* is significant as a robust confessional statement although it took little notice of developing critical trends. In this respect, the contribution of William Arthur (1819–1901) as an apologist grappling with the intellectual issues of his time is of major importance, as is now being realized.

Latterly Methodism has been more productive of biblical scholars than of theologians as such, although mention must be made of John Scott Lidgett (1854–1953), who sought in particular to relate the NT concept of divine fatherhood* to the doctrine of the atonement, and of Geoffrey Wainwright (b. 1939), whose recent *Doxology* breaks relatively new ground in attempting to interpret theology through the praise of God in worship,* doctrine and life (see Doxology;* Liturgical Theology*). The Methodist understanding of Christian perfection was set in the context of ongoing tradition by Robert Newton Flew (1886–1962). By and large it may be said that interest in a specifically Wesleyan approach to theology is less in evidence in Britain than among American holiness groups. Such widely used manuals as those by A. M. Hills (1848–1935) and H. Orton Wiley (1877–1962) are now supplemented by a symposium edited by Charles W. Carter.

See also: CALVINISTIC METHODISM.

Bibliography
R. W. Burtner and R. E. Chiles (eds.), *A Compend of Wesley's Theology* (Nashville, TN, 1954); W. R. Cannon, *The Theology of John Wesley* (Nashville, TN, 1956); C. W. Carter (ed.), *A Contemporary Wesleyan Theology*, 2 vols. (Wilmore, KY, 1983); R. E. Davies, *Methodism* (Harmondsworth, 1963); T. A. Langford, *Practical Divinity: Theology in the Wesleyan Tradition* (Nashville, TN, 1984); W. E. Sangster, *The Path to Perfection: An Examination and Restatement of John Wesley's Doctrine of Christian Perfection* (London, 1943); C. W. Williams, *John Wesley's Theology Today* (London, 1960); M. B. Wynkoop, *Foundations of Wesleyan-Arminian Theology* (Kansas City, KS, 1967).

A.S.W.

METZ, JOHANNES BAPTIST (b. 1936), professor at the University of Mainz, and a leading Roman Catholic representative of political theology.* A student of Karl Rahner,* some of whose earlier works he has reissued, his theology is particularly concerned with the political dimensions of Christian faith and theological reflection. Strongly opposed to any reduction of religion to a merely private option in secular society, he understands Christian faith, and its expressions in corporate life and theological activity, as a force of critical and liberating potential. In particular, he envisages theology as not simply a discipline internal to Christianity but as a constructive critique of social reality, and in this way he sees theology as a dialogue with the world over the future shape of society. The relationship of theology to politics is not one of consequence or application; politics is intrinsic to the theological exercise. Moreover, theology has a critical role in the church, in so far as it enables the identification of ideological elements within the hierarchical forms of church life, and so contributes to the emergence of a 'post-bourgeois church'. Much of this theology rests on the basis of a powerful doctrine of creation* and on an understanding of salvation* as concerned primarily with man in his bodily, corporate and political existence.

Bibliography

Faith in History and Society (ET, London, 1980); *Theology of the World* (ET, London, 1969).

R. D. Johns, *Man in the World. The Political Theology of Johannes Baptist Metz* (Chico, CA, 1976).

J.B.We.

MILLENNIUM. The term refers to the period of 1,000 years mentioned in Rev. 20:2–7 as the time of the reign of Christ and the saints over the earth. Although the term 'millenarianism' has come to be used much more loosely, in this article we are concerned with millennial belief in the strict sense, referring to interpretations of the millennium of Rev. 20. Three main views of the millennium are usually distinguished (premillennialism, postmillennialism and amillennialism), but these views as they have emerged in the history of Christianity can be best understood as five traditions of interpretation:

1. Premillennialism (or chiliasm) in the early church

Many of the early fathers, including Papias (c.

60–c. 130), Justin (c. 100–c. 165), Irenaeus,* Tertullian,* Victorinus of Pettau (d. c. 304) and Lactantius (c. 240–c. 320), were premillennialists, *i.e.* they expected the personal coming of Christ in glory to inaugurate a millennial reign on earth before the last judgment* (see Eschatology*). This belief was not only an interpretation of Rev. 20, but also a continuation of Jewish apocalyptic* expectation of an interim messianic kingdom. The framework of Rev. 20 was filled with content derived from Jewish apocalyptic and especially from OT prophecies, with the result that the millennium was understood primarily as a restoration of paradise. Amid the abundant fruitfulness of the renewed earth and peace between the animals, the resurrected saints would enjoy 1,000 years of paradisal life on earth before being translated to eternal life in heaven. The 1,000 years were explained either as the originally intended span of human life on earth or as the world's sabbath rest at the end of a 7,000-years' 'week' of history. It was the materialistic nature of this millennialism which made it objectionable to others of the fathers, including Augustine,* whose highly influential rejection of it led to the virtual disappearance of premillennialism until the 17th century.

2. Augustinian amillennialism

The interpretation of Rev. 20 which held the field for most of the medieval period and remained influential down to the present was pioneered by the 4th-century Donatist* Tyconius, whose ideas were taken up by Augustine. According to this view the millennial reign of Christ is the age of the church, from the resurrection of Christ until his parousia. Augustine took the figure 1,000 itself to be symbolic, not the actual length of time. This interpretation of Rev. 20 is often called amillennialist, because it rejects belief in a *future* millennium. For the earthly kingdom expected by the chiliasts, it substituted a twin emphasis on the present rule of Christ and other-worldly eschatological hope.

The Protestant Reformers adopted a modified form of this view. They took the millennium to be an actual period of 1,000 years in the past (variously dated), during which the gospel flourished. Satan's release at the end of this period (Rev. 20:7) marked the rise of the medieval papacy.* For the future, the Reformers expected the imminent coming of

Christ, leading at once to the last judgment and the dissolution of this world.

3. Joachimism and Protestant postmillennialism

The ideas of the 12th-century abbot Joachim* inspired a new form of eschatological expectation which in the later Middle Ages and the 16th century was the major alternative to the Augustinian view. Before the end of history there would be an age of the Spirit, a period of spiritual prosperity and peace for the church on earth, which was identified with the millennium of Rev. 20, though not primarily derived from that text. This expectation can be called postmillennialist, since it held that the millennium would be inaugurated by a spiritual intervention of Christ in the power of his Spirit, not by his bodily advent, which would follow the millennium.

Joachimism appealed to some early Protestants, who saw in the success of the Reformation gospel the dawning of a new age of prosperity for the church. Joachimist influence, Protestant optimism about the trends of history, and exegesis of Revelation combined to produce Protestant postmillennialism, whose first influential exponent was Thomas Brightman (1562–1607) and which first flourished in the 17th century. In this view, the millennium would come about through the Spirit-empowered preaching of the gospel, resulting in the conversion of the world and the world-wide spiritual reign of Christ through the gospel.

The 18th century was the great age of postmillennialism, which played a key role in the development of missionary thinking. The revivals were seen as the first ripples of the movement of conversion which would engulf the world, and a view which gave human activity a significant role in God's purpose of establishing his kingdom was a major stimulus to missionary activity. But in the 19th century, postmillennial expectation increasingly approximated to the secular doctrine of progress* and merged into liberal theology's* identification of the kingdom of God* with moral and social improvement. The modern decline of postmillennialism coincides with the loss of Christian credibility that doctrines of progress have suffered.

4. Protestant premillennialism

Protestant premillennialism originated in the early 17th century, especially under the influence of Joseph Mede (1586–1638). It differs from postmillennialism in expecting the personal advent of Christ and the bodily resurrection of the saints to precede the millennium, and therefore tends to stress the discontinuity between the present and the millennial age more than postmillennialism does. It enjoyed a major revival in England in the 1820s, from which its modern forms derive. Whereas postmillennialism thrived on observing hopeful signs of the approaching millennium, premillennialism gained popularity in circles whose view of the current situation was deeply pessimistic. Not the influence of the church, but only the personal intervention of Christ could establish his kingdom on earth.

Premillennialists have taken many views on the character of the millennial reign, but 19th-century premillennialism tended towards a literal interpretation of prophecy, including OT prophecies applied to the millennium. This tendency reached extreme form in the dispensationalist* theology pioneered by J. N. Darby,* in which a 'secret rapture' of the church, preceding the coming of Christ, is to bring the age of the church to an end, while the millennium functions as the time of fulfilment for the OT prophecies to Israel.

5. Symbolic amillennialism

Many proponents of views 2, 3 and 4 above have taken the figure 1,000 in Rev. 20 to be a symbolic number, but have still interpreted the millennium as a period of time. A view found occasionally in the modern period takes the millennium to be a symbol, not of a period at all, but of the complete achievement of Christ's kingdom and his total victory over evil at the parousia.

The various views are, of course, based in part on the debated details of exegesis, but in a broader sense they represent differing attitudes to the relationship between the kingdom of Christ and the history of this world. In all its forms, millennial belief represents, in opposition to a completely other-worldly eschatology, the conviction that it is part of God's purpose to realize his kingdom in this world.

Bibliography

O. Blöcher, G. G. Blum, R. Konrad, R. Bauckham, 'Chiliasmus,' TRE VII, pp. 723–

745; R. G. Clouse (ed.), *The Meaning of the Millennium: Four Views* (Downers Grove, IL, 1977); J. Daniélou, *The Theology of Jewish Christianity* (London, 1964); P. Toon (ed.), *Puritans, the Millennium and the Future of Israel* (London, 1970).

R.J.B.

M INISTRY. The term is used in both a wider and a narrower sense. In its wider sense it refers to service rendered to God or to people. In its narrower usage it denotes the officially recognized service of persons set apart (usually by formal ordination) by the church.

The ministry of Jesus Christ

The ministry of Jesus was initially one of preaching the good news about the kingdom of God,* of teaching, of healing* and of prayer* (Mk. 1 *passim*). He came not to receive service but to give it: the characteristic terms used to describe his ministry are *diakonia* and its cognates, which are associated particularly with waiting at table. This emphasis appears in all four gospels (Mt. 20:28; Mk. 10:45; Lk. 22:27; *cf.* Jn. 13:4–17, where the even more lowly title of *doulos*, slave, is used). Such a ministry of dedicated service entailed the offering of his whole life to God, culminating in his crucifixion which the NT writers understand as a priestly, sacrificial act to make atonement* for human sin (Heb. 10:5–14; *cf.* Rom 5:2; Eph. 2:13–18; 3:12; 5:2; 1 Jn. 2:1–2). Thus Jesus of Nazareth, a 'layman' in Jewish terms, acted as both rabbi and priest in performing what his followers came to understand as a divine ministry of reconciliation for the world (2 Cor. 5:18–19).

The ministry of the early church

The Christian priesthood. The whole Christian community continued Jesus' ministry of reconciliation: his own offering for sin was final and complete, but it opened the way for his followers to perform acceptable priestly and sacrificial duties (Heb. 10:12, 19–22). Sacerdotal and liturgical terminology from the OT is freely used by NT writers to describe the ministry of the church, both as a priestly community (1 Pet. 2:5, 9; Rev. 1:5–6) and also as a group of individuals (Rom. 12:1). The sacrifices offered are not ritual ones but the daily acts by which God is honoured and

his grace proclaimed among men (Rom. 15:16; Phil. 4:18; 2 Tim. 4:6; Heb. 13:15–16). This priesthood is basic to membership of the Christian community (*laos*, see Laity*) and is never applied in the NT to a restricted group or a particular office in the church (see Mediation*).

Mutual service. Like Jesus, his followers were to undertake *diakonia:* they were to serve him in the persons of the needy (Mt. 25:31–46) and to use their gifts (*charismata*) for the benefit of others (1 Pet. 4:10). Paul uses the analogy of a human body, with various limbs and organs each having a different function (Rom. 12; 1 Cor. 12; Eph. 4). As the body of Christ the whole community is inhabited by the Spirit who bestows particular gifts* upon each member. Where lists of ministries are given these do not describe different offices or orders within the church but give examples of the different functions which the Spirit, through distinctive 'charisms', enables to happen.

Apostles, prophets,* evangelists.* The followers of Jesus were commanded to testify to his resurrection* as the event by which God had vindicated and honoured his ministry. Among these the Twelve had a special place as those who had been most closely associated with Jesus' earthly ministry, and more especially as chosen witnesses (although not the only ones) of the resurrection (Acts 1:8, 21–22). This role admitted of no successors (Judas was replaced, but none of the others when they died), but the apostolic and missionary task of founding churches was soon shared with others, especially Paul whose apostolic commissioning by the risen Lord was independent of the Twelve. Later Paul and Barnabas were set apart by the church at Antioch, but this was clearly no ordination in the modern sense, as they were already numbered among the prophets and teachers there (Acts 13:1–3). It was Paul's practice to travel with a team of fellow workers (who were sometimes called 'apostles'; Rom. 16:7), and other groups of itinerant ministers are mentioned in the NT (*e.g.* prophets in Acts 11:27). In the following period the *Didache* (*c.* 100) indicates the continuing peregrinations of 'apostles and prophets'.

Overseers, elders, deacons. The infant church was a 'flock' under the care of Jesus the good shepherd. It appears that Simon Peter among the Twelve (Jn. 21:15–17) and later others in each community (1 Pet. 5:2–4) were given responsibility for shepherding the flock. In the earliest documents, however, these leaders do not have a very high profile and it is not clear how they were appointed. Paul's early letters refer to workers who lead and guide the church (1 Thes. 5:12) but no offices with titles appear apart from a single reference to overseers (*episkopoi*) and deacons at Philippi (Phil. 1:1). Remarkably there is no reference to any such officers or their duties in the whole discussion on 'church order' in 1 Cor., where the description of worship is given in the context of the charismatic ministry already described. Moreover, nowhere in the NT is a particular office associated with the ministry of the Lord's Supper (see Eucharist*). Acts mentions the appointment of elders (*presbyteroi*) in the churches founded by Paul and his companions, and a similar group appears at Jerusalem (Acts 14:23; 15:2; 21:18). Elders and overseers (presbyters and bishops) were probably alternative names for the same leaders in these local churches (see Acts 20:17, 28). There is no clue as to why the titles came to indicate separate offices later on. Elders may literally have been the older men at first, or at any rate the seniors among the early converts who were thus likely to be more mature and able to accept responsibility for the nurture of those newly born in the faith. Elders or overseers are always referred to as a group in each place.

Deacons appear in the Pastorals along with the overseers/elders as officers in the congregation. They probably included women (Rom. 16:1). There is no explanation why this general term for ministry became appropriated to a particular office. It is doubtful whether the appointment of the Seven in Acts 6:1–6 was the origin of this office: they were to be 'deacons of tables' so that the Twelve could be 'deacons of the word', but the gifts of the Spirit subsequently prompted other avenues for their ministry.

An ordered ministry. Very soon after the end of the NT period the 'official' ministry came into much greater prominence in many places. Reasons for this probably included the deaths of the apostles and their immediate companions, and dangers from false prophets and apostles. Already in *e.g.* the Pastorals and the letters of John the need for leaders to protect the flock and their formal appointment for this purpose are evident. Clement of Rome (*c.* 96), who knows only the corporate leadership of overseers/elders and deacons, is much concerned with an orderly succession in ministry (*cf.* Paul, who makes no mention of the appointment of successors to the elders at Ephesus in Acts 20). Ignatius of Antioch (*c.* 110) reveals that in some places (but not apparently at Rome as yet) a single overseer (bishop) has emerged as a safeguard for the unity of the church. He likens the bishop and the presbyters to Christ and his apostles, and the bishop to God.

The development of orders

Not all local churches developed their 'official' ministry at the same rate or necessarily in the same direction. In Alexandria the presbyters consecrated a new bishop from among their own number as a kind of chairman at a time when in other places a new bishop could be consecrated only by other bishops. In time each town with a sizeable Christian community would have a bishop, and there were some 'country bishops' (*chōrepiskopoi*) also who acted in a subordinate capacity. The presbyters formed a kind of advisory board while the deacons emerged as a 'professional' ministry assisting the bishop with liturgical as well as administrative functions: bishops were often chosen from their ranks. Women as deaconesses assisted at the baptism of females. An important change occurred when bishops began to preside over more than one eucharistic community which in effect meant that individual presbyters became attached to particular congregations to preside on behalf of the bishop.

After 200, in writers such as Tertullian* and Hippolytus,* the ordained ministry, especially that of the bishop, began to be described in sacerdotal terms. Developments in eucharistic theology prompted the application of language about a priestly offering of prayers and worship to a more specific offering of the bread and wine. With Cyprian* there emerged a Christian sacrificing priesthood offering the body and blood of Christ. Some later writers (*e.g.* Lactantius, *c.* 240–*c.* 320, and Eusebius)* continued to employ a more general idea of priesthood in the church. With the full development of the medieval doctrine of transubstantiation by the beginning of the 13th century, priesthood became the essential order of the church's ministry.

Private absolution by a priest, originating in Celtic monasticism, became the prerequisite of admission to communion. Minor liturgical orders of door-keeper, reader, exorcist* and acolyte had existed since the 3rd century, but these, along with deacon and subdeacon, became in practice but stepping-stones along the path to full admission to the priesthood. The requirement of celibacy for priests became effective from the 11th century in the West, but in the East married men have always been eligible for the priesthood though not for the office of bishop. Medieval theology included orders as a sacrament* and it was believed that ordination, like baptism, imparted an indelible character to the recipient, which meant that under no circumstances was readmission to the same order permissible. The sacramental character of the lower orders remained obscure.

Ministry in the Reformed churches

The Reformers rejected the concept of a sacerdotal priesthood as a separate order upon which the church was dependent for its existence through a sacramental ministry. They maintained a pastoral and teaching office with high professional standards which in practice perpetuated a distinction between clergy and laity (*cf.* Milton's dictum that 'new Presbyter is but old Priest writ large'). This was challenged by more radical groups (*e.g.* the Quakers*) who viewed preaching as a gift which was not dependent upon ordination. Differences of order between the Protestant* churches affected the manner in which pastors were chosen and ordained, and the rights of local congregations (or groups of elders within them) to appoint and dismiss their ministers. Some churches established a separate and distinct diaconal ministry. The Church of England observed a threefold division of bishops, priests and deacons which was believed to have existed 'from the Apostles' time' (*Book of Common Prayer*). The bishops continued to have charge of large dioceses and there was a prayer for deacons that they might be found worthy to be called 'unto the higher ministries'. The Anglican ministry therefore retained the medieval structure shorn of its sacerdotal functions. This continuity was made into a virtue by the Anglo-Catholic* movement of the 19th century which claimed validity for Anglican orders through an unbroken succession of episcopal ordinations.

In 1896 Pope Leo XIII ruled in the bull *Apostolicae Curae* that the intention had changed because the Anglican Ordinal does not empower priests to offer sacrifice, and Anglican orders were therefore null and void. Fifty years later it was still maintained by representatives of the Anglo-Catholic school that 'a valid ministry is one which . . . proceeds in due succession from the apostles by the laying on of hands of the Essential Ministry [*i.e.* bishops in due succession]; and that should such a ministry fail, the apostolic Church, which is the Body of Christ in space and time, would disappear with it' (K. E. Kirk, ed., *The Apostolic Ministry*, London, 1946, p. 40).

Modern developments

In recent times almost all churches have been affected by a renewed theological understanding of the scriptural basis of ministry which has emphasized two aspects: 1. that no modern pattern of ordained ministry can claim to conform to what little we know about 'official' ministry in the NT, and therefore to claim biblical authority for a particular pattern is hazardous; 2. that if the functions of ministry in the NT as distinct from its organization are taken seriously then every member of the *laos* is actively involved in its exercise. Ecumenical discussion of these matters has produced important agreed statements (see Bibliography), but differences of organization, and the theological rationale behind them, continue to prove a stumbling-block to reunion negotiations.

See also: COLLEGIALITY AND CONCILIARITY.

Bibliography
R. S. Anderson (ed.), *Theological Foundations for Ministry* (Edinburgh, 1979); Anglican-Roman Catholic International Commission, *ARCIC: The Final Report* (London, 1982); *Baptism, Eucharist and Ministry*, Faith and Order Paper No. 111 (Geneva, 1982); J. M. Barnett, *The Diaconate – A Full and Equal Order* (New York, 1981); C. K. Barrett, *Church, Ministry and Sacraments in the New Testament* (Exeter, 1985); A. T. and R. P. C. Hanson, *The Identity of the Church: A Guide to Recognizing the Contemporary Church* (London, 1987); R. P. C. Hanson, *Christian Priesthood Examined* (Guildford, 1979); H. Küng, *Why Priests?* (London, 1972); P. C. Moore (ed.),

Bishops – But What Kind? Reflections on Episcopacy (London, 1982); D. M. Paton and C. H. Long (eds.), *The Compulsion of the Spirit: A Roland Allen Reader* (Grand Rapids, MI, 1983); A. Russell, *The Clerical Profession* (London, 1980); E. Schillebeeckx, *The Church with a Human Face: A New and Expanded Theology of Ministry* (London, 1985); E. Schweizer, *Church Order in the New Testament* (London, 1961); M. Thurian, *Priesthood and Ministry: Ecumenical Research* (London, 1983).

J.T.

MIRACLE. The word 'miracle' comes from the Lat. *miraculum*, meaning a wonder. It suggests supernatural* interference with nature* or the course of events. In the history of the church, miracles have been seen not only as extraordinary expressions of God's grace, but as divine attestation of the person or the teaching of the one who performs the miracle.

With the rise of science* and historical criticism miracles have come under increasing attack. The classic objections to miracles were summed up by David Hume* in his *Enquiry Concerning Human Understanding* (1748), section 10. Hume argued that 'A miracle is a violation of the laws of nature; and as a firm and unalterable experience has established these laws, the proof against a miracle, from the very nature of the fact, is as entire as any argument from experience can possibly be imagined.'

Hume went on to argue that the actual testimony to miracles was weak. The witnesses were frequently ill-educated persons of doubtful reputation. The alleged miracles generally happened in obscure parts of the world. Hume noted the common human propensity to exaggerate, and also argued that miracles in different religions cancel each other out. In view of all this, miracles cannot be used to establish the truth-claims of Christianity. Instead of providing reasons for belief, miracles are themselves the object of a credulous faith.

Hume's argument sounds plausible, but it begs key questions. Hume was in effect ruling out the possibility of events for which the science of his day (or any day) could not provide an explanation. By defining miracles in terms of violations of the laws of nature, Hume was excluding the possibility that some miracles might be events in which God controlled the forces of nature.

The attempt to deny miracles in the name of science is itself an act of faith which presupposes that the world is a system of natural causes which is closed to supernatural intervention. The 'laws' of science, however, are generalizations based on repeated, testable experience. They are provisional to the extent that they are open to modification and correction in the light of further understanding. Hume's argument amounts to a refusal to entertain testimony to any unusual event which lies outside the scope of such provisional generalizations.

Hume's arguments concerning the type of testimony to miracles were arbitrary and generalized. It is arbitrary to require as a prerequisite of credibility that witnesses should possess certain educational and cultural qualifications and that miracles should occur only in certain places. Recognition that some people are inclined to exaggerate does not mean that all people exaggerate. In dealing with miracles it is arbitrary to assume that all witnesses are naturally prone to exaggerate and fantasize. If a witness is sceptical to begin with but is convinced by experience, the testimony of that witness gains in credibility.

The argument that miracles in different religions cancel each other out would be valid if rival religions could adduce comparable miracles to establish their truth-claims. Some religions, however, do not appeal to miracles at all, while others recognize miracles but do not associate them with truth-claims. No major religion claims a miracle comparable with the resurrection* of Jesus.

The credibility of miracles depends upon the world-view within which we view them. If we view the world as a natural closed system, we may recognize unusual events, but we shall refuse to see them as divine miracles. If we see the world as God's creation* which is open to his personal interaction, miracles are feasible.

While some biblical miracles may be seen as expressions of God's control over nature, *e.g.* the events connected with the exodus (Ex. 7 – 14) and some cases of healing,* other miracles may represent the breaking into our present world-order of the order of the world to come. The resurrection of Christ is not only his restoration to life and the Father's vindication of him. It is also the manifestation of God's new order in our world (1 Cor. 15).

In Scripture, miracles are not uniformly distributed throughout biblical history. They occur at certain times associated with God's special saving work, such as the exodus, the conflict with paganism in the time of Elijah and Elisha (1 Ki. 17; 2 Ki. 4 – 5), and the ministry of Jesus.

Scripture also recognizes that false prophets may also perform signs and wonders (Dt. 13:1–5; Mt. 7:22; 24:24; Mk. 13:22; 2 Thes. 2:9). Such signs are to be ignored. An indirect but important testimony to the fact that Jesus performed miracles may be seen in the attitude of Jewish leaders to Jesus. They viewed him as a blasphemous impostor who performed signs and wonders in order to lead the people astray, and accused him of being in league with Satan (Mt. 12:22–32; Mk. 3:6, 20–30; Lk. 11:14–23; Jn. 7:12, 20, 25; 8:59; 10:20, 33; 11:47–53). Under the law such activity was punishable by death (Dt. 13:5; cf. Dt. 18:20).

The resurrection of Jesus represents God's reversal of the verdict passed on Jesus by the Jewish leaders. It confirms the character of his works which were the work of the Father and the Holy Spirit through the Son (Mt. 12:18, 28, 32–32; Mk. 3:29; Lk. 4:18; 11:20; Jn. 5:20–29, 36; 8:28; 9:4; 10:37–38; 14:10–11; 15:24; 17:2–10, 21; Acts 2:22; 10:36–38). As such, the miracles of Jesus not only attest Jesus as the Christ, the Son of God; they also point to the Trinity.*

The argument that miracles ceased with the apostolic foundation of the church was forcefully advanced by B. B. Warfield.* It has been increasingly challenged, *e.g.* by convictions about healing* among Pentecostals* and in the traditional denominations, and by the claims of the charismatic renewal movement about the gifts of the Spirit.* A 'signs and wonders' approach to evangelism has emerged (appealing especially to Mk. 16:15–20), evincing a possibly manipulative approach to miracles and an unbiblical overemphasis on physical well-being and prosperity. At the same time, the recovery of a holistic understanding of salvation* has also contributed to a lively interest in what Scripture should lead the contemporary church to expect from God.

See also: POWER.

Bibliography

C. Brown, *Miracles and the Critical Mind* (Grand Rapids, MI and Exeter, 1984); *idem*, *That You May Believe: Miracles and Faith – Then and Now* (Grand Rapids, MI, 1985); H. C. Kee, *Miracle in the Early Christian World* (New Haven, CT, and London, 1983); C. S. Lewis, *Miracles: A Preliminary Study* (London, 1947); H. van der Loos, *The Miracles of Jesus* (Leiden, 1968); L. Monden, *Signs and Wonders: A Study of the Miraculous Element in Religion* (New York, 1966); C. F. D. Moule (ed.), *Miracles; Cambridge Studies in their Philosophy and History* (London, 1965); A. Richardson, *The Miracle-Stories of the Gospels* (London, 1941); R. Swinburne, *The Concept of Miracle* (London, 1970); G. Theissen, *The Miracle Stories of the Early Christian Tradition* (Edinburgh and Philadelphia, 1983); B. B. Warfield, *Counterfeit Miracles* (1918; repr. Edinburgh, 1972), also repr. as *Miracles: Yesterday and Today, True and False* (Grand Rapids, MI, 1953).

C.B.

MISSIOLOGY is the ordered study of the Christian church's mission. As such it is a discipline within theology, incorporating a number of strands. Biblical study investigates the basis of the church's mission in the *missio Dei*, the calling of Israel to be a light to all nations (Is. 49:6) and Jesus' commission to his disciples to be his witnesses to the ends of the earth and the end of time (Mt. 28:18–20; Acts 1:8). Historical study surveys the growth and expansion of the church at various periods and assesses its impact on different societies and cultures. Systematic theology* studies the interaction of Christian faith both with secular philosophies and ideologies and with other systems of belief. Ethical studies are incorporated into missiology where the church has a reponsibility to declare God's will for the whole of life (see Ethics;* Social Ethics*). Pastoral theology* seeks ways to intruct new converts and integrate them into the church.

Because of the wide scope of missiology it has an important role to play in the integration of other areas of theology. Put another way, every aspect of theology has an inescapably missiological dimension, for each one exists for the sake of the church's mission.

In popular imagination mission is often misconceived as Christians crossing national frontiers to spread the gospel. This view reflects a past age when Christians tended to divide the world neatly into Christian and non-Christian. Today, however, 'the missionary frontier runs round the world. It is the line which separates belief from unbelief.' Mission takes place from and to all continents and within each nation.

Some Christians want to restrict missions to evangelism,* understood as proclaiming the good news about Jesus Christ and inviting people to believe in him for salvation. Most students of mission, however, see it in wider terms (see Lausanne Covenant*).

'Mission' conveys the biblical idea of 'being sent', classically expressed in Jesus' saying, 'As the Father has sent me, I am sending you' (Jn. 20:21). The parallel between God sending Jesus and Jesus sending his disciples describes both the method and the content of mission. The church's mission, then, encompasses everything that Jesus sends his people into the world to do. It does not include everything the church does or everything God does in the world. Therefore, to say the church *is* mission is an overstatement. Nevertheless, to ignore or compromise the commission to go into all the world as Jesus' representatives shows a defective life. 'A church exists by mission as a fire exists by burning.'

The church's mission can be summed up in five general tasks. The order in which they are listed is not intended to suggest priorities. Biblically speaking each is vitally important. By stressing one more than the others, different groups of Christians have tended to see them as alternatives. God, however, allows us no choice.

1. It is to be involved in stewarding* the material resources of creation.* This means encouraging a wise and harmonious use of the natural order created by God, by engaging in the numerous aspects of conservation and the elimination of pollution (see Nature, Theology of*). The church will point to the creator's gift of life for all which implies renouncing greed, and a restrained enjoyment of material goods by all in such a way that future generations will find life sustainable on earth.

2. It is to serve human beings without distinction and whatever their need. It has a compassionate task to aid refugees and the victims of drought and famine and to help set up development schemes, literacy campaigns, health education and housing programmes. It has a particular responsibility to minister to the needs of the handicapped, old people, the bereaved, children at risk and families in tension, and to rehabilitate offenders against the law, alcoholics, drug-addicts and chronic gamblers.

3. It must bear witness to 'the truth as it is in Jesus' (Eph. 4:21). This includes a number of tasks, sometimes separated into apologetics,* pre-evangelism and evangelism. Bearing witness means both the verbal communication of the apostolic gospel and visual demonstration of its power to bring new life and hope to human relationships and communities.

4. It should be engaged in seeing that God's justice is done in society (see Righteousness;* Society, Theology of*). In particular, the church will be active in promoting and defending the integrity of family* life against easy divorce (see Sexuality*), abortion,* casual or abnormal sexual relationships, pornography, the exploitation of women and children, and experimentation on early human life (see Bioethics*). It will also seek alternatives to policies which give rise to more homeless, badly educated, undernourished and unemployed people. It will fight for human rights* and against human discrimination (especially racism; see Race*). Finally it will challenge the inexorable build-up of weapons of mass destruction and the increasing arms trade between rich and poor nations (see War and Peace*).

5. It has a responsibility to show what it means in practice to be a reconciled and liberated community in the midst of a corrupt, distressed and despairing world. It is sent to demonstrate the reality of God's unmerited grace* by practising forgiveness (see Guilt*), the sharing of goods and resources, by eliminating prejudice and suspicion, and by exercising power* as servanthood, not as domination and control. The church is to be both a sign and an agent of God's purpose to create a new order where his peace and justice will reign.

Missiology engages in serious theological reflection on all these aspects of the church's mission. In addition it has, in recent years, focused on a number of specific issues to do with the implementation of its task. Is it right for Christians to be involved in violence to overthrow non-elected, repressive regimes (see

Revolution, Theology of*)? What is the right approach in sharing Christ with people of other faiths – dialogue, proclamation or simply presence among them? Should churches of ethnically and culturally homogeneous groups be encouraged for the sake of church growth?* What role, if any, should mission agencies, which exist independently of any church, play in evangelism, relief or development? How may human and financial resources be shared in genuine Christian partnership between different parts of the worldwide church in a way which commends the gospel?

Bibliography

D. Bosch, *Witness to the World: the Christian Mission in Theological Perspective* (Basingstoke, 1980); O. Costas, *Christ outside the Gate. Mission beyond Christendom* (New York, 1983); R. Padilla, *Mission Between the Times* (Grand Rapids, MI, 1985); W. Scott, *Bring Forth Justice* (Grand Rapids, MI, 1980); J. R. W. Stott, *Christian Mission in the Modern World* (London, 1975); J. Verkuyl, *Contemporary Missiology: an Introduction* (Grand Rapids, MI, 1978).

J.A.K.

MOBERLY, ROBERT CAMPBELL (1845–1903), creative Anglo-Catholic* theologian. The son of Bishop G. H. Moberly of Salisbury (1869–85), Moberly was Oxford's regius professor of pastoral theology from 1892 until his death. Educated at Winchester and New College, Oxford, he was principal of St Stephen's House, Oxford (1876), the Diocesan Theological College, Salisbury (1878), and incumbent at Great Bedworth, Cheshire (1880–92). Moberly was self-consciously a writer and is remembered primarily for his theological works. A liberal* Anglo-Catholic, Moberly contributed an essay 'The Incarnation as the Basis of Dogma' to the controversial Oxford publication *Lux Mundi* (1889). His influential *Ministerial Priesthood* (London, 1897) reflects a High Anglican justification of Anglican orders and centres on Christ's priesthood as determinative of the basis and nature of a 'ministerial priesthood' in the church (see Ministry*). *Atonement and Personality* (London, 1901) is a more significantly liberal reinterpretation of the atonement,* based on Hegelian* views of personality and the redemptive power of Christ's exemplary life and satisfaction* for sin. His other noteworthy works are *Sorrow, Sin and Beauty* (London, 1889), *Christ our Life* (sermons, London, 1902), *Undenominationalism as a Principle of Primary Education* (London, 1902) and *Problems and Principles* (collected papers, London, 1904).

Bibliography

Appreciations by A. Clark, *DNB, Second Supplement 1901–11*, vol. 2, pp. 624–626; W. H. Moberly, *JTS* 6 (1905), pp. 1–19; W. Sanday, *JTS* 4 (1903), pp. 481–499.

R. S. Franks, *A History of the Doctrine of the Work of Christ*, vol. 2 (London, 1918); M. Hutchison, 'Classics Revisited: *Ministerial Priesthood*, R. C. Moberly', *Anvil* 2 (1985), pp. 247–253; T. A. Langford, *In Search of Foundations. English Theology 1900–1920* (Nashville, TN, and New York, 1969).

C.D.H.

MODELS. 'Model' has only recently become a technical term in theology, having been borrowed from the scientific world. In science a model is a kind of 'visual aid' – a set of ideas, or a natural process, or some other series of known phenomena, which can be used as a guideline for investigating relatively unknown areas. A simple example of this is the old picture of the nervous system as similar to a network of ropes, levers and pulleys. This example also serves to show that as scientific knowledge advances certain models have to be discarded as inadequate, and replaced by others – for example, the picturing of the nervous system as a series of electrical impulses.

Theology has in fact always needed to use models, for the reality being described transcends the world, from which language is taken and used to describe that transcendent reality. A classic example of a model in theology is the use of 'word' in the OT and John 1, and from the history of doctrine we could take the Logos* concept of the Apologists,* Augustine's* Trinitarian analogies, or the body-soul picture of the union of natures in Christ. One of the major issues in Christology* today is whether language about 'two natures' is itself a model that needs to be discarded, or at least revised. There is the danger, however, that the introduction of new models can lead, not to a greater understanding of the mystery of Christ, but to the elimination of that mystery, as Christ is reduced to the status of a mere man.

See also: ANALOGY; PARADIGM; RAMSEY, IAN THOMAS.

Bibliography
I. G. Barbour, *Myths, Models and Paradigms* (London, 1974); J. McIntyre, *The Shape of Christology* (London, 1966); I. T. Ramsey, *Models and Mystery* (London, 1964).

M.D.

MODERNISM, CATHOLIC. Roman Catholic modernism is the term applied to a loose-knit movement at the end of the 19th and beginning of the 20th century in which scholars, working in a number of different fields, tried to bridge the gap between Christianity as traditionally understood by the Roman Catholic Church and the world of modern thought and knowledge. Since the Counter-Reformation Rome had increasingly presented Christian truth as a logically watertight, scholastic system. Against this static, unhistorical understanding, and against the authoritarianism by which it was imposed, a diverse group of scholars protested. They claimed that crucial questions about the historical origins of the Bible, the development* of doctrine, the self-understanding of the church and the relation of religion to science* were going unheard. The 'modernists', as they were called by Rome, and as some of them came to call themselves, insisted that these questions had to be faced. Pope Leo XIII (1878–1903) appeared to give some encouragement in the attempt.

Alfred Loisy (1857–1940) was a brilliant biblical scholar who dedicated himself to the application of modern, critical methods. In 1890 he became professor of holy Scripture at the Institut Catholique in Paris. Loisy taught, as 'permanent acquisitions of knowledge', that the Pentateuch in its present form cannot be the work of Moses, that the first chapters of Gn. do not contain an exact and reliable account of the beginnings of mankind, that the historical books of the Bible, including those of the NT, were composed 'in a looser manner than modern historical writing' and that there is a real development of doctrine within Scripture. Through the ineptitude of his rector, he lost his job in 1893 and became chaplain of a girls' school for five

years. When Adolf Harnack* published his classic liberal Protestant account of Christian origins, *What is Christianity?* (1900), Loisy already had to hand all the material for a comprehensive refutation, which was critical of Harnack's individualistic understanding of the gospel and his rejection of apocalyptic,* but in some respects was even more radical than Harnack on questions of gospel criticism. In *L'Evangile et l'eglise* (Paris, 1902), Loisy stressed the continuity between the ministry of Jesus and the life of the church: 'Jesus foretold the Kingdom* and it was the church that came.' The sharp distinction he made between history and faith, and the concession he allowed at the historical level, were unacceptable to Rome. Loisy made his meaning even clearer in a second book, and five of his works, including *L'Evangile et l'église*, were placed on the *Index* in 1903. Understandably, Loisy could not accept the condemnation as a comment on his historical work, but, largely because of political relations between France and Rome, he was not excommunicated until 1908.

A second important name is that of the British Jesuit,* George Tyrrell (1861–1909). He was not a scholar in the same sense as Loisy, but was the most gifted writer of the movement. In a series of brilliantly readable books and articles on devotion, ethics and apologetics, written between 1897 and 1909, he pleaded for a new synthesis between Christianity and 'science' and particularly history. He became an ever more outspoken critic of the rationalist and authoritarian mentality of Rome. From 1900, he was in serious conflict with his Jesuit superiors. In 1906 he was dismissed from the Jesuits, and when, in 1907, he published in *The Times* a searing critique of the anti-modernist encyclical *Pascendi*, he was excommunicated. Tyrrell, like Loisy, rejected the notion that the dogmas* of the church had been revealed in propositional form. He stressed 'revelation* as experience' and dogma as the human attempt to speak about that experience. The function of dogma is not primarily to inform the mind, but to promote the life of charity. The key to religious life is not theology, but prayer and love, and the test of religious truth is pragmatic, the truth of dogma being measured by its power to promote sanctity.

An important influence upon both Loisy and Tyrrell was the philosopher Maurice

Blondel (1861–1949). In *L'Action* (Paris, 1893), he presented a phenomenology* of man as an integrated being, active in the world. It was Blondel, with Lucien Laberthonnière (1860–1932), who showed how the supernatural* could be regarded not as an alien element imposing itself from without upon the natural, but as the transcendental presupposition of all human action. The supernatural is not 'extrinsic' to the natural life of man, but discerned *within* the natural by 'the method of immanence'.

If there was a coherent Catholic 'modernist movement' in France, Italy and England, the common factor among the scholars involved was friendship with Baron Friedrich von Hügel,* himself a biblical scholar and critical historian of mysticism.* Von Hügel sought them out, corresponded with them, and brought them into touch with each other. Like Blondel, he eluded condemnation.

From the accession, in 1903, of Pius X, a man of simple and intolerant devotion, scholars such as these were regarded as a deadly threat to the Catholic faith. In 1907, the encyclical *Pascendi* warned against 'the doctrine of the modernists', and presented the picture of a composite 'modernist' who, as philosopher, founded his religious philosophy on agnosticism; as believer, rejected the notion of propositional revelation; as theologian, believed that dogmas represent divine reality only in 'symbolical' fashion; as historian, was a rationalist who excluded the miraculous; as critic, believed that Scripture is a human summary of religious experiences; and as apologist, tried to promote religious experience,* not the acceptance of religious truth. 'Modernism' (which was never a system) was branded as 'the synthesis of all heresies', and from 1910 an anti-modernist oath was imposed on Roman Catholic clergy. Not until after Vatican II (1962–65) did Roman Catholic scholarship recover confidence in critical study of the Bible and of Christian origins.

Bibliography

A. F. Loisy, *L'Evangile et l'église* (Paris, 1902), ET, *The Gospel and the Church* (London, 1903); *idem*, *Mémoires pour servir à l'histoire religieuse de notre temps*, 3 vols. (Paris, 1930–31); E. Poulat, *Histoire, dogme et critique dans la crise moderniste* (Paris, ²1979); G. Tyrrell, *Christianity at the Cross-roads* (London, 1909); A. R. Vidler, *The Modernist Movement in the Roman Church* (Cambridge, 1934).

N.S.

MODERNISM, ENGLISH, was a school of late 19th- and early 20th-century theology loosely united by the belief that the proper response to modern thought is to make radical alterations in Christian doctrine. This is an assumption on which much religious thinking has proceeded since the Enlightenment,* but in modernism the assumption became an explicit principle.

The name was first given to a school of Roman Catholic theologians, represented in France by A. F. Loisy (1857–1940) and in Britain by Baron F. von Hügel* and by G. Tyrrell (1861–1909), which was condemned by the Church of Rome in 1907. It adopted a far-reaching biblical criticism* and a sceptical attitude towards Christian origins and traditional dogma,* emphasizing ethical conduct and, sometimes, mystical* devotion (see Modernism, Catholic*).

In the different context of English Protestantism, modernism displayed many of the same features. There was the same rationalistic demolition of biblical authority and traditional doctrine, the same emphasis on ethics (the moral example and moral teaching of Jesus being particularly emphasized), and in some writers, notably Dean W. R. Inge (1860–1954), the same concern for mystical devotion. The affirmation of human goodness and of historical progress* in rational and moral thought, and the denial of any real distinction between the natural and the supernatural* or between Christianity and other religions, were frequent themes. The divinity of Jesus was often explained as different only in degree from the divinity of every person made in the image of God.

Though theology of this kind had many representations in the Free Churches, it attracted most notice in the Church of England, where its proponents were linked together by the Modern Churchmen's Union (founded 1898), and where one of them, E. W. Barnes (1874–1953), became in 1924 Bishop of Birmingham. In this position he gained notoriety by his attacks on what he regarded as Anglo-Catholic superstition and especially by the publication of his sceptical book *The Rise of Christianity* (London, 1947), after which the archbishops of both Canterbury and York publicly called on him to resign. Modernism was by this date rapidly declining. Its ideas of human goodness and progress had been discredited by the experience of Nazism, culminating in the events of the Second World War, and its Anglican representatives had always had conscientious problems with the supernaturalism of the *Book of Common Prayer* and especially with the obligation to use the creeds.* The radicalism that arose in the 1960s, when the War was sufficiently far past and the Prayer Book revision had started, brought back many of the ideas of the modernists, but not their strong ethical emphasis (*cf.* Robinson, John Arthur Thomas*).

In many ways the most distinguished of the English modernists was Hastings Rashdall (1858–1924), teacher of philosophy at Oxford and afterwards dean of Carlisle. Apart from his standard history of the European universities, he wrote a great variety of theological works, notably *The Theory of Good and Evil* (Oxford, 1970), propounding a modified utilitarian ethics, *Philosophy and Religion* (London, 1909), defending idealism* as a basis for religious philosophy, and *The Idea of Atonement in Christian Theology* (London, 1919), upholding the Abelardian* or exemplarist theory of the atonement,* and rejecting the idea of substitutionary* sacrifice* as abhorrent to modern conceptions of justice. Rashdall was also strongly opposed to mysticism, thus demonstrating the variety of opinion possible among modernists.

Bibliography

H. P. V. Nunn, *What is Modernism?* (London, 1932); A. M. G. Stephenson, *The Rise and Decline of English Modernism* (London, 1984); A. R. Vidler, *The Modernist Movement in the Roman Church* (Cambridge, 1934).

R.T.B.

MÖHLER, JOHANN ADAM

(1796–1838), Catholic theologian and church historian, who taught at Tübingen and Munich. He gained an early acquaintance with the work of leading contemporary Protestant theologians, notably J. A. W. Neander (1789–1850) and Schleiermacher,* and much of his work is implicitly concerned to mediate between Catholicism and Protestantism, most especially in his *Symbolik* (Mainz, 1832; ET, *Symbolism, or Exposition of the Doctrinal Differences . . .* , 2 vols., London, 1843), where established confessional divergences are deliberately de-emphasized. His other chief works are *Die Einheit der Kirche* (*The Unity of the Church*) (Tübingen, 1825), *Athanasius der Grosse* (*Athanasius the Great*) (Mainz, 1827) and *Neue Untersuchungen* (*New Enquiries*) (Vienna, 1834). His earlier work drew charges of unorthodoxy, notably in its assertion of the priority of spiritual church unity over institutional unity guaranteed by communion with the ecclesiastical hierarchy. Later writings shift towards a more positive evaluation of visible, institutional forms of organization, possibly under the influence of Hegel's* theory of religion. Many Catholic modernist* theologians drew inspiration from Möhler's work, which remains one of the decisive influences on post-Enlightenment* Catholic thinking.

Bibliography

J. Fitzer, *Möhler and Baur in Controversy* (Tallahassee, FL, 1974); R. H. Nienaltowski, *J. A. Möhler's Theory of Doctrinal Development* (Washington, 1959).

J.B.We.

MOLTMANN, JÜRGEN (b. 1926),

Reformed theologian, who since 1967 has been professor of systematic theology at Tübingen. He is best known for his earlier work, comprising *Theology of Hope* (London, 1967), which has been one of the most influential theological works of the post-World War II period, not only in the West but also in the Third World; *The Crucified God* (London, 1974), which is one of the most important modern studies of the cross; and the political theology* with which in numerous collected essays he drew out the implications of his dogmatic* theology for Christian praxis* in the world.

Especially in his earlier books, Moltmann's theology has its determining centre in a dialectical* understanding of the cross and the resurrection,* according to which they represent total opposites – Godforsakenness and the nearness of God – and Jesus has his identity in this contradiction. In *Theology of Hope* the focus is on the resurrection, which Moltmann interprets as God's promise for the future of the world, thereby restoring to theology the dimension of eschatological* hope*. As Jesus in his death was identified with the present state of the world in all its negativity, so his resurrection, which contradicts the cross, is a promise for the total transformation of the whole of reality. Moltmann's is therefore a dialectical and universalistic* eschatology. Moreover, since the promise is for the transformation of the whole of this-worldly reality by God in the future, it is also an incentive for world-transforming activity in the present. *Theology of Hope* opens theology and the church simultaneously towards the future and towards the world, in hope and in hopeful praxis.

From the resurrection and hope, *The Crucified God* shifts the focus to the cross and suffering* love* (see Cross, Theology of the*). The death of Jesus, forsaken by his Father, is interpreted as God's act of loving solidarity with all the godless and the Godforsaken, by which the salvific presence of God, promised in Jesus' resurrection, is mediated to them. This leads Moltmann both into the doctrine of God and into the question of theodicy.* As an event between the Father and the Son, and as an event of divine suffering, the cross requires a Trinitarian* theology and a doctrine of divine passibility. As God's act of loving identification with all who suffer, it takes the problem of suffering up into God's Trinitarian history in hope for the eschatological overcoming of all suffering.

Moltmann's major trilogy is completed by *The Church in the Power of the Spirit* (London, 1977), in which he develops an ecclesiology in the context of a doctrine of the Spirit* as working out the dialectic of cross and resurrection in a process leading to the eschatological kingdom.* The church* is seen as an open society of friends, a charismatic community of committed disciples, in fellowship with the poor and oppressed.

The three books of the trilogy complement each other as different angles on a single theological vision. But Moltmann now sees them as preparatory work for a second series of major books, comprising studies of particular doctrines. Two of these have so far appeared: *The Trinity and the Kingdom of God* (London, 1981), which propounds a strongly social doctrine of the Trinity deeply involved in and affected by the world, and *God in Creation* (London, 1985), in which the doctrine of the Spirit in creation* is related to ecological concerns (*cf.* Nature, Theology of*). Throughout all these major works and many minor ones Moltmann combines a creative faithfulness to the central themes of biblical and historical Christianity with a critical and praxis-orientated openness to the realities of the modern world.

Bibliography

The Experiment Hope (London, 1975); *On Human Dignity* (London, 1984); *Religion, Revolution and the Future* (New York, 1969).

M. D. Meeks, *Origins of the Theology of Hope* (Philadelphia, 1974); R. Bauckham, 'Bibliography: Jürgen Moltmann', *MC* 28 (1986), pp. 55–60; *idem, Moltmann: Messianic Theology in the Making* (London, 1987).

R.J.B.

MONARCHIANISM. In the 3rd century, under the general name 'monarchianism', the heresies of ebionism and docetism* of the 2nd century reappeared. Its basic doctrine that God is one, the sole principle of all existence, was itself an accepted truth of the ethical monotheism of the OT of which Christianity was heir. The term *monarchia* applied to God had an honourable history. It was used by Plato and Aristotle, and with a more religious connotation by Philo.* Tertullian,* who first gave the name 'monarchianism' to its specific heresy, declares, after examination of its Greek and Latin usage, that *monarchia* has no other meaning than 'single and individual rule' (*Against Praxeas* 3).

The heresies of monarchianism developed naturally as a consequence of their initial interest. Where the theological concern was the stronger, it was found necessary to stress the *oneness* of God against pagan polytheism. The tendency here was to exalt the unity of God at the expense of Christ's divinity. The result was the elaboration of a new form of ebionism, or as now designated 'dynamic monarchianism'. Christ is here conceived as the subject of a special influence or 'dynamis' (Gk. 'power') of the one monarchia which came to reside in the man Jesus. For introducing this 'God-denying heresy' that 'Christ was a mere (indwelt) man', Theodotus of Byzantium was expelled from the church in

Rome *c.* 190. Its most formidable exponent was, however, Paul of Samosata, bishop of Antioch 260–72. For him only a matter of degree marked the difference between Jesus and other men. Jesus entered progressively into such an ethical relationship with God that he became the more penetrated with the divine *ousia* (see Substance*) until 'out of man he became God'. Paul was condemned by a synod of Antioch in 268. He used the word *homoousios* to deny that the Son and the Father were distinct beings.

Modalist monarchianism, otherwise designated patripassianism and Sabellianism, started from a firm conviction of Christ's divinity free from all compromising emanationisms and subordinationisms. However, it called in question the integrity of Christ's body and thus verged towards docetism. It sought to unite the deity of the Son and the oneness of God by declaring the designations Father and Son to be modes, or expressions of manifestation, of the one divine being. The view was first elaborated by Noetus of Smyrna (*c.* 200–25), who 'introduced a heresy from the tenets of Heraclitus' (according to Hippolytus*), and was developed by the anti-Montanist* Praxeas, who brought in the Holy Spirit as the third mode of representation of the one God and thus 'did a twofold service to the devil at Rome: he drove away prophecy and brought in heresy; he put to flight the Paraclete, and crucified the Father' (Tertullian, *Against Praxeas* 1).

The name of Sabellius (in Rome *c.* 198–220) is now identified with modalist monarchianism. In the interest of strict monotheism Sabellius declared that, although the names Father, Son and Holy Spirit were biblical, they were attached to the one being. Thus God as a single monad is manifest in three distinct and successive operations of self-revealing. The unity of God is thus secured at the expense of the divine triunity of persons within the Godhead. The Son and the Holy Spirit are but temporary modes of self-expression of the one Father of all. It was the Father who became incarnate as the Son and was crucified (patripassianism – lit. 'Father-suffering'). Origen's* strong assertion of the Logos* as at once eternal with, yet subordinate to, the Father gave the decisive blow to monarchianism.

See also: ADOPTIONISM; TRINITY.

Bibliography

J. F. Bethune-Baker, *An Introduction to the Early History of Christian Doctrine* (London, 1903); J. N. D. Kelly, *Early Christian Doctrines* (London, ⁵1977); G. L. Prestige, *God in Patristic Thought* (London, 1956).

H.D.McD.

MONASTIC THEOLOGY.

In the 5th century, Western Europe was overrun by successive waves of barbarian invasions. In 476 the last Western emperor was deposed by a barbarian Gothic king and the Western Roman Empire had effectively ceased to exist. The ensuing period, until about 1000, can aptly be called the Dark Ages. But while Western European intellectual life was at a low ebb, theology and learning continued in the relative security provided by the monastic communities (see Asceticism;* Benedict and the Benedictine Tradition*). This was the age of monastic theology.

The term 'monastic theology' refers not just to the local setting of the theologians but to the approach that they adopted. They worked in an atmosphere of commitment and devotion, within the framework of the monastic life. Their goal was not the pursuit of knowledge for its own sake, but edification and worship.* Their approach was one of contemplation, meditation and adoration. The theologian was not a detached academic observer studying his material from outside, but a committed, involved participant. As the Dark Ages came to an end, there arose another form of theology – scholastic* theology. Theology came to be studied outside of the cloister – in the university and other 'secular' (non-monastic) settings. The goal was objective intellectual knowledge. The approach was one of questioning, logic, speculation and disputation. Theology had become a detached objective science. This approach did not eliminate the older monastic approach, but it displaced it from the front line of theology. Bernard of Clairvaux* has been called 'the last of the fathers' (see Patristic Theology*) and he was the last really great representative of monastic theology.

Three great names dominate the age of monastic theology: Augustine,* Gregory* and Benedict.* Augustine, the greatest of the Latin fathers, wrote shortly before the disintegration of the Western Empire and summed up much of the teaching of the earlier fathers of the church. Pope Gregory I, the greatest of the monastic theologians in the Dark Ages, was a much-loved master of the spiritual life. Indeed, J. Leclercq could state that 'in the realm of theological analysis of the Christian experience, nothing essential has been added to Gregory the Great'. The Augustinianism* of the Dark Ages was by and large the teaching of Augustine as filtered through Gregory. Monastic theology was lived, preached and written in the monastery and the monastic life was focused on the Rule of Benedict. But it was only in the 8th century, through the labours of his namesake Benedict of Aniane (*c.* 750–821), that Benedict's Rule became widely adopted within Western monasticism. In 817 a synod at Aachen made it the official rule for all monks.

Monastic theology was above all a theology of experience (see Religious Experience*), a theology of the spiritual life (see Spirituality*). The writings of Augustine were prized especially for their spiritual teaching. Among the greatest achievements of monastic theology is the mystical* teaching of Gregory and Bernard, who followed the Augustinian tradition of Neoplatonic mysticism (see Platonism*). Monastic theology was based primarily on Scripture which, together with the fathers, was read daily in the *lectio divina* ('divine reading'). Although Scripture was central, the aim was not a literal, scientific exegesis. Nevertheless, monastic exegesis was disciplined. There was a strong emphasis on the study of grammar as a preparation for handling the sacred text. Scripture was interpreted by Scripture, especially through relating together passages where the same words appear. But the interpretation of Scripture was heavily allegorical (see Hermeneutics*). The aim was not to analyse the text in a scientifically precise manner but to apply the message of salvation to the hearer. The book which was most often read and expounded was the Song of Solomon, interpreted as an account of the relation between God and the individual soul. It is noteworthy that Reformers such as Calvin,* who opposed allegory, none the less saw in monastic theology the preservation of a purer form of Augustinian theology which was later corrupted by scholasticism.

Bibliography
C. Butler, *Western Mysticism: The Teaching of Augustine, Gregory and Bernard on Contemplation and the Contemplative Life* (London, ³1967); J. Leclercq, *The Love of Learning and the Desire for God* (New York, 1961).

A.N.S.L.

MONISM. As a philosophical theory, monism is the view that all reality is ultimately one, not twofold (as in dualism*) and not many. The one, however, may be understood either quantitatively or qualitatively. In the first sense everything is numerically one, and any plurality that appears is either illusory (*e.g.* Parmenides and the Greek Eleatic school, 6th–5th centuries BC) or else a transitory mode of operation of the underlying one (*e.g.* Spinoza*). In the second sense everything is of one kind, which may be either physical (as in naturalism and materialism*), or immaterial and spiritual (as in idealism*), or else neutral with regards to the matter-spirit distinction. Quantitative monism applied to religion erases the God-creation distinction that is basic to theistic* belief, thereby leading to forms of pantheism* or panentheism* as in Neoplatonic and Hegelian* theology. Qualitative monism applied to religion takes theism to be a kind of metaphysical idealism (*e.g.* Berkeley*) or else a panpsychism (*e.g.* process theology*).

The difficulty with monism is that when everything is treated as one, the over-generalization involved elides important distinctions, and so tends to a reductionist position. Mind or spirit is reduced to a by-product of physical processes, individuality is diminished, any ultimate distinction between good and evil is eroded, and the transcendence of God (either numerically or qualitatively) is lost. In some Eastern religions, and in F. H. Bradley (1846–1924), God is therefore one manifestation of the all-inclusive Absolute Being, rather than himself the one eternal reality.

A.F.H.

MONOPHYSITISM. The seeds of monophysitism, that the person of the incarnate Christ was of one nature only (*monos*, 'single', *physis*, 'nature'), are present in Cyril of Alexandria's* polemic against Nestorius.* Cyril's *That Christ is One* affirms that 'there is one nature (*mia physis*) of God the Word incarnate, but worshipped with his flesh as one worship'. While, according to

Harnack,* Cyril's theory is pure but unintentional monophysitism, he cannot be said to state the view precisely. That was done by Eutyches, the aged anti-Nestorian monk of Constantinople (c. 378–454). Eutyches supported Cyril against Nestorius at the Synod of Ephesus, 431, but was himself accused by Eusebius of Dorylaeum in 448 of confounding the two natures and was deposed by Flavian, bishop of Constantinople (d. 449). By court support Eutyches had Flavian's decision reversed at the Latrocinium (Robber Synod) of Ephesus, 449. Both put their case to Leo* of Rome for judgment. Leo's decision went against Eutyches and his doctrine was consequently repudiated at Chalcedon (451; see Christology;* Councils*) and Eutyches again deposed and exiled.

Eutyches' view was simply a reaction from Nestorianism in favour of Apollinarianism.* Faced with the question whether he confessed two natures in the incarnate Christ, Eutyches declared 'our Lord to have become out of two natures before the union. But I confess one nature after the union.' He conceived of Christ as a mingling of two natures, which constituted him a *tertium quid*. In the union the divine had the major share, the humanity being merged with deity as a drop of honey mingled with the ocean.

Leo's *Tome* in which he repudiated Eutyches's monophysitism became one of the bases of the dogma of Chalcedon. Chalcedon declared for the two natures after the union, but gave no explanation of how they unite in the one Christ. The Chalcedonian Definition was not, however, well received everywhere in the East. The Cyrilline formula, 'one nature of the Word made flesh', had popular allegiance and was sometimes defended with outbursts of violence.

After Chalcedon monophysitism diverged into two main streams. The more moderate, the Severans, following Severus the monophysite Patriarch of Antioch (c. 460–538), adhered closely to Cyril, considering the two natures to be a mere ideal abstraction. They strongly asserted the humanness of the resultant nature which they declared capable of corruption in itself like ours. Monophysites of this type were sometimes called *phthartolatrai*, worshippers of the corruptible, by their opponents. The other group, the Julianists, after Julian, bishop of Halicarnassus (deposed c. 518) adopted the stance of Eutyches. For them Christ's human body was so modified by union with the divine as to be rendered incorruptible. Christ suffered by an act of his own will, and not because he possessed a corruptible human nature. They were consequently referred to as the *aphthartodokētai*, 'teachers of the incorruptible' or as the *phantasiastai*, declarers of Christ's body as merely phantasmal.

Another group, who flourished c. 519 in Constantinople and taught that 'one of the Trinity suffered in the flesh', were called *theopaschitai* by their opponents for teaching that 'God suffered'.

The usurper Basiliscus' (d. 477) *Encyclion* of 476, pressing on all Eastern sees the 'one nature' doctrine, and the Emperor Zeno's *Henoticon* of 482, declaring the Nicene Creed as alone binding, served merely to intensify opposition to and support for Chalcedon. In the 6th century Leontius of Byzantium (see Hypostasis*), by interpreting Chalcedon in a Cyrilline sense, succeeded in bringing most of the East and West finally to concur in affirming the Chalcedonian dogma.

Monophysitism remains the official interpretation of Christology in the Syrian Jacobite, Coptic* and Ethiopian* churches.

Bibliography

W. H. C. Frend, *The Rise of the Monophysite Movement* (London, 1972); A. A. Race, *Monophysitism, Past and Present* (London, 1920); W. A. Wigram, *The Separation of the Monophysites* (London, 1923).

H.D.McD.

MONOTHEISM is the belief that there is only one God.* The term commonly refers to Israel's belief in one God, taken over by the Christian church. Contrasted with animism* (worshipping nature spirits), polytheism* (recognizing many gods), and henotheism/monolatry (recognizing that many gods exist, but accepting a personal commitment to only one), it then characterizes Israel's religion over against those of other Western Asian peoples, or Israel's religion at its most developed over against its earlier stages.

It needs to be noted, however, that at all periods the OT affirms that Yahweh has unrivalled power and wisdom, and that his being is uniquely unoriginate and eternal. Gn. 1, for instance, describes God's creative activity in absolute terms. Distinguishing him from nature and cosmos, and leaving no room for the existence of other beings of his stature, it subverts the polytheisms of Babylon and Canaan and – by anticipation – the emanations of Gnosticism.* Ex. 1 – 15 relates God's redemptive work in similar absolute terms, asserting his power in history and over natural forces in such a way as to imply a claim to an exclusive deity. The Psalms and Job declare that Yahweh is Lord over all forces of chaos and evil and implicitly exclude any metaphysical dualism* (cf. Is. 45:7).

At the same time, the OT also accepts the existence of other 'gods' at all periods, though demoting these to the status of Yahweh's aides, beings whose divinity is not absolute as his is (cf. 1 Cor. 8:4–6). The OT does not develop from animism or polytheism to monotheism. Further, some of the OT's monotheistic-sounding affirmations (e.g. Dt. 6:4) are primarily concerned to summon Israel to an exclusive commitment to Yahweh; and in general, the distinctive feature of biblical faith is the conviction that the God of Israel who is also the God and Father of our Lord Jesus Christ is (the one) God, rather than merely that God (whoever he be) is one. This latter belief would in any case not be peculiar to Israel, its clearest expression elsewhere being in Akhenaten's Egypt.

Monotheism became an explicit theological theme in the early Christian centuries in the form of an emphasis on God's *monarchia* (see Monarchianism*). Here the biblical testimony to the unique deity of Israel's redeemer and the Father of Jesus came to be associated with Platonic* and Aristotelian* convictions regarding the one divine monad. The commingling of biblical and philosophical perspectives made it possible to work out the implications of the scriptural testimony regarding the uniqueness of God, but it also hindered the development of Trinitarian theology. Indeed, the word 'monotheism' in its earliest usage denotes non-Christian or sub-Christian beliefs which contrast with Trinitarianism.

Bibliography

C. Geffré and J.-P. Jossua (eds.), *Monotheism* (*Concilium* 177, Edinburgh, 1985); J. N. D. Kelly, *Early Christian Doctrines* (London, ⁵1977); P. Lapide and J. Moltmann, *Jewish Monotheism and Christian Trinitarian Doctrine* (Philadelphia, 1981); J. Moltmann, *The Trinity and the Kingdom of God* (London, 1981); H. H. Rowley, *From Moses to Qumran* (London, 1963); J. F. A. Sawyer, 'Biblical Alternatives to Monotheism', *Th* 87 (1984), pp. 172–180; O. Weber, *Foundations of Dogmatics*, vol. 1 (Grand Rapids, 1981).

J.G.

MONOTHELITISM, see CHRISTOLOGY.

MONTANISM was a prophetic movement originating *c.* 170 in Phrygia, where a Christian named Montanus began to utter prophecies* in a state of convulsive frenzy. He and his supporters claimed that his ecstatic condition was a sign that he was totally possessed by the Holy Spirit, who was inaugurating a new dispensation of divine revelation. They demanded unhesitating recognition for the new prophecy.

Others demurred at this because the ecstatic mode of prophecy was contrary, they said, to recognized church tradition. Some, believing Montanus to be demon-possessed, even tried to have him exorcized,* but they were frustrated by his supporters. Several local church councils did condemn the Montanist prophecies, but were powerless to prevent the Montanist movement running its course and creating a split within the churches. The Montanists looked exclusively to Montanus and two women, Prisca and Maximilla, as their prophets, and saw to the widespread circulation of their oracles. They did not suggest that every believer should claim the prophetic gift. Indeed, when the last of these prophets, Maximilla, died *c.* 189, she left a prophecy that there were to be no further prophets before the end of the age. Thereafter in Phrygia the movement turned into a cult in memory of the three prophets and their writings. Elsewhere the movement gained some acceptance in a diluted form. It was taken as one piece of evidence that God had new revelation to give to his people. In this form the 'new prophecy', as it was termed, gained its most outstanding convert in the African writer, Tertullian.*

Tertullian was attracted to the movement by its strict discipline. For example, the prophecies proscribed remarriage after being widowed as unlawful, and added both to the length and frequency of those fasts which had become statutory within the church. Tertullian believed that this development was directly in line with the teaching in Jn. 16:12–13 that the Holy Spirit had further truth to bestow. The church by Tertullian's time had reached such maturity that it could tolerate standards previously beyond its capacity. But opponents of Montanism contended that these developments were innovations contrary to Scripture.

The influence of Montanism on the church lasted about a generation. At first it provoked an inconclusive debate on the validity of ecstatic prophecy, but attention later turned to the more important issue of whether the church was to expect further revelation after the apostolic era. Montanism failed in the end to convince the church that it was a valid addition to recognized Scripture. For one thing, the movement lost the phenomenon of prophecy in its directly inspired form, while its position on second marriage was considered contrary to Scripture. The mainstream church was left with a heightened appreciation of the apostolic teaching, and prophecy in all forms virtually disappeared from the church.

Bibliography

H. von Campenhausen, *Ecclesiastical Authority and Spiritual Power in the Church of the First Three Centuries* (London, 1969); *idem, The Formation of the Christian Bible* (Philadelphia, 1972).

G.A.K.

MOONIES, see NEW RELIGIONS; SECTS.

MORAL REARMAMENT (MRA) originated through Frank Buchman (1878–1961), an American Lutheran. After an experience of conversion while at Keswick (see Higher Life Theology*) for the convention in 1908, he gradually became concerned about reforming the world. He founded the Oxford Group in 1929, and this became MRA in 1938. The movement spread beyond the Christian faith, and welcomed any who sought to change society through practising the four absolutes, namely absolute purity, absolute unselfishness, absolute honesty and absolute love. Every legitimate means was used to spread the message and enrol supporters. Groups and houseparties were used from the beginning, and the general public were reached through plays and films,

the Westminster Theatre in London being a centre for plays.

Buchman himself received many honours from world leaders, and after his death his place was taken by Peter Howard (1908–65), who himself wrote some of the MRA plays. At Howard's death control of the movement passed to directors in USA, but there are strong local centres at Caux in Switzerland, in Japan and other countries.

The absolutes accord with Christian ideals, but MRA members remain in their own religion, generally, but not always, Christianity. Some evangelicals who, like Buchman, already have a clear experience of salvation in Christ and his death, have held that in MRA they are united in a corporate expression of Christian standards. Others believe that there is no need for a separate organization to promote Christian values; and the promotion of values, without basic Christian doctrines, is not the NT gospel.

Bibliography

K. D. Belden, *Reflections on MRA* (London, 1983); G. Ekman, *Experience into God* (ET, London, 1972); P. Howard, *The World Rebuilt* (Poole, 1951); C. Pignet and M. Sentis, *World at the Turning* (ET, London, 1982).

J.S.W.

MORAL THEOLOGY. Although theology, especially in the West, has always been concerned with questions of Christian morality, the recognition of moral theology as an independent discipline dates from the late 16th century. The expression *theologia moralis* is found a century earlier in connection with the medieval confessionals, which elaborate the purpose of the penitentials of the early Middle Ages: to give guidance to the priest on suitable penances* for various sins. With the moral theology of the Counter-Reformation (see Reformation, Catholic Counter-*) the concern is more profound and the theological roots more extensive. It aims to guide the perplexed conscience* of the individual believer confronted with complex practical deliberations. It draws on the theology of law and psychology of moral judgment developed by Thomas Aquinas,* on the canon law,* and on the common theological understanding of man's orientation to God as the *summum* *bonum* which derived from Augustine.* It attended closely to the detailed examination and analysis of moral cases – hence the modern word 'casuistry'.* In the 17th century, as theological concern shifted from the doctrinal questions of the Reformation, English Protestantism was attracted by this orientation to deliberative questions, and major contributions to moral theology were made in English by Puritans* (*e.g.* William Perkins, 1558–1602) as well as by Laudians (*e.g.* Jeremy Taylor, 1613–67).

The validity of traditional moral theology has been a matter of controversy. It is typical in many ways of the 17th century in which it flowered: individualist in its conception of the conscientious agent, lay-orientated in its concern for life in the world; yet looking to impose order upon subjective moral perceptions not by appeal to the Scriptures so much as by the authoritative guidance of the institutional church. (This last point applies less to Protestant contributions to the genre.) Modern critics (*e.g.* Barth)* have objected to its authoritarianism; contemporaries (*e.g.* Pascal*) objected to its accommodation to lax standards. Both criticisms have some justice. So do objections to its formalist analysis of moral problems, its focus on the pathological and exceptional phenomena of the moral life, and its scholastic traditionalism. Nevertheless, it contributed enormously to an understanding of the type of discernment required in the interpretation of particular situations of moral decision; and so pointed towards a Christian moral thinking that was neither legalistic nor subjective. The tradition fell into disrepute in Protestant circles in the 18th century. In Roman Catholicism it reached its height in the early 18th century with the work of Alphonsus Liguori (1696–1787), and achieved a renewed vigour in the 19th, only to lose favour in the 20th.

Protestant thinkers turned increasingly to philosophical sources for their moral guidance, and from the end of the 18th century were under the influence of the ethics of Kant.* The resulting tradition of 'Christian ethics'* has been marked by a persistent anxiety about how the Kantian doctrine of ethical autonomy can be made at home in a theological context. It has never been as successful as moral theology in the detailed analysis of recurrent moral situations, so that in the face of new social challenges it has often

appeared to be at a loss, limited to edifying reflections about Christian motivation and driven back upon a pragmatic consequentialism in matters of ethical substance. The moral-theological tradition, for all its weaknesses, has yielded valuable insights into such questions as the conduct of war,* medical practice and the role of labour in industry.

There have been frequent calls for a reformation of moral theology (or Christian ethics, for the distinction has no more than a historical usefulness) into a more wide-ranging intellectual enterprise with a greater responsiveness to Scripture than either tradition has displayed in the past. How effectively this demand is being met it is too soon to say. The following points may be taken as recommendations rather than descriptions.

1. Moral theology is distinct from 'spiritual theology' (the study of prayer* and worship;* *cf.* Liturgical Theology;* Spirituality*) and from 'pastoral theology'* (the study of the tasks of Christian ministry), being concerned with questions that are more worldly than the one and more lay-orientated than the other. Yet there will always be interaction between these three fields.

2. The primary task of moral theology is to clarify *Christian moral concepts*, showing how the distinctive Christian ways of posing moral questions (in terms of the command of God [see Law*], love* for the neighbour, the freedom* of faith, the sanctification* of the believer, the forms of created orders, *etc.*) arise from the Scriptures, and comparing them with other ways in which moral questions may be put.

3. Moral theology has to develop in detail certain aspects of *the Christian doctrine of human nature*, especially of society* and government, of sexuality,* and of life and death.* This continues the work of systematic theology* in these areas, and draws upon the relevant biblical commands and injunctions in reaching a systematic view.

4. Moral theology must address the *deliberative questions* faced by individuals or societies in a way that applies what has been learned. These questions will often present themselves in three forms: a. asking about the conduct of the individual believer who has to make a decision for himself (the agent perspective); b. asking about how a believer or the church may advise others who have particular decisions to make (the counselling

perspective); c. asking about the form of an appropriate social rule that might govern practice (the legislative perspective). When these three forms of deliberative questioning are not kept distinct, confusion results.

5. There is no value in the division of moral theology into 'personal' and 'social ethics'* – which fosters the mistaken conception that the personal and the social constitute separate *fields* of moral enquiry, whereas every serious deliberative matter has both personal and social *aspects* to it, as outlined by the threefold distinction in 4. above.

Bibliography

Barth, CD III.4; J. Gustafson, *Protestant and Roman Catholic Ethics* (London, 1979); B. Häring, *The Law of Christ*, 2 vols. (Cork, 1963–67); S. Hauerwas, *The Peaceable Kingdom: A Primer in Christian Ethics* (London, 1984); J. Macquarrie and J. Childress (eds.), *A New Dictionary of Christian Ethics* (London, 1986); H. R. Niebuhr, *Christ and Culture* (New York, 1951); O. O'Donovan, *Resurrection and Moral Order* (Leicester, 1986); P. Ramsey, *Deeds and Rules in Christian Ethics* (New York, 1967); H. Thielicke, *Theological Ethics*, 3 vols. (Grand Rapids, 1966–81).

O.M.T.O'D.

MORMONS, see SECTS.

MURRAY, ANDREW (1828–1917), South African religious leader, evangelist, educator, author of over 250 books and numerous articles on theology, missionary strategy, pastoral concerns and personal devotion. The son of a Scottish Dutch Reformed Church (DRC) minister, he was born in Graaf-Reinet, South Africa, and educated at Aberdeen and Utrecht. He was ordained in 1849 and returned to South Africa to become the first regular DRC minister north of the Orange River. After nine years on the frontier he returned to the Cape Colony where he engaged in a series of theological and legal disputes with liberal clergymen. In 1860 a revival* movement began in his Worcester pastorate which quickly swept through South Africa. Murray became known as a 'revivalist' preacher, and in 1879 began a series of highly successful evangelistic tours throughout South Africa, Europe and America. He is best remembered for his books on personal piety

such as *With Christ in the School of Prayer* (London, 1885), *The New Life* (London, 1891) and *Absolute Surrender* (London, 1895), as well as for his study of Hebrews, *The Holiest of All* (London, 21895).

Although not a Pentecostal* in the modern sense, Murray was deeply influenced by Methodist* holiness* tradition, and through his books *The Spirit of Christ* (London, 1888), *The Second Blessing* (Cape Town, 1891), *The Full Blessing of Pentecost* (London, 1907), and *Divine Healing* (London, 1900), he helped shape modern Pentecostalism.* Bengt Sundkler has argued, in *Zulu Zion and Some Swazi Zionists* (London, 1976), that Murray's teachings and emphasis on Christian experience contributed to the rise of African independent churches.* His works clearly influenced the rise of interdenominational movements such as Inter-Varsity (Christian) Fellowship in the USA and UK, and the theology of the Chinese Christian leader Watchman Nee (1903–72). Nee's work, in turn, has encouraged the growth of transdenominational 'Bible' churches in North America which are similar in many ways to 'independent church' movements in Africa and the Third World.

Although he preached a pietist* message, Murray was involved in South African social life and strongly opposed the growing Afrikaner nationalist movement as well as British imperialism. He was a gifted and unusual man whose influence is still felt in evangelical Christianity.

See also: DUTCH REFORMED THEOLOGY.

Bibliography

J. Du Plessis, *The Life of Andrew Murray of South Africa* (London, 1919).

I.He.

MURRAY, JOHN (1898–1975), Scottish Presbyterian theologian. After fulfilling a promise to teach for one year (1929–30) at his *alma mater* Princeton Theological Seminary, Murray joined the faculty of the newly formed Westminster Seminary, Philadelphia, which J. G. Machen* and others had founded (following the appointment to the Princeton Board of two signatories of the Auburn Affirmation, 1924, which was essentially a plea for the toleration of theological diversity within the Presbyterian church).

An eloquent and thoughtful advocate of the

classical orthodoxy of the Westminster Standards, Murray married that theology to strong personal piety and a deep appreciation of the significance of biblical theology* for dogmatic* thought (an element in his work traceable to the influence of the teaching of G. Vos;* see *Collected Writings*, vol. 2, pp. 1ff.). Murray's teaching and writing were consequently often marked by the close exegetical and theological argument characteristic of his *Commentary on Romans* (Grand Rapids, vol. 1, 1960; vol. 2, 1965).

Of special interest in his thought are: 1. his understanding of biblical covenants* as oathbound promises, which led to his reticence to adopt the classical dual covenant thought of Reformed theology* (*Covenant of Grace*, London, 1954; *Collected Writings*, vol. 2, pp. 49–50); 2. his rooting of the Christian ethic* in the ordinances of creation (*Principles of Conduct*, Grand Rapids, 1957); 3. his exposition of immediate imputation (*The Imputation of Adam's Sin*, Grand Rapids, 1959; see Adam;* Sin*); and 4. his reworking of the doctrine of sanctification* to reflect more fully its definitive as well as progressive character (*Collected Writings*, vol. 2, pp. 277–317).

A deeply committed churchman, Murray served as Moderator of the General Assembly of the Orthodox Presbyterian Church, USA, in 1961.

Bibliography

Collected Writings, 4 vols. (Edinburgh, 1976–83), including I. H. Murray, *The Life of John Murray*, vol. 3, pp. 1–158; Bibliography, vol. 4, pp. 361–375.

S.B.F.

MYSTICAL THEOLOGY, like mysticism, has been defined in so many ways that it is necessary to distinguish its various connotations.

1. It can mean, as it did in the Middle Ages, simply personal experience of God and reflection upon it (see Religious Experience*). In this sense every medieval theologian was a mystic because he wrote about what he himself experienced. Thus Karl Rahner* can affirm that 'the devout Christian of the future will either be a "mystic", one who has "experienced" something, or he will be nothing at all' (*Theological Investigations*, vol. 7, London, 1971, p.15). Theology and

mysticism are equally inseparable in Eastern Orthodox* theology: 'If the mystical experience is a personal working out of the content of the common faith, theology is an expression, for the profit of all, of that which can be experienced by everyone' (Vladimir Lossky, *The Mystical Theology of the Eastern Church*, London, 1957, p.9).

Writers who understand mystical theology in this way as a loving awareness or knowledge of God* see nothing unusual in describing Jesus* and Paul* as mystics and their teaching about prayer,* union* with God and Christ, or life in the Holy Spirit,* as mysticism. They will also point out how deeply steeped in Scripture are mystics like Teresa of Avila and John of the Cross (see below).

2. A more restricted usage of the term confines it to the higher stages of mystical prayer which, like other gifts of the Spirit,* are given as God wills to some and not to others. In this sense mystical theology is distinguished from ascetical* theology, which describes the stages of prayer from the beginnings to the prayer of 'loving attention' or 'simple regard' that goes beyond words. Many writers on prayer consider that this latter type of contemplation is open to every Christian.

3. Protestant writers, though well aware of the relationship between theology and experience of God, have usually been reluctant to speak of mystical theology. The term 'mystical' has suggested confusion with the Graeco-Roman mystery religions, identification with the Neoplatonism of the *Mystical Theology* of Dionysius,* and the errors of Gnosticism* and quietism.* It has also been maintained that mystical theology overlooks the prominent prophetic or ethical element in Scripture (cf. A. Nygren,* *Agape and Eros*, 3 vols., London, 1932–39; G. Ebeling,* *Word and Faith*, London, 1963). Some mystics may have laid themselves open to such charges, sometimes through their attempts to describe the indescribable, but it is impossible to categorize all mystical theology in this way. Each example must be examined in context and assessed on its own merits.

A survey of Western mystical theology down to the 13th century would include the fathers from Augustine* to Bernard of Clairvaux*, Francis of Assisi* and his disciple and biographer Bonaventura,* not forgetting the mystical side of Thomas Aquinas.* Bernard's devotion to the humanity of Christ, maintained in the writings of Aelred of Rievaulx (1110–67), had lasting influence in European mysticism. The other major influence was the apophatic* theology of Dionysius, translated from Greek into Latin by Eriugena* in the 9th century and into a modified English version in the late 14th century by the anonymous author of *The Cloud of Unknowing*. *The Cloud* (which also introduced English readers to the third contemporary influence in European mysticism, the school of St Victor; see Victorines*) appeared *c.* 1370, between the works of Richard Rolle of Hampole (*c.* 1295–1349) and the other flowers of English mysticism: *The Scale of Perfection* of Walter Hilton (d. 1396), the *Showings* or *Revelations of Divine Love* to the anchoress Julian of Norwich (*c.* 1342–1416) and *The Book* of Margery Kempe (*c.* 1373–1433).

Mysticism also flourished during this period in movements of spiritual renewal in Germany and Flanders inspired by Meister Eckhart (*c.* 1260–1327), John Tauler (*c.* 1300–61) and Henry Suso (*c.* 1295–1366). The three were involved with the Rhineland Friends of God (which produced the *Theologia Germanica*, an anonymous plain man's guide to mysticism which Luther* later printed) and indirectly contributed to the Brethren of the Common Life in Flanders by their influence on Jan van Ruysbroeck (1293–1381). Ruysbroeck's disciple Gerard Groot (1340–84) founded the Brethren, thus promoting a spirituality which achieved lasting expression the following century in the writings of Thomas à Kempis (1380–1471; see Imitation of Christ*).

If some of the writings mentioned above suggest that a mystic is concerned only with the inner life of the soul, such an impression would be corrected by a study of the lives of Italian and Spanish mystics such as Catherine of Siena (1347–80), Catherine of Genoa (1447–1510), Ignatius of Loyola,* or Teresa of Avila (1515–82), the Carmelite reformer who produced, like her disciple the poet John of the Cross (1542–91), analyses of the stages of the mystical life which have never been surpassed.

Twentieth-century wrestlings with the relation between prayer and action stretch from Bonhoeffer* to recent liberation theology.* It is a substantial theme in Thomas Merton (1915–68; *cf. Contemplation in a World of Action*, London, 1971), whose work is also important as a pioneering contribution

to the increasingly pressing question of the relationship between mystical theology and religious experience in Christianity and other religions.

Bibliography
Individual volumes in the *Classics of Western Spirituality* series (London and New York, 1978–); A. Bancroft, *The Luminous Vision* (London, 1982); L. Bouyer (ed.), *A History of Christian Spirituality*, 3 vols. (London, 1963–69); P. Grant, *A Dazzling Darkness* (London, 1985); G. Gutiérrez, *We Drink from Our Own Wells* (London, 1984); W. Johnston, *The Wounded Stag* (London, 1985); A. Louth, *The Origins of the Christian Mystical Tradition* (Oxford, 1981); S. Tugwell, *Ways of Imperfection* (London, 1984); G. S. Wakefield (ed.), *A Dictionary of Christian Spirituality* (London, 1984); R. Williams, *The Wound of Knowledge* (London, 1979). Earlier literature, including the classic studies by Otto,* Underhill* and von Hügel* may be traced through the bibliography in R. Woods (ed.), *Understanding Mysticism* (London, 1981).

P.N.H.

MYTH is a confusing and slippery term in theology; it is used in so many ill-defined ways by individual theologians that it would be no bad thing if its use were prohibited. In popular parlance the word is used to refer to stories that are fictional and hence it has come to have a pejorative sense. Traditionally it refers to invented stories about the gods in which they behave like human beings with superhuman powers. Closely associated with this sense of the word is its usage to refer specifically to the stories which may accompany and allegedly form the basis for religious rituals. Thus the Greek myth of Demeter and her daughter Persephone (who married Pluto and spent six months of each year in the underworld with her husband and six months with her mother on earth) was recited in the rites of the mystery religion celebrated at Eleusis near Athens, and was regarded as the justification for performing them. A number of modern writers would argue that such myths reflect in some ways fundamental aspects or modes of human thinking.

As the term is used technically in theological discussion it seems to have four nuances, any or all of which may be present at any one time. 1. A myth may be a story which attempts to explain the origins of things without the use of modern historical and scientific investigation. Myth can thus be represented as pre-scientific thinking, and this may lead to a negative evaluation of it. 2. A myth may depict some aspect of human experience in the form of a story about the past. The story of an original 'social contract' which expresses the structure of society by a fictitious example of 'how it began' would be a myth of this kind. 3. A myth may be a story which is presented in terms of some symbolism and thus has a poetic or emotional appeal and is capable of reinterpretation in the light of fresh experiences. Some of the deepest feelings of people about the human predicament may find expression in mythical form. 4. The term is often used to refer to any kind of story which involves the gods or other supernatural actors.

The story of the fall* of man in Gn. 3 can be seen to function in these ways. 1. It is meant to explain how sin and disobedience came into the world. 2. It is expressive of the present fallen state of mankind, summed up in the statement 'Each of us has become our own Adam' (2 Baruch 54:19). It describes *our* plight in the form of a story. 3. The language contains symbolism that is capable of further development and that may evoke fresh ideas and deeper understanding. 4. The story includes among its actors God and a serpent who miraculously speaks.

To say that this story performs the functions of a myth enables us to recognize a number of facts. 1. To say that a story is a myth is not to pronounce on its historical truth or falsity; it is to say something about how it functions (just as a parable may be historical or fictional). A myth may or may not employ historical materials. For example, F. F. Bruce has commented on the way in which Ex. 1 – 15 functions as the *mythos* of the annual Passover ritual in Israel: 'But – and herein lies the whole *differentia* of Israel's faith as contrasted with the surrounding religions of Old Testament days – the *mythos* in this instance is . . . the recital of something that really happened in history, interpreted as the mighty, self-revealing act of Israel's God' (in C. Brown, *op. cit.* below, p. 80). 2. The important question about a myth is whether it is valid or invalid in the point that it makes:

a myth which tells us that man is fallen is clearly valid whereas a myth asserting that man is not really sinful would be invalid. 3. Myth is a well-recognized literary genre, and there is no reason in principle why the Bible should not contain mythical material. The question regarding the historical truth of a myth must be separated from the question of its validity; a myth may well be valid even though the story is fictitious, just as in the case of parables. A verdict on the literal truth or historicity of Genesis 3, for example, will depend on general considerations regarding the nature of the story and how it came to be composed and also on how we evaluate the NT references to Adam* as a historical person.

The question of the presence of myth in the Bible raises various problems. Some of the NT writers themselves reject the use of what they call 'myths' (1 Tim. 4:7; 2 Pet. 1:16), and thereby indicate that the substance of Christian belief is not akin to pagan myths. So far as the OT is concerned, the writers on the whole did not take over pagan mythology, although, as we have seen, the use of material functioning as myth should not be excluded. One can find some parallels in pagan mythology to biblical concepts and stories in the NT, but again the influence, if any, is marginal.

Difficulties arise when material which appears to be historical is labelled as myth in the sense of being unhistorical. A powerful body of opinion extending from D. F. Strauss* to R. Bultmann* and then to the 'myth of God incarnate' school has argued in one way or another that some central affirmations of Christian faith – the incarnation,* sacrificial death (see Atonement*), resurrection* and second coming of Jesus (see Eschatology*) – are mythical in this sense. Some scholars simply reject such myths and argue that they must be dropped from Christian theology; others hold that these myths 'really' express an understanding of humanity which must be released from its mythological expression (*i.e.* demythologized) and then re-expressed in other terms which will be intelligible to modern men and women who cannot believe in the supernatural.

This proposal is open to basic objections. Fundamentally, it assumes that the modern scientific, materialistic frame of reference is to be the criterion by which the truth of biblical teaching is to be assessed, and it does not sufficiently recognize that such a godless understanding stands judged by biblical teaching. Further, as a result of the slipperiness of the term, it may lump together as 'mythical' a whole set of varied concepts and fail to differentiate between them. For example, the 'three-decker' view of the world held by many ancient people is not essential to the expression of biblical truth and need not be shared by modern people. But to reject this as being 'mythical' or 'pre-scientific' is quite different from rejecting the truth of the incarnation. The danger is to argue that stories involving God are 'mythical' like the three-decker universe, and to fail to recognize that, if myth is defined in terms of 'stories involving God', it is not possible to dispense with myth. To say that the myths are 'really' expressions about the nature and existence of humanity is to fail to recognize that the biblical writers were making the point that any expressions about the existence of humanity must inevitably also be statements about the nature and existence of God. This is not to deny that we may need to find ways of translating the biblical expressions to make them intelligible to modern people; but the whole point of translation is that it faithfully renders in our language what was originally said in another. It would be better to recognize that much of what is often called mythical language is really analogical* or symbolical* language in which we talk about the God who lies beyond the grasp of ordinary literal expressions in terms of analogy with human persons.

Bibliography

H.-W. Bartsch (ed.), *Kerygma and Myth* (London, 1972); C. Brown (ed.), *History, Criticism and Faith* (Leicester, 1976); D. Cairns, *A Gospel Without Myth?* (London, 1960); J. D. G. Dunn, 'Demythologizing – the problem of Myth in the NT', in I. H. Marshall (ed.), *New Testament Interpretation* (Exeter, 1977); R. Johnson, *The Origins of Demythologizing* (Leiden, 1974); G. Stählin in *TDNT* IV, pp. 762–795.

I.H.Ma.

—————N—————

NARRATIVE THEOLOGY. A good deal of the church's difficulty, down the centuries, in finding a method of interpreting the Bible has been experienced particularly in relation to narrative – which constitutes, indeed, a large part of it. Interpretation of narrative has resorted variously to allegory, to an over-exclusive concern for historicity and to a tendency to view it as a quarry of doctrinal statements. Narrative theology, reacting against the last two, is part of a perfectly correct modern concern to do justice to narrative in its own terms, a concern which has produced a dramatic change of interest in the direction of literary appreciation, especially among OT scholars. Narrative theology, in particular, seeks to draw upon modern insights into the way in which narrative has meaning, and to appropriate those insights for theology.

There are two major problems for exponents of narrative theology.

1. In principle it takes for its subject-matter stories drawn from sources beyond as well as within the Bible. A problem of authority* is thus immediately raised. On what grounds do the *biblical* stories commend themselves as sources? And why do the interpretations of *any* stories attain the status of theology?

2. It is undeniable that stories convey truth in a way that is different from that in which theological propositions convey truth; that is, they do it by engaging the imagination.* This means that there is a sense in which the reader must be prepared to perceive 'new' truth – *i.e.* both hitherto unperceived by himself and not expressly contained in the doctrinal statements of the church. The twin problems here are first that there is inevitably a degree of subjectivity about any reader's reading of a piece of narrative, and secondly that it does not seem to be necessary to suppose that the kind of 'openness' that is appropriate in reading narrative entails a rejection, even provisional, of the church's traditional doctrinal statements.

In reading biblical narrative, the question of whether a sensitivity to its character as literature involves a rejection of traditional truth-claims, or merely enriches a traditional understanding of the faith, seems to be a matter of personal or philosophical commitment. The problem is really a form of the perpetual and universal hermeneutical* dilemma: How can one be open to Scripture, while remaining true to 'the faith once delivered'?

Bibliography

D. J. A. Clines, D. M. Gunn and A. J. Hauser, *Art and Meaning* (Sheffield, 1982); H. Frei, *The Eclipse of Biblical Narrative* (New Haven, CT, 1974); R. W. L. Moberly, 'Story in the Old Testament', *Them* 11:3 (1968), pp. 77–82; G. W. Stroup, *The Promise of Narrative Theology* (London, 1984); G. Theissen, *On Having a Critical Faith* (London, 1979).

J.G.McC.

NATURAL LAW, see LAW.

NATURAL THEOLOGY is the attempt to attain an understanding of God and his relationship with the universe by means of rational reflection, without appealing to special revelation* such as the self-revelation of God in Christ and in Scripture.

Three main types of argument for the existence of God have been developed which avoid appealing to special revelation. The ontological argument argues that God's existence is a rational necessity. The cosmological and teleological arguments posit a creator as the ground of cause and purpose in the world. The moral argument traces experience of moral values and obligations to a personal moral creator.

The *ontological argument* was developed by Anselm* in his *Proslogion*. It was restated by rationalist philosophers in the 17th and 18th centuries, and has been much discussed in recent philosophy. It attempts to demonstrate the logical necessity of God's existence by reason alone. In its simplest form the argument defines God as 'that than which no greater can be thought'. To exist in reality is greater than to exist merely in thought. Therefore, 'that than which no greater can be thought' must exist both in reality and in thought.

The argument is generally considered to be fallacious because of its tautological nature.

Merely to define an entity as existing does not provide grounds for inferring its existence. As Kant* pointed out, a merchant cannot increase his wealth merely by adding noughts to the figures in his accounts. Just as the merchant requires justification for the figures in his accounts, so the argument requires justification for defining God as an actually existing 'that than which no greater can be thought'. However, the argument fails to provide such justification. It treats existence as a predicate or quality which makes an actually *existing* 'that than which no greater can be thought' superior to a merely *thought* 'that than which no greater can be thought'. But existence is not a quality which makes an entity which possesses it greater than one which does not. Existence is either there, or it is not there at all. The addition of existence to the definition of God does not, in itself, provide reasons for believing in the existence of God.

The cosmological and teleological arguments figure in the so-called 'Five Ways' of Thomas Aquinas* (*Summa Theologica* I:2:3) which were five ways in which God's existence could be shown. They go back to Aristotle* who taught that God was the First Cause and the Last End of the world. Both arguments appeal to the observed features of human experience.

The *cosmological argument* argues for the existence of a first cause of the cosmos. It asserts that the things we observe in the world all have antecedent causes. Nothing is totally self-caused. We have to posit a self-caused first cause somewhere in the chain of cause and effect. Otherwise, the process of cause and effect would never start. This self-caused first cause is identified with God.

The *teleological* argument (which is sometimes called the physico-theological argument) gets its name from the Gk. word *telos*, meaning 'end'. It observes that things in our experience appear to serve ends beyond their devising or control. Evidence of purpose may be observed in nature. But purpose implies a cosmic mind outside nature with the capacity to implement its purposes. This cosmic mind is identified with God.

The *moral argument* draws attention to the fact that people of different cultures and beliefs recognize certain basic moral values and obligations. These values cannot be reduced to mere convention. Nor can they be derived from the material world. Material things exist on a purely material plane. Moral values imply a dimension of reality which transcends the merely physical. They posit a personal, moral being as the source of all moral values and as the one to whom all moral beings are ultimately responsible. This supreme moral being is identified with God.

The cosmological, teleological and moral arguments each make significant points. But they remain inconclusive as proofs of the existence of the God of the Christian or of any other religion. In and of themselves they do not show that they are talking about the same God. It is an assumption to presuppose that the universe is a single system which must have only one cause, identical with the designer who gave it its purpose. Again, it is an assumption to conclude that the God of any of these arguments is the same as the God of any particular religious faith. Evolutionary theory sets a question mark against the idea that all creatures were created from the beginning with a particular purpose in mind. There are many things in the world for which we cannot specify a purpose. No-one is in a position to say on the basis of observation what is the over-all purpose of the world. The most that we can say is that it bears evidence of structure.

Although some Protestant theologians have made use of natural theology, it has figured much more in Roman Catholic theology than in Reformed theology. Calvin* did not use the above arguments for the existence of God. However, he believed in a general revelation of God in nature and providence,* and spoke of our human 'sense of divinity' or 'sense of God' which was 'the seed of religion' (*Institutes*, I.iii.4). Although marred and corrupted by sin, this awareness of God has not been obliterated. For sure and certain knowledge of God we must turn to the word of God in Scripture.

Natural theology was advocated by the deists* in the 18th century who saw rational religion as the alternative to the mysteries and priestcraft based on revealed religion. The idealism* of Hegel* and F. W. J. von Schelling (1775–1854) in the 19th century, together with Tillich's* existential ontology in the 20th century, are further forms of natural theology. They replaced the transcendent God of Christian theism with a philosophy of being. God ceases to have an existence that is independent of the world. He is viewed as the immanent ground of all being. Christian faith is then adapted to this view of reality.

A major source for the study of natural theology is the Gifford Lectures,* established by Lord Gifford in the 19th century with that end in view. Courses of Gifford lectures have been delivered in the Scottish universities since 1888, and are available to a wider public in their published form.

A contemporary form of natural theology is process theology* which owes its main inspiration to A. N. Whitehead. It has found followers chiefly in North America. Process theology rejects the biblical view of the transcendent God, in favour of a view which makes God a finite factor within evolutionary process.

Karl Barth* rejected all natural theology on the grounds that God reveals himself in his word. It was therefore pointless to look elsewhere for revelation. This view was questioned by Emil Brunner,* who believed that Barth had overstated his case. Brunner pleaded for a Protestant natural theology which he wanted to base on such ideas as the image of God, general revelation, preserving grace, divine ordinances, point of contact, and the contention that grace does not abolish nature, but perfects it.

The Bible itself does not contain arguments for the existence of God. It assumes that God is already known, however imperfectly, and that God makes himself known through his word. His word corrects our distorted knowledge and gives a knowledge which could not be known naturally. General revelation is mentioned in Ps. 19; Rom. 1:18–32; 2:12–16 (though this may refer to Gentile Christians); Acts 14:16–17; 17:27ff. However, the context of these passages shows that this general knowledge needs correcting and supplementing by special revelation. Knowledge that the world was created by the word of God is not inference based on observation but a truth known by faith (Heb. 1:2–3; *cf.* Gn. 1).

If natural theology is seen as an attempt to lay foundations for a revealed theology, the results will prove disappointing. Its arguments will appear fallacious, inconclusive and misleading. On the other hand, recognition of the radical lack of creaturely self-sufficiency at all levels of finite existence poses metaphysical and theological questions which can be answered only on the basis of revelation. The cosmological, teleological and moral arguments do not prove the existence of the God revealed in Scripture. However, they draw attention to the fact that the ultimate question concerning cause, purpose and moral values in the universe cannot be answered by the universe itself. To find answers to the ultimate questions posed by nature, we need to look to the self-revelation of God.

Bibliography

J. Baillie, *Our Knowledge of God* (Oxford, 1939); *idem, The Sense of the Presence of God* (Oxford, 1962); J. Barnes, *The Ontological Argument* (London, 1972); K. Barth and E. Brunner, *Natural Theology* (London, 1946); G. C. Berkouwer, *General Revelation* (Grand Rapids, MI, 1955); F. H. Cleobury, *A Return to Natural Theology* (Cambridge, 1967); W. Craig, *The Cosmological Argument from Plato to Leibniz* (London, 1980); Austin Farrer, *Finite and Infinite* (London, 1943); A. Flew, *God and Philosophy* (London, 1966); J. Hick, *Arguments for the Existence of God* (London, 1970); *idem* and A. McGill (eds.), *The Many-Faced Argument* (London, 1968); B. Lonergan, *Insight* (London, 1957); E. L. Mascall, *He Who Is* (London, 1943); *idem, The Openness of Being: Natural Theology Today* (London, 1971); T. McPherson, *The Argument from Design* (London, 1972); B. S. Mitchell, *The Justification of Religious Belief* (London, 1973); H. P. Owen, *The Moral Argument for Christian Theism* (London, 1965); *idem, The Christian Knowledge of God* (London, 1969); *idem, Concepts of Deity* (London, 1971); A. Plantinga (ed.), *The Ontological Argument* (London, 1968); G. F. Stout, *God and Nature* (Cambridge, 1952); R. Swinburne, *The Coherence of Theism* (Oxford, 1977); *idem, The Existence of God* (Oxford, 1979); *idem, Faith and Reason* (Oxford, 1981); A. E. Taylor, *The Faith of a Moralist*, 2 vols. (London, 1937); W. Temple, *Nature, Man and God* (London, 1934).

C.B.

NATURE, THEOLOGY OF. The term 'nature' translates the Gk. *physis*. If it is taken to connote underived self-existence, it is in opposition to the biblical concept of creation,* according to which nothing comes to be of itself, but only by God's word (*cf.* Jn. 1:3). Understood, however, in the sense of

454

'that which exists prior', *i.e.* prior to some supervening activity, it is used extensively in Christian theology, with two main references: 1. that which is prior to human cultural activity, *i.e.* the natural world; and 2. that which is prior to God's saving grace, *i.e.* human nature.

Nature prior to human culture

In some classical Gk. thought *physis* and *nomos* ('law' or 'convention') are in opposition: *physis* in this connection refers to the human nature common to all, a given constant admitting only of simple acceptance; *nomos* designates the sphere of moral, social and political practice, which may differ between cultures. Another strand of Gk. thought, however, intimates that of itself nature is shaped by law.* Biblical teaching resembles this latter, differing from it in ascribing the law in nature to divine promulgation. Thus Paul's dictum that 'Gentiles who have not the law (*nomos*) do by nature (*physis*) what the law requires' (Rom. 2:14, rsv) assumes an embodiment of God's law in human nature: the application of the same principle to the non-human world may be inferred from certain passages in the OT (*e.g.* Ps. 19).

The divine declaration that creation is 'very good' (Gn. 1:31) establishes the natural world as the proper context for human fulfilment. Mankind's vocation* is to be found in respect for nature and the stewardship* of its order, not in escape from it to a 'higher' freedom. The denial of the goodness of the material universe, contrary to the biblical view, was a feature of certain 2nd-century Gnostic* sects and of the Manichaean* heresy (3rd–5th centuries): they typify the recurrent tendency in the West to assert a radical opposition between inert nature and imposed human ordering. In the modern period the idealist* polarization of nature and spirit and the rejection of the medieval sacralization of nature have frequently led to the denial that the natural order is either knowable or valuable. At the same time the understanding of human vocation has shifted from stewardship of a God-given order to technological manipulation of a recalcitrant environment. Similarly, values have come to be grounded in the purposes imposed on an indifferent universe by the historical creativity of the human spirit (*cf.* Teilhard de Chardin's* doctrine of universal 'hominization'). This relocation of the ground of morality has been rationalized in terms of the supreme value of freedom and the alleged impossibility of deriving 'values' from 'facts'. The discussion of ecological problems and of the character of stewardship demands serious reconsideration of the biblical teaching concerning an inherent order of value in creation. The natural world bears an intrinsic dignity and ordering anterior to its usefulness for human purposes: it may not be treated simply as raw material to be exploited at the convenience of a technologically minded civilization.

The incorporation of law within nature also suggests a role for natural law (see Law*) within Christian ethics,* though the concept is admittedly fraught with difficulties. There are common threads within the many Christian and non-Christian conceptions of natural law: 1. moral and legal precepts are 'objective' (*i.e.* true independently of the will or affections of human agents); 2. they are founded on nature; and 3. they are known to all through reason (however these terms are construed). Thus human morality, despite its apparent diversity, is fundamentally homogeneous; to be human is to share in certain basic conceptions, however much they may be denied through self-interest, passion or corrupt sophistication. Natural law therefore stands against accounts that identify moral reasoning with the mere articulation or expression of preferences (subjectivism and emotivism), the prediction of consequences (utilitarianism), the unguided response to necessarily particular situations (situationism), or the reflection on untranscended communal tradition (communitarianism).

In the classic Christian exposition of natural law (that of Thomas Aquinas,* in *Summa Theologica* II:1:90–105), only a part of moral knowledge is derived from unassisted human reason, namely the basic principles: these comprise the law of non-contradiction and the principle that the good is to be pursued and the bad avoided; also primary precepts concerning murder, lying, stealing, duty to parents, *etc.* The greater part of the substance of moral teaching is provided by divine law (revealed in Scripture*) and conventional human law. But natural law also has a function here: it explains how we can *recognize* moral truths as necessary implications of the basic principles once we have received instruction in them from revelation or culture.* Thus

the doctrine of natural law is not meant to explain how we come by all our moral insights or even (since it is admitted that culture plays a role) how we come by those that are widely accepted. Moreover, it can be given an interpretation compatible with the claim that all knowledge is ultimately dependent on grace.

Nature prior to divine action

In Protestant* theology 'nature' refers most commonly to the unfitness of mankind for God's presence prior to God's intervening act of grace.* Thus 'we were by nature children of wrath' (Eph. 2:3, RSV). In this context the term points to the fallen condition of human nature originally created good but now corrupted. Failure to set the fall* within the context of creation has sometimes left theology misleadingly polarized. Catholicism on the one hand has avoided an unacceptable severance of God the redeemer from God the creator through its division of human nature into a 'natural' part (which is substantially unaltered by the fall) and a 'supernatural' part (which is bestowed by grace), but has been tempted to a Pelagian* optimism about human capacity for good. Protestantism on the other hand has recognized that every part of human nature has been corrupted by sin,* but in its proper emphasis on the absolute human dependence on grace has leant towards a Manichaean denial of creation.

However, the limits of human nature prior to grace, even regardless of the fall, must also be stressed. Against naturalism Christian theology teaches that human beings are not self-sufficient, but require the gracious self-disclosure of God in order to achieve the goal of their existence. Debate about revelation and the possibility of natural theology* must be set within this perspective. Through his work of salvation God gave himself to humankind in a new way, not already implicit in creaturely human existence. The knowledge of God is given as a 'mystery hidden for ages . . . but now . . . manifest' (Col. 1:26, RSV): in the person of Christ is imparted the fullness of grace and the promise of glory. Human nature is called to fulfilment in the supernatural, which transcends but does not abolish or destroy it. The same may be said about created nature as a whole: it is God's plan to 'unite all things in [Christ], things in heaven and things on earth' (Eph. 1:10, RSV).

455

Bibliography
K. Barth, *CD*, III.1–2; J. Finnis, *Natural Law and Natural Rights* (Oxford, 1980); C. S. Lewis, *The Abolition of Man* (Oxford, 1943); Jürgen Moltmann, *God in Creation* (London, 1985); D. J. O'Connor, *Aquinas and Natural Law* (London, 1967); O. O'Donovan, *Resurrection and Moral Order* (Leicester, 1986).

O.M.T.O'D. and R.J.S.

NEO-ORTHODOXY. This title is applied to a 20th-century development in theology, which is 'orthodox' inasmuch as it emphasizes key themes of Reformed theology, but 'neo-', *i.e.* 'new', inasmuch as it has taken serious account of contemporary cultural and theological developments. It originated with continental theologians: Barth,* Brunner,* Bultmann* and Friedrich Gogarten (1887–1967) but others have become associated with it such as Aulén,* Nygren,* Tillich,* C. H. Dodd,* Richardson,* J. Baillie,* D. M. Baillie,* Reinhold Niebuhr* and H. Richard Niebuhr.* It was in no sense an organized movement, and precise definitions or boundaries are impossible.

Neo-orthodoxy emerged in reaction against the liberal* Protestantism which had dominated the end of the 19th century and the beginning of the 20th. In particular, it rejected the notion that historical investigation could provide absolute certainty as to the events recorded in Scripture,* upon which scholars had hoped to build secure theology. Further, it renounced the attempt to make man's experience of God a starting-place for theology (*cf.* Religious Experience*). The crisis in human culture* epitomized by World War I precipitated a recognition of the bankruptcy of a theology which had been naively optimistic.

In searching for a new way to do theology, the work of Kierkegaard,* the rediscovery of Luther,* and the novels of the Russian author Fyodor Dostoevsky* became influential. Driven back to the Bible, and spurred on by the need to be able to engage with contemporary social issues, a new method of theology was developed which nevertheless could not ignore the discoveries which had been made by the application of the historical-critical method to Scripture (see Biblical Criticism;* Hermeneutics*).

Neo-orthodoxy affirmed the absolute transcendent 'otherness' of God whom man cannot know except God reveal himself. This he has done primarily through Jesus Christ but also in the events of salvation-history* to which Scripture bears witness. Neo-orthodoxy accepted the results of historical inquiry showing Scripture to be a human, fallible and errant document, because its certainty was thought to lie in the fact that God has chosen to make himself known through it. It is theologically reliable as a means whereby God in Christ may be encountered.

This foundation seemed a more secure basis for theology than questionable historical events or religious experience capable of alternative secular explanations.

On the basis of an encounter with the word of God, incarnate, written and preached, the neo-orthodox theologians affirmed the sinful predicament of humanity redeemed through the grace* of God in Christ alone. Receptive faith* was the only way to enter a saving relationship with God; indeed only those who believe can know God, or know how to please him. They thus espoused the key Reformation* principles of *sola gratia* and *sola Scriptura*.

While some common theological features characterized those dubbed neo-orthodox, sharp disagreements arose as to how to work these out in a systematic theological way. For example Tillich and Bultmann were prepared to be influenced by contemporary philosophy more than Barth thought permissible; and Brunner's espousal of general revelation* (*cf.* Natural Theology*) caused a sharp dispute.

Classic critiques of this position suggest: 1. Neo-orthodoxy can offer no justification for basing itself on God's revelation known only by faith (lest faith become sight), since this renders its foundation impervious to verification* or falsification. 2. The emphasis on the transcendent 'otherness' of God led to extreme scepticism about whether talk about God was possible, and indeed whether such a God any longer existed (*cf.* Death-of-God Theology*). 3. Pannenberg* and others challenged its view of secular history as essentially uncertain, susceptible of differing interpretations and separable from God's activity in the world, for they regarded revelation as history. 4. Neo-orthodoxy can have no reply to those who claim to have encountered God through other religions and would therefore adopt an alternative basis to their theology.

Bibliography

G. C. Berkouwer, *A Half Century of Theology* (Grand Rapids, 1977); J. Livingston, *Modern Christian Thought* (London, 1971); H. R. Mackintosh, *Types of Modern Theology* (London, 1937); W. Nicholls, *Pelican Guide to Modern Theology*, vol 1: *Systematic and Philosophical Theology* (Harmondsworth, 1969); S. Sykes, *The Identity of Christianity* (London, 1984).

C.A.B.

NEO-PLATONISM, see PLATONISM.

NESTORIUS (*fl.* 428–*c.* 451), Patriarch of Constantinople, as an extreme exponent of the Antiochene* Christology* has his name attached to the heresy of the two persons, a divine and a human, existing in juxtaposition in the incarnate Christ. A pupil probably of Theodore of Mopsuestia (*c.* 350–428), Nestorius was a monk and presbyter at Antioch before his elevation to the see of Constantinople by Theodosius II. His Christology, for which he was eventually condemned, was elaborated in relation to the question of the legitimacy of the term *theotokos* ('bearer of God', commonly translated 'mother of God') in reference to the Virgin Mary.* His chaplain at Constantinople, Anastasius, objected to its increasing usage, especially by monks. Nestorius gave him his support and himself declared the designation unscriptural and going 'best with those who deny Christ's true humanity'. Instead Nestorius preferred *anthropotokos* ('bearer of man') or *Christotokos* ('bearer of Christ'). In his structure of Christ's person Nestorius made a clear-cut distinction between the human and the divine natures (which he seems to have equated with 'persons') in Christ, denying any real organic union between the man Jesus and the indwelling divine Logos.*

The extant fragments of his sermons and his 'Twelve Counter-Anathemas' reiterate, 'Not one nature but two are we constrained to concede to Christ' (*Fragments* 216). The theme is constant, Christ 'is not divided', 'the Son of God is double in his natures'. Throughout, the *theotokos* issue is discussed and the conclusion restated, 'The Virgin bore indeed the Son of God, but since the Son of God is twofold in his nature, she bore the manhood, which is Son because of the Son who is joined thereto' (*Sermons* x).

Cyril of Alexandria's* vehement opposition and his 'Twelve Anathemas against Nestorius' brought about the patriarch's condemnation by the Council of Ephesus (431). He died in exile somewhere in the East.

Nestorius maintained his orthodoxy, declaring that the Scriptures show Christ to have been truly divine and as such not involved in human suffering and change. The same Scriptures present Christ as having lived a truly human life of growth, temptations and suffering. The only way to understand the relation of these two distinct elements, that of full Godhead and of full manhood, is to acknowledge their separate presence in a 'common *prosōpon*' of union. 'Christ is indivisible in that he is Christ, but he is twofold, in that he is both God and man, he is one in his Sonship, but he is twofold in that which takes and in that which is taken. In the *prosōpon* of the Son he is an individual, but as in the case of two eyes he is separate in the natures of manhood and Godhead' (*Fragments* 297).

Although Nestorius was condemned for heresy by the excessive zeal and vindictiveness of Cyril, the question of his actual unorthodoxy has persisted. The discovery of Nestorius' *The Bazaar of Heracleides* in a Syriac translation in 1910 reopened the issue. Opposing verdicts have been returned. J. F. Bethune-Baker declares that Nestorius was no Nestorian; while F. Nau upholds his condemnation. *The Bazaar* is consistent in its rejection of the designation 'Mother of God', while strongly asserting the full manhood of Christ as necessary for salvation. Cyril's objections are countered one by one and his monophysitic* statements rebutted. Nestorius denies that he admits only a moral union of the two natures, by declaring it to be 'syntactic' and 'voluntary'.

Nestorius' defence of his orthodoxy was accepted by several Eastern bishops who continued to acknowledge his primacy after the Council of Ephesus and united to form a separate Nestorian Church. The Nestorian Christians, characterized by a vigorous missionary zeal, carried the gospel to India and Arabia. In the 13th and 14th centuries their adherents suffered greatly in the Mogul invasions. Groups of 'Assyrian Christians' survive who consider themselves Nestorians and prohibit the designation 'Mother of God'.

Bibliography

G. R. Driver and L. Hodgson (trs.), *Bazaar* (Oxford, 1925); A. Grillmeier, *Christ in Christian Tradition*, vol. 1: *From the Apostolic Age to Chalcedon AD 451* (London, ²1975); R. V. Sellers, *Two Ancient Christologies* (London, 1940).

H.D.McD.

NEW ENGLAND THEOLOGY. This is a general name for the theological tradition which stretched from Jonathan Edwards* to Edwards Amasa Park (1808–1900). Although the New England theologians all called themselves Calvinists,* they did not share entirely similar beliefs. Rather, it was a common approach to theology combining practical morality with philosophical speculation and a common fascination for issues like the freedom of the human will which set the tradition apart.

Jonathan Edwards' efforts to describe and defend the revival in colonial America known as the Great Awakening defined the distinctive concerns of the New England theology. To an unusual degree, Edwards brought together penetrating insight into religious experience,* sophistication in the use of current philosophy, and firm commitment to Calvinistic convictions. His books such as *The Freedom of the Will* (1754) and *Original Sin* (1758) defended divine sovereignty* in salvation* over against contemporary views arguing for autonomous moral action. His works of practical divinity such as *A Treatise on the Religious Affections* (1746) and *The Nature of True Virtue* (1765) provided tests to judge the reality of spiritual experiences. The major emphases of Edwards' theology were the greatness of God, total dependence upon God for salvation, and the intrinsic value of the holy life. By promoting these concerns through careful attention to both practical Christianity and recondite philosophical argumentation, he marked out the path for his followers.

Two of Edwards' students, Joseph Bellamy (1719–90) and Samuel Hopkins (1721–1803), provided a transition to the major New England theologians of the 19th century. Bellamy defended at length Edwards' belief that church membership should be reserved for those who made credible profession of saving faith. Hopkins developed Edwards' ethics* into an entire system of what he called 'disinterested benevolence'. But as they adopted their teacher's ideas, they also began subtly to change them. Bellamy gave more emphasis to a governmental view of the atonement* whereby God's sense of right and wrong, rather than his wrath, was the key to understanding the work of Christ. Hopkins came to regard sin* as a quality not so much of human character as of human action.

The New Englanders who came after Bellamy and Hopkins made still further alterations in the Edwardsean legacy, but like them they shared Edwards' twin commitment to revival and theological precision. Jonathan Edwards, Jr. (1745–1801) more firmly set aside the view of God as jealous sovereign. Timothy Dwight (1752–1817), a grandson of Edwards, placed greater stress on the reasonableness of Christian faith and on the natural powers of the human will. Dwight's most influential student, Nathaniel William Taylor (1786–1858), became the most prominent exponent of New England views during the mid-19th century. From his position in the chair of theology at the Yale Divinity School, Taylor reversed the elder Edwards on the will by contending for a natural power of free choice. The last major theologian of this school, E. A. Park, held forth over a long career from Andover Theological Seminary near Boston. He attempted to draw back closer to Edwards, but still held views on natural human capacity and the character of sin which were more characteristic of his century's moral optimism than of Edwards' moral realism.

All of the New England theologians were 'close' reasoners. This strength could sometimes lead to dry preaching, but it could also result in a fruitful conjunction of practical piety and learned theology. In the 1930s when theologians like Joseph Haroutunian (b. 1904) and H. Richard Niebuhr* rediscovered this tradition, they concentrated their attention on Edwards rather than his successors. To them, Edwards had seen more clearly the dangers to Christianity of optimistic opinions about human nature. Historians since Haroutunian and Niebuhr have not so much altered their judgments as pointed out the care and intelligence with which Edwards' successors also went about their work.

See also: EDWARDS, JONATHAN; NEW HAVEN THEOLOGY; WILL.

Bibliography
A. C. Cecil, *The Theological Development of Edwards Amasa Park: Last of the Consistent Calvinists* (Tallahassee, FL, 1983); J. A. Conforti, *Samuel Hopkins and the New Divinity Movement* (Grand Rapids, MI, 1981); F. H. Foster, *A Genetic History of the New England Theology* (Chicago, IL, 1907); J. Haroutunian, *Piety Versus Moralism: The Passing of the New England Theology* (New York, 1932); B. Kuklick, *Churchmen and Philosophers: From Jonathan Edwards to John Dewey* (New Haven, CT, 1985); H. R. Niebuhr, *The Kingdom of God in America* (New York, 1937); B. B. Warfield, 'Edwards and the New England Theology,' in *The Works of Benjamin B. Warfield*, vol. IX: *Studies in Theology* (New York, 1932), pp. 515–540.

M.A.N.

NEW HAVEN THEOLOGY was the last important stage of the New England theology* which had begun with the work of Jonathan Edwards.* Its name derived from the Divinity School at Yale College in New Haven, Connecticut. The first professor of theology at that seminary, Nathaniel William Taylor (1786–1858), was also its most influential proponent.

Taylor's background included several divergent aspects of New England's theological history. He grew up in an 'Old Calvinist' community which questioned the rigorous views promoted by Jonathan Edwards. He then attended Yale College, where a grandson of Edwards, Timothy Dwight (1752–1817), was president. Dwight was not only a winsome individual and a solid theologian in his own right; he was also an ardent promoter of revival in the manner of his grandfather. In his later work, Taylor would reflect this early training. He was wary of traditional Calvinistic* (or Augustinian*) solutions to problems such as the nature of sinfulness, the innate capacity of the human will, and the character of divine justice, but he was also fervently committed to revival and societal reform.

Timothy Dwight's theological work helped prepare the way for Taylor. Dwight's concern for revival led him to emphasize the natural human ability to respond to the gospel more heavily than Edwards had. And his efforts to defend the faith reasonably gave it more of a rationalistic tone than had been the case with his famous grandfather.

Taylor, first as pastor of an influential Congregational church in New Haven and then as Yale's professor of theology, engaged in lengthy polemics against both the emerging Unitarian* party and Calvinists who were more conservative than himself. Although Taylor still regarded himself as a successor of Edwards, he went even further than Dwight in modifying Edwards' views, especially in regard to human nature. In his day Taylor was best known for his argument that people always had a 'power to the contrary' when faced with the choice for God. He also contended that human sinfulness arose from sinful acts, not from sinful nature inherited from Adam.* Everyone did sin, Taylor held, but this was not a result of God's predestinating action or the imputation of Adam's guilt.

One of the things that explains Taylor's theological convictions is the fact that he was much impressed with the Scottish philosophy of common sense.* Unlike the Presbyterian Calvinists of Princeton Seminary in New Jersey, who used the Scottish philosophy mostly as a guide to theological method, Taylor made the Scottish conception of an internal 'moral sense' a critical feature of his ethics.* For Taylor, the intuitive deliverances of this 'moral sense' – for example, that the will had a self-determining power – constituted conclusive theological demonstration.

The New Haven theology became a powerful engine for revival and reform when it was taken up by activists such as Taylor's friend, Lyman Beecher (1775–1863). Beecher and like-minded revivalists used its principles in evangelizing the western United States and in promoting the moral reform of the country. The New Haven theology traced its origins to a colonial Calvinist, Jonathan Edwards, but it exerted its greatest influence in an America which had largely set aside the earlier Calvinistic convictions of its Puritan ancestors.

See also: NEW ENGLAND THEOLOGY; REVIVAL, THEOLOGY OF.

Bibliography
F. H. Foster, *A Genetic History of the New*

England Theology (Chicago, IL, 1907); B. Kuklick, *Churchmen and Philosophers: From Jonathan Edwards to John Dewey* (New Haven, CT, 1985); S. E. Mead, *Nathaniel William Taylor: A Connecticut Liberal* (Chicago, IL, 1942); N. W. Taylor, *The Moral Government of God* (New York, 1859).

M.A.N.

N EW RELIGIONS is the more neutral name of groups commonly called 'cults' or 'sects'.* The problem with the word 'cult' is that it lacks theoretical definition and has been used by the media to refer to many groups considered legitimate by evangelical Christians. Thus American Jewish groups have labelled 'Jews for Jesus' and other evangelical Jewish groups 'cults', while humanists have attacked Campus Crusade and the Navigators as cultic.

The sociologist Rodney Stark suggests that a cult is either a 'new faith' which has been 'imported from another society' or the result of 'cultural innovation'. Generally, however, evangelicals have used the term 'cult' to refer to religious groups which deviate from some recognized standard of evangelical orthodoxy. Given the confusion created by the popularization of the term 'cult' in the media, most social scientists prefer to talk about 'new religious movements'.

Many evangelical books such as J. K. van Baalen's *The Chaos of the Cults* (1936) and Walter Martin's *The New Cults* (1980) give extensive historical and doctrinal descriptions of specific religious movements such as the Mormons and The Way. But although this approach is useful it has the great weakness that the popularity of new religions is constantly changing. In the mid-1960s Transcendental Meditation was the most popular group, in the early 1970s the Divine Light Mission rose to prominence, then in the mid-1970s the Unification Church (Moonies) seemed to be the fastest-growing movement. But by the early 1980s the Rajneeshies were the largest new religion in America, excluding the various fundamentalist-type groups like The Way and the Local Church which were still growing. Each of these groups experienced a period of rapid growth followed by spectacular decline. Therefore the likelihood of meeting members of a new and relatively unknown group is high. For this reason, it is better to understand in general how groups grow and the dynamics of religious belief systems, rather than learning specific details about groups which may already be dying out.

At the core of new religions lies a realm of experience which reflects the spiritual needs of individuals (see Religious Experience*). This core includes experience such as revelatory dreams, visions, pre-cognition, extra-sensory perception, a sense of awe, a sense of presence, ghosts, dread, *etc*. In assessing these experiences, all we are required to do is recognize that people believe them to be real.

Secondly, in addition to the experiential core, new religions thrive on what may be labelled 'the new mythology', which is a collection of largely unconnected beliefs representing the folk religion of our society. This mythology includes belief in things like UFOs, mystic healings, astrology (see Occult*), reincarnation (see Metempsychosis*) and a host of similar ideas which are un-Christian and relatively new in Western society. The importance of these myths is that they provide a conceptual framework within which supposed 'spiritual' experiences can be interpreted.

Thirdly, all new religions draw upon the great religious traditions to provide them with a sense of philosophy and a basic theology. The great religious traditions may be phenomenologically divided into two main types: the Abramic and the Yogic. The Abramic represents the religions of Abraham: Christianity, Islam and Judaism. The Yogic represents religions of Indian origin, which have the practice of yoga or meditation at their core. The two most important Yogic religious traditions are Hinduism and Buddhism.

The final element in the analysis of new religions is the role played by a belief in science or modernity. All new religions claim in one way or another to represent a 'true science', even though, like the Hare Krishna Movement, they may reject modern science. This belief in 'true science' functions as a pseudo-religion which is encouraged by popular ideas about evolution and the tendency to 'believe in' rather than understand science. Thus faith-in-science replaces the scientific method in the lives of many people; and they are easy targets for the extravagant claims of new religions, which mingle psychic healing, extra-sensory perception, UFOs and a host of other credulous ideas with claims about revelations and doctrines drawn from the great religious traditions.

The synthesis of traditions can be seen in groups like the Unification Church which combines Abramic beliefs with Korean folk religion and a faith in technology. Hare Krishna on the other hand represents a Yogic tradition in a relatively pure form, while Scientology is primarily a religion of modernity which draws upon Yogic ideas to strengthen its religious appeal. Each of these new religions is reinforced by elements of the new mythology and a strong experiential core which builds on the life experience of their members.

Contrary to the claims of books like *Snapping* (1978), members of new religions are not brainwashed. In fact the idea of brainwashing as an explanation of conversion was first popularized by William Sargant in *Battle for the Mind*, and was intended to explain evangelical conversion. Although *Snapping* deals primarily with members of the Unification Church, and therefore has appealed to many evangelicals, the authors make it very clear that they consider evangelicals to be a prime example of brainwashing (*cf. Snapping*, p. 46).

Sociologists David Bromley and Anson D. Shupe present evidence against the brainwashing thesis in *Strange Gods* (1982), as do a number of other authors including the Ontario Government's special investigator in in his report *Study of Mind Development Groups, Sects and Cults in Ontario* (1980). More importantly, as psychiatrist Saul V. Levine of the University of Toronto shows in various articles, people who join new religions do so because the group concerned meets a psychological need.

Considerable evidence now exists to show that membership of new religions depends on conversion experiences and individual choice rather than mysterious psychological control. It is true that strong social pressures are exerted to encourage membership and discourage people from leaving. But it is a fact that most people who join new religions leave of their own choice after a relatively short time.

Essentially people join new religions because those religions meet real needs. In this sense, van Baalen's observation that 'the cults are the unpaid bills of the church' still holds true. Anyone wishing to communicate with members of a new religious group must, therefore, take the converts' conversion seriously and attempt to discover what it was that caused them to convert and why they found that particular group attractive. The process of encouraging someone who has joined a new religion to reveal why they did so is usually a long one, and requires considerable tact and understanding. But unless Christians are prepared to enter into real dialogue prior to presenting the Christian message, communication will inevitably break down and each party will lose respect for the other. In dealing with members of new religions, principles of personal evangelism apply at least as much as they do in other situations. Unfortunately, the label 'cult' often obscures this fact and charges of 'brainwashing' provide an excuse for hasty rejection and name-calling. Such an approach is both un-Christian and counter-productive. For this reason, understanding the logic of the beliefs of new religious movements, and the psychology which led to a given individual's conversion, is important if Christians are to participate in an increasingly important arena of discussion and evangelism.

Bibliography

J. K. van Baalen, *The Chaos of the Cults* (Grand Rapids, MI, 1936); D. Bromley and A. D. Shupe, *Strange Gods* (Boston, MA, 1982); F. Conway and J. Siegelman, *Snapping: America's Epidemic of Sudden Personality Change* (Philadelphia, 1978); I. Hexham and K. Poewe, *Understanding Cults and New Religions* (Grand Rapids, MI, 1986); D. G. Hill, *Study of Mind Development Groups, Sects and Cults* (Toronto, 1980); W. Martin, *The New Cults* (Santa Ana, CA, 1980); W. Sargant, *Battle for the Mind* (London, ²1959); R. Stark with W. S. Bainbridge, *The Future of Religion: Secularization, Revival and Cult Formation* (Berkeley, CA, 1985); S. M. Tipton, *Getting Saved from the Sixties* (Berkeley, CA, 1982).

I.He.

NEW TESTAMENT THEOLOGY is of comparatively recent origin as a recognized subject within theological studies.

1. History

The discipline of NT theology emerged at the beginning of the 19th century, largely as the result of the influence of the Enlightenment*

461

on biblical studies. (The four-volume work in German, of G. L. Bauer, 1800–02, is apparently the first NT theology.) Earlier, biblical theology* had originated in 17th-century Protestant orthodoxy to aid dogmatics* (systematic theology*) by presenting the biblical passages supporting the various doctrines of the church, and then in pietism* to renew the theology and life of the church by purging its doctrinal formulations of what were perceived to be speculative, philosophically foreign elements. In the context of the Enlightenment, however, biblical theology took on a radically different cast (cf. the epoch-making inaugural lecture of J. P. Gabler on the difference between biblical and dogmatic theology, 1787). The Enlightenment's fundamental commitment was to the autonomy of human reason ('Man, the measure of all things'). This involved rejection of the verbal inspiration and final authority of Scripture, which was to be treated like any other book of purely human origin, subject to the then-emerging 'historical-critical' method of interpretation (see Biblical Criticism*). This denial of inspiration meant further that the canonical integrity of Scripture could no longer be maintained (cf. the influential multivolume work of J. S. Semler on the 'free investigation' of the canon, 1771–75). Consequently, the unity of the OT and NT was increasingly called into question, and the search for a biblical theology (in the sense of a single theology of the whole Bible) gave way to considering each testament separately. With this development NT theology as a particular discipline was born.

Denial of verbal inspiration inevitably led to a disjunction between revelation* (truth) and the Bible; what the human authors teach cannot simply be equated with the word of God. NT theology, therefore, soon perceived that it had to distinguish between a *descriptive* task (what do the various NT writers in fact teach and wish to have believed?) and a *normative* task (what after all in the NT is to be taught and believed today?). Consequently, throughout the course of the 19th century, NT theology unfolds as an ongoing effort to ascertain the abiding validity and authority of the NT. The position of F. C. Baur (1792–1860; see Tübingen School*) was an especially bold attempt to join the descriptive and normative tasks in one: the NT, analysed as comprising flatly contradicting theological

viewpoints at its core (Jewish-Petrine in conflict with Gentile-Pauline Christianity), documents the advance of 'spirit' (Geist) to the freedom of self-consciousness; Christianity is the absolute religion because, especially in its earliest history (Jesus and Paul), it embodies the unparalleled manifestation of the absolute.

This viewpoint was bound up with the speculative metaphysics of Hegel,* including his dialectical view of history, and its direct influence gradually waned. Toward the end of the century NT theology for the most part became a purely descriptive discipline. The predominant approach was to identify the controlling 'doctrinal concept' (Lehrbegriff) for each of the NT authors and then to note the similarities and differences between them. The tendency of this approach was to draw the conclusion, similar to that of Baur, that the NT is marked by competing, or at least conflicting, theologies (e.g., H. J. Holtzmann [1832–1910], in 1897). The normative element was located almost invariably in the teaching of Jesus (reconstructed primarily out of Mark), who, despite the application of historical-critical principles, premised on respect for the historical distance between the interpreter and the text, ended up sounding suspiciously like a neo-Kantian moralist (see Liberalism, German*).

A programmatic essay by Wilhelm Wrede (1859–1906) on the task and methods of NT theology (1897) proved to be extremely important because it convincingly clarified the path NT theology had chosen to travel since the Enlightenment, and so shaped the course of subsequent developments in this century to the present. For Wrede the designation 'NT theology' is a total misnomer (the essay's title refers to 'so-called NT theology'). The NT is not a record of abstract theological reflections, but of living religion; it does not contain various doctrinal concepts about faith, hope, love, etc., but expresses the writers' *actual* believing, hoping, loving, etc. Moreover, confining attention to the NT as a complete or closed collection is arbitrary; canonicity is a subsequent imposition on the NT documents. In reality they are the surviving literary fragments of earliest Christianity, and belong together in a continuum, with other early Christian literature (see Apostolic Fathers*), as well as contemporary non-Christian religious writings. Wrede was an advocate of the 'history-of-religions'* approach. This represented rigorous outworking of autonomous historical method, and sought to explain the origin of Christianity exhaustively in terms of religious and cultural factors already resident within the 1st-century Mediterranean world. Consequently, Wrede insisted that, if NT theology would remain faithful to its Enlightenment roots, it must be an exclusively descriptive discipline with a purely historical approach. When it becomes oriented to the normative concerns of a modern statement of faith (systematic theology), it tends to falsify its task.

The most imposing and influential response so far to Wrede's challenge is that of Bultmann.* The task of an interpreter is to understand an author better than the author himself. This basic hermeneutical* stance, in turn, gives rise to a distinction between what the NT writers *said* and what they *meant*. The diverse, often self-contradictory teaching of the NT focuses on the person and activity of Jesus, cast in the language and concepts of a long-outdated, mythical* view of the world. But the *intention* of this teaching – to give expression to the contingent freedom of man, the openness of human existence to the experience of transcendence, and the authentic eschatological existence effected in the cross of Jesus – this (demythologized) intention is thoroughly relevant to modern man and the concerns of contemporary Christian faith. Bultmann's NT theology (1948–53) represents the effort to do full justice to the demands of a purely historical approach, but in a way that, without compromising autonomous historical reconstruction, puts it in the service of an interpretation of the NT that has something to say to the present.

Bultmann's programme has been challenged, especially because his interpretation of the NT (demythologization) was so heavily dependent on the categories of modern existentialism.* The work of O. Cullmann (b. 1902) exemplifies the opposite pole of reaction to Bultmann. Although Cullmann believes that both Jesus and the apostles mistakenly expected his imminent return, he maintains that the various NT writers all share the same basic salvation-historical* outlook and that this outlook is in large measure directly applicable to the present. As the 20th century draws to a close, however, the search for a single, unified NT theology

has largely been abandoned as demonstrably unattainable. The accent falls on the NT as comprising ('canonizing') doctrinal divergence and theological tensions, in which the slender unifying thread is continuity between the historical Jesus and the exalted Christ (*e.g.*, E. Käsemann,* J. D. G. Dunn).

Outside the dominant historical-critical tradition, works on NT theology are few and relatively recent. This in large measure is due to the persistent, widespread influence of the perception, originating with the Enlightenment, that recognizing the historical conditioning of the biblical documents necessitates denying their verbal inspiration. G. Vos* led the way in effectively challenging this perception and the dilemma it poses by outlining the programme for, and then developing, a biblical theology premised on the verbal inspiration and canonical unity of Scripture. Major NT theologies in this tradition are those of G. E. Ladd (1974) and D. Guthrie (1981). The discussion that follows is confined to this approach to NT theology.

2. Structure and content

NT theology, a major subdivision of biblical theology, presupposes, in this tradition, the verbally inspired origin and canonical unity of the NT. These presuppositions, in turn, are confirmed in carrying out its task, which is to set forth the teaching present in the NT as a whole.

Several factors serve to clarify this task:

a. Progressive revelation. The Bible did not originate in one piece as a doctrinal handbook or a manual of ethics. Rather, made up of diverse literary genres, it is a record of the history of special revelation,* a history of which its own production (inscripturation; see Scripture*) is a part. This long history begins as early as the garden of Eden and, after the fall,* continues as God's ongoing redemptive* activity, accompanied by his own attesting and interpreting word, primarily in his covenantal* dealings with Israel, until its culmination in the person and work of Christ. Biblical revelation, then, is essentially redemptive, or covenantal-historical, and the concern of biblical theology is to explore and clarify this historically progressive and differentiated character of special revelation.

b. The end-point of revelation. The concern of the NT is not so much with the process of revelation as it is with the end-point of that process. Ongoing development and progress is, rather, a structural mark of the OT. This difference is reflected in the observation that the OT is written over a span of approximately 1,000 years and covers a period considerably longer, while the NT is completed in a little more than one generation and focuses on the ministry of Jesus and its immediate historical consequences. Further, in view of the eschatological* nature of this ministry, and so of the NT focus on it, the NT is the eschatological end-point of the revelation process (cf. Heb. 1:1–2, where, following on the ongoing process of old covenant revelation 'at many times and in various ways', the Son is God's final, 'last days' revelation). This is not to deny an element of progression in NT revelation (the ministry of John the Baptist → the earthly ministry of Jesus → the founding of the church). This progression is in fact basic to the message of the NT; the gospel stands or falls with the historical sequence from the humiliation (sufferings and death) to the exaltation (resurrection and ascension) of Christ. But development within these basic phases is not highlighted, and a detailed pattern is difficult to establish convincingly, especially for the apostolic church. The NT writers are much more concerned, each in his own way, with the reality of Christ's death and resurrection, together with his still future return, as the consummation of redemptive history. Their attention centres, variously, on this great event-complex and on its implications for the life of the church in the world. As the record of the redemptive-historical end-point, the NT is basically a composite of (verbally inspired) testimonies to Christ from a post-resurrection perspective; the NT is a diverse and essentially synchronic witness to the crucified and now exalted Jesus.

c. Jesus and the NT writers. The teaching of Jesus is not a canon within the canon, as if his teaching, because of his incomparable person and work, were somehow the most pure and profound expression of truth in the NT, in relation to the peripheral, less important teaching of the apostles.* The relationship between Jesus, including his teaching, and the apostles (and other NT writers) is 'in general that between the fact to be interpreted and the subsequent interpretation of this fact' (G. Vos, *Biblical Theology*,

p. 325). The organic unity of the NT is such that the teaching of Jesus and the teachings of the apostles are incomplete and ultimately unintelligible apart from each other. The latter are the necessary amplification and expression of the former, especially as they are from a post-exaltation perspective; the former is the indispensable presupposition and roots of the latter.

d. Unity and diversity. How the unmistakable diversity of NT teaching is assessed is crucial. This diversity is not simply the relative, human, historical side of the NT, in contrast or even in tension with its unity or divinity (revelation, truth, abiding validity) somehow present within the diversity. Diversity is certainly a function of the multiple human authorship of the NT, but ultimately and even more properly it stems from the unique divine origin of the NT (cf. 1 Thes. 2:13, where Paul says of his teaching, indelibly stamped as it was by his own personality and capacities, 'not . . . the word of men, but as it actually is, the word of God'). To explore the diversity of the NT is not merely to be occupied with its humanity, but is to be involved directly in the varied riches of God's revelation. The tendency to suppress or ignore the historical particularity of NT teaching and to harmonize or unify prematurely, perhaps out of the apologetically motivated fear that to stress diversity will relativize or otherwise undermine unity, is wrong; it does a serious disservice to the NT, because ultimately it obscures 'the manifold [many-sided, multi-faceted; *polypoikilos*] wisdom of God' (Eph. 3:10). The unity of the NT is unity in diversity; better, reflecting the person of God himself, it is unity *as* diversity.

e. Analytic or thematic method? There are two basic ways to present a NT theology: either in terms of the specific and perhaps distinctive teachings, in turn, of each of the various writers; or in terms of the major themes of NT teaching as a whole. Neither of these methods excludes the other. The thematic approach should take into consideration the particular contributions of each author; the analytic approach should show the interrelationships and coherence among the various groups of writings. On the whole, however, the analytic method is preferable for at least two reasons: i. It safeguards adequate attention to the diversity of the NT, which the thematic approach tends to minimize; ii. It makes NT theology more serviceable than does the thematic method to systematic theology, which in its unifying topical (thematic) approach has to take into consideration not only the teaching of the NT but also that of the OT, as well as developments in the history of doctrine. A thematic NT theology can easily become competitive with systematic theology, thus confusing the over-all theological task of the church.

f. An analytic NT theology. In brief outline, this will begin with the pre-ascension ministry and proclamation of Jesus, as presented in the four gospels. The gospels, to be sure, are not impartial, chronicle-like records; written from the 'bias' of faith in Christ (e.g. Jn. 20:31 – 21:25) and in the light of his exaltation, each reflects post-ascension circumstances and concerns of the church. Within the narration it is probably not possible to distinguish every instance of the evangelists' editorial activity. Still, Luke intends his Gospel to be read as an account of 'all that Jesus began to do and to teach' (Acts 1:1), *prior* to the ascension, and the other evangelists share this intention (*cf.* Mk. 1:1; Jn. 20:30–31; 21:25). The gospels, then, present themselves as trustworthy accounts of Jesus' earthly ministry, in distinction from the post-ascension situation of the church.

According to the synoptic gospels, the central theme of Jesus' proclamation is the kingdom of God:* the kingdom is the comprehensive saving rule of God over creation (Mt. 28:18), which has at last arrived, as the fulfilment of the OT promises (Mt. 13:16–17; Lk. 10:23–24; Mk. 1:15), in the person and work of Jesus, the Messiah (Mt. 16:16; Mk. 8:29; Lk. 9:20); this eschatological order, relative to Christ's coming, is not only present (Mt. 11:11–12; Lk. 16:16; Mt. 12:28; Lk. 11:20) but also future, both immediately (Mt. 4:17; 16:28; Mk. 9:1; Lk. 9:27) and more indefinitely (Mt. 8:11–12; Lk. 13:28–29; Mt. 25:31–34, 41). In John's Gospel, the vocabulary of the kingdom recedes (but see 3:3, 5; 18:36), the focus from the outset is on Jesus as the Son of God (1:34, 49; 3:16–18), and on his work as the outcome of his person, primarily in the form of longer discourses in which Jesus presents salvation as essential components of his being, such as life, light, truth (6:35; 8:12, 32; 11:25; 12:35, 36, 46; 14:6; *cf.* 1:4–5, 7–9, 14, 17).

The axis between Jesus* and Paul* makes up the substantial core of NT theology. Paul 'does nothing but explain the eschatological reality which in Christ's teaching is called the kingdom' (H. Ridderbos, *When the Time Had Fully Come*, Grand Rapids, MI, 1955, pp. 48–49). As for Jesus, the kingdom of God is the great eschatological reality which is both future (1 Cor. 6:9–10; Gal. 5:21) and present (Rom. 14:17; 1 Cor. 4:20), but explicit references to the kingdom are relatively infrequent. Instead, Paul's focus is on the death and resurrection of Christ (Acts 17:2–3; 1 Cor. 15:3–4), the climax of all four gospel narratives and anticipated by Jesus himself as the great turning-point in the coming of the kingdom (Mt. 16:21–28; Mk. 9:1, 31; Lk. 18:31–34). Jesus' death and resurrection inaugurate the eschatological age-to-come/new creation which overlaps this age/old creation until his return (*e.g.* Rom. 12:2; 1 Cor. 1:18 – 2:9; 10:11; 2 Cor. 5:17; Gal. 1:4; Eph. 2:1–10). This eschatological fulfilment is actualized, in the church, by the presence of the Holy Spirit (Rom. 8:23; 2 Cor. 1:22; 5:5; Eph. 1:14), as the correlate of the exalted Christ (Rom. 8:9–10; 1 Cor. 15:45b; 2 Cor. 3:17–18), and is further explicated by major themes such as reconciliation (2 Cor. 5:10 – 6:2; Col. 1:19–23), righteousness* (Rom. 1:17 – 6:23; Gal. 2:16 – 3:22), adoption (Rom. 8:14–30, Gal. 3:23 – 4:7), and the Holy Spirit* (Rom. 8:1–17; 2 Cor. 3:3–18; Gal. 5:16–26).

The other NT writings share this focus on the eschatological setting of Christ's death and resurrection (Acts 2:14–36; Heb. 1:2, 9:26; Jas. 5:3; 1 Pet. 1:20; 2 Pet. 3:3; 1 Jn. 2:18; Jude 18; Rev. 1:1–7), and contribute in various, sometimes distinctive ways to the major axis (Jesus–Paul) of NT theology.

Bibliography.

History: H. Boers, *What Is New Testament Theology?* (Philadelphia, 1979); R. Bultmann, *Theology of the New Testament*, vol. 2 (London and New York, 1955); L. Goppelt, *Theology of the New Testament* (Grand Rapids, MI, 1981); D. Guthrie, *New Testament Theology* (Leicester, 1981); G. Hasel, *New Testament Theology: Basic Issues in the Current Debate* (Grand Rapids, MI, 1978); G. E. Ladd, *A Theology of the New Testament* (Grand Rapids, MI, 1974); R. Morgan, *The Nature of New Testament Theology* (London, 1973).

Structure and content: D. Guthrie, *New*

Testament Theology (Leicester, 1981); A. M. Hunter, *Introducing New Testament Theology* (London, 1957); G. E. Ladd, *A Theology of the New Testament* (Grand Rapids, MI, 1974); H. Ridderbos, *The Coming of the Kingdom* (Philadelphia, 1962); *idem, Paul. An Outline of His Theology* (Grand Rapids, MI, 1975); G. Vos, *Biblical Theology* (Grand Rapids, MI, 1948); *idem, The Pauline Eschatology* (Grand Rapids, MI, 1953).

R.B.G.

NEWMAN, JOHN HENRY (1801–90), Anglican and Roman Catholic theologian and philosopher. Undergoing at fifteen a gradual intellectual conversion which he later described as an experience of falling 'under the influence of a definite creed', Newman wrestled continually with the doctrine of the church* and questions about its authority* and apostolic role as the guardian and teacher of Christian truth, finding much inspiration in the patristic studies he began in his first book, *The Arians of the Fourth Century* (London, 1833).

Newman's *Parochial Sermons* at St Mary's, Oxford, had considerable spiritual impact on hearers and readers, and his contributions to *Tracts for the Times* (London, 1834–41) played a significant role in the formation of the Anglo-Catholic theology* of the Oxford Movement. He supported for a while the theory that the Church of England was the true heir of the early church and a *via media* between the errors of Rome and Protestantism, but gradually changed his mind. Shocked by public and ecclesiastical condemnation of his attempt in *Tract 90* (1841) to reconcile the Thirty-nine Articles with official Roman Catholic teaching, Newman retired to nearby Littlemore. Here he lived a semi-monastic life and worked on his *Essay on the Development of Christian Doctrine* (London, 1845), which appeared soon after Newman was received into the Catholic Church in 1845.

The high feelings aroused in both Anglicans and Catholics by Newman's conversion were cooled by the honesty of his spiritual autobiography, *Apologia Pro Vita Sua* (London, 1864), but his independent habits of mind found little recognition in a Catholic Church moving towards Vatican Council I and the definition of papal* infallibility (1870). New-man was convinced about papal supremacy and the pope's place as the divinely appointed and visible centre of unity in the church. But he did not equate authority with authoritarianism and absolutism, or confine the church's teaching office to papal pronouncements. However, Newman's suggestions 'On Consulting the Faithful in Matters of Doctrine' (1859) earned him the reputation at Rome of being the most dangerous man in England. His argument for a creative inter-relationship between the church's prophetical (teaching), priestly (worshipping) and kingly (ruling) functions – which was outlined in the preface to the third (London, 1877) edition of *Lectures on the Prophetical Office of the Church* (London, 1837), now retitled *The Via Media of the Anglican Church*, vol. 1 – was almost a century too early.

Although Newman was made a cardinal in 1879 and officially cleared of modernism* in 1908, his theology was generally neglected or misunderstood until Vatican Council II (1962–65) focused the whole Roman Catholic Church's attention on many parallel issues. It then became clear that Newman had touched on many questions of enduring importance, even if his own answers had proved to be fragmentary, illustrative rather than explanatory, inspirational rather than definitive. Newman's relevance to recent theology can be seen in two of his works in particular: the *Essay on the Development of Christian Doctrine* (London, 1845, [8]1891) and *An Essay in Aid of a Grammar of Assent* (London, 1870).

The first of these, although primarily the intellectual cause and justification of Newman's conversion to Catholicism, had the much wider function of pioneering the idea of development* in doctrine, fifteen years before Darwin's *Origin of Species* popularized the concept of evolution. It also, in its final (1878) form, made a significant contribution to the question of defining the essence* of Christianity, a question now often discussed in terms of contextualization.*

The second essay, which contains Newman's analysis of the movement from implicit to explicit belief, may be criticized for assuming that faith* is chiefly a matter of believing theological propositions, and for describing 'assent' in terms of an act of will towards a truth that we grasp, rather than a truth that grasps us. Elsewhere, however, in his *Lectures on Justification* (London, 1838), in his sermons and in hymns such as 'Lead, kindly light,' Newman does emphasize divine grace. But the *Grammar of Assent*'s focus on what Newman called an 'illative sense' or instinctive capacity to make sense of a mass of diverse evidence, determining 'the limit of converging probabilities, and the reasons sufficient for a proof' was an important step towards present recognition of the significance of intuition. Lonergan* has acknowledged his debt to Newman and sought to explain more fully what Newman described. Wittgenstein's* *On Certainty* (Oxford, 1984) and H.-G. Gadamer's *Truth and Method* (ET, London, ²1979) have made major contributions in this area. Many other studies on the place of imagination* in faith and the relationship between faith and doubt* have found inspiration in Newman's *Grammar of Assent.*

Bibliography

Many editions of *Apologia Pro Vita Sua, Essay on the Development of Christian Doctrine, Idea of a University* (1852), and poem *The Dream of Gerontius* (1865); *On Consulting the Faithful in Matters of Doctrine*, ed. J. Coulson (London, 1961).

Studies: Biography by M. Trevor (1962), abridged as *Newman's Journey* (Glasgow, 1974); life after 1845 from C. S. Dessain *et al.* (eds.), *The Letters and Diaries of John Henry Newman*, vols. XI-XXVI (London, 1962–74); general introductions to Newman's thought: O. Chadwick, *Newman* (Oxford, 1983) and J. M. Cameron, 'John Henry Newman and the Tractarian Movement' in N. Smart *et al.* (eds.), *Nineteenth Century Religious Thought in the West*, vol. II (Cambridge, 1985), pp. 69–109; specialist works: J. Coulson, *Newman and the Common Tradition* (Oxford, 1970) and *Religion and Imagination* (Oxford, 1981); N. Lash, *Newman on Development: The Search For an Explanation in History* (London, 1980); P. Misner, *Papacy and Development* (Leiden, 1976); T. J. Norris, *Newman and his Theological Method* (Leiden, 1977); D. A. Pailin, *The Way to Faith* (London, 1969); R. C. Selby, *The Principle of Reserve in the Writings of John Henry, Cardinal Newman* (Oxford, 1975); S. Sykes, *The Identity of Christianity* (London, 1984).

P.N.H.

NEWTON, ISAAC (1642–1727).

Professor of mathematics at Cambridge (from 1699) and president of the Royal Society (1703–27), Newton was the most eminent physicist of his day. His most far-reaching achievement was to formulate the universal law of gravitation to explain the motion of the planets and the behaviour of everything in the solar system. The publication of his theory in *Principia Mathematica* (1687) heralded great advances in science. The universe was seen no longer as an irrational chaos or the place of God's constant and unpredictable intervention. It functioned according to laws that could be calculated and, in principle at least, all its secrets could be discovered by patient and logical inquiry.

Although Newton himself, a deeply religious man like many of his scientific contemporaries, believed he was discovering laws established by the creator and that it was necessary for God to intervene from time to time to correct irregularities in the solar system that would otherwise occur due to loss of energy, this view did not prevail long. As the 18th century progressed it was increasingly felt that any apparent irregularities would be accounted for in due course by refinements of scientific theory. The 'God of the gaps' would disappear, along with any concept of miracle* or providence.*

While Newton's scientific views were revolutionary, his religious beliefs were unremarkable for the period. He maintained the convention of not linking science* and religion in public debate, and kept his researches into biblical and world chronology, prophecy and alchemy to himself, along with his doubts about the doctrine of the Trinity.* Newton's private papers suggest that he did not see himself as a Unitarian,* as he criticized Arius* as well as Athanasius* for being among the many before and since who had corrupted the plain meaning of Scripture with metaphysics.* Newton does not seem to have been aware that his difficulty in taking the incarnation* seriously was entirely consistent with his understanding of space and time. For if, as Newton held, absolute space and time are attributes of God, God becomes the 'container' of the universe and his incarnation in it becomes unthinkable.

By the beginning of the 19th century experiments with magnetism and electricity were calling in question the universal application of

Newtonian principles and paving the way for relativity theory and quantum mechanics. It remains to be seen if and to what extent the scientific revolution associated with Albert Einstein (1879–1955) produces a new climate of thought favourable to the Christian understanding of creation as contingent and open, 'finite and unbounded' (Torrance*).

Bibliography

S. L. Jaki, *Science and Creation* (Edinburgh, 1974); F. E. Manuel, *A Portrait of Isaac Newton* (Oxford, 1968); idem, *The Religion of Isaac Newton* (Oxford, 1974); J. Moltmann, *God in Creation* (London, 1985); T. F. Torrance, *Divine and Contingent Order* (Oxford, 1981); idem, *Space, Time and Incarnation* (London, 1969); R. S. Westfall, *Science and Religion in Seventeenth-Century England* (New Haven, CN, 1958).

P.N.H.

NICAEA, see COUNCILS.

NICENE CREED, see CREEDS.

NICHOLAS OF LYRA (c. 1265–1349) was the most influential biblical exegete of the late Middle Ages. Born in Normandy, he entered the Franciscan* order before studying theology at the University of Paris and then teaching there. An able Hebraist, he was familiar with Jewish commentaries on the OT. He was appointed provincial of his order in France and later in Burgundy. He became involved in a controversy about the beatific vision,* in reaction against the view of Pope John XXII that the souls of those who die in grace do not enjoy this until after the last judgment. Lyra had a profound concern for the conversion of Jews, as is reflected in both his preaching and writing.

He was the author of numerous works, some of which still remain unpublished. His major achievement lay in his contribution to hermeneutics* as represented by his commentary on the whole Bible in two parts, the first (written 1322–31) expounding the literal sense and the second (1339) the mystical or moral. These *Postillae* established themselves as recognized text books widely cited by other biblical scholars. When published (1471–2) they had the distinction of being the first printed commentary on Scripture and soon ran through several editions. Lyra also produced a tractate comparing the Vulgate OT with the Hebrew text, and two treatises contesting Jewish interpretations of Christ.

Lyra's *Postillae* were so highly regarded as to be adopted as a supplement to the standard *Glossa Ordinaria* and indeed to be set alongside it in some editions. These two commentaries are looked upon as the crown of medieval exegesis. In the prologue to his first volume Lyra declared that the primary function of Scripture is to reveal divine truth; he described it as the sole source of theology. He conceded that Scripture may bear more than one meaning, but insisted nevertheless that the literal sense is basic and that other senses depend upon it. He therefore proposed to avoid the confusing variety of interpretations which had so hampered the scholastic* approach, and to use the historical-grammatical meaning as the over-all criterion.

With this principle to guide him, Lyra realized how important it was to recover the authentic biblical text which had been obscured by the carelessness of copyists and the ineptitude of some emendations. He stressed the need to get behind the Vulgate to the Hebrew original as a corrective. Lyra's indebtedness to Rashi (Rabbi Solomon ben Isaac, 1040–1105) has been the subject of much discussion. He was not the first Christian expositor to pay attention to Rashi, but he did so more thoroughly, if cautiously, than others. Latterly his independence grew more apparent.

He displayed a similar attitude to church tradition, claiming that the opinions of the fathers were not to be accepted as definitive in themselves but were subject to the final jurisdiction of Scripture. In this, as in his insistence on the primacy of the literal sense, Lyra anticipated Luther* and the other Reformers. Luther, in turn, often referred to him, ranking him among the most useful commentators because his aim was to discover the exact meaning intended by the biblical writers themselves.

Bibliography

H. Labrosse, 'Biographie de Nicolas de Lyre', *Etudes Franciscaines* 17 (1907), pp. 489–505, 593–608; A. Skevington Wood, 'Nicolas of Lyra', *EQ* 33 (1961), pp. 196–206.

A.S.W.

NIEBUHR, H. RICHARD (1894–1962), who taught at Yale from 1931 to his death, and was Reinhold Niebuhr's* brother, represented the left wing of American neo-orthodoxy.* He aimed at a holistic and critical Christian world view.

Niebuhr's most important theological work was *The Meaning of Revelation* (1941), which advocates 'perspectival relativism'* and counsels Christians to adopt a 'confessional' stance. He maintains that any perception of truth is historically and culturally conditioned, but he repudiates agnosticism.* He holds that in revelatory experiences we truly perceive the Absolute, but our perception itself is not absolute. Thus we need not disparage other revelations and faiths in order to affirm our own. Revelation* is primarily personal, not propositional. Meaning, not information, is revealed, and different meanings have been revealed to others. The task for Christians is to view all of life according to the 'pattern' of Jesus Christ.

Niebuhr pursued this task in his famous *Christ and Culture* (1951). He delineates five possible models for relating the two: 1. 'Christ Against Culture' rejects the world as evil. Believers must retreat to the elect community, shunning politics, art, the military, and worldly entertainments. Revelation is preferred to 'the whole Reason.' Christ has given the law of the kingdom in the Sermon on the Mount, and his disciples must live as sojourners in a foreign land. 2. 'The Christ of Culture' makes Christ the figurehead of one's culture,* embodying the culture's values yet providing a basis for culture's critique. Revelation is accommodated to reason, the line between God and world is blurred, and Christ's salvation is mere 'moral influence'. 3. 'Christ Above Culture' describes a schema like Thomas Aquinas',* wherein cultural institutions are grounded in 'natural law' (see Law*), which is yet limited in scope. Christ's *super*natural law is revealed to enable us to reach salvation. Nature is supplemented and fulfilled by grace, both coming from Christ. 4. 'Christ and Culture in Paradox' proposes the world as radically corrupt yet not abandoned by God, who has set up social structures to stem the tide of chaos. We live in this world of necessary evils as sinners justified by grace, resulting in a predominantly private, personal Christian morality. 5. 'Christ the Transformer of Culture' sees the world as fallen, but capable of sanctification, both socially and personally.

In his third major theological work, *Radical Monotheism and Western Culture* (based on lectures given in 1957), Niebuhr calls for an integrative approach to culture, politics, science, religion, *etc*. We ought to reject 'polytheism'* (the fragmented pursuit of many distinct value centres) and 'henotheism' (partisan championing of one finite value centre, *e.g.*, one country, sect, or political party, against others) in favour of 'monotheism'* (a trusting and loyal adherence to Being-itself, the source and integration point of all penultimate value centres).

Niebuhr's other works all evidence both his integrative vision and his gift for creating helpful typologies.

Bibliography

L. A. Hoedemaker, *The Theology of H. Richard Niebuhr* (Philadelphia, 1970); J. Irish, *The Religious Thought of H. Richard Niehbuhr* (Atlanta, GA, 1986); D. F. Ottali, *Meaning and Method in H. Richard Niebuhr's Theology* (Lanham, MD, 1983); P. Ramsey (ed.), *Faith and Ethics: The Theology of H. Richard Niebuhr* (New York, 1957).

R.M.P.

NIEBUHR, REINHOLD (1892–1971). The development of Christian thought in the face of the social and political challenges of the middle years of the 20th century in Western history was dominated by Reinhold Niebuhr. Senior politicans on both sides of the Atlantic and across the political parties have spoken of their debt to his thinking.

After graduating in 1914 from Yale, Niebuhr took a pastorate in the Presbyterian Church in Detroit. His experience of ministry among Ford workers and in the face of the developing corporate power of the motor industry profoundly transformed his thinking. He abandoned the social ideas of liberal Protestantism which had been dominant in the early years of the century. Its utopianism seemed inadequate in the face of the hard realities of collective power in the contemporary world. After the publication of his first book *Does Civilization Need Religion?* (New York, 1927) he left Detroit to become Professor of Applied Christianity at Union Theological Seminary, New York. He remained there until his retirement. 1932 saw the publication of one of his most influential books, *Moral Man and Immoral Society* (New York). In it he demolished liberal Protestant responses to the social structures of the age, and set about constructing a theology of justice as the true response of biblical faith to the realities of power. In coming to terms with the structural issues of social order and political life, Niebuhr showed a sympathy for aspects of Marxist* analysis. He sometimes described himself as a Christian Marxist. However, the roots of his growing theological work could be found in the developing neo-orthodoxy* represented by Barth* and Bonhoeffer* in Europe. In many ways he stood in the tradition of Calvin* and Augustine,* demanding a full, structured statement of the transcendence and righteousness* of Christ to meet the forces of power which threatened such disastrous consequences for human experience in the middle years of the 20th century. *The Nature and Destiny of Man* (1941 and 1943, 2 vols.) (his Gifford lectures of 1939), is the fullest theological statement he made. It was regarded as a masterpiece of contemporary exposition of fundamental Christian themes.

Niebuhr has been criticized, in his stress on the corporate manifestations of power, for being too pessimistic about human nature and for overstressing the fallenness of humanity. It was for these reasons, so the criticism runs, that he could not see a way to relate the radically Christian understanding of *agapē* (see Love*) directly to social issues. This is why he interposed the notion of justice as the only way Christian faith could relate to the collective issues of the time.

After the Second World War he became increasingly concerned with the effects of the Cold War. His book *Children of Light and Children of Darkness* (London, 1945) attempts to provide a fuller and more substantial justification of democracy than could be provided in liberal thought: 'Man's capacity for justice makes democracy possible; but man's inclination to injustice makes democracy necessary' (p.xiii). He foresaw the weakness of the optimism of liberal notions of democracy and the dangers of the optimism of Marxist ideas of social order. Throughout, he kept a vision of world community and the need, in the face of the Cold War, to find

practical realistic understandings and policies to move the world towards it.

No serious 20th-century political theology* can avoid either Niebuhr's contribution or the issues he sought to tackle in his work.

Bibliography

E. J. Carnell, *The Theology of Reinhold Niebuhr* (Grand Rapids, MI, 1951); G. Harland, *The Thought of Reinhold Niebuhr* (New York, 1960); R. Harries (ed.), *Reinhold Niebuhr and the Issues of Our Time* (London, 1986); C. W. Kegley and R. W. Bretall (eds.), *Reinhold Niebuhr: His Religious, Social and Political Thought* (New York, 1956); D. B. Robertson, *Reinhold Niebuhr's Works* (Syracuse, NY, ²1976).

J.W.G.

NIETZSCHE, FRIEDRICH (1844–1900). German philologist and philosopher, son of a Lutheran minister, he began his own university studies in theology. As his interests changed, he undertook a career in philology, becoming a full professor at Basel at the age of 26. Plagued by bad health, dissatisfied with his academic duties, and critical of the current state of both religion and culture, he in time gave himself to philosophical writing.

Nietzsche's *Ecce Homo* (1888) exalts self-assertion in the face of the cultural and religious passivity of the day. The philosopher Arthur Schopenhauer (1788–1860), pessimistic about all that life could offer, had advocated a morality of self-renunciation. Christianity, Nietzsche holds, is hostile to bodily life, depreciates the aesthetic and, by its emphasis on universal moral law, says 'no' to instinct. Furthermore, the theory of natural selection would have us placidly adjust to external circumstances rather than change and exploit them by the force of human will.

To all of this Nietzsche strongly reacts. In place of Schopenhauer's renunciation of the will to live, he asserts a will to power that can transform human values and create a new *Übermensch* (superman). In place of natural selection and the regularities of natural law, he turns to biological vitalism with its unleashing of creative energies. In face of an otherworldly Christianity overly identified with the cultural *status quo*, *Thus Spake Zarathustra* (1883) dramatically announces that the death of God opens up new and vast horizons for those with strength of will to meet the challenge.

Two attitudes to life thus come into conflict. In *The Birth of Tragedy* (1872) Nietzsche calls them the Dionysian and the Apollonian, the former assuming a primordial unity with nature that finds expression in vitality and instinctual activity, the latter calling for individual self-restraint in the interest of cosmic and cultural form and order. Two moralities result, and conflict: a slave morality, egalitarian, democratic, acquiescing in supposed absolutes; and a master morality that asserts itself with a will to power. Nietzsche calls for the self-creation of the strong-willed. The truth will be whatever enhances power, their morality deliberately egoistic, for only in this way can an effete culture be revitalized and the human race delivered from decline.

Although the Nazis appealed to Nietzsche for their concept of a super-race, he himself would undoubtedly have repudiated such extremes. His actual influence is better seen in the novels of Thomas Mann (1875–1955) and Hermann Hesse (1877–1962), in the existentialism* of Sartre and Albert Camus (1913–60), and in the gropings of the 'death of God'* theology for a more vital religion than liberalism provided. Nietzsche in effect climaxes the modern revolt against the Enlightenment,* on behalf of a radical Romanticism* which makes human freedom the virtually divine deliverer from all that drags humankind down.

Bibliography

Works: *The Birth of Tragedy*, tr. F. Golffing (Garden City, NY, 1956); *Thus Spake Zarathusa*, tr. T. Common (London, ⁶1967); H. W. Riechert and K. Schlechta, *An International Nietzsche Bibliography* (Chapel Hill, NC, 1960).

Studies: F. C. Copleston, *Friedrich Nietzsche: Philosopher of Culture* (London, ²1975); W. Kaufmann, *Nietzsche, Philosopher, Psychologist, Antichrist* (Princeton, NJ, ³1968).

A.F.H.

NOMINALISM designates a philosophical trend culminating at the close of the Middle Ages. Originally the term referred to the question of what sort of reality 'universals' possessed. When reference is made to a group or class of individual things, is that class or universal itself real (hence the position of the Realists, inspired by Platonism*), or is it merely a convention or name (*nomen*), with no existence apart from the individuals themselves?

While all medieval theologians agreed that divine revelation* could be ultimately understood only through faith,* there were differences over the value of preliminary rational organization of theological insights as an aid to their acceptance by faith (see Faith and Reason*). The older Augustinian*/Franciscan* tradition put greater emphasis upon faith in terms of willing acceptance of what God had willed to reveal, while the newer Thomistic*/Dominican* approach saw greater value in rational organization of theological truths, as an appropriate response to divine rationality. From that perspective nominalism could be regarded as a variety of voluntarism (see Will*). The essence of nominalism* does not consist merely in employing universals in the recognition that they possess no independent existence; rather it extends to a recognition of all divine activity without requiring physical evidence.

This is especially the case in the question of individual salvation.* While all theologians were committed to the value of sacramental* grace,* it was equally apparent that such grace was valueless without the presence of a preliminary grace to produce the proper disposition for the reception of the sacraments. The greater the emphasis that was placed upon this Augustinian prevenient grace, the less necessary were the sacraments and indeed the church* that administered them. Prevenient grace was to be found not through sacramental causality, but rather through mystically* or morally 'doing the best one could,' *i.e.* by meriting* grace congruently (see Augustinianism;* Jesuit Theology;* William of Ockham*).

Towards the end of the period these tendencies polarized. The more Thomism was seen as rationalistic, the more extreme became the Franciscan response. God's graciousness was increasingly perceived as arbitrariness. While the language of cause and effect was still employed, increasingly it came to take on the modern sense of statistical correlation, or regularity of observation. Nominalism may then be regarded as contributing to the general scepticism of the age preceding the Reformation.* It is not surprising to hear late-medieval Augustinians such as Gregory* of Rimini and Thomas Bradwardine* denouncing nominalism as Pelagian.*

The Reformation's understanding of nominalism is vigorously negative, linked as it was with congruism. Luther* identified himself as a nominalist but also spoke of the foolishness of nominalistic speculation. Probably this should be taken as appreciation of the work nominalism had done in exposing the speculative character of previous theology, combined with his conviction that nominalism itself had nothing to offer.

Calvin's* rejection of speculation about God is similar (cf. Institutes I. ii. 2; x. 2; III. ii. 6). That did not mean a new enthusiasm for Thomistic rationalism on the part of the Reformers. Instead a new interest in the historical character of the Christian faith replaced both philosophical directions, expressed most vigorously in the Reformed* emphasis on the doctrine of the covenant.* Divine causality is not so much rational as covenantal. God has *bound himself* by his word of promise.

It is possible to see Protestant interest in the ways of God in the secret work of regeneration,* with consideration of the significance of the probable effect certain human actions have upon it, as a revival of congruism. This was the view of the Dutch Reformed theologian Herman Bavinck.*

See also: BIEL, GABRIEL.

Bibliography

E. Gilson, *History of Christian Philosophy in the Middle Ages* (London, 1955); E. A. Moody, *Truth and Consequence in Medieval Logic* (Amsterdam, 1953); H. Oberman, *The Harvest of Medieval Theology; Gabriel Biel and Late Medieval Nominalism* (Grand Rapids, MI, ²1967); P. Vignaux, *Le Nominalisme au XIVᵉ siècle* (Montreal, 1948).

D.C.D.

NOVATIAN (*fl.* 249–51) was a highly educated priest, theologian and writer, who led the Roman clergy during the vacancy between popes Fabian and Cornelius in 250–51. During this time he corresponded with Cyprian* of Carthage. After the Decian persecution when many believers lapsed from the faith, Novatian opposed any readmission of these people into the church. Because his severe denial of reconciliation was opposed to

Catholic practice, Novatian was excommunicated by a Roman synod. He set up a schismatic church, which lasted to the 8th century.

According to Jerome,* Novatian wrote several works, including *On the Passover, On the Sabbath, On Circumcision, On the Priesthood, On Prayer, On Standing Fast, On Jewish Foods*, and many others (some of which are extant), 'especially a great volume on the Trinity'.

In his *On the Trinity*, Novatian's theology advances beyond Tertullian's* earlier thought in maintaining the eternal Sonship of Christ (cf. Christology*). Novatian gives a clear explanation of biblical anthropomorphisms* in terms of God's accommodation* to human language. He uses the doctrine of Trinitarian circumincession, and anticipates what later theology came to call the 'hypostatic union' of the two natures of Christ in one person, and the 'communication of idioms' between the natures.

Bibliography

Works, ed. G. F. Diercks (*CCL* 4, 1972); tr. R. J. DeSimone (*FC* 67, 1974); *De Trinitate*, ed. W. Y. Fausset (Cambridge, 1909), tr. H. Moore (London, 1919).

D.F.K.

NUMINOUS, see OTTO, RUDOLF.

NYGREN, ANDERS (1890–1977) served the Swedish Lutheran Church as bishop and professor of theology in Lund. Along with that of Gustav Aulén,* his work represents a Scandinavian parallel to German dialectical theology* in the 1920's and 1930's, especially in its critical attitude towards the then dominant liberal* theology. Nygren, however, was more interested than either Barth* or Bultmann* in the analysis of Christianity as a human religious system, and became one of the few significant Lutheran philosophers of religion. His method of analysis is usually labelled 'motif-research', in that it attempts to uncover basic distinguishing motifs of Christianity by historical analysis and contrast with other religious systems. His best-known work along these lines is the now classic *Agape and Eros*, which presents an historical account and theological analysis of the contrast between the motif of *agapē* (Gk., unmotivated self-giving love) and that of *erōs* (Gk., love which desires to attain a higher good). The presentation of these motifs offers Nygren the opportunity to discuss basic theological issues in such areas as revelation, atonement and ethics. The book's historical analysis has been the subject of much debate, as has its sharp distinction between *agapē* and *erōs*. Critics suggest that Nygren lacks interest in love* as a human phenomenon, and that his theology shows a general deficiency in the area of the doctrine of creation. Behind the motif analysis there certainly lies a strong theology of grace as a divine accomplishment requiring no human ethical response. Such emphasis on the priority of divine action is also expressed in a brief work on the doctrine of the atonement, *Essence of Christianity*, and is pervasive throughout the *Commentary on Romans*. Nygren's philosophy of religion can be studied in more detail in his *Meaning and Method*.

Bibliography

Agape and Eros, 2 vols. (ET, London, 1932–39); *Commentary on Romans* (ET, London, 1952); *Essence of Christianity* (ET, London, 1960); *Meaning and Method* (ET, London, 1972).

C. W. Kegley (ed.), *The Philosophy and Theology of Anders Nygren* (Carbondale, IL, 1970); G. Wingren, *Theology in Conflict* (ET, Edinburgh, 1958).

J.B.We.

OBEDIENCE OF CHRIST. A biblical concept of particular importance in Reformed* theology and piety.

Filial obedience

The NT clearly depicts Jesus' whole life as one of perfect, sinless and conscious obedience to God as his Father (*e.g.* 1 Jn. 2:2; 3:5; 1 Pet. 2:22), whose will for his life was learned through prayerful meditation on OT Scripture (Mt. 3:15; Lk. 22:37; Jn. 8:29, 46). Such obedience was based on trust and love of the Father, and it involved a real experience of temptation by Satan, acting both directly and through others, to try to make him doubt the Father's goodness and deviate from his plan

for his life (Mt. 4:1–11; 16:22–23; 26:53–54). Such temptation was overcome by the spiritual weapons of prayer, the word of God and fasting, in a genuinely human life of faith. John emphasizes that Christ's ministry and teaching were all based on obedience to what his Father showed him and gave him to do and say. A military background enabled a Roman centurion to perceive that such submission to God was the source of Jesus' authority over evil and disease (Mt. 8:8–10; Jn. 5:19–20; 7:16).

While Christ's obedience also included submitting himself to other God-given human authorities, even when imperfectly exercised (Mk. 14:61–62; Lk. 2:51; Jn. 19:11; 1 Pet. 2:23), his obedience to God involved a resolute adherence to the Father's specific will in every situation, sometimes rejecting another morally allowable course in order to see that perfect will done in his life and death.

Representative obedience

As man and as Messiah, Jesus learned the meaning and cost of obedience in experience through what he suffered (Mk. 8:31; Heb. 5:7–9), and became obedient even to death on a cross (Phil. 2:5–8). This was a conscious and voluntary act of obedience right up to the point of death itself (Jn. 10:17–18; 19:30). Since Satan and evil had no place in his righteous life, death could not in fact hold on to him (Jn. 14:30; 16:10–11; Acts 2:24; Rom. 1:4). Paul contrasts the obedience of Jesus with the disobedience of Adam,* seeing the two as representative figures acting on behalf of the old and the new humanity. Christ's obedience right to the cross won justification* and eternal life for the many people on whose behalf he lived and died (Rom. 5:18–19; *cf.* also 1 Cor. 15:20–22, 45–49).

Christ's obedience as understood by the Christian church

Jesus' obedience and sinless life have been drawn upon in at least four ways by the church down the years: 1. As the example of perfect obedience by a Son of the Father, his life gives inspiration to all God's children to live obedient lives (1 Pet. 2:18ff.); 2. The one who was tempted and did not yield can help us when we are tempted (Heb. 2:18; 4:14–16); 3. Only his righteous life could be laid down on behalf of sinners as an effective atoning sacrifice (2 Cor. 5:21; Heb. 7:26–27;

1 Pet. 3:18; 1 Jn. 2:2); 4. The Holy Spirit* of Christ dwells within Christians to reproduce Christ's life and image in them (Rom. 8:9–30). Calvin rightly states that we are saved by 'the whole course of his obedience' (*Institutes* II. xvi. 5). In keeping with this, Reformed theologians have often distinguished between Christ's *active* obedience (his life of filial obedience to the Father) and his *passive* obedience (his suffering of the Father's judgment against covenant-breakers). These terms were not intended to denote that Christ was at any point inactive ('passive') in his obedience. Passive is used here in the Latinate sense (*patior*: suffer, submit). Nonetheless, the *fullness* of his obedience is now commonly clarified in terms of his *preceptive* and *penal* obedience.

Bibliography

G. C. Berkouwer, *The Person of Christ* (Grand Rapids, MI, 1954); L. W. Grensted, *The Person of Christ* (London, 1934); D. Guthrie, *New Testament Theology* (Leicester, 1981); J. Murray, *Collected Writings*, vol. 2 (Edinburgh, 1977), pp. 151–157; B. B. Warfield, *The Person and Work of Christ* (Philadelphia, 1950).

J.P.B.

OCCULT. This term, meaning 'hidden', is applied to practices which are below the surface of normal life. They may be contacts with the evil spirit world, deliberately sought through (black) magic or Satanism. Or they may be the fostering of experiences that occasionally come to Christians or non-Christians alike, such as second-sight, prevision and telepathy. Such experiences may come spontaneously, and, although they are neutral in themselves, they should be committed to God to use or to take away. Otherwise they may be fostered for self, or be used as a substitute for spiritual experience, or used against God, and thus serve Satan's cause. The way of the world is to bolster pride; the way of Satan is to cloud the vision of God and obedience to God.

The Bible has little or nothing to say about neutral paranormal experiences, but it recognizes that true spiritual experiences may be copied by occult forces. Thus false prophets are a psychic copy of prophets inspired by the Spirit of God. True and false appeared the same, but Jeremiah knew that the false spoke

'delusions of their own minds' (Je. 23:26). Similarly the early Christians had to distinguish true from false prophecy* by the content of the message about the person of Jesus Christ (1 Jn. 4:1–3; 1 Cor. 12:1–3).

A list of prohibited occult practices is given in Dt. 18:10–11. NIV translates these as divination, sorcery, omens, witchcraft, spells, mediumship, spiritualism, and consulting the dead. Other modern translations are not essentially different. None of these is allowed in the NT, and converts who had previously practised magic burnt their textbooks (Acts 19:19).

Today divination is practised by tarot cards or crystal ball. Sorcery exists as magic (not in the sense of conjuring tricks). Omens are the superstitious use or avoidance of certain practices. Witchcraft flourishes in secret covens, and often invokes pagan gods. Individual witches and magicians mobilize psychic forces to cast spells. But the restrictions on mediumship and consulting spirits are held by some to be lifted today. Attempts are made to show that the descriptions in the Bible are of something different from modern mediumship. Nonetheless the final summing up of 'one who enquires of the dead' is all-embracing.

Astrology is a form of divination. It has developed into the use of complicated tables of planets and houses which mark out the present and future of clients. In a chapter on idolatry Jeremiah tells God's people not to 'be terrified by signs in the sky' (10:2). Isaiah mocks the Babylonian 'stargazers who make predictions month by month' (47:12–15). The heavenly bodies were intended as calendars (Gn. 1:14).

NEB translates 'magi' as 'astrologers' (Mt. 2:1), but they were not astrologers in the modern sense. Probably they were wise men who had learnt from exiled Jews to expect a star as the sign of the messianic king (Nu. 24:17).

See also: DEVIL AND DEMONS.

Bibliography

R. Palms, *The Occult: a Christian View* (London, 1972); J. Stafford Wright, *Understanding the Supernatural* (London, 1971).

J.S.W.

OCHINO, BERNARDINO (*c.* 1487–1564). Italian Reformer, popular evangelist and author, Ochino was born in Siena, joined the Franciscans* at the age of eighteen and studied medicine at Perugia. Transferring to the newly founded Capuchins in 1534, he was elected Vicar-General of the Order in 1538 and 1541.

His preaching was directly inspired by the gospels and won rapturous response throughout Italy, particularly delighting Charles V at Naples in 1536. Many turned to Christ. But his 'Lutheran' doctrine began to arouse suspicion, and in July 1542 he was summoned to appear before the recently reconstituted Inquisition in Rome. Instead he quit Italy for Geneva, his flight causing a national sensation.

In 1547 Cranmer invited him to England, and he spent six years in London: here he wrote his most ingenious work, *Tragoedie* (1549), which influenced Milton. He pastored exiled Italian communities in Germany and Switzerland, but his questing and questioning mind made him an uncomfortable bedfellow. No orthodoxy satisfied him, and he was suspected of anti-Trinitarianism. A stream of published sermons and speculative dialogues – such as *Labyrinthi* (1561) – culminated in *Dialogi XXX* (1563), which included the scandalous *Dialogus de Polygamia*.

Banished from Bullinger's* Zurich, denied asylum in Nuremberg, he sought refuge in Poland, was again banished and died an outcast from Christendom in Moravia.

Bibliography

R. H. Bainton, *Bernardino Ochino, esule e riformatore senese del cinque cento, 1487–1563* (Florence, 1940); C. Benrath, *Bernardino Ochino of Siena* (London, 1876).

P.M.J.McN.

OECOLAMPADIUS, JOHN (1482–1531), German Reformer. Born in Weinsberg in Württemberg, he attended Heidelberg University and was soon in touch with a humanist* circle which included Jacob Wimpfeling (1450–1528), John Reuchlin (1455–1522), Melanchthon* and Bucer.* After a period as a tutor to the children of Landgrave Philip I of the Palatinate, he became a preacher at Weinsberg (1510). Further study at Tübingen University led to a mastery of Greek, Latin and Hebrew and thence to work with Erasmus* on his NT (1515). In 1518 he was awarded his doctorate at Basel. He rapidly became a considerable patristic scholar, particularly interested in the Greek fathers. In 1518 he was appointed penitentiary in the Münster at Basel. His studies continued and for a short time in 1521 he entered a Brigittines Monastery at Altomünster. He was, however, moving in a Reformed direction and soon left. In 1522 he returned to Basel and published the first of his translations of Chrysostom.

Already under the considerable influence of Zwingli,* he soon became the leading figure of the Reformed cause in Basel. In 1525 he was made professor of theology and, in typical Swiss fashion, furthered the Reformation cause by formal disputations. In Basel he was successful; in Catholic Baden (1526), faced by John Eck (1486–1543), much less so, but later in Berne (1528), and with the help of Bucer, Zwingli and Wolfgang Capito (1478–1541), he was part of the process which won Berne to the Reformation cause.

In the following year, under his influence, Basel committed itself to the Reformation. He made proposals for setting up a body composed of pastors, town councillors and church elders which sought to avoid the dependence for church discipline* upon the council, which characterized Zurich. These were a foretaste of later developments by Bucer and Calvin.*

Oecolampadius' theology developed towards a view of Christ's spiritual presence in the eucharist.* Though he followed Zwingli at this point, he had an independent mind and cited patristic sources to support his convictions. He was involved in the Colloquy of Marburg (1529). Like Zwingli, he found himself troubled by the Anabaptists* and in 1529 disputed with them. They were driven from Basel.

He died shortly after the battle of Kappel (1531). A scholarly, retiring man, he was a significant Reformation figure in Switzerland. He had continued to work in close collaboration with Erasmus in translating Chrysostom. His role in keeping Erasmian and patristic learning within the early Reformation circle is important.

Bibliography

G. Rupp, *Patterns of Reformation* (London, 1969).

C.P.W.

OFFICES OF CHRIST. During the inter-testamental period, Jewish expectations of a coming deliverer and king who would usher in the kingdom of God* came regularly to use the term 'the anointed one' to describe this eagerly awaited figure (Heb. *māšîaḥ*, Messiah; Gk. *christos*, Christ). While not using it regularly himself, Jesus accepted this title and acknowledged that he was the Christ at his trial, although he had a very different understanding of the Messiah's mission and kingdom from that commonly held amongst his Jewish contemporaries (Mk. 8:27–33; 14:61–62). From Pentecost onwards, the church used the title 'Christ' of Jesus and attached it to his personal name, as 'Jesus [the] Christ', or 'Christ Jesus', and his followers were soon called Christians (Acts 2:36; 11:26).

Christian theology has often reflected on the meaning of this title as applied to Jesus. In the OT anointing* was normally with oil, and denoted consecration to an office by God. It implied an empowering for the task by the Spirit of the Lord. In Is. 61:1ff. this is made explicit in relation to the Messiah, and Jesus applied this prophecy to himself early in his ministry (Lk. 4:16–21). In post-NT times, many Christian writers up to Luther observed that, just as in the OT high priests as well as kings had been anointed, so the title Christ points to Jesus as a royal priest, *i.e.* to a (high) priestly and kingly office. Luther* developed this more fully and biblically than anyone before him, but it was Calvin* who saw further that prophets (*e.g.* Elisha) had also been anointed on occasion, and the work of the Spirit in and upon them was often mentioned. This led him in the final edition of the *Institutes* fully to develop a threefold understanding of the offices of Jesus Christ as the mediator between God and man, *viz.* prophet, priest and king. (This idea had actually been mentioned by Bucer* in 1536, and was first alluded to by Eusebius.*) Reformed theology* and all the Protestant churches have followed him in this ever since.

1. The anointed prophet

The proclamation of good news was a major part of the coming Messiah's work (Is. 61:1–2). The disciples of Jesus called him 'teacher', and the NT church preserved his teaching as the Lord's word, and saw in him the prophet like Moses *par excellence* foretold in Dt.

18:15ff. (*e.g.*, see Acts 3:22–23; 7:37). A major part of Jesus' earthly ministry was his teaching on the kingdom, God as Father, faith, discipleship and the true meaning of the law. In him the ministries of the teacher and the prophet coalesce perfectly; he supersedes all the OT prophets, including John; his words will never pass away and will judge all men at the last day (Mk. 13:31; Jn. 12:48). He continues to teach the church by his Holy Spirit (the same anointing, in principle, which was upon him), in the first instance through the apostles; and the Spirit continues in every age the ministry of Jesus Christ as prophet in his body, the church, which is called to proclaim his word and gospel to all people.

2. The anointed priest

The classic exposition of the theme of Jesus Christ as our great high priest is the Epistle to the Hebrews, especially the central section, 4:14 to 10:25 (or 39). The writer stresses: a. Jesus' divine appointment to that office; b. the tasks of priesthood, especially representative action on our behalf towards God in offering a sacrifice* for sins; c. Christ's fitness for the office through his human experience, suffering, and sinlessness, and because of his consequently indestructible life; d. his belonging to a different and better order of priesthood than the old Levitical one, namely that of Melchizedek (after Ps. 110 and Gn. 14), requiring neither physical descent from the family of Aaron, nor any co-occupant or successor in office; e. his mediation* of a better and eternal covenant,* based on better promises (whereas the old could never bring assurance of forgiveness, containing only foreshadowings of the coming reality); f. his offering a single, perfectly adequate, effective and unrepeatable sacrifice for all sins, in his own death at Calvary, which God accepted; and g. his entry, having finished making the sacrifice, into God's presence (the 'true tabernacle') on our behalf, as our forerunner, where he 'ever lives to intercede for us'.

Jesus (our forerunner) is described as our advocate with the Father (1 Jn. 2:2). From the ascension* onwards, he is looking after our interests with the Father in heaven, or pleading our cause. Heb. 7:25 and Rom. 8:34 speak of him 'making intercession for us'. But how is this to be construed? Is it secured merely by his presence there as man, or is he actually praying to the Father for his people?

Both ideas have received support, but the idea of his needing to pray for us seems gratuitous, since a. he specifically appears to deny this in Jn. 16:25–26; b. he is himself over God's kingdom, with all authority in heaven and earth and all judgment committed to him by the Father (Mt. 28:18–20; Jn. 5:22–23); and c. he does not need to persuade the Father to be gracious to us, since his saving work proceeded from the Father's grace.

A true understanding of Jesus' high-priesthood will guard the church against medieval misrepresentations of the Lord's Supper (see Eucharist*), and against wrongly sacerdotal views of the ordained presbyter/elder. There is a priesthood of all believers,* but this is only of a more general kind, to have access to God through Christ's death, and to offer acceptable worship and service through him. It is *not* i. a representative priesthood to make atonement for sin, *nor* ii. a tenure of office in the Melchizedek priesthood, *nor* iii. any special order of ministry* within the church.

3. The anointed king

The reign of the Messiah as God's king is clearly predicted in the OT (*e.g.* Pss. 2; 110; Is. 11, *etc.*). While Jesus rejected any worldly kingdom or idea of kingship (Mt. 4:8; Jn. 6:15; 18:33–38), he nevertheless spoke of himself on occasion as king in God's kingdom, and the Son of Man is a regal figure in several of his sayings (with a background of Dn. 7). Jesus' coming brought in the kingdom, which is a spiritual one of truth, righteousness, faith and love, in which God rules in human life, and the devil's works are judged and cast out. His ascension is seen as his investiture or coronation as the Father's vice-gerent, and his reign began then, according to the NT, not at some future date (millennial* or otherwise). The present process is one of his enemies progressively being made his footstool (see 1 Cor. 15:25, Heb. 10:12–13, following Ps. 110:1; and Rev.). He rules his church by his word and Spirit, and calls Christians to reign with him and share his victory over evil. Every knee will eventually bow to his kingly dominion, and at his glorious return the kingdom will be consummated, evil banished, the dead raised, and the new creation ushered in in its full splendour, physical as well as spiritual. Then, with every other rule subjected to his, he will hand over the kingdom to the Father, his mediatorial work completed (1 Cor. 15:21–28; Rev. 11:15).

The anointed healer?

Since the rite of anointing is preserved in the NT only in connection with healing,* and the Messiah's work plainly featured healing prominently in Is. 35 and 61 and in the gospels, some have felt a fourth office (that of 'healer') should be added. This is possible, but not necessary, since a. it can be subsumed under his work as prophet (miracles) and king (the judging and expelling of evil in human life), and b. while people were anointed to be healed, they never seem to have been anointed as healers in OT or NT.

To conclude, Christians are to learn from Jesus Christ the Son of God as prophet; to approach God confidently trusting in his perfect atoning sacrifice for sins as our great high priest (and through him to offer themselves in worship and service); and to submit gladly to his rule as king, to pray and work for the spread of his kingdom, and as his subjects to defeat evil in his name.

Bibliography

L. Berkhof, *Systematic Theology* (Grand Rapids, MI, 1953); J. Calvin, *Institutes* II. xvi; C. Hodge, *Systematic Theology* (Grand Rapids, MI, 1952); I. H. Marshall, 'Jesus Christ, Titles of' in *IBD*.

J.P.B.

OLD TESTAMENT THEOLOGY. For 200 years, 'biblical theology'* has been a programmatic term for a new and independent method of approaching the Bible in theological research. Ever since Johann Philipp Gabler's inaugural address, 'On the Proper Distinction Between Biblical and Dogmatic Theology and the Specific Objectives of Each,' at the University of Altdorff on 30 March 1787, this new biblical discipline has flourished.

However, in spite of the voluminous bibliography and ingenious labours of 200 years, OT biblical theology has produced few, if any, final answers. OT theology is a discipline in search of a definition, a methodology, an organizing centre or motif, and a permanent berth in the curriculum of divinity.

Gabler (1753–1826) was the first to face theoretically most of the issues currently troubling OT theological scholarship. The programme he advanced had these steps: 1. collect all key ideas from the biblical corpus based on a careful exegesis of the text, 2. arrange these ideas according to the historical periods from which they come, 3. weed out all the historically conditioned words and ideas that reflect the times and situations in which they were written, 4. concentrate on those which express timeless truths and universal notions or concepts, and 5. arrange those timeless and universal ideas from each of the biblical eras into a theology of the Bible.

So strongly did Gabler stress a strict historical order that his example tended to push this emerging discipline in the direction of the history of religion and a purely descriptive task. The OT theologies of the next fifty years, therefore, exhibited a heavy rationalistic bent. Among their authors were men such as C. F. Ammon (1792), G. L. Bauer (1796), G. P. C. Kaiser (1813), W. M. L. De Wette (1813), L. F. O. Baumgarten-Crusius (1828), C. P. W. Gramberg (1829) and D. C. von Cölln (1836). Towards the end of this period emerged the influence of the philosopher Hegel* (who relegated Israel, in his philosophy of religion, to a mere point in the development of Christianity) and the theologian Schleiermacher* (who stressed religious feelings and the subjective aspect of religion).

These movements were not without their sporadic interruptions, for in the middle of the 19th century a number of conservative OT theologians entered the discussion, such as: E. W. Hengstenberg (1829–35), G. L. Oehler (1845, 1873), H. A. C. Hävernick (1848), J. L. S. Lutz (1847), H. Ewald (1871), J. C. K. von Hofmann (1841–44), M. Baumgarten (1843–44), Franz Delitzsch (1881 etc.), and C. F. Keil (1853).

Nevertheless, by the end of the century, the history-of-religion* type of OT theology once again gained the dominant position in the field, principally under the influence exerted by Julius Wellhausen's Prolegomena to the History of Israel (1878).

It was only after World War I that the discipline was able to shake off this influence sufficiently to experiment with combinations of existentialism* and neo-orthodoxy.* The ensuing 'golden age' of OT theology was marked by two monumental works by W. Eichrodt (1933) and G. von Rad (1957, 1962). Between these two giants came L. Köhler (1936), P. Heinsch (1940), M.

Burrows (1946), Th. C. Vriezen (1949), O. Procksch (1950), G. E. Wright (1952), P. Imschoot (1954, 1956). E. Jacob (1955), E. J. Young (1958), G. A. F. Knight (1959) and J. B. Payne (1962).

OT theology did not disappear in the post-von Rad era as many had predicted; if anything it accelerated its activity and diversity. No less than eleven new OT theologies appeared in one decade: G. E. Wright (1970), M. G. Cordero (1970), C. K. Lehman (1971), G. Fohrer (1972), J. L. McKenzie (1974), D. F. Hinson (1976), W. Zimmerli (1978), W. C. Kaiser, Jr. (1978), C. Westermann (1978), R. E. Clements (1978), and S. Terrien (1978).

In spite of all this activity, W. Brueggemann concluded, 'It is clear that the organization of an OT Theology is now a quite open and unresolved question' (CBQ 47, 1985, p. 28). The prevailing mood of OT scholarship is to prefer the new paradigm* of a dialectic to organize the variety of OT materials.

Accordingly, in an attempt to move beyond what many regard as the totalitarianism of the search for a centre or Mittelpunkt for OT theology (e.g. Eichrodt), or the lean historicism of a history-of-religions or traditions approach (e.g. von Rad), some have experimented with the use of a dialectic approach. Thus the bi-polarities of 'blessing/deliverance', 'aesthetic/ethical', 'cosmic/teleological', and 'Grosskult/Kleinkult' were each set forth in 1978 by C. Westermann, S. Terrien, P. Hanson, and R. Albertz respectively (W. Brueggemann, JSOT 18, 1980, pp. 2–18; idem, CBQ 47, 1985, pp. 28–46; see also J. Goldingay, VT 34, 1984, pp. 153–168).

But the function of OT theology is not merely confessional or descriptive (B. S. Childs, HBT 4, 1982, pp. 1–12) or dialectical. As long as OT theology continues to be used in the singular, it must be systematic (R. P. Knierim, HBT 6, no. 2, 1984, pp. 47–48), 'because theology by definition has to do with the systematic ordering of thought, it involves comparison and contrast, the relating of this understanding or practice to that one, and the critical evaluation of life, thought, and ethos in light of the claims made within the tradition as to the truth and the fundamental meaning of it all' (W. Harrelson, HBT 6, no. 1, 1984, pp. 60–61). Harrelson continued, 'The demand then for some qualitative and quantitative modalities of the relation of Yahweh to reality that will show themselves to be central, all-inclusive, and capable of being shown by critical thought, to be central and all-inclusive *derives from this understanding of theology as a systematic endeavor*' (emphasis his).

As a contribution to this search for an organizing paradigm, we would urge all future OT theologies to take a 'diachronic' shape, *i.e.* to examine the OT in its chronological and historical sequence by eras, along with an inductively derived 'focal-point' that will supply the organizing centre to which the writer of Scripture implicitly or consciously contributed as it emerged from a germ idea to a fully developed concept.

The best contender for a textually derived 'focal-point' is what eventually the NT referred to as the 'promise' (*epangelia*; see W. J. Beecher, *The Prophets and the Promise*, Grand Rapids, MI, 1963, pp. 175–194), but which the OT knew under a constellation of terms (F. R. McCurley, Jr., *Lutheran Quarterly* 22, 1970, p. 402, n. 2) and a network of interlocking features. The 'promise' was most frequently embedded in the contents of the various covenants or as an accompanying word to a revelatory event.

This 'promise' was God's word of blessing to be or to do something for his people Israel and thereby to be or to do something for all the people of the earth (Gn. 12:3). Throughout some eleven OT eras, this 'oath,' 'pledge,' 'given-word' or declaration of God continued to unfold with increased variegation and specification.

The following eras featured these enlargements of the promise theme: 1. The prolegomena to the promise: blessing (Gn. 1:22, 28; 8:17; 9:1, 7), a seed (Gn. 3:15), a race (Gn. 9:27), and the gospel (Gn. 12:3); 2. The patriarchal era: the three basic provisions of the promise, *viz.*, an heir (Gn. 12:7; 13:14–16; 15:4), an inheritance (Gn. 12:1, 7; 13:15, 17; 15:7–8, 18; 17:8; 24:7; 26:3–4; 28:13–15), and a heritage of the good news (Gn. 12:3; 18:18; 22:18; 26:4; 28:14); 3. The Mosaic era: the people of the promise who were a holy nation (Ex. 4:22; 19:5), and a royal priesthood (Ex. 19:6); 4. The pre-monarchical era: the place of the promise: a place of rest (Nu. 10:33; Dt. 28:65; Jos. 21:44–45); 5. The monarchical era: the king of the promise who was David's heir (2 Sa. 7:12, 14) and who would inherit David's 'dynasty' (2 Sa. 7:11, 19, 25, 26, 27, 29) and 'kingdom' (2 Sa. 7:12, 13, 16) as an 'everlasting' promise (2 Sa. 7:13,

16, 24, 25, 26, 29); 6. The wisdom era: life in the promise which begins in the 'fear of the Lord' (Pr. 1:7, 29; 2:5; 8:13; 9:10; 10:27; 14:26–27; 15:16, 33; 16:6; 19:23; 22:4; 23:17) and leads to living life according to the path laid down by the law of the Lord (Pr. 2:19; 5:6; 10:17; 15:24) and to acquiring wisdom (Pr. 1:7, 29; 2:5; 8:13; 15:33); 7. The 9th-century prophets: the day of promise (Joel 3:2, 12; Ob. 15); 8. The 8th-century prophets: the servant of the promise (Is. 41:8; 43:5; 44:3; 45:19, 25; 48:19; 53:10; 54:3; 59:21; 61:9; 65:9, 23; 66:22); 9. The 7th-century prophets: the renewal of the promise (Je. 31:31–34); 10. The 6th-century prophets: the kingdom of the promise (Dn. 2:34, 44–45; 7:13–14; Ezk. 37:7–30); and 11. The post-exilic prophets: the triumph of the promise (Zc. 14).

Bibliography

B. S. Childs, *Biblical Theology in Crisis* (Philadelphia, 1970); W. Dyrness, *Themes in Old Testament Theology* (Downers Grove, 1979); J. Goldingay, *Theological Diversity and the Authority of The Old Testament* (Grand Rapids, MI, 1987); G. Hasel, 'A Decade of Old Testament Theology: Retrospect and Prospect', *ZAW* 93 (1981), pp. 165–183; J. Hayes and F. Prussner, *Old Testament Theology: Its History and Development* (Atlanta, GA, 1985); W. C. Kaiser, Jr., *Toward an Old Testament Theology* (Grand Rapids, MI, 1978); E. A. Martens, *Plot and Purpose in the Old Testament* (Leicester, 1981); J. Sandys-Wunsch and L. Eldredge, 'J. P. Gabler and the Distinction Between Biblical and Dogmatic Theology: Translation, Commentary and Discussion of His Originality', *SJT* 33 (1980), pp. 133–158; J. D. Smart, *The Past, Present and Future of Biblical Theology* (Philadelphia, 1979).

W.C.K.

OMAN, JOHN WOOD (1860–1939), Presbyterian theologian. Born in Orkney and educated at Edinburgh and Heidelberg, Oman was minister at Alnwick 1889–1907 before becoming professor at, and principal of, Westminster College, Cambridge. Deeply concerned about the crisis for Christianity brought about by the Enlightenment,* he developed an interest in Schleiermacher* and in the inner authority of truth* which verifies and helps elucidate all other experiences. But this inner illumination is not just absoluteness of value: it attaches itself to that objective reality we call the super-natural.* Oman's 'sacredly discerned' seems not unlike R. Otto's* 'idea of the holy', though Oman criticized the latter, probably unfairly. Oman believed strongly in man's progress to ultimate freedom and exalted the individual religious conscience* at the expense of all external authority,* including the creeds* and the church.* In his thinking the kingdom of God* has a similar primacy: his doctrine of the church and ministry is thus rather impoverished. In all, he wrote thirteen books, notably *The Natural and the Super-natural* (1931), but the Germanic cast of his thought does not make for easy reading. Oman's pupil, H. H. Farmer (1892–1981), went on to stress the personality of the super-natural, feeling that his teacher had not done justice to this aspect of deity.

Bibliography
G. Alexander and H. H. Farmer, in J. Oman, *Honest Religion* (Cambridge, 1941), pp. xv-xxxii (memoirs); F. G. Healey, *Religion and Reality: The Theology of John Oman* (Edinburgh, 1965); Y. Woodfin, *John Wood Oman (1860–1939): A Critical Study of His Contribution to Theology* (unpublished dissertation, New College, Edinburgh, 1962).

I.S.

ORANGE, COUNCIL OF, see SEMI-PELAGIANISM.

ORDINATION, see MINISTRY.

ORDO SALUTIS (Lat. 'order of salvation') is the systematic ordering of the various elements in personal salvation.* It answers the question: How are, for example, regeneration,* faith,* repentance,* justifi-cation,* sanctification* and glorification related to each other?

The term is common in Reformed theo-logy,* but first appeared in the Lutheran* dogmaticians Franz Buddeus (*Institutiones Theologiae Dogmaticae*, 1724) and Jakobus Karpov (*Theologia Revelata Dogmatica*, 1739). The concept, however, has an older pedigree, stretching back into pre-Refor-mation theology's attempt to relate the various experiential and sacramental steps to salvation (see Penance*). In this context

Luther's* personal struggle may be viewed as a search for a truly evangelical *ordo salutis*.

The *ordo salutis* seeks to establish, on the basis of Scripture, a pattern common to all believers, although experienced with different degrees of consciousness by each individual. The *order* involved is logical, not chrono-logical (even if certain temporal implications seem to be implied).

Controversies over apparently isolated issues of soteriology are frequently related to contrasting expositions of the *ordo salutis*. This is well illustrated by the desire of some theologians (*e.g.* A. Kuyper*) to safeguard the justification of the *ungodly* by placing justifi-cation prior to regeneration in the *ordo*, and teaching a justification from eternity. Others, meanwhile, seek to safeguard man's responsi-bility by giving faith priority over regener-ation, while yet others give regeneration (God's sovereign work) priority over conver-sion* (man's response) in order to safeguard divine sovereignty.*

Important (though often neglected) in such discussions is the recognition of the fluidity of theological language. Not all theologians have used their terminology in the same way. For example, Calvin* uses 'regeneration' to denote the whole process of renewal, repent-ance, mortification and vivification (new life), in contrast to later evangelical theology's use of the term in an inaugural sense (new birth).

In recent years the concept has come under widespread criticism because: 1. It is heavily dependent on a passage (Rom. 8:28–30; *cf.* W. Perkins' [see Puritan Theology*] 'Golden Chain') which does not reflect on the order, but rather on the fullness of salvation (*e.g.* O. Weber, Berkouwer*).

2. It distorts the basic NT (Pauline) emphasis on *historia salutis*, substituting for it a less than biblical emphasis on personal experience (H. N. Ridderbos). It transforms the NT's *via salutis* (Christ, Jn. 14:6) into a 'psychologizing' (Barth*) or 'spiritualizing' (Weber) of salvation. This subjective focus means that man's basic orientation as *incur-vatus in se* ('turned in on himself', Luther) is unresolved.

3. It reduces to one level (*ordo*) elements belonging to disparate dimensions of salvation (the divine activity and human responsibility). This 'lowest common denominator' approach minimizes the riches of God's grace* and virtually nullifies the NT emphasis on the

eschatological* (already/not yet) character of Christian experience.

Some of these criticisms are salutary, but: 1. We cannot avoid thinking about salvation in a coherent (order-ly!) fashion. H. Berkhof* is correct to say of Barth that 'he too needs a kind of logical order' (*The Christian Faith*, p. 479). 2. Following Calvin, we should stress that the disparate elements in soteriology all have their centre in Christ. All evangelical blessings are ours only in him (Eph. 1:1–14). Union* with Christ must therefore be the dominant motif in any formulation of the application of redemption and the dominant feature of any 'order' of salvation.

Bibliography

K. Barth, *CD* IV.2; G. C. Berkouwer, *Faith and Justification* (Grand Rapids, MI, 1954); J. Calvin, *Institutes,* III; R. B. Gaffin, *The Centrality of the Resurrection* (Grand Rapids, MI, 1978); A. A. Hodge, 'The *Ordo Salutis;* or Relation in the Order of Nature of Holy Character and Divine Favor', *PTR* 54 (1878), pp. 305–21; J. Murray, *Redemption – Accomplished and Applied* (Grand Rapids, MI, 1955); O. Weber, *Foundations of Dogmatics*, vol. 2 (Grand Rapids, MI, 1983).

S.B.F.

ORIGEN (*c.* 185–*c.* 254). As learned exegete, creative philosopher, master of the spiritual life, and active churchman, Origen was one of the great figures of the ancient church. He was born in Alexandria* of Christian parents. After the martyrdom of his father in the Severan persecution (202), Origen supported the family by teaching. When he was asked to instruct catechumens preparing for baptism, he gave up secular teaching and adopted an ascetic* life. Devoting himself to the study of Scripture, he was often called to other places to participate in theological discussions. On a trip to Palestine (*c.* 215) he was invited to preach by the bishops of Caesarea and Jerusalem. His bishop Demetrius, perhaps spurred by jealousy of Origen's influence, took exception to this. On a later visit to Palestine (*c.* 230) he was ordained a presbyter so that there would be no objection to his preaching. Demetrius was furious, and Origen chose to move his teaching activities to Caesarea. His pupil, Gregory Thaumaturgus (*c.* 213–*c.* 270), in his *Panegyric on Origen*, described his edu-

cational methods: he provided an encyclopedic education, encouraged the reading of all the non-atheistic philosophers, employed the Socratic method, and taught more by example than by instruction. Imprisoned and tortured during the Decian persecution, Origen died not long after at Tyre.

Origen's great work of scholarship was the *Hexapla*, a study edition of the OT, presenting in parallel columns the Hebrew text, a Greek transliteration, and the translations of Aquila, Symmachus, the Seventy (Septuagint), and Theodotion. His exegetical work found expression in *scholia* (brief notes) on difficult passages, numerous homilies preached regularly in Caesarea and directed to ordinary believers, and full-scale scholarly commentaries on major books (significant portions of John and Matthew surviving). The climax of Christian apologetic* literature in Greek was reached in his *Against Celsus*; in replying to this pagan critic's *True Word*, Origen, in addition to the usual themes of Christian apologetics, made extensive use of the argument from the moral excellence of Jesus and the beneficent influence of Christian teaching. The treatises *On Prayer* and *Exhortation to Martyrdom* show the saintly spirituality and fervent faith of a man often remembered only as a scholar and theologian. Origen's major work of theology was *On First Principles*, treating in four books God and heavenly beings, the material world and human beings, free will and its consequences, and the interpretation of Scripture. Opposition to his teachings on the pre-existence of souls (see Soul, Origin of*) and universal* salvation, climaxing in their condemnation at the Fifth Ecumenical Council in Constantinople (553), adversely affected the circulation of his works, many of which survive only in Latin translations of sometimes doubtful accuracy.

Origen was educated in the milieu of emerging Neoplatonism (see Platonism*), and his theological construction works with its philosophical concepts. His basic presuppositions are the unity and benevolence of God and the freedom of his creatures. Origen contributed significantly to the doctrine of the Trinity* with his teaching on the eternal generation of the Son by the Father. This assured that the Son was eternally of the same nature as the Father but derived from him. The Holy Spirit,* whose exact relation to the Father and Son is not clear, is in the third rank as the chief of spiritual beings. The universe includes a variety of functions united as in a body, so there are various ranks of angels and demons, their nature determined by their free choice. Some spiritual beings by choosing evil became demons; others whose transgression was not so serious fell into bodily existence, becoming the souls of human beings. Origen seems to make a more significant division between being which are pure spirits (bodiless) and those having bodies, than between uncreated and created beings. Jesus Christ was a union of the Logos,* a soul that had not fallen into sin, and a human body.

In his doctrine of redemption* Origen drew on traditional Christian themes, such as the victory of Christ over the wicked spiritual powers, but at other times he described it as an educational process. The process continues in successive worlds, in which punishment is disciplinary and corrective (see Metempsychosis*). The love of God eventually triumphs in the salvation of all beings, who finally choose freely to love God. The church is important as the school of Christ. As with the human nature of Christ, the material aspect of the sacraments is not neglected, but the emphasis is on the spiritual aspect and what benefits the soul of the recipient. The true leaders of the church are concerned with the care of souls.

Origen's most enduring influence on the practice of the church was his biblical interpretation (see Hermeneutics*). Scripture is inspired by the Holy Spirit, which means that every text has a spiritual meaning whether it has a literal meaning or not. The same Spirit must be in the interpreter for him to discern this meaning, and divine power must be added to the words to make them effective. Not every part of Scripture appears to have a lofty spiritual sense, because God has accommodated it to human language and not every person is at the same stage of spiritual growth. Problems in the text are to make the reader look beyond the literal to a non-literal sense. Since the human being is body, spirit, and soul (see Anthropology*), so Scripture has three senses: the actual story, the meaning for the church and Christian doctrine, and the moral lesson. This is Origen's normal order, and in his homilies in church he went directly from the historical sense to the application to the souls of his hearers. The non-literal meanings were justified on the basis that since Scripture is spiritual, it must have a meaning worthy of God and be inerrant in spite of apparent difficulties. Controls on the non-literal interpretation were provided by the history of salvation and the articles of faith, but the understanding of the nature of man and God allowed philosophical ideas to influence the interpretation. The allegorical (spiritual) interpretation was elevated to prominence by Origen's followers, who thereby lost the control exercised by the moral purpose.

Bibliography

H. Crouzel, *Origène et la philosophie* (Paris, 1959); idem, *Théologie de l'image de Dieu chez Origène* (Paris, 1956); J. Daniélou, *Origen* (London, 1955); B. Drewery, *Origen and the Doctrine of Grace* (London, 1960); W. Fairweather, *Origen and Greek Patristic Theology* (Edinburgh, 1901); E. de Faye, *Origène, sa vie, son oeuvre, sa pensée*, 3 vols. (Paris, 1923–28); R. P. C. Hanson, *Allegory and Event* (London, 1959); idem, *Origen's Doctrine of Tradition* (London, 1954); M. Harl, *Origène et la fonction révélatrice du Verbe Incarné* (Paris, 1958); H. Koch, *Pronoia und Paideusis: Studien über Origenes und sein Verhältnis zum Platonismus* (Berlin, 1932); P. Nautin, *Origène: sa vie et son oeuvre* (Paris, 1977); R. B. Tollinton, *Selections from the Commentaries and Homilies of Origen* (London, 1929); J. W. Trigg, *Origen: The Bible and Philosophy in the Third-Century Church* (Atlanta, GA, 1983).

E.F.

ORIGINAL RIGHTEOUSNESS, see FALL.

ORIGINAL SIN, see SIN.

ORR, JAMES (1844–1913). Scottish theologian, apologist and polemicist, Orr was educated for the most part at Glasgow University, where he distinguished himself in philosophy and theology. After seventeen years of pastoral ministry, he delivered a lecture series which was published as *The Christian View of God and the World* (1893). This work, which proved to be his *magnum opus*, was widely acclaimed and launched him on a prolific academic career. He was the leading United Presbyterian theologian at the time of the United Free Church

of Scotland union of 1900, and he came to exercise a significant influence in North America.

Orr's adult life corresponded to a particularly dynamic period in Protestant theology, and within this milieu he sought to defend evangelical orthodoxy in the face of various challenges. He was one of the earliest and principal British critics of Albrecht Ritschl's* thought. In *The Ritschlian Theology and the Evangelical Faith* (1897) and elsewhere, Orr insisted that Ritschlianism was opposed to genuine Christianity, and was intellectually untenable because of its limitation of the role of reason in Christian thought and experience. He also opposed Julius Wellhausen's documentary hypothesis on the Pentateuch. In *The Problem of the Old Testament* (1905), Orr argued for the 'essential Mosaicity' of the Pentateuch, and for the traditional construction of OT history. Further, Orr treated Charles Darwin's theory of man's origin as a serious threat to the Christian doctrines of man and sin. Initially he appeared comfortable with theistic evolution (see Creation*), but later, in *God's Image in Man* (1905), he stressed the necessity of supernatural interruptions of the evolutionary process to account for man as an embodied soul, and still later, in *Sin as a Problem of Today* (1910), he argued that the idea of moral evolution undermined the seriousness of sin and man's accountability for it.

There are some distinctive elements in Orr's apologetical thought. In *The Progress of Dogma* (1901), for example, Orr tried to counter Adolf Harnack's* negative verdict on the history of dogma by arguing that it has unfolded according to a recognizable inner logic. By regarding this logical movement as a manifestation of God's hand in history Orr sought to vindicate the orthodox doctrines that the movement produced. With respect to Scripture,* Orr affirmed its plenary inspiration and remarkable accuracy, but regarded inerrancy as apologetically 'suicidal' (see *Revelation and Inspiration*, 1910). Finally, in such works as *The Virgin Birth of Christ* (1907), Orr defended theologically as well as biblically the virginal conception of the Mediator.

The significance of Orr's theological contribution lies in neither its brilliance nor its originality, but in the breadth of his grasp of orthodox theology, the exhaustiveness of the reading upon which his conclusions were based, and the vigour with which he defended and diffused his views. His voice seemed omnipresent in his day, and his last great work as editor of *The International Standard Bible Encyclopaedia* (1915) constituted a substantial and enduring means of extending conservative orthodoxy's line of defence. He was also a contributor to the twelve-volume series *The Fundamentals* (1910–15).

Three themes pervade Orr's work. The first is an appreciative insistence that evangelical orthodoxy offers a unified and coherent world-view, a satisfying *Weltanschauung*. The second follows from the first: since Christian doctrine is an interconnected unity, no part can be negated or even altered without serious consequences for the whole. This determined Orr's apologetic agenda, and he ranged with remarkable competence across many disciplines in his efforts to buttress orthodoxy. The third decisive theme is the conviction that virtually all modern deviations from evangelical orthodoxy are prompted by anti-supernatural presuppositions.

Bibliography

J. Rogers and D. McKim, *The Authority and Interpretation of the Bible* (San Francisco, CA, 1979); G. G. Scorgie, *A Call for Continuity: The Theological Contribution of James Orr* (PhD thesis: University of St Andrews, 1986); P. Toon, *The Development of Doctrine in the Church* (Grand Rapids, MI, 1979).

G.G.S.

ORTHOPRAXIS, see Praxis.

OSIANDER, ANDREAS (1498–1552), Lutheran theologian. Born at Guzenhausen near Nuremberg, he studied Hebrew at the University of Ingolstadt and became an able Hebraist. Osiander was ordained in 1520, joined the Augustinians,* and taught Hebrew in Nuremberg. He revised the Lat. Vulgate in the light of the Heb. (1522). He attached himself to the Reformation cause and became an ardent advocate of Lutheran* doctrinal and liturgical principles in Nuremberg.

He had a difficult personality and irritated others remarkably easily. Nonetheless his ability ensured that he was present as a Lutheran representative at the Colloquy of

Marburg (1529). He was aggressive by temperament and had little sympathy with the irenic compromises of Melanchthon* at Augsburg (1530). It was not thought appropriate that he should take part in the delicate negotiations at the Colloquy of Regensburg (1541).

In 1542 he went to the Palatinate to further the Lutheran Reformation. After the Leipzig Interim (1548), with which he did not agree, he went to Königsberg (1549) and joined the theological faculty. It was from there that he became involved in a controversy with Melanchthon* over justification.* He argued that Melanchthon* overstated imputation. He maintained correctly that Luther spoke not only of external imputation but also of a real union* with Christ. However, he exaggerated the point so that he taught that genuine righteousness* was achieved, and thus lost the Lutheran tension (*simul peccator, simul justus*, 'always a sinner, always justified'). His emphasis was on the indwelling of the divine Christ, at the expense of the justifying consequences of the human death of Christ. The human nature of Christ and his work consequently receded in importance.

Characteristically Osiander conducted the controversy with much invective and won considerable opprobrium. Calvin* attacked both his view of justification and his understanding of the image of God* in man. His writings 'prove him to have been perversely ingenious in futile inventions' (*Institutes* I. xv. 3). On the Lord's Supper (see Eucharist*) he was a strong Lutheran. He was also very interested in science. He wrote the anonymous preface to Copernicus's *De Revolutionibus Orbium Caelestium* (*Revolutions of the Celestial Spheres* 1543). It has been argued that by speaking of Copernicus' theory as a 'hypothesis', Osiander was undermining his work. He was in reality seeking to find a way round the opposition and was using a well-accepted philosophical word.

Bibliography

J. Dillenberger, *Protestant Thought and Natural Science: a Historical Interpretation* (London, 1961); D. C. Steinmetz, *Reformers in the Wings* (Philadelphia, 1971).

C.P.W.

O TTO, RUDOLF (1869–1937), German Lutheran theologian, professor of theology at Breslau (1914–17) and at Marburg (1917–29). A man of profound religious experience, he found his intellectual roots in Luther,* Kant* and Schleiermacher.*

His overriding concern was to defend the integrity of religious experience* as opposed to other types of human experience. He began by defending it from the threat posed by materialistic science but then went on to explore its essential nature. To this end he visited India in 1911 and took up serious study of Sanskrit.

The main fruit of this inquiry was *Das Heilige* (1917; ET, *The Idea of the Holy*, Oxford, 1923), one of the classic studies of religion* in the 20th century. The sub-title is *An inquiry into the non-rational factor in the idea of the divine and its relation to the rational*. Otto was concerned to reject the rationalistic emphasis of comparative religion or the history of religion, and to stress the non-rational and irreducible element in religion. For him there was at the heart of religion an experience which could not be reduced to any other category. This he described as the experience of the holy.

In Kantian terms he argued for the addition of the holy to the categories of the understanding and the categorical imperative. However, he was not perfectly at ease with the term 'holy', since it had become too identified with the moral category; so he coined the term *numinous* (Lat. *numen;* spirit, divinity) to replace it. Since, for Otto, this experience of the numinous is essentially supra-rational, all religious language is an attempt to express the inexpressible. He also recognizes that any terms he might use to describe this experience can but point towards or evoke it. Thus his famous formula describing the numinous as *mysterium tremendum et fascinans* is to be taken as a series of ideograms and not a rational definition. But in attempting to evoke the numinous experience Otto is not completely subjective. For example, he considered Schleiermacher's definition of religion too subjective since it does not point clearly enough to the presence of the numinous object as the ground of the numinous experience. Thus the experience of the *mysterium* is described in terms of creature-feeling, the feeling of dependence upon that which stands over and above man as 'wholly other'. This *mysterium* is, on the one hand, absolutely unapproachable or awe-inspiring (*i.e. tremendum*), overpowering and replete with energy or life, while on the other hand, there is something in it that entrances and attracts (*i.e.* the aspect of *fascinans*), which is expressed conceptually in terms of love, mercy, pity and comfort.

While emphasizing that this numinous experience is the foundation of all religion, Otto also emphasizes the necessity of constructing a rational superstructure upon it, if it is to be of any benefit to mankind. To be a blessing, mere feeling must be transmitted into belief; and belief is only possible in rational terms. Thus the comparison of religions is possible, and Otto goes on to argue for the superiority of Christianity because of its superior conceptualization of the numinous.

Bibliography

Works: The Idea of the Holy (Oxford, 1923); *Mysticism East and West* (London, 1932); *The Philosophy of Religion* (London, 1931); *Religious Essays, A Supplement to 'The Idea of the Holy'* (Oxford, 1931).

Studies: P. C. Almond, *Mystical Experience and Religious Doctrine* (Berlin, NY, 1982); D. A. Crosby, *Interpretive Theories of Religion* (Berlin, NY, 1981), pp. 115–160; R. F. Davidson, *Rudolf Otto's Interpretation of Religion* (Princeton, 1947); R. R. Marett, *The Threshold of Religion* (London 1909); N. Smart, *Philosophers and Religious Truth* (London 1964). See also 'The Piper at the Gates of Dawn', in K. Grahame, *The Wind in the Willows* (London, 1908).

D.A.Hu.

OUSIA, see SUBSTANCE.

OWEN, JOHN, see PURITAN THEOLOGY.

OXFORD MOVEMENT, see ANGLO-CATHOLIC THEOLOGY.

P

PAEDOBAPTISM, see BAPTISM.

PALEY, WILLIAM (1743–1805). Paley is chiefly remembered for his use of the analogy of the watch and the watchmaker as a defence of the existence of God. He studied at Christ's College, Cambridge, of which he eventually became a Fellow, leaving in 1775 to take up an ecclesiastical career in the diocese of Carlisle. In an age when the universities were at something of a low ebb, Paley was a gifted and conscientious teacher whose lectures were popular.

Paley's theology was in the tradition of latitudinarianism,* and he wrote a number of apologetic works against the prevailing scepticism of the 18th century which had its roots in deism.* He was not an original thinker, but had the great virtue of being a clear one, and his writings are more in the nature of textbooks than original treatises. His major theological works were *A View of the Evidences of Christianity* (1794), *Natural Theology, or Evidence of the Existence and Attributes of the Deity Collected from the Appearances of Nature* (1802), and *Principles of Moral and Political Philosophy* (1785). This last is one of the clearest statements of the utilitarian morality propounded by the latitudinarian divines of the 17th century, anticipating many of the arguments of Jeremy Bentham (1748–1832); though Paley appeals, as Bentham does not, to the supernatural sanction as an inducement to moral behaviour. His definition of virtue was 'doing good to mankind, in obedience to the will of God, and for the sake of everlasting happiness'.

Despite his rejection of scepticism, however, Paley's own theological views appear to have been tinged with Unitarianism.* Early in his career as a university lecturer he took the view that subscription to the Thirty-nine Articles of the Church of England could only be construed as an action of 'peaceableness', since they included, on his estimate, 'some 240 distinct propositions, many of them inconsistent with each other'. On these grounds he continued to adhere nominally to the creeds, although on a conservative interpretation of them his views were at odds with the Christian understanding of the incarnation. He was, however, entirely sincere in his belief that the doctrines he did accept were logically demonstrable.

The watchmaker analogy, which appears in his *Natural Theology,* is a classic statement of the argument from design (the teleological argument) for the existence of God (see Natural Theology*). Paley introduces it by

485

comparing his likely reaction in crossing an empty heath to discovering, on the one hand, a stone, and, on the other, a watch. One might reasonably account for the stone in terms of its having always been there, but no-one would account for the watch in that way. Watches evidence purpose and design. In short they are mute testimonials to the existence of a watchmaker, and this is the conclusion any sensible person would infer from the discovery of one. The conclusion is not invalidated by the discoverer never having seen a watch made, nor by the watch not being accurate, nor by parts of it having an unknown function; neither could its existence be satisfactorily explained by appeals to impersonal laws or chance. What it demonstrates is the fact of design. Paley concludes, 'Every indication of contrivance, every manifestation of design, which existed in the watch, exists in the works of nature . . .', and the conclusion is therefore irresistible that nature too has its maker.

It is one of the ironies of history, and an example of the gap that frequently occurs between the discussions of theologians and philosophers, that twenty-three years before the publication of Paley's *Natural Theology*, David Hume* had already published the classic critique of the argument from design in his *Dialogues Concerning Natural Religion*.

Bibliography
M. L. Clarke, *Paley: Evidence for the Man* (Toronto, 1974); D. L. LeMahieu, *The Mind of William Paley* (Lincoln, NE, 1976).

D.D.S.

PANENTHEISM is the view that the universe is God, though God is more than the universe. It should be clearly distinguished from pantheism,* in which God and the universe are strictly identical. For the panentheist God has an identity of his own, that is, he is something which the universe is not. On the other hand, the universe is part of the reality of God. It is God.

The actual term was first used by contemporary process theology,* but it could be used of several earlier theories. Plotinus (c. 205–70; see Platonism*), who influenced early medieval theology, held that the world emanates from God. It is an overflow of his creative being. God creates out of himself, not out of nothing.

Some idealists,* for example George Berkeley,* held that the world has reality only as a thought of God's mind. The very reality of the universe consists in its being the contents of God's ideas, and is, therefore, God himself. Though very different from Plotinus' view, here too, God has his own reality but the universe is real only as God.

Alfred North Whitehead and Charles Hartshorne each developed slightly differing versions of panentheism which have become the philosophical basis of process theology.* For Whitehead this view is demanded by his general view of causality, coupled with the insistence that God cannot be an exception to the basic principles of reality, but must rather be their chief example. Whitehead thought of reality as composed of multiple series of events, not objects. Since only actual entities can be causes, and since each preceding event is past and not actual, events must determine themselves. And yet something must create the possibility of each event. This, Whitehead argued, must be God. Causal relations, including that of knowing, are real connections. They are events, hence God who creates and knows each event cannot be separate from them. They are just his experience, and he is just the subjectivity that feels all events.

Charles Hartshorne supplies a more detailed view of God. In his earlier writings especially, he begins by arguing for a new concept of perfection. If God is related by inclusion to all events, then he cannot be perfect in the classical sense of being unaffected by the limitations of the universe. Rather, God is perfectly relative. He is all he can be because he feels and retains all there is. And, by constantly including novel events, God is in perpetual change in new and more complex states. God grows in a creative advance as he experiences the universe he includes.

Hartshorne and his theological followers often compare God's relation to the universe to a person's relation to his body. I depend on my body as the source of my experience, but I also transcend it. Just so, while God depends on his body, the universe, he also transcends it as a mind that knows all of the possibilities for future events.

Bibliography
D. Brown, R. James, G. Reeves (eds.), *Process Philosophy and Christian Thought*

(Indianapolis, 1971); C. Hartshorne, *Omnipotence and other Theological Mistakes* (New York, 1984); L. Ford, *The Lure of God* (Philadelphia, 1978); A. N. Whitehead, *Religion in the Making* (London, 1926).

W.D.B.

PANNENBERG, WOLFHART (b. 1928). A German Lutheran born in Stettin, Pannenberg studied philosophy and theology, first at Göttingen (1948) under Nicolai Hartmann (1882–1950), then at Basel (1950) under K. Jaspers (1883–1969) and Karl Barth.* Later at Heidelberg (1951–58), having gained his doctorate under Edmund Schlink (1903–84), two men in particular influenced him: post-Bultmannian* scholar Günther Bornkamm (b. 1905), with the 'new quest' of the historical Jesus,* and Hans Von Campenhausen (b. 1903), through his 1947 rectorial address, 'Augustine and the Fall of Rome'. Pannenberg helped form a 'working circle' of graduate students and with them began searching for a unique theological interpretation or concept of history.* From 1958 he has occupied chairs in systematic theology* at Wuppertal and Mainz (1960).

Concerning revelation,* Pannenberg says theology must go beyond Barth's formula, 'the Word became human flesh'. We must add 'became human and *historical* flesh'. Otherwise, God's self-revelation still risks being dissolved into myth* or Gnosticism.* Within a context of universal history, theology must seek a Hegelian* vision of the historical movement and total unity of God's revealed Word of truth. This takes proper theological form, however, only when theology stresses the eschatological* goal which draws all history towards God, that which Pannenberg calls 'the ontological priority of the future'. Or, to speak of Christ, Christ represents the final (though provisional or proleptic) manifestation of the coming God.

Christology,* Pannenberg believes, is best approached through the historical drama of Jesus'* message and destiny. This he says is 'a Christology "from below", rising from the historical man Jesus to the recognition of his divinity' (*Jesus – God and Man*, p. 33). Pannenberg insists that going back behind the apostolic proclamation to the historical Jesus is not only possible but necessary. He rejects what, since Martin Kähler (1835–1912), has become standard practice, namely, approaching Christology through the post-Easter proclamation of the church. He also rejects the modern idea that the apocalyptic* framework of Jesus' teaching is an embarrassment. Jesus through his teaching, death and resurrection* anticipated the end of history and the life to come. His pre-Easter claims, which amounted to being one with God, were fully confirmed by God when he raised Jesus from the dead. Pannenberg says the resurrection thus confers upon the earthly Jesus, through its inherent 'retroactive power', his full title as divine Son and Messiah.

Pannenberg's theological method represents a swing of the pendulum away from the Barth–Bultmann tradition, back to history and reason. Pannenberg speaks of the 'historicality' of knowing. Faith* and knowledge (*cf.* Epistemology*) are rooted in their own history. Biblical history he defines as 'event suspended between promise and fulfilment'. However, because in the OT he sees no wedges being driven between event and interpretation or historical fact and its meaning, Pannenberg says there is a basic hermeneutical principle at work in Scripture whereby the received tradition of Israel* is constantly being revised in the light of new experience and new expectations for the future. For Pannenberg, therefore, hermeneutics* and critical history are really one science. All he asks is that, when assessing the biblical truth-claim, critical history must use the language of historical analogy* fairly and not exclude, by definition, a divine entering into history.

In apologetic terms, Pannenberg believes there can be no purely subjective defence of the faith (see Apologetics*). Theology can and must defend its objective claim on truth before the bar of critical reason. In fact, had proper lessons been learned from the efforts of the patristic writers to defend the faith (see Apologists*), modern theology might have faced the rising tide of intellectual atheism which followed in the wake of the Enlightenment* with more courage. But by failing to defend, for example, the existence of God as the necessary presupposition of all truth and of all human dignity and freedom, 19th-century theology simply abandoned the whole idea of God; it became progressively anthropologized, whilst the notion of truth became merely a creative possibility within man. Clearly, in Pannenberg's thinking lie interesting possibilities for developing a new apologetic programme.

Bibliography

Works: *Anthropology in Theological Perspective*, tr. M. J. O'Connell (Edinburgh, 1985) lists Pannenberg's works; *The Apostles' Creed* (London, 1972); *Basic Questions in Theology*, vols. I-III (London, 1970–3); *Christian Spirituality* (Philadelphia, 1983); *The Church* (Philadelphia, 1983); *Ethics* (Philadelphia and London, 1981); *Faith and Reality* (London and Philadelphia, 1977); *Human Nature, Election and History* (Philadelphia, 1977); *The Idea of God and Human Freedom* (Philadelphia, 1973); *Jesus – God and Man* (Philadelphia, 1982); *Revelation as History*, ed. Pannenberg *et al.* (London, 1969); *Spirit, Faith and Church* (Philadelphia, 1971); *Theology and the Kingdom of God* (Philadelphia, 1971); *Theology and the Philosophy of Science* (London, 1976); *What is Man?* (Philadelphia, 1970).

Studies: P. J. A. Cook, 'Pannenberg: A Post-Enlightenment Theologian', *Churchman* 90 (1976) pp. 245–264; A. D. Galloway, *Wolfhart Pannenberg* (London, 1973); B. O. MacDermott, *The Personal Unity of Jesus and God according to Wolfhart Pannenberg* (St Ottilien, West Germany, 1973); D. McKenzie, *Wolfhart Pannenberg and Religious Philosophy* (Lanham, MD, 1983); H. Neie, *The Doctrine of Atonement in the Theology of Wolfhart Pannenberg* (Berlin, 1979); J. M. Robinson and J. B. Cobb, Jr. (eds.), *Theology as History* (New York and London, 1967) with focal essay by Pannenberg; E. F. Tupper, *The Theology of Wolfhart Pannenberg* (Philadelphia, 1973).

P.J.A.C.

PANTHEISM derives from Gk. *pan* (all) and *theos* (God). Literally, it means 'all is God'. Specifically, pantheism's metaphysic, its view of reality, affirms two things: the unity of all reality and the divineness of that unity. Pantheism parallels naturalism on the first point in that both assert only one reality. But in contrast to naturalism, it calls reality divine. Pantheism is like theism* on the second point, for both recognize that the world depends on God. But unlike theism, it does not hold the world's existence to be separate from God's.

Pantheism often teaches that logical opposites coalesce in the divine being. Conceptual pairs like good/evil, personal/impersonal, and even A/non-A cannot be separated in God. These function only at the level of logical thought. At the highest levels of reality, conceptual distinctions break down because they treat as divided what is actually undivided. Since language depends on logic, pantheists usually assert God* to be ineffable or indescribable.

Epistemologically,* in their ways of knowing, pantheists fit into two general categories. Religious pantheists are often mystical.* Mysticism teaches a communion with God which bypasses discursive thought. Through ascetic* or meditative practices, mystics claim to experience God directly, intuitively, and/or ineffably. Philosophical pantheists often use rationalism, the method of reason unadulterated by sense-data, for knowledge of God. Representatives of this latter group include Benedict Spinoza* and Georg W. F. Hegel.*

Religious pantheisms appear in each of the world's five major religions. Most prominently, major religions which sprang from India, Hinduism* and Mahayana ('Greater Vehicle') Buddhism,* presuppose the pantheism of the ancient Hindu scriptures, the Upanishads. Modern proponents include the Hindu Sarvepalli Radhakrishnan (1888–1975), and the Zen Buddhist D. T. Suzuki (1870–1966). But pantheists have also been found among the theistic religions, Judaism, Christianity, and Islam. In Christianity, mystics like John Scotus Eriugena,* Meister Eckhart (*c.* 1260–1327), and Jacob Boehme* at least border on pantheism because of the influence of the Neoplatonic mystic, Plotinus (*c.* 205–70; see Platonism*).

Theists, however, have generally resisted pantheistic expressions. They often hold that pantheism destroys God's personality and goodness for it affirms that God is beyond such conceptual opposites as personality/impersonality and good/evil. They also criticize pantheism for implying that life in this world, including ethics, has little importance. Biblical Christianity in particular finds pantheism unacceptable, for it blurs the distinction between the creator* and his creatures.

Philosophers who argue against pantheism raise several questions. What empirical evidence could ever count for pantheism's claim of unity? Further, what reasons could be given to call this unity divine?

Bibliography

Texts: Jacob Boehme, *Works*, ed. C. J. Barber (London, 1909); G. W. F. Hegel, *Lectures on the Philosophy of Religion*, tr. E. B. Speirs and J. B. Sanderson, 3 vols. (London, 1962); Meister Eckhart, *Meister Eckhart: The Essential Sermons, Commentaries, Treatises, and Defense*, tr. E. Colledge and B. McGinn (New York, 1981); S. Radhakrishnan, *Indian Philosophy*, 2 vols. (London, 1929); B. Spinoza, *The Chief Works*, tr. R. H. M. Elwes, 2 vols. (New York, 1951).
Studies: N. Geisler, *Christian Apologetics* (Grand Rapids, MI, 1976); C. Hodge, *Systematic Theology* (1872–3, repr. Grand Rapids, MI, 1981); H. P. Owen, *Concepts of Deity* (New York, 1971); D. T. Suzuki, *Essays in Zen Buddhism*, 3 vols. (New York, 1949).

D.K.C.

PAPACY. The Vatican II Constitution on the Church declares, 'The Roman Pontiff, as the successor of Peter, is the perpetual and visible source and foundation of the unity of the bishops and of the multitude of the faithful' (*Lumen Gentium*, 23). The papacy (from Lat./Gk. *papa(s)*, meaning 'father') is intended to exercise a ministry of cohesion within the church by preserving its apostolic message and mission and its catholic, or universal, identity. Current ecumenical developments have focused attention on the possible role of such a ministry.

In the early church, importance was attached to certain sees, such as Alexandria* and Antioch,* which was felt to invest their bishops with special authority. The determining factor was their part in the apostolic mission and witness. This was notably the case with Rome, where the apostles Peter and Paul were said to have been martyred. In these apostles were brought together the Jewish and Gentile missions. Their witness was crowned with the supreme seal of martyrdom. Irenaeus* speaks of the Roman church's 'more powerful origin' and the consequent need for other churches to agree with her (*Against Heresies* III.3.3). This gave a significant boost to the acceptance of Pope Leo I's* letter on Christology* at the Council* of Chalcedon in 451. Clearly the political importance of the city of Rome also enhanced its bishop's prestige.

Claims for the bishop of Rome based on the Petrine texts (Mt. 16:18, 19; Lk. 22:31, 32; Jn. 21:15–17) began in the 3rd century; Tertullian may reflect an application of 'You are Peter' to Roman primacy. Subsequent church leaders, including Augustine,* were much more hesitant, preferring to use the Lucan text, 'Strengthen your brothers'. An analogy was drawn between the role of Peter among the apostles and that of his vicar, or successor, in the see of Rome among the other bishops. At best this Petrine office was regarded as a ministry* of service, not of domination. It is clear that the earliest Christian communities regarded Peter as first among the Twelve. He was the first to be called by Jesus (Mt. 4:18, 19), first in the list of apostles (Mt. 10:2), first to confess Jesus to be the Messiah (Mt. 16:16), the first apostle to see the risen Lord (1 Cor. 15:5) and the first to proclaim the good news (Acts 2:14). Yet Peter on occasion had been in the wrong and in need of reproof (Gal. 2:11), and there is a large gap between the recognition of the importance of Peter's role and the claim that the bishops of Rome are his successors. Contemporary Catholic theology tends to make less demanding claims of the Petrine texts than was often the case in the past, while continuing to emphasize the importance of the Petrine office.

From the early centuries the history of the papacy is one of growth in political power and spiritual claims. The trappings of imperial rule were gradually assimilated by the bishops of the capital city. Tension grew between loyalties to lay rulers and to the Roman pope. Gregory VII (1073–85) won the battle for the church's right to make appointments without lay interference, culminating in the humiliating appearance of the German emperor Henry IV at Canossa (1077). He even claimed complete temporal power in Western Christendom. But the conflict persisted. Boniface VIII (1294–1303) in 1300 had two swords carried before him to symbolize his temporal and spiritual power. His bull *Unam Sanctam* (1302) not only declared that there was no salvation or forgiveness outside the one church, but that this church was to be identified with the Church of Rome under the headship of Peter and his successors. The Greek church in the East, from which the

West had become divided in the 11th century, was explicitly shown to be excluded. All this was a far cry from the early centuries of the Church of Rome. Not until the papacy was divested of the Papal States in the 19th century could the politicization of the Roman see begin to be reversed. The concept of temporal authority died hard.

The spiritual authority of the bishop of Rome became a major source of dispute in the Conciliar controversy of the 15th century. At a time of schism with two or more popes, an ecumenical council seemed the ultimate solution. Had not Honorius I been formally anathematized for heresy at the Council of Constantinople in 681? However, the Council of Florence (1438–45) finally came down on the side of the superiority of the pope over councils,* reversing the decision of the Council of Constance some thirty years earlier.

This uneasy situation was especially evident in France, where an independent spirit within the church showed itself from the 13th century. Gallicanism, as the body of doctrine was called, stood for the independence of the Catholic Church in France from the ecclesiastical authority of the papacy. The Gallican Articles (1682) reaffirmed the superiority of councils over popes, thus upholding the decrees of the Council of Constance. They also maintained that the judgment of the pope was not irreformable until confirmed by a general council. Many French supporters of Jansenism, a French Catholic movement with some Protestant overtones (see Augustinianism*), appealed to a future council when the papal bull *Unigenitus* (1713) condemned their beliefs. The Articles also denied the claims of the pope to have dominion over civil rulers or that he could dispense their subjects from allegiance to them.

Movements like Gallicanism led increasingly to a reaction that was called Ultramontanism. Suspicion of breakaway groups with their heretical lapses caused many to wish to invest more and more authority in the centralized system of the papal curia. The anti-Christian and liberal developments after the French Revolution in 1789 came to a head in the 19th century. The climax of Ultramontanism was the declaration of papal infallibility at the First Vatican Council* in 1870. Pius IX (1846–78) gave the papacy for the first time a personal and approachable image,

now so familiar. But there was bitter division at the Council over this heightening of papal authority.

Vatican I declared that the pope spoke infallibly on matters of faith and morals when speaking *ex cathedra* to the whole church. A large number of safeguards were written in, which make it virtually impossible to judge retrospectively which papal pronouncements were intended to be infallible. The only statements known to fulfil the conditions are the dogmas concerning the Immaculate Conception of the Virgin Mary* (1854) and her bodily Assumption (1950). Both lack scriptural or historical warrant and neither could be described as matters of urgency that could not wait for a council. The Council used the language of 'divine right' of the successors of Peter, though there is no uniform interpretation today of this language. Universal jurisdiction was also claimed for the papacy. The abrupt termination of the Council, when Italian soldiers seized Rome, prevented any further qualifying statement about the role of the bishops.

While not denying the claims of Vatican I, Vatican II (1962–5) qualified them by emphasizing the whole 'college' of bishops, where the bishop of Rome is 'the first among equals' (see Collegiality*). He acts with them and as their spokesman, not independently. He is thus intended to be a focus of faith and of communion. For non-Catholics the chief difficulties remain papal claims that lack scriptural support, the difference between the ideal and the actual working of the papacy, together with serious doubt whether it is possible, or desirable, for one person to fulfil such a role within the universal church.

Bibliography

W. M. Abbott (ed.), *The Documents of Vatican II* (London, 1966); R. E. Brown, K. P. Donfried and J. Reumann (eds.), *Peter in the New Testament* (London, 1974); C. Butler, *The Vatican Council 1869–70* (London, 1930); D. W. O'Connor, *Peter in Rome* (New York, 1969); B. Tierney, *The Origins of Papal Infallibility, 1150–1350* (Cambridge, 1972); J. M. R. Tillard, *The Bishop of Rome* (London, 1983).

J.W.C.

PARADIGM. 1. Literally, an example, especially a normative example, in the light of which the whole class is to be understood. In 1 Cor. 15:45–49, Paul treats Adam and Christ as paradigms, in this sense, of mankind.

2. In philosophy, 'paradigm case' arguments are sometimes used against sceptical positions, *e.g.* if it is denied that free will exists by arguing that 'freedom' is to be understood in terms not of some abstract definition, but of paradigm cases such as lovers deciding to marry. Such cases certainly exist; so therefore does freedom. Critics reply that this would have 'proved' the reality of witchcraft. Moreover, concepts so defined are of limited use: is 'freedom' thus understood the 'freedom' relevant to moral responsibility?

3. Martin Dibelius (1883–1947) used the term for gospel passages used by early Christian preachers as examples of 'that which Jesus was and brought into being' (*e.g.* Mk. 2:23–28). Paradigms end in thoughts useful for preaching purposes, usually a saying of Jesus. Dibelius thought paradigms historically valuable, though sometimes modified by preachers or evangelists.

Bibliography

G. Carey, *I Believe in Man* (London, 1977), ch. 4; E. Gellner, *Words and Things* (London, 1959), ch. 2, sect. 4; P. Schilpp (ed.), *The Philosophy of G. E. Moore* (New York, ²1952), pp. 343–368; M. Dibelius, *From Tradition to Gospel* (ET, London, 1934), ch. 3.

R.L.S.

PARADOX IN THEOLOGY. Paradox, *i.e.* the unexpected and seemingly irrational or impossible (from Gk., *para* and *doxa*, 'against opinion'), occurs in human thought at three levels.

1. *Verbal* paradox is a use of words which, by linking ideas that look incompatible, challenges fresh thinking and prompts new questions. Examples are: 'Whose service is perfect freedom' (*Book of Common Prayer*); 'He who finds his life will lose it' (Mt. 10:39); see also 2 Cor. 6:9–10. Verbal paradoxes are resolved by explanation and reformulation. Theologians frequently use verbal paradox to catch attention and provoke reflection, *e.g.* 'simultaneously righteous and a sinner' (Luther); that the Son of God died is 'to be believed, because it is absurd' (Tertullian); the resurrection 'is certain, because it is impossible' (*idem*). Such statements depend on specific explanations of the words used, and can be replaced by non-paradoxical statements at will.

2. *Logical* paradox is apparent self-contradictoriness in assertions about matters of fact. Logical paradoxes have fascinated philosophers ever since Zeno the Stoic argued that, since distance is infinitely divisible and you must pass through each segment of it before reaching the next one, the hare can never overtake the tortoise. Or again: In affirming that I always lie, can I be telling the truth? (If yes, then no.) Techniques of philosophical analysis are needed to resolve paradoxes of this kind.

3. *Ontological* paradox is the seeming incompatibility of statements describing reality, or inferences drawn from those statements. Kant* called this an *antinomy*. In theology, taking Scripture as the touchstone for the reality of God, sample ontological paradoxes are: tri-personality within God's unity and uniqueness (see Trinity*); 'our God contracted to a span, incomprehensibly made man' (Charles Wesley's focusing of the incarnation*); faith* as man's act and equally God's gift; God ordaining and overruling all human action without destroying human liberty and answerability, or becoming the author of sin in a morally blameworthy sense (see Providence;* Sovereignty of God*); God determining the words of prophets, apostles, and biblical writers without impeding their freedom and spontaneity in self-expression (see Scripture*). Since none of these realities can be made transparent to the human mind, a better name for them than 'paradoxes' (which suggests that they are only verbal or conceptual) is 'mysteries' – that is, objective states of affairs which we know to be real, without knowing how they *can* be real. It should not surprise us to find aspects of the existence and activity of our creator incomprehensible, *i.e.* beyond our creaturely grasp.

Neo-orthodox* theologians, standing on Kierkegaard's* shoulders, have often embraced paradox as a paradigm* of the dialectical* method of theologizing (affirmation-within-negation and vice versa). This method was thought to lead beyond the rationalism of armchair theologians who domesticate God, boxing him into their own thoughts, to a dynamic faith that encounters the free, living, sovereign, transcendent creator in the crisis of commitment and decision. The strength of this fashion of thought ('the theology of paradox' as it was once called) lay in its recognition that creator and creature, eternal and temporal, infinite and finite, are not commensurate; further, that sin twists our natural thinking about God out of true, so that we cannot expect good theology and real faith to seem other than irrational to the secular world. The corresponding weakness, however, was an unwillingness to be bound by the consistent rationality of Scripture; this resulted in much real irrationality and incoherence. The theology of paradox is now, in some quarters, somewhat *passé*.

Bibliography

C. F. H. Henry, *God, Revelation and Authority*, vol. 1 (Waco, TX, 1976), chs. 11 – 15; R. W. Hepburn, *Christianity and Paradox* (London, 1958); H. R. Mackintosh, *Types of Modern Theology* (London, 1937).

J.I.P.

PAROUSIA, see ESCHATOLOGY.

PASCAL, BLAISE (1623–62). Pascal, whose early genius emerged in mathematics, experimental physics and practical inventions, was converted to Jansenism (see Augustinianism*) at Rouen in 1646. He participated in the social, intellectual and cultural life of Paris until his 'night of fire' (1654), an experience of intense assurance, joy and peace through Christ, leading to the total consecration of his life to God. Visiting the Jansenist community at Port-Royal, he was invited to rally public support for their leader, Antoine Arnauld, accused of heresy by the Sorbonne. In fourteen months he wrote a series of anonymous pamphlets, ten addressed to a provincial priest and eight to the Jesuits. With biting satire *The Provincial Letters* exposed the intellectual dishonesty of Arnauld's opponents and the moral hypocrisy of the Jesuits, who were the leading faction.

His chief legacy is an apologia* of the Christian religion, aimed at the educated unbeliever of his day. Ill health restricted it to sketches, some developed, others telegraphic, which the Jansenists published posthumously as the *Pensées*. Pascal eschews the traditional proofs for the existence of God, based on pure reason or deduced from the cosmos. Human reason is faulty, affected by instincts, illnesses and delusions, subject to pride, incapable of establishing first principles (*contra* Descartes*), let alone of bringing us to a knowledge of God and of our eternal destiny; at best it establishes only an abstract God and is powerless to move the heart (in the biblical sense, Ps. 119:36) – the highest order of human awareness, which is persuaded by grace alone. Instead, Pascal the empiricist* starts with the data, notably the inexplicable phenomenon of mankind: unquestionably corrupt, subject to inconstancy, boredom, anxiety and selfishness, doing anything in the waking hours to divert the mind from human wretchedness, yet showing the vestiges of inherent greatness in the mind's realization of this condition. Mankind is also finite, suspended between the twin infinities revealed by telescope and microscope, and aware of an inner emptiness which the finite world fails to satisfy. No philosophy makes sense of this. No moral system makes us better or happier. One hypothesis alone, creation in the divine image followed by the fall, explains our predicament and, through a redeemer and mediator with God, offers to restore our rightful state. Pascal proceeds to challenge his reader to commitment to Christ and to eternal life, particularly in his famous 'wager' passage, and then presents evidence for the truth of Christianity by showing its perpetuity from the first man until the end of time and Christ's excellence as mediator in perfectly combining human greatness with human degradation on the cross; further, the whole OT finds fulfilment in him, whose redemption relieves despair, humbles pride and empowers us to do good while not rendering us totally sinless.

The *Pensées* remain striking by their almost unique approach to apologetics, their deep, compassionate understanding of mankind without God and the persuasive prose of some of the developed sections. Their readership has multiplied in our affluent, anxious generation; many 20th-century writers who reject Pascal's solution show the influence of his analysis of the human condition.

Bibliography

A. Krailsheimer (ed.), *The Provincial Letters* (Harmondsworth, 1967); *idem* (ed.), *Pensées* (Harmondsworth, 1966).

J. H. Broome, *Pascal* (London, 1965); A. Krailsheimer, *Pascal* (Oxford, 1980); J.

Mesnard, *Pascal, His Life and Works* (London, 1952).

D.G.P.

PASCHAL CONTROVERSIES, see EASTER.

PASCHASIUS RADBERTUS (*c.* 785– *c.* 860), theologian, was the first explicit proponent of transubstantiation. Monk, and for a time abbot, of the Benedictine monastery at Corbie in modern France, he issued in 831 the first separate treatise on the doctrine of the holy communion, *De Corpore et Sanguine Domini (On the Body and Blood of the Lord)*. It brought to a head the tendencies of the immediately preceding centuries, by interpreting the emphatic language of many of the fathers about the presence of Christ in the sacrament, or in the elements, in a strictly literal sense, as meaning that the true body and blood of Christ which suffered on the cross, are present, through being made out of the substance of the bread and wine – though without altering the appearance or taste of the latter (see Eucharist*). The doctrine of transubstantiation was defined by the Fourth Lateran Council (1215) (see Councils*), and Paschasius is a saint of the Roman calendar. He seems to have expected opposition, and the revised edition of his book (844) was given by King Charles the Bald to Ratramnus,* and perhaps to John Scotus Eriugena,* for them to answer. Paschasius wrote various other works, including a long commentary on Matthew.

Bibliography

Works: in *PL* 120; extracts, with translations, in C. Herbert, *The Lord's Supper: Uninspired Teaching* (London, 1879); discussion in N. Dimock, *The Doctrine of the Lord's Supper* (London, 1910).

R.T.B.

PASTORAL THEOLOGY. Although obviously taking its cue from the biblical imagery of the shepherd, pastoral theology is notoriously difficult to define with precision. Pastoral theology has to do with the mutual relationship between theology and pastoral work. It provides the theological foundation for pastoral ministry, stimulates theological reflection on pastoral experience and at the same time reflects on theology from a pastoral perspective.

Problems of definition arise because of the ambiguous nature of its boundaries with related disciplines. Practical theology, a discipline which emerged in the 19th century, has to do with the skills needed to conduct a ministry and so relates to subjects such as worship,* homiletics, missions and administration. Applied theology relates to ethics* or moral theology* which, together with the provision of spiritual direction, have always been closely allied to pastoral theology, especially within Catholicism. More recently it has often been wrongly identified with pastoral psychology. Ecclesiology in its broadest sense, meaning not only the doctrine of the organization of the church but contemporary understanding of the church's role and mission, is also a close relation of pastoral theology. Pastoral theology both draws on these disciplines and contributes to them but is not itself limited by them and concentrates on the interface between theology and pastoral experience. Hence from the theological standpoint, it raises questions and provides direction regarding the nature of ministry; and from the pastoral standpoint, it looks to theology for understanding and interpretations of human experience.

The Bible rarely presents an explicit pastoral theology although it may be said to be doing so in Ezk. 34; Acts 20:13–38; 2 Corinthians and the Pastoral Epistles. But much of the Bible is an implicit pastoral theology; even the gospels may contribute to our understanding of pastoral theology if the pastoral motives which lie behind them, and not simply their evangelistic purpose, are noted. In the early centuries several outstanding works were written on the nature of pastoral ministry, among which are Gregory of Nazianzus'* *Oration* II, John Chrysostom's *On the Priesthood* and Gregory the Great's* *Pastoral Rule*. Others, while not writing systematically about pastoral work, provide examples of early pastoral theology, such as Augustine's* *City of God*.

Few developments took place during the Middle Ages, and it was not until the Tridentine reforms of the 16th century and the writings of the Reformers that renewed interest was demonstrated. The chief systematic exponent of pastoral theology among the Reformers was Martin Bucer.* The effect of

493

the Reformation was not limited to the development of Puritan* spiritual direction but was widely felt in the raising of the standards of the ministry. Even so, the effects were most clearly marked in Richard Baxter's* *The Reformed Pastor*.

The increasing need to provide an adequately trained ministry led to the emergence of pastoral theology as a separate discipline in a more modern sense in the late 18th century. During the following century numerous works were published which drew on contemporary science and philosophy in an attempt to provide a systematic and comprehensive understanding of ministry. At the turn of the century, however, a decline had set in and works on pastoral theology had become practitioners' handbooks rather than works of theological depth.

The 20th century witnessed major developments in the discipline, initially through the work of A. T. Boisen (1876–1966) who introduced the clergy to clinical training. His pupil Seward Hiltner (b. 1909) was to have an even more marked effect and, in his book *Preface to Pastoral Theology*, was to reorganize the discipline around the concerns of healing, sustaining and guiding. In doing so he stressed that traditional pastoral theology which dealt with spiritual life in a psychological, social and cultural vacuum was to be rejected and replaced by an approach to the whole person. He stamped the discipline with a psychological trade-mark and firmly bound pastoral training to psychological training. Since Hiltner, there have been many attempts to correlate psychology with theology. Among the best have been those of Don Browning (b. 1934), James N. Lapsley (b. 1930), Thomas Oden and Daniel Williams (1910–73). Their concern was not so much to translate the language of religion into the language of psychology as to show the theological assumptions and implications of psychology.

Subsequent developments have moved away from this approach for a number of reasons. First, there has been a concern to break the 'psychological captivity' in which pastoral theology was held. Equal emphasis is now placed on man's social and political situation. Many see recent liberation theologies* as the latest expression of pastoral theology, since they seek to provide theological understanding and direction for those who are socially and economically oppressed.

Secondly, there has been a concern to establish pastoral theology as a credible academic discipline in its own right rather than as an adjunct to psychology. Thirdly, and most significantly, there has been a reassertion of the need for pastoral theology to have moral and theological foundations. Under Hiltner the theological dimension was liberal and the moral dimension relativist, if not at times altogether absent.

A recent evangelical exponent of pastoral theology is Eduard Thurneysen (1888–1974), who in his thorough book *A Theology of Pastoral Care* deals expertly and biblically with the human need for forgiveness and marks out the distinctive pastoral, as opposed to psychological, approach to human need. Its limitation lies in the fact that it confines itself to that subject alone, whereas pastoral theology must demonstrate wider concerns, however central that issue is. The wide spectrum of recent literature suggests that the future for pastoral theology is promising.

See also: PRACTICAL THEOLOGY.

Bibliography

P. H. Ballard (ed.), *The Foundations of Pastoral Studies and Practical Theology* (Cardiff, 1986); R. Baxter, *The Reformed Pastor* (1656; Edinburgh, 1974); D. S. Browning (ed.), *Practical Theology* (New York, 1983); S. Hiltner, *Preface to Pastoral Theology* (Nashville, TN, 1958); B. Holifield, *A History of Pastoral Care in America: From Salvation to Self-Realization* (Minneapolis, MN, 1983); J. T. McNeill, *A History of the Cure of Souls* (New York, 1977); H. R. Niebuhr and D. D. Williams (eds.), *The Ministry in Historical Perspective* (New York, 1956); E. E. Shelp and R. Sunderland (eds.), *A Biblical Basis for Ministry* (Philadelphia, 1981); M. Taylor, *Learning to Care* (London, 1983); E. Thurneysen, *A Theology of Pastoral Care* (Atlanta, GA, 1962); D. Tidball, *Skilful Shepherds* (Leicester, 1986); F. Wright, *The Pastoral Nature of the Ministry* (London, 1980).

D.J.T.

PATRISTIC THEOLOGY is strictly the theology of the fathers (Lat. *patres*), *i.e.* the teachers and writers of the early church, expressed not only in their individual works but also in communal forms such as church orders and conciliar definitions. The phrase was first used in the 17th century, in distinction from biblical, scholastic, symbolic and speculative theology.

There is no agreed end to the patristic period. The doctrinally most creative era reached its peak in the Council of Chalcedon (451), and the collapse of Roman power in the West also suggests a historical break in the later 5th century; but many would make Gregory the Great* or Isidore of Seville (d. 636) the last of the Western fathers – or even Bernard,* the last great pre-scholastic church teacher. In the East, where Roman rule continued unbroken, John of Damascus* sums up the patristic era, followed by the last of the early councils,* Nicaea II in 787. But Eastern Orthodoxy* dislikes sharp divisions, and Gregory Palamas was honoured as a father and doctor of the church soon after his death in 1359.

The traditional doctors (*i.e.* teachers) of the Western church are Ambrose,* Jerome,* Augustine* and Gregory,* and of the eastern, Basil,* Gregory of Nazianzus* and John Chrysostom, with Athanasius* added later. But medieval and modern theologians are also recognized as church doctors in the West. The category is both wider than that of fathers (in not being restricted to the early centuries) and narrower (in including only the most eminent, and requiring more formal ecclesiastical designation). Another distinction has been made between fathers, marked by orthodoxy of doctrine and sanctity of life, and ecclesiastical writers, such as Tertullian* and Origen,* who belong to Christian antiquity but enjoy only qualified church approval.

The appeal to the fathers in virtually the modern sense began in the late 4th to early 5th centuries, chiefly in the Christological* controversies. The Orthodox churches draw no dividing line between the Bible and the church's theological tradition. The faith has come down, ultimately from God through Christ, in an unbroken continuum, received by the church 'from Holy Scripture, and from the teachings of the holy fathers and from the definitions of one and the same faith by the four sacred councils' (Constantinople II, 553). In Roman Catholicism, the early conciliar definitions, which endorsed patristic doctrine, have the infallibility of the church's magisterium, while a less precise authority belongs to the general consensus of other patristic

teaching. According to Vincent of Lérins (d. before 450), the catholicity* of the faith is recognizable by its universality, antiquity and consensus.

The Reformation churches all paid special attention to the early fathers, not as authorities on a par with Scripture but as godly interpreters of the apostolic faith in a united and largely uncorrupted church. The church's 'fall' into medieval error and superstition was often dated by the Reformers *c.* 600. The Anabaptists placed it in the time of Constantine, and were able to disregard the councils and creeds, even appealing to the pre-Nicene fathers against later patristic dogma. The Anglican tradition has always evinced a particularly high regard for the fathers, but all the Magisterial Reformers shared it to a marked degree.

The fathers were productive in most fields of theology: apologetic* (*e.g.* Justin, Tertullian, Origen, Augustine), moral* (*e.g.* Clement of Alexandria, Ambrose, Gregory the Great), biblical* (especially Irenaeus), dogmatic* (*e.g.* Athanasius, the Cappadocians, Augustine, Cyril of Alexandria), mystical* (*e.g.* Gregory of Nyssa, Pseudo-Dionysius), ascetic* (*e.g.* the Alexandrians, Cassian, Evagrius Ponticus, Basil), sacramental* (*e.g.* Cyprian, Augustine), liturgical* (*e.g.* Cyril of Jerusalem), philosophical* (*e.g.* Augustine).

Their major contributions were to the elucidation of the Trinity, Christology, and the doctrines of church and sacraments, and sin and grace. On these a clear consensus emerged, in West or East if not throughout the church, to which Reformation theology could appeal with little hesitation. But no patristic consensus was reached on atonement, anthropology, eschatology, the work of the Spirit and other topics.

The distinctive features of patristic theology may be broadly defined as follows:

1. *It was church theology.* Patristic theologians were churchmen (Origen and Tertullian are not exceptions to this) and teachers of the church. Many were bishops (a common meaning of 'father'). There were no theological seminaries or faculties! In Vincent's canon, truth and church belonged together, as did error and schism. The catechumenate was an important setting for systematic doctrinal teaching. Patristic theology was therefore a corporate enterprise.

2. *It was based on the spiritual exegesis*

495

of Scripture. Sermons and commentaries were important media of patristic teaching. Convinced of the total inspiration of Scripture but often lacking in historical perspective, the fathers readily resorted to forms of spiritual exegesis, especially allegory and extended typology, particularly in dealing with the Old Testament (see Hermeneutics*). The Antiochene school* followed a more grammatico-historical approach.

3. *It was shaped by worship and piety.* The fathers cited the *lex supplicandi* or *orandi* ('law of praying') to establish the *lex credendi* ('law of believing'). Augustine argued from the practice of infant baptism to the doctrine of original sin. Basil discussed the dogmatic significance of different doxologies, and others (*e.g.* in the Pelagian* controversies) the doctrinal implications of prayer. Devotion to Christ as *theotokos* ('God-bearer') was a starting-point in the Christological disputes.

4. *It was a developing tradition.* The fathers built on their predecessors' foundations – hence the embarrassment when Cyprian's non-recognition of schismatic baptism had to be abandoned. Orthodox theologians were held to be merely unfolding what the apostles taught in brief; it was heretics who produced novelties. Augustine's anti-Pelagian theology probably could not satisfy Vincent's criterion of antiquity, but he was anxious to refute Pelagius' appeal to earlier teachers.

5. *It was pervasively otherworldly.* Most of the great fathers espoused ascetic* ideals. Platonic* influences imparted a strong spiritualizing tendency to much of their theology. The values it most characteristically affirms belong to the inner world of the spirit or the transcendent realm of heaven.

6. *It interacted with secular philosophy.* From the 2nd century Apologists* onwards, the fathers made philosophy the handmaid of theology. The influence of eclectic Platonism and Stoicism,* in particular, was widespread. The fathers engaged critically with pagan thought, and spoke intelligibly to the pagan mind. But today they are often faulted for failing to distinguish between Greek philosophical theology and Judaeo-Christian beliefs.

Bibliography
B. Altaner, *Patrology* (Freiburg, 1960); J. N. D. Kelly, *Early Christian Doctrines* (London, ⁵1977); J. Pelikan, *The Christian Tradition*, vol. 1: *The Emergence of the Catholic Tradition (100–600)* (Chicago and London, 1971); G. L. Prestige, *Fathers and Heretics* (London, 1954); B. Ramsey, *Beginning to Read the Fathers* (London, 1986); H. Von Campenhausen, *The Fathers of the Greek Church* (London, 1963); *idem, The Fathers of the Latin Church* (London, 1964); M. F. Wiles, *The Christian Fathers* (London, 1966).

D.F.W.

PAUL. This article presents an overview of Paul's life and work, his theology, place in early Christianity, and significance for today.

1. Life and work

The apostle Paul, a Jew from the tribe of Benjamin, was born a Roman citizen, in Tarsus of Cilicia, with the Heb. name Saul. Paul was most probably one of his Roman names. Brought up as a Pharisee, he became highly skilled in Jewish law and tradition (Gal. 1:14). While engaged in a violent persecution of the church, he was confronted, on the road to Damascus, with a blinding vision of the risen Jesus. He continued to Damascus, and there regained his sight and was baptized *c.* AD 34 (Acts 9:3–19). In obedience to his new Lord he began at once to preach Jesus as Messiah in the synagogues, and became in his turn the object of Jewish persecution (Acts 9:19–25; *cf.* 1 Thes. 2:14–16).

At this point he apparently spent some time in Arabia (Gal. 1:17), returning to Damascus for three years before going to Jerusalem (Acts 9:26–29). Persecution again followed, and Paul went to his home town, Tarsus, until brought by Barnabas to help in the growing multi-racial church in Antioch (Acts 11:19–26). From there the two made a further trip to Jerusalem (Acts 11:30) in order to provide famine relief (*c.* 46). It is fairly likely that this is the same trip as that described in Gal. 2:1–10, though some have identified the latter with the visit of Acts 15.

Back in Antioch, Barnabas and Paul were called by the Spirit to an itinerant preaching ministry (Acts 13 – 14), whose very success led to controversy over the terms of admission of non-Jews into the people of God (Gal.; Phil. 3:2–11; see Acts 15). Paul made two subsequent journeys with Silas and others, spending considerable time in Corinth on the first journey and Ephesus on the second (Acts

16 – 19). On his return to Jerusalem he was arrested and tried before the Sanhedrin and two successive Roman governors, a process which ended only when Paul used his right as a Roman citizen to appeal to Caesar. He was thereupon taken to Rome by boat, being shipwrecked *en route* off Malta (Acts 20 – 28). The narrative of Acts ends with Paul preaching openly in Rome, mentioning neither trial nor execution. Later church accounts fill in the gap, telling of Paul's martyrdom under Nero, *c.* 64.

The surviving letters formed a vital part of Paul's ministry, being the principal means by which he could, even when absent, exercise pastoral authority over the churches he had founded. These letters raise three major questions: a. How is his theology to be understood? b. What role did he play in the development of early Christian thought? and c. How is he to be appropriated in the contemporary church?

2. Paul's theology

Some have put justification* at the centre of Paul's thought: others, his doctrine of 'being in Christ' (see Union with Christ*). Neither solution solves all the problems. A better way forward is to see Paul as having rethought his pharisaic theology in the light of Jesus Christ, as follows.

a. Paul's background. The basic affirmations of Jewish theology are monotheism* (there is one God, the creator of the world) and election (this God has chosen Israel to be his people). This double doctrine finds classic expression in the covenant,* whose focal point was the law* (Torah). Israel's task was to be faithful to God by keeping the Torah, and God for his part would be faithful to the covenant ('righteous'*) by delivering Israel from her enemies. As a Pharisee, Paul believed that this deliverance would take the form of a new age breaking in to the present (evil) age: Israel would then be vindicated ('justified', *i.e.* declared to be truly within the covenant) and those who had died faithful to the covenant would be raised from the dead to share in the new world order. In the meantime, Israel's one hope lay in fidelity to Torah, and in consequent exclusiveness and separation from defilement, particularly through contact with Gentiles. It was the apparent loosening of these covenant obligations by the early Christians that led Paul to persecute them. His

vision of the risen Jesus caused a total upheaval not only in his personal life, through his acknowledgment of Jesus as Lord, but also in his thinking. If God had raised Jesus from the dead, that meant that Jesus was the Messiah, Israel's representative. This realization led at once to the reassessment of Paul's whole theological scheme and practical vocation.

b. God and Jesus. Paul's view of Jesus caused, and shaped, the revolution in his view of God. If God had vindicated the crucified Jesus as Messiah, then in him – in his suffering and vindication – God's action to save his people had already occurred. Since the OT saw that action as essentially God's own, Paul concluded that Jesus himself *was* God in action: 'God was in Christ reconciling the world to himself' (2 Cor. 5:19, RSV). What Jesus did on the cross is something only God can do: so Jesus, who before becoming human was 'in the form of God', did not regard that equality with God as something to take advantage of, but revealed the true character of God by his self-abnegation, incarnation and death (Phil. 2:6–8). The resurrection is God's affirmation that this self-giving love is indeed the revelation of his own life and character (Phil. 2:9–11; *cf.* Rom. 1:4). The God who would not share his glory with another has shared it with Jesus (Is. 45:22–25; *cf.* Phil. 2:9–11). Monotheism is thereby redefined, not abandoned: Paul draws on the Jewish metaphor about the 'wisdom* of God' by which God made the world, to ascribe that agency in creation, as well as in new creation, to Jesus (1 Cor. 8:6; Col. 1:15–20), placing Jesus alongside 'the Father' in formulations which are themselves restatements of Jewish monotheism over against pagan polytheism. This striking new vision of God, highlighting especially the divine love, is filled out further by Paul's view of the Spirit* at work in men and women to accomplish that which God intends, the giving of true life (Rom. 8:1–11; 2 Cor. 3:3, 6, 17–18). Finally, Paul recognizes that monotheism cannot remain content with dividing the world into two halves. If there is one God, and one Lord, there must be one people (Rom. 3:27–30, 10:12; Gal. 3:19–20). His new view of God thus points to a new view of God's people (*cf.* Church*).

c. The new covenant. In recognizing Jesus as Messiah ('Christ' in Gk.), *i.e.* as the one in whom God's purposes for Israel* had been summed up, Paul was compelled to rethink the place of Israel, and of her law, in God's over-all purposes. Unless God had changed his plans (which was unthinkable), that which had happened in Christ must have been God's intention all along. The cross and resurrection gave Paul the clue: since the Messiah represents Israel, Israel herself must 'die' and be 'raised' (Gal. 2:15–21). Reading the Scriptures again with this in mind, Paul discovered that, in the very passage where the covenant promises were first made (Gn. 15), two themes stood out: God's desire that 'all nations' should share in the blessing of Abraham, and the faith of Abraham as the sign that he was indeed God's covenant partner (Rom. 4; Gal. 3). But this meant that Israel's understanding of her role in God's plan had been wrong. She had mistaken a temporary stage in the plan (her land, her law and her ethnic privileges) for the final purpose itself. The law, however, although coming from God and reflecting his holiness, could not be the means of life, because of sin. But now Christ, not Israel, took centre stage: and in Christ, God's plan for a worldwide family was being enacted. Israel's political enemies were merely a metaphor or symbol for the real enemies of God, namely sin and death (1 Cor. 15:26, 56), which held sway over not merely Israel but the whole world.

These ultimate enemies had been overcome in the cross and resurrection. As the innocent representative of Israel, and hence of the human race, the Messiah had allowed sin and death to do their worst to him, and had emerged victorious. Sin's power had exhausted itself by bringing to his death the one human being who, himself without sin, could properly be vindicated by God after death (2 Cor. 5:21). The cross thus stands at the heart of Paul's theology, as the basis of his mission (2 Cor. 5:14–21), and of his redefinition of the people of God. The fact of universal sin (Rom. 1:18 – 3:20) demonstrates the necessity for a saving act of pure grace (3:21–26): the divine wrath (1:18 – 2:16) is turned aside, as at the exodus, by the blood of sacrifice (3:24—6). Had Israel herself not been captive to sin, covenant membership would have been definable in terms of law and circumcision: but in that case Christ would not have needed to die (Gal. 2:11–21).

The resurrection provides the basis for the true definition of God's people. God has vindi- cated Jesus as Messiah, and has thereby declared that those who belong to him, who in the Heb. idiom are 'in Christ' (*cf.* 2 Sa. 19:43 – 20:2), are the true Israel. The marks of new covenant membership are the signs of the Spirit's work, *i.e.* faith* in Jesus as Lord, belief in his resurrection, and baptism* as the mark of entry into the historical people of God (Rom. 10:9–10; Col. 2:11–12). 'Justifi- cation' is thus God's declaration in the present that someone is within the covenant, a declar- ation made not on the basis of the attempt to keep the Jewish law but on the basis of faith: because faith in Jesus is the evidence that God has, by his Spirit, begun a new work in a human life which he will surely bring to completion (Rom. 5:1–5; 8:31–39; Phil. 1:6; 1 Thes. 1:4–10). The present divine verdict therefore correctly anticipates that which will be issued on the last day on the basis of the entire life of the Christian (Rom. 2:5–11; 14:10–12; 2 Cor. 5:10). This double verdict is thus based on two things – the death and resurrection of Jesus and the work of the Spirit: Christ and the Spirit together achieve 'that which the law could not do' (Rom. 8:1– 4). 'Justification' thus redefines the people of God, and opens that people to all who believe, whatever their racial or moral background.

The whole world is thus the sphere of God's redeeming action in Christ, and men and women without distinction are summoned by the gospel to submit to Jesus' lordship and so to enjoy the blessings of life in the covenant community, both in the present world and in that to come. God's people form, in Christ, that true humanity which Israel was called to be but by herself could not be. Paul expresses this appropriately by referring to the church, the people of the Messiah, as 'the body of Christ' (Rom. 12; 1 Cor. 12). This member- ship in Christ must be lived out by individual Christians allowing the Spirit to direct their actions, enabling them to live in the present as appropriate for the heirs of God's future kingdom (Rom. 8:12–25; Gal. 5:16–26; Col. 3:1–11). Since they are already thus partici- pating in the new age, the final return of Christ may be soon or late, but should find them 'awake', not asleep in sin (1 Thes. 5:1– 11; *cf.* Phil. 3:17–21). And when that day comes, not only human beings, but the whole creation, will share in the renewal which the one God has planned for his world (Rom. 8:18–25).

d. The righteousness of God. This picture of the renewal of all creation through the work of Christ and the Spirit completes Paul's picture of God himself. In the letter to Rome, Paul takes the standard Jewish question concerning God's righteousness (If Israel is the people of God, why is she suffering?), intensifies it in the light of universal sin (If all, Israel included, are sinful, how can God be true to the covenant?), and answers it in the light of the gospel. The cross and resurrection, he declares, demonstrate that God is in the right: he has been true to the covenant with Abraham, he has been impartial in his dealings with Jew and Gentile alike, he has dealt with sin on the cross, and he now saves those who cast themselves on his mercy. The further question, whether God is righteous in thus apparently allowing the original covenant people to miss the messianic salvation, is answered in Rom. 9 – 11. God has been true to his promise, which always spoke of a worldwide family: Israel's present casting away is a necessary part of the over-all divine purpose, since only so can Gentiles be welcomed in and Jews themselves saved, as they will continue to be, by grace alone. Paul explains the apparent oddities of the divine plan as the outworking of God's love and mercy in the face of human, including Jewish, sin.

Paul's theology thus effects a redefinition of monotheism and election, based on the death and resurrection of Jesus and the work of the Spirit. This theology is at every point characterized by love: the love of God for his world and his human creatures; the love of Jesus in his atoning death; and the love for God and for one another with which, by his Spirit, God is transforming the corporate and individual lives of his new covenant people, so that they become the fully human beings God intends, reflecting his own image, which is Jesus himself (2 Cor. 3:18; Col. 3:10).

3. Paul in early Christianity

It thus becomes clear that Paul was not responsible for the 'Hellenization'* of early Christianity, *i.e.* the transformation some have postulated from a pure Jewish faith into a philosophical construct. Nor, on the other hand, was he simply using rabbinic methods to perpetuate a Jewish system of thought. He was putting into effect that Jewish redefinition of Judaism which came about through Jesus,

allowing the cross and resurrection constantly to inform the Jewish message of worldwide salvation which he preached. He came to be mistrusted by those Christians who felt bound to uphold the special status of Jews even within the new covenant. Conversely, his ideas were misused by others (*e.g.* Marcion*) to denigrate the Torah and portray the church as a purely Gentile entity. His work and writing nevertheless formed a key part of the foundation for the life and thought of the second, and subsequent, generations of the church.

4. Paul for today

Since the Reformation, it has been customary to read Paul as the enemy of 'legalism' in religion (see Law and Gospel*). Though important in its own way, this issue does not represent Paul's central thrust. Instead, the contemporary church would do well to learn from Paul the true significance of Christ-shaped monotheism and of the new covenant in the Spirit, which together provide the basis, rationale, content and pattern for the church's life and, particularly, its responsibility for world-wide mission.

Bibliography

F. F. Bruce, *Paul, Apostle of the Free Spirit* (Exeter, 1977); W. D. Davies, *Paul and Rabbinic Judaism* (Philadelphia, 1980); E. Käsemann, *Perspectives on Paul* (London, 1969); S. Kim, *The Origin of Paul's Gospel* (Grand Rapids, MI, 1982); W. A. Meeks, *The First Urban Christians: The Social World of the Apostle Paul* (New Haven, CT, 1983); H. N. Ridderbos, *Paul: An Outline of His Theology* (Grand Rapids, MI, 1975); E. P. Sanders, *Paul and Palestinian Judaism* (London, 1977).

N.T.W.

PELAGIANISM was a current of teaching in the ascetic* movement in the West in the 5th century, of which Pelagius is commonly regarded as the fountain-head. Its theological outlook was characterized by: an insistence on the adequacy of created human nature, essentially unimpaired by Adam's fall,* to fulfil the will of God; the denial of original sin* as either guilt* or corruption transmitted from Adam* to all mankind; the highest moral and spiritual expectations of the baptized Christian who must be capable of a life of perfect holiness, because God commands him thereto; and an understanding of the gifts of grace that excludes, or at best drastically minimizes, that enabling power without whose inner working we can do nothing acceptable to God.

In reality the Pelagian movement was neither uniform nor united by Pelagius' sole inspiration. Nevertheless the traditional terminology remains useful. The label 'Pelagian' is often loosely invoked to damn any doctrine felt to threaten the primacy of grace, faith and spiritual regeneration over human ability, good works and moral endeavour.

Pelagius was a British layman who gained acceptance in Rome *c.* 400 as a teacher of Christian asceticism. He wrote letters of ascetic counsel, some treatises (including a credally orthodox *Faith in the Trinity*) and a commentary on the Pauline Epistles. These works drew on several Christian sources, including Origen,* Ambrosiaster and Augustine.* Strongly persuaded of the goodness of the created order, he opposed whatever denigrated it, such as Manichaeism* and even Jerome's* more extravagant asceticism. One gift of grace was God's inviolable endowment of the human creature with self-determination. Although the fall set in train a habit of sinning, to the detriment of subsequent generations, the created abilities (*posse*) of the will,* though overlaid with inveterate custom or obscured by forgetfulness or ignorance, remained as God made them, and needed only our act of will (*velle*) to make the accomplishing of God's will a reality (*esse*). To this end was added the grace of revelation and illumination, by both law* and gospel.* In conversion-and-baptism (assumed to be that of the responsible believer), the grace of the forgiveness of past sins was assured (unlike Paul, Pelagius wrote explicitly of justification* 'by faith *alone*'). Thereafter, however, the Christian was deemed capable of realizing the potential of his created powers. Above all there was no room for the dismal defeatism or fatalism in the face of sin that Pelagius claimed to find in Augustine's *Confessions*. The church must be a community zealous for Christian perfection.

The Gothic advance on Rome in 410 dispersed Pelagius and his supporters, southwards to Sicily and Roman Africa, and eastwards to Palestine in particular. His associate Celestius was the first 'Pelagian' to incur the censure of the church, at Carthage in 411. Similar in background to Pelagius, he was nevertheless a more combative and possibly less guileful spirit. He clumsily offended received Catholic beliefs in Africa by asserting that Adam was mortal before his fall, which injured no-one but himself, and that infants were baptized not for the remission of sin (for there was no original sin) but to obtain sanctification or the kingdom of heaven. These opinions of Celestius were apparently disowned by Pelagius in Palestine in 415, when he was acquitted by two synods of eastern bishops. Celestius had himself appealed to one Rufinus 'the Syrian' in defence of his denial of the transmission of sin. This shadowy figure (not to be confused with Rufinus of Aquileia) illustrates both the diversity of 'Pelagian' views (for, unlike Celestius, he taught that Adam would not have died had he remained sinless) and the ultimate eastern roots, or at least affinities, of Pelagian ideas (although his role is exaggerated by the writer who depicts him as the inspirer of Pelagius himself). Rufinus rejected the traducianist theory of the origin of the soul,* which suited belief in the transmission of original sin, and was a sharp critic of Origen.* The disputes about Origen's speculative doctrines, not least the pre-existence of souls, were a powerful undercurrent in the Pelagian controversy.

The condemnation of Celestius and Pelagius was spearheaded by the African episcopate instructed by Augustine. The Council of Carthage in 418 anathematized the following teachings: the natural, rather than penal, mortality of Adam; the denial of infant baptism, and of original sin derived from Adam and requiring cleansing in baptism for the new-born; the restriction of justifying grace to the remission of past sins, excluding its help against committing future sins; the restriction of the aid that grace gives against sinning to the enlightening of the understanding, to the exclusion of the implanting of love which enables us to delight in and obey the will of God; the assertion that grace merely enables us to do more easily what we could still do without it, albeit with greater difficulty; and the denial of the plain statements of 1 John 1:8–9 and the implications of the Lord's Prayer ('forgive us our debts') in order to claim that one is in reality without sin.

African pressure was largely instrumental in eliciting a conclusive condemnation of Pelagian teachings from pope Zosimus later in 418. Its terms are only partly recorded, but it certainly affirmed the universal transmission of sin from Adam, resulting in that captivity to sin from which all need to be set free through baptism, which has the same force for infant and adult alike. The (third ecumenical) Council of Ephesus in 431 also condemned any who shared the opinions of Celestius.

A group of Italian bishops led by Julian of Eclanum in South Italy (c. 386–c. 455) refused to subscribe to Zosimus' verdict. Julian now became the protagonist for Pelagian beliefs, conducting an increasingly bitter controversy with Augustine until the latter's death. Fragments of his works survive largely in Augustine's replies. Extant expositions of Job and of Hosea, Joel and Amos are with considerable probability ascribed to Julian.

This phase of the controversy is important more for elaborations in Augustine's thought (which in turn provoked the anti-Augustinian reaction known misleadingly as Semi-Pelagianism*) than for significant new teachings expounded by Julian. He attributed Augustine's account of humanity's bondage to sin to his incurable Manichaeism, and generally systematized Pelagian doctrines, which made him a more formidable opponent than either Pelagius or Celestius. More central to this phase of the controversy were predestination (Julian charged Augustine's God with injustice), the sinful concupiscence persisting in the Christian after baptism, and sexual intercourse between inevitably concupiscent partners as the medium for the transmission of original sin.

Pelagianism was important for provoking new or sharper clarification of Catholic beliefs on issues untouched by earlier controversies in the East, where they were inadequately understood. Modern study has rescued Pelagius and his fellows from the ranks of the moralists and humanists, recognizing their serious religious intent and their claim to be faithful to earlier tradition in areas where much was undefined. But the Pelagian assessment of the effects of Adam's fall and understanding of grace cannot be squared with Scripture, although the church, in decisively rejecting Pelagian views, did not wholly endorse Augustine's refutations.

Bibliography

T. Bohlin, *Die Theologie des Pelagius und ihre Genesis* (Uppsala, 1957); G. Bonner, *Augustine and Modern Research on Pelagianism* (Villanova, 1972); *idem*, 'How Pelagian was Pelagius?', *SP* 9 (1966), pp. 350–358; P. Brown, *Religion and Society in the Age of St Augustine* (London, 1972); R. F. Evans, *Pelagius: Inquiries and Reappraisals* (London, 1968), and *Four Letters of Pelagius* (London, 1968); J. Ferguson, *Pelagius. A Historical and Theological Study* (Cambridge, 1956); G. de Plinval, *Pélage: ses écrits, sa vie et sa réforme* (Lausanne, 1943); D. F. Wright, 'Pelagius the Twice Born', *Churchman* 86 (1972), pp. 6–15.

D.F.W.

PENANCE. The Gk. noun *metanoia*, which is frequently found in the NT, is usually rendered in English as 'repentance'. The Vulgate Lat. rendering, however, is *poenitentia*, which came to be understood in terms of the medieval sacrament* of penance, with a connotation very different from that of *metanoia*. The result was that, when the Vulgate translated the Gk. verb 'Repent' *Poenitentiam agite* (in Mt. 3:2), the Baptist was taken to mean 'Do penance; for the kingdom of heaven . . .' (Douay Version).

This curiosity of translation thus encouraged the medieval understanding that there was a defined and God-given sacrament called 'penance'. It appeared in the 'Canon' of seven sacraments in Peter Lombard,* and regularly thereafter. The discipline* of excommunication and (in certain circumstances) restoration practised by the early church had led in the Middle Ages to the belief that the priest, simply by virtue of his orders, had power to absolve from sins confessed privately to him. The systematization included the necessity for confession of this sort to precede reception of communion (which was rare in the Middle Ages), and especially so if the penitent had committed mortal sin since his or her last confession. It also relied upon Jn. 20:23 ('if you forgive anyone his sins, they are forgiven . . .') on which the form of absolution was based, and also some unclarities about the 'matter' of the sacrament. The Jn. 20:23 material also passed into the Roman ordination service, in a subsidiary role, in the early Middle Ages.

The Reformation* began with a protest

against the sale of indulgences (see Merit*) – a practice closely connected with the confessional – which meant that from the outset questions were raised over the priest's power to forgive. Nevertheless, the sacrament of penance proved more enduring than others of the five additional so-called sacraments. It is, for instance, the only one of the five to be listed with baptism and communion as a sacrament in the Ten Articles of religion of the Church of England of 1536. It was reinforced in the Act of the Six Articles in 1539, and provision of an optional sort was still made for it in the 1548 and 1549 English liturgical innovations. In the 1552 *Book of Common Prayer*, however, 'auricular confession' disappeared; all main services now had 'general' confessions, and the absolutions provided were of a declaratory or precatory kind. For the dying, provision was still made, in the Visitation of the Sick, for confession and for an absolution in the pre-Reformation style ('I absolve thee from all thy sins . . .'). And for all persons opportunity was made for taking a troubled conscience to a 'discreet and learned minister of God's Word', that 'by the ministry of God's Word' they might receive the 'benefit of absolution'. All the wording here was significantly changed from the 1549 form. The Reformers also retained the use of Jn. 20:23 at the laying on of hands in ordination – indeed they made it central. But they did not expound the passage as leading to the sacrament of penance. And they translated *metanoia* in the NT as 'repentance'.

Lutheran and Anglican Churches have sometimes allowed the continued use of auricular confession by scrupulous individuals, though the discipline of these churches has never required it of the members. In the 19th century the 'Catholic revival' in the Anglican Church (see Anglo-Catholic Theology*) led to a new emphasis among some clergy upon the importance of regular use of the confessional, and a linking of the words in the ordination rite and the provision for the absolution of the dying (both of which are described above) to demonstrate that Anglican clergy are true Catholic priests with the powers and duties of priests to administer 'penance'. A strong reaction was set up among more Protestant Anglicans, and the division on the issue still continues.

Since Vatican II (1962–65) there have been changes in Roman Catholic practice. In particular, the rite is now called 'The Reconciliation of a Penitent', and there has been experimental use of a semi-corporate way of administering it. There has also arisen a much greater concern about the pastoral and counselling use of the relationship between priest and penitent. But the theological question about the ultimate propriety of the priest's personal absolution of the penitent remains.

Bibliography

T. W. Drury, *Confession and Absolution* (London, 1903); J. Macquarrie, *The Reconciliation of a Penitent* (London, 1987); R. C. Mortimer, *The Origins of Private Penance in the Western Church* (Oxford, 1939); J. R. W. Stott, *Confess your Sins* (London, 1964).

C.O.B.

PENTECOST, see BAPTISM IN THE SPIRIT; HOLY SPIRIT.

PENTECOSTALIST THEOLOGY.

Pentecostalism is one stream within Arminian* evangelicalism* with distinctive emphases upon a further experience after conversion,* namely, the baptism* in the Holy Spirit as an enduement of power signified by speaking in tongues (glossolalia); and upon the gifts* of the Spirit listed in 1 Cor. 12:8–10.

Pentecostal theology has its roots in various aspects of 19th-century fundamentalism* in America: holiness* groups which taught that one could receive after conversion an experience of entire sanctification* (see Methodist Theology*), sometimes called the baptism of the Spirit, and an enduement of power by some key leaders such as Charles Finney,* Asa Mahan (1800–89) and Phoebe W. Palmer (1807–87); the teaching of R. A. Torrey (1856–1928) and others who claimed that the baptism of the Spirit was a post-conversion enduement of power primarily for witness and service, not sanctification; the teaching of A. B. Simpson (1843–1919) and A. J. Gordon (1836–95) and others that divine healing* was to be received by faith; and the premillennialism (see Millennium*) and the need to live in expectation of the imminent return of Christ taught by J. N. Darby,* C. I. Scofield (1843–1921) and many others. These streams all contributed to the 'four-square' emphases of Pentecostal preaching: Christ the saviour,

Christ the baptizer in the Holy Spirit, Christ the healer and Christ the coming king.

Origins and spread

The origins of Pentecostalism may be dated to 1 January 1901, when Miss Agnes Ozman, a student at Bethel Bible College, Topeka, Kansas, spoke in tongues after the principal, Charles Fox Parham (1873–1929), laid hands on her and prayed for her to receive the power of the Spirit. Henceforth, for Pentecostals, the supreme sign of being baptized in the Spirit would be speaking in tongues. This is considered to be the gateway to vivid experience of God, lively worship, the gifts of the Spirit, especially divine healing, and power for Christian witness and service.

Within a few years Pentecostalism had spread widely in the USA, especially through the influence of the Azusa Street Apostolic Faith Mission in Los Angeles. It soon reached Europe, where there was a ready response to its message among some affected by recent spiritual awakenings in Wales and elsewhere. Pentecostalism gained a strong foothold in Scandinavia and subsequently spread worldwide.

Pentecostalism gave rise to considerable controversy among evangelicals in the first half of the 20th century, especially over baptism in the Spirit as a second experience after conversion and the availability today of the supernatural gifts of the Spirit, especially speaking in tongues and divine healing. Although it originated in the holiness movement, the majority of holiness leaders rejected Pentecostalism, although some joined the growing movement after contact with those influenced by the Azusa Street mission. Having taught that sanctification was a 'second blessing' prior to their Pentecostal experiences, some of these holiness teachers described the baptism of the Spirit with glossolalia as a 'third blessing'. Most Pentecostals, however, argued that sanctification* was a progressive work following conversion and so the baptism in the Spirit was a 'second blessing'. Some groups have maintained the Wesleyan doctrine of entire sanctification (see Perfection, Perfectionism*).

More serious controversy occurred in America at the time of World War I when some Pentecostals taught an anti-Trinitarian 'oneness' or 'Jesus only' doctrine, namely, that God is one person manifest as Father, Son and Spirit and that water baptism was valid only if performed in the name of Jesus alone. A few groups have continued to maintain this teaching, but the vast majority have adhered to traditional Trinitarian doctrine, some practising threefold immersion in baptism.

Over the years Pentecostal denominations have been formed throughout the world, due sometimes to schism but more often to the growth of indigenous churches. Considerable growth occurred after World War II in North and South America, Africa and Scandinavia. The World Pentecostal Conference first met in 1947 in Zurich, and has since met triennially. In the 1960s and 1970s Pentecostal teaching and experiences were introduced into most Protestant* denominations through the charismatic movement (see Gifts of the Spirit*), although the Pentecostals tended, apart from some notable exceptions, to stand aloof from these developments as well as from the newer 'house-church' movements. But in the 1980s the Pentecostals were more open to fellowship with these movements. Since 1967 the charismatic movement has extended into the Roman Catholic Church, but, apart from two series of Roman Catholic–Pentecostal dialogues at the Vatican in 1972–76 and 1977–82, there has, in general, been little attempt amongst Pentecostals to foster fellowship with Roman Catholics. According to the *World Christian Encyclopedia* (ed. D. B. Barrett, Nairobi, 1982), by 1980 the Pentecostal movement had grown to 51 million and a further 11 million were included in the charismatic movements in the traditional mainline denominations.

Distinctive doctrines

In support of their distinctive doctrine of baptism in the Spirit, Pentecostals argue that the disciples of Jesus, like the OT saints, were regenerate* before the day of Pentecost. How could Jesus have sent out unregenerate men to preach, heal the sick, cast out demons and raise the dead (Mt. 10:1, 8)? Jesus described his disciples as spiritually clean (Jn. 13:10; 15:3), with peace from God (Jn. 14:27; 20:19, 21), obedient to God's word (Jn. 17:6, 8, 14) and belonging to him, not the world (Jn. 15:19; 17:6, 10, 16). Thus, they were already regenerate *before* Pentecost, when they were baptized in the Holy Spirit (Acts 1:5), endued with power (Lk. 24:49; Acts 1:8), filled with the Spirit, enabled to speak in other tongues, and empowered as effective and courageous witnesses to the risen Lord (Acts 2:4, 37, 41, 43).

Pentecostals likewise argue that in the Acts of the Apostles the Samaritan converts and the Ephesian disciples were regenerate before they were baptized in the Spirit. The Samaritans had responded with joy to the gospel and been baptized before Peter and John prayed that they might 'receive the Holy Spirit' (Acts 8:6, 8, 12, 15). The Ephesian 'disciples' (a term used for Christians elsewhere in Acts) responded to Paul's teaching about Jesus and were baptized before 'the Holy Spirit came on them' (19:4–6). Thus 'to receive the Holy Spirit' (Acts 2:38; 8:15, 17, 19; 10:47; 19:2) is 'the same gift' (Acts 11:17; 15:8) as the baptism by Jesus in the Holy Spirit (Acts 1:5; 11:16) which the disciples received at Pentecost. The Holy Spirit is described as 'coming' or 'falling' upon believers (1:8; 8:16; 10:44; 11:15; 19:6) with observable results (2:5–13; 8:18) such as speaking in tongues (2:4; 10:46; 19:6). In the case of Cornelius and his household the baptism in the Spirit appears to have accompanied their reception of the gospel (Acts 10:44).

1 Cor. 12:13 can be legitimately paraphrased as 'We were all baptized in one Spirit in order that we might manifest the unity of the body of Christ. . . .' It does not necessarily refer to regeneration and its ambiguity means that it cannot be used as the governing principle by which to interpret the receiving of the Spirit in Acts. (See Baker, *Baptized in One Spirit*, p. 18.)

Pentecostals further distinguish between the indwelling of the Holy Spirit as the source of saving faith (Rom. 8:9, 11; 1 Cor. 3:16; 6:19; 2 Tim. 1:14) and the outpouring of the Spirit that empowers for Christian witness (Lk. 24:49; Acts 1:5, 8; 4:31; Rom. 15:19; 1 Cor. 2:4; 1 Thes. 1:5). Supernatural gifts and miracles abounded throughout the apostolic period (Acts 2:43; 4:30; 28:9; 1 Cor. 12:7–10; 14:1, 18, 26; Gal. 3:5; Heb. 2:4), and this is still Christ's will for his people (Mk. 16:17–18; Jn. 14:12–14). Supernatural gifts will cease 'when perfection comes', namely, when we see God 'face to face', and not before (1 Cor. 13:10, 12). Just as Jesus was anointed 'with the Holy Spirit and with power' (Mt. 3:16; 12:15, 18; Mk. 1:10; Lk. 3:22; 4:14, 18, 21; Jn. 1:32–33; Acts 10:38), so believers need the empowering of the Spirit. This is a manifestation of Jesus' messianic lordship and his exaltation to the Father's right hand (Jn. 7:39, literally 'for Spirit was not yet, because Jesus was not yet glorified'; Acts 2:33, 36), and thus baptism in the Spirit is grounded in the ascension* of Christ, just as forgiveness of sin and new life are grounded in the death and resurrection of Christ respectively. The gift of the outpoured Spirit is thus integrated with God's saving acts in Christ.

Pentecostals have traditionally acknowledged speaking in tongues as the principal sign of being baptized in the Spirit (Acts 2:4; 10:46; 19:6; presumed to be what Simon Magus 'saw', 8:18), but many now recognize other gifts as signs of this experience. They also acknowledge that Christians may share this experience without using the Pentecostals' terminology to describe it. Pentecostals adhere to the general evangelical consent to the need to be continuously filled with the Spirit (Eph. 5:18).

Along with other evangelicals, Pentecostals have stressed the importance of preaching the biblical gospel of salvation through faith in Christ alone. The penal substitution theory of the atonement* is generally held. Sometimes there has been a tendency to a Pelagian* view of man, with a denial that we are born sinners or have Adam's sin imputed to us. In general the Bible is interpreted literally and preaching is forceful and emotional.

Pentecostals have regarded their movement as a restoration of the apostolic Christianity of the NT, hence the frequence use of 'apostolic' in denominational titles. Some groups recognize particular leaders as apostles or prophets* in conscious implementation of Eph. 4:11. More generally, the ministry of the evangelist has been widely recognized. Members of Pentecostal churches are usually expected to engage in personal evangelism, to manifest personal holiness of life, and to give up smoking, alcohol and secular dancing. Services are characterized by lively singing with the opportunity at communion services for extemporary prayer and the exercise of the gifts of tongues, interpretation and prophecy by church members.

Pentecostals have invariably rejected paedobaptism and adhered to the practice of adult water baptism* as a public profession of faith after conversion. It is regarded as the normative NT pattern that the baptism in the Spirit, in answer to prayer, should follow water baptism. A purely symbolic (Zwinglian*) view of the sacraments* has usually predominated, along with an emphasis upon the priesthood* of all believers. Church government* usually takes congregational* or presbyterian* forms. A more recent influence derived from the 'house-church' movement is greater recognition of the local church as the body of Christ with implications for seriously committed mutual fellowship, and with lay elders having an important governing and pastoral role in the local assembly alongside the pastor.

Prayer for the sick accompanied by the laying on of hands* has been a regular practice of Pentecostals in both evangelistic campaigns and weekly church services. Miracles* are reported and testimonies to conversion and healing are encouraged. Pentecostals have often adhered to the 'healing in the atonement' doctrine in which Christ is regarded as having borne our sicknesses as well as our sins. More recently some have not accepted this view, holding to a less dogmatic doctrine of divine healing.

Preaching on the second coming of Christ, often presented as imminent, has been frequent and most Pentecostals still hold to a premillennial view of Christ's return. Many have adhered to the dispensational* eschatology* of J. N. Darby and C. I. Scofield. But such dispensationalism is much less widely accepted today.

For much of its early history Pentecostalism was led mainly by evangelistically orientated activists with little concern for academic biblical scholarship, extended theological education or social care. But these are now generally accepted as part of the work and mission of the church. The training of pastors is usually undertaken at full-time colleges, and some churches run their own day schools or social care and rehabilitation centres. Having become conscious of its own history, Pentecostalism is now producing its own biblical scholars and church historians.

Bibliography

Pentecostal: P. S. Brewster (ed.), *Pentecostal Doctrine* (Cheltenham, 1976); C. Brumback, *What Meaneth This? A Pentecostal Answer to a Pentecostal Question* (Springfield, MO, 1947); D. Gee, *Concerning Spiritual Gifts: A Series of Bible Studies* (London, ²1967); S. M. Horton, *What the Bible Says about the Holy Spirit* (Springfield, MO, 1976); W. H. Horton (ed.), *The Glossolalia Phenomenon* (Cleveland, TN, 1966); P. C. Nelson: *Bible Doctrines: A Series of Studies Based on the Statement of Fundamental Truths as Adopted by the General Council of the Assemblies of God* (Springfield, MO, ²1948); E. S. Williams, *Systematic Theology*, 3 vols. (Springfield, MO, 1953).

Charismatic: J. P. Baker, *Baptized in One Spirit: The Meaning of 1 Corinthians 12:13* (London, 1967); I. Cockburn, *The Baptism in the Spirit: Its Biblical Foundations* (London, 1971); H. M. Ervin, *Conversion-Initiation and the Baptism in the Holy Spirit* (Peabody, MA, 1985) – a reply to Dunn (see below); K. McDonnell (ed.), *Presence, Power, Praise: Documents of the Charismatic Renewal*, 3 vols. (Collegeville, MN, 1980); J. A. Schep, *Spirit Baptism and Tongue Speaking according to Scripture* (London, 1970); J. R. Williams, *The Gift of the Holy Spirit Today* (Plainfield, NJ, 1980).

Non-Pentecostal: D. Bridge and D. Phypers, *Spiritual Gifts and the Church* (London, 1973); F. D. Bruner, *A Theology of the Holy Spirit* (Grand Rapids, MI, 1970); J. D. G. Dunn, *Baptism in the Holy Spirit* (London, 1970); J. R. W. Stott, *Baptism and Fullness: The Work of the Holy Spirit* (London, 1975); M. F. Unger, *The Baptism and Gifts of the Holy Spirit* (Chicago, IL, 1974).

J.W.W.

PERFECTION, PERFECTIONISM.

The basis of the Christian concern with perfection is the biblical injunction to holiness, repeated in many forms but summarized by Peter: 'Just as he who called you is holy, so be holy in all you do; for it is written, "Be holy because I am holy" ' (1 Pet. 1:15–16). At all times Christians have been faced with the tension between this calling to reflect in their lives and conduct the perfect holiness of God, and the fact, all too evident to experience, of the continuing presence within the personality of the sinful tendencies of their former lives. It is hardly surprising that, from time to time, Christian teachers have argued for the attainability of such a perfection in the present life as a way of dealing with this tension. Such perfectionist teachings, however, have generally been regarded as heterodox.

Although a variety of forms of perfectionism has occurred in the church since earliest times, so far as modern Protestant churches are concerned the main impetus towards the elaboration of perfectionist ideas came from John Wesley.* The form in which he stated the perfectionist thesis reappears repeatedly: a parallel is drawn between justification* and sanctification,* in which each is regarded as a *gift* given by God, to be appropriated by an act of faith. They are distinguished, however, in time, occurring always in sequence, and each therefore appropriated by its own separate act of faith. According to this formulation the parallel is complete: sanctification (holiness) is *received* just as is justification, and it is received complete, so that a person who has entered into this second stage of Christian experience through the necessary act of faith can properly be described as 'perfect'. Wesley often used the expression 'perfect love' to describe the second stage of Christian experience, and a number of perfectionist teachers have referred to the experience through which this state of grace is entered as a 'baptism of/in the Holy Spirit'.*

A major problem for the perfectionist, however, concerns the moral verifiability of the perfection he claims. Very few have actually suggested that all moral defectibility is expunged in the state of perfection. More commonly the claim to perfection is made on the basis of a careful and specific limitation of what is meant by sin. Wesley defined sin as 'conscious transgression of a known law of God', and understood perfection as freedom from sin so defined, though he spoke also of 'involuntary transgressions' which required the atoning blood of Christ just as much as sin, without being included within it. A consequence of this limitation of sin is that perfectionists tend to assert the 'moment by moment' character of perfection, as a state that must be consciously maintained through 'abiding in Christ'. Another consequence is that a significant reduction occurs in the moral stature of the perfection which is sought.

Many perfectionists have attempted to avoid the use of the term 'perfection', preferring 'entire sanctification' or a similar form. One reason for this is that some perfectionists have taught that the Christian in the state of perfection is actually secure from sin whatever he does, so that actions which were morally culpable before his sanctification are so no longer. Such teachings have sometimes been associated with sexual deviations and marital infidelity. Antinomianism (see Law and Gospel*) of this kind was something of which Wesley had a deep horror, and it has been rejected by all responsible perfectionist groups.

Perfectionist ideas had a profound influence within English-speaking evangelicalism in the 19th and early 20th centuries. They were widespread and popular in America, where they were vigorously promoted by the evangelist Charles Finney,* who eventually developed his own peculiar form of the doctrine, based on his concept of 'the simplicity of moral action'. A number of visiting evangelists promoted perfectionism in England, the most noted of whom was Robert Pearsall Smith, who was influential in the founding of the Keswick convention (see Higher Life Theology*). Perfectionism played an important part in the thought of William Booth, the founder of the Salvation Army,* and it is perhaps not entirely surprising that it was in American perfectionist circles that modern Pentecostalism,* with its emphasis on a two-stage Christian experience and the baptism of the Spirit, first appeared. In the contemporary church the influence of perfectionism has waned in the face of the spread of the charismatic movement (see Gifts of the Spirit*).

See also: HOLINESS MOVEMENT; PENTECOSTALIST THEOLOGY.

Bibliography
S. Neill, *Christian Holiness* (London, 1960); J. C. Ryle, *Holiness* (Cambridge, 1956); B. B. Warfield, *Perfectionism* (Philadelphia, 1967); J. Wesley, *Thoughts on Christian Perfection* (London, 1759).

D.D.S.

PERICHORESIS, see TRINITY.

PERKINS, WILLIAM, see PURITAN THEOLOGY.

PERSEVERANCE. The doctrine of the *perseverantia sanctorum* (perseverance of the saints) in Reformed* theology teaches that true believers will certainly keep their faith to the end through all tests and temptations, and will finally come into their heavenly inheritance. Heaven and the believer are thus being kept for each other (1 Pet. 1:4–5), and Christ pledges that all who believe will certainly be raised by him at the last day (Jn. 10:28–30, cf. 6:39, 40).

Similar promises are quite clear in the NT. Jesus taught that, unlike the seed snatched away in the parable (Mt. 13:19), believers cannot be snatched from his grip (Jn. 10:29). Paul too was convinced that God will sustain and keep believers to the end (1 Cor. 1:8–9; Phil. 1:6; 1 Thes. 5:23–24). Perseverance, moreover, logically follows from the nature of the believer's union* with Christ (Col. 3:1–4) and from his justification* (Rom. 8:30; cf. Rom. 5:1–2; Tit. 3:7). Most fundamentally, however, it is grounded in the doctrine of election* (Rom. 8:28–30; Eph. 1:12–14).

A number of passages seem to envisage a possible falling away from salvation (Heb. 3:21; 6:1–9; 10:1, 2; 2 Pet. 2:20), but these may be explained in context as warnings against a superficial Christianity, or as purely hypothetical arguments *ad hominem*, or as urgings to seek a surer ground in holiness for Christian confidence (2 Pet. 1:3–11).

It was Augustine* who first clearly elaborated a doctrine of perseverance, in consequence of his convictions concerning predestination,* but later theology, like some earlier thought, entertained the possibility of a falling from grace. The sacraments* assumed a crucial role in any restoration of the lapsed, so that the pre-Reformation clergy came to wield an awesome power.

Luther* was equivocal about perseverance because of the tension in his thought on grace and law, but Calvin* clarified and consolidated the Augustinian doctrine, tracing all the effective stages of Christian life to the 'predestination to glory'. The opposing scheme of Dutch Arminianism,* conversely, rejected the doctrine of perseverance as did later the English Arminians and Wesleyans.*

Those opposed to the tenet of final perseverance often take this stance out of concern for the biblical emphasis upon the contingency of final salvation, believing that the doctrine may encourage complacency. If it has any evils, however, it has been the provoking of excessive preoccupation with *assurance* of final perseverance. In general the result of the Calvinist conviction has not been lack of zeal, any more than non-Calvinists have, on the whole, lacked a strong Christian hope. The purpose of the teaching in the NT is to direct attention away from the always incomplete nature of Christian experience to the complete faithfulness and reliability of the God of all grace, and to strengthen the believer for the conflict with sin in the service of God. It emphasizes that the ultimate destiny of the Christian is achieved by God's grace through an enduring faith. Calvin, it is true, recognized that the confidence of this faith will be sometimes as a light that flickers and even seems to go out altogether. But it will certainly burst into flame again and burn unextinguished to the end.

Bibliography

G. C. Berkouwer, *Faith and Perseverance* (Grand Rapids, MI, 1958); J. Calvin, *Institutes*; J. S. Whale, *The Protestant Tradition* (London, 1955).

R.K.

PETRINE THEOLOGY. The two epistles ascribed to Peter in the NT are addressed to special situations and do not supply a systematic Petrine theology. At best it is possible to note the most significant emphases.

1 Peter provides a strong combination of theology and ethics. It is an essentially practical letter and yet it is far from being moralistic. It roots its practical advice in Christian experience. It deals with the way in which a Christian ought to behave in view of what God has done for him. Perhaps nowhere else in the NT is the inextricable connection between theology and ethics* more clearly brought out.

Everywhere God is active in the lives of his people. The fact that he chose them and sanctified them (1:1) is stressed in the introductory words. Moreover it is God's power that keeps them (1:5). They are God's own people (2:9–10). God is concerned for them in their suffering (2:19–20). It is his will that should govern them (3:17; 4:2). God is a God both of power (5:6) and of grace (5:10, 12). He has prepared a glorious future for his people (1:4; 5:10).

But Jesus Christ is equally active on the part of his people. Their regeneration is through his resurrection (1:3; 3:21); their redemption is through his blood (1:19). They are a holy priesthood acceptable to God through Christ (2:5). They are a spiritual house of which Christ is the cornerstone (2:6). He is an example to them when they suffer (2:21; cf.

4:1; 5:1). He is to be reverenced as Lord (3:15). He died for their sins once for all (3:18). It is through him that God is glorified (4:11). He is seen as the shepherd and guardian of his people (2:25; 5:4).

It is striking that what Peter says about the atonement* arises from essentially practical concerns. It is after mentioning that Christ is an example that he introduces the idea that he bore our sins in his body on the tree (2:24). In other words, an ethical need gives rise to a theological statement. A similar occurrence is the introduction of the ransom theme in 1:18. There is no doubt that the atoning work of Christ is seen as essential to man's deliverance. There is equally no doubt that Christ's redeeming work was accomplished because of his own sinlessness. The lamb was without blemish (1:19) and the righteous died for the unrighteous (3:18).

The purpose of the epistle is to encourage those who are suffering. The most essential feature is that suffering can be according to God's will (4:19). In addition to this emphasis, there is concentrated practical advice in chapter 5. In spite of the many assurances of God's care for his people, the readers are nevertheless called on to do their part. They are to resist the devil; they are to be watchful; they are to humble themselves before God; they are to cast their cares on God (5:6–9). In this way, the divine initiative is linked closely with human responsibility.

Some have seen baptism* as a key theme of 1 Peter, but there is only one specific reference to it (3:21). One of the peculiarities of the letter is the obscure reference to the preaching to the spirits in prison (3:19) and to the dead (4:6), but the difficulties of interpretation do not affect the over-all thrust of the theology.

Many scholars do not regard 2 Peter as Petrine, but there are good reasons for including this letter in a statement of Peter's theology, since it is attributed to his name. While the main interest of the epistle is to deal with false teachers who are troubling the believers, there are some significant theological statements. God is seen to be just in his judgments (2:4ff.). He nevertheless knows how to deliver the godly (2:9). He is not slow concerning his promise (3:8). His person is glorious (1:17). Moreover believers, as in 1 Peter, have responsibility to work things out (1:5ff., 10), although God will ensure that they receive an entrance into his kingdom*

(1:11). In the course of this letter, an important statement is made about the Scriptures* (1:20, 21), which has exerted a powerful influence on Christian thought.

See also: PAPACY.

Bibliography

R. J. Bauckham, *Jude, II Peter* (Waco, TX, 1982); J. N. D. Kelly, *A Commentary on the Epistles of Peter and Jude* (London, 1969); E. G. Selwyn, *The First Epistle of St Peter* (London, 1946); A. M. Stibbs, *The First Epistle General of Peter* (London, 1959).

D.Gu.

PHENOMENOLOGY deals with *phenomena* (a Gk. word meaning 'things which appear') in different senses and in various ways in philosophy, psychology, sociology and religious studies. Descartes* had said, 'I think, therefore I am,' but Husserl (1859–1938) extended the 'Cartesian doubt' further, arguing that in the first place, if I think, all I am sure of is that there is thought, or a stream of consciousness. That must therefore be the philosophical starting-point: an examination of man's consciousness. It must be consciousness of something. The contents of consciousness were called 'phenomena', apparent objects, or appearances. Husserl introduced the Gk. term *epochē* to describe the bracketing off, or suspension of judgment, on questions of the validity of the phenomena and whether they gave actual knowledge of the external world. The first stage was the collection of data. This was not objective, but subjective, as the data were the appearances in the consciousness.

As the stream of consciousness flowed into the mind from perceptions, the mind would reduce the variety to general forms. This was termed 'eidetic reduction', or 'eidetic vision', from the Greek *eidos*, meaning 'what is seen', or 'form'. 'Intentionality' indicated that the mind, as subject, directed itself towards certain objects. If the mind found some unity in the perceptions, that was meaning. If other minds besides mine found this unity, that showed that the meaning was not just subjective, but intersubjective. Thus Husserl claimed to reach the real world.

Husserl did not claim success in his religious philosophy, saying that his mistake had been to seek God without God. An intelligible account of Husserl's difficult philosophy (*cf.*

The Paris Lectures, The Hague, 1969) is given by John Bowker, *The Sense of God* (Oxford, 1973).

The term 'phenomenology of religion', was used first by Chantepie de la Saussaye in 1887. He was trying to look at religion in both its essence and its manifestation, and was engaged in bringing together groups of religious phenomena (sacred items or actions) in various cultural settings, as the basic elements of religion. This is 'descriptive phenomenology' (Eric Sharpe, *Comparative Religion: A History*, London, 1975).

Nathan Söderblom (1866–1931) considered that holiness was an essential part of any real religion, but that it was evident in different ways in different religions. Two important points arise here: first, this is a *religious* study of religions, by a man who himself held deep religious convictions, and secondly, he studied religions, rather than religion. It is not self-evident that there is one thing called 'religion', and that all particular religions manifest this one thing. If this really is the case, then it needs to be proved from the evidence, and not just assumed.

Gerardus van der Leeuw (1890–1950) was a major figure in the phenomenology of religion (*Phänomenologie der Religion*, 1933; published in English as *Religion in Essence and Manifestation*, London, 1948.) For him the subject involved not just description and categorization, but also discussion and understanding; it should lead to finding the 'essence' of religion. Here are both eidetic vision and *epoché*; it was left to theology to evaluate the truth.

Since the publication of *Religious Education in Secondary Schools: Schools Council Working Paper 36* (London, 1971), many in England have insisted that school religious education must be 'objective or "phenomenological" ' (p. 43). But thus to equate 'objective' and 'phenomenological' is to deny the nature of the phenomenology of religion. Sharpe (*op. cit.*, p. 248) speaks of 'a regrettable tendency to seize on the term "the phenomenology of religion" and use it in all manner of approximate senses'. In schools, it simply means looking at the phenomena of religions without any expression of personal commitment. One method of study has been to examine the 'six dimensions of religion' (Ninian Smart, *The Religious Experience of Mankind*, London, 1971); namely ritual, mythological, doctrinal, ethical, social and experiential. But a seventh dimension of history needs to be added. Smart's inclusion of history in mythology may suit Hinduism, but is quite unsatisfactory for Christianity (see W. Pannenberg, *Basic Questions in Theology*, vol. 3, London, 1973).

K.G.H.

PHILO (*c*. 20 BC – *c*. AD 50). A Hellenistic Jew and a leading citizen of the Jewish community in Alexandria, Philo was a prolific writer who through allegorical interpretation (see Hermenentics*) of the Pentateuch was able to find the doctrines of Plato* and the Stoics* already present in the words of Moses. His writings can be divided broadly into those that deal directly with the biblical text and those that do not. The latter include *On The Contemplative Life* (a treatise describing the life of a monastic order called the Therapeutae, who claimed that they experienced the vision of God*), and *Against Flaccus* and *The Legation to Gaius* (documents dealing with the anti-Jewish actions of the emperor Gaius Caligula in AD 38). The writings concerned with the biblical text consist of the major divisions entitled 'The Exposition of the Law', which proceeds according to various subjects (*e.g. On the Life of Moses, Concerning Abraham, On the Decalogue, On Rewards and Punishments*), 'The Allegory of the Law' (a series of free-flowing expositions of specific passages drawn from Genesis), and finally 'Questions and Answers' (concerning Genesis and Exodus).

Philo is important not only for his use of allegorical interpretation of the OT, but also because of his attempt to synthesize Greek philosophy with the world of Hebrew thought. In both regards Philo has been seen as an important precursor of Christianity (see Apologists;* Hellenization of Christianity;* Platonism*). Although this observation has some truth to it, it can also be misleading. Philo's influence is far more important for later Alexandrian* Christianity (*e.g.* Clement* and Origen*) and for allegorical exegesis and theology generally, than for the emergence of NT Christianity itself. Early Christianity's Christological* understanding of the OT is only superficially like Philo's allegorical exegesis; the theology of the NT, for all its newness, is not primarily the result of the amalgamation of two different worlds of ideas, Jewish and Greek, but is fully explainable within a Jewish framework alone.

Philo's goal is not philosophy, but the practice of religion, culminating in the mystic* vision of (*i.e.* communion with) God. His eclectic appropriation of Greek philosophy is mainly an attempt to communicate the truth of Judaism to his enlightened Hellenistic contemporaries. Basic to Philo's entire approach is the fundamental dualism* between material and non-material. It is the latter, the intelligible world, which is ultimately all-important to Philo, who by his allegorical exegesis presses consistently beyond the material, whether in matters of understanding or conduct, to Plato's transcendent realm of Ideas. Philo borrows the Stoic concept of the Logos* as the mediating factor between the transcendent God and the material world (*e.g. Who is the Heir of Divine Things*, 205f.).

How Philo is to be related to Palestinian (*i.e.* rabbinic) Judaism, and to the writings of the NT, has been hotly debated. Two great Jewish scholars disagreed on the former question, E. R. Goodenough alleging that Philo's Judaism had become essentially a Greek mystery religion, H. A. Wolfson maintaining that Philo held to a variant form of Pharisaic Judaism. S. Sandmel, another Jewish scholar, is right when he concludes that Philo, for all his uniqueness, is a representative of Hellenistic Judiasm. Philo's possible relation to NT writings is an even more complex question. There has been much discussion of Philo's possible influence upon the epistle to the Hebrews, Spicq arguing that the author had been a student of Philo, but Williamson denying any direct influence. Because of its use of 'Logos' in the prologue, and its frequent contrasting of the material and the spiritual – with the former being symbolic of the latter – the gospel of John* has also been described as heavily influenced by Philo. Scholars have also found parallels to Philo in Paul's* main epistles and the Pastoral Epistles. If we keep in mind the enormous differences between Philo and the NT writers, however, probably the best conclusion is that none of the NT writings reflects direct dependence on Philo, and that the similarities that have been observed reflect instead the general milieu of Hellenistic ideas so pervasive throughout the Mediterranean world of the 1st century.

Bibliography

H. Chadwick, 'Philo and the Beginnings of Christian Thought', in *CHLGEMP*, pp. 137–192; *idem*, 'St Paul and Philo', *BJRL* (1965–66), pp. 286–307; E. R. Goodenough, *An Introduction to Philo Judaeus* (New Haven, CT, 1940); S. Sandmel, *Philo of Alexandria: An Introduction* (Oxford, 1979); C. Spicq, 'Le philonisme de l'Epître aux Hébreux', *RB* 56 (1949), pp. 542–572; and 57 (1950) pp. 212–242; R. Williamson, *Philo and the Epistle to the Hebrews* (Leiden, 1970); R. McL. Wilson, 'Philo and the Fourth Gospel', *ExpT* 65 (1953), pp. 47–49; H. A. Wolfson, *Philo* (Cambridge, MA, 1947).

D.A.Ha.

PHILOSOPHICAL THEOLOGY. Philosophy is the critical examination of the meaning, truth* and grounds of ideas, and of the methods by which ideas are arrived at. Philosophy of religion* is the critical examination of religious ideas in general. By contrast, philosophical theology pursues such an examination of the ideas of a theology associated with a particular religion.

Philosophy is not a subject which has its own autonomous subject-matter, as does astronomy, biochemistry, English literature or international law. It is an ancillary discipline which examines the ideas, truth-claims, and methods practised in a discipline, and seeks to elucidate and evaluate their nature. Thus there is philosophy of science, behaviour (see Ethics*), art (see Aesthetics*), knowledge (see Epistemology*), history,* education, logic, and religion. In each case philosophy is not a short cut to achieving the results otherwise arduously obtained in the discipline concerned. It is rather an attempt to clarify and reflect critically on what is entailed in the truth-claims and methods of the discipline. Christian philosophical theology takes the Christian faith as its starting-point and examines it philosophically.

Among the questions examined by philosophical theology are the following:

Grounds for belief in the existence of God. This includes discussion of the traditional arguments for the existence of God: the ontological, the cosmological, the teleological and the moral arguments (see Natural Theology*). It also examines the nature and validity of appeals to experience and revelation* (*cf.* Religious Experience;* Scripture*) as well as the claim that belief in God is a necessary presupposition for making sense of the world and our experience. It takes account of arguments for agnosticism* and disbelief in God (cf. Atheism*).

The identity of God and God's relation with the world. This includes evaluation of the competing claims of theism,* deism,* idealism,* pantheism,* and panentheism.*

*Religious language.** Discussion of the structure, meaning and use of religious language has been a major preoccupation in philosophical theology since the advent of logical positivism.* However, the problem of using ordinary language to describe transcendent reality was a concern of the Neoplatonists (see Platonism*) and the medieval thinkers. Logical positivism claimed that religious language is meaningless, since it is not open to verification in the way that scientific claims are verifiable. This gave rise to much discussion of verification,* falsification and ways of testing meaning and truth-claims. Even scientific claims are not always strictly verifiable. Words for God are not literally true, since God is not an object in time and space. Meaningful talk about God presupposes analogy* rather than direct literal correspondence. Recent investigation into religious language has drawn attention to the richness of its variety and use, and to the complexity of symbolism.

History and religion. This includes the way God may be thought of as acting in history,* the question of miracles,* and the clarification of the distinction between history and myth.*

Revelation, faith and reason. This includes discussion of revelation* as a form of knowledge, the role of faith* in cognition, assent, trust and interpretation, and the role of reason in apprehending, discerning and explaining (see Epistemology*).

Evil. How can the existence of physical and moral evil* be reconciled with belief in an almighty, loving God (cf. Theodicy*)?

Freedom. In what sense may we speak of freedom* and free will,* in the light of theological considerations concerning the sovereignty* of God and philosophical considerations concerning human beings who are products of their physical environment and whose activities are capable of explanation in terms of physical processes?

Human identity. Are human beings more than bodies? What is meant by the mind, the self and the soul? What is the relationship between the brain and the mind and between the body and the self?

Life after death. What grounds are there for belief in life after death, and what are its possible forms?

Prayer. What sort of an activity is prayer?* What are the logic and implications of intercessory and other forms of prayer?

The relation of Christianity to other faiths. This includes examination of the conflicting truth claims of different religions and ways of testing them.

Bibliography

C. Brown, *Philosophy and the Christian Faith* (London, 1969); M. J. Charlesworth, *Philosophy of Religion* (London, 1972); A. Flew and A. MacIntyre (eds.), *New Essays in Philosophical Theology* (London, 1955); B. Davies, *An Introduction to the Philosophy of Religion* (Oxford, 1982); S. T. Davis, *Logic and the Nature of God* (Grand Rapids, MI, 1983); C. S. Evans, *Philosophy of Religion* (Downers Grove, IL, 1985); F. Ferré, *Basic Modern Philosophy of Religion* (New York, 1967); N. L. Geisler, *Philosophy of Religion* (Grand Rapids, MI, 1974); J. Hick, *Faith and Knowledge* (London, ²1966); idem, *Philosophy of Religion* (Englewood Cliffs, NJ, ³1983); idem (ed.), *Classical and Contemporary Readings in the Philosophy of Religion* (Englewood Cliffs, NJ, ²1970); G. MacGregor, *Philosophical Issues in Religious Thought* (Boston, 1973); H. A. Meynell, *God and the World* (London, 1971); B. S. Mitchell, *The Justification of Religious Belief* (London, 1973); B. S. Mitchell (ed.), *The Philosophy of Religion* (London, 1973); N. Smart, *Philosophers and Religious Truth* (London, ²1969); R. Swinburne, *The Coherence of Theism* (Oxford, 1977); idem, *The Existence of God* (Oxford, 1979); idem, *Faith and Reason* (Oxford, 1981); K. E. Yandell, *Christianity and Philosophy* (Leicester and Grand Rapids, MI, 1984).

C.B.

PHILOSOPHY AND THEOLOGY. As

philosophy involves a fundamental inquiry into the nature of reality and of human thought about it, and as Christian theology is concerned with the nature of God, mankind and the non-human creation, it may seem to be inevitable that theology would find

511

expression in the philosophical categories of the day. Inevitable, perhaps, but desirable? There seems always to have been a strand in the history of Christian theology, from Tertullian* to Karl Barth,* which has been mistrustful of, or suspicious of, any positive link between Christian theology and the findings or concerns of secular philosophy. What has Athens to do with Jerusalem?

Yet, while Christian theologians are right to question anything that would impair or compromise the distinctiveness of the faith, and while the efforts of philosophers have sometimes been bent towards such compromise, there is nothing intrinsic to philosophy which is inimical to the Christian faith. There is much that may be of benefit to it. Even those who inveigh against philosophy may be found, in their systematic theology, to be making unwitting use of some of its concepts.

From the first, Christians have been urged to give a reason for their hope (1 Pet. 3:15) and to distinguish revealed truth from heresy (1 Jn. 4:1); and they have been found using the language of, and even appealing to the insights of, non-Christian thinkers (Acts 17). Unless the church is to be restricted in these activities to a literal repetition or close paraphrase of passages of Scripture, she will invariably be drawn into adopting, and adapting, current philosophical forms of thought in order to probe more deeply, or to explain or vindicate some aspect of the faith. This is the process of 'faith seeking understanding', in Anselm's influential phrase.

The Christian philosophical theologian is under two constraints which are not easily reconcilable. The first is the belief that basic conceptual questions must have answers. God is, presumably, either timeless or in time. The other constraint is that Scripture often appears to be undetermined on such questions. In fact the situation is even more complex than this, for much of the language of Scripture is figurative. For example, is the statement 'I make known the end from the beginning' (Is. 46:10) a figurative expression of God's timelessness, or a literal expression of the fact that God is in time?

Besides such a positive and accommodating relation between philosophy and theology, it is possible to discern two other historically influential relationships of a less positive kind.

Philosophical argument is based upon reason alone, the appeal to the standards of deductive and inductive logic. But 'reason' has also come to have a normative meaning: that which seems 'reasonable' to a person at a particular time. Thus Descartes* came to hold that he ought to believe only what is 'clearly and distinctly perceived', seen by rational insight and intuition. Such 'rationalism', as it came to be called, led Descartes to the conclusion that he could only be sure of God's existence because he was sure of his own. Other variants of rationalism led to the pantheism* of Spinoza* and the optimism of Leibniz,* who held that there is good reason to believe that this world is the best of all possible worlds. In a parallel way, Locke* held that it is only reasonable to believe what sense-experience informs us of, or renders probable.

While such general appeals to reason – to what all or most people find reasonable – are attractive (for none of us likes to be considered unreasonable), they ought nevertheless to be viewed with reserve. The theological danger posed by rationalism is that of being a priori about theology, rather than allowing the data of revelation to speak on its own terms.

Such a danger is heightened still further in the case of those approaches to Christian theology and theological method inspired by the Enlightenment.* Here it is not just a question of reason placing limits on revelation but of recasting the whole of Christian theology in a rational manner, and actively discarding those elements which do not fit the mould. A notable example is Kant* who denied on philosophical grounds the possibility that God could be known by either reason or revelation, but held that the existence of God must be postulated on moral grounds.

The constriction of theology by philosophy reaches its zenith in the claim by logical positivists* that theological utterances are cognitively meaningless, incapable of stating anything which could be either true or false.

It is important to bear in mind that these various philosophical attacks upon either the superstructure or the foundations of Christian theology are themselves open to philosophical critiques of various kinds. This fact exemplifies another possible relationship between philosophy and theology, that in which philosophy 'makes a space' for theology by attempting to rebut philosophical objections to its possibility.

Even this limited use of unaided human reason in theology is discounted by the religious approach to philosophical issues known as fideism. According to fideism, matters of faith and theology have their own justification because of the insufficiency or inappropriateness of human reason to inquire into, or debate, such matters. Sometimes such a position has been supported by argument, sometimes it has been assumed in dogmatic fashion. Such fideism has sometimes been combined with claims to have a mystical contact or union with the divine. The dangers of relativism, and of sheer irrationalism, are very great.

P.H.

PHILOSOPHY OF RELIGION

PHILOSOPHY OF RELIGION is to be distinguished from both philosophical theology* and apologetics.* Unlike philosophical theology, which is concerned with ontological and logical reflection on the doctrine of God (and which has as a matter of historical fact been closely tied to the Judaeo-Christian tradition), the philosophy of religion is concerned with religion* as a pervasive feature of human culture. And unlike the apologist, the aim of the philosopher of religion is to understand and evaluate religion from a philosophical standpoint rather than to defend religion, or a particular religion, by philosophical argument. This is not to say that the work of the apologist is of no interest to the philosopher of religion. Thomas Aquinas'* *Summa contra Gentiles*, intended as a manual for missionaries to Islam, contains material of the greatest importance to the philosopher of religion.

Sometimes 'religion' is used in a wide sense, to include all that any person commits himself to basically or unreservedly. Thus Marxism or atheistic materialism are sometimes, perhaps with justification, dubbed 'religions'. Generally speaking, however, the philosopher of religion is not concerned with religion in this broad sense, but in religions which involve belief in a God or gods. His interest is in two aspects of such religion, and at two levels.

Scope

He is interested, in the first place, in the subjective human states which are recognized as religious, for example, worship, prayer, religious belief, in fact the whole range of phenomena which are gathered together rather loosely under the rubric of 'religious experience',* from visions to convictions. In the second place, the philosopher of religion is interested in the claims about objective reality made by various religions. Central to these claims is, of course, the claim that God exists. But the philospher of religion's interest extends beyond this one basic question (in which his work impinges most closely on that of the philosophical theologian) to others: If God exists, how does he interact with his creation? Could polytheism be true? Are there miracles? Is there a providential ordering of events? Does the idea of miracle conflict with science? How does the idea of divine providence comport with human intention and responsibility and the seeming randomness and pointlessness of much that happens?

The philosopher of religion is interested in these subjective states and objective claims at two levels. In the first place, he seeks to clarify what it *means to say* that someone has seen a vision, or that a miracle has occurred, or that God exists and is infinitely wise. What any of these things means is partly a matter of the logical implications of a particular proposition. For example, is saying that God exists like saying that there is a moon? Is God an object in space, as the moon is? If so, where is he located? If God is not in space, how is his existence to be understood? Is it like the existence of an abstract object, such as goodness or beauty? But God acts. Are goodness and beauty capable of acting? Is something called a miracle simply because it makes us wonder? Is 'miracle' what we call an event which we cannot explain? What if a physical explanation of 'the miracle of the resurrection' were discovered? Would it cease to be a miracle? What is religious belief? Is it like the belief that I have a left hand? Or is it more like a gamble, a leap in the dark? Such questions, which can obviously be asked across the whole range of religious phenomena, are conceptual questions, asked in an effort to gain understanding about the basic categories and ontological commitments of religion and its theology. Discovering meaning is also a question of determining how various terms and sentences function distinctively within religion or a particular religion to witness, praise, confess, petition. The balance between these two aspects of meaning is itself a matter of controversy, both in philosophy in general and in the philosophy of religion.

Besides studying the concepts and propositions of religion in an effort to gain insight into what they mean, the philosopher is also concerned about how one might reasonably be said to believe or know that some particular religious or theological proposition was or was not true. Here the connections between the philosophy of religion and mainstream philosophical positions become more apparent. Three broad answers to this question are discernible, though these are not to be regarded as exclusive of each other.

First, certain basic theological propositions may be known to be true by reason alone, *a priori*, by rational reflection upon the concept of God (Anselm;* Descartes*) or by argumentation from propositions known to be true by any rational man (Thomas Aquinas). The main questions which arise here are over the legitimacy of such a programme, its tendency to rationalism, and questions about the soundness and validity of particular arguments.

Second, certain basic theological truths may be known by experience, either by direct experience, through personal encounter, vision or inspiration, or by indirect experience, by rational reflection on one or other aspect of nature. The chief problems here concern the ambiguity of the adequacy of experience alone to provide reasonable grounds for believing that God, the transcendent ground of experience, exists; the legitimacy of appealing to experience; and the particular problems arising from the analogical* character of the 'argument from design', the threat of anthropomorphism* and reductionism.

A third broad approach may be termed 'fideistic'. It can embrace at one extreme an unthinking irrationalism and at the other a reasoned reliance upon divine revelation. 'A reasoned reliance upon divine revelation' is not a contradiction in terms. The reasoning in question may involve a consideration of the inadequacies of both rationalism and empiricism;* an appeal to the categories of the candidate revelation itself; personal categories of reliance and confidence; and also more general considerations of personal insight, self-knowledge and explanatory coherence. It is a mistake to think that no general reasons can be given for the view that the justification of religious belief does not consist in the provision of general reasons. But such

reasoned fideism as has been described clearly depends on accepting the trustworthiness of the human reason and senses, and this is so even where it is claimed that the biblical revelation is the presupposition which alone makes it reasonable to trust one's reason and senses.

These epistemological* concerns about the justification of knowledge-claims, including claims to know truths about God, have been much more dominant since the 17th century than they were in the medieval period and before, when the reliability of reason and the senses was taken for granted, and when the authority of the church was so dominant. Even Aquinas' celebrated 'Five Ways' play a much more subordinate role in his philosophical and theological system than the prominence given to them in subsequent discussion may suggest.

An important watershed in the philosophy of religion is marked by the position of Immanuel Kant.* Kant dismissed all natural or rational theology because in his view the very questions it raised marked an illegitimate extension of human natural enquiry beyond its rational boundaries, and claimed that it was necessary to 'deny *knowledge*, in order to make room for *faith*'. By faith here Kant meant a 'pure moral faith', not an assent to propositions, whether the propositions of natural or revealed theology, but rather a confidence both that God exists and that he is the rewarder of virtue and the punisher of vice. Kant's position became important and influential in post-Kantian Protestant theology from Ritschl* to Barth,* gaining the status of an unquestioned assumption.

Contemporary emphases

Present-day philosophy of religion, particularly in the English-speaking world, has been characterized by controversies about the meaning of religious language. The logical positivists* of the 1930s claimed that, apart from the analytic, purely tautological propositions of mathematics and logic, to be cognitively meaningful a proposition must be capable of verification* (or falsification) by means of the senses. It was alleged that theological propositions were unverifiable (or unfalsifiable) and hence cognitively meaningless, that is, incapable of expressing propositions which were either true or false. The sentences of theology, it was alleged, are pseudo-propositions.

This challenge evinced diverse reactions. Some were content to accept the logical positivists' argument, and endorsed some version of reductionism. Others counter-argued that the verification principle, the heart of logical positivism, was incapable of being stated in such a way that satisfied the logical positivists themselves. Laws of science, for example, are unverifiable, but the positivists themselves wished to regard these as paradigms* of meaning. Others have attempted to show that theological sentences are verifiable in principle, while still others have argued that religious language has distinctive functions and purposes, and that, following Wittgenstein,* it forms a distinctive language-game or 'form of life' irreducible to the language-game of science or of anything else. The danger with such an appeal is a certain sort of conceptual relativism.

Apart from this preoccupation with meaning, much modern philosophy of religion is characterized by work of great technical rigour and sophistication unmatched since the medieval and post-Reformation periods and by an interest in a very wide range of problems, including issues raised by religions outside the Judaeo-Christian tradition, by drugs and by allegedly para-normal phenomena.

Justification

Can the philosphy of religion be justified as a legitimate area of interest for the Christian? The Christian scholar must perforce take an interest in the philosophy of religion because of its influence upon the historical development of theology. But is the philosophy of religion itself a legitimate enterprise for the Christian? There has been a tradition which has given an emphatic 'No' to this question, claiming that philosophy in general and the philosophy of religion in particular involves a corrupting intrusion into the purity of the biblical faith.

While there is always the danger of contaminating or corrupting the faith, such a reaction is too negative. The philosopher's questions, 'What do you mean?' and 'How do you know?', when applied to the Christian faith, *may* be taken as sceptical challenges, the response to which would involve an implicit if not explicit denial of the faith; just as, when applied to other non-religious claims, they may be taken to be implicitly sceptical about

the possibilities of human communication, or the reliability of the senses. But they *need not* be taken as sceptical insinuations, but rather as calls to reflect rationally upon how the statements and other utterances of a religion are to be understood, and how they are to be justified. These are questions which a Christian must ask for himself, and which therefore it is no hardship to have pressed upon him by the philosopher.

If the questions are legitimate, what answer ought the Christian to give? Here it is important to recognize that, as with many scientific and theoretical questions – if not with all – the Bible, and the basic creeds and confessions of the church, are by the current standards of philosophical rigour undetermined both as to meaning and to truth. As the Bible is not a textbook of the natural sciences, neither is it a philosophical textbook. Yet while on the one hand it is clearly mistaken to interpret the central affirmations of the Christian faith as non-cognitive pictures or 'bliks' (a term coined by R. M. Hare in a paper published in 1955), it is equally wrong to interpret them wholly literalistically, with no element of analogy* or modelling* about them. They are not statements of science, nor are they reducible to statements about the states of mind of the first disciples. But within these broad but definite limits it is up to the church and the individual Christian to articulate the faith philosophically as best they may. Similarly, while total scepticism and rationalism are excluded as theories of knowledge, it is not clear that some appeal to what may be obviously true without the benefit of divine revelation may not help to ground acceptance of that revelation.

Bibliography

B. A. Brody (ed.), *Readings in the Philosophy of Religion* (Englewood Cliffs, NJ, 1974); A. Flew, *God and Philosophy* (London, 1966); A. Plantinga, *God, Freedom and Evil* (London, 1974).

P.H.

PIETISM has been one of the least understood movements in the history of Christianity. The word comes from *pietas* (piety, devotion, religiousness), the Lat. rendition of the Gk. *eusebeia* and the Heb. *ḥāsîd* (kind, benevolent, pious, good). Appearing over a dozen times in the NT, *eusebeia* has been translated as 'godliness,' 'piety' or 'religion.' The English word 'piety' *etc.* has a positive meaning but may also denote vain and hypocritical characteristics, as in 'a pious hope'. Such was true of *Pietismus*, the German nickname given to the reform movement within Lutheranism* by its enemies. The name possibly surfaced in response to the title Phillip Jacob Spener (1635–1705) gave to his introduction of a book of sermons by Johann Arndt (1555–1621) in 1675, *Pia Desideria (Pious Wishes*, tr. Th. Tappert, Philadelphia, 1964).

Spener is commonly regarded as the father of pietism. In German-speaking circles his religious significance is judged second only to Luther*. As the senior minister of the famous Paulskirche in Frankfurt, the young pastor expressed his concern about the corrupt state of the church. He was reacting against the polemical orthodoxy that was sterile amid the immorality and terrible social conditions following the Thirty Years' War (1618–48). Hoping for better times, Spener set forth his 'pious wishes' for the reformation of the church. He advocated: 1. more intensive Bible study, individually and in *collegia pietatis* (conventicles); 2. the exercise of the universal priesthood of believers through increased lay activity; 3. the practice of Christianity in daily life and works of unselfish love; 4. dealing with unbelievers and heretics with sincere prayers, good example, persuasive dialogue and the spirit of love instead of compulsion. These proposals quickly became the focus of a growing controversy.

One of Spener's spiritual sons, August Hermann Francke (1663–1727), attempted to implement these concerns at the University of Leipzig during 1689. The young lecturer instigated meetings for the purpose of entering more deeply into exegetical studies. The *collegium philobiblicum* soon attracted many students and citizens, their numbers and enthusiasm growing to the extent that the authorities dissolved the society. A faculty opponent stated publicly, 'Our mission is to make students more learned and not more pious.' In response a professor of poetry defended the movement in a little poem favourably describing a 'pietist'.

As pastor and professor Francke also founded many *Stiftungen*, philanthropic and educational institutions related to the newly formed University of Halle. Among other enterprises, these included an orphanage, a Bible society, and a home for widows. Francke emerged as the organizational genius of pietism. Halle became an international centre for the dissemination of pietist literature, missionaries and beliefs to Russia, Scandinavia, Britain and the New World.

Because this widespread influence continued through subsequent expressions in many denominations and religious awakenings, some historians employ the term 'pietism' to encompass a wide spectrum which includes Dutch Pietism, Puritanism,* the Wesleyan* revivals and the Great Awakening. Others delimit the name more narrowly to the reform movement stemming from the activities of Spener, Francke, Bengel,* Count von Zinzendorf (1700–60) and others. A growing consensus acknowledges the many legacies and influences of pietism on British and American Christianity.

Although pietism is viewed as having roots in mysticism,* Anabaptism* and Reformed groups in Holland, and was followed by more radical and separatist manifestations, pietist motifs are probably more fairly defined through examining the thought of the early leaders. The mystical and spiritualist themes of Jacob Boehme,* Gottfried Arnold (1666–1714) and others should more properly be called radical pietism. Early and contemporary critics accuse pietists of a subjectivism which exalts self above God and derives religious norms from the experience and needs of persons. The resultant individualism is often said to undermine sound doctrine. The pietists insisted, however, that the necessary reformation of doctrine by Luther must lead to a *reformation of life*. They believed they were entirely Lutheran in insisting that faith must become active in love. Their insistence that credal formulations must be tested by biblical theology, together with their more democratic proposals, tended to undermine the authority of the church. But the pietists desired *reformation of* and not *separation from* the church. The pietist emphasis on careful study of the texts in the original languages combined with the devotional use of the Bible was no doubt vulnerable to the perils of private interpretation. But in general this served to revive the Reformation emphasis on biblical authority. From the beginning pietism faced a legalistic temptation. Nevertheless, Spener and Francke remained Lutheran in insisting that regeneration* be an integral part of an experience of justification.* Contrary to the meritorious works of medieval Catholicism, pietism stressed the gift of sanctifying grace. The theology of pietism led in some cases to an excessive emotionalism. However, for the early leaders the experience of the Spirit was seen as an appropriation of, rather than a substitution for, revelation.

In spite of their opposition to many degenerate currents of the fallen world, Spener's interpretation of the book of Revelation led pietists to hope for better times through participation in God's work of changing human lives. Pietism's otherworldliness and ascetic* tendencies must be viewed in the light of Francke's global concerns and charitable endeavours. In general, Spener and Francke attempted to walk the middle way between dogmatic rigidity and emotional warmth, between faith and works, between justification and sanctification, and between forsaking the fallen world and affirming it through love of neighbour, enemies and God's good creation.

Bibliography
Works ed. P. Erb in *Classics of Western Spirituality* series (London and New York): *Pietists: Selected Writings* (1983); *Johann Arndt: True Christianity* (1979); *Jacob Boehme: The Way to Christ* (1978).

Studies: Dale W. Brown, *Understanding Pietism* (Grand Rapids, MI, 1978); F. E. Stoeffler, *The Rise of Evangelical Pietism* (Leiden, 1965); *idem, German Pietism During the Eighteenth Century* (Leiden, 1973).

D.W.Br.

PLANTINGA, ALVIN (b. 1932). Plantinga is an American analytic philosopher, a member of the Christian Reformed Church and a Professor at the University of Notre Dame in Indiana. He is best known for his work on the theistic proofs and on the problem of evil. He has argued that 1. the evidence for God's existence is as good as that which each of us has for the existence of other human persons (*God and Other Minds*); 2. the ontological argument can be given a sound formulation (*The Nature of Necessity*); and 3. God's omnipotence, omniscience, and goodness are logically consistent with the existence of evil (*God, Freedom and Evil*; *The Nature of Necessity*) nor does the existence of evil render

God's existence improbable ('The Probabilistic Argument from Evil'). His treatment of the problem of evil includes a sophisticated version of the classic 'free-will defence'.

Other works of theological interest include *Does God Have a Nature?* (the 1980 Aquinas lectures which discuss God's simplicity and his supposed identity with his attributes), and several papers on Christian epistemology* and ontology. One thesis of these papers is that belief in God is 'properly basic'; that is, it is natural to us (sin aside), and is the kind of belief we are justified in holding without appeal to other beliefs as evidence for its truth.

Bibliography
Does God Have a Nature? (Milwaukee, WI, 1980); *God and Other Minds* (Ithaca, NY, 1967); *God, Freedom and Evil* (Grand Rapids, MI, 1974); 'How to be an Anti-Realist', *Proceedings of the American Philosophical Society* 56 (1982), pp. 47–70; *The Nature of Necessity* (London, 1974); 'On Reformed Epistemology', *RJ*, vol. 32, no. 1 (1982), pp. 13–17; 'The Probabilistic Argument from Evil', *Philosophical Studies* 35 (1979), pp. 1–53; 'Reason and Belief in God', in Plantinga and Wolterstorff (eds.), *Faith and Rationality* (Notre Dame, IN, and London, 1983).

J. E. Tomberlin and P. van Inwagen (eds.), *Alvin Plantinga* (Dordrecht, 1985).

D.W.C.

PLATONISM. The tradition of philosophy deriving from Plato of Athens (*c.* 429–347 BC), one of the most significant figures in the history of human thought, has had a major influence on Christian theology, especially through its last creative development known as Neoplatonism.

Plato's work rests on the impressive life and death of his fellow-Athenian Socrates (469–399 BC), perhaps the first Greek thinker to devote critical philosophical attention to the bases of morality (and, for his adherence to conviction even unto death, the favourite pagan hero of early Christianity). For his last forty years, Plato taught at a grove outside Athens which gave the name 'the Academy' both to his school (which lasted until Justinian's final dissolution of pagan schools in AD 529) and to the Platonic tradition in general. He produced some twenty-five works, nearly all in dialogue form, with Socrates often a leading participant. The most significant for Christian thought come from his middle and later periods, notably the *Phaedo, Republic, Timaeus* and *Laws*.

True understanding is pursued by dialectical argument. The so-called Socratic method, best observed in *Meno* (and known from the Gk. word as 'maieutic' because the philosopher acts as 'midwife'), demonstrates that we have innate knowledge (*epistēmē*) of basic realities, awareness of which is elicited by question and answer, not imparted by teaching. By such reasoning we may attain explicit knowledge of the 'forms' (*ideai*), one of Plato's most distinctive contributions to philosophy. He emphasizes that sense experience yields only fallible opinion (*doxa*), not firm knowledge, for the observed world is in perpetual flux, and easily deceives. Behind the impermanent phenomena lie the changeless archetypal 'forms', the originals, of which all particular things are imperfect copies. Thus there exists a 'form' of the human person above and apart from all individual human beings, their perfect and eternal model, by sharing in which they are what they are. The same applies to artefacts (*e.g.* tables and the 'form' of the table) and to abstract realities such as beauty and wisdom. Knowledge of the 'forms' is the basis of morality and practical life.

The supreme 'form' is that of the good, which Christian thought has easily identified with God, although Plato distinguishes them. Normally the 'forms' are independent of God, but in *Timaeus* they appear as his thoughts. This work had a long influence on Christian thought (later in Chalcidius' Lat. translation and commentary, *c.* AD 400), for it presents an outline cosmology. The world was fashioned by the Demiurge ('craftsman'), who is apparently God, imprinting the pattern of the 'forms' on chaotic matter. The world is both soul and body, and so in a true sense both divine and corruptible. *Laws* gives the earliest version of the cosmological argument for God's existence (see Natural Theology*), based on the necessity for a 'perfectly good soul' as the source of all motion.

Plato believed in the immortality* of souls (*Phaedo*), which belong to the realm of the 'forms'. While subject to their imprisoning bodies they gain knowledge of the 'forms' by recollection (*anamnēsis*) from their previous existence. Souls are liable to reincarnation (see

Metempsychosis*) until, finally released by death, they find fulfilment after judgment in a supra-mundane heaven.

The similarity of certain Platonic ideas to Judaeo-Christian beliefs was highlighted by early Christian apologists.* At the same time Platonic dualism* deeply tainted Christian attitudes, with its depreciation of the body and the physical world in favour of the soul and the realm of true reality accessible to reason alone.

One element in Plato's thought was developed by Arcesilaus and Carneades (3rd–2nd centuries BC) into philosophical scepticism. Knowledge was impossible; probability must serve as guidance for living. This position heavily influenced Cicero and evoked Augustine's* *Against the Academics*.

It was the Middle Platonism of the first two centuries AD (especially Albinus, Plutarch and Numenius) that most directly influenced early Christian writers such as Justin (see Apologists*) and Clement of Alexandria.* Religious concerns predominated, and Plato was mixed with elements of Aristotelian,* Stoic,* Pythagorean and even Jewish origin. (Numenius described Plato as 'Moses speaking Attic Greek'.) Middle Platonism heightened God's transcendence, leaving him describable only negatively (*cf.* apophatic theology*) and active in creation only through intermediaries (*e.g.* Logos,* planetary powers, world-soul). Plato's 'forms' are now unambiguously thoughts in the divine mind, and speculations about the cause of evil relate it in different ways to matter itself. Such tendencies fed into Gnosticism* as well as orthodox Christianity. An eclectic Platonism pervasively coloured early Christian theology, most conspicuously in the Christian Platonists of Alexandria,* where Philo* the Jew had led the way.

The last phase of the tradition was Neoplatonism (3rd–6th centuries), which developed out of Middle Platonism (especially Numenius) but took its shape from the creative genius of Plotinus (*c.* 205–270), a contemporary of Origen* at Alexandria who later taught at Rome. By *c.* 400 Neoplatonism had taken over the Athenian Academy itself, with Proclus (410–485), the most encyclopaedic Neoplatonic teacher, its leading light. The Syrian Iamblichus (*c.* 250–*c.*325) accommodated Neoplatonism to polytheism,* magic and divination, while Porphyry (*c.* 232–303), the pupil, editor, biographer and even popularizer of Plotinus, gave it an anti-Christian twist. His *Against the Christians* was shrewd and weighty enough to demand responses from several major Christian writers.

In Plotinus' Platonism, dualism is subsumed within a higher monism,* and philosophy approaches religion and mysticism. The source and goal of all existence is the One, which is beyond not only description but even being itself. It is accessible only by ascetic* abstraction above the world of sense and even thought, culminating in rare moments of ecstatic vision in which the self is united with the One. From the One's creative overflow emanates a hierarchy of levels of being, tending towards multiplicity and inferiority and aspiring to return to the One. The first emanations are Mind and Soul, cosmic principles respectively of intelligence and animation. All being as such is good, even bare matter at the lower limit of the 'great chain of being' (hence Plotinus' polemic against Gnosticism). Evil* is strictly non-being – a real possibility for those who turn away from the One.

Although it inspired ancient paganism's last major intellectual challenge to Christianity, Neoplatonism proved enormously attractive to Christian thinkers from Origen's successors onwards. The Cappadocian Fathers, Ambrose,* Victorinus Afer,* Augustine* and Pseudo-Dionysius the Areopagite* were all deeply indebted to it. Through Dionysius it became perhaps the most formative factor in Christian mystical theology* in both East and West (see Eastern Orthodox Theology*). Through Augustine it coloured virtually the whole medieval tradition in the West. Other peaks of Christian Platonism or Neoplatonism include Boethius,* Eriugena,* the school of Chartres, Hugh of St Victor (see Victorines*) and Nicholas of Cusa (c. 1400–64).

Although the rediscovered Aristotle* became 'the philosopher' of scholasticism,* Platonic and Neoplatonic influence lived on. The Renaissance witnessed renewed interest, both in Italy (especially in Marsilio Ficino's (1433–99) Florentine Academy) and in England (e.g. John Colet, c. 1466–1519). Platonic ideas were current in some streams of the Radical Reformation.* Anglicanism has been particularly receptive, from Hooker* through the Cambridge Platonists* and the Christian Socialists* to B. F. Westcott* and

W. R. Inge (1860–1954; see Modernism, English*). In the 20th century, despite widespread reactions against dualism* and Greek metaphysics,* the vitality of Platonism is evident in writers as diverse as A. E. Taylor (1869–1945), A. N. Whitehead (b. 1919; see Process Theology*), John Baillie,* Tillich* and Iris Murdoch. Universalism* often betrays Neoplatonic influence at work.

Bibliography

A. H. Armstrong and R. A. Markus, *Christian Faith and Greek Philosophy* (London, 1960); *CHLGEMP*; E. Cassirer, *The Platonic Renaissance in England* (Edinburgh, 1953); J. Daniélou, *Gospel Message and Hellenistic Culture* (London and Philadelphia, 1973); J. Dillon, *The Middle Platonists* (London, 1977); W. R. Inge, *The Platonic Tradition in English Religious Thought* (London, 1926); J. B. Kemp, *Plato* (Nottingham, 1976); J. M. Rist, *Plotinus* (Cambridge, 1967); N. A. Robb, *Neoplatonism of the Italian Renaissance* (London, 1935); P. Shorey, *Platonism Ancient and Modern* (Berkeley, CA, 1938); R. W. Southern, *Platonism, Scholastic Method and the School of Chartres* (Reading, 1980); A. E. Taylor, *Plato* (London, ⁶1949); *idem*, *Platonism and Its Influence* (London, n.d.); D. P. Walker, *The Ancient Theology: Studies in Christian Platonism from the Fifteenth to the Eighteenth Century* (London, 1972); R. T. Wallis, *Neo-Platonism* (London, 1972).

D.F.W.

PLOTINUS, see PLATONISM.

PNEUMATOMACHI, see ARIANISM; HOLY SPIRIT.

POLANUS, AMANDUS, see REFORMED THEOLOGY.

POLANYI, MICHAEL (1891–1976), scientist and philosopher. Hungarian by birth, British by adoption, Polanyi came to prominence as a scientist after World War I. Stimulated on the one hand by the new physics of Einstein, and on the other by contacts with fascism and Marxism before his move to Britain, he devoted his later years to a wide-ranging investigation of philosophical, social and cultural questions.

His major book, *Personal Knowledge* (London, 1958), charts a path between the epistemological extremes of subjectivism and objectivism which, although bequeathed by classical philosophy, had been especially polarized since the Enlightenment.* For Polanyi faith and knowledge are not be set in opposition, even in the physical sciences, but are properly combined in a concept of *personal* knowledge. This new epistemology* is established by reference to a wide range of examples and arguments, and helps to unify a spectrum of knowledge from science to the arts. Although he did not extend his arguments substantially into the domain of theology, he recognized the validity of this enterprise, in which theologians, most notably T. F. Torrance,* have been engaged.

After *Personal Knowledge*, besides refining his epistemological ideas in *The Tacit Dimension* (London, 1967), he began to explore corresponding questions of ontology: in what ways does the actual structure of reality affect our search for an understanding of it? His last writings, summarized in *Meaning* (Chicago, 1975), present a stratified world which human beings, with their mental activity, indwell, personally and objectively. Polanyi's analysis of the multi-levelled structure of reality may throw interesting light upon various aspects of the relationship between divine and human activity in the world.

Bibliography

For a general introduction to Polanyi's thought, see R. Gelwick, *The Way of Discovery* (Oxford, 1977). For its application to theology, see T. F. Torrance (ed.), *Belief in Science and in Christian Life* (Edinburgh, 1980); articles by R. L. Hall *et al.* in *Zygon*, 17 (1982), pp. 3–87; J. V. Apczynki, *Doers of the Word: Toward a Foundational Theology Based on the Thought of Michael Polanyi* (Chico, CA, 1982).

P.R.F.

POLITICAL THEOLOGY is a term which has had a wide range of meanings in the history of religions, reflecting different attempts to relate a religion to the political character of the society in which it exists. Its present prominence dates from the mid–1960s when the West German Roman Catholic theologian, Johann Baptist Metz,* revived the term and later referred to 'the new political theology'. Many have followed his lead, some

520

using the term in a broader sense for a group of related theological emphases.

Older forms of political theology

Augustine* drew on Stoic* use in order to criticize the 'civil theology' of earlier, official Roman civic religious cults which legitimated and sanctified the political system (see his *City of God* 6:5–12). However, the same tendency had already entered the Christian church, notably in the 'court theology' of Eusebius* with its adulation of Constantine and then in the 'Christian Empire' of Theodosius. There are traces of it even in the earlier part of the *City of God*, but Augustine was moving to the apolitical reaction of its later books which gave rise to the Augustinian tradition of a spiritual, inner kingdom separate from politics. This was continued in Luther's* doctrine of the two kingdoms. But the political theology of civil religion* was equally persistent and approved of by Machiavelli and Hobbes. It reached full formal expression in the 'political theology' of Carl Schmitt with its eulogy of German nationalism in the 1920s and 1930s which encouraged the 'German Christians' in their legitimizing of Hitler. At the time this was condemned as 'political monotheism' by Eric Peterson – an abuse of theology to justify political injustice (see the development of this critique by Jürgen Moltmann,* in *The Trinity and the Kingdom of God* (London, 1981), pp. 192–200).

The new political theology of J. B. Metz

According to Metz not only 'political monotheism' but also most recent theology stands in need of correction. In the case of civil theology a false equation of the kingdom with a political system left the church open to the Enlightenment* tradition, especially through Hegel* and Marx,* which criticized it for being merely the ideological superstructure of particular social patterns and power structures. Much modern theology, on the other hand, has an extreme privatizing tendency, stressing the individual, the transcendental and the existential, dismissing the social aspects of life as secondary, viewing charity as a private virtue, and centring religion on the 'I-Thou' relationship (see Buber*) with faith reduced to 'the timeless decision of the person'. This, of course, does have definite political implications, leaving the status quo unquestioned or tacitly approved. Thus, for

Metz, 'the deprivatizing of theology is the primary critical task of political theology' (*Theology of the World*, London, 1969, p. 110). This is not to deny the NT message to the individual. In fact, Metz believes that the first 'critical liberating function' of the church is to protect the individual 'from being considered exclusively as matter and means for the building of a completely rationalized technological future' (p. 118). However, political theology emphasizes that all the NT promises of the kingdom,* *e.g.* freedom, peace, justice, reconciliation, 'cannot be made radically private affairs . . . cannot be entirely interiorized and spiritualized as corresponding to the individual's longing for freedom and peace. They make the individual free with regard to the political society around him, in the sense of committing him to it in a free critique of it' (art. on 'Political Theology' in *SM*, New York, 1970, vol. 5, p. 36). In several of his writings Metz makes the important general statement: 'the so-called hermeneutical problem of theology was not really a problem of the relationship between systematic and historical theology or between dogma and history, but rather a problem of the relationship between theory and praxis* or between the understanding of faith and social praxis' (1969, p. 112; 1970, pp. 35–36; and *Faith in History and Society*, London, 1980, p. 52). It should be agreed that Scripture requires this concern, with its witness to Jesus in moral conflict with the religious and political leaders of his society, his cross set up in public, and his church called, as bearer of his eschatological message, to similar encounters with the political world. The church is an institution within society with a series of critical, liberating tasks: first, concern for the individual, especially the person who is a victim of impersonal technology devoted to bettering the future of the rich; secondly, a message that the future depends on God; thirdly, love expressed in social terms by bringing justice and peace to all, even in extreme situations to the extent of calling for revolutionary change for the sake of the victims of present systems; and fourthly, a changed view of itself which accepts internal criticism of its leadership (a problem for the Roman Catholic Church especially), welcomes truth from outside and is prepared to oppose the political powers that be.

Political theologies

Metz forms part of a widespread trend in contemporary theology with several features in common: a. a rejection of the earlier concentration on denominational orthodoxy in confessional theology; b. an opposition to the preoccupation with personal decision in existential theology; c. a concern with how beliefs actually affect and are affected by what is, or is not, done to change society, *i.e.* with praxis, a term deriving from Marx's concept or critique which asserts the interdependence of theory and practice as they relate to the changing of society, advocating 'orthopraxis', a word popularized by Metz, to emphasize that all good theology has to be action-oriented; d. a stress on the essentially *public* nature of the gospel, so that Christianity is not a private matter but involves a new community which challenges all societal structures; e. a critical opposition to most present societies and to institutionalization of the church, in the sense used by the social philosopher Jürgen Habermas, *i.e.* one which does not pretend to be neutral or value-free but which is open to future change and committed to encouraging more just social relationships; f. a shared conviction that *politics* has a mediating role in good theology, in that a connecting link which affects the expression of Christian faith is made by involvement in politics.

A wide range of theologians include themselves in the above grouping, not only all black,* liberation,* theology of revolution,* most African,* and Asian,* many Indian* and feminist* writers, but also people working on fundamental theology,* the theology of secularization,* spirituality,* poverty* and Marxism and Christianity.* (See the useful discussions in *The Militant Gospel* by Alfredo Fierro, London, 1977, and Alistair Kee's *Reader in Political Theology*, London, 1974, and *Scope of Political Theology*, London, 1978.) Significant recent books include *Agenda for Prophets: Towards a Political Theology for Britain*, ed. Rex Ambler and David Haslam (London, 1980), Sri Lankan theologian Tissa Balasuryia's *Planetary Theology* (London, 1984), *The True Church of the Poor* by Jon Sobrino from El Salvador (London, 1985), and *Black and Reformed*, by the South African Christian leader Alan Boesak (New York, 1985), related to which is *The Kairos Document* (London, 1985), an important theological comment by Christians involved in active resistance to apartheid. They distinguish a valid 'prophetic theology' from 'state theology', their term for civic theology (see above), and from 'church theology', which resembles the 'bourgeois' theology criticized by Metz (see *The Emergent Church*, London, 1981, and above).

Responses

The reaction from 'bourgeois' theology has ranged from cautious agreement, *e.g.* Peter Hinchliff in *Holiness and Politics* (London, 1982), through outright condemnation of any 'politicization', *e.g.* Edward Norman in *Christianity and the World Order* (Oxford, 1979), to a revived 'political monotheism' in South African apologias for apartheid, *e.g. Human Relations and the South African Scene in the Light of Scripture* (Cape Town, 1976), or the theology of the 'new religious right', *e.g.* Rousas Rushdoony's *Politics of Guilt and Pity* (Nutley, NJ, 1970), or *The Kindness that Kills*, ed. Digby Anderson (London, 1984). There is a corresponding range of views among those evangelicals who are beginning to contribute to the growing discussion of political theology. Richard Mouw is generally sympathetic in *Politics and the Biblical Drama* and *When the Kings Come Marching In* (Grand Rapids MI, 1976 and 1983). Haddon Willmer's response to Norman, in *Christian Faith and Political Hopes*, by C. Elliott *et al.* (London, 1979), is positive while stressing the need to do justice to the nature of forgiveness. More substantial development of an evangelical political theology can be found in Orlando Costas, *Christ Outside the Gate* (New York, 1982), and Nicholas Wolterstorff, *Until Justice and Peace Embrace* (Grand Rapids MI, 1983).

Conclusion

The world-wide nature of the church and of the theological enterprise at a time of a widening gap between rich and poor, with the majority of Christians and of the unevangelized being among the poor, should oblige any forward-looking theology to be political in the sense intended by Metz, yet not at the expense of leaving out the challenge to personal commitment and obedience to Jesus Christ.

522

See also: CIVIL RELIGION.

C.W.

POLYTHEISM. The belief in and worship of many gods. Earlier in the 20th century it was believed to be a stage in the evolution of religion* from animism* to monotheism.* This view is now generally rejected, and polytheism is seen as the fruit of pre-scientific response to the natural world, since most of the gods are linked to some aspect of nature. Thus the sky, sun, moon, planets, earth, fire, water, animals and even plants have been considered divine, as well as identified with various characteristics of individual and social life. With the personification of natural phenomena as superhuman beings polytheism is born. The world's mythologies are the accounts of the deeds of the gods which often sink to the level of the grossest immorality. Each god has a cult, the centre of which is the god's image. This can be a human being, an animal, a statue, a tree, a fire, a phallus *etc.* Within polytheism one god or goddess is sometimes singled out by a particular group, and elevated to the position of supreme deity, though the existence of other gods is not denied. This is called henotheism or monolatry and some have argued that OT patriarchal religion was this type of polytheism. Generally, however, the OT condemns the image-worship of polytheism as false attempts to represent God. The NT confirms this condemnation, and Paul even identifies the Corinthian gods with demons (Rom. 1:22f.; 1 Cor. 8:4–6; 10:19f.).

Bibliography

J. H. Bavinck, *The Church Between the Temple and the Mosque* (Grand Rapids, MI, n.d.); A. Daniélou, *Hindu Polytheism* (London, 1964); M. Eliade, *Patterns in Comparative Religion* (London, 1958); P. Grimal (ed.), *Larousse World Mythology* (London, 1965); W. B. Kristensen, *The Meaning of Religion* (The Hague, 1960).

D.A.Hu.

POSITIVISM. A philosophy and humanist 'religion' originating with Auguste Comte (1798–1857). Individuals, he held, and mankind in general, begin by being 'theological', ascribing events to supernatural powers; develop to a 'metaphysical' stage where they ascribe them to abstractions like 'force', which rename rather than explain; and finally reach the 'positive' stage where both these are abandoned, knowledge being recognized as of facts alone, or, in the sciences, regularities among facts. This progress is inevitable. It is matched by parallel progress in society; and Comte proposed a new science of sociology, to study mankind and enable society to be organized rationally and peacefully by a scientifically trained élite.

God, as an explanatory hypothesis, is unnecessary; religion should be based on worship of humanity as a whole. Comte devised a complete positivist 'church' with its saints, ceremonies and so on: this never became widely popular, nor did Comte's philosophy as a whole, but he influenced many who were not styled positivists, in philosophy of science, sociology, and the growth of 'scientific humanism'.

See also: LOGICAL POSITIVISM.

Bibliography

L. Kolakowski, *Positivist Philosophy from Hume to the Vienna Circle* (London, 1968); F. Copleston, *History of Philosophy*, vol. 9 (Tunbridge Wells, 1975), chs. 5 and 6.

R.L.S.

POVERTY AND WEALTH. The Bible gives attention, not to wealth and poverty as the accumulation or lack of riches as a commodity, but to the relationships between people which poverty and wealth express. We will therefore look at how the Bible views and addresses economic relationships between people.

First, 'poor' in the Bible basically refers to people's physical condition. The poor in spirit are those who because of their condition in this world are dependent on, and have turned to, God. The term does not refer to spiritual deadness, atheism, or humility.

Secondly, the focus of God's work in bringing deliverance to all is upon the poor.

The focus of God's work

When God addresses the deformation which human sin brought into the world, he begins with those suffering most deeply from greed, selfishness and the exercise of wrong dominion over others – Hebrew migrant labourers in Egypt. He rescues them from Pharaoh's oppression. 'Let my people go that they may serve me' (Ex. 3 – 5). God's deliverance of Israel focused and defined what he was doing in the world (Dt. 26:1–10). It identified some aspects of rebellion against God, *e.g.* Pharaoh's ruthless oppression. It showed what God cared about – that all people together should be stewards* of the resources of earth (Gn. 1:27–28; Ex. 3:8). It demonstrated how God worked in the world to bring redemption – by choosing what was least, to shame human boasting (Dt. 7:7–8; 1 Cor. 1:21–31).

One clear goal of the Mosaic law was to prevent such injustice ever arising again among God's people (Dt. 6:20–25), so that there should be no poor among them (Dt. 15:4). However, the institution of the monarchy centralized power and wealth and impoverished large sections of Israelite society (1 Sa. 8:10–22; 1 Ki. 12:4; Am. 2:6–8). The king who was meant to protect the poor from exploitation (Pr. 31:1–8) became one of its chief agents (*e.g.* Ahab, 1 Ki. 21). So the prophetic hope grew of a king who would bring justice to the poor (Is. 11:4).

Good news to the poor

Jesus' focus was also on the poor. He himself became poor (2 Cor. 8:9). His ministry in Galilee (a place of the dispossessed and the outcast) was a judgment on the powerful of Jerusalem; his ministry was with the sick, the Samaritans, those branded as 'sinners' and the socially rejected. It was not confined to such, but he identified its nature by reference to them; his proclamation and demonstration were good news to the poor (Lk. 4:18; 7:22). The meaning of Jesus' ministry among the poor would give the meaning of what he was doing among everybody else. The significance of the good news for the rich was to come through what Jesus was doing among the poor. How a tax-collector (socially poor) experienced forgiveness was to determine how the Pharisee ought to experience it (Lk. 18:9–14), not vice versa.

Thus the good news of the whole gospel of the kingdom* is to be introduced to a whole community through the poor. How a community treats its poor is, for the Bible, the acid test of its life (Jas. 2:1–7). And the way a community will be changed is through the poor. In the Bible the grace of God is universally available to all. But in the OT its reality and nature are to be revealed through what it means to Israel. The OT concentrates on what it means in economic relationships (*e.g.* Lv.

523

25). In the NT the poor replace Israel as the focus of the gospel. As the poor experience the good news of the kingdom, the real nature of the gospel becomes evident to others. The NT gives special attention to what that means in terms of children, women, Samaritans, social outcasts, the sick, the 'lost sheep of the house of Israel'.

Thus the issue of poverty and wealth is not about economic relationships separate from the experience of the kingdom of God or the proclamation of the gospel. The good news is defined for all by what it means to the poor – the new identity as sons of God that they are given, in a society which gives them no value or even treats them as rubbish; the undeserved forgiving grace of God for those who deserve nothing; the new community into which he welcomes those who have been excluded; the power which he makes available to the power-less. By these criteria the problem of wealth is that it can blind people to their need to depend on God and their responsibility to care for the needs of the poor (Lk. 12:13–34; 16:19–31).

Paul says that the fact that not many of the Corinthian Christians were wise or powerful or of high social standing demonstrated the nature and power of the gospel (1 Cor. 1:28). 'Has not God chosen those who are poor in the world to be rich in faith and heirs of the kingdom which he has promised to those who love him?' (Jas. 2:5).

The content of the gospel

The content of the gospel will be best displayed in its reality among the poor. In the gospels Jesus said that the groups which best demonstrated the gospel in its fullness are the poor and the 'sinners'. The self-righteous Pharisees would learn the true nature of the gospel only as they too ate with 'sinners', and learnt what the gospel meant to them. Only as they experienced helplessness and alienation* themselves would they be transformed by the gospel and experience its true power.

The power of the gospel

When those who are 'righteous' and 'rich' do experience the content of the gospel as defined by what it means to the poor, then the power of the gospel is shown. When the rich young ruler turned away, Jesus commented: 'How hard it is for rich people to enter the kingdom of God ... What is impossible for man is possible for God' (Lk. 19:24–27).

This biblical perspective confronts the view that the poor need the generosity of the wealthy as endless receivers of aid. Rather the wealthy need the poor, to learn from them the nature and meaning of the deliverance God brings to both. The basis of the sharing is when those separated by distorted relation-ships discover that they both equally need each other. Only Jesus Christ can bring this about. 'Accept one another as Christ has accepted you' (Rom. 15:7).

Bibliography

B. C. Birch and L. Rasmussen, *The Predica-ment of the Prosperous* (Philadelphia, 1977); R. Holman, *Poverty: Explanations of Social Deprivation* (London, 1978); Lausanne Committee for World Evangelization, *Chris-tian Witness to the Urban Poor* (London, 1982); S. C. Mott, *Jesus and Social Ethics* (Nottingham, 1984); *idem*, *Biblical Ethics and Social Change* (New York, 1982); K. Nurnberger, *Affluence, Poverty and the Word of God* (Durban, 1978); V. Samuel and C. Sugden (eds.), *The Church in Response to Human Need* (Grand Rapids, MI, 1986); *idem*, *Evangelism and the Poor* (Exeter, 1983), has an extensive bibliography; D. Sheppard, *Bias to the Poor* (London, 1983); R. J. Sider, *Lifestyle in the Eighties* (Exeter, 1982); *idem*, *Rich Christians in an Age of Hunger* (London, 1978); P. Wogaman, *The Great Economic Debate* (Philadelphia, 1977).
C.M.N.S.

POWER is an everyday reality which is much talked about, but little understood. It is hard to define satisfactorily, and yet we all experience it. Among other things, power is expressed in the *freedom* and ability to make choices and act on them. It is also invested in certain *possessions* – like wealth, status, knowledge, qualifications, personal gifts, the membership of certain groups and the loyalty one can command.

The Bible acknowledges that power in human affairs is a fact of life. It is possessed by rulers (Ec. 8:4; Mk. 10:42), by groups of people (Jos. 17:17) and by individuals who are able to help their neighbours (Pr. 3:27–28). Exercising power is right and good, for ultimately it comes from God who delegates it to human agents (2 Chr. 1:12; Is. 40:10–17, 22–26; Jn. 19:11). It is given for a variety of circumstances: to govern (power is the authority of office), to denounce evil, to pray and to demonstrate wisdom and understanding (Ps. 8:5–8; Rom. 13:1–7).

The NT speaks particularly of the power (or authority) of Jesus in the coming of the kingdom (Lk. 4:14; 5:17; 11:20): the power to call disciples, interpret Scripture, heal sick people, drive out evil spirits, raise the dead, control nature, forgive sinners in his own name, rebuke religious and political leaders and associate with the outcasts of society. The chief evidence of God's power is the resurrection of Jesus from the dead (Rom. 1:4; Eph. 1:19–20) and the raising of dead sinners to new life in the Spirit (Rom. 8:11; Eph. 2:5–6; Col. 2:13). It is his ability to overcome all Christ's enemies (1 Cor. 15:24–27), and to create a new heaven and a new earth of justice and righteousness (2 Pet. 3:13; Rev. 21:5). Some hold that the power manifested in 'signs and wonders' (Acts 8:6–7; 14:3; Heb. 2:4) should accompany the preaching of the gospel in every age. Others believe it was given once only, to confirm the apostolic message.

Power in human hands, however, is easily corrupted. It is used by some to oppress others (Ec. 4:1; 8:9; Mi. 2:1–2; Jas. 5:1f.). The God-given gifts to create wealth and beauty and to bring order and harmony to the world are used to exploit and humiliate others. In the spiritual realm 'the power of the Spirit' (Rom. 15:13) has been falsely understood as an impersonal force and used to manipulate people in ways which deny their integrity and dignity (*cf.* Acts 8:18–23).

Behind the corruption of power there are evil forces at work ('principalities and powers'). They owe their origin to Christ (Col. 1:16), but now their power is directed against his purposes. The destructive results of their activity may be seen particularly in the political realm (Acts 13:27; 1 Cor. 2:6, 8), in intellectual life (Col. 2:8), in religious observance (Gal. 4:3; Col. 2:20f.), and in the struggle to maintain a faithful witness to Christ (Eph. 6:12f.).

Jesus Christ transforms the use of power. The gospel itself is power, in that it reverses the common, distorted view of its meaning (Rom. 1:16; 1 Cor. 1:18). When human beings use such examples of power as human intelligence, religious practices, social status, political privilege and wealth as grounds of boasting, they are unable to receive salvation as a gift of God (1 Cor. 1:26–29).

Power, then, takes its clearest meaning from the central fact of salvation – Jesus' crucifixion. It is the freedom that Jesus gives to his disciples, to let go of all that hinders a life of sacrificial love (Mk. 10:42–45; Jn. 10:17–18; 13:1; Phil. 2:5f.). It is the use of gifts and possessions given by God in serving the spiritual and material needs of others (Rom. 15:26–27). It is the conquest of internal and external forces (temptation, sin and evil), which cause us to be in bondage to falsehoods and unbelief, and to destructive and oppressive spiritual, moral, intellectual, emotional, political and social influences.

Bibliography

O. Betz, C. Blendinger in *NIDNTT* II, pp. 601–616, and G. Braumann, *ibid.* II, pp. 711–718; F. Bockle and J. M. Pohier (ed.), *Power, Domination, Service* (*Concilium*, n.s. 10:9, Dec. 1973); W. Foerster in *TDNT* II, pp. 560–575, and W. Grundmann, *ibid.* II, pp. 284–317; M. Hengel, *Christ and Power* (Philadelphia, 1977); J. Moltmann, *Power of the Powerless* (London, 1983); C. D. Morrison, *The Powers that Be: Earthly Rulers and Demonic Powers in Romans 13.1–7* (London, 1960); K. Rahner, 'The Theology of Power', *Theological Investigations*, vol. IV (London, 1966), pp. 391–409; W. Wink, *Naming the Powers* and *Unmasking the Powers* (Philadelphia, 1984, 1986), vols. 1 and 2 of trilogy, *The Powers*.

J.A.K.

PRACTICAL THEOLOGY, an umbrella term concerned to relate theology to the practice of ministry.* The term is recognized especially in Scottish theological education and elsewhere. Traditionally, its subject-matter was preaching,* worship* and liturgy,* education and catechetics and pastoral care. Although Schleiermacher* and others attempted to provide it with a disciplined and systematic theological foundation, in which the application was informed by theology, the field tended to become handy tips for ministers.

More recently the discipline has broadened in a number of respects. The relationship between theology and practice is no longer regarded as one-sided but rather a mutual relationship where a genuine dialogue between theology and its application takes place. It is no longer devoted exclusively to the role and task of the ordained minister but is concerned with the ministry of the whole church. Furthermore, its subject matter has broadened not only to include new applied subjects such as administration, communication and church growth* but also, more fundamentally, to give a central place to ethics,* to relate pastoral care to contemporary psychology and to include within its scope social and political dimensions (cf. Liberation Theology*), thus recognizing that God's interest is not confined within the limits of the church.

See also: PASTORAL THEOLOGY; PRAXIS.

Bibliography

P. H. Ballard (ed.), The Foundations of Pastoral Studies and Practical Theology (Cardiff, 1986).

D.J.T.

PRAYER, THEOLOGY OF. Prayer is communication with God in worship. Prayer is possible because the triune God is personal, and has so revealed himself that men and women, made in his image, may address him by name. Because God is holy, sin breaks the fellowship in which prayer is acceptable to him. God's gracious work of salvation restores and renews that fellowship through Jesus Christ.

Jesus, the incarnate Son of God, prayed to his heavenly Father in unbroken communion. He began his public ministry in prayer (Lk. 3:21). He prayed in solitude before dawn (Mk. 1:35), and marked the turning points of his ministry with periods of prayer (Lk. 5:16; 6:12; 9:18). Before he went to the cross he agonized in prayer, submitting to his Father's will (Mt. 26:36–44). He who as the Priest prayed for his people (Jn. 17), became the sacrifice to die for them (Heb. 9:24–26). As the heavenly High Priest, the risen Christ lives to make intercession for the saints (Rom. 8:34; Heb. 7:24,25; 1 Jn. 2:1). Only in the name of Jesus, and by that way which he has opened, do sinners have access to the Father (Jn. 14:6). The Holy Spirit, sent by the Father, unites us to Christ in saving faith and gives us the confidence to call God 'Abba', Father, as Jesus did (Mk. 14:36; Rom. 8:14–17). We do not know the plan by which God wills all things to work together for our good; we do not know, therefore, how to pray according to that plan. Yet the Spirit aids our weakness:

he prays for us with inarticulate groanings (Rom. 8:26–28).

The Lord promises to hear and answer our prayers as we pray according to his will (1 Jn. 5:14, 15). To pray according to God's will means to make God's word the guide for our prayers, to seek that his revealed will should be done on earth as in heaven. Prayer seeks God's will in faith, believing in his power to answer in his created universe (Mt. 21:21, 22). Faith does not use prayer as a technique to alter consciousness, but as an address to the living God. On the other hand, prayer is not made pointless by the sovereign power of God. Our prayers, no less than their answers, are part of his design. It is God's will and promise: prayer changes things in his world (Jas. 5:16–18).

Awareness of God's presence shapes the response of prayer. In adoration we praise God for what he does and who he is. 'Hallowed be your name' asks that God be God, a petition that seeks blessing not for us, but for him. God's holiness demands confession of sin; his grace invites supplication for pardon. We seek his will, not our own, as we bring our petitions for guidance, provision, deliverance, and vindication. The communion of prayer deepens faith and love for God, not only as we draw near to him, but as we reach out in intercession for fellow Christians and for a lost world.

God hears and blesses both individual and corporate prayer (Mt. 18:19). Since prayer looks to God alone, faith is its key (Mt. 21:22). By faith we know that our prayers in Jesus' name are heard. In the communion of prayer we express our love for God and offer to him the tribute of our lives. Our awareness of God's love and our understanding of his purpose draw us to pray with fervent urgency for the spread of the gospel and the coming of his kingdom of righteousness, both now, and with the return of Christ. Prayer is reverent, but also shameless and persistent, not because God is unwilling to hear, but because we struggle to ask according to his will and are driven by the eternal issues at stake.

Prayer is the living breath of Christ's church. By prayer the church resists the assaults of Satan (Mt. 26:41; Eph. 6:13–20); receives fresh gifts of grace (Acts 4:31); seeks deliverance, healing and restoration for the saints (Eph. 6:18; Jas. 5:15; 1 Jn. 5:16);

supports the witness of the gospel (Col. 4:3, 4); seeks the return of the Lord (Rev. 22:20); and, above all, worships him of whom, through whom and unto whom are all things.

The practice of prayer, its methods and forms have been considered through the centuries. The church has used the Lord's prayer, the language of the Psalms and other fixed forms to pray in unison; the 'richly indwelling word of Christ' has produced a concert of prayer, formal and free, around the globe and across the years. Forms of prayer may be abused, as in 'vain repetition' (Mt. 6:7). An opposite danger is formless and wordless prayer that seeks mystical absorption into deity rather than living and personal fellowship with the Father through Jesus Christ. The witness of the Spirit grants inexpressible joy to Christians in prayer, yet prayer does not seek to gain ecstasy for ourselves, but to give joy and glory to God.

Bibliography

D. G. Bloesch, *The Struggle of Prayer* (New York, 1980); J. Bunyan, *Prayer* (repr. London, 1965); J. Calvin, *Institutes*, III. xx; F. L. Fisher, *Prayer in the NT* (Philadelphia, 1964); O. Hallesby, *Prayer* (London, 1961); J. Hastings, *The Doctrine of Prayer* (Edinburgh, 1915); F. Heiler, *Prayer: a Study in the History and Psychology of Religion* (New York, 1966); J. Jeremias, *The Prayers of Jesus* (London, 1967); E. Lohmeyer, '*Our Father,*' *An Introduction to the Lord's Prayer* (New York, 1966); D. M. M'Intyre, *The Hidden Life of Prayer* (Minneapolis, MN, 1969); J. Murray, *The Heavenly Priestly Activity of Christ* (London, 1958); J. Owen, 'A Discourse of the Work of the Holy Spirit in Prayer', *Works* (London, 1967), vol. 4, pp. 235–350; B. M. Palmer, *Theology of Prayer* (Richmond, VA, 1984); W. R. Spear, *The Theology of Prayer* (Grand Rapids, MI, 1979).

E.P.C.

PRAXIS AND ORTHOPRAXIS.
'Praxis' essentially means 'action'. Traditionally, the concept refers to the application of theory or socially innovative human behaviour. Its long history begins with Aristotle* but the concept achieved contemporary prominence through Marx,* who used it in various ways but, most commonly, to mean revolutionary action through which the world was changed.

In theology it has gained currency through liberation theology.* Theology usually emphasizes orthodoxy, *i.e.*, right belief or conceptual reflection on truth. Political theology* balances this with an emphasis on action (praxis) and right action (orthopraxis). Gutiérrez typically complains that 'the church has for centuries devoted her attention to formulating truth and meanwhile did almost nothing to better the world'. It not only advocates action but questions whether knowledge can be detached; and it insists that truth can only be known through action. Knowing and doing are dialectically related, and right action becomes the criterion for truth.

The danger is, as Miguez Bonino has observed, that theology is reduced to ethics, the vertical dimension equated with the horizontal and the concept built on Marxism. Positively, however, it can claim biblical roots. God communicates with his world, not through a conceptual frame of reference, but in creative activity; in John's gospel knowing truth is contingent on doing it (Jn. 3:21).

Bibliography

L. Boff, *Jesus Christ Liberator* (London, 1980); G. Gutiérrez, *A Theology of Liberation* (London, 1974); J. A. Kirk, *Liberation Theology: An Evangelical View from the Third World* (London, 1979); J. Miguez Bonino, *Revolutionary Theology Comes of Age* (London, 1975).

D.J.T.

PREACHING, THEOLOGY OF. In the
Bible, preaching plays a major part. This is true of the OT (*cf.* Prophecy*), but in particular of the NT. One may even say that the NT itself is the result of preaching. Both the gospels and the epistles are fully kerygmatic.* Jesus* himself continually proclaimed the coming of the kingdom of God.* Even more, in his preaching and healing* activities the kingdom was already present. In his cross and resurrection God's eschatological act of redemption took place. This is also the reason why after his resurrection and the outpouring of the Spirit Jesus himself is the main content of the apostolic proclamation. It is therefore not surprising to see that the New Testament uses more than thirty verbs to denote the activity of preaching. The apostles, commissioned by the risen Lord, preached this message as the very word of God (*cf.* 2 Thes.

2:13). The Pauline Epistles frequently use such expressions as 'the word of God' or 'the word of the Lord' or, in an even shorter formula, 'the word' (*cf.* 1 Thes. 1:6, 8; 3:1; Col. 4:3; 2 Tim. 2:9; 4:1; etc.). In all these passages the terms refer to the *preached* word (*cf. TDNT* IV, 116). This is also the reason why the word preached by Paul and the others is effective. This efficacy is not due to the talents of the preacher, but the secret lies in the genitive: it is the word *of God* or *of the Lord*. In the apostolic message (the emphasis being always on *the content*) the voice of the living God is being heard.

This emphasis was shared by the Reformers. Both Luther* and Calvin* were convinced that, when the message of the gospel of Jesus Christ is being proclaimed, God himself is heard by the listeners. In chapter 1 of the Second Helvetic Confession (1566) Heinrich Bullinger,* the successor of Zwingli,* summarized the position of the Reformers in one terse statement: *Praedicatio verbi Dei est verbum Dei* – the preaching of the word of God *is* the word of God. In the next sentence he interprets this statement as follows: 'Wherefore when this word of God (=Scripture*) is now preached in the church by preachers lawfully called, we believe that the very word of God is proclaimed, and received by the faithful.'

The indispensable condition for true preaching is the faithful proclamation of the message of Scripture. Yet preaching is not a simple repetition of this message. It must also be actualized into the present. If preaching is to be true and relevant, the message of Scripture must be addressed to people in their concrete historical situation. The biblical message may not be *adapted* to the situation of today, but it must be 'accommodated' (Calvin) to the situation. As in Christ God stooped down to take upon himself our flesh (see Accommodation,* Incarnation*), so in the preaching of the word the Holy Spirit stoops down to reach people in their situation. The preacher therefore must be an exegete of both Scripture and of his congregation, so that the living word of God for today will be heard at the intersection of text and situation.

Bibliography

E. P. Clowney, *Preaching and Biblical Theology* (London, 1961); C. H. Dodd, *The Apostolic Preaching and Its Developments* (London, 1936); H. H. Farmer, *The Servant of the Word* (London, 1950); D. W. Cleverley Ford, *The Ministry of the Word* (London, 1979); P. T. Forsyth, *Positive Preaching and the Modern Mind* (London, 1949); D. M. Lloyd-Jones, *Preaching and Preachers* (London, 1971); K. Runia, *The Sermon Under Attack* (Exeter, 1983); *idem*, 'What is preaching according to the New Testament?', *TynB* 29, 1978, pp. 3–48; J. R. W. Stott, *I Believe in Preaching* (London, 1982).

K.R.

PREDESTINATION. The apostle Paul in Rom. 8 and 9 and in Eph. 1 definitely teaches a doctrine of predestination. As a result the church through the ages has laboured to understand what Paul and other biblical writers meant by predestination.

Many have in effect defined predestination as identical with God's foreknowledge. God in his omniscience has foreseen how all individuals will respond to the offer of the gospel and has predestined to eternal life those whom he has foreseen responding in faith and obedience.

Another definition of predestination can be traced back to Augustine.* Reflecting on his study of Scripture and the experiences of his own life, Augustine came to believe that the individual left to himself is so lost in sin* and rebellion against God that he will not seek God. His fallen will* is so corrupted that he cannot seek salvation. In that sense humanity has no free will. So if there is to be salvation for man, it must come at God's initiative. God's grace* seeks, restores, saves and preserves the sinner. But then why are some saved and not others? Augustine and others in his tradition argue that it cannot be for anything in men and women – for some residual goodness or moral superiority in those saved over those who are lost. The Augustinian doctrine of sin precludes that answer. So the reason that some sinners are saved and others are lost must be in God. It is according to God's sovereign purpose, his eternal decree, that some sinners are rescued and others are left in their sin. The foundation of this divine decree is simply the good pleasure or will of God.

The Augustinian doctrine of predestination has certain clear attractions. It gives full prominence to a biblical doctrine of sin and it magnifies the grace of God in salvation.*

That is why most of the Western church in the 5th century supported Augustine against Pelagius'* doctrine of free will and the natural ability to find salvation apart from grace. The church could eagerly respond to the teaching that salvation is a result of sovereign grace alone.

The problem came with the negative side of predestination, commonly known as reprobation. The doctrine of reprobation teaches that God, according to his sovereign will, passes over some sinners, leaving them in their sins, and at last condemns them for their sins. To many this doctrine seems harsh, unjust and determinist. Therefore some (like many Lutherans* who hold to the Formula of Concord) accept the positive, saving side of the doctrine of predestination, but reject the doctrine of reprobation. Those who reject reprobation in this manner are often said to believe in single predestination rather than double predestination.

Those who defend double predestination (predestination and reprobation) argue that reprobation is biblical (e.g. Rom. 9:10–23) and displays the justice of God just as salvation displays his mercy. They argue that it is not unfair or unjust for God to leave sinners in their sin. Nor does double predestination result in fatalism since God has appointed preaching, evangelism and the church as the means by which he will accomplish his saving purposes. Further they argue that the doctrine of single predestination is inherently unstable theologically, tending again to make something in us the ultimate factor in salvation.

In the Middle Ages many theologians like Thomas Aquinas* and Gregory of Rimini* followed the Augustinian doctrine of predestination. Others like William of Ockham* called themselves Augustinian while actually tending to identify predestination with foreknowledge.

The leading Protestant Reformers, Luther,* Zwingli* and Calvin,* taught the full Augustinian* doctrine of predestination. It also became the official teaching of the Church of England as summarized in the Thirty-nine Articles. There were also defenders of an Augustinian view of predestination including Cardinal Gasparo Contarini (1483–1542), some Dominican* theologians and the Jansenists (see Augustinianism*).

The late 16th-century Jesuit Robert Bellarmine* suggested a compromise position on predestination that has come to be known as congruism, but is in fact not fully Augustinian. Congruism teaches that God has elected certain specific individuals to salvation but that God saves those individuals by offering them sufficient grace in circumstances that he has foreseen will result in their freely accepting that grace (see Merit*). Augustinianism, by contrast, teaches that salvation comes to the elect through efficient grace sovereignly given to the elect individual.

Predestination came to have a special prominence and role in the theology of John Calvin* and his followers. Calvin made predestination an integral element in Christian experience, insisting that believers should be assured that they are elect because they are in Christ. Since they are elect, their lives should be characterized by a joyous, confident service of God and others. For Calvin, predestination was a doctrine of comfort and assurance* and should liberate the Christian from morbid introspection or debilitating insecurity.

Among Calvinists a disagreement arose over the logical order of the decrees of predestination in the mind of God. There were two basic positions, supralapsarianism and infralapsarianism. Supralapsarians held that God first decreed to save some and to condemn others and then decreed the fall* and the work of Christ as means to that end. They followed Theodore Beza* in his interpretation of Rom. 9 and in following the Aristotelian principle that what is last in action must be first in thought. The infralapsarians, always a majority among the Calvinists, held that God first decreed or permitted the fall and then decreed to save some and to condemn others.

Within the Reformed* churches there were various reactions to Calvin's doctrine of predestination. Some Puritans,* for example, held to the doctrine but made assurance of election the result of a lengthy process or struggle for the Christian. They created an excessively introspective kind of Calvinism. Others in Reformed churches rejected the doctrine of predestination. The most famous was the 17th-century Dutch theologian Jacobus Arminius* who tended like earlier theologians to identify predestination with foreknowledge. His name was taken by later Protestants who as Arminians rejected the

Augustinian doctrine of predestination. John Wesley's* Methodist* Church officially adopted the Arminian theology. Most Baptists in the 17th and 18th centuries were Augustinian on predestination. They were known as regular or particular Baptists. Later many Baptists became Arminian or general Baptists.

The contemporary evangelical church has become largely Arminian often as a result of anti-doctrinal bias rather than careful theological reflection. The historic Augustinian doctrine of predestination remains biblically and theologically compelling. Karl Barth* propounded an influential reinterpretation, making Christ in effect the one who experienced both election and reprobation for all humanity.

See also: DETERMINISM; SOVEREIGNTY OF GOD.

Bibliography
G. C. Berkouwer, *Divine Election* (ET, Grand Rapids, MI, 1960); J. Calvin, *Institutes* III.xxi-xxiv; *idem*, *Concerning the Eternal Predestination of God*, tr. J. K. S. Reid (London, 1960); C. Hodge, *Systematic Theology*, vol. 3 (London, Edinburgh and New York, 1873); P. Jacobs, H. Krienke, *NIDNTT* I, pp. 692–697; C. H. Pinnock (ed.), *Grace Unlimited* (Minneapolis, MN, 1975); B. B. Warfield, *Biblical Foundations* (London, 1958).

W.R.G.

PRESBYTERIANISM denotes both a form of church government* by elders (presbyters), and a system of scriptural doctrine. Contemporary Presbyterianism originated in the Protestant Reformation,* particularly in Calvin's* Geneva. The unity of Presbyterian doctrine and order appears in John Calvin's *Institutes of the Christian Religion*. Calvin turns to Scripture to formulate principles for the order of the church as well as the doctrines of the faith of the church. In the *Institutes*, as in the later Presbyterian and Reformed tradition, the key to both the doctrine and the order of the church is found in God's sovereignty.*

The doctrinal distinctives of Presbyterianism are expressed in the Reformed creeds of the 16th century, but the Presbyterian churches have adopted the Confession of Faith and the catechisms of the Westminster Assembly (1643–9). All these Reformed confessions* make God's glory the supreme end of man's creation, so that all of life is in trust for him. In sin humanity is guilty before God and hostile to him; salvation no less than creation must be God's work (Rom. 11:36). God's salvation springs from the free choice of his electing love. It is accomplished by the gift of God's eternal Son, who by his perfect obedience merited eternal life for God's elect, and who died on the cross as their representative, atoning for their sins and securing their salvation. The Holy Spirit, sent from the throne of the Lord Christ, applies his salvation to those given him of the Father, regenerating them so that they are persuaded and enabled to embrace Christ as he is freely offered in the gospel, and giving them grace to persevere in faith. Human choice has eternal consequences, but sinners can choose Christ only because he has first chosen them.

Presbyterians regard these doctrines as biblical, and note how the apostle Paul answered obvious objections to them (Rom. 9:14, 19). They hold, therefore, that they stand in a tradition of apostolic teaching that has never been fully eclipsed in the history of the church.

In similar fashion Presbyterianism has sought to restore a biblical church order. Jesus Christ, exalted as Lord over all, is the one king and head of the church, the only mediator between God and man. He rules in his church directly by his word and Spirit, but he has ordained government in his church, revealed its principles in his word, and promised his presence in the midst of the church as the keys of the kingdom are used in his name. All office in the church exists by his appointment; he calls and equips all office-bearers for their ministry.* In choosing officers, the church does not grant them authority, but recognizes Christ's authority and calling. Church government must conform to the scriptural pattern. In those circumstances not specifically ordered by Scriptures the church must observe the general rules of the word: all things are to be done 'decently and in order' to the glory of the Lord, for the edification of the saints, and in witness to the world. The scriptural pattern of government is necessary for the well-being of the church, but is not essential for its existence. Presbyterians recognize that many degrees of faithfulness to Scripture exist in their own and other churches; Reformed churches must be ever reforming.

Christ's rule of the church through his word and Spirit requires that all church power be ministerial and declarative. No church officer or council can legislate novelties of faith or worship, but can only minister the word of the Lord.

Final judgment is committed to Christ; he has not given the sword of justice to the officers of his kingdom (Jn. 18:36). All church power is wholly moral and spiritual. Church officers possess no civil jurisdiction; they may not inflict civil penalties nor seek the aid of the civil power in the exercise of their jurisdiction. They recognize the divine authorization of civil government (Rom. 13:1–7; 1 Pet. 2:13–17); they support and pray for its effectiveness in keeping peace.

The church is the body of Christ: Presbyterian order reflects the fact that salvation is corporate as well as individual. The church is not composed first of clergy possessing unique gifts to dispense sacramental grace. It is a body of believers and their children, a covenantal community called of Christ and endued with the Spirit to join in a mutual ministry of worship, edification, and witness. The gifts of the members differ from the gifts of officers not in kind but degree.

Those chosen by the church to join in its government are ministers of the word, or teaching elders, and others with gifts for rule, called ruling elders. Since the inspired authority of the foundational office of the apostles has not been continued, all elders rule in parity. ('Bishop' and 'presbyter' are synonymous terms in the New Testament.) The Presbyterian recognition of the ruling elder is based on the distinction of teaching and ruling gifts (1 Tim. 5:17; Rom. 12:8; 1 Cor. 12:28), and the divinely authorized role of the elders of the people in the Old Covenant (Nu. 11:16, 17), continued in the New (Acts 11:30; *cf.* Mt. 13:52; 23:34).

Presbyters govern jointly in the local assembly (session, consistory), regional assembly (presbytery, classis), and in wider assemblies (synod, general assembly). This system of graded assemblies or courts reflects the unity of the church catholic, regional, and local. The concern of each assembly is determined by its scope. Christ grants gifts of rule for the whole church; they may be legitimately used in broader assemblies of those acknowledged by the saints as those set over them in the Lord.

The office of the deacon is one of ministry rather than spiritual government. It is charged with the service of mercy to the poor and needy among the saints, and, as God grants opportunity, to the world. While the Pauline Epistles restrict the governing role in the family of God to male elders (1 Tim. 2:12), the place of women in ministries of mercy is clear. Some Presbyterian churches appoint women to the diaconal office (Rom. 16:1; 1 Tim. 3:11).

Bibliography

J. L. Ainslie, *The Doctrines of Ministerial Order in the Reformed Churches of the Sixteenth and Seventeenth Centuries* (Edinburgh, 1940); A. C. Cochrane (ed.), *Reformed Confessions of the Sixteenth Century* (London, 1966); J. M. Gettys, *What Presbyterians Believe: An Interpretation of the Westminster Standards* (Clinton, SC, 1953); G. D. Henderson, *Presbyterianism* (Aberdeen, 1954); J. H. Leith, *Introduction to the Reformed Tradition* (Atlanta, GA, 1977); J. A. Mackay, *The Presbyterian Way of Life* (Englewood Cliffs, NJ, 1960); J. Moffatt, *The Presbyterian Churches* (London, 21928); J. H. Nichols, *Corporate Worship in the Reformed Tradition* (Philadelphia, 1968); E. W. Smith, *The Creed of the Presbyterians* (Toronto, 1901).

E.P.C.

PRIESTHOOD OF ALL BELIEVERS, a doctrine ultimately of biblical origin but classically formulated by Luther,* affirming the common dignity, calling and privilege of all Christians before God. Israel was distinguished from other peoples as 'a kingdom of priests and a holy nation' for God (Ex. 19:6; *cf.* Is. 61:6), and the church is likewise described (1 Pet. 2:9; Rev. 1:6; 5:10), being called to 'offer spiritual sacrifices acceptable to God through Jesus Christ' (1 Pet. 2:5), including praise and the service of Christian love (Heb. 13:15–16; *cf.* Rom. 15:15–16). The NT does not explicitly connect this royal priesthood of Christians to the priesthood of Christ (but *cf.* Heb. 10:19–22), in whom the OT priesthood was fulfilled and hence superseded (*cf.* Heb. 6:20–10:25). There is no NT warrant for ascribing any special qualification of priesthood to ordained persons within the common priesthood of the church (as argued by, *e.g.*, T. F. Torrance,* *The Royal Priesthood*, Edinburgh, 1955).

The early fathers spoke of Christians as 'a (high-) priestly race' presenting pure sacrifices to God (*cf.* Mal. 1:11). But the designation of bishops and presbyters as sacrificing mediatorial priests in OT terms, promoted especially by Cyprian* in the mid–3rd century, increasingly obscured the general priesthood of Christians. In the Middle Ages, Christians who were not clergy or monks were in effect relegated to second-class status.

Against such distortions Luther protested that 'our baptism* consecrates us all without exception and makes us all priests. . . . We all have the same authority in regard to the word and the sacraments, although no one has the right to administer them without the consent of the members of his church.' In particular, 'those who exercise secular authority have been baptized like the rest of us. . . . They are priests and bishops. They discharge their office as an office of the Christian community', and so may advance the reform of the church. All human callings are acceptable before God. 'Every shoemaker can be a priest of God, and stick to his own last while he does it.' 'By virtue of his priesthood, the Christian exercises power with God, for God does what he asks and desires.'

This doctrine was fundamental to the whole Reformation.* In Calvin* it was more firmly grounded in the one priesthood of Christ. Yet the Reformation did not abolish ministerial order, leaving somewhat uncertain the relationship between the two. In modern theology the common priesthood of Christians is generally acknowledged but often muted in the interests of a special priesthood of the ordained. This is frequently depicted as of a different order altogether from the general priesthood ('in essence and not only in degree' – Vatican II), or as a representative focus of the priesthood of all. It remains true that 'no single Church has been able to express in its worship, work, and witness, the full richness of this doctrine' (C. Eastwood).

Bibliography

E. Best, 'Spiritual Sacrifice: General Priesthood in the New Testament', *Int* 14 (1960), pp. 280–290; J. H. Elliott, *The Elect and the Holy: An Exegetical Examination of 1 Peter 2:4–10 and the Phrase* βασίλειον ἱεράτευμα (*Suppl. to NovT* 12; Leiden, 1966); C. East-wood, *The Priesthood of All Believers. An Examination of the Doctrine from the Reformation to the Present Day* (London, 1960); for Luther, see *LW*, vols. 35, 36, 39.

D.F.W.

PRINCETON THEOLOGY was a major expression of conservative Calvinism (see Reformed Theology*) in America during the 19th and early 20th centuries. It owed its force to the remarkable series of theologians who taught at the Presbyterian seminary in Princeton, New Jersey, and to the significance of that institution within the denomination and the country at large. The three most important Princeton theologians were Archibald Alexander (1772–1851), founding professor of the school, Charles Hodge,* who taught over 3,000 students in his over fifty years as a Princeton professor, and Benjamin Breckinridge Warfield,* who upheld Old Princeton positions during a period of fading evangelical influence. These three were joined by a host of other important figures, including Hodge's son, Archibald Alexander Hodge (1823–86), two sons of Alexander, James Waddel (1804–59) and Joseph Addison (1809–60), and the New Testament scholar and apologist, J. Gresham Machen.*

The Princeton theologians upheld Reformed confessionalism, defended high views of biblical inspiration and authority, organized their thinking with the aid of the Scottish philosophy of Common Sense,* and had a surprisingly large place for the role of the Holy Spirit in religious experience. The theologians of Old Princeton were jealous guardians of Calvinistic views on the divine pre-eminence in salvation, the unity both of the race in Adam's guilt and of the elect in the work of Christ, and the moral inability of humans apart from God's grace. They upheld these positions against continental romanticism* and rationalism, against domestic forms of subjectivity, against the excesses of enthusiastic revivalism, against all varieties of theological liberalism* and against evangelical perfectionism.* One of the Reformed positions which the school held most doggedly was the infallibility* of the Bible. This was a central theme in the apologetics of Alexander, it was an essential foundation for Charles Hodge's *Systematic Theology* and for the polemics which he carried on in the *Princeton*

Review, and it provided Warfield with the position that he defended in countless essays toward the end of the 19th century. The well-known monograph on 'Inspiration' in 1881 by Warfield and A. A. Hodge summed up the Princeton position: the church's historic belief in the verbal infallibility of the Bible should be maintained both because of external proofs for Scripture's divine character and because of the Bible's own testimony concerning itself.

Principles of the Scottish philosophy of Common Sense provided guidelines for the Princeton theologians in their organization of scriptural material and for their approach to theology. In this they reflected the teaching of two Scottish-born presidents of Princeton College, John Witherspoon (1723–94) and James McCosh (1811–94), whose work influenced all of the major Princetonians directly or indirectly.

At Princeton Seminary, the Scottish philosophy was not so much a guide for convictions about the native powers of the 'moral sense', as was the case among New England* Calvinists. It provided rather a confidence in empirical science and simple inductive procedures by which to chart a theological course. The opening pages of Charles Hodge's Systematic Theology provide the clearest illustration of these procedural commitments. But even as the Princetonians adopted the scientific standards of the Scottish philosophy, they always retained a large place for distinctly spiritual influences. The major Princeton theologians were all powerful preachers. Although they distrusted unrestrained revivalism, they worked for renewal in the church. Charles Hodge especially, in his commentaries and some of his polemics, could write as movingly about the inward effects of the Holy Spirit as any of his contemporaries.

The Princeton theologians embodied their beliefs in powerful institutions. The seminary itself trained more ministers than any comparable institution in the United States during the 19th century. The Princeton Review and its successor journals were mighty organs, not only among northern Presbyterians but across denominational boundaries. And the school was a force to be reckoned with in the denomination, both when its positions dominated significant segments of the church and when its views became a minority position.

Critics of the Princetonians accuse them of scholastic rationalism and a mechanical bibli-

cism. While these claims are not without a particle of truth, the larger reality is that the theologians of Old Princeton were faithful representatives of historic Calvinism, who energetically adopted their confessional position to the needs and opportunities of the American experience.

Bibliography

C. Hodge, 'Retrospect of the History of the Princeton Review,' Biblical Repertory and Princeton Review. Index Volume, no. 1 (1870), pp. 1–39; A. W. Hoffecker, Piety and the Princeton Theologians: Archibald Alexander, Charles Hodge, and Benjamin Warfield (Phillipsburg, NJ, 1981); T. M. Lindsay, 'The Doctrine of Scripture: The Reformers and the Princeton School,' The Expositor, Fifth Series, Vol. 1, ed. W. Robertson Nicoll (London, 1895), pp. 278–293; M. A. Noll (ed.), The Princeton Theology 1812–1921: Scripture, Science, and Theological Method from Archibald Alexander to Benjamin Warfield (Grand Rapids, MI, 1983); J. C. Vander Stelt, Philosophy and Scripture: A Study in Old Princeton and Westminster Theology (Marlton, NJ, 1978); J. D. Woodbridge and R. Balmer, 'The Princetonians and Biblical Authority,' in Scripture and Truth, eds. Woodbridge and D. A. Carson (Grand Rapids, MI, 1983).

M.A.N.

PRISCILLIANISM, named after Priscillian, a Spanish nobleman, was an ascetic* movement which emerged within the churches of Spain and Aquitaine in the 370s. It emphasized virginity, voluntary poverty, and vegetarianism as sure means of attaining greater spiritual heights, particularly the gift of prophecy.* For the Priscillianists this meant the ability to discern special meaning both in the Scriptures and in various aprocrypha. While Priscillian, who became Bishop of Avila, accepted the current canon of Scripture, he was convinced divine revelation was not confined to this. He also took some interest in occult literature in the belief that a successful spiritual life involved a close knowledge of the enemy and his strategy.

Priscillianism neither challenged the church authorities directly nor fostered monastic foundations, though some informal fraternities were established. Certain bishops, however, became suspicious that the activities and doctrines of the Priscillianists smacked of Manichaeism* and sorcery. Matters came to a head when these charges were brought against Priscillian and some associates before the Emperor Maximus at Trier in 385. This led to their execution – the first and almost only occasion in antiquity when a heretic suffered this fate at the hand of a civil ruler. At the time the greatest indignation was reserved for those bishops who had pressed capital charges.

After these executions there was a temporary reaction in favour of Priscillian, who in some quarters was regarded as a martyr.* A schism* was threatened within the Spanish church, but this was avoided by vigorous action from the Council of Toledo in 400. At a popular level Priscillianism continued to exercise some influence right up to the 6th century.

Bibliography

H. Chadwick, *Priscillian of Avila* (Oxford, 1976).

G.A.K.

PROCESS THEOLOGY is the theological system that has been developed on the basis of the philosophy of Alfred North Whitehead and Charles Hartshorne. The name itself derives from the central tenet of both of these philosophers that reality is a process of becoming, not a static universe of objects. From this, a unique concept of both God and man is derived, and from that in turn a complete theology.

Whitehead (1861–1947) began, in 1925, a series of publications which culminated in *Process and Reality* (1929). Here he developed an original metaphysical* system based on the primacy of events. The notion of events combines into one the previously separated notions of space, time and matter, as indicated by Einstein's physics. These events (Whitehead called them actual occasions) are the atoms of the cosmos. Each atom is a point in the process, which takes from the past and incorporates new possibilities into a new event which, in turn, contributes to the future. The highest principle in this process is that of creativity. It continuously brings about novelty in a creative advance that maximizes good.

Hartshorne (b. 1897), beginning with several major works in the 1940s, has developed a complete process philosophical theology, detailing especially a full concept of God.

These views have seen extensive elaboration in succeeding decades by theologians and philosophers such as John Cobb (b. 1925), David R. Griffin (b. 1939), Schubert Ogden (b. 1928), Daniel Day Williams (1910–73) and Lewis Ford (b. 1933) in the United States and Norman Pittenger (b. 1905) in England, to name just a few.

Most process theology is rooted in process theism.* God, according to Whitehead, is the primary example of metaphysical truths as well as the one who supplies initial direction to every event. Hence neither the general nature of reality nor the free actions of history* are comprehensible apart from him.

The process view of God has been described as panentheism.* It differs from theism in identifying God and the universe, but it differs also from pantheism* in seeing God as more than, or existing beyond, the universe. Hartshorne and Ogden use the analogy of a person's relation to his body. I am my body, but I am more than it.

In Whitehead and Hartshorne, God's existence is necessitated by two different factors which produced a dipolar concept. God in his 'primordial', eternal, absolute nature as mind contributes the novel aims or possibilities to each succeeding event. God in his 'consequent' changing and growing nature physically experiences the process, knowing and loving it. But experiencing involves a real relation or union, hence the cosmic process is God.

For Whitehead God is conceived of as himself a single event who in one act is comprehending the whole process. More recently, John Cobb and others have developed a view of God as being like a human person, that is, a series of comprehending events, identified by common characteristics which continue in the transition.

The doctrine of Christ (see Christology*) has presented process theologians with a difficult problem. Every event in history is God's activity and being inserting itself. In this sense every occasion is incarnation,* and hence no single event can be so exclusively. Yet it remains true that God cannot determine events. As a result, no event is only God's action, and therefore the deity of Christ is impossible in any strict sense.

Process Christologies, as in David Griffin,

Norman Pittenger and Lewis Ford, generally attempt to show that Christ's life was God's in the sense that it was lived in complete obedience, that is, that Christ most perfectly followed the 'lure' of God. Others have done so to a high degree, but in Christ obedience was so complete that a whole new subjectivity, a way of human living, is inaugurated.

The result of the life and death of Christ is the emergence of a new kind of community, the church.* This is the meaning of resurrection:* the body of Christ is born. For Ford this is seen as a major step in human evolution. Man is now radically different.

Add to this the view that the Holy Spirit* is to be understood as God's contribution of initial aims, and we see that process theology is unitarian,* not Trinitarian.

The twofold character of all events as both incarnational and autonomous also defines the process theologian's view of revelation.* Because all events, including human actions, are given their initial design by God, they are each a revelation of his character. As a result the traditional distinction between general and special revelation breaks down. There is only special revelation; direct, intentional and conscious acts of God. But every event has this quality.

On the other hand, because every event is self-determined in its actuality, God cannot ensure that any revelation truly represents him. The future is never known, always free and open. Until it decides itself, it has no reality and cannot be predicted, even by God. Consequently, revelation could never be inerrant. Some expressions will be more characteristic than others, but none can be guaranteed true.

Hermeneutics* is seen as an attempt to retrace the revelational process to discover God's original 'lure'. Thus, it has both objective and subjective components, and is possible only in the interaction of the reader.

The general features of process philosophy imply a view of man that is very close, if not identical, to that of Heidegger, Bultmann* and other existentialists.* Ogden has been the principal figure in developing this point. A person is a series of separate events. Each point is autonomous not only in relation to all others in the series but also to God. It is self-determinative. Thus, it is also dependent on its own existential decision. I am what I am now deciding to be.

As a result, the redemptive activity of God consists in his willingness to accept past evil, transform it into good and continue to lure each individual toward a self-authenticating acceptance of true value. A person's salvation consists in his recognition of disloyalty to communality (Ford, Cobb and Griffin) and his willing acceptance of God's lure to be a member of the body of Christ.

The process-God's ability to preserve each event as an 'eternal object' adds an eschatological* dimension to the theological system. Not only does God's continuing knowledge preserve the reality (in a subjective sense) of each occasion, but his use of the past in presenting new possibilities to the future also gives meaning to former events. Ogden and others have used this concept in Whitehead as a way of spelling out the biblical idea of eternal life and heaven. Nothing is forgotten to the love of God, all is preserved and continues to affect the future meaningfully. It should be noted, however, that this is not conscious personal continuance, and also that it is universal in application.

Ford, Cobb and others have done much to develop a general eschatology as well. It follows from their view of the church as the emergence of a higher state of human evolution (see Creation*). This understanding permits us to look forward to a time when God's aims will finally overcome the individual evil events, and bring about a true community of love and peace. Hartshorne roots this in the biblical view of love as true union.

There is among process theologians wide diversity of concern to preserve a biblical Christianity. Some, like Lewis Ford and many Roman Catholics, indicate a strong desire to remain scriptural, but most are concerned only to remain within a broadly understood Christian tradition. Some, like Hartshorne, are impressed with many process-like insights in Buddhism* and other religions and will explicitly reject some Christian ideas in their favour. Hence an evangelical response to process theology is bound to be varied.

In general, however, several major flaws can be indicated. First, its general metaphysics negates the biblical view of creation* and providence* with its radical distinction between infinite creator and finite cosmos. Some, like Hartshorne, have argued that the traditional view is not Hebrew but a Greek addition and to be rejected. Others have attempted to modify Whitehead to allow for the distinction.

Second, its universal view of incarnation has so far prevented any ontological, rather than functional, concept of the deity of Christ. Likewise, it prevents any judicial or truly redemptive view of salvation. Finally, the hermeneutic of process theology eliminates any concept of inerrancy (see Infallibility*). God cannot bring about such an event, neither could words have purely objective meaning (Hartshorne).

Bibliography

D. Brown, R. E. James, G. Reeves (eds.), *Process Philosophy and Christian Thought* (Indianapolis, IN, 1971); J. Cobb and D. R. Griffin, *Process Theology: An Introductory Exposition* (Philadelphia, 1976, and Belfast, 1977); L. Ford, *The Lure of God* (Philadelphia, 1978); D. R. Griffin, *A Process Christology* (Philadelphia, 1973); C. Hartshorne, *Man's Vision of God and the Logic of Theism* (Chicago, 1941); S. Ogden, *The Reality of God* (London, 1966); Norman Pittenger, *The Word Incarnate* (New York, 1959); S. Sia, *God in Process Thought* (Dordecht, Netherlands, 1985); A. N. Whitehead, *Process and Reality* (London, 1929).

Response: R. Gruenler, *The Inexhaustible God* (Grand Rapids, MI, 1984).

W.D.B.

PROCESSION (OF HOLY SPIRIT), see HOLY SPIRIT; TRINITY.

PROGRESS, IDEA OF. The idea most characteristic of 19th-century thinking was that of progress. There were many reasons for this. Britain's industrial revolution became the pattern for rapid economic growth and social development throughout the West. Scientific discovery and its application in such practical developments as techniques of mass production and advances in public health helped generate an optimistic and forward-looking cast of mind, which was fostered by the spread of civilization by the European empires and across the continent of North America. At the same time, the wide influence of Hegel's* dialectical rationalism provided the seed-bed in which was sown the theory of evolution (see Creation*).

The idea of evolutionary progress as the explanatory hypothesis of reality was therefore antecedent to the development of Darwin's theory of evolution (itself not the first scientific theory of its kind). But Darwinism seemed to provide a scientific basis for the philosophical ideas which were already popular, and the use of biological evolution as the key to all historical development reached its high-water mark in the extensive writings of Herbert Spencer (1820–1903). It was typical of the mind-set of the mid–19th century that his scientific hypothesis should be made the basis for general philosophical constructions. Scarcely any thinker, Christian or not, avoided being influenced by the idea of evolutionary progress, in which the development of human society and the moral development of man were seen as continuous and essentially analogous with the supposed upward progress of biological evolution.

More recently, the Jesuit anthropologist Teilhard de Chardin* has attempted a full-blooded marriage of Darwinism and the Christian view of man and redemption. Spencer's later contemporary Henry Drummond sought in popular evangelical terms to do something similar in his *Ascent of Man* (1894).

An immediate implication of this way of thinking was found in the writing of history, in which an evolutionary progress was traced, and since the Christian Bible is largely an historical account there were dramatic repercussions for the way in which the Scriptures were assessed. A classic instance is William Robertson Smith's *Religion of the Semites* (1889), which attempts to find revelation in a naturalistic reading of history. It was of course not new for a naturalistic explanation to be given to the biblical history, since from the first days of the church those who were sceptical of its claims had their own way of reading its Scriptures. Yet such was the absorption with evolutionary progress that in the mid- and later 19th century the church itself began to adopt such a reading of its canonical Scriptures.

The Bible does not speak of man's history as an evolutionary progress. It tells of an original perfection from which man has fallen (see Fall*), and the story which follows is that of failed attempts to set matters right (Babel, flood, exile), with a constant regress on the part of man. Progress comes only from the side of God. The idea of a natural evolutionary progress is therefore the precise antithesis of the biblical picture of man and his religion, so the attempt thus to re-interpret the biblical history has to adopt the violent methods of Procrustes, and subordinate the data to the theory. This single fact explains in large measure the subsequent history of OT scholarship, which despite later renunciation of an evolutionary paradigm* is still undergirded by the inversion of the order of the law and the prophets which the theory required (since prophetic religion was held to be more simple and therefore earlier).

More recent social developments, beginning with the First World War and coming to a head in the nuclear threat, have dealt a death-blow to essentially progressive views of man, and returned ideas of evolution to the laboratory where they may or may not prove fit to survive. Man's economic and technological progress have been shown to be tenuous and by no means inevitable, and question-marks put against the claim that he has advanced morally since his earliest days. Redemption, far from being a product of evolution, can only be by revolution in man's continually regressive moral and spiritual story. The only true idea of progress is that of the progress of God in salvation-history.*

See also: BIBLICAL CRITICISM.

Bibliography

C. Dawson, *Progress and Religion. An Historical Enquiry* (London, 1945); C. S. Lewis, 'The Funeral of a Great Myth', in *Christian Reflections* (London, 1967).

N.M.deS.C.

PROOFS OF GOD'S EXISTENCE, see NATURAL THEOLOGY.

PROPHECY, THEOLOGY OF. Prophecy may be defined as (1) a way of knowing truth; and as such, may be compared and contrasted with philosophy. In its biblical manifestation it forms a part of (2) the theology of the Holy Spirit* and is represented as (3) one mode of the divine revelation* of God's truth or, in a broader sense, the totality of that revelation. Prophecy may be expressed in (4) a variety of literary forms and in (5) both canonical and non-canonical contexts. Each part of this definition may be expanded as follows.

1. Like philosophy, prophecy purports to offer truth about God, man and the world, and its concerns may also be framed within well-known philosophical categories: What is the real? How do we know truth? How shall we act? Unlike philosophy, its starting-point is God and its source of knowledge is divine revelation – truth received, rather than truth achieved by autonomous human reason or experience. Thus, prophecy presupposes a transcendent world-view; that is, a creator and a spirit world, realities that are separate from but nonetheless impinge upon and communicate with the natural creation, specifically, with man. Prophecy is the mode and the content, and the prophet the human agent of that communication.

Prophecy not only represents a distinctive approach to truth but also, in the commentary on Scripture in 1 Cor 1:18–3:20, is given an exclusive claim to it. There Paul denies that autonomous human reason is a valid alternative way to truth, and his indictment against the wisdom of the Greeks must, in the context, have included philosophical thought (Godet; *cf. sophia*, 'wisdom', in 1 Cor.1:19–21; 1 Cor. 2:11–12). By this a redemptive natural revelation or insight is excluded (*cf.* O. Weber, Barth*).

2. Prophecy has its source in the 'Spirit of God.' This is clear in the NT where it is represented as the gift or act of the Spirit (Rom. 12:6; 1 Cor. 12:10; *cf.* 1 Cor. 12:28; Eph. 4:8; 1 Thes. 5:19f.) and the prophet is identified as 'a man of the Spirit' (*pneumatikos* = 1 Cor. 14:37; *cf.* Hos. 9:7). But it is also true of prophecy in the OT (1 Sam. 19:20; 2 Ki. 2:15; 2 Ch. 15:1; Ne. 9:30; Mi. 3:8; *cf.* 2 Pet 1:20f.), even if in some books the role of the Spirit is lacking, unstressed or undifferentiated from that of Yahweh (Lindblom, *Prophecy*). The hope of Moses (Nu. 11:16, 29; *cf.* Lk. 10:1) that 'all the Lord's people [might be] prophets' and the prophecy of Joel (2:28) that 'God will pour out his Spirit on all flesh' find their specific import in the prophecy of the Baptist (Mt. 3:11) and their fulfilment in the post-resurrection church (Acts 2:16, 33).

3. The varieties of divine revelation are described in Je. 18:18 as 'the law . . . from the priest, counsel from the wise [and] the word from the prophet' (*cf.* Is. 28:7; 29:10, 14). While prophets might live together in communities or guilds (2 Ki. 2:3ff.; 6:1), others were attached to the temple and some

537

were probably themselves priests; for example, Samuel, Elijah, Ezekiel (1:3) and (?) Jeremiah (1:1). At the same time priests had a 'prophetic' function in interpreting, transcribing and updating the Law (Is. 28:7). Thus, the roles of the OT prophet and priest in mediating God's word were not so distinct as some have thought (Pedersen, Johnson).

The wise man and wisdom teachers were also regarded in Israel as the recipients and mediators of a divine gift (Gn. 41:38f.; 2 Sa. 14:20, 17; 16:23; 1 Ki. 3:9, 12, 28; von Rad), and they have certain other affinities with the prophet. In later OT and intertestamental writings, wisdom and prophecy manifest increasing affinities with one another and are sometimes involved in what was also a traditional priestly function, the interpretation of the Scriptures. Moreover, they are embodied in the same persons, such as Daniel, the wise teachers (*maśkîlîm*) at Qumran and the equivalent pneumatics (*pneumatikoi*) in the Pauline churches (1 Cor. 2:15; Ellis, *Prophecy*). When 'prophecy' is employed in this broader sense as the revelatory teaching of various types of inspired persons (though the term is not so used by Paul; 1 Cor. 14:6), it may mean the totality of divine revelation (2 Pet 1:19ff.; *cf.* Lk. 11:50f.; Acts 2:16ff.; Jas. 5:10f.).

4. Prophecy has been classified in terms of literary forms and of modes of revelation (*cf.* Aune, Rendtorff-Meyer-Friedrich). However, it probably cannot be defined or limited in terms of literary type since it was recognized to be multiform in its OT expression by both Judaism (Josephus, *Against Apion* I, 38–42) and early Christianity (Mk. 12:36; Acts 2:30; 7:37). There is also evidence that the enterprise underlying and culminating in the NT was, in all its literary variety, recognized to be the work of prophets, that is, persons with prophetic gifts (Ellis, 'Gospels'; *cf.* Lindblom, *Gesichte*). The different written forms of prophecy are matched by the variety of revelatory experiences mediating the prophetic word, experiences which for Christians found their prototype in considerable measure in the earthly Jesus (Hengel).

5. The prophet was not the final judge of the validity of his message. As the conflict between prophets in both the OT (1 Ki. 22; Je. 23; 28) and the NT (2 Cor. 11:4, 13; 1 Jn. 4:1–3) shows, his word was 'tested,' for example, for its prophetic character (1 Cor.

14:29) and for its agreement with the teaching of Moses (Dt. 13:1–5) or of Jesus (Mt. 7:15; 24:11; 2 Pet 2:1). It was given unquestioned authority only after it was vetted (*cf.* 1 Thes. 5:19–21). Even when it was recognized to be a divine word, it did not necessarily become canonical word. Prophecy had (and has) important uses for its immediate recipients, but it was given canonical status only when it was recognized also to be normative revelation for future generations and a touchstone by which future prophecies might be tested.

See also: GIFTS OF THE SPIRIT; OFFICES OF CHRIST.

Bibliography

D. E. Aune, *Prophecy in Early Christianity* (Grand Rapids, MI, 1983); K. Barth, 'No,' in *Natural Theology* (London, 1950), pp. 90ff.; E. Cothenet, 'Prophetisme dans le Nouveau Testament', *DBS* 8 (1967–72), pp. 1222–1337; E. E. Ellis, 'Gospels Criticism', in *Das Evangelium und die Evangelien*, ed. P. Stuhlmacher (Tübingen, 1983), pp. 27–54; *idem, Prophecy and Hermeneutic* (Tübingen and Grand Rapids, MI, 1978); F. Godet, *Commentary on First Corinthians* (1889; Grand Rapids, MI, 1977); M. Hengel, *The Charismatic Leader and his Followers* (New York, 1981); D. Hill, *New Testament Prophecy* (London, 1979); A. R. Johnson, *The Cultic Prophet and Israel's Psalmody* (Cardiff, 1979); J. Lindblom, *Gesichte und Offenbarungen* (Lund, 1968); *idem, Prophecy in Ancient Israel* (Oxford, 1967); J. Panagopoulos (ed.), *Prophetic Vocation in the New Testament and Today* (Leiden, 1977); J. Pedersen, 'The Role Played by Inspired Persons . . . ,' *Studies in Old Testament Prophecy*, ed. H. H. Rowley (New York, 1950), pp. 127–142; G. von Rad, *Wisdom in Israel* (London, 1972); R. Rendtorff, R. Meyer, G. Friedrich, *TDNT* VI, pp. 796–861; O. Weber, *Foundations of Dogmatics* (Grand Rapids, MI, 1981), vol. 1.

E.E.E.

PROPITIATION, see ATONEMENT; SACRIFICE; WRATH.

PROTESTANTISM. The word derives from the *Protestatio* of the pro-reform representatives at the Diet of Speier (1529) against Roman Catholic practices. It soon came to cover all those within the Christian tradition outside of Roman Catholicism and Orthodoxy.

The origins of Protestantism, then, lie in the teaching and actions of both the magisterial Reformers, chiefly Luther,* Zwingli* and Calvin,* and the leaders of the Radical Reformation (see Reformation, Radical*). Though there were sometimes bitter divisions between these seminal figures, a number of leading convictions can be seen to characterize the vast majority.

*1. Justification by faith.** The central question of Protestantism related to salvation. Luther's 'discovery' that righteousness depended not on merit earned by man but on God's saving act in Jesus Christ was crucial to Protestant thinking. It marked a basic difference in theological approach between the Roman Catholic understanding of justification as analytic – arising from something in the person justified – and the Protestant understanding of it as synthetic – arising from something provided from outside. The issue of justification remained until the 20th century one of the great areas of controversy between Roman Catholics and Protestants.

*2. Scripture.** The Reformers were united in their commitment to Scripture as the only authority in matters of doctrine. The magisterial Reformers retained a high respect for tradition, particularly that of the fathers (see Patristic Theology*) and councils* of the early church. They rejected, however, any subordination of Scripture to tradition (see Scripture and Tradition*). The Radical Reformers had far less respect for tradition and tended to regard Scripture as the sole important reference point.

*3. Church and state.** The Reformation, and therefore Protestantism, made no claims to wield direct political power in the way medieval Catholicism had done. The magisterial Reformers rather sought to instruct the rulers in their spiritual responsibility. Some of their Protestant successors, particularly Lutherans and Anglicans,* were open to the charge of Erastianism (see State*). The Radical Reformers sought a sharp separation between church and state.

*4. The priesthood of all believers.** This doctrine was universally held. It had immense implications leading to the demolition of the hierarchical ministerial structure and of the clergy/lay division of medieval Catholicism. Generally speaking ministry* was understood by Protestants in a functional rather than an ontological sense. At the same time Anglicans and some Lutherans retained ministerial structures which enabled later apologists to claim continuity with a more traditional Catholic interpretation.

While the emphasis on the priesthood of all believers did radically alter the layman's perception of the role of the ordained minister in relation to his access to God and salvation, its implications with respect to gifts in the body of Christ were generally not followed. Within much mainline Protestantism the sense of divide between minister and laity was perpetuated almost as strongly by the preaching ministry of the highly trained parson as it had been by the remote sacramental functions of the slightly trained medieval priest. Lay discontent was a major factor in the Radical Reformers' dissatisfaction with the magisterial Reformation and in that of many subsequent movements of dissent within Protestantism. Generally speaking, however, such reforming movements quite quickly developed ministerial institutions comparable to those against which they had protested.

*5. The sacraments.** Protestantism firmly rejected the seven sacraments of Catholicism and emphasized only those with dominical warrant – baptism* and the Lord's Supper. All rejected a sacrificial interpretation of the eucharist* and accepted communion in both kinds, but there remained considerable debate within Protestantism as to the meaning of the Lord's Supper. Luther emphasized the real corporeal presence, Calvin a spiritual presence, while Zwingli was more inclined to dwell on the Lord's Supper as a communion of believers to remember the Lord's death. Protestants have most often tended towards a Zwinglian interpretation, although in Anglicanism, Lutheranism and sections of the Reformed tradition higher views of the Supper have prevailed.

World Protestantism

After the considerable spiritual and institutional creativity and formulation of the Reformation period, the development of Protestantism has been much less dramatic in subsequent centuries. Numerically and territorially it has followed emigration from Europe to America, Canada, Australia and New Zealand, and the considerable achievements of the missionary movement from

Europe and America in the 19th and 20th centuries to Africa, Asia and South America. In broadest terms it can be divided into seven main families – the Lutheran* (with about 54 million adherents), the Anglican* (50 million), the Baptist* (48 million), the Presbyterian* or Reformed (40 million), the Methodist* (30 million), the Congregationalist* (3 million), and those standing in the heritage of the radicals of the Reformation and having the characteristics of the 'sect', rather than the 'church' (in the categories of Troeltsch*) or 'denomination'. The Pentecostalists* belong partly to this last category.

If Protestantism is defined broadly in the sense suggested, it had a total world community in 1980 of 408 million. Some Anglicans would, however, be unhappy to be labelled as Protestants. Their reservation scarcely does justice to the historical realities, as most Anglicans did not question the description until the Oxford Movement (see Anglo-Catholic Theology*). These family groupings in some senses hide the enormous fissiparous tendency of Protestantism. They do however, at the same time, point to common origins and to some sense of common identity. Within the mainline denominations there are also increasing movements in a more ecumenical direction. These are reflected in the World Council of Churches, which of course includes Orthodox Churches, and in a variety of united churches such as the United Church of Canada, the Church of South India and the Church of North India.

Tensions: objective and subjective

From the Reformation onwards, Protestantism has tended to oscillate between an objective, deductive approach looking to the biblical revelation as its starting-point and a subjective, inductive one which looks rather at personal experience. Early indications of this tension can be seen in Luther's struggle with the 'Enthusiasts' (Schwärmer).

The century following the break from Rome was marked by a period of confessional orthodoxy in which a distinctive Protestant scholasticism* emerged. It was, like its Catholic counterpart, heavily intellectualized. Towards the end of the 17th century it was challenged by pietism,* which underscored experience as determinative and gave its stimulus to the active outworking of Christian commitment as in the missionary work of Count Zinzen-

dorf. The Enlightenment* with its confidence in reason brought a considerable challenge to Protestantism. This was answered, but to a large extent in the philosophical and rationalist terms of the Enlightenment. For example, the substantial work of figures such as Bishops Berkeley* and Butler* did little to satisfy the needs of ordinary people in Ireland and England. Partly in reaction to this, the Evangelical* Revival emphasized the importance of experiential religion. It was immensely influential.

In similar reaction against Enlightenment rationalism and influenced by both pietism and romanticism,* Schleiermacher* sought to develop a theology which reflected the human experience of faith. Starting from the feeling of absolute dependence and using the inductive method, he constructed a theology which was extremely influential and typical of much of liberalism* in that it considerably reduced the significance of revelation* and the supernatural.* The challenges of history and science in the 19th century accentuated the problems for Protestant intellectuals by posing the question whether the Christian revelation was in any meaningful sense divine and distinctive. Liberalism as reflected in the works of Ritschl* and Harnack* continued Schleiermacher's tradition, emphasizing the centrality of Jesus as one who taught the fatherhood of God and brotherhood of man.

Throughout the 19th century, liberalism was criticized by many conservatives, for example in England by the Evangelicals and the Tractarians (see Anglo-Catholic Theology*). In the 20th century, existentialist* thought and the experience of the First World War had underminded liberal optimism. Karl Barth* became the most significant opponent of liberalism. He reasserted the importance of starting from the word of God rather than from the experience of man. He pointed to the radical discontinuity between natural religion and its confidence that it could find God, and the word of God which declared that man had no such capacity. Only through the gift of grace could man experience God.

Barth thus polarized the divide between natural* and supernatural theology, between reason and faith and between secular and sacred history. More contemporary theologians such as Pannenberg* and Moltmann* reject these sharp contrasts and see revelation as including God's activity through world history. They are at the same time committed to a biblical understanding, and the Trinity* and the resurrection,* for example, remain crucial, along with eschatology,* in their theologies. A more immanentist view is reflected in Britain in the work of Macquarrie.*

Bultmann* rejected liberalism almost as vigorously as Barth and also stressed the word of God as decisive. He interpreted its message in existentialist categories but was extremely sceptical about the historical reality of the events it described. Contemporary theologians of the new hermeneutic* retain Barth's and Bultmann's emphasis on the crucial centrality of the word of God.

Many Protestants have been impatient with the conclusions of the radical theologians and reacted strongly against the consequent attenuation of belief which they have detected in the mainline denominations. This led to numerous confrontations with liberal elements – for example, Spurgeon* and the 'Downgrade Controversy' in the late 19th century, and the debate in America over *The Fundamentals* in the early part of the 20th century, and to an increase in Protestant divisions. Others of equally conservative inclinations, but perhaps with a more developed theology of the church, have felt the importance of staying within the historic denominations.

Bibliography

J. Dillenberger and C. Welch, *Protestant Christianity Interpreted through its Development* (New York, 1954); M. E. Marty, *Protestantism* (London, 1972); J. H. Nichols, *Primer for Protestants* (New York, 1947), republished as *The Meaning of Protestantism* (London, 1959); W. Niesel, *Reformed Symbolics: A Comparison of Catholicism, Orthodoxy and Protestantism* (Edinburgh, 1962); P. Tillich, *The Protestant Era* (Chicago, IL, 1948); J. S. Whale, *The Protestant Tradition* (Cambridge, 1955).

C.P.W.

PROVIDENCE. The idea of providence is implicit in any notion of God as the supreme being. An adequate definition of the idea of God requires his overlordship of the history of all that is. But the Christian doctrine of the providence of God rests not upon such metaphysical speculation, but on the teaching of the Bible.

Providence is the beneficent outworking of God's sovereignty* whereby all events are directed and disposed to bring about those purposes of glory and good for which the universe was made. These events include the actions of free agents, which while remaining free, personal and responsible are also the intended actions of those agents. Providence thus encompasses both natural and personal events, setting them alike within the purposes of God.

Providence has been carefully distinguished from creation.* The upholding and directing of all things is understood in Scripture to be subsequent to, and distinct from, their having been made. The distinction is partly sequential: first God created, then he sustained and directed. But it also has moral significance, since Christian theodicy* has emphasized the goodness of the original creation (Gn. 1) and recognized the radical transformation which that creation underwent with the fall.* The providence of God is largely concerned with the history of a fallen order, and the confounding of this with creation would immediately attribute sin to the creative goodness of God. While it can be argued that theistic evolutionism is compatible with the doctrines of creation and providence, any theory which is unable to preserve the distinction between the two is untenable.

The doctrine of providence provides a bulwark against three major errors.

1. *Deism.** The deists conceived of God as detached from the present workings of the universe, since he had created it and then left it to operate like a machine. Providence asserts the personal involvement of God in every turn of human affairs, and his constant upholding of all natural process. Natural law therefore represents merely the constancy and regularity of the divine purposes. The natural order no less than the human expresses God's *personal* control.

2. *Fatalism.* This pagan notion is regaining wide currency through popular astrology. While providence personalizes nature, fatalism de-personalizes man. His free actions are free no longer, since the horoscope's predictions (unlike the prophet's) make no allowance for personal response. Providence never denies free personal agency, though it asserts a higher order of purpose alongside it.

3. *Chance.* Providence asserts the directional and purposeful character of history, and so provides hope to a fallen world. God's hand, as Calvin says, is at the helm. It is customary to speak of providence as general and special (this latter when directed to a specific beneficent end), but too much should not, perhaps, be made of the distinction. Scripture speaks of a particular divine concern for the ephemera of nature (*e.g.* the sparrows of Mt. 10:29–30). Miracle* is a special case of providence, when the normal ordering of natural affairs is set aside for a particular purpose.

The providence of God displays his benevolence (Mt. 5:45), especially to the believer, who is comforted to be told that all things work together for his good (Rom. 8:28). It is therefore in this doctrine that the sovereign character of God becomes the ground of practical hope and comfort to all who trust him.

Bibliography

G. C. Berkouwer, *Providence* (Grand Rapids, MI, 1952); J. Calvin, *Institutes* I.xvi, xvii.

N.M.deS.C.

PSEUDO-DIONYSIUS THE AREOPAGITE
(5th/6th centuries), the unknown author, probably a Syrian, of an extremely influential group of Greek theological works in the tradition of Christian Neoplatonism (see Platonism*).

The writings in question comprise four treatises and ten letters addressed to persons of the apostolic age (though hints are also made in these texts about the existence of other works which, presumably, have not survived). *The Divine Names* explains God's attributes on the basis of the divine names supplied in the Bible. *The Heavenly Hierarchy* deals with angels* and their triadic hierarchical divisions and functions (*i.e.* seraphim–cherubim–thrones, dominions–authorities–powers, principalities–archangels–angels, and the threefold function of purification–illumination–perfection). *The Ecclesiastical Hierarchy* deals with the church's hierarchical structures (*i.e.* hierarchs–priests–liturgists and therapeutes (monks)–laity–catechumens) and their liturgical/sacramental functions. *The Mystical Theology* deals with the mystical union of the human soul with God achieved by means of cataphatic and apophatic* procedures.

Clearly the addressees of the *Epistles* and the claims of the author point to his identity with Dionysius the Areopagite of Acts 17:34. This view prevailed by 649, when the Lateran Council, summoned in Rome against Monotheletism (see Christology*), appealed to the writings as accredited theological witnesses. This view had been already accepted by such distinguished church authors as Gregory the Great,* Leontius of Byzantium (see Hypostasis*) and Maximus* the Confessor. Once it became accepted Dionysius' writings were rapidly disseminated, exerting a profound influence, both in the East and in the West, for centuries to come.

At the close of the Middle Ages their authenticity was questioned by Lorenzo Valla (*c.* 1406–57) and especially by Erasmus,* but without procuring a universal consensus, though from now on their authorship remained in dispute. This was true both at the time of the Reformation and during the 19th century, until in 1895 Joseph Stiglmayr and Hugo Koch, arguing independently on internal grounds and especially from their literary dependence on Proclus (411–85) and clear reference to later liturgical forms, established that the writings belong to an author who lived in late-5th-century Syria. Since then, many attempts have been made to identify the author but without success. The only sure point of an emerging consensus is that he must have been either a Monophysite* or a Monophysite sympathizer.

The obvious question how an unknown writer could exert such a tremendous influence on theologians of all contexts and ages can be adequately answered only by reference to the profound content and exceptional quality of his thought. It represents an answer to the two great challenges to early Christianity of Gnosticism* and Neoplatonism, which is based not on the development of a dialectical antipode to either of these but on a vision of catholic wholeness which includes and transcends both. Against Gnosticism it maintains that God is unknowable (*anōnymos*) and against Neoplatonism that he is knowable (*polyōnymos*, with many names, or *apeirōnymos*, of infinite names). In other words, God is both transcendent and immanent in relation to the world, the former relating to his being and the latter to his acts and powers. This view is defended on the basis of the Scriptures as understood by spiritual masters and of a true knowledge of the natural world, and finds its anthropological presupposition in the Christian ascetical* life.

The work of Pseudo-Dionysius is in fact a theology or a philosophy of theology (this is still much debated), which comprises three stages, the cataphatic, the symbolic and the mystical. These are respectively related to the three persons of the Trinity* (theological dimension), to the soul's ascent to the Trinity (anthropological* dimension) through purification, illumination and glorification (or deification* or union with God), and also to the threefold structure of the cosmos.

The cataphatic theology, developed in *The Divine Names*, refers to man's knowledge* of God in his acts (or energies or attributes). The symbolic theology, developed in *The Heavenly Hierarchy*, *The Ecclesiastical Hierarchy* and *Epistle IX*, refers to the threefold knowledge of the world in which God's revelation* (*theophaniai*) is granted (*i.e.* the sensible world together with the earthly world of human beings and the heavenly world of angels*) and to the soul's movement from the sensible to the ecclesiastical (purification), from the ecclesiastical to the heavenly (illumination) and from the heavenly to the divine (deification). This last stage is developed in *The Mystical Theology*.

Though none of his works represents a comprehensive system of theology, the whole teaching of Pseudo-Dionysius presents a remarkable coherence and systematic structure. The terminology is full of neologisms and superlatives. The style leaves much to be desired. The Christology* seems to fall in line with Zeno's *Henotikon* (482) and it is interesting that its central notion is that of 'a new theandric energy' (*Epistle IV*) instead of the traditional 'one' or 'two natures'. Despite the problems surrounding Pseudo-Dionysius, the study of his teaching is indispensable for historical theology in both East and West.

Bibliography

English translations: T. L. Campbell, *Dionysius the Pseudo-Areopagite, The Ecclesiastical Hierarchy* (Lanham, MD, 1981); J. D. Jones, *Pseudo-Dionysius Areopagite, The Divine Names and Mystical Theology* (Milwaukee, WI, 1980).

Studies: A. Louth, *The Origins of the Christian Mystical Tradition from Plato to Denis* (Oxford, 1981); R. Roques, in *DSp* 3, cols. 244–286; D. Rutledge, *Cosmic Theology, The Ecclesiastical Hierarchy of Pseudo-Denys: An Introduction* (London, 1964); I. P. Sheldon-Williams, 'The pseudo-Dionysius', in *CHLGEMP*, pp. 457–472.

G.D.D.

PSYCHOLOGY OF RELIGION. There is no single 'psychology of religion' but several. The reason is that psychologists today have interests ranging from studies of the biological bases of behaviour to the social psychological factors affecting attitude and behaviour change. Such diversity is mirrored in the diverse psychological accounts given of how religious behaviour arises and of how religious beliefs and attitudes are formed. Broadly speaking, psychologists have concentrated upon the roots and the fruits of religion.* L. S. Hearnshaw (*A Short History of British Psychology, 1840–1940*, London, 1964, pp. 292–295) identified four influences which converged at the end of the 19th century to provide the basis for later psychological studies of religion. These were: Galton's studies of the manifestations of religion (*e.g.* prayer*); studies by anthropologists, such as Fraser, of comparative religion and the origins of religions; the writings of theologians, such as Inge (1860–1954), on mysticism* and religious experience;* and finally the beginnings of a systematic psychology of religion, best illustrated by E. D. Starbuck's *The Psychology of Religion* (London, 1899). These culminated in William James' classical work *Varieties of Religious Experience* (1902; ed. M. E. Marty, Harmondsworth, 1983).

While debates continued about what distinguished religious from non-religious or irreligious activity, William James (1842–1910) differentiated between institutional religion and personal religion. Institutional religion, he said, is concerned with 'theology, ceremony and ecclesiastical organization' and personal religion with 'the inner disposition of man himself, his conscience, his deserts, his helplessness, his incompleteness'.

Psychologists' aims and achievements in the study of religion can best be illustrated by briefly reviewing the work of leading contributors to the field.

One of William James' lasting contributions was his classification of religion into 'healthy-minded' and 'morbid-minded'. These, he thought, were related to factors of temperament and personality. Like Starbuck, James saw conversion* as a normal aspect of adolescent development in which sub-conscious maturing processes in individuals lead on towards unification of the self. J. B. Pratt (*The Religious Consciousness*, London, 1924) identified stages of religious development from the primitive to the intellectual and the emotional, believing that these stages were present in all religions. By contrast, J. H. Leuba (*Psychological Study of Religion*, New York, 1912) presented an analysis which was more critical of religion, treating it from a naturalistic standpoint and contending that the religious life can be explained exclusively in terms of certain fundamental principles of general psychology. According to Leuba, man, through religion, searches for ways of satisfying his needs and desires for a better life. Unlike William James, who strongly affirmed the reality of there being a higher power in life, Leuba declared that there is no objective transcendent agent or source connected with man's religious experience. According to his view, belief in a personal God will, in time, disintegrate.

R. H. Thouless (*An Introduction to the Psychology of Religion*, Cambridge, 1923) broadly followed the example set by William James. He studied in detail the factors which were involved in religious belief and the part played by both conscious and unconscious processes. He also had an interest in specific phenomena, including prayer, conversion and mystical experiences. As Thouless indicated when his book was reissued in 1961, his interest was in religious consciousness rather than religious behaviour, and he paid more attention to case history material than to statistical enquiries. His confidence in the reality of the ultimate mysteries lying behind faith was reiterated in his 1961 book.

Freud on religion

The views of Sigmund Freud (1856–1939) may be divided into those on primitive religion and on developed religion. In *Totem and Taboo* (London, 1913) he attributed the origins of religion to the psychological connection between his 'Oedipus complex' and 'totemism' as it existed in small primitive groups. Freud had given the name 'Oedipus complex' to the idea of an unconscious hostility that young men have to their fathers.

He supposed that the young men of a primal horde had killed their father in order to possess his wives. According to this theory, 'the Totem Feast was the commemoration of the fearful deed from which sprang man's sense of guilt* (the original sin) in which was the beginning at once of social organization, of religion and of ethical restriction'. This, thought Freud, gave some clues to the way in which primitive religions had developed, especially those that showed some forms of patriarchal totemism. When he wrote *Totem and Taboo* anthropological knowledge was limited. Today, it is clear that many of the so-called 'facts' upon which Freud bases his theory were incorrect. It is perhaps, therefore, not surprising that his theory was misleading. In *Moses and Monotheism* (London, 1939) Freud ventured yet further into his speculative theories about the origins of religion; but with the development of anthropology his speculative views fell more and more into disrepute (*e.g.* see B. Malinowski, *Sex and Repression In Primitive Society*, London, 1927, and *The Foundations of Faith and Morals*, London, 1936).

Freud's views on developed religion are summarized in *The Future of an Illusion* (London, 1934) and *Civilization and Its Discontents* (London, 1939). For Freud, an 'illusion' stands for any belief system which is based on human wishes. He was careful to point out that such a basis does not necessarily imply that the system is false, but as far as Christianity was concerned, he clearly believed that it was. He did not deny that religion had served a useful purpose in providing a sense of security for man in the face of a hostile environment and, at the same time, had proved an important reservoir for ethical standards as civilization had developed. On his view, however, the time had come when such a basis could no longer usefully serve the needs of modern man, who must replace it by some rational grounds for living a civilized life.

Freud concluded that religion is an interim social neurosis which man must grow out of if he is to become educated and able to cope with reality. For this reason he emphasized how, in the past, religion had offered a means of escape from the realities of life. Thus, faced with the challenges and puzzles of the natural world and the restraints imposed upon individuals by organized society, religion for

Freud offered, on the one hand, an explanation of these puzzles, and on the other, an escape from the constraints. The idea of religion as a means of protection and escape is closely associated with Freud's view that the function of gods is that they are substitute ideal fathers. Religion thus became the projection of the child's relationship with its earthly father so that gods in all their different guises were simply magnified father-figures.

Jung on religion

Carl Gustav Jung (1875–1961), who for a while worked closely with Freud, also developed his views from within the psychoanalytic tradition. During his association with Freud, he produced a small work which made it clear that his views on the significance of the father-figure were very much those of Freud. Soon thereafter, his views were to undergo a considerable change and he was to put forward his view that all religions have their psychological roots in what he called the 'collective unconscious' of the human race. Religion for Jung is not a matter of theological concepts but primarily of experience, since it is only through these experiences that concepts can be formulated. That does not mean that for Jung God is nothing but a psychic event in the unconscious. He was careful to point out that what exists in the human psyche, in his judgment, exists in reality. Jung frequently refers to God as the God-Imago or God-symbol. In this respect, he claims to be in the tradition of Meister Eckhart (1260–1327) who maintained that 'God's being is of the soul, but his Godhead is of himself' (cf. Mystical Theology*). For Jung, therefore, the God that is in the soul (God-Imago) is the reality that is met in a religious experience; whilst the Godhead is beyond our experience and beyond all human comprehension and – on this psychology – can have nothing to say. These views led Jung to comment on the divisions in Christendom from a psychological, as well as from an historical and theological, viewpoint. For him, the Reformation* began with the kinds of assertions that were implied by Meister Eckhart's declaration that we know God only as an experience. Hitherto, the church had been a psychological necessity as an institution. It was the means whereby man's religious life could be protected against archetypal invasions from the collective uncon-scious. This view of the church gives great importance to symbols as a means of spiritual communication and experience and also gives to the church, as a spiritual community, the context in which the individual can enjoy a safe and proper experience of reality. Jung took the view that both of these beliefs were rejected by the Protestant Reformation. The great positive characteristic of Protestantism* in Jung's estimation is its feature as a great spiritual adventure. Thus he could write, 'the Protestant is left to God alone . . . if a Protestant survives the complete loss of his church and still remains a Protestant, that is a person who is defenceless against God no longer protected by walls or communities, then he has a unique spiritual opportunity for immediate religious experience' (Psychology and Religion: West and East, in Collected Works, vol. 11, London and New York, 1958, p. 48). For Jung, for a man to be an integrated personality (or, as he would put it, a spiritually happy soul), he must have some purpose to live for, some object to be united with; and herein lay, for Jung, religion's essential role for mankind. How these psychological facts may be related to objective truths remained for him an unanswered question.

Freud and Jung, as on other psychological matters, were soon to differ radically about the role of religion in a person's life. While Freud, according to Jung, was inclined to interpret the nature of man too exclusively in terms of his defects, Jung would take a more optimistic view of man. Freud, according to Jung, was unable to understand the real nature of religion because he would always interpret everything in terms of the neurotic mind. There were, thus, quite fundamental differences between Freud and Jung in their attitudes towards religion. While for Freud, psychology pointed to religion as a neurosis which in time could be dispelled and the patient cured, for Jung religion is an essential activity of man and the task of psychology is not to explain away religion but to try and understand how man's nature reacts to situations normally described as religious. Summing up the difference between the Freudian and the Jungian views, G. S. Spinks very aptly wrote that 'for Freud religion was an obsessional neurosis, and at no time did he modify that judgment. For Jung it was the absence of religion that was the chief cause of adult psychological disorders. These two sentences indicate how great is the difference between their respective standpoints on religion' (*Psychology and Religion*, London, 1963).

Other psychological studies of religion

Though much less well-known than either Freud or Jung, a significant contribution to the field of psychology of religion was made by G. W. Allport (*The Individual and His Religion*, London, 1950). He traced the way in which religion develops from childhood and adolescence through into maturity, thus underlining the way in which belief in God functions differently for people at different times in their lives. His account is well substantiated with the results of empirical studies of religious beliefs and behaviour. Another significant contribution to the field are the books of M. Argyle (*Religious Behaviour*, London, 1958, and, with B. Beit-Hallami, *The Social Psychology of Religion*, London, 1975), which are a mine of information summarizing empirical studies of social psychological aspects of religious behaviour.

Others whose views have received wide publicity are Dr William Sargant and Professor B. F. Skinner. Sargant's views appeared in *Battle for the Mind* (London, 1957) and *The Mind Possessed* (London, 1973). While writers like Argyle evaluated psychological theories of religion against empirical data, Sargant concentrated on the psycho-physiology of religious behaviour. Most noteworthy were his attempts to link psychological studies of brainwashing with religious conversion. He argued that suggestion and brainwashing are operative in some large evangelistic campaigns. Some of the effective ingredients in such campaigns he identified as an evangelist, given wide publicity and a prestige build-up, speaking with great fervour, conviction and authority to a crowded meeting which had begun with the repetitive singing of emotional hymns and choruses. Added to this, there may be bright lights, mass choirs and stirring music, the latter often with a rhythmic beat. In such circumstances, argued Sargant, physical and psychological stresses are skilfully applied to produce dramatic changes in both behaviour and beliefs. Sargant contended that these are less florid examples of those which occur in extreme forms in the meetings, for example,

of the snake-handling sects of the southern states of America. There, emotional exhaustion leads to heightened suggestibility at which point beliefs can most readily be implanted. Perhaps one day we shall be able to understand a little more of the psycho-physiology of the processes whereby such beliefs are implanted, but, as we shall see later, this will tell us nothing one way or the other about the truth or falsehood of the beliefs thus arrived at.

Skinner, encouraged by earlier successes achieved using a wide variety of techniques for modifying behaviour, speculated about how similar processes could be harnessed to shape the future of our society (*Beyond Freedom and Dignity*, London, 1972). He believed that his principles of learning, based on the effects of rewards and punishment, offer an explanation of how the practices of religion function psychologically. Thus, he contends, 'A religious agency is a special form of government under which "good" and "bad" become "pious" and "sinful". Contingencies involving positive and negative reinforcement, often of the most extreme sort, are codified – for example as commandments – and maintained by specialists, usually with the support of ceremonies, rituals and stories' (p. 116). He later described how he thought that the good things personified in a God are, in his terms, reinforcing, whereas the threat of hell is an aversive stimulus to shape behaviour. Underlying the whole of Skinner's approach is a reductionist presupposition. At times he speaks of concepts of God being 'reduced to' what we find positively reinforcing. O. H. Mowrer, an equally distinguished behavioural scientist, took issue with Skinner to the extent that he believed Skinner had, in fact, arrived 'at a theory of political dictatorship which seems to be conditioned more by personal predilection than by logical necessity' (*Contemporary Psychology* 17:9 (1972), p. 470).

What of the future?

L. B. Brown (ed.), *Advances in the Psychology of Religion* (Oxford, 1985), reported a conference aimed at identifying current and new directions in the psychology of religion. He noted that most current work still relies heavily on correlational analyses and that the participants agreed that more experimental methods should be used in the psychological study of religion. 'Natural experiments' are taking place, but often the opportunity for careful study is being missed. Thus, for example, while religious education and the selection and training of clergy have been altered, few careful, systematic assessments have been made of the effects of such changes. Instead, opinions have been based upon intuitions of committee members and those in authority who sanction such changes.

Developments in cognitive psychology have affected new ways of studying how people conceive God (L. B. Brown and J. P. Forgas, *JSSR* 19, 1980, pp. 423–431). Studies of the effects of religion on behaviour have led to attempts to identify actual differences between the behaviours of religious and non-religious people, their morality and moral judgments. The use of hallucinogenic drugs has shown how religious experiences may be artificially induced, thus raising the question of how these are related to normal but similar non-drug induced experiences. Attempts have even been made to link results of studies of cerebral asymmetries to religious behaviour (J. Jaynes, *The Origin of Consciousness in the Breakdown of the Bicameral Mind*, Boston, MA, 1976). The field is open to systematic studies of the new cults* (J. T. Richardson, 'Psychological and Psychiatric Studies of New Religions', in *Advances in the Psychology of Religion*), and how they benefit, or otherwise, their adherents as measured, for example, by their mental health.

Evaluating psychological accounts of religion

Any aspect of religious behaviour may, in principle, be investigated by psychologists. This is well illustrated by examining some of the psychological explanations given of conversion. Some have concentrated on the formative influence of the social and cultural environment, and how the family and the church shape the conversion experience and prescribe the beliefs of the convert (*e.g.* Argyle, 1958). Others have offered psychophysiological accounts of conversion* (*e.g.* Sargant, 1957). Yet others have speculated about the functions of gods in the lives of human beings (*e.g.* Freud). That different people come to faith in different ways is clear from Scripture. A cursory study of the Acts of the Apostles indicates that the conversions described there differed widely in their cir-

cumstances (M. A. Jeeves, *Psychology and Christianity: The View Both Ways*, Leicester, 1976).

To focus on the psychological aspects of conversion does not mean that one either ignores or denies that it is the truth gripping the mind of the hearer rather than the stirring of the emotions that is ultimately the prime ingredient in any conversion experience. It is also clear that the concern of Scripture is with the God who initiates and over-rules these events. Thus, man responds to the gospel only because God has first begun to work in him (Acts 8:26, 29; 9:6, 15; 10:3, 44; 16:14).

Although some who have written on the psychology of religion (*e.g.* Freud and Skinner) have taken the view that in offering an explanation of religious behaviour and the roots of religious beliefs, they are explaining away those beliefs, such a view is not accepted by the majority of psychologists. Argyle states quite categorically that 'it does not follow that because a belief has psychological roots it is therefore false', and that 'there needs to be no relation between a psychological basis for a belief and the truth of that belief' (in 'Seven Psychological Roots of Religion', *Th* 67 (1964), pp. 333–339). While a person who is converted will describe his experience in personal terms involving a new relationship with God in Jesus Christ, a non-Christian may always say that he finds that particular kind of explanation superfluous or that interpretation meaningless. No amount of arguing can produce incontestable proofs that the non-Christian is right and that the Christian is wrong or vice versa. At the same time, to regard the psychological account as in competition with the personal religious account is to make a category mistake (*Psychology and Christianity: The View Both Ways*, pp. 140–144). Psychology can no more explain away religious experience than the study of the physics of sound can explain away the aesthetic experience of listening to music.

M.A.J.

See also: DEPTH PSYCHOLOGY.

PUNISHMENT. The definition of punishment is customarily taken to have three elements: 1. the infliction of suffering upon an offender, 2. on the grounds of a particular offence, 3. administered by a legitimate authority. Punishment is therefore

547

distinguished from any form of rehabilitation of offenders in which suffering is incidental; from other legitimate inflictions of privation or pain, such as taxation or surgery; and from personal vengeance. All punishment is retributive in the weak sense that it is visited upon an offender for an offence; but not all theories of punishment are 'retributivist' in the stronger sense that they regard the practice of retribution as self-justifying and sufficient to support the institution of punishment to which it gives rise.

It has usually been held that a theoretical account of punishment must show how retributive punishment fulfils the general requirements of justice. Optionally, it may also try to show what specific modes or applications of punishment best fulfil these requirements. Such an account is not usually expected also to show what other concerns legitimately determine the treatment of offenders (such as the wish to see them profess Christian faith, or the desire to mitigate social and psychological evils that may result from punishment): this is the concern of wider social theory. Nor is it obliged to consider whether punishment is justified in any particular case, which is a matter for ordinary judicial enquiry.

Of the three formal theories of punishment traditionally acknowledged in the West, two proceed from the assumption that retributive punishment is not self-justifying. The oldest theory attempted to justify punishment as a moral benefit to the offender. Plato* (Gorgias 476–7) argues that since a just punishment is 'a good', the person who suffers it has good done to him: he is freed from injustice of soul. The theory was influential in antiquity, and a strand of Christian thought (later regarded as heterodox) interpreted eternal fire in these terms (see Origen,* Gregory of Nyssa*). The weakness of the theory lies in its assumption that a just punishment in itself makes the sufferer just.

The second theory is associated with the rise of modern contractarian political thought in the 17th century. According to this view, the purpose of punishment is the security of other members of society through the restraint of the offender and deterrence of other likely offenders. Since, on the contractarian account, individuals have surrendered certain freedoms to the state in exchange for protection of their rights, the rationale of punishment lies in its claim to safeguard potential victims. The deficiency of this theory is that deterrence and restraint do not seem to afford a sufficient justification for the limited scope of retributive punishment (as indicated by points 1. and 2. above). Nor does the theory provide a convincing account of the intuition that just punishment must be proportionate to the offence.

The third theory, associated in modern times with Kant,* Hegel* and Schleiermacher,* and building on an Aristotelian* conception, treats the practice of retribution as inherently self-justifying. It is therefore often designated the 'retributivist' theory, though it might be better termed a theory of penal 'satisfaction' or 'annulment'. For its root notion is that the damage inflicted by the offence is cancelled out, or annulled, through the imposition of a comparable injury. The theory deals more effectively than the others with the question of providing a rationale for the proportionate character of just punishment. It characteristically faults other accounts for failing to affirm the dignity of the offender as the bearer of moral responsibility. However, the theory sometimes stresses the notion of equal return to such an extent as to insist on the lex talionis, or 'eye for eye' principle; moreover, its emphasis on the absolute justice of proportionate retribution allows little room for mercy and forgiveness.

The limitations of the traditional theories arise from their failure to treat punishment within a wider account of justice in society. The Scriptures have little to say about punishment as such, but a great deal about 'judgment'* (the active noun is more typical than the abstract 'justice'; see Righteousness*). Judgment gives public affirmation to those values on which the common life of society depends. The retributive form which judgment takes is derived in the OT from the natural phenomenon of blood-vengeance (e.g. Gn. 4:10–11; 9:6). The role of the human judge (as appears especially in the paradigm case of the cities of refuge, Nu. 35; Dt. 19; Jos. 20) is to assume communal responsibility for vindicating the victim's claim and so to transfer the rights and duties of vengeance from the private to the public sphere. By giving judgment, and thus discriminating between innocence and guilt* and rewarding the offender proportionately to his offence, the judge transforms the originally blind and impassioned act of vengeance into an occasion for public disclosure of the truth. Proportion need not entail the arbitrary *lex talionis*, nor need it imply a supposedly precise equilibrium of liability and penalty. Rather, the practice of retribution is moulded into a symbolic language of proportionate response which allows a high degree of flexibility about methods and degrees of punishment.

The derivation of retribution from the wrath of the injured party helps to explain the persistent ambivalence with which it is viewed. It can neither be dismissed nor absolutized, for it is a feature of human judgment which takes place under the broken social and cosmic conditions of the fall.* Scripture does, of course, use retributive concepts of the final judgment* of God also, and so admits the general conception that justice must include an appropriate penalty for offence. Yet by characterizing divine judgment also as the free justification* of sinners, it prevents the unqualified application of the norms of human retribution to the divine. To explore the interaction of these two concepts in the eschatological sphere would require a discussion of the atoning death of Christ – the ultimate punishment for sin, which is, at the same time, the decisive act of forgiveness.

Bibliography

Historical: Thomas Aquinas, *Summa Theologica* II:1:87; H. Grotius, *The Right of War and Peace* (London and New York, 1964), book 2, chs. 20, 21; G. W. F. Hegel, *The Philosophy of Right* (ET, Oxford, 1967), sections 88–103; T. Hobbes, *Leviathan* (London, 1914), ch. 28; I. Kant, *The Metaphysical Elements of Justice*, section 49E, Part I of *The Metaphysics of Morals* (ET, Indianapolis, IN, 1965); W. Perkins, *Epieikeia: or a Treatise of Christian Equitie and Moderation* (London, 1604); H. Rashdall, *The Theory of Good and Evil* (Oxford, 1907), book 1, ch. 9; F. de Suarez, *De legibus ac Deo legislatore* (London, 1679), book 5, chs. 1–12.

Contemporary: W. Berns, *For Capital Punishment. Crime and the Morality of the Death Penalty* (New York, 1981); Lord Longford, *The Idea of Punishment* (London, 1961); W. Moberly, *Responsibility* (London, 1951); O. O'Donovan, *Measure for Measure: Justice in Punishment and the Sentence of Death* (Bramcote, Nottingham, 1977); *Punishment*, Report of Working Party of the Church of England's Board for Social Responsibility (London, 1963); J. H. Yoder, *The Christian and Capital Punishment* (Newton, KS, 1961).

O.M.T.O'D. and R.J.S.

PURGATORY. In Roman Catholic theology, a supposed middle state between heaven and hell (*cf.* Eschatology*). As the Councils* of Florence and Trent defined it, purgatory is not simply a place of cleansing (the sort of intermediate state between death and resurrection which even some Protestant theologians have envisaged) but a place of punishment, though of temporary punishment, not eternal. This belief is not based on the canonical Scriptures. Support for it is hard to find in the early centuries of church history, it has never been accepted by the Eastern Church, and at the Reformation it was rejected by the Reformed churches in the West as well.

The idea of purgatory can easily appeal to a legalistic mentality, which supposes that salvation is by works, that God reaches his judgment upon us by balancing our good works against our bad, and that some special provision is necessary for those in whose case the balance is fairly even. The Jewish rabbis often thought in these terms. The defined doctrine of purgatory is more subtle, however. It recognizes that salvation is by grace, but claims that a temporal penalty has to be paid by the sinner, even when the eternal penalty of his sins has been remitted by forgiveness. If, by acts of penitence (see Penance*), he has fully paid this penalty in the present life, on dying he goes, with the saints,* straight to heaven; if he is impenitent, he goes straight to hell; but if he has partially paid the penalty, he pays the rest of it in purgatory.

The souls in purgatory can be helped, and their term there shortened (so it is held), by the acts of the living. Prayers and almsgifts can be made for them, the propitiatory sacrifice of the mass (see Eucharist*) can be offered for them (as a requiem mass), and indulgences (see Merit*) can be obtained for them. In Roman Catholic practice, the old custom of praying for the faithful departed has been wholly transferred to praying for the souls in purgatory. Indulgences are based on the belief that the church has the right to dispense benefits from the 'treasury of merits',* accumulated by Christ and the saints. The sale of indulgences by authorized pardoners was one of the chief precipitating causes of the Reformation.

Bibliography
J. Le Goff, *The Birth of Purgatory* (London, 1984); C. H. H. Wright, *The Intermediate State and Prayers for the Dead* (London, 1900).

R.T.B.

PURITAN THEOLOGY. Theology, according to William Ames, 'is to us the ultimate and the noblest of all exact teaching arts. It is a guide and master plan for our highest end, sent in a special manner from God, treating of divine things, tending towards you, and leading man to God. There is no precept of universal truth relevant to living well in domestic economy, morality, political life, lawmaking which does not rightly pertain to theology' (*Marrow of Theology*, 1623).

This comprehensive vision grew out of encounter with the God who called mankind to repentance and faith in Christ through the written and preached word, and who energized them to holiness through his Spirit. Though 'Puritan' was initially a term of abuse, historians use it for those concerned for the further reform of the Elizabethan and Stuart Church of England, because of their particular religious experience* and commitment to Reformed theology.* Their faith was shaped by their struggle with popular religious culture and Roman Catholicism.

Puritans such as Thomas Cartwright (1535–1603), Dudley Fenner (c. 1558–87) and Walter Travers (c. 1548–1643) had, by the 1580s, given Reformed theology in England a strong emphasis on purity of biblical worship and polity, as part of continued reformation. A small minority saw no hope of reformation without separation from the Church of England, into a covenanted church of saints. Robert Browne (c. 1550–1633), Henry Barrow (c. 1550–93), John Greenwood (d. 1593) and Francis Johnson (1562–1618) provided the initial theology for this movement, but their practice and conclusions were rejected not only by the authorities, but also by most of the Puritans who were firmly committed to a national church.

Henry Smith (c. 1550–91), Richard Greenham (c. 1535–c. 1594), Richard Rogers (c. 1550–1618) and William Perkins worked for reformation within the Church of England and developed a theology which had increasing popular appeal among a cross-section of the nation. These preacher-theologians wrote in detail about the way God's grace could be identified in human experience, penetrating behind formal religion to an inner transformation from death in sin to life in Christ, based on full faith. Puritan diaries and autobiographies reveal how intense this struggle could be, and how personalized were the great themes of Catholic and Reformed theology.

Theologians in the Puritan tradition did not neglect the work and being of Father, Son and Spirit, or the great themes of election, calling, justification, adoption, sanctification and glorification, but their emphases on religious experience and practical piety gave their writings an accent which was unusual among Reformed theologians in other parts of Europe. J. Bunyan's* *Pilgrim's Progress* (1676) is a striking example of this difference.

Though P. Helm rightly insists that differences from Calvin should not be exaggerated, shifts of emphasis in the doctrines of predestination* and assurance* reflect use of the work of Beza* and Zanchius (1516–90), as well as expansion of the use of a theology of law and covenant.* By the time the masterly Westminster Confession and Savoy Declaration were written, the stream of Reformed theology had cut some fresh channels, including revolutionary and apocalyptic ones. The practical emphasis of Puritan theology led to detailed attention being paid to personal and social ethics in cases of conscience, discussions of vocation* and the relationship between family,* church and commonwealth in the redeeming purpose of God.

Reform of worship and popular religious observance, hearing and obeying the word of God and sanctification of time intersected in the development of sabbatarianism, a unique function of 17th-century British Christianity, which was one of the most enduring legacies of applied Puritan theology. The enthusiasm with which this was taken up by many gentry and town corporations indicates how powerfully the religious seriousness of the Puritans and their theological vision of sabbath* rest integrated with more secular aspirations such as control of leisure and the discipline of the socially marginal and disorderly.

The theology of William Perkins (1558–1602) was the first major example of a synthesis reflecting Augustinian* and Reformed* theology applied to the transformation of Elizabethan society, church and individuals. His earliest writings were on popular piety. By 1590, he expounded the Reformed tradition in *Armilla Aurea (The Golden Chain)* around the theme of theology as 'the art of living well', using the logic of P. Ramus* to order his themes in memorable visual charts. 'Living well' was explored in Perkins' other prolific writings on worship, ministry, family life, vocation and conscience, as well as in published sermons, anti-Roman polemic and detailed biblical commentaries. Perkins sought to give insight into the majesty of God's order and its social and personal implications.

As a preacher he was reported to be able to make his auditors' hair stand up and hearts fall down. That same intensity shines through his writing, which was translated into Dutch, German, French, Czech and Hungarian, making him the first Elizabethan theologian with an international reputation. His writing on predestination inspired Arminius* to write a refutation, which in turn precipitated one of the most important theological debates of the 17th century, whose reverberations are still faintly heard. Perkins' personal influence won some important disciples, who helped the further development and popularization of Puritan theology in the British Isles, New England and the Netherlands, where it helped to shape the beginnings of Reformed pietism.*

William Ames (1576–1633), Perkins' most distinguished disciple, also wrote prolifically, but his forceful criticisms of the Church of England led to his exile to the Netherlands and the banning of his books in England, until the collapse of censorship under the Long Parliament. Teaching at Franeker gave him opportunity to demonstrate his theological gifts to a wide audience. His *Marrow of Theology* (1623) and *Cases of Conscience* (1630) were his best-known works, but his writings on congregational polity and covenant were also very influential. Ames died just before his intended migration to Massachusetts, but his influence there and in the Netherlands lasted into the 18th century. Like Perkins, he drew deeply on the Augustinian and Reformed tradition, but also read widely in the fathers and scholastics to refute Roman Catholic criticisms of Protestant novelty. Ames' practical divinity gave a comprehensive perspective of how every part of life ought to be dedicated to the glory of God, for exact understanding of divine truth must be reflected in the appropriate meaning of every detail of daily life.

By the outbreak of civil war in Scotland, Ireland and England, many with Puritan sympathies had migrated to New England, for they saw little future for their theological tradition in the Church of England. The policy of Charles I and the Laudian bishops cut across Puritan convictions on worship, ministry and conscience. Arminian theology with its rationalizing and anti-Calvinist emphases appeared to threaten foundation doctrines. Nevertheless, Puritan theology still had some formidable expositors such as Richard Sibbes (1577–1635), Thomas Goodwin (1600–80), John Owen (1616–83). Their power as preachers, leaders and theologians gave Puritan theology both popular influence and scholarly depth, complementing the influence of popular devotional manuals like *A Plain Man's Pathway to Heaven* (1601) by Arthur Dent (d. 1607), which set out themes of Puritan theology in very accessible form. Indeed, one of the great strengths of Puritan theology was that it was popularized without being trivialized. As a result, its reading of the Scriptures penetrated every level of British society.

Sibbes, for example, was the son of a wheelwright who studied as a sizar at St John's College, Cambridge, before becoming a Fellow, Preacher at Gray's Inn and then Master of Catherine Hall. His preaching and life gave him wide influence in the legal profession, but his educational achievements in Cambridge were also considerable. According to Izaak Walton, 'Heaven was in him, before he was in heaven.' His telling imagery and deep spiritual insight rested on solid theological foundations. He exemplified the synthesis between biblical depth and pastoral sensitivity which characterized Puritan theology at its best. His writings are practical rather than systematic, but show clearly why Puritan emphases were so thoroughly assimilated by many laity. He underlined the authority of Scripture. 'Were not faith founded on the word of an infinite God, thoroughly appeased, the soul would sink in great temptations.' Being under

Christ's government was essential to profiting from God's promises. That meant the pulling down of human achievement before the temple of God could be built. Pessimistic about the natural man, theologians like Sibbes sensitively explored the relation of grace and freedom in the redeemed. Every aspect of life had to be scrutinized by constant self-examination, so that the temptations to sin were hated as sin itself. Such strenuous and precise piety could become a caricature of evangelical freedom, sinking into joyless legalism (see Law and Gospel*), but, at its best, its insights into personal and corporate holiness have been unmatched. Sibbes' writings such as *A Christian's Portion* and *Christ's Exaltation Purchased by his Humiliation* reveal deep insights into creation and incarnation, not just a sharp focus on soteriology.

Goodwin was influenced by both Sibbes and John Preston (1587–1628) and seemed assured of a distinguished ecclesiastical career when he became vicar of Holy Trinity, Cambridge in 1632. He resigned in 1634 after being persuaded by John Cotton (1584–1652) of the rightness of independency. He was in the Netherlands briefly after continuous harassment by the English authorities, but in 1641 his sermon *A Glimpse of Syons Glory* showed that he was deeply influenced by expectations of a new divine ruler, led by the Spirit. He played an important role as an advocate of independency in the Westminster Assembly and was one of the authors of *An Apologetical Narration* (1643), which underlined the need for reformation in polity and life. He remained an orthodox Calvinist, but rejected a national church for covenanted churches freely associated by consultation. He played a prominent part in Cromwell's regime and was president of Magdalen College, Oxford. With John Owen he counter-attacked critics of the intellectual tradition of Puritan theology, warned against the dangers of the Racovian Catechism (published in England 1652) and sought to bring unity between Independents and Presbyterians in *Christ the Universal Peacemaker* (1651). Goodwin's deep personal meeting with Christ permeated all his writings and he came close to reasoning from experience rather than Scripture in some contexts. He was more interested in biblical exposition than in systematic theology, so that his many books are occasional pieces, rather than an ordered exposition of all the great themes of Puritan theology.

It was John Owen who was, with Richard Baxter,* the great systematic thinker in the Puritan theological tradition. Educated at Oxford and thoroughly grounded in the Aristotelian tradition there, he had a long spiritual struggle for assurance that ended about 1642. His formidable intellectual gifts were given to the parliamentary cause. *A Display of Arminianism* (1643) was a vigorous exposition of classical Calvinism. Initially of presbyterian views, he was converted to independency by J. Cotton's *Keyes of the Kingdom of Heaven* (1644) and became an influential advocate of toleration for the orthodox in *Of Toleration* (1648). His experience as an army chaplain gave him a vivid insight into the problems of a religion of inner light, but in *Christs Kingdom and the Magistrates Power* (1652) he sought to show the differences between civil and religious authority.

His definition of biblical authority and the unity of the Scriptures can be seen in his massive commentary on Hebrews (1668–84). A firm opponent of Quaker* teaching on the Inner Light, he also rejected attempts to give a more weighty role to reason in the formulation of theology by his critique of Socinian* and Grotian* reinterpretations of the atonement and divinity of Christ in books such as *The Death of Death in the Death of Christ* (1647). Owen's exposition of the high-priestly office of Christ and his classic work on the Holy Spirit make his contribution to British Trinitarian theology of permanent importance. To the end of his life he worked for a more comprehensive national church and reconciliation of rival dissenters.

Puritan theology remained influential among some British dissenters such as C. H. Spurgeon* until the end of the 19th century. Many of the major Puritan theologians were republished in more accurate editions. Likewise in New England their direct influence was still strong in the 18th century through scholars such as Jonathan Edwards.* There has been some revival of interest among Evangelicals such as D. M. Lloyd-Jones* and J. I. Packer (b. 1926). The intellectual strength and coherence of this theological tradition is increasingly recognized by historians, despite its eclipse during the heyday of liberal theology. Its success in interpreting the 17th-century world has made adaptation difficult in an intellectually different era. But the faithfulness of Puritan theology to the scriptural revelation, its comprehensiveness, its integration of theology with other kinds of knowledge, its pastoral and spiritual depth, its success in creating a lasting tradition of worship, preaching and lay spirituality make it a tradition of permanent importance in English-speaking Christianity and in the wider Reformed churches, despite its distrust of the arts, its over-emphasis on individualism and its tendency to devalue the sacraments into mere symbols.

Bibliography

F. J. Bremer, *The Puritan Experiment* (New York, 1976); P. Christianson, *Reformers and Babylon* (Toronto, 1978); J. T. Cliffe, *The Puritan Gentry* (London, 1984); P. Collinson, *English Puritanism* (Historical Association pamphlet, London, 1983); P. Helm, *Calvin and the Calvinists* (Edinburgh, 1982); E. B. Holifield, *The Covenant Sealed* (New Haven, CT, 1974); P. Miller, *The New England Mind* (New York, 1939; Boston, MA, 1954); E. S. Morgan, *Visible Saints* (Ithaca, NY, 1975); R. S. Paul, *Assembly of the Lord* (Edinburgh, 1984); K. L. Sprunger, *The Learned Dr William Ames* (Urbana, IL, 1972); P. Toon, *God's Statesman* (Edinburgh, 1971); D. D. Wallace, *Puritans and Predestination* (Chapel Hill, NC, 1982); B. R. White, *The English Separatist Tradition* (Oxford, 1971); G. Yule, *Puritans in Politics* (Appleford, 1981); D. Zaret, *The Heavenly Contract: Ideology and Organization in Pre-Revolutionary Puritanism* (Chicago, IL, 1985).

I.B.

Q

QUAKER THEOLOGY. The Quakers (the Religious Society of Friends) grew out of the religious controversies of the 1650s in England. There are now 20,000 Friends world-wide, but there is no central religious authority.

Early Quaker theology contained both Puritan* and Anabaptist* elements. George Fox (1624–91) taught the apostasy of the visible church from NT times (2 Tim. 3:1–5), and claimed that Christ had now come to gather the true church. Outward belief was powerless to save, for the universal Inward Light (Jn. 1:9–18) was the only way to Christ. The Light led Christians into unity, continually revealed scriptural truth (Jn. 16:13), and enjoined non-violence, strict equality and a disuse of all conventional forms of address. It was active savingly also in non-Christians.

Outward sacraments were rejected as survivals of the old covenant inappropriate to the pure inward worship instituted by Christ (Jn. 4:24). Friends considered creeds to have been created by limited and defective human intellects not under the guidance of the Light and rejected such doctrines as imputed righteousness, total depravity, and the Trinity. The true church met for worship in silence, waiting for the Holy Spirit to inspire extempore prayers, sermons or testimonies. Ministry, unpaid and unordained, was open to all, regardless of sex.

The *Apology for the True Christian Divinity* by Robert Barclay (1648–90) provided structure and coherence for Quaker theology. Scripture and the fathers were used to argue the distinctive Quaker testimonies as the central truths of NT Christianity, from which all other formal doctrines derived their cogency. So convincing was this work that no serious theological development occurred among Friends until they were forced to drop their quasi-Anabaptism and come to terms with a different intellectual climate at the beginning of the 19th century.

Largely due to the influence of Joseph John Gurney (1788–1847), over half the world's Quakers are now Evangelicals. Scriptural inerrancy and the divinity of Christ can be harmonized with traditional Quakerism, but continuing revelation, doctrinal pacifism and atonement through the Light are harder to accommodate to evangelical principles. This branch of the Quakers calls, but does not ordain, pastors. It has adopted programmed worship, while maintaining the testimony against ordinances. Holiness movements* have had some influence. The Richmond Declaration (1887) is the standard statement of evangelical Quaker belief.

The modern non-evangelical branch combines rational, mystical and liberal tendencies deriving partly from 18th-century quietist* Quakerism. The doctrine of the universal Light is extended, incarnational doctrine is attenuated and the basic harmony of all religions asserted. The sense of the oneness of humanity leads this branch to be as active in peace work and social concerns as the other branch is in mission.

What divides the branches is often rival interpretations of what the original message can be understood to mean in changed circumstances. Contemporary liberal and evangelical Quakers are both being challenged by a movement to be found within both groups which takes the original message of Fox, Barclay and William Penn (1644–1718) as its datum rather than more contemporary theologies.

Bibliography
R. Barclay, *Apology for the True Christian Divinity* (Amsterdam, 1676); L. Benson, *Catholic Quakerism* (Philadelphia, 1966); J. J. Gurney, *Observations on the Religious Peculiarities of the Society of Friends* (London 1824); W. Penn, *Primitive Christianity Revived* (London, 1696); W. Pollard, F. Frith, and W. Turner, *A Reasonable Faith* (London, 1885); G. Richards, *On Being Incarnate* (London, 1979).

J.A.P.

QUEST FOR HISTORICAL JESUS, see HISTORICAL JESUS, QUEST FOR.

QUIETISM. The term quietism derives from the belief that God is only pleased to work in the heart of a person whose whole being is passive or quiet. It may be applied generally or specifically. In a general sense it denotes an attitude, found in many religions and at all periods of the history of the church, which suggests that one should 'Let go and let God' or 'Stop thinking and empty your mind of everything' and withdraw, individually or corporately, from concern with the world.

Such tendencies or teaching may have threatened orthodox belief most seriously in the Middle Ages, when they attracted the denunciation of the Flemish mystic Ruysbroeck (1293–1381); but the term quietism is usually reserved for the 17th-century controversy which received papal censure. The teaching of the Spanish priest Miguel de Molinos (1628–96) was condemned by Innocent XI in 1687; and the more orthodox 'semi-quietism' of the French nun Madame de Guyon (1648–1717), which was defended by Archbishop Fénelon (1651–1715), was condemned by Innocent XII in 1699.

Molinos was condemned for holding that 'one must totally abandon one's whole self in God and thereafter remain like a lifeless body', since 'natural activity is the enemy of grace and it hinders God's action and true perfection, because God wishes to act in us without us'. This may seem a very spiritual regard for grace and a rejection of works, but in fact it is the opposite. The 'natural' activities of the believer which are discarded include petitionary prayer, self-examination, worship with fellow-believers and participation in the Lord's Supper. All ordinary means of grace are rejected in favour of an infallible short cut: if the believer makes himself passive, God *must* raise his soul to union with himself.

Quietism also taught that such an experience of union with God was not a momentary ecstasy, nor a temporary stage on the path of prayer, but a permanent stage of 'pure love'. Furthermore, because in this 'mystical death' God was everything and the believer nothing, the believer was not only unconcerned about his own behaviour, but – on the grounds that all his acts were God's acts – he could hold that his acts were sinless by definition, even if they caused actual harm to others. Thus quietism represents an individualistic approach to salvation and an ethic similar to that found in pantheism.*

Quietism is a distortion of orthodox mystical theology,* but official condemnation of the one produced deep suspicion about the other. In Catholicism, uncertainty lasted throughout the 18th century and caused a virtual suspension of serious reflection on religious experience.* The effect on Protestantism was even more extended. Quietism had some influence on pietism's understanding of the Christian life as one of sanctification* and union with Christ.* But Ritschl's* rather unsympathetic *Geschichte des Pietismus* (*History of Pietism*, 3 vols., Bonn, 1880–86) did nothing to dissuade subsequent Reformed theologians from feeling that all so-called Christian mysticism was as suspect as quietism.

Bibliography
J. Aumann, *Christian Spirituality in the Catholic Tradition* (London and San Francisco, 1985); E. Herman, 'Quietism', *ERE* 10,

pp. 533–538; D. Knowles, *What is Mysticism?* (London, 1967); R. A. Knox, *Enthusiasm* (Oxford, 1950); E. Underhill, *Mysticism* (London, 1911).

QUMRAN, see DEAD SEA SCROLLS.

R

RABBINIC THEOLOGY. The most important sources are the Mishnah, the Palestinian and Babylonian Talmuds, the Midrashim and the Targums. None of these, not even the Mishnah and Talmuds with their division into tractates, attempts a systematic rabbinic theology. The unity of God and his attributes of mercy and justice (these latter associated with the divine names Yahweh and Elohim respectively) are universally affirmed; most other basic tenets are subject to a diversity of interpretations which, in the Mishnah, Talmuds and Midrashim, are often presented in an unresolved dialectic. In general, the divine attributes of omnipresence, omnipotence and omniscience are acknowledged – the first represented by the concept of *šᵉkînâ*, the radiance, presence or glory of God ('There is no place without *šᵉkînâ*', Midrash on Exodus ii. 9), and the last two balanced by a belief in human freedom ('All is foreseen, but freedom of choice is granted', Mishnah Aboth iii. 16). The extent of an individual's piety or impiety determines whether the *šᵉkînâ* is experienced as near or far.

Tôrâ ('law') is the privileged possession of Israel and what sets her apart from other nations. According to one view, it is the Jews' obedience to *tôrâ* that will decide the precise time of the Messiah's coming; others held that the time had already been appointed by God regardless of such considerations. That the Messiah would be an essentially human figure is the predominant rabbinic view, based partly on the Hebrew Scriptures and perhaps also conceived in reaction to Christians' claims about their Messiah. The principal function of the Messiah would be to relieve Israel of foreign oppression and raise her to her true status in the world (*cf.* Targum Is. 53:8).

The rabbis attributed the human proneness to sin to the 'evil inclination' which infects human nature from birth, if not before. For Jews, however, there is the countervailing 'good inclination' which becomes operative at the bar mitzvah stage, a ceremony which marks the initiation of a boy at the age of thirteen into the Jewish religious community and into observance of the precepts of the Torah. As for the expiation of sins, repentance is effective in averting, or at least delaying, punishment in all manner of circumstances (Mishnah Yoma viii. 8). Study of *tôrâ* and regular prayer are regarded as the particularly appropriate exercises of the faithful in an age when temple and cultus are denied even to those resident in the land of Israel. Such meritorious acts could cancel out a weight of guilt and ensure divine acceptance at the last for the one who performed them. One might also derive benefit from the meritorious deeds of someone more righteous, while, on a national scale, the merits of the fathers (patriarchs) were reckoned among the causes of prevenient grace to the people of Israel. An earthly paradise was the prospect for those, principally within Israel, who merited divine favour on the day of judgment; for those who did not, Gehenna had long since been prepared, but rabbinic humaneness is well illustrated by the tendency to limit the duration of punishment therein to a finite period, twelve months being especially favoured.

Bibliography

I. Epstein, *Judaism* (London, 1959); R. A. Stewart, *Rabbinic Theology* (Edinburgh, 1961).

RACE is a concept used to distinguish different groups of human beings. Distinctions are made according to a number of criteria, which always include physical appearance and its underlying genetic structure, but which may also include cultural, social, political and economic factors.

This method of distinguishing people is quite alien to Scripture, where the primary assertions are 1. of the unity of the human race, both in creation (Gn. 1:28; 5:1, 2; Acts 17:26) and in the scope of salvation (Gn. 12:3; Mt. 28:19; Col. 3:11; Rev. 5:9); and 2. that the main type of sub-division of mankind is that of 'ethnicity' or 'peoplehood', where the reference is mainly cultural, though religion may be a major factor. Therefore while at times the writers of both the OT and NT refer to peoples with a darker skin colour than their own (Nu. 12:7; Song 1:5; Je. 38:7; Acts 8:27; 13:1) no further significance is seen in the fact. Likewise, most modern scientists refuse to extrapolate from genetic formation to other human characteristics. On the other hand, the existence of 'peoples' is constantly acknowledged. The beginning of Israel's special calling follows from a list of surrounding nations (Gn. 10), and a major theme of both her historians and prophets is her interplay with other peoples. Her calling to be a blessing to all peoples is seen in the NT as fulfilled in Jesus, with the gospel spreading to all peoples, whose cultures are recognized (see the numerous incidental ethnic references in Acts) and affirmed (Rev. 21:24–26), while recognizing that individuals transcend cultures (1 Cor. 9:19–23) and that ethnic identity has idolatrous potential (Phil. 3:4–9).

Biblical reflection on 'race' in the present world, therefore, eliminates the simply physical and genetic emphasis, and affirms, in a restrained way, its cultural aspect. There is however a further and major element in the meaning of 'race' in the modern world: namely that differences in economic well-being and political power at both the international level and within particular nations bear a definite though not absolute correlation to differences in appearance. Such injustice is sustained either by overt ideologies of racial superiority (as in apartheid), or by unacknowledged assumptions, resulting in discriminatory and oppressive behaviour. In judgment on this situation there is a mass of biblical material about God's hatred of social and international injustice, his concern for the oppressed, and his call to establish justice in the world (cf. Liberation Theology,* Political Theology*).

Any attempt, therefore, to justify treating people differently on the grounds of their appearance falls foul of biblical teaching. In particular, attempts to produce a theological defence of apartheid err in the following ways. 1. They treat 'race' rather than ethnicity as the main determinant (taking Israel's relations with her neighbours as paradigmatic would logically lead to separating Afrikaans- and English-speaking, not African and European). 2. They treat racial and cultural identity as

fixed, when Scripture and history show how they develop, borrow, fragment and re-form within the God-given flux of history. 3. They are blind to the ungodly brutality, oppression and economic disparity which is inseparable from the actual implementation of apartheid.

See also: BLACK CONSCIOUSNESS; BLACK THEOLOGY; DUTCH REFORMED THEOLOGY.

Bibliography
J. A. Kirk, 'Race, Class, Caste and the Bible', Them 10:2 (1985), pp. 4–14.

J.B.R.

R AHNER, KARL (1904–84) was a Jesuit* who taught theology in Germany and Austria, a prolific author, and probably the most important and influential Roman Catholic theologian of the 20th century.

At the basis of all Rahner's theological work is a theological anthropology,* which he developed under the influence of the transcendental Thomism* of Joseph Maréchal (1878–1944) and in dialogue with the existential* philosophy of Martin Heidegger. He adopts what he calls a 'transcendental and anthropological method of theology', which makes human experience the key to all theological meaning and focuses on 'transcendental experience', i.e. a universal, a priori and pre-reflective experience which is the condition for all other human experience. Such transcendental experience becomes conscious only when we reflect on the conditions for the possibility of human knowledge and activity, but such reflection reveals a human transcendence of the finite world in which humanity as such is open to the infinite mystery beyond the world, which religion calls God. Rahner's analysis of transcendental experience means that a pre-reflective experience of God is present in all human experience. Human nature is self-transcendence into God.

On this basis Rahner's work aims to reinterpret the traditional dogmas of the church, so that, instead of appearing fossilized formulations in the language of the past, they can be seen to have existential* meaning in terms of universal human experience and its specifically modern conditioning. The message of Christianity is that the infinite Mystery, towards which human existence is intrinsically orientated, while always remaining a mystery, gives himself in absolute self-communication to human experience. This grace of divine self-communication is present in the transcendental experience of all human beings as an offer which can be accepted or rejected, though it grounds human freedom and determines human existence even when it is rejected. Thus, for Rahner, grace* is already present in human nature, and therefore the possibility of salvation is given by God in human experience as such; it can be realized without knowledge of the historical Christian revelation and, without explicit faith in Christ, by 'anonymous Christians'. These may be adherents of other religions, or may even be professed atheists who fail to thematize their transcendental relatedness as relation to God, but have not rejected it. Rahner's Christology* interprets Jesus primarily as the absolute fulfilment of human destiny in acceptance of God's self-communication, and as such God's offer, in history, of the divine self-communication to all other men and women. This 'transcendental Christology' makes the need for such an 'absolute bringer of salvation' intrinsic to human existence.

Rahner has made very important and influential contributions on a wide range of specific dogmatic topics, such as the Trinity,* the nature of Scripture* and tradition, and ecclesiology. He has also written extensively on the theology of the spiritual life, where he marries his own theological approach to the Jesuit tradition of Ignatian* spirituality.*

Bibliography

Foundations of Christian Faith (London, 1978); *Theological Investigations*, 20 vols. (London, 1961–81).

G. S. McCool (ed.), *A Rahner Reader: A Comprehensive Selection from Most of Karl Rahner* (London, 1975); L. J. O'Donovan, *A World of Grace: An Introduction to the Themes and Foundations of Karl Rahner's Theology* (New York, 1984); C. J. Pedley, 'An English Bibliographical Aid to Karl Rahner', *Heythrop Journal* 25 (1984), pp. 319–365; H. Vorgrimler, *Understanding Karl Rahner* (London, 1986); K.-H. Weger, *Karl Rahner: An Introduction to His Theology* (London 1980).

R.J.B.

RAMSEY, IAN THOMAS (1915–72). Ordained in 1940, Ramsey became a fellow of Christ's College, Cambridge, in 1944, professor of the philosophy of the Christian religion at Oxford in 1951, and Bishop of Durham from 1966. In his philosophy, Ramsey saw the characteristically religious situation as one combining on the one hand a discernment, in which 'the penny drops' and we become aware of something that includes the visible elements of the situation but goes beyond them; and on the other, a total commitment arising from that discernment. God can be the 'objective reference' of such a 'disclosure'. In these cases we find that any appropriate language has logical oddities; typically, it uses models* drawn from other contexts but qualifies them so as to differentiate them from their normal use and stress the element of transcendence. Thus God is *infinitely* wise, *eternal* Father, *first* cause, and so on.

Bibliography

Principal writings (*cf. Bibliography* by J. H. Pye, Durham, 1979): *Christian Discourse* (London, 1965); *Christian Empiricism* [collected papers] (London, 1974); *Freedom and Immortality* (London, 1960); *Models and Mystery* (London, 1964); *Models for Divine Activity* (London, 1973); *On Being Sure in Religion* (London, 1963); *Religion and Science* (London, 1964); *Religious Language* (London, 1957). For critical assessment see J. H. Gill, *Ian Ramsey: To Speak Responsibly of God* (London, 1976).

R.L.S.

RAMUS, PETRUS. Pierre de la Ramée (1515–72), a French humanist, was educated at the College of Navarre, part of the University of Paris. He was appointed regius professor in 1551. He became a Protestant *c.* 1561 and was murdered during the St Bartholomew's Day massacre. He advocated comprehensive reform of the academic curriculum, which had been long dominated by universal dependence on Aristotelian* logic.* His stress was on method, on practical utility, on simplification. His method of dichotomous division, whereby any subject could be distributed into ever smaller components and then arranged in diagrams, enabled the whole topography of knowledge to be displayed for instant comprehension. This simplifying diagrammatic method was part of a major intellectual and cultural revolution marking the boundary between the medieval and modern worlds. The invention of printing was already dissociating knowledge from discourse and reconstructing it in spatial, visualist terms. The humanist development of *loci* (places from which knowledge in any given subject could be surveyed) had further facilitated this shift from auditive to visual categories of thought. Ramus brought this process into pedagogy.

Ramism spread rapidly, having a major impact on educational practice until *c.* 1650. Germany was its principal centre, 133 editions of Ramus' *Dialectic* and 52 editions of his *Rhetoric* being published there from 1573 to 1620. Ramist method was applied to biblical exposition by Johannes Piscator (1546–1625) and to systematic theology by Amandus Polanus (1561–1610; see Reformed Theology*). J. H. Alsted (1588–1638) applied it to everything. Indeed, a line can be drawn from Ramus through Alsted to Diderot and modern encyclopaedism. Ramist influence was felt in Holland and also England, where Cambridge Puritanism* had its own stress on practical utility. In 17th century New England* it became firmly established at Harvard and Yale.

Despite his support of congregationalism,* which brought him into conflict with Theodore Beza,* Ramus' influence on theology was indirect, his one theological work (*Commentary on the Christian Religion*, 1576) being of meagre interest. His redefinition of theology, in line with practical utility, as '*doctrina de bene vivendo*' (the doctrine of living well) and its major consequent dichotomy of faith and observance was later developed by Puritan* Ramists such as William Ames. It represented a new foundation in man's faith rather than in objective revelation and so prepared the way for pietism.* Ramus' method also became associated with the emergent covenant theology,* its rigorous dichotomizing possibly accelerating acceptance of the double covenant idea, with a pre-fall covenant of works additional to the covenant of grace. Ramist focus on the visual could be seen as diverging from the Reformation* stress on the word. Its persistent sub-division, in imposing an arbitrary structure on theology, focused on distinctions and divisions rather than internal connections and, by its rigorous simplification, tended to obscure theology's richness and multiform complexity.

Bibliography

W. S. Howell, *Logic and Rhetoric in England 1500–1700* (Princeton, NJ, 1956); R. W. Letham, 'The *Foedus Operum*: Some Factors Accounting for its Development', *The Sixteenth Century Journal* 14 (1983), pp. 457–467; J. Moltmann, 'Zur Bedeutung des P. Ramus für Philosophie und Theologie in Calvinismus', *ZKG* 68 (1957), pp. 295–318; W. J. Ong, *Ramus, Method, and the Decay of Dialogue* (Cambridge, MA, 1958); idem, *Ramus and Talon Inventory* (Cambridge, MA, 1958); K. L. Sprunger, *The Learned Doctor William Ames* (Urbana, IL, 1972).

R.W.A.L.

RASHDALL, HASTINGS, see MODERNISM, ENGLISH.

R ATRAMNUS (d. 868), who was known to the Reformers as 'Bertram', was an opponent of the eucharistic* teaching of Paschasius* Radbertus. Other distinguished contemporaries of Paschasius have left writings at variance with his teaching, namely John Scotus Eriugena* and Rabanus Maurus (d. 856), but Ratramnus, monk of Corbie, devoted a formal treatise to the matter, at the request of King Charles the Bald. Like the treatise of Paschasius (who was abbot of Ratramnus' own Benedictine monastery), it is entitled *De Corpore et Sanguine Domini* (*On the Body and Blood of the Lord*). Corbie had for fifty years been a centre of Augustinian* teaching, and Ratramnus considered that he could appeal to the teaching of both Augustine* and Ambrose* against that of Paschasius. His positive teaching is not as clear as Eriugena's, though he emphasizes the role of symbolism* and faith; but, negatively, he firmly denies that the sacramental body of Christ is identical with the body born of Mary. Many passages from his treatise were borrowed by the Anglo-Saxon writer Aelfric (d. *c.* 1020), whose works were published at the Reformation by Archbishop Matthew Parker; but it had a strong direct influence as well, especially on Ridley (see English Reformers*) and in 1559 it was put on the *Index*. Various English translations have been published, from 1548 onwards. Ratramnus wrote also on predestination* (on the side of Gottschalk*) and on the controversy with the Eastern church. His recently discovered treatise on the soul is to be found in D. C. Lambert (ed.), *Analecta Mediaevalia Namurcensia* 2 (1951).

Bibliography

Works in *PL* 121; J. N. Bakhuizen van den Brink (ed.), *De Corpore* (Amsterdam, ²1974) (critical edition); A. J. Macdonald (ed.), *The Evangelical Doctrine of Holy Communion* (Cambridge, 1933).

R.T.B.

R AVEN, C. E. (1885–1964). One of the most distinguished Anglican scholars of the 20th century, Raven's origins in the 19th are reflected in the diversity of his interests, which included theology, biological science and history. A clergyman who preached throughout his long life, Raven was a prodigious author. His achievements included a major biography of John Ray (1628–1705, 'the father of English natural history') and books on ornithology, botany, the ordination of women and pacifism (he was a supporter of both the latter causes). He occupied the Regius Chair of Divinity at Cambridge and was vice-chancellor for a period.

Raven's theology was deeply influenced by his scientific interests and in particular by his enthusiastic use of the theory of organic evolution to provide an interpretative framework for religion as well as for science. So he saw an evolutionary background even to the incarnation, and sought to understand the God-man as himself within the 'evolutionary series'. Such an extended use of evolutionary theory, common in the earlier part of this century, has fallen out of fashion more recently. It is interesting that Raven's books include a volume on Teilhard de Chardin*, for like Teilhard (though with more modest proposals) he saw himself as seeking to re-interpret orthodoxy in line with what he took to be the new science.

Bibliography

Evolution and the Christian Concept of God (London, 1936); *Natural Religion and Christian Theology*, 2 vols. (Gifford Lectures, 1951–52; Cambridge, 1953); *Science and the Christian Man* (London, 1952).

F. W. Dillistone, *Charles Raven, Naturalist, Historian, Theologian* (London, 1975).

N.M.deS.C.

R EBAPTISM. Mainstream Christian theology has generally held that baptism* is unrepeatable – or more strictly, ought not to be repeated. Although often based on a misreading of Eph. 4:5 (where 'one baptism' refers to the *common* baptism shared by all) and an unhistorical appeal to the Nicene Creed ('one baptism for the remission of sins', which relates to the controversy over post-baptismal sin and could not have encompassed infant baptism), this teaching has its proper grounding in the once-for-all character of Christ's work of redemption and hence of the baptismal initiation into him.

Nevertheless, rebaptism (which is what its critics call it, although for clarity it is unavoidable) has not infrequently been practised and defended, chiefly for the following reasons:

1. *Denial of the validity of an earlier baptism.* In the patristic era, Donatists* and other movements rejected Catholic baptism, which they regarded as administered by the fatally defiled clergy of an apostate church. The Donatists appealed to the earlier Catholic practice (*cf.* Cyprian*) which refused to recognize baptism given outside the Catholic fold and hence rebaptized, but by the Council of Arles (314) this position had been abandoned. Optatus of Milevis (*fl. c.* 370) and Augustine* provided the theological justification for this reversal.

Baptism has commonly been treated as null and void if any essential feature (notably, a flow of water and the Trinitarian name) is lacking. In cases of uncertainty, some churches (*e.g.* Roman Catholic) have conditionally (re)baptized ('If you have not been baptized, I baptize you . . .').

Several churches at different periods have not recognized some other churches' baptism and have accordingly rebaptized 'converts'. Southern Presbyterians in the USA took this view of Roman Catholic baptism.

2. *Denial of infant baptism as true Christian baptism.* The Anabaptists* (literally, 'rebaptizers') and other Radical Reformers* pioneered this position (with only insignificant medieval precedents), but since that 16th-century divide such rebaptism has been common, both in new churches holding to believers' baptism only and in individual cases.

In recent times, especially in the context of charismatic renewal, a second baptism has been sought by those unable to regard their infant baptism as meaningful – *e.g.* because of their parents' apparent lack of faith. Such requests raise acute pastoral problems, but also touch on basic issues of baptismal theology – *e.g.* the relation between baptism and faith (or experience).

Bibliography

R. S. Armour, *Anabaptist Baptism* (Scottdale, PA, 1966); A. Aubry, 'Faut-il rebaptiser?', *NRT* 99 (1967), pp. 183–201; C. Buchanan, *One Baptism Once* (Bramcote, Nottingham, 1978); T. H. Lyle, 'Reflections on "Second Baptism"', *IJT* 21 (1972), pp. 170–182.

D.F.W.

RECONCILIATION, see ATONEMENT.

REDEMPTION is a concept found in the OT to express the action of a relative in setting free a member of his family or buying back his property (Lv. 25:25ff.) or in general that of purchasing something for a price. A ransom-price is paid to secure the release of what would otherwise be under forfeit (*e.g.* Ex. 21:30). Religiously God acts as redeemer by powerfully delivering his people from captivity (Ex. 6:6–7; Is. 48:20) or even from sin (Ps. 130:8). A ransom may also be paid to God in the form of a sacrifice or offering, to deliver people whose lives would otherwise be forfeit (Ex. 13:13). There is dispute whether, when the action of redeeming is ascribed to God, he is regarded as paying a price to set his people free; certainly cost and effort are applied, but the thought of a price being received by somebody from him is absent (Is. 43:3 is metaphorical; *cf.* 52:3). The term was also applied to the setting free of slaves in the Graeco-Roman world on the payment of a ransom to their owners; this could be done in various ways, one of which involved a religious ceremony in which the slave was the object of a fictitious purchase by a god so that he was free of earthly masters. The terminology used is somewhat different from that employed in the NT, and has led recent scholars to doubt whether the origin of the NT metaphor lies in this area; nevertheless, the manumission of slaves would surely have formed an excellent and relevant illustration of redemption.

In the NT the starting-point for the use of the concept is found in the sayings of Jesus, which state that no-one can give anything in exchange for his life (Mk. 8:37; *cf.* Ps. 49:7–

9), but that the Son of Man came to give his life a ransom for many (*i.e.* for all; Mk. 10:45 as paraphrased in 1 Tim. 2:6; *cf.* Tit. 2:14). Jesus thus does what God alone can do (Ps. 49:15) by giving his own life, and the use of the noun *lytron* makes it quite clear that he gives his life in exchange for those whose lives are forfeit and thus sets them free. The death of Jesus is thus conceived as the sacrifice (Acts 20:28; Rom. 3:24; 1 Pet. 1:18) through which we are set free from our sins and their consequences, in other words through which we receive forgiveness (Col. 1:14; Eph. 1:7). Redemption is by faith in Christ (Rom. 3:24f.), and there is no longer any need to keep the law, as the Jews supposed, to secure salvation (Gal. 3:13; 4:5). Believers, however, can also be said to have been purchased by God to become his people; he has paid the price for them (1 Cor. 6:20; 7:23). Thus the term 'redemption' can be used in quite a broad sense to express the general concept of salvation and deliverance (*e.g.* Lk. 24:21).

Bibliography

F. Büchsel, *TDNT* IV, pp. 328–56; D. Hill, *Greek Words and Hebrew Meanings* (London, 1967), ch. 3; L. Morris, *The Apostolic Preaching of the Cross* (London, [3]1965), ch. 1; J. Schneider and C. Brown, *NIDNTT* III, pp. 177–223; B. B. Warfield, *The Person and Work of Christ* (Philadelphia, 1950), pp. 325–348, 429–475.

I.H.Ma.

REFORMATION, CATHOLIC COUNTER-. The name Counter-Reformation, though now generally accepted, is a misnomer. What we now call the Reformation* was that movement, beginning with Luther,* which sought to *re*-form a Christendom *de*-formed, and to effect this on the lines of biblical scholarship, sound tradition and clear reason. The movement called the Counter-Reformation did not arise to counter this Reformation, but was essentially a movement to recover the Catholic Church from the hammer-blows of Protestant criticism directed at her theological and spiritual penury, her secularization and her corruption. The true Catholic reformers were silenced, the evangelical Reformers excluded: the former effected nothing, the latter gave us what we now call Protestantism.* The Counter-Reformation, therefore, may be described as arising with those scholars who engaged in debate with Luther from the 1520s on, culminating in the Jesuits,* the Inquisition, and the Council* of Trent, reaching its decline and conclusion in the Thirty Years War and the Treaty of Westphalia in 1648. The Counter-Reformation is properly speaking the Catholic idea of reformation: the Reformation proper runs counter to this movement.

By the end of the 15th century all groups in society – except those in whose interest it was to maintain the Roman curia – regarded the unreformed papacy* as the running sore of Europe. The grounds of their complaints were mainly the secularization and corruption of the church which had caused it to lose its *raison d'être*, namely, the preaching of the gospel and the cure of souls, and to become a sordid, money-making, power-seeking institution. More than this, people chafed under the scandals arising from the benefit of clergy; the right of sanctuary; the domination of civil law by canon law; clerical absenteeism . . . the list was long. There were the humanists,* too, who brought forward a different idea of reform, namely, a repudiation of scholasticism* and a return to the simple Christian philosophy of the early Christian centuries. The true Reformers, the theological teachers, sought to re-establish the pure gospel, the authority of Scripture, believing that the traditions, the corruptions, the scandals, the superstitions, all that the common man experienced as Christianity would fall away like dross – as they did.

The clearest insight into the nature of Catholic reformation can be seen in Spain. There the medieval reformers of the church conceived of reformation on the lines of a measure of secular control of the church, the enforcement of canon* law to effect the reformation of clerical morals, a measure of humanist scholarship, the maintenance of scholastic* theology, the preservation of the hierarchy and the rites and usages of the medieval church, together with a ruthless suppression of heresy or criticism. King Ferdinand V (1452–1516) and Queen Isabella (1451–1504) virtually effected this kind of reformation with the support of Pedro González de Mendoza (1428–95), Hernando de Talavera (1428–1507), and Francisco Ximénes de Cisneros (1436–1517) in particular. The saintly Ximénes, after purifying the morals of the Spanish clergy, set about their theological

and cultural education, establishing universities and seminaries: the theology of these institutions was that of early scholasticism (Thomism*) rather than later (Duns Scotus* and William of Ockham*), with a touch of Augustinian* theology and a dash of Erasmian learning. In the early stages they read Erasmus* and even welcomed Luther's early attack on the scandals of the day, though they shrank back from his powerful and disturbing evangelical theology. It was this Spanish idea of reformation which Emperor Charles V (1500–58) sought, and Pope Adrian VI (1522–23), too. It was these three forces which met at Worms in 1521 – the theological reformation (represented by Luther), the Spanish kind of reformation (represented by Charles V), and the stolid refusal of the papal curia to countenance any kind of reformation whatsoever (represented by the papal envoy Girolamo Aleander, 1480–1542). Luther's idea of reformation was to quicken the church through a fresh awareness of God's work in Christ, and for the priesthood* of all believers to stand on its own feet in the strength of a biblical theology and spiritual experience, even at the cost of severence from the papacy. The Spanish idea was a revival of church life, leaving unchanged the sacerdotal ministry, the power of the pope and Catholic tradition, with the authority of the secular arm to purge, persecute and punish any and every deviant.

Italy provides a further insight into the nature of the Catholic Counter-Reformation. The peasants were little more than superstitious pagans; in the cities groups of people earnestly desired the reformation of morals and manners of clergy and townspeople alike; the intellectuals realistically saw the church as a political institution, almost a necessary evil, of no help whatever to anybody genuinely religious. Nevertheless, there was an important group of Catholic reformers, organized well enough to be called the Oratory of Divine Love, with which were associated the devout and upright Gasparo Contarini (1483–1542), Giovanni Pietro Caraffa (1476–1559, later Pope Paul IV, 1555–59), as well as quite a number of distinguished women, *e.g.* Renée, Duchess of Ferrara (1510–74), Vittoria Colonna (1490–1547), Caterina Cibo (1501–57). In Naples Juan de Valdés* was the centre of a reforming circle that included Peter Martyr Vermigli.* Another force making for reform was the revival of the monastic orders, *e.g.* the Capuchins (Franciscans*), and also the renewal of the secular clergy by the new Theatines. The accession of Paul III (1534) gave new hope to all these movements. He summoned selected cardinals to report to him on the reformation of the church, but their report (1538) was so scathing an indictment that he refused to make it known, and though the cardinals urged steps to be taken, the long-hoped-for council was yet again postponed. In pursuance of reformation, Contarini went to the Diet of Regensburg (1541) whence he brought back from a discussion with the Protestants an agreed statement, but it was a semantic rather than a theological agreement, later abrogated by the pope. At this point the ideal of Catholic reformation died, the idea of Counter-Reformation took sole command: in 1542 Paul III re-organized the Inquisition in Italy.

It was the revival of missionary zeal under Ignatius* Loyola, whose Company of Jesus (Jesuits*) had already been established in Italy by Paul III in 1540, which kindled the enthusiasm for the Counter-Reformation to take the offensive. He set himself a threefold task: to reform the church from within, chiefly by means of education; to preach the gospel to the lost outsider and to the heathen; and to fight against Protestantism in any shape or form, by any means, with any weapon. By its zeal, devotion and spirituality the movement made considerable progress, for the multitude proved itself more willing to accept a general tidying up, which it wanted in its own interest anyway, than face the profound evangelical reformation of Luther in all its consequences. Loyola showed a deep pastoral concern when in Italy by tackling three major social evils of his day, namely, the discarding of unwanted children, beggary, and prostitution. With the support of his disciples, his missionary zeal furthered the church with remarkable effectiveness in the New World, in Africa and in the Far East. The decisive impress of the Jesuits on the Counter-Reformation was their demand of a blind, fanatical obedience to an infallible church headed by an infallible pope. This lasted until the later 20th century, when in Vatican II (1962–65) some idea of the true Catholic reformation of the 16th century emerged.

It was the Society of Jesus, accompanied by the now universal Inquisition, which gave the driving force to the Council of Trent (1545–63; see also Councils,* Roman Catholic Theology*). Trent was the most impressive embodiment of the ideals of the Counter-Reformation. Its doctrinal and internal reforms sealed the triumph of the papacy over both those Catholics who wished for conciliation with the Protestants and those who opposed papal claims. The Council provided a new look to doctrine, by modifying late scholasticism and opposing evangelical theology root and branch. It formulated afresh its own intellectual basis and on this established a proper and respected hierarchy. It provided a system of gradual reformation which was to free the church from many of the evils and corruptions which had given substance to the Protestant protest. It made provisions for an educated clergy. It also had the effect of making Catholicism both Roman and anti-Protestant. A succession of reforming popes sustained the movement – Pius V (1566–72), Gregory XIII (1572–85) and Sixtus V (1585–90) – and, supported by the Inquisition, extended a Spanish conception of ecclesiastical discipline to Italy and elsewhere; while Philip II (1527–98), a bigoted and fanatical Catholic ruler with the one idea of extending Catholicism and extirpating Protestantism, set himself up as the secular arm of the Counter-Reformation throughout Europe. Nevertheless, it was not all persecution and torture and intolerance. The Frenchman, Francis of Sales (1567–1622) and the Italian, Charles Borromeo (1538–84), showed great pastoral zeal, and the Spanish mystics deep spirituality, and a remarkable blossoming of theology, music, spiritual literature and fine architecture was the outcome.

The zeal of the Jesuits, the activity of the papacy, the *Index of Prohibited Books*, the skilful political handling of the constitution of the Holy Roman Empire and the secular support of Catholic princes and monarchs, were all factors which played an important part in the new power Catholicism began to display in relation to Protestantism. It regained its hold over the Rhineland, Austria, Southern Germany and Poland, but lost the Netherlands eventually though retaining Belgium; it held its own in Spain, France and Italy, yet lost the whole of Northern Europe to Protestantism. The outcome of all this was that the Catholic Church now became 'Spanish', and was striving to re-clericalize the whole Western world and to subject it to

Roman police, the Inquisition and censorship. It everywhere sought to stifle and crush, by its authoritarian reaction, every movement and every person who struggled to maintain the free spirit of enquiry of the early years. It amounted to a re-conquering crusade of a monarchical and bureaucratic church. Its hierarchical structure and sacerdotalism, in alliance with most oppressive dynastic courts, proved a disastrously reactionary mixture. Rome's answer to Luther at Trent (already nearly fifty years after Luther had raised his questions) was little more than a defiant re-assertion of what the Reformers had regarded as paganism. We now see not less pomp but even more lavish pomp, cults and rites; more hagiography; more worship of the Virgin Mary* and the saints;* more miracles and wonder-working images; more processions; more monastic orders; more devotion to the Catholic prince as the secular arm of the church: all this and more, but with less preaching from the Scriptures, stricter prohibition of their translation, tighter control of the clergy, strict censorship of thought and publication. This is what the Counter-Reformation amounted to, defiantly proud in its new baroque splendour. Only half of Christendom saw the significance of prophetic Luther, and even that half has largely forgotten him and his fellow Reformers.

Vatican II has afforded a glimmer of hope that Catholicism has not totally forgotten its own reformers of the 16th century, and that she may yet arrive at a sounder reassessment both of the Reformation and of the Counter-Reformation.

Bibliography

J. C. H. Aveling, *The Jesuits* (London, 1981); J. Delumeau, *Catholicism between Luther and Voltaire* (London, 1977); P. Janelle, *The Catholic Reformation* (Milwaukee, WI, 1949); G. V. Jourdan, *The Movement towards Catholic Reform in the Early Sixteenth Century* (London, 1914); B. J. Kidd, *The Counter-Reformation 1550–1600* (London, 1933); D. Mitchell, *The Jesuits* (London, 1980); A. R. Pennington, *The Counter-Reformation in Europe* (London, 1899); H. Tüchle *et al.*, *Réforme et Contre-réforme* (Paris, 1968); A. D. Wright, *The Counter-Reformation* (London, 1982).

J.A.

REFORMATION, RADICAL. This term has been used to describe those who desired a more far-reaching Reformation* than that sought by the main-line or magisterial Reformers (Luther,* Zwingli* and Calvin*). Some historians prefer the term 'left-wing' to describe the phenomenon under study. Recent research has pointed to a measure of continuity between the radicals and late mediaeval apocalyptic* groups. Erasmus* was also a particularly important source, because he took the Bible seriously and yet reached very different conclusions from those of the magisterial Reformers.

Origins

The origins of radicalism can be traced back to the demands for an acceleration of change in Wittenberg in 1522 made by Carlstadt (*c.* 1477–1541) and the Zwickau prophets. They wanted an abolition of Catholic liturgical practices; they preached that infant baptism was wrong, and the prophets claimed to have direct revelations from God. Thomas Müntzer (*fl.* 1490–1525), who preached in revolutionary apocalyptic terms and was savagely critical of Luther for putting too much reliance on a learned ministry and for giving insufficient place to the Holy Spirit's leading of ordinary people, was very influential in encouraging the confident but hopeless resistance of the Peasants' Revolt. Finally a group emerged in Zurich which was critical of Zwingli, and it became clear that its concerns were not only the question of how speedily the Reformers could achieve their objectives but also what was the nature of those objectives. They sought both a total break with non-biblical traditions and a separation of like-minded people from those who 'compromised' the faith.

G. H. Williams in his definitive study has noted three very broad radical groupings, though within these further sub-groupings can be detected.

The *Anabaptists** emphasized believers' baptism, separation from the world (including the refusal to be involved in the institutions of the state) and a very literal biblicism. They are sometimes helpfully distinguished from the Reformers as those who sought a very precise 'restoration' or 'restitution' of NT Christianity (for example, sometimes advocating communism) as opposed to a 'reformation' according to NT principles.

Somewhat unfairly, the activities of a revolutionary element among the Anabaptists – who sought to set up a rule of the godly based on a rigid and authoritarian interpretation of the OT law in Münster in 1534 – became a symbol, for most contemporaries, of the dangers of radicalism. By and large they were not a threat to the state, and the followers of Menno Simons (1496–1561) and Jacob Hutter (d. 1536) survived through the centuries as significant groupings (see Mennonite Theology*).

The *Spiritualists* put a considerable emphasis on the leading of the Spirit, sometimes at the expense of the Bible. This could lead towards a mystical understanding of the faith and a concentration on the indwelling Word. Caspar Schwenckfeld* scandalized all orthodox believers by suggesting that there should be a moratorium on the Lord's Supper as it had become so divisive.

The *Evangelical Rationalists* put reason on a par with Scripture, and often stood rather loose to doctrine, favouring a unitarian* theology. Socinianism* developed from the teaching of Laelius Socinus (1525–62) and his nephew Faustus Socinus (1539–1604).

Characteristics

It is possible to identify eight characteristics of the radicals, though the movement was so diverse that exceptions abound.

1. An emphasis on sanctification rather than justification. Luther, they said, put too much emphasis on the Christian's continued sinfulness (*semper peccator*). Some held out, by contrast, the possibility of reaching a perfect state. Many thought that Paul's description in Romans 7 ('O wretched man that I am') did not apply to Christians.

2. A reaction against an over-intellectual faith. There was a strong conviction that the Reformers had over-intellectualized the faith in the emphasis they gave to theology and to learned ministers. What was much more important was the witness of the Spirit within.

3. A conviction that it was possible to establish a holy church. All the Reformers accepted that the visible church could not be an exact replica of the true church. The radicals had a greater confidence in the possibility of creating a church of real believers and to this end put a great emphasis on excommunication ('the ban').

4. A determination to be separate from the world. In particular they stressed that the state was for non-Christians and their members should have as little to do with it as possible. They consequently caused great perturbation by refusing to serve as magistrates or soldiers and thus appeared to challenge the fabric of society which was based, in both Catholic and orthodox Protestant theory, on a close relationship between church and state.

5. The importance of believers' baptism. Most of the radicals were strongly against infant baptism, and hence practised rebaptism.*

6. A tendency to theological heterodoxy. The restorationist emphasis meant that the great credal formulations of the church were ignored. The result was a tendency to unorthodox theological views particularly in relation to the Trinity* and Christology.* Many, for example, believed that Christ did not take our human flesh but brought his own divine body to earth ('the celestial flesh of Christ').

7. A passionate commitment to evangelism. They had a strong sense of the continuing force of the great commission which the Reformers had tended to limit to the apostolic era. This, together with their lack of interest in political boundaries and their willingness to face persecution, made them very courageous evangelists.

8. A growing conviction about toleration. Though it is undoubtedly true that the fierce reaction they aroused within both Protestantism and Catholicism had the effect of undermining any idea of toleration, the radicals did in time have an important part to play in extending the idea that religious opinion should be left to the individual to decide without any pressure from church or state.

In background the radicals, though often led by men of education and position, were generally simple people, often peasants and craftsmen, manifestly seeking an identity and a medium of self-expression which the Reformers' doctrine of the priesthood* of all believers had promised, but had not, it was contended, delivered. They often met in simple and informal settings. They were very prone to division. Sometimes their emphasis on the leading of the Spirit produced dangerously emotional and aberrant moral behaviour.

The existence of the radicals and their particular emphases is a good example of the not infrequent tensions in the Christian church between enthusiasm and order; between Spirit and word; between Scripture and tradition;* between seeing the church* as a communion of saints or a school of sinners; and between understanding the priesthood of all believers as giving equal ministry* to all or ministries to all but with a special ministry, involving authority, to some.

Bibliography

C. P. Clasen, *Anabaptism: A Social History, 1526–1618* (Ithaca, NY, and London, 1972); J. S. Oyer, *Lutheran Reformers against Anabaptists* (The Hague, 1964); G. H. Williams, *The Radical Reformation* (Philadelphia, 1962); *idem* and M. M. Angel, *Spiritual and Anabaptist Writers* (London, 1957).

C.P.W.

REFORMATION THEOLOGY. The Protestant* Reformation produced a theology that was a massive reassertion of the centrality of God,* the glory of his sovereignty,* and the primacy of his grace* in the salvation* of humanity through Jesus Christ.*

Basic principles

To Martin Luther* it was a revolutionary discovery that the righteousness* of God is 'the righteousness by which we are made righteous' (*LW* 25, p. 151). Medieval thinkers, he believed, had led Christendom astray by teaching that human persistence in doing good moral and ritual actions would earn merit* in the eyes of God and enable sinners to achieve salvation. But the appalling consequences of sin* had so paralysed the will* that sinners could not take the least step towards pleasing God. Close study of the teaching of Paul, however, led Luther to the conviction that through faith* in Jesus Christ – a faith which is itself God's gift – a sinner is granted free and full pardon. He is justified* by faith, not by his own achievements but because Christ bestows upon him the merits that he (Christ) has won through his victory over sin,* death,* the law* and the devil,* the 'tyrants' which have held sinful humanity in thrall. So justification is a forensic declaration of pardon which in no way depends upon human merit.

All the magisterial Reformers followed Luther in this matter. Calvin* indeed did insist that the hidden work of the Holy Spirit,* in bringing a sinner to exercise faith, also regenerated* him into a new life, because to believe in Christ of necessity means coming into personal union* with him. The righteousness of faith thus manifests itself in the good works that spring from that union. But this so-called 'double justification' did not jeopardize the emphasis on primary justification by faith alone. Rather was it a way of understanding the connection between justification and sanctification.* The Reformers had no wish to minimize the role of morality in Christian living, but they were adamant that it was the product of justification, not its cause.

The Reformers were also agreed upon the authority of Scripture.* For Luther, Scripture is the word of God. Its human authors wrote under the inspiration of the Holy Spirit, and that ensured its accuracy – not only in its general teaching, but also in its verbal details. This did not preclude a critical attitude to the transmitted text; knowledge of Hebrew and Greek was necessary in order to get as close as possible to the original autographs. The Bible is the possession of the whole people of God and so translation into the various national languages is a necessity, for how could the public acquire a knowledge of the truth, asked William Tyndale, 'except ye scripture were playnly layd before their eyes in their mother tonge?' (Foreword to the Pentateuch).

God the Holy Spirit is the true expositor of the Bible, as Zwingli* explained in his book, *The Clarity and Certainty of the Word of God* (1522). The pope could claim no monopoly in expounding it. The key of interpretation, said Luther in his appeal *To the Christian Nobility of the German Nation* (1520), was given not to Peter and his successors at Rome, 'but to the whole community'. Calvin gathered into a more systematic form the insights of his predecessors. He emphasized the self-authenticating character of the Bible (*Institutes* I. vii. 2–4), as its objective witness is confirmed by the internal testimony of the Holy Spirit in the believing heart. The relation between the Holy Spirit and the Bible is therefore a very close one. To separate them from each other is to embrace either a lifeless biblicism or the vagaries of spiritual enthusiasm.

Application

The application of these two principles, *sola fide* and *sola Scriptura*, led to striking

565

consequences. It led to a critical modification of medieval belief and practice. Church tradition could no longer be acknowledged as a standard independent of the Bible. That meant a severe curtailment of the luxurious growth of allegorical interpretation and an insistence that biblical exposition should be grounded upon the literary and historical meaning of the text. The belief in purgatory* was abandoned for lack of scriptural proof. The cults of the saints and of the Virgin Mary* were demolished in the light of the doctrine that Christ is the sole mediator between God and man.

On the other hand, those doctrines and declarations of faith that were consonant with Scripture were retained. Thus the classical doctrines of the Trinity* and the incarnation* were retained, as well as the definitions which expressed them, such as the Apostles' Creed, the Nicene Creed and the Definition of Chalcedon. Soon the Reformers set to it to expound their own understanding of theology. Although Luther produced no systematic exposition of his theology, he made a massive contribution in a large number of publications, among which his treatises of 1520, together with his commentaries on Galatians and Romans, are crucial to an understanding of his thought. Philip Melanchthon* attempted the first systematic exposition of Lutheran theology in his *Loci Communes* (1521), and the Lutheran movement produced as a definitive exposition of its faith the Augsburg Confession (1530). Zwingli had produced the most mature expression of his theology, *True and False Religion*, in 1525. But pride of place must be given to Calvin's *Institutes of the Christian Religion*. The first edition of 1536 was expanded over the years to become the impressive masterpiece of the 1559 edition. While using the pattern of the Apostles' Creed as his framework, Calvin meant his book to be a manual for Bible readers. It is unwise therefore to seek to expound his thought in terms of one dominating doctrine, such as predestination or divine sovereignty. The work is characterized by a well-balanced treatment of complementary doctrines, each contributing towards a harmonious integration of the richness of biblical teaching.

So the Protestant Reformation released a vast amount of creative theological energy which is only partially suggested by the tags,

'faith alone', 'Scripture alone', 'Christ alone', 'grace alone' and 'to God alone be glory'.

Different emphasis

Even in those theological areas where the Reformers accepted the formulations of classical Catholic orthodoxy, there were variations of emphasis. Thus, with regard to the doctrine of God, there was a new dynamism. Luther, in his exposition of the 'theology of the cross',* introduced penetrating insights as he expounded the paradox of the glorious God who reveals himself, and yet conceals himself (see Hidden and Revealed God*), in the mystery of abasement and suffering*. For Calvin similarly, God is no remote and static divinity, but one who intervenes in a dynamic and revolutionary way in human history.* For both of them divine grace is not an impersonal quality, as it so often was in medieval theology, but a personal involvement.

In Christology* again there were differences of emphasis amongst the Reformers. Luther was always concerned to accentuate the oneness of Christ's person, while Zwingli and Calvin underlined the distinction between the two natures. In the case of Calvin, his exaltation of Christ's divinity did lay him open to the charge of minimizing his human nature. On the other hand, some Anabaptists* such as the Melchiorites rejected the teaching of the Chalcedonian Definition and maintained that Jesus' body was composed of 'celestial flesh', a unique product of the Virgin's womb, substantially different from ordinary human flesh.

Yet another area where differences of emphasis emerged was in the understanding of the relationship between law and gospel.* All the magisterial Reformers took a sombre view of the radical effects of sin and rejected the medieval doctrine that man's natural gifts were only partially affected by the fall.* On the contrary, man's will had become enslaved through sin, as Luther demonstrated in his *Bondage of the Will* (1525), and his mind darkened. For Luther, the chief function of the law was to convict man of his sin. It accused but could not save. Only the gospel could save. So Luther, and his colleague Melanchthon, distinguished sharply between law and gospel. Calvin did not dismiss the accusatory aspect of the law in revealing the need for a saviour, but for him the chief function of the law was to inspire the justified sinner to aim at moral perfection. So gospel and law are to work hand in hand, for the covenant* of grace provides the setting for the law. It was this conviction that injected into Calvinism its moral activism both in the life of the individual and in society*.

According to the Augsburg Confession, the church 'is the congregation of the saints, in which the gospel is rightly taught and the sacraments rightly administered'. And Calvin agrees with this definition (*Institutes* IV. i. 8). Indeed, Luther and Calvin were in close agreement about the nature of the church.* The true church, known to God alone, is a company of justified sinners. But the visible church at Geneva or Wittenberg also contained hypocrites who lacked saving faith. It follows that the visible church is a mixed company, but as long as it ensures the right preaching of the gospel and the right administration of the sacraments,* it is still a true church. Calvin, unlike Luther, believed that in view of this it was necessary for the church to submit itself to constant self-examination. Its members must accept a system of pastoral discipline* to purify it, just as its ministers should be diligent to test their doctrine by the word of God. The reformation of the church is not an act but a process. The reformed church must be a reforming church, not a church which emulates Rome's boast that it is *semper eadem*, always the same.

The sacraments

It was by the stringent application of scriptural standards that the Reformers came to reject the sacramental system of the Church of Rome. The attack upon it had been launched by Luther in *The Babylonian Captivity of the Church* (1520). Christ's sacrifice* on Calvary was a complete and final oblation for the sins of the world. The doctrine that the mass was an unbloody repetition of that sacrifice had therefore to be rejected. Nor should the offering of the mass be considered a meritorious work. Holy communion is Christ's gift to his people, and it is their offering to him only in the sense that it is an offering of praise and thanksgiving. Although Luther in 1520 still listed penance* as a sacrament (but only in a severely qualified sense), the Protestant consensus was that Christ had instituted only two sacraments, baptism and the eucharist. With this radical transformation of the concept of sacrament, the Roman

Church's claim to be the sole dispenser of grace was nullified, and the priesthood stripped of its quasi-magical pretensions.

Further, the Reformers sought to eradicate the Roman Catholic distinction between priest and layman. Luther put the point with characteristic vigour: 'It has been devised that the pope, bishops, priests and monks are called the spiritual estate; princes, lords, artificers and peasants are the temporal estate. This is an artful lie . . . all Christians are truly of the spiritual estate' (*To the Christian Nobility*, 1520). This is the principle of the 'priesthood of all believers'.* All offices in the church are functions of the common ministry of the community of faith.

Despite the fact that the Reformers were of a common mind in their criticisms of the Roman Catholic doctrines of the sacraments,* they were unable to agree about the precise nature of the biblical doctrines that should replace them. Luther and Calvin were agreed that baptism* involves washing in water in the name of the Trinity, that it is a sign of God's pledge to forgive sin, that it is to be closely connected with the death of Christ and his resurrection,* and that baptism is a commitment to life-long repentance.* They were also agreed that it was appropriate to baptize infants on the grounds that the benefits of God's covenant with the parents applied to their offspring, and that Jesus had blessed infants and declared that 'of such is the kingdom of heaven'; also (in the case of Calvin) because the Holy Spirit may well act secretly even in the personality of an infant, as was the case with John the Baptist and Jesus (*Institutes* IV. xvi; Luther, *The Holy and Blessed Sacrament of Baptism, LW 35*; Zwingli, *On Baptism* and *Exposition of the Faith*).

The validity of infant baptism was challenged by the Anabaptists.* For them, baptism with water is of no avail unless it is preceded by the inner baptism of the Spirit.* Water baptism is the external sign of the commitment of faith. Since infants are incapable of exercising faith, they cannot be appropriate subjects for baptism. This was the position which drove George Blaurock and Conrad Grebel to reject infant baptism, and so to initiate the Anabaptist movement by rebaptizing those who adopted their convictions. Much was involved in their protest, because baptism on profession of faith became for them the door of entry into the church. They consequently challenged the principle, enunciated by the magisterial Reformers, that the church was a 'mixed company'. Rather, it must be a covenanted community of sincere believers. Such a position aroused the intense opposition of the authorities; it led directly to a denial of the concept of an established church in which people, by virtue of their citizenship, were also under the pastoral jurisdiction of the church.

Similarly there was bitter acrimony among Protestants about the eucharist. In article 15 of the confession signed by the participants at the Colloquy of Marburg (1529) to seek a common mind on the subject, it was agreed that the Lord's Supper should be celebrated in both kinds, that the mass was not to be deemed a good work which ensured pardon for the living and the dead, and that it is the sacrament of the very body and blood of Jesus Christ. But they failed to agree about the precise nature of Christ's presence in the sacrament. Luther held that 'in the Supper we eat and take to ourselves Christ's body truly and physically' (*That These Words of Christ, 'This is my body' &c., Still Stand Firm*, 1527). Zwingli, supported by Oecolampadius,* denied this physical presence 'in, with and under' the elements. They held that Christ's body is in heaven and could not be ubiquitous. His divine nature, however, is ubiquitous, and to be nourished by the sacrament is to partake of Christ's spirit through faith in the heart. So Zwingli did not deny Christ's presence in the sacrament, but he insisted that it was a real spiritual presence. Luther, however, was adamant. When Christ said, 'This is my body', he meant the word 'is' to be taken in a literal and not a figurative sense. The differences remained unresolved.

Calvin was dissatisfied with both positions. In Book IV of the *Institutes* he carefully expounded his own position. The sacrament has no efficacy when dissociated from the gospel. Word and sign go together. Moreover, the sacrament is made efficacious by the operations of the Holy Spirit in the heart of the participant. This is to say that in the eucharist there is a personal, not mechanical, relationship between God and the believer. Christ is the true substance of the sacrament, and the bread and wine are signs of the invisible food which he provides; namely, his body and blood. Christ's physical body is not

ubiquitous and there is no question of its being brought down from heaven to the table by the words of institution. Rather is it true to say that, thanks to the work of the Holy Spirit, the communicants are raised to the heavenly places to share communion with their Lord. So there is a real, but spiritual and personal, presence of Christ in the eucharist. But none of these solutions commanded general support among Protestants.

A theology of grace which emphasizes that salvation is entirely God's work is compelled to pay close attention to the biblical doctrine of divine predestination.* Salvation is entirely God's work. Faith itself is God's free gift. Is unbelief therefore also willed by God? The leading Reformers were agreed that God elected believers to eternal life and ensured their ultimate salvation on the basis of his own gracious decision, not because of any qualification in them. It was Calvin who made the most careful study of divine election. But he confessed that he could not see how it was possible to acknowledge election to life 'except as set over against reprobation' (*Institutes* III. xxiii. 1). Yet he does not put them on an equal basis. God actively elects those whom he saves but 'passes over' the reprobate. Even so, Calvin was convinced that even this 'passing over' was according to the divine plan, for the reprobate 'have been raised up by the just but inscrutable judgment of God to show forth his glory in their condemnation' (*Institutes* III. xxiv. 1–4).

Those who stood on the radical* wing of the Reformation found this predestinarianism unacceptable. Thus Melchior Hofmann (c. 1495–1543) in *The Ordinance of God* argued that those who were in covenant with God would through perseverance* attain election. Similarly, Balthasar Hübmaier (?1485–1528) in *On Free Will* developed the thesis that, despite the effects of sin, man is not entirely deprived of the capacity to choose: 'God gives power and capacity to all men in so far as they themselves desire it.'

The theology of the Protestant Reformation is an imposing intellectual achievement; it was to have a profound influence upon modern civilization.

Bibliography

Works: see under individual Reformers, and Reformers, English;* Confessions.* *LCC* vols. XV–XXVI presents writings by all the leading Reformers. The *Documents of Modern History* series (London, 1970–83) includes volumes on Luther, Calvin, Zwingli. Note also: H. J. Hillerbrand, *The Reformation in its Own Words* (London, 1964).

Studies: see under individual Reformers, *etc.* Note also: G. W. Bromiley, *Historical Theology: an Introduction* (Edinburgh, 1978); W. Cunningham, *The Reformers and the Theology of the Reformation* (Edinburgh, 1862); R. T. Jones, *The Great Reformation* (Leicester, 1986); E. Léonard, *A History of Protestantism*, 2 vols. (London, 1965–67); J. T. McNeill, *The History and Character of Calvinism* (New York, 1954); W. Pauck, *The Heritage of the Reformation* (Glencoe, IL, ²1961); J. Pelikan, *Reformation of Church and Dogma (1300–1700)* (*The Christian Tradition* 4; Chicago and London, 1983); B. M. G. Reardon, *Religious Thought in the Reformation* (London, 1981); G. H. Williams, *The Radical Reformation* (London, 1962).

R.T.J.

REFORMED THEOLOGY.

The classic representative statements of Reformed theology are found in the catechisms* and confessions* of the Reformed Churches; *e.g.* the French Confession (1559), the Scots Confession (1560), the Belgic Confession (1561), the Heidelberg Catechism (1563), the Second Helvetic Confession (1566), the Thirty-nine Articles of the Church of England (1562, 1571), the Canons of the Synod of Dort* (1619), the Westminster Confession of Faith and Catechisms (1647) and the Formula Consensus Helveticus (1675). On a secondary level are the writings of the leading representative theologians of those churches; *e.g.* Ulrich Zwingli* and Heinrich Bullinger* of Zurich, Martin Bucer* of Strasburg and Cambridge, John Calvin* and Theodore Beza* of Geneva, Peter Martyr Vermigli* of Strasburg, Oxford and Zurich, together with later great synthesizers such as Amandus Polanus (1561–1610) and Francis Turretin (1623–1687).

Historical emergence

Reformed theology developed within 16th-century Protestantism* in distinction from Lutheranism.* Initial disagreement between Luther and Zwingli emerged on the eucharist,* coming to an open breach at the Colloquy of Marburg (1529). Luther's so-called consubstantiation was based on his radical, innovative view of the *communicatio idiomatum* ('interchange of properties' between Christ's divine and human natures; see Christology*) as it found expression in the ubiquity of Christ's humanity. Other differences existed but were more of emphasis or else less divisive; *e.g.*, Lutheranism tended to posit more discontinuity between law and gospel,* to allow greater autonomy to the civil magistrate and to focus more narrowly on soteriology than did the Reformed. Yet agreement was immensely more extensive. Together with Rome and Constantinople, both held to the ecumenical dogmas* on the Trinity* and Christology.* On the central affirmations of the Reformation* (justification by faith,* the denial of transubstantiation, the number of sacraments,* the authority* of Scripture*) both were at one. Yet all attempts to achieve theological and ecclesiastical unity failed.

Principal characteristics

The centrality of God is a theme that pervades Reformed theology, which developed under the compelling demand of God's self-revelation in Scripture, its ultimate focus being on the Trinity with a more immediate focus on Jesus Christ as mediator. In distinction from Lutheranism, in which Luther's personal struggles for forgiveness bequeathed a concentration on soteriology narrowly focused on justification, the Reformed attempted to bring the whole of reality under the sway of the supremacy of God. This can be seen as eminently biblical, while avoiding the perils of faddish 'emphases'. The dominance of the doctrine of God comes to expression in a number of ways:

1. Human self-knowledge is attained only in the light of the knowledge of God. For Calvin, we are able to recognize who we are only when confronted by the supreme majesty and transcendent holiness of the living God as he makes himself known to us in his word by his Spirit. Thereby we are made cognizant of our sin and wretchedness, of the depravity that pervades our entire being. This Augustinianism* represents in reality a high view of man, since we are seen as moral beings responsible to God, known only in the light of God. Our deep-rooted alienation is floodlit by the greatness of God. Our true identity is as the image of God.*

2. Salvation in its entirety is the work of God. Because of the pervasive impact of sin we stand under the condemnation of God, unable to change our status or condition. Hence, Reformed theology has consistently testified to the sole and sovereign activity of God in salvation. Its origin is God's eternal purpose, his sovereign election of his people in Christ before the foundation of the world (Eph. 1:4), a choice made without regard to anything intrinsic in man. Correspondingly, although divergently nuanced, sovereign reprobation was consistently recognized. Therefore, Christ's purpose in incarnation* and atonement* was to save his people from their sins. His death was not intended to atone for every human being; for then either he would have failed, or the road would lead to universalism,* uniformly rejected as unbiblical. Nor did the cross provisionally atone for all while intrinsically accomplishing nothing, leaving atonement in suspense, contingent upon believing appropriation of Christ. Rather, Christ made effective atonement for the sins of all his people (see Atonement, Extent of*). Similarly, the Holy Spirit draws us invincibly to Christ. Since we were dead in sin (Eph. 2:1) and unable because unwilling to trust Christ, faith (indeed, all Christian virtue) is entirely a gift of God. The Spirit not only brings us to Christ but keeps us there. The whole process of sanctification* and perseverance* requires our strenuous effort in faith, but that effort itself is the Spirit's gift. Thus, Reformed theology maintained with vigour at Dort that none of the elect can finally fall away from grace so as to be lost.

Frequently, the mnemonic TULIP (Total depravity, Unconditional election, Limited atonement, Irresistible grace, Perseverance) is used to summarize the Canons of Dort and Reformed theology generally. However, this can present a truncated picture, an abridgement of the panoramic grandeur of the Reformed view of church and cosmos.

3. The whole of personal and corporate life is to be subjected to God. Reformed theology has consistently sought to order the whole of life according to the requirements of God in Scripture. From its beginnings in Zurich, Strasburg and Geneva, strong efforts were made to model civic as well as ecclesiastical life in this way. Reformed theology has been linked with the rise of both capitalism and socialism, with the spread of education, with literacy and science, besides revolution in France, the Netherlands, England, Scotland and the American colonies. Correspondingly, greater stress was laid on sanctification and the ongoing role of the law* in the Christian life than in Lutheranism. Consequently, Reformed theology has always sought to do justice to the corporate dimension of the gospel and, while increasingly influenced by individualism as time passed, nevertheless maintained this more effectively than other branches of Protestantism. Covenant theology* exerted a strong impact in this direction within Reformed theology, since, although the covenant of grace was related to individual soteriology, the notion of the covenant of works made by God with Adam before the fall was increasingly applied, from 1600, to the civic and political responsibilities of nations to God on the basis of a permanent and universally binding law of creation.

Christocentricity. In early Reformed theology, exemplified by Calvin, Knox* and Zanchius (1516–90), a consistent focus was evident on Christ as the ground of our knowledge of God, as the subject and object of election and, precisely because of the centrality of God, as the immediate focal centre of theology. Later, the impact of scholasticism, with its rigid logical deductivism, and covenant theology, with its preponderant use of the covenant concept (see below), led to the intrusion of other factors which then assumed a place of dominance. At times, attempts have been made to reassert a Christocentric Trinitarianism, in extreme form by Karl Barth.* A merit of such proposals has been to call attention to tendencies to depart from Reformed theology's roots.

Pluriformity. Reformed theology is not, nor has been, monolithic. It has possessed creative vitality sufficient to encompass diversity within an over-all consensus. For instance, before Dort differences existed on the question of limited atonement. Calvin was somewhat ambiguous, if not contradictory, on the matter, and may have leaned towards universal atonement. His successor Beza opposed the common formula (sufficient for all, efficient for the elect) on the grounds that it weakened the biblical stress on limited, or definite atonement. Dort, in fact, fashioned a compromise agreement between the powerful British delegation's universalizing tendency and the majority's particularizing concern.

The development of covenant theology indicates diversity too. Begun with Zwingli, Oecolampadius* and Bullinger, developed by Zacharius Ursinus (1534–83) and Kaspar Olevianus (1536–87), the movement came to maturity with Robert Rollock (1555–99) and was further elaborated by Johannes Cocceius (1603–69). While increasingly dominant in the 17th century, not all were covenant theologians in the sense of using the concept to structure their theology. Still more was this so before 1600. Differences existed on the nature of the covenant of grace: was it a unilateral and unconditional imposition by God or a bilateral pact with conditions to be fulfilled by man? Most early covenant theologians had one covenant, the covenant of grace. Later, the idea of the pre-fall covenant of works emerged. From 1648 a third, pre-temporal covenant was proposed. Each suggestion had its adherents. Additionally, diversity existed on questions of piety. Puritanism* in old and new England was oriented towards praxis,* sanctification and pastoralia, increasingly tending to anthropocentrism. Similar developments occurred in the Netherlands and Scotland. This represented a contrast with earlier Reformed theology and with the more scholastically oriented tradition. This pluriformity did not extend to Arminianism,* which was proscribed by Dort for undermining the gratuitous theocentricity of salvation.

Calvin and Calvinism

Reformed theology is often called 'Calvinism' due to the towering impact of John Calvin. However, this is not an entirely satisfactory term. First, owing to the above pluriformity Calvin neither could nor did impose his views on others. The autonomy of the various Reformed centres saw to that. For instance, his theology is not shaped by the covenant concept in the manner of later Reformed theology, yet after his death covenant theology became increasingly influential. Second, it is doubtful whether Calvin's distinctive theology, rooted in biblical exegesis, was properly grasped by many who came later. A recrudescence of Aristotelian* scholasticism led to a greater reliance on reason and bred a markedly different theological climate, characterized by clarity of definition, rigorous deductivism, greater use of causal analysis and liberal employment of the syllogism. Calvin's more fluid biblicism

went into eclipse. Consequently, many scholars posit a dichotomy between Calvin and the Calvinists. This can be overplayed, for, whatever the differences, the parties concerned saw themselves as colleagues not competitors. Despite his antipathy to Aristotle, Calvin did use Aristotelian causal analysis on occasion. However, the reintroduction of Aristotelian logic by Beza, Zanchius and Vermigli may well have encouraged the eventual ossification of Reformed theology by the late 17th century. The living biblical dynamic of earlier days, exemplified by a flood of biblical commentaries and Trinitarian-grounded systematic treatises based on the Apostles' Creed (Calvin's *Institutes* was one), became straight-jacketed in a rigid, logical, causal system. In fact, the ground was prepared for deism,* since God became simply the First Cause behind an immanent causal chain. Despite this, there was still a major contribution to the renewal of Reformed theology in 18th-century North America by Jonathan Edwards.*

Later developments

A revival of Reformed theology occurred in the 19th century in America, where the Princeton theology,* spearheaded by Charles Hodge,* A. A. Hodge (1823–86) and B. B. Warfield,* followed and adapted the scholastic Calvinism of Turretin. In Holland, Abraham Kuyper* and Herman Bavinck* also made a profound impact. Kuyper took his theology into public life, founding a university, a daily newspaper and a political party, eventually becoming prime minister.

In his massive reaction to liberalism, Karl Barth's debt to the Reformed theology of the 16th and 17th centuries is obvious on almost every page of *CD*, seen in his welcome, if exaggerated, Christocentricity and his vigorous repudiation of anthropocentrism. However, he never entirely eradicated the existentialism* so evident in his *Romans* commentary, and represented something of a truce between Reformed theology and neo-Kantianism.

The 20th century has witnessed major application of Reformed thinking to philosophy by, *e.g.*, Herman Dooyeweerd,* and the development of a unitary theology interacting with modern physics by T. F. Torrance.* Beyond that, Reformed theology shows an ongoing capacity for self-criticism and renewal which bodes well for the future, for, as Warfield argued, the future of Christianity is inseparable from the fortunes of the Reformed faith. Its concern for consistent theocentrism, its comprehensive world-view, and its at least implicit Christocentricity all exemplify its rigorous theological exploration of the gospel, its pursuit of 'faith seeking understanding', and its movement towards the integration of creation and redemption in Christ. Indeed, whenever prayer is offered the church is engaging in Reformed theology, acknowledging what on other occasions its theology and praxis may sometimes deny.

Bibliography
J. W. Baker, *Heinrich Bullinger and the Covenant: the Other Reformed Tradition* (Athens, OH, 1980); J. W. Beardslee (ed.), *Reformed Dogmatics* (New York, 1965); W. R. Godfrey, *Tensions within International Calvinism: the Debate on the Atonement at the Synod of Dort, 1618–1619* (PhD dissertation, Stanford University, 1974); B. Hall, 'Calvin against the Calvinists', in G. E. Duffield (ed.), *John Calvin* (Appleford, Abingdon, 1966); H. Heppe (ed.), *Reformed Dogmatics: Set Out and Illustrated from the Sources* (London, 1950); J. T. McNeill, *The History and Character of Calvinism* (New York, 1954); B. B. Warfield, 'Calvinism', in *Calvin and Augustine* (Philadelphia, 1974); H. E. Weber, *Reformation, Orthodoxie und Rationalismus*, Teil 2 (Gütersloh, 1937).

R.W.A.L.

REFORMERS, ENGLISH. The success enjoyed by the Protestant Reformation in England during the 16th century was the result of many factors, intellectual, political, theological and social, but at its heart was the work of a group of men who were personally devoted to the Protestant doctrines and fervently advocated them even at the cost of their own lives. Most prominent among their leaders were Thomas Bilney (*c.* 1495–1531), Hugh Latimer (1485–1555), Cranmer, Frith, Tyndale, Ridley, Robert Barnes (1495–1540), John Rogers (*c.* 1500–55) and John Bradford (1510–55). All of these men were burned at the stake as heretics* between the years 1531 and 1556. During the subsequent reign of Elizabeth I (1558–1603), however, the cause of Protestantism triumphed, and, largely through the writings of John Foxe (1516–

87), the testimony of the martyrs* made a profound impression on the English Christianity of the next four centuries. The writings of Tyndale, Frith, Ridley and Cranmer are of particular theological significance, and helped to shape the Protestantism which eventually took root in England. In their turn they clearly owed a great debt to the continental Reformation,* with Luther's* early influence being moderated by the growing prestige of the Reformed* scholars of Switzerland. At the same time, the native traditions of Wyclif* and the Lollard movement had their effect as well.

The first priority for the reformation of the church was given to the accurate translation* and dissemination of the Bible. William Tyndale (*c.* 1494–1536) devoted most of his labours to this end. His translation of the NT and parts of the OT laid the foundation for English versions to this day. In pursuing his goal so relentlessly, Tyndale exemplified the Protestant belief that the reform of the church and the salvation of men and women depended upon dispelling spiritual ignorance through a knowledge of the sure word of God. The practical consequences of their belief in the authority and sufficiency of Scripture* can be judged by the assault on those beliefs and practices they did not find in the Bible. Using the category of 'superstition' the Reformers dismissed such elements of Catholic religion as purgatory,* the use of images* in devotion, prayers for the dead, the veneration of saints* and the belief in sacred objects and contemporary miracles.* At the same time there was a deep commitment to the Christian tradition (see also Scripture and Tradition*), especially in the writings of the early church fathers. Councils* and fathers (see Patristic Theology*) were regarded as providing a guide to the interpretation of Scripture, although they were also thought to err on occasion and their judgments could be and were dissented from.

The doctrine of justification* by faith alone was the second great concern of the Reformers. John Frith (*c.* 1503–33), the brilliant younger friend and associate of Tyndale, illustrated its controlling influence, for example, in his work *A Disputation of Purgatory* (1531). It was not only the lack of scriptural support which caused Frith to dismiss purgatory; it was its inconsistency with the Pauline* view of grace,* especially that sinners are justified by faith in the merits of

Jesus Christ alone, not by works. Any other view brings discredit to the cross of Christ, for it assumes that the blood of Christ is ineffective to secure forgiveness of sin (see Guilt and Forgiveness*). It also underestimates the gravity of sin* and its grip on the human personality. To trust in the message of the cross is to be truly purged. The tribulation of the Christian life is also a purgatory, but it is completed at death when all are fully purified. Frith, like the other Reformers, completed his teaching on grace by espousing a doctrine of election in which God's initiative in salvation was thoroughly secured.

The doctrines of Scripture and grace thus provided the standard by which all was to be reformed. The charge levelled by their opponents that their doctrine of grace was antinomian (see Law and Gospel*) led to a constant emphasis by the Protestants on the need for good works as a fruit of faith. In Tyndale, for example, this found particular expression in a use of the theme of covenant,* for which he has been somewhat unjustly suspected of legalism. Thomas Cranmer (1489–1556) used different language but with the same purposes in his classic Homily of Salvation, where he described justification by faith alone as 'the strong rock and foundation of Christian religion' and pressed home the necessity of obedience to God as the fruit of a true faith, without which a person is not saved.

The greatest controversies of the English Reformation revolved around the doctrine of the mass (see Eucharist*). It was at this point above all that the understanding of Scripture and faith held by Cranmer, Frith and Ridley reached its most perilous expression in their own society. Holding the views of Scripture and justification which they did, they could not but differ from Roman Catholic theology* at a point regarded by Catholics of prime significance. For this they suffered the consequences at the stake.

Nicholas Ridley (c. 1500–55) argued that the whole debate on the mass could be reduced to one key issue: whether the matter of the sacrament* was 'the natural substance of bread, or the natural substance of Christ's own body'. If this question was answered in terms of Christ's body, there would follow the idea of transubstantiation, with the devotional honour due to the sacrament, the sacrificial offering of Christ by the priest on the altar,

and the reception of the flesh and blood of Christ by the unworthy. Such consequences were at odds with the Christology and soteriology of the Reformers, and they asserted that the body of Christ was and remained in heaven, the bread and the wine being the sacrament or sign of the body, and that the faithful person (and he alone) fed on Christ spiritually by faith. These were the views of the mature Cranmer, and it is they which are encapsulated liturgically in the Book of Common Prayer, especially the 1552 revision, and in the Thirty-nine Articles of Religion (see Confessions*).

Another focus for debate was the doctrine of the church.* The struggle with Roman Catholicism over the role of the papacy* was increasingly understood in terms of the war between God and antichrist,* with the pope supplying the latter role. This gave the Reformers a way of interpreting the history of the church and offering theological insights about the significance of current events. There remained, however, the difficult problem of the state.* Cranmer had to attempt to give royal authority a rightful place in the affairs of the church, without acceding to unlawful constraints. Tyndale strongly declared in his Obedience of the Christian Man the necessity of obedience to all lawful authority, but with the caveat that the Christian most obey God rather than men. At times this teaching created an alliance with the Tudors; at times its constraints proved difficult and even fatal. Ultimately, for the major Reformers, as for many others, faithfulness to Christ as the head of the church over which he rules through the Scriptures demanded an example of obedience which has resounded even to the present day.

Bibliography

R. Bauckham, Tudor Apocalypse (Appleford, 1978); A. G. Dickens, The English Reformation (London, 1964); G. E. Duffield, The Work of William Tyndale (Appleford, 1964); P. E. Hughes, Theology of the English Reformers (Grand Rapids, ²1980); D. B. Knox, The Doctrine of Faith in the Reign of Henry VIII (London, 1961); M. L. Loane, Masters of the English Reformation (London, 1954); J. I. Packer and G. E. Duffield, The Work of Thomas Cranmer (Appleford, 1965); T. H. L. Parker (ed.), English Reformers (LCC 26; London, 1966); A. Townsend (ed.), Writings of John Bradford, 2 vols. (1848,

1853; repr. Edinburgh, 1979); N. T. Wright, *The Work of John Frith* (Appleford, 1978).

P.F.J.

REGENERATION. This important concept relates the Christian to God and to fellow believers.

1. Biblical evidence

'Regeneration' or 'new birth' (Tit. 3:5; Jn. 3:3; 1 Pet. 1:3) describes the inner renewal by the Spirit of God, which takes place when a person becomes a Christian. The decisive historical grounds for this renewal are the coming of Jesus Christ and his vicarious death (Tit. 2:12; 3:4,6; Jn. 3:16). A person receives forgiveness of sins through belief in Christ, and is born again to a life characterized by faith, love and hope.

The biblical teaching on regeneration includes the following emphases: a. It is not the result of human endeavour, but a creative act of God's Spirit (Jn. 1:13). b. It is a once-for-all event, in which God substantially intervenes in a person's life (Tit. 3:5, 'saved'; *cf.* the contrast between the past and the present in vv. 3–5). c. It involves being added to the family of God: the regenerated person becomes a child of God, and is also incorporated into the fellowship of the children of God.

2. History of the doctrine of regeneration

Baptism and regeneration are linked in the NT (Tit. 3:5). Because infant baptism became a general practice in the early church, and it was assumed that regeneration came about at the same time, the biblical understanding of regeneration was forgotten. The Reformers, by contrast, emphasized that without personal faith (where appropriate), baptism* would hold no benefit. But it was only with the rise of the Anabaptists,* the development of pietism* and the Evangelical Awakenings that special emphasis was placed on regeneration as the individual *starting point* of the Christian life. (Calvin himself saw regeneration as a *life-long* process.) In the Roman Catholic Church and in some Protestant denominations (*e.g.* the Lutheran Church), the doctrine of baptismal regeneration is still represented. Liberal theology tends to understand regeneration as an educational process of personal development. Dialectical theology* interprets regeneration as a trans-subjective word encounter,

and, influenced by this, the theology of revolution* sees regeneration as social renewal and the amelioration of political realities towards achieving the kingdom of God.*

3. The doctrine of regeneration in systematic theology

A biblically orientated theology of regeneration must emerge from the biblical evidence itself. Thus regeneration is a verbal illustration of the spiritual renewal of people at the beginning of their Christian lives. It describes the same event as conversion.* If regeneration is placed first, it leads to sacramentalism or mysticism; if placed afterwards, it leads to synergism. At regeneration both justification* and sanctification* take place, but whereas regeneration and conversion inaugurate the Christian life, the state of justification and the process of sanctification characterize that life in its entirety (Phil. 3:12).

Regeneration is the beginning of the Christian life of fellowship* with God as heavenly Father, a fellowship characterized by freedom from fear and by loving gratitude. At the same time, however, regeneration places the believer in a God-given spiritual relationship to all fellow Christians as brothers and sisters. Regeneration is therefore an organic start for the realization of human fellowship free from selfishness.

Bibliography
H. Burkhardt, *The Biblical Doctrine of Regeneration* (Exeter, 1978); B. Citron, *New Birth: A Study of the Evangelical Doctrine of Conversion in the Protestant Fathers* (Edinburgh, 1951).

H.B.

REINCARNATION, see METEMPSYCHOSIS.

RELATIVISM. To say that truth is relative is to claim that it varies from one time, place or person to another, and that it depends on the changing conditions they bring: that there is no universal truth, valid for all peoples at all times and places. This claim has been repeated throughout history. Protagoras, the Greek sophist, asserted that each man is the measure of all things.

Relativism today is to be found in most areas of enquiry. Ethical relativists see moral standards as culturally relative; situational ethics rejects universally binding moral rules in favour of decisions dependent on their peculiar contexts. Religious relativists view different religious beliefs and practices as legitimate products of different historical and cultural settings. Relativism has even arisen in the natural sciences, with the realization that the growth of scientific knowledge is in measure a function of personal and sociological, rather than just experimental or mathematical, factors. Wherever subjective or sociological influences are admitted, as distinct from the objective and universal, there relativism is likely to make its appearance.

A number of historical developments have encouraged this trend. Twentieth-century studies in the sociology of knowledge have uncovered influences on human learning which were previously overlooked. The extension of evolutionary concepts to the history of religion and of ethics has popularized the notion that changing ideas are historically dependent. Yet running through these developments is the over-all secularization* process, which turned Western culture from its theistic way of thinking to a naturalistic world-view lacking any transcendent point of reference. Theism had provided a transcendent locus for universally valid truth, in the wisdom of the eternal, self-revealing God. Without an adequate substitute for its divine locus, truth is dislocated and becomes relative to changing natural conditions.

Critics of relativism point out that even if beliefs are as diverse as the relativist claims, this does not mean that they *ought* to be so; many of our differences in fact yield to reason and evidence. But the diversity seems greatly overstated, for similarities plainly exist between different cultures; common human concerns arise from generic aspects of human nature and of the world in which we all live. The supposed dependency of human beliefs on cultural and historical conditions is likewise exaggerated, for critical and creative thought transcends in measure the ideas we inherit from others. Indeed, if all human beliefs vary and depend totally on local conditions, so too will belief in relativism. Total relativism cannot be unchangingly true: it is a self-refuting position. But if not all beliefs vary and not all are totally dependent, then at least some universal truths are valid for all times and places.

Relativism therefore boils down to epis-temological* questions. Is there any objective locus for truth? Can human knowledge transcend its subjective and historical conditions sufficiently to apprehend universally valid truth? Does divine revelation give us access to universal truth?

Bibliography
N. L. Gifford, *When in Rome* (New York, 1983); J. Rachels, *The Elements of Moral Philosophy* (New York, 1986), ch. 3; R. Trigg, *Reason and Commitment* (Cambridge, 1973).

See also Bibliography for Truth.

A.F.H.

RELIGION. Although the meaning of the term may seem obvious, there is no generally agreed definition and it is used in widely differing senses by different writers. In its original Latin usage (*religio*), Cicero defined it as the giving of proper honour, respect and reverence to the divine, by which he meant the gods (Cicero, *The Nature of the Gods*, 2.3.8, and *Invention*, 2.53.161). He distinguished 'religion', a dutiful honouring of the gods, from 'superstition', an empty fear of them (*The Nature of the Gods*, 1.4.2).

It is useful to start with this narrower definition of religion as belief in God or gods, together with the practical results of such a belief as expressed in worship, ritual, a particular view of the world and of the nature and destiny of man, and the way someone ought to live his daily life. It is also useful to distinguish, as Cicero did, between religion itself and other things which may be associated with it or are a part of it.

The widest possible usage of the term is seen in *Discovering an Approach: Religious Education in Primary Schools* (London, 1977), which claims to use it 'both in the strict sense to refer to a particular religion and in a looser sense to embrace religious and non-religious belief systems'. This is very confusing and quite unjustified.

The term 'implicit religion' is used in religious education to cover the study of things which are not religious in themselves, but can have religious significance for religious people. Thus the beauty of flowers is in itself solely aesthetic, but may be viewed religiously as the handiwork of God, and thus become part of explicit religion.

It is disputed whether a faith such as

575

Buddhism* is a religion or not. In its broader forms, where there is worship of gods, and perhaps of the Buddha himself, it is clearly a religion. But in its narrower form it may be considered as a philosophy of life. Some (such as Donald Horder) would insist on changing the definition of religion to include Buddhism.

Some further distinctions will help to define religion. Theology is an intellectual, systematic and theoretical study, while religion refers to the whole man and his practice. Religion is the practice; theology is the theory. Politics, as such, deals with this-worldly affairs, while religion has a divine reference. But a religious person's political view will naturally be shaped by his religious views and his religious scale of values.

Ethics deals with a way of living and of treating people, and can be entirely non-theistic. Religion includes a way of living, but it is related to the divine. Ceremony and ritual of themselves are purely external actions, whereas religion is both internal and external; religion may be expressed in ceremonials and rituals, but ceremonials and rituals do not necessarily express religion.

Sport may produce very great enthusiasm on a human level. Religion may produce a similar enthusiasm and emotional excitement, but it has a divine reference. Whether the strong feelings in religion come directly from God, or whether they are generated at least in part by association with others of similar persuasion, they are at any rate linked with religious belief. To a psychologist, the emotions involved in sport and in religion may be very similar; but that does not justify including sport in the category of religion, as some do. The similarity is only superficial and at one level.

A distinction was made by Barth* between religion – even the Christian religion – and faith, which comes from divine revelation. Barth stressed the sovereignty of God so much that he denied any possibility of knowing God at all by human effort, and he considered that all religion was a human activity. God could only be known by his self-revelation in Christ, and that could be accepted only by faith. So Barth spoke of 'the judgment of divine revelation upon all religion' (*CD*, I.2, p. 299). 'Apart from and without Jesus Christ we can say nothing at all about God and man and their relationship one with another' (IV.1, p. 45).

Brunner* similarly said that 'revelation – in the Christian sense of the word – means something entirely different from all forms of religion and philosophy' (*The Mediator*, London, 1934, p. 202). But 'no religion in the world, not even the most primitive, is without some elements of truth'; this, however, 'is not half the truth but distorted truth' (p. 33). 'In distinction from all other forms of religion the Christian religion is faith in the one Mediator' (p. 40).

The study of religion, or religious studies, has become increasingly popular as an academic subject. It has a different scope from theology, and is more closely related to anthropology, in that it examines human experience.

Bibliography

J. Bowker, *The Sense of God* (Oxford, 1973); E. Brunner, *The Mediator* (London, 1934); H. Gollwitzer (ed.), *Karl Barth: Church Dogmatics. A Selection with Introduction* (Edinburgh, 1961); H. Kraemer, *Religion and the Christian Faith* (London, 1956); E. Sharpe, *Comparative Religion: A History* (London, 1975); N. Smart, *The Religious Experience of Mankind* (London, 1971).

K.G.H.

RELIGIONS, THEOLOGY OF. Even though Christianity has been in some contact with other religions throughout its history, it is only in the last two centuries that a thorough knowledge of the great non-Christian religions has become available in the Christian world. With increased contact between adherents of various faiths and Christians the relationship between Christianity and other religions and the status of other religions have become pressing questions for many theologians. It is such questions that give rise to various theologies of religion. Alan Race suggests three main types, *viz.* the inclusivist, the pluralist and the exclusivist.

The *inclusivist* believes that God can be known through each of the world's religious traditions, but that full and complete knowledge of him is to be found only in Christianity. This idea of Christianity as the fulfilment of man's quest for the truth has an ancient pedigree in the Logos* theology of Justin Martyr, the 2nd-century Christian apologist,* and was revived in the last century by some of the founders of the modern study of religion such as F. Max Müller (1823–1900). This position is also clearly expressed in the work of J. N. Farquhar (1861–1929), the liberal Protestant missionary of the Indian YMCA. Since Vatican II (1962–65) it has become popular among some Roman Catholic theologians, the most famous being Karl Rahner.* While accepting the Catholic dogma that there is no salvation outside the church, Rahner broadens the meaning of the church* to include those within non-Christian religions who belong spiritually though not actually to the church and whom he describes as 'anonymous Christians'.*

The *pluralist* believes that God can be known through each of the world's religious traditions and that Christianity must, therefore, take its place by the side of other religions as an authentic way to God. Earlier liberal Protestants such as Troeltsch* and W. E. Hocking (1873–1966) saw this as the only logical conclusion of abandoning the traditional view of revelation.* Among the contemporary exponents of this view are John Hick,* Ninian Smart (b. 1927) and W. Cantwell Smith (b. 1916). Hick, *e.g.*, calls for a Copernican revolution in theology so that, just as people eventually had to accept that the sun is the centre of the universe, so modern men and women will have to accept that God and not Christianity is the centre of the religious universe, and that people everywhere worship the same God though by means of differing ideas and practices. Obvious results of adopting this stance are the removal of Christ as the central figure of revelation and the replacing of mission or proclamation by dialogue as the appropriate mode for inter-religious relationships.

The *exclusivist* view is that there is only one way to God, and that that way is to be found in Christianity. The non-Christian religions are, therefore, false attempts to find God. This is essentially the orthodox Christian view, and it can be found sensitively developed in the context of our modern situation by authors such as H. Kraemer,* J. H. Bavinck,* S. Neill (1900–84), L. Newbigin (b. 1909) and J. N. D. Anderson (b. 1908). The most impressive modern statement is probably to be found in Karl Barth.* Barth contrasts religion and revelation. All religion, including Christianity, is by definition unbelief, or man's futile quest to find God by means of his own resources.

Revelation, on the other hand, contradicts all man's effort and throws him back absolutely upon the grace of God in Jesus Christ. All exclusivists share this heavy emphasis upon the centrality and uniqueness* of Jesus Christ compared with the inclusivists, who tend to an idealist conception of Christ, and the pluralists, who abandon traditional Christology altogether.

See also: CHRISTIANITY AND OTHER RELIGIONS.

Bibliography

J. N. D. Anderson, *Christianity and World Religions* (Leicester, 1984); K. Barth, *CD* I.2; J. H. Bavinck, *The Church Between the Temple and the Mosque* (Grand Rapids, MI, n.d.); J. Hick and B. L. Hebblethwaite (eds.), *Christianity and Other Religions* (London, 1980); E. J. Hughes, *William Cantwell Smith: A Theology for the World* (London, 1986); P. Knitter, *No Other Name? A Critical Survey of Christian Attitudes towards the World Faiths* (London, 1985); L. Newbigin, *The Open Secret* (Grand Rapids, 1978); A. Race, *Christians and Religious Pluralism* (London, 1983); W. C. Smith, *The Meaning and End of Religion* (London, 1978); *idem, Towards a World Theology* (London, 1980).

D.A.Hu.

RELIGIOUS EXPERIENCE. It is sometimes maintained that we can only believe in God *in spite of* experience, as 'we walk by faith, not by sight' (2 Cor. 5:7, RSV). But this view, it may be argued, besides forgetting that we do at least 'see' partially (*cf.* 1 Cor. 13:12), neglects the fact that walking by faith is itself a religious experience. The witness of Jeremiah, Job, or Jesus in the garden of Gethsemane, suggests that even experience of God's absence is a real experience, as real as estrangement from a loved one or a bereavement. Furthermore, the laments in the Psalms remind us that God's absence can be experienced corporately (*cf.* Pss. 44; 60; 74; 79; 80) as well as individually, whenever his people, perhaps under persecution or the pressures of secularism, find themselves forced to ask 'How shall we sing the Lord's song in a foreign land?' (Ps. 137:4, RSV).

These contrasting views stem from different understandings of religious experience. The first view defines it quite strictly in terms of particular and often dramatic or unusual events which are recognizable from Scripture or mystical theology,* or from certain characteristics like the senses of 'encounter' with the 'Holy' identified by Buber* and Otto.* The second view defines religious experience more generally in terms of the responses of people who are open to understanding any part of their experience of life and the world around them in a religious way, whether or not it occurs in a religious context. If interpretation of such experiences can be integrated with other religious beliefs it can form an important element of an individual's personal theology, or even be shared and systematized as the theology of the church or a substantial part of it. Reflection on experience played an important part in the early church's definitions of the person of Christ and the doctrine of the Trinity (see Creeds*). It is also a significant aspect of recent trends in theology. Interest in spirituality* and calls for contextualization,* liberation theology* and narrative theology* are, at least in part, protests against theologies which seem divorced from experience and unaware that religious reflection without religious experience is empty.

However, as it is also true that religious experience without religious reflection is blind, every claim to an experience of God requires examination, whether it appears to be direct and objective (the first view, above) or more indirect and subjective (the second view). Since all human experience has both an objective and a subjective side, every religious experience invites assessment of its source, nature and interpretation.

The NT writers present Christianity as a way of life to be experienced and not just a theory to be believed, yet they are not naive or uncritical about the compelling nature of religious experiences. Jesus and the apostles were not the only miracle-workers of their time. Even within the church it was necessary from the beginning to 'test the spirits', to see if they were from God, in terms of their effect on love, truth and unity in the fellowship (cf. 1 Cor. 12 – 14; 1 Thes. 5:21; 1 Jn. 4). Such doctrinal and ethical tests have been applied ever since to both individual and corporate religious experience. For since Christianity has no concept of religious experiences that do not have doctrinal or ethical consequences, or of experiences of God that do not involve a human response, it considers religious com-

mitment without discernment as harmful as discernment without commitment.

Right from the time of the desert fathers (cf. Asceticism and Monasticism*) mystical theology* has underlined the importance of assessing the source and nature of religious experience and has assumed that it would all, whether apparently ordinary or extraordinary, be discussed with one's spiritual director. Protestants have tended to stress the individual's direct access to God, but there is a tradition of personal direction or counselling of a more occasional and less authoritative kind in the letters of some of the Reformers and Puritans. Noteworthy too is the Quaker and early Methodist practice of group discernment which has been revived in some modern Christian communities.

Movements within the church which stress the importance of experience (cf. R. A. Knox, *Enthusiasm*, Oxford, 1950) also invite assessment. Jonathan Edwards,* for example, chronicled the New England Awakening in his *Narrative of Surprising Conversions* (1737), and later in *A Treatise Concerning Religious Affections* (1746) gave his mature reflections on its significance. His careful discrimination between its positive and negative features was a forerunner of William James' approach in *Varieties of Religious Experience* (1902; ed. M. E. Marty, Harmondsworth, 1983), which set the tone for modern studies. These supplement theological concerns with psychological and sociological criteria, philosophical analysis and comparison with drug-induced experiences, as well as widening the field to include other religions beside Christianity.

This last development raises the question of truth-claims between religions and the place of religious experience in validating them. If a religious experience is judged to be valid and significant within the religion in which it occurs, does it make that religion more true than another? Debate on this issue continues between those who claim that all religious experience is fundamentally the same (although inevitably interpreted within the religious context in which it happens), and those who point out that many Christian claims to direct experience of God are specifically Trinitarian in character and could not be confused with experiences of 'union with the One' in other religions.

A single interpretation or classification of religious experience is also difficult to square with evidence that some experiences are destructive or demonic, and other positive experiences of bliss or ecstasy occur outside any religious context to people who have no religious beliefs. It might be more helpful in the latter case to distinguish between, say, nature mysticism and religious mysticism, than to dilute the concept of religious experience to include everything. Yet such verbal distinctions, however useful and necessary, could not replace assessment of the religious value of an experience on criteria derived from one's understanding of revelation* and natural theology.*

See also: PSYCHOLOGY OF RELIGION.

Bibliography

C. D. Batson and W. L. Ventis, The Religious Experience (New York, 1982); J. Bowker, The Sense of God (Oxford, 1973); idem, The Religious Imagination and the Sense of God (Oxford, 1978); A. Hardy, The Spiritual Nature of Man (Oxford, 1979); M. Kelsey, Encounter with God (London, 1974); H. D. Lewis, Our Experience of God (London, 1959); A. O'Hear, Experience, Explanation and Faith (London, 1984); H. P. Owen, The Christian Knowledge of God (London, 1969); N. Smart, The Religious Experience of Mankind (London, 1971); R. Woods (ed.), Understanding Mysticism (London, 1981).

P.N.H.

RELIGIOUS LANGUAGE. This naturally comes in many forms: commandments, questions, moral judgments, historical statements, praise, prayer and so on. Most of these it has in common with non-religious language. There are, however, two ways in which it has been thought special problems arise, particularly where statements are made about God.

One has been recognized for centuries. God cannot be described in human words without apparently making him out to be less than he truly is. Language developed to describe the created, not the creator (cf. Anthropomorphism*). Yet we have no other words, and if we invented some, even if they were not false to Scripture, how should we understand them except by defining them in terms of words we understand already?

Various solutions have been proposed which deny the literal truth of certain religious assertions but maintain their truth in some non-literal yet still supposedly adequate sense. One such is the theory of analogy:* words applied to God are to be taken as meaning something analogous to their normal meaning, but differing in that they are being used of so different a subject.

Another is that religious terms are symbolic. This is an extremely vague word, variously used. 'Symbol'* may perhaps best be understood as a kind of metaphor which cannot be rendered into non-metaphorical terms. According to the view of C. A. Campbell (1897–1974), the emotions we feel on encountering or contemplating God (e.g. adoration) feel like, point in the same direction as, emotions like love or admiration directed towards humans, and in the opposite direction to emotions like contempt or hate. Qualities which we love and admire in humans, like goodness, can therefore act as symbols for the divine qualities to which they correspond. Rather similarly, C. S. Lewis* pointed to the way that poets achieve their effects by arousing in us emotions appropriate to the subject of the poem, and so indirectly describe something we have never even experienced; some, though not all, religious language works in the same way.

The views of H. L. Mansel (1820–71) and Edwyn Bevan (1870–1943) were 'symbolist' in a different way. Human notions of God must be inadequate; but those revealed in Scripture are the best available, and enough to guide our lives, though probably not to allow speculation. (A problem here is whether 'revelation'* itself is an inadequate concept.)

A less radical approach is to hold that concepts applied to God are in fact the 'human' concepts, but with all defects found in human examples removed, and the qualities themselves conceived to be in complete perfection. Thomists* regard this as a form of analogy. Duns Scotus,* on the other hand, and surely correctly, thought it was to use the words in their natural sense – so that our original difficulty was perhaps unwarranted after all.

More recently, debate has arisen over problems raised originally by logical positivism*, which claimed that all statements (other than tautologies) must, to have meaning, be verifiable through the senses. Many statements made by Christians seemed to fail this test: how could 'Jesus Christ is my saviour', for instance, be so verified? Even though logical positivism proper did not last, questions of meaning in religious language remained. Words and sentences, it was pointed out, can be used in many ways apart from reporting facts, and some philosophers (*e.g.* R. Braithwaite, R. M. Hare (b. 1919), D. Z. Phillips, b. 1934) have contended that religious assertions are not claims about matters of fact at all. What they *are* is disputed: they may express a resolve, or a way to understand the world; or, in terms derived from Wittgenstein,* religion may be seen as a 'form of life' or 'language-game'. Debate *within* the 'form of life' is legitimate, but about the form itself there can be none; either it is adopted or it is not. Since no facts are asserted, all religions become immune to criticism, and, equally, impossible to defend with apologetics.* (So, some hold, do other 'language-games' such as science – or astrology.) The obvious difficulty with such theories is that few professed believers have realized there was no factual content to what they said; they have supposed that in believing in God, or Christ's salvation, or eternal life, they believed in something true. (And, equally, unbelievers have thought Christians believed in something false which could be criticized for its falsity.)

More moderate philosophers have argued that while everyday sensory experiences may not justify religious assertions, there are other experiences which can and do. Thus Ian Ramsey* suggested that religious situations involved special discernments associated with total commitment, and it was hardly surprising that odd language was needed to talk about them. This language, he thought, often took the form of using a 'model'* and qualifying it, *e.g.* by describing God as *infinitely* loving – a notion fairly close to that of analogy. John Hick* and I. M. Crombie have pointed out that Christianity (like many other religions) believes that this life is not the only one, and that Christian assertions which cannot be checked now will be checkable hereafter.

It seems quite possible that believers' statements do not normally need to be thought of as using special language. (There are, of course, special 'technical' words confined to religious or theological contexts, but this is true of many other disciplines, from biochemistry to football.) What *are* special about them are the enormously important subjects about which they are made, and the commitment which normally accompanies their assertion.

Bibliography

E. R. Bevan, *Symbolism and Belief* (London, 1962); C. A. Campbell, *On Selfhood and Godhood* (London, 1957); J. Duns Scotus, *Philosophical Writings*, ed. A. Wolter (London, 1962), pp. 19–25; J. Hick (ed.), *The Existence of God* (London, 1964); A. Keightley, *Wittgenstein, Grammar and God* (London, 1976); C. S. Lewis, *Christian Reflections* (London, 1967); E. Mascall, *Words and Images* (London, 1957); D. Z. Phillips, *Faith and Philosophical Enquiry* (London, 1970); I. Ramsey, *Religious Language* (London, 1957); R. Trigg, *Reason and Commitment* (London, 1973). See also Bibliography on Analogy.

R.L.S.

RENAISSANCE, see HUMANISM.

REPENTANCE. The OT often speaks of repentance to describe Israel's turning back to their God (*e.g.* 2 Ch. 7:14), in response to a promise of restored fortunes for the nation. In the NT, however, the preaching of repentance is greatly heightened and given specific content for the individual. This feature starts with the preaching of John the Baptist (Mt. 3:5–12; Lk. 3:7–14). The Gk. words used throughout the NT are mainly forms related to the verb *metanoein*, 'to change one's mind'. This small phrase, however, describes a radical change in the individual's *disposition*, for the change of mind concerns his judgment upon himself and his sin together with an evaluation of God's demands upon him. The transformation implied, therefore, is not a matter merely of mental judgment, but of new religious and moral attitudes (a turning to *God*, 1 Thes. 1:9) and of new behaviour (Acts 26:20), as John's preaching spelt out.

Since repentance is God-directed and affirms newly received principles, it is inseparable from faith* by which alone comes the knowledge of God. It is a serious misrepresentation of Scripture to separate repentance and faith as if the former were in any sense a condition of receiving the latter. This is clear from the fact that apostolic preaching sometimes summoned people to repent (Acts 2:38; 17:30; 26:20) but on other occasions to believe (Acts 13:38–41; 16:31). Equally, forgiveness of sins follows upon either repentance or faith (Acts 2:38; 3:19; 10:43). Repentance and faith, therefore, are simply two aspects of the same movement, though it is true that, in the case of faith, the NT emphasizes consciousness of Christ (Acts 20:21). Hence repentance, like faith, is regarded as a gift of God (Acts 5:31; 11:15–18; 2 Tim. 2:25).

The importance of repentance is seen from the early preaching of the apostles and from its place as a first principle of the Christian message (Heb. 6:1). Although there is in conversion a decisive change of mind, the renewing of the mind towards God is a *continuous* process (Rom. 12:2; Eph. 4:23) just as faith is to be increased. Turning, and renewal of faith in the Christian's life, are the active side of the process called sanctification,* of which regeneration* and preservation are the passive aspects.

Due to the increased emphasis on penitence (sorrow for sin) associated with repentance, the idea of confession and penance* came to overshadow the sense of 'changing one's mind', and it was Luther* who rediscovered the NT Gk. word, *metanoein*. With this he replaced the prevailing Latin Vulgate rendering of 'do penance', and allied repentance closely to faith.

It cannot be stressed too much that repentance is a moral act involving the turning of the whole person in spirit, mind and will to consent, and subjection, to the will of God. It is in a very real sense a moral miracle, a gift of grace. Terms often confused with repentance, such as penitence, remorse or penance,* do not do justice to the impact of grace which we call repentance.

Bibliography

F. Lauback and J. Goetzmann in *NIDNTT* I, pp. 353–362; J. Murray, *Redemption – Accomplished and Applied* (Edinburgh, 1973); W. Telfer, *The Forgiveness of Sins* (London, 1959).

R.K.

REPRESENTATION, see Substitution and Representation.

REPROBATION, see Predestination.

RESURRECTION, GENERAL. Belief in a resurrection of persons from the dead finds expression in at least eight OT passages (Jb. 19:26; Pss. 17:15; 49:15; 73:24; Is. 26:19; 53:10–12; Dn. 12:2, 13), while resurrection terminology is borrowed on two notable occasions (Ezk. 37:1–14; Ho. 6:2) to portray a future national and spiritual restoration brought about by a return from exile.

Five types of resurrection may be distinguished in NT usage: 1. the past physical resurrection of certain individuals to renewed mortal life (*e.g.* Lk. 7:14–15; Jn. 11:43–44; Heb. 11:35); 2. the past bodily resurrection of Christ to immortality* (Rom 6:9); 3. the past spiritual resurrection of believers to new life in Christ (Col. 2:12); 4. the future bodily resurrection of believers to immortality (1 Cor. 15:42, 52); 5. the future personal resurrection of unbelievers to judgment* (Jn. 5:29; Acts 24:15). Occasionally, then, resurrection refers to mere reanimation, but it generally also implies transformation (1 Cor. 15:52, 'raised immortal') and exaltation (Acts 2:32–33; 5:30–31). In its fullest sense, resurrection is God's raising of persons from the realm of the dead to new and unending life in his presence. It is an event leading to a state.

The resurrection of Christ is both the pledge and the paradigm of the bodily resurrection of believers (1 Cor. 6:14; 15:20, 23, 48–49; Col. 1:18). Moreover, believers are now raised 'with Christ' (Eph. 2:6; Col. 2:12; 3:1) in that they share his victory over sin and his risen life (Rom. 6:4, 10–11). The Holy Spirit* also is closely associated with believers' resurrection, being 'the Spirit of life' (Rom. 8:2) who 'imparts life' (2 Cor. 3:6). According to Paul, the Spirit is the pledge and means of a future resurrection transformation and the one who sustains resurrection life (Rom. 8:10–11; 2 Cor. 5:5; 13:4; Eph. 1:13–14).

Redeemed humanity's resurrection is linked to the whole creation's renewal in Rom. 8:18–25; 1 Cor. 15:20–28; Phil. 3:20–21. As at the fall, so in the restoration, what affects man affects all of creation. 'New heavens and a new earth' (2 Pet. 3:13; *cf.* Rev. 21:1, 5) correspond to our new, resurrection body.

Only a few characteristics of the resurrection body of believers are mentioned in Scripture. It is of divine origin (1 Cor. 15:38; 2 Cor. 5:1–2); it is 'spiritual' (1 Cor. 15:44, 46), not meaning 'composed of spirit', but 'animated and guided by the spirit', fully responsive to the Christian's perfected spirit which in turn will be completely swayed by God's Spirit, and also free from sinful inclinations and without physical instincts (1 Cor. 6:13–14); it is imperishable, glorious and powerful (1 Cor. 15:42–43), that is, free from sickness or decay, and of unparalleled beauty and endless energy; it is angel-like (Mk. 12:25; Lk. 20:36), without sexual passions or procreative powers, and deathless; it is heavenly (1 Cor. 15:40, 47–49), perfectly suited to the ecology of heaven.

Jn. 5:29 distinguishes 'a resurrection that leads to life' from 'a resurrection that issues in judgment' (cf. Acts 24:15; Rev. 20:4–6). All persons will be subjected to the divine assessment of their works as the evidence of their belief or unbelief (Jn. 3:36; Acts 10:42; Rom. 2:12–16; 1 Pet. 1:17; Rev. 20:12–13) but two distinct verdicts will be entered – eternal life, or condemnation to eternal perdition (Mt. 25:46; 2 Thes. 1:8–9). A universal judgment implies a universal resurrection, although the unrighteous are 'raised' only in the sense that by divine power they are reanimated and appear before God in some undisclosed personal form.

In the Western Church the confessional formula 'the resurrection of the flesh' was used. Although some have argued that 'flesh' here means 'complete humanity' of 'the person himself', more probably it was intended to denote 'the body of flesh' as distinct from the soul. In the Eastern Church, after the Council of Constantinople (381), the biblical phrase 'the resurrection of the dead' was customary. Both of these traditional expressions stress the personal continuity between the pre- and post-resurrection states, but neither phrase denies the need for the transformation of the body before the kingdom of God is inherited (1 Cor. 15:50).

See also: ESCHATOLOGY; IMMORTALITY; INTERMEDIATE STATE.

Bibliography

H. C. C. Cavallin, Life After Death, part I (Lund, 1974); R. B. Gaffin, The Centrality of the Resurrection (Grand Rapids, MI, 1978); M. J. Harris, Raised Immortal (London, 1983); idem, 'Resurrection and Immortality', Them 1 (1976), pp. 50–55; R. Martin-Achard, From Death to Life (Edinburgh, 1960); J. A. Schep, The Nature of the Resurrection Body (Grand Rapids, MI, 1964).

M.J.H.

RESURRECTION OF CHRIST. This two-part article considers the resurrection of Christ from the standpoints of biblical and of systematic theology.

1. Biblical theology

According to Acts 13:30ff., Jesus Christ was raised from the dead in order to fulfil God's promises to the fathers, specifically 'the holy and sure blessings promised to David'. Closely related is Rom. 1:3–4: the 'power' phase of Christ's kingship has commenced with the resurrection. His endowment with the Holy Spirit* has ushered in an unprecedented stage of power and dominion (Mt. 28:18; 2 Cor. 13:4; Eph. 1:19–20). Our Lord foresaw this when he spoke of the kingdom* coming in power (Mk. 9:1 and par.) by his resurrection, exaltation and the outpouring of his Spirit (Acts 1:8; 2:33).

Jesus' resurrection marked a turning-point in his identity as the last Adam.* In his rising from the dead he assumed a new mode of existence as 'life-giving Spirit' (1 Cor. 15:45; 2 Cor. 3:18), thereby undertaking a role virtually synonymous with that of the Spirit of God. Christ, then, is present in his church by the Spirit (Mt. 28:20; 1 Cor. 5:4), becomes one spirit with his people (1 Cor. 6:17) and dwells in their hearts by faith (Eph. 3:17).

Our Lord's resurrection introduced a new creation. He died to the old age dominated by sin and entered a new era in which he now lives to God (Rom. 6:9–10). His emergence from the tomb at the dawning of the day is symbolic of this truth. As the old creation, the new creation signalled its arrival by the intrusion of light into the darkness.

What Christ inaugurated by his resurrection he continues by his exaltation at the right hand of God (Eph. 1:20–21; Heb. 1:3–4). If he ever lives to make intercession for us (Heb. 7:25), it is because of his 'indestructible life' (Heb. 7:16), which is resurrection life (Rom. 5:10).

The NT makes an apologetic* use of the resurrection. Acts 2:23–24; 13:27ff. maintain that God vindicated his Son by delivering him from the hands of his murderers (cf. 1 Tim. 3.16; Jn. 10:17–18). The same event verifies the future judgment of the world in righteousness (Acts 17:31).

When Christ rose from the dead he did so in a representative capacity as the 'firstfruits of those who have fallen asleep' (1 Cor. 15:20).

Hence: i. We have been raised with Christ (Rom. 6:4; Col. 3:1) and caused to sit with him in the heavenly places (Eph. 2:6). ii. Christ is our life (Phil. 1:21; Col. 3:4; Jn. 11:25–26), and henceforth we live to him (Col. 3:1; 2 Cor. 5:15). Having come under the reign of the risen Son of David (Rom. 1:3–4), we render to him 'the obedience of faith' (Rom. 1:5, RSV). iii. The believer has entered the new creation (Rom. 6:4–5; 2 Cor. 4:6; 5:17) by his rebirth through the resurrection of Jesus Christ from the dead (1 Pet. 1:3). iv. In his own 'spiritual body' the Christian will bear the image of the heavenly man (1 Cor. 15:44–49) and receive his own vindication as ensured by the risen and living Christ (Rom. 5:9–10).

The resurrection of Christ concentrates the whole of salvation* into a single event. It is the turning-point of the ages and the centre of time. Henceforth not only time but life itself can never be the same.

Bibliography

J. D. G. Dunn, *Jesus and the Spirit* (London, 1975); R. B. Gaffin, *The Centrality of the Resurrection* (Grand Rapids, 1978); W. Künneth, *The Theology of the Resurrection* (London, 1965); G. E. Ladd, *I Believe in the Resurrection of Jesus* (Grand Rapids, MI, and London, 1975); E. Lövestam, *Son and Saviour: A Study of Acts 13:32–37* (Lund, 1961); A. M. Ramsey, *The Resurrection of Christ* (London, 1945); H. N. Ridderbos, *Paul: An Outline of his Theology* (Grand Rapids, 1975).

D.Ga.

2. Systematic theology

Christ's resurrection is decisive for our general understanding of Christianity.

a. The nature of Christianity. First of all, Christ rose not in the minds of the disciples but in time and space, and this immediately establishes Christianity as a religion based on history and vulnerable to critical historical scholarship.

Secondly, the resurrection is a statement about Christianity's attitude to the material world. It expresses God's commitment to redeeming it, first in the body of Christ, then in the bodies of believers and finally in the cosmos as a whole.

Thirdly, the resurrection underlines the fact that Christianity is a religion of cataclysm.

The empty tomb does not evolve out of anything which has gone before. It is a divine perforation of history.

Fourthly, the resurrection confirms that in Christianity the *forensic* principle has primacy over the *transforming*. The cross was rooted in a forensic principle: Christ was the guilty sin-bearer. Equally, the resurrection was rooted in the forensic principle. He was raised because, having died the death due to sin, he was justified. His exaltation and transformation were God's response to the Saviour's new righteousness.

b. The person of Christ. The resurrection is also significant for the person of Christ. It means, for example, that in his present state he possesses a full humanity. He has not returned to his pre-incarnate state of being only divine. Nor does he exist in an incorporeal state. He is still man: and the manhood he now possesses is physical as well as spiritual. Yet it is not in the state in which it was before his death. Precisely because risen, it is glorified and perfected. It has new might and majesty. Once so vulnerable, it is now inviolable.

The resurrection obviously has a very close connection with the divine sonship of Christ (Rom. 1:4), but not as the point when he *became* Son. He is sent into the world as Son (Rom. 8:3; Gal. 4:4). Indeed, it is the pre-existent sonship which gives point to such passages as Jn. 3:16 and Rom. 8:32, which emphasize the cost of our salvation to God the Father. The AV(KJV) translation of Rom. 1:4 is too weak. The usual meaning of the verb translated 'declared' here (Gk. *horizō*) is 'to determine' or 'to delimit' (see Lk. 22:22; Heb. 4:7). What is being said, however, is not that he was appointed Son of God, but that he was appointed Son of God *with power*. The contrast is between a time when he was the weak and humiliated Son of God and a time when he became the Son of God in full majesty and authority. The resurrection marks the end of his poverty and *kenōsis*.* It was a *coronation*, not an adoption (*cf.* Heb. 2:9).

c. The work of Christ. The resurrection is no less significant for the work of Christ. The interval between his first and his second coming is filled with redemptive activity. This is clear in John 17:2: 'You granted him authority over all people, that he might give eternal life to all those you have given him.' We find the same perspective in Acts, the story of what

583

Jesus continued to do and to teach (*cf.* 1:1). It is the risen Lord who pours forth his Spirit at Pentecost (Acts 2:33), apprehends Saul on the Damascus road (Acts 9:5), opens the heart of Lydia (Acts 16:14) and directs Paul to continue his missionary work at Corinth (Acts 18:9).

This post-resurrection activity embraces all three aspects of Christ's work as priest, prophet and king (see Offices of Christ*). As *priest* his work of atoning for human sin is over, but his intercession continues and is specifically grounded in the fact that 'he always lives' (Heb. 7:25). By virtue of the resurrection, this intercession takes place 'with the Father' (1 John 2:1, RSV), and thus partakes of the authority proper to his exaltation.

So far as his work as *prophet* is concerned, the risen Lord was clearly the source of the apostolic message. Paul makes this plain in 1 Cor. 11:23, 'I received from the Lord what I also passed on to you' (*cf.* Gal. 1:12). The result is that in the apostolic teaching we have 'the mind of Christ' (1 Cor. 2:16, AV(KJV)) and 'the command of the Lord' (1 Cor. 14:37, Gk.). Nor was it only a matter of revelation. The risen Christ was also the one who gave the insight and open-mindedness necessary to receive the Christian message. It was the Lord who opened Lydia's heart (Acts 16:14). Both his work as illuminator and his work as revealer would be impossible apart from the resurrection.

But it is on Christ's *kingship* that the resurrection bears most strikingly. His post-resurrection sovereignty differs from the pre-resurrection in several important respects.

It differs, first, in its range. Until the resurrection the dominion given to the Son as mediator was limited to Israel. Now the uttermost parts of the earth are his possession (Ps. 2:8). He has *all* the authority in heaven and on earth (Mt. 28:18). This is the background to the teaching of the Apocalypse that Satan no longer binds the Gentiles with his deception (Rev. 20:3).

It differs, secondly, in its close relation to the ministry of the Spirit: John can even say that before Jesus was glorified 'the Spirit was not yet' (Jn. 7:39, Gk.). The mission of the Comforter depended not only on Jesus' death but on his exaltation (*cf.* Jn. 16:7). Through his Spirit the risen Christ leads his people and governs the world.

Thirdly, the post-resurrection sovereignty is one modified by the experience of the Lord's incarnate life. In its pre-resurrection phase the sovereignty of the Son of God had all the advantages of his love, pity and omniscience. It retains these but is now enriched by his involvement in the common lot of men and women during his life on earth. Today the memories of Nazareth and Cana, of poverty and pain, of temptation and suffering, Gethsemane and Calvary, are imprinted indelibly on the Lord's memory and contribute to the way he runs his administration. He knows our humanness from the inside and having himself lived on the outer limits he can ensure that we are not tested above what we can bear.

d. The Christian life. The resurrection has implications for the Christian as well as for Christ. For one thing, it makes possible our union* with him. The NT uses a wide range of *incorporative* terminology, portraying the church* as the body of Christ, a vine, a temple, a bride. All these presuppose a living Christ in whom Christians *are*, by whom they are indwelt and with whom they form one body. This is the secret of the Christian's power. He can do all things *in* the one who strengthens him (Phil. 4:13).

Furthermore, the transformation undergone by the Christian is patterned on that experienced by Christ. Just as for him there was a chasm between pre-resurrection and post-resurrection existence, so there is for the believer between pre-Christian and Christian life: 'I no longer live, but Christ lives in me' (Gal. 2:20).

But the NT emphasizes not only that we are in Christ but equally that he is in us. It also speaks of him as being with us. In the very context in which he charges the church with the apparently impossible task of evangelizing the world he promises to be with her always. All this is clearly impossible apart from the resurrection. The same is true of the eucharistic* presence of Christ, however that is to be defined. It is quite impossible (although the attempt is made often enough) to graft a Christology which denies the resurrection on to Catholic sacramentalism. How can we experience or encounter Christ in the eucharist if his life ceased on the cross?

e. The moral universe. Finally, the resurrection gives assurance that we live in a world governed by absolute standards of rectitude; and in a world, too, where, at last, right will triumph. At first glance, the cross proclaims the triumph of evil and lawlessness. But in the resurrection God responds to the glory of Christ's service. Death had rights over him, through sin. Now that he has once for all died to sin, death no longer has rights. Right is now on the side of Christ and his people. When we look at the empty tomb we are looking at the triumph of righteousness.

The resurrection, set in the middle of history, is God's pledge that its end will be peace. Indeed, this is part of the offence of the cross. Those human eyes which think they see farthest and deepest protest that all optimism is shallow. Realism, they say, means pessimism. But the wisdom/folly of the Bible, with the empty tomb as its symbol, is committed to a Happy Ending.

Bibliography

R. B. Gaffin, *The Centrality of the Resurrection* (Grand Rapids, MI, 1978); G. E. Ladd, *I Believe in the Resurrection of Jesus* (Grand Rapids, MI, and London, 1975); W. Milligan, *The Resurrection of Our Lord* (London, 1913); O. O'Donovan, *Resurrection and Moral Order* (Leicester, 1986).

D.M.

R EVELATION refers to the disclosure or unveiling of something. In that sense, reality is constantly revealing itself to probing minds as they seek to comprehend it. We approach the world as those who expect the hidden to be revealed, and the unknown to become known. According to the Bible, God himself has satisfied man's quest for intelligibility by revealing himself, his divine power and his will for mankind, so that we might come to know him.

Two species of revelation

Ps. 19 calls our attention to the two varieties of divine revelation. On the one hand, 'the heavens are telling the glory of God' in such a way that it is impossible for anyone not to know it. And on the other hand, there is a testimony granted to Israel which conveys more specific information about the gift and the demands of God. We call the first 'general' revelation because it is universally available, and the second 'special' revelation because it is a particular disclosure about how mankind can find favour with God – a disclosure given at first to particular people chosen by God but intended in the end for the whole human race. Although there are differences between general and special revelation in terms of their completeness and orientation, we should not draw the contrast too sharply. After all, there is only one God whose Logos* is spreading the knowledge of the Lord everywhere. The two species of revelation stand together in a complementary relationship. We should not forget that God is the source of revelation in both cases, and that the two types of revelation work together to the same goal. The creational light 'that enlightens every man' orients us toward the Word become flesh (Jn. 1:9, 14). General revelation alerts us to the reality of God, while special revelation urgently summons us to make peace with God. The two species belong to the one overarching unity of divine revelation.

General revelation

God is a mystery, and some in modern times have supposed that he is unknowable by man. Kant* developed an epistemological* theory in which God could not be an object of human knowledge. For some this spells simple atheism,* but for others it has led to a denial of general revelation. Karl Barth,* for example, has denied the reality of revelation outside of Jesus Christ. But this is not a scriptural position. Even though he is transcendent, God 'has never left himself without witness' (Acts 14:17). No-one can honestly say that he does not know what the term 'God' refers to. The Bible tells us that God's eternal power and deity can be clearly perceived in the things God made (Rom. 1:20). It also informs us that God is sovereign over human history and that often we are able to trace God's hand in events. In particular the reality of God is detected in human nature, for example, in the moral realm. This moral impulse which characterizes all human beings points to the moral God who brought us into existence (Rom. 2:1–16). God's existence is also attested in man's religious nature, in that people everywhere have always believed in a reality higher than themselves. Barth was right to worry about the bad uses to which general revelation was put in liberal theology, but that cannot be an excuse for denying a dimension of the actual revelation of God.

One can list several points of real value which reside in general revelation. First, it means that there is common ground between believer and unbeliever. Everyone already has a certain knowledge of God which can serve as a starting point in an evangelistic discussion. Some of the truth is already known, whether welcome or not (see Christianity and other Religions*). Second, it means that we can be hopeful about discovering God's truth outside the sphere of special revelation in the wider world. This might even be true amidst the rubble of man's religious strivings. God has placed truth throughout the whole extent of his creation, and it is there to be uncovered.

If there indeed is an objective general revelation, does this mean that natural theology* is possible and justified? The majority opinion in the history of apologetics* has answered affirmatively. Men such as Thomas Aquinas* and Jonathan Edwards* have tried to show by an appeal to certain features of the world that theism* is a rational belief, indeed the only belief which can make sense of things. Some Protestants have been more cautious, worrying that this exercise might be making assumptions about the integrity of human reason which should not be made. Nevertheless, given the objective reality of general revelation, together with the practical need to establish common ground, it is likely that natural theology has a future. If God is the creator, one would expect the world to reveal its maker. The Bible itself confirms this expectation; therefore, Christians are likely to continue to explain how this is so to those they want to convert.

If we posit a basic unity between general and special revelation, does it not follow that both possess saving potential and that a sinner might turn to God and trust God in the context of general revelation alone if he were limited to it? Many Evangelicals are very wary about giving an affirmative answer to this question, because to do so would seem to imply that salvation is possible anywhere, with or without the knowledge of Christ. I think it may be possible to answer affirmatively in a way that would allay such fears. God's grace is meant for the whole human race, and Christ has provided for the salvation of all in his universal atonement (1 Jn. 2:2). Surely we may assume, with support from Scripture in the form of what one might call the Melchizedek factor, that the person who turned to God in the light of whatever revelation he had would become eligible, as it were, for the fuller revelation and the salvation

implied in it. We do not need to suppose that a person can enjoy Christ's salvation without Christ, but only that a person who turns to God for mercy on the basis of only general revelation will surely receive it.

Special revelation

An obvious limitation of general revelation is that while it calls attention to a moral and religious defect in us, it does not highlight a solution for it. A person might cast himself upon God for mercy on the basis of general revelation, but not be assured that there is mercy available for him. One is led to hope for and anticipate additional revelation which would address the painful tension between our moral and religious obligation and our moral and religious shortcomings. One would hope against hope that the God who made the world would have done or said something to alleviate this desperate situation.

None of this remains hypothetical for those who recognize that special revelation which culminates in the incarnation.* The Word has become flesh; the divine person has joined to himself our human potential for selfhood, thus surpassing the gulf that separates us. Furthermore, in this incarnation the problem of our moral guilt was effectively solved by a sacrifice which satisfies God's moral law and provides for our moral regeneration. Thus at the heart and centre of special revelation is a divinely initiated solution to the universal moral and religious predicament of man which takes the form of the incarnation of the Son of God. As Jesus told Philip, 'He who has seen me has seen the Father' (Jn. 14:9).

Stepping back from the mountain peak of special revelation, let us reflect on the features of that revelation in a more general way. The creation witness does not involve verbal revelation, and leaves us to figure out from the outside what is going on. There is a certain amount that we can learn from observing a person's behaviour and appearance, but this does not begin to compare with what we can know if the person involved is willing to open himself up to us. When it comes to self-directing persons as distinct from inert objects, revelation can only proceed if the willingness to share one's inner thoughts is present. If we are really to get to know God, it is absolutely necessary that God should reveal to us who he is. Otherwise, we would be left largely in the dark. This is why the

586

Bible stresses so enthusiastically the self-revelation of God.

This revelation is personal. God reveals himself by telling us his name. He enters into covenant* with us, and gives himself to be known by us. God himself, and not just universal truths about God, is what is revealed. Further, in revelation God stoops to make himself known in ways we can grasp and understand. He comes to us in categories of thought and action which make sense to us.

Of particular significance in addition to the incarnation are two modes of special revelation: revelation in historical events, and revelation in divine speech. First, the narrative line of the biblical gospel is structured around a recital of the works God has performed in human history. The mighty deeds of the Lord are repeatedly praised. He brought his people Israel out of the land of bondage, and he sent his Son to accomplish an even greater redemption. It is not enough to think of the deeds of God as ordinary events, construed in a religiously insightful way by people with faith. Nor is it enough to say that God presents himself to us personally through events, as if to minimize the deeds themselves as revelation. In the resurrection, for example, God did something outside ourselves and our experiences. In this miracle, God gave an objective witness to all mankind, in validating Christ's own claim to be God's anointed (Acts 17:31; Rom. 1:4). Jesus was attested by signs and wonders, and although put to death by evil men he was raised up by God and set at his right hand as Lord (Acts 2:22–36). The Christian proclamation rests, then, on solid historical reality when it calls people to consider its claim to revelation.

Second, and of equal importance, there is a verbal component to special revelation. God gave his law through Moses, and speaks to us through Jesus Christ, along with the apostles and prophets. Divine speech as well as divine action plays a crucial role in revelation. As the writer to the Hebrews says, 'In many and various ways God spoke of old to our fathers by the prophets, but in these last days he has spoken to us by his Son' (Heb. 1:1–2). God's acts by themselves, while meaningful, would be relatively mute, unless accompanied by verbal commentary giving insight into the character and purposes of God. God not only raises the crucified Christ from the dead, but also explains to us the redemptive significance of that action, as when Paul writes: 'Christ died for our sins according to the Scriptures' (1 Cor. 15:3). Jesus was not merely another Jewish martyr dying for his faith, but the divinely appointed substitute of us all putting away our sins. The divinely given interpretation of the cross is practically as important to us as the cross itself, at least as far as our being able to appropriate its benefits intelligibly is concerned. In the biblical account, the divine speech is every bit as central to revelation as the divine action. Revelation is to be found both in God's deeds and in God's words.

If it is true that special revelation conveys propositional truth and verbal communication from God, then it is natural to expect the deposit of truth to be settled into written form. It would be very surprising if this were not so, given the verbal character of revelation, not to mention the linguistic nature of human beings themselves. It is more than reasonable to expect that divine revelation would find expression in written form. Only written documents are capable of preserving the insights communicated in revelation over time and making them available to the people who come later. Again, none of this remains hypothetical because we find in the Bible a claim concerning inscripturated revelation which answers to this need (see Scripture*).

Bibliography

J. Baillie, *The Idea of Revelation in Recent Thought* (New York, 1956); G. C. Berkouwer, *General Revelation* (Grand Rapids, MI, 1955); idem, *Holy Scripture* (Grand Rapids, MI, 1975); J. Cottrell, *What the Bible Says about God the Creator* (Joplin, MO, 1983); B. A. Demarest, *General Revelation, Historical Views and Contemporary Issues* (Grand Rapids, MI, 1982); M. J. Erickson, *Christian Theology* I (Grand Rapids, MI, 1983); C. F. H. Henry, *God, Revelation and Authority* I–VI (Waco, TX, 1976–83); H. D. McDonald, *Ideas of Revelation, An Historical Study 1700–1860* (London, 1959); idem, *Theories of Revelation, An Historical Study 1860–1960* (London, 1963); C. H. Pinnock, *Biblical Revelation, The Foundation of Christian Theology* (Chicago, IL, 1971); idem, *The Scripture Principle* (New York, 1985).

C.H.P.

REVIVAL, THEOLOGY OF. Revival, as Protestant theology has used the word for 250 years, means God's quickening visitation of his people, touching their hearts and deepening his work of grace in their lives. It is essentially a corporate occurrence, an enlivening of individuals not in isolation but together. 'Revive' is the AV(KJV) word for this process of spiritual reanimation (Ps. 85:6; Hab. 3:2); 'revivedness' would be the appropriate term to describe its result. The Reformation, the Evangelical Revival in Britain, the first and second Great Awakenings in America, the Welsh Revival of 1904–05, and the East African Revival still continuing after half a century, are seen as instances. The narrower American use of 'revival' for a concentrated evangelistic campaign, and of 'revivalist' for its leader, stems chiefly from the ministry pattern of Charles G. Finney,* as delineated in his brilliant and still influential *Lectures on Revivals of Religion* (1835).

The recurring pattern of revival appears in many descriptions and anticipations of spiritual movements throughout the Bible. In its NT form the pattern is seen in the narratives of evangelism and early church life found in Acts, and in the spiritual conditions that the apostolic letters to churches reflect or seek to promote. In revival God is said to arise and come to his people, in the sense of making his holy presence felt among them (Ps. 80; Is. 64; Zc. 2:10; *cf.* Hab. 3; 1 Cor. 14:24–25), so that his reality becomes inescapable, and the infinite ugliness, guilt, ill-desert and pollution of sin are clearly seen (Acts 2:37, *cf.* 5:1–11). The gospel of redeeming love and free forgiveness through the cross is valued as the best news ever, and the exercises and gestures of repentance whereby believers distance themselves from their sins (confession to God and others, restitution, public renunciation of vices) become vigorous and violent (Mt. 3:5–10, 11:12; Acts 19:18–19; 2 Cor. 7:9–11; Jas. 5:16). God works fast through the gospel (*cf.* 2 Thes. 3:1) in saving, sanctifying, and stabilizing, and there is an evangelistic overflow to those around (Zc. 8:23; Acts 2:47), despite human and Satanic opposition (Acts 4; Eph. 6:10–13).

The pioneer theologian of revival was Jonathan Edwards.* After seeing revival in his own church in 1735 and in the Great Awakening of 1740, Edwards wrote *The Distingu-* ishing Marks of a Work of the Spirit of God (1741), *Thoughts on the Revival of Religion in New England in 1740* (1742), and *A Treatise on the Religious Affections* (1746), setting forth a cyclical view of revival as a work of grace that under God's sovereignty recurs periodically, like the breaking of successive waves, and is in fact God's major means of extending his kingdom. God initiates revival by first stirring up prayer for it; Satan seeks to counterfeit it and corrupt it into heretical and antinomian fanaticism at every stage. J. Edwin Orr (1912–87), gifted chronicler of revivals, has maintained Edwards' view today.

Finney's Arminian* – Pelagian* theology allowed him to reconceive Edwards' morphology of revival as illustrating what he took to be the law of revival, namely that the church's praying, repenting, and seeking God guarantees an outpouring of the Holy Spirit in revival blessing; just as, under God's kindly providence, the farmer's sowing and caring for his field guarantees a crop. The thought that revival is God's immediate will whenever his servants pay the price in passionate prayer and penitence has been potent in popular evangelical piety since Finney's day, though the finding has not been commensurate with the seeking.

More recently the idea has become current that revival, meaning powerful Christianity as exhibited in Acts, is a permanent norm for the church, and will automatically be continuous where obstacles to it (unbelief, misbelief, apathy, sin) are removed and right goals are aimed at. This, too, seems to assume an Arminian concept of God. The charismatic renewal, like original Pentecostalism,* is sometimes interpreted as continuous revival in this sense.

Bibliography

J. Edwards, *Works*, 2 vols. (London, 1974, reprint); C. G. Finney, *Lectures on Revivals of Religion*, ed. W. G. McLaughlin (Cambridge, MA, 1960); R. F. Lovelace, *Dynamics of Spiritual Life* (Downers Grove, IL, 1979); J. I. Packer, *Keep in Step with the Spirit* (Leicester, 1984).

J.I.P.

REVOLUTION, THEOLOGY OF. 'Revolution' is used in the political sphere to describe the destruction of one social system and its replacement by another. It is more than the transference of power between rival political groups; it represents a new way of ordering society. By changing values and creating new political and economic structures and institutions, revolutionary groups believe that it is possible to eliminate the injustice and conflict of present societies.

Revolution is associated with the slogan, 'liberty, equality and fraternity', with Marx's view of the class struggle, Engels' withering away of the state, Lenin's belief that capitalism was doomed to devour itself, and Trotsky's permanent vigilance against state bureaucracy (see Marxism and Christianity*). Revolution flows from the utopian dream that human beings can act as historical midwives bringing to birth a qualitatively new human society.

A theology of revolution may possess or combine any one of three different strands. It may be a systematic theological reflection on the basis, nature and implications of revolution. It may seek to draw out the revolutionary characteristics of Christian faith. And it may help direct the church's legitimate response to revolutionary movements.

Though revolution in a distinctively modern sense dates from the 18th century, there had been political eruptions in previous centuries, which had produced (or were sometimes caused by) theological thought: the English Peasants' Revolt of 1381, the Taborites of the early 15th century, Münster in 16th-century Germany (see Reformation, Radical*) and the Levellers and Diggers of 17th-century Puritan* England. Both Calvinists* and Jesuits* in the 16th and 17th centuries argued for the justice of rebellion in certain contexts.

The church in the 19th century was almost uniformly hostile to the ideas that sprang from the French Revolution. There were some exceptions: theologians such as Bruno Bauer (1809–82) and David Strauss* belonged for a time (the late 1830s) to the circle of political radicals called 'the Young Hegelians'; F. D. Maurice, C. Kingsley and others formed the Christian Socialists* in 1850, and at the end of the century Rauschenbush in America and Ragaz in Switzerland were leaders in a movement called the Social Gospel.*

In the present century, at least four major groups have developed Christian thinking on revolutionary change. R. H. Tawney (1880–1962), the British economist, is representative

of influential thinkers in the Western world who have challenged the capitalist economic system from a Christian basis. The Czech theologian, Josef L. Hromadka (d. 1969), was a foremost exponent after World War II of those who challenged Christians to come to terms with a socialist state. Some theologians in Africa and Asia have given thought to the way in which decolonization and movements of national liberation impinge on Christian faith. Most recently, Christian leaders in Latin America (see Liberation Theology*) and South Africa (see Black Theology*), speaking on behalf of peoples oppressed by neo-fascist and racist regimes, have been reflecting theologically on social change.

Theologies of revolution have a number of characteristics in common. They are critical of the official church's tendency to remain non-committal when challenged to endorse sweeping political changes at times of severe social dislocation. They believe that theological reflection has to begin with the real circumstances of the poor (see Poverty and Wealth*). Further, they are convinced that social analysis is a necessary part of the hermeneutical* task of making Christian obedience concrete in specific situations. Finally, they hold that theological work cannot be divorced from ideological commitment, for no intellectual discipline is neutral towards social conflict.

These theologies hold the following basic themes in common. The Exodus story of God's liberation of oppressed people from Egypt is interpreted as a paradigm* of his liberating activity throughout all history.* God continues to hear the cries of those suffering from repressive government. He does not surrender to human intransigence.

Justice (see Righteousness*) is the supreme category for knowing God; it is his action on behalf of oppressed people. Only those who take 'an option for the poor' can know him truly. Jesus,* in his life and ministry, as he inaugurated the kingdom, incarnated God's justice. He seals God's intention to deliver the poor from their oppression. He died as a result of resisting the religious and political complex of power. His resurrection* displays God's triumph over all forces of death. It is the sign of hope that the economic and military idols of our time can be destroyed and a new way of justice and peace inaugurated.

Theologies of revolution represent one type

589

of Christian response to the innate human desire to be free of external constraints to political and economic self-determination. They express the evident antagonism of the God of the Bible to the abuse of power which grinds defenceless people into the dust. They articulate God's saving work in social terms, believing that in the coming of Jesus a power has been unleashed which can break apparently invulnerable, closed, political and economic systems.

They draw their inspiration from the hope that a better world can be realized within history. This, it is argued, will not happen because history is bound to unfold in a predetermined direction, but because groups of people, motivated by the conviction that God's power is greater than the forces which cause death in today's world, struggle for change.

Two main weaknesses are apparent in this form of theological reflection. First, in the sphere of political analysis diagnosis tends to be confused with cure. A right solution to the present suffering of the poor does not spring automatically from a correct analysis of its causes. Evil is more extensively present in the world than its operation in political and economic institutions and policies.

Secondly, a new kind of society cannot emerge without people, spiritually regenerated,* walking in the new life which God offers exclusively through Jesus Christ. However, the NT emphasis on grace,* enabling people to be free of guilt,* corruption and selfishness for a life of selfless love,* is not prominent enough in theologies of revolution. Grace tends to be seen as an addition to human power* (supplementing nature*), when people are not able to eliminate power that is against change. Revolution will certainly bring change. Almost as certainly it will not bring real human transformation, unless the regenerating power of God's grace is active in human communities.

See also: POLITICAL THEOLOGY.

Bibliography

G. Gutiérrez, The Power of the Poor in History (London, 1983); A. Kirk, Theology Encounters Revolution (Leicester, 1980); J. Miguez Bonino, Revolutionary Theology Comes of Age (London, 1975); J. Moltmann, The Power of the Powerless (London, 1983);

N. Wolterstorff, Until Justice and Peace Embrace (Grand Rapids, MI, 1983).

J.A.K.

RICHARDSON, ALAN (1905–75), a leading Anglican theologian and ecumenist, and one of the chief exponents of the biblical theology* movement in Britain. Richardson was a distinguished contributor to systematic and philosophical theology in the third quarter of the 20th century. Much of his earlier work (such as The Miracle Stories of the Gospels, London, 1941, The Biblical Doctrine of Work, London, 1952, and commentaries on Genesis and John) focuses on recovering the distinctiveness and unity of the biblical message. His more technical Introduction to the Theology of the New Testament (London, 1958) was very widely influential, and was, along with the Theological Wordbook of the Bible (London, 1950) which he edited, an important monument of the biblical theology movement. Richardson's more strictly theological work made some important moves towards detaching theology from the positivism* and empiricism* of much of the philosophical climate of his day, starting with Christian Apologetics (London, 1947), and culminating in his major work, the Bampton Lectures* on History, Sacred and Profane (London, 1964). The latter work developed the notion of history* as an apologetic* platform for explaining the biblical kerygma,* making use of historiographers such as Dilthey* and R. G. Collingwood (1889–1943) to expound the nature of revelation,* resurrection* and divine action in the world. Much recent work in both theology and philosophy has moved away from Richardson's concerns, and in particular recent developments in hermeneutical* theory and epistemology* have been such that his work has a decidedly dated air.

Bibliography

J. J. Navone, History and Faith in the Thought of Alan Richardson (London, 1966). Cf. R. H. Preston (ed.), Theology and Change: Essays in Memory of Alan Richardson (London, 1975).

J.B.We.

RIGHTEOUSNESS. The basic meaning of 'righteousness' and its cognates in the Bible derives from the Hebrew *ṣedeq*, which was usually translated in the LXX as *dikaiosynē*. It thus denotes not so much the abstract idea of justice or virtue, as right standing and consequent right behaviour, within a community. English translates this semantic field with two different roots: 'right', 'righteous', and 'righteousness' and 'just', 'justice', 'justify' and 'justification'. In Heb. and Gk., however, these ideas all belong together linguistically and theologically.

In the OT (upon which the NT idea is based) two fields of thought give specific shape to the idea:

1. The lawcourt setting gives 'righteousness' the idea of the standing of a person in relation to the court's decision. In the Hebrew court there were no public prosecutors: all cases had to be brought by a plaintiff against a defendant. Righteousness is the status which results, for either party, if the court finds in his favour. Since the standard of judgment is the covenant* law* of God, 'righteousness' can acquire the sense of 'behaviour in conformity with the covenant requirements', bringing about the possibility that right covenant standing can be observed in ordinary behaviour. In addition, the judge, or king, must conform to a different sense of righteousness: he must try cases fairly, *i.e.* he must be true to the law and/or the covenant, must condemn evil, show no partiality, and uphold the cause of the defenceless. This complex meaning explains the occasional instances when the Septuagint uses *dikaiosynē* to translate not *ṣedeq* and its cognates but other roots such as *ḥesed* (grace, covenant mercy), *mišpāṭ* (judgment, justice), *etc.*

2. The covenantal setting merges with that of the lawcourt: this is due partly to the fact that the law (Torah) is the covenant charter. Though sometimes God himself is seen as Israel's adversary at law, the more frequently encountered picture is of God as judge or king, with Israel as either plaintiff (pleading her cause against her enemies) or defendant (on trial for failure to keep the covenant). God's righteousness is then invoked as the reason why he can be expected to deliver his people: he is committed by covenant to do so. When this is apparently called into question (in the exile, and later in the Maccabean revolt and the fall of Jerusalem in AD 70), the writers of these periods reply that God is righteous in judging his sinful people; that he is righteous in waiting before judging their enemies,

granting time for repentance; and that he will show himself righteous in restoring the fortunes of his people, in renewing the covenant (Dn. 9; Ezr. 9; *etc.*). The book of Job can be seen as a long lawcourt scene in which Job pleads his righteousness, imagining that God is his adversary, only to discover that God cannot be brought into court: the first two chapters reveal Satan (see Devil*) as the real prosecutor, with Job's comforters as his unwitting assistants.

These two settings (lawcourt and covenant) combine to produce the developed covenantal theology which underlay Judaism at the time of Jesus. To have 'righteousness' meant to belong to the covenant, the boundary marker of which was the Torah, and the hope of which was that God, in accordance with his own righteousness, would act in history to 'vindicate', to 'justify', his people (*i.e.* to show that they really were his people) by saving them from their enemies. These meanings are reflected particularly in Matthew, where 'righteousness' is shorthand both for the saving plan of God (Mt. 3:15) and for the covenantal obligations of his people (5:20; 6:1), and Luke, which emphasizes the 'righteous' standing of many of the key actors in the drama (Lk. 1:6; 2:25; 23:50; Acts 10:22). Jesus himself is sometimes called 'the righteous one', in virtue of his being the one designated by God as his true covenant partner (*e.g.* Acts 3:14; 7:52, 22:14, Jas. 5:6). The Jewish belief that God would judge the world justly is echoed repeatedly in the NT, *e.g.* 2 Thes. 1:5–6; Rom. 2:1–16; Heb. 12:23. But the fullest development comes in Paul, particularly with his exposition in Romans of the righteousness of God.

Paul saw that the Jewish problem of God's righteousness (if the creator of the world is Israel's covenant God, why is Israel still oppressed?) had been answered in a new and striking way in the death and resurrection of Jesus Christ. The answer had, in fact, forced a restatement of the question, demonstrating as it did the universal sinfulness of Jews as well as pagans. The gospel, Paul declares, proves that God is in the right despite appearances: he has kept covenant with Abraham, has dealt properly with sin, has acted and will act without partiality, and upholds all those who cast themselves, helpless, on his mercy (Rom. 1:16–17; 2:1–16; 3:21 – 4:25). God has, in other words, shown 'righteousness' in

591

the sense appropriate for the judge and the Lord of the covenant. He is thus able to anticipate the verdict of the last day (Rom. 2:1–16) and to declare in the present (Rom. 3:21–26) that all who believe the gospel are already within the covenant community (see Justification*).

The view that 'the righteousness of God' refers to a righteousness which God gives to, bestows upon, or recognizes in human beings came initially from Augustine, but gained its force (in terms of the development of modern theology) from Luther's reaction against a *iustitia distributiva*. The term *iustitia*, as found in the Latin Vulgate, had indeed pulled the understanding of texts such as Rom. 1:17 in the (false) direction of a merely 'distributive' justice, in which God simply rewards virtue and punishes vice. Luther's alternative, however fruitful in opening new worlds of theology to him, was in some ways equally misleading, for it directed attention away from the biblical notion of God's covenant faithfulness and instead placed greater emphasis upon the status of the human being. In the period after Luther, Protestant theology largely returned to the notion of the distributive justice of God: because God is righteous, he must in fact reward virtue and punish sin, and this satisfaction of divine justice took place in Christ.

According to the NT, the people of God do indeed have 'righteousness'. This is not, strictly speaking, God's own righteousness (though *cf.* 2 Cor. 5:21), but that which is proper to the person in whose favour the court has found; within the covenant context, it is the right standing of a member of the people of God. 'Righteousness' thus comes to mean, more or less, 'covenant membership', with all the overtones of appropriate behaviour (*e.g.* Phil. 1:11). The terminology plays a central role in Paul's debate with those who sought to keep the covenant community within the bounds of physical Judaism: they, Paul says, are ignorant of God's righteousness (*i.e.* of what God is righteously accomplishing, of how he is fulfilling his covenant) and are seeking to establish a righteousness of their own (*i.e.* a covenant membership for Jews alone), whereas in God's plan Christ offers covenant membership to all who believe the gospel (Rom. 10:3–4). (See further Paul.*)

The central biblical discussions of righteousness thus principally concern membership in the covenant and the behaviour appropriate to that membership. Since, however, these passages depend on a theology in which God is creator and judge of all the earth, and in which God's people are to reflect God's own character, it is not illegitimate to extrapolate from them to the 'justice' which God desires, and designs, for his world. The church is to be not only an example of God's intended new humanity, but the means by which the eventual plan, including the establishment of world-wide justice, is to be put into effect. Lack of emphasis here in older theological writing, due sometimes to individualism and sometimes to a dualistic split between church and world, has led to a reaction (*e.g.* in some liberation theology*) in which 'justice' as an abstract virtue has been elevated in an unbiblical manner (*e.g.* at the expense of mercy). This should not prevent a balanced orthodox view of world-wide justice from regaining, and retaining, its place in the church's teaching and practice.

Bibliography

On 'justice': P. Marshall, *Thine is the Kingdom: A Biblical Perspective on Government and Politics Today* (Basingstoke, 1984); R. J. Mouw, *Politics and the Biblical Drama* (Grand Rapids, MI, 1983); N. Wolterstorff, *Until Justice and Peace Embrace* (Grand Rapids, MI, 1984); J. H. Yoder, *The Politics of Jesus* (Grand Rapids, MI, 1972). On 'righteousness' see under Justification.

N.T.W.

RIGHTS, ANIMAL. The increasing interest shown today in the relationship between human beings and animals is all too obvious in the violent activities of such movements as the Animal Liberation Front in Britain, and also in the voluminous literature being produced by the animal rights camp on both practical and philosophical matters concerned with human use or abuse of animals. Sadly, little effort has been made on the part of evangelicals to look at the biblical basis for an understanding of our dealings with the animal world.

This lack of emphasis is not reflected in the Bible. Indeed, since, in a primarily agricultural society, the relationship between human beings and the animal world is a very close and everyday one, it is not surprising that the creation narrative in the early chapters of

Genesis places great importance on teaching about this interaction. Adam is to rule over the beasts and subdue the earth (Gn. 1:26–30). While the Heb. terminology here is used elsewhere in the OT of kings coercing nations into servitude, of treading grapes or even of rape we should not follow the environmentalists of the 1960s such as Ian McHarg and Lynn White (b. 1907) in their conclusion that this portrays an unacceptable domination of the non-human world and justifies the modern-day pillage of the environment. For this 'dominion' language must be seen in the context of these chapters. Adam is assigned the role of the gardener tending God's creation and making it productive (Gn. 2:15). Furthermore, as von Rad has noted, the idea of man made in the image of God is intimately related to his relationship with the world, for, 'just as powerful earthly kings, to indicate their claim to dominion, erect an image of themselves in the provinces of their empire where they do not personally appear, so man is placed on earth as God's sovereign emblem. He is really only God's representative, summoned to maintain and enforce God's claim to dominion over the earth' (*Genesis*, London, 1961, p. 58). This must mean that our rule over the earth is to emulate God's righteous rule. This is reflected in the OT where both man and beast were to rest on the sabbath (Ex. 23:12), and provision was to be made for both the rescue of animals on the sabbath and the welfare of animals while they were working (Dt. 25:4). 'A righteous man cares for the needs of his animal' (Pr. 12:10). The animals are even included in God's covenant with Noah (Gn. 9:8–17).

It would be easy on the basis of this to suggest that we should only look after the animals in our care and not use them for our own ends. However, we are given the animals both to use alive and also to kill for food, with the clear understanding that the animal is God's and not ours. The shedding of blood in Gn. 9:4 is instituted that Noah might realize that the life of the animal is God's gift and not something with which he can do as he likes. Barth goes as far as suggesting that we may be guilty of 'murdering' an animal if we kill it without understanding that it does not belong to us but to God (*CD* III.4, pp. 353–355).

It has been argued that the provision in Gn. 9:2 is merely a concession to fallen meat-eating men and women. There is no evidence for this in the text or in the way that the NT writers viewed meat. For while Christ made clear that, for instance, the divorce regulations were given 'because your hearts were hard' (Mt. 19:1–9) and were thus not the ideal, the fact that he ate fish (Lk. 24:43) and in all probability meat also, at the passover meal, suggests that it is legitimate for us to do so also. Paul was not talking about moral vegetarianism when he wrote 'nothing is to be rejected if it is received with thanksgiving' (1 Tim. 4:4; *cf.* 1 Cor. 8:7–10; Rom. 14:1–4). Nevertheless it is clear that he considered meat-eating to be acceptable for a Christian.

Jesus plainly taught that although birds and sheep are cared for by God, human beings are valued a great deal more (Mt. 6:26; 12:12). This is in complete variance with the animal rights movement for whom animals and men and women have the same value. For them the ultimate wrong is to use animals; cruelty merely compounds that wrong. For Christians, although it is right to use animals, it is wrong to cause them to suffer unjustifiably. But what is unjustifiable suffering? The idea of an animal having the right not to suffer is unhelpful when conflicts of rights are considered. It would be much more biblical to see us as having a duty to prevent animal suffering but a greater duty to alleviate human suffering. Thus medical experimentation causing animal suffering might be justifiable while animal use to produce cosmetics could be considered unacceptable. However, the practical issues involved in relating the biblical principles above to laboratory and agricultural use of animals are very complicated and beyond the scope of this article. What is clear is that animals can be used by men and women within the bounds of 'responsible stewardship'.*

Bibliography

A. Linzey, *Animal Rights* (London, 1976); *idem, The Status of Animals in the Christian Tradition* (Birmingham, 1985); *idem, Christianity and the Rights of Animals* (London, 1987); D. L. Williams, 'Assault and Battery', *Third Way* 9:7 (July, 1986), pp. 25–28; R. Griffiths, *The Human Use of Animals* (Bramcote, Nottingham, 1979).

D.L.W.

R IGHTS, HUMAN. In order to avoid vague ideological thinking, clear definitions are required. Human rights regard individual persons as unique beings. They do not denote those rights which a person has as a member of a community, *e.g.* a political vote, but those which he or she has over against a community. They are a radical rejection of every form of totalitarianism – political, industrial, trade-union, ecclesiastical, *etc.*

The doctrine of human rights received its first spiritual impulse from Renaissance humanism,* in the idea of the fundamentally free, autonomous and self-determining human person. Locke* and Kant* translated this into the political terms of the liberal state, which has as its only task the protection of the freedom and rights of its individual citizens. The state has to refrain as much as possible from interference with society. This idea was translated into economic terms by the founders of the so-called classical theory, Adam Smith (1723–90) and David Ricardo (1772–1823), and in modern times by Milton Friedman (b. 1912) and others. This liberal, individualistic concept of the state was often combined with an implicit or explicit deism.* If social and economic forces were left to operate freely, as though moved by an 'invisible hand', a perfect harmony would automatically be established.

Explicit *Christian thinking* about and articulation of the idea of human rights is of more recent origin. But the issue itself is long-standing. From a *biblical viewpoint*, human rights are founded not in the fundamental freedom of humanity, but in the revealed truths that: 1. men and women are the fruit of the everlasting word of creation* (Gn. 1:26–27), as confirmed in the person and work of Jesus Christ (Rom. 8:29; Eph. 4:24; Col. 1:15), and as the bearers of God's image* have a dignity and worth guaranteed by their creator (Gn. 9:6; Jas. 3:9); 2. they are called and enabled by that same creative word to be stewards* of God's creation (Gn. 1:28; 9:1, 2; Ps. 8:6–9); and 3. for that reason they have a momentum in themselves and a responsibility towards themselves and others before God (Mt. 22:35–40). This responsibility stands alongside and, if necessary, may need to be exercised even over against the communities of which they are part (*e.g.* Acts 4:19; 5:29). Their rights may need to be claimed over against, *e.g.* states (*cf.* 1 Ki. 21:3; Acts 16:37) or families (*cf.* Mt. 8:21–22).

The individualistic concepts of human freedom and rights and of the state were implemented in various Western countries in the 19th century. They failed to produce, however, the predicted harmony. Since they were only formal in nature, they did not offer a substantial basis for freedom for everyone, and in particular not for manual labourers. The consequence was a process of proletarianization, a basic denial of humanity. This necessitated labour legislation by governments to protect workers and their families against bad conditions of work and inadequate wages, in order to guarantee a minimum level of livelihood. This process accelerated rapidly after World War II, at least in the highly industrialized countries, and a fundamental shift took place. Regulations were sought, not only to protect individuals against unworthy conditions of work but also to augment their possibilities for wider development.

The result has been that, next to classical human rights (freedom of religion, conscience, expression of opinion, press, association, and disposal of property, equality before the law, security of the person), new social, economic and cultural human rights were formulated, a number of which found a place in international documents such as the United Nations' Universal Declaration of Human Rights (1948) and, with a more positive effect, the European Convention on Human Rights (1953), and in several national constitutions. These new rights include the right to life, food, clothing, housing, integrity of the human body, health insurance, unemployment benefit, old-age pensions, education, participation in culture, democracy in industry, *etc.*

A key question became, 'Who is to guarantee these rights?' The answer of many has been that the state has the primary responsibility. This whole development, however, has caused 1. a far-reaching individualization and even fragmentation of society, with a process of 'massification' as a consequence; 2. a tendency towards a totalitarian democracy in the name of freedom and equality, in the spirit of Jean Jacques Rousseau (1712–78; *cf.* his 'social contract'); 3. a denial of a basic plurality and diversity of communities in human life (*e.g.*, families, industries, trade unions, artistic companies, cultural organizations, schools, churches, universities), each of which has, within the general cultural mandate given to mankind (Gn. 2:15), its specific task and responsibilities. Human rights can flourish only in such a pluralist, non-totalitarian society, in which groups of people have the freedom to organize, at least in part, their own communal life and in which the individual has a certain freedom to move from one community to another.

Bibliography

J. N. D. Anderson, *Liberty, Law and Justice* (London, 1978); J. Gladwin, 'Human Rights', in D. F. Wright (ed.), *Essays in Evangelical Social Ethics* (Exeter, 1979); P. Marshall, *Human Rights Theories in Christian Perspective* (Toronto, 1983); A. O. Miller (ed.), *A Christian Declaration of Human Rights* (Grand Rapids, MI, 1978); J. Moltmann, *On Human Dignity* (London, 1984); Reformed Ecumenical Synod, *Testimony on Human Rights* (Grand Rapids, MI, 1983); M. Stackhouse, *Creeds, Society and Human Rights* (Grand Rapids, MI, 1984); J. R. W. Stott, *Issues Facing Christians Today* (Basingstoke, 1985); *Theological Aspects of Human Rights* (WCC Exchange 6; Geneva, 1977); C. J. H. Wright, *Human Rights: A Study in Biblical Themes* (Bramcote, Nottingham, 1979).

J.D.De.

RITSCHL, ALBRECHT (1822–89), German systematic theologian, professor at Bonn (1852–64) and Göttingen (1864–89). Through his own writings and those of his disciples, especially Herrmann* and Harnack,* Ritschl was probably the most influential continental Protestant theologian between Schleiermacher* and Barth,* certainly during the period 1875–1930, the heyday of liberal* Protestantism.

Ritschl followed Kant* in rejecting metaphysical knowledge of God and stressing the ethical elements of religion. God was to be known not in himself, but in his effects on mankind, understood in terms of Christian experience of justification* and reconciliation (see Atonement*) and progress towards the kingdom of God. In proposing this approach, most clearly expressed in vol. 3 of *The Christian Doctrine of Justification and Reconciliation* (1874; ET, Edinburgh, 1900), Ritschl rejected certain kinds of religious experience.* He judged Schleiermacher's sense of 'absolute

dependence' too subjective, and ruled out all mysticism* and pietism* as individualistic, amoral and not distinctively Christian. God was to be known rather through the gospel witness to Jesus and his unique vocation to fulfil God's will for the world by inaugurating the kingdom, which Ritschl defined as the 'organization of humanity through action inspired by love'. Thus Jesus has the 'value' for us of God, and demonstrates that Christianity is like an ellipse, with justification and reconciliation as one focus and the kingdom of God* as the other.

Ritschl has been criticized for maintaining an ethical rather than a religious view of justification and reconciliation, reading Luther* very differently from someone like Otto.* His assertion that all religious doctrines are 'value-judgments' that affirm or deny man's worth or value has seemed to many to drive an unacceptable wedge between fact and value, history and interpretation, objective and subjective salvation. Yet in insisting on the need for justification and reconciliation and locating them primarily in the church (rather than the heart of the believer), Ritschl moved some way beyond Schleiermacher's individualistic optimism. He may even have contributed, via Herrmann, to Barth's interest in Christology and decision to undertake a church dogmatics.

Barth himself, however, always stressed his differences with Ritschl and the Ritschlian school, seeing in his own theological teachers' support of Germany's declaration of war in August 1914 proof that their approach produced a dangerous confusion between the values of German civilization and the values of the kingdom of God. Yet the fact that Ritschlian theology produced an inadequate understanding of a this-worldly kingdom need not be allowed to obscure Ritschl's achievement in correctly identifying the kingdom of God as a central concern of the teaching of Jesus.

It can also be argued that Barth's well-known repudiation of Ritschl (*cf. Protestant Theology in the Nineteenth Century*, London, 1972) is an insufficient basis for neglecting Ritschl's influence in other areas of theology. Yet the contribution of Ritschl's concept of value-judgments to Bultmann's* existential* theology has been largely overlooked, and Pannenberg* is one of the few contemporary theologians who has given Ritschl's pioneering attempt 'to build his Christology on the question about the divinity of the historical man Jesus' (*Jesus – God and Man*, Philadelphia, 1968, p. 37) the kind of attention, and reasoned disagreement, that Barth afforded to Schleiermacher.

Bibliography

H. R. Mackintosh, *Types of Modern Theology* (London, 1937); D. L. Mueller, *An Introduction to the Theology of Albert Ritschl* (Philadelphia, 1969); B. M. G. Reardon, *Liberal Protestantism* (London, 1968); J. Richmond, *Ritschl: A Reappraisal* (London, 1978).

P.N.H.

ROBINSON, JOHN ARTHUR THOMAS (1919–1983), Anglican bishop and theologian. A prolific and controversial writer, Robinson made significant scholarly contributions in the areas of NT, systematic theology,* apologetics,* Christian ethics,* and liturgics.* He began his career as a fellow and Dean of Clare College, Cambridge (1951–59), achieved fame as the suffragan Bishop of Southwark (South London) with responsibility for Woolwich (1959–69), and ended his days as Dean of Trinity College, Cambridge (1969–83). *Honest to God* (London, 1963), which sold more than 1,000,000 copies, was an attempt to commend the Christian faith to the modern man who, he thought, was unable to receive the gospel when presented with it in traditional terms. The book infuriated most orthodox churchmen, and Robinson became England's best-known (if most radical) theologian.

His most substantial contributions were to NT studies, where many of his views were surprisingly conservative (by the standards of contemporary critical scholarship). In a series of studies on John's Gospel, culminating in the Bampton Lectures* he was preparing at the time of his death (*The Priority of John*, ed. J. A. Coakley, London, 1985), he argued for both the essential historicity and early date of the book. In *Redating the New Testament* (London, 1976) he defended the view that all four gospels should be dated prior to the destruction of Jerusalem (AD 70) and expressed equally conservative views on other critical issues. On the other hand, *Jesus and His Coming* (London, 1957) was an influen-

tial statement of the view that Jesus did not teach or expect his future second coming (see Eschatology*), and *In the End, God* (London, 1950) propounded universalism.* His doctrine of the church was sacramentalist (see *The Body: A Study in Pauline Theology*, London, 1952), his ethics opposed love to law, while his Christology* and essential theology were modernist (see *The Human Face of God*, London, 1973).

Bibliography

Current Biography Yearbook 1984 (New York, 1985); *The Annual Obituary 1983* (Chicago and London, 1984); R. P. McBrien, *The Church in the Thought of Bishop John Robinson* (Philadelphia, 1966).

W.W.G.

ROMAN CATHOLIC THEOLOGY. Different schools of theology arose very early in the church,* but it remained essentially united for a thousand years despite schisms,* heresies* and bitter controversies. During this period the prominence of the see of Rome steadily increased (see Papacy*). Its authoritarian claims were well advanced by the 11th century and certain doctrinal emphases became increasingly clear. It is only with the division between the Eastern and Western churches formalized in 1054 (the 'Great Schism') that we can speak more precisely of a Roman Catholic theology. The 16th-century rift with Protestantism* at the Reformation* sharpened its distinctiveness.

Roman Catholic theology is so comprehensive that it cannot easily be summarized. It is necessary to distinguish between official teaching and the opinions expressed by the many schools of theology. The teaching office of the church, the *Magisterium*, presents a far more monolithic structure than the diversity of the schools might suggest. There was, for instance, a major clash in the Middle Ages between the followers of Duns Scotus* and those of Thomas Aquinas.* It has been the role of the bishops of Rome and of ecumenical councils* to sift the findings of the various theological schools. This was a significant part of the work of the Council of Trent (1545–63), which not only took a firm stance in the face of the challenge of Protestantism,* but also anathematized many of the opinions that had been debated in medieval theology. Even then a large number of options were left open.

Yet even papal pronouncements and conciliar definitions are recognized to be historically conditioned. They are constantly open to fresh interpretation and application by the living authority* of the church. This results in a remarkable elasticity in elucidation, which can be a source of bewilderment to non-Catholics. It also points up a fundamental factor in Roman Catholic theology, which is its emphasis on a centralized priestly authority. This is focused in the bishop of Rome in his responsibility for the universal church, supported by the college of bishops. Though it has been variously interpreted, apostolic succession in the ministry* requires ordination in the line of the successors of Peter and being in communion with the see of Rome. Sacramental graces are bestowed through the priesthood, which thus exercises a very great authority in the church's life. The Second Vatican Council (1962–65) sought to rediscover the role of the laity,* to which the Catholic Church has always paid lip-service, but clerical control is firmly built into the doctrine of the priesthood.

There is, nevertheless, much common ground with Christians of other traditions. Roman Catholics accept the same Scriptures* as normative, though they include the writings in the Apocrypha: they hold to the same early creeds:* they believe in the doctrine of the Trinity* and the divinity of Christ.* But the teaching authority of the church enables them to extrapolate from the Scriptures through a belief in doctrinal development,* ably expounded by Newman* in the 19th century. What therefore appears to be unacceptable dogma* to the outsider will still be claimed as scriptural. The Marian dogmas of the immaculate conception and of the assumption illustrate the point (see Mary*). The claim to papal infallibility only compounds the problem.

Early medieval theology was evolved largely in a monastic setting (see Monastic Theology*). The Rule of Benedict* (c. 540) had a long-lasting influence, where the 'divine office' (worship at regular hours) was the inspiration for the work, study and private prayer that filled the rest of the day. Theology in such a context aimed at holiness and dedication of life. A radical change came with scholasticism* in the eleventh century. This was a largely new method, of which Anselm* was regarded as father, though some of its prin-

ciples were traced back to Augustine.* It held that reason had some access to the truths of faith, so faith should be shown to be reasonable even for the unbeliever. Anselm was not a rationalist: faith was still supreme over reason.

Meanwhile Peter Abelard* was formulating many of the questions that would be faced by the scholastics. Their supreme achievement was the *Summa Theologica* of Thomas Aquinas in the 13th century. The rediscovery of Aristotle* turned theology into a scientific discipline. Reason and faith were sharply differentiated. Philosophy was now the tool of theology, with the consequent danger of theology becoming increasingly divorced from experience. So fundamental did Aquinas become to Catholic theology that philosophical training has for centuries played a far more important part in preparation for the priesthood than scriptural studies. Only recently has this pattern begun to be reversed.

Philosophical categories can quickly become dated. When they have been hallowed by theological use, they can become a serious hindrance. For example the concept of 'transubstantiation' in the mass (see Eucharist*), whereby the bread and wine are understood to become the body and blood of Christ, was originally used to try to correct a physical literalism. Ultimately it had the reverse effect. At the Reformation* it became a major subject of dispute. To all appearances the priest at the mass was offering again the sacrifice of Christ. Although such an interpretation would be hotly denied by most Catholics today, liturgical language still uses the words 'We offer Christ'. Contemporary theologians find the Aristotelian categories of 'substance' and 'accidents' a very inadequate theological tool.

The central theological debate at the Reformation concerned the nature of grace.* The situation was confused by the fact that when Catholics spoke of justification,* they also included sanctification,* whereas Protestants sharply differentiated between the two. Catholic theology has long been concerned with the question of human freedom* – what part does man play in his salvation,* if he is at all a responsible agent? It was such issues that the Council of Trent sought to clarify (see Reformation, Catholic Counter-*). This Council was held to be ecumenical by the Catholic Church. It confirmed the seven sacraments* as instituted by Christ, the doctrine of transubstantiation, the equal authority of Scripture and tradition* as sources of truth, and the right of the church to declare how the Bible should be interpreted. Its stance against the Reformation pervaded Catholic theology well beyond Vatican I (1869–70) and affected Catholic opposition to the whole trend of the 18th-century Enlightenment.*

Modern developments in Catholic theology include the liturgical* movement and the return first to patristic* studies and then to the Bible. The Second Vatican Council opened the door to ecumenical* dialogue and laid the foundations for the construction of liberation theology* in Latin America.

At the heart of Roman Catholic theology lies its exclusive understanding of the church and its authority. Its teaching authority stands over that of the Bible and its interpretation. Its priestly authority has control over the church's sacramental life. Yet there is great diversity of opinion among individuals, discernible even in the documents of a Council such as Vatican II. Far from being unchanging, the Catholic Church is constantly in process of development: it is the direction that it will take which remains unpredictable.

Bibliography

G. C. Berkouwer, *The Conflict with Rome* (Philadelphia, 1957); *idem*, *The Second Vatican Council and the New Catholicism* (Grand Rapids, MI, 1965); G. Carey, *Meeting of the Waters* (London, 1985); F. Copleston, *A History of Philosophy*, vol. 2 (London, 1950); R. Haight, *The Experience and Language of Grace* (Ramsey, NJ, 1979); D. Knowles, *The Evolution of Medieval Thought* (London, 1962); W. Niesel, *Reformed Symbolics: A Comparison of Catholicism, Orthodoxy and Protestantism* (Edinburgh, 1962); K. Rahner, H. Roos, J. Neuner (eds.), *The Teaching of the Catholic Church* (Cork, 1966); V. Subilia, *The Problem of Catholicism* (London, 1964); P. Toon, *Protestants and Catholics* (Ann Arbor, MI, 1984).

J.C.

ROMANTICISM. The term 'romanticism' is found in common usage in almost every sphere of human thought and action – religion, philosophy, history, politics, poetry, architecture, music, art. Despite its wide usage, it is very difficult to define with any agreed precision. According to A. O. Lovejoy (1873–1962), it 'has come to mean so many things that by itself, it means nothing. It has ceased to perform the function of a verbal sign' ('On the Discrimination of Romanticisms', 1924; repr. in *Essays in the History of Ideas*, Baltimore, MD, 1948). An agreed definition is problematic because the word assumes many shades of meaning within the same discipline, and varies in usage as we move across national frontiers as well as from one generation to the next. Despite these complications, the term is increasingly accepted as a label embracing a cluster of principles and ideas which came into growing prominence toward the end of the 18th and during the course of the 19th century. Even Lovejoy speaks of a 'Romantic period' between 1780 and 1830.

Few of those we consider 'Romantics' ever thought of themselves as such. They would have resented the thought of being party to a Romantic movement, for one of their most cherished principles was that of particularity and individuality. Another common feature was their rejection of classicism. A. W. von Schlegel (1767–1845) published a series of articles in 1809–11 in which he compared romanticism and classicism with the antitheses of 'organic-mechanical' and 'plastic-picturesque'. For others, this was synonymous with the difference between death and life. Life, and a meaning for existence, were to be found in a rediscovery of a sense of the infinite and an exploration of the irrational element in the human personality.

The Romantics reacted fiercely against the rational categorizations of the Enlightenment* which, they believed, had so distorted the nature of the spiritual dimension that it was in danger of destroying people's interest and involvement therein. Ridiculing the concept of an absentee God and a mechanistic universe, Coleridge* condemns the attempt to construct proofs for the existence of God, Schleiermacher* diverts the emphasis from rationalistic doctrinal assertions to individual feeling or experience, and William Blake (1757–1827) and William Wordsworth (1770–1850) mould nature once more into a garden in which one can sense the nearness of God. The creator is immanent in everything that exists as its life-giving force.

The same immanentism permeates the Romantic view of man. He is part of an infinity which surrounds but does not submerge him. Consciousness of, and participation in, the infinite fall within the capacity of every man. The limitations imposed by the Enlightenment on the scope of the discursive reason are surmounted by means of a special faculty or ability called 'the illative sense' by J. H. Newman,* 'Reason' (as distinguished from 'Understanding') by Coleridge, and 'feeling' by Schleiermacher. According to Coleridge, this faculty enables people to discern 'invisible realities or spiritual objects'. Reason is the source of transcendental ideas. For Schleiermacher, theology is the reading-off of our experiences.

Romanticism served to provoke many searching questions concerning the very essence of religion. For theology its most beneficial legacy was threefold. First, it required that theologians undertake a radical reappraisal of the relationship between truth and its verbal statement. Secondly, it demanded an overhaul of the assumed connection between religious experience and the statement of truth. Thirdly, it produced a devastating and convincing critique of the seemingly immovable inertia which clung tenaciously to inflexible theological models of previous centuries.

Bibliography

M. H. Abrams, *The Mirror and the Lamp* (New York, 1953); *idem, Natural Supernaturalism* (New York 1971); H. N. Fairchild, *Religious Trends in English Poetry*, 5 vols., esp. vols. 3 and 4 (New York, 1939–62); L. Furst, *Romanticism in Perspective* (London, 1969); W. T. Jones, *The Romantic Syndrome* (The Hague, 1961); S. Prickett, *Romanticism and Religion* (Cambridge, 1976).

J.H.E.

RULE OF FAITH, see CREEDS.

RUSSIAN ORTHODOX THEOLOGY.

Within the Eastern Orthodox* theological tradition Russian Orthodox theology has developed specific characteristics of its own.

1. From the beginnings to c. 1800

The conversion of the two most populous Slavic nations, the Poles and the Russians, began with the baptism of the Polish prince Mieszko I in 966 and was followed 22 years later by that of Grand Prince Vladimir of Kiev

(979–1015). An apparently insignificant difference in these two conversions was to influence profoundly the development of theology in the two nations. The Poles accepted their Christianity from Latin-speaking Christians of the West, and their resulting Latin orientation integrated them into Western Europe. The Russians, however, accepted the Christian faith from Constantinople, the capital of the still vigorous 'Roman' Empire (usually called, somewhat inexactly, the Byzantine Empire), where Greek was spoken. The first Greek missionaries to the Slavs, Cyril (826–69) and Methodius (c. 815–85), devised the so-called Glagolithic alphabet (the forerunner of the Cyrillic alphabet used for Russian and several other Slavic languages). Cyril's translations of biblical and liturgical texts laid the foundation for Old Church Slavonic, once widely spoken and still used in the liturgy of Slavic national churches. The use of Slavonic proved a great asset in the conversion of the Slavs, but it was later to make theology and even liturgy less accessible to the Russian masses.

For about 700 years from the conversion of Vladimir to the 18th century, the Russian Church produced no substantial original theological literature, despite the richness of its ethical and spiritual life. A number of factors contribute to this apparent stagnation. The two most prominent are 1. the wealth of the heritage of Greek patristic* theology entering Russia in Slavonic translation, and 2. the centuries-long isolation of Russia from the outside world, particularly the West, caused by the schism of 1054 between Constantinople and Rome, the more than two centuries of Mongol rule in Russia after 1237, and the capture of Constantinople by the Muslim Turks in 1453. The flood of theological and spiritual works translated from Greek into Slavonic simply submerged the Russian Church and made original work seem superfluous. The isolation of Russia kept it largely unaware of theology as a science until well into the 17th century.

Nevertheless, one note of continuing significance for Russian theology through the centuries was sounded early, by the first non-Greek metropolitan bishop of Kiev, Ilarion (*fl.* 1037–54), who produced a confession of faith as well as a classical sermon, 'On Law and Grace', around 1051. It is the sermon that foreshadows the future: Ilarion sets Russia in

599

redemptive history, giving it an eschatological* role. In addition, he takes what will come to be a typically Russian stand concerning the relationship between faith and good works – a strong theoretical emphasis on the sufficiency of faith coupled with a very practical insistence on good works, particularly on asceticism* and charity. But for centuries Ilarion stands virtually alone as an original writer.

In the West, where it was done in Latin, theology was in constant, productive ferment from the beginning of the 11th century, producing great thinkers such as Anselm* of Canterbury, Peter Abelard,* Thomas Aquinas* and Duns Scotus,* as well as a host of lesser figures. Russian theology, done in Slavonic, oriented towards Constantinople, and, for centuries hampered by the Mongol yoke, lacked the stimulus of contact with the West. Greek theology, which it did know, was itself highly conservative and developed largely in the area of mysticism* and the ascetic life; in the East there was no counterpart to the flourishing scholastic* theology of the West.

As Russia emerged from Mongol subjugation in the reign of the Grand Prince of Moscow, Ivan III (1462–1595), Constantinople had fallen to the Turks. Russia, with Moscow as its new power centre, self-consciously assumed the mantle of empire from Constantinople. The Russian Church appropriated Greek theology in large doses (see Eastern Orthodox Theology*), but it was not to develop this theological heritage until it began to feel the shock of the Protestant Reformation and the pressure of Catholic expansion in the Counter-Reformation two centuries later. Ivan married the Byzantine princess Zoé Paleologus, the niece of the last Byzantine emperor, and took up the fallen imperial mantle. This continuity was given a theological interpretation by Abbot Filofei of Pskov (fl. c. 1540). Vassily III (1479–1534), Ivan's successor, was the first Russian ruler to take the title of tsar (from the Roman and Byzantine title 'caesar') and to appropriate the Byzantine double eagle, the symbol of empire. Filofei likened the new tsar to Constantine the Great, the founder of New Rome (i.e. Constantinople), and wrote to him, 'Two Romes have fallen, a third stands, and a fourth shall not be.' This signalled the beginning of a remarkable subservience of Russian theology to tsarist ideology, partly explicable because of the fact that Russian theology derives from Constantinople rather than from Rome. Constantinople was never without a Christian emperor (apart from the brief reign of Julian the Apostate, 361–63) from its establishment to its fall in 1453. Consequently the patriarch of Constantinople could never claim to be the head of all Christendom as the pope did, for he always stood in the shadow of the 'sacred' emperor and his quasi-divine office. The patriarchy of Moscow was established in 1589, bringing the number of Eastern patriarchs back to the traditional early-church number of five (Rome being no longer counted).

At this time, Rome firmly set the direction for Russian theology for two centuries by attempting to bring the Russian church under its influence, since Russia could no longer look to Turkish-ruled Constantinople. The project was facilitated by the fact that most of what is now western Russia then belonged to Poland, or, more properly, to Lithuania, in the commonwealth of Poland-Lithuania. Poland itself was just recovering from an affair with Protestantism, in which the majority of the nobility briefly embraced the Reformation. Having brought most of the Protestants back into its fold, Catholicism turned east, where a few Polish and Lithuanian Catholics lived in the midst of an Orthodox majority. The flood of Catholic propaganda called forth an Orthodox reaction: Prince Konstantin Ostrozhsky (1526–1608) established a printing-house to publish classical Byzantine theological works in translation, and in 1581 it brought out the Ostrog Bible, the first complete Bible in Slavonic.

King Zygmunt (Sigismund) III of Poland-Lithuania convened a church council at Brest in 1596. The resulting Union of Brest established the uniat Eastern Church (i.e. churches in communion with Rome but retaining their own language, liturgy, etc.) and, with mixed success, placed the Russians and Ukrainians in Zygmunt's realm under papal hegemony. Leading the opposition to this union was the Cretan Cyril Lucaris (1572–1638), later to become patriarch first of Alexandria, then of Constantinople. Lucaris spent five years in Poland-Lithuania in an attempt to prevent the submission of the Orthodox to Rome. Lucaris' role illustrates the interplay of Greek Orthodox and Protestant ideas in the development of Russian theology, which continued to be receptive rather than creative, in reaction rather than in action. During his years in Poland-Lithuania, Lucaris became acquainted with Protestant* (chiefly Reformed*) theology and theologians. Consequently, he promoted Protestant ideas in Russia as well as in the Near East, initiating the Protestant connection that produced a two-centuries-long, three-way conflict in Russian theology. The struggle to preserve a distinctive Orthodox tradition was waged at times in alliance with Protestantism against Roman Catholic influence, at times against Protestantism under Roman Catholic influence, and at times against both. The period which began in 1453 with the fall of Constantinople, may conveniently be seen to close with the accession of Tsar Alexander I in 1801, for under this charismatic ruler (1801–25), who was strongly influenced by German and Baltic Protestant pietism* and eschatological speculation, the Protestant influence appeared to predominate. Eventually Alexander's patronage of Protestant and biblical piety would stimulate, largely as a reaction, the real flowering of Russian Orthodox theology in the 19th century.

To the generation following Ostrozhsky and Lucaris belongs the greatest name in Orthodox theology in the 17th century, that of Peter Mogila (1596–1646), who was born in Moldavia in 1597 and educated at the Latin school of L'vov in Polish Galicia. In 1640 he published his Confession of Faith, containing Protestant emphases. This confession was translated and revised by another Cretan, Melitios Syrigos (d. c. 1667), somewhat undoing the Protestant influence of Lucaris. It was accepted in this form at the Synod of Jassy in 1643 as the confession of the Eastern churches. Mogila also published a Small Catechism in 1645, somewhat in response to Syrigos' revisions, as well as a liturgical handbook, the Euchologion, both of which again promoted Protestant tendencies. Thus the situation prevailing at the end of the 17th century was one in which Russian theology, without changing its officially anti-Roman and anti-Protestant stand, was permeated with Protestant influences. Patriarch Nikon (1605–81) of Moscow had revised the Orthodox liturgy in 1660, sparking the schism of the Old Believers (raskolniki, fallen-away ones) in reaction; it is significant that the major religious controversy of this period was based not on theological differences but on liturgy. (The Old Believers soon developed pronounced ascetic, separatist, and chiliastic tendencies, which are beyond the scope of our consideration here.)

Tsar Peter the Great (1682–1721) promoted the Westernization of Russian religion in the context of his efforts to Westernize all of Russian life. A small group of theologians in Moscow resisted Protestantizing tendencies, among them Stefan Iavorsky (1658–1722), who enjoyed Peter's favour until he produced his anti-Protestant polemic, Kamen' very (The Rock of Faith) in 1713 (banned in Russia). Peter turned to Feofan (Theophanes) Prokopovich of Kiev (by then in Russian hands) to counter Iavorsky's anti-Protestant polemics, which in Peter's eyes tied Russia to the past. Prokopovich was a typical Russian theologian of his day, in that he relied heavily on two orthodox Lutherans, J. A. Quenstedt (1617–88) and Johann E. Gerhard (1582–1637). In his Introductio ad Theologiam, Prokopovich followed the Protestants in excluding the OT apocrypha from the Bible, but in his major treatise, On the Gratuitous Justification of Sinners through Christ Jesus, he rejected the Protestant doctrine of the bondage of the will. Although we are 'saved by faith alone,' faith is never 'lonely,' but must be accompanied by good works as Ilarion had taught 600 years earlier.

Opposed by the Moscow theologians around Iavorsky, at the tsar's request Prokopovich drafted the new church constitution, the Ecclesiastical Regulations of 1721. It abolished the patriarchate and created the 'Holy Synod' in its stead, a move that placed the Russian Church thoroughly under imperial control. Peter was visited by the ecumenically-minded German mathematician G. W. Leibniz,* who saw in Russia the predestined mediator between China and Europe. Leibniz unsuccessfully promoted the idea of an ecumenical council, to be summoned by Peter the Great as the successor to the first Christian emperor, Constantine the Great (just as Filofei of Pskov had said a century before!). Less spectacular but more pervasive was the influence of the German pietist* theologian and educator August Hermann Francke (1663–1727), exercised through the intermediary of the German minority in Russia as well as through Swedish prisoners of war there;

Russian diplomats regularly visited Francke in Halle *en route* to and from western Europe.

Later in the 18th century, Platon Levshin (1737–1812), rector of the Moscow Academy and later metropolitan (not patriarch!) of Moscow, perpetuated the Protestant tendencies of Prokopovich, like him relying heavily on the Lutheran theologian Quenstedt. Although Levshin followed the Orthodox tradition in denouncing 'popery, Calvinism, and Lutheranism' as 'devastating heresies', in fact he held Lutheran views on the sole authority of Scripture as well as on the church as the company of believers rather than an institution. Nevertheless, Levshin's major work (*Orthodox Teaching or a Brief Christian Theology*, Moscow, 1765) marks the first attempt at a theological system in Russian (ET by R. Pinkerton, *The Present State of the Greek Church in Russia . . .*, Edinburgh, 1814, and G. Potessaro, *The Orthodox Doctrine of the Apostolic Eastern Church*, London, 1857). At this time, Russian theological education and writing were strongly coloured by Western models, Roman Catholic as well as Protestant. Such an imported theology remained a fragile transplant and could not strike deep roots in Russia. Not until the end of the period would Juvenal Medvedsky (1767–1809) compose the first truly Russian systematic theology.

As always in Russia, where theology remained more mystical and practical than speculative, the ascetics were more influential than the Protestantizing theologians, as for example in the case of the two monks, St Tikhon of Zadonsk (1724–83) and Paisy Velichkovsky (1722–94). Tikhon relinquished an episcopate in Voronezh for the monastery of Zadonsk. He promoted a practical love ethic based on mystical reflection on the passion of Christ. Velichkovsky gave a new impetus to the hesychast* (quietist) spirituality of the Byzantine Church, which had long been popular in Russia, by publishing the hesychast spiritual and devotional handbook *Philokalia (Love of the Good)* in Slavonic. The *Philokalia* emphasizes an intense personal devotion to Jesus based on the frequent repetition of the 'prayer of the heart' or 'Jesus prayer' – the short ejaculation, 'Lord Jesus Christ, Son of God, have mercy on me!'

Although the non-dogmatic and internationalist ideas of freemasonry enjoyed a certain vogue during the reign of Catherine the Great (1762–96), Russian spirituality soon turned back to its fascination with the Russian role in the end times. The German physician Johann Heinrich Jung-Stilling (1740–1817) contributed to the nationalistic tendencies of Russian theological speculation with his conviction that the antichrist had been at work in the French Revolution and that all true Christians were called to gather in the East, in Russia, to withstand him. Thus a note first sounded by Metropolitan Ilarion of Kiev in 1051, namely the conviction that Russia has an important role to play in initiating the last days, continued to resound for three-quarters of a millennium: Alexander I would be seen as the 'angel flying through the midst of heaven' of Rev. 8:13. Indeed, the conviction that Russia must play a central role in the last days would continue to be heard in both tsarist and communist Russia (in secularized dress) to the present day, and to echo in an altered form in the West in the speculations of those who see the Soviet Union not as God's agent but as the opposite – the apocalyptic, anti-Christian power of the end times.

Russian Orthodox theology has been consistently a conservative force, but while it preserved major elements of patristic Gk. thought, it treated them as though they were Russian. From its very beginnings it had strongly nationalistic and eschatological overtones, assigning Russia a prominent role in the conversion of the world and in the culmination of salvation-history.* In the 17th and 18th centuries, Russian theology was deeply influenced by Protestantism, first by Lutheran scholasticism, and then by pietism. Throughout the period 1453–1801, it was never original or independent, but always borrowing, first from the Greeks, then from the Germans. Nevertheless, it has consistently been eager to claim a special destiny for Moscow and the Russian people, whether in terms of the 'third Rome' (Filofei of Pskov), of the conversion of Asia (Leibniz), or in the ultimate conflicts of the end times (Jung-Stilling). Not being productive of original ideas, it has also produced very little heresy – which may help to explain the survival of the Russian Church through almost seven decades of communist oppression.

Bibliography

G. P. Fedotov, *The Russian Religious Mind*,

2 vols. (Cambridge, MA, and London, 1946, 1966); G. Florovsky, *Ways of Russian Theology* (Belmont, MA, 1979); P. Kawerau, *Die Christentum des Ostens* (Stuttgart, 1972); G. A. Maloney, *History of Orthodox Theology since 1453* (Belmont, MA, 1976).

H.O.J.B.

2. From the 19th century to the present

The finest flowering of Russian Orthodox religious thought began in the later 19th century. Its roots lay in the more liberal atmosphere following the rigid rule of Nicholas I (1825–55), in the revival of ascetic spirituality led by disciples of Velichkovsky (with an influential centre at Optina) and richly exemplified in St Serafim of Sarov (1759–1833), and in the renewal of theological learning seen in the vigorous church leader, Metropolitan Filaret* of Moscow, and in Alexis Khomyakov (1804–60). The latter's work, anchored in the Eastern patristic tradition, developed a strong emphasis on organic unity and community (cf. *The Church is One*, Willits, CA, 1974; see Sobornost*) as the distinctive genius of Orthodoxy. Khomyakov thus became one of the inspirers of the Slavophil movement, which focused attention on the originality and resources of Russian Orthodox religious culture.

The Russian intelligentsia in the 19th century was identifiable as a stratum of individuals within society concerned to write and speak about the social and political development of their country. By the 1860s positivist* ideas, mostly of Western origin, had established predominance among them, and during the second half of the century all the different strands of the intelligentsia were unified by atheism and a critical stance towards the Russian Orthodox Church. Yet the same period also saw the championing of spiritual values by such isolated geniuses as Tolstoy* and Dostoevsky,* and the drawing together by the lay Orthodox philosopher Vladimir Solovyov (1853–1900) of a wide range of elements in the Orthodox heritage to produce a comprehensive religio-philosophical system. This system in turn acted as a catalyst among certain sections of the intelligentsia, producing the turn-of-the-century phenomenon known as the 'new religious consciousness' or the 'Russian religious renaissance'.

Solovyov was one of a number of philosophers who had become disillusioned with positivism and had turned back to Orthodoxy – not, however, simply to the 'official' Orthodoxy of the church fathers, but to an individualistic and creative reinterpretation of the faith in the light of modern realities. He was well versed in modern scientific developments and wanted to include the fruits of science in his own religio-philosophical scheme. He has been called Russia's first systematic philosopher. His system drew together elements of critical philosophy and Eastern religion: empiricism,* rationalism and mysticism, science and poetry. All are reconciled in a tremendous edifice bound together by the concept of the 'total-unity' of all reality. Among other things, he reconciled on a religious level the two main tendencies of early 19th-century Russian intellectual life, Slavophilism and Westernism. He has had an influence on almost every non-Marxist philosopher of the 20th century.

The fundamental concept in Solovyov's system of 'positive total-unity' is that of 'Godmanhood'. Through the incarnation, God sanctified all creation, including matter. The whole of creation strives for reunion with God. Such reunion is being achieved in an evolutionary manner through the exercise of creative love, which is the motive power of the Trinity.* Solovyov adapted certain concepts derived from the Slavophils, such as Kireyevsky's (1806–56) 'integral knowledge' and Ivan Khomyakov's '*sobornost*' (best defined as 'individual diversity in free unity'), but developed them to their logical conclusion to the extent that his system is vulnerable to the charge of pantheism.*

During the 1890s, the most comprehensive and rigorously scientific positivist world-view so far adopted by the Russian intelligentsia – Marxism* – began to attract an extensive following. Solovyov's own system was of a stature to challenge Marxism, and influenced a whole new generation of the intelligentsia who were growing disillusioned with Marxism's dogmatic materialism.* Politically aware idealistic liberals such as Pyotr Struve (1870–1944), Sergei Askoldov, Semyon Frank (1877–1950), Nikolai Lossky (1903–58), Sergei Bulgakov (1871–1944) and Nikolai Berdyayev (1874–1948) stressed the absolute value and primacy of the individual in political and social progress. Many of these people had been Marxists in their youth, and had been trained in critical techniques; now, turning their criticism against the ethical relativism of Marxism, they looked for an objective ethical system in Kant,* and then moved quickly on to the ethical teachings of Orthodoxy – again, not to academic official Orthodoxy but to a creative reinterpretation in the tradition of the Slavophils and Solovyov. The brothers Trubetskoy, Sergei (1862–1905) and Yevgeni (1863–1920), while remaining true disciples of Solovyov, laid greater stress than he had done on *sobornost* and hence on individual freedom. At the other end of the spectrum, symbolist and decadent poets, artists and writers in the 'new religious consciousness' movement, such as Dmitri Merezhkovsky (1865–1944), Dmitri Filosofov (1872–1940), Zinaida Gippius (1869–1945) and Andrei Bely (1880–1935), acknowledged an extensive debt to Solovyov too, not so much as a philosopher but as a mystic, poet and visionary. From within Marxism, the 'God-builders' such as Maksim Gorky (1868–1936) and Anatoli Lunacharsky (1875–1933) believed that socialism itself must be made into a religion; conversely, the famous philosophers Bulgakov and Berdyayev were examining the revolutionary and socialist potential of religion under the direct influence of Solovyov, as an alternative to the all-embracing Marxist analysis.

Bulgakov has been called the father of Christian socialism in Russia. He became involved with providing a Christian alternative to Marxist socialism and with founding a Christian Socialist party. After 1906, however, he became steadily more disillusioned about the possibility of gradual political change in Russia, and devoted himself more and more to theology, becoming a priest in 1918. Berdyayev moved in a different direction, from Kant to Nietzsche,* formulating an ethics of creativity and a form of Christian anarchism.

In 1922 over a hundred intellectuals who were unsympathetic to Marxism were banished from the Soviet Union to the West. They included a large proportion of the heirs of Solovyov whom we have been discussing. The establishment of the seminary of St Serge in Paris and later that of St Vladimir in New York provided centres where these thinkers could continue their activity and train a new generation of Russian philosophers in exile. It is paradoxical that while the ruling ideology in the USSR, Marxism, is of Western origin,

the emigré Orthodox philosophy which continues to be formulated in the West is derived from the Russian tradition. The mutual cross-fertilization of the Orthodox heritage and the Catholic and Protestant traditions in the West which has taken place since 1922 is beyond the scope of this article.

The most influential exile of 1922 was Berdyayev. It was a happy coincidence that he should arrive in the West at a time when existentialism* was growing in popularity: mutual enrichment followed. Berdyayev's mature outlook is existential and eschatological. From the Slavophils he derives his overriding concern for the person as a creative spirit, in contrast to the 'bourgeois' socialized role-playing individual. He distinguishes two realms of reality: spirit, which is living and free; and nature or being, which is passive, the product of the fall.* Humanity's free creative love of God is to be the source of the salvation of humankind and the world.

Bulgakov's mature philosophy continued to take him in a different direction. He sees the created world as a total unity, bound together by 'Sophia' – the Wisdom of God – as the principle of creation. The world and the Absolute remain distinct, but Sophia relates them, and hence participates in both divine and created nature. Hence Sophia is a third being between God and the world and from here it is a short step to positing the existence of a fourth person of the Trinity. For his teachings Bulgakov was accused of heresy by the Moscow Patriarchate.

In the Soviet Union, the Russian Orthodox Church today is severely restricted by the state, and while it possesses theological educational establishments it can engage in no study which would relate Orthodoxy to the modern world. Over the last twenty years, young converts to Orthodoxy in the USSR have been more and more concerned to apply their faith to Soviet reality and to tackle problems in their lives with spiritual weapons. Their mentors are some powerful Orthodox thinkers who have been converted in Soviet Russia, such as Aleksandr Solzhenitsyn and Anatoli Levitin; but beyond them they are reaching back to Berdyayev and to Bulgakov, and to Solovyov and the Slavophil tradition he enclosed within his own far more comprehensive system.

Bibliography

J. Billington, *The Icon and the Axe: an Interpretive History Of Russian Culture* (New York, 1966); J. M. Edie, J. P. Scanlan, M.-B. Zeldin, G. L. Kline (eds.), *Russian Philosophy*, vol. 3 (Chicago, IL, 1965), G. Kline, *Religious and Anti-Religious Thought in Russia* (Chicago, IL, 1968); G. E. Putnam, *Russian Alternatives to Marxism: Christian Socialism And Idealistic Liberalism in Twentieth-Century Russia* (Knoxville, TN, 1977); D. Treadgold, *The West in Russia and China: Religious and Secular Thought in Modern Times*, vol. 1: *Russia 1472–1917* (Cambridge, 1973); N. Zernov, *The Russian Religious Renaissance of the Twentieth Century* (London, 1963).

P.M.W.

RUTHERFORD, SAMUEL (1600–61). Scottish Covenanter* and writer.

Born near Jedburgh, Rutherford graduated at Edinburgh in 1621 and was later appointed regent of humanity there. This office he demitted in 1625 when some moral misdemeanour was alleged against him. Its insubstantial nature did not prevent him being accepted as a divinity student and inducted in 1627 to the parish of Anwoth, Galloway.

This was done 'without giving engagement to the Bishop', though episcopacy (see Ministry*) had since 1612 been the national church policy. In Rutherford's view, episcopacy brought Arminianism.* He wrote forcibly against that danger in his *Exercitationes Apologeticae pro Divina Gratia* (*Apologetical Exercitations for Divine Grace*, 1636), published in Amsterdam. This led to invitations to chairs in Dutch institutions, but also to a summons from the notorious Court of High Commission which was incensed by the author's persistent nonconformity.

He was deprived of his pastoral office, forbidden to preach, and exiled to Aberdeen – 'the first in the kingdom put to utter silence', he mourned. Aberdeen to him was full of 'Papists or of men of Gallio's naughty faith'. When in 1638 most Scots rebelled and drew up the National Covenant against Charles I's duplicity and Laud's liturgy, Rutherford hurried down from the north to subscribe his name. In 1639 he became professor of divinity at St Andrews.

His *Lex Rex* (1644), written in reply to the 'divine right of kings' theory, caused a furore, not least at the Westminster Assembly, to which he made influential contributions. This work asserts the supremacy of the people; that the law, and no royal tyrant, is king; and that unlimited power pertains to God only. With the Restoration the author (though not the book itself) barely escaped the hands of the public hangman. Its doctrine became the constitutional inheritance of democratic countries in modern times, but not before many Covenanters had died for the only King to whom unswerving loyalty was due.

In 1649, with the principle of religious toleration* beginning to find acceptance in England, Rutherford's *Free Disputation against Pretended Liberty of Conscience* argued that such toleration was against Scripture and common sense. It allowed two religions side by side, and was outrageous ecclesiastically and sinful civilly. The magistrate as God's vicegerent sent offenders to the scaffold, not with the idea of producing spiritual results, but to strengthen the foundations of the civil order.

Rutherford did not recognize the existence of religious minorities; the contempt he expressed for Independents and others in *A Free Disputation* provoked Milton's charge that 'New Presbyter is but Old Priest writ large.' Rutherford nonetheless came to have misgivings about the assumed infallibility of the ruling Covenanting party.

While there has been a resurgence of interest in his political views in North America, he is now chiefly remembered not for his political theory but for his *Letters*. Addressed to correspondents of all classes, they still offer spiritual counsel that is both biblical and insightful, thought-provoking and imaginative; and they do so with true compassion born of experience and understanding.

Cited to answer a charge of treason, the dying Rutherford sent the Privy Council notice of non-appearance, stating that he had a prior summons from 'a Superior Judge and Judicatory'.

Bibliography

A. A. Bonar (ed.), *Letters of Samuel Rutherford* (repr., Edinburgh, 1984); G. D. Henderson, *Religious Life in Seventeenth-Century Scotland* (Cambridge, 1937); A. T. Innes, in *The Evangelical Succession*, second series (Edinburgh, 1883); M. L. Loane, *Makers of*

Religious Freedom in the Seventeenth Century (London, 1960); A. Smellie, *Men of the Covenant* (repr. Edinburgh, 1975).

J.D.Do.

S

SABBATH. Scripture contains numerous references to the sabbath. In view most often is the weekly, seventh-day sabbath (*e.g.* Ex.20:10; Mk. 2:27). In the OT there is also the pattern of sabbath years occuring every seven years and culminating every fifty years in the Year of Jubilee (Ex. 23:10–11; Lv. 25). The sabbath institution is integral to the life of Israel; it is a sign of Israel's identity as God's covenant people (*e.g.* Ex. 31:13; Ezk. 20:12).

The primary provision/demand of the weekly sabbath (the word comes from Heb., related to the verb *šabat*, 'to cease', 'to rest') is that the day be kept holy to the Lord by resting from the activities, especially labour, of the other six days (Ex. 20:8–11; 31:14–15; Is. 58:13). One of the major indictments in the later OT books is that Israel has desecrated the sabbath by conducting business as usual (*e.g.* Ne. 13:15–18; Je. 17:19–23).

Sabbath-rest, however, is not simply idleness or inactivity but is oriented towards worship. The sabbath is 'a day of sacred assembly' (Lv. 23:3); the sacrifices appointed for the tabernacle are increased on the sabbath (Nu. 28:9–10). How Israel as a whole worshipped on the sabbath during OT times is difficult to say. Some indications at least are found in the later custom of weekly synagogue worship which most likely developed from more ancient practices (*cf.* Lk. 4:16; Acts 15:21; 17:2).

Rev. 1:10 is the only explicit mention of the Lord's Day in Scripture. Efforts to find in this verse a reference either to the eschatological Day of the Lord (the final judgment) or to Easter Sunday (an annual day) are not convincing. There can be little doubt that the first day of the week is intended. The adjective translated 'Lord's' (Gk. *kyriakos*) describes the first day, no doubt because the day of Christ's resurrection was in some way set apart by and marked out for the Lord, just as

the only other NT occurrence of the adjective in 1 Cor. 11:20 describes the eucharistic meal instituted by the Lord to commemorate his death (v. 26). In this light Acts 20:7 and 1 Cor. 16:2 are best read as alluding to the church's regular practice of gathering for corporate worship on Sunday.

Is the Lord's Day the Christian sabbath? This has been a matter of perennial debate in the church, especially since the Reformation. Those who answer negatively argue primarily 1. that the sabbath was not instituted until the time of the exodus and then only for Israel, and 2. that the sabbath has been abolished because it was a sign or 'shadow' anticipating the salvation-rest already realized by the work of Christ (Mt. 11:28; Col. 2:17). Of greater weight, however, are the principal arguments for an affirmative answer: 1. that the weekly sabbath is a 'creation ordinance', that is, based on the action of God in blessing, hallowing and himself resting on the seventh day at creation, before the fall (Gn. 2:3; Ex. 20:11; 31:17); 2. that the sabbath commandment, because it is included in the Decalogue (Ex.20:8–11; Dt. 5.12–15), is part of God's enduring moral law; 3. that the writer of Hebrews teaches that the weekly sabbath-sign points to the eschatological rest-order, anticipated by God already at creation and secured, in view of the fall, by the redemptive work of Christ, but which will not be entered by the people of God until Christ's return (Heb. 4:3b–4, 9–11; 9:28).

Bibliography

R. T. Beckwith and W. Stott, *This is the Day* (London, 1978); D. A. Carson (ed.), *From Sabbath to Lord's Day* (Grand Rapids, MI, 1982); J. Murray, *Collected Writings*, vol. 1 (Edinburgh, 1976), pp. 205–228.

R.B.G.

SABELLIANISM, see MONARCHIANISM.

SACRAMENT (Lat. *sacramentum*, military oath) has been commonly used by the Christian church to denote rites or ceremonies used in Christian worship, which have both an outward sign and an inner signification. It is not a word used in Scripture, or one with a settled meaning in the early church. It has come to denote a distinctive class of ceremonies, though there has also been disagreement on how the distinctiveness should be defined. The original definition of a sacrament is attributed to Augustine,* summed up in *The Book of Common Prayer* as 'an outward and visible sign of an inward and spiritual grace'. Augustine's categorization included, however, around thirty ceremonies as *sacramenta*, among which were, for instance, the making of the sign of the cross as well as baptism* and communion.*

The number of the sacraments was systematized by Peter Lombard* in his *Libri Quattuor Sententiarum*. The fourth book distinguishes between sacraments, of which there are seven, and 'sacramentals' which are lesser rites with some sacramentality about them. The seven became the norm for medieval Christendom, and were further systematized by Thomas Aquinas.* They were: baptism; confirmation,* communion, matrimony, penance,* (extreme) unction (see Anointing*), and ordination (see Ministry*). These varied somewhat between themselves and it was not at all clear whether there was in truth an outward sign in penance, or *what* it was in confirmation and ordination, or whether it was a *churchly* ministration in matrimony.

The Reformers viewed these definitions as encrusted by a traditionalism which cried out for reform. Thus the definition was sharpened by the addition to the definition of 'ordained of Christ our Lord in the Gospel' (*cf.* Article XXV of the Thirty-nine Articles). This established baptism and the Lord's Supper as the only two 'sacraments of the gospel' – the only two rightly called sacraments. The other medieval sacraments were downgraded as 'those five commonly called sacraments'. The two remaining sacraments had explicit command of Christ (*cf.* Mt. 28:19–20; Lk. 22:19–20), and were thus clearly differentiated from the five. They corresponded to circumcision and the passover in the old covenant,* one once-for-all-for-life sacrament of initiation, one repeatable sacrament of consolidation and growth. On this analogy the two also have a complementary role in relation to each other, in which baptism may be regarded as admitting to communion (*cf.* Acts 2:37–47; 1 Cor. 10:1–2), although in Protestantism practice has rarely been so straightforward (see Confirmation*).

The Reformers not only corrected the medieval systematization, but also revised the understanding of the means by which God works through the use of sacraments. They denied the doctrine of *ex opere operato* (the understanding that God works simply through the act or deed of administering the outward element) and laid greater emphasis upon the efficacy of a sacrament depending upon its being received with faith. The medieval doctrine was, of course, always qualified by the proviso 'unless the recipients present a barrier (*obex*) to God's grace' – which may actually lead to a doctrine nearer to the Reformers' understanding than either side would have been happy to concede. The Reformers compared sacramental efficacy closely to that of the ministry of the word, which enabled them to ascribe power to the ministry of the sacraments as being akin to the ministry of the word. The more rigorous Reformers confined the ministry of both to the ordained ministers of the church because they saw correspondence between the two kinds of ministry of God's grace or found them linked in Mt. 28:19–20. And the Reformers generally retained a 'high' view of the benefits conferred by God in his sacraments, varying from the medieval and Counter-Reformation authors not so much in this question as in the setting out of the conditions under which God might be expected to confer that grace. Particular issues arose about the two sacraments separately, such as whether infants should continue to be baptized (see Baptism*), and what the Lord meant by 'this is my body'. Many such issues have relevance to general questions about the sacraments (*e.g.*, their relation to OT ordinances).

In recent times the liturgical movement and the ecumenical movement have both emphasized a factor which is present in the 16th-century discussions, but not to the forefront of them. This is the sacraments' ecclesial significance, particularly in the face of an unbelieving world. The sacraments incorporate believers into the visible people of God (see Church*) and sustain them in that membership. They thus represent to the recipients their calling to fulfil the loving, peace-making, missionary and other tasks of God in the world. Their significance is impaired in a divided church, but they stand as a witness to the catholic and undivided character of the people of God in the scriptural revelation against which we have to measure ourselves. They are understood by being done, and it is in the context of obeying the Lord's commands and celebrating the liturgical acts – in other words, in our sacramental worship – that we may expect to be led into a true understanding of the sacraments.

Bibliography

D. Baillie, *The Theology of the Sacraments* (London, 1957); G. C. Berkouwer, *The Sacraments* (Grand Rapids, MI, 1969); J. Calvin, *Institutes* IV. xiv–xix; N. Clark, *An Approach to the Theology of the Sacraments* (London, 1957); P. T. Forsyth, *The Church and the Sacraments* (London, 1917); B. Leeming, *Principles of Sacramental Theology* (London, 1956); O. C. Quick, *The Christian Sacraments* (London, 1927).

C.O.B.

S ACRIFICE. In antiquity, sacrifice was the universal religious observance. The way sacrifice was offered varied, but in Israel there were sacrifices of cereals or liquids (mostly wine), while the most important sacrifices were those of animals. Here we may discern six stages. 1. The bringing of the animal to the altar. 2. The laying of worshippers' hands on the head of the animal. (At least in later times this was accompanied by the confession of sin.) 3. The killing of the animal by the worshipper. 4. The manipulation of the blood of the victim (done by the priest). 5. The burning of parts of the animal on the altar (the whole carcass in a burnt offering). 6. The disposal of the rest of the animal. In sin and guilt offerings this was done by the priests, in peace offerings the priests took a part and the worshipper ate the rest.

Why were sacrifices offered? There may be something in the contention that a prime reason was the promotion of fellowship with God, but there can be no doubt that in the Old Testament the significant element was the putting of the sinful person right with God. Sacrifices were 'to make atonement'* (Ex. 30:10; Lv. 1:4; 4:20; *etc.*). Sin* had put the worshipper in the wrong with God and now sacrifice was offered to atone.

Sin brought the wrath* of God on the sinner: 'you shall not go after other gods . . . lest the anger of the LORD your God be kindled against you' (Dt. 6:14–15, RSV): 'his anger mounted against Israel; because they had no faith in God' (Ps. 78:21–22, RSV). The divine wrath is roused by sin of every kind, and many sins are specifically mentioned

including violence (Ezk. 8:17–18), afflicting widows and orphans (Ex. 22:22–24), adultery (Ezk. 23:27), and covetousness (Je. 6:11–13). With more than 580 references to the wrath of God in the OT, the Israelite was left in no doubt as to the strong divine opposition to every form of evil.

But he was left in no doubt either as to the love of God. That love was shown in many ways, specifically in the sacrificial system which was God's gracious provision for his sinful people, as the repeated commands laid down in Leviticus make abundantly clear. Of the blood on the altar it is specifically said, 'the life of the flesh is in the blood; and I have given it for you upon the altar *to make atonement* for your souls . . .' (Lv. 17:11). The same could be said of the whole of the sacrificial system.

It has frequently been held that the words about *blood* and *life* give us the key to the understanding of the sacrificial approach. The death of the victim (on this view) is seen as a regrettable necessity; it takes place only because that is the one way to get the life in a form in which it can be presented to God. The life of the worshipper is stained by sin, but God allows the substitution of the pure life of a victim without spot. This view, however, does not take account of the strong biblical connection of blood with death;* in the majority of its OT occurrences it refers to violent death (*e.g.* Gn. 9:6; 37:26; 1 Ki. 2:5). Lv. 17:11 refers to the life given up in death and not the life set free by death.

In the NT, worshippers offer no such sacrifices; their sacrifices are spiritual (1 Pet. 2:5), the offering of their bodies as living sacrifices (Rom. 12:1), and generally the doing of good (Heb. 13:15–16; *cf.* Phil. 2:17; 4:18). There is no place for any other sacrifice because Christ has offered the perfect sacrifice that put away sin once and for all.

The NT writers clearly see the death of Jesus as fulfilling perfectly all that the OT sacrifices foreshadowed. It is impossible for the blood of animals to put away human sin (Heb. 10:4), but the willing offering of Jesus does this (Heb. 10:10). Sometimes Jesus' death is described with reference to a particular sacrifice, such as the Passover (1 Cor. 5:7), but more commonly the reference is a general one such as 'Christ loved us and gave himself up for us, a fragrant offering and sacrifice to God' (Eph. 5:2, RSV).

From one point of view Christ by his sacrifice of himself put away the wrath of God from sinners. Paul and John speak of him as a 'propitiation' (Rom. 3:25 and 1 Jn. 2:2, AV; Gk. *hilastērion*). In modern times scholars who reject the idea of the wrath of God suggest that we should understand such passages to mean expiation rather than propitiation (*cf.* RSV). But the linguistics are against this (the *hilaskomai* word group is used for the turning away of wrath, not for expiation). Furthermore, Scripture requires the concept. Expiation is an impersonal term; we expiate a sin or a crime. But propitiation is a personal word; we propitiate a person. And the problem in bringing about our salvation is that by our sin we have put ourselves in the wrong with the living God. We have aroused his wrath, that is exercised against all evil, and this must be reckoned with. Hence one biblical way of looking at Christ's saving work is to see it as averting the divine wrath, that is to say, as a propitiation.

Sacrifice brings out five things in particular. 1. Sin is defiling; the sinner is not fit to approach a holy God. 2. The sacrifice of Christ cleanses sinners from their sin. 3. The death of Christ really deals with sin and puts it away for ever. 4. Our salvation is at cost to God. 5. Those for whom the sacrifice is offered respond by upright living, offering their bodies as a living sacrifice.

Bibliography

L. L. Morris, *The Atonement* (Leicester, 1983), pp. 43–105; R. de Vaux, *Ancient Israel* (London, 1961).

L.L.M.

SAINT. In the OT, God's people are from time to time called 'saints', 'holy ones', as being set apart to the holy God. In the NT 'saints' (*hagioi*) becomes the commonest title used of Christians in general, for the more particular reason that they have been consecrated to God by the atonement of Christ and the gift of the Holy Spirit. This is a status which they already enjoy, and not simply one at which they aim. However, it is not surprising that the expression came in time to be applied especially to people who showed conspicuous marks of their consecration to God, or of the influence of the Holy Spirit upon them, by their character or conduct.

The inclusion of saints in the liturgical calendar* began in the 2nd century. Originally these were local observances of the death-days of martyrs.* The dedication of churches to saints began in the same way, with churches built over the tombs of martyrs. As the fame of martyrs and saints spread, observance of their festivals became more widespread, and universal calendars of saints for the Western and Eastern churches eventually resulted. Biblical saints who were not already commemorated as martyrs were inserted, and in the East this included OT saints. After the Nestorian* controversy, feasts of the Blessed Virgin Mary,* as being the *theotokos* (bearer of God), became especially numerous and popular.

In the Church of Rome, a saint qualifies for inclusion under that title in the calendar when he or she has been canonized by the pope. The requirements for canonization are heroic virtue and miracles wrought in response to the saint's intercession. Heroic virtue contributes to the 'treasury of merits'* (see Purgatory*). Miracles are believed to occur at the saint's tomb or through his relics or images,* or at shrines where the saint is said to have appeared, and these miracles are attributed to the saint's intercession.

Direct requests to a saint for his or her intercession or for other benefits are what is meant by 'the invocation of saints'. The practice implies that the saints can hear such requests and know how to answer them. The practice was certainly in existence by the 4th century, and was eventually introduced into the liturgy, both Eastern and Western. It was abolished by the Reformers, as equivalent to prayer, and tending to treat the saints as gods, and hence inconsistent with the sole mediatorship* of Christ.

Because of the vast numbers of saints' days, and the legends and abuses associated with them, the Reformers were inclined to remove saints from the calendar altogether, but in England and Sweden festivals of NT saints and All Saints' Day were retained.

See also: COMMUNION OF SAINTS; SANCTIFICATION.

Bibliography

W. E. Addis and T. Arnold, *A Catholic Dictionary* (London, 1960); K. Donovan, 'The Sanctoral', in C. P. M. Jones *et al.* (eds.), *The Study of Liturgy* (London, 1978); M.

Perham, *The Communion of Saints* (London, 1980).

R.T.B.

SALVATION. 'Salvation' is the most widely used term in Christian theology to express the provision of God for our human plight. The word-group associated with the verb 'save' has an extensive secular usage which is not sharply differentiated from its theological usage. It can be used of any kind of situation in which a person is delivered from some danger, real or potential; as in healing a person from illness (Mk. 5:28), from enemies (Ps. 44:7) or from the possibility of death (Mt. 8:25). The noun 'salvation' can refer positively to the resulting state of well-being and is not confined to the negative idea of escape from danger. In the OT the verb 'save' expresses particularly God's actions in delivering his people; in the context of his saving Israel from their enemies, the noun can be translated as 'deliverance' (Ps. 3:8, RSV). But it is also used in a very broad sense of the sum total of the effects of God's goodness on his people (Ps. 53:6). Thus the OT understanding of salvation is quite concrete and often covers more than spiritual blessings.

In the gospels the word-group is used of the mighty works of Jesus* in healing* people from disease. But the terminology developed a distinctive sense which was based largely on the OT understanding of God and his gracious action towards his people. By the time of the later writings of the NT it was common to give both God and Jesus the title of 'saviour'. (1 Tim. 1:1; 2 Tim. 1:1), and it would not be unfair to say that this title summed up the Christian doctrine of God in relation to his people. The name 'Jesus' is etymologically 'Yahweh is salvation', and this meaning must have been known to Christians (Mt. 1:21). But salvation is now understood in a new way. The sense of rescue or deliverance is still uppermost, but the reference is to deliverance from sin and from the wrath of God as the ultimate fate which awaits the sinner (Rom. 5:9–10). Christians are those people who are certain that they will be saved, and it has sometimes been held that this concept of a future salvation is primary in the NT (Acts 2:21; Rom. 13:11; 1 Cor. 5:5; Heb. 9:28: 1 Pet. 1:15). However, Christians are also described as 'those who are being saved' (Acts 2:47; 1 Cor. 1:18; 2 Cor. 2:15) and indeed as 'those who have been saved' (Eph. 2:5, 8). Thus the moment of conversion is regarded as the moment of salvation (Tit. 3:5).

The use of the term in itself indicates that the thought is of an action from the outside by God who is the saviour; human beings cannot save themselves by their own efforts (Tit. 3:5). Thus salvation is dependent on the grace of God. It is effected through the action of Jesus Christ whose incarnation and atoning death took place in order that he might save sinners (1 Tim. 1:15). It is revealed in the Scriptures (2 Tim. 3:15), and it becomes effective for individuals through the preaching of the gospel (1 Cor. 1:21), provided that they respond to the gospel message with faith and repentance; those who call on the Lord are saved (Rom. 10:9–10). Thus the word becomes a technical term in NT theology to describe God's action in rescuing people from their sins and their consequences and in bringing them into a situation where they experience his blessings. Salvation is then understood comprehensively as the sum-total of the benefits bestowed on believers by God (Lk. 19:9; Rom. 1:16). Although it will not be fully realized until the consummation of the new age, nevertheless it is a real experience in the here and now (2 Cor. 6:2; Phil. 2:12).

During the history of the church since NT times the doctrine of salvation has constantly been in danger of misunderstanding and corruption. Most commonly, salvation has been thought of as something that people must earn or merit by doing actions that please God and win his favour. At the Reformation, the Protestants insisted that the doctrine of justification* by faith is the indication of whether the church is standing or falling from the truth of the gospel. They realized that salvation is the gift of God and that the church must not usurp his place in declaring who can be saved, even if it is true that the church is appointed to proclaim the gospel. More recently other errors have arisen. Salvation has sometimes been separated from the person of Jesus, who is then regarded as little more than a teacher of morality; the recognition that God was in Christ to reconcile a sinful world to himself has been lost, and salvation has been thought of as exclusively deliverance from ignorance of God and not also as cleansing from sin and its guilt.

The scope of salvation has also been a

matter of dispute. The OT usage of the term to express God's action in saving his people from their enemies has been taken as normative, and salvation has been understood as freeing people from hunger, poverty and the threat of war so that they may live a whole life in this world; the thought of spiritual salvation has retreated into the background. But while there can be no doubt that Christians should be working for these desirable ends, the unfortunate effect can be that the distinctive theological emphasis of the term, which lies at the centre of the NT message, is lost. People fail to realize that the major need of humanity is for reconciliation with God, and that it is only when there is peace between God and humanity that lasting peace between the peoples of the world is possible; in other words, spiritual salvation is not simply a small and dispensable part of a broader 'salvation' but is the basis of a new attitude between people. Granted that the task of the church is to care for the spiritual and the physical needs of people, the NT sees the spiritual task, which is inseparable from material concern, as fundamental.

Bibliography

W. Foerster and G. Fohrer, *TDNT* VII, pp. 965–1024; E. M. B. Green, *The Meaning of Salvation* (London, 1965); C. R. Smith, *The Bible Doctrine of Salvation* (London, 1942); D. F. Wells, *The Search for Salvation* (Leicester, 1978).

I.H.Ma.

SALVATION ARMY. The foundation deed of the Salvation Army (1878) states that in the year 1865 William Booth 'commenced preaching the Gospel in a tent erected in the Friends Burial Ground, Thomas Street, in the parish of Whitechapel in the county of Middlesex and in other places in the same neighbourhood', and that he formed a company of likeminded people 'to bring under the Gospel those who were not in the habit of attending any place of worship' – a society known first as the East London Revival Society, and afterwards as the East London Christian Mission. Later, as groups proliferated, they were united under the name 'The Christian Mission', which became 'The Salvation Army' in 1879, with Booth as its first General.

Born in 1829 in Nottingham, Booth was converted in 1844, associated first with the reformed movement of the Methodist Church, and became a preacher in it in 1852. He entered the New Connection in 1854, became an evangelist in 1855, and married Catherine Mumford in the same year. He resigned in 1862 after ministries in Brighouse and Gateshead, and spent the next three years in evangelistic endeavours in Cornwall and the provinces, before establishing the East London Christian Mission.

The growth of the new movement was phenomenal. In a time of general spiritual awakening, it was 'an idea whose hour had come'. Preaching stations proliferated, full-time evangelists multiplied, and by 1884 the Army had established more than 900 corps. Its development seemed to thrive on fierce, sometimes brutal, opposition and rioting.

Overseas expansion began, first in the USA in 1880, then in Canada and India in 1882. Social work was an inevitable development, in a time when social deprivation was an open sore on British society: involvement in the exposure of white slave traffic, hostels for the homeless and destitute, soup kitchens, unemployment and missing persons' bureaux, prison work, unmarried mothers' homes, besides medical outreach in more than thirty territories world-wide. Today it is at work in over seventy countries, and numbers some 2,000,000 members, with over 2,500 full-time officers and some 100,000 corps workers.

The theology of the Salvation Army is basically Arminian,* traceable to Booth's Methodist* origins, with strong emphasis on human free will,* holding that it is possible for the Christian to lose his salvation, through lack of watchfulness, moral or spiritual failure, or other evidences of backsliding, in marked contrast to the Reformed* doctrine of the final perseverance* of the saints. The Methodist influence is also evident in the Army's doctrine of 'holiness',* which has been developed in its literature both as an experience subsequent to conversion, and as meaning and implying 'entire or complete sanctification',* a state in which a believer no longer commits sin.

The Army regards itself as part of the one church, and has fraternal (observer) status in the World Council of Churches, but is non-sacramental. Booth decided to abandon the sacraments* on the grounds that 1. he could see no scriptural warrant for the view that they were essential to salvation or to be perpetuated and 2. they proved divisive among Christians. Controversial questions should be avoided, he said, as being 'the very poison of hell'.

The Army shared in the widespread spiritual awakening in Britain in the second half of the 19th century as one of a number of movements caught in the floodtide of revival, and its world-wide influence can certainly be traced to the spiritual impetus of that time. With other movements and denominations, however, in the late 20th century, it needs to recapture the fire and inspiration of earlier days.

Bibliography

J. Coutts, *The Salvationists* (Oxford, 1977); St John Ervine, *God's Soldier: General W. Booth*, 2 vols. (London, 1934); R. Sandall *et al.*, *The History of the Salvation Army*, 6 vols. to date (London, 1947–73); B. Watson, *A Hundred Years' War* (London, 1964).

J.P.

SALVATION-HISTORY. At the present time there are two main interpretations of the relation of the biblical message to the events of history. For R. Bultmann,* the historical basis underlying the Christian gospel or 'kerygma'* is not accessible to the historian because of what he regards as the lack of reliable evidence; in any case, to enquire after it is illegitimate for the theologian, because that would mean that faith* would be dependent on the findings of historians. Therefore, the gospel is seen as a message which announces the bare fact of the coming of the Christ, but which is essentially a challenge to the hearer to respond to the possibility of authentic existence by making himself open to the future. This 'demythologized' version may appear to conserve the bare minimum of the gospel, namely that justification* is by faith alone in Christ who is God's word of grace* to sinful man; but the appearance is deceptive. It requires us to accept a bare word which is independent of history, and, for all Bultmann's emphasis on the fact of Christ, there is no real saving event and hence no real act of grace. Over against this view, which in effect confines revelation to the word, stands the view which sees revelation as taking place in words and events.

'Salvation history' (Ger. *Heilsgeschichte*) is a term which refers to the series of historical events which are interpreted by Christian faith as the specific acts of God to save his people. The terminology is particularly associated in the past with J. C. K. von Hofmann (1810–1877) and Adolf Schlatter,* but in post-World War II theology its main protagonist has been Oscar Cullmann (b. 1902) who deliberately presented an alternative understanding of the Bible to that of Bultmann. Cullmann insists that the structure of biblical thinking is historical, and that revelation* takes place through a series of events in which God is active. What actually happened matters, for the believer. To be sure, Cullmann insists that the recognition of the events as salvation-history is a matter of faith and not of historical proof, but this does not affect the point that God is now seen to be active in the world in the historical incarnation, sacrificial death, resurrection and parousia of his Son. Thus the biblical story tells of a pattern of events in which God is active, stretching from creation to the consummation, with Christ's coming as the midpoint of time, the pivot of history. Although Bultmann's followers continue to deny that salvation-history is a category used by the biblical writers (or at least by the ones whom they regard as offering the kernel of biblical teaching), there can be little doubt that this is the correct framework for the interpretation of the Bible. It has been found particularly congenial by evangelical scholars, who have seen in it a viable alternative to the Bultmannian existentialist,* demythologizing approach which dissolves history away.

The most notable evangelical attempt to write a NT theology* from this standpoint is that of G. E. Ladd (1911–82). Ladd insists that revelation takes place through events, but only as they are interpreted by the word. In this way justice is done to the two modes of divine revelation in deed (supremely in Jesus Christ) and in word. Since a limitation of revelation to the word would be to deny the reality of the events of the incarnation and atonement, evangelical theology cannot do other than recognize the insights of the salvation-historical approach.

Bibliography

O. Cullmann, *Christ and Time* (London, 1951); *idem, Salvation as History* (London, 1967); G. E. Ladd, *A Theology of the New*

Testament (Grand Rapids, MI, 1974); D. H. Wallace, 'Oscar Cullmann', in P. E. Hughes (ed.), *Creative Minds in Contemporary Theology* (Grand Rapids, MI, 1966), pp.163–202.

I.H.Ma.

SANCTIFICATION. In biblical religion, the concept of the holiness of God is of paramount importance. It signifies his unblemished righteousness as well as his singular and radiant majesty. The Holy One cannot have communion with the unholy. Sinful humans can only approach him if they are sanctified, *i.e.* made to correspond to his holiness (Lv. 19:2). In the OT, the term sanctification is primarily a technical term of cult ritual. It connotes both *cleansing* (*e.g.* the washing of garments in preparation for an encounter with God's presence, Ex. 19:10, 14), and *consecration*, dedication to the service of God (of priests, the vestments, cult implements, Ex. 19:22; warriors in preparation for holy war, Is. 13:3; first-born, Dt. 15:19; and gifts for the temple, 2 Sa. 8:11).

However, in the OT the meaning of sanctification and holiness also extends beyond the ritual to the moral sphere. Some describe this as the struggle of 'prophetic *vs.* cultic religion' (referring, *e.g.*, to Joel 2:13: 'Rend your hearts and not your garments') or as the supersession of animal sacrifice by the 'sacrifice' of prayer, thanksgiving and a contrite heart (Ps. 50:13ff.; 51:16ff.). The addition of the figurative (moral) understanding of santification can also be observed in the 'Holiness Code' (Lv. 19ff.) where (self-)sanctification consists of observation of God's laws both ceremonial and moral (*cf.* Lv. 11:44 with 20:7–8). It is understood (negatively) as abstention from defilement as well as (positively) implementation of God's commandments. Lv. 20:7 moreover shows human self-sanctification and God's sanctification of man as its cause, side by side, both the imperative and the indicative, in dialectical harmony. Humans must not only sanctify themselves, they can also 'sanctify God' (Nu. 20:12; Ezk. 20:41) or his institution (*e.g.* the sabbath, Ex. 20:11) through obedience. In sum, sanctification is the act or process by which people or things are cleansed and dedicated to God, ritually and morally.

Although there are occasional echoes of the cultic sense of sanctification (Mt. 23:19) or consecration (1 Cor. 7:14; 1 Tim. 4:5), the NT concepts of holiness and sanctification emphasize their moral meaning. This is programmatic in Jesus' confrontation with the Pharisees and scribes over their rules of purification (Mt. 15:19–20). Correspondingly, the apostles hold that people must be sanctified by a cleansing of the heart (Acts 15:9) and conscience (Heb. 9:14) as well as actively living out sanctification in moral conduct (1 Pet. 1:15, *cf.* 1 Thes. 4:1ff.). The figurative (moral) understanding applies also to the NT continuation of the two elements of sanctification in the OT: *cleansing* (*hagiazein* with *katharizein*, Eph. 5:26; Heb. 9:13–14) and dedication to God (*hagiasmos* with *parhistēmi*, Rom. 6:19). Paul appropriates the technical language of cult and ritual for the spiritual commitment of man to God and his service (Rom. 15:16; Col. 1:28): to him, sanctification is the moral equivalent to sacrifice (Rom. 12:1–2).

Believers have been chosen and called for sanctification. It is God's will for them (1 Thes. 4:3), for without it, no-one will see the Lord (Heb. 12:14). Thus, for the rest of their lives, they must no longer live by human passions, but by the will of God (1 Pet. 4:2). Sanctification pertains to soul and body, and it is expressed in 'doing good' (1 Pet. 2:15, 20; 3:6, 17; 3 Jn. 11), and in 'good works' (2 Tim. 2:21; 1 Pet. 2:12; and see Mt. 25:31–46) which, indeed, are the goal of God's salvation for them (Eph. 2:10; Tit. 2:14; 3:1).

In consonance with the moral understanding of the concept, sanctification of believers in the NT is seen primarily as the work of God (*cf.* Jn. 10:36), of Christ (Jn. 17:19; 1 Cor. 1:30; Eph. 5:26; Heb. 2:11; 10:10, 14; 13:2) and especially of the Holy Spirit (Rom. 15:16; 2 Thes. 2:13; 1 Pet. 1:2 and *cf.* 1 Cor. 6:11). It is understood first as a saving event in the past in which believers were sanctified 'once and for all' (Heb. 10:29, looking to the cross of Christ; and 1 Cor. 6:11, looking to their baptism). Thus they can now regularly be addressed as *hēgiasmenoi*, the sanctified (1 Cor. 1:2; Acts 20:32; 26:18; Rom. 15:16; referring to an individual in Heb. 10:29 and 2 Tim. 2:21), or as 'saints'* (*hagioi*). Sanctification is, however, also seen as an ongoing and future work of God (1 Thes. 5:23; Rev. 22:11, *cf.* Jn. 15:2). Beyond that, sanctification is even understood as a realm of human action. Therefore, *hagiasmos* (the Gk. term meaning holiness just as much

613

as sanctification) can denote a state *in which* believers find themselves (2 Thes. 2:13; 1 Pet. 1:2; 1 Thes. 4:7, *cf*. Eph 1:4) and in which they must remain (1 Tim. 2:15; 1 Thes. 4:7) by living in correspondence to their given holiness (*cf*. Eph. 5:3), as well as to a state *to which* they must strive (Rom. 6:19, 22), which they must 'pursue' (Heb. 12:14), or 'complete' (2 Cor. 7:1) in order to attain it (Heb. 12:10). Believers are thus both passive and active in their sanctification. Whereas the two associated verbs denoting cleansing and dedication are used with man as passive and active (2 Tim. 2:21; *cf*. 1 Jn. 3:3), the verb *hagiazein* (to sanctify) may occasionally be used in an active sense with man as subject, in a construction similar to Nu. 20:12, speaking of the sanctification of God, or Christ, in the hearts of the believers (1 Pet. 3:15); but it never seems to connote human self-sanctification – except in the case of Jesus (Jn. 17:17; in Rev. 22:11 it is – like Mat. 6:9 – characteristically imperative passive). In sum, sanctification is seen as a one-time event and as a process, the believers *being* and *becoming* holy and *acting* correspondingly.

In the primitive church, the NT doctrine of sanctification and holiness at first is still very much present. Sanctity is holiness of the heart (*1 Clement* 29:1). Christians are called to be saints (*1 Clem.* Prologue; 59:3; Hermas, *Shepherd*, Visions 3:1; *Didache* 10:5). Because they *are* holy, they aim to 'do all that belongs to sanctification' (*1 Clem.* 30:1; *cf*. *Barnabas* 15:7). This includes personal discipline (*1 Clem.* 32:2) but especially good works of caring for the poor and needy (Hermas, *Shepherd*, Mandates 8:9f.; 2:4). Christians will be highly visible in their pagan environment – theirs is a holiness in the midst of the world (*Diognetus* 5f.), therefore they must witness to God and glorify him by their daily behaviour (2 *Clem.* 13:22ff.; Ignatius, *Eph.* 14:2; Polycarp, *Ep.* 10:2f.; Aristides, *Apology* 15:4ff.). At this point, sanctification is both a soteriological and an ethical concept.

Later, in the Greek church, sanctification continues as a soteriological concept linked to baptism but its moral meaning disappears, yielding to the indigenous terminology of 'virtue'. At the same time, its ritual usage strongly returns, denoting the consecration of priests, liturgical vestments, the elements of the eucharist, water, oil and buildings. Sanctification here is soteriological or ritual.

For Clement of Alexandria* the 'saint' is still the Christian, in so far as his body and soul are the temple of the holy God and he continues to be sanctified in the school of the saviour. His good works lie in the spiritual and material uplifting of his brethren. For that, he does not have to leave his situation; as a pilgrim, he 'lives in the city as if it was the desert' (*Strom*. VII. 7, 3). Two hundred years later, for Theodoret of Cyrrhus (*c*. 393– *c*. 458) the 'saints' are the small band of athletes in asceticism* who, preferably living in the desert, have distinguished themselves by brilliant feats of abstinence which are recommended for imitation. Not only has the term sanctification disappeared; its biblical contents have also changed out of recognition.

Among Latin writers, Tertullian* resumes the moral concept of sanctification and straightforwardly identifies it with sexual abstinence, 'either from birth or from rebirth', and especially with the rejection of a second marriage of the widowed. Augustine* re-emphasizes the soteriological aspect: accusing the Pelagians* of the reduction of justification* to forgiveness of sins (the believer looking after his future moral life himself), he claims that God's saving grace comprises two gifts, forgiveness and the infusion of love (Rom. 5:5), which restore and equip man for his future moral life. For the Latin ear, 'justification' (making righteous) can never denote a merely declarative forgiveness of sins, it includes the effective transformation of the person. Thus, in the tradition of Augustine, Catholic theologians normally include sanctification with justification, indeed defining the latter as if it were the former (*cf*. the Council of Trent, Session VI), and emphasizing the reality and evidence of change in man.

In the Middle Ages, both Bernard of Clairvaux* and Thomas Aquinas* recognize and support Paul's translation of the ritual meaning of sanctification into a moral one. Like Tertullian, Bernard equates sanctification with continence. Thomas, however, recovers the richer content of the term. He expounds it as threefold: purification from sin, confirmation in the good and dedication to the service of God (*Summa Theologica* I/II: 102: 4; II/II: 81: 8).

The Protestant Reformation was sparked by the ambivalence of the Latin concept of justification, as its ingredient of sanctification could be understood as embracing human works necessary for salvation. Luther* re-emphasized declarative justification as forgiveness of sins, but desired to link it closely with sanctification or regeneration leading to good works. We must be made good in order to do good, not do good in order to become good (*Christian Liberty*; *cf.* Melanchthon's *Apology*). Luther originally insisted that good works would follow from faith automatically, as fruit from a tree, whereas Melanchthon* (and Calvin*) urged the continuing necessity of exhortation, the 'third use of the law'. Later in his life, Luther resolutely fought against the 'Antinomians' (see Law and Gospel*) who failed to teach sanctification as the necessary consequence of justification. The Reformation determined civil vocation* as the field of sanctification, good works and Christian perfection* (Augsburg Confession, article 27) and – against popular misconceptions – postulated a progress in sanctification although perfection would never be attained here on earth.

Calvin described the Christian life which follows justification and regeneration* or repentance in terms of mortification, meditation on the future life and the study of piety. In his *Institutes* III. iii. 14 and III. xiv. 9, he defines sanctification as the process by which we are 'more and more' being 'consecrated to the Lord in true purity of life' and 'our hearts formed to obedience to the law' by the indwelling of Christ through the Holy Spirit. Although Calvin has no separate chapter on sanctification the whole thrust of his theology is such that he has been dubbed 'the theologian of sanctification'.

Reformational orthodoxy in the 17th century elevated sanctification to the status of a separate theological topic and spent much energy trying to determine the *ordo salutis** (order of salvation) and sanctification's place in it. It held to the biblical concept of a dual agency of God and man in its process. Puritanism* strongly directed Christian attention to the practice of sanctification. Similarly, pietism* reacted against the intellectualism of some Lutheran* orthodoxy, fighting the 'twin pernicious errors that sanctification was neither possible nor necessary at this time' (Spener). Methodism* shared this concern for sanctification. John Fletcher of Madeley (1729–85) wrote his famous 'Checks to Antinomianism' holding that 'Christ is not a minister of sin but a saviour from sin'. John

Wesley* himself stressed sanctification to the extent that he would speak of 'full sanctification' as a 'second grace' by which believers are being made perfect, not only with 'holiness begun but finished holiness' (*cf.* sermon 35 of his *Forty-four Sermons*, and Charles Wesley's hymn 'God of all power, and truth, and grace'). From here, there is development to the holiness (Keswick) movement* of the 19th and 20th century which stresses 'victorious living' not by human effort but by complete reliance on the strength of Christ living in the believer (see Higher-Life Theology*).

Contemporary theologians sometimes ignore the topic, or often give it only a weak treatment or arbitrarily stress individual aspects, excluding others. For example, Karl Barth* sees sanctification strictly as a work of God only, denying the participation of man as well as the idea of progress; he complements his treatise, however, with a highly original paragraph on vocation to witness, in which he calls for the synergism of the believer with Christ. Emil Brunner* presents a balanced view but again, like Paul Tillich,* rejects the commandments as guiding principles for sanctification.

Theology today should recover and present the whole range of aspects of the biblical teaching: Christians are called to sanctification. It is part of the purpose of their election and remains the indispensable condition of their communion with God. As the complement of justification (forgiveness of sins) it is, in the first place, a work of God, more specifically of the Holy Spirit, both as a one-time act, valid for all time, imputing and imparting holiness, and as an ongoing, progressive work. In the latter sense, it also becomes a human work. It takes place in our earthly lives, as a moral and spiritual cleansing and dedication of soul and body, harnessing and deploying all human faculties in the service of God, for the upbuilding of Christian fellowship and the implementation of God's will in the world. Holiness means to be at God's disposal; it is task-orientated. Sanctification will find expression in a life of prayer and spiritual warfare and discipline, *i.e.* in acts of asceticism, as well as in good works that benefit people for time and eternity. It is the restoration of the image of God* in man, the gradual assimilation of the believer to Christ and 'the mind of Christ', and the 'demonstration of the Spirit and of power' (2 Cor.

2:4). Directed by the double commandment of love of God and love of neighbour as the fullest description of human dedication, it works by the instruction and drive of the Holy Spirit through which we fulfil the requirements of God's law (Rom. 8:14, 4) and obey the NT exhortations. Finally, sanctification, the eager pursuit of holiness in the midst of an unholy world, is the positive alternative to secularism, the attitude of a world turning away from God.

Bibliography

K. Barth, *CD* IV. 2. ch. 66; IV. 3. ch. 71; L. Berkhof, *Systematic Theology* (Grand Rapids, MI, 1938); G. C. Berkouwer, *Faith and Sanctification* (Grand Rapids, MI, 1952); D. G. Bloesch, *Essentials of Evangelical Theology*, vol. 2 (New York, 1982); E. Brunner, *Dogmatics* (London, 1949–62), vol. 3; H. G. A. Lindström, *Wesley and Sanctification* (London, 1961); S. Neill, *Christian Holiness* (London, 1960); J. C. Ryle, *Holiness* (²1877; repr. London, 1956); O. Weber, *Foundations of Dogmatics* (Grand Rapids, MI, 1983), vol. 2.

K.Bo.

SARTRE, JEAN-PAUL, see EXISTENTIALISM.

SATAN, see DEVIL.

SATISFACTION pertains to the work Christ accomplished on the cross in bearing the punishment demanded by the law. Scripture teaches that God's justice (see Righteousness*) was violated and his wrath* aroused by the sin of his creatures. His holy nature required that sin be punished by death. In the plan of God, Christ endured the penalty of death on the cross thereby satisfying God's justice and averting his wrath. Satisfaction is related to atonement,* as cause is to effect.

Satisfaction is not strictly a biblical term, although the idea is woven into the fabric of both testaments. According to the AV (KJV) rendering of Nu. 35:31, God commanded Moses to 'take no satisfaction for the life of a murderer' (*cf.* v. 32). The Heb. *kōper* means a price paid as compensation, *i.e.* a satisfaction. The entire OT sacrificial* system involved the idea of satisfaction. As the victim was slain and its blood sprinkled on the altar, God's wrath against sin was temporarily

appeased. In the NT Christ emerges as the fulfilment of the Jewish sacrificial system. Thus Christ is the lamb that was slain to remove the world's sin (Jn. 1:29). He is the sin offering (Rom. 8:3; 2 Cor. 5:21), the sweet-savour offering (Eph. 5:2), the peace offering (Eph. 2:14) and the passover lamb (1 Cor. 5:7). Is. 53:4–6 speaks the language of satisfaction. Humankind lay under the curse of self-actualized sin. However, the 'punishment' (*mûsār*) due to us was heaped on the Lord's servant, with the result that sinners experience God's 'peace,' *i.e.* forgiveness and spiritual healing.

The principal NT text teaching satisfaction is Rom. 3:21–26. In response to universal sin and to demonstrate his justice 'God presented him (*i.e.* Christ) as a sacrifice of atonement (*hilastērion*), through faith in his blood' (v. 25). The use of *hilasmos* in 1 Jn. 2:2 and 4:10 indicates that Christ renders God propitious by bearing the punishment of sins not his own. According to 2 Cor. 5:21 God purposed that Christ should take the place of sinners, suffer the penalty of their sins, and so enable them to be made righteous before a just God. Paul makes the same point of satisfaction wrought by penal substitution in Gal. 3:13.

Fathers such as Origen,* Athanasius* and Augustine* maintained in the spirit of the above scriptures that Christ offered satisfaction to God by bearing the penalty of the world's sins. It was Anselm,* however, who developed at length the satisfaction theory of the atonement. He argued that since *man* had sinned, *a* man must repay what was owed to God. But no-one save God could make full satisfaction for the sins of the whole world. Hence the death of the God-man provided the infinite merit that made full satisfaction for sins. The Council of Trent (1545–63) concurred that Christ made satisfaction for sinners by his death on the cross. However, for sins committed after baptism the individual makes satisfaction for sins by works of penitence (Canons of Trent, XIV.8).

Orthodox theologians such as Luther,* Calvin,* Owen and Hodge* upheld the view of satisfaction wrought by penal substitution, as do the Belgic Confession, article XXI, the Westminster Confession, ch. VIII. v, and the Thirty-nine Articles, article XXXI. Liberals such as Ritschl,* Harnack* and W. N. Clarke (1841–1912) focus not on satisfaction rendered to an offended God by the sufferings of

Christ, but on the cross as a display of the divine love that constrains sinners to exercise love in their lives.

Bibliography

J. Calvin, *Institutes*, II. xvi-xvii; L. Morris, *The Apostolic Preaching of the Cross* (London, 1965); J. R. W. Stott, *The Cross of Christ* (Leicester, 1986); O. Weber, *Foundations of Dogmatics* (Grand Rapids, MI, 1983), vol. 2.

B.D.

SAUMUR, see Amyraldism.

SCHAEFFER, FRANCIS AUGUST (1912–84). Francis Schaeffer was born in the USA, studied under C. Van Til* and others at Westminster Theological Seminary, Philadelphia, was ordained to the ministry of the Bible Presbyterian Church and in 1948 moved to Switzerland. Eventually at Huemoz (Vaud) he established the 'L'Abri' community which he led until his death. His special ministry was to all who had begun to realize the hopelessness of humanistic ideals and also to Christians who were in danger of drifting with the tides of existentialism* into a relativistic* position. He restored to many Christians a fresh confidence in the truth of God. He spoke of 'true truth'. An orthodox Calvinist, he placed special emphasis on the reliability and authority of the Bible. His apologetic* approach has been described as 'cultural apologetics'. It laid more stress on common grace than did the apologetics of Van Til and the Dooyeweerdians,* and he helped the Christian to argue with the non-Christian and expose the inadequacy of his world-view as well as affirm the objective truth of Christian doctrine and ethics. He collaborated closely with Professor Hans Rookmaaker (1922–77) in the examination of art history as a portrayal of philosophical and religious trends. His many books started to appear in 1968 and, along with his films and public seminars in USA and Europe, gave him a world-wide influence. He did much to restore the confidence of educated evangelicals in an orthodox theology. He helped many to understand cultural trends and thereby to have both a more positive view and use of the arts and an awareness of what was seductive in humanistic culture.

Bibliography

Complete Works, 5 vols. (Westchester, IL, ²1985); *Escape from Reason* (London, 1968); *The God Who is There* (London, 1968); *He is There and He is Not Silent* (London, 1972); *How Should We Then Live?* (London, 1980); *True Spirituality* (London, 1972); *Whatever Happened to the Human Race?* with C. E. Koop (London, 1983). L. T. Dennis (ed.), *Letters of Francis Schaeffer*, vol. 1 (Eastbourne, 1986).

L. T. Dennis, *Francis A. Schaeffer: Portraits of the Man and His Work* (Westchester, IL, 1986); R. W. Ruegsegger (ed.), *Reflections on Francis Schaeffer* (Grand Rapids, MI, 1986); E. Schaeffer, *L'Abri* (London, 1969).

O.R.B.

SCHILLEBEECKX, EDWARD (b. 1919), progressive Roman Catholic theologian. Schillebeeckx is Belgian by birth and a member of the Dominican* order. Until his retirement in 1982 he was professor of dogmatics and the history of theology in the University of Nijmegen in the Netherlands. A prolific writer in all fields of dogmatic theology, his most important work has been on the sacraments, ecclesiology, Christology and hermeneutics.

His influential early work on sacramental* theology proposed a move away from mechanical and impersonal interpretations (as in the idea of transubstantiation) towards a more existential* view of the sacraments as embodiments of the personal presence of Christ and hence a means of encounter with God in Christ.

Schillebeeckx' work is controlled by his view of the hermeneutical* task of theology. This is the task of mediating between past interpretations of the Christian experience of salvation in Christ (in the Bible and tradition) and the cultural situation in which the gospel must be reinterpreted today. The substance of the faith cannot be had in a non-historical form, but only in the fluid, historical forms which it assumes in changing cultural contexts. Thus the tradition from the past cannot be the only norm for theology, but must be creatively reinterpreted in the light of an interpretation of the modern experience of the world. Into the outworking of this hermeneutic enter two further basic principles of Schillebeeckx' approach to theology. 1. He refuses to draw a sharp distinction between nature* and grace.* There is a universal history of God's salvific presence in human experience, which the Christian history of revelation only makes explicit. 2. Especially under the influence of the Frankfurt School,* Schillebeeckx insists that a theology which is to avoid functioning as a mere ideology must be closely related to liberating Christian praxis.* These two principles also help to make the political dimension of experience an important, though not the only, sphere of soteriology and praxis.

In his great work on Christology* (to be completed in three volumes) Schillebeeckx therefore sees the task of Christology as one of relating two sources: the early Christians' interpretations of their experience of salvation through Jesus, and the experience, both Christian and non-Christian, of living in the modern world. To this end he studies in great detail the ways in which the early church interpreted Jesus within its own cultural context, in order to distil certain principles which are constant structures of Christian experience and which must still structure our own understanding of praxis of Christian faith in the very different cultural context of today. Much of the criticism of Schillebeeckx' work on Christology has focused on the significance he gives to a speculative reconstruction of the earliest Christian interpretations of Jesus, which he thinks developed out of the original interpretation of Jesus as the eschatological prophet. This interpretation is important because it preserves the significance of the message and praxis of the historical Jesus, and Schillebeeckx therefore uses it as a critique of later Christologies which neglect these features of Jesus. While he does not consider the development of an incarnational Christology in the Johannine tradition and the fathers to be illegitimate in itself, he judges it one-sided to the extent that it left behind Jesus the eschatological prophet, with the challenge of his message and praxis.

Bibliography

Works: Christ: The Christian Experience in the Modern World (London, 1980); Christ the Sacrament (London, 1963); The Church with a Human Face (London, 1985); Jesus: An Experiment in Christology (London, 1979); The Understanding of Faith (London, 1974).

J. Bowden, Edward Schillebeeckx (London, 1983).

R.J.B.

SCHLATTER, ADOLF (1852–1938), Swiss-German theologian. Born in St Gall, Switzerland, where his father was a pharmacist and lay preacher in an independent church (though mother and children attended the state Reformed church), he studied in Basel and Tübingen (1871–75). Following brief pastoral charges in Zurich and Kasswill-Uttwill (near Lake Constance), he taught NT at Berne (1880–88), systematic theology at Griefswald (1889–93), theology in Berlin (1893–98), and NT at Tübingen (1898–1930). He was the most important figure in the faculty of theology in Tübingen during his time, and also the most influential teacher of a generation of German pastors. His biblical-historical theology and exegesis was in stark contrast to the history-of-religions* approach (see Bultmann*) and liberal theology* (see Harnack*) of others. Rooted firmly in a careful study of language and historical data, with special emphasis on the Jewish context of the NT, he sought to ground both systematic and contemporary theological concerns in the biblical text, rather than in speculative hypotheses. He resisted the call to separate faith and history, criticism and preaching, theology and life. He came to the study of the Bible quite conscious of the fact that he was a Christian theologian. Although he gave due weight to the differences between the OT and NT, he insisted on their underlying unity. Central to his work was the conviction that Jesus was 'the Christ of God' and the heart of the biblical revelation, and that this was the essential hermeneutical* key to the two testaments.

Schlatter's writings were prolific; unfortunately, few are available in English. Perhaps his greatest work is his massive study of faith in the NT (1885), in which he attempted to correct the hyper-Lutheran understanding of justification* by faith. He wrote a series of popular commentaries on the entire NT, alongside more technical and extensive volumes on Matthew (1929), John (1930), Luke (1931), James (1932), the Corinthian epistles (1934), Mark (1935), Romans (1935), Timothy and Titus (1936) and 1 Peter (1937). Those on Matthew and Romans (entitled The Righteousness of God) are the most important. He also wrote a two-volume NT theology (1909), a history of the primitive church (1926; ET, *The Church in the NT Period*, London, 1955), as well as major works on dogmatics (1911) and ethics (1914).

Bibliography

W. W. Gasque, 'The Promise of Adolf Schlatter,' *Crux* 15:2 (June 1979), pp. 5–9; R. Morgan (ed.), *The Nature of New Testament Theology: The Contribution of William Wrede and Adolf Schlatter* (London, 1973) – includes ET of *The Theology of the New Testament and Dogmatics;* P. Stuhlmacher, 'Adolf Schlatter's Interpretation of Scripture', *NTS* 24 (1978), pp. 433–446.

W.W.G.

S**CHISM,** from the Gk. *schisma*, a division in (*cf.* 1 Cor. 1:10), or split from, the church. In the early centuries no clear distinction obtained between schism, an offence against unity and love, and heresy,* error in doctrine. Heretics were assumed to be, in reality or tendency, outside the church (*i.e.* schismatics) and vice-versa. Greater clarity came in response to schismatic movements, *e.g.* Novatianism* and Donatism,* recognized as orthodox in faith and divided only on points of discipline or order. Whereas Cyprian* regarded separation from the institutional church as spiritual death, and sacraments* given in schism as worthless, later theology – especially Augustine* grappling with Donatism – accepted the reality if not the benefit, of schismatic sacraments. Traditional Roman theology has until recently treated bodies out of communion with the papacy (*e.g.* the Eastern church from 1054, and the Reformation churches, including Anglicanism*) as outside the church of Christ; but most Protestant and ecumenical theology has come to view the 'one church' of the creeds as internally in schism. Reunion thus requires not the reintegration of non-church schisms into the church, but the reconciliation of fellow churches to each other.

Bibliography

G. C. Berkouwer, *The Church* (Grand Rapids, MI, 1976); S. L. Greenslade, *Schism in the Early Church* (London, ²1964).

D.F.W.

S**CHLEIERMACHER, FRIEDRICH DANIEL ERNST** (1768–1834), German Protestant theologian commonly thought to be the founding father of liberal* Protestantism, though he transcends that movement and is more properly ranked with the great Reformation divines.

Born into a devout family, Schleiermacher experienced a religious conversion under Moravian influences, but whilst attending a Moravian seminary found his youthful pietist* theology intellectually inadequate. He went to study philosophy at Halle, where he immersed himself in Kant* and Plato.* During his studies there, and his early work as a tutor and pastor, he began the process of reconstructing his account of the Christian faith. His mature years were spent in Halle and later Berlin, as professor, preacher and political activist. He is chiefly known to English-language theology through the third edition of his *On Religion: Speeches to its Cultured Despisers*, and the second edition of his dogmatics, *The Christian Faith*, a formidably difficult work which, along with Barth's* *Church Dogmatics*, is the most important Protestant theological text since Calvin's* *Institutes*. His other significant writings include the methodological sketch *Brief Outline on the Study of Theology*, the posthumous *Hermeneutics* and a large body of sermons, along with translations of Plato, and a *Dialektik* and an *Ethik* which, with much of the important biographical material, remain untranslated.

Schleiermacher's theology is self-consciously *church* theology. He invisages theology as an intellectual exercise which has its origins in the concrete forms of the religious life. Because Christian theology is related to the corporate piety of the Christian community, it is empirical rather than speculative: the Christian faith is not primarily conceptual, and doctrines are a second-order conceptualization of its primary religious truth. In making piety central, Schleiermacher is partly seeking an alternative base for religious knowledge in response to the restrictions placed upon speculative theology by the critical philosophy of Kant and others. His account of revelation* in *The Christian Faith* is thus of a knowledge of God mediated through the corporate experience of redemption rather than of a body of doctrine propositionally revealed. Hence Schleiermacher's perspective on doctrines clearly distinguishes between their dogmatic form and the corporate realities of the religious life to which they give secondary expression, and thus they may be alternatively expressed.

The core of Schleiermacher's understanding of the phenomena of piety lies in his much-disputed notion of the 'feeling of absolute dependence'. He proposes that the primal structure of the religious life, Christian or otherwise, is the consciousness of self as determined by that which transcends the self. In talking of a 'feeling' of dependence, Schleiermacher does not mean 'emotion': much more is he talking of a fundamental structure of personal existence, prior to emotion, action or thought. Self-consciousness is consciousness of dependence, and thus consciousness of God as the 'whence' of the feeling. And so consciousness of the self as dependent is the primary locus of God's self-disclosure to his human creation.

In *The Christian Faith*, this universal understanding of piety is given a distinct Christological* shape. Whereas in the *Speeches on Religion* Schleiermacher sought primarily to commend religion as the implicit backcloth to science and art, and was only peripherally concerned with Christianity, his dogmatics explores how the Christian consciousness of God is determined at every point by the redemptive work of Christ. He understands redemption as the impression made by Jesus' unclouded consciousness of God upon the Christian community, as their own impoverished God-consciousness is repaired through the God-consciousness of Jesus. The relationship of Christ as the archetype of God-consciousness to the history of Jesus is not clear in Schleiermacher, and has been the subject of much criticism since F. C. Baur (see Tübingen School*). Schleiermacher's manner of approaching Christology by a soteriological route means, moreover, that he discards much of the apparatus of classical Christology as an inadequate expression of the Christian self-consciousness.

Schleiermacher consistently refuses to move behind the analysis of the conditions of piety to discuss the objectivity of God in and for himself. Thus in his doctrine of God in *The Christian Faith* he passes over Trinitarian* dogma, since all talk of distinctions within the Godhead is speculation divorced from piety: 'We have no formula for the being of God in

itself as distinct from the being of God in the world' (172.2). Thus the doctrines of creation* and preservation are accorded prior treatment, since they relate immediately to man's consciousness of dependence, and the doctrine of the Trinity is assigned to an appendix (a move which Barth carefully reverses at the beginning of his *Church Dogmatics*).

The relation of dogma to piety is paralleled in Schleiermacher's hermeneutics,* a subject whose contemporary prominence owes much to Schleiermacher's work, notably the recently published posthumous material. Whilst his earlier hermeneutical writings focus on the objectivity of language, he later understands the act of interpretation as *psychological* rather than *grammatical*, piercing through the text to the consciousness of the author to which it affords access.

Like his whole theology, Schleiermacher's hermeneutics have frequently attracted the charge of subjectivism. It is argued that by underlining the primacy of psychological interpretation, he gives priority to questions of meaningfulness rather than truth and locates the text's referent in subjective consciousness rather than objective states of affairs. Similarly, on a broader canvas, he is often thought so to emphasize the religious self-consciousness that he undervalues the objective ground of religious life and thought. Hence he is sometimes charged with initiating the process (completed by Feuerbach*) of reducing theology to anthropology.* This line of criticism was powerfully stated by Barth who nevertheless had far deeper respect for and proximity to Schleiermacher than many who made Barth's earlier repudiation of his predecessor a fixed norm for Schleiermacher interpretation, in a way which Barth himself left behind. This critique is seriously undermined by the fact that Schleiermacher understood the 'feeling of absolute dependence' as *intentional*, *i.e.* referring to an external ground. The religious self-consciousness apprehends a world which transcends the self, so that through piety the 'whence' of the religious life is disclosed. This latter interpretation suggests that Schleiermacher is restating a Reformation emphasis on the coinherence of God and the life of faith, such as can be found in passages from Luther.* It remains, none the less, an open question whether Schleiermacher's theology can support any notion of God's action and presence as other than immanent. This might be borne out by his ambivalence towards miracles* and providence.* Moreover, it is debatable whether his refusal of speculative language about God's own being, in and for himself, betrays a loss of confidence in the possibility of revelation from outside the processes of human history.

After its hostile reception by many under the influence of Barth, Schleiermacher's work has attracted more positive evaluation recently, notably in Germany where a new critical edition is harvesting scholarly inquiry into the development of his thought. It is certainly no longer possible to maintain the easy stereotypes by which Schleiermacher has often been dismissed. He remains the quintessential exponent of an alternative Reformation tradition from that articulated in Calvin and Barth, namely one preoccupied with human religion* as a response to God's self-disclosure. And he constitutes a type of response to Enlightenment* critiques of the possibility of theology, a response in which the reality of God is located in human historical experience.

Bibliography

Works: *Kritische Gesamtausgabe* (Berlin, 1980–); *Brief Outline on the Study of Theology* (Richmond, VA, 1966); *The Christian Faith* (Edinburgh, 1928); *Christmas Eve* (Richmond, VA, 1967); *Hermeneutics* (Missoula, MT, 1977); *On Religion: Speeches to its Cultured Despisers* (London, 1894); *Selected Sermons* (London, 1890).

Studies: K. Barth, *The Theology of Schleiermacher* (Edinburgh, 1982); *idem, Protestant Theology in the Nineteenth Century* (London, 1972); R. B. Brandt, *The Philosophy of Schleiermacher* (New York, 1941); B. A. Gerrish, *A Prince of the Church: Schleiermacher and the Beginnings of Modern Theology* (London, 1984); *idem*, in N. Smart (ed.), *Nineteenth Century Religious Thought in the West* (Cambridge, 1985), vol. 1, pp. 123–156; H. R. Mackintosh, *Types of Modern Theology* (London, 1937); R. R. Niebuhr, *Schleiermacher on Christ and Religion* (London, 1964); M. Redeker, *Schleiermacher* (Philadelphia, 1973); S. W. Sykes, *Friedrich Schleiermacher* (London, 1971); R. R. Williams, *Schleiermacher the Theologian* (Philadelphia, 1978).

J.B.We.

SCHOLASTICISM. 'Scholastic' was used first by humanists* and 16th-century historians of philosophy to describe the philosophers and theologians of the Middle Ages. It was a negative, derogatory term meant to indicate a tradition-bound, logic-chopping mentality, involving a slavish adherence to Aristotle.* While echoes of the old usage remain, today the term usually refers simply to the dominant form of philosophy and theology in the central and later Middle Ages. There is also a modern scholasticism, dating from about 1550 to 1830 and associated with the age of 'confessional orthodoxy', which was influential in both Protestant and Catholic universities of Western Europe. Finally, among contemporary Catholics there is a neoscholasticism which traces its roots to the Middle Ages, especially Thomas Aquinas* (see Thomism*).

When political order began to be restored in Western Europe, from the 9th century onwards, education was also fostered and with it the people in the West began the task of assimilating classical culture, an intellectual tradition far richer than that of the West in that era. Consequently, much of the teaching in the monastic* and cathedral schools, and later in the universities, was built on reading and explication of classical texts. Since the schools were founded and maintained by Christians to foster their faith, a faith rooted in the Bible as an authoritative text, a text-based method was natural to them.

The medievals were convinced that divine revelation* made available to us truth* that otherwise surpassed our understanding (see Faith and Reason*). Hence, Scripture, accepted as divinely inspired, was studied and commented on. It clarified spiritual things but also illumined the understanding of man* and the world.* With the rediscovery of all of the writings of Aristotle (see below), both a more sophisticated dialectical method and an alternative account of reality appeared on the scene. More than anything else, the problem of coming to terms with Aristotle dominated the debates in the medieval schools. Faith still remained prior, and the theologians accepted Anselm's* view that one should not seek to understand in order to believe but believe in order to understand.

The earliest example of the kind of rational analysis of doctrine that became characteristic of scholasticism is found in Boethius'* work *On the Trinity*. Of much greater influence was Abelard,* who sought to provide explanations of the statements of faith. In his *Yes and No* he advanced theological method by making the resolution of disagreements among authorities a part of the theologian's task. Peter Lombard's* *Sentences* become the most widely used textbook in theology. It was a collection of texts from the Bible and the fathers of the church (see Patristic Theology*) on the topics of God, creatures, the incarnation,* redemption,* the sacraments* and last things (see Eschatology*). Written about 1150, this work was still being used and commentaries being written on it at the time of the Reformation* in the 16th century.

In the 13th century, study of the biblical text continued, but gradually the masters also began to treat difficult questions by themselves. So there developed the 'disputed question', a comprehensive examination of a single topic based on the Bible, the fathers and the philosophic tradition. These questions treated such topics as truth, God's power, his will and free choice. The crowning achievement of scholasticism was the *Summa*, which was an orderly presentation of theological issues. Best known of these is Thomas Aquinas' *Summa Theologica*, which he wrote for beginners in theology. In it Aquinas discusses issues in an order appropriate for beginners, treating each topic more briefly than he does in his disputed questions.

Like earlier medieval thinkers in the West, Abelard and his contemporaries in the 12th century had access only to Aristotle's logical writings, but in the 13th century the remainder of Aristotle's writings became available in the West. Instead of Aristotle the dialectician, Aristotle the philosopher challenged Christian thinkers. In Aristotle's *Physics*, *Metaphysics*, *Ethics*, and other works the medievals found an account of reality which was far superior to anything they had known. The difficulty was that this sophisticated account was fundamentally opposed to Christian teaching on such points as the eternity of the world, the nature of the human soul, and the end of human existence. William of Auvergne (c. 1180–1249), Albertus Magnus,* Bonaventura,* Roger Bacon (c. 1214–92), and Thomas Aquinas are the most prominent among the many masters who sought to articulate a Christian position in the

context of the new Aristotle. Each of them has his own solution. In the last century historical criticism has shown that scholasticism was not a single theology or philosophy, but rather consisted of a multiplicity of positions which attempted to deal with a common problem, the challenge of Aristotle's thought.

Around 1270 the situation at Paris was complicated by the fact that certain members of the arts faculty were promoting the interpretation of Aristotle advanced by the commentator Averroes,* who held, for example, that there is only one intellectual soul for all men. Most famous of these arts masters was Siger of Brabant (c. 1235–c. 1282). He and others seem to have thought that, so far as reason goes, Aristotle had given the final word. Siger presented the thought of Aristotle without claiming that it was true but also without challenging it where it contradicts revelation. Because he did not show that Aristotle had erred, he gave the impression that natural reason inevitably contradicts revelation. This led opponents to suggest that he held a double-truth theory, the view that one thesis can be true for philosophy and its opposite true for faith. More satisfactory was the approach taken by Aquinas, who not only insisted, in principle, that all truth is one, but also criticized Aristotle and his commentators, so showing that reason does not contradict faith.

The threat of an unrestrained rationalism, as manifested in Siger and others, led to the condemnation of 1277. The bishop of Paris condemned 219 propositions. Most were those held by Averroes and his followers, but a variety of others, including some held by Aquinas, were included. More important than the content of this condemnation is the reaction which followed it. The conviction of Aquinas and others that philosophy can serve faith gave way to doubts on this score. In Duns Scotus* and William of Ockham* one sees the collaboration of faith and reason beginning to fall apart.

By 1350 scholasticism was in decline. Lectures on the Bible were no longer mandatory and study of the writings of the church fathers had also declined. Dialectical subtleties became more and more the focus. This development worsened what was already a weakness in scholasticism – its lack of historical sense. Later scholastics tended to confine themselves to extracts from the ancients and so lost the historical context and much of the meaning of the original writings. Also, there developed a tendency among these later scholastics to group themselves into schools, and then to focus on the relatively minor issues on which they differed. Ockhamists, Scotists and Thomists battled with one another, and theology became more and more remote from the life of the church. In this context it is little wonder that Erasmus* wanted to return to the simple gospel, that Luther* had no use for Aristotle, and that Calvin* repeatedly attacks the fictions of the schoolmen.

After the Reformation, nominalist, Scotist and Thomist schools continued in the Catholic universities. The most influential new thinker was Francisco de Suarez (see Jesuit Theology*), whose *Metaphysical Disputations* influenced Leibniz,* Christian Wolff (1679–1754) and other philosophers. Among Protestants Melanchthon* employed a humanist Aristotelianism in his theology, while Peter Ramus* promoted an anti-metaphysical humanism. Even so, among Protestants, too, Suarez was influential. In spite of Calvin's anti-scholasticism, Francis Turretin (1623–87) and other Reformed* theologians adopted the scholastic method in their theology.

Contemporary scholasticism is an extensive movement in Catholic circles which started in the early 19th century and flowered after Leo XIII's encyclical *Aeterni Patris* (1879), in which he called for the restoration of Christian philosophy, and singled out the teachings of Thomas Aquinas for special consideration (see Thomism*). Institutes were established and journals founded in both Europe and America. Better-known members of this movement include E. Gilson,* J. Maritain (1882–1973), K. Rahner* and B. Lonergan.*

A weakness of scholasticism has been noted, but it should be added that often the schoolmen have been condemned unheard. They have sometimes been ridiculed (as by Erasmus), and more often ignored, but seldom refuted. Some opponents of scholasticism are repelled by its analytical mode of thought which by its precision places a heavy demand on the reader. But precise definitions and careful arguments are as appropriate in theology as in any other area. Historically it is the scholastics who considered most carefully the relation of faith to reason (see Faith and Reason*) and of theology to the other

sciences. For these reasons the scholastics remain a source of inspiration for philosophers and theologians even today.

Bibliography

M.-D. Chenu, *Nature, Man, and Society in the Twelfth Century* (Chicago, 1968); F. C. Copleston, *A History of Philosophy*, vols. II and III (Westminster, MD, 1950, 1953); E. Gilson, *A History of Christian Philosophy in the Middle Ages* (London, ²1980); *idem, The Spirit of Medieval Philosophy* (New York, 1936); N. Kretzmann, A. Kenny and J. Pinborg (eds.), *Cambridge History of Later Medieval Philosophy* (London, 1982); P. O. Kristeller, *Renaissance Thought: The Classic, Scholastic, and Humanist Strains* (New York, 1955); A. Maurer, *Medieval Philosophy* (New York, 1962); J. Pieper, *Scholasticism: Personalities and Problems of Medieval Philosophy* (New York, 1960); F. van Steenberghen, *Aristotle in the West* (Louvain, 1955); G. Van Riet, *Thomistic Epistemology* (St Louis, 1963).

A.V.

SCHWEITZER, ALBERT (1875–1965). Born in Alsace, Schweitzer was a human dynamo possessing the combined talents, energy and accomplishments of many individuals. He earned doctorates in philosophy, theology, musicology and medicine. At the age of thirty he became a missionary doctor in French Equatorial Africa in obedience to Jesus' command to 'lose his life for my sake and the gospel's'. Through many adversities, including both World Wars, he laboured among the people, eventually building his own hospital. He periodically returned to Europe to give lectures and organ recitals, and during the whole period he continued the writing career which he had begun in student days.

In *The Quest of the Historical Jesus* (1906; ET 1909) Schweitzer demonstrated how all the modern 'historical' reconstructions of the life of Jesus simply attributed to Jesus the liberal theology of their authors. Schweitzer held that Jesus believed the apocalyptic* kingdom* of God would momentarily appear, in response to the zealous piety of himself and his disciples. Thus Jesus taught an 'interim ethic', the need for absolute righteousness* if one hoped to enter the kingdom. Jesus' values of 'higher righteousness', love and faith (described in liberal terms) called for extreme application because of the extremity of the times. One must renounce possessions, turn the other cheek and endure persecutions. In the imminent tribulation Jesus and his disciples would die and rise again, Jesus as the Son of Man.

When the end tarried, Jesus concluded that he must undergo the tribulation alone, on his followers' behalf, and thus usher in the kingdom. Later, Paul reasoned that Jesus' messianic reign had indeed begun, albeit invisibly, and so had the resurrection of his predestined elect. Paul's views of sacraments,* ethics,* the law* and justification* were all a function of his eschatology,* and not influenced by the mystery religions, as many scholars held.

In *The Philosophy of Civilization* (1923) Schweitzer set forth his ethical theory of 'reverence for life', which he saw as the only way to unite world-affirmation with inner moral devotion. All creatures share the 'will to live' but only humans can recognize this common bond. We must cherish the lives of all beings equally and should try not to kill even insects and plants, though of course often we cannot avoid doing so. Schweitzer regarded 'reverence for life' as the principle implicit in the ethic of Jesus. As a child he had felt protective of all animal life, and it is possible that his study of the Hindu and Jainist doctrine of *ahimsa* (non-harm) strengthened him in these feelings.

Bibliography

J. L. Ice, *Schweitzer: Prophet of Radical Theology* (Philadelphia, 1971); O. Kraus, *Albert Schweitzer* (London, 1944); G. N. Marshall, *An Understanding of Albert Schweitzer* (New York, 1966).

R.M.P.

S CHWENCKFELD, CASPAR (1489–1561). A lay theologian and Radical Reformer. From Silesia, Schwenckfeld became a Lutheran in 1518 and from 1522 to 1529 was the chief adviser of Duke Frederick II in the promotion of the Reformation.* By 1524 he had embraced eucharistic* views that were unacceptable to Luther,* and he went into voluntary exile. His theology as it developed put him in the ranks of the Spiritualists among the Radicals (see Reformation, Radical*).

The eucharist played a formative role in his thinking. The true eucharist, he held, is not outward participation in the rite but an inward, spiritual, feeding on the heavenly bread which is the celestial flesh of Christ. Such inward feeding ensured that the communicant was transformed by full participation in the divine nature. As a result, the will, previously paralysed by sin, is liberated to exercise the love to God and man commanded by Christ. This spiritual absorption of the celestial flesh of Christ is made possible by justifying faith which incorporates the believer in the second Adam. Even those, such as Abraham, who lived before the incarnation, were equally partakers of the spiritual Christ if they exercised faith, and are to be deemed Christians. Schwenckfeld rejected Luther's forensic understanding of justifying faith, by linking faith closely with a continuous feeding upon Christ. In this way justification* is closely tied to progressive deification.* It harmonized with his sombre view of sin and his yearning to see the Reformation producing an improvement in morality.

His Christology* matches his eucharistic teaching. He held that the human nature of Christ, although received from Mary, was 'begotten, not made'. He conceived of man's human nature, like his divine nature, progressing from a state of humiliation in the earthly ministry to a glorification which is virtually deification. He insisted that Christ suffered on the cross in his divine, as well as in his human, nature. In this way, Christ's celestial flesh became available for believers by means of the eucharist. It is difficult to discern the difference between the two natures in the state of glorification, and that is why Schwenckfeld was accused by Luther of Eutychianism (see Monophysitism*).

The contrast between 'outer' and 'inner' runs throughout Schwenckfeld's theology. The 'outer' word of God in Scripture* is contrasted with the 'inner' or spiritual word in the heart. The true church is not the outward institution but the company of people who feed spiritually upon Christ. 'Outer' baptism* with water is nothing apart from the 'inner' baptism of the Holy Spirit.* Because of his conviction that the Holy Spirit cannot be fettered by institutions and ceremonies, Schwenckfeld withdrew from communion with other churches but without yielding his irenical belief that God's true spiritual church had members in all communions. It followed that he was a protagonist of toleration.* He argued for the separation of church and state* and yet believed that the Christian had a creative role to play in civil government.

Although he rejected infant baptism, he is not to be confused with the Anabaptists.* The differences between him and them were sharply defined in his long controversy with Pilgram Marpeck (c. 1495–1556).

Bibliography

W. Loetscher, *Schwenckfeld's Participation in the Eucharistic Controversy* (Philadelphia, 1906); P. Maier, *Caspar Schwenckfeld on the Person and Work of Christ* (Assen, Netherlands, 1959); S. G. Shultz, *Caspar Schwenckfeld von Ossig (1489–1561): Spiritual Interpreter of Christianity, Apostle of the Middle Way* (Norristown, PA, 1946); G. H. Williams, *The Radical Reformation* (Philadelphia, 1962).

R.T.J.

SCIENCE AND THEOLOGY.

In this article 'science' is taken to mean the systematic study of the natural world, an activity at once intellectual, practical and social. It is thus to be distinguished from the vast corpus of empirical 'facts' accumulated by that activity and often called 'science' by the layman. The precise character of the scientific enterprise and its methodology have varied with time. 'Modern science' may be said to have originated in Western Europe at about the time of the Renaissance and Reformation. Since then its relationship with theology has been conceived in a variety of ways.

1. Models of the relationship between science and theology

Some have imagined a model of *total independence*, thus eliminating any of the possibilities (and problems) discussed below. Such a zero-interaction model is irreconcilable with historical evidence, which points to a continuous series of strong interactions over many centuries.

Secondly, there is a *conflict* model which was assiduously developed after Darwin by those who wished science to snatch cultural supremacy from the church in late-Victorian Britain. On the basis of undeniable episodes in which scientific evidence did undermine received traditions that were apparently based on the Bible (*e.g.* Galileo and Darwin), a generalized, triumphalist image for science was cultivated, owing much to the positivist* philosophy that only scientific knowledge was ultimately meaningful. Despite much evidence for the gross historical distortions introduced by such a pre-emptive generalization, its survival in popular literature even today testifies to its hold on the public mind.

A third model is that of *complementarity* which (though not by that name) may be dated back to Francis Bacon (1561–1626) in the 17th century. He spoke of 'two books', the book of nature and the book of Scripture, each of which had to be read and understood. Because both came from the same author they could not be in conflict. But because each had a different purpose it was idle to mix 'philosophy' (science) and divinity, and to seek scientific data in the pages of Scripture. Problems arose, however, where biblical and scientific evidence appeared to clash, and in those circumstances it was necessary to recognize the complementarity of their modes of explanation. Calvin,* drawing on the Augustinian* concept of 'accommodation',* assumed that the Holy Spirit accommodated his language to that of common speech in order to teach spiritual principles. Hence biblical accounts of the days of creation,* of the structure of the cosmos, of the sun (as opposed to the earth) standing still and of a literally universal flood would be susceptible to a non-literal interpretation. In other words, the biblical and scientific accounts of natural phenomena have purposes that are complementary rather than contradictory, the Bible's concerns being spiritual and eternal. This approach has continued to our own day and may be fruitfully applied to later problems, not least the creation debate.

For all its merits the 'complementarity' model by itself fails in a number of respects, particularly by ignoring the considerable network of relationships between science and theology disclosed by recent historical scholarship. A fourth model which takes these into account may be termed *symbiosis*. This recognizes that historically, scientific and theological thinking have owed much to one another and that their growth has been mutually promoted. It conforms with a widespread acknowledgment that much human knowledge is culture-dependent, but it does not prejudice the independence of data either in the Bible or in the natural world. It merely recognizes that in the interpretation of such data, theological and scientific ideas are often intermingled in one brain, as they are indeed in one society. Hence one might expect some degree of mutual influence; and such turns out to be the case.

2. Influence of science on theology

The responses of theology to science have been legion. One of the earliest was *natural theology.** From Robert Boyle (1627–91) to Paley,* English literature is replete with attempts to make discoveries of science the basis of a Christian apologetic; it has been argued, somewhat doubtfully, that underlying such efforts lay a quest for social stability which might be bolstered by a strong Anglican church. Its unchanging formularies were to be confirmed by the unchanging laws of science. Be that as it may, the 'argument from design' survived, albeit in a weakened form, even the onslaughts of Darwinism. With today's greater knowledge of the intricacies of the natural world, attempts have been made to revive it, though not with conspicuous success.

It was in fact the awesome regularity of the mechanical universe as emphasized by Isaac Newton* that raised urgent questions of divine intervention. Did God intervene in the running of the machine he had created, or did he not? The dilemma was crystallized in the (probably apocryphal) remark by Laplace (1749–1827) that he had 'no need of that hypothesis (God)' in his cosmology. Thus arose a powerful stimulus to the growth of *deism** and its derivatives such as unitarianism.* A recognition that all natural events (not merely those explicable by known scientific laws) must be seen as God's activity was not absent in the late 18th century. But a God-in-the-gaps theology proved surprisingly resilient and represents another popular misunderstanding of the science/religion relationship.

A third response of theology to science has come in the area of *biblical interpretation*. It goes at least as far back as Galileo's famous quip of 1615 that, in Scripture, 'the intention of the Holy Ghost is to teach us how one goes to heaven, not how heaven goes' – a response engendered at least in part by his own telescopic discoveries in vindication of Coper-

nicus. Since that time the discoveries and theories of science have not infrequently led to a revision of traditional interpretations of Scriptures. These include ancient views on the age of the earth, the structure of the universe, the extent of Noah's flood and the origins of biological species (including human beings). Few commentators disagree when this happens over cosmology, but application of an identical methodology to questions of human origins is still controversial.

It is important not to imply a unique role for science in the reinterpretation of Scripture, but it cannot be neglected. Where a theological response to science has been claimed with much less justification is in the 'demythologization' (see Myth*) programme prescribed by Bultmann* and others. The assertion that 'miracle'* is incredible in a scientific age is as unphilosophical as it is unhistorical. It ignores the fact that science is, by definition, concerned only with regularities and can therefore make no pronouncement on their breach; and it neglects to note that, at the very time when demythologization came into vogue, old-fashioned, positivistic scientific dogmatism was in decline. For this a variety of causes may be cited, notably the demise of the deterministic* world of Newtonian mechanics in the face of successive challenges by thermodynamics, relativity and quantum theory.

Finally it may be briefly noted that the *process theology** of Whitehead, Hartshorne and others sprang, at least ostensibly, from a concern to understand God's relationship to the world of nature as studied by science.

3. Influence of theology on science

The origins and growth of science may be fruitfully considered in terms of a response to biblical insights liberated at, and since, the Reformation (Hooykaas, Russell). This response may be seen in the writings of many men of science and in the morphological similarity between scientific and religious theories. Five such insights may be identified:

1. The elimination of myth* from nature: an animate, even 'divine', nature is not susceptible to scientific enquiry, nor compatible with biblical injunctions to treat nature instead as a dependent creation of God (Pss. 29, 89, 104, 137, *etc.*) who alone is to be worshipped (Dt. 26:11; Is. 44:24; Je. 7:18; *etc.*). The replacement of an organismic by a

mechanistic universe (nature's own 'demythologization') coincided with a renewed awareness of such teaching.

2. The laws of nature: the emergence of 'laws of nature' in the 17th century has been shown by Zilsel (*Physical Review* 51, 1942, pp. 245–279) as a derivative of biblical doctrines, citing *inter alia* Jb. 28:26 and Pr. 8:29. Later writers (Whitehead, Oakley, *etc.*) have strengthened this thesis.

3. The experimental method: both in English Puritanism* and continental Calvinism* the questioning manipulation of nature was strongly encouraged as an alternative to the abstract reasoning of ancient pagan cultures. It was seen as fully compatible with biblical injunctions to 'test' all things (1 Thes. 5:21; Rom. 12:2; Ps. 34:8; *etc.*).

4. Controlling the earth: Bacon and his followers saw in Scripture (Gn. 1:26; Ps. 8:6–8, *etc.*) a clear mandate for altering the natural world for human benefit.

5. To the glory of God: that scientific research could add lustre to the divine name was believed even by patristic writers, but it most strongly emerged in the 17th century. Thus John Kepler (1571–1630), in studying those heavens which declared the glory of God (Pss. 8, 19, 50), exclaimed he was 'thinking God's thoughts after him'. This of itself was a powerful motive for the scientific exploration of nature.

If science may, without exaggeration, be seen as historically dependent for its emergence on Christian theology, then, in an age when this has been largely forgotten, biblical theology has an even more important contribution to make. This is in the area of *ethical direction*. Crucial to such an impact is a renewal of the biblical concept of stewardship* which may be seen as the only key to current dilemmas over areas of concern ranging from the pollution of the biosphere to a possible nuclear holocaust. All of these arise from a technology now made possible by science. Moreover, many aspects of modern science have been seen as eroding human dignity and worth, whether in the extrapolations of biological science to the so-called 'sociobiology', or in the naive reductionism that, in the manner of the Greek atomists, sees all phenomena in purely material terms. To an allegedly 'scientific' world-view so devoid of comfort and hope theology surely has much to say.

See also: MacKay, Donald M.; Nature, Theology of; Polyani, Michael; Torrance, Thomas F.

Bibliography

I. G. Barbour, *Issues in Science and Religion* (London, 1966); J. Dillenberger, *Protestant Thought and Natural Science* (London, 1961); R. Bube, *The Human Quest* (Waco, TX, 1971); R. Hooykaas, *Christian Faith and the Freedom of Science* (London, 1957); idem, *Religion and the Rise of Modern Science* (Edinburgh, ²1973); M. A. Jeeves (ed.), *The Scientific Enterprise and Christian Faith* (London, 1969); D. M. MacKay, *The Clockwork Image: A Christian Perspective on Science* (London, 1974); idem, *Human Science and Human Dignity* (London, 1979); H. Montefiore (ed.), *Man and Nature* (London, 1975); A. R. Peacocke, *Creation and the World of Science* (Oxford, 1979); A. Richardson, *The Bible in the Age of Science* (London, 1964); C. A. Russell, *Crosscurrents: Interactions between Science and Faith* (Leicester, 1985).

C.A.R.

SCIENTOLOGY, see Sects.

SCOTS CONFESSION, see Confessions of Faith.

SCRIPTURE

SCRIPTURE (Lat. *scriptura*, rendering the Gk. *graphē*, which means 'a writing' and is used some 50 times in the NT for some or all of the OT) is the historic Judaeo-Christian name for the specific literature, that the church receives as divine instruction, that is, as God's own witness to himself in the form of human witness concerning his work, will, and ways, and how mankind should worship him. 'Bible', by contrast, is a latter-day Western coinage, the fruit of a medieval misreading of the Gk. *biblia* ('books') as a feminine singular Lat. noun. 'Scripture' is used in essentially the same sense in both the singular and the plural: 'the Scriptures' are all the items that make up the Bible, viewed as carrying divine content, and 'Scripture' is the same material viewed as one organic unit of divine teaching.

1. Scripture and canon

Scripture expresses and mediates the authority of God, which means, formally, his right to be believed when he speaks and obeyed when he commands; and, materially, the sum total of declarations and directives by which he requires us to live. Hence Scripture is called 'canonical' (Gk. *kanōn*, a rule, measure, or standard). The use of 'canon' for a list of books that are canonical in the defined sense is secondary and derivative. The church has always known, more or less clearly, that it did not create a canon by discretionary fiat but received the canon that God created for it. The OT canon (*i.e.* the 39 books of the 1st-century Palestinian canon, Jesus' Bible) came to the church from the hands, as it were, of Christ and the apostles, for whom Christianity's credentials presupposed the divine authority of the Jewish Scriptures which the Christian facts fulfilled (Mt. 5:17; 26:56; Lk. 4:21; 18:31; Acts 3:18; 13:27–33; Rom. 1:2; 16:25–27; 1 Pet. 1:10–12; 2 Pet. 1:19–21; *etc.*). The NT canon came from the same source, for it was the Holy Spirit whom Christ sent who enabled the apostles to speak and write divine truth about Jesus and who all along has brought about recognition of apostolic documents containing this truth as canonical. The basis of that recognition was and is a. apostolic authorship or authentication, b. Christ-honouring doctrinal content, in line with the known teaching of other apostles, and c. continuous acknowledgment and spiritually fruitful use of the books within the church from the apostolic age on – a consideration that becomes weightier and more compelling with every passing year. The Protestant* claim, that the Holy Spirit decisively authenticates the canonical Scriptures by causing them to impose themselves on believers as a divine rule for faith and life, should be understood in corporate terms – as meaning that at no time has the great body of the church rejected any book now in the canon, and that divine authority is constantly experienced by the faithful when canonical Scripture is read and preached in the congregation.

On the extent of the canon there has not been perfect unanimity: Protestants hold to the list of 66 books found in Athanasius's *Festal Letter* of 367, in Jerome, and in the canons of the provincial council that met at Carthage in 397; the Council of Trent defined 12 apocryphal (OT) books into the Roman Catholic canon in 1546; the Synod of Jerusalem defined four of these (Judith, Tobit, Wisdom, and Ecclesiasticus) into the Eastern Orthodox canon in 1672; Luther rejected James; and so on. But in truth these are small matters: Luther's trouble was simply that he misunderstood James, supposing him to contradict Paul, and the Apocrypha is not important for doctrine. Much more important is the fact that the principles of canonicity to which, however unconvincingly, appeal was made each time, remained constant throughout. Thus, b. above was Luther's warrant for rejecting James and c. was the Catholic and Orthodox warrant for canonizing apocryphal books which, though no part of Christ's Bible, had been both in the LXX (the Gk. version of the OT, which the church took over in the apostolic age) and in the Vulgate.

2. Scripture and revelation

The historic Christian view, that Scripture is verbal revelation* in writing, is largely out of favour today; most theologians will only speak of Scripture as a human record, exposition, and celebration of God in history which is also the instrumental means of God's self-revealing encounter with us in the present. This formula, though true so far (unless 'human' is taken to imply inadequacy, incoherence, or incorrectness), is theologically incomplete. That Scripture is intrinsically revelation must also be affirmed (see next section). But when this affirmation is not related to God's saving work in history and to the illumining and interpreting work of the Spirit, it too is theologically incomplete. Bible writers depict revelation as a complex work of grace, whereby the creator-become-redeemer brings sinners into relational saving knowledge of himself, and the nature of Scripture as revelation has to be understood within this functional frame of reference.

In revelation, according to Scripture itself, God acts at three linked levels. Level one is revelation *on the public stage of history*, in a series of redemptive events of which God's verbal predictions and explanations at each stage formed part. This series reached a penultimate climax in the incarnation, atonement, and enthroning of the Son of God and the Pentecostal outpouring of the Spirit. Awaited now is the final climax of Christ's return for judgment and cosmic renewal, which will end history as we know it.

Within this frame emerged level two, revelation *in the public records of Scripture.*

Written public records (Calvin's description of Scripture) are for accuracy and permanent availability. As redemptive revelation unfolded, God caused narrative, explanatory, celebratory, and anticipatory writing to be done that would preserve and spread true knowledge of, and evoke response to, his ongoing work of grace. Canonical Scripture is a providentially given collection of such material in two parts, the OT spanning many centuries as it looks forward and leads up to the Christ who was to come, and the briefer NT garnering the one generation of apostolic witness to the Christ who came and will come again.

Level three is revelation *in the personal consciousness of individuals:* that is, the gift to sin-blinded humans of a responsive understanding of the God of history and Scripture, whom Jesus disclosed (Mt. 11:25–27; 16:17; 2 Cor. 4:6; Gal. 1:12–16; Eph. 1:17–20; 1 Jn. 5:20). This present and continuing reality of revelation through each believer's life occurs under the enlightening ministry of the Holy Spirit, who interprets to us the contents of Scripture, however these are met. The Reformers rightly insisted that as only Scripture, unaugmented from any philosophical or religious source, can bring us to know God, so it is only as the Spirit opens Scripture to us and write its teachings on our hearts that this knowledge becomes reality for us.

Undergirding Scripture's instrumental function at level three is the total trustworthiness that its divine origin guarantees (see Infallibility and Inerrancy*). Were the 'public records' incoherent and misleading, the knowledge of God based on them would be correspondingly incoherent and uncertain too. The many who nowadays affirm this to be the case call in question not only the veracity of God as Scripture's primary author, but also his wisdom and competence in communication. If documents designed to make God in Christ known to all generations are untrustworthy and thus inadequate for their purpose, God has indeed failed badly. But only liberal,* modernist,* existentialist,* and process theologies* ever require such a conclusion.

3. Scripture and inspiration

The historic description of Scripture as inspired means not that it is inspiring (although it is) but that it is 'God-breathed' (*theopneustos*, 2 Tim. 3:16), a product of the creator-Spirit's work, always to be viewed as the preaching and teaching of God himself through the words of the worshipping human witnesses through whom the Spirit gave it. Both testaments view the words of Scripture as God's own words. OT passages treat Moses' law as God's utterance (1 Ki. 22:8–16; Ne. 8; Ps. 119; *etc.*); NT writers view the OT as a whole as 'oracles of God' (Rom. 3:2), prophetic in character (16:26; *cf.* 1:2; 3:21), written by men whom the Spirit moved and taught (2 Pet. 1:20–21; *cf.* 1 Pet. 1:10–12). Christ and the NT constantly quote OT texts not merely as recording what men such as Moses, David or Isaiah said through the Spirit (Mk. 7:6–13; 12:36; Rom. 10:5, 20; 11:9), but also as recording what God has said through men (Mt. 19:4–5; Acts 4:25; 28:25; 1 Cor. 6:16; 2 Cor. 6:16; Heb. 1:5–13; 8:5, 8), or what the Holy Spirit says (Heb. 3:7; 10:15). Paul's citing of God's promise to Abraham and threat to Pharaoh as the utterance of *Scripture* to both (Gal. 3:8; Rom. 9:17) shows how completely he equated statements of Scripture with words of God. And when Paul taught and commanded in Christ's name (2 Thes. 3:6), claiming Christ's authority because he was Christ's apostle (1 Cor. 14:37) and maintaining that both his matter and his words were Spirit-given (1 Cor. 2:9–13), he presented a paradigm* of apostolic inspiration that requires the same attitude towards the NT writings that the NT teachers took towards the OT (*cf.* Christ's own promise and expectation regarding apostolic teaching, Jn. 14:26; 15:26–27; 16:13–15; 17:20, where the present tense is inchoative – 'are shortly to believe', 20:21–23). As Scripture, being God-given, 'cannot be broken' (Jn. 10:35), so with apostolic testimony: whether oral or written, it is the guaranteed truth of God, which those who know God and are 'of God' will hear (1 Jn. 4:6; *cf.* 2:7, 20, 27).

Since the God who created Scripture by sanctifying the authorial efforts of his servants is true and no deceiver, biblical infallibility* becomes an article of faith. It was no more necessary that the Bible, being human, should be wrong sometimes than it was for Jesus, being human, to go astray in conduct or teaching. Those who confess a sinless Christ (see Sinlessness of Christ*) cannot consistently dismiss this analogous belief in an inerrant Bible. To treat the witness of Christ and the apostles to the nature of Scriptures as not settling the matter, and to go against them on the point, is in itself illogical, irreverent, and indefensible, quite apart from the way that it undermines the concept of revelation stated above. The right path is to deal with the phenomena of Scripture on the assumption that, being God-given, it is faithful to physical, moral and spiritual fact; for that is the approach that Christianity's founders modelled in their own ministry and authoritatively taught their followers.

4. Scripture, authority and interpretation

Authority* is the basic theological issue into which discussions of revelation, inspiration, infallibility and inerrancy, and the necessity, sufficiency, and clarity of Scripture (three classic themes), and also of biblical interpretation, eventually run. What is at issue is the nature and extent of the control that canonical Scripture should exercise over the doctrine, discipline, and devotion of the church and its members. That Scripture mediates the authority of the God who gave it and the Christ to whom it testifies, that it does this by presenting the realities of salvation-history* in their universal significance, and that it cannot have authority further than it is in an appropriate sense true (for falsehood has no right to rule) are points of widespread agreement. That the church has no right to read into Scripture, or graft on to it, traditional ideas that cannot be read out of it, and that the individual Christian has no right ever to back his judgment against the Bible, are principles that ought to be generally conceded, though sometimes they are not. (Nor is the helpfulness of the church's heritage of interpretation always recognized, nor is the obligation to maintain rational coherence when interpreting always heeded.) But none can deny that only when rightly interpreted does Scripture actually exercise its rightful authority. A false approach to interpretation will frustrate that authority completely. So some comment on interpretation is needed to round off this article (see also Hermeneutics*).

The interpreter's task is to draw from Scripture and apply to thought and life today that body of universal truths about God, humanity, and their mutual relations that the texts yield. Since the biblical books are occasional writings addressed to people and situations of long ago, interpretative method involves unshelling those truths from the particular applications in which we find them embedded and reapplying them to ourselves. But to travel thus from what the text meant historically, to what it means as a word from God for today, is not always easy, certainly not when accuracy is a concern.

To grasp what the text meant (the first step in interpretation) requires grammatico-historical exegesis that takes account of the text's linguistic idiom and literary genre, its geographical, cultural and historical milieu, and the particular life-situation of both writer and first readers, so far as this can be known. One therefore needs to ask where, when, by whom, for what reason, to what end, and with what resources, each book and each part of each book was written. These are the questions of biblical criticism,* which thus at a certain level becomes everyone's concern. Answers that treat scriptural writers as deceitful or deluded, however, as a number of critical theories do, should be dismissed as needless and unjustified.

Discerning what the text means in application today (the second step in interpretation), then requires of us two things. The universal truths excavated by exegesis should first be checked to make sure that they square with the covenantal, Christocentric, redemptive, holiness-oriented framework of canonical revelation as a whole (only so dare one believe that one has perceived them aright). Then they should be set to interrogate us 'for reproof, for correction, and for training in righteousness' (2 Tim. 3:16) as they confront our inadequacies, clarify to us our calling and our hope, and animate us to the activities whereby God's truth is obeyed.

The help of the Holy Spirit must be sought throughout, for only the Spirit enables us to see the meaning and bearing of scriptural principles and to realize the reality of God as the texts set him forth. Without the ministry of the Spirit as authenticator and interpreter of the Scripture that he authored, we shall at best be locked into a barren and mechanical biblicism. Through the Spirit, however, life under the authority of Scripture becomes what it was meant to be – namely, realized communion with the Father and the Son (cf. 1 Jn. 1:3). Living under biblical authority is a prescription not only for theological rectitude but also for spiritual life.

Bibliography

R. Abba, *The Nature and Authority of the Bible* (London, 1958); J. Barr, *The Bible in the Modern World* (London, 1973); K. Barth, *CD* I.1–2; D. A. Carson and J. Woodbridge (eds.), *Scripture and Truth* (Leicester, 1983); *idem, Hermeneutics, Authority and Canon* (Leicester, 1986); N. Geisler (ed.), *Inerrancy* (Grand Rapids, MI, 1979); R. Laird Harris, *The Inspiration and Canonicity of the Bible* (Grand Rapids, MI, 1957); C. F. H. Henry, *God, Revelation and Authority*, vols. I–IV (Waco, TX 1976–79); *idem* (ed.), *Revelation and the Bible* (Grand Rapids, MI, 1958); A. Kuyper, *Principles of Sacred Theology* (Grand Rapids, MI, 1954); B. M. Metzger, *The Canon of the New Testament* (Oxford, 1987); J. I. Packer, *God Has Spoken* (London, 1979); C. Pinnock, *Biblical Revelation* (Chicago, IL, 1971); *idem, The Scripture Principle* (San Francisco, CA, 1984); E. Radmacher and R. Preus (eds.), *Hermeneutics, Inerrancy, and the Bible* (Grand Rapids, MI, 1984); A. C. Thiselton, *The Two Horizons* (Exeter, 1980); B. Vawter, *Biblical Inspiration* (London, 1972); B. B. Warfield, *The Inspiration and Authority of the Bible* (Philadelphia, 1948).

J.I.P.

SCRIPTURE AND TRADITION. The relationship between Scripture and tradition cannot be studied in isolation. They interact with one another only through a third party: the contemporary church.* It might help to define the two terms. 'Scripture'* refers to the canonical writings of both testaments. The early Christians inherited the Jewish (OT) Scriptures, but did not immediately acquire a parallel body of Christian Scriptures. Early moves toward it (*e.g.* 2 Pet. 3:15f.) came to fruition by the time of Irenaeus,* by when there was a clear concept of a *New* Testament alongside the Old. The acceptance of Christian Scriptures posed the question of the relation between these writings and the Christian tradition, which included the teaching of the apostles* handed down in other ways in the church. 'Tradition' is sometimes understood narrowly to refer solely to extra-scriptural or even un-scriptural traditions. Such clearly exist, but our present concern is with tradition in the broader sense of the Christian faith as it is handed down to us from the past. Such a broad definition could logically *include* Scripture, but since our concern is with the relation between Scripture and tradition, it is better to follow normal usage and to exclude Scripture from the definition. Every Christian group has to grapple with the relationship between these two. There is no Christian group, however informal, that has no tradition. Similarly, every Christian group, however informal, has some authority structure, some standards of what is and is not 'Christian'. It is this element, the contemporary teaching authority of the church, which must not be forgotten in considering the relation between Scripture and tradition.

The relationship between Scripture, tradition and church has been seen differently over the ages. The earliest view may be called the *coincidence view;* the church teaches what the apostles taught, which it receives from the apostolic Scriptures and from the apostolic tradition. Scripture, tradition and church are assumed to teach the same one apostolic message. There is no conflict between them, and the whole Christian message is found in each. It is this approach that was adopted by Irenaeus* and Tertullian* against Gnosticism.* The Gnostics appealed to their own scriptures and to their own secret traditions. Irenaeus responded with the claim that the apostles' teaching, found in their genuine writings, was handed down in an open public tradition of teaching in those churches which they had founded, where it was still taught. This threefold cord provided the most effective answer to the Gnostic claims.

In time, the coincidence view came to be overshadowed by the *supplementary view:* tradition is needed to supplement Scripture, to provide teaching not found in Scripture. The belief that apostolic tradition supplements Scripture as a guide to *practice* is found early, but it was some time before theologians came to defend *beliefs* which they acknowledged not to be in Scripture. An important step in this direction was taken by Basil of Caesarea* in his defence of the deity of the Holy Spirit, where he states that some Christian beliefs are not found in Scripture. This approach became more common in the Middle Ages, with the emergence of unscriptural doctrines, such as those concerning Mary.* But the coincidence view was never lost sight of. With the use of allegory there is never the need to admit that a doctrine is not found in Scripture!

The supplementary view could be invoked to justify beliefs with no scriptural basis. But what of beliefs actually *contrary* to Scripture? As the Middle Ages drew to a close, various groups began to raise this charge against some Roman Catholic doctrines. These charges came to a head in the Reformation. The most fundamental issue in the Reformation was not justification* by faith, not the role of tradition, but the relationship between Scripture and the church. The Reformers rejected the teachings of the Roman Church in the name of the scriptural gospel. In turn, they faced the charge of heresy for rejecting church doctrine. The issue was simple: Does the gospel define the church, or vice versa? The Reformers branded the Roman Catholic Church a false church for suppressing the gospel. Rome called the Reformers heretics for rejecting the teaching of holy mother church. The Reformers did not believe in 'private judgment', with every man his own theologian. But they did believe that all church teaching needs to be tested by Scripture. They had a deep respect for tradition, especially the teaching of the early fathers. But tradition must not add to Scripture and must be tested by Scripture.

The Council of Trent (see Reformation, Catholic Counter-*) responded to the Reformers in its *Decree on Scripture and Tradition* (1546). It stated that 'the truth and discipline [of the gospel] are contained in the written books and in unwritten traditions – those unwritten traditions, that is, which were either received by the apostles from the mouth of Christ himself or were received from the apostles themselves (having been dictated by the Holy Spirit) and have come down even to us, having been transmitted as it were hand by hand'. Furthermore, Scripture and tradition are to be venerated 'with equal affection of piety and reverence'. It used to be believed that this committed Rome to the supplementary view, but in recent years J. R. Geiselmann (b. 1890) and others have challenged this assumption. It is now widely accepted that Trent does not foreclose the question of the material sufficiency or otherwise of Scripture. In other words, Trent allows the view that all Catholic doctrine is found in Scripture. What is quite clear in the teaching of Trent is the role of the church. No-one shall 'presume to interpret [the Scriptures] contrary to that sense which holy mother Church, to whom it belongs to judge of their true sense and interpretation, has held and holds, or even contrary to the unanimous teaching of the Fathers.'

Many changes have taken place since the 16th century. Historical criticism has affected the church's approach to the Bible (see Biblical Criticism*) and has also shown how doctrine has changed over the years. Today the fact of the development* of doctrine is widely accepted by both Roman Catholic and Protestant theologians. But despite these changes, the fundamental issue, the relationship between Scripture and the church, remains much the same. At the Second Vatican Council (1962–65), the dogmatic constitution on *Divine Revelation* expounded, in the second chapter, the relationship between Scripture, tradition and church. Due to the efforts of J. R. Geiselmann and others the question of the material (in)sufficiency of Scripture was left open. The apostolic teaching of the gospel is transmitted to us through both Scripture and tradition, which 'are to be accepted and venerated with the same sense of devotion and reverence'. Development of doctrine is acknowledged: 'there is a growth in the understanding of the realities and the words which have been handed down'. But the final authority is neither Scripture nor tradition but the teaching office of the church: 'The task of authentically interpreting the word of God, whether written or handed on, has been entrusted exclusively to the living teaching office of the church, whose authority is exercised in the name of Jesus Christ.' Among Protestants today there is a greater willingness than before to acknowledge the importance of tradition and to ascribe to it a high role. This is seen very clearly in the report *Scripture, Tradition and Traditions* of the Fourth World Conference on Faith and Order of the WCC, which met at Montreal in 1963. But there are no signs that Protestants are willing to submit their interpretation of Scripture to 'the living teaching office of the church'.

Tradition cannot be escaped. A sermon in church, a book read at home, sharing one's faith with a friend – all of these are tradition in action. Tradition is inevitable – and also desirable. The adage that 'those who are ignorant of history are condemned to repeat it' holds true in the history of theology. Those who have arrogantly despised tradition have often ended by relearning some of the most basic lessons that the past can teach us. Karl Barth* aptly stated that the correct attitude to tradition is summarized in the fifth commandment: honour your father and mother. We must honour our theological forbears and listen with respect to the voice of the past, but we are not bound by it. With tradition, as with parents, there are times when we should say 'we must obey God rather than men'. Tradition is worthy of respect, but is subject to the word of God in the Scriptures.

The Reformers coined the slogan *sola Scriptura*: Scripture alone. What does this mean? It does not mean that we should use nothing but the Bible – that there is no place for dictionaries of theology and the like. It does not mean that we should learn Christian doctrine only directly from the Bible, which would make sermons and other books redundant. It does not even mean that we should recognize no other authority than the Bible in our Christianity. Tradition and the church inevitably and properly function as authorities in some sense. But the Bible remains the decisive and *final* authority, the norm by which all the teaching of tradition and the church is to be tested.

Bibliography

F. F. Bruce and E. G. Rupp (eds.), *Holy Book and Holy Tradition* (Manchester, 1968); Y. M. J. Congar, *Tradition and Traditions* (London, 1966); P. C. Rodger and L. Vischer (eds.), *The Fourth World Conference on Faith and Order* (London, 1964), 3:II, 'Scripture, Tradition and Traditions'; G. H. Tavard, *Holy Writ or Holy Church: The Crisis of the Protestant Reformation* (London, 1959).

A.N.S.L.

SECTS are distinguished from the mainstream denominations, which basically accept the orthodox creeds* (see Sociology of Religion*). Individuals may adopt unorthodox views of the Trinity* and the incarnation,* but, if they attract a body of like-minded followers, they may formulate their beliefs, and worship as an exclusive sect.

It is impossible to discuss the ramifications of the many sects that exist (now often referred to as 'cults') but one can classify a few of the main ones on the basis of their source of authority and their attitudes

towards the Trinity and the incarnation, whether or not their moral standards approximate to the Christian ideal. Thus we have the premises on which we can begin to discuss our differences. Admission to their beliefs would mean that God had allowed the Christian church to be in fundamental error for nearly 2,000 years before raising up a true witness. But which true witness out of many claimants?

1. The Bible as the sole authority, but freshly interpreted

Jehovah's Witnesses hold that the Bible does not teach the full deity of Jesus Christ. By selected texts they adopt the Arian* heresy that Christ was the first created being, and is not the eternal Jehovah. In practice their interpretations of Scripture and rules of life are prescribed by their headquarters in America. They stem from Charles Taze Russell (1852–1916).

Christadelphians originated with an Englishman, Dr John Thomas (1805–71), but his successor, Robert Roberts, gave them the slogan, *Christendom Astray from the Bible*, in his book of that title. They believe that the Son came into existence only when the Virgin Mary* gave birth to Jesus. Previously he existed potentially in the divine will. After his resurrection his humanity was transformed into divinity.

2. The Bible plus a further written revelation

Mormons (The Church of Jesus Christ of Latter Day Saints). These originated with an American, Joseph Smith (1805–44), who claimed to have translated the so-called *Book of Mormon* from golden plates in ancient Egyptian. Later he produced two other books which he claimed were inspired, *Doctrines and Covenants* and *Pearl of Great Price*. The books sometimes use orthodox language, but teach that God has a physical body. All humans, including Jesus Christ, were begotten by God in the beginning before being born on earth. Jesus has become God, and we also may become gods.

Christian Science regards *Science and Truth with Key to the Scriptures* as supremely authoritative, and it is read alongside the Bible in the services. It was written by the founder, Mary Baker Eddy (1821–1910). The Trinity is summarized as 'God the Father-Mother;

Christ the spiritual idea of sonship; divine science or the Holy Comforter.' A basic belief is that spirit and matter are such opposites that they cannot exist together. Hence matter, illness and even sin are errors of 'mortal mind'. 'Jesus is the name of the man who, more than all other men, has presented Christ, the true idea of God.' At the ascension 'the human, material concept, or Jesus, disappeared, while the spiritual self, or Christ, continues to exist'.

3. The Bible with psychic or visionary interpretations

Swedenborgianism. Emanuel Swedenborg (1688–1772), scientist, philosopher and a psychic, did not found a church, but his followers formed the Swedenborg Society and also the New (Jerusalem) Church. He saw visions of angels and of the departed, but claimed that his revelations of spiritual truth came from God alone. There is one God, with three essentials corresponding to soul, body and action in man. At the incarnation the one divine Being took up the human into himself, and finally at the cross his human became the divine. Swedenborg denies vicarious atonement and justification by faith. Salvation comes through a life lived according to love. Scriptures are interpreted by their correspondence with inner spiritual truths. Books lacking the 'internal sense' are rejected, *i.e.* Chronicles, Song of Solomon, Acts and all the epistles.

Anthroposophy. Founded by Rudolf Steiner (1861–1925), an Austrian scientist with psychic gifts. He has attracted some Christians by the centrality that he gives to Jesus Christ and his crucifixion and to the cosmic Christ as Lord of the universe. He believes in God the Father and God the Holy Spirit, but concentrates his thinking on union with Christ. He believes in many rebirths (see Metempsychosis*) for ordinary people, but that the pure soul born in Jesus had been kept intact down the ages. At Jesus' baptism the divine Christ united with the human soul, and went on to deliver mankind from bondage to evil spiritual world rulers. Steiner thus differs from theosophists, with whom he was once associated, who postulate various reincarnations for Jesus Christ, without lifting him above the human plane.

Moonies (The Unification Church). Their interpretation of the Bible is guided by the teachings of the founder, Sun Myung Moon (b. 1920), which were received in a series of visions, in which he was called to complete the unfinished work of Jesus Christ. The teachings were set out in *The Divine Principle*. 'Jesus is a man in whom God is incarnate. But he is not God himself.' He achieved spiritual salvation for mankind, but, by failing to marry and raise a family, he did not achieve the physical salvation which would spread more and more perfect families through the world.

4. Fringe movements with secondary use of the Bible

The Church of Scientology was founded by L. Ron Hubbard (1911–86). It is hardly a church, but an expensive course in psychiatry to open up the mind, with God somehow tacked on. Jesus is only one of several great teachers seeking the truth which Scientology reveals.

Spiritualism. There are several spiritualist groups, with varying beliefs. The spirit communicators speak with differing voices, but never with the confident joy of the presence of Christ which we find in the NT. Some deny the truth of the deity and atoning sacrifice of Jesus Christ. Those who meet as churches have a high respect for Jesus as leader, but, in speaking of his divinity, they do not always mean his deity.

See also: NEW RELIGIONS.

Bibliography

M. C. Burrell, *The Challenge of the Cults* (Leicester, 1981); *idem*, *Wide of the Truth: A Critical Assessment of the Mormon Religion* (London, 1972); *idem*, booklets *Learning About the Mormons; Jehovah's Witnesses; the Unification Church (the Moonies)* (Oxford, 1983); M. C. Burrell and J. Stafford Wright, *Some Modern Faiths* (Leicester, ²1983) (repr. as *Today's Sects* (Grand Rapids, MI, 1983); Horton Davies, *Christian Deviations* (London, ³1972); A. A. Hoekema, *The Four Major Cults* (Exeter, 1964) (incl. Christian Science, Jehovah's Witnesses, Mormons); J. Stafford Wright, *Understanding the Supernatural* (London, ²1977).

J.S.W.

SECULARIZATION. The term had its
origin in the Peace of Westphalia (1648), designating the transfer of ecclesiastical prop-

erty into princely hands. It helps to bear this early meaning in mind, as the loss of the churches' temporal power is one of the most important dimensions of 'secularization'. The concept is bedevilled by controversy, some of which may be defused by distinguishing different definitions.

First, secularization has to do with the splitting apart of church and state which has occurred since medieval times. Although this has happened in various ways (the USA hardly ever had strong church-state collusion, France abolished such collusion with a revolution, Britain still has national churches, but also a large denationalized sector), the result is similar. Other voices vie for attention in the marketplace of ideologies. Organized Christianity has little say in the affairs of state, or, indeed, in public life in general. However much their modern history owes to the stimulus or support of Christianity, contemporary science, industry, education, commerce and art operate without reference to Christian values or practice.

Secondly, secularization often refers to the way in which modern societies, in contrast with previously more transcendentally-orientated ones, are said to be preoccupied with purely temporal concerns. Max Weber* pointed to the rational, calculating mentality typical of modern capitalism and bureaucracy, and suggested that its consequence was a 'disenchantment' of the world. People lose their sense of awe and worship. Prediction and planning take over from prayer and providence.

This dimension of secularization may simply be a feature of the way in which modern societies are organized. (Who needs Hannah's prayer when fertility pills may be prescribed?) But it may also be a result of another dimension: secularization as a conscious policy. Since the European Enlightenment* some notions of 'rationality' have been set over against 'religion', begetting for example the 'science versus faith' type of hostility. Better termed 'secularism', this may have an impact on the pace and pattern of secularization. But whereas Christians may justly regard 'secularism' as an enemy, 'secularization' as such is not.

The confusion arises from yet another connotation, that of secularization as 'worldliness' *within* the church. Culturally isolated within society (because of that church-state

split), and spending a large part of waking time in contexts (particularly employment) where cost-benefit analysis and the clock rule supreme, Christians often lead lives little different from the 'secular' world. The salt of the earth becomes bland, blending innocuously with its surroundings. If the religion–society split gives rise to the feeling that Christianity has nothing to say beyond individual salvation, and no distinctive world-view affecting education, politics and business, then in this sense secularization is corrosive of Christianity. Some theologians (*e.g.* J. A. T. Robinson,* Harvey Cox (b. 1929), R. Gregor Smith, 1913–68), further muddied the waters of 'secularization' in the 1960s by arguing that secularization actually expresses Christian truth. To this end they appealed to some utterances of Dietrich Bonhoeffer.* In so far as this emphasis highlighted human tasks of responsibly opening up the creation, *under God* (for instance as early science *desacralized* nature with Puritan encouragement; see Science and Theology*), the insight is sound. But in slogans such as 'man [*sic*] come of age', another agenda rears its head. Disenchantment, and preoccupation with purely temporal affairs, with which the church should be so uneasy, is innocently wheeled in as a theologically blessed Trojan horse.

In the mid-20th century, social scientists boldly predicted the demise of religion, often using declining adherence to religious institutions as evidence for this 'secularization'. Less confidence is expressed today. For one thing, although the strength of traditional Christianity in the West is less easy to gauge since the advent of such phenomena as 'house churches', it is clear that a certain robust resilience obtains, especially in the more 'conservative' sectors. Add to that the tremendous growth around the 'Pacific rim', and persistence within hostile 'iron curtain' countries, and the picture is far from consistently gloomy.

But even where church decline is apparent, secularization does not spell the death of all religious or sacred concern. New religious movements proliferate in East and West, many still orientate their lives by a residue of pre-Christian superstition and belief which have been bypassed by the more overt aspects of secularization, and, as biblical people might expect, many items of temporal life are granted sacred significance, becoming cultural symbols which give life meaning.

Secularization explains nothing; the term rather alerts us to a cluster of related themes which connect religion and society. Pluralism, the retreat of 'religion' to the private sphere of life, the stranding of the church on the social margins, and even the making of new 'idols', are closely bound up with secularization.

Bibliography

O. Chadwick, *The Secularization of the European Mind in the Nineteenth Century* (Cambridge, 1975); O. Guinness, *The Gravedigger File* (London, 1984); P. Hammond (ed.), *The Sacred in a Secular Age* (Berkeley, CA, 1985); D. Lyon, 'Secularization: The Fate of Faith in Modern Society?' *Them* 10:1 (1984), pp. 14–22; *idem*, 'Rethinking Secularization: Retrospect and Prospect', *Review of Religious Research* 26:3 (1985), pp. 228–243; *idem*, *The Steeple's Shadow: the Myths and Realities of Secularization* (London, 1985); D. Martin, *A General Theory of Secularization* (Oxford, 1978); B. Wilson, *Religion in Sociological Perspective* (Oxford, 1982).

D.L.

SEMI-PELAGIANISM, a largely monastic movement of reaction against Augustine's* developed anti-Pelagian* teachings (and hence more fittingly called Semi-Augustinianism; 'Semi-Pelagian' is found no earlier than the 16th century). This 'revolt of the monasteries' began in Roman Africa in 427, evoking from Augustine *Grace and Free Will* and *Correction and Grace* in response to critics of his *Letter* 194. When he heard of monastic disaffection in South Gaul, where John Cassian's teaching breathed an Origenist* optimism (*cf.* P. Munz in *JEH* 11, 1960, pp. 1–22), he wrote *The Predestination of the Saints* and *The Gift of Perseverance*. Controversy continued after his death (430), with his weightiest critic, Vincent of Lérins (see Catholicity*), whose famous *Commonitory* implicitly faults his 'non-catholic' doctrine, and Prosper of Aquitaine (*c.* 390–*c.* 463) his tireless champion. Later Faustus of Riez (*c.* 408 – *c.* 490) and Fulgentius of Ruspe (468–533) represented the two positions.

Eventually bishop Caesarius of Arles (*c.* 470–542) convened the Second Council of Orange in 529, which condemned Semi-Pelagian (and Pelagian) doctrines and endorsed a qualified Augustinian theology. Its deliverances, compiled by Caesarius partly from Prosper's digest of Augustine, rejected predestination* to evil, affirmed that with God's grace* we can fulfil his will, and were silent on such issues as irresistible grace, the fate of unbaptized infants and the manner of transmission of original sin.

The initial point of difference concerned 'the beginning of faith'.* Augustine's critics insisted that this was an act of unaided human freedom, although grace instantly strengthened incipient faith. Augustine held that 'the will is prepared by God' by prevenient grace alone. The assault soon extended to the 'fixed quota' who were alone predestined to salvation and granted such grace, the abandonment of the rest of the 'mass of perdition' to just condemnation, the irresistibility of grace in the elect and their infallible perseverance* to the end. Objection was also taken to Augustine's denial that God 'willed all people to be saved', which even Prosper eventually abandoned.

This anti-Augustinianism arose in part out of a monastic spirituality anxious lest fatalism should encourage lethargy (monastic accidie) and make rebuke and exhortation, not to say prayer and evangelism, pointless. Although Augustine feared a recrudescence of Pelagianism proper, these 'semi-Augustinians' affirmed original sin and the necessity of grace for salvation, but sought a balanced antinomy between grace and freedom, disliked the resort to God's hidden counsels in election and doubted whether a just predestination could avoid being based on foreknowledge.

The doctrinal issues opened up in these decades have reappeared regularly, especially in the 16th to 18th centuries (see Jesuit Theology*) and in the ceaseless 'Calvinist* vs. Arminian'* debate in modern evangelicalism.

Bibliography

Prosper's works, tr. P. De Letter, *ACW* 14 (1952) and 32 (1963); P. Brown, *Augustine of Hippo* (London, 1967); N. K. Chadwick, *Poetry and Letters in Early Christian Gaul* London, 1955); O. Chadwick, *John Cassian* (Cambridge, ²1968); G. Fritz in *DTC* 11 (1931), cols. 1087–1103; J. Pelikan, *The Christian Tradition*, 1: *The Emergence of the Catholic Tradition (100–600)* (Chicago, IL, 1971); G. Weigel, *Faustus of Riez* (Philadelphia, 1938); E. Amann in *DTC* 14 (1941), cols. 1796–1850; F. H. Woods, *The Canons of the Second Council of Orange* (Oxford, 1882).

D.F.W.

SESSION OF CHRIST, see ASCENSION.

SEVENTH-DAY ADVENTISM. The Seventh-day Adventist Church had its official beginning in 1863, when its first General Conference was held. William Miller (1782–1849), a lay Bible student (later a Baptist preacher), predicted that Christ would return to earth some time between 21 March 1843 and 21 March 1844. One of Miller's followers postponed the date to 22 October 1844. When Christ did not return on that day, however, there was 'great disappointment'.

The following three groups of 'Millerites' later combined to form the Seventh-day Adventist Church: first, the group around Hiram Edson (1806–82), who on the morning after 'the great disappointment' had a vision of Christ entering a heavenly sanctuary – which he interpreted to be the real meaning of Miller's prophecy; second, a group who followed Joseph Bates (1792–1872), a retired sea captain, who through his study of the Bible became convinced that the seventh day was the proper sabbath;* third, the followers of Ellen G. White (1827–1915), who began to have visions confirming various teachings later to be adopted by Adventists, and who was recognized as having a prophetic gift.

Though the first headquarters of the Seventh-day Adventist Church were in Battle Creek, Michigan, in 1903 they were moved to Takoma Park, a suburb of Washington, DC. World membership was 4,863,047 in 1985. Four out of five Seventh-day Adventists reside outside of North America. The Adventists maintain an ambitious missionary programme, and are very active in educational and medical enterprises.

Seventh-day Adventists share with evangelicals such doctrines as the Trinity, the deity of Christ, Christ's atoning work and his second coming. They also hold teachings which set them apart from evangelical Christianity. One of these is the teaching that the proper Christian day of rest is the seventh day. Another is the doctrine of the so-called 'investigative judgment' – that after a person's death there will occur an investigation of his life to deter-

mine and reveal whether he or she will be deemed worthy to have a part in the 'first resurrection' (the resurrection of believers). It is further taught that the Seventh-day Adventist Church is the 'remnant church' – that is, the last remnant of God's commandment-keeping people. One of the marks of the remnant church is said to be the gift of prophecy* which was given to Ellen G. White; her teachings are still considered authoritative for Adventist theology. Many dietary laws are observed; the strictest Adventists are vegetarians.

Is Seventh-day Adventism to be considered a branch of evangelical Christianity? This is not at all clear. The Adventist claim to be the remnant church implies that all other Christians are walking in some degree of darkness. Mrs White once said that the observance of the seventh-day sabbath distinguishes God's loyal subjects from transgressors. Many Adventists today would like to be thought of as evangelical Christians, and in recent years there has been considerable internal discussion on central doctrinal issues. But the doctrine of the remnant church, still official Adventist teaching, would seem to make identification with main-stream evangelicalism impossible.

Bibliography

Seventh-day Adventists Answer Questions on Doctrine (Hagerstown, MD, 1957); D. M. Canright, *Seventh-day Adventism Renounced* (1889; repr. Grand Rapids, MI, 1961); J. Craven, 'The Wall of Adventism', *CT* 28 (1984), pp. 20–25; A. A. Hoekema, *The Four Major Cults* (Exeter, 1963); G. Land (ed.), *Adventism in America: A History* (Grand Rapids, MI, 1986); G. J. Paxton, *The Shaking of Adventism – A documented account of the crisis among Adventists over the doctrine of justification by faith* (Grand Rapids, MI, 1978).

A.A.H.

SEXUALITY. Human sexuality is a much larger concept than sexual behaviour. Its focus falls more on what people are than on what they do.

This comes out clearly in the Bible's account of creation.* There, the making of man and woman as sexual beings is specifically linked with their creation in God's image* (Gn.

637

1:27). Biblically, therefore, sexuality is integral to human personhood.

Scripture's creation teaching also highlights the relational value and purpose of sexuality. In Gn. 2, woman is made as God's provision for man's need of relationship (vv. 18–25). And though the primary reference is to marriage, the expressions used to describe the way a husband relates to his wife are applied in the rest of the Bible to relationships of a far broader kind.

For example, the evocative phrase 'bone of my bones and flesh of my flesh' is used later in the OT by a man appealing to his extended family and by the tribes of Israel responding to their national leader (Jdg. 9:2; 2 Sa. 5:1); while the strong word 'united' describes not only a husband and wife's intimacy but the inseparable affection a woman feels for her mother-in-law and the close loyalty the people feel for their king (Ru. 1:14; 2 Sa. 20:2). Though we shrink from describing any of those relationships as 'sexual', the Bible's language presents them as belonging peripherally to the expression of sexuality.

Scripture, then, is overwhelmingly positive in its treatment of sexuality. The theology of creation strongly affirms the goodness of sex and gives the lie to any ascetic* ideal which denies its value (cf. Pr. 5:18–19; Song).

The NT's witness to sexuality's positive value is even more impressive than the OT's because the ascetic alternative was being openly canvassed in many of the young churches to which the epistles were addressed. Paul in particular (in spite of his misogynist image), is lucidly blunt in condemning those who despised marriage, and in bracketing an affirmation of body-life with a positive attitude towards sex which has no room for either abuse or withdrawal (cf. 1 Tim. 4:1–5; 1 Cor. 6:12–15; 7:3ff.).

It is against this backcloth that the Bible's veto on extra-marital sexual intercourse must be seen. Any behaviour which breaks the links between sex, personhood and relationship is symptomatic of disorder. Moreover, the doctrine of creation was widely understood in NT times as limiting the legitimacy of intercourse to permanent, exclusive heterosexual relationships. Hence the specific biblical ban on prostitution, pre-marital intercourse, adultery and homosexual behaviour (1 Cor. 6:13–18; Eph. 5:3; 1 Thes. 4:3; Ex. 20:14; Rom. 1:26–27).

The history of the church betrays a far less positive attitude to sexuality than the Bible's. In its earliest days, the church was confronted by a powerful philosophical dualism* which taught (among other things) the superiority of the mind and spirit over the body. Theologically, this was identified as heresy and vigorously resisted. Its influence on Christian thinking about sexuality, however, was far more insidious, and it was not long before ascetic idealism gained a strong grip on Christian behaviour.

With very few exceptions, patristic and medieval writers condemned the sensual pleasure of intercourse as sinful. Their attitude to marriage, too, was at best ambivalent. They certainly regarded celibacy as preferable – and mandatory for clergy.

Attitudes to women at this time reveal a similarly negative approach. There was a strong tendency to blame Eve for man's fall into sin.

The Reformers did much to redress the balance. With their Bibles open, they condemned compulsory celibacy for the clergy and upheld marriage as a gift of God confirmed by his word and safeguarded by the authority of his law. It is in their writings, too, that we see the beginnings of a recall to the biblical emphasis on the relational aspect of marriage and family life.

Contemporary scholars are virtually unanimous in giving pride of place to the relational values of sexuality. Nevertheless, they take their places on a broad spectrum of theological opinion and their conclusions about sexual behaviour often differ sharply. On the one hand, conservative writers strongly affirm the relational aspect of sex in marriage while maintaining, equally firmly, the biblical veto on all extra-marital intercourse. Situationists, on the other hand, see no need to be tied to biblical or traditional hitching-posts. In their view, the demands of love-in-relationship must always override rules and regulations, whether those are enshrined in 'a Bible or a confessor's manual' (J. Fletcher, *Situation Ethics*, London, 1966, p. 18).

Such divergent conclusions are clearly discernible in modern debates about issues related to sexuality. For example, on divorce and remarriage the main (though not the only) division is between those who assert – on the basis of Scripture or tradition – that marriage is indissoluble, and those who believe that divorce 'is what Christ would recommend' (J. Fletcher, *op. cit.*, p. 133) when a marriage relationship is irretrievably broken.

Discussions about homosexuality illustrate the same polarization. Here, the voices of Scripture and tradition merge in a consistent condemnation of all homosexual acts (*cf.* Lv. 18:22; 20:13; Rom. 1:24–27; 1 Cor. 6:9–10; 1 Tim. 1:9–10). But some modern writers defend stable, affectionate homosexual relationships on the ground that the only valid criterion by which to judge any sexual behaviour is love.

Scholarly disagreements about the parameters of legitimate sexual expression highlight the different ways 'love' can be defined and applied. A. Nygren,* in *Agape and Eros*, distinguished *agapē* (love as giving) from *erōs* (love as getting). His thesis, popularized by C. S. Lewis* in *The Four Loves* (Glasgow, 1960), has been attacked as an over-polarization. Nevertheless, it has been highly influential in exposing the inadequacy of an *erōs* approach to sexuality which sees a sexual functionary where a person should be.

The Bible does not teach that *agapē* supplants erotic love. But it does teach very clearly that the erotic finds fulfilment only in the context of *agapē*. So the test of love in marriage, according to Paul, is the *agapē* relationship between Christ and the church (Eph. 5:22–33). While *erōs* responds to something lovable, *agapē* creates and sustains lovableness (in the case of marriage) by 'loving out' latent qualities in the partner.

See also: ANTHROPOLOGY; FEMINIST THEOLOGY.

Bibliography

J. Dominian, *Proposals for a New Sexual Ethic* (London, 1977); L. Smedes, *Sex in the Real World* (Tring, 1979); H. Thielicke, *The Ethics of Sex* (London, 1964).

D.H.F.

SHEPHERDING MOVEMENT. This movement arose primarily within the house churches which sprang up in the 1960s and 1970s, though it has influenced charismatic congregations within major denominations (see Gifts of the Spirit*).

Observing the failures of more traditional churches – low commitment, poor sense of community, copying the world's values and little if any discipline* – the movement is concerned with discipling, for growth into spiritual maturity. It desires to restore the church (God's kingdom*) by introducing what it perceives to be biblical patterns of leadership and accountability. All Christians must be shepherded and thus subject to kingdom authority. Each church member is made accountable to a house-group leader who is to make sure that the member is properly discipled: *i.e.* growing spiritually, suitably employed, using his or her gifts in the church and becoming a responsible member. The house-group leaders are in turn accountable to the elders of the church with regard to both their own lives and the lives of those under their care. The elders are answerable to pastors and the pastors to apostles,* who may be seen as church planters or the equivalent of bishops with a 'diocese' under their care, but whose ministry* is sometimes compared to that of NT apostles (see Church Government*). These apostles are to be subject to one another 'in the Lord'.

To ensure that shepherding is adequately implemented, 'covering' may be adopted. 'Covering' means that a church member must have any important decision, and sometimes less important ones, 'covered' or approved by their house-group leader, elder or pastor. This approval for decisions is required so that right choices may be made and the devil can gain no foothold. Examples of decisions for covering by an elder or more mature Christian are: moving home, employment, marriage, even an appointment with the doctor. Covering may also be required for any new ministry or gift-exercise that an individual may feel called to undertake. In some churches, prophecy* may be required for new directions for churches, families and individuals. Prophetic words are sometimes given a place of almost equal importance with Scripture.

Shepherding churches are often characterized by strong community, zeal for the Lord's work, readiness to obey Scripture, vibrant worship and lively prayer – in short, by many characteristics of true discipleship.

It is difficult to trace the origin of the concepts of shepherding and covering. Some see the emphasis of the Argentinian, Juan Carlos Ortiz, on discipling as a possible source. Others point to the Fort Lauderdale (Florida, USA) group of house churches and the teaching of Bob Mumford, Derek Prince, Charles Simpson, Don Basham and Ern

Baxter who claim an apostolic authority. Yet Watchman Nee (1903–72) was teaching a similar system of accountability to his Little Flock churches in China in the 1920s and 1930s. Nee himself had been influenced by the Brethren movement on his visits to Britain. Whatever the source, the motivation is clearly to bring moral accountability and spiritual maturity into the church in an age of immorality, irresponsibility and selfish individualism.

There are dangers, however. The teaching of the NT apostles was binding on the whole church (Jn. 14:26; 15:26–27; 16:13; 20:21; Acts 1:22; Gal. 1:1), but no such group exists today. All believers are priests* through Christ and thus have equal access to the Father (1 Pet. 2:9; Heb. 4:15–16). The Spirit and wisdom are given richly to everyone who asks (Lk. 11:13; Jas. 1:5). Advice may be sought, community and support must be encouraged, but no single individual has an exclusive right to claim to know God's particular will for another believer. Discipline must be applied only for doctrinal and moral disobedience to Scripture, not for questioning prophecy or 'covering'. Spiritual immaturity rather than true discipleship results from excessive authority.

Bibliography
J. Barrs, *Freedom and Discipleship* (Leicester, 1983); J. C. Ortiz, *Disciple* (London, 1976); D. Watson, *Discipleship* (London, 1983).

J.B.

SHINTOISM AND CHRISTIANITY.
Shintoism is a naturalistic cosmic religion, an animistic* polytheism.* It represents the original world-view and way of life of the Japanese. Its central concept is *kami*. (The Chinese character pronounced *kami* on its own is pronounced *shin* in combination.) *Kami* is usually translated as 'god' or 'gods', but also means 'above', 'superior', or 'divine'. *Kami* means anything sacred and/or extraordinary which arouses man's fear or respect (see R. Otto*). Shintoism claims that there exist 800 million *kami*, being manifested in the beneficent beauties of nature – mountains, trees, beasts, and birds. Shinto shrines are dotted around the countryside. Humankind is also a part of this world, and can never be separated from it. Every being is part of the community of the entire universe and all share

kami nature. When a person is purified (*harai*), he recovers his *kami* nature and restores his true self. In Shintoism, the heavenly and earthly realms are not sharply separated, nor the realms of life in this world and life after death. In many homes dead relatives are worshipped as *kami*, through syncretism* with ancestor worship.

The Shinto myths trace the origin of heaven and earth to the marriage of a male deity (Izanagi, he who invites) and a female deity (Iznami, she who is invited). This resulted in the birth of the sun goddess Amaterasu Oominokami. Her children came down to the human domain and their descendant, Jimmu, is said to have been the first *tenno* (heavenly emperor) of Japan.

In the early history of Japan (5th century AD), several clans fought to establish themselves as the political centre. Each clan possessed its clan *kami*, to whom the whole clan turned in the time of need. The leader of the clan acted as both chief priest and military commander. The *tenno* clan (whose leader has been *tenno* up to the present day) eventually united the whole country. This meant that the goddess of *tenno* was invincible. As a result, Shintoism came to play the central role in Japanese history as a patriotic imperial cult.

In the 5th and 6th centuries, Shintoism was influenced by Confucianism* and Buddhism,* which supplied respectively the ethics and the philosophy which Shintoism lacked. Shinto's simple naturalistic faith and practice became more theoretical and ritualistic. In the 9th century, a Buddhist interpreted the Shinto *kami* as local manifestations of the universal Buddha. This provided the philosophical explanation for the co-existence of these two religions (known as *Ryobu Shinto*), which lasted until the 19th century. Buddhist concepts of repeated rebirths (see Metempsychosis*) and of success and failure as the result of sins in earlier lives were syncretized with underlying Shinto beliefs.

Christianity came to Japan on three occasions in history as the religious element of foreign aggression. It was first introduced to Japan by the pioneer Jesuit Francis Xavier (1502–52) in 1549. At that time, Japan was nominally ruled by *tenno*, but was actually divided among feudal lords. In such a situation, Christianity spread rather rapidly and claimed several Christian feudal lords. After the Tokugawa Shogunate consolidated its political power (1603), it severely persecuted Christians because they pledged allegiance to God rather than to Shogun. It also isolated the country to prevent Christian influence.

As soon as Japan reopened after 250 years of seclusion (1854), Protestant Christian missionaries arrived and were initially successful. In 1868, the Tokugawa Shogunate was overthrown and the Meiji imperial government was established. This government introduced several Western social, educational, political and military structures, including monarchy. The leaders of the government argued that Christianity was too individualistic for the Japanese Empire and Buddhism too weak to solidify the country. They chose Shintoism to play the role which Christianity had played in European monarchies. This was the origin of state Shintoism in Japan. A rescript read daily in schools between 1889 and 1945 declared that Japan was 'the nation of the *kami*'. When nationalists and militarists thus utilized state Shintoism to enhance Japanese nationalism, Christians were again faced with the choice between worshipping God or the emperor, as were the Christians in the early Roman Empire. The defeat of the Japanese Empire in 1945 was seen as the failure of the *kamikaze* ('divine wind') to protect the country. This caused a serious loss of face for the *kami*, and weakened Shinto for a time.

The 20th-century interdenominational mission also began with some success, but today Japanese Christians see attempts to reinstate Shinto as the state religion as threatening. They feel that any check on Japan's economic empire might mean a return to militarism sanctioned by Shinto as a nationalist patriotic movement.

Most Christian services in Japan begin with reference to seasons or weather, which may be either desirable contextualization* in recognition of the true creator or syncretism with Shinto! The Christian concepts of sin and cleansing are difficult to understand if one holds Buddhist preconceptions, but the Shinto ideas of defilement and ritual cleansing (perhaps explaining why the Japanese bathe far more frequently than other humans) provide a helpful way of illustrating how the Bible thinks of sin and cleansing. Outward cleansing of the body is meant to be accompanied by a cleansing of the heart.

Little theological cross-fertilization has taken place between Christianity and Shinto. The anti-Buddhist Shinto restorationist, Hirata Atsutane (1776–1843), was partly influenced by a Christian understanding of God, and some Christian elements have been incorporated into sect Shinto. An extreme 'Japanese Christianity' has only rarely been advocated. K. Kitamori's (b. 1916) *Theology of the Pain of God* (1946; ET, Richmond, VA, 1965) is a deliberate theological attempt to speak to Japanese culture.

Another writer whose theology has sought to be explicitly sensitive to Japanese tradition and experience, particularly after the atomic bombing of Hiroshima, is Kosuke Koyama, notably in *Mount Fuji and Mount Sinai: A Pilgrimage in Theology* (London, 1984).

Bibliography

Agency for Cultural Affairs, *Japanese Religion* (Tokyo and Palo Alto, CA, 1972); H. B. Earhart, *Religion in the Japanese Experience* (Encino and Belmont, CA, 1974); R. Hammer, *Japan's Religious Ferment: Christian Presence amid Faiths Old and New* (London, 1961); J. M. Kitagawa, *Religion in Japanese History* (New York and London, 1966); C. Michalson, *Japanese Contributions to Christian Theology* (Richmond, VA, 1965); S. D. B. Picken, *Shinto: Japan's Spiritual Roots* (Tokyo and New York, 1980).

S.P.K. and M.C.G.

SIBBES, RICHARD, see PURITAN THEOLOGY.

SICKNESS, see HEALING.

SIN. Scripture employs a variety of words to speak of sin, with meanings ranging from 'the missing of a mark or goal' or 'the breach of relationship' to 'ungodliness', 'perversion' or 'rebellion'. Yet the common theme of every biblical expression of the nature of sin is the central idea that sin is a state of our being that separates us from the holy God; biblically, sin is ultimately sin against God.

According to Augustine* sin ought not to be considered in positive terms, but negatively, as a privation of the good. He defined the essence of sin as concupiscence (*concupiscentia*), a word used to translate the biblical words for desire and understood by Augustine as the perverted self-love which is the opposite of love for God. But to define sin as selfishness surely fails to do justice to its seriousness in biblical terms as being primarily against God. Calvin* argued that sin ought not merely to be conceived of as a privation of good but as a total corruption of man's being; desire itself is sin which defiles every part of man's nature, but the root of this corruption is not merely self-love but disobedience inspired by pride. At first glance Barth's* definition of sin as 'nothingness', an 'impossible possibility', may appear to be similar to Augustine's idea of a 'privation of the good', but Barth is not speaking merely of 'privation'. 'Nothingness' is not 'nothing'; it is that contradiction of God's positive will and that breach of his covenant which can exist only under the contradiction which is his judgment. Thus sin is the human pride which is the contradiction of God's humbling of himself in Christ; it is the human sloth that is the contradiction of God's desire to exalt man in Christ; it is the human falsehood that is the contradiction of God's pledge to man in Christ.

If the narrative of Gn. 3 is to be interpreted not only as the historical account of Adam's* sin, but also as an account of the origin of sin, then the sin of Adam must be recognized as the primary biblical definition of the essence of sin – i.e. a grasping for spiritual and moral autonomy rooted in unbelief and rebellion. It may have become common to think of an inner disposition towards sin as being passed on through society and its structures, through the influence of parents, environment or education. Yet such an analysis fails to give sufficient seriousness to the sinful state of humanity as the Bible depicts it. Traditionally the church has accounted for this inner disposition by reference to the concept of original sin as a means of defining the manner in which the sin of Adam affects all human beings. On the basis of Ps. 51:5, Augustine defined original sin as inherited sin; he considered that the fallen nature of Adam was transmitted biologically through sexual procreation. Although Anselm* considered original sin to be original in each individual rather than in reference to the origin of the race, he also understood this original guilt and pollution to be passed from father to child; all were germinally present in Adam and therefore actually sinned in Adam. The weakness of this approach is that if all are guilty of Adam's sin through this organic

connection, are they not also guilty of the subsequent sins of all their ancestors? For Calvin and Barth, Ps. 51:5 is not to be interpreted as a reference to this inherited sin, but as a recognition that from the very first the psalmist is conscious of his own sin and corruption: 'From his very conception he carries the confession of his own perversity' (Calvin, *Institutes*, II.i.5).

Both Luther* and Calvin understood original sin not as an external constraint but as the internal necessity which is rooted in the perversity of human nature; yet while Calvin speaks of 'a hereditary depravity and corruption of our nature' (*Institutes*, II.i.8), he relates original sin not so much to heredity as to an ordinance of God, a judgment of God passed on all mankind whereby Adam's sin is imputed to all in the same manner as Christ's righteousness is now imputed to all believers. This notion was subsequently developed by Beza* and enshrined in the Westminster Confession in terms by which Adam is recognized not merely as the natural head of the human race but also as its federal representative (federalism); all are born corrupt because they are representatively incorporate in the sin and guilt of Adam. It is this representative incorporation that is the root of each person's inherent disposition to sin, a federal relationship that all confirm by their own sinful acts: a person is not a sinner because he sins, he sins because he is a sinner.

Thomas Aquinas* had argued that for a person to be held guilty of sin it was necessary for him to be a rational being; and that therefore the fall* could not have involved the loss of human reason, which Aquinas identified as the image of God* in which man and woman were created, but rather must have involved the loss of that supernatural endowment (*donum superadditum*) which enabled a person's reason to be subject to God. According to the Reformers, however, the fall resulted in the corruption of human nature in its entirety. Reason and every aspect of his being have become totally depraved as a consequence of Adam's sin. This doctrine of total depravity is not intended to imply that fallen humanity is incapable of good works, but rather that there is no aspect of human being that is unaffected by sin: there is no 'relic or core or goodness which persists in man in spite of his sin' (Barth, *CD* IV.1, p. 493). Since even good human actions may spring from mixed motives, human religion, ethics, art and creativity have all become occasions for his unbelief and pride.

While a person may certainly be conscious of immoral acts and false motives, the reality of man's sinful state can never be perceived merely by self-knowledge. The totality and inclusiveness of Adam's sin and the consequent depravity of all is an issue that is only truly made known in the cross: 'In that He takes our place it is decided what our place is' (Barth, *CD* IV.1, p. 240). The cross of Christ and the condemnation of human sin that it represents reveals the objectivity and total depravity of our sinful state just as it reveals the utter inadequacy of existentialist* reductions of our sin in terms of 'unauthentic existence', anxiety or despair.

See also: ANTHROPOLOGY.

Bibliography

K. Barth, *CD* IV.1, pp. 358ff.; G. C. Berkouwer, *Studies in Dogmatics: Sin* (Grand Rapids, MI, 1971); J. Calvin, *Institutes*, II. i – ix; M. Luther, *The Bondage of the Will* (ET, Cambridge, 1957); B. Milne, *Know the Truth: A Handbook of Christian Belief* (Leicester, 1982).

J.E.C.

SINLESSNESS OF CHRIST.

The belief in the sinlessness of Christ appears in all the major witnesses of the NT (Paul, 2 Cor. 5:21; John, 1 Jn. 3:5; Peter, 1 Pet. 3:18; the writer to the Hebrews, Heb. 4:15). Its theological significance is primarily soteriological. Christ must be sinless in order to achieve the redemption of the sinful human race (see the discussion in Heb. 7:23–28 concerning the nature of Christ as high priest; *cf.* Offices of Christ*).

Given its wide biblical base and critical function in NT theology, it is not surprising that this doctrine was universally affirmed in the patristic church. Unfortunately, it underwent developments which, although intending to heighten the doctrine, in fact contradicted its biblical foundations and undermined its theological significance. This occurred in two stages. First, primarily through Augustine,* the discussion shifted from the extraordinary faithfulness of Jesus in resisting temptation (stressed in the temptation narratives and Hebrews), to the metaphysical conditions necessary for Christ to be sinless from birth.

Thus, the virgin birth* was given in Augustine the significance of breaking the bond of sexually transmitted original sin.* The force of that argument, however, led to further discussions about the status of Jesus' mother and the development of the doctrine of her immaculate conception (see Mary*).

The second development was the shift from affirming the fact that Christ *did* not sin to affirming that he *could* not sin. This was an extension of Augustinian ideas, and it shows how far the tradition had departed from the NT. Not only did this belief result in some theologians (*e.g.* Basil*) asserting that Christ did not take on a human nature identical to ours but only one which was analogous, but it also demanded that some account be given of how Christ's 'impossible' temptations could be meritorious.

In modern theology the idea of the sinlessness of Christ has taken a number of interesting turns. Classic liberal theology, while denying that Jesus was incapable of sinning, if anything placed a greater emphasis on the fact that Christ did not sin. In the followers of A. Ritschl,* the sinlessness of Christ becomes the one proof of his divine status, made all the more significant since the other signs of his divinity – his virgin birth, miracles, and resurrection – were called into question.

But it is in radical theologies that the underlying religious significance of the sinlessness of Christ is most clearly revealed. J. A. T. Robinson's* and G. W. H. Lampe's (1912–80) fear of docetism* required them to reject any element of traditional Christology* which would separate Jesus from the rest of humanity, yet they both affirmed his sinlessness. While this might appear utterly incongruous in the light of the fact that sinfulness is a universal human characteristic, their belief has a fundamental logic. So long as Jesus is regarded as worthy of religious devotion, it is psychologically impossible to attribute sin to him, even if the rest of one's theology would seem to demand it.

Bibliography

W. Pannenberg, *Jesus – God and Man* (Philadelphia, 1968); C. Ullmann, *The Sinlessness of Jesus* (Edinburgh, 1870).

B.E.F.

SLAVERY,

a social institution justifying the involuntary servitude of individuals who are treated as the property of others. The social arrangements and degree of oppression have varied greatly throughout history and in different cultures. Although very widely accepted in the ancient world reflected in the Bible, many Christians came to regard slavery as unnatural and undignified. But it was not until the late 18th and early 19th century that a determined Christian movement developed for its abolition. However, despite considerable successes throughout the 19th century, the Anti-Slavery Society in London reports that slavery exists in many parts of Africa and Asia today, even though governments may officially deny that it is practised.

The ancient Hebrews accepted and even traded in slaves (Gn. 24:35; 26:14; Jb. 1:3; Gn. 14:14; 17:23, 27). In theory at least Hebrew slavery was comparatively humane. It lacked the harshness found in many other cultures to the extent that slaves were accorded some protection under the law (Ex. 12:44; 21:26–27, 20–21). To what extent these laws were enforced in actual cases is hard to determine.

In ancient Greece, slaves enjoyed considerable privileges when they were household slaves; but in Rome rigid severity was more often the rule. To a large extent the treatment of slaves depended on chance, although the Stoic* doctrine of the equality of all people slowly influenced both Greek and Roman thinking on the subject. There appears to be little evidence that either Christianity or Judaism modified Graeco-Roman views of slavery.

In the Hebrew Bible the idea of slavery was used to illustrate the relationship between God and his people Israel. The Israelites were pictured as being redeemed from Egyptian slavery by the historic deeds of Yahweh (Ex. 22:2; Dt. 5:6). As a result the Hebrews believed that they had become the slaves of God and were dependent on him for their being. For this reason they could neither live for themselves alone nor worship other gods (Lv. 25:42, 55; Ex. 20:2–6).

A similar use of the imagery of slavery is to be found in the NT where Christians were described as slaves of God (Rom. 1:1; 1 Pet. 2:16). Practically, however, Christians owned slaves and the institution as such was not condemned in the NT (Mt. 18:23; 1 Cor. 7:21; Phm). Some writers argue that, despite the acceptance of slavery, early Christian writings display a significantly changed attitude towards the slave which reveals a new awareness of slaves as people made in the image of God (cf. Hermas, Shepherd; Eph. 6:5ff., Col. 3.22; 4:1; Tit. 2:9–10).

Despite these arguments the Council of Agde in S. Gaul in AD 506 forbade abbots or bishops to free slaves, lest they reduce the wealth of their churches. The monastic orders, on the other hand, received slaves into their numbers as free men and refused to own slaves of their own. By the 12th or 13th century slavery had practically disappeared in north-western Europe although the new system of serfdom had replaced it. Only in 1031 did Pope Conrad II forbid traffic in slaves. Yet despite this, Pope Paul III confirmed the right of clergy to own slaves as late as 1548.

The abuse of slavery by supposedly Christian people reached its greatest heights in the 17th and 18th centuries with the transatlantic slave trade. Between 1579 and 1807 over 15,000,000 slaves were transported to the Americas from Africa. The majority of the human cargoes on slave ships often died in transit. Upon arrival in the Americas these slaves were destined for a harsh existence on the plantations of the West Indies. Slave revolts were frequent and were suppressed with the utmost severity.

In the 18th century various Christian writers sought to develop a theological defence of slavery. Probably the first of such works to be written in America was John Saffin's A True and Particular Narrative... and A Brief and Candid Answer.... Both tracts were published in Boston in 1701 and concerned the affairs of Saffin and his slave Adam. Saffin sought to justify slavery as a perpetual institution created by God and ordained in Scripture. He also attempted to refute the anti-slavery arguments of Judge Samuel Sewall who had attacked both Saffin and the institution of slavery in his work The Selling of Joseph... (Boston, 1700). He argued that all people were united in Christ by the bond of love.

Throughout the 18th and 19th centuries many other theological defences of slavery appeared. In 1772 Thomas Thompson produced The Trade in Negro Slaves on the African Coast in Accordance with Humane Principles and with the Laws of Revealed Religion. Later, in the 1850s Samuel A.

Cartwright could argue that 'to expect to civilize or Christianize the negro without the institution of slavery is to expect the impossible' (quoted in E. N. Elliot's book *Cotton is King, and Pro-Slavery Arguments*, Augusta, GA, 1860, p. 596). In defending slavery numerous arguments were developed such as those linking black Africans with the curse of Ham (Gn. 9:22–27) and the notion that slaves were receiving a 'just' punishment for their 'vicious, evil nature, dishonesty, treachery, lowmindedness and malice . . .' Josiah Priest even argued, in his *Bible Defence of Slavery* (Glasgow, KY, 1852), that Lv. 18:8 indicated that Ham had committed 'abuse and actual violation of his own mother' and that the 'horrors' associated with the name Ham could be seen 'agreeing, in a most surprising manner, with the color of his skin . . .' (p. 3). All these arguments, however, eventually gave way before the force of the philosophical criticism of slavery and the zeal of evangelical reformers.

The writings of Jean Jacques Rousseau (1712–78) and Tom Paine (1739–1809) led the philosophical attack on slavery but it was evangelical Christians who pursued the cause of abolition with the utmost vigour. In 1772, Granville Sharp (1735–1813) began a campaign for the suppression of slavery. John Wesley* and the Methodists took up the challenge as did William Wilberforce (1759–1833) and the Anglican Clapham Sect in England. Quakers, Presbyterians and Baptists all campaigned against slavery which was outlawed in Britain in 1807, and in 1808 the foreign slave trade was prohibited in the United States. In 1833 slavery was abolished in the British Empire and the Royal Navy engaged in a vigorous campaign to suppress it at sea. On land, missionaries such as David Livingstone (1813–73) exposed the realities of the internal African slave trade and fought for its abolition. Much of the late 19th-century missionary endeavour in Africa, such as the founding of Blantyre in Malawi, was part of a strategy aimed at the abolition of the Arab slave trade. In America slavery was finally abolished after the Civil War in 1865. Today, slavery still exists in many societies although it receives little attention and is generally considered a dead issue.

See also: THORNWELL, J. H.

Bibliography
D. B. Davis, *The Problem of Slavery in Western Culture* (New York, 1966); G. D. Kelsey, *Racism and the Christian Understanding of Man* (New York, 1965); J. O. Buswell III, *Slavery, Segregation and Scripture* (Grand Rapids, MI, 1964).

I.He.

SOBORNOST. In Russian *sobor* means both 'church' and 'synod' or 'council'. No single English word can do justice to *sobornost*. Its use to characterize Orthodoxy's distinctive vision of the church* dates from the Russian Orthodox lay theologian Alexis S. Khomyakov (1804–60). In his view the genius of Orthodoxy lay in avoiding the polar weaknesses of Romanism (unity imposed externally from above) and of Protestantism (individualistic liberty), in a unique synthesis of freedom and unanimity, diversity and unity. This *sobornost*, or communal unity by free association in Christ, finds significant expression in the church council,* where harmony is attained by free consultation. Khomyakov also made much of the 'reception' of conciliar decisions by the church as a whole. The *sobornost* of the church is a kind of organic spiritual catholicity and conciliarity. In ecumenical discussion *sobornost* has become almost a shorthand description of Orthodoxy's distinctive approach to ecclesiology. Somewhat comparable concepts in Anglican and Roman usage are koinonia* and (in more limited contexts) conciliarity and collegiality.*

See also: RUSSIAN ORTHODOX THEOLOGY.

Bibliography
S. Bulgakov, *The Orthodox Church* (London, 1935); N. Zernov, *Three Russian Prophets* (London, 1944).

D.F.W.

SOCIAL ETHICS. The aim of social ethics is to clarify the underlying values and principles which should inform practical understandings of and responses to social matters. Christians will approach the task by seeking help in identifying such perspectives from Christian faith and thought. The reason for talking specifically about *social* ethics is the experience we have of corporate social life. Christians believe that social experience is basic to being human and is an important aspect of what God's creation wills for people. The practical effect of the task of social ethics is to enable the church to form judgments and to take action in the realm of social life.

There are three aspects to the social ethical enterprise. First, there is a need for as full an understanding of the social question as may be available. The Christian community cannot form adequate judgments if it does not make use of all the information and current evaluation open to it. Good social ethics often requires detailed, lengthy and painstaking work in grasping the nature of the subject-matter. Second, there is a need for continual reflection upon the Christian tradition. There are a number of aspects to this. There is the search for biblical models* which bear some relation to the matter being discussed. No serious Christian discussion of the family* or of war,* for example, can take place without considering biblical models of family life and biblical experience of, and teaching on, war. The theological task is not complete, however, if it is limited to textual comparisons. Christian social thought must go on to reflect on the basic themes of biblical faith and their implications for Christian values. Here theology is continually trying to hold in balance the beliefs 1. that the world and its history are created by God, 2. that nevertheless the world and human life within it have been spoilt and corrupted by human sin, 3. that in God's purpose in Jesus Christ there is salvation and restoration, and 4. that the future is to be one of hope, of the transformation of our life and our world and of the unity of all things reconciled to God and to one another in Jesus Christ. This theological task is assisted by a careful consideration of how the church has dealt with social questions throughout its history.

The final aspect of social ethical work is the forming of the Christian mind and judgment on the issues. In bringing together our understanding of what is happening in the social order with the living world of the gospel, the Christian church is equipped to begin to set out the shape of a social ethic which can undergird practical social experience.

The Christian church has produced a wide range of different approaches to this work. These have included a number of views which do not accept that it is possible to relate the gospel directly to the social order. The task of Christian ethics is to explore the middle and

bridging ground of values. In the Roman Catholic tradition especially, there has been an emphasis upon the natural-law (see Law*) tradition as providing the necessary bridge from faith to society. (Thomas Aquinas* is the classic Catholic theologian in this tradition.) There are certain inbuilt natural principles to which society must conform, if it is to live within the boundaries of the purposes of God. Others have stressed the need continually to search for and elucidate middle-order axioms which both make good sense of Christian faith and can help us live practically and humanly in the contemporary social order. In recent English thought, Ronald Preston's (b. 1913) work is an example of this approach. Yet others have stressed the impossibility of relating the elevated Christian ethic of love to the corrupt world of society and social practice. We need a value which can bind the forces of collective life to human aims. Reinhold Niebuhr's* work is the classic 20th-century example of the attempt to expound justice as the key value derived from Christian faith which can have this effect.

Others are more confident that it is possible to move more directly from biblical faith to social ethics. Alan Storkey's A Christian Social Perspective (Leicester, 1979) is an example of such a tradition whose roots are partly in continental Calvinist* theology and partly in the Anabaptist* tradition.

These differences are important. Nevertheless, they are also all examples of the attempt of Christian thought to make sense of our social vocation in the light of our belief in Jesus Christ. Furthermore, they all seek to help the church form specific judgments on the basic social-order matters of the day and thus to witness to the meaning of Christ's reign in our social history as well as in our personal experience.

Bibliography

Grove Booklets on Ethics (Bramcote, Nottingham, 1974–); R. Niebuhr, *Moral Man and Immoral Society* (New York, 1934); W. Temple, *Christianity and Social Order* (Harmondsworth, 1942); D. F. Wright (ed.), *Essays in Evangelical Social Ethics* (Exeter, 1979).

J.W.G.

SOCIAL GOSPEL. The Social Gospel was a loosely organized movement in North

America from roughly 1880 to the start of the Great Depression (1929) which attempted to formulate a Christian response to the rapid social changes of the period. Its origins were both domestic and foreign. The strong link in the American revival tradition between personal holiness and social reform contributed to the movement; as did also the newer concern for scientific study of social problems that accompanied the rise of modern America after the Civil War. In addition, the example of Britons, like Thomas Chalmers* in Scotland or the Christian Socialism* of F. D. Maurice (1805–72), who attempted innovative Christian responses to the problems of industrial society, also influenced Americans desiring a Christian social reform.

Early expressions of the Social Gospel included the work of Washington Gladden (1836–1918), a Congregationalist minister in Springfield, Massachusetts, and Columbus, Ohio. While still in Massachusetts he had published *Working People and Their Employers* (1876), an appeal for fairness to workers. In his Ohio congregation were mine owners whose labourers struck twice in the mid–1880s for better wages and working conditions. Gladden's belief in the justice of their demands led to a more insistent appeal for the rights of labour and the application of the 'Golden Rule' to industrial organization. A different expression of the Social Gospel appeared in the work of Charles Sheldon (1857–1946), a clergyman from Topeka, Kansas, whose best-selling novel *In His Steps* (1897) presented a picture of what could happen in a community torn by social dissension if Christians would only ask themselves in every decision, 'What would Jesus do?'

The most important exponent of the Social Gospel was Walter Rauschenbusch (1861–1918), a German-American Baptist who ministered for ten years in New York City's 'Hell's Kitchen' before becoming a professor of church history at Rochester Seminary in the state of New York. Rauschenbusch's first-hand experience of industrial exploitation and governmental indifference to workers made him a convinced critic of the established order. His fruitful relationships with New York City socialists like Henry George (1839–97) offered alternative models for social organization. But Rauschenbusch's main concern was to search the Scriptures for a message to the troubled circumstances of industrial society.

The results of this search were published in 1907 as *Christianity and the Social Crisis*, a work that recalled the prophetic denunciations of OT prophets against social callousness as well as NT injunctions about the dangers of mammon. Rauschenbusch followed this work with other influential volumes, including *Prayers of the Social Awakening* (1910), *Christianizing the Social Order* (1912), and *A Theology for the Social Gospel* (1917). In these works Rauschenbusch combined a prophetic ideal of justice (see Righteousness*) with a commitment to building the kingdom* of God through the power of Christ.

The Social Gospel is often identified with theological liberalism,* and with some justice. Gladden, for example, was a popularizer of biblical higher criticism, and Rauschenbusch, though much more realistic about the intractably fallen* character of human nature, yet reinterpreted some traditionally supernatural elements of Christian doctrine. At the same time, however, themes of social service associated with the Social Gospel were also prominent among evangelical bodies such as the Salvation Army* or in individual evangelical leaders like A. J. Gordon (1836–1895) in Boston. Since the 1930s the Social Gospel has disappeared as a movement in its own right, but its influence remains, both in the more liberal, mainline denominations and in the renewed social concern displayed by American evangelicals since the 1960s.

See also: SOCIAL ETHICS; SOCIETY, THEOLOGY OF.

Bibliography

P. A. Carter, *Decline and Revival of the Social Gospel . . . 1920–1940* (New York, 1956); R. T. Handy (ed.), *The Social Gospel in America, 1870–1920* (New York, 1966); C. H. Hopkins, *The Rise of the Social Gospel in American Protestantism 1865–1915* (New Haven, CT, 1940); W. S. Hudson (ed.), *Walter Rauschenbusch: Selected Writings* (New York, 1984); R. C. White, Jr., and C. H. Hopkins (eds.), *The Social Gospel: Religion and Reform in Changing America* (Philadelphia, 1976).

M.A.N.

SOCIETY, THEOLOGY OF. The
concept 'society' is used to describe an organized group held together by common ties

of membership. Membership may be thought of in a number of ways. We may think of the common life of the people who live within certain borders – 'British society' being about the common life of all who live in Britain. We may think in terms of citizenship – 'British society' being about the common life of British citizens. We may think in terms of nationhood or even or race* – 'English society' being about the English nation or the English as a race of people. Thus we are invariably using the term 'society' about the common experience of a group whose membership we have delineated in one way or another.

We may have a number of different things in mind when we talk about 'society'. We frequently use such language when we want to talk about cultural* identity. There are certain features which, in general, mark out this particular society from that. This is not necessarily to suggest that all the members have any or all these features but that there is sufficient of a preponderance of these features in that society viewed as a whole to make it out in a distinctive way. Similarly we may have political or national identity in mind when we talk in society terms.

Much of the discussion of the philosophy and practice concerning society has been concerned with the question of the merits of open and closed societies. Karl Popper's (b. 1902) famous thesis *The Open Society and its Enemies* (2 vols., London, ²1952) is a formidable rationale for open societies and an attack on closed ones. Open societies seek to maintain only the most minimal of conditions of membership. Closed societies are much more rigorous and may require political, religious or racial conformity to allow full membership to individuals to that particular society. Another aspect of the same debate concerns the question of plurality in society. Those who argue against plurality do so on many grounds, often out of a fear of what plurality will do to the cultural cohesion of society. Whilst it is not the purpose of this brief article to comment on its desirability, for much of the history of the church Christianity has been identified in different ways with closed and uniform societies. For centuries it was only small sects,* Anabaptist* groups and dissenters (non-conformists) whose presence and theology challenged the predominant model of a Christian society equalling a society conforming to a particular form of church order (see Christendom;* Reformed Theology*). Christian theology has, in the main, abandoned attempts at justifying such concepts. Not only are they no longer pertinent to much of the modern world, they seem in danger of threatening some important Christian insights. Whilst Christian theology has not the resources to produce a blueprint for a Christian society (even the organized church, while called to reflect the NT picture of the body of Christ, is not given a fixed form of order in the NT), it does provide some sharp critical perspectives on different sorts of society. For example, Christian theology is rigorous in its opposition to societies which exclude people on the ground of race, sex, or religious belief. There is a counter-stress on the dignity of all individuals (see Rights,* Human) and the need for society to be organized on a basis of equal recognition of this truth. Similarly Christian thought has been very wary of secret societies and of societies organized on the basis of deliberately keeping many of its members ignorant of basic matters which are properly their concern. The Christian commitment to truth and to the 'open secret' of Jesus Christ is a force for openness and accountability. Similarly Christian belief in God as the one to whom all, equally and without exception, give account works to deflate excessive claims for particular societies. Attempts at deifying certain forms of society are a denial of the unique sovereignty* of God.

So thus the effect of Christian belief, properly understood, is to reduce extravagant claims and thus to humanize society by affirming inclusive, participatory and accountable concepts of membership.

See also: CIVIL RELIGION; STATE.

Bibliography

F. Catherwood, *A Better Way: The Case for a Christian Social Order* (Leicester, 1975); V. A. Demant, *Theology of Society* (London, 1947); T. S. Eliot, *The Idea of a Christian Society* (London, 1942); J. W. Gladwin, *God's People in God's World: Biblical Motives for Social Involvement* (Leicester, 1979); R. Niebuhr, *Moral Man and Immoral Society* (New York, 1934); A. Storkey, *A Christian Social Perspective* (Leicester, 1979); W. Temple, *Christianity and Social Order* (Harmondsworth, 1942); E. Troeltsch, *The Social Teaching of the Christian Churches*, 2 vols. (London, 1931); N. Wolterstorff, *Until Justice and Peace Embrace* (Grand Rapids, MI, 1982).

J.W.G.

SOCINUS AND SOCINIANISM. Two

lay theologians of this name (Italian, Sozini, or Sozzini), Lelio (1525–62) and his nephew Faustus (1539–1604), had wide influence because of their persuasive reconstruction of early Christianity. The elder was one of many gifted Italian Protestant exiles. He travelled widely and discussed theology with Calvin,* Melanchthon* and Bullinger.* His learning, social status and attractive personality gave him many friends, though Calvin warned him about the spiritual dangers of his penchant for asking questions. His *Confession of Faith* (1555) used orthodox terms, but in an open-ended and enquiring manner which made some Protestants uneasy.

Faustus, largely self-educated, was a prolific writer of anonymous manuscripts. Though he did not attract the attention of the Holy Office while at the court of Isabella de Medici (1565–75), his early works show he had moved far from orthodoxy. As early as 1562 his *Explicatio* raised questions about the divinity of Christ and in 1563 he rejected the natural immortality* of the soul. He defended the authority of the Scriptures on rational and historical grounds, rather than on the testimony of the Holy Spirit. In Basel, his *De Jesu Christo Servatore* (unpublished until 1594) dramatically reinterpreted the person and work of Christ, underlining their exemplary character.

He arrived in Poland in 1579, finding a congenial environment in the 'Minor Church'. Their simple biblical piety and quest for holiness had led to deep divisions. Socinus gave unifying leadership, which profoundly influenced younger ministers. He appears not to have been a church member for he refused rebaptism,* but by his death he was its most authoritative spokesman. They began to be called Socinians. He was able to moderate their other-worldliness and rejection of the state, but repudiated any political resistance. Though he agreed with their anti-Trinitarian theology, he guided them into a more coherent and reasoned theological position, which is well expressed in the Racovian *Catechism* (1605). Drawn up by Socinus' colleagues, it was very influential among Socinian churches

and beyond. Emphasis on correct knowledge as the key to salvation was basic to its content. At many points, it differed from mainstream Protestantism. Jesus did not die for satisfaction* of sin. His role was to inspire disciples to follow his example, for only those who persevered in obedience were raised from the dead.

As a system of belief and life, Socinianism appealed not only in Poland and Hungary, but to many distressed by bitter theological warfare, who sought a simpler biblical and more tolerant Christianity. The publication of Socinus' works gave his ideas wide currency. The move from a substitutionary understanding of atonement,* apologetic emphasis on Jesus' miracles and greater emphasis on non-dogmatic interpretation of the Scriptures aroused bitter hostility. Nevertheless, the leavening influence of Socinianism continued to grow in the 18th century, especially with the rise of a more historical and critical approach to the Scriptures and the search for a rational rather than a revealed Christianity. By the end of the 19th century, Socinianism was no longer seen as one of the major threats to orthodoxy.

Bibliography

H. J. McLachlan, *Socinianism in Seventeenth Century England*, (Oxford, 1951); M. Martini, *Fausto Socino et la pensée socinienne* (Paris, 1967); E. M. Wilbur, *History of Unitarianism*, 2 vols. (Cambridge, MA, 1945–52); G. H. Williams, *The Polish Brethren*, 2 vols. (Chico, CA, 1980).

I.B.

SOCIOLOGY OF RELIGION. In its

19th-century origins, the sociology of religion was often hostile to Christianity. French founders Claude Saint-Simon (1760–1825), Auguste Comte (1798–1857), and Emile Durkheim* each viewed sociology as a possible replacement for outmoded theology as a source of ethics. Max Weber,* who above all has given his name to this discipline, seemed to hold out little hope for the survival of religion in the modern age, despite Christianity's enormous influence on the course of Western civilization. And Edward Tylor (1832–1917), whose anthropology of religion has informed sociology, set the trend of *evolutionary* explanations. For him, religion would become socially extinct as a feature of a fading phase of development.

Of course, not all were rationalists or evolutionists. Ernst Troeltsch,* who may also be regarded as a founding father, made the analytically helpful distinction between 'church' (that is, 'established' or 'national' church) and 'sect'. Although his work has been qualified by others since (such as Bryan Wilson, b. 1926), the distinction still aids our understanding of religious organization. Churches tend to be conservative and traditional, whereas sects are voluntary protest groups, either reviving some forgotten orthodoxy or purveying some new or ancient heresy. During the 1920s H. Richard Niebuhr* took this idea further, arguing that in the USA sects tend to become *denominations* as they organize educational programmes, acquire property, and so on.

It would seem that those who sought an over-all explanation of the role of religion in modern society were heard as being antagonistic to religion, whereas those who developed 'ideal types' in order to investigate the inner dynamics of religious life could show that their studies had practical payoff in the social self-understanding of the churches. But this simple contrast no longer obtains. While it is true that up until the 1960s one still encountered sweepingly global accounts of religion-and-society (often in terms of secularization,* from the pens of Peter Berger, b. 1929, and Bryan Wilson), some such studies may today be far more sympathetic to Christianity (*e.g.* David Martin's *A General Theory of Secularization*, Oxford, 1978). Conversely, many social studies of church life are undertaken for no other reason than intellectual curiosity.

The sociology of religion attempts to place religious phenomena (see Religious Experience*) in their social context, to examine the effects of that context on the shape and direction religion takes, and to analyse the social impact of religion. While Christian people seem fairly content with the latter enterprise, they have often been suspicious of the former. Weber's famous study, *The Protestant Ethic and the Spirit of Capitalism* (1904–5; ET, London, 1930), for example, has sometimes been taken as a vindication of a noble role for Christianity (despite Weber's own highlighting of Protestant misgivings about central capitalist tenets!). On the other hand, Peter Berger's proposal that ecumenism* is a kind of ecclesiastical equivalent of the business merger, and guided by a similar rationale, is taken to underplay the sincerity of the participants in such ventures. Such apparent sociological reductionism appears to match the naive psychological reductionism of William Sargant's *Battle for the Mind* (London, 1957; see Psychology of Religion*).

The role of social factors *is* sometimes exaggerated in the sociology of religion. For instance, Berger's stress on what he calls 'plausibility structures' seems to imply that the credibility of a doctrine is very heavily dependent on the presence of a supporting group who agree to its veracity. While it is almost self-evident that it is easier to believe when surrounded by others who share that belief, this consideration may amount, if taken too far, to a denial of the importance of the truth of a given doctrine for its survival.

Berger does little to allay such fears when he dubs his basic approach 'methodological atheism'. The sociologist of religion should, he counsels, 'bracket' personal commitments when engaging in social investigation. This hygienic precaution sounds fine, but in practice, Berger's own (Schleiermacherian*) stance shows through his sociology (for instance in *The Heretical Imperative*, London, 1980), just as Bryan Wilson's wistful traditionalism protrudes provocatively round the margins of his professed neutrality.

This problem is unsolved as yet, and is possibly insoluble. Robert Bellah's (b. 1927) pleas that sociologists take seriously their own religious stances, while welcome as an antidote to the 'neutrality' theorists, themselves lead up a blind alley (see Epistemology*). For it then seems difficult to produce a sociology which is in any way truly *critical*. All religion becomes equally 'true'. Another way forward would be to admit frankly one's religious commitments at the outset, and to allow them to guide one's choice of theory, while simultaneously observing scholarly canons of honesty, parsimony, accuracy, and so on.

Critical comments on method should in no sense be taken as dismissive of the worth of sociology of religion. Unencumbered by both evolutionary and sociolog*istic* views, which variously minimize the role of conscious human agents, see 'fate' in 'trends', or treat religion as a social epiphenomenon, the distinctive focus on the *social* dimensions of faith* and practice is invaluable. The apparent congruence between ecumenism and the quest of commercial economies of scale could stimulate some well-placed heart-searching among those tempted to soft-pedal truth in the interests of 'unity'. Furthermore, the clergy may also be helped towards self-understanding and appropriate strategy through the sociologically-inspired realization that their status as 'professionals' is very ambiguous. Lacking the 'real' credentials of other 'professionals', clergy experience the pull of other designations (social worker, therapist, and so on), which may eventually draw them away from the biblically central tasks of 'pastors'.

But the sociology of religion is not to be sequestered as a handmaiden of the churches (still less an exercise in the manipulation of sacred statistics), valuable though its lessons are for Christian mission.* It has a wider remit, namely the interpretation of religion-and-society* relationships. Meshing with historical and cultural analysis, the sociology of religion addresses such issues as the pattern of church-state liaisons (this is the burden of Martin's above-mentioned book), and the tremendous growth of 'new religious movements' in East as well as West, over recent decades (see New Religions;* Sects*).

Less obviously 'religious' in the conventional sense (but hardly escaping that category biblically) is another area claiming increasing attention, the study of 'implicit', 'common', or 'customary' religion. In this case interest narrows to what people *actually* believe, and what difference this *actually* makes in their lives. Such investigations may, from a churchly point of view, reveal rifts between pulpit 'orthodoxy' and the *mélange* of pew-level interpretations of belief and justifications of practice. Broadened out to include the study of 'civil religion'* and 'ideology', explorations like this may expose the true 'treasures' of a society, and thus where its heart really lies.

Bibliography

P. Berger, *The Social Reality of Religion* (Harmondsworth, 1966), repr. as *The Sacred Canopy* (New York, 1967); R. Gill, *Theology and Social Structure* (Oxford, 1977); D. Lyon, *Sociology and the Human Image* (Leicester, 1983); J. A. Walter, *A Long Way from Home* (Exeter, 1980), repr. as *Sacred Cows* (Grand Rapids, 1980); B. Wilson, *Religion in Sociological Perspective* (London, 1982).

D.L.

SOELLE, DOROTHEE (b. 1929), radical German theologian, who now divides her time between Hamburg and New York, where she is visiting professor at Union Theological Seminary. The major characteristics of her theology are her rejection of traditional theism* and her political hermeneutic. Her deep concern with the issues raised by Auschwitz (see Holocaust*) both led her to Christian faith and made the idea of God as omnipotent ruler of the world inconceivable. She shares the Marxist* criticism of traditional theism as putting people in a position of alienated dependence and encouraging the acceptance of suffering, instead of protest and political activity to abolish suffering. For Soelle, God is loving solidarity, not omnipotent superiority. She pursues this reconception of God to the extent that, in her work, God often seems to be only a symbol for human love, liberation and hope. In this she is continuing Bultmann's* programme of demythologizing (see Myth*), but she rejects Bultmann's existential* privatization of Christianity in favour of a political hermeneutic of the gospel. Existential concerns cannot be separated from the need for concrete application of the gospel to the oppressive realities of international politics. Soelle's passionate advocacy of a radical political theology* has been matched by personal involvement, most recently in base communities and in the peace movement, which she sees as the most important religious event of the 1980s.

Bibliography

Christ the Representative (London, 1967); *The Inward Road and the Way Back* (London, 1979); *Political Theology* (Philadelphia, 1974); *Suffering* (London, 1975).

R.J.B.

SOLOVYOV, VLADIMIR, see RUSSIAN ORTHODOX THEOLOGY.

SONSHIP. As a theological term 'sonship' carries several shades of meaning, depending on whether the subject is the angels, human beings, or Jesus Christ in the three phases of his existence (pre-incarnate, earthly and exalted). We may conveniently adopt these divisions.

1. Angels*

The phrase 'sons of (the) God' is used a few

times in the OT in reference to heavenly beings (Gn. 6:2, 4; Jb 1:6, 2:1; 38:7; Ps. 82:6; Dn. 3:25). Not all these allusions are precisely to the angelic order, *i.e.* members of Yahweh's heavenly court, and it is not clear whether the term 'God' always means Israel's God. Sometimes 'sons of the gods' is the best translation. But what is common is the reference to other worldly beings, of whom a divine nature is predicated. But there is no clear case of physical paternity (as in the Greek and Roman pantheon where Zeus/Jupiter is the father of sons and daughters). In Hebraic thought the clear distinction between God and his creation, even angelic, is maintained.

2. Human beings

Several groups of individuals are dignified with the title 'son(s) of God', not always in connection with the Israelite people (*e.g.* Nu. 21:29). In the main, however, it is Israel* that claims this relationship to her God. Sometimes, the bond is more metaphorical and descriptive than literal, *e.g.* Pr. 3:11, 12. Even in those passages where the link is more realistic, there is still no idea of direct paternity. God chose Israel to be his own (Ex. 4:22: 'Israel is my son, my first-born'; Dt. 14:1, 2; Je. 31:9); and evidence of this election is seen primarily in the exodus (Ho. 11:1: 'Out of Egypt I called my son'). Israel is claimed as Yahweh's people and summoned to live as those who share his holy nature (Dt. 14:2). For that reason where there is apostasy from the covenant, sonship is broken (Dt. 32:5, 6), but with the promise of restoration (Ho. 1:2–10). Hope became centred on a messianic king who would embody the nation's obedience and loyalty, as David and his successors mirrored this ideal (2 Sa. 7:14). Pss. 2:7 and 110:3 both speak of royal sonship as vested in the Israelite king who enjoyed a special relationship to God (Ps. 89:19–29). In the inter-testamental period two lines of development are clear: the restorer of Israel's fortunes will act, in God's name, to chastise the people as 'sons of God' (Psalms of Solomon 17:30, 18:4), and in the Wisdom of Solomon chs. 2 – 5 the 'righteous man' in Israel is called 'son of God' (2:18). Both ideas are important for the NT.

The writers of the NT place Israel's election (Rom. 9:4) high on the list of the nation's privileges. But they interpret the calling in a new way to relate to the fulfilment of Israel's destiny for the blessing of all peoples (Gn. 12:2, 3; Gal. 3:6–25; Rom. 4:1–25). So 'sonship' is re-interpreted as promising to all nations a place in God's family of faith, extended to the Gentiles along with the Jews (1 Pet. 2:4–10). The coming of Jesus as God's Son and Israel's Messiah has made this possible. He is hailed as the 'first born' (Rom. 8:29; Col. 1:15; Rev. 3:14), and so the 'elder brother' in a world-wide divine family that is called to enter into personal relationship by faith in God who is revealed uniquely and finally in his life, death and triumph.

The process of becoming 'sons of God' (in non-sexist language as we see in 2 Cor. 6:18) is called 'adoption', a term found only in Paul (Rom. 8:15, 23, 9:4; Gal. 4:5; Eph. 1:5). Closely linked with this act is the work of the Holy Spirit who, as the Spirit of adoption, permits believers to invoke God under the 'nursery' title of Abba, 'dear Father'* (Rom. 8:16; Gal. 4:6), and to await their final salvation (Rom. 8:23–25).

Sonship as a term in later theology is best viewed as an aspect of regeneration.* As God brings new life to those who formerly were dead in sins (Eph. 2:1), so he is described as their Father who regards them as adopted children in his family of grace. When grace is denied or demoted as the central distinctive of God's dealings with sinful humanity, as in much medieval thought, adoption tends to be downplayed. The scholastics devised a distinction which was later to be an important one for Luther* between 'servile fear' (from which Christ sets us free) and 'filial fear', which is believers' continuing awareness of their creaturely dependence on God as both creator and Father, an important facet in Calvin's *Institutes* (III.xxiv). In the 18th century the Wesleys were to make assurance one of the main emphases of the early Methodists, and to celebrate, in both sermon and hymn, the Christian's privilege as one who had received the 'spirit of adoption' (based on Rom. 8:15) to replace the 'spirit of bondage' which is legalism (see John Wesley's Sermon IX in *Sermons on Several Occasions*; and Charles Wesley's couplet which is typical: 'He owns me for His child/I can no longer fear'). Modern evangelicalism has fully endorsed this truth as part of the believer's heritage of faith as a child of God.

3. Jesus Christ

He is the Son of God *par excellence*. The title takes us back to his eternal being (Jn. 1:18, NIV), but it is especially the descriptive term of his incarnate life seen as expressing a deep filial union from his baptism as the elect one (Mk. 1:11 par.) onwards. The high points of filial awareness are seen in Mk. 9:7; 12:6; 14:36, with the later churchly confession attested by 15:39 as the centurion became the first witness (Acts 8:27, NIV mg.). Christ's mediatorial kingdom is exercised in his role as Son (1 Cor. 15:25–28), one day to merge into the perfected kingdom of God.

Bibliography

B. Byrne, *'Sons of God'* – *'Seed of Abraham'* (Rome, 1979); G. Cooke, 'The Israelite King as Son of God', *ZAW* 73 (1961), pp. 202–225; M. J. Lagrange, 'La paternité de Dieu dans l'Ancient Testament', *RB* 5 (1908), pp. 481–499; W. H. Rossell, 'New Testament Adoption – Greco-Roman or Semitic?', *JBL* 71 (1952), pp. 233–234; M. W. Schoenberg, 'Huiothesia: The Word and the Institution', *Scripture* 15 (1963), pp. 115–23; J. Swetnam, 'On Romans 8, 23, and the Expectation of Sonship', *Biblica* 48 (1967), pp. 102–108.

R.P.M.

SOUL, see ANTHROPOLOGY.

SOUL, ORIGIN OF. The origin of the soul in the descendants of Adam is a question that long resisted an agreed explanation among Christian theologians, largely because their discussions assumed an anthropology* which regarded the soul as an entity different from the body.

To the early fathers, three main options were at hand:

1. *Pre-existence.* Platonism* inspired the belief that souls enjoyed some higher existence prior to their entry into individual human bodies. This view often coexisted with notions of a pre-cosmic fall and of the transmigration (see Metempsychosis*) of souls. Among Gnostics* and others, it presented the soul as an emanation from the divine substance itself. Although championed by Origen,* it was widely condemned in the 5th and 6th centuries.

2. *Traducianism* (also often called *generationism*). This argues that, like the body, the soul is derived from our parents by the process of procreation. It was advocated by Tertullian,* who, under Stoic* influence, believed the soul to be material. Traducianism most easily sustained the doctrine of our solidarity in original sin* 'in Adam' (and hence was denied by the Pelagians*), and became the teaching of Lutheranism.*

3. *Creationism.* This standpoint has enjoyed the widest support, asserting that God creates a soul *ex nihilo* for each human being. (It invites the further question about when God implants the soul – at conception, or at some later point in gestation?) Creationism is the official teaching of Roman Catholicism (it was reaffirmed in 1950 in the encyclical *Humani Generis* against evolutionism) and has generally appealed to Reformed theologians (*cf.* H. Heppe, *Reformed Dogmatics*, 1861, repr. London, 1950, pp. 227–231). It more readily preserves the differentiation of the soul (*e.g.* as immortal,* immaterial, indivisible) from the body, and also Christ's possession of a human soul free from sin. (Apollinarianism* assumed a traducianist position.) Creationists find biblical support in texts such as Gn. 2:7; Ec. 12:7; Zc. 12:1 and Heb. 12:9.

Preferences on this question have been heavily influenced by different understandings of original sin and its impact upon human nature. This is evident in Augustine's lifelong struggles with the issue. He remained undecided to the end, but only the transmission of sin kept him from espousing the creationist account. The differing views of Reformed and Lutheran also relate to different approaches to the fallenness of man created in God's image.

In the modern era, biblical theology's large-scale rejection of all dichotomist anthropologies appears to favour traducianism, but in reality overturns an assumption common to all traditions. 'Soul' (a word used sparingly in modern translations of the Bible) is not a part of human nature but characterizes it in its totality, just as 'flesh' and 'spirit' do (*cf.* Intermediate State*). A separate or different origin for 'soul' no longer enters the picture. But if we owe our whole being to our parents, biblical faith also denies that God is no longer actively creating (as traducianism claimed, citing Gn. 2:2). The whole human person, soul as much as body, is a wonderful divine creation (*cf.* Jb. 10:8–12; Pss. 33:4; 139:13–16; *etc.*), even in its very formation in a human womb.

Bibliography

G. C. Berkouwer, *Man: The Image of God* (Grand Rapids, MI, 1962).

D.F.W.

SOUTHERN BAPTIST THEOLOGY.

The Southern Baptist Convention (founded 1845) has distinguished itself more for practical Christian activity than profound theological writing. Nevertheless, its missionary activity has not proceeded within a theological vacuum. John L. Dagg (1794–1884), the convention's first writing theologian, contributed theological, ecclesiological, ethical, and apologetic works giving identity and direction to Southern Baptists. His *Manual of Theology* (1858) is a devotional, yet theologically cogent, exposition of evangelical Calvinism* founded upon the fundamental principle of every man's duty to love God. J. P. Boyce (1827–88), founder of the first Southern Baptist theological seminary, wrote *Abstract of Systematic Theology* as a textbook. Reflecting Boyce's Princeton* education, it gives voice to the consistent Calvinism of his Southern Baptist contemporaries. B. H. Carroll (1843–1914), though not a systematic theologian, had great conserving effect on Southern Baptist theology through pulpit, print, classroom, personal relations (G. W. Truett, 1867–1944, and L. R. Scarborough, 1870–1945), and the founding of Southwestern Baptist Seminary (1908). E. Y. Mullins (1860–1928) retained Calvinistic views of election, the precedence of new birth to faith, justification by faith, and perseverance, but his book, *The Christian Religion in its Doctrinal Expression*, made universal Christian experience one of the major sources of theological method, thus introducing pragmatism into 20th-century Southern Baptist theology. W. T. Conner (1877–1952) taught systematic theology at Southwestern Seminary for thirty-nine years. His *Revelation and God* and *The Gospel of Redemption* show a clear indebtedness to Mullins and A. H. Strong.* Dale Moody's (b. 1915) *The Word of Truth* shows a highly eclectic relationship with modern trends in theology, a cordial receptivity to biblical criticism,* and a general rejection of historic Baptist Calvinism.

Theological controversy within Southern Baptist life has focused on two issues – ecclesiology (See Church*) and Scripture. The Land-

mark movement, led by J. R. Graves (1820–93), so defined Baptist origins and ecclesiology that members of non-Baptist fellowships were not embraced as Christian brethren nor their ministers as Christian ministers. Mainstream Southern Baptists rejected the most radical features of Landmarkism.

Controversy over Scripture arose from the gradual introduction of biblical criticism into the seminaries, countered by a growing awareness of its destructive implications for the doctrines of revelation and inspiration. The C. H. Toy controversy at Southern Seminary (1879), the evolution controversy (1923–27), the controversy over Ralph Elliott's book *The Message of Genesis* (1961–63), and the *Broadman Commentary* controversy (1970ff.) were actually individual eruptions produced by the tension of this one conflict. The 1980s have seen a continuous display of debate on this issue.

See also: BAPTIST THEOLOGY.

Bibliography

R. A. Baker, *The Southern Baptist Convention and its People* (Nashville, TN, 1974); L. R. Bush and T. J. Nettles, *Baptists and the Bible* (Chicago, IL, 1980).

T.J.N.

SOVEREIGNTY OF GOD.

The sovereignty of God is not that of an abstraction or impersonal force but of the God and Father of our Lord Jesus Christ. Jesus himself is at the heart of the sovereignty. Because he and the Father are *the same in substance* (*homoousios*; see Trinity*) there cannot be in the sovereignty of God any un-Christlikeness at all. It is holy, wise and powerful, gracious, loving and merciful. Furthermore, not only is the sovereignty marked by the eternal qualities of the Son, it is also enriched by his earthly experience. He stands in the midst of the throne as the Lamb who was slain. Nothing we can say of the divine sovereignty may contradict this. Foreordination, election, government, reprobation, judgment, must all be consonant with the way God has defined himself in Christ.

The biblical idea of God's sovereignty includes all that is involved in the divine kingship and this means at least three things:

1. *Ownership*. The Heb. word for lord (*'ādôn*) and the two Gk. words, *kyrios* and *despotēs*, all imply this. In addition, the Bible

asserts it constantly. All things are God's: the earth, the heavens, the silver, the gold and, above all, Christians themselves.

2. *Authority.** God has an absolute right to impose his will on all his creatures. But his commands are never arbitrary. They express his own character as righteous and holy love. They accord fully with his relationship to us as redeemer and Father. Yet his authority is categorical, and when confronted with it, people have no right to temporize or negotiate, let alone disobey.

3. *Control.* God is master of his universe. At times he is displeased with it and at times angry. But it never baffles or frustrates or threatens him.

Sovereignty in foreordination

The foundation of this control is God's fore-ordination (see Predestination*). Nothing in the universe is outside his plan. He works all things according to the counsel of his will (Eph. 1:11). He has foreordained fortuitous occurrences, such as the fall of the dice (Pr. 16:33); laudable human actions, especially the good works of Christians (Eph. 2:10); and even sinful actions such as David numbering the people (1 Ch. 21:1ff.) and Jews crucifying their Messiah (Acts 2:23).

Christian orthodoxy has hedged this doctrine about with two indispensable safeguards.

1. God's foreordination of all things does not mean that he is the author of sin.* Sin, by definition, is lawlessness (*anomia*). Nothing can justify it – not even the fact that God overrules it and brings good out of evil. It absolutely ought not to be.

2. Foreordination does not mean that God overrides or violates the will of his creatures. God has given some of his creatures (men and angels) the faculty of choice. Foreordination does not destroy that faculty. God furthers his plans through the free decisions of human beings. Even at the point of conversion,* where his intervention is at its maximum, he deals with us in such a way that we come most freely. Human choices are real choices.

Behind these two caveats there lies an insistence that we must distinguish between fore-ordination and causality. God foreordains all things and he is the cause of many things, but not of *all* things. Our unbelief, for example, is *our* unbelief; and our coming to Christ is *our* coming to Christ. As a result, while the

Christian can speak perfectly properly of the sovereignty of God, he cannot, like the Muslim and the pantheist,* speak of the omnicausality of God. He is not the All-Cause. We, too, are causes and our causality is not illusory but real.

Sovereignty in creation

So far as creation* is concerned, God's sovereignty means not only that the decision to create is entirely God's, but that in the actual work of creating, he operates with complete freedom. One indicator of this is the curious fact that the Hebrew verb for creating (*bārā'*) is never used with an accusative of materials. The human artist or craftsman is always limited and often frustrated by the materials with which he works. But not God. For him, the materials are irrelevant. He creates his own, and moulds and fashions them at his will.

The sovereignty of God in, and over, creation is the ultimate guarantee of the rationality of the universe and hence of the possibility of science. The world was made by the word and wisdom of God and therefore reflects the coherence and order of his mind. It is logical with the logic of the Logos,* benign and rational because it is always *his*. We can therefore research it not only with a good conscience but with good courage because we can never come up against a truth which contradicts the mind of Christ.

Sovereignty in revelation

As in creation, so in revelation* the initiative rests with God. Creation itself is revelatory. God's works reveal him – a point on which the Bible is most emphatic (Ps. 19:1; Rom. 1:18ff.). Creation cannot, however, reveal God's mystery or secret. The marvel that 'there is forgiveness!' can be known only from a special word of God. That word is given to us by his authorized and accredited spokesmen, the prophets* and the apostles.* The manner, timing and contents of this revelation are always under God's control. So are its limits. Even when the revelation is completed, there are 'secret things' (Dt. 29:29). Scripture insists on this (Mk. 13:32; Acts 1:7). There is much about the earthly life of our Lord which was undoubtedly revelatory and yet has not been recorded (Jn. 21:25). And Paul indicates that more was revealed to him personally than he was permitted to pass on to the church

(2 Cor. 12:4). The net result is that what we have in revelation is God telling us only as much about himself as he thinks it good for us to know.

Sovereignty in redemption

The divine sovereignty appears most clearly in redemption.* In the conception, accomplishment and application of our salvation, the initiative always belongs to God, who acts with complete freedom and decisive effect.

Scripture highlights this sovereignty in several different ways.

1. It constantly ascribes our salvation to God's mercy. The exercise of mercy is in its very nature discretionary. It is an act of clemency. The gift of Christ as saviour is traceable to this source (Tit. 3:4) and so are our own calling* (Gal. 1:15) and our regeneration, justification and entire salvation (Tit. 3:5ff.).

2. Our salvation begins with regeneration* or new birth. Without this, no-one enters the kingdom (Jn. 3:3). Yet it is always God's gift. We are born from above by the action of the breath of God blowing where it wills (Jn. 3:8). We contribute no more than we do to our natural conception and birth. It is as much – and as entirely – God's act as the creation of light (2 Cor. 4:6) or the regeneration of heaven and earth.

3. God's redemptive sovereignty appears in the fact of election (see Predestination*). This is the channel in which his mercy runs and through which his regenerating grace operates.

Sovereignty in evangelism

The sovereignty of God has often been made an excuse for not evangelizing.* From a biblical point of view this is absurd. God commands us to evangelize and the more clearly we see his sovereignty the more anxious we shall be to obey (cf. Isaiah, Paul, the early disciples: Is. 6:1; Acts 9:3ff.; Mt. 28:18–20).

But God's sovereignty is not only a motive to obedience. It is also our supreme encouragement in evangelism. Humanly speaking, preaching the gospel is futile. Yet, in this apathetic, hostile, unresponsive world, God has his people. That is the one factor which can sustain Christian mission.

See also: GOD.

Bibliography

J. I. Packer, *Evangelism and the Sovereignty of God* (London, 1961); A. W. Pink, *The Sovereignty of God* (London, 1961).

D.M.

SPINOZA, BENEDICT (BARUCH) DE (1632–77). A complex, original, Dutch thinker, prominent in public affairs, Spinoza was of Jewish origin, but was expelled from his synagogue (1656) for his unorthodox views, which were pantheistic.* There is only one reality or 'substance', which can be called equally 'God' or 'Nature'; all other things are modifications of this (similarly, mind and body are aspects of a single human unity.) Since God/Nature exists necessarily, all else follows necessarily; human freedom is simply acting rationally rather than as a slave of the passions. Our greatest good is to know and love God; but God, being perfect in himself, neither loves nor hates, save in us. The common idea of immortality* is a mistake; yet in necessary knowledge we are aware of an eternal, timeless aspect of the mind.

According to Spinoza, religions such as Judaism and Christianity do not express philosophical truth; they are primarily ways of conveying moral truths to those incapable of seeing them by reason. Any religion which helps in this way should therefore be tolerated. In seeking to study the Bible dispassionately (and dating many OT books later than tradition) Spinoza has also been seen as a forerunner of biblical criticism.*

Bibliography

Ethics and *De Intellectus Emendatione* (ET, London, 1910); S. Hampshire, *Spinoza* (Harmondsworth, 1951).

R.L.S.

SPIRITUALISM, see SECTS.

SPIRITUALITY is a word that has come into vogue this century. French Catholic in origin, it is now common to Protestantism as well. The term has no direct equivalent in Scripture and did not emerge historically as a well-defined branch of theology until the 18th century, when Giovanni Scaramelli (1687–1752) of the Society of Jesus established ascetical* and mystical* theology as a science of the spiritual life.

The term 'spirituality' is used in various senses by different scholars and Christian traditions, partly because the spiritual life is itself so complex. Here we will attempt to provide a broad definition of the term and illustrate some of the major issues involved in attempting to understand the spirituality of any particular group.

Christian spirituality involves the relationship between the whole person and a holy God, who reveals himself through both testaments – and supremely in the person of his unique Son, Jesus Christ. This relationship began at creation, but was broken by sin* and can only be restored through faith* in Jesus Christ (see Salvation*). The test of Christian spirituality is conformity of heart and life to the confession and character of Jesus as Lord (1 Cor. 12:3). The guarantee of Christian spirituality is the presence and power of the Holy Spirit in the life of the believer (resulting in conformity to God's revealed will). Jesus described the ultimate test for Christian spirituality when he told his first followers 'all men will know that you are my disciples if you love one another . . . as I have loved you' (Jn. 13:34, 35; see Imitation of Christ*).

Spirituality as a term is necessarily more synthetic than analytic, since the Bible knows nothing of the fragmentation of the divine-human relationship into sacred and secular, religious and social, etc. Contemporary usage of the term in Protestant circles seeks to integrate theological disciplines without denying their importance or utility.

The study of Christian spirituality allows one's understanding and imagination to be lifted beyond the limits commonly placed upon the Holy Spirit by contemporary practice. Some familiarity with the various forms and styles of spirituality developed across the ages and around the world can help prevent a myopic vision limited to one's own religious tradition.

Historically, Christian spirituality may be broadly divided into Eastern and Western – and into Protestant and Catholic within the West. (See Eastern Orthodox Theology;* Roman Catholic Theology;* Protestantism;* Religious Experience;* Asceticism;* Anglicanism;* Evangelical Theology;* Lutheranism;* Mennonite Theology;* Methodism;* Mystical Theology;* Pietism;* and Russian Orthodox Theology.*)

One of the important insights offered by the study of spirituality comes from observing the interaction between doctrine, discipline, liturgy and life. *Doctrine* has to do with what is believed (about the self, others, the world and the supernatural). *Discipline** has to do with the source(s) of authority, the structure of corporate life and the consequences of deviant behaviour. *Liturgy** has to do with the corporate life of worship and praise. Music, prayer, the sacraments and various patterns of public acts in worship have a major impact upon the attitudes, actions and lifestyles of the worshippers. *Life* refers to the individual lifestyle of the believer; not only in prayer, study and devotion but also at work, at play and in one's involvement with society. Woven together, these four factors provide the basic pattern for understanding the fabric of any given spirituality.

Some scholars would suggest that doctrinal theology both forms and informs spirituality (*e.g.* Pourrat and Bouyer). Other 20th-century writers maintain that spirituality gives shape and substance to theology (R. N. Flew, *The Idea of Perfection*, London, 1934; G. Wainwright, *Doxology*, London, 1980). As one becomes aware of the interaction between belief and behaviour within the context of Scripture and contemporary culture it becomes easier to appreciate differing patterns of authentic Christian spirituality. Antony of Egypt, Thomas à Kempis and William Law may be taken as examples of three classic patterns.

Antony of Egypt (*c.* 250–356) based his spirituality on Jesus' admonition to go and sell all in order to be a disciple (Lk. 18:18–24). One of the early leaders of the monastic* tradition, Antony believed the way to salvation was narrow and hard (Mt. 7:14) and that celibacy was more in keeping with Paul's highest model of discipleship (1 Cor. 7:8). Other aspects of Antony's spirituality included long periods of solitude, extreme physical austerity and willingness to counsel those seeking help.

Thomas à Kempis (1379/80–1471) was powerfully influenced by an informal community of cenobitic monks known as the Brethren of the Common Life. His devotional classic, *The Imitation of Christ*, comprises four books. Book One ('Counsels of the Spiritual Life') is concerned with growth in self-knowledge on the part of the believer and a progressive detachment from secular values.

Book Two ('Counsels on the Inner Life') develops the theme of meditation upon the passion of Christ as a means of spiritual growth. The third book ('On Inward Consolation') is a series of dialogues between Christ and the disciple. The rich insights into human nature and Christian psychology found here are a significant factor in the work's enduring popularity. The final book is concerned with the eucharist,* emphasizing the need for careful preparation and frequent participation in the sacrament.

William Law,* one of the best known of the latter Nonjurors, was intensely individualistic and uncompromising in his early view of what authentic Christianity required. His *Serious Call to a Devout and Holy Life* (1728) is a forceful exhortation to embrace the Christian life in all its moral fullness, every activity being directed toward the glory of God. Daily acts of temperance, humility and self-denial are illustrated in this work through the attitudes and actions of skilfully drawn characters. Unfortunately, the proportion of human activity that can validly be directed to the glory of God is severely limited by Law – learning is suspect, relaxation is slothful and culture dangerously close to the world.

Bibliography

J. Aumann, T. Hopko and D. G. Bloesch, *Christian Spirituality, East and West* (Chicago, IL, 1968); L. Bouyer *et al., History of Christian Spirituality*, 3 vols. (London, 1963–69); R. J. Foster, *Celebration of Discipline* (New York, 1978); C. Jones, G. Wainwright and E. Yarnold (eds.), *The Study of Spirituality* (London, 1986); R. F. Lovelace, *Dynamics of the Spiritual Life* (Exeter, 1979); P. Pourrat, *Christian Spirituality*, 4 vols. (Westminster, MD, 1953–55); G. S. Wakefield (ed.), *The Westminster Dictionary of Christian Spirituality* (Philadelphia, 1983) = *Dictionary of Christian Spirituality* (London, 1983).

T.R.A.

SPURGEON, CHARLES HADDON (1834–1892), Baptist preacher. Born into an Essex Congregational home, Spurgeon experienced a dramatic conversion in his early teens and sought baptism as a believer. After a successful short ministry in rural Cambridgeshire he became Baptist minister at New Park Street Chapel, London, which later moved to the Metropolitan Tabernacle to accommodate the vast congregations which came to hear him preach. His popularity was greatly enhanced by the weekly publication (from 1855 onwards) of his sermons, the sale of which in England and the USA helped to finance the theological college he had established in 1856. The sermons give rich expression both to his firmly held Calvinistic* convictions and evangelistic concern. In 1864 his sermon on 'Baptismal* Regeneration' brought him into theological conflict with paedobaptists, including some evangelicals. Later, when liberal* theological ideas were gaining ground, he affirmed his unqualified allegiance to biblical doctrine. During his own denomination's 'Downgrade' controversy (1887–89) he expressed alarm concerning unorthodox views and in 1887, 'with the utmost regret', withdrew from the Baptist Union. His voluminous writings (135 books), which frequently reflect his indebtedness to 17th-century Puritanism,* continue to be published, maintaining his immense spiritual influence throughout the evangelical world.

See also: BAPTIST THEOLOGY.

Bibliography

J. C. Carlile, *C. H. Spurgeon: An Interpretative Biography* (London, 1933); H. F. Colquitt, *The Soteriology of Charles Haddon Spurgeon* . . . (unpublished dissertation, New College, Edinburgh, 1951); I. H. Murray, *The Forgotten Spurgeon* (London, 1966); G. H. Pike, *The Life and Work of Charles Haddon Spurgeon*, 6 vols. (London, 1892–3); H. Thielicke (ed.), *Encounter with Spurgeon* (London, 1964).

R.B.

STATE. The question of how Christians were to understand and relate to temporal power confronted the church from earliest times. It was the political demands of Rome that set Jesus'* birth in Bethlehem; it was against the background of political unrest and national aspiration characteristic of an occupied territory that his ministry unfolded; and it was on the orders of the 'secular' power that he was executed. Jesus faced the issues which, for the modern Christian, are summed up in the phrase 'church and state', both in his confrontation with the religious authorities of the Jews, and in his response to the political implications of the Roman presence in Judaea.

NT writers, accordingly, address the subject both explicitly and implicitly, taking account of the realities of the church's relations with 'secular' power at the time they wrote.

Faced with the political and theological question 'Is it right to pay taxes to Caesar or not?', Jesus replies, 'Give to Caesar what is Caesar's and to God what is God's' (Mt. 22:21), without further specifying what the distinction entails. For Paul the Roman authorities 'have been established by God. Consequently he who rebels against the authority is rebelling against what God has instituted' (Rom. 13:1, 2). The magistrate is 'God's servant to do you good' as well as 'to bring punishment on the wrongdoer' (v. 4). Similarly Peter requires submission to the emperor and his representatives (1 Pet. 2:13, 14). Later in the NT, however, the writer of Revelation presents a more radical theology of Rome as 'Babylon . . . the mother of harlots . . . drunk with the blood of the saints' (Rev. 17:5, 6), in whose fall heaven and the church rejoice (ch. 18). Paul was prepared to appeal to Caesar as a Roman citizen (Acts 25:11), but argued that the Christian's citizenship was in heaven (Phil. 3:20). Similarly Hebrews presents the heroes of the old covenant as men and women who were not thinking of an earthly country but looking for a heavenly one (Heb. 11:15, 16). These different strands in the NT underlie the subsequent development of the theology of the state, as well as considered appeals to the position of Israel and its kings in the OT.

The modern Christian, however, must beware of bringing to that development inappropriate assumptions and expectations. The modern state is, with relatively rare exceptions, a secular* entity. Even where, as in England or Scotland, the Christian church is in some sense 'established', the state remains secular and pluralistic. The phrase 'church and state' presents the modern reader with an implicit conflict – between a community of faith with ideals and aspirations focused upon the ultimate and eternal power of God, and a community of unbelief whose aims and objectives are strictly limited to the sphere of time, only to be realized through 'the art of the possible'. For such a secular entity, religious faith cannot be more than one of the opinions of which the organs of power must take note.

In the world of the NT, however, and until comparatively recently, a secular state was unthinkable. Every state was religious, supporting and supported by the particular religious tradition which expressed its ideals and objectives. This was particularly true for the Jews, from among whom the first disciples came, but also for every community in the ancient world. In encountering the Roman state the early church confronted a religious phenomenon, and this explains the conflict that developed between them. Roman religion was, in fact, pluralistic. Any cult was tolerable that did not offend against public decency and whose adherents were prepared to express their loyalty to Rome by participating in Roman worship, but Christians believed that to do so was idolatry, and their refusal was understood as a symbol of defiance.

The church's theological response to the consequent persecution broadly followed two lines, each drawn from the NT. Those who, like Paul, affirmed the powers of the state, sought to present the case for the toleration of Christianity without the condition of participation in the Roman cults. They argued, in effect, that the Christian must always be the best of citizens because of his perception of the divine origin of temporal power: obedience to God ensures commitment to the commonwealth. Those, on the other hand, who looked to the traditions of Jewish apocalyptic,* including the book of Revelation, for their inspiration, developed a theology in which the Roman empire was strongly rejected as the embodiment of evil and idolatry. The objective for the Christian was not rapprochement with the world, but martyrdom* – the victory by which the believer prepared the way for the ultimate overthrow of earthly states by the kingdom of Christ.

But the religious character of states in the ancient world also helps explain the eventual outcome of the conflict between Rome and the church. Once a Roman emperor became an adherent of Christianity it was inevitable, in the absence of any concept of the secular, that Christianity must become the official cultic expression of his faith to his subjects. The eventual result of the conversion of Constantine in AD 312 was that the church changed places with the official pagan cult of Rome. In effect, the Christendom* of the Middle Ages was inaugurated. In many ways this marked the triumph of the moderate, world-affirming theology over the martyr

659

tradition. Some adherents of the latter, the Donatists,* continued to reject the state, now identifying the established church with idolatry and evil. The majority, however, turned to other-worldly patterns of spirituality* in the growing ascetic* movement.

For the next thousand years, as either ideal or reality, the identification of church and state was to be the most pervasive feature of European society. In many ways the medieval church *was* the state: it had a coherent structure, a single head (the pope), an effective administration and a body of law; it had its own courts and it controlled all learning and most communications, so that even such civil power as was able to survive depended upon it. Medieval Europe was, in effect, a church-state (see Theocracy*), and relations between church and state were largely a matter of manoeuvres between laymen and ecclesiastics to exercise effective power within it. Theologically, society was a descending pyramidal power-structure with the pope (see Papacy*) at the apex as God's representative, the earthly source of all authority, both spiritual and temporal. The state continued to be an essentially religious institution, undergirded by the effective unity of the the medieval church, and in turn supporting that unity by using its temporal power to dispose of any dissent from it on the part of heretics; an activity which now looks like persecution, but which then appeared no more than obvious religious duty.

The medieval pattern survived as long as the representatives of civil power accepted the validity of this theological rationale and its ultimate sanction – excommunication. Only when an intellectual climate in which it could be questioned began to obtain in the aftermath of the Renaissance (see Humanism*) did significant shifts appear in the church-state balance. Even then, in the 16th-century Reformation* such change as took place affected the patterns of relationship rather than fundamental concepts. Most Reformers seem to have accepted the basic notion of the religious character of the state, for which they found biblical support in the OT for the most part. In the search for a legal foundation for their church reforms they were often left dependent on the civil powers. Princes and city councils, on the other hand, were in search of a theological rationale for disputing the claims of the papacy to the stewardship of civil authority. The alliance between the two often led (as in England) in the direction of Erastianism, the subjection of the church to the authority of the state, even in matters of faith and discipline (though Thomas Erastus himself (1524–83) was a Zwinglian layman who merely opposed the power of the church elders at Heidelberg to excommunicate without reference to the city council). In the Protestant concept of the godly magistrate called to legislate for the community of faith of which he was a member, the Reformers continued to build on the Constantinian foundation. The more radical Reformation divines, however, included a number who did begin to question the role of the civil power in the church (see Reformation, Radical*). There are examples among the English Puritans,* but it was, in particular, the Anabaptists* who, in the same spiritual tradition as the 4th-century Donatists, insisted on the separation of church and state, and the voluntary principle of church membership. It was, however, only in the aftermath of the 18th-century Enlightenment,* when the ground had been prepared for a new perception of the state as a secular entity by both statesmen and churchmen, that the idea of the church as a voluntary association for religious purposes rather than as the state viewed from its religious aspect began to gain widespread currency.

Such voluntarism, however, has its own dangers, arising from the concentration of attention on relationships between state and *church* rather than state and *kingdom*. The gospel of Jesus Christ is about the kingdom of God* (Mk. 1:15) – *i.e.* God's administration of power. Its ultimate vision is of the kingdoms of this world becoming 'the kingdom of our Lord and of his Christ' (Rev. 11:15). This should warn Christians against any theology of church and state which may encourage the church to abrogate its responsibility to confront the stewards of secular power with the demands of God's kingship for all of human society. At the same time, it must be recognized that, in the interim before the kingdom comes in its fullness, it is to the church, not to the state, that people ought to be able to turn for the models of God's kingly rule. In an age when the state now makes the omnicompetent claims of the medieval church, Christians are rightly insisting increasingly on the ultimately inalienable authority of Christ in the church to order its life and proclaim the good news of the kingdom.

Bibliography
W. H. C. Frend, *Martyrdom and Persecution in the Early Church* (Oxford, 1965); D. Sceats, '*Quid Imperatori cum Ecclesia?* The Contemporary Church and the Royal Supremacy', *Churchman* 93 (1979), pp. 306–320; R. W. Southern, *Western Society and the Church in the Middle Ages* (Harmondsworth, 1970); W. Ullmann, *The Middle Ages* (Harmondsworth, 1965); L. Verduin, *The Reformers and their Stepchildren* (Exeter, 1964).

D.D.S.

STAUPITZ, JOHN, see AUGUSTINIANISM.

STEWARDSHIP. The principle of stewardship is closely linked to the concept of grace: everything comes from God as a gift and is to be administered faithfully on his behalf. There is thus both stewardship of the earth and stewardship of the gospel (*cf.* J. Goetzmann, *TDNT* II, pp. 253–256); stewardship of personal resources of time, money and talents, and stewardship of the resources of church and society. Along with questions of mission strategy and support there are issues of personal and corporate lifestyle, just wages and fair prices, poverty and wealth,* all related to explicit or implicit theologies of the kingdom of God,* work* and nature.*

The theme of stewardship as a recognition of the unity of creation and the consequent need to care for the whole earth can be traced in Eastern Orthodoxy and in Western theology down to Calvin. Nevertheless it can be argued that in practice a more prevalent understanding of 'dominion' (Gn. 1:28) as domination rather than stewardship has been a justification, if not a cause, of much exploitation. However, international consciousness of the relationship between ecological and political exploitation and the need to seek what the World Council of Churches has called a 'just, participatory and sustainable society' has grown steadily since the publication of *Only One Earth* by Barbara Ward and René Dubois (London, 1972) and the Brandt Commission report *North–South: A Programme for Survival* (London, 1980), with much attention inside and outside the chur-

ches paid to the arms race and nuclear disarmament. More recently, at least in Western Europe, the stewardship of human resources has become a major concern as churches seek to respond at a personal, community or national level to the social consequences of unemployment and technological change in industry.

Bibliography
R. Attfield, *The Ethics of Environmental Concern* (Oxford: 1983); Church of England Board of Social Responsibility, *Our Responsibility for the Living Environment* (London, 1986); D. J. Hall, *Imaging God: Dominion as Stewardship* (Grand Rapids, MI, and New York, 1986); R. Mullin, *The Wealth of Christians* (Exeter, 1983); WCC publications (all Geneva): P. Gregarios, *The Human Presence: An Orthodox View of Nature* (1978); *Faith, Science and the Future* (1978); *Faith and Science in an Unjust World* (2 vols., 1980); H. Davis and D. Gosling (eds.), *Will the Future Work?* (1985); World Evangelical Fellowship publications: R. J. Sider (ed.), *Lifestyle in the Eighties: An Evangelical Commitment to Simple Lifestyle,* and *Evangelicals and Development: Towards a Theology of Social Change* (both Exeter, 1981); The Wheaton '83 Statement in *Transformation* 1 (1984), pp. 23–28; C. Sugden (ed.), *The Church in Response to Human Need* (Exeter, 1987). Earlier literature from C. Sugden, *Radical Discipleship* (London, 1981).

P.N.H.

STOICISM was founded by Zeno (335–263 BC) who taught in Athens in a *stoa* (porch), from which his school derived its name. He was succeeded by Cleanthes (331–232 BC), who breathed a more personal spirit into the Stoic conception of deity, as in his 'Hymn to Zeus'. Chrysippus (*c.* 280–207 BC) gave Stoicism its completed form and logical defence.

The Stoic world-view may be characterized as materialistic* pantheism.* Matter, however, comes in two kinds: a grosser kind, corresponding to the ordinary conception of matter, and a more refined kind, described as breath or spirit and diffused throughout reality. The latter is the ruling power and guiding force of reality and corresponds to deity, for it exercises providence, making this the 'best of all possible worlds'. The human being too is composed of these same two kinds of material reality as is the cosmos. The present world derived from fire and will return to fire (the world conflagration), after which the same world will re-emerge to repeat the cycle (the regeneration, *palingenesia*). The ruling spirit is rational, and the Stoics contributed to logic by their efforts to represent reality rationally and to defend their system. The Stoics developed the allegorical method of interpretation as a way of attaching their physical theories to classical mythology. Their philosophy provided a defence of the traditional religion, including divination and astrology, on the basis of the interconnectedness of the universe.

The lasting influence of Stoicism came not from its pantheism and rationalism but its moral teaching and attitude toward life. The goal of life is virtue, and virtue is to live in accord with the rational nature of reality. The emotional life was disparaged as irrational and unnatural. The only important thing in life is virtue: therefore, one is to remain unmoved by external affairs, anything that is not within one's own power, and concentrate on the attitudes and character that are within one's control. Since according to the Stoic view of providence and the cyclical nature of reality, everything is determined, a person should accept things as they are. One cannot control circumstances, but he can control the way he looks at them. Everything outside of virtue is indifferent, but in the development of later Stoic ethics more and more attention was paid to what was preferred and not preferred among indifferent things.

This change in ethical concern came with the Middle Stoa of Panaetius (*c.* 185–109 BC), who adapted Stoicism to the Romans by giving more attention to political theory and allowing a greater place to emotional and aesthetic concerns. Posidonius (*c.* 135–50 BC) further broadened Stoicism to include scientific experiment, and through the theory of sympathetic relationship between all parts of the world contributed to the understanding of kinds of unity. He likened the universe to the unity of a living body. The later Stoics allowed a greater independence to the life of the soul and so weakened the earlier monism.

Roman Stoicism represented almost exclusively ethical concerns. Seneca (*c.* AD 1–65) laid bare the wickedness in human nature, and in his moral exhortations he more nearly

approximated to Christian teaching than any other classical philosopher. Musonius Rufus (AD 30–101) and Epictetus (AD 55–*c.* 135) use language comparable to that in the NT. Stoicism ascended the imperial throne with Marcus Aurelius (AD 131–180), an introspective and melancholy yet noble man. Thereafter we do not hear about Stoicism as a school, but it was not extinct, for its significant moral insights had become common property, one of the permanent legacies of the ancient world to western civilization.

Many points of contact between Stoicism and the NT have been noted. For instance, Paul in Acts 17:28 quotes a Stoic commonplace from the *Phaenomena* of Aratus (*c.* 315–240 BC), a pupil of Zeno. Many terms in the NT were at home in Stoicism: spirit, conscience,* *logos*,* virtue, self-sufficiency, reasonable service. Even the substantive similarities, however, are set in different worldviews. Stoicism did not have a fully personal god, a creator, personal immortality, or a saviour. In ethics, where the similarities were the closest, there were fundamental differences. Stoicism told one to have the attitude to self that one has towards others; Christianity reversed the outlook. The motivation was different: in Stoicism, living in accord with the higher self; in Christianity, response to the love of God in Christ.

The pervasive influence of Stoicism in the ethical thought of the early Empire, including that of the 1st-century Jewish philosopher, Philo,* meant that early Christian ethical writings showed contact with Stoicism. This is evident, for example, in Clement of Alexandria's* *Instructor* (*Paedagogus*). Ambrose's* treatise *On the Duties of the Clergy* is a Christian adaptation of Cicero's *On Duties*, itself influenced by Panaetius. The Stoic view of anthropology* influenced Tatian (2nd century) and Tertullian's* *On the Soul*, which gives a more 'material' view of the soul than Platonism* did.

As assimilated into Christian thought, aspects of Stoicism became a part of the Christian heritage. Independent revivals of elements in Stoicism occurred in the Renaissance and early modern period. The Stoic attitude that inner character is superior to and indifferent to external affairs has continued to have appeal. Where morality has been sought apart from religion the Stoic view that virtue is sufficient for happiness has given encouragement. The Stoic stimulation of the idea of a natural religion and its humanitarianism and cosmopolitan universalism have been absorbed into Christian thought.

Bibliography
L. Edlestein, *The Meaning of Stoicism* (Cambridge, 1966); R. MacMullen, *Enemies of the Roman Order* (Cambridge, MA, 1966), ch. 2; M. Pohlenz, *Die Stoa*, 2 vols. (Göttingen, 1955–59); J. M. Rist, *Stoic Philosophy* (Cambridge, 1969); F. H. Sandbach, *The Stoics* (London, 1975); J. N. Sevenster, *Paul and Seneca* (Leiden, 1962); M. Spanneut, *Le Stoïcisme des pères de l'Église de Clément de Rome à Clément d'Alexandrie* (Paris, 1957); R. M. Wenley, *Stoicism and its Influence* (New York, 1963); E. Zeller, *Stoics, Epicureans, and Sceptics* (London, 1880).

E.F.

STRAUSS, DAVID FRIEDRICH

(1808–74) was born at Ludwigsburg in Württemberg, South Germany, and studied at Tübingen under Ferdinand Christian Baur (see Tübingen School*). After further study in Berlin, he was appointed tutor in the theological seminary at Tübingen, where he wrote his most famous work, *The Life of Jesus*. From its appearance in 1835 we may date the open emergence of the historical-critical investigation of the Bible (see Biblical Criticism*).

The key to understanding this work is not merely Strauss's Hegelian* ideas, but rather his underlying non-miraculous and non-supernatural presuppositions. Strauss to the end of his days explicitly denied the existence of a God who was both transcendent and personal. It followed logically from this that there could be no divine miracles, and that every miraculous story in the NT must be *ipso facto* unauthentic. Thus the gospels were regarded by him as fictitious accounts, elaborated solely to prove that Jesus was the Messiah. If it was prophesied that the Messiah would heal the blind and raise the dead, then such miracles had to be claimed for Jesus by the evangelists in order to show that he had fulfilled these prophecies. If Enoch and Elijah were taken up to heaven, then Jesus also had to have an ascension. The gospel stories reflected the myth-making power of his followers' piety which was steeped in OT expectations. This mythical* approach had

been suggested by some of Strauss's predecessors, but Strauss was the first to apply it consistently to every part of the NT. It is quite independent of the Hegelian philosophy, and only in his concluding attempt at a positive reconstruction of Christianity was the Hegelian philosophy employed. Jesus demonstrates the realization of the Absolute in the human race.

As a consequence of his attack on historic Christianity Strauss was dismissed from his position at the seminary. Nomination to a professorship of theology at Zurich in 1839 came to nothing, and Strauss spent the remainder of his life writing historical biographies with renewed forays into the theological field. In 1864 he produced his revised *Life of Jesus for the German People*, and in 1872 came his last work, *The Old Faith and the New*, in which he accepted a scientific materialism, rejected life after death, and espoused Darwinian evolution, the first theologian to do so.

Strauss was undoubtedly one of the most significant theological figures of the 19th century. His *Life of Jesus* set in motion the whole 'Quest' for the historical Jesus, and precipitated the continuing critical examination of the NT sources. Throughout the theological and ecclesiastical world, not only in Germany but also abroad, he was widely regarded as the leader of the attack against the Bible.

See also: HISTORICAL JESUS, QUEST FOR.

Bibliography
R. S. Cromwell, *David Friedrich Strauss and his Place in Modern Thought* (Fairlawn, NJ, 1974); H. Frei, 'David Friedrich Strauss', in N. Smart *et al.* (eds.), *Nineteenth Century Religious Thought in the West* (Cambridge, 1985), vol. 1, ch. 7; H. Harris, *David Friedrich Strauss and his Theology* (Edinburgh, 1982).

H.H.

STRONG, AUGUSTUS HOPKINS

(1836–1921), Baptist minister, theologian, and seminary professor. Rochester, New York, was the scene of his birth, death, and the majority of his ministry. Strong received his BA from Yale in 1857, graduated from Rochester Seminary 1859, and spent 1859–60 in study in Berlin. He was minister at the First Baptist Church, Haverhill,

Massachusetts, 1861–65, and at the First Baptist Church, Cleveland, Ohio, 1865–72. He served from 1872 to 1912 as president and professor of systematic theology at Rochester Seminary, and was president emeritus from 1912 to 1921. His mature thought is reflected in *Christ in Creation and Ethical Monism* and the 1907 edition of his *Systematic Theology*. Strong sought to maintain traditional orthodoxy within the Calvinistic framework while adopting both evolutionary thought and biblical higher criticism. The radical immanence of Christ in creation became his key for balancing this tension. His views of creation, providence, inspiration, human sinfulness, divine justice, atonement, and world missions were shaped by this principle.

See also: SOUTHERN BAPTIST THEOLOGY.

Bibliography
C. F. H. Henry, *Personal Idealism and Strong's Theology* (Wheaton, IL, 1951); G. Wacker, *Augustus H. Strong and the Dilemma of Historical Consciousness* (Macon, GA, 1985).

T.J.N.

STRUCTURALISM is the name commonly applied to a movement that emerged within a circle of French linguistic philosophers following the publication of Ferdinand de Saussure's *Cours de linguistic générale* in 1916. Saussure (1857–1913) and those who follow him argue that language reflects certain universal patterns or structures, which in turn reflect universal orders within the human brain. From this it was concluded that all narrative, especially the more unconscious or 'folk' literature, will reflect in some way the settled 'deep structures' by which societal consciousness is governed.

Biblical studies

Although most French structuralists have been far more interested in primitive mythology than in biblical studies, their work has inspired a number of experiments by students of Scripture, in which the methods more than their philosophical underpinnings have been applied to biblical texts. These studies are commonly known by the name 'structural analysis', a broad umbrella term that has come to signify any approach to Scripture which looks at the material 'synchronically' (relationships are to be found *within* the text), rather than 'diachronically' (relationships are to be found in various historical stages of the development of the text), as in traditional biblical criticism.*

An important distinction must be made between the true structuralist, whose philosophical bent has frequently led to an abandonment of history as a category of meaning, and the various practitioners of structural analysis in biblical studies circles in the late 20th century. Very few biblical scholars share the rejection of history which marks true structuralism, and some of the most fruitful work being done today looks for synchronic relationships, but couples the study with diachronic research as well.

A further concern of 'semiology', as structuralism is often called, is to trace the dynamics operative in the process 'text to reader', in place of traditional biblical studies' concern for the process 'author to text'. A common conviction holds that not only the structures of societal thinking which are found in the mythologies of the past, but also the 'deep structures' of the society or group which in a later age receives the message, are important. For a full linguistic picture, then, one must look at the original mythological structures, and then the structures operative in the receiver society, comparing the two and tracing the development of the myth in that light.

Method

The object of true structuralist research is not primarily to reveal meaning in the text itself, but rather to discover how the text, as a reflection of the deeper structures which transcend time and circumstances, conveys a symbolic and timeless structure or meaning. This has led structuralists, as opposed to the biblical 'structural analysts', frequently to prefer the category 'myth'* over the study of historical narrative, and has in turn led to some rather eccentric approaches to biblical material.

Claude Levi-Strauss (b. 1908), one such structuralist, grouped together all the mythological texts of a given culture, finding in those texts 'variations of a basic myth', reducing the events of each story studied to short sentences which he calls 'mythemes'. The mythemes are then grouped together, and from them the more comprehensive 'view of reality' emerges

(C. Levi-Strauss, 'The Structural Study of Myth,' in *Structural Anthropology*, ET, Garden City, NY, 1963). Applying the methods of Levi-Strauss, Edmund Leach (b. 1910) gives an example of how biblical studies might look from a structuralist viewpoint, in his *Genesis as Myth and Other Essays* (London, 1969), a series of essays which amply illustrate the reasons why biblical scholars have generally rejected the method in its purest form.

Turning to more traditional biblical studies, one finds a growing body of material. From an initial critique of Leach ('Some Comments on Structural Analysis and Biblical Studies,' *Supplements to VT* 22 (Congress Volume, Uppsala, 1971), Leiden 1972, pp. 129–142, and 'Structural Analysis: Is it Done with Mirrors?' *Interpretation* 28, 1974, pp. 165–181), R. C. Culley proceeded to apply the method to various groups of biblical stories, while making it clear that his philosophical and methodological approach varied significantly from that of the structuralists. (See Culley's *Studies in the Structure of Hebrew Narrative*, Philadelphia, and Missoula, MT, 1976.)

Additional biblical scholars have taken up the task, most of whom readily argue for a sharp modification of French structuralist presuppositional and methodological approaches. Some of the new work is probably little more than a shift from historical to internal structural concerns in looking at the text, but some fresh insights in how to study the Bible have emerged in the wake of the new discipline. If nothing else, the text itself, rather than some putative form of reconstructed earlier version, has again become the focus of attention, surely a needed emphasis in contemporary biblical scholarship.

Bibliography
C. E. Armerding, *The Old Testament and Criticism* (Grand Rapids, MI, 1983); J. W. Rogerson, *Myth in Old Testament Interpretation* (Berlin and New York, 1974).

C.E.A.

SUBORDINATIONISM, see TRINITY.

SUBSTANCE the word most commonly used in Christian theology to denote the objective reality of the one being of God. Strictly speaking, it derives from the Latin equivalent (*substantia*) of the Greek word *hypostasis*,* which means 'an objective reality capable of acting'. Greek theology, however, following Origen,* claimed that there were three *hypostaseis* in God, which caused confusion when Hilary of Poiters* translated this word as *substantiae* (plural) in his *De Trinitate*.

Latin usage had been determined by Tertullian*, who used *substantia* to refer to what the Greeks usually called *ousia* (essence, being). This was almost certainly because he equated *ousia* with *hypostasis*, as the single objective reality in God. Behind the confusion of terms, therefore, there lies a different approach to theology, one which seeks to discover the Trinity* in the unity of God, rather than the other way round. In the creed of the Council of Nicaea (325), *homoousios*, a compound of *ousia*, was used to affirm the full divinity of the Son as 'of one substance' with the Father (see Trinity*).

The term *ousia* was widely used in pre-Christian philosophy, where its meaning was roughly equivalent to 'real thing'. However, philosophical usage was elastic, and though it certainly influenced Christian thinking, it did not possess a single, well-defined concept of *ousia*. Christians were undoubtedly convinced, primarily from the Scriptures, that the word should be used of God. This was because the God of the Bible was called by the name I AM, or He Who Is (*ho ōn*; Ex. 3:14; *cf.* Jn. 8:58).

Certain branches of the Christian mystical* tradition have held that the essence of God is in some sense visible, but most theologians have maintained that it is unknowable by any creature. Its attributes were listed by John of Damascus* as 'anarchy' (*i.e.* without beginning), uncreatedness, unbegottenness, imperishability, immortality, eternity, infinity, limitlessness, boundlessness, omnipotence, simplicity, uncompoundness, incorporeality, immutability, impassibility, unchangeability, unalterability and invisibility.

This list was simplified and systematized by Thomas Aquinas,* whose teaching has become the foundation of classical Western theism.* The Reformers accepted this on the whole, though they dismissed speculation about God's substance and urged the church to concentrate instead on knowing him in his persons.

In modern times, the traditional language

of divine substance has come under severe attack. In particular, process theology* accuses it of conveying a static view of God, even though Marius Victorinus,* and the Augustinian tradition after him, believed that God's being was motion (*esse=moveri*). Process theology follows the tradition of natural theology* in trying to understand the *ousia* of God in philosophical and scientific terms, but this cannot be done successfully. If we are to speak of the divine substance today, we must do so in the light of the Bible's teaching about God as the I AM, which is not bound to any philosophical system of interpretation.

Bibliography

J. B. Cobb, *A Christian Natural Theology* (Philadelphia, 1966); E. L. Mascall, *The Openness of Being* (London, 1971); A. Plantinga, *Does God have a Nature?* (Milwaukee, WI, 1980); G. C. Stead, *Divine Substance* (Oxford, 1977); R. Swinburne, *The Coherence of Theism* (Oxford, 1977).

G.L.B.

SUBSTITUTION AND REPRESENTATION.

It is generally accepted among Christian theologians that Jesus acted as our representative in his work of atonement. By this is meant that his life, death, resurrection and continuous intercession accrue to our benefit. His work is for us. There is also, however, in the Scriptures a dimension of substitution in the atonement of Christ and specifically with reference to his death. In Rom. 3:23–26 Christ is said to suffer in our place as a substitutionary bearer of the judgment which we deserve. This presented answers to the question of how God can be just and yet justify* the ungodly when his wrath is revealed against all ungodliness and unrighteousness of men. God the Son endures judgment as our substitute and becomes the propitiation whereby God is able to receive sinners. This emphasis is reinforced when Christ is identified as the suffering servant: 'He was wounded for our transgressions . . .' (Is. 53:5, RSV). Two passages also speak of him as a ransom. In Mk. 10:45, the Son of man gives his life a ransom for many, and in 1 Tim. 2:6 Christ is said to have given himself as a ransom for all. The ransom concept has a powerful substitutionary connotation. Similarly, the application of the OT symbolism of

the scapegoat (Lv. 16:8) to Jesus is undoubtedly substitutionary (Heb. 9:7, 12, 28).

Apart from Romans, there are two primary verses on which this view is based. In 2 Cor. 5:21, Paul argues that Jesus, who is sinless, identifies with sin to such a degree that mysteriously he is said to be made sin for our sake. The concept of substitution is perceived in that he is treated not on the basis of what he is, but what we are. He became our substitute. In Gal. 3:13, Paul argues that in order for Jesus Christ to redeem us from the curse of the law, he himself must endure, in our place, the curse of sin which we deserve.

Those scholars who reject this concept of the atonement do so for at least three reasons.

1. Vincent Taylor (1887–1968), for example, argues that Paul consistently does not use the substitutionary preposition *anti* ('instead of, in place of') but rather the representative *hyper* ('on behalf of, for the sake of') in expounding the death of Jesus. (He rejects 1 Tim. 2:6 as non-Pauline.) In response, it has been pointed out that *hyper* can have the force of *anti* in Hellenistic Gk. and that, for example, in Rom. 3:25 where it is used with *hilastērion* (propitiation) it is clearly substitutionary in intent.

2. The concept of God's personal wrath* is questioned by C. H. Dodd,* who finds it incongruous to his inherent love and pleads for the wrath of God to be seen as inevitable and inherent consequences of man's rebellious spirit. The object of atonement is therefore said to be man *and his sin*, not God and his wrath. *Hilastērion* is then translated 'expiation', which is focusing upon sin and its consequences for man, rather than 'propitiation' which has, as its focus, the fulfilment of the justice of God. In reply, it must be said that wrath, in biblical terms, is not uncontrolled pique but the inevitable response of personal pure love to that which is unholy. Again, although wrath may be the need for atonement, love is the ground of atonement. God takes the initiative not only in dealing with sin (in expiation) but in removing the personal opposition to our access into his righteous presence (propitiation). Love and wrath are not therefore contradictory in God.

3. The idea of transactional guilt, *i.e.* of someone else being asked to carry our responsibility in order to make reconciliation, is said to be essentially immoral. It has to be

recognized that at times the notion of Christ's substitution has been presented crudely and devoid of mystery. Nevertheless, this element in the work of Christ can be seen as a corollary of grace whereby God secures for us totally and incomprehensibly what we cannot do for ourselves.

There is more to the atonement than an objective substitution by Christ in the place of sinners. This is one of a number of complementary motifs used by the biblical writers, which subjectively increases our security and excites our worship. The confidence that in Christ we cannot be condemned because he has been condemned in our stead, leaves the Christian in humble and speechless wonder.

Bibliography

R. W. Dale, *The Atonement* (London, 1894); J. Denney, *The Death of Christ*, ed. R. V. G. Tasker (London, 1951); C. H. Dodd, *The Epistle of Paul to the Romans* (London, 1932); R. S. Franks, *A History of the Doctrine of the Work of Christ* (London, 1918); E. M. B. Green, *The Empty Cross of Jesus* (London, 1984); L. Morris, *The Apostolic Preaching of the Cross* (London, ³1965); *idem, The Cross in the New Testament* (London, 1965); J. K. Mozley, *The Doctrine of the Atonement* (London, 1915); J. R. W. Stott, *The Cross of Christ* (Leicester, 1986); V. Taylor, *The Atonement in New Testament Preaching* (London, 1940).

T.W.J.M.

SUFFERING. The reality of suffering, especially that of the helpless or innocent, is a problem for anyone who posits the existence of an omnipotent and benevolent Deity. The Bible, however, says little about suffering as an intellectual conundrum (see Theodicy*). Gn. 1 – 3 shows that evil* entered the world through sin.* The first sufferings, which were emotional and the immediate consequence of disobedience, were followed by God's curse (Gn. 3:16–19), which promised pain, toil and death.* Although suffering results from sin (a moral evil), it is not itself a moral but a physical (or material) evil, for God is frequently presented in Scripture as its dispenser (*e.g.* Jos. 23:15; Jb. 2:10; Is. 45:7; Je. 25:29; Mi. 2:3), sending it either as punishment* of individuals and nations (both historically and eschatologically) or as chastisement of his people (see Eschatology;* History;* Judgment*).

While Scripture says very little about the sufferings of humanity generally, it does speak extensively about the suffering of God's people, and it is in respect to the latter only that a theology of suffering may be formulated. Suffering assumes a distinctly negative character in much of the OT owing to the nature of the Mosaic covenant,* which stipulated for the children of Israel health, prosperity and success for obedience and a variety of afflictions for disobedience (*e.g.* Ex. 15:25, 26; 23:25, 26; Lv. 26; Dt. 28 – 30). The corporate and material nature of the Mosaic covenant gives to its blessings and cursings a quality distinct from that of any prosperity or suffering that does not have as its ultimate cause a covenantal relationship contingent upon covenantal faithfulness. Hence the suffering that was the consequence of violating the Mosaic covenant was devoid of mystery. In spite of this apparent clarity of cause and effect, however, the wicked within Israel often prospered and afflicted the righteous, causing the latter's consternation regarding God's purposes (*e.g.* Pss. 37; 73). God's judgment of national apostasy was often withheld for a time, and when it came both the wicked and the righteous were swept away by the same calamities. This evoked a feeling of helpless frustration (*e.g.* Ps. 44).

Even during periods of national faithfulness, God's people were still sinners who could benefit from discipline.* God told Abraham that his descendants' sojourn in Egypt would be a time of discipline (Gn. 15:13–16; *cf.* 5:15; 26:5–9). After reminding the people that the Lord had humbled and tested them in the wilderness, Moses says, 'Know then in your heart that as a man disciplines his son, so the Lord your God disciplines you' (Dt. 8:5; *cf.* Pr. 3:11–12; for individual examples, see Pss. 94:12; 119:67, 71, 75).

At other times the afflicted are perplexed by their suffering since they can find no explanation for it. The OT only gradually developed the concept of suffering as a mystery, as God's people were slowly weaned from the temporal to the eternal, from the material to the spiritual. Even the most spiritually sensitive and mature believers in the OT, though they saw the Lord as their ultimate reward, did not see tribulations as experiences in which they should exult. It was not until after the resurrection of the Suffering Servant that those in close communion with God could grasp fully that as co-heirs with him they were to share his sufferings as a prerequisite to sharing his glory.

That this lesson was not part of the Jewish consciousness at the time of Christ is well illustrated by the tendency to view specific sin as the immediate cause of suffering (e.g. Lk. 13:1–5; Jn. 9:1–12) and by the persistent failure of Jesus' disciples to understand the redemptive nature of his mission (e.g. Mt. 16:21; 17:12; Lk. 17:25; 22:15; Jn. 2:19–22). Not until after his resurrection did his followers grasp the necessity of the Lord's atoning suffering (see especially Lk. 24:13–35). Once understood, his suffering became the focal point of apostolic evangelism (e.g. Acts 2:23; 3:18; 17:3; 26:22–23) and a frequent emphasis in the epistles (e.g. 1 Cor. 5:7; 2 Cor. 5:21; Eph. 5:2; 1 Pet. 1:10–11, 9; 3:18). While the OT promised prosperity for obedience, Christ expected affliction (e.g. Mt. 5: 10–12; 10:24–25; Mk. 10:28–30; Jn. 15:20), as did the apostles (e.g. Acts 14:22; Rom. 8:17–18; 2 Cor. 1:3–7; Phil. 1:29; 2 Tim. 3:12; Heb. 12:5–11; Jas. 1:2–4; 1 Pet. 4:1–2, 12–16).

The sufferings that Christians experience can be divided into two categories. 1. Suffering can be the direct result of grace. Only Christians can experience the civil war of spirit and flesh, described by Paul in Gal. 5:17, and graphically personalized in Rom 7:14–25. Furthermore, when Christians are persecuted for Christ's sake, they are experiencing a type of suffering that in its cause and purpose is distinct from anything that the unregenerate suffer.

2. Christians also suffer as a consequence of sharing in a fallen humanity in a fallen world. Here their suffering does not differ qualitatively from that of the unregenerate. They too can bring suffering on themselves by their own errors. They also experience sorrow, poverty, sickness and death. Christians are saved in such suffering and not from it. They share with all mankind the experience of and vulnerability to it. The vital and spectacular difference is God's use of it and their response to it. Heb. 12:5 admonishes Christians not to be indifferent to affliction or discouraged by it, because God's purpose in disciplining his children is to refine them and to equip them for kingdom service.

The suffering Christian is sustained by the fact that Christ not only suffered for his people but also suffers with them (e.g. Acts 9:4–5; 1 Cor. 12:26–27). He is their High Priest who can sympathize with their weaknesses (Heb. 4:15; cf. 2:18) as they also share his sufferings (Rom. 8:17; 2 Cor. 1:5; Heb. 13:13; 1 Pet. 4:13). Thus to suffer with Christ is a prerequisite to being glorified with him (Rom. 8:16; cf. 1 Pet. 1:16–17; 4:13; 5:10). Hence Christians can rejoice in afflictions (Acts 5:41; Rom. 5:3; 1 Thes. 1:6; Jas. 1:2).

While the suffering to which believers respond aright contributes to their spiritual growth and fellowship with Christ, it is also a form of witness – to each sufferer of his own salvation; to the unsaved for their conviction; to fellow Christians for their edification, encouragement and comfort; to principalities and powers in accordance with God's mysterious purposes. Thus, suffering 'produces a harvest of righteousness and peace for those who have been trained by it' (Heb. 12:11). The Christian's capacity to receive the comfort of the Holy Spirit in the midst of suffering is commensurate with an appreciation of the paternal sovereignty* of God, who is the ultimate cause of a bewilderingly diverse variety of proximate causes that can impinge upon their lives, until God 'will wipe every tear from their eyes' (Rev. 21:4).

Throughout history, attitudes toward the purpose of suffering have been diverse. The NT presents Christ as the believer's example in all things (Phil. 2:5) including suffering (1 Pet. 2:21; Heb. 12:3; Lk. 9:23). Applying the imitatio Christi (see Imitation of Christ*) to the realm of suffering, however, presents various problems, since Christ's sufferings were expiatory and unique in kind, degree and cause. Nevertheless, during the early centuries of Christianity the sufficiency of Christ's atoning sufferings was increasingly seen as limited to the remission of the penalty of eternal damnation, thus leaving sinners liable to satisfy God's justice by suffering temporal punishment in this life (cf. Penance*) or, by the late Middle Ages, in purgatory.* This theology has fostered a variety of aberrations based on the supposed merit of self-inflicted suffering. Such are now quite rare.

Different aberrations confront the church today. Process theology* sees human suffering as contributing to God's ongoing development. Along more orthodox lines, theologians have paid new attention to the suffering of God in Christ, *e.g.* in Moltmann's* influential *The Crucified God* (London, 1974) and K. Kitamori's *Theology of the Pain of God* (1946; ET, Richmond, VA, 1965). This concern has been partly stimulated by reflection on the Holocaust,* in an endeavour to theologize sensitively in the light of Auschwitz (*cf.* U. Simon, *A Theology of Auschwitz* (London, 1967). Some modern presentations of the gospel leave little room for suffering as an aspect of the Christian life. Toleration of religious diversity together with materialism, prosperity and medical sophistication that encourage an analgesic mentality in the West have conditioned many evangelicals to regard most suffering as an intrusion on the tranquil life that they feel is their God-given due (*cf.* Healing*). To all such aberrations the biblical teaching acts as a health-giving corrective.

Bibliography

T. Boston, *The Crook in the Lot: The Sovereignty and Wisdom of God in the Afflictions of Men* (1737, repr. Grand Rapids, MI, 1978); J. S. Feinberg, *Theologies and Evil* (Lanham, MD, 1979); J. Hick, *Evil and the God of Love* (London 1966); H. E. Hopkins, *The Mystery of Suffering* (London, 1959); C. S. Lewis, *The Problem of Pain* (London, 1948); H. W. Robinson, *Suffering Human and Divine* (London, 1940); E. F. Sutcliffe, *Providence and Suffering in the Old and New Testaments* (London, 1953); P. Tournier, *Creative Suffering* (London, 1982).

D.W.A.

SUNDAY, see SABBATH.

SUPEREROGATION, see MERIT.

SUPERNATURAL. In the OT there is no Hebrew word equivalent to our word 'natural', nor is there any concept of an unbreakable natural order independent of God. The world is continually dependent upon God in every respect. That which we refer to as 'nature',* the OT perceives as the outworking of God's gracious providence* in history. It is God who directly causes the seasons to change, the rain to fall and the grass to grow (Gn. 8:22; Jb. 38:22ff.; Pss. 65:9ff.; 147:8f.). In such a context any idea

of the supernatural as the interruption of an unbreakable natural order of cause and effect would be totally foreign. A 'miracle'* is not an event with a 'divine cause' as distinct from a 'natural cause', but is rather an event in which God's power is particularly (and sometimes unusually) evident; a 'sign' in which the grace and judgment of God's redemptive purpose are especially revealed.

The inheritance of Greek metaphysics* and the notion of God's 'otherness' led inevitably to an implicit dualism* between God and the world, the supernatural and the natural, faith and reason. In the context of Newtonian* physics the world was considered as a closed system of cause and effect, a system in which a 'supernatural' event must be viewed as an unwarranted intrusion. The removal of God from a closed natural order through deism* and his identification with it through panentheism* both imply a dismissal of the supernatural, a demythologizing of Scripture and a rejection of the possibility of present-day miracle.

The use of the term 'supernatural' (other than in the colloquial sense of 'extraordinary') with its dualistic connotations is therefore neither helpful nor scriptural but an unnecessary diversion from a biblical faith in the transcendently immanent God whose actions reveal both the covenantal faithfulness and the sovereign freedom of his grace.

Bibliography

C. E. Gunton, 'Transcendence, Metaphor, and the Knowability of God', *JTS* 31 (1980), pp. 501–516; J. Oman, *The Natural and the Supernatural* (Cambridge, 1950); T. F. Torrance, *Theological Science* (Oxford, 1969).

J.E.C.

SUPPER-STRIFE, see EUCHARIST.

SUPRALAPSARIANISM, see HYPER-CALVINISM; PREDESTINATION.

SWEDENBORGIANISM, see SECTS.

SWISS CONFESSION, see CONFESSIONS OF FAITH.

SYMBOL. A symbol has characteristics of a sign: it stands for, points to (indicates); in short, it signifies something. Characteristic of a symbol, however, is that it draws together facets of meaning of that which it symbolizes, concentrating or compressing them in a pregnant fashion. A sign can also function in this way, when it serves *e.g.* as a token or a portent.

Thus credal statements are called 'symbols'. They pregnantly summarize the beliefs of a confessional group, standing for the whole and compressing it into a brief pronouncement. A symbol is often contrasted with what it symbolizes, as symbol to reality. The provisions of the OT dispensation, seen from the vantage-point of the final revelation in the NT, are symbols. They foreshadowed that which was to come, the reality of salvation in Jesus Christ, anticipating it in germ.

The idea of symbol has been prominent in recent thought. In psychology, conscious states have been regarded as symbolic of deeplying irrational forces; economic systems have been regarded as symbols of class warfare; the facets of a society have been regarded as symbols of that society's spirit. In contemporary theology there is talk of 'unfounded symbol', *i.e.*, symbol that does not have a referent that is distinguishable from it; and ultimate reality is supposed to be discerned only through symbols. According to some Christian philosophy, symbolization is confined to the created cosmos; it is not to be confused with the pointing (meaning) that characterizes the creation as a whole, in its lack of self-sufficiency in relation to its creator.

Bibliography
E. Bevan, *Symbolism and Belief* (London, 1938); F. W. Dillistone, *Christianity and Symbolism* (London, 1958); E. L. Mascall, *Theology and Images* (London, 1953); K. Rahner, 'Theology of the Symbol', *Theological Investigations*, vol. 4 (London, 1966), pp. 221–252.

R.D.K.

SYMEON, see MACARIUS.

SYMEON THE NEW THEOLOGIAN, see EASTERN ORTHODOX THEOLOGY.

SYNCRETISM. The term was first used by Plutarch, referring to the ability of Cretan warring factions to unite against a common enemy. In the 17th century it was applied to those such as Georg Calixtus

(1586–1656), who sought unity between Protestant denominations. In the 19th century it was adopted by the history-of-religions school* to describe any religion that was the result of fusing two or more religions. Sikhism, which is a fusion of Hinduism and Islam, would thus be described as a syncretistic religion. Biblical scholars of this school have argued that both OT and NT religion are syncretistic in this sense – that OT religion is a fusion of Babylonian and Hebrew (Hermann Gunkel, 1862–1932) or Phoenician-Canaanite and Hebrew (Ivan Engnell, 1906–64) religion, whereas NT religion is a fusion of Hellenistic Judaism and the primitive religion of Jesus (Bultmann*). It is also used in a broader sense to describe the process of borrowing elements by one religion from another in such a way as not to change the basic character of the receiving religion. It is questionable, however, whether such a broad definition is helpful, since it makes every religion syncretistic to some extent.

Bibliography
H. Ringgren, 'The Problems of Syncretism', in S. Hartman, *Syncretism* (Stockholm, 1969).

D.A.Hu.

SYNERGISM, see WILL.

SYRIAC CHRISTIAN THEOLOGY. Roman Syria, in its wider sense, was an extensive area centred on Antioch, but embracing Mesopotamia. Much of it was bilingual, with Greek being used as well as dialects of Aramaic of which Syriac was an eastern dialect, spoken in northern Mesopotamia around Edessa and Nisibis. It was distinguished from other dialects of Aramaic by its script, but was basically similar. For some Syriac writers, it was their sole language.

Syria bordered on Palestine (and in the wider sense included Palestine), and also contained more Jews than any other country outside Palestine. For these reasons, as well as because of the common Aramaic language, Syriac Christianity had peculiarly close links with Palestinian Christianity and with Judaism. (Some scholars have suggested the influence of the Essene Judaism of Qumran on early Syriac Christianity.) Most of the early Christian literature from Palestine and West Syria is in Greek, and though it shows clear marks of Semitic culture (*cf.* Antiochene

School*), the marks are naturally clearer in literature written in the Semitic language of Syriac. The influence of Syriac Christianity is also evident in the early Christian literature of Armenia and Georgia.

The old Syriac translation of the Bible, the *Peshitta* ('plain'), probably originated in a Syriac targum on the Pentateuch, made for the kingdom of Adiabene, after its conversion to Judaism in the first century AD. Chronicles also is thought to be a Jewish translation, but the other OT books as well as the NT were translated by Christians. The canonical OT books and Ecclesiasticus were translated from Hebrew, but the rest of the Apocrypha from Greek, somewhat later than the rest. There is an older translation of the gospels than the *Peshitta* (the 'Old Syriac'), but the oldest of all was the *Diatessaron* (harmony) of Tatian (*fl. c.* 150–72), on which Ephraim (c. 306–73) wrote an extant commentary.

Gnosticism* was very active in Syria, and some of the oldest Syriac Christian literature, notably the *Odes of Solomon* (perhaps translated from Greek) and the *Acts of Thomas*, has lesser or greater Gnostic tendencies. Orthodox Syriac literature survives from the 4th century onwards. Aphrahat (*fl.* 330–50), the author of twenty-two *Demonstrations* (short treatises on biblical and ecclesiastical subjects), and Ephraim, both date from that century. Ephraim wrote many biblical commentaries and controversial works, but is chiefly remembered as a poet and hymn-writer. His hymns are markedly theological as well as devotional in content, and he leans strongly to asceticism.* Asceticism had been a marked feature of Syriac Christianity from early times. Celibacy was even a condition of baptism, and Marcion's* teaching had wide appeal.

After the Nestorian* and Monophysite* controversies of the 5th century, Syriac-speaking Christianity was largely out of communion with catholic Christianity, but retained many older traits. The Nestorian liturgy of *Addai and Mari* (the legendary apostles of Edessa) is an important witness to the early evolution of the eucharistic liturgy.

Bibliography

S. P. Brock, *The Harp of the Spirit* [ET of eighteen poems of Ephraim] (London, 1983); J. Neusner, *Aphrahat and Judaism* (Leiden, 1971); I. Ortiz de Urbina, *Patrologia Syriaca* (Rome, 1965); R. Murray, *Symbols of Church and Kingdom* (Cambridge, 1975); Selections of works of Ephraim and Aphrahat, tr. J. Gwynn, are in *NPNF*.

R.T.B.

SYSTEMATIC THEOLOGY, as a discipline within the science of knowing God, makes two assumptions. 1. Man, made in God's likeness, is a reasoning being and in response to the revelation which God has made, must use his rationality to apprehend God. 2. According to the 'analogy of Scripture', the Bible reveals not only the character of God and his purposes of grace in Jesus Christ, but that there is harmony and coherence in the mode of God's unveiling.

The method employed by the systematic theologian is to seek to organize thematically the various dimensions and emphases of Scripture and in particular to show their inter-relatedness as they communicate the word of God. This aspect of 'theology'* is dependent upon exegesis to discern the meaning of Scripture, biblical theology* to grasp the historical-redemptive process of particular themes and historical theology* to perceive how elements of truth have become formulated and later developed. Systematic theology is therefore best engaged in through corporate dependence upon the other disciplines within the theological encyclopaedia, and in a humble spirit of prayerful submission to the authority of Scripture.

The result will inevitably reflect the cultural ethos of the community out of which the systematic theology has emerged and the issues before the church at any particular era. It is, however, interaction with the church catholic and a recognition of extra-biblical influences upon our formulations which will produce a more biblically balanced systematic theology. Even then it will be fallible. The Scriptures of the OT and NT are the *only* infallible rule of faith and practice.

T.W.J.M.

SYSTEMATIC THEOLOGY, HISTORY OF. This is the development which has organized specific theological principles and beliefs into a coherent whole, in which each part is shown to have direct bearing on and relevance to the others. Christians have always recognized that the Bible does not contain a systematic theology, but they have generally argued that it is implied by the unity of God and his consistency in the working out of his plan of salvation. On the other hand, experience has shown that many different types of systematic theology are possible, and the great masters of the discipline have each created schools of thought which reflect and develop their particular method.

The beginnings of theological systematization can be traced to the writings of Tertullian* and Origen*, and the first theological systems are those of the great creeds,* especially the Athanasian Creed. But although the ancient church admitted the principle of systematization, no ancient divine worked out a complete system of his own. Most theological writing was confined to works in defence of a particular doctrine (*e.g.* the Trinity), and this pattern remained standard until the 13th century.

Systematic theology as we know it owes its origins to medieval scholasticism, in particular to the work of Thomas Aquinas.* Thomas wanted to develop philosophical arguments for the existence of God, which led him and his successors to an ever-greater elaboration of their first principles. Their method was the classical one of proceeding from a question to an answer, which would bring into play the whole range of theological speculation. Thus a question like whether Adam had a navel, or how many angels could dance on the head of a pin, would be used to explain the doctrine of creation, the nature of man and the relationship between the spiritual and the material worlds.

The Reformers of the 16th century generally rejected this method, and preferred to develop a systematic theology based on biblical evidence, rather than philosophical speculation. The classic example of this was the *Institutes of the Christian Religion*, written by John Calvin* as an aid to understanding his biblical commentaries. Later generations of both Protestants and Catholics pursued their respective principles in ever greater detail, developing a systematic theology designed to support the position of a particular confession. The usual method was to state a position in the form of an 'article', and then to back up the assertion with proof-texts from the Bible or, in the case of Roman Catholics, from the fathers of the church as well.

The heyday of systematic theology of this type lasted until the 18th century, and even later, one of its last great representatives being Charles Hodge.* By that time however, traditional systematics was fighting a losing battle against a rising tide of scepticism. In the 19th century, many leading theologians regarded their discipline as non-scientific, more akin to art and literature than to philosophy, and they argued against the tradition of systematics which they had inherited.

In modern times, systematic theology continues to flourish in conservative circles, and Karl Barth* made a determined attempt to reintroduce it to the mainstream of academic theology in his great *Church Dogmatics*. But despite the enormous influence which Barth has had, he did not succeed in restoring systematic theology to the place which it occupied in the 17th century, and opposition to it is as strong today as it was in the last century. Whether it can ever be revived without a corresponding revival of belief in the authority of the Bible as the repository of a single theological system is doubtful. Today the whole weight of emphasis is placed on relativistic, comparative studies of religions and beliefs, an outlook which can use systematic theology as a resource tool, but which is fundamentally hostile to it as a serious intellectual discipline.

Bibliography

H. Blamires, *A Defence of Dogmatism* (London, 1965); B. Hebblethwaite, *The Problems of Theology* (Cambridge, 1980); J. Macquarrie, *Principles of Christian Theology* (London, 1966).

G.L.B.

TAOISM AND CHRISTIANITY.

Taoism was founded in China by Lao Tzu (604–531 BC), who lived in a period of war and political disorder during the Middle Chou Dynasty (771–474 BC). He tried to find a solution to end the struggles in China through searching for Tao (the Way), that is, the moral and physical laws of nature.

Taoism is mainly divided into two distinct

movements: philosophical Taoism and religious Taoism.

The teaching of Taoism is developed in the book, *Tao Te Ching* by Lao Tzu, and in later writings of Chuang Tzu, his follower (399–295 BC). The basic idea of the *Tao Te Ching* is the doctrine of inaction ('*wu-wei*', literally, 'not doing') in the attempt to harmonize with nature. For Lao Tzu the best way to deal with pillage, tyranny, and killing was to do nothing, because in human relations force defeats itself and produces reaction. 'The more laws and regulations are given, the more robbers and thieves there are.' Lao Tzu advocated the natural and spontaneous way in opposition to artificial regulations, organizations, and ceremonies. This is why he vigorously attacked all formalities and artificialities. '*Wu-wei*' does not mean that an individual should avoid all action in life, but that he should avoid all hostile and aggressive actions against others.

This philosophical Taoism began to decline in the 4th century when Buddhism* spread in China. Buddhists adopted Taoist terminology to express their philosophy, while Taoists borrowed religious ideas, such as the transmigration of souls (see Metempsychosis*) and salvation, and divinities and cults from Buddhism. Taoists incorporated the animistic practices of the Chinese folk religion into their beliefs. Thus, Buddhism, Taoism and folk religion fused in the common people's thinking. This popular type of religious Taoism absorbed local nature deities, and adopted magic, fortune-telling, animism* and the control of spirits.

Taoism, Buddhism and Confucianism* are the three significant religions of the Far East. While Taoism and Buddhism are more religiously oriented, Confucianism's chief significance is mainly in the area of ethics. Buddhism appeals effectively to people with its doctrine of salvation (*nirvana*) from suffering, while Taoism gives the people gods of nature and national heroes to worship.

In contrast with Christianity, the Taoist concept of God is polytheistic.* The many gods to which the people pray include the gods of agriculture, medicine, literature, birth, city and land, the goddess of the sea, and also national heroes. Praying to each god is believed to bring help and blessings to those with special needs. Because of their doctrine of inaction, many Taoists are fatalists. Apart from the ethical values of Taoism found in the Five Precepts (against killing, drinking alcohol, stealing, lying, adultery) and the Ten Virtues (piety, loyalty, love, patience, self-sacrifice, remonstration of evil deeds, helping the poor, advocating a life of freedom, planting trees and building roads, and teaching the unenlightened), Christianity and Taoism are very far apart.

These three religions, Taoism, Buddhism and Confucianism, are all human-centred in that men and women reach out to please their gods. Christianity is in direct contrast, for it teaches that God reached out to save humanity through Christ.

Bibliography

Ching Feng (quarterly), Hong Kong; H. G. Creel, *What is Taoism?* (Chicago, IL, 1970); A. F. Gates, *Christianity and Animism in Taiwan* (San Francisco, 1979); Lao Tzu, *The Way of Lao Tzu*, tr. Wing-Tsit Chan (New York, 1963); H. Welch, *Taoism: The Parting of the Way* (Boston, 1965).

B.R.R.

TEILHARD DE CHARDIN, PIERRE (1881–1955). Born in France, Teilhard de Chardin trained as a Jesuit* and as a palaeontologist. He clashed with his superiors in the Roman Catholic Church in the mid-1920s and was forbidden to continue teaching as a geologist because of his unorthodox ideas on original sin and its relation to evolution. From 1926 he lived in China where he carried out palaeontological work, making important contributions to the study of one form of early man, Sinanthropus (Peking Man). On his return to France in 1946 he was forbidden to publish or teach on philosophical subjects. In 1951 he moved to New York where he worked until his death.

At the time of his death Teilhard's influence was limited. With the publication of *The Phenomenon of Man* (ET, London, 1959), his influence spread rapidly. Within a few years a spate of further books and collections of his writings appeared, including devotional works (*Le Milieu Divin*; ET, London, 1960), palaeontological writings, collections of his letters and largely speculative writings (*The Future of Man*; ET, London, 1964).

Teilhard's aim was to construct a phenomenology* of the universe, based upon scientific thinking, and providing a coherent explanation for the world. His synthesis incorporated immense evolutionary ideas, and brought together science, philosophy and theology. For him, evolution was a general condition to which all theories and systems must conform, and within which there was movement towards increasing complexity and consciousness converging ultimately towards a supreme centre, Omega.

Underlying much of Teilhard's thinking was the basic postulate that matter, like human beings, possesses a form of consciousness. All matter has a 'within' as well as a 'without'. Evolution is an ascent towards consciousness, which is supremely manifested in humanity.

Teilhard's thought consists of three main components, cosmic, human and 'Christic'. God was viewed as an integral part of the evolutionary process, since God and the evolving universe are united. Evolution therefore has a 'Christic' centre and mankind's duty is to advance this 'Christification'. The third component, the human, links the cosmic and the 'Christic', constituting the thinking layer (noosphere), which lies between the living layer (biosphere) and the ultra-human (Omega, Christ or God). Underlying Teilhard's vision was an intense optimism, an ardent desire to bring together his science and his Christianity, a strong mystical* sense, and a rejection of any form of dualism* of mind and matter. Ultimately, therefore, he viewed Christ as the organic centre of the cosmos, with Christ's body being equivalent to the cosmos itself.

Teilhard retained the basic concepts of Roman Catholic doctrine, although they were understood in terms of a world in evolution; hence his emphasis on the cosmic role of Christ rather than his redemptive role. His Christology was in the tradition of incarnational theology with Christ as the goal and crowning-point of the natural order.

Evil and sin became by-products of evolution, with sin being viewed as part of the evolutionary process and the fall as a symbol of the world's incompleteness. The incarnation of Christ took on universal evolutionary significance with limited meaning at the levels of individuals. Salvation was equated with the efforts of mankind to complete the mystical body of Christ.

See also: CREATION; SCIENCE AND THEOLOGY.

Bibliography

C. Cuenot, *Teilhard de Chardin* (London, 1965); R. Hooykaas, 'Teilhardism, a Pseudo-scientific Delusion', *etc.*, *Free University Quarterly* 9 (1963), pp. 1–83; D. G. Jones, *Teilhard de Chardin. An Analysis and Assessment* (London, 1969); H. de Lubac, *The Faith of Teilhard de Chardin* (London, 1965); E. Rideau, *Teilhard de Chardin. A Guide to His Thought* (London, 1968); C. Van Til, 'Pierre Teilhard de Chardin', *WTJ* 28 (1966), pp. 109–144; J. J. Duyvené du Wit, in P. E. Hughes (ed.), *Creative Minds in Contemporary Theology* (Grand Rapids, MI, 1966), pp. 407–450.

D.G.J.

TEMPLE, WILLIAM (1881–1944), philosopher, theologian and churchman; Bishop of Manchester (1921–29), Archbishop of York (1929–42), Archbishop of Canterbury (1942–44). A many-sided figure active far beyond the Church of England, Temple believed that 'it is in the sacramental view of the universe, both of its material and of its spiritual elements, that there is given hope of making human both politics and economics and of making effectual both faith and love' (*Nature, Man and God*, Gifford Lectures, London, 1934). His thought had a strong central focus on the incarnation.* Recognized as much for his skill as a chairman at bringing out the best from other people as for his own attainments in philosophy and theology (*cf. Mens Creatrix*, London, 1917; *Christus Veritas*, London, 1924) or personal piety (*cf. Readings in St John's Gospel*, 2 vols., London, 1939–40), Temple applied himself to many causes.

He was president of the Workers' Educational Association (1909); member, and chairman from 1925, of the commission that produced *Doctrine in the Church of England* (1938); chairman of the interdenominational Conference on Christian Politics, Economics and Citizenship (COPEC) held in Birmingham (1924); and of a similar Anglican conference held at Malvern (1941). The latter conference inspired *Christianity and Social Order* (Harmondsworth, 1942), a widely-read paperback described as 'one of the foundation piers of the welfare state' (D. L. Munby). As chairman of the second world conference on Faith and Order, Edinburgh (1937), and president of the provisional committee for the formation of the World Council of Churches (1938), Temple embraced the world-wide church as 'the great new fact of our time'.

Bibliography

R. Craig, *Social Concern in the Thought of William Temple* (London, 1963); F. A. Iremonger, *William Temple, Archbishop of Canterbury* (London, 1948); J. F. Padgett, *The Christian Philosophy of William Temple* (The Hague, 1974); A. M. Ramsey, *From Gore to Temple* (London, 1960); A. M. Suggate, *William Temple and Christian Social Ethics Today* (Edinburgh, 1987).

P.N.H.

TEMPTATION. The note of testing rather than seducing is uppermost in biblical teaching. In the OT Yahweh tests his own people to see (really to show) whether or not they will be true to their place in the covenant (Dt. 8:2, 16; 13:3; Jdg. 2:22). It is significant that it is Israel and not the heathen whom he puts on trial. Such tests of faith and obedience are integral to the special relationship involved (Dt. 8:5–6; *cf.* Heb. 12:4–11). God brings those he most values into testing situations either directly (Gn. 22:1–2, 12) or indirectly (Jb. 1:12), to refine obedience (Ps. 119:67, 71; Zc. 13:9) and to strengthen trust (Ps. 66:10–12).

Satan too tests, but only to damage or destroy faith and obedience and to provoke to exasperation and rebellion against God (Gn. 3:1–4; Jb. 1:12; *cf.* Lk. 22:31). Israel herself is said to have put God to the test repeatedly, by challenging his wisdom and his power; a standing warning to us all, says the NT (Dt. 6:16; *cf.* 1 Cor. 10:9–11; Heb. 3:7–12).

Jesus himself was tested and subtly tempted to abandon God's way of redemption and to strike out on his own programme of Messianic conquest, seeking peace by power not by suffering (Mt. 4:1–11; 16:21–23; 26:36–41; *cf.* Jn. 12:27, 38). Both Jesus' own relationship with God and God's inherent righteousness were thus brought into question (Jn. 5:19–20; Phil. 2:8; Rom. 3:26).

Throughout the NT 'avoidable suffering' is the great test and one for which to be prepared (Mt. 6:13). Uncompromising obedience to the faith brought the early Christians into situations of great temptation (Heb 2:1; 10:34; 12:4). God's 'way out' did not, and does not, lie in sinful compromise or even, necessarily, in change of circumstances (1 Cor. 10:13–14), but in determined faith (Heb. 10:37–39), triumphant joy (Jas. 1:2–4) and unvanquishable grace (1 Pet. 1:5–7). A view of Christ in temptation, suffering and glory is the supreme antidote to the discouragements of the hour (Heb. 4:14–16; 7:25; 12:2–4; *cf.* Lk. 22:31).

Besides those temptations peculiar to times of persecution, Christians daily face temptation from Satan (2 Cor. 2:11; 11:14; 12:7; I Thes. 2:18), from a godless society (Ps. 1:1; Jn. 17:14–16; 1 Jn. 2:15–17), and above all from indwelling sin (Gal. 5:16–18; Eph. 4:22–32; Col. 3:8; Jas. 1:13–15; 1 Jn. 2:15–17). Failure to face, resist and overcome temptations to sin disrupts our communion with God, weakens our power to obey and dishonours the name of our Lord. John Owen (see Puritan Theology*) in his devotional classic *Of Temptation*, explores the words of Christ in Gethsemane: 'Watch and pray so that you will not fall into temptation', as the believer's refuge in times of fierce assault.

Bibliography

D. Bonhoeffer, *Temptation* (London, 1955); C. S. Lewis, *The Screwtape Letters* (London, 1942); J. Owen, *Of Temptation* (1658), in W. H. Goold (ed.), *The Works of John Owen* (London, 1850–55), vol. VI; J. I. Packer in *NBD*, pp. 1173–1174; W. Schneider, C. Brown and H. Haarbeck in *NIDNTT* III, pp. 798–811; H. Seesemann in *TDNT* II, pp. 23–36.

P.H.L.

TERESA OF AVILA, see MYSTICAL THEOLOGY.

TERTULLIAN (*fl. c.* 196–*c.* 212) began writing in Carthage, North Africa, towards the end of the 2nd century, his undisputed works dating from *c.* AD 196 to *c.* AD 212. Some scholars claim to detect fresh doctrinal distinctives in his later work when he was sympathetic to Montanism.* He has been characterized both as 'the last of the Greek apologists'* and as 'the first of the Latin fathers'. Both descriptions are appropriate, since he preserves in his work a compendium of mainstream Christianity, while significantly foreshadowing the Latin Church's preoccupation with power* and

675

stressing such legal themes as confession, penance,* renunciation and merit.*

Tertullian concentrated much of his fire against 'Christian' options tolerant of dualism,* most cogently in his *Against Marcion*.* Other dualistic systems attacked were Gnosticism* and the philosophy of Hermogenes who, in Tertullian's view, raised the status of primeval matter to the level of the unique God.

Tertullian claimed throughout his writings that he defended the doctrinal *regula fidei* (rule of faith) universally held by churches in the apostolic tradition (*Against Praxeas* 2; *Prescription of Heretics* 13, 36; *Veiling of Virgins* 2). The pillars of this confession, shared by his great predecessor Irenaeus* of Lyon, affirmed one creator of all things, the incarnation* of the divine Word and the ultimate resurrection* of the dead. When we begin, however, to unpack this simple scheme, we meet a comparable commitment to significant implied details. The creator,* accordingly, forms the universe from nothing (*creatio ex nihilo*), since only this guarantees his uniqueness as God and protects the intrinsic worth of the creation product itself. Hence, in his opposition to docetism,* Tertullian was able to deem the 'flesh' or humanity of Christ a worthy vehicle of God's presence (*Against Marcion* 2:4, 3:10, 5:14; *Flesh of Christ* 6, 16), and boldly identified the gracious God at work in Christ with the very creator-deity whom Marcion dismissed as malevolent or weak. Tertullian went even further and included Christ himself in the functions of creation and judgment, thus effectively placing him on the divine side of the creator-creation division (*Against Marcion* 4:20, 29, 30 *etc.*), while still repeatedly underlining the reality of Christ's human nature (*ibid.* 2:27, 5:14; *Flesh of Christ* 5, 16).

The case for future general resurrection equally rested on the doctrine of creation. The power which made all things from nothing could similarly recall persons from the dissolution of death and weave a new resurrection order in nature (*Resurrection* 7, 42, 57).

The feeling for divine power pervasively present in Tertullian's thought did not mean that he had no vision of divine grace. The incarnation for him was no mere display of God's might and majesty, but an essentially *saving* operation (*Against Marcion* 4:37, 5:14, 17; *Flesh of Christ* 5, 14). The power

which undertook our salvation reached even to the cross where Christ 'reigned from the tree' (*Against Marcion* 3:18, 19, 21). Similarly the Holy Spirit,* by virtue of his powerful role in creation, was the re-creating Spirit of grace who was at work in sanctification* (*Against Praxeas* 12), in the sacraments* (*Baptism* 3, 4), in prayer (*Prayer* 1), and in forgiveness (*Purity* 21).

Tertullian is chiefly famous, however, for his formulations of the Trinity,* at their most mature in his work *Against Praxeas*, directed at 2nd-century Monarchianism.* For the Monarchians there existed only one undifferentiated divine ruler who assumed, in succession, appropriate roles in the work of redemption. Tertullian freely conceded the principle of one rule, but held this rule to be administered through the Son and the Holy Spirit as co-regents of the Father. Despite this equality of status, Tertullian nevertheless recognized a *delegation* of the power of the kingdom to the Son in his redemptive self-humbling. He thereby supplied a concrete distinction between Father and Son, at least in the economy (see Trinity*), which broke the tight monotheistic mould of Monarchianism.

In his Trinitarian doctrine Tertullian made varied and complex use of the term *substantia* (substance).* Most scholars are agreed that the later Trinitarian theology of Athanasius* and the ecumenical councils* should not be read into Tertullian's use of the term. The Latin term signified for him the uniquely divine spirit-substance of which the Son and Spirit partook mainly by virtue of their emergence out of the one God as agents in the work of creation. Underlying this dynamic, economic Trinity was the Logos* theology inherited from earlier apologists* and which was highly subordinationist.

Balancing the *substantia* was the term *persona* (person), which primarily highlighted the Johannine* conversations of the Father and Son, thus establishing real distinctions between them in the economy of redemption. One should not assume a formulation in Tertullian's mind of all that may go with the modern word 'person' (such as self-consciousness, self-determination, *etc.*), though the biblical setting makes some such conception natural (*cf.* Hypostasis*).

Tertullian's Trinitarian doctrine has, rightly, been called an 'economic Trinity' since all his formulations are set within the works of creation and redemption, hardly addressing at all a Trinity within the divine nature quite apart from God's activity. This is typical of his theology generally, which bore many marks of the Latin world's practicality and functional thinking. For Tertullian, God was active rather than abstract.

In considering the death and resurrection of the Son of God, Tertullian comments that 'it is certain because it is impossible'. This apparently irrational statement highlights his famous alleged antipathy towards philosophy. Evaluation of Tertullian on this score, however, should take account of the fact that he constantly, though very selectively, plundered contemporary sources (especially Stoicism*), was severely rationalist in many of his discourses and was concerned mainly to oppose syncretistic expressions of the Christian faith rather than philosophy in general.

Although Tertullian's originality as a theologian is sometimes questioned, and although dependence on earlier apologists is freely admitted by him (*Against Valentinians* 5), his marshalling of the material and his own trenchant presentation of it produced not only an invaluable compendium of 2nd-century thought, but many original formulations which justify his celebrated position in the history of Christian doctrine.

Bibliography

R. H. Ayers, *Language, Logic and Reason in the Church Fathers: A Study of Tertullian, Augustine and Aquinas* (New York, 1979); J. Daniélou, *A History of Early Christian Doctrine Before the Council of Nicaea*: vol. 3, *The Origins of Latin Christianity* (London, 1977); E. Evans, *Tertullian's Treatise Against Praxeas* (London, 1948); *idem, Tertullian's Treatise On The Incarnation* (London, 1956); *idem, Tertullian's Treatise On The Resurrection* (London, 1960); J. Morgan, *The Importance of Tertullian in the Development of Christian Dogma* (London, 1928); R. E. Roberts, *The Theology of Tertullian* (London, 1924); W. P. Saint, *On Penitence and On Purity*, in *Tertullian: Treatises on Penance* (London, 1952).

R.K.

THEISM. In a broad sense, theism is synonymous with belief in God, usually one God, as in monotheism.* This usage does not distinguish it from deism* and pantheism,* nor does it look beyond philosophical theory to historical religions. In a more specific sense, then, theism refers to the belief in a personal creator-God, distinct from the world (*contra* pantheism) yet constantly active in it (*contra* deism), who is therefore worthy of worship. As creator, the God of theism is both intelligent and powerful. As personal, he is capable of self-revelation, a moral being with just and benevolent concerns for his creatures. As alone transcendent, he is free to act sovereignly in the creation.* In this immanent activity, he seeks his own good purposes for history in general and for individual persons.

In this more specific sense, three major theistic religions may be identified: Islam,* Judaism* and Christianity. Each affirms one personal creator-God, self-revealing, active in creation, and worthy of worship. Of these three, Christianity gives the fullest account of God's involvement in his creation, in terms of the incarnation and redeeming work of the eternal Son of God.

Theism as a philosophical position may be traced to Plato* in the West. It was carefully developed by medieval Moslem, Jewish and Christian thinkers, among the latter notably Augustine,* Thomas Aquinas* and Duns Scotus.* In modern times, theologians such as John Calvin* and philosophers such as Descartes* and Kant* shaped the tradition. Current advocates include Basil Mitchell (*The Justification of Religious Belief*, Oxford, 1981), Richard Swinburne (*The Coherence of Theism*, Oxford, 1977) and Alvin Plantinga* (*God, Freedom and Evil*, Grand Rapids, MI, 1978).

A.F.H.

THEOCRACY. A theocracy, strictly speaking, is a society ruled by God. The term is often used more loosely, however, of communities where there is a union of church and state, or where the civil power is dominated by the ecclesiastical (properly, a *hierocracy*).

The purest example of a theocracy is OT Israel.* Yahweh was King (Dt. 33:5), Israel was his army (Ex. 7:4) and their wars were his wars (Nu. 21:14). But the concept was not only a military one. Legislative and judicial power also lay in the hands of God. A great leader like Moses did no more than mediate it (Ex. 18:16) and even the king was only God's vice-regent (Dt. 17:15). In his capacity as 'theocratic deputy' he not only had to fight Yahweh's battles (2 Sa. 8:5–20) but to promote the faith, destroy God's enemies and carry out (as Josiah did) major reforms. In all his actions, however, he remained subject to divine direction and scrutiny: a fact expressed especially in the way the great seers (Samuel, Nathan and Ahijah, for example) relentlessly stalk the monarch. He was never allowed to forget that 'Yahweh is our judge, Yahweh is our ruler, Yahweh is our king: He will save us' (Is. 33:22).

The concept of the theocracy is closely bound up with two other fundamental concerns of the Old Testament: 1. The covenant. The promise, 'I shall be your God and you shall be my people,' brought every Israelite face to face with the will of God. Life in the theocracy was intensely theonomous, *i.e.* lived under the terms of divine law. 2. Eschatology. As Th. C. Vriezen argues, the theocentric outlook on life created not only a theocratic society but also a teleological concept of history. Out of this arose Israel's hope and that hope was itself focused on a theocracy: 'God will establish His theocracy, if not among the present Israel, then among a new Israel which He will constitute from "the remnant." And if the present house of David proves unwilling God will bring forth a new rod from the stem of Jesse, which shall rule in the theocratic kingdom' (*An Outline of Old Testament Theology*, Oxford, 1960, p. 229).

It is against this background that we must see the NT. The theocracy appears to have vanished. The elect are scattered, stateless and disorganized (1 Pet. 1:1). Yet the difference from the OT is more apparent than real. The church is the new Israel,* possessing all the essential characteristics of the old (1 Pet. 2:9). If it is not itself exactly the kingdom* of God it has a very close connection with it (Mt. 16:18f.). In essence it is a theocracy. Christ, as its head, is the source of all authority (Eph. 5:23). Discipline is exercised only in his name and in his presence (1 Cor. 5:4). The church has leaders, but only in the Lord (1 Thes. 5:12). To him they must give account (Heb. 13:17) and the charismata by which they function are his gifts* (Eph. 5:11). His will is as binding for the new Israel as the will of Yahweh was for the old.

In the looser sense, of a society dominated by the church (or by its clergy), scholars have found examples of theocracy in medieval Catholicism, Calvin's Geneva, Cromwell's England and the teaching of the Westminster Confession (see Confessions*): 'The civil magistrate hath authority, and it is his duty, to take order that unity and peace be preserved in the church, that the truth of God be kept pure and entire, that all blasphemies and heresies be suppressed, all corruptions and abuses in worship and discipline prevented or reformed, and all the ordinances of God duly settled, administered and observed' (ch. XXIII. iii). What J. T. McNeill said of Calvin's Geneva is probably true of all of these: 'Certainly the system was a theocracy in the sense that it assumed responsibility to God on the part of secular and ecclesiastical authority alike and proposed as its end the effectual operation of the will of God in the life of the people' (*The History and Character of Calvinism*, New York, 1954, p. 185). In the Protestant tradition, however, this never meant the subordination of the civil power to the church. On the contrary, the Westminster Confession is adamant that 'ecclesiastical persons' are not exempted from the magistrates' power, even though they be infidels (ch. XXIII. iv). Conversely, however, the state, as much as the individual, is subject to the will of God. As such it has no right to be either indifferent or hostile to the church, but is bound to support and protect it. The unlikelihood of such protection in a pluralistic society does not falsify the principle itself.

Today, however, not even those churches most loyal to the Westminster Confession would be happy with the way it expresses this principle. It would have to be supplemented by a due emphasis on liberty of conscience and by a firm disavowal of all that savours of persecution and intolerance.

Bibliography

W. Eichrodt, *Theology of the Old Testament*, vol. 2 (London, 1967); T. S. Eliot, *The Idea of a Christian Society* (London, 1939); C. Hodge, *The Church and its Polity* (London, 1879); H. Höpfl, *The Christian Polity of John Calvin* (Cambridge, 1982); J. T. McNeill, *The History and Character of Calvinism* (New York, 1954); J. B. Payne, *The Theology of the Older Testament* (Grand Rapids, MI, 1962);

T. M. Parker, *Christianity and the State in the Light of History* (London, 1955).

D.M.

THEODICY (from Gk. *theos*, 'God', and the root *dik-*, 'just') seeks to 'justify the ways of God to man' (Milton), showing that God is in the right and is glorious and worthy of praise despite contrary appearances. Theodicy asks how we can believe that God is both good and sovereign in face of the world's evil* – bad people; bad deeds, defying God and injuring people; harmful (bad) circumstances, events, experiences and states of mind, which waste, thwart, or destroy value, actual or potential, in and for humankind; in short, all facts, physical and moral, that prompt the feeling, 'This ought not to be'.

All theodicies view evil as making for a good greater than is attainable without it. Thus, Leibniz* (who coined the word 'theodicy' in 1710) argued that a world containing moral and physical evil is better, because metaphysically richer, than one containing good only, and that God must have created the best of all possible worlds. Hegel,* a closet pantheist,* held that all apparent evil is really good in the making; it looks and feels bad only because its character as good is as yet incomplete. Process theologians* picture their finite God struggling against evil in hope of mastering it some day. Biblical theists,* however, reason differently. Affirming with Augustine* that evil is a lack of good, or a good thing gone wrong, they begin by agreeing that:

1. Pain, though it hurts, is often not really evil. The stab of pain acts as an alarm, and living with pain can purge, refine, and ennoble character. Pain may thus be a gift and a mercy.

2. Virtue (choosing good) is only possible where vice (choosing evil) is also possible. An automaton's programmed performance is not virtue, and lacks the value of virtue. In making man capable of choosing the path of grateful obedience, God made him capable of not doing so. Though not sin's author, God created a possibility of sin by creating the possibility of righteousness.

3. Moral growth and maturity are only possible when the consequences of action are calculable. Since God means this world to be a school for moral growth, he gave it physical regularity so that consequences might be foreseen. Frustrations through miscalculation, and natural events called disasters because they damage humans, are therefore inevitable. Unfallen man would have experienced them. In fact, we mature morally through coping with them.

Beyond this point in theodicy, speculations intrude. John Hick* posits universal* salvation, arguing that nothing less can justify all the evil that God for soul-building purposes permits in his world. Advocates of the 'free-will defence' (of God, against the charge of being the source of evil) speculate that God cannot prevent humans from sinning without destroying their humanity – which would mean that glorified saints, being still human, may sin. Some Calvinists envisage God permissively decreeing sin for the purpose of self-display in justly saving some from their sin and justly damning others for and in their sin. But none of this is biblically certain. The safest way in theodicy is to leave God's permission of sin and moral evil as a mystery, and to reason from the good achieved in redemption, perhaps as follows:

a. In this fallen world where all have turned from God and deserve hell, God has taken responsibility for saving individuals and renewing the cosmos, at the cost to himself of the death of Jesus Christ his Son (see Atonement;* Redemption;* Substitution*). The cross shows how much he loves sinners (Rom. 5:8; 8:32; 1 Jn. 4:8–10), and induces responsive love in all whom he calls to faith.* b. God enables believers, as forgiven sinners, to relate to all evil (bad circumstances, bad health, bad treatment, even their own bad past) in a way that brings forth good – moral and spiritual growth and wisdom, benefit to others by example and encouragement, and thanksgiving to God; so that facing evil becomes for them a value-creating way of life. c. In heaven, where the full fruit of Christ's redemption* will be enjoyed, earth's evils will in retrospect seem trivial (Rom. 8:18), and remembering them will only increase our joy* (Rev. 7:9–17). Thus through God's sovereign goodness evil is overcome; not theoretically, so much as practically, in human lives.

This unspeculative, confessional, pastoral theodicy leaves with God the secret things (*cf.* Dt. 29:29), justifies and glorifies God for what is revealed, calls forth wonder and worship, and resolves the feeling, 'This ought not to be,' into the contented cry, 'He does all things well!' – which is a supremely positive declaration that God is in the right, and is to be praised. Meantime, logic declares it possible, and faith, reasoning as above, thinks it certain, that the final state of things will demonstrably be better than anything God could have achieved by taking a different course at any stage.

See also: SUFFERING.

Bibliography
M. B. Ahern, *The Problem of Evil* (London, 1971); S. T. Davis (ed.), *Encountering Evil: Live Options on Theodicy* (Atlanta, GA, 1986); P. T. Forsyth, *The Justification of God* (London, 1916); P. T. Geach, *Providence and Evil* (Cambridge, 1977); J. Hick, *Evil and the God of Love* (London, 1966); J. W. Wenham, *The Goodness of God* (London, 1974; revised ed., *The Enigma of Evil*, Leicester, 1986); J. S. Whale, *The Christian Answer to the Problem of Evil* (London, 1939).

J.I.P.

THEODORE OF MOPSUESTIA, see ANTIOCHENE SCHOOL.

THEODORET OF CYRRHUS, see ANTIOCHENE SCHOOL.

THEOLOGY is derived from the Gk. *theologia*, compounded of two words, meaning basically an account of, or discourse about, gods or God. Among the Greeks, poets such as Homer and Hesiod were called *theologoi*. Their stories about the gods were categorized as 'mythical theology' by Stoic* writers, who spoke also of 'natural or rational theology', which was close to Aristotle's 'theological philosophy' – broadly what today would be referred to as philosophical theology* or metaphysics.*

Although Philo* called Moses a *theologos*, *i.e.* one who speaks of God, God's spokesman, no form of the Gk. word appears in the LXX of the OT or in the NT. (A few manuscripts entitle its last book 'The Revelation of John the Theologos'.) Its Christian usage begins with the Apologists,* for whom the verb sometimes means 'ascribe divinity to, call God', a meaning which it frequently has in the later disputes about the deity of Christ (see Christology*) and of the Holy Spirit.* But by AD 200 both the Gk. and its Lat. transliteration were being used of teaching, normally Christian teaching, about God. Athanasius* applies *theologia* to knowledge of God in his own being, as distinct from his dealings with the world, and others such as Augustine* restrict it to teaching about the Godhead. Only occasionally in the fathers does 'theology' refer to a broader range of church doctrine. It belongs within the community of faith, and no separation is made between teaching about God and knowledge (*i.e.* apprehension and experience) of God. *Theologia* can even mean 'praise of God'.

It was chiefly through the scholastic* writers and the new universities of Europe that theology became a more systematic exercise, a field of study and teaching, even a discipline or a science. This usage was not entirely new – it picked up pre-Christian Gk. uses and some in the fathers also, but it foreshadowed the development of theology as an academic discipline no longer necessarily located in the Christian community. At the same time, the schoolmen increasingly distinguished between different kinds of theology, alongside a common distinction between theology and philosophy, which broadly corresponded to their distinction between faith and reason.* Although the Reformers were generally impatient of the distinctions beloved of the schoolmen, their successors in the age of confessional orthodoxy or Protestant scholasticism adopted or developed an extensive categorization of different kinds of theology.

In the modern world, 'theology' is often used in a comprehensive sense, embracing all the disciplines involved in a university course or in training for church ministry (*i.e.* including the biblical languages, church history, homiletics, *etc.*). It may thus be an academic discipline alongside, for example, English literature or physics. More precisely, the word denotes teaching about God and his relation to the world from creation to the consummation, particularly as it is set forth in an ordered, coherent manner. (It is rarely used solely of the doctrine of God himself.) It is normally made more specific by one or more of a wide range of qualifiers, which may indicate the church or tradition it belongs to (*e.g.* monastic,* Roman Catholic,* Reformed,* evangelical,* ecumenical*), its material basis (*e.g.* natural,* biblical,* confessional, *i.e.* grounded in a church confession,* symbolic, *i.e.* based on a church's 'symbols', which here means creeds,* *etc.*), its doctrinal content (*e.g.* baptismal,* Trinitarian*), its organizing centre or dominant motif or focus (*e.g.* covenant,* liberation,* incarnational, feminist,* theology of the cross* – each of which denotes more than mere subject-matter), its purpose as determined by its audience (*e.g.* apologetic,* polemical), *etc.*

Among the main disciplines of theological study today must be counted biblical,* historical,* systematic,* philosophical,* pastoral* and practical* theology, and others pursued less widely, such as dogmatic,* liturgical* and fundamental* theology. Most kinds of theology have less and less a confessional or denominational character.

The acid test for all theology was well expressed by Thomas Aquinas:* 'Theology is taught by God, teaches of God, and leads to God'.

Bibliography
G. F. van Ackeren, in *NCE* 14, pp. 39–49 (a Catholic discussion, including 'positive' and 'speculative' theology); G. Ebeling, in *RGG* VI, cols. 754–769; R. Hedde, in *DTC* 10, cols. 1574–1595; F. Kattenbusch, 'Die Entstehung einer Christliche Theologie: Zur Geschichte der Ausdrücke Θεολογία, Θεολογεῖν, Θεολόγος,' *ZTK* n.s. 11 (1930), pp. 161–205; F. Whaling, 'The Development of the Word "Theology" ', *SJT* 34 (1981), pp. 289–312.

D.F.W.

THEOPHANY. As the Gk. etymology implies, theophany refers to an 'appearance of God' to man. The OT records numerous theophanies, beginning with the early chapters of Genesis which record that God talked to Adam and walked in the garden (3:8). God manifested himself to man in three forms – human (see Anthropomorphism*), angelic* and non-human. The form of each theophany correlates to its function.

When God comes in judgment, he appears in a threatening guise. For instance, God presented himself as an irresistible warrior immediately preceding the conquest of Jericho (Jos. 5:13–15). Judgment theophany, though always threatening, brings both curse and fear to God's enemies and blessing and comfort to God's people (Na. 1:1–9).

The frequently encountered warrior theophany demonstrates that God often appeared in human-like form. Of course, God assumes various roles in the many OT theo-phanies. For example, in Gn. 18:1–15, a passage in which God confirmed his covenant promises to Abraham, he appeared as a messenger.

A second type of theophany occurred when God revealed himself to people in the form of an angel. Manoah and his wife received news of the birth of Samson from an angelic figure whom they later recognized as God himself (Jdg. 13). Many, if not most, evangelical scholars believe that the angel of the Lord is a pre-incarnation appearance of the second person of the Trinity.* This is true as well of other theophanies in human form. Occasionally, these theophanies are more specifically referred to as 'christophanies'. Neither the OT nor the NT directly identifies Jesus Christ with the angel of the Lord. Scholars, though, reason backward from the teaching of the NT (Jn. 1:18) that no-one has seen God the Father.

A third form of theophany occurs on those occasions when God appeared among men and women in non-human form. At the critical juncture of the establishment of the Abrahamic covenant, God passed between divided animal carcasses in the form of a 'smoking fire pot with a blazing torch' (Gn. 15:17).

The theophany *par excellence* is the advent of Jesus Christ (Jn. 1:1–17; 14:9; Col. 1:15). In the NT theophany becomes christophany, and is superseded by actual incarnation. Believers today look forward to the last days when 'the Lord himself will come down from heaven' (1 Thes. 5:16).

Bibliography
J. A. Borland, *Christ in the Old Testament* (Chicago, 1978); J. Jeremias, *Theophanie: die Geschichte einer Alttestamentlichen Gattung* (Neukirchen-Vluyn, 1965); J. K. Kuntz, *The Self-Revelation of God* (Philadelphia, 1967).

T.L.

THIELICKE, HELMUT (1908–85). Born in Barmen, Thielicke graduated PhD in 1931 and ThD in 1934. He first pastored and taught in Württemberg. Having offended the Nazi regime by questioning the so-called 'orders' of race* and people, he was for a time forbidden to speak, write or travel except in a small area. Yet he had a powerful pulpit ministry during the war years and immediately after. In 1945 he took up a professorship at Tübingen and in 1954 transferred to Hamburg, where he served as Rector in 1961. Famous as a preacher, he continued to preach to large congregations and sponsored an indirect evangelistic venture to spread Christian knowledge by discussion, pamphlets, and radio and television talks.

His main contribution, however, came through his writings, most of which have been translated into English. Even under Hitler's ban he managed to smuggle an early version of his work on death out of the country in a diplomatic bag. After the war he published selections of sermons (e.g. The Silence of God, The Final Dereliction), in which he delivered a prophetic message for an apocalyptic situation. His academic programme, apart from some early works, began with the many volumes of the Theological Ethics, available in three volumes in English. The three volumes of The Evangelical Faith developed his dogmatic thinking, and Modern Faith and Thought offered a commentary on recent theological history, especially in Germany. Among works designed for more general readers The Hidden Question of God, Living with Death, and an essay in anthropology* entitled Being Human – Becoming Human, deserve special mention. Reminiscences (Zu Gast auf einem schönen Stern) provide valuable insights into his life, thought, and times.

As a preacher Thielicke addressed the deep questions of life that emerge in days of crisis. His response to them was to press through to the final issues of human nature and destiny that lie behind immediate problems. He thus reformulated the questions, so as to point to the higher divine purpose fulfilled in Christ. Proclamation of the word of Christ forms the church's primary task, in the discharge of which preachers* tread a fine line between irrelevance and false accommodation. They best achieve this by combining expository and topical material and relying on the self-evident truth of the message as it is applied by the Spirit. The issues raised in the crises of life include many ethical* problems, e.g. lying to protect victims of persecution, political assassination, and the new questions of sex and medicine (see Bioethics*). Tackling such issues first in his scholarly work, Thielicke laid bare the theological truths which underlie their solution, namely, creation* in God's image,* the fall, the relation of indicative and imperative in the new life, the role of natural

law,* the tension of law and gospel,* the question of compromise in living the Christian life in a fallen world, and the continuing need for forgiveness as we are righteous in hope (spe) but sinners in fact (re).

Discussion of ethical problems brought Thielicke to the heart of the gospel, and in The Evangelical Faith he explored God's answer to the plight of human alienation which comes to expression in the modern cleavage of the religious and the secular. God himself initiates restoration by accepting solidarity with us in Christ and bringing us to new life through the Spirit. Utopias hold out only false promises, and social reconstruction is impossible without individual renewal. Yet the new aeon has dawned, advance is thus possible, and by God's action, mediated by the word and Spirit, the race may again become, and be, human, notwithstanding every threat. Participating in this mediation is the church's first responsibility; on its fulfilment depends the church's life or death.

Readers may often find Thielicke wordy, repetitive, and provocative, and at times obscure. Yet for those who use discernment he makes a notable contribution to preaching, ethics, and dogmatics.* He raises crucial issues, displays their final significance as he pushes through them to the issue of God, and indicates their one authentic solution in the work that God has done, and does, through Christ and the Spirit.

Bibliography

G. W. Bromiley, 'Helmut Thielicke', in D. G. Peerman and M. E. Marty (eds.), A Handbook of Christian Theologians (Nashville, TN, ²1984).

G.W.B.

THIRTY-NINE ARTICLES, see Confessions of Faith.

THOMAS AQUINAS (1225–74). The greatest of the 13th-century scholastic theologians, known both for his theological and philosophical work, Aquinas was born the son of the Count of Aquino at Roccasecca, near Naples. As a young man he joined the Dominicans,* a new mendicant order, in spite of strong opposition from his family who wanted him to become a traditional Benedictine* monk. The Dominicans emphasized both a return to the gospel and academic learning, for their mission was to preach and hear confessions. Aquinas was immediately sent to the University of Paris to study. He spent the rest of his life teaching theology, at Paris (1256–59 and 1269–72), Rome, Naples, and Viterbo.

The major problem facing the 13th century was that of dealing with the recently rediscovered thought of Aristotle.* Aristotle gave a much richer account of the natural world than the West had yet known; but as interpreted by Arab commentators, he also held positions opposed to Christianity, such as the eternity of the world and the existence of one agent intellect for all. Some theologians responded by rejecting Aristotle completely; others accepted him uncritically, holding that what is true in philosophy does not always agree with what is true in theology. By contrast, Aquinas welcomed what was true in Aristotle but systematically revised what he found to be inadequate or in error. Since all truth is from God, it is one. In principle there can be no conflict between faith and reason.* Where Aquinas found conflict, he sought to show that it was because of errors in human understanding.

With regard to the eternity of the world, Aquinas argues that reason cannot prove that the world is eternal, but the fact that it has a beginning and will end is known from revelation.* On the issue of personal immortality,* Aquinas deepens Aristotle's psychology significantly, showing how man (see Anthropology*) is a single substance composed of matter and form, but his form is immaterial and so immortal. On this basis he attacked the view that there is only one soul for all people, the interpretation of Aristotle given by Averroes* and his followers. At the same time Aquinas was modifying the traditional anthropology in the Christian West, which, following Augustine,* had tended to be dualistic. Because Aquinas adapted Aristotelian methods and principles in organizing theology, he was looked upon, and even opposed, as an innovator.

Like other scholastic theologians, Aquinas began his career by writing a commentary on Peter Lombard's* Sentences. Because of opposition to his order at Paris his licence to teach was delayed, but was soon granted on order from the pope. Throughout his career Aquinas gave lectures on Scripture to students. Some of these have come down to us in the form of commentaries. Better known are his 'disputed questions', On Truth, On the Power of God, On Evil, On Spiritual Creatures, and On the Soul, which are the product of university courses and formal disputations. In addition, Aquinas wrote commentaries on works of Boethius* and the Dionysian work, On the Divine Names. His greatest works as a commentator were his commentaries on the major works of Aristotle, including the logical works, Physics, On the Soul, Metaphysics and Ethics. Aquinas is best known, however, for two works produced apart from his teaching, the Summa contra Gentiles and Summa Theologica. The latter, which was intended as a summary of theology for beginners, has three parts: the first contains the doctrine of God* and how things come from God; the second treats how human creatures return to God, dealing first with moral matters in general and then giving a detailed account of the virtues and vices; the third part considers the incarnation* and sacraments.* Aquinas had completed about half of the third part when he stopped writing and died a few months later.

In the Aristotelian account of the sciences, the highest part of philosophy included theology, considering such matters as the first movers. While acknowledging this theology and using some of its results, such as the proofs of God's existence, Aquinas argues nevertheless that there is need for sacred theology in addition to the theology of the philosophers. Sacred theology is based on revelation* and it makes known truths about man's end that cannot be known through reason. In addition, it also reveals truths that reason *can* grasp, because these truths are necessary for salvation;* but through reason only a few could grasp them, and then only after much study and still mixed with many errors.

For Aquinas, sacred theology is a science unlike any other; for while all others are based on human reason, it is based on what God has revealed. A wide variety of matters are considered in sacred theology, but they are all considered from the point of view of being revealed. Because sacred theology is founded on divine knowledge which cannot err, it possesses greater certitude than any science founded on human reason. Nevertheless, because of the weakness of our ability to understand divine things, they may appear doubtful to us, even though they are certain in themselves. Because of its origin in revelation, the strongest argument in this science is to appeal to authority* – the weakest argument in the other sciences. Aquinas denies that it is possible to argue to the articles of faith, which are the principles of this science, but one can answer objections rooted in misunderstanding. It is wrong to try to use reason as a basis for believing, but it is meritorious to try to understand what one has believed (see Faith and Reason*).

In discussing issues, Aquinas consistently employs the works of the fathers and the ancient philosophers, adopting Paul's use of the poets as his model. Thus the best arguments of the philosophers show that there is a first mover, first efficient cause, *etc.*, and Aquinas concludes in each case that this is what everyone understands to be God. Of course, God is much more than just a first mover, so from this beginning Aquinas goes on to show that God is one, good, infinite, eternal, and Trinity.* Similarly with regard to the end of man,* Aquinas accepts the view of the ancient philosophers that man's end is happiness, but he argues that it is to be found only in heaven, in the vision* of God of the blessed. In this life there is only imperfect happiness, which is what the philosophers grasped to a greater or lesser degree. In his discussion of law,* Aquinas argues for a natural law which is in man, a participation in the divine law and a guide for the formation of the laws made by human legislators. The decalogue, as given to the Israelites, is held to be a divinely given formulation of the content of the natural law. For Aquinas, nature* is from God and so is good, but – because of sin* – divine aid is needed in order both to regain the good of nature and to return to God.

Within fifty years of his death, the Dominicans* had adopted Aquinas as the doctor of their order. Centres of Thomistic scholarship have flourished in many countries from the 15th century on. Today he remains the most influential theologian of the medieval church.

Bibliography

Works: *Summa contra Gentiles*, tr. A. C. Pegis *et al.*, *On the Truth of the Catholic Faith*, 5 vols. (Garden City, NY, 1955–57); repr. as *Summa . . .* (Notre Dame, IN, 1975);

Summa theologica, ET in 59 vols + index (London, 1964–81).

Studies: M. D. Chenu, *Toward Understanding St Thomas* (Chicago, 1964); E. Gilson, *Le Thomisme* (Paris, 61965); R. McInery, *St Thomas Aquinas* (Boston, 1977); F. van Steenberghen, *Thomas Aquinas and Radical Aristotelianism* (Washington, DC, 1980); A. Vos, *Aquinas, Calvin and Contemporary Protestant Thought* (Grand Rapids, MI, 1985); J. A. Weisheipl, OP, *Friar Thomas D'Aquino* (Garden City, NY, 1974). See also Bibliography under Thomism.

A.V.

THOMISM AND NEO-THOMISM.
Thomism is the theological tradition which springs from Thomas Aquinas* and his followers.

1. Aquinas' theological views

The wide-ranging writings of Aquinas covered the whole gamut of Christian thought.

*a. Faith and reason.** Like Augustine,* Aquinas based faith in God's revelation in Scripture. Support for faith was found in miracles and rational arguments. Aquinas presented 'five ways' to prove the existence of God (*Summa*, I:2:3). Since he believed sin obscures human ability to know, however, belief (not proof) is necessary for most. While belief is never *based* on reason, nonetheless believers should reason *about* and *for* their faith. Aquinas' reasons for belief that God existed were spelled out in his famous 'five ways'. He argued 1. from motion to an unmoved mover, 2. from effects to a first cause, 3. from contingent beings to a necessary being, 4. from degrees of perfection to a most perfect being, and 5. from design to a designer. In addition to truths which are in 'accord with reason', there are some (*e.g.*, Trinity,* Incarnation*) which go 'beyond reason' and can be known only by faith.

*b. Epistemology.** Thomas held that all knowledge begins in experience. There is nothing in the mind which was not first in the senses, except the mind itself. For we are born with an *a priori*, innate capacity to know. All knowledge is dependent on first principles, such as 1. identity (being is being), 2. noncontradiction (being is not non-being), 3. excluded middle (either being or non-being), 4. causality (non-being cannot cause being), and 5. finality (every being acts for an end). Once these principles are properly known they are seen to be self-evident, or reducible to the self-evident.

c. Metaphysics.* It is the task of the wise person to know order. The order reason discerns in its own acts is *logic*. The order it produces in acts of will is *ethics*. The order produced by reason in external things is art. But the order reason contemplates but does not produce, is *nature*. Nature contemplated as sensible is called *physical science*. Nature understood, in so far as it is quantifiable, is *mathematics*. And nature viewed in so far as it is being is *metaphysics*.

The most important affirmation of Thomas' metaphysics is: 'Act in the order in which it is act is unlimited and unique, unless it is conjoined with passive potency.' Only God is pure actuality. All creatures are composed of actuality and potentiality. God has no form, but is pure actuality. Angels are completely actualized potencies (pure form). And the human being is a composition of form (soul) and matter (body) with progressive actualization.

d. God.* God alone is pure Existence (the 'I Am'). He *is* Being; everything else *has* being. God's essence is to exist. He is a Necessary Being. All else is contingent. God cannot change since he has no potentiality for change. Likewise, since time involves change (from a before to an after), God is a-temporal or eternal. God is simple (indivisible) since he has no principle (potency) for division. He is also infinite (not-finite), having no potency to limit him. Besides these metaphysical attributes, God is also morally perfect (just, good) and infinitely wise.

e. Religious language.* Our language about God is analogous (see Analogy*). It cannot be univocal, since God's knowledge is unlimited and ours is limited. Neither can it be equivocal; since creation must resemble the creator, the effect is like its efficient cause (*cf.* Ps. 19:1; Rom. 1:19–20). Nonetheless, there are great differences between an infinite God and finite humanity. Hence, the way of negation (*via negativa*; see Apophatic Theology*) is necessary. We can apply to God only the perfection signified (*e.g.*, goodness, truth), but we must negate the finite mode of signification by which these perfections are found in creatures.

f. Creation.* God created out of nothing (*ex nihilo*). An eternal creation is logically possible, because there is no logical contradiction in a cause causing from eternity. Nonetheless, by revelation we know that the universe began. No time existed before creation. God did not create *in* time; rather, there was a creation *of* time with the world.

g. Humanity. Following Aristotle, Aquinas held that the human being (see Anthropology*) is a hylomorphic unity of body and soul. Despite this unity of soul-body there is no identity between them. Rather, the soul survives death and awaits reunion with the body at the resurrection. God creates directly each individual human soul in its mother's womb (see Soul, Origin of*).

h. Ethics. There are first principles not only of thought, but also of action (called laws*). Eternal law is the plan by which God governs all creation. Natural law is the participation of rational creatures in this eternal law. Human law is the application of natural law to local communities. And divine law is the revelation of God's law through the Scriptures and the church.

There are two types of virtue: natural and supernatural. The former are the classic virtues of prudence, justice, courage, and temperance. The latter are faith, hope, and love.

2. Thomism and Neo-Thomism

Thomism is a movement which follows the thought originating with Thomas Aquinas. Upon his death, his teachings were adopted by various individuals, most notably by his Dominican* brothers. Several propositions of Aquinas were condemned by church authorities in 1277, but primarily due to Dominican* efforts his system was eventually established. Aquinas was canonized in 1323.

Thomists used an Aristotelian* mode of thought and expression, in contrast to Franciscans* who were more Platonic.* This led to lively debates between the orders through the ages.

A central figure in developing Thomism was Thomas de Vio Cardinal Cajetan (1469–1534) who opposed Luther.* Cajetan held several distinctive interpretations of Aquinas. Notable is his view that analogy is best understood as the possession of an attribute by two essences, rather than properly by only one. He also thought more in terms of abstract essences than existing substances. Finally, he raised doubts concerning the provability of God's existence and man's immortality.

By the 16th century Thomism became the leading school of Catholic thought. The Jesuit* order (approved in 1540) aligned itself with Aquinas and in many of its pronouncements the Council* of Trent consciously expressed itself in Thomistic phrases. In the 17th century John of St Thomas (1589–1644) was a major representative of Thomism. But it became ingrown in the 18th century and faded. Thomism experienced a revival in the 19th century, however, due largely to its emphasis on human dignity in the face of the Industrial Revolution. By the time of Vatican I (1869–70), Thomism was again in vogue and triumphed in 1879 when Pope Leo XIII, in *Aeterni Patris*, gave official recommendation to it, which gave impetus to a movement known as Neo-Thomism.

Neo-Thomism is a 20th-century revival of Thomistic thought. Two main groups emerged. 1. The Transcendental Thomists, such as Joseph Maréchal (1878–1944), Bernard Lonergan,* and Karl Rahner,* adapted Thomism to Kantian* thought. 2. Others under the leadership of Reginald Garrigou-Lagrange (1877–1964), Etienne Gilson,* and Jacques Maritain (1882–1973) sought to expound Aquinas himself. Thomism crossed denominational lines and included Anglicans such as E. L. Mascall (b. 1905) and even many non-Catholics.

The distinctive teaching of Neo-Thomism is the maxim that 'existence precedes essence'. By this it is meant that one knows by intuition *that* something exists before one knows *what* it is. For this reason Maritain claimed that Thomism is the origination of existentialism.*

The Neo-Thomist tradition is carried on by notables such as Frederick Copleston (b. 1907) in Great Britain, Joseph Owens (b. 1908) in Canada, and James Collins (b. 1917) and Vernon Bourke (b. 1907) in the United States.

Bibliography

V. J. Bourke, *Thomistic Bibliography: 1920–40* (St Louis, MO, 1945); T. L. Miethe and V. J. Bourke, *Thomistic Bibliography: 1940–78* (Westport, CN, and London, 1980). F. Copleston, *Aquinas* (Harmondsworth, 1955); K. Foster, *The Life of St Thomas Aquinas: Biographical Documents* (London and Baltimore, MD, 1959); E. Gilson, *The Christian Philosophy of St Thomas Aquinas* (New York, 1956); M. Grabmann, *The Interior Life of St Thomas Aquinas* (Milwaukee, WI, 1951); J. Maritain, *Distinguish to Unite, or the Degrees of Knowledge* (New York, 1959); *idem, Scholasticism and Politics* (London, ²1945); A. Walz, *Saint Thomas Aquinas, a Biographical Study* (Westminster, MD, 1951). See also Bibliography under Thomas Aquinas.

N.L.G.

THORNTON, L. S., see ANGLO-CATHOLIC THEOLOGY.

THORNWELL, JAMES HENLEY (1812–62), eminent theologian, teacher, minister within the Presbyterian Church in the United States (PCUSA), and one of the founders of the Presbyterian Church in the Confederate States of America (1861). As a minister he served at Lancaster, SC (1835–38) and Columbia, SC (1840–41; 1855–61). In 1847 the General Assembly elected him as moderator, the youngest man ever to be so elected. From 1841 to 1851 he was professor at South Carolina College, and its president 1852–55. He taught didactic and polemic theology at the seminary in Columbia, SC, 1855–62. Thornwell was a strong and able defender of the Westminister standards. His polemical ability arose from a passion for truth rather than native pugnacity.

Before the PCUSA divided between North and South, the most severe conflict engaged in by Thornwell was with Charles Hodge.* The conflict culminated with an encounter in 1860, at Rochester, New York, on the issue of the administration of missions. The issue expanded into concerns over the nature of Presbyterianism,* with special reference to the importance of the regulative and constitutive principles of Scripture, the legitimacy of virtually autonomous boards for the support of benevolent activities, and whether a ruling elder is to be considered a presbyter. Thornwell contended that church government* was no less a matter of revelation than doctrine. Hodge argued that the details of the system were not given in Scripture. Thornwell contended that committees of the presbytery, rather than boards, should control church benevolences; Hodge saw nothing unscriptural in boards. Thornwell saw ruling elders as full presbyters, acting for the church in the courts, while he felt Hodge's theory distinguished too radically between clergy and laity* and created a hierarchy.

Concerning the most volatile issue of his day, slavery,* Thornwell believed that from a study of the biblical material one could not conclude that slavery *per se* was immoral. Moreover, it had become so highly politicized that he defended the justness of the Confederate cause and supported the separation of Southern churches to serve the new nation.

Bibliography

The Collected Writings of James Henley Thornwell, 4 vols. (New York, 1871–72; repr. Edinburgh, 1986); E. B. Holifield, *The Gentleman Theologians: American Theology in Southern Culture, 1795–1860* (Durham, NC, 1978); B. M. Palmer, *The Life and Letters of James Henley Thornwell* (Richmond, VA, 1875; repr. Edinburgh, 1974); T. W. Rogers, 'James Henley Thornwell', *Journal of Christian Reconstruction* 7 (1980), pp. 175–205; L. G. Whitlock, 'James Henley Thornwell', in D. F. Wells (ed.), *Reformed Theology in America* (Grand Rapids, MI, 1985).

T.J.N.

TILLICH, PAUL (1886-1965). Writing as a philosophical theologian, Tillich sought to mediate between Christian theology and secular thought. He viewed his task as one of apologetics,* provided that we define apologetics in his own way, as an 'answering theology' which is offered on the basis of a shared area of common ground. He studied and subsequently taught in several German universities, and although he emigrated to the United States when Hitler came to power in 1933, his thought remains firmly rooted in German philosophical traditions. He is indebted to the Romantic* movement (*e.g.* to Schleiermacher* and to F. W. J. von Schelling, 1775–1854) but also to the phenomenology* of Edmund Husserl (1859–1938) and Martin Heidegger (1889–1976). He also drew heavily on the psychology of Jung, especially in his work on symbols (*cf.* Depth Psychology;* Psychology of Religion*).

Tillich's major mature work was his three-volume *Systematic Theology* (1951, 1957, 1963). Its central principle is the method of correlation: 'In using the method of corre-lation, systematic theology proceeds in the following way: it makes an analysis of the human situation out of which existential questions arise, and it demonstrates that the symbols used in the Christian message are the answers to these questions' (*Systematic Theology* I, p. 70). Tillich's work is then organized around five major correlations: reason and revelation; being and God; concrete human existence and Christ; life in its ambiguities and the Spirit; the meaning of history and the kingdom of God. Tillich acknowledges that these questions and answers may influence each other in their formulations. For this reason many secular philosophers have expressed suspicions about the genuineness of the 'questions', while many theologians criticize the 'answers' as representing accommodations towards the questions. But Tillich sees his own role as that of a theologian of mediation. He seeks to mediate between theology and philosophy; between religion and culture; between Lutheranism and socialism; between the traditions of Germany and those of America. He insists that no isolated system of doctrine or theology can embrace the whole truth. Fragmentation and compartmentalizing are symbols of the demonic; wholeness points to God.

This is bound up with what Tillich has termed 'the Protestant* principle'. Since no single system of thought can encompass the reality of God, theology can never be final. It must always be in process and correction. God remains above and beyond all formulations in theology, including the formulations of the Bible itself. Pastorally, Tillich sees this principle as a defence against idolatry (see Images*). It is possible to think that we have either found or rejected God, when in reality we have encountered only a reduced image of him. The God who is truly God is ultimate. In Tillich's language, he is 'ultimate concern'. Tillich attempts to argue that an attitude of ultimate concern can have only the Ultimate as its object. 'Ultimate concern' thus has a double meaning, describing both the attitude and the reality to which it is directed. By this means Tillich seeks to replace the traditional criteria of theological content by the test of an attitude of ultimate seriousness. But this double meaning of ultimate concern can seem plausible only within a particular German philosophical tradition.

Theology, Tillich insists, uses the language

of symbol.* Symbols point to that which they symbolize, but they also participate in it in the kind of way that the American flag is said to participate in the dignity of the nation. In particular, Tillich stresses the power of symbols to create or to destroy, to integrate or to fragment. They open up dimensions of reality, but also resonate with the pre-conscious depths of the human mind. Following Jung, Tillich stresses the creative and healing power of symbols which well up from the unconscious. While cognitive statements have the effect of reducing God to 'a' being alongside other beings, Tillich believes that symbols point beyond themselves to God who is the ground of being. Symbols are born and die, as human experience changes. But although he rightly stresses their power, Tillich provides no adequate criterion to test their truth, and his theory of symbols is insufficiently grounded in a comprehensive account of language and meaning.

Bibliography

Main works include: The Courage to Be (New Haven, CN, London, 1953); The Protestant Era (Chicago, 1947); Systematic Theology, 3 vols. (Chicago, 1951, 1957, 1963); Theology of Culture (New York, 1959).

R. C. Crossman (ed.), Paul Tillich: A Comprehensive Bibliography and Keyword Index of Primary and Secondary Writings in English (Metuchen, NJ, 1984).

Critical discussions include: J. L. Adams, Paul Tillich's Philosophy of Culture, Science, and Religion (New York, 1965); D. M. Brown, Ultimate Concern – Tillich in Dialogue (New York, 1965); J. P. Clayton, The Concept of Correlation (Berlin, 1980); K. Hamilton, The System and the Gospel (London, 1963); C. W. Kegley and R. W. Bretall (eds.), The Theology of Paul Tillich (New York, 1952); D. H. Kelsey, The Fabric of Tillich's Theology (New Haven, CT, 1967); W. and M. Pauck, Paul Tillich (New York, 1976); J. Heywood Thomas, Paul Tillich: An Appraisal (London, 1963).

A.C.T.

TIME AND ETERNITY. While the relationship between time and eternity is perhaps not readily recognized as a fundamental issue for theology, what could be more fundamental than God's relatedness to time

and space? Every major doctrine of Christian faith is expressed within the framework of time and eternity.

In the Bible, eternity is not an abstraction or a timeless concept: the Gk. word aiōn is not a non-temporal term but the most comprehensive temporal term. The phrase ho aiōn tōn aiōnōn could be translated 'the age of the ages'. The living God is not non-temporal, but is revealed as active in the flow of man's time. The temporal distinction between God and man is that he is enduring and changeless in time; God possesses lasting time in contrast to man's fleeting and passing time (Ps. 90:1ff.).

The conception of eternity as timelessness was the eventual outcome of the attempt to express Christian truth within the framework of Greek metaphysics.* God's transcendence came to be considered in terms of his absolute otherness to time, ultimately expressed by Kant* in his definition of God as noumenal, an unknowable object of thought. How can such a philosophical abstraction, imprisoned in transcendent otherness, be identified with the living God of the Bible who reveals himself in time and space in Jesus Christ?

For this reason Oscar Cullmann (see Salvation–History*) rejects the abstract Greek conception of eternity, and argues that the biblical understanding of eternity is that of time indefinitely prolonged in endless linear duration. But is the element of duration a sufficient identification of the distinction between eternity and time? Does God's time differ from man's time simply in terms of quantity?

Perhaps the most significant feature of Karl Barth's* treatment of the doctrine of God is his determination to deal exclusively in dynamic rather than static terms. God's transcendence is not his absolute otherness to time and space, but his self-motivated freedom to be immanent to man in time and space. Eternity is not to be conceived negatively as God's timelessness but positively, as God's time, his authentic temporality. This authentic temporality is distinguished from human time not merely by its duration (in contrast to Cullmann) but by what Barth defines as its pure simultaneity. God is not dominated by the succession and division of past, present and future but possesses time in that pure simultaneity in which past, present and future coinhere without the blurring of the distinctions between them. God's constancy does not consist in some abstract immutability, but in his faithfulness in time as the living God. This authentic time of God is the prototype and source of humanly perceived time and, in Jesus Christ, this true time has occurred amidst fallen time as the fulfilment of time. God's eternity is real time in contrast to unreal or fallen human time; God has time, we only experience time in the fleetingness of its distinctions.

Boethius* defined eternity as *interminabilis vitae tota simul et perfecta possessio*, 'the total, simultaneous and complete possession of unlimited life'. Barth accepts this definition, not as a reference to abstract eternity, but specifically as referring to the eternity of the living God, the *possessor interminabilis vitae*, the one who possesses life in freedom. Abstract classical conceptions of timelessness and immutability must be recognized as foreign to faith in the living God of the Bible.

Bibliography
K. Barth, *CD* II. 1, pp. 608ff.; III. 1, pp. 67ff.; III. 2, pp. 437ff.; O. Cullmann, *Christ and Time* (London, 1962); T. F. Torrance, *Space, Time and Incarnation* (London, 1969).

J.E.C.

TOLERATION is the recognition that a community can permit religious pluralism and be enriched. It is a modern idea, and only possible in societies which deny ultimate authority to state or church, cherish the liberty of the individual conscience* to reach different conclusions, and legally uphold freedom of enquiry and speech. The drawing of these boundaries is never completed. Christians with power to persecute have rarely resisted the temptation.

The beginnings of toleration are found in the 16th–18th centuries. These are varied – the desire of Reformation Christians to worship outside Roman Catholicism, unhappiness about intolerance of national churches which led to partial separation of church and state,* pleas of individuals for an end to persecution, development of theories of natural law (see Law*) and personal rights and recognition of the tragic consequences of religious war, which destroyed the foundations of religion and society.

Sebastian Castellio (1515–63) raised important objections against the persecution of heretics such as Servetus, but his pleas fell on deaf ears. Jacobus Acontius (1492–*c.* 1566) sought to undermine intolerance by setting out the basic oneness and simplicity of Christian faith, deploring fierce debates about the fine points of dogma. Arguments* for limited toleration were urged by persecuted Protestants and Roman Catholics alike, but only in Poland and France was this tried, ending in 1660 and 1685 respectively with the expulsion of Protestants from both countries. In Holland, remarkable toleration of variety within Protestantism emerged, and this provided a haven for religious refugees from all over Europe. Thinkers such as Grotius* and Spinoza* gave theological and philosophical justification for this. In England, the rejection of religious unity within the Church of England led to the emergence of Independents, Baptists* and Quakers,* who pleaded for liberty of conscience and religious equality. This was granted in limited form during the Commonwealth and Protectorate and was largely achieved by the early 20th century. The American colonies of Rhode Island and Pennsylvania provided the most remarkable and lasting experiments in toleration, inspired by the convictions of Roger Williams (*c.*1603–83) and William Penn (1644–1718), which ultimately made the USA a haven for religious and political refugees during the 18th and 19th centuries.

Thinkers such as Locke,* Pierre Bayle (1647–1706), Lessing* and J. S. Mill (1806–73) also provided important rational justifications of toleration, far in advance of existing law. This secular approach to toleration gained momentum during the 19th and 20th centuries, when revolutions and political change steadily undermined the coercive power of national churches.

Growing relativism* has increased toleration based on secular assumptions, but contemporary repression of dissent demonstrates how fragile are the intellectual and political foundations of toleration. Developing a positive theology and commitment to toleration, which does justice to the tragedy of the Holocaust,* as the supreme example of Christian intolerance, is an awesome task. Equality before the law is essential, as is legal protection for the religious freedom of ministries and individuals. Toleration, for Christians, must be grounded in creation and redemption. All bear the image of God. That is developed uniquely through Christ's new creation. The gift of inner freedom before God must be complemented by outer freedoms which enhance the potential of others before God.

Bibliography

R. H. Bainton, *The Travail of Religious Liberty* (Philadelphia, 1951); W. K. Jordan, *The Development of Religious Toleration in England*, 4 vols. (London, 1932–40); H. Kamen, *The Rise of Toleration* (London, 1967); E. Käsemann, *Jesus Means Freedom* (London, 1969); J. C. Murray, *The Problem of Religious Freedom* (London, 1969); W. J. Sheils (ed.), *Persecution and Toleration* (Oxford, 1984); P. J. Wogoman, *Protestant Faith and Religious Liberty* (Nashville, TN, 1967).

I.B.

TOLSTOY, LEO (1828–1910),

Russian novelist and social reformer. Early in his life he lost both his parents and was brought up by aunts on the family estate near Tula. A child of the aristocracy, he knew wealth and social prestige from the beginning. He had little interest in university life and withdrew without taking a degree, but he read widely and became absorbed in the social theories of Jean Jacques Rousseau (1712–78). To study educational systems and municipal governments he made trips to Europe in 1857 and 1860. In 1861 he liberated his serfs. The following year he married Sonya (Sofya) Andreyevna Bers, who bore thirteen children.

The appearance of *War and Peace* (1860), one of the great novels of Western literature, brought Tolstoy wide acclaim. *Anna Karenina* (1877) is a masterly study of a strong but unhappy woman. In his fiction Tolstoy stresses the tension between moral restraint and the natural desire to live without the constraints of society. He is a master of large panoramic scenes, character study, and penetrating moral insights.

Fame failed to bring inner peace to Tolstoy, however, and he cast in his lot with the peasants following a mystical experience c. 1880. He disowned his title, quarrelled with the Orthodox Church (which excommunicated him in 1901), and turned over his wealth to his wife and children. Setting out on a journey by rail with his daughter Alexandra, he died *en route*.

With genuine zeal Tolstoy fashioned his own religion, incorporating some Christian elements and urging love and charity toward all mankind. He rejected Christian supernaturalism in favour of an inner power in human nature, and took his basic principles from an adaptation of the Sermon of the Mount, emphasizing especially non-resistance and simplicity of life. His rejection of ecclesiastical and civil authority has been described as 'Christian anarchism'.

See also: RUSSIAN ORTHODOX THEOLOGY.

Bibliography

Several works in ET, *e.g. The Kingdom of God is Within You*, 2 vols. (London, 1894); *My Confession and the Spirit of Christ's Teaching* (London, 1889); *What I Believe* (London, 1885).

A. H. G. Craufurd, *The Religion and Ethics of Tolstoy* (London, 1912); H. Troyat, *Tolstoy* (Garden City, NY, 1967).

P.M.B.

TORRANCE, THOMAS F. (b. 1913)

was born the son of missionary parents in Szechwan, Western China. A. E. Taylor (1869–1945), Norman Kemp Smith (1872–1958) and John Macmurray (1891–1976) were his teachers in philosophy, and he studied theology under H. R. Mackintosh* and Karl Barth.* Torrance was professor of Christian dogmatics at New College, Edinburgh, from 1952 to 1979, a founding editor of the *Scottish Journal of Theology*, and Moderator of the General Assembly of the Church of Scotland in 1976. He was joint editor of the English edition of Barth's *Church Dogmatics* and of a translation of Calvin's NT commentaries, and has published over twenty books.

Torrance's theology, deeply influenced by the Greek fathers (especially Athanasius* and Cyril of Alexandria*), by Calvin,* and by Barth, is strongly Christocentric and Trinitarian. He focuses particularly on the 'vicarious humanity' of Christ, who assumed our fallen humanity precisely in order to redeem and sanctify it. Incarnation* and atonement* are thus inseparable. Salvation pivots on Christ and not on our faith or decision or piety. In Christ, God has acted in 'unconditional grace' objectively completing salvation for all mankind. Yet, for Torrance, this does not imply universalism.*

Torrance's main thinking has been in the area of theological method,* and in the relationship between theology and science.* In his view, much theology (and in particular, biblical criticism*) has become trapped in analytical and dualist* ways of thinking made obsolescent by advances in modern physics. Instead of tearing apart 'self and the world, subject and object, fact and meaning, reality and interpretation', modern science since James Clerk Maxwell (1831–79) and Albert Einstein (1879–1955) works with unitary, integrative, relational modes of thought. Thus, true scientific objectivity lies not in detachment from reality (the object of study), but in a relationship to reality in which our ideas are called in question.

So in theology we begin like any scientist with faith,* which is a fully rational, cognitive, intuitive apprehension of reality. Reality in this case is the Lord God who gave himself in grace to be known in his articulate Word made flesh. God's self-revelation in Jesus is identical with God himself (for the Son is consubstantial with the Father) so that we know God only as we are reconciled to him in Christ.

Like all sciences, theology is distinctive in developing its own peculiar method appropriate to its object, and its own peculiar logic and structures. The great dogmas of the church, particularly the declaration of the Nicene Creed (see Creeds*) that the Son is consubstantial (*homoousios*) with the Father (see Trinity*), are analogous to the great scientific constructs, such as Einstein's theory of relativity. They are open-ended structures of thought giving insight into a reality which greatly and mysteriously transcends our knowing of it.

When theology is vigorously faithful to the truth of God's revelation, it will call in question our culture-bound formulation of doctrine, and is thus bound to be integrative and ecumenical. Not only so, but as integrative modes of thought gain ground, Torrance sees a massive new synthesis emerging in which all scientific endeavour is set in its theological context and man fulfils his God-given role as the 'priest of creation', humbly articulating the mysterious intelligibility of the universe to the praise of the creator.

Bibliography

Works: *Christian Theology and Scientific Culture* (Belfast, 1980); *Divine and Contingent Order* (Oxford, 1981); *God and Rationality* (Oxford, 1971); *The Ground and Grammar of Theology* (Belfast, 1980); *Reality and Evangelical Theology* (Philadelphia, 1982); *Space, Time and Incarnation* (Oxford, 1969); *Space, Time and Resurrection* (Edinburgh, 1976); *Theological Science* (Oxford, 1969); *Theology in Reconciliation* (London, 1975); *Theology in Reconstruction* (London, 1965); *Transformation and Convergence in the Frame of Knowledge* (Belfast, 1984).

Studies: A. I. C. Heron, *A Century of Protestant Theology* (Cambridge, 1980), pp. 209–214; T. A. Langford, *SJT* 25 (1971), pp. 155–170; D. S. Klinefelter, *JR* 53 (1973), pp. 117–135; M. Shuster, *Studia Biblica et Theologica* 3 (1973), pp. 50–56.

T.A.N.

TRADUCIANISM, see Soul, Origin of.

TRANSCENDENCE, see God.

TRANSMIGRATION OF THE SOUL, see Metempsychosis.

TRANSUBSTANTIATION, see Eucharist.

TRENT, COUNCIL OF, see Councils; Reformation, Catholic Counter-; Roman Catholic Theology.

TRINITY. The Christian doctrine of God,* according to which he is three persons (see Hypostasis*) in one substance* or essence. The doctrine of the Trinity is sometimes attacked as being insufficiently monotheistic,* but Christians have always denied this. The doctrine developed in the early church because it was the only way in which the NT witness to Jesus* and to the Holy Spirit* could be adequately accounted for. Far from being a covert invasion by pagan philosophical and religious influences, it would appear that the doctrine of the Trinity has survived against precisely these temptations, which have occasionally threatened to push the church into a practical and even a theoretical unitarianism.*

The appearance of the Trinity in the NT raises the familiar problem of later interpolation, but although this has certainly been the case in 1 Jn. 5:7, it does not appear to be true elsewhere. Even the words of Jesus in Mt. 28:19, though they are frequently attacked as spurious, bear the authentic hallmark of the most primitive Trinitarianism, which was connected with baptism. Similar early Trinitarian theology appears in 2 Cor. 13:14, the famous 'Grace', which is peculiar in that the person of Christ is mentioned first. There are however a large number of indirect references to the Trinity, of which Gal. 4:6 may be cited as perhaps the most primitive. It is also apparent from what is said in Acts 8 and elsewhere, that Trinitarian baptism goes back to the earliest days of the church, when it was felt that baptism in the name of Christ alone was insufficient.

Whether the Trinity appears in any form in the OT has been much debated. Scholars have often noted the apparent personification of the Word and of the Spirit of God, but these are generally believed to fall short of personal existence in the NT sense. Nevertheless it is worth bearing in mind that for many centuries it was believed that the appearance of the three men to Abraham (Gn. 18) was an instance of the epiphany of the Trinity, a view which goes back in part to the pre-Christian exegesis of Philo.*

The main passages of the Bible which have been used in the construction of Trinitarianism are to be found in John's Gospel, especially chs. 14 – 16. Nevertheless, it must be borne in mind that the fathers of the church made great use of the Pauline Epistles as well, so that to erect an opposition between John and Paul on this score is highly misleading.

Trinitarian speculation begins in the 2nd century, with Athenagoras (*fl. c.* 177), who defends the doctrine as an essential part of the church's faith (see Apologists*). It was expounded at length by Tertullian,* who was largely responsible for the method and vocabulary which the Western tradition now uses. Tertullian argued that there was one God, in whom could be found three persons. His thought was influenced by what is known as economic Trinitarianism, the belief that God the Father brought forth his two hands, the Son and the Holy Spirit, to serve as mediators in creating the world. This approach related to the three successive phases of God's dealing with the world from creation onwards. The economy (Gk. *oikonomia; cf.* Eph. 1:10; 3:9) was this ordered plan of God. Human history could be divided into three periods, each of which belonged to a different person of the Godhead. The OT was the age of the Father, the gospel period the age of the Son and the time since Pentecost the age of the Holy Spirit. This view was unsatisfactory because it tied the Trinity to the time and space framework, and because it lent itself to modalism, the belief that the one God appeared to man in three different modes. As creator he appeared as the Father, as redeemer he appeared as the Son and as sanctifier he appeared as the Holy Spirit. These views, which were a form of Monarchianism,* were later attributed, somewhat unfairly, to Sabellius, a 3rd-century heretic, and are now known as Sabellianism.

In reality, Sabellius held a doctrine which was more subtle than this. His view was apparently designed to overcome the objection to modalism, that it made the Father suffer and die on our behalf (patripassianism). Sabellius posited two poles of opposition and attraction in God – the Father and the Son. Both became incarnate in Jesus Christ, but on the cross they separated, as the Son cried out 'My God, my God, why have you forsaken me?' However, the love of the Father could not endure this separation, and so he brought forth the Holy Spirit as a kind of glue, to weld the Son back to him. This teaching appears extraordinarily crude, but it contains elements which returned in later Western Trinitarianism. Chief among these are the link between the Trinity and the atonement, and the tendency to regard the Holy Spirit as in some way impersonal and inferior to the Father and the Son.

Western Trinitarianism was matched by its Eastern rival, which is associated with the name of Origen.* Working quite independently of Tertullian, Origen developed a doctrine of the three *hypostaseis* of Father, Son and Holy Spirit, which were revealed to share the same divine *ousia* (essence). Origen arranged these in hierarchical order, with the Father as God-in-himself (*autotheos*), the Son as his exact image, and the Holy Spirit as the image of the Son. He insisted that this order existed in eternity, so that there could be no question of saying that there had been a time when the Son had not existed. But he also maintained that the Son had always been subordinated to the Father in the celestial hierarchy.

This view was later questioned by Arius,* who argued that a subordinate being could not be co-eternal with the Father, since co-eternity would imply equality. He was countered by Athanasius* and others who replied that the Son was indeed co-eternal with the Father, but not subordinate to him, except in the context of the incarnation. Classical Trinitarianism developed in earnest after the Council of Nicaea (325). There it had been stated that the Son was consubstantial (homoousios) with the Father, but soon afterwards this key term and the doctrine it embodied were widely rejected in favour of compromise formulae, such as homoiousios, 'of a similar substance'. Athanasius, almost alone in the East, but after 339 with the support of the West, battled for an understanding (reflected in homoousios as he read it) which would make the Son numerically identical with the Father. The Son was not to be regarded as a part of God, nor was he a second deity; he was simply God himself, in whom the fullness of divinity dwelt (Col. 2:8) and in whom the Father himself was to be seen (Jn. 14:9). Eventually his viewpoint was secured, but not before controversy had broken out over the Holy Spirit.

This controversy concerned the biblical evidence for the Spirit's divinity. Many assumed that because he did not have a 'personal' name, like the Father and the Son, he must be an inferior being. This was countered first by Athanasius and then by Basil of Caesarea,* who argued at great length that the Holy Spirit was God because Scripture called him the Lord and life-giver, said that he proceeded from the Father (Jn. 15:26), and gave him the honour of being worshipped alongside the Father and Son.

Basil's theology was declared orthodox at the Second Ecumenical Council* (Constantinople, 381), since which time it has been the basis of Trinitarian theology in the Eastern Church. In the West however, there was considerably more speculation, much of it based on Basil's work and associated with the name of Augustine.* Augustine inherited Tertullian's theology, which he explored at length in his masterly work on the Trinity, De Trinitate, composed between 399 and 419.

In this work Augustine developed his doctrine of Trinitarian relations, which was to become a major element of difference between his thought and that of the Cappadocians. The Greeks generally thought in terms of causal origins for the persons of the Trinity. The Father was unbegotten, the Son begotten, and the Holy Spirit proceeding. As a result, unbegottenness, begottenness and procession became the distinguishing marks of the persons in relation to each other.

Augustine did not reject this way of thinking, but modified it considerably. For him, the one primordial God was not the Father, but the Trinity. The different persons found their cause not in some generation or procession, but in an inherently necessary interior relationship with each other. He developed this view by using a number of analogies,* of which the most significant are mind and love. A mind knows itself because it conceives of its own existence; what is more, it must also love its self-conception. A lover cannot love without a beloved, and there is of necessity a love which flows between them but which is not strictly identical with either. From this, Augustine deduced that God, in order to be himself, had to be a Trinity of persons, since otherwise neither his mind nor his love could function.

The implications of this way of thinking were manifold and far-reaching. Causality was eventually replaced altogether by pure relations, existing of necessity in the very being of God. The Holy Spirit was likewise seen to be the fruit of the mutual love of Father and Son, the bond of unity which tied the Trinity together and revealed its essence, which was spirit. This in turn made it necessary for Augustine to affirm that the Spirit proceeded from both the Father and the Son (a Patre Filioque), whereas the Eastern tradition had affirmed a procession from the Father only. This was to provoke great controversy in the Middle Ages, and to contribute to the eventual separation of the Eastern and Western Churches. To this day it remains as a characteristic feature of Augustinian theology.

After Augustine, the West generally accepted his teaching without question, though in practice it was elaborated considerably. The most significant figure in the Middle Ages was Richard of St Victor (d. 1173; see Victorines*). Richard argued for a social Trinity, in which the relationship of the persons was paradigmatic of human society on earth. His views were not given serious consideration until quite recently, but modern research is re-establishing him as a major medieval theologian.

At the Reformation, the traditional Western doctrine was reaffirmed, but John Calvin* began a new development of thought in the work of the different persons. The Cappadocians had stated that the works of the Trinity outside the Godhead (ad extra) were undivided, i.e. the God who created the world was the Trinity. But Calvin, following Anselm,* who had stressed the fact that the atonement was a work of God inside the Trinity (ad intra), said that Christians are admitted, through the Holy Spirit, to participation in the inner life of the Godhead. We are sons of God, not as Christ was, by nature, but by the grace of adoption. As a result of this, the Reformed tradition witnessed an explosion of works dealing with the work of Christ and the work of the Holy Spirit, in a depth which had previously been unknown.

The doctrine of the Trinity suffered eclipse in the deistic* atmosphere of the 18th century, when many theologians became Unitarians.* By the time of Friedrich Schleiermacher* it had become an embarrassment, and the way was open to dismiss it as a philosophical construction by the early church. In the 20th century, however, thanks largely to the work of Karl Barth,* the doctrine of the Trinity is once more at the centre of the church's concerns. Basing himself on the Word of God as the principle of all theology, Barth reworked Augustine, and spoke of a revealer, of the thing revealed, and of revelation as the constituent elements of the Trinity. Like Augustine he was uncomfortable with the term 'person', and for this he has been criticized, especially from the Eastern standpoint.

Barth's revival of Trinitarianism has borne fruit in all the churches, and the classical doctrine has been restated in different ways by Roman Catholics such as Karl Rahner* and Bernard Lonergan,* by Protestants such as Jürgen Moltmann* and Eberhard Jüngel,* and by Orthodox such as Vladimir Lossky (1903–58) and Dumitru Staniloae (b. 1903). There has been intense discussion of the Filioque cause in the context of ecumenical relations, and it seems certain that the doctrine of the Trinity will be explored even further in the near future. Whether this will add anything of permanent value to the traditional deposit, however, remains to be seen.

Bibliography
E. J. Fortman, *The Triune God* (London, 1972); J. Moltmann, *The Trinity and the Kingdom of God* (London, 1981); L. Vischer (ed.), *Spirit of God, Spirit of Christ* (Geneva, 1981); A. Wainwright, *The Trinity in the New Testament* (London, 1962).

G.L.B.

TRITHEISM is the belief that the Trinity is not one God but three. It can arise if the persons of the Trinity are regarded as substantial* beings in their own right, sharing a common divinity only in the sense that people share a common humanity.

Tritheism has never been the official teaching of any church. It is at best an error which some Christians may have fallen into in their attempts to explain the Trinity. Jerome* accused the Greek Church of holding a form of tritheism, on the ground that the Greeks referred to the persons of the Trinity as *hypostaseis*, which he took to mean 'substances'; but he was mistaken in this and had to be corrected. Christians today are sometimes accused of tritheism by Jews, and particularly by Muslims, and also by such sects* as Jehovah's Witnesses, though the accusation has always been strenuously denied and does not in fact reflect any major strand in Christian theology.

Bibliography
J. N. D. Kelly, *Jerome* (London, 1975), pp. 52–55.

G.L.B.

TROELTSCH, ERNST (1865–1923). A wide-ranging scholar who worked in the areas of history, theology, philosophy and sociology, Troeltsch taught theology in the Universities of Bonn (1892) and Heidelberg (1894) and philosophy in the University of Berlin (1915). He was the systematic theologian of the history-of-religions* school, and was chiefly influenced by Kant,* Hegel,* Schleiermacher,* Ritschl* and Dilthey.* His main concern was to deal with the problem of relativism* which arose through the new understanding of history.* He and others were convinced of the influence of culture on the formation of religion, but that discovery threatened the normative nature of moral and religious values and the absoluteness of Christianity.

He first approached the problem in 1902 in *The Absoluteness of Christianity and the History of Religion* and last dealt with it in lectures which he would have delivered in England but for an untimely death. These were subsequently published under the over-generalized title of *Christian Thought: its History and Application* (1923). He both feared and was fascinated by the problem of historical relativism. He tried to resolve the problem by positing that man was irreducibly religious and that religion itself could not be reduced to non-religious factors. He argued for the superiority of the Christian religion on the grounds that it gave the greatest value to human personality through its belief in a personal God and therefore was of a higher form than Eastern religions, which devalued the human personality. He himself became less convinced of the absoluteness of Christianity as his studies progressed, and he became increasingly uneasy about the validity of Christian missions.

He is best remembered for *The Social Teaching of the Christian Churches* (1912, ET, 1931), in which, with massive historical insight, he related the churches' ethics to their cultural situation. He developed the idea that Christianity has three basic organizational orientations, namely church,* sect* and mysticism.* His formulations, which were much influenced by the German sociologist Max Weber,* have had a profound effect on the development of the sociology* of religion.

Troeltsch was a significant churchman of a liberal Protestant persuasion and an active politician, being at one stage a government minister for education. His ideas have recently come back into favour since in many ways they laid the foundations for theologies which believe that man has come of age. For most, however, his answers to the problems of historical relativism are unsatisfactory, not least because they sacrifice much which is essential to Christian faith.

Bibliography

R. H. Bainton, 'Ernst Troeltsch – Thirty Years After', *Theology Today* 8 (1951), pp. 70–96; J. P. Clayton (ed.), *Ernst Troeltsch and the Future of Theology* (Cambridge, 1976); B. A. Reist, *Toward a Theology of Involvement: The Thought of Ernst Troeltsch* (London, 1966).

D.J.T.

TRUTH. In the OT, '*emet* signifies faithfulness, reliability, a moral attribute ascribed both to God (*e.g.* Pss. 86:15; 132:11; Je. 42:5) and to humans (*e.g.* Ex. 18:21; Jos. 24:14). This primary usage underlies the ascription of truth to sayings or teachings (*e.g.* Pss. 15:2, 25:5; Ze. 8:16). The NT *pistos* continues the idea of faithfulness (*e.g.* Mt. 24:45; 1 Cor. 1:9) more explicitly than does *alētheia;* the latter term and its cognates are more frequently applied to reliable sayings and true teachings (*e.g.* Mt. 22:16; Jn. 3:33; 8:44–46). Yet significantly the antithesis of truth is not just error, but a lie or deception (*e.g.* Rom. 1:25; Eph. 4:25; Tit. 1:4). A true statement is not just accurate, eliciting a detached kind of assent: it is reliable, worthy of personal commitment and trust.

Western philosophy has given more attention to truth as a property of statements than to the biblical sense of truth as a personal attribute. This had given rise to an emphasis on objective inquiry and detached assent more than whole-personal trust. Kierkegaard* is the major exception. Resulting from this Western emphasis, truth is usually defined as the correspondence of idea to object, a positive correlation between a proposition and that state of affairs to which it refers. The Enlightenment* therefore brought quasi-scientific expectations for precision and proof to all questions of knowledge and truth. Hegelian* idealists* broke with this tradition, defining truth instead as the coherence of a concept within the over-all concept of Being. From a theistic* standpoint, however, in which an ultimate referent for truth exists in God's perfect knowledge, and in which God transcends the creation he knows to perfection, some kind of correspondence theory seems more appropriate. The biblical emphasis on reliability and trustworthiness should still be distinguished from Enlightenment expectations of precision and personal detachment.

Truth as correspondence stresses the extramental and extra-linguistic reference of what is thought or said. To provide this point of reference for universal (as distinct from particular) truths, the medievals spoke of *ontological* truth: the objective reality of ideal universal archetypes, as distinguished from the particulars which exemplify them (see Platonism*). Thus, to speak of justice or of human nature is to refer to their ideal forms, as in Greek philosophy, rather than to offer empirical generalizations or mental abstractions. The medievals, however, went beyond the Greeks in locating these universals in the mind of God – the ultimate theistic referent for truth.

Three senses of truth result: 1. moral or personal truth; 2. cognitive or propositional truth; 3. ontological truth – the Greek and medieval way of giving universal truths an extra-mental point of reference.

See also: EPISTEMOLOGY.

Bibliography
A. F. Holmes, *All Truth is God's Truth* (Leicester, 1977); R. Nicole, 'The Biblical Concept of Truth', in D. A. Carson and J. D. Woodbridge (eds.), *Scripture and Truth* (Grand Rapids and Leicester, 1983); A. C. Thiselton, *NIDNTT* III, pp. 874–902; G. Quell *et al.*, *TDNT* I, pp. 232–250; Thomas Aquinas, *Summa Theologica* I: 15–17.

A.F.H.

TÜBINGEN SCHOOL. Tübingen is a university town in Württemberg, south Germany. The name 'Tübingen School' refers to a small group of NT scholars who, in the middle years of the 19th century, were associated with Ferdinand Christian Baur (1792–1860), Professor of Theology at the University. Prominent members of the School were Eduard Zeller (1814–1908), Baur's son-in-law, and Albert Schwegler (1819–57). More loosely attached were Albrecht Ritschl,* Adolf Hilgenfeld (1823–1907) and Gustav Volkmar (1809–93).

Although Baur is recognized as head of the school, the significance of the name 'Tübingen' begins with Strauss'* *Life of Jesus*, for it was its appearance in 1835 which caused the name 'Tübingen' to become almost synonymous with 'unbelief'. Henceforward the investigations into the NT by Baur and his disciples were regarded with extreme scepticism by the orthodox, since the non-miraculous theological position of Strauss was maintained by the entire school. 'With a miracle' wrote Baur, 'all explanation and understanding ceases.' This non-miraculous viewpoint may be called the Tübingen *theological*

perspective. From this presupposition, there began a concentrated investigation into the authorship and dating of all the books in the NT.

Within this over-ruling theological perspective there was a more limited *historical* perspective, first developed by Baur during the 1830s. This envisaged the history of the early church as a struggle between two rival parties – the Jewish Christian party led by Peter, and the Gentile Christian led by Paul. For a century these two parties stood over against each other in bitter hostility, and only towards the end of the 2nd century did they become reconciled in a higher irenic and mediating movement in which both were ultimately absorbed. In accordance with this historical perspective all the NT books were now assessed in order to ascertain their 'tendency' (*Tendenz*) – whether Petrine, Pauline or mediating. Once their tendency had been established, their authorship and dating were more accurately determined by fitting the books into the historical framework which Baur had already worked out. Only five books of the NT were regarded as authentic – Romans, 1 and 2 Corinthians, Galatians and the Apocalypse of John. All other books were ascribed to unknown hands, mostly in the 2nd century.

The high-point of the school was reached in 1846 with Schwegler's two-volume work, *The Post-apostolic Age*, which provided a comprehensive portrayal of the school's position. But from the following year the school slowly began to break up, and with Baur's death in 1860 it may be said to have reached its end. Baur's historical perspective gradually revealed itself as untenable; the historical framework into which he fitted his tendencies was based in part on a misunderstanding of the historical evidence. The *Clementine Homilies*, in which Baur perceived a caricature of the apostle Paul in the person of Simon the magician, were composed later (3rd or 4th century) than Baur's 2nd-century estimate, and did not portray Paul in disguise. The investigation of the Ignatian letters (see Apostolic Fathers*) by Theodor Zahn and J. B. Lightfoot in the 1870s drove the final nail into the Tübingen coffin, in that these letters, written by Ignatius in the early 2nd century, revealed no trace of the bitter controversy which Baur had postualted as raging between Jewish and Gentile Christians in Ignatius' day.

Other evidence also disproved the late dating which Baur had assigned to the NT books.

In its influence on NT scholarship the Tübingen School was undoubtedly the most important movement in 19th-century theology, in that non-miraculous presuppositions constituted the basis of its methodology. Prior to 1835, biblical scholarship had examined historical and theological questions under the implicit presupposition of the authenticity and general veracity of the biblical records. With Strauss that theological perspective was completely overturned, in that no miracle was henceforth to be admitted. Christianity in its origin and development was to be regarded as completely *un*supernatural. With Baur this same position was maintained – a non-supernatural theological and historical perspective determined all biblical interpretation.

Bibliography
H. Harris, *The Tübingen School* (Oxford, 1975); P. C. Hodgson, *The Formation of Historical Theology* (New York, 1966); R. Morgan, 'Ferdinand Christian Baur', in N. Smart *et al.* (eds.), *Nineteenth-Century Religious Thought in the West* (Cambridge, 1985), I, chapter 8.

H.H.

TYCONIUS, see DONATISM.

TYNDALE, WILLIAM, see REFORMERS, ENGLISH.

TYPOLOGY, see HERMENEUTICS.

—————U—————

ULTRAMONTANISM, see PAPACY.

UNDERHILL, EVELYN (1875–1941), in private life Mrs Hubert Stuart Moore. She was an Anglo-Catholic* expositor of mysticism (see Mystical Theology*) and Christian spirituality.* In her copious writings, as in her own Christian pilgrimage, she wrestled with the problem of relating personal spiritual experience (which, she believed, underlies every living religion) to the formal theology of the church. Her classic

analytical survey *Mysticism* (London, 1911; [12]1930) presented Christian doctrines as symbolic maps or diagrams of subjective encounters, both individual and corporate, with 'ultimate reality'; but under the influence of the Roman Catholic theologian Baron Friedrich von Hügel* she came to see these doctrines as expressing objective truth about God's historical and ongoing interaction with his creation, and as thereby holding together the experiential, biblical, liturgical and sacramental channels of divine revelation* to which they provide an interpretative key. This position was perhaps most clearly articulated in *Man and the Supernatural* (London, 1927) and *The School of Charity: Meditations on the Christian Creed* (London, 1934), but was also reflected in many other writings of her later years, which culminated in the magisterial study *Worship* (London, 1936). Her thesis that mystical experience and orthodox Christian theology are mutually complementary, together with her tireless ministry as a retreat conductor, spiritual counsellor, religious journalist, public speaker and broadcaster, contributed significantly to the revival of widespread British interest in the interior life of faith during the first half of the 20th century.

Bibliography
C. J. R. Armstrong, *Evelyn Underhill* (Oxford, 1975); L. Barkway, 'Evelyn Underhill in her Writings', in L. Menzies (ed.), *Collected Papers of Evelyn Underhill* (London, 1946), pp. 7–30, repr. in E. Underhill, *The Mount of Purification* (London, 1960), pp. 135–158; M. Cropper, *Evelyn Underhill* (London, 1958); C. Williams (ed.), *The Letters of Evelyn Underhill* (London, 1943).

S.J.S.

UNIFICATION CHURCH, see SECTS.

UNION WITH CHRIST. Christian worship and devotional literature down the ages have rightly and understandably made much of the believer's and the church's union with Jesus Christ. The Christian's knowledge, experience and enjoyment of God are through Christ, his baptism is into Christ, his standing and every blessing are in Christ, and his destiny is with Christ. The church is to be one with her Lord, as he is one with his

Father, and as he calls his followers to be with one another. Different traditions in the church and in Christian theology have concentrated on various strands of this rich theme, which has at least five aspects to it.

1. Incarnational union

The foundation of our union with Christ is his taking of our nature, our flesh, at the incarnation. The Eastern Orthodox* tradition has always stressed that in Christ God becomes one with us in order to make us one with him; he stooped to take our nature, in order that we might be restored to become partakers of his nature. (Sometimes the Orthodox even refer to his 'deifying'* our nature – a phrase somewhat open to misunderstanding.) The theological basis on which this whole process and its interpretation rest is that humanity was made in the image of God,* and that Jesus Christ is the perfect image of the Father, into which image he restores us by his incarnation, passion, *etc.*, and through the Holy Spirit.

2. Covenantal union

The NT takes up the OT theme of the covenant* between God and humanity as the framework within which the Christian's and the church's relationship with God through Christ is understood. Christians are united with him in a covenant relationship grounded on better promises and a surer foundation through Christ's work on our behalf. The marriage picture, used by some OT prophets to describe God's covenant with his people, is taken over in the NT and applied to Christ (the Bridegroom) and the church (his bride). This underlines the nature of the covenant union as one of committed mutual love, respect, trust and faithful allegiance. (Other family-relationship pictures are also used, as father/son, and the older brother and other children.) The Puritans,* among others, especially loved this theme.

Within the general covenant character of God's dealings with man in Christ, one aspect of Paul's teaching, sometimes called *federal union*, has been especially noted and developed within the Reformed* theological tradition. The way in which men and women are dealt with by God 'in Christ' is seen to parallel his dealings with mankind 'in Adam'. He deals with the many through a representative man (or 'federal head') in each case,

imputing Adam's sin to his descendants and Christ's obedience and atonement to his followers (*cf.* Rom. 5:12–21; 1 Cor. 15:45–49), with all that flows from that in both cases. This is part of the meaning of a person's being 'in Christ', or of his union with him. The basis for God's dealing with his people on this representative footing is seen to have been laid in his dealings with humanity in Adam* from the first.

3. Sacramental union

The Catholic tradition has always laid great stress on the sacramental nature and means of initial and continuing union with Christ. In the NT the Christian's incorporation into Christ, by which he or she becomes a member of his body, is through baptism* as the outward sacramental rite of initiation, coupled with repentance and faith in Jesus as Messiah, saviour and Lord as the inner means of appropriation. Baptism in Christ's name speaks of the uniting of those baptized with Jesus Christ, especially in his death, burial and resurrection. Equally the Lord's Supper or holy communion, as the covenant rite or sacrament of continuance in Christ and his body, is designed to help Christians to nurture, deepen and strengthen their relationship or union with Christ, and with one another in him. While not necessarily speaking directly of this sacrament, John 6 stresses in the strongest possible language the necessity of such feeding on Christ. Communion focuses especially on Christ's death as the demonstration of his love and the source of Christians' new life in him.

4. Experiential union

Jesus became man and underwent the full range of human experience in life, death and resurrection, to unite Christian people with him in the full range of his experience, calling and destiny. Having died to sin and the old life of self-centredness with him at Calvary, and risen to a new life with him, Christians share his status, relationship and calling as sons and daughters of God, and are called to suffer with him, to pass through physical death to ultimate physical resurrection, and to reign with him in glory. He has gone as their forerunner into the Father's more immediate presence in heaven, the guarantor of the eventual arrival of all his people there also. His inheritance as man is also theirs. *En route* to that goal, he calls all Christians into progressive conformity to his own image, continually renewing and transforming their characters into God's likeness by the power of his Holy Spirit within, and by the application of God's word to every department of their life. The evangelical and Catholic traditions both make much of this union of calling, standing, experience and destiny. The believer has to enter into, and live out in experience, the position that is now his in Jesus Christ by God's free gift.

5. Spiritual or mystical union

The final important aspect, stressed particularly by the mystical,* pietist* and charismatic traditions within the church, is the Christian's spiritual union with Christ, with whom he who is joined 'is one spirit' (1 Cor. 6:7). This is sometimes called 'mystical union', and is rooted in the mystery of the encounter of the spirit of man and the Spirit of God or of Christ. It originates in a new birth brought about within a person by the Holy Spirit, and centres thereafter on the hidden life of prayer, meditation (based especially on God's word from Scripture), contemplation and worship. The object of such spiritual disciplines is to deepen one's knowledge of the Lord, love-relationship with him and submission of the whole life to him in trust and obedience, knowing that such a submission of love in response to love is the route to true wholeness of spirit and being. Although the Holy Spirit grants various illuminations and experiences on occasion, the Christian must not seek any particular mystical experience for its own sake, nor any special experiences apart from the over-all goals of knowing and delighting in the Lord with his whole being, and of moral conformity to God's will. The ultimate Christian goal of complete union with the Lord, the unclouded vision of God,* has no necessarily 'ecstatic' content in the pagan or occult sense at all, although it will totally satisfy the soul; and it does not involve the loss of individual personal identity in any Buddhist-type absorption into the infinite reality or universal consciousness. Those fully renewed in God's image will enjoy unfettered and unclouded fellowship with him, freed from every delusion of independence which would block the free flow of pure love, truth, trust, co-operative obedience and delight between

themselves, their creator and the other creatures.

Bibliography

L. Berkhof, *Systematic Theology* (Grand Rapids, MI, 1953); D. Guthrie, *New Testament Theology* (Leicester, 1981); J. Murray, *The Epistle to the Romans*, vol. 1 (Grand Rapids, MI, 1959); J. I. Packer, *Knowing God* (London, 1975); J. K. S. Reid, *Our Life in Christ* (Philadelphia, 1963); L. B. Smedes, *Union with Christ* (Grand Rapids, MI, 1983); J. S. Stewart, *A Man in Christ* (London, 1935).

J.P.B.

UNIQUENESS OF CHRIST. It is not in the subjective sense of personal allegiance only that the Christian confesses that 'Jesus is Lord' (1 Cor. 12:3), for he believes that Christ is in fact Lord of the whole world, whether people recognize it or not. It is true, no doubt, that, strictly speaking, every individual is 'unique'; but in the usual sense of the term, 'without like or equal', it is supremely true of Jesus alone.

He was unique in his teaching (with his matchless parables and his intimate knowledge of both God and human nature) and in the influence it has had all down the centuries. He was unique in his life and character, as supremely the 'Man for others', with an infinite compassion for the poor, the outcast and the sinful. And he was unique in the combination of personal humility and gentleness with an authority appropriate to God alone. Of whom else could his most intimate friends testify that 'he committed no sin' (1 Pet. 2:22; *cf.* 1 Jn. 3:5)?

What compelled his followers, however – convinced monotheists* as they were – to feel free to worship him, pray to him and apply to him some of the great monotheistic statements in the OT which originally referred, without doubt, to Israel's covenant God, was his resurrection* from the dead.

This was no resuscitation of a corpse but a transformation of a lifeless human body into a spiritual body. This is clear not only from the accounts of the empty tomb and resurrection appearances recorded in the gospels, but also from the epistles (*cf.* Rom. 6:9; 1 Cor. 15:42–49; Phil. 3:21). It was the fact that God had raised him from the dead which not only proved to them what they had previously believed (that he was the Messiah), but which added a whole new dimension to their view of the very term 'Messiah'.

It was the resurrection, too, which proved to them that his death on the cross 'in weakness' (2 Cor. 13:4) was not that of a martyred reformer but an atoning* sacrifice* for his people's sins. He 'who had no sin' had been 'made sin [or 'a sin-offering'] for us, so that in him we might become the righteousness of God' (2 Cor. 5:21). The fact that 'there was no other good enough to pay the price of sin' is true, but wholly inadequate; for it is unthinkable that God would allow one who was *only* a wonderful human being to bear 'our sins in his body on the tree' (1 Pet. 2:24). Nor would it have been possible for Paul to state that 'God demonstrates his own love for us in this: While we were still sinners Christ died for us' (Rom. 5:8), had there not been a basic identity between the Father who sent and the Son who died.

It is in the light of his life, death and resurrection that we should view his unique birth, or conception. To this the gospels pay unequivocal witness, although it was not, apparently, part of the apostolic 'proclamation'. While it is true that pagan mythology is full of legends of a hero born as the result of intercourse between a god and a human woman, it is equally true that 'the Jewish mind (and Mt. 1 and Lk. 1 are intensely Jewish) would have been revolted by the idea of physical intercourse between a divine being and a woman' (Richardson). Virgin birth is, moreover, undeniably congruous with his pre-existence (Jn. 8:58; 17:5; Phil. 2:6–7).

Bibliography

J. N. D. Anderson, *Christianity and World Religions: The Challenge of Pluralism* (Leicester, 1984); idem, *Jesus Christ: the Witness of History* (Leicester, 1985); S. Neill, *The Supremacy of Jesus* (London, 1984); A. Richardson, 'Virgin Birth', in Richardson (ed.), *A Dictionary of Christian Theology* (London, 1969); W. H. Griffith Thomas, *Christianity is Christ* (London, 1925).

J.N.D.A.

UNITARIANISM. Though Unitarians reject creeds* and have a wide spectrum of beliefs, they stress the oneness of God and deny the divinity of Jesus Christ and the Holy Spirit. They are committed to freedom, reason

and tolerance as the context essential to a religion that is truly personal and social. Organized ecclesiastically only since the Reformation, they have some precursors such as the Monarchians* and Arians.*

Renewed attention to the literal meaning of the Scriptures led scholars such as Juan de Valdés,* Bernardino Ochino* and Michael Servetus (1511–53) to claim that Trinitarian* theology had little biblical foundation. Servetus believed that purging Christiany of such corruptions would complete the restitution of primitive Christianity and hasten the conversion of Jews and Muslims. His views were widely rejected, but his execution in Geneva did nothing to prevent other radicals raising similar issues in Hungary and Poland, where anti-Trinitarian ideas were widely held.

In Holland and England, the influence of Socinianism* and reaction against Calvinist orthodoxy led to important questions being raised about the relation of Scripture and dogma by such distinguished thinkers as Grotius* and John Milton (1608–74). Unitarian ideas were taught by John Biddle (1616–62), but he was severely dealt with by the authorities and died in prison. His concern for purifying doctrine of unbiblical additions went with deep concern for holiness of life. This seriousness was an abiding note of the Unitarian way.

Convictions about the credibility of the doctrine of the Trinity were weakened as many dissenters rejected subscription to creeds and confessions* as unscriptural. In the Church of England, many moved to a loosely 'Arian' position, because, like Samuel Clarke (1675–1729) they could find no scriptural justification for the doctrine of the Trinity. While denial of the Trinity was an offence until 1813, many simply ceased to preach and teach what they did not believe, rather than risk the penalties of public denial. Many Presbyterian congregations in England and Ireland moved steadily away from Westminster orthodoxy into a less dogmatic, more simply biblical Christianity. Richard Price (1723–91) and Joseph Priestley (1733–1804) rejected foundation doctrines such as the divinity of Christ and the inspiration of Scripture. That opened up entrance to new philosphical, scientific and religious ideas, where the authority of reason and experience was given increasing weight.

A different tributary of Unitarianism came

from Theophilus Lindsey (1723–1808), who resigned from the Church of England because of his anxieties about worship being corrupted by pagan philosophical additions. He drew up a new liturgy for his followers, and came to believe that the narratives of Jesus' birth were legendary and that Jesus was fully and solely human. For these early Unitarians worship was to be addressed only to the Father. They reverenced Jesus and underlined his religious authority, but argued that correct understanding of the Scriptures led to a necessary distinction between the Father and Jesus in worship.

As they became more aware of German biblical criticism,* their use of Scripture as authoritative changed. They had to search for a new basis for religious authority. Thomas Belsham (1750–1825) organized the first general Unitarian Society in 1791 and specifically excluded Arians. From this time onwards the term 'Unitarian' developed a more particular ecclesiastical meaning in Britain and more slowly, in the USA, as well as indicating a wide range of theological positions. In England there were two major strands of thinking. One stressed human religion rather than God's reality and was politically radical. The other had mystical tendencies and emphasized the intrinsically divine character of Christianity. James Martineau (1805–1900) was especially important in this area; he did much to deepen the theology and spirituality of Unitarian congregations. Reason's place was one of the distinctive features of Unitarianism by the end of the 19th century. Unitarians found it hard to balance generous fellowship and definite teaching. They were deeply involved in parliamentary and civic reform, social welfare, education, and intellectual life, but in the 20th century their religious influence has steadily waned with the decline of the free churches. Sustaining a distinctive religious community without boundaries has proved an almost impossible task.

Similar trends occurred in the USA, where many Congregational churches moved into a non-dogmatic Arian position, rejecting Calvinistic emphases on original sin, atonement and predestination in favour of convictions about the perfectibility of mankind. The liberalizers won control of Harvard early in the 19th century, and, with leaders like William Ellery Channing (1780–1842), who sought to free Christianity from past corrup-

tions so it could perfect human nature, the movement gathered momentum. More radical leaders such as Theodore Parker (1810–60), who shocked conservative Unitarians by his insistence that Christianity did not depend on the historical existence of Jesus, but on the truth of his teaching, had a powerful influence.

Unitarian views seemed to many educated Americans the growing edge of Protestantism. Convictions about the unipersonality of God were only a part of the movement's appeal. Openness to new knowledge and commitment to social reform helped to Christianize post-revolutionary and scientific optimism in the USA, as well as providing a sympathetic approach to other religions. Their emphasis on Jesus' humanity, and their rejection of traditional soteriology and worship, led to Unitarianism becoming a liberal religion of self-improvement and benevolence, free from credal and ecclesiastical boundaries.

Its influence has declined in the 20th century, as the theistic and biblical heritage has become less formative, and it has been more and more shaped by the American social context. In an increasingly illiberal and pessimistic world, the varied Unitarian message seems increasingly limited culturally. The lack of denominational identity in the Unitarian Universalist Association, formed in 1961, may make survival difficult, for Unitarians have never displayed a strong missionary spirit. Nevertheless, they have played a significant role in the liberalization of Protestant orthodoxies by their approach to revelation, their emphasis on reason and experience, their passion for freedom of theological enquiry and their distrust of human creeds and organization as an adequate context for the best insights of Jesus.

Bibliography
C. G. Bolam et al., The English Presbyterians from Elizabethan Puritanism to Modern Unitarianism (London, 1968); H. McLachlan, The Unitarian Movement (London, 1934); E. M. Wilbur, A History of Unitarianism, 2 vols. (Cambridge, MA, 1946–52); C. Wright, The Liberal Christians (Boston, MA, 1970).

I.B.

UNIVERSALISM. The word 'universalism' has been used in two senses in Christian theology. Of these, the first is generally accepted, and the second usually rejected, in orthodox thinking.

1. In reference to biblical thought, 'universalism' frequently denotes the view, common to OT and NT, that the purposes of God are not limited to any one nation or race, but extend world-wide. Based on monotheism,* this idea comes to expression in the world-wide scope of the promises to Abraham (Gn. 12:3, *etc.*), in the welcome afforded to those coming into the people of God from other nations (Rahab, Ruth, *etc.*), and above all in the frequent prophetic vision of the nations of the world coming within the scope of that salvation planned by God for his people. This last takes two forms in particular. a. The Gentiles will come and worship Israel's God on Mount Zion (Is. 2:1–5, *etc.*). b. Salvation will extend beyond the borders of Israel, out into the pagan world (Mal. 1:11, 14, *etc.*). In the NT this belief in the world-wide scope of salvation comes to expression in the mission to the Gentiles, which Paul bases explicitly on monotheism itself (Rom. 3:27–30; 10:12–13), understood in the light of Christ and the Spirit. The emphasis here is that people from every nation, race, tribe, language (and indeed every moral background) are welcome in the kingdom of God; there is 'neither Jew nor Greek, slave nor free, male or female, for you are all one in Christ Jesus' (Gal. 3:28). The one God has one family. This doctrine has come under attack since the Second World War from those who maintain that God has two covenants,* one for Jews and one (the Christian one) for everybody else, but this position has no basis in Scripture.

2. The second use of the word denotes the belief that all human beings, without exception, will eventually attain salvation. This belief has taken various forms. a. In the patristic period it was maintained by Origen* and others, with varying degrees of certainty, that God would eventually restore the entire created order, including Satan himself, to a perfect state (hence the Gk. *apokatastasis*, 'restoration', is often used to designate this belief). Though this can claim some apparent biblical foundation (*e.g.* Col. 1:18–20), it was seen to be more Platonic* than biblical, and was condemned at the Council of Constantinople in 553.

b. The powerful influence of Augustine* ensured that this form of universalism did not regain popularity until the Reformation,*

when it was embraced by some of the extreme Radical Reformers (see Reformation, Radical*), being condemned again in ch. 17 of the Augsburg Confession.

c. Contemporary universalism stems largely from Schleiermacher* (with some predecessors in the 17th century). He argued i. that the sovereign love of God is bound to save all eventually, and ii. that heaven would be spoilt if its inhabitants were forced to witness the eternal sufferings of the damned. Nineteenth-century English theology debated this topic with some acrimony. Many theologians broke away from the traditional doctrine of hell without forming one consistent alternative, some opting for 'conditional immortality', which avoids Schleiermacher's second argument, others for the idea of a second chance after death, which allows for his first. The notion of continued spiritual growth and development, which has influenced much contemporary universalism, has a good deal in common with the evolutionism of the Romantic* movement. Some universalist groups founded new churches in the 19th century, some of whose members later (1961) joined with Unitarian* groups.

d. In the present century universalism has spread further, partly due to a relaxing of biblical authority. Although, strictly speaking, neither Barth* nor Brunner* taught universalism proper, both held it to be a possibility for which one might hold out hope. Tillich* regarded hell as a symbol which had lost its character of 'eternal damnation'. Recently J. Hick* has argued that only universalism i. makes sense of world-wide suffering and ii. prevents Christianity from becoming triumphalistic in its attitude to other faiths. In some modern Roman Catholic theology the adherents of such faiths are regarded as 'anonymous Christians'* (Rahner*), either despite the fact that they are in error or because their religions are really disguised versions of the truth. In modern universalism appeal is often made to the apparent teaching of such passages as Rom. 11:32, held to be in tension with passages predicting judgment,* and recourse is often had to the idea of the limitless ages of future time, after death, during which the love of God will eventually draw all people freely to accept the proffered salvation. In writers such as Hick the doctrine is allied to a considerable relativizing of traditional Christian claims about, *e.g.* the divinity of Christ.

Arguments which can be marshalled against this second kind of universalism are as follows.

a. The biblical evidence for the certainty of future judgment and condemnation of at least some is extremely strong, strong enough to function as a warning even for professing Christians (1 Cor. 3:12–15; 10:12), and the texts commonly held to teach universalism can be shown to admit of other, more probable, explanations. There is no biblical warrant for the idea of a 'second chance' after death.

b. The second sort of universalism undercuts the first (which is clearly scriptural), in that it makes Christianity one way, one family, among many. This is to compromise Christology,* the doctrine of the Holy Spirit,* and monotheism itself (by providing at best a radically different alternative to biblical monotheism, seeing all the gods worshipped in the world, including the God of Abraham, Isaac and Jacob, the Father of Jesus, as different manifestations of the one god who lies behind all, a view which has some echoes at least of the sin of the golden calf (Ex. 32:4)).

c. The responsibility of human beings to choose to obey their creator God is seriously undercut by universalism. (This is more than simply to say that universalism cuts the nerve of evangelism* and moral exhortation, though that can also be true.) A doctrine of hell can thus be part of an affirmation of God's intention to let his human creatures exercise their human responsibility. Orthodox Christianity need not lapse into the dualism,* rightly rejected in universalism, of seeing hell as a kind of concentration camp in the middle of heaven. To choose that which is not God is to choose that which distorts, fragments and ultimately destroys genuine humanity itself.

d. Universalism, particularly the modern variety, tends to reduce the seriousness of sin.* In a century which continues to witness moral evil of frightening proportions and dimensions, a failure to condemn absolutely would be evidence of basic moral blindness.

e. Although a biblical theology does not forbid the notion that some may worship the true God, and genuinely serve him, without ever hearing the message of the gospel (so, according to some, Rom. 2:14–16), it does not encourage the idea that there will be a large company of such people.

See also: CHRISTIANITY AND OTHER RELIGIONS; ESCHATOLOGY.

Bibliography

R. Bauckham, N. T. Wright *et al.* in *Them* 4:2 (1979), pp. 48–69; J. Hick, *Evil and the God of Love* (London, ²1977); *idem*, *God and the Universe of Faiths* (London, ²1977); *idem*, *Death and Eternal Life* (London, 1976); C. S. Lewis, *The Problem of Pain* (London, 1940); J. A. T. Robinson, *In The End, God* (London, ²1968); G. Rowell, *Hell and the Victorians* (Oxford, 1974); D. P. Walker, *The Decline of Hell* (London, 1964).

N.T.W.

V

VALDES, JUAN DE (*c.* 1498–1541), Spanish Catholic author of evangelical writings. He was born at Cuenca, studied at Alcalá de Henares, corresponded with Erasmus* and became one of Spain's leading Erasmians. Falling foul of the Spanish Inquisition with *Diálogo de Doctrina Cristiana* (1529), he was declared a heretic,* but escaped the consequences by leaving Spain for Rome. Here he found favour with Pope Clement VII and was ordained. On the election in 1534 of Pope Paul III (whom he detested) he settled in Naples, where he remained in communion with the Roman Catholic Church until his death. The unique and deepening spirituality of his later years followed some profound experience when 'Christ was revealed' to him; it is first sensed in *Alfabeto Cristiano* (1536) and fully felt in his commentaries on Scripture (Mt., Rom., 1 Cor., *etc.*). He lived like an other-worldly recluse, yet exerted incalculable influence on a select circle of society ladies, humanists* and distinguished clerics: Pietro Carnesecchi (1508–67), Celio Secundo Curione (1503–69), Marc Antonio Flaminio (d. 1550), Ochino,* Vermigli* and countless others came under the fascination of his teaching. The linchpin of his doctrine was justification* by faith (with a pre-Quaker emphasis on inner light), and he drew on Protestant sources,

703

especially Calvin's *Institutes*. His major work is his *The Hundred and Ten Considerations* (*c.* 1540; ET, Oxford, 1638), of which the Spanish original has not survived.

See also: REFORMATION, CATHOLIC COUNTER-.

Bibliography

J. C. Nieto, *Juan de Valdés and the Origins of the Spanish and Italian Reformation* (Geneva, 1970).

P.M.J.McN.

VAN TIL, CORNELIUS (1895–1987), Reformed theologian and presuppositional apologist. Van Til was born at Grootegast in the Netherlands to a pious Calvinist family, who migrated to the United States in 1905 and became active in the Christian Reformed Church (which was Dutch in origin).

He studied at the Christian Reformed Calvin College and Seminary in Grand Rapids, MI, and continued his education at Princeton Seminary and University. There he studied under Geerhardus Vos,* Casper W. Hodge (1870–1937), Robert Dick Wilson (1856–1930), Oswald T. Allis (1880–1973) and J. Gresham Machen.* At the university, he studied under the personalist idealist philosopher, A. A. Bowman (1883–1936). Also influential in his Princeton training was the biblical and dogmatic theologian B. B. Warfield.*

In 1925, Van Til married Rena Klooster (d. 1978). In 1927, he was ordained and called by the Spring Lake Church of Classis Muskegon in Michigan, his first and only pastorate. Van Til taught apologetics* at Princeton Seminary in 1928, but, along with Wilson, Allis, and Machen, he resigned from the Seminary in 1929 owing to its reorganization under a theologically more liberal board of directors. That same year, Van Til became one of the original professors of the newly organized Westminster Theological Seminary in Philadelphia, which carried on the conservative Reformed tradition of Old Princeton. He remained at Westminster as professor of apologetics until his retirement in 1975. He joined the Orthodox Presbyterian Church soon after its inception in 1936.

From the 1940s until the late 1970s, Van Til was a most prolific writer. His major contribution was in the area of apologetics with particular reference to the foundational questions of introductory theological methodology* and structure. Van Til's distinctive approach is 'presuppositionalism', which may be defined as insistence on an ultimate category of thought or a conceptual framework which one must assume in order to make a sensible interpretation of reality: 'The issue between believers and non-believers in Christian theism cannot be settled by a direct appeal to "facts" or "laws" whose nature and significance is already agreed upon by both parties to the debate. The question is rather as to what is the final reference-point required to make the "facts" and the "laws" intelligible. The question is as to what the "facts" and "laws" really are. Are they what the non-Christian methodology assumes they are? Are they what the Christian theistic methodology presupposes they are?' (*Defense of the Faith*, Philadelphia, ³1967).

Not only to 'prove' biblical Christianity, but to make sense of any fact in the world, Van Til holds that one must presuppose the reality of the 'self-contained' triune God and the self-attesting revelation of the Scriptures. From this basis, the redeemed person then reasons 'analogically',* attempting 'to think God's thoughts after him'. This means humans may know reality truly (for God, in whose image they are created, knows it truly), but not exhaustively (for God is infinite and they are finite).

The presuppositionalist endeavours to convince the unregenerate first by demonstrating that, on unregenerate presuppositions of chance occurrence in an impersonal universe, one cannot account for any sort of order and rationality. Next, he tries to show that life and reality make sense only on the basis of Christian presuppositions.

Van Til vigorously criticized the traditional apologetic approach of both Catholics and Protestants as failing to challenge the non-Christian view of knowledge, as allowing sinners to be judges of ultimate reality, and of arguing merely for the probability of Christianity. He considered himself in the line of Kuyper* and Bavinck* in his presuppositionalism, and opposed the 'evidentialism' of Thomas Aquinas,* Joseph Butler* and Warfield.

Both Van Til's apologetic stance and his stringent critique of Karl Barth* (as a 'new modernist') have created continuing controversy. G. C. Berkouwer,* James Daane (b. 1931), J. W. Montgomery (b. 1931), John Gerstner and others in the evangelical and Reformed traditions have written at length against Van Til's position as lacking in exegesis of Scripture, and as tending to irrationalism, fideism and 'reasoning in a circle'. Other students of Van Til have sought to develop his insights and apply them to theology and ethics.

Bibliography

J. Frame, *Van Til the Theologian* (Phillipsburg, NJ, 1976); E. R. Geehan (ed.), *Jerusalem and Athens* (Nutley, NJ, 1971) – includes bibliography; R. C. Sproul *et al.*, *Classical Apologetics* (Grand Rapids, MI, 1984); D. Vickers, *Cornelius Van Til and the Theologian's Theological Stance* (Wilmington, DE, 1976); W. White, *Van Til, Defender of the Faith* (Nashville, TN, 1979).

D.F.K.

VATICAN COUNCILS, see COUNCILS; PAPACY; ROMAN CATHOLIC THEOLOGY.

VERIFICATION AND FALSIFICATION.

Verification is simply the procedure carried out to determine whether a statement is true or false. The usual tests of a statement's truth are coherence, correspondence with reality, and pragmatism. The coherence view stresses that a statement is true because it fits in or coheres with all other statements. The correspondence theory argues that true statements are those which accurately correspond to or picture reality as it is. The pragmatic theory stresses that what is true is what works in practical terms. In modern philosophy, the logical positivist* school based on the Vienna Circle has produced a programme for verification and falsification.

Logical positivism and empiricism

The positivists, following the empiricist* approach to knowledge, stressed that for any sentence to be meaningful it must express a statement or proposition which is either analytic (true by definition, by necessity, or *a priori*) or empirically verifiable. The empirically verifiable statements were thus *a posteriori*, concerned with contingent facts known only by sense-experience. This division was used by the positivists to dismiss theology and metaphysics as meaningless using the 'verification principle'.

Verification principle (principle of verifiability)

This declared that a statement is meaningful if, and only if, it can be verified by sense-experience. Statements in logic* and mathematics were meaningful on an analytic basis for they were true by definition, though they gave no information about the real world. Statements of science or empirical fact were meaningful, for they could be tested by sense-experience. Statements of ethics and aesthetics were not literally meaningful, but rather expressed feelings, attitudes, taste and one's emotional response. This approach developed in positivism and empiricism the 'emotive' theory of ethics, which suggested that all ethical judgments were expressions of feeling and attempts to arouse similar feelings in others. Statements of metaphysics (*e.g.* about reality or creation) or theology were literally meaningless. They were either expressions of personal taste or nonsensical. They could not be true and were not objective according to the verification principle. Philosophy was no longer to make claims beyond the clearly observable, but only to clarify meaningfulness in the here-and-now realm of scientific fact.

This position seemed to give victory to the empiricist and to dismiss religion's and theology's claims to truth. However, the verification principle was soon seen to have problems. It was debated whether it applied to sentences, statements or propositions and how one separated out these different levels. The status of the principle was highly doubtful. If the verification principle was itself subjected to its own canon, then it failed the test. Thus it was literally meaningless. It could not be argued that the statement was true by definition, for it can be doubted or rejected without contradiction. The positivists tried to safeguard it as a recommendation for action or an assumed first principle, but this smacks of special pleading.

The principle also excluded areas which the positivist/empiricist wanted to include. Historical statements, such as 'Caesar crossed the Rubicon', could not be tested, for they were in the past. Likewise, and more seriously, all claims of a universal form could not be verified. This meant that all statements or general scientific laws could not be totally verified, for we never exhaust all possible sense-experiences and an exception may be waiting in the next sense-experience. Thus in excluding religion, theology and metaphysics, historical and scientific statements were also ruled out.

This led to attempts to adapt the principle from a strong sense of verification to a weaker sense. This argued that a statement is meaningful if, and only if, we know how to verify it by sense-experience *in principle*. This weaker version seemed to pose less of a threat, for as long as some kind of verification was available then this would satisfy the 'in principle' condition.

A. J. Ayer (b. 1910) and R. Carnap (1891–1970) tended to move verification in the direction of testability and confirmability. Karl Popper (b. 1902) stressed falsifiability.

Falsification principle

Following the model of natural science, Popper realized that universal statements could not be verified but could be falsified by counter-examples. Indeed, the natural progression in science was to develop hypotheses with a view to testing them, by attempting to disprove them by one or more negative instances. In a sense, the more falsifiable the hypothesis, the more valuable it is likely to be. If no negative instances are found, then we may have confidence in the truth of the hypothesis. Built into this move is a recognition that both acceptance and rejection of hypotheses are incomplete and provisional. This procedure cannot establish the truth of scientific laws, and says nothing about non-scientific areas such as theology and metaphysics except that they are not science. The most that can be claimed for scientific laws by the method of falsification is probability, which is very far short of the certainty which was the initial aim of the logical positivist and empiricist.

Recent moves

While theology has continued to be attacked and defended on the basis of the verification and falsification principles, modern philosophy has tended to move away from strict verification to a much wider approach to linguistic and conceptual analysis. In philosophy of religion, much has been made of the 'Don't ask for the meaning, ask for the use' approach based on the later Wittgenstein.*

This appears to allow religion and theology to function on their own terms immune from external criteria or criticism. It is within the theological circle that meaning and truth are to be found. The Bible, however, is not afraid of seeing the Christian faith in terms of truth or falsity. Christians make claims for faith and offer evidence in support of their faith. Paul argues that if Christ did not rise from the dead, then Christianity is pointless and Christians are to be pitied. This would be a clear case of falsification. Christians need to develop appropriate criteria for truth and falsity, orthodoxy and heresy,* which will allow truth claims to be made and reinforce the spreading of the gospel and the defence of the faith.

See also: RELIGIOUS LANGUAGE.

Bibliography

A. J. Ayer, *Language, Truth and Logic* (London, ²1946); K. Popper, *Logic of Scientific Discovery* (ET, London, 1959); F. Waismann, 'Verifiability' in A. Flew (ed.), *Logic and Language* (Oxford, 1951); J. Wisdom, *Philosophy and Psycho-analysis* (Oxford, 1953). See also Bibliography for Logical Positivism.

E.D.C.

VERMIGLI, PETER MARTYR (PIETRO MARTIRE) (1499–1562),

Italian Protestant Reformer, was born in Florence and died in Zurich. The son of a shoemaker, he entered the Canons Regular of St Augustine of the Lateran Congregation at Fiesole in 1514 and was professed in 1518. His most formative years (1518–26) were spent at Padua University, where he taught himself Greek and received his doctorate: he later learned Hebrew at Bologna.

While Abbot of S. Pietro ad Aram in Naples (1537–40) he came under the influence of Juan de Valdés,* who taught him the way of God more perfectly. Elected in 1541 Prior of S. Frediano at Lucca, a position of considerable importance, he initiated a series of far-reaching reforms both educational and ecclesiastical; but, called to account for his actions, he chose to renounce his vows and fled to Zurich and the Protestant camp in 1542.

After five years with Bucer* at Strasburg, where he expounded the OT and married an ex-nun from Metz, he was invited to England by Cranmer (see Reformers, English*) in 1547 and was appointed Regius Professor of Divinity at Oxford and a canon of Christ Church. Here his lectures on 1 Corinthians provoked in May 1549 the public disputation on the eucharist described in John Foxe's *Acts and Monuments*. The following year he was involved in the vestiarian controversy. He assisted Cranmer in the revision of the Anglican liturgy (part of the 1552 Communion service is his), the reform of the ecclesiastical laws and the formulation of the Forty-two Articles (the statement on predestination is attributed to him). On Mary's accession he was allowed to return to Strasburg.

In 1556 he was invited to Zurich, where he occupied the chair of Hebrew until his death. His last venture abroad was to attend the Colloquy of Poissy in 1561, when he spoke in Tuscan to persuade his fellow-Florentine, Catherine de Medici.

Vermigli influenced the Reformation's course in ways both hidden and apparent, for unlike most of his exiled compatriots he became, and remained, a bastion of biblical orthodoxy. He was the friend and confidant of Bullinger* and Calvin,* and a father in God to many of the Marian exiles from England – especially John Jewel (1522–77), who lived with him at Strasburg and Zurich. Because of his calm, informed and balanced judgment, his opinion was sought on many issues of the day. The influence he exerted on Queen Elizabeth and the English Reformation settlement is attested but imponderable.

Deeply skilled in the three classical languages, he excelled in patristic* learning, while his Aristotelian* training at Padua made him a formidable controversialist. He was a voluminous writer and erudite exegete, his commentaries on Scripture remaining standard works of Protestant reference for generations. His major contribution to the Reformation was in the arena of eucharistic* doctrine, and his *Defensio* (against Stephen Gardiner) has been judged the weightiest treatise of the era on this subject. Calvin declared that 'the whole [doctrine of the eucharist] was crowned by Peter Martyr, who left nothing more to be done'.

Vermigli taught that a sacrament* is a work of God from beginning to end, and consists of a dynamic *relatio* between two distinct realities rather than a given *quid*. In the eucharist the two realities are the *funda-* *mentum* (the bread and wine on the table) and the *terminus* (the body of Christ in heaven). The sacrament is created by the concurrence of three factors: Christ's historic institution, God's word in consecration, and the Holy Spirit's power in reception. Employing a subtle but consistent distinction, he maintained that the believer truly and spiritually (but not 'really' and corporeally) feeds on Christ's glorified flesh and blood in partaking of the consecrated elements. These suffer no change of *substantia*, yet become, not Christ's body and blood, but the sacrament of his body and blood. The *signa* of bread and wine are raised to the dignity of visible words of God by being transformed into the instrument of the Spirit. But *sacramentum est tantum in usu* ('the sacrament exists only in its use') means that the eucharist is an event that happens rather than an object to be venerated or reserved, and it happens when it is received by faith: hence the *manducatio impiorum* ('eating by the ungodly') is sacramentally a non-event. But for the believer there is a *duplex manducatio* ('twofold eating'): with his mouth he eats the outward symbols, yet by the same act with his spirit he eats the true body of Christ in heaven.

Bibliography

M. W. Anderson, *Peter Martyr, A Reformer in Exile (1542–1562): A Chronology of Biblical Writings in England and Europe* (Nieuwkoop, 1975); S. Corda, *Veritas Sacramenti: A Study in Vermigli's Doctrine of the Lord's Supper* (Zurich, 1975); J. P. Donnelly, *Calvinism and Scholasticism in Vermigli's Doctrine of Man and Grace* (Leiden, 1976); R. M. Kingdon, *The Political Thought of Peter Martyr Vermigli: Selected Texts and Commentary* (Geneva, 1980); J. C. McLelland, *The Visible Words of God: An Exposition of the Sacramental Theology of Peter Martyr Vermigli, AD 1500–1562* (Edinburgh and London, 1957); idem (ed.), *Peter Martyr Vermigli and Italian Reform* (Waterloo, Ontario, 1980); P. M. J. McNair, *Peter Martyr in Italy: An Anatomy of Apostasy* (Oxford, 1967).

P.M.J.McN.

VICTORINES. A 12th-century group of commentators, poets, exegetes and mystical writers who were part of the staff of the Abbey Church of St Victor in the suburbs of Paris. They lived in community and followed a collection of ascetic* instructions attributed to St Augustine.* The school was founded in 1108 by William of Champeaux (c. 1070–1121; teacher of Abelard*), and adopted its own *Book of Rules* under its first abbot Gilduin (1135–53). The Victorines had a widespread influence on communities and monasteries in France, Italy, Germany, England, Denmark and Ireland. Aiming at a balance between monastic life and devotion to scholarship, these priests served the student population of Paris and tried to create a synthesis of the new learning of the medieval schools with the traditional approach of the fathers. These activities, they believed, should find their focus in contemplating and loving God.

The most famous representatives of the school were Adam of St Victor (c. 1110–c. 1180), a lyric poet and liturgist; Hugh of St Victor (c. 1096–1141), a biblical commentator who laid out a method of scriptural study in his *Didascalion;* Richard of St Victor (c. 1123–1173), a spiritual writer who emphasized the mystical meaning of Scripture; and Andrew of Wigmore (d. 1175), an exegete who concentrated on the literal study of the Bible.

Bibliography

F. Copleston, *A History of Philosophy*, vol. 2:1 (Westminster, MD, 1950); J. Leclerq *et al.*, *A History of Christian Spirituality*, vol. 2 (London, 1968); B. Smalley, *The Study of the Bible in the Middle Ages* (Oxford, ²1952).

R.G.C.

VICTORINUS (AFER), CAIUS MARIUS (fl. 350–365) was a Christian Neoplatonist from Africa (hence distinguished as 'Afer'). He became a famous rhetorician in Rome, and as a pagan wrote rhetorical and logical works (mostly lost), including translations of, or commentaries on, Aristotle, Cicero and the Neoplatonists Plotinus and Porphyry (see Aristotelianism;* Platonism*). He was thus an important link between Greek and Latin worlds of thought. His bold conversion to Christianity in mature life (c. 355) later impressed Augustine* (*Confessions* VIII, ii. 3 – v. 10), who had read his Neoplatonic translations. Victorinus lost his professorship under the pagan emperor Julian in 362.

His surviving Christian works comprise three against Arianism* (*To Candidus, on the Generation of the Divine Word*; *Against Arius*; *The Acceptance of Homoousios*), a commentary on Paul's Galatians, Ephesians and Philippians, and a few hymns. He also wrote against Manichaeism* and on Scripture. He was perhaps the first systematic theologian of the Trinity* (*cf.* P. Henry, *JTS*, 1950, pp. 42–55), primarily in metaphysical rather than scriptural terms, and including a 'psychological Trinitarianism' akin to Augustine's. His importance lies in his pioneering Christian–Neoplatonic synthesis, in which he stretched Neoplatonism in an attempt, which was not wholly successful, to accommodate the faith of Nicaea (see Councils*). Despite the obscure complexity of his thought, he blazed the trail for Christian Platonism in the West.

Bibliography

Trinitarian works in *Sources Chrétiennes* 68–69, ET in *FC* 69; Pauline commentary A. Locher (ed.), *Bibliotheca Teubneriana* (Leipzig, 1972) – no ET; R. A. Markus in *CHLGEMP*, pp. 329–340.

D.F.W.

VINCENT OF LERINS, see CATHOLICITY.

VIRGIN BIRTH. In accordance with popular usage, the term 'virgin birth' will be used in this article to refer to the virginal *conception* of Jesus, the belief that he was conceived by the Virgin Mary* without sexual intercourse. There is also, in the Catholic tradition, a later belief that Mary's virginity was physically preserved during the actual birth process – *i.e.* that the hymen was not broken. This belief is found in Leo's* *Tome*, which was officially accepted by the Council of Chalcedon. Today it is questioned by at least some Roman Catholic scholars, such as Karl Rahner.*

The virgin birth is taught clearly in only two NT passages: Mt. 1:18–25 and Lk. 1:26–38. Others are sometimes cited (such as Mk. 6:3; Jn. 1:13 – on which see below; Gal. 4:4) but there is no certain reference to the virgin birth in any of these latter passages. The paucity of references in the NT is sometimes given as an argument against the historicity of the doctrine. But it should be noted that the virgin birth is almost the only point in common between the two infancy narratives, a clear indication that it is based on an earlier, common tradition. It should also be noted that, in view of the gospel record, the alternative to the virgin birth is not a normal birth within wedlock (for which there is *no* evidence) but an illegitimate birth (which seems to be the charge in Jn. 8:41 and which is countered in Mt. 1:18–25).

The virgin birth is common to all mainstream orthodox Christian confessions. In the early church it was questioned only by ebionites (who denied Jesus' deity) and by docetists* (who denied his true humanity). It was included in the early creeds* and is affirmed today in the Apostles' and Nicene Creeds. With the rise of liberal* theology it has increasingly come to be questioned. This is largely because the normative status of Scripture is denied, and sometimes also because the possibility of the miraculous is denied. Because of its inclusion in the creeds and because of confusion between the virgin birth and the incarnation, the doctrine of the virgin birth has often become a central point of controversy. It has thereby been given a prominence out of proportion to its place in the NT or its theological significance.

The NT teaches that Mary remained a virgin 'until she gave birth to a son' (Mt. 1:25). But in the following century the belief emerged that she remained *perpetually* a virgin, that her marriage with Joseph was never consummated. This view was opposed by some – notably Tertullian* and some of the 4th-century opponents of asceticism.* But the dominant majority view in the early church was that Mary remained a perpetual virgin and that Jesus' 'brothers' were either Joseph's children from a previous marriage or Jesus' cousins (Jerome*). This doctrine was not at first opposed by the Reformers. Calvin* reserved judgment on the question and the strongly Protestant Geneva Bible (1560) repeatedly defends the doctrine. But more significant than the numerical support for this belief is the lack of *early* evidence for it and the dogmatic motivation behind it, namely an unbiblical belief that sexual intercourse is defiling.

In the popular mind the virgin birth is often confused with the incarnation. This confusion has been encouraged by some of the literature on the subject. The doctrine of the incarnation states that the eternal Son, the second person of the Trinity, became man. The doctrine of the virgin birth states that this man Jesus did not have a human father. It does *not* state that God was his father. The virgin birth is not to be confused with pagan myths about gods mating with beautiful women. The virgin birth means that Jesus' conception was miraculous, that he had no human father. This is not to be confused with the belief that he was the eternal Son of God become man.

Granted that the virgin birth and the incarnation are distinct, do they logically entail one another? No. The virgin birth does not of itself prove the deity of Christ. Arians* (who deny Christ's deity), adoptionists* (who deny the incarnation) and Muslims have all traditionally believed in the virgin birth. The virgin birth is a supernatural conception which shows Jesus to be someone very special. It does not *prove* his deity. Conversely, while it can be argued that the incarnation required a supernatural birth, this does not necessarily mean a *virgin* birth. Scripture tells that Jesus was as a matter of fact conceived by a virgin. It never tells us that this was the only possible way for him to have been conceived.

What then is the relationship between the virgin birth and the incarnation? The virgin birth is not meant to be a biological explanation of the incarnation. It has sometimes been expounded in such terms, and it is at least partly for that reason that Brunner* and Pannenberg* both rejected the doctrine. The virgin birth is better seen, as by Barth,* as a sign pointing to the incarnation. It is fitting and congruous with the incarnation, to which it bears witness; Jesus' miraculous birth points to the fact that he was a unique person.

The virgin birth is criticized by J. A. T. Robinson,* among others, because it makes Jesus different from us, not truly human. (It is ironical that those who have the most to say about functional Christology often take diametrically opposed positions when it comes to Jesus' *humanity*.) In response, R. F. Aldwinkle has fairly stated that 'it is not the method by which a human being comes to be such which is decisive but the end product itself, namely a human being'. But there is a deeper issue here. The role of Christ requires that there should be both continuity and discontinuity between him and us; that he should be one of us (Heb. 2:10–18) and yet also different from us. Jesus is the second

Adam* – one of the human race, yet inaugurating a new redeemed humanity. The virgin birth points to this combination of continuity and discontinuity.

Traditionally it has often been held that the virgin birth is necessary for the sinlessness* of Jesus Christ. This idea was introduced by some of the early fathers (especially Augustine*) because of their beliefs about original sin.* Augustine held that *lust* is involved in all intercourse in fallen humanity. If this is so, then the virgin birth clearly protects Christ from being the product of sinful activity. But such a theory has no biblical basis. A modern variant of this argument is found in the claim that original sin is transmitted through the male line. This theory serves to explain how the virgin birth exempts Jesus from original sin, but there is no biblical basis for it.

Karl Barth discerned in the virgin birth a denial of humanity's natural capacity for God, a favourite Barthian theme. According to this view, the significance of the virgin birth is the absence not of the sex act or of human lust, but of *active* human participation. Humanity is involved, but only as a 'non-willing, non-achieving, non-creative, non-sovereign, merely ready, merely receptive, virgin human being' (*CD* I.2, p. 191). Men rather than women are the active agents in the history of the world, and therefore the male must be set aside in the conception of Christ. This view is open to various objections. In addition to its sexist overtones, it appears to teach the total depravity of all males! But Barth is not without justice in applying the doctrine of the virgin birth to the realm of grace.

There is a variant reading of Jn. 1:13 which affirms that Christ was 'born not of natural descent, nor of human decision or a husband's will, but born of God'. This is all but universally agreed not to be the original reading, but the verse is not without relevance. It is highly likely that John knew the tradition of the virgin birth and it is possible that he was deliberately drawing a parallel between the virgin birth and regeneration. In conversion, as in the virgin birth, the initiative and the sovereignty lie with God.

Bibliography

T. Boslooper, *The Virgin Birth* (London, 1962); R. E. Brown, *The Virginal Conception and Bodily Resurrection of Jesus* (London, 1974); D. Edwards, *The Virgin Birth in History and Faith* (London, 1943); A. N. S. Lane, 'The Rationale and Significance of the Virgin Birth', *Vox Evangelica* 10 (1977), pp. 48–64; J. G. Machen, *The Virgin Birth of Christ* (London, 1930); H. Von Campenhausen, *The Virgin Birth in the Theology of the Ancient Church* (London, 1964).

A.N.S.L.

VISION OF GOD. The vision of God, also called the beatific vision, is one of the classic theological definitions of the eschatological* goal of humanity.

The idea that the ultimate destiny of the righteous is to see God face to face has its roots in the OT (Ps. 17:15) and was known in intertestamental Judaism (4 Ezra 7:98), whence it was taken up in the NT. It owes something to the oriental court, in which the king was normally inaccessible, but his close personal attendants were privileged to enjoy his immediate presence (Rev. 22:3–4). There is also a contrast between the indirect, fragmentary and obscure knowledge of God which we have in this life, and the direct, clear apprehension of God as he really is, to which we aspire (1 Cor. 13:12). The moral qualifications for enjoying the vision of God are stressed (Mt. 5:8; Heb. 12:15; 1 Jn. 3:3). Finally, the NT belief that the glory of God has been revealed in Christ (Jn. 14:9; 2 Cor. 4:6) makes the revelation of Christ at his parousia the vehicle for the eschatological vision of God (1 Jn. 3:2).

The pagan world into which early Christianity spread also aspired to the vision of God in the form in which this was envisaged in the Platonic* tradition (*cf.* Neoplatonism). This influenced the development of patristic and medieval thinking about the vision of God, with some unfortunate results. Instead of the context of personal fellowship with God in which the biblical notion of the vision belongs, Platonic influences promoted a more purely intellectualist and individualist understanding of the vision, as intellectual contemplation of eternal being, anticipated in this life in solitary mystical* ecstasy. With it came the Greek distinction between contemplation and action, which created a tension in medieval Christianity between the pursuit of the vision of God in the contemplative life, which required withdrawal from society, and the practice of neighbourly love in the active life. The Platonic form of the vision of God also tended to relativize the incarnation. Because the beatific vision was considered simply as the goal of monastic flight from the world, of ascetic discipline and of all-too-Platonic forms of mysticism, the Reformers, followed by most Protestant theology, largely neglected the notion; but in doing so they neglected an important element in the eschatological hope of the NT and lost some of the valuable insights of medieval theology and spirituality.

In medieval Western theology the beatific vision was defined as the direct, intuitive, intellectual vision of the essence of God, whereas the Eastern church denied that God can be seen in his essence (see Eastern Orthodox Theology;* Hesychasm;* Iconoclastic Controversies*). The Council of Vienne (1311–12) and scholastic* theology insisted that the natural powers of the created intellect are incapable of the vision of God, which is a supernatural gift of God's grace to the faithful after death. Controversy over the views of Pope John XXII (1316–34) led to the decree of the Council of Florence (1439) to the effect that the beatific vision is already enjoyed by the redeemed in heaven before the last judgment.

Properly understood, the doctrine of the vision of God teaches that God himself is the ultimate goal of human life, that he will be known by the redeemed in heaven in an immediate relationship involving their whole persons, endlessly satisfying both the love of beauty and the love of truth, the object of all their attention and the source of all their joy. As Augustine (City of God XXII.29) well recognized, the vision of God will not exclude but will include the corporate life of the redeemed and the reality of the new creation; for in the new creation all things and people will reflect God's glory and he will be seen in all.

Bibliography

G. C. Berkouwer, The Return of Christ (Grand Rapids, MI, 1972); A. E. Green, NCE II, pp. 186–93; K. E. Kirk, The Vision of God (London, 1931); V. Lossky, The Vision of God (London, 1963); J. Moltmann, Theology and Joy (London, 1973).

R.J.B.

VOCATION, in the OT a call from God to a selected person or persons, e.g. Abraham, Moses, the prophets, the people of God; in the NT, a call to follow Jesus, or to salvation.

The problem is how to fulfil that call in the world. Luther,* in particular, wrestled with this issue, and rejected three false solutions: 1. the medieval, monastic distinction between precepts (for monks) and counsels (for laity); 2. the sectarian repudiation of law and contracting out of the responsibility of government; 3. the political role of the medieval church as a secularized power structure. He argued for the NT distinction between the kingdom of God* and the kingdom of this world (God and Caesar). In the kingdom of God only faith obtains; in the kingdom of the world, love to neighbour. In the kingdoms of this world God has ordained peace and order, but, because of the sin of man, this rule can be maintained only by the sword. Nevertheless, this rule of force is still a blessing, for it provides the necessary temporal blessings of peace, order and prosperity.

It is precisely in those offices to which a Christian is called in his worldly station, e.g. father, farmer, craftsman, teacher, soldier, judge, mother, milkmaid, that he or she fulfils the Christian vocation, and exercises love to neighbours. It is through these offices that God actually rules his world. Therefore, a Christian has a calling both into the kingdom of God but in the kingdom of the world: he holds them together in their distinctiveness by prayer, wherein God exercises his re-creative power in his world. To confuse these two kingdoms produces the most miserable confusion possible (as the papacy had done; as Zwingli* and the peasants were doing; and as has been done frequently since). Calvin* held a view similar to Luther's (Institutes III.x.6), though some of his followers have modified his theology according to a Zwinglian tendency.

In the usage of the secularized modern world the term 'vocation' has been drained of its theological content and significance, and virtually invalidated.

See also: WORK.

Bibliography

E. G. Rupp, The Righteousness of God (London, 1953); P. Watson, Let God be God (London, 1947); G. Wingren, The Christian's Calling (Philadelphia, 1957).

J.A.

VOLTAIRE (FRANÇOIS-MARIE AROUET) (1694–1778). The 18th century in Europe witnessed the release on a portentous scale of a blistering attack on traditional Christianity and its clerical representatives. Amongst the detractors none was more eloquent than Voltaire. A scintillating writer, able to represent with devastating skill much of his age's hostile discontent with the establishment, he conducted a passionate literary crusade in the cause of justice and humanity against the damaging superstitions and malpractices of the received faith. His authorship was prolific and wide-ranging in style and subject-matter, and its unity can be variously described; but the religious question figures prominently in his productions. He early came under the influence of the English deists,* and this, together with continental sources, abetted the development of his own deism. Voltaire was not a systematic or profound philosopher or theologian; but he was effective enough to enjoy outstanding acclaim as a writer in his native France, and Europe generally, by the end of his turbulent life.

In Voltaire's writings, we meet the standard criticisms made in his day against Christianity's claims to be a revealed religion. The Bible was perceived to contain absurdities, contradictions, errors and immoralities and thus to be a shabby candidate for status as divine revelation.* Its depiction of God, especially in the OT, could be singularly unworthy of the supreme being. Yet Voltaire was neither atheistic* nor merely negative. His God was real, but freed from the tyrannous caprice of his usual representation; the atheistic materialism* of d'Holbach (1723–89) drew forth from Voltaire, late in his life, a defence of theism.* The appropriate substitute for revealed religion was natural religion, whereby the moral virtues of benevolence and fraternal love would resolve many of the social ills generated in Europe by erroneous belief.

However, Voltaire was no shallow optimist. In the wake of the Lisbon earthquake and in the course of the Seven Years War (1756–63), he grappled with the problem of suffering and earthly injustices. *Candide* (1759), his most widely known work, attacks (among other things), the philosophical optimism which holds this to be the best of all possible worlds. Less trenchant and less idealistic,

perhaps, than his contemporary Jean Jacques Rousseau (1712–78), Voltaire was not blinded by the promise of humanity to its perplexities. Ultimately only a vigorous struggle to change the world, not an essay in speculative metaphysics,* would achieve the desired ends.

Voltaire died, as he put it, 'worshipping God, not hating my enemies, loving my friends, detesting superstition'. This endeavour was undertaken resolutely outside the traditional framework. While debate about that framework continues, Voltaire's contribution will be neglected by many, but few who agree with him that 'never will twenty folio volumes produce a revolution; it is the portable little books of thirty sous which are to be feared' will underestimate it.

Bibliography

T. Besterman, *Voltaire* (Oxford, 1976); H. Mason, *Voltaire* (London, 1975); R. Pomeau, *La Religion de Voltaire* (Paris, 1969); N. L. Torrey, *Voltaire and the English Deists* (New Haven, CT, 1930).

S.N.W.

VOLUNTARISM. A theory or doctrine is voluntaristic when it gives explanatory emphasis to the will* at the expense, particularly, of the intellect or of moral character. For example, in discussions of the relation between morality and divine authority, certain writers (*e.g.* Duns Scotus* in the medieval period, and Samuel Rutherford* in the Puritan period), in an effort to do justice, as they see it, to divine sovereignty,* have maintained that a principle is morally good or obligatory simply in virtue of the fact that God has willed it (and not because, say, it accords with God's moral nature). Thus Rutherford held that, had he so willed, God could have pardoned sin without an atonement. In criticism it may be said that such a debate proceeds on too abstract and speculative (and perhaps too anthropomorphic*) a view of the divine nature. A voluntarist account of faith emphasizes the role of free will and of personal trust at the expense of the apprehension of and assent to truth, and is characteristic of Arminianism* but more especially of modern irrationalism.

Voluntarism is to be distinguished from voluntaryism, the idea that the Christian church is distinct from the state and that which church one joins and supports is a matter of personal choice.

Bibliography
Duns Scotus, *The Oxford Commentary on the Four Books of the Sentences*, II.xxxvii, tr. D. J. Walsh, in A. Hyman and J. J. Walsh (eds.), *Philosophy in the Middle Ages* (Indianapolis, IN, 1973); J. Owen, *A Dissertation on Divine Justice* (1653), in *Works*, ed. W. H. Goold (1850–55; repr. London, 1965–68), vol. X; P. Quinn, *Divine Commands and Moral Requirements* (Oxford, 1978).

P.H.

VON HÜGEL, FRIEDRICH (1852– 1925). Baron Friedrich von Hügel was one of the leading Roman Catholic intellectuals of his day and widely influential in cultured religious circles in England, where he settled after 1867. A man of the broadest intellectual interests, embracing philosophy, theology, history, spirituality and science, and of wide religious sympathies with diverse traditions, von Hügel was acquainted with leading thinkers of his day, notably the Roman Catholics George Tyrrell (1861– 1909) and Maurice Blondel (1861–1949), and the Protestant historian and theologian Troeltsch.* He was an early supporter of critical views concerning the OT, and became associated with Roman Catholic modernism* in the early part of the present century, although his own work was not condemned like that of others more central to that movement. His chief literary legacy, apart from a voluminous correspondence with scholars and those seeking spiritual counsel, is his book *The Mystical Element in Religion*, which, through a study of Catherine of Genoa (1447– 1510), argues that the religious life needs to hold together emotional, institutional and intellectual elements. His thought is developed in a number of directions in his once widely known *Essays and Addresses*.

Bibliography
Essays and Addresses (First Series: London, 1921; Second Series: London, 1926); *Eternal Life* (Edinburgh, 1912); *The Mystical Element in Religion* (London, 1908); *The Reality of God* (London, 1931).
L. F. Barmann, *Baron Friedrich von Hügel and the Modernist Crisis* (Cambridge, 1972); M. de la Bedoyère, *The Life of Baron von Hügel* (London, 1951).

J.B.We.

VOS, GEERHARDUS (1862–1947). Born in the Netherlands, Vos was professor of biblical theology, Princeton Theological Seminary, NJ, 1893–1932.

Vos is important for his pioneering work in biblical theology,* based on a conviction of the plenary inspiration and supreme authority of Scripture. He is among the first, and certainly the most gifted, in Protestant orthodox tradition to grasp the fundamental significance of the fact that God's special, redemptive revelation comes as an organically unfolding historical process, and to draw methodological (hermeneutical*) consequences from this fact. A controlling thrust of his life's work is that the Bible is not merely a collection of postulates about God, man, the world, *etc.*, but that post-fall verbal revelation* is a function of redemption; revelation is invariably focused on, and patterned by, the ongoing history of God's redemptive acts which has its centre and consummation in Christ. An important effect of this stress on the historical, covenantal* character of biblical revelation has been to point the way toward maintaining a properly high view of Scripture,* without falling into the unduly intellectualistic understanding of Christian faith which has tended to accompany that view.

Bibliography
R. B. Gaffin, Jr. (ed.), *Redemptive History and Biblical Interpretation: The Shorter Writings of Geerhardus Vos* (Philadelphia, 1980) – contains an account of Vos's life and complete bibliography.

R.B.G.

WALDENSIANS (also called Waldenses or Vaudois), adherents of a 12th-century evangelical movement that began in the context of Catholicism, was rejected by successive popes, became schismatic and suffered severe persecution from church and state both before and after the Reformation. It survives to this day, mainly in the Cottian Alps west of Turin. Similar in style and inspiration to the Franciscan* movement a generation later, it was founded by Peter Waldo, a rich merchant of Lyons who in 1173 was moved by Christ's words in Mt. 19:21 to sell all he had and give to the poor. He caused the Vulgate NT to be translated into the vernacular, and from 1177 gathered round him men and women dedicated to obey and preach the gospel to the letter. Catholics said of them: 'They go about in twos, barefoot, in woollen clothes, owning nothing but holding all things in common like the apostles.'

Banned by Pope Lucius III in 1184 for unauthorized preaching, these 'Poor Men of Lyons' organized themselves into an alternative church that spread widely through Latin Christendom. Ministers (called barbes) were ordained as bishops, priests and deacons with vows of poverty, chastity and obedience. At first they deviated little from Catholic orthodoxy, but later they forbade all swearing and military service, rejected purgatory* and indulgences (see Merit*), requiem masses and works performed by the living for the dead. Yet they kept the seven sacraments of Catholicism, celebrating the eucharist once a year, practising auricular confession, doing penance, and invoking Mary with certain saints. Women preached. Catholic repression was intense: in 1211 alone about eighty men and women disciples were burnt alive in Strasburg.

In their biblicism, their evangelical life-style and their condemnation of the abuses and worldliness of medieval Catholicism they were proto-Protestants, and at Chanforans in 1532 they made common cause with the Reformers, giving up the vestiges of Roman practice and adopting the Genevan doctrine of predestination.* Since then they have remained a Protestant denomination, known in Italy as 'la Chiesa Evangelica Valdese'. After murderous opposition – such as the massacre of 1655 that provoked Milton's sonnet and Cromwell's intervention – they were granted religious freedom in 1848. Today they number about 20,000.

Bibliography

E. Cameron, *The Reformation of the Heretics: the Waldenses of the Alps, 1480–1580* (Oxford, 1984); E. Comba, *History of the Waldenses of Italy, from their Origin to the Reformation* (London, 1889); Th. Kiefner, *Die Waldenser auf ihrem Weg aus dem Val Cluson durch die Schweiz nach Deutschland 1532–1755*, 2 vols. (Göttingen, 1980, 1985); M. D. Lambert, *Medieval Heresy: Popular Movements from Bogomil to Hus* (London, 1977); G. A. Leff, *Heresy in the Later Middle Ages* (Manchester, 1967); *Storia dei Valdesi*: vol. 1, A. Molnar (1176–1532); vol. 2, A. A. Hugon (1532–1848); vol. 3, V. Vinay (1848–1978) (Turin, 1974–80); G. Tourn, *The Waldensians – The First Eight Hundred Years*, ET, Camillo P. Merlino (Turin, 1980); G. B. Watts, *The Waldenses in the New World* (Durham, NC, 1941).

P.M.J.McN.

WAR AND PEACE. One of the great social problems ranking with poverty* and racism (*cf.* Race*), war has evoked a variety of responses from Christians, ranging from non-violent pacifism to the idea of the just war and the concept of the crusade. The reasons for such a variety of opinions include the problem of harmonizing the OT with the NT and the difficulty of applying some of the ethical teachings of Jesus. In the OT many passages endorse armed conflict, such as Dt. 7 and 20 and the war narratives of Joshua, Judges and Samuel. Although these are used by some Christians to justify their participation in war, others point out that Israel* was a theocratic state, and that in NT times there is no state where God is king, but rather that he deals with humanity through an international body, the church,* distinct from any political unit and composed of individuals from all races and nationalities who profess faith in Jesus Christ. Another problem arises, however, over the directions that Jesus gave to his followers. He seems to indicate that they must be non-violent, in such statements as 'But I tell you, Do not resist an evil person. If someone strikes you on the right cheek, turn to him the other also' (Mt. 5:39) and 'But I tell you, Love your enemies and pray for those who persecute you' (Mt. 5:44). Because Christians are citizens of national states in addition to being members of the church, it has seemed to most of them that these words should be interpreted in a way that allows believers to fight for their country.

With these considerations as a basis, it is helpful to consider the reaction of Christians to war and peace during the history of the church. Because of the difficulty in applying the biblical comments about war, some believe that Christians should try to find their model for conduct in the early church. Those who support non-resistance have pointed out that there is no evidence of believers serving in the Roman legions before c. AD 170. The problem is partly a lack of evidence for this early period. The Roman empire did not have universal conscription, and this seems to have resulted in little discussion of the issue. During the closing years of the 2nd century there is evidence of Christians serving in the army, despite the protests of church leaders. The *Apostolic Tradition* of Hippolytus,* a 3rd-century guide for church discipline, indicates that military life might be acceptable if the individual does not kill anyone. This seemingly contradictory statement is explicable in the light of the fact that, during the period of the *Pax Romana* (roughly 30 BC – AD 235), soldiers provided services that are performed by the police and fire departments of modern times. In this era it was possible to serve in the army and not kill anyone.

During the 4th and 5th centuries Roman society was progressively Christianized following the conversion of the emperor Constantine. Eusebius* wrote about Constantine's campaigns as holy wars. The growth in the church made it difficult to maintain pacifism because Christians were no longer a minority in society. Also, the danger posed by the barbarian invasions made defensive war seem necessary. Augustine* led the way in revising Christian attitudes toward war by formulating a series of rules to regulate violence and permit believers to fight for the empire. He combined the OT with the ideas of Aristotle,* Plato* and Cicero into a Christian doctrine of the just war. According to his view, war should have as its goal the establishment of justice and the restoration of peace. It must be fought under the authority of the legitimate ruler and be conducted in a just manner, which included keeping one's promise to the enemy and refraining from looting, massacre and burning, so that noncombatants would not be injured. Also, those engaged in God's service such as monks and priests should be exempt from military service. Despite his grudging acceptance of war there was a genuine respect for pacifism in Augustine's view. His statements on military life are characterized by the same gloom and resignation that pervades his whole outlook on civil government.

It was left to the medieval church to reject pacifism completely, leaving it the view of some minor heretical sects. During this period the majority of theologians supported the ideal of the Christian knight, and religious and military practices were interwoven. The influx of German barbarians into Europe with their martial outlook encouraged the church to adjust to the new situation. This attitude is illustrated in the series of crusades that were launched to free the Holy Land from Islamic control. Beginning in 1095 these campaigns, fought under the auspices of the church for a holy ideal, were characterized by a vicious attitude toward the enemy who were considered to be the representatives of the evil one. Consequently, the counsels of moderation of the just-war theory were suspended, and torture and rapine became the order of the day.

The pacifist, just-war, and crusading interpretations of armed conflict had all been clearly articulated by the close of the Middle Ages and have continued to be followed by Christians in modern times. The Wars of Religion, which accompanied the Reformation, led believers to think once more about issues of war and peace. Generally, the Lutherans* and Anglicans* adopted the Augustinian position of the just war, the Reformed* and many Roman Catholics* felt themselves to be engaged in a crusade, while pacifism was the approach of the Anabaptists* and Quakers.*

With the development of large national armies and the ideology of nationalism during the 19th and 20th centuries, the problem of armed conflict became even more urgent. During this period a number of societies were founded that worked for peace. For example, the Fellowship of Reconciliation, founded in the USA in 1915 as an international pacifist body, continues today its efforts to encourage co-operation and understanding among the nations of the world. The period between the two World Wars also saw a revival of pacifist sentiment both inside and outside the church. Their efforts found expression in the League of Nations (forerunner of the United Nations) and the movement for independence in India led by Mohandas Ghandi. In the years that have followed World War II the balance of terror between the East and West based on nuclear weapons has led many in the Roman Catholic Church and the major Protestant denominations to advocate pacifism, in some cases nuclear pacifism rather than total pacifism. Two examples are Vatican Council II's 'Pastoral Constitution on the World', which recognized pacifism as compatible with Catholic teachings; and the statement of the United Presbyterian Church (USA), 'Peacemaking, the Believer's Calling'.

Bibliography

P. Brock, *Pacifism in Europe to 1914* (Princeton, NJ, 1972); *idem, Twentieth-Century Pacifism* (New York, 1970); C. J. Cadoux, *The Early Christian Attitude to War: A Contribution to the History of Christian Ethics* (London, 1919); R. G. Clouse (ed.), *War – Four Christian Views* (Downers Grove, IL, 1981); P. C. Craigie, *The Problem of War in the Old Testament* (Grand Rapids, MI, 1978); V. Eller, *War and Peace from Genesis to Revelation: King Jesus' Manual of Arms for the Armless* (Scottdale, PA, 1981); J. Ellul, *Violence: Reflections from a Christian Perspective* (New York, 1969); G. F. Hershberger, *War, Peace and Nonresistance* (Scottdale, PA, 1944); A. F. Holmes (ed.), *War and Christian Ethics* (Grand Rapids, MI, 1975); F. D. Kidner, I. H. Marshall, D. F. Wright and G. L. Carey, articles on 'Perspectives on War', in *EQ* 57 (1985), pp. 99–178; G. H. C. Macgregor, *The New Testament Basis of Pacifism* (London, 1958); Reinhold Niebuhr, *Moral Man and Immoral Society: A Study in Ethics and Politics* (New York and London, 1932); G. F. Nuttall, *Christian Pacifism in History* (Oxford, 1958); P. Ramsey, *War and the Christian Conscience: How Shall Modern War be Conducted Justly?* (Durham, NC, 1961); M. Walzer, *Just and Unjust Wars: A Moral Argument with Historical Illustrations* (New York, 1977); R. A. Wells (ed.), *The Wars of America: Christian Views* (Grand Rapids, 1981); J. H. Yoder, *Nevertheless: A Meditation on the Varieties and Shortcomings of Religious Pacifism* (Scottdale, PA, 1971); *idem, The Politics of Jesus* (Grand Rapids, MI, 1972).

R.G.C.

WARFIELD, BENJAMIN BRECKINRIDGE (1851–1921), was the last great theologian of the conservative Presbyterians at Princeton* Theological Seminary, New Jersey. His activity as a theologian coincided with the period when higher-critical views of Scripture* and evolutionary conceptions of religion were replacing evangelical convictions in most of America's major institutions of higher learning. Warfield distinguished himself as a scholarly defender of Augustinian* Calvinism,* supernatural Christianity, and the inspiration of the Bible. Some of his views, especially on biblical inerrancy (see Infallibility*), continue to play an important role among Evangelicals at the end of the 20th century.

Warfield was born into a wealthy Virginia family and received his early education privately. He entered Princeton College in 1868, the year that James McCosh, last of the major proponents of the Scottish philosophy of Common Sense,* began his service as president. Warfield then studied at Princeton Seminary where he came under the influence of the ageing Charles Hodge.* Warfield had pursued scientific interests avidly before deciding to train for the ministry, and he continued to be an eager amateur reader of scientific literature throughout his entire life. Perhaps for this reason, Warfield had less difficulty than many of his evangelical contemporaries in making peace with the scientific aspects of Charles Darwin's evolution (see Creation*). He may also have been helped in this direction by the example of McCosh, who was both a forthright Calvinist and an unembarrassed theistic evolutionist. After graduating from seminary in 1876, Warfield married, travelled in Europe, served a brief pastorate in Baltimore, and was then called to teach NT at a Presbyterian seminary in Allegheny, Pennsylvania. In 1887 he succeeded Archibald Alexander Hodge (1823–86) as Professor of Didactic and Polemic Theology at Princeton.

Unlike several other Princeton theologians, Warfield was not an active churchman. His concerns were almost entirely intellectual and theological. His reserved personality, and perhaps the long years of care for his invalid wife, contributed to what his brother called 'a certain intellectual austerity, a loftiness and aloofness' (Ethelbert Warfield, 'Biographical Sketch', in *Works*, I, p. viii). Throughout his years at Princeton, Warfield wrote an incredible number of essays, reviews, pamphlets, and monographs for both scholars and the laity. (He also regularly published hymns and poetry.) His scholarship was detailed and precise. He laboured to provide accurate summaries of his opponents, but could be astringent in pointing out their errors. Although he probably had the keenest intellect of any Old Princeton theologian, the nature of the times, especially with the growing diversification of academic life, gave his work a somewhat more fragmentary quality than that of his greatest predecessor, Charles Hodge. Warfield's primary contribution lay in three areas: the Bible, Calvinism, and the nature of religious experience.

When higher critical views of Scripture (see Biblical Criticism*) gained popularity in America, Warfield joined with other conservatives to define more exactly the divine inspiration and total truthfulness of Scripture. In 1881 he published with A. A. Hodge a famous essay on 'Inspiration' which set forth his position. Over the centuries, this piece argued, the Bible had received the most convincing demonstrations of its divine origin. The church's historic belief that the letter as well as the spirit of Scripture came from God was still a valid position. In this article, as in several other important essays, Warfield painstakingly investigated the Scriptures' testimony concerning themselves. His conclusion was that when the Bible spoke, God spoke. This 1881 essay placed somewhat greater emphasis on 'proofs' for Scripture than Charles Hodge had usually done, and it made more of the fact that the inspiration of Scripture (and its consequent freedom from error) applied, strictly considered, only to the original autographs of the text. But in general, Warfield was only restating in response to contemporary criticism the kind of confidence in Scripture that had once been commonplace in both Catholic and Protestant circles. In over 100 further writings on Scripture, Warfield drew attention repeatedly to the Bible's testimony about its own authority. He also asserted that terms like 'inerrancy' did not imply a mechanical process of inspiration. Warfield held rather that biblical inspiration involved a process of *concursus* whereby human actions and the working of the Holy Spirit coincided. This meant that historical study of the Bible was appropriate, just so long as such study did not presuppose an exclusively human origin for Scripture.

Warfield's convictions about the Bible had wide currency in his own day and have continued to be studied seriously in the present. Not so well known is his adherence to the theology of the Reformation.* When at the end of the century American Presbyterians debated whether to amend the Westminster Confession (see Confessions;* Reformed Theology*), Warfield responded with a series of careful studies on the meaning of that document. His own opinion never wavered: the Reformers of the 16th and 17th centuries had provided sound guidelines for the church. To tamper with these in favour of modern views of human betterment or divine immanence would be fatal. Warfield penned several careful monographs on the Confession, many penetrating studies of Calvin's thought, and a number of academic treatises on figures in the early church (especially Augustine). All testified to his belief that the theological principles of these earlier periods were fully sufficient for the present. In 1904 he summed up the burden of these historical exercises: 'Calvinism is just religion in its purity. We have only, therefore, to conceive of religion in its purity, and that is Calvinism' (*Selected Shorter Writings*, I, p. 389).

Warfield's convictions on religious experience* were the product of his high view of Scripture and his fervent Calvinism. He saw two major opponents to orthodoxy in his day: the modernism which exalted the spirit of the age over Scripture and over confessional traditions, and the popular piety which treated Jesus as merely a motivational force and the Holy Spirit as a private possession for personal manipulation. Against the first tendency, Warfield tried to rebut efforts at grounding religion in evolutionary optimism or the romantic* sense of the self. Against the latter he wrote tracts decrying the shallowness of modern fundamentalism,* and many works pricking the pretentions of 'perfectionism'.* In all of these efforts, Warfield held to the objectivity of God's work. God had objectively given his word in Scripture. He had objectively given the church as the means to offer grace through preaching, prayer, and the sacraments. Those who relied on inward subjectivity, whether of the right or the left, to find what God had offered objectively were deluding themselves as well as scorning the work of God.

Warfield ranks with his contemporaries, the Dutchmen Herman Bavinck* and Abraham

Kuyper,* and the Scot James Orr,* as the greatest of modern conservative Calvinist theologians. His works are not popular with the theological community at large, nor are they taken too seriously by Evangelicals, except where they refer to Scripture. Yet they remain a reservoir for those who, with Warfield, revere the work of God in Scripture and the history of the church and who value careful intellectual labour applied to an understanding of that work.

Bibliography
The Works of Benjamin B. Warfield, 10 vols. (New York, 1927–32; repr. Grand Rapids, MI, 1981); *Selected Shorter Writings of Benjamin B. Warfield*, ed. J. E. Meeter, 2 vols. (Phillipsburg, NJ, 1970, 1973); J. E. Meeter and R. Nicole, *A Bibliography of Benjamin Breckinridge Warfield 1851–1921* (Nutley, NJ, 1974); J. H. Gerstner, 'Warfield's Case for Biblical Inerrancy', in *God's Inerrant Word*, ed. J. Warwick Montgomery (Minneapolis, MN, 1974); W. A. Hoffecker, 'Benjamin B. Warfield', in *Reformed Theology in America*, ed. D. F. Wells (Grand Rapids, MI, 1985); T. F. Torrance, Review of Warfield's *Inspiration and Authority of the Bible*, *SJT* 7 (1954), pp. 104–108.

M.A.N.

WEALTH, see POVERTY AND WEALTH.

WEBER, MAX (1864–1920), German sociologist who, with Emile Durkheim,* is often called a founder of modern sociology. Bred in the German idealist milieu with its historical emphasis, he was particularly interested in social change and studied religion as a factor in such change. His most famous work in this context was *The Protestant Ethic and the Spirit of Capitalism* (1904–05; ET, London, 1930) in which he argued that the this-worldly asceticism* of Calvinists,* which was a consequence of the doctrine of predestination,* was an important factor in the formation of capitalist societies. This study was explicitly directed against the economic determinism of Marxist* theory and initiated a debate which is not yet finished, particularly since the technological revolution has intensified interest in the Protestant work* ethic.

Weber, however, was not consistent in his opposition to social determinism. In support of his thesis in *The Protestant Ethic*, he engaged in a series of studies of world religions which was left uncompleted when he died. The main contribution of his *Sociology of Religion* (1922) is considered to be the development of a system for classifying different types of religious leader in terms of their social significance, *i.e.* the type of person who would be attracted to a particular type of leader, and the sort of organization established by them. This last facet was developed by Weber's close friend, Ernst Troeltsch.*

Weber's influence is still very apparent in the sociology* of religion, which has persisted with his attempt to establish natural laws in the area of sociology while clinging to belief in human self-determination.

Bibliography
R. Bendix, *Max Weber* (London, 1960); S. Budd, *Sociologists and Religion* (London, 1973); J. Freund, *The Sociology of Max Weber* (London, 1968).

D.A.Hu.

WESLEY, JOHN (1703–91) was born in the rectory of Epworth, Lincolnshire, the fifteenth child of Samuel and Susannah Wesley. Together with his younger brother Charles (the hymnwriter) he gave leadership to the 18th-century Evangelical Revival and particularly to the Methodist* movement.

Wesley was raised in a family with deep religious convictions. His grandfathers had distinguished themselves as Puritan* nonconformists. His father was educated in dissenting academies before deciding to return to the Established Church and attend Exeter College, Oxford. John's mother would have been an exceptional woman in any century.

John left home for school at Charterhouse in London when he was ten years old (1714), and went on to Christ Church, Oxford, in 1720 (BA, 1724; MA, 1727). He did not decide 'to make religion the business of his life' until 1725. This was his religious or moral conversion, and was no less real or important than his evangelical conversion thirteen years later. That same year he was ordained deacon, and the following year was elected fellow of Lincoln College. Through the influence of a 'religious friend' Wesley was guided to the writings of Thomas à Kempis (see Imitation of Christ*), Jeremy Taylor

(1613–67) and later William Law.* In the summer of 1727 he left Oxford to serve as his father's curate in Wroot where he was ordained presbyter in 1728.

In 1729 he returned to Oxford at the request of Lincoln College and soon became spiritual leader of the small group of students his brother Charles had gathered. This band was called the 'Holy Club' by other students; later they were known as 'Methodists'. Together they studied the Greek NT, abridged numerous theological and devotional works, fasted twice a week, partook of the sacrament weekly and regularly visited those sick or imprisoned.

After their father's death in 1735, John and Charles left Oxford for Georgia. The two primary benefits of the brief mission came through contact with the German Moravians and the new practice of giving special religious instruction to small groups of the most committed parishioners (men and women). Shortly after John's return to England in 1738 he met Peter Böhler, a Moravian minister who stressed the importance of justification* by faith alone accompanied by an inner assurance* of salvation and victory over all known sin. Convinced by Böhler's arguments from Scripture, historic Christianity and the experience of several witnesses, Wesley began to seek and to preach justification by faith alone.

On 24 May 1738, at a small Moravian meeting in Aldersgate Street in London, Wesley felt his 'heart strangely warmed' while listening to the reading of Luther's preface to Romans. Modern scholars do not agree as to the exact nature of this evangelical experience, but history attests to the fact that nothing in Wesley was left untouched by it. The warmth of his evangelical experience was united with that of his brother Charles and another member of the Holy Club (George Whitefield*) to produce the flame of the Evangelical Revival and catch the attention of London, Bristol and the press.

The evangelical stress on a personal experience of salvation by faith alone was considered 'new doctrine' and unnecessary by most leaders of the Church of England (who maintained that a person was sufficiently saved by virtue of infant baptism). Established churches were soon closed to the Methodist preachers, forcing them into the open air. In April 1739 George Whitefield invited John to Bristol to organize the multitude of new converts among the Kingswood coal miners into small groups for Christian nurture and discipleship (one of Wesley's great talents).

The centre of Methodist theology was love: the love* of God for all persons and the grace* of God available to all through faith in Jesus Christ alone for salvation.

This view of (prevenient) grace maintained that God reaches out to each person offering a personal relationship and ensuring each one a valid opportunity to respond. Justification or saving faith was also a result of grace. Conversion* was understood as one experience with two inseparable parts: justification, in which the righteousness* of Christ was attributed (or imputed) to the believer; and the new birth or regeneration,* in which the Spirit began to produce (or impart) the righteousness of Christ. Sanctifying grace described the work of the Holy Spirit in the life of the believer between conversion and death. Wesley understood this activity to be both instantaneous and progressive. Because it is a work of grace received by faith alone, sanctification* could be instantaneous. Yet 'entire sanctification' was primarily understood as love for God and others. Therefore, sanctification was the infinite and dynamic love of God at work in a finite believer. In this sense sanctification could never be a static state of 'absolute perfection' (which Wesley always denied) but rather must, in some sense, always be progressive (see Perfection, Perfectionism*).

John Wesley's Methodism was more than just a theology. It was an understanding of the Christian life which stressed a joyful personal relationship with a loving Father. This relationship found expression through worship toward God and loving action toward others. Love for those who were lost meant 'offering them Christ' in evangelism.* Love for the poor meant social concern – homes for widows and orphans, free health clinics, help with food and clothing, schools and Sunday Schools, etc. Love for the newly converted meant provision for discipleship – small nurture groups; opportunities to receive the sacrament of communion when they were excluded from the parish church; books of hymns and sacred poems; Bible study notes; books of prayers; tracts; children's prayers, lessons and hymns; adult Christian literature (both theological and devotional); a monthly

Christian magazine; in all over 400 different publications in his lifetime. Love for others in the Christian community meant honest attempts to put aside prejudice and focus on winning the lost (*e.g.* 'Letter to a Roman Catholic'), along with an ecumenical* willingness to appropriate genuine spiritual contributions from every tradition. Love for all nations caused Wesley to say 'the world is my parish'. His own evangelistic travels took him to Georgia, Germany, Wales, Ireland and Scotland. Wesley sent Methodist preachers to North America from 1769 onward, and, after the war with Britain, ordained them to continue their work on the frontier.

Wesley's personal efforts were formidable. During his fifty-two years as an itinerant he averaged 4,000 miles annually, and preached more than 40,000 sermons in all. Yet the real genius of his work was in his ability to enlist, organize and develop the spiritual talents of others, both men and women. Through a growing structure of small groups, local leaders, and travelling preachers, Wesley was able to maintain both the passion for evangelism and its fruit. He never lost sight of the need to nurture and disciple those newly won to Christ. In a real sense, John Wesley's Methodism was a revival of pastoral care and a product of lay* ministry (both male and female), as well as a response to evangelical theology and preaching. Through Wesley and Methodism, a viable Christian spirituality* was available to the masses of industrial labourers in 18th-century Britain.

See also: METHODISM.

Bibliography
Works: *Journal*, ed. N. Curnock, 8 vols. (London, 1938); *Letters*, ed. J. Telford, 8 vols. (London, 1931); *Sermons*, ed. E. H. Sugden, 2 vols. (London, 1921); *Sermons*, ed. A. C. Outler (Nashville, TN, 1984); *Works*, ed. T. Jackson, 14 vols. (Grand Rapids, MI, 1975); *Works*, ed. F. Baker *et al.* (Oxford, 1975–). *Studies*: V. H. H. Green, *The Young Mr Wesley* (London, 1961); R. P. Heitzenrater, *The Elusive Mr Wesley*, 2 vols. (Nashville, TN, 1984); H. Lindström, *John Wesley and Sanctification* (London, 1946); A. C. Outler (ed.), *John Wesley* (New York, 1964); M. Schmidt, *John Wesley: A Theological Biography*, 2 vols. in 3 (London and Nashville, TN, 1962–73); R. G. Tuttle, *John Wesley, His Life and Theology* (Grand Rapids, MI, 1978); L. Tyerman, *Life and Times of John Wesley*, 3 vols. (London, 1873); C. W. Williams, *John Wesley's Theology Today* (London, 1960).

T.R.A.

WESTCOTT, BROOKE FOSS (1825–1901).

NT scholar and bishop, best known for his partnership at Cambridge (where he was Regius Professor of Divinity from 1870) with J. B. Lightfoot (1828–89) and F. J. A. Hort (1828–92) on a NT commentary based on a reliable Greek text. Although the project was not completed, Hort's introduction to the Westcott and Hort *New Testament in the Original Greek* (1881–2) remains a classic statement of the principles of textual criticism, and Westcott's commentaries on John (1880), the Johannine epistles (1883) and Hebrews (1889) are still valued for their spiritual insight and pioneering application of patristic exegesis, even if the text is sometimes over-translated. (Lightfoot produced his own equally famous commentaries on Galatians (1865), Philippians (1868) and Colossians with Philemon (1875), as well as critical editions of some of the apostolic fathers* – Clement of Rome, Ignatius and Polycarp.)

Less remembered now, but perhaps more significant at the time for the Church of England and the public's perception of her interests, was Westcott's concern for social issues. He was the first president of the Christian Social Union (founded 1889) and, like Lightfoot before him, was called from academic life to be Bishop of Durham (1890–1901). There he used his influence and administrative skills to mediate in the 1892 coal strike and developed an incarnational theology sharing much with the Christian Socialism* of F. D. Maurice in his sermons and addresses around the diocese.

Several of the Bishop Westcott Memorial Lectures deal with aspects of Westcott's thought.

Bibliography
S. Neill, *The Interpretation of the New Testament 1861–1961* (London, 1964); F. Olofsson, *Christus Redemptor et Consummator: A Study in the Theology of B. F. Westcott* (Uppsala, 1979).

P.N.H.

WESTMINSTER CONFESSION, see CONFESSIONS OF FAITH.

WHEATON DECLARATION, THE

was issued by an ecumenical conference of evangelical missionaries who met at Wheaton College in Illinois on 9–16 April 1966. This 'Congress on the Church's Worldwide Mission', called by the Interdenominational Foreign Mission Association and the Evangelical Foreign Missions Association, attracted over 900 missionaries and national leaders, and was the largest evangelical gathering of the kind in North America to that date. The Congress's 'Declaration' called for greater cooperation and for more research about evangelistic work. It also confessed that evangelicals had not applied biblical teaching to many of the great critical issues of the modern world, including race* relations, family* decay, war,* social revolution, and communism (see Marxism*). On directly theological matters, it affirmed that the Bible, 'the only authoritative, inerrant Word of God,' was the proper source of all missionary strategy. It denied that other religions* led truly to God (see Christianity and Other Religions*) while at the same time acknowledging that 'cultural* accretions' sometimes compromised evangelical proclamation of the gospel. It reaffirmed the reality of eternal punishment (see Eschatology*) and repudiated the idea that all people would some day be redeemed (see Universalism*). And it warned about the danger of treating the Roman Catholic Church as a sister church. The Wheaton Congress helped pave the way for even larger international gatherings of evangelicals at Berlin (1966), Lausanne* (1974), and elsewhere.

Bibliography

H. Lindsell, 'Precedent-Setting in Missions Strategy,' *CT*, 29 April (1966), p. 43; 'The Wheaton Declaration', *CT*, 13 May (1966), p. 48.

M.A.N.

WHITEFIELD, GEORGE (1714–70),

English evangelist, was born at Gloucester. While an undergraduate at Oxford he was converted and experienced the call to the ministry of the Church of England. Following his ordination he preached his first sermon and it was said to have driven fifteen hearers mad. Tremendous congregations flooded the churches to hear him, but being denied the constant use of these buildings he resorted to the open air. Needing help, he influenced John (and Charles) Wesley* to undertake the outdoor ministry too. He preached twice and sometimes three times a day and proved able to make himself heard by crowds of 20,000, and this was his manner of life from the age of twenty-two until he died at fifty-five.

He carried his message throughout most of the English-speaking world of that time. Important in this labour were his seven visits to America and fifteen to Scotland, together with his frequent ministry in Wales. He preached repeatedly in almost all the counties of England, founded two large churches in London and ministered regularly to the nobility at the home of Lady Huntingdon. At first he organized his followers into societies, and during his lifetime he was known as 'The leader and founder of Methodism'.*

Whitefield was drawn toward Calvinist* theology even before his conversion and thereafter increased in his understanding of its doctrines. But John Wesley, in addressing a congregation of Whitefield's people, preached a severe sermon against predestination.* He published the sermon and Whitefield produced a reply. He wrote graciously, but Wesley was offended and broke off fellowship. Methodism was thereby divided into two branches, the Calvinistic (see Calvinistic Methodism*) and the Arminian.*

Whitefield sought to effect a reconciliation but soon realized there was little hope of doing so as long as he remained at the head of his branch of the work. He determined to relinquish his leadership and allow Wesley to have first place. To the many who urged him to retain his prominence he replied, 'Let the name of Whitefield perish, but Christ be glorified!' He became 'the servant of all', and throughout the rest of his life he helped any evangelical minister and especially assisted Wesley.

His ministry presents an unparalleled example of declaring the sovereignty of God combined with the free offer of salvation to all who would believe on Christ. A powerful urgency characterized his delivery; he often broke into copious tears as he pleaded with sinners. His major themes were the holiness of God and the sinfulness and helplessness of man, and justification through the atonement of Christ. He was a man of holy life, and as Wesley suggested when preaching at his funeral, history records none 'who called so many myriads of sinners to repentance'.

Bibliography

The Works of the Rev. George Whitefield, 6 vols. (London, 1771); *George Whitefield's Letters* (Edinburgh, 1976).

A. Dallimore, *George Whitefield*, 2 vols. (Edinburgh and Westchester, IL, 1970, 1980); L. Tyerman, *The Life of the Rev. George Whitefield*, 2 vols. (London, 1876).

A.D.

WHITEHEAD, A. N., see PROCESS THEOLOGY.

WILL. It is a fundamental characteristic of human beings that they are capable of taking decisions about what they should do, and of carrying them out. According to Scripture such powers are an important part of the *imago Dei* ('image of God'). But what, more exactly, is the power to decide and how does it relate both to the divine will, and to the effects of sin* and divine grace* upon human nature?

Some have thought that the will is confined to the power to execute what the understanding believes that it is best, in all relevant circumstances, to do. The person expresses such preferences by appropriate mental acts, 'volitions', which bring about physical actions unless prevented by other circumstances, *e.g.* physical weakness or the compulsion of others. While some attribute to the will in this sense the power of acting against the understanding, what is sometimes called the power of contrary choice or the freedom of indifference, others have argued that such a theory is incoherent. Augustine* thought of the will in more dispositional terms, as the metaphysical and ethical directedness of human nature, as a set of preferences which, if not hindered by external factors, will express itself in actions of a certain character.

On either view there is a *prima facie* problem of reconciling the activity of the human will with the divine. Those who have attributed powers of contrary choice or self-determination to the human will have often attempted to effect such a reconciliation by limiting the scope of the divine decree in some

respect, *e.g.* by denying that God *foreordains* all human actions, while allowing that he *foreknows* them (*cf.* Predestination*). Others have rested content with maintaining that while God foreordains all human actions he is not the author of sin; either because, since sin is a deficiency, God cannot be its author, or by holding that since to be free is to do what one wants to do, the occurrence of such wanting guarantees freedom and responsibility, whatever the exact nature and scope of the divine decree.

The question of the effects of sin upon human nature raises moral rather than metaphysical issues (*cf.* Fall*). No-one in the central Christian tradition has asserted that sin changes human nature into a nature of another kind. And yet if human beings are in bondage to sin, and cannot live in such a way as to please God by keeping his law, then divine grace is needed to renew them, and the question arises how divine renewal of such strength and depth can be efficacious if the human will is metaphysically free to resist and to reject it. So how the divine will in its savingly gracious operations harmonizes with the human will is a special case of the more general question of the relation between the human will and the divine will. Even if it is said that such divine grace constitutes a *rescue*, it is still nevertheless a rescue which does not violate the distinctive powers of human nature but rather restores and redirects them. Such radical conclusions have been disputed by adopting less radical views of human need and of the divine provision.

Besides these metaphysical issues the effect of sin on the human will also raises ethical questions, particularly the question whether a person without grace is ethically free.

Discussion is sometimes confused because of a failure to distinguish the moral from the metaphysical dimension; at other times the biblical teaching on the bondage of the will to sin is resisted on the grounds that it is mistaken to make a distinction between the moral and the metaphysical. Rather it is asserted that the power of contrary choice *is* the supreme moral value. But it is clear that according to Scripture redemption in principle secures the restoration of a particular ethical directedness lost at the fall. The freedom* that Christ brought is not so much an increase in the range of possible human powers, as a change in that range through release from the corrupting and enslaving power of sin.

In the history of Christian theology Augustinianism,* both in its pre-Reformation and post-Reformation phases, has equally stressed the all-encompassing nature of the divine decree, and the bondage of the human will (*voluntas*) to sin, while still maintaining that God is not the author of sin, neither is violence done to the human will in gracious conversion. Those who, like Jonathan Edwards,* are in the Augustinian tradition, but who have adopted a non-Augustinian view of the will, have tried not altogether successfully to mitigate the consequences of this position for human responsibility by distinguishing between *moral* and *natural* ability and inability, arguing that while sin disables morally, it does not do so naturally.

One attempt to mediate between Augustinian and Pelagian* conceptions of the will has emphasized the idea of *co-operation* (sometimes called synergism) between the human and the divine will. But such a proposal is inherently unstable, being liable to lapse into a monergism of either the divine or the human will. It is not clear how, metaphysically, such a co-operation could be effected, nor is it easy to see how such a view could do justice to the biblical teaching already noted.

If, on the Augustinian view, the will is wholly dependent on the coming of enlivening grace, could it prepare itself for such a grace (*cf.* Semi-Pelagianism*)? Debate on 'preparationism' has been plagued by unclarity of the central terms. Clearly, no consistent Augustinian could hold that a person might prepare himself to be renewed, for such preparation is encompassed in any renewal. But this is not to say that a person may not, unknowingly, be prepared by grace for conversion, or that he ought to adopt a policy of total passivity when faced with the overtures of the gospel.

Bibliography

Augustine,* *Enchiridion, Free Will,* and other works; D. and R. Basinger (eds.), *Predestination and Free Will: Four Views of Divine Sovereignty and Human Freedom* (Downers Grove, IL, 1986); V. J. Bourke, *Will in Western Thought* (New York, 1964); J. Edwards,* *The Freedom of the Will* (*Works*, vol. 1; New Haven, CN, 1957); J. Ellul,* *The Ethics of Freedom* (London, 1976); A. Farrer,* *The Freedom of the Will* (London, 1958); E. Gilson,* *The Christian Philosophy of St Augustine* (London, 1961); *idem, The Spirit of Medieval Philosophy* (London, 1936); J. N. Lapsley (ed.), *The Concept of Willing* (Nashville, TN, 1967); M. Luther, *The Bondage of the Will,* tr. J. I. Packer and O. R. Johnston (Cambridge, 1957); D. Müller, *NIDNTT* III, pp. 1015–1023.

P.H.

WILLIAM OF OCKHAM, 14th-century scholastic* theologian and philosopher (1280/5–1349). Ockham joined the Franciscan* order and studied at Oxford. Following the usual programme in theology, he first lectured on the Bible and then on the *Sentences* of Peter Lombard* (probably 1317–19). Before he received the licence to teach, charges of heresy were brought against him by the chancellor of his university. Ockham was called to the papal court at Avignon in 1324 to defend himself. Articles of censure were drawn up, but the inquiry was never completed. While at Avignon, Ockham was drawn into his order's dispute with the pope concerning evangelical poverty. In 1328 he fled to Pisa where emperor Lewis of Bavaria, an opponent of the pope, was residing. Excommunicated after leaving Avignon, Ockham stayed at the imperial court for the rest of his life. He died in Munich, probably in the Black Death.

Ockham's flight from Avignon divides his career: before, he was an academic, writing theological and philosophical works; after, he became a polemicist defending his order and the emperor and condemning the pope for heresy and abuse of spiritual power.

The *Commentary on the Sentences* presents the most complete account of Ockham's thought, but he revised and edited only the first book (the *Ordinatio*). The other three books are available only in an unrevised 'report' (*Reportationes*). Also important is the *Summa Logicae,* since it is a more mature expression of his logic.

Ockham is the most important figure in the development of the 'modern way,' the nominalist* or terminist movement, as opposed to the moderate realism of the 'ancient way' represented by such theologians as Bonaventura,* Thomas Aquinas,* and Duns Scotus.* While some interpreters have held that Ockham was a destroyer who upset the careful balance between faith and reason worked out by the earlier schoolmen, other interpreters have seen authentic Christian concern as the source of his position.

The root of his thought is an awareness that everything depends on God* as creator and conserver for both its existence and its place in creation. The logical implications of this dependence are worked out in his teaching that God has the power to conserve, destroy, create separately or differently everything found in experience or held on faith. This does not mean that Ockham distrusts the reliability of nature or God; rather he accepts the regularities of nature and the constancy of moral norms but shows the limitations of natural certainty in the light of God's omnipotence. This opposition to all necessity in creation is a Christian response to a natural determinism* that had become prominent in the arts faculty in Paris around 1270. So for Ockham God is omnipotent and free, able to do everything that does not involve a logical contradiction, and the world is totally contingent.* True statements about finite things are contingent truths dependent on the divine will.

For Ockham, only individuals exist. The immediate awareness of individuals, intuitive knowledge, is the basis of knowledge of individuals. The objects of intuitive knowledge are not limited to material things, for there is intuitive knowledge of acts of desiring and will. Both sense-perception and introspection are sources of natural knowledge of reality. Through generalization other individuals of the same nature can be known, and this is the basis of the knowledge found in universal propositions.

Ockham insists that only propositions in the mode of possibility can be necessary. Hence it is not possible to infer the existence of what is not known, including the existence of God, from what is known. Where prior schoolmen had analysed diverse aspects of being, Ockham replaced such metaphysical* analyses with a logical analysis of the use of terms, their significative or non-significative role in propositions, and connections in arguments. Ockham does not deny the principle of causality or reduce it to the idea of regular sequence, but says we can discover the cause of an event only through experience. In general, Ockham rejects most of the metaphysical teachings of the earlier schoolmen.

In his political tracts, Ockham was mainly concerned with curbing the abuses that stemmed from the pope's claim to absolute power (*plenitudo potestatis*). He did not seek to subordinate either ecclesiastical or temporal power to the other, but wanted freedom from total ecclesiastical power. He sought to achieve this by restricting each power to its own sphere. True spiritual power is displayed in Christ, who renounced all possessions and attempts to make him a temporal king and lived on alms and exercised only a spiritual mission. Ockham made non-involvement in temporal matters the criterion of legitimate spiritual power; the pope errs when he claims temporal power where Christ refused to exercise such authority. Neither the pope, nor civil rulers, nor the clergy alone, but wise men who sincerely love justice and are guided by the gospel are competent to judge what is legitimate for the church.

Bibliography

Works: Philosophical Writings, ed. and tr. P. Boethner, OFM (Nashville, TN, 1957); *Ockham's Theory of Terms: Part I of the Summa Logicae*, tr. M. J. Loux (Notre Dame, IN, 1974); *Ockham's Theory of Propositions: Part II of the Summa Logicae*, tr. A. J. Freddoso and H. Schuurman (Notre Dame, IN, 1980); *Predestination, God's Foreknowledge and Future Contingents*, tr. M. McCord Adams and N. Kretzmann (East Norwalk, CT, 1969).

Standard histories of medieval philosophy contain an introductory account of Ockham's work. See also G. Leff, *William of Ockham* (Manchester, 1975); E. A. Moody, 'William of Ockham' in *EP* 8, pp. 306–317.

A.V.

WILLIAMS, CHARLES WALTER STANSBY (1886–1945), English

novelist, poet, critic, and lay theologian. He grew up in St Albans and was educated at St Albans Grammar School, University College, London, and the Working Men's College, London. He worked as a proofreader and editor at the Oxford University Press from 1908 until his death. He produced seven novels, ten volumes of his own poetry besides editing many others, six biographies, many verse plays (most of which were privately printed), four volumes of literary criticism, several volumes of theology (which are difficult to number, since some, *e.g. Religion and Love in Dante*, London, 1941, and *The Figure* of *Beatrice*, London, 1943, are as much literary criticism as theology), and one brief and idiosyncratic history of the church, *The Descent of the Dove* (London, 1939). Williams is best remembered for his novels (*e.g. Descent into Hell*, London, 1937, and *All Hallows' Eve*, London, 1945), and his cycle of Arthurian poems, published in two volumes, *Taliessin Through Logres* (Oxford, 1938), and *The Region of the Summer Stars* (Oxford, 1944). In his fiction and poetry as well as in his essays, Williams expounds his 'theology of romantic love,' the key idea deriving from Dante's vision of Beatrice as an image of beauty that beckoned him on to God, the perfection of all beauty. Williams stresses the notions of 'exchange', 'substitution', and 'co-inherence', as summing up the law of 'the City' [of God]. An early interest in Rosicrucianism, and brief membership in the Order of the Golden Dawn, do not appear to have compromised his lifelong Anglican orthodoxy.

Bibliography

G. Cavaliero, *Charles Williams: Poet of Theology* (Grand Rapids, MI, 1983); L. Glenn, *Charles W. S. Williams: A Checklist* (Kent, OH, 1975); A. M. Hadfield, *Charles Williams: An Exploration of His Life and Work* (Oxford, 1983); T. Howard, *The Novels of Charles Williams* (Oxford, 1983).

T.H.

WINGREN, GUSTAV (b. 1910). Gustav Wingren succeeded Anders Nygren* as Professor of Systematic Theology at Lund in Sweden, and his work is in close dialogue both with that of his predecessor and, through him, with that of Aulén.* Of the three major Swedish theologians of the century, Wingren is the least well known, probably because his work is less richly dramatic and more cautious and corrective than that of Nygren and Aulén.

His published work is especially notable for its attempt to hold together the doctrines of creation and redemption in a way which Protestant theology has traditionally found very difficult. His affirmation of creation and the moral law as starting-points for Christian theology is intended to serve as a corrective to both Nygren's exclusive concentration on the descent-motif of 'agape' and Barth's* Christocentrism and hostility to all talk of a relatively independent order of creation. In this way, he is enabled to give fuller weight to human reality outside the gospel. In Christology,* Wingren draws heavily on Nygren and Irenaeus,* but places especial emphasis on the humanity of Jesus, the agent of salvation, once again underlining the significance of human action.

Bibliography

The Christian's Calling (Edinburgh, 1958); *Theology in Conflict* (Edinburgh, 1958); *Man and Incarnation* (Edinburgh, 1959); *Creation and Law* (Edinburgh, 1961); *Gospel and Church* (Edinburgh, 1964).

B. Erling, 'Swedish Theology from Nygren to Wingren', *Religion in Life* 30 (1960–61), pp. 206–208; S. P. Schilling, *Contemporary Continental Theologians* (London, 1966), pp. 161–182.

J.B.We.

WISDOM IN EARLY CHRISTO-LOGY. On a few occasions the NT speaks of Christ in terms which echo OT and intertestamental references to Wisdom. These parallels should not be pressed too far. Although a number of texts in Jewish Wisdom literature appear to 'personify' the concept of Wisdom, this should be seen as a literary device rather than as an indication that Wisdom was believed to be a 'divine being' separate in some sense from Yahweh himself. (*Cf.* the personification of the 'name', 'glory', 'power' or 'arm' of the Lord.) The Christian doctrine of the pre-existence of Christ as the Son of God is not merely an adaptation of a supposed Jewish hypostatization of divine Wisdom. There is no evidence that the NT Church saw Jesus (or that Jesus saw himself) as the incarnation of 'Wisdom' in the sense of a distinct divine being mentioned occasionally and prophetically in the OT.

In its Christology* the NT makes little explicit use of either the expression 'Wisdom' (of God) or the OT Wisdom passages. Nevertheless this concept is not altogether absent. In particular the cosmic role of Christ is presented in terms which remind us of the creative role ascribed to Wisdom. Passages such as Jn 1:1–18 (where, it seems, John deliberately chooses 'Word' (Logos*) in preference to 'Wisdom'), 1 Cor. 8:5–6; Col. 1:15–17 and Heb. 1:1–3 bear some resemblance to Prov. 3:19–20 and 8:22–32. In Proverbs, Wisdom is portrayed as the agency whereby God creates and sustains his world. In 1 Cor. 1:24 Paul speaks of Christ as 'the power of God and the wisdom of God', and underlying Paul's teaching on the person and work of Christ is the idea that the power and wisdom of God, seen in creation and providence, achieve their fullest and clearest expression in Christ. The association of Wisdom with Christ implied in certain NT passages emphasizes the link between creation and redemption.

In patristic* Christology the concept of Wisdom, and in particular the Wisdom passage in Pr. 8:22–32, becomes more prominent than in the NT. Although some writers identify Wisdom and the Holy Spirit (*e.g.* Irenaeus,* *Against Heresies* IV.xx.3), this is not typical of the fathers in general. Justin Martyr (*Dialogue with Trypho* 61, 129) quotes Pr. 8 as part of his argument that the Word (who is the divine Wisdom) is distinct yet inseparable from God. Athenagoras (*Embassy* 10) and Tertullian* (*Against Praxeas* 7) quote from Pr. 8 as part of their presentation of a 'two-stage' history of the Logos:* there is the Word immanent in the mind of God from all eternity and there is the Word expressed or sent forth for the purposes of creation. By the time of the Arian* controversy, the idea that the OT Wisdom passages spoke directly of Christ was so well established that Pr. 8:22ff., which in the LXX speaks of Wisdom as 'created', 'established', 'made' and 'begotten', became a major storm-centre. Arius used this passage as one of his chief proof-texts. However, like earlier writers, both he and his opponents missed the point of this and other Wisdom passages, which speak poetically of a divine attribute and not concretely of a divine person.

Bibliography

J. D. G. Dunn, *Christology in the Making* (London, 1980); S. Kim, *The Origin of Paul's Gospel* (Tübingen, 1981; Grand Rapids, MI, 1982); T. E. Pollard, *Johannine Christology and the Early Church* (Cambridge, 1970); M. Simonetti, 'Sull'interpretazione patristica di Proverbi 8, 22', *Studi sull'arianesimo* (Rome, 1965).

M.D.

W**ISLØFF, CARL FREDRIK** (b. 1908). Born in Drammen, Norway,

Wisløff graduated from the Free Faculty of Theology, Oslo, in 1931. In 1958 he defended his PhD thesis *Nattverd og Messe* at the University of Oslo (ET, *The Gift of Communion: Luther's Controversy with Rome on Eucharistic Sacrifice*, Minneapolis, MN, 1964). Ordained in 1932, he became rector of the Practical Theology Department of the Free Faculty of Theology in 1940, and Professor of Church History in 1961.

Wisløff has been one of the most outstanding representatives of evangelical Christianity in Scandinavia. A convinced Lutheran,* he has also co-operated with Evangelicals from different denominations, for instance in his current collaboration on a new translation of the Bible into Norwegian. Wisløff's vigorous defence of the inspiration and authority of *all* Scripture* has been a source of tension between him and colleagues. Justification* by faith* is one of the main themes in his theology.

Wisløff's paper on the World Council of Churches (1952) gave Norwegian Christians guidelines for a critical attitude to the theological relativism advocated by the WCC. (The Norwegian Missionary Council withdrew from the International Missionary Council at the merger of the IMC and WCC in 1961.) Wisløff has also strongly emphasized the priesthood* of all believers and urged freedom for Christian organizations and societies within the Church of Norway.

Wisløff has for many years been a leading figure in the Norwegian Evangelical Student Movement and the International Fellowship of Evangelical Students. He is the author of more than 30 books, the best known being *Jeg vet på hvem jeg tror* (ET, *I Know on Whom I Believe*, Minneapolis, MN, 1946), a dogmatics* translated into more than 13 languages.

N.Y.

W**ITTGENSTEIN, LUDWIG JOSEF JOHANN** (1889–1951). Wittgenstein explored two distinct philosophical approaches to the problem of language, meaning, and logical necessity. His importance as a creative thinker extends not only to philosophy, but also less directly to theology, hermeneutics,* and questions of method in the social sciences. He was deeply influenced by the intellectual and cultural climate of Vienna, where he was born, but in 1908 he moved to England to study engineering, and after 1930 taught philosophy at Cambridge for much of his remaining life. His passionate concern to understand the foundations on which any subsequent problem rested drove him from engineering to mathematics, from mathematics to logic, and from logic to the philosophy of logic, which he studied at Cambridge under Bertrand Russell (1872–1970). His earlier thought (roughly 1913–29) is dominated by the problem of logical necessity, the limits of language, and the nature of propositions. In his later thought (especially after 1933) he finds the foundation of language not in abstract logic but in the ongoing stream of human life in its varied forms.

Wittgenstein's earlier thought is available in his *Notebooks* and in the brief but rigorous *Tractatus Logico-Philosophicus*. This work begins by distinguishing things (or logical objects) from facts (or determinate states of affairs). A name may refer to a thing; but a proposition depicts a state of affairs. The combination of logical elements within an elementary proposition corresponds structurally with the combination of things which constitute facts, or states of affairs. Wittgenstein alludes to the proceedings of a Paris lawcourt, in which dolls and other models were set up in various formations to depict alleged states of affairs relating to a car accident. He comments, 'In the proposition a world is, as it were, put together experimentally' (*Notebooks*, p. 7). 'A proposition is a model of reality as we imagine it' (*Tractatus*, 4.01). 'A thought is a proposition with a sense' (4). Hence, if we could combine all fact-stating propositions within a single logical system, we could comprehensively describe the whole world, articulate all determinate thoughts and thus reach the very limits of language. His last proposition in the *Tractatus* reads: 'What we cannot speak about, we must pass over in silence' (7). Unlike Russell and A. J. Ayer (b. 1910), Wittgenstein did not make this part of a positivist doctrine. Indeed, what could not be 'said' might still be profoundly important.

From 1929 onwards, however, Wittgenstein became increasingly aware that 'the crystalline purity' of the fact-stating language of the logician's classroom was 'a pre-conceived idea'; one which can only be removed 'by turning our whole examination round' (*Philosophical Investigations*, section 108). As a logician he had said, 'There *must* be . . .' But if we actually '*look* and *see*' (66), there comes before our eyes a wide *variety* of uses of language, each of which serves a concrete and particular situation. 'The speaking of language is part of an activity, or of a form of life' (23). Wittgenstein employed the term 'language-game' to draw attention to several points: that often (though not always) meaning depends on use; that meaning arises from the wholeness of language and 'the actions into which it is woven' (7); and that concepts change when there are changes in the situation in life which gives them their particular grammar. The richness and fruitfulness of this later angle of approach can be seen only when we follow Wittgenstein in attending to the concrete instances which he investigates. These are all language-uses which have significance for philosophy, but many also arise in theology and hermeneutics: understanding, meaning, intending, believing, thinking, fearing, expecting, loving, and many more. The 'grammar' of *believing*, for example, cannot be separated from the speaker's own stance in life. Thus: 'If there were a verb meaning "to believe falsely", it would not have any significant first person present indicative'. Wittgenstein develops this approach further by examining the importance of shared practices and shared language-using behaviours. This has far-reaching consequences for the technical notion of 'private' language. Wittgenstein laid the foundation for work on language which we now take for granted, such as speech-act theory, and also re-enforced the importance of questions about community, context, and tradition, in hermeneutics and the social sciences.

See also: LOGICAL POSITIVISM; RELIGIOUS LANGUAGE.

Bibliography

Works: *Tractatus Logico-Philosophicus* (London, 1961); *Philosophical Investigations* (Oxford, ³1967); *Zettel* (Oxford, 1967); *On Certainty* (Oxford, 1969); *Remarks on the Foundations of Mathematics* (Oxford, 1956); *Lectures and Conversations on Aesthetics, Psychology, and Religious Belief* (Oxford, 1966).

Studies: A. Janik and S. Toulmin, *Wittgenstein's Vienna* (London, 1973); A. Kenny, *Wittgenstein* (London, 1975); N. Malcolm,

Ludwig Wittgenstein. A Memoir (Oxford, 1958); H. Morick (ed.), *Wittgenstein and the Problem of Other Minds* (New York, 1967); D. Pears, *Wittgenstein* (London, 1971); G. Pitcher, *The Philosophy of Wittgenstein* (Englewood Cliffs, NJ, 1964); R. Rhees, *Discussion of Wittgenstein* (London, 1970); Royal Institute of Philosophy Lecture VII: *Understanding Wittgenstein* (London, 1974); A. C. Thiselton, *The Two Horizons* (Exeter, 1980).

A.C.T.

WOMAN, see ANTHROPOLOGY; FEMINIST THEOLOGY.

WORK. In the Gn. narrative, work is depicted as a basic dimension of human existence. Its character is shaped, first, by the fact that human beings are made in God's likeness (Gn. 1:26) with the capacity to participate actively in the wider creation. Their commission is to rule over it and administer God's gifts. Secondly, work acquires the character of a burdensome necessity because of the Fall.* The curse which followed man's disobedience to God (Gn. 3:17) means that human survival depends on 'painful toil'. These are the twin themes of the OT view of work. Throughout, it is assumed that work is part of the divine ordering of the world. Although frustrated by human sinfulness, work is something to be accepted willingly as a means of God's blessing (Ps. 128:1ff.). The meaning of work, however, is not defined solely by its character as a divine ordinance. Both God's work of creation and human work also have an extrinsic purpose which is expressed in God's rest on the seventh day of creation (Gn. 2:2) and in the commandment to keep the sabbath (Ex. 20:11). In contrast to the modern conception of leisure, this rest is not a state of idleness but a higher form of activity which involves worship of God and the enjoyment of his creation.

The NT values work in the same way as the OT, and sets it in the light of Christ's 'work': his ministry, miracles and work of redemption (Jn. 4:34). The incarnation of God as the carpenter of Nazareth is the perfect fulfilment of the teaching that work is necessary and good. But the work of Christ takes his people beyond the mundane realm of necessity into the joy and freedom of serving God. The gospels condemn any approach to work which would make it or its products a substitute for God's kingdom, while the advice of the epistles is to treat work and everyday life as the sphere in which service to God is rendered. Christians are seen as 'co-workers' with God (1 Cor. 3:9) and their first priority is the furtherance of the gospel. Therefore, the motive for working diligently and well is not merely duty or obedience to the law, but a grateful response to the work of Christ.

The Christian's 'calling' or 'vocation' is to new life in Christ. This word does not refer in the first instance to a profession or occupational role. However, in resisting the tendency of medieval Catholicism to elevate the monastic orders to a 'divine vocation', the Reformers employed the concepts of profession (*Beruf*) and vocation* (*vocatio*) to show that 'ordinary' stations in life could be a means to glorify God. Luther,* Calvin* and others were reasserting the NT view that ordinary work is an integral part of Christian living, not a hindrance to it. It has been argued, notably by Max Weber,* that the Reformers' idea of 'vocation' to a divinely ordained task or occupation was one important element in the 'Protestant work ethic', the others being abstinence from worldly pleasures, a strong propensity to save and a disciplined use of time. Weber's thesis that there was a close affinity between this work ethic and early capitalist entrepreneurship in parts of Europe is not capable of convincing historical demonstration. But there is no doubt that these values (or secular versions of them) did play a significant part in Western attitudes to work and employment, and continue to do so among some sections of the working population. Weber's contribution draws attention to the important place of values, including religious values, both in the individual's commitment to work and in its social organization.

The doctrine of work is spelt out in Scripture against the background of the types of economic activity which prevailed in the eastern Mediterranean between 2000 BC and AD 100. These societies were either nomadic or agrarian. Work was organized on a family or household basis and closely linked to rights over land. Present-day industrial societies based on capitalist accumulation and a free market for labour are quite different and present particular problems for the theology of work. First, there is the tendency for work to become synonymous with paid employment. Work in this restricted sense becomes the measure of worth. It devalues the contribution of those whose work is mainly within the home or in the voluntary sector. The second problem is that labour markets are an imperfect mechanism for allocating work, leaving many people either without a useful occupation or in an ill-suited one. Third, industrialism entails a complex division of labour which reduces many tasks to repetitive and meaningless routines. Instead of being the subjects of the work process, human beings become the objects of technical and organizational systems. All these aspects of work in Western industrial society have attracted much criticism, but the theological response has been sluggish. Indeed, certain narrow interpretations of work and vocation still lend support to a business ethic which stresses achievement and material success as a sign of God's favour. Increasingly however, biblically informed approaches to work, employment and unemployment acknowledge the need for just and peaceable relationships in the social organization of work. This, rather than the individual's commitment to work *per se*, is the dimension which is historically and culturally most variable and fraught with difficulties of interpretation.

A theology of work will recognize the continuing and fundamental importance of work for human existence and well-being. The mandate is for every human being, for every generation, at every stage of economic development. However welcome the release from drudgery which automation may bring, a 'leisure society' is not a valid goal. There is no end to useful work within the created world. The theology of work has also to consider the intrinsic value of work in the light of the problems of authority,* control, technology and alienation.* It has to engage with contemporary critiques in order to develop an appropriate ethic for these times. Finally, theology has to face the challenge of the social (dis-)organization of work, especially mass unemployment. Where the means of livelihood, social identity and participation are obtained or denied largely through the labour market, the social right to useful work must be established as a matter of priority. A theological understanding can no longer be developed, as previously, in

relation to the individual worker. It is called to express the interdependence of human relationships under God in the world of work no less than in the family, the church or the state.

See also: VOCATION.

Bibliography
R. Clarke, *Work in Crisis* (Edinburgh, 1982); A. Richardson, *The Biblical Doctrine of Work* (London, 1952); M. Weber, *The Protestant Ethic and the Spirit of Capitalism* (London, 1930).

H.H.D.

WORLD. In a few biblical passages the word 'world' (*kosmos*) is used in the sense of mankind. In Jn. 3:16, for instance, we are told of God's love for 'the world' in this sense. When this is what is meant, then the Christian duty to love mankind is clear.

It is in the other, and more usual, sense that there are problems. In this wider sense 'the world' usually means 'the environment of humanity'. That is to say, it includes not only the natural environment and all its varied resources, but also the cultural and social environment brought into being by sinful humanity. In this sense, the devil is described as the 'prince' or 'ruler of this world' who was condemned and cast out by the power and work of Christ (Jn. 12:31; 16:11; Eph. 6:12). 'The whole world lies in the power of the evil one' (1 Jn. 5:19).

When these passages about the rule of the devil over the world are added to verses like 1 Jn. 2:15–17, where we are warned to love neither 'the world nor the things in the world', there is a *prima facie* case for a negative attitude to both material goods and to man's cultural and other natural abilities such as marriage.

On the other hand, 'everything created by God is good', even in a fallen world. We are to receive all these gifts with thanksgiving if we 'believe and know the truth'. A negative view of food and marriage, and even money and the things that it can buy, is roundly condemned by the NT, especially in the Pastoral Epistles (notably 1 Tim. 2:1–4; 4:1–10; 5:8–23; 6:17–19, and Tit. 3:8–14).

The church down the ages has wrestled with these two apparently competing emphases. Inevitably the surrounding climate of thought has influenced Christian thinking. When, for instance, Gnosticism,* with its negative view of the body, was a common part of religious thinking, it was easy for Christians to absorb at least a little of this spirit. Monasticism and even more the cult of the hermit life owed something to this and resulted in an ascetic* tradition that regarded poverty, celibacy and fasting as in themselves spiritually superior. The Protestant Reformation made a major break with this ascetic tradition. Finding in the Bible a positive attitude to the body, to God-given natural abilities, to manual work and to the good things of life, the Reformers encouraged clerical marriage, the joys of family life and enjoyment of God's gifts in the whole of the natural and cultural environment. This certainly contributed to the development of economic life and of science and technology.

As long as a living biblical theology controlled the use of these gifts in the Western world the abuses were not too prominent. By the 20th century, however, we find the secularized version of this in the idolization of sex, artistic freedom, materialism and *laissez-faire* economics without respect to ethical principles. The controls of 'by the word of God and prayer' given in 1 Tim. 4:4 have been abandoned. Pleasure, sex, material prosperity and success are the new idols of a formerly Christianized society.

The result is that a new asceticism is attractive to Protestants. If one has to choose between a piously disguised greedy misuse of the world and a negative attitude to it, the latter certainly seems the more Christian. The Bible, however, condemns both. On the one hand we are never to '*love* the world or the things in the world', neither on the other are we to deny that food, marriage, good government and physical health are good gifts of God. They are, as 1 Tim. 4:8 has it, 'for this life only', and therefore may be set aside for eternal things, but Christians are *stewards** of these gifts for God's glory. 'All things are yours . . . the world . . . – all are yours, and you are of Christ . . .' (1 Cor. 3:21–23). Because of sin, the world is never perfect, and can be seductive to sinful man, but 'to the pure all things are pure' (Tit. 1:15), and we do not honour God by pretending that his creation is evil when it is ourselves that we must blame for 'lust' or greed of what is good. We should rather be thankful that the world, although fallen, is far from being hell and has

many excellent features for us 'richly to enjoy' in accordance with 'the word of God and prayer'.

Bibliography

O. R. Barclay, *Developing a Christian Mind* (Leicester, 1984); R. Morgenthaler *et al.*, *NIDNTT* I, pp. 517–526; H. R. Niebuhr, *Christ and Culture* (London, 1952); H. Sasse, *TDNT* III, pp. 867–898; R. V. G. Tasker, 'World', *IBD* 3, pp. 1655–1656.

O.R.B.

WORLD COUNCIL OF CHURCHES, see ECUMENICAL MOVEMENT.

WORSHIP. Man's sense of awe in the presence of the magnificent, the frightening or the miraculous illustrates something of what is meant by 'worship'. His response may be one of speechlessness, paralysis, emulation or dedication.

Revelation and response

At the heart of Christian worship is God himself. In order truly to worship two fundamental elements are needed: revelation, through which God shows himself to man, and response, through which awe-stricken man responds to God. Martin Luther claimed that 'to know God is to worship him'. In so saying, he succinctly embraced both aspects of worship. He also insisted that worship is not an optional extra for the godly person, but an essential symptom or expression of that knowledge.

God makes himself known in a number of ways: through his works in creation (Ps. 19:1); through his written word (Ps. 19:7); supremely, through Jesus Christ (Jn. 1:18); and through the Holy Spirit (Jn. 16:13).

Christian worship will depend on that revelation. It is therefore founded on theology – the knowledge of God. The shortest route to deeper and richer worship is a clearer theology. This will enable the worshipper to know who, and how great, God is. Further, it will inform the worshipper how God wants worship to be expressed.

Service

The biblical words used for worship convey significant insights into its nature. One of the most common Heb. words comes from the root *'ebed*, meaning 'servant'. This contains

730

the idea of service of every kind, acts of adoration as well as doing the chores (*e.g.* Ex. 3:12; 20:5; Dt. 6:13; 10:12; Jos. 24:15; Ps. 2:11). The occasional use of *hištaḥªwâ* (prostrate, religiously or in the course of duty), refers exclusively in OT to ritual acts (Gn. 27:29; 49:23). The Gk. equivalent, *proskyneō*, is used more extensively in the LXX and in the NT (*e.g.* Mt. 4:9–10; 14:33; Mk. 15:19; Acts 10:25).

The two most important words for worship in the NT are: 1. *latreia*, meaning 'service' or 'worship'. Its exact translation depends on the context (see particularly Rom. 12:1 and commentary discussion; also Mt. 4:10; Lk. 2:37; Acts 26:7; Heb. 8:5; 9:9). 2. *leitourgia*, a word taken from secular life, means service to the community or state, frequently without charge or wage (Lk. 1:23; 2 Cor. 9:12; Phil. 2:30; Heb. 9:21; 10:11). The implication is that Christian worship and service are essentially one.

According to the Bible, God alone is to be worshipped or served (Ex. 20:1–3). He is to be served with man's whole being (Dt. 6:5; Lk. 10:27). Mind as well as emotions, physique as well as feelings are to combine in God's praise. The very nature of God, overwhelming in his attributes, demands everything of man. Personal, individual worship is practised (*e.g.* Psalms) and corporate acts are described (*e.g.* 2 Ch. 7). Wesley's 'O for a thousand tongues to sing/My great Redeemer's praise' reflects this fact: that God is so great that no one person can adequately worship him.

God, transcendent and immanent

The tension between God's transcendence (his wholly otherness) and immanence (being at hand) has frequently brought dissension. In both testaments these attributes are explicit (Ex. 19:10; Jb. 38–41; Ps. 8; Is. 40:12ff.; Jn. 1:1–14; Heb. 1 – 2; and Gn. 3:8; Dt. 7:21–22; Ps. 23; Is. 43:1–2; Mt. 1:23; 28:20; Phil. 4:19). From the OT it is clear that sin* cuts people off from God, but through sacrifice he brings about a new oneness (Gn. 3; Lv. 16; *cf.* Redemption*). With the ultimate atonement* made by Jesus'* own sacrifice,* the rituals of Exodus, Leviticus, Numbers and Deuteronomy are no longer relevant; but their careful exposition is still important since they reveal abiding principles of worship. For example, sincerity, purity and holiness are constant requirements, as is the offering of what is best to God (*e.g.* Ex. 24 – 40; Lv. 1 – 10; 16; 21 – 27; Nu. 7; 15; 28; 2 Ch. 3 – 4).

In the NT the commands of Jesus embrace a comprehensive understanding of worship and service (*e.g.* fellowship, Jn. 13:34; ordinances, Mt. 28:19–20; 1 Cor. 11:23–24 and evangelism, Mt. 28:19–20). The fulfilment of these commands is worship – 'in the beauty of a holy life' (Ps. 96:9, RSV).

With the giving of God's Spirit in fulfilment of prophecy (Joel 2:28–32; Jn. 14:26; 16:7) at Pentecost upon all who believe in Christ (Acts 2), the church was empowered as a 'kingdom and priests to serve . . . God' (Rev. 1:6; Ex. 19:6). From time to time in its history, the church has been engaged in divisive controversies about the nature of the gifts* of the Spirit, but without exception Christians agree that the Spirit's enabling is vital to worship-service.

Worship in history

From the outset the Christian church recognized herself as a people who worship and not so much a place of worship. In the early church Christians normally worshipped in homes (Acts 2:46; 11; 12:12), public halls (Acts 19:9), synagogues (Acts 13:14ff.; 14:1; 17:1–2) and at the Temple (Acts 2:46; 3). Evangelism was conducted in those places and in the open (Acts 16:13–14; 17:22–23). The conversion of emperor Constantine (AD 312) brought greater freedom to build basilicas for corporate worship.

Music and singing were an important part of the worship of biblical Judaism (*e.g.* Pss; 1 Ch. 16:7ff.; 25). Together with the reading and explaining of the Scriptures and prayer, this constituted the heart of synagogue worship and stood alongside the sacrificial aspects of Temple worship (1 Ch. 22:17–19; 2 Ch. 6:12ff.; Ne. 8:1–8). The early Christians included music and singing in their corporate gatherings (Col. 3:16; Eph. 5:19) as well as in personal devotion (Acts 16:25), though history shows considerable differences of opinion about the place of music and other creative arts in worship.

The division between the Church of the East and that of the West in the 11th century reflected tensions in approaches to worship, to which the stronger mystical element of the East and the rational element of the West contributed.

With the Reformation* in the West, religious practice was largely released from superstition, and from what had become merely ceremonial or ritual. The Reformation's emphasis on the word as central to worship led to the Protestant emphasis on preaching* as the royal sacrament and as the highest *raison d'être* of corporate worship. In the context of mind-stretching, relevant and passionate exposition of Scripture, the liturgy of music and prayer become simpler and less ritualistic. Together with an emphasis on the need for the Holy Spirit to enliven preacher and congregation, this emphasis has undergirded evangelical worship until today. Tensions continue between those who look for a common liturgy, uniting churches wherever they meet, and those who depend on the spontaneous expression of faith. Many have found the need to be free to use both forms. What is central to Christian worship is not 'forms' but the presence of the triune God, who through his word, the Bible, and by his Holy Spirit, enlivens, enlightens and enables all who believe in order that they may worship-serve him in spirit and in truth.

Bibliography

J. J. Von Allmen, *Worship – Its Theology and Practice* (London, 1965); O. Cullmann, *Early Christian Worship* (London, 1953); R. P. Martin, *The Worship of God* (Grand Rapids, MI, 1982); N. Micklem, *Christian Worship* (Oxford, 1936); J. I. Packer, *Keep in Step with the Spirit* (Leicester, 1984); R. Otto, *The Idea of the Holy* (Oxford, 1923); E. Underhill, *Worship* (London, 1948). Articles in *HDB*, *ERE*.

P.D.M.

WRATH OF GOD. It is a necessary part of moral character to abhor evil as well as to love good. God is actively and strongly opposed to all forms of evil; and the biblical writers express this opposition, in part at least, by speaking of the wrath of God. Hundreds of biblical passages refer to the divine wrath. God is 'a God who expresses his wrath every day' (Ps. 7:11); 'our God is a consuming fire' (Heb. 12:29).

In modern times, this is rarely emphasized. Indeed attempts have been made to eliminate the concept altogether, by suggesting that God is not personally angry with sinners. An impersonal process is operating, it is argued, by which sin is inevitably followed by unpleasant consequences, and the ancients called this process 'the wrath of God'.

While it is true that human anger often involves passion and loss of temper, such emotions are out of place in a consideration of the anger of God. When we speak of God's wrath we must supply the qualification 'without the imperfections we see in human anger at its best'. In fact we must supply that qualification when we ascribe any quality to God, even love. Even in human life, furthermore, there is a 'righteous indignation' which is not sinful.

The denial of God's wrath does not solve the imagined moral problem. For what would be the meaning of an impersonal process in a genuinely theistic* universe? God has created a moral universe in which people reap what they sow. Since he is also active in the universe, we cannot deny that involvement by depersonalizing his wrath.

Moreover, if there is no wrath there is no salvation. If God does not take action against sinners, then sinners are in no danger and do not need salvation. Only when we take seriously the wrath of God against sinners do we put real meaning into the salvation that Christ wrought on Calvary.

The idea that God is not angry with sinners belongs neither to the OT nor to the NT; it is neither Jewish nor Christian, but an alien intrusion from the Greek world of thought. For a healthy religion, we need the concept of a God who is unalterably opposed to evil and who takes action against it.

Bibliography

A. T. Hanson, *The Wrath of the Lamb* (London, 1957); L. Morris, *The Apostolic Preaching of the Cross* (London, [3]1965); H. Schönweiss and H. C. Hahn, in *NIDNTT* I, pp. 105–13; R. V. G. Tasker, *The Biblical Doctrine of the Wrath of God* (London, 1951).

L.L.M.

WYCLIF, JOHN (*c.* 1329–84). In his numerous books Wyclif discussed philosophy, politics and theology. His participation in contemporary political life was guided by the doctrine of 'dominion' which he expounded in *De dominio divino* (*Divine Lordship*, 1375) and *De civili dominio* (*Civil Lordship*, 1376). God is the supreme Lord but he endowed humanity at creation with a derivative and conditional lordship over the world. Humanity is God's steward but the stewardship* is entirely of grace and is forfeited if man falls into moral sin even though he may continue to hold possessions and exercise rule. But he who is in grace has a right to lordship even though he be destitute. In so far as the church is guilty of innumerable sins it should forfeit its lordship and the state may strip it of its wealth.

The interest in Wyclif's theology centres upon its similarity to the thinking of the Protestant Reformers. The most striking resemblance is in his attitude to Scripture.* Scripture proceeds, as he puts it in *De veritate Sacrae Scripturae* (*The Truth of Sacred Scripture*), 'from the mouth of God'. It is the everlasting truth in written form and provides in essence all that needs to be known of law, ethics and philosophy. Scripture is superior in authority to the pope, the church and the teaching of the church fathers. It is the 'law of God' and its focus throughout is upon Christ. Wyclif's reverence for the Bible as the supreme authority for Christian thought and life is amply shown in his innumerable references to it as well as in his resolve to have it translated into English and made available to the public at large.

Using the Bible as his standard, he launched an increasingly violent attack upon the wealth, power and decadence of the church. In *De ecclesia* (*The Church*, 1378) he explains that the members of the church are God's elect, for predestination* is the foundation of the church. But no-one, not even the pope, can be certain of his election, for the visible church includes the 'foreknown', that is the reprobate as well. But all true Christians have direct personal access to God and enjoy a common priesthood.* Wyclif lays heavy stress on moral character as a mark of the true Christian, and the immorality, the lust for temporal power and wealth amongst the clergy led him to call for the abolition of the monastic orders and the papacy.* By the same token he elevated the dignity of the true Christian layman to the extent of arguing that a priest was not necessary to administer holy communion.

He rejected the medieval doctrine of transubstantiation (see Eucharist*) and argued in *De Eucharistia* (*The Eucharist, c.* 1380) that the body of Christ is 'sacramentally concealed' in the elements. Similarly, he condemned indulgences (see Merit*) and the cult of the saints,* though reverence should be accorded to the Virgin Mary.*

Although Wyclif's thought was expressed in a typically medieval scholastic idiom, his teaching on Scripture and the primacy of preaching, as well as his condemnation of transubstantiation and his elevation of lay spirituality justifies calling him 'the morning star of the Reformation', provided allowance be made for the greater clarity and sophistication of the Reformers' evangelical theology.

Bibliography

The works of Wyclif were published by the Wycliffe Society of London, 1843ff.; selections in ET, *LCC* 14, ed. M. Spinka, *Advocates of Reform* (London, 1953).

E. A. Block, *John Wyclif: Radical Dissenter* (San Diego, CA, 1962); K. B. McFarlane, *John Wycliffe and the Beginnings of English Nonconformity* (London, 1952); J. Stacey, *Wyclif and Reform* (London, 1964); H. B. Workman, *John Wyclif*, 2 vols. (Oxford, 1926).

R.T.J.

YEAR, CHRISTIAN, see Calendar, Liturgical.

ZION. A suggestive and evocative theme in Scripture and Christian theology.

1. Old Testament

The walled citadel of the kingdom of David, its geographical, political and economic capital, was at the same time the site where God lived in his 'house'. In the story of salvation, this small acropolis called Zion occupies a prominent position because it made visible God's covenant* commitment to live among his people, and to be Father to the

Davidic dynasty. 'Zion' can also personify the Jerusalem populace.

Three factors contribute to the language used about Zion: formative events in Israel's experience; God's words of promise backed by miracles; and polemic engagement with the alternative city/temple theologies of Canaan and Babylon.

a. Formative events. David's capture of Jerusalem from the Jebusites and transference of the ark there, the experience of empire and tribute during the united monarchy and the inauguration of Temple worship in Solomon's reign, Sennacherib's siege and retreat from Jerusalem, destruction of city and Temple by Nebuchadnezzar, and its post-exilic re-consecration in the time of Haggai and Zechariah all left their mark in history books, psalms and prophecy.

b. Words of promise. God's choice of Zion and his choice of David's dynasty are linked in Pss. 2 and 132, reflecting the oracle given through Nathan (2 Sa. 7:11–16). Spectacular miracles marked Zion as the chosen site for entering the presence of the heavenly king – fire from heaven on the altar of burnt offering set up by David on Araunah's threshing floor (1 Ch. 21:26), and theophanous* glory and fire when Solomon settled the ark of the covenant in the Holy of holies and dedicated the Temple (2 Ch. 5:13–14; 7:1). These miraculous demonstrations lie behind the colourful poetry with which Zion's role is celebrated in psalm and prophetic eschatology.

The cluster of theological ideas associated with Zion finds expression in parallel phrases. It is 'the city of David' (2 Ch. 5:2); 'the city of God' (Ps. 46:4); his 'resting place' (Ps. 132:13–14); his 'holy hill' (Ps. 2:6; Dn. 9:16); 'the holy city' (Is. 48:2, 52:1, Ne. 11:1) and 'holy mountain' (Dn. 11:45).

c. Polemic engagement. Because Mount Zion is a low hill compared with known mountains such as the snow-capped Lebanon range, there is more to its description as a mountain than the experience of pilgrims going uphill to 'ascend the hill of the LORD' and 'stand in his holy place' (Ps. 24:3) at the time of national festivals. The spatial symbolism of height is dramatically exploited by hymn writer (Ps. 48) and prophet (Is. 2; Mi. 4). Zion is outstanding in all the earth.

Baal texts locate his mythical palace on top of Mount Zaphon, his 'chosen site' and 'mountain of victory' from which his voice thunders forth, putting his enemies to flight. Ps. 48 clearly asserts the supremacy of Mount Zion, championing Yahweh's true kingship against Canaanite beliefs about Baal. Similarly, Ps. 46 affirms that Yahweh as El Elyon (v. 4) rules cosmos and nations from 'the city of God' with its stream of water (cf. Ezk. 47:1), counteracting Canaanite claims for El's rule from his mountain tabernacle at the source of the two rivers. 'The city of the great King' (Ps. 48:2) at the centre of the promised land symbolized Yahweh's historic victories as cosmic warrior (Ex. 15; Jdg. 5; cf. Is. 49; 51 – 52; 60 – 63). To 'walk about Zion' inspecting its fortifications (Ps. 48:12ff.) meant the strengthening of faith, a deep sense of security, national identity, and enjoyment of God's presence. But Zion with Baal worship and without a right covenant relationship spelled false security and judgment (Je. 7).

Isaiah 40 – 55 proclaims the return of Yahweh to Zion after the Judean exile. Neo-Babylonian royal inscriptions show that Nebuchadnezzar, his father and his successors saw Babylon as cosmic centre of warrior-creator Marduk's global empire with tribute pouring into it. The prophecies about Zion in national and political terms (e.g. Is. 24; 45:14ff., 49:22ff.; 51, 54, 60ff.) are best read as counteractive, contextualized theology affirming the kingship of Israel's God in Zion against all counterclaims.

2. New Testament

The NT describes Zion in terms which leave behind the ethnic, territorial and economic framework of David's kingdom. Instead of a physical Temple and acropolis to make visible the reality of God's kingdom, there is Jesus (cf. Jn. 4:20ff.). By entering the new covenant, believers have already joined heavenly worshippers and 'have come to Mount Zion, to the heavenly Jerusalem, the city of the living God' (He. 12:22; cf. Rev. 14:1). There is no sacred city, shrine or site on earth which gives access to God's presence as did OT Zion.

Though Paul foresees the national conversion of Jews when 'the delivery will come from Zion' (Rom. 11:26), the NT knows nothing of Zion as a re-built earthly Temple or world capital, or focus of national ideology. When dispensational* theology reads OT Zion eschatology in a literalist manner, it appears to misconstrue its poetic symbolism, its contextual polemic, and its re-interpretation by Jesus and the NT. 'The heavenly Jerusalem' and all forms of earthly Zionism are disconnected by the NT.

Bibliography

W. D. Davies, *The Gospel and the Land* (London, 1974); B. C. Ollenburger, *Zion, the City of the Great King* (Sheffield, 1986); J. D. Pentecost, *Things to Come* (Grand Rapids, MI, 1958).

D.C.T.S.

ZOROASTRIANISM AND CHRISTIANITY.

Zoroastrianism, the Persian religion associated with Zoroaster, is an ancient and complex faith which has evolved through many stages. Its modern adherents, the Parsees (*i.e.* Persians), who are found mainly in the region of Bombay, India, though numbering only 100,000, exercise influence out of proportion to their numbers because of their cohesion, wealth, and education. Their ancestors migrated to north-west India in the 7th and 8th centuries after the Muslim conquest of Iran. About 20,000 Zoroastrian Gabars are still left in Iran, concentrated in Tehran, Kirman, and Yazd.

Numerous scholars have argued that Zoroastrianism influenced Judaism in the post-exilic period in the areas of demonology (see Devil*) and eschatology.* Others have seen parallels between the dualism* of Zoroastrianism and of the Dead Sea Scrolls.* A few (*e.g.* J. R. Hinnells) have argued that the Zoroastrian concept of the *soshyant* ('saviour') influenced Christianity. To assess these claims one must consider the dates of the sources for our knowledge of Zoroastrian teachings.

1. The sources

Though many scholars have accepted the traditional date from Arabic sources that Zarathustra (Gk. Zoroaster) lived in the Achaemenid era (569–492 BC), a growing consensus has placed his *floruit* before 1000 BC because of the evidence of the *Gathas*, the seventeen hymns which are universally acknowledged to originate from the prophet.

The next oldest source is known collectively as the *Younger Avesta*. These texts may date from either before the Achaemenid era or mainly after it. Handed down orally for centuries, we have perhaps only one quarter of the originally extant traditions preserved. These are mainly works used in the various rituals.

The Zoroastrian works which deal with such subjects as cosmology, demonology, and eschatology are written in Pahlavi (Middle Persian) and date from the 9th century AD, though they are believed to preserve traditions from the Sasanid era (AD 226–651), when Zoroastrianism was made the Iranian state religion. Of the fifty-five Pahlavi texts the two most important are: the *Bundahishn* (*The Creation*) and the *Denkard* (*Acts of Religion*), an encyclopaedia which includes a legendary life of Zoroaster.

Unfortunately from the Parthian epoch (247 BC to AD 225), the crucial period for both Judaism and Christianity, almost no Persian text survives. Philosophers such as Aristotle* were interested in the Persian doctrines. Greek traditions placed Zoroaster 6,000 years before Plato.*

2. Teachings

The *Gathas* indicate that Zoroaster was concerned about the worship of Ahura Mazda ('The Wise Lord') and the care of 'cattle'. Though many have taken the latter in the literal sense, as in the closely related Hindu traditions, some scholars have argued that 'cattle' should be taken metaphorically for the good 'vision'. Whether Zoroaster's teachings were originally monotheistic* or dualistic,* with Angra Mainyu (Pahlavi Ahriman) as the primal evil being, is a matter of dispute among scholars. During the Sasanid period Zurvanism, a poorly attested heresy, exalted Zurvan, the god of time, as the father of the twin spirits, Ahura Mazda and Angra Mainyu. The Parsees, who have been influenced by the West and Christianity, emphatically stress the monotheistic character of Ahura Mazda.

Man, who is naturally good, must choose between Angra Mainyu and Ahura Mazda. By choosing the side of truth instead of the lie, man can aid in the eventual triumph of Ahura Mazda. Man is saved according to his deeds. At the day of judgment he must cross the Cinvat Bridge, which expands for the righteous to pass into paradise but contracts to a razor's edge for the wicked, who plunge into hell.

Ritual is very important to the Parsees. Prayer is constantly offered in the presence of a fire fed by sandalwood, and sacred texts are recited from memory. Parsees must wear the *sudreh* (a special shirt) and the *kusti* (a holy cord). When polluted they undergo purification with bull's urine in the *bareshnum* ceremony. Their dead are exposed to vultures in a Tower of Silence so as not to defile the sacred elements of earth, fire or water.

While the *Gathas* used the word *soshyant* to describe Zoroaster and his supporters as 'redeemers', the late Pahlavi texts speak of the coming of a future *Soshyant*, born of a virgin from the seed of Zoroaster which had been preserved in a lake. He will smite the demons, resurrect the dead, and restore paradise.

While many parallels between Judaism* and Zoroastrianism may be noted, the very late sources which must be used to reconstruct the teachings of the latter cast considerable doubt on many alleged cases of Zoroastrian influence upon Judaism and Christianity. One demonstrable case of borrowing is the appearance of the demon Asmodeus in the book of Tobit, formed from the Iranian demon Aeshma.

Bibliography

K. Aryanpur, *Iranian Influence in Judaism and Christianity* (Tehran, 1973); M. Boyce, *A History of Zoroastrianism*, 2 vols. (Leiden, 1975, 1982); J. W. Boyd and D. A. Crosby, 'Is Zoroastrianism Dualistic Or Monotheistic?', *JAAR* 47 (1979), pp. 557–588; J. Duchesne-Guillemin, 'The Religion of Ancient Iran,' in C. J. Bleeker and G. Widengren (eds.), *Historia Religionum I: Religions of the Past* (Leiden, 1969); J. R. Hinnells, 'Christianity and the Mystery Cults', *Th* 71 (1968), pp. 20–25; *idem*, 'The Zoroastrian Doctrine of Salvation in the Roman World', in E. J. Sharpe and J. R. Hinnells (eds.), *Man and His Salvation* (Manchester, 1973); *idem*, 'Zoroastrian Saviour Imagery and Its Influences on the New Testament', *Numen* 16 (1969), pp. 161–185; S. Shaked, 'Iranian Influence on Judaism: First Century BCE to Second Century ACE', in W. D. Davies and L. Finkelstein (eds.), *The Cambridge History of Judaism, I: Introduction: The Persian Period* (Cambridge, 1984); R. E. Waterfield, *Christians in Persia* (New York, 1973); J. E. Whitehurst, 'The Zoroastrian Response to Westernization: A Case Study of the Parsis of Bombay', *JAAR* 37 (1969), pp. 224–236; D. Winston, 'The Iranian Component in the Bible, Apocrypha, and Qumran', *HR* 5 (1965–66), pp. 183–216.

E.M.Y.

ZWINGLI, ULRICH (1484–1531),

Swiss Reformer. Born at Wildhaus on 1 Jan. 1484, Zwingli, the pioneer of the Swiss Reformation, received his education at Basel, Berne and Vienna. He emerged with renaissance enthusiasm, especially for Erasmus,* and perhaps some knowledge of the doctrines of grace, acquired from Thomas Wyttenbach. Ordained in 1506, he became rector of Glarus, where he was a diligent pastor, effective preacher, affectionate colleague, and industrious student. Chaplaincy service in the papal army brought him a pension but plunged him into opposition to the mercenary system. This caused tension in Glarus that led him to the new charge of Einsiedeln in 1516.

At Einsiedeln Zwingli ministered to the many pilgrims to the famous shrine of Mary. He enjoyed the resources of the Abbey library and had leisure to immerse himself in Erasmus' Greek New Testament (1516). The study of the original text gave him new insights into the gospel which were to affect all his future life, thought and work.

A vacancy at Zurich in 1519 opened the door to his reforming activity. Appointed people's priest in spite of opposition, he used the Great Minster pulpit for a systematic exposition of the NT, and later the OT. This preaching alerted both preacher and people to the wide gap between Scripture and contemporary belief and practice. A plague in 1520, which claimed Zwingli's brother and almost cost him his own life, added depth to his ministry. Quickly gathering adherents, he initiated the radical programme of reform which rapidly changed the ecclesiastical life of the city, the canton, and neighbouring cities such as Schaffhausen, Basel and Berne. Prominent changes included the ending of the Mass, the rejection of the papacy* and hierarchy, the suppression of the monasteries, the translation of the Bible and liturgy, the pruning of customs and practices according to Scripture, the improvement of the theological training, the establishment of synodal ministry, the enhancing of the role of the laity* and the introduction of a tighter disciplinary* system.

After 1525 Zwingli unfortunately found himself not only at odds with Roman Catholic adversaries but also embroiled with the

Anabaptists* and Lutherans.* Controversies diverted resources and weakened the force of reform. The growing isolation of Zurich, the implacable hostility of the Swiss Forest Cantons and the possibility of Austrian intervention made the failure of the Marburg Colloquy (1529; see Eucharist*) a serious setback. The Forest Cantons caught Zurich unprepared at Kappel in October 1531, and Zwingli fell in the defeat which halted, although it did not reverse, the Reformation in German Switzerland.

Zwingli lived a busy life during the days of reform and reorganization, but he still found time to publish several important works. *The Clarity and Certainty of the Word of God* came out in 1522. In 1523 the *Sixty-Seven Theses*, for which he also composed a commentary, constituted the first Reformation confession. To the same period belonged the sermon *On Divine and Human Righteousness* and the essay *On the Canon of the Mass*. Perhaps his most significant theological treatise was his *Commentary on True and False Religion* (1525). The works *On Baptism* and *On the Lord's Supper* marked the beginning of the sacramental debates among the Reformers, each of them followed by further polemical treatises. In 1530 Zwingli published his Marburg address *The Providence of God*, and also prepared a statement, *Fidei Ratio*, for the Diet of Augsburg. In 1531 he wrote his very similar final work, *Exposition of the Faith*, in a vain effort to win over the king of France to the reforming cause.

Zwingli died prematurely, but not before he had launched the Reformation in Switzerland and helped to give it a distinctive stamp. Naturally he shared many of Luther's* concerns, *e.g.* for justification* by faith, for vernacular Bible translation, for correction of abuses, for biblical learning and for the primacy of Scripture. He went beyond Luther, however, in radical application of the biblical rule. In a less autocratic society, he gave the city's councils a bigger voice as representatives of the church's laity. He devised a simpler liturgy. He acted more effectively to secure an educated ministry by the establishment of a theological college and by the so-called prophesyings at which pastors would study Scripture in the original tongues. He took sharper measures for discipline,* with a special body including lay delegates. He moved toward a presbyterian* system in taking over supervision from the distant bishop of Constance.

Theologically, too, Zwingli steered the Swiss churches into courses which would distinguish the Reformed* family. Thus he gave a special emphasis to the primacy of Scripture as the rule of faith and conduct. The Berne Theses (1528) express his point that, as the church is born of God's word, so it can rule only on this basis. Sharing with Luther a firm belief in the efficacy of the word, he asserted with added strength that, although the word has instrinsic clarity, only illumination by the Holy Spirit enables us to pierce the thicket of misinterpretation and know and accept its saving truth. Prayer* is thus a hermeneutical* prerequisite.

In debate with the Anabaptists and Lutherans, Zwingli developed two important doctrines. As regards baptism, he turned to the covenant theology* of the OT, which in turn fed his strong views on election (see Predestination*) and controlled his understanding of church and society. He agreed with Luther in rejecting the eucharistic* sacrifice but saw in the Supper no necessary equation of sign and thing signified in virtue of the presence of Christ's humanity, which is now in fact at the right hand of the Father. Faith alone, he thought, perceives the presence and receives the benefits.

Zwingli is often depicted as a humanist Reformer with little theological perspicacity or spiritual profundity. Overdue reappraisals, however, have noted the crises at Einsiedeln and Zurich resulting from his problems with celibacy, his study of the NT, and his almost fatal sickness, which combined to give him an acute awareness of divine grace and divine over-ruling. He often adopts a rational style of argumentation, but closer analysis of his works reveals a sharper Trinitarian* and Christological* focus. The eucharistic teaching initially suggests a weak memorialism, but it was clearly gaining in content as Zwingli came to appreciate the divine presence of Christ, the concept of the visible word, and the role of the sacrament in the confirming of faith. Even what might often seem to be a compromise with civil religion* takes on a new aspect when set in the biblical context of covenant and election. If Zwingli did not himself develop all the emphases that characterize the reformed churches, he sketched many of the outlines both practically and theologically. For this reason his brief and more localized ministry has a broad and lasting significance.

Bibliography

Works: ETs in G. W. Bromiley, *Zwingli and Bullinger* (London, 1953); G. R. Potter, *Huldrych Zwingli* (London, 1978) – documents; S. M. Jackson, *Selected Works . . .* (New York, 1901); *idem, The Latin Works and the Correspondence . . .*, 3 vols. (New York and Philadelphia, 1912, 1922, 1929).

Studies: G. W. Bromiley, *Historical Theology* (Grand Rapids, MI, 1978); G. W. Locher, *Zwingli's Thought: New Perspectives* (Leiden, 1981); G. R. Potter, *Zwingli* (Cambridge, 1976); J. Rilliet, *Zwingli* (London, 1964); W. P. Stephens, *The Theology of Huldrych Zwingli* (Oxford, 1986).

G.W.B.